Encyclopedia of Sociology

Second Edition

Editorial Board

Encyclopedia of Sociology

Second Edition

VOLUME 3

Edgar F. Borgatta
Editor-in-Chief
University of Washington, Seattle

Rhonda J. V. Montgomery
Managing Editor
University of Kansas, Lawrence

Macmillan Reference USA
an imprint of the Gale Group
New York • Detroit • San Francisco • London • Boston • Woodbridge, CT

Encyclopedia of Sociology
Second Edition

Macmillan Reference USA
an imprint of The Gale Group
1633 Broadway
New York, NY 10019

Library of Congress Catalog in Publication Data
Encyclopedia of Sociology / Edgar F. Borgatta, editor-in-chief, Rhonda Montgomery, managing editor.—2nd ed.
    p. cm.
    Includes bibliographical references and index.
    ISBN 0-02-864853-6 (set: alk paper)—ISBN 0-02-864849-8 (v. 1: alk. paper)—0-02-864850-1 (v. 2)—0-02-86485-1 (v. 3)—0-02-864852-8 (v. 4)—0-02-865581-8 (v. 5)
      1. Sociology—Encyclopedias. I. Borgatta, Edgar F., 1924- II. Montgomery, Rhonda J. V.

HM425 .E5 2000
301'.03—dc21
                                      00-028402
                                          CIP

Printed in the United States of America by the Gale Group
Gale Group and Design is a trademark used herein under license.

Staff
Publisher
Elly Dickason

Project Editors
Timothy Prairie
Pamela Proffitt

Editorial Assistants
Shawn Beall
Wayne Yang

Assistant Manager, Composition
Evi Seoud

Buyer
Rhonda Williams

Senior Art Director
Michelle DiMercurio

J

JAPANESE SOCIOLOGY

Japanese sociology divides roughly into four stages of development: pre–World War II, with emphasis on theoretical and philosophical orientations, influenced primarily by European (especially German) sources; post–World War II, with growing emphasis on empirical orientations, influenced primarily by the United States; diversification, with emphases on both theoretical and empirical orientations (on various aspects of the history of Japanese sociology, see, e.g., Halmos 1966; Koyano 1976; Odaka 1950); and globalization, with emphasis on theoretical orientations and an increasing number of empirical orientations, some encompassing cross-national and foreign area studies. In a general sense, the development of Japanese sociology reflects the country's social and cultural change, as well as shifting national policies. The significant Western influence generally exhibits a time lag in terms of its expression in Japanese sociology.

PRE–WORLD WAR II STAGE (1893–1945)

Japanese sociology began as a European import and reflected a conservative stance. This occurred shortly after the Meiji Restoration of 1868. E. F. Fenollosa (1853–1908), an American professor, first taught sociology at the University of Tokyo in 1878. Three years later, Masakazu Toyama (1848–1900) began teaching at the same university; in 1893 (just one year after the founding of the University of Chicago's sociology department), he became the first professor of sociology in Japan and is regarded as the founder of Japanese sociology. Toyama, and later Nagao Ariga (1860–1921), a student of Fenollosa and the first sociologist in Japan to publish, both introduced aspects of Herbert Spencer's organic analogy for society. The works of Spencer and John Stuart Mill were particularly significant during these early years and were translated frequently.

Tongo Takebe (1871–1945), successor to Toyama in 1898, introduced Auguste Comte to Japan, combining Comte's positivism with Confucian philosophy and social thought to fit Japanese society. In 1913 Takebe also founded the Japan Institute of Sociology, an organization replaced by the Japan Sociological Society in 1924. A new approach began to take hold in the 1910s—the psychological approach initiated by Ryukichi Endo (1874–1946), who drew on Franklin Giddings's theory of consciousness of kind to explain social phenomena.

During the 1910s, other Western sociological theories came to Japan, largely through the work of Shotaro Yoneda (1873–1945). Yoneda, who looked at society and culture from a sociopsychological perspective, was an important teacher who introduced the ideas of many Western sociologists to Japan, including those of Gabriel Tarde, Emile Durkheim, Georg Simmel, and Franklin Giddings. Yoneda laid the groundwork for the subsequent strong influence of the German school of sociology.

From this point forward, until the end of World War II, the German school dominated

Japanese sociology. There were two major divisions that grew out of the German school: *formale Soziologie* (formal sociology) and, later, *Kultursoziologie* (cultural sociology). The major proponent of the former was Yasuma Takata (1883–1972), a student of Yoneda. Takata (1922, 1989) successfully changed the view of sociology from that of a synthesis of the social sciences to one in which sociology stood as separate and independent, drawing in particular on the work and influence of Max Weber, Georg Simmel, Ferdinand Tönnies, and Robert MacIver.

New influences, however, emerged in the 1920s. Formal sociology was deemed abstract and out of touch with the real world. As a consequence, cultural sociology gained a stronger foothold in both Germany and Japan. Pioneering the work in cultural sociology in Japan was Eikichi Seki (1900–1939). No doubt a reaction to the Depression of 1929, cultural sociology gained popularity for its closer ties with the social realities of the day. Although a theory of cultural sociology fitting the Japanese society seemed imminent, it never really unfolded.

While there were also French and American influences on Japanese sociology during the prewar period, they were minor compared with those of Germany. Jyun'ichiro Matsumoto (1893–1947) saw a need to synthesize formal and cultural sociology into what he would call "general sociology." At the same time, Masamichi Shimmei (1898–1988) sought to take Matsumoto's thoughts and combine them with Simmel's general sociology and the thinking of Karl Mannheim.

Because Western theory and thought dominated Japanese sociology in the prewar period, little of the work analyzed Japanese society. There were, however, a handful of notable empirical studies, especially in family and rural sociology, a tradition begun at the University of Tokyo by Teizo Toda (1887–1955). Toda had studied at the University of Chicago, where he learned about survey methodologies being used in the United States. Toda analyzed statistics on the Japanese family structure, using census and other then-current and historical data. Kizaemon Aruga (1897–1979) worked in the area of rural sociology, linking his findings with previous folklore studies and working toward clarifying the condition of social strata in prewar Japan. Lack of financial support,

however, hindered the development of empirical research during this time.

Two phenomena in particular worked against the development of Japanese sociology prior to World War II. First, Japanese sociology focused on European sociology rather than on studies of its own society. The second phenomenon, bolstered by government officials and scholars inclined toward nationalistic militarism, involved a distorted public image: that sociology and sociologists were associated with socialism because of the two words' similarity in the Japanese language ("sociology," *shakaigaku*; "socialism," *shakaishugi*). Many thought that sociology was the study of socialism or social revolution and that sociologists were socialists and, therefore, a sinister threat to national security. As World War II grew closer, and during the war, publications were often censored, academic freedom was severely curtailed, and meetings and conventions were forbidden.

POSTWAR STAGE (1946–1960s)

Defeat and U.S. occupation brought drastic social changes to Japan. The traditional family system collapsed, and land reform became the order of the day. Favorite prewar survey subjects centering on village and family were replaced by issues related to land reform and revision of traditional family values. Indeed, the traditional Japanese value system was pulled out from under the nation. "Democratization" was the new buzzword. The term "sociology" was released from taboo. Educational reforms in the 1950s now required sociology courses as part of the general university education, especially for freshmen and sophomores. More and more departments of sociology or sociology programs within other departments were formed, particularly at private colleges and universities. Suddenly, many sociologists were needed. American influences were rampant in all areas of Japanese society, and sociology was no exception. Many American sociological theories came to influence Japanese sociology, the strongest being that of Talcott Parsons.

As the importance of empirical study was growing in the United States, Japanese sociologists also began to develop a strong interest in empirical work. Social research, positivism, and functionalism were key words. Marxism had significant impact on Japanese sociology as well. "Democratization" and "modernization" were major fundamental themes in sociological studies. Japanese sociologists studied American research methods, ultimately leading to a rapid increase in surveys and research based on the results of these surveys. To many, the empirical studies of Japanese sociology moved the entire discipline from one of art and humanity to one of social science. However, many surveys were carried out for fact-finding purposes rather than hypothesis testing for theory construction.

Tadashi Fukutake (1917–1989) significantly influenced the postwar stage and the subsequent stage of Japanese sociology. Fukutake's studies focused on rural sociology (see, e.g., 1967) in the context of Japanese society's postwar democratization. Also influential was Kunio Odaka (1908–1993), a positivist, who played an important role in industrial sociology (see, e.g., 1975) as well as general sociology, especially during the period of extraordinary economic development from 1955 through 1965. Odaka and Fukutake were two of Japan's leading empirical researchers conducting field research in real social settings during this stage in the development of Japanese sociology.

Mentioned earlier, the Japan Sociological Society is a nationwide organization for Japanese sociologists. It holds annual meetings and publishes a journal, and it joined the International Sociological Association (ISA) in 1950. Two years later, a survey on social stratification and mobility was conducted under the auspices of the Japan Sociological Society, led by Odaka, in cooperation with the ISA. This survey was repeated three years later on a nationwide scale and subsequently every ten years.

In 1954, the Institute of Statistical Mathematics in Tokyo began a nationwide time-trend survey of the Japanese national character, a survey conducted every five years since, with the objective of analyzing changes (or lack thereof) in general social attitudes among the Japanese since World War II (Hayashi 1998). This ongoing survey pioneered the use of identical questions over time and as such became a model for the General Social Survey of the National Opinion Research Center at the University of Chicago. Both these ongoing surveys continue as the most well-known nationwide social surveys in Japan.

Although the postwar period saw great social change in Japan, within academic circles, senior sociologists, most of whom belonged to the prewar generation, prevailed. A generational change among leading Japanese sociologists occurred in the 1960s, marking the end of the postwar period (Koyano 1976).

DIVERSIFICATION STAGE (1960s–1990s)

Since the 1960s, American sociology has gained an ever-stronger influence on Japanese sociology. With the exception of Talcott Parsons and his structural-functionalism, however, no major American sociologists have significantly influenced the theoretical aspects of Japanese sociology. Whereas Marxist sociology had tended to influence many of the younger Japanese sociologists from a theoretical perspective, "the entire history of [Japanese] sociological development to the 60s was criticized and thrown into examination by more or less radical criticism. . . . Thus many talented younger sociologists turned from Marxism to structuralism or structuralist social theory . . . [or] alternately accepted rather subjective methodologies and theories such as phenomenological sociology, symbolic interactionism and ethnomethodology . . . [i.e.] phenomenological trends" (Shoji 1996). Interests among some Japanese sociologists also shifted from macro- to micro-sociological analyses. Multidimensional paradigms became prevalent, such as those of Michel Foucault, Jürgen Habermas, Niklas Luhmann, Pierre Bourdieu, Anthony Giddens, and Alfred Schutz, all of whom have consequently influenced Japanese sociology. Much as the prewar emphases of the theoretically oriented Japanese sociologists tended toward the purely theoretical, the new attractions continued the inclination toward speculative and interpretive theory—more like social philosophy—as against the empirical science tradition represented by Fukutake and Odaka. Though Japanese sociologists have been quite keen on the general trends in Western social and sociological thought, there is about a ten-year lag from introduction to translation and analysis of the works of Western sociologists.

Along with the vast changes in Japanese society in the postwar period came a nearly unlimited number of topics for sociological study and investigation, particularly from an empirical standpoint. This, too, accounted for diversification in Japanese sociology and signaled the establishment of a number of subdisciplines in the field. Thus, as a result of American influences, economic development, and a host of other factors, Japanese sociology continuously diversified from the early 1960s on. This is partially attributable to the fact that the industrialization of Japan, into the early 1970s, led to serious social and environmental problems, which in turn led to student uprisings, increases in delinquency and other expressions of social unrest, and, in response, the emergence of environmental-protection, feminist, and other movements, even though many of these social phenomena and movements waned in the 1980s.

These circumstances brought forth a wide variety of challenging research topics for sociologists and coincidentally created a situation in which there are no especially influential figures in Japanese sociology, although each subdiscipline does have its major proponents. These scholars include, among others, Eiichi Isomura (1903–1997) in urban sociology; Michio Nagai, who later became Japanese Minister of Education, in the sociology of education (cf. 1971); Kazuo Aoi in the field of small groups; Kiyomi Morioka in the sociology of religion and the sociology of the family (cf. 1975); Saburo Yasuda (1925–1990) in sociological methodology (cf. 1964); Akira Takahashi in social movements; Joji Watanuki in political sociology (cf. 1976); Ken'ichi Tominaga in social stratification (cf. 1969); and Tamito Yoshida in communication.

From the 1960s on, the number of sociologists in Japan grew markedly, to the point where, based on memberships in national sociological organizations, there are more sociologists in Japan than in any other country except the United States. While there were about 300 sociologists teaching at colleges and universities in Japan in the 1970s, their number grew to about 1,000 by the late 1980s. The Japan Sociological Society's membership rosters totaled 870 in 1957; 1,931 in 1985; 1,945 in 1988; 2,200 in 1990; 2,450 in 1992; and 3,034 in 1999.

In 1988, Japanese sociology had about thirty subdisciplines. On the basis of first-, second-, and third-choice subdiscipline selections by the 1,945 members of the Japan Sociological Society at that time, the most prominent were: (1) rural sociology

and community studies, 17.7 percent; (2) sociology of the family, 17.2 percent; (3) general sociological theories, 16.4 percent; (4) social welfare, social security, and medical sociology, 16.2 percent; (5) social thought and the history of sociology, 14.9 percent; (6) management, industry, and labor, 13.0 percent; (7) social pathology and social problems, 12.5 percent; (8) culture, religion, and morality, 12.4 percent; and (9) the sociology of education, 11.6 percent. Among other things, we see that sociology of the family and rural sociology held their significance from the prewar era.

Sociologists who study industrial sociology—including management; urban sociology; and social welfare, social security, and medical sociology—have increased in number continuously since World War II. And, over time, foreign sociologists have shown more and more interest in industrial sociology; the sociology of education; and social welfare, social security, and medical sociology, as these are seen as particularly successful elements of Japan's economic and social development.

Derived from lists of publications in the *Japanese Sociological Review* between 1984 and 1988, publication of articles originating from the various subdisciplines broke down as follows: (1) sociology of the family, 7.4 percent; (2) social thought and the history of sociology, 7.2 percent; (3) general social theories, 6.5 percent; (4) the sociology of education, 6.5 percent; (5) urban sociology, 6.2 percent; (6) rural sociology and community studies, 5.8 percent; (7) industrial sociology and management, 5.2 percent; (8) social pathology and social problems, 5.1 percent; and (9) social welfare, social security, and medical sociology, 5.1 percent. Articles totaled 7,426 (books, 927) during the five-year period, most of which appeared in Japanese.

Unlike in the United States, in Japan there is no rigid screening or referee system for publications, with the exception of a few well-known journals such as the *Japanese Sociological Review* (*Shakaigaku Hyoron*, the official journal of the Japan Sociological Society), *The Study of Sociology* (*Shakaigaku Kenkyu*), and *Sociology* (*Shoshioroji*). With regard to presentations at meetings of the Japan Sociological Society, the five regional associations, and the associations of the various subdisciplines, there have been, in many cases, no rigid referee systems. Heated debate is rare, and thus academic stimulation from published or presented controversies is quite limited.

By the late 1980s, 33 of Japan's 501 colleges and universities had doctoral programs in sociology. The major institutions with such programs included the public universities of Hokkaido, Tohoku, Tokyo, Hitotsubashi, Tokyo Metropolitan, Nagoya, Kyoto, Osaka, Kobe, and Kyushu, and the private universities of Waseda, Keio, and Hosei. Also during the period, there were about 700 graduate students studying sociology, 490 of whom were doctoral candidates (see Committee on Education for Sociology 1988). In general, two years are required to obtain a master's degree and an additional three years to finish coursework for doctoral programs. A much higher percentage of those who complete a master's program at public universities go on to a doctoral program than do those at private universities. Most who obtain master's degrees do not complete their doctoral theses within three years. Rather, after finishing their doctoral coursework, they obtain teaching or research positions and often complete their doctorates at a later stage in their careers. Forty-one persons obtained doctoral degrees in sociology during the period 1977–1986. During this time, there was a surplus of sociology graduates versus the number of teaching positions available. In the late 1980s, of those teaching at Japanese universities who obtained their doctoral degrees from Japanese universities, twenty-four sociology professors held doctoral degrees in literature, about thirty held doctoral degrees in sociology, and several others held doctoral degrees in related fields. Compared to other social sciences such as economics, the number of professors who obtained their doctoral degrees in sociology from foreign educational institutions is limited. For instance, only about twenty Ph.D. holders who taught at Japanese colleges and universities in the late 1980s obtained their degrees in the United States, although their numbers have been increasing.

GLOBALIZATION STAGE (1990s AND BEYOND)

As a whole, Japan has recently seen substantial movement toward globalization (or internationalization), and Japanese sociology is no exception. However, before exploring the implications of globalization for Japanese sociology, it is appropriate to look at the changes that took place in the 1990s.

In 1997, out of 586 universities and colleges in Japan, 65 had master's programs and 47 had doctoral programs in sociology. In 1997, more than forty-five Ph.D. degree holders (obtained from non-Japanese universities) in sociology were teaching at Japanese universities and colleges. Also, more than sixty-five doctoral degree holders (obtained from Japanese universities) in sociology were teaching at various universities and colleges in Japan. It should be noted that these numbers are not at all significant compared to those in the West.

The Japan Sociological Society polled its members in 1998 for their preferred subdisciplines and research fields. They identified (1) general sociological theories, 15.6 percent; (2) sociology of the family, 15.2 percent; (3) communications and information, 15.1 percent; (4) social thought and the history of sociology, 14.7 percent; (5) social welfare, social security, and medical sociology, 14.3 percent; (6) culture, religion, and morality, 13.6 percent; (7) social psychology and social attitudes, 13.1 percent; (8) rural sociology and community studies, 12.2 percent; and (9) cross-national and foreign area studies, 11.3 percent. Note that the first three choices, including communications and information, are effectively tied for first place. We can see, compared with the figures from 1988, that management, industry and labor, social pathology and social problems, and the sociology of education all dropped out of the top nine fields, having been replaced by communications and information, social psychology and social attitudes, and cross-national and foreign area studies. That communications and information made such a showing is particularly notable and reflects the changes in information infrastructure (the Internet, among others) that are in large part responsible for globalization.

During the period 1989–1996, publication of articles originating from the various subdisciplines broke down as follows: (1) social thought and the history of sociology, 8.7 percent; (2) the sociology of education, 7.2 percent; (3) sociology of the family, 6.6 percent; (4) general sociological theories, 6.6 percent; (5) urban sociology, 6.2 percent; (6) communications and information, 5.6 percent;

(7) culture, religion, and morality, 5.6 percent; (8) management, industry, and labor, 5.4 percent; and (9) rural sociology and community studies, 5.2 percent. These figures were derived from lists of publications in the *Japanese Sociological Review*. Notice that, compared to the publications listed from 1984 through 1988, social pathology and social problems and social welfare, social security, and medical sociology dropped from the top nine while communications and information, and culture, religion, and morality appeared. That communications and information did not rise to the top here is not surprising, as publishing traditionally carries with it varying degrees of time lag.

As in the United States and western Europe, aging has become a serious issue; in 1998, about 16 percent (i.e., 20 million persons) of the Japanese population was over 65. Therefore, more and more sociologists are involving themselves in this field and contributing to national and local policy formation.

In Japan, there are no major university research centers such as the Institute for Social Research at the University of Michigan or the National Opinion Research Center at the University of Chicago, nor does Japan have any colleges or universities that are especially well known for their sociology departments or programs. However, there are some survey sections within organizations (e.g., research institutions, government organizations, the press and mass media) that have carried out major surveys since the 1950s, some on a continuing basis, including surveys targeting trends in social attitudes. Among others, these include the Japanese Prime Minister's Office; the Institute of Statistical Mathematics, as mentioned above; the Mainichi Press; Jiji Press; and Nippon Hoso Kyokai, a Japanese broadcasting organization (see Sasaki and Suzuki 1991). Each one of these endeavors is independent and generally does not provide its data to outside researchers, making secondary analysis of such data a difficult task in Japan. This hinders those in graduate training, as they often lack access to such data for thesis work.

On occasion, surveys, including cross-national studies, are funded by agencies such as the Japanese Ministry of Education, the Japan Society for the Promotion of Science, and the Toyota Foundation. On a regional or local basis, funds are sometimes provided by prefectural or municipal governments. Findings from some of these studies have had significant impacts on policy formation at the local and national levels. Most research grants for sociologists, for both domestic and international (cross-national and foreign area) studies, are provided by the Japanese Ministry of Education. The Japan Society for the Promotion of Science provides grants for foreign area and cross-national research projects, for joint research conferences and seminars, as well as travel allowances for visiting scholars.

Japanese sociology does not enjoy a wide-ranging reputation in the rest of the world. This has been attributed to lack of integration and coordination, as well as a descriptive rather than analytic focus. Indeed, Japanese sociology has relied substantially on foreign influence, particularly that which is *au courant*, and has not excelled in the development of original theoretical or empirical ideas, rather having a stronger commitment to theory interpretation than theory testing and theory building. With the exception of a few research groups doing cross-national studies, in general Japan's sociologists have had limited contact with researchers in other nations. This can be attributed primarily to the language barrier and lack of experience in exchanging ideas. Despite these apparent shortcomings, sociology is comparatively popular in Japan, where there is a strong demand for books on the subject. As a consequence, Japanese scholars often feel little need to publish in foreign languages.

Broader publication—in English, in particular—will be essential to the mutual exchange of ideas and research results now and in the future, as well as to enhancing the reputation of Japanese sociology. To encourage scholars, the Japan Sociological Society has published the *Bibliography of Japanese Sociological Literature in Western Languages* in 1982, 1986, 1990 and 1994 (see Japan Sociological Society 1982, 1986, 1990, 1994). Research Committee meetings of the ISA have been held from time to time in Japan, and occasionally Japanese sociologists have served as ISA Executive Committee members. Japanese sociologists will need to host, and invite their foreign colleagues to, more international meetings and conventions, as occurred in 1991 when the 30th World Congress of the International Institute of Sociology (IIS; founded in 1893 and the oldest sociological association in the world) met in Kobe, Japan, for the first time in the history of Japanese sociology. In 1998, a Japanese sociologist became the first IIS president ever elected from Asia.

Japan's globalization has fostered opportunities for sociologists through studies of Japanese communities with growing contingents of foreign workers and studies of communities with Japanese administrative and managerial personnel in foreign countries. In these instances, Japanese sociologists are able to examine social, ethnic, and multicultural issues stemming from these circumstances. In this respect, Japanese sociologists are able to contribute to policy implications for community formation in the globalizing environment. Recently, too, the number of Japanese sociologists conducting cross-national and/or foreign area studies has increased (see, e.g., Japan Sociological Society 1997). In 1992, the Japan Sociological Society began publishing the *International Journal of Japanese Sociology*, its only English-language journal and one of the few in Japan to employ a referee system.

Although the language barrier also hinders foreign scholars from coming to Japan to study, again, this is changing, and more and more such activity has been observed recently. In 1998, there were about 340 Japanese sociologists who reported internationally comparative sociological research or foreign area studies as one of their top three research interests, although many of these were not officially collaborating with other nations' researchers. Of these, the most popular areas of emphasis were ethnicity and nationalism; rural sociology; community studies; social history and ethnology; and sociology of the family, culture, and religion. The popular locations for study were Asia, the United States, and western Europe.

There are also less pragmatic reasons why Japanese sociology has not enjoyed a wide-ranging reputation in the rest of the world. Despite a history now spanning more than a century, Japanese sociologists have made few efforts to integrate their considerable empirical research findings with sociological theory. Japanese sociology has had a long history of importing "fashionable" theories from the West. Japanese sociologists with theoretical orientations have tended more toward social philosophy, with its emphasis on pure theory. Japanese sociological researchers, on the other hand, have tended to limit their studies to specific features of Japanese society, often without sufficient hypothesizing aimed at investigating the underlying social structures and processes thus potentially revealed. This lack of originality, this reluctance to carry through to a complete synthesis of empirical findings and structures and processes, has contributed to Japanese sociology's limited outside appeal. The foreign influences inevitable in and attendant with globalization will no doubt encourage Japanese sociology to finally integrate empirical research results with original thought about Japanese social structures and processes, toward the construction of viable theories of Japanese society as well as society as a globalizing whole. This suggests the need for greater theoretical and methodological training—in the context of their synthesis—in Japanese graduate sociology programs.

While Japanese sociology commands a significant amount of useful empirical data, it is nonetheless disparate. The establishment of a central data archive would be imperative for secondary analysis, graduate training, and empirical study in general. As data gathering becomes increasingly expensive, the usefulness and need for such archives will become even more important.

In conclusion, in terms of the disciplines within Japanese sociology that will take on greater and greater importance, cross-national and foreign area studies will certainly become more popular. Along these same lines, time-trend studies will increase in popularity, in an effort to discover what changes and what does not change in society. Major research funding is likely to continue to center around empirical studies, both within Japan and comparatively with other nations. Finally, whereas Japanese sociologists traditionally have seldom been consulted in the industrial, business, and governmental environments, this will change as Japanese sociologists acquire greater methodological skills and theoretical knowledge, as well as empirical research experience and findings. And, from a strictly practical standpoint, growth in the number of teaching positions in sociology has not kept pace with the growth of sociology's popularity in Japan, nor with the output of sociologists from Japanese and foreign graduate schools, forcing many to seek teaching positions in junior high and high schools or nonacademic positions in government, research institutes, and industry. This diffusion of the discipline outside the traditional academic environment will no doubt impact Japanese society as a whole, and it could well become a two-way medium for idea exchange.

While Japanese sociology will no doubt become more pervasive and useful in Japanese society, it will nevertheless take time. The same is true outside of Japan, as Japanese sociology becomes more internationalized and demonstrates greater tangible offerings to the sociological community in the rest of the world. Certainly more and better cross-national and foreign area studies will emerge, as this is an area where Japanese sociology has already made particularly beneficial contributions. In turn, in the tradition of comparativists such as Machiavelli, Marx, Weber, and Durkheim, who sought to construct universalized theory based on comparison, Japanese sociology may finally be able to make its mark. Given the methodological expertise demonstrated by Japanese sociology, these efforts may ultimately assist Japanese sociologists in positing social theories of use to the rest of the world's sociological community. Of course, such a vision requires that Japanese sociology strive to broaden its horizons internationally—for Japanese sociologists to recognize that they must cooperate and join with the global sociological community to achieve these objectives.

REFERENCES

Committee on Education for Sociology, Japan Sociological Society 1988 "Research Report on a Survey of the Problem of Post-Graduate Students." *Japanese Sociological Review* 39:314–334. (In Japanese)

Fukutake, Tadashi. 1967 *Japanese Rural Society*. Ithaca, N. Y.: Cornell University Press.

Halmos, P., ed. 1966 "Japanese Sociological Studies." *Sociological Review Monograph*, No. 10. Keele, U.K.: University of Keele.

Hayashi, Chikio. 1998 "The Quantitative Study of National Character: Interchronological and International Perspectives." In Masamichi Sasaki, ed. *Values and Attitudes Across Nations and Time*. Leiden: Brill.

Japan Sociological Society 1982, 1986, 1990, 1994 *Bibliography of Japanese Sociological Literature in Western Languages*. Tokyo: Japan Sociological Society.

—— 1997 "Japanese Sociology: Its Continuous Efforts for the Development of Inter-Societal and Inter-Cultural Knowledge and Information." *International Journal of Japanese Sociology* 6:1–162.

Koyano, Shogo 1976 "Sociological Studies in Japan: Prewar, Postwar and Contemporary Stages." *Current Sociology* 24(1):1–196.

Morioka, Kiyomi 1975. *Religion in Changing Japanese Society*. Tokyo: University of Tokyo Press.

Nagai, Michio 1971 *Higher Education in Japan*. Tokyo: University of Tokyo Press.

Odaka, Kunio 1950 "Japanese Sociology: Past and Present." *Social Forces* 28:400–409.

Odaka, Kunio 1975 *Toward Industrial Democracy*. Cambridge, Mass.: Harvard University Press.

Sasaki, Masamichi, and Tatsuzo Suzuki 1991 "Trend and Cross-National Study of General Social Attitudes." *International Journal of Comparative Sociology* 31:193–205.

Shoji, Kokichi 1996 "Institutionalization of Sociology in Japan." In Su-Hoon Lee, ed., *Sociology in East Asia And Its Struggle for Creativity*, Proceedings of the ISA Regional Conference for Eastern Asia, Seoul, Korea, November 22–23, 1996. Madrid, Spain: International Sociological Association, pp. 33–43.

Takata, Yasuma 1922 *Shakaigaku Gairon*. Tokyo: Iwanami Shoten. (In Japanese) Translated into English and published in 1989 as *Principles of Sociology*. Tokyo: University of Tokyo Press/New York: Columbia University Press.

Tominaga, Ken'ichi 1969 "Trends Analysis of Social Stratification and Social Mobility in Contemporary Japan." *The Developing Economy* 7(4):471–498.

Watanuki, Joji 1976 *Politics in Postwar Japanese Society*. Tokyo: University of Tokyo Press.

Yasuda, Saburo 1964 "A Methodological Inquiry into Social Mobility." *American Sociological Review* 29:16–23.

MASAMICHI SASAKI

JUVENILE DELINQUENCY AND JUVENILE CRIME

The twentieth century ended amid an explosion of violence in all corners of the globe. However, juvenile violence has probably been center stage more in the United States than in any other industrialized nation. As the 1998–1999 school year ended, we had just experienced a massive display of violence by two young men at a high school in Littleton, Colorado. Both seniors, these two killed twelve of their fellow students and a teacher before turning their assault weapons on themselves. The decade of the 1990s ended in the way it started, with a public grown increasingly apprehensive of its youth. This increase was not limited to the United States; it has been detected in many other countries—England, Spain, France, Italy, and Germany, among others.

It is important to note here also that this anxiety and disquiet induced by youth is not limited to the modern area. Citing the code of Hammurabi, which dates back to 2270 B.C., Regoli and Hewitt (1991) note that "legal prohibitions of specific behavior by juveniles is centuries old" (p.6). Still, they note that in the Middle Ages "little distinction was made between juveniles and adults who were older than 12" (p. 6). In a comment made in 1959, but which is still relevant to those who are intrigued, frightened, or perplexed by the "heedlessness" of today's youth, Teeters and Matza (1959) stated: "It has always been popular for each generation to believe its children were the worst" (p. 200). We are also reminded by them that "Sir Walter Scott in 1812 deplored the insecurity of Edinburgh where groups of boys between the ages of 12 and 20 years scoured streets and knocked down and robbed all who came in their way" (p. 200). Apropos of delinquency, such remarks underscore the relativity of opinions and the brevity of trends. They also remind us that while juvenile delinquency is a relatively new legal category that subjects children to court authority, it is also a timeless and ubiquitous part of life. Regoli and Hewitt (1991) suggest that postcolonial American delinquency was similar to that found in Spain in the seventeenth century and in Britain in the eighteenth century. By the mid-1800s, teenage gangs were frequently found in the larger cities in the United States. "The habits of hanging out on street corners, verbally abusing pedestrians, and even pelting citizens with rocks and snowballs were among the least threatening of their behaviors. More serious were the violent gangs of juvenile robbers" (p. 7). They also note that "the latter decades of the nineteenth century saw a number of changes in the public's understanding of the causes of delinquency and [of] appropriate approaches to its control and treatment . . . the

common law distinction between child and adult had changed for purposes of criminal prosecution" (p. 7). The change contrasted greatly with practices in the early part of the century: In America, children as young as three years of age could be brought before the court, while in England a girl of seven was hanged. In Massachusetts, in 1871, 1,354 boys and 109 girls were handled by the courts. Reform schools proliferated during the nineteenth century and were criticized for failing to prevent the apparent increase in delinquency. Reformers—called "child savers"—believed that juveniles required noninstitutional treatment that would reflect the natural family (Platt 1969). This legal and humanitarian concern for the well-being of children led to the establishment of the first juvenile court in Cook County, Illinois, in 1899. By 1925, all but two states had followed the Illinois example. Thus, it seems fair to say that the idea of "juvenile delinquency" is a relatively modern construction, a notion shared by writers such as Gibbons and Krohn (1991), Empey (1982), and Short (1990). The data on delinquency, however, are not limited to the legal status of "juvenile delinquent," because sociologists are just as interested in unofficial as in official acts of delinquency. More specifically, it is well known that much of the behavior defined by law as delinquent is not detected, not reported, or not acted on by legal agents.

Moreover, different jurisdictions have different legal definitions of delinquency. In the United States, for example, while the statistics defining delinquency are similar in the fifty states and District of Columbia with respect to age and type of offense requiring juvenile court control, there are more differences than similarities. First, laws vary in terms of the age limits of juvenile court jurisdiction: thiry-one states and the District of Columbia set seventeen years of age as the upper age limit, twelve states set sixteen years, six set fifteen years, and one sets eighteen years. Moreover, in many states the delinquency laws empower the juvenile court to remand youths under the maximum juvenile court age to criminal courts. In such cases, the offenses are often those for which adults may be arrested: index crimes (see below). In addition, some states have passed legislation that requires certain cases, such as homicides, or youths charged with other serious offenses, to be dealt with by the criminal court. In these cases, the juvenile acquires the legal status of criminal. Finally, it should be noted that all U.S. state jurisdictions contain an omnibus clause or provision, referred to as status offenses, that awards the court jurisdiction over youths who have behaved in ways not forbidden by criminal law. While these provisions differ from state to state, it is of interest to note a few examples of these conditions. They include engaging in indecent behavior, knowingly associating with vicious or immoral persons, growing up in idleness or crime, being incorrigible, and wandering the streets at night. Critics note that these behavior categories are so vaguely defined that nearly all youngsters could be subjected to them.

Such different procedures and practices caution us against making easy generalizations both within and between countries when examining official data. Indeed, other shortcomings likewise warn against drawing firm conclusions when unofficial data are examined. Although methodological shortcomings may exist in the study of delinquency, there may be advantages in utilizing all the data of delinquency (official and unofficial) in pursuit of its understanding. Thus, the study of official delinquency data places much of the focus on the actions of official agents of control (the police, the courts), while the study of unofficial—including hidden—delinquency often allows students to examine the processes leading to the behavior. Moreover, as Vold and Bernard (1986) and others have noted, unofficial data, especially self-reports, frequently focus on trivial offenses, while the more serious offenses often do not appear in self-reports but are limited to reports of official agencies.

In sum, our concern here will be to discuss those topics of delinquency that are of the greatest concern: the frequency, severity, and duration of delinquency. Attention will also be devoted to trends. In the following section, the focus is on the extent of delinquent behavior.

EXTENT OF AND TRENDS IN DELINQUENCY

In addressing the matter of the extent of delinquency, it is important to note the admonitions of Empey and Erickson (1966), Hirschi (1969), Matza (1964), and others that delinquency is not only transient but also widespread. Many juveniles engage in delinquency only occasionally, but some engage in it more frequently. Gibbons and Krohn (1991) call delinquency "a sometime thing," while Matza (1964) describes the process of drifting into and out of delinquency. Moreover, it should be kept in mind that some acts of delinquency are serious acts of criminality and others are petty, trivial acts. As we consider both official and unofficial data on juvenile delinquency and juvenile crime, we will encounter these various clarifying factors.

Official Delinquency. The most serious crimes committed by youths and adults in the United States are referred to as index crimes; data on them are compiled by the FBI, based on reports of law enforcement agencies throughout the country. These index crimes, reported in Uniform Crime Reports, are divided into two major types: violent (homicide, rape, robbery, and aggravated assault) and property (burglary, larceny-theft, motor-vehicle theft, and arson). Nonindex offenses are those considered to be relatively petty, such as liquor law violations, disorderly conduct, sex offenses (except forcible rape, prostitution, and commercialized vice), and drug-abuse violations.

Readers are warned that various official reports of offenses should be treated with caution since there are inconsistencies in reporting processes. While great efforts are being made by federal agencies to improve reporting mechanisms, it is well to remember that the number of reporting agencies fluctuates regularly, and the number of cases involving persons with unknown characteristics (such as age, sex, and race) also fluctuates (sometimes by as much as 30 percent). In 1987, the U.S. Department of Justice reported that there were 10,747 contributing agencies covering approximately 84 percent of the U.S. population. This number appears to be higher than the number reporting in 1996. Moreover, the news media have occasionally reported that some jurisdictions have been accused of irregular reporting habits in apparent efforts to demonstrate improved efficiency.

Index crimes are reported annually by the FBI; sometimes estimates for the United States as a whole are derived from a sample of reporting agencies. In 1996 the FBI's Uniform Crime Reports (UCR) indicated that of all arrests in the United States in 1996, approximately 18.9 percent were of youths under eighteen years of age; 18.7 percent of the arrests for violent crimes in 1996 (murder, manslaughter, forcible rape, robbery, and aggravated assault) were of persons under eighteen years of age. For property crimes, youth under 18 years of age comprised 35 percent of offenders. For index crimes as a whole, the FBI Uniform Crime Report indicates that 30.9 percent were contributed by persons under 18 years of age in 1996. (U.S. Department of Justice 1996).

Perhaps it is surprising to learn that over the last quarter of the twentieth century, contrary to fears, delinquency has declined. According to the *Sourcebook of Criminal Justice Statistics* for 1997, in 1971 arrests of youths under age 18 comprised 45 percent of all arrests for index crimes reported to the UCR program, 23 percent of violent crime arrests, and 51 percent of property crime arrests. In 1996 persons under age 18 comprised 31 percent of index offense arrests, 18.8 percent of violent crime arrests, and just 35 percent of property crime arrests. Thus juvenile crime, as measured by arrest data, has decreased driving this quarter-century.

During this same period, a number of criminologists have argued that fluctuations in the delinquency crime rates are due to changes in the age structure of the population. The UCR presented data showing a substantial decrease in delinquency arrests between 1979 and 1988, following an increase in such arrests between 1965 and 1977. Kratcoski and Kratcoski (1990) suggest that this dramatic change could be due to "movement of the 'baby boom' segment of the population through the high offense years during the mid-70s followed by a reduction in the under 18 population since 1978" (p. 15). Gibbons and Krohn (1991) also suggest that such trends may be due to shifts within the delinquency-eligible youth group. Further, the latter authors suggest that such trends may reflect increased or decreased concern about youthful misconduct.

There was apparently a substantial increase in juvenile crime between 1988 and 1991, followed by another dip in rates after 1991. Blumstein (1995) suggests that a projected increase in the proportion of the population in the high-crime-rate age group will probably lead to higher crime rates by early in the twenty-first century. Still, the FBI UCR for 1996 suggests that there has been a strong decline in juvenile delinquency in recent years.

Juvenile Crimes of Violence. In contrast to this apparent improvement, an examination of murder and non-negligent manslaughter shows a different picture. While the national murder rate in 1996 (7.4 per 100,000 inhabitants) was down 11 percent since 1987, the proportion of murder and non-negligent manslaughter offenders who were under age 18 increased from 9.7 percent in 1987 to a whopping 15.2 percent in 1996, an increase of about 50 percent. Editors of the *Sourcebook of Criminal Justice Statistics* for 1997, and other analysts such as Conklin (1998), Gall and Lucas (1996), and Blumstein (1995) have commented on the increasingly serious nature of crimes by juveniles.

Conklin (1998), reviewing data presented by Fox (1995) and by Blumstein (1995), says that between 1985 and 1993 "the homicide arrest rate for people twenty-five and over declined by 20 percent, while the rate for eighteen-to-twenty-four year olds increased by 65 percent and the rate for fourteen-to-seventeen year olds rose by 165 percent" (p. 124). An increasing number of researchers fear that there will be a continued surge in violent crimes by the under-eighteen population.

This increase in youth violence in the United States has apparently been mirrored in a number of industrialized nations. In a study of juvenile violence in Great Britain, Oliver (1997) states that the number of violent juveniles increased by 34 percent between 1987 and 1993, an increase he attributes to the growth of inequality and family stress in Britain. In France, Bui-Trong (1996) has written about the recent escalation of juvenile violence, noting especially the increased severity of scale. This author, noting a decline in family morals, predicts that this problem can be expected to worsen. During the 1980s even Japan experienced an increased rate of juvenile delinquency, which some observers attributed to the stress of competition for academic success (Conklin 1998).

School violence has been most dramatic, of course, in the United States and is a focus of great national attention. Presenting data gathered by the National School Safety Center, the *Boston Globe* reported in 1999 that since the 1992–1993 school year there had been 248 deaths from violent acts in schools. ("U.S. Police Chiefs" 1999). Although many school shootings and other violent acts have not resulted in deaths, they *have* resulted in injuries and heightened fears. The 248 school deaths between 1992 and 1999 included cases of multiple deaths in seventeen states. Many of these incidents involved the use of assault weapons. This increase in school violence has elicited a spate of explanations, including weakened parental supervisions, ostracism by schoolmates, bullying and its effects (Farrington 1993), the easy availability of guns, and the poor examples set by our leaders. The search for the causes of violence among the young will, no doubt, have to be accompanied by an examination of violence in the adult population as well. Certainly the official data on violence show that the population over age eighteen is also engaged in a substantial amount of violent behavior.

Cohort Study. One of the first longitudinal studies of delinquency was conducted by Wolfgang and colleagues (1972) in Philadelphia. They traced the police contacts of all boys born in 1945 who lived in the city between their tenth and eighteenth birthdays. One of their aims with this cohort of 9,945 was to trace the volume and frequency of delinquent careers up to age eighteen. They found that 35 percent of these boys (3,475) were involved with the police at least once between their tenth and eighteenth birthdays. Of these 3,475 boys with police contacts, 54 percent were repeaters. The total number of delinquent events (offenses) for the 3,475 delinquent boys amounted to 10,214 through age seventeen. It is clear that the number of offenses far outnumbers the number of offenders in the cohort. One must note, then, that longitudinal (i.e., over an extended period) studies of delinquents yield data with important differences from those obtained when cross-sectional (i.e., single point in time) studies of persons arrested are conducted. Examples of other longitudinal studies include the Provo Study, the Cambridge-Somerville Study, the Vocational High Study, and, in Britain, the National Survey of Health and Development.

Self-Reports: Offender Reports and Victim Reports. Official reports of crime and juvenile delinquency have been criticized for years because they are widely believed to underreport the volume of offenses. Moreover, many scholars, especially those with a conflict perspective, believed that official reports underreported middle-class crime and delinquency. In an effort to detect "hidden" delinquency, sociologists developed a technique designed to produce a more accurate picture. The technique used by Short and Nye

(1958) in a number of studies of hidden delinquency consisted of having juveniles in a school or other population complete questionnaires on the extent to which they engaged in law-violating behavior. They found that delinquency was widespread throughout the juvenile population. Subsequently, Williams and Gold (1972) and Empey and Erickson (1966) embarked on studies employing self-reports. These writers found that 88 percent and 92 percent of their study groups, respectively, had engaged in violations. Hindelang and colleagues (1981) present a similar volume of law-violating behavior in their Seattle study. Criticisms of the self-report method followed many of these studies, centering on issues of respondent misrepresentation, respondent recall, and inappropriateness of study groups. A major criticism (by Nettler, 1984, for example) was that self-reports elicited admission of only minor or petty infractions for the most part. Because of its obvious utility, the self-report technique has been greatly improved in recent years, becoming an important, if not the dominant, method of measurement in studies focusing on the extent and cause of delinquency.

A number of students of delinquency agree that many of the improvements in self-report studies have been contributed by Elliott and Ageton (1980): (Bartol and Bartol 1989; Gibbons and Krohn 1991; Regoli and Hewitt 1991). Elliott and colleagues have created a panel design that employs periodic interviews instead of questionnaires. The study, called the National Youth Survey (NYS), utilized a 5-year panel design with a national probability sample of 1,726 adolescents aged eleven to seventeen and covered more than a hundred cities and towns in the United States. In contrast with earlier self-report studies, Elliott asked his respondents about a full range of activities designed to get at serious as well as minor infractions. In addition, his respondents were asked whether they were caught when engaging in delinquent and criminal activities.

Another attempt to ascertain the volume of delinquency in the United States is represented by the National Crime Survey (NCS). This survey, an effort to determine the extent of victimization in the population of the United States, was begun in 1973 after an initial study sponsored by the President's Commission on Law Enforcement and Administration of Justice in 1967. Interviews are conducted semiannually by the Bureau of the

Census with a large national sample of 60,000 households (Bartol and Bartol 1989). The survey was intended to supplement the Uniform Crime Report data and measures the extent to which persons and households are victims of rape, robbery, assault, burglary, motor-vehicle theft, and larceny. Binder and colleagues (1988) note that one of the major findings of the 1967 study of victims by the President's Commission was the revelation that "actual crime was several times that indicated in the UCR" (p. 34). In the current victim interviews, if the respondent has been victimized, he or she will be asked questions about both self-characteristics and characteristics of the offender. Binder and colleagues warn about the difficulties of age discrimination by a victim under stress and suggest that this method cannot be relied on too heavily in measuring delinquency.

Nevertheless, Laub (1983) has found NCS data useful in addressing the issue of the extent and change in delinquency volume. In an analysis of NCS data obtained between 1973 and 1980, he found no increase in juvenile crime over those years. He further noted that data from the National Center for Juvenile Justice supported this conclusion. It would seem, then, that the NCS data, UCR data, and juvenile court data have been fairly consistent regarding the volume of delinquency. While self-report data indicate that violations are consistently widespread in American society, it is important to note that these reports involve primarily minor violations. Indeed, to the extent that almost everyone engages in minor violations, it may make sense to focus mainly on serious violations. Nettler (1984), noting that self-report studies find a large number of minor infractions, suggests that such violators are best described as lying on a continuum rather than as being "delinquent" or "nondelinquent." The cohort studies of Wolfgang and colleagues (1972) show that only a small proportion of the study groups were involved in serious violations.

FACTORS RELATED TO DELINQUENCY

Age and Gender. In the United States, Britain, and other European countries where delinquency is recognized and studied, there is general agreement that it peaks in adolescence (ages fifteen to eighteen) rather than in childhood. (This is not to

say, however, that delinquency is not on the increase among younger children. A study by the FBI in 1990 found that the arrest rate for rape among males aged twelve years and under had more than tripled since 1970 (Parmley 1991). The UCR shows that 18.9 percent of all arrests in 1996 involved persons under eighteen years of age. This age group accounted for 31 percent of arrests for index crimes, however. Male arrests peaked at age eighteen in 1996 and female arrests at age sixteen. Earlier studies and analyses by Empey and Erickson (1966), Wolfgang (1983), and Braithwaite (1981) are consistent with this picture, with age sixteen being the peak year for juvenile misconduct.

It has consistently been found that males outnumber females in UCR arrest data. Thus in both 1988 and 1989, among those under eighteen, males were arrested four times more frequently than females. For those under eighteen in both 1988 and 1989, males outnumbered females 8-to-1 in arrests for violent offenses. In 1990, Short pointed out that the gender ratio had declined substantially. Between 1980 and 1989 violent crime increased by 4.5 percent for males under eighteen and by 16.5 for comparable females. Considering all arrests for males and females under eighteen, males showed a *decline* of 8.5 percent between 1980 and 1989, while females showed an *increase* of 1.1 percent for the same period.

Indeed, as reported in the Uniform Crime Reports, female delinquency, compared to male delinquency, has been rising steadily since the 1960s. In 1960, there was a 6-to-1 ratio of male to female juvenile arrests. The ratio has declined steadily since then and in 1987 was 3.4-to-1. In 1996 the FBI data revealed a male-female ratio of just 3-to-1.

Moreover, the ratio for violent offenses has dropped from 8-to-1 in 1989 to 5.5-to-1 in 1996, according to FBI data reported in the *Sourcebook* for 1997. Finally, it must be mentioned that FBI data reveal a decline of 15.3 percent in the murder and manslaughter charges for males under age 18 between 1995 and 1996 but reveal no change for females in that age group. It should also be noted, however, that for those aged thirteen to nineteen, 92 percent of murder offenders in the UCR in 1996 were males and only 8 percent were females. Also sobering is the fact that 29 percent of all murder victims in the under-eighteen age group were females in 1996.

Perhaps Hagan's power-control theory is relevant here. Hagan and colleagues (1987) suggest that child-rearing styles in the home (the power structure) are determined in part by the nature of the parents' occupations. The two main types of child-rearing styles are patriarchal and egalitarian. The two types of occupations are command (managerial) and obey (subject to others' authority). In the egalitarian family where both parents work in authority positions, the mother's authority means she has a substantial amount of power in the home, and this leads to daughters having increased freedom relative to sons. This situation is reversed in patriarchal families, which are controlled by fathers and sons. In the egalitarian family, the adolescent daughter has an increased willingness to take risks. Hagan assumes that willingness to take risks is a fundamental requirement for delinquency. He also predicts that female delinquency will be high in mother-only homes. The absence of a father leaves a void in male power, allowing the adolescent girl more freedom, greater risk taking, and an increased tendency to deviate. The theory needs to be tested more fully.

With respect to self-reports, the reports of the NYS suggest that gender was not strongly related to involvement in delinquent acts. Although males admitted to more infractions than did females, the differences were much less pronounced than those seen in the UCR. Again, it should be emphasized that efforts are being made to enhance the ability of self-report studies to elicit information on more serious infractions.

Race and Class. UCRs for 1985 and 1989 present data on arrests by race in the United States. Among persons arrested and under eighteen years of age, the number of blacks increased from 23 percent in 1985 to 28 percent in 1989, but declined slightly to 27 percent in 1996; the number of whites decreased from 75 percent in 1985 to 70 percent in 1989 and remained at 70 percent in 1996. The remainder of the arrests were categorized by race as Native Americans, Asians, Pacific Islanders, and Alaskan Natives. The proportion of violent index crimes committed by blacks under age eighteen increased from 52 percent in 1985 to 53 percent in 1989 but declined to 47 percent in 1996. The comparable proportions for whites were

46 percent, 45 percent, and 50 percent. Also of interest are the figures for murder and non-negligent homicide. Here, blacks under eighteen accounted for 51 percent, 61 percent, and 57.5 percent of these crimes in 1985, 1989, and 1996, respectively; whites accounted for 48 percent, 37 percent, and 39 percent during the same three years. This slight decline in the proportion of murder and non-negligent manslaughter accounted for by blacks under eighteen is accompanied by the fact that the number of such crimes increased by 25 percent for blacks and by 18 percent for whites under eighteen during the period between 1988 and 1996. This is a decided improvement over the period between 1985 and 1989, when there was a doubling of the number of such crimes for blacks and a 30 percent increase for whites under age eighteen. Aggravated assaults also increased substantially during this period for both whites and blacks under eighteen, increasing for blacks by 25 percent and for whites by 50 percent during the eight-year period ending in 1996. Forcible rapes by blacks under age eighteen showed an improving picture, declining by 12 percent between 1988 and 1996. On the other hand, forcible rapes by whites under age eighteen increased by 15 percent during this time frame. Overall, despite short-term improvements in the murder rate for those over age 18, there is no denying the fact that serious and violent crime increased among those under age 18 between 1988 and 1996. This violence has been growing among white youth as well as black youth.

William J. Wilson (1996) and other sociologists have long suggested that social class and inequality are important concepts in the attempt to understand the increase in violence among blacks. The move of businesses to suburban locations with consequent loss of job opportunities, educational inequities, and the growth of female-headed households have combined to limit the coping resources in inner cities where most black youth reside. Wilson suggests that the resulting stresses hit lower-class blacks particularly hard and contribute to the high rates of violent crime in these areas. In addition, Bernard (1990) suggests that anger is reinforced by the social isolation that comes from being confined to communities that have high rates of crime. Policies by local departments of justice with respect to police routines, bail practices, and sentencing as these apply to blacks have also come in for considerable comment (Teele 1970b). In 1999 news media reported that the U.S. Department of Justice was investigating allegations of racial profiling—targeting minorities for an unjustified amount of police attention—by police in New Jersey, Michigan, and Florida ("US Police Chiefs" 1999).

While there are those who say that the nation has not paid enough attention to the causes of black teenage violence, an increasing number of analysts say that we have paid a lot of, perhaps too much, attention to black violence in urban areas while ignoring the rising tides of violence by white youths in suburban and rural areas. While income inequality has seemed appropriate to an explanation of urban violence, it may appear less relevant in the analysis of violent behavior in our affluent suburban areas. This situation brings to mind Toby's (1967) classic work on delinquency in affluent society as well as Durkheim's (1951) discussion of rising expectations in his theory of anomie.

In Toby's case, he was trying to account for the rise in theft crimes in a variety of countries. Although he took special note of adolescent crime in industrial countries such as Japan, Sweden, and Great Britain, he also included developing countries such as Nigeria and India in his analysis. Toby suggests that the resentment of poverty is likely to be greater among the relatively poor in an affluent society than among the poor in a poor society. He suggests, however, that envy is at work not only in the more affluent societies, such as Japan, but also in countries with rising standards of living, such as India and Nigeria. Moreover, he suggests that not only adults but also the young are subject to rising expectations. It may be that relative deprivation can account for at least some of the rise in youth violence in the United States. Toby's work also suggests that the presence of such envy could be heightened where the inhibiting effect of schools or families or jobs is missing in either affluent or developing societies. Here Toby's thesis greatly resembles control theory. The increase in single-parent families among blacks, persisting educational inequalities for blacks, and chronic employment problems for black youth may tend to lessen social controls and could be factors in the greater increase in violence among them.

Toby's discussion of "resentment" seems somehow applicable to the school violence discussed earlier, but with a different twist. There seems present in these cases something besides income inequality—especially since in many of these instances the youth are from apparently affluent families, as in the Littleton, Colorado, case. While assault weapons were certainly available and parents seemed loathe to invade their sons' privacy, there was at school, perhaps, a certain intolerable inequality that alienated the assaulters and pulled them into circles of violent schemes, feelings, and, eventually, behavior. Most of the youths—usually white—felt rejected by their peers, their teachers, their parents, or their girlfriends. In Colorado they resented the athletes and those who were generally in the "in crowd." There apparently were feelings of jealousy toward those who did not invite them to join their group. While such feelings, involving relative deprivation, seem to be far removed from considerations of wealth, they fit the phenomenon of inequality. This form of inequality is probably anathema to children who are deprived of neither their basic needs nor considerable luxuries.

Social class has been by far the most controversial of all the factors studied in connection with juvenile delinquency. The argument seems to revolve around both method and theory. Some argue about the impact of social class, others debate the measurement of social class, and a few argue about both. Several writers have attempted to review the research on class and delinquency or crime. Tittle and colleagues (1978), noting that nearly every sociological theory of crime or delinquency had class as a key factor, reviewed thirty-five such studies. Their findings suggested that the class and crime–delinquency connection might be a "myth" because the relationship could not be confirmed empirically.

Subsequently, Braithwaite (1981) criticized Tittle's study not only as incomplete but also as having come to the wrong conclusions. He reviewed fifty-three studies that used official data and forty-seven studies that used self-reports in the study of delinquency. Braithwaite forcefully argues that the class–crime relationship is no myth. Of the studies using official records, Braithwaite found that the vast majority (forty-four) showed lower-class juveniles to have substantially higher offense rates than middle-class juveniles. Of the forty-seven self-report studies, he concluded that eighteen found lower-class juveniles reported higher levels of delinquent behavior, seven reported qualified support for the relationship, and twenty-two found no relationship. Braithwaite is critical of self-report studies when (1) they do not closely examine the lowest group on the social-class continuum (the lumpen proletariat) and (2) they do not include serious offenses and chronicity in their data gathering. While the argument may continue, Braithwaite and others seem to be less critical of self-report studies when they correct these apparent shortcomings.

Apparently the work of Elliott and Ageton (1980) has done much to defuse this issue. They found, for example, that the relationship between class and self-reported delinquency is totally a consequence of the difference between the lowest class group and the rest of the sample, with no difference between the working and middle classes. Writers such as Messner and Krohn (1990), Hagan and Palloni (1990), and Colvin and Pauly (1983) have apparently profited from these debates; their work shows an inclination to refine the "objective" measure of class, using insights from conflict theory as they formulate explanations of delinquency. Indeed, it is safe to say that social class is alive and well, but it is more broadly conceptualized now; many of the new theories include patterns of child rearing, job experiences, and family structure that are incorporated into the framework of a more radical neo-Marxist perspective. The effort by sociologists in the United States and in other countries to better understand juvenile delinquency appears to have entered a new and more urgent phase.

REFERENCES

Bartol, Curt, and Anne Bartol 1989 *Juvenile Delinquency: A System Approach.* Englewood Cliffs, N.J.: Prentice-Hall.

Bernard, Thomas J. 1990 "Angry Aggression Among the 'Truly Disadvantaged.'" *Criminology* 28:73–96.

Binder, Arnold, Gilbert Geis, and Bruce Dickson 1988 *Juvenile Delinquency: Historical, Cultural, Legal Perspectives.* New York: Macmillan.

Blumstein, Alfred 1995 "Violence by Young People: Why the Deadly Nexus?" *National Institute of Justice Journal* (August):2–9.

Braithwaite, John 1981 "The Myth of Social Class and Criminality Reconsidered." *American Sociological Review* 46:36–57.

Bui-Trong, Lucienne 1996 "Resurgence de la Violense en France." *Futuribles* 206:5–20.

Colvin, Mark, and John Pauly 1983 "A Critique of Criminology: Toward an Integrated Structural-Marxist Theory of Delinquency Production." *American Journal of Sociology* 89:513–551.

Conklin, John E. 1998 *Criminology*, 6th ed. Boston: Allyn and Bacon.

Durkheim, Emile 1951 *Suicide*, trans. J.A. Spaulding and George Simpson. New York: Free Press.

Elliott, Delbert, and Suzanne Ageton 1980 "Reconciling Race and Class Differences in Self-Reported and Official Estimates of Delinquency." *American Sociological Review* 45:95–110.

Empey, Lamar T. 1982 *American Delinquency*, rev. ed. Homewood, Ill.: Dorsey.

——, and Maynard Erickson 1966 "Hidden Delinquency and Social Status." *Social Forces* 44:546–554.

Farrington, David 1993 "Understanding and Preventing Bullying." In Michale Tonry, ed., *Crime and Justice: A Review of Research*, vol. 17. Chicago: University of Chicago Press.

Fox, James A. 1995 "A Disturbing Trend in Youth Crime." *Boston Globe* (June 1):9.

Gall, Timothy, and Daniel Lucas (eds.) 1996 *Statistics on Weapons and Violence*. New York: Gale Research.

Gibbons, Don, and Marvin Krohn 1991 *Delinquent Behavior*, 5th ed. Englewood Cliffs, N.J.: Prentice-Hall.

Hagan, John, and Alberto Palloni 1990 "The Social Reproduction of a Criminal Class in Working-Class London, Circa 1950–1980." *American Journal of Sociology* 96:265–299.

——, J. Simpson, and A. R. Gillis 1987 "Glass in the Household: A Power-Control Theory of Gender and Delinquency." *American Journal of Sociology* 92:788–816

Hindelang, M. J., Travis Hirschi, and Joseph Weis 1981 *Measuring Delinquency*. Beverly Hills, Calif.: Sage.

Hirschi, Travis 1969 *Causes of Delinquency*. Berkeley: University of California Press.

Kratcoski, Peter, and Lucille Dunn Kratcoski 1990 *Juvenile Delinquency*, 3rd ed. Englewood Cliffs, N.J.: Prentice-Hall.

Laub, John 1983 "Trends in Serious Juvenile Crime." *Criminal Justice and Behavior*. 10:485–506.

Matza, David 1964 *Delinquency and Drift*. New York: Wiley.

Messner, Steven, and Marvin Krohn 1990 "Class, Compliance Structures, and Delinquency: Assessing Integrated Structural-Marxist Theory." *American Journal of Sociology* 96:300–328.

Nettler, Gwynn 1984 *Explaining Crime*, 3rd ed. New York: McGraw-Hill.

Oliver, James 1997 *Juvenile Violence in a Winner–Loser Culture: Socio-Economic and Familial Origins of the Rise of Violence Against the Person*. London: Free Association Books.

Parmley, Suzette 1991 "Children Who Molest Children." *Boston Globe* (January 14):25.

Platt, Anthony M. 1969 *The Child Savers*. Chicago: University of Chicago Press.

Regoli, Robert, and John Hewitt 1991 *Delinquency in Society*. New York: McGraw-Hill.

Short, James. 1990 *Delinquency in Society*. Englewood Cliffs, N.J.: Prentice-Hall.

——, and F. Ivan Nye 1958 "Extent of Unrecorded Juvenile Delinquency: Tentative Conclusions." *Journal of Criminal Law, Criminology and Police Science* 49:296–302.

Sourcebook of Criminal Justice Statistics 1997 Washington, D.C.: U.S. Government Printing Office.

Teele, James E. 1970 "Social Pathology and Stress." In Sol Levine and Norman Scotch, eds., *Social Stress*. Chicago: Aldine Press.

Teeters, Negley, and David Matza 1959 "The Extent of Delinquency in the United States." *Journal of Negro Education* 28:200–213.

Tittle, Charles R., Wayne Villemez, and Douglas Smith 1978 "The Myth of Social Class and Criminality: An Empirical Assessment of the Empirical Evidence." *American Sociological Review* 43:643–656.

Toby, Jackson 1967 "Affluence and Adolescent Crime." *1967 President's Commission on Law Enforcement and Administration of Justice: Task Force Report on Juvenile Delinquency and Youth Crime*. Washington, D.C.: U.S. Government Printing Office. Reprinted in James E. Teele, ed., *Juvenile Delinquency: A Reader*. Itasca, Ill.: Peacock, 1970.

U.S. Department of Justice 1997 *Crime in the United States, 1996*. Washington, D.C.: U.S. Government Printing Office.

"U.S. Police Chiefs Examining Race, Traffic Stops" 1999 *Boston Globe* (April 10):11.

Vold, George, and Thomas Bernard 1986 *Theoretical Criminology*. New York: Oxford University Press.

Williams, Jay, and Martin Gold 1972 "From Delinquent Behavior to Official Delinquency." *Social Problems* 20:209–229.

Wilmot, Peter 1966 *Adolescent Boys in East London*. London: Routledge and Kegan Paul.

Wilson, William J. 1996 *When Work Disappears*. New York: Random House.

Wolfgang, Marvin 1983 "Delinquency in Two Birth Cohorts." *American Behavioral Scientist* 27:75–86

——, Robert Figlio, and Thorsten Sellin 1972 *Delinquency in a Birth Cohort*. Chicago: University of Chicago Press.

JAMES E. TEELE

JUVENILE DELINQUENCY, THEORIES OF

The topic of juvenile delinquency is a fertile area for construction of sociological theory. Three major sociological traditions, including structural functionalism, symbolic interactionism, and conflict theory, contribute to the explanation of delinquency. Much of the work in this area seeks to explain why officially recorded delinquency is concentrated in the lower class, or in what is today more often called the underclass. This entry considers the most prominent theories of delinquency under the theoretical rubrics noted above.

STRUCTURAL FUNCTIONALISM AND DELINQUENCY

Structural-functional theories regard delinquent behavior as the consequence of strains or breakdowns in the social processes that produce conformity. These theories focus on institutions, such as the family and school, that socialize individuals to conform their behavior to values of the surrounding society and on the ways in which these institutions can fail in this task. Wide agreement or consensus is assumed about which behaviors are valued and disvalued in society. The question structural-functional theories try to answer is: Why do many individuals during their adolescence behave in ways that challenge this consensus? That is, why do many adolescents violate behavioral norms that nearly all of us are assumed to hold in common?

Anomie Theory. The roots of functional theory are found in Durkheim's notion of *anomie* ([1897] 1951). To Durkheim, this term meant an absence of social regulation, or normlessness. Merton (1938, 1957) revived the concept to describe the consequences of a faulty relationship between goals and the legitimate means of attaining them. Merton emphasized two features of social and cultural structure: culturally defined goals (such as monetary success) and the acceptable means (such as education) to their achievement. Merton argued that in our society success goals are widely shared, while the means of or opportunities for attaining them are not.

Merton's theory is used to explain not only why individual adolescents become delinquents but also why some classes are characterized by more delinquency than others. Since members of the lower- or underclass are assumed to be most affected by the disparity between the goals and the means of attaining success, this class is expected to have a higher rate of delinquent behavior. Merton outlined a number of ways individuals adapt when faced with inadequate means of attaining their goals. Among these, *innovation* revolves substituting illegitimate for legitimate means to goal attainment; it is the resort to this adaptation that is thought to account for much theft among adolescents from the underclass.

Subcultural Theory. Group-based adaptations to the failure to attain success goals involve the *delinquent subculture.* Cohen (1955) suggests that children of the underclass, and potential members of a delinquent subculture, first experience a failure to achieve when they enter school. When assessed against a "middle-class measuring rod," these children are often found lacking. A result is a growing sense of "status frustration." Underclass children are simply not prepared by their earliest experiences to satisfy middle-class expectations. The delinquent subculture therefore emerges as an alternative set of criteria or values that underclass adolescents can meet.

Cohen argues that these subcultural values represent a complete repudiation of middle-class standards: the delinquent subculture expresses contempt for a middle-class lifestyle by making its opposite a criterion of prestige. The result, according to Cohen, is a delinquent subculture that is "nonutilitarian, malicious, and negativistic"— an inversion, of middle-class values. Yet this is only one possible type of subcultural reaction to the frustration of failure. As we see next, many subcultural responses are elaborated in the theoretical tradition of structural functionalism.

Differential Opportunity Theory. Cloward and Ohlin (1960) argue that to understand the different forms that delinquent and ultimately criminal behavior can take, we must consider the different types of illegitimate opportunities available to those who seek a way out of the underclass and where these opportunities lead. Different types of community settings produce different subcultural responses. Cloward and Ohlin suggest that three types of responses predominate, each one leading to its own respective subculture: a stable criminal subculture, a conflict subculture, and a retreatist subculture.

The *stable criminal subculture* offers, as its name suggests, the most promising (albeit still illegitimate) prospects for upward economic mobility. According to Cloward and Ohlin, this subculture can emerge only when there is some coordination between those in legitimate and in illegitimate roles—for example, between politicians or police and the underworld. One pictures the old-style political machine, with protection provided for preferred types of illegal enterprise. Only in such circumstances can stable patterns be established, allowing opportunities for advancement from adolescent to adult levels of the criminal underworld. When legitimate and illegitimate opportunity structures are linked in this way, the streets become safe for crime, and reliable upward-mobility routes can emerge for aspiring criminals.

Violence and conflict, on the other hand, disrupt both legitimate and illegitimate enterprise. When both types of enterprises coexist, violence is restrained. However, in the "disorganized slum," where these spheres of activity are not linked, violence can reign uncontrolled. Cloward and Ohlin see these types of communities as producing a *conflict subculture.* A result of this disorganization is the prevalence of adolescent street gangs and their violent activities, making the streets unsafe for more profitable crime.

The *retreatist subculture* includes adolescents who fail in their efforts in both the legitimate and illegitimate opportunity structures. These "double failures" are destined for drug abuse and other forms of escape.

Cloward and Ohlin's theory played a role in encouraging the Kennedy and Johnson administrations of the 1960s to organize the American War on Poverty, which attempted to open up legitimate opportunities for youth and minorities in the underclass (see Moynihan 1969). However, another important variant of structural-functional theory argued that the most important cause of delinquency was not a strain between goals and means but rather a relative absence of goals, values, commitments, and other sources of social control.

Social Disorganization Theory. The earliest North American efforts to explain crime and delinquency in terms of social control focused on the absence of social bonds at the community level. Entire neighborhoods were seen as being socially disorganized, as lacking the cohesion and constraint that could prevent crime and delinquency. This work began in the late 1920s, when Clifford Shaw and Henry McKay (1931, 1942) sought to identify areas of Chicago that were experiencing social disorganization. They explored the process that characterized these communities. What they found were indications of what they assumed to be social disorganization— truancy, tuberculosis, infant mortality, mental disorder, economic dependency, adult crime, and juvenile delinquency. In Chicago, the rates of these conditions were highest in the slums near the city center; they diminished in areas farther away from the center. Since these problems were assumed to be contrary to the shared values of area inhabitants, they were taken as indications that these areas were unable to realize the goals of their residents. In other words, they were taken as indicators of social disorganization.

Shaw and McKay also attempted to determine the sorts of community characteristics that were correlated with delinquency so that they could infer from these characteristics what the central components of social disorganization were and how they caused delinquency. Three types of correlates were identified: the economic status of the community, the mobility of community residents, and community heterogeneity. The implication was that poverty, high residential mobility, and ethnic heterogeneity led to a weakening of social bonds or controls and, in turn, to high rates of delinquency. All of this was being said of the neighborhoods Shaw and McKay studied; it was left to later theories to spell out the meaning of weakened neighborhood bonds or controls for individuals.

Control Theory. At the level of individuals, to have neither goals nor means is to be uncommitted and thus uncontrolled. Hirschi (1969) has argued that the absence of control is all that really is required to explain much delinquent behavior. There are other types of controls (besides *commitment* to conformity) that may also operate: *involvement* in school and other activities; *attachments* to friends, school, and family; and belief in various types of values and principles. Hirschi argues that delinquent behavior is inversely related to the presence of these controls. Alternatively, as these controls accumulate, so too does conformity. According to control theory, the more committed, attached, involved, and believing individuals are, the greater is their bond to society. Again, Hirschi's point is that no special strain between goals and means is necessarily required to produce delinquent behavior; all that is required is the elimination of the constraining elements of the social bond.

In each of the theories that we have considered thus far, values or beliefs play some role in causing delinquency. It is argued that the presence of success goals or values without the means to obtain them can produce deviant behavior, as can the absence of these goals or values in the first place. It is an emphasis on these values, and the role of the school and family in transmitting them, that ties the structural-functional theories together.

SYMBOLIC INTERACTIONISM AND DELINQUENCY

Symbolic-interactionist theories of delinquency are concerned less with values than with the way in which social meanings and definitions can help produce delinquent behavior. The assumption, of course, is that these meanings and definitions, these symbolic variations, affect behavior. Early versions of symbolic-interactionist theories focused on how adolescents acquired these meanings and definitions from others, especially peers; more recently, theorists have focused on the role of official control agencies, especially the police and courts, in imposing these meanings and definitions on adolescents. The significance of this difference in focus will become apparent as we consider the development of the symbolic-interactionist tradition.

Differential Association Theory. Edwin Sutherland (1939, 1949) anticipated an emphasis of the symbolic-interactionist perspective with his early use of the concept of *differential association*. This concept referred not only to associations among people but also, and perhaps even more important, to associations among ideas. Sutherland's purpose was to develop a general theory that explained delinquency as well as adult criminality. He argued that people violate laws only when they define such behavior as acceptable and that there is an explicit connection between people and their ideas (that is, definitions). So, for example, delinquent behavior is "learned in association with those who define such behavior favorably and in isolation from those who define it unfavorably," and this behavior occurs when "the weight of the favorable definitions exceeds the weight of the unfavorable definitions."

Although Sutherland intended his theory to be general and explicitly to include the explanation of delinquency, his best-known applications of the theory were in his famous studies of professional theft and white-collar crime. Nonetheless, Sutherland's emphasis on white-collar illegality was important for the study of delinquency because it stressed the ubiquity of criminality, and, as we see next, it helped to mitigate delinquency theory's preoccupation with underclass delinquency.

Neutralization Theory. While most of the theories we have considered to this point portray the delinquent, especially the underclass delinquent, as markedly different from "the rest of us," Sykes and Matza (1957, 1961) follow Sutherland's lead in suggesting that the similarities actually outnumber the differences. Their argument is based in part on the observation that underclass delinquents, like white-collar criminals, usually exhibit guilt or shame when detected violating the law.

Sutherland had argued that individuals become white-collar criminals because they are immersed with their colleagues in a business ideology that defines illegal business practices as acceptable. Sykes and Matza (1957) argue that the delinquent, much like the white-collar criminal, drifts into a deviant lifestyle through a subtle process of justification. "We call these justifications of deviant behavior techniques of neutralization," they write, "and we believe these techniques make up a crucial component of Sutherland's definitions favorable to the violation of law" (p. 667).

Sykes and Matza list four of these *neutralization techniques:* denial of responsibility (e.g., blaming a bad upbringing), denial of injury (e.g., claiming that the victim deserved it), condemnation of

the condemners (e.g., calling their condemnation discriminatory), and an appeal to higher loyalties (e.g., citing loyalty to friends or family as the cause of the behavior). Sykes and Matza's point is that delinquency in the underclass, as elsewhere, is facilitated by this kind of thinking. A question lingered, however: Why are these delinquencies of the underclass more frequently made the subjects of official condemnation?

Labeling Theory. Franklin Tannenbaum (1938) anticipated a theoretical answer to this question. He pointed out that some aspects of juvenile delinquency—the play, adventure, and excitement—are a normal part of teenage street life and that, later in their lives, many nostalgically identify these activities as an important part of their adolescence. But others see such activities as a nuisance or as threatening, so they summon the police.

Tannenbaum's concern is that police intervention begins a process of change in the way the individuals and their activities are perceived. He suggests that there is a gradual shift from defining specific acts as evil to defining the individual as evil. Tannenbaum sees the individual's first contact with the law as the most consequential, referring to this event as a "dramatization of evil" that separates the child from his or her peers for specialized treatment. Tannenbaum goes on to argue that this dramatization may play a greater role in creating the criminal than any other experience. The problem is that individuals thus singled out may begin to think of themselves as the type of people who do such things—that is, as delinquents. From this viewpoint, efforts to reform or deter delinquent behavior create more problems than they solve. "The way out, "Tannenbaum argues, "is through a refusal to dramatize the evil." He implies that the less said or done about delinquency the better.

Sociologists have expanded Tannenbaum's perspective into what is often called a labeling, or societal reactions, theory of delinquency and other kinds of deviance. For example, Lemert (1967) suggests the terms *primary deviance* and *secondary deviance* to distinguish between acts that occur before and after the societal response. Acts of primary deviance are those that precede a social or legal response. They may be incidental or even random aspects of an individual's general behavior. The important point is that these initial acts have little impact on the individual's self-concept. Acts of secondary deviance, on the other hand, follow the societal response and involve a transformation of the individual's self-concept, "altering the psychic structure, producing specialized organization of social roles and self-regarding attitudes." From this point on, the individual takes on more and more of the "deviant" aspects of his or her new role (Becker 1963, 1964). The societal response has, from this viewpoint, succeeded only in confirming the individual in a deviant role; for example, by potentially making adolescent delinquents into adult criminals through the punitive reactions of the police, courts, and others.

In the end, symbolic interactionists do not insist that all or even most delinquent behavior is caused by officially imposed labels. Being labeled delinquent is thought, rather, to create special problems for the adolescents involved, often increasing the likelihood that this and related kinds of delinquent behavior will be repeated. The point is that not only the actor but also reactors participate in creating the meanings and definitions that generate-delinquency. The symbolic interactionists note that poor are more likely than the rich to get caught up in this process. This point is further emphasized in conflict theories.

CONFLICT THEORY AND DELINQUENCY

The most distinctive features of conflict theories include attention to the role of power relations and economic contradictions in generating delinquency and reactions to it. For example, conflict theories have focused on the role of dominant societal groups in imposing legal labels on members of subordinate societal groups (Turk 1969). The fact that subcultural groups typically are also subordinate groups ties this work to earlier theoretical traditions discussed above.

An Early Group-Conflict Theory. George Vold (1958) was the first North American sociologist to write explicitly about a group-conflict theory of delinquency. He began with the assumption that criminality involves both human behavior (acts) and the judgments or definitions (laws, customs, or mores) of others as to whether specific behaviors are appropriate and acceptable or inappropriate and disreputable. Of the two components, Vold regarded judgments and definitions as more significant. His salient interest was in how groups impose their value judgments by defining the behaviors of others as illegal.

Vold regarded delinquency as a "minority group" behavior. For example, he argues that "the juvenile gang . . . is nearly always a 'minority group', out of sympathy with and in more or less direct opposition to the rules and regulations of the dominant majority, that is, the established world of adult values and powers" (p. 211). In this struggle, the police are seen as representing and defending the values of the adult world, while the gang seeks the symbolic and material advantages not permitted it under the adult code. At root, Vold argues, the problem is one of intergenerational value conflict, with adults prevailing through their control of the legal process.

A Theory of Legal Bureaucracy. According to this viewpoint, determining which groups in society will experience more delinquency than others may be largely a matter of deciding which laws will be enforced. Chambliss and Seidman (1971) observe that in modern, complex, stratified societies such as our own, we assign the task of resolving such issues to bureaucratically structured agencies such as the police. The result is to mobilize what might be called the primary principle of legal bureaucracy. According to this principle, laws will be enforced when enforcement serves the interests of social control agencies and their officials; and laws will not be enforced when enforcement is likely to cause organizational strain. In other words, the primary principle of legal bureaucracy involves maximizing organizational gains while minimizing organizational strains.

Chambliss and Seidman conclude that a consequence of this principle is to bring into operation a "rule of law," whereby "discretion at every level . . . will be so exercised as to bring mainly those who are politically powerless (e.g., the poor) into the purview of the law" (p. 268). Theoretical work of this kind coincided with important research on the policing of juveniles (e.g., Reiss 1971). According to the conflict theorists, poor minority youth appear disproportionately in our delinquency statistics more because of class bias and police and court prejudice than because of actual behavioral differences.

Recent Structural Theories. Some recent theories of delinquency have combined conflict theory's structural focus on power relations with etiological questions about sources of delinquent behavior as well as reactions to it. Thus Spitzer (1975) begins the formulation of a Marxian theory of delinquency (and deviance more generally) with the observation, "We must not only ask why specific members of the underclass are selected for official processing, but also why they behave as they do" (p. 640).

One effort to answer behavioral questions with insights from conflict theory is an "integrated structural-Marxist theory" proposed by Colvin and Pauly (1983). This theory integrates elements of control theory and Marxian theory. The theory is comprehensive, and only some of its most striking features can be outlined here. These features include a Marxian focus on working-class parents' experiences of coerciveness in the workplace, which Colvin and Pauly suggest lead to coerciveness in parenting, including parental violence toward children. In turn, Colvin and Pauly argue that such children are more likely to be placed in coercive control structures at school and to enter into alliances with alienated peers. All of these experiences make delinquent behavior more likely, including the violent and instrumental kinds of delinquent behavior that may be precursors of adult criminality.

Power-control theory is another recent structural formulation (Hagan 1989) that attempts to explain large and persistent gender differences in delinquency by taking power relations into account. Power relations in the family are the starting point of this theory. The cornerstone of the theory is the observation that, especially in more patriarchal families, mothers more than fathers are involved in controlling daughters more than sons. A result of this intensified mother–daughter relationship is that daughters become less inclined to take what they perceive as greater risks of involvement in delinquency. Police and other processing agencies act on stereotypes that extend these gender differences in officially recorded delinquency. Power-control theory generally predicts that in more patriarchal families, sons will be subjected to less maternal control, develop stronger preferences for risk taking, be more delinquent, and more often be officially labeled for being so. More recently, this theory has been elaborated to emphasize that in less patriarchal families mothers may become more involved in the control of their

sons and this can reduce their sons' involvement in risk taking and delinquency (McCarthy and Hagan 1999).

These structural approaches illustrate an ongoing trend toward theoretical integration in this tradition and elsewhere in the study of delinquency (e.g., Hagan and McCarthy 1997; Messner et al. 1989; Sampson and Wilson 1995; Tittle 1995). These integrations involve theories that are often thought to be in apposition if not opposition to one another. Yet the trend toward integration in delinquency theory has been apparent for more than a decade, and it seems likely to continue.

TROUBLESOME QUESTIONS

Despite the richness of sociological theories of delinquency and the emerging sense of convergence among previously competing theoretical traditions, there is a new awareness that delinquency theories remain incomplete in their capacity to explain and sometimes even address basic micro- and macro-level questions. For example, a classic issue that persists despite its recognition is the question of why most delinquents discontinue their delinquency before or during their transition to adulthood. We know that most delinquents "age out" of deliquency, but we have not adequately explained why this happens (Hirschi and Gottfredson 1983). Our theories are much more attentive to why young people become delinquent than to why they stop being so.

A seemingly related but only more recently apparent question involves the decline since the early 1990s in the violent forms of delinquency, such as robbery and homicide, that we are best able to measure and monitor statistically over time. This trend is strikingly apparent as we head toward the millennium (see, e.g., Blumstein and Rosenfeld 1998). None of the prominent sociological theories of delinquency predicted or can easily account for this decline in violent delinquency. Again, our theories have focused more on increases in delinquency than on its decline. Sociological theories of delinquency confront new as well as continuing questions in the new century.

(SEE ALSO: *Crime, Theories of; Criminology; Juvenile Delinquency and Juvenile Crime*)

REFERENCES

Becker, Howard 1963 *Outsiders: Studies in the Sociology of Deviance*. New York: Free Press.

——1964 *The Other Side: Perspectives on Deviance*. New York: Free Press.

Blumstein, Alfred, and Richard Rosenfeld 1998 "Explaining Recent Trends in U.S. Homicide Rates." *Journal of Criminal Law and Criminology* 88:1175–1216.

Chambliss, William, and Robert Seidman 1971 *Law, Order and Power*. Reading, Mass.: Addison-Wesley.

Cloward, Richard, and Lloyd Ohlin 1960 *Delinquency and Opportunity: A Theory of Delinquent Gangs*. New York: Free Press.

Cohen, Albert 1955 *Delinquent Boys*. New York: Free Press.

Colvin, Mark, and John Pauly 1983 "A Critique of Criminology: Toward an Integrated Structural-Marxist Theory of Delinquency Production." *American Journal of Sociology* 89(3):512–552.

Durkheim, Émile (1897) 1951 *Suicide*, trans. John Spaulding and George Simpson. New York: Free Press.

Hagan, John 1989 *Structural Criminology*. New Brunswick, N.J.: Rutgers University Press.

——, and Bill McCarthy 1997 *Mean Streets: Youth Crime and Homelessness*. New York: Cambridge University Press.

Hirschi, Travis 1969 *Causes of Delinquency*. Berkeley: University of California Press.

——, and Michael Gottfredson 1983 "Age and the Explanation of Crime." *American Journal of Sociology* 89:552–584.

Lemert, Edwin 1967 *Human Deviance, Social Problems and Social Control*. Englewood Cliffs, N.J.: Prentice-Hall.

McCarthy, Bill, and John Hagan 1999 "In the Company of Women: An Elaboration and Further Test of a Power-Control Theory of Gender and Delinquency." *Criminology* in press.

Merton, Robert 1938 "Social Structure and Anomie." *American Sociological Review* 3:672–682.

——1957 *Social Theory and Social Structure*. New York: Free Press.

Messner, Steven, Marvin Krohn, and Allen Liska 1989 *Theoretical Integration in the Study of Deviance and Crime: Problems and Prospects*. Albany: State University of New York Press.

Moynihan, Daniel P. 1969 *Maximum Feasible Misunderstanding.*, New York: Free Press.

Reiss, Albert 1971 *The Police and the Public*. New Haven, Conn.: Yale University Press.

Sampson, Robert, and William Julius Wilson 1995 "Toward a Theory of Race, Crime, and Urban Inequality." In John Hagan and Ruth Peterson, eds., *Crime and Inequality*. Stanford, Calif.: Stanford University Press.

Shaw, Clifford, and Henry McKay 1931 *Social Factors in Juvenile Delinquency*. Washington, D.C.: National Commission of Law Observance and Enforcement.

——1942 *Juvenile Delinquency and Urban Areas*. Chicago: University of Chicago Press.

Spitzer, Steven 1975 "Toward a Marxian Theory of Deviance." *Social Problems* 22:638–651.

Sutherland, Edwin 1939 *Principles of Criminology*. Philadelphia: Lippincott.

——1949 *White Collar Crime*. New York: Dryden.

Sykes, Gresham, and David Matza 1957 "Techniques of Neutralization: A Theory of Delinquency." *American Sociological Review* 26:664–670.

——1961 "Juvenile Delinquency and Subterranean Values." *American Sociological Review* 26:712–719.

Tannenbaum, Frank 1938 *Crime and the Community*. Boston: Ginn.

Tittle, Charles 1995 *Control Balance: Toward a General Theory of Deviance*. Boulder, Colo.: Westview Press.

Turk, Austin 1969 *Criminality and the Legal Order*. Chicago: Rand McNally.

Vold, George 1958 *Theoretical Criminology*. New York: Oxford University Press.

JOHN HAGAN

K

KINSHIP SYSTEMS AND FAMILY TYPES

Kinship systems are mechanisms that link conjugal families (and individuals not living in families) in ways that affect the integration of the general social structure and enhance the ability of the society to reproduce itself in an orderly fashion. Kinship performs these social functions in two ways. First, through relationships defined by blood ties and marriage, kinship systems make possible ready-made *contemporaneous networks* of social ties sustained during the lifetimes of related persons and, second, they enable the *temporal continuity* of identifiable family connections over generations, despite the limited lifespan of a family's members. Variations in norms governing the structure of contemporaneous networks and the modes of temporal continuity compose the basis for the typologies of kinship systems described in this article.

In conceptualizing connections between kinship systems and family types, social scientists have applied either of two approaches. Some have developed typologies from historical analyses (and evolutionary schemes) that depict the transition of Western societies from ancient or medieval origins to modern civilizations. Other social scientists construct typologies that cut across diverse historical periods. Each historical era then constitutes a unique medium in which the structural typologies are expressed.

MODERNITY, FAMILY PATTERNS, AND KINSHIP SYSTEMS

There are at least three ways to develop historical typologies related to kinship and family. One way is to hypothesize a linear historical progression, which includes a family type existing at the beginning point in time, a particular historical process that will act upon the family and kinship structures (e.g., urbanization or industrialization), and a logical outcome at the end of the process. A second approach builds upon the above approach by positing a transitional family type that emerges during the historical process and gives way in the final stages of the process to another family type. A third approach, which includes devising a family type based upon a configuration of attributes peculiar to a particular historical era (e.g., the Victorian family, the American colonial family), implies that any historical era represents a unique convergence of diverse factors.

Bipolar Typologies. By and large, sociologists have drawn a connection between kinship and family on the basis of a distinction between traditionalism and modernity. Generally, this distinction draws upon Henry Maine's ([1861] 1963) depiction of the transformation of social relations in early societies. Maine argued that social relations changed from those based on ascriptive status (deriving from birth) to relations created and sustained through voluntary contractual arrangements. Maine's theory has evoked a series of typologies that, in large measure, refine the status–contract distinction. For instance, an ideal type developed by Ferdinand Toennies ([1887] 1957) has provided a backdrop for later typologies. The Toennies typology itself refers to a shift from *Gemeinschaft* (community) as a form of social organization based upon an existential will (*Wessenwille*), which is suited to feudalism and peasant society, to *Gesellschaft* (society) as a social form based upon rational will (*Kurwille*), which fits an urban environment under modem capitalism. Contemporary family typologies, in building upon Toennies's conceptual scheme, portray a weakening of kinship obligations and constraints.

One position, rooted in George P. Murdock's (1949) analysis of cross-cultural archives, has resulted in the main sequence theory of social change in kinship structure (Naroll 1970). Main sequence theory pertains to the way differential gender contributions to production of material resources affects the use of kindred as human resources/ property. This theory holds that basic changes in kinship are initiated by a shift in the relative importance of men and women to the economic life of the society. First, there is a modification in the economic division of labor by gender. (For example, in hoe cultures, women tend to do the farming; when plows are introduced, men become the farmers.) Second, the shift in sexual division of labor generates a change in married couples' choices of residence, the major alternatives being near the husband's relatives (patrilocal), the wife's (matrilocal), or anywhere the couple desires (neolocal). (Plow cultures tend toward patrilocal residence.) Third, the change in choice of residential site affects the line of descent and inheritance favored in the kinship system: the husband's side (patrilineal), the wife's (matrilineal), or both sides (bilateral). (In line with the shift in residence, plow cultures show a greater inclination toward patrilinearity than do hoe cultures.) Fourth, the transfer to lineage affiliation generates a change in kinship terminology, particularly in ways that show tribal or clan membership, or, in modern societies, the dissolution of larger kinship structures. As applied to the emergence of modernity, main sequence theory predicts a continual emancipation from kinship constraints. An increase in the proportion of women in the labor force will produce a trend toward neolocal residence, which in turn will lead to increased emphasis upon bilaterality, weakening sibling ties and obligations to both

sides of the extended family, and in the long run to changes in kin terminology and identity [e.g., voluntarism in choice of surnames as an indicator of preference as to line(s) of descent].

In a variation of main sequence theory, urban sociologists such as Wirth (1956) and Burgess and associates (1963) wrote on the effects of transferring the economic base of societies from the land to urban centers. The theme of their work is to be found in the German proverb "Stadt Luft macht frei" ("city air makes one free"). For example, Burgess and associates described a progression from what they named the institutional family to the companionship family. In this conceptualization, the institutional family, embedded in a larger kinship group, is characterized by patriarchy, clearly defined division of household labor by sex, and high fertility. Its unity is derived mainly from external constraints—social mores, religious authority, fixity in location, position in the social structure, and the value of familism (i.e., values giving priority to the collective welfare of the family over that of individual members). Burgess and associates regarded the institutional family as an adaptation to relatively immobile, rural, agricultural societies and believed its way of life was fixed over time. By way of contrast, urban society, which is characterized by mobility, anonymity, and change, makes inoperative the social control mechanisms developed to maintain stable, rural societies. With the withering of these external controls on rural family life, Burgess, Locke, and Thomes proposed that the companionship family is bound together by internal forces—mutual affection, egalitarianism, a sense of belonging, common interests—and affords freedom from the demands of traditional family and kinship ties.

Unlike the urban sociologists, structural functionalists such as Talcott Parsons (1954) place considerable emphasis on the interaction of subsystems in the larger social system. In part, structural functionalists are concerned with economic and kinship factors in structuring nuclear family relationships. Parsons described American kinship as "a 'conjugal' system in that it is made up exclusively of interlocking conjugal families" (1954, p. 180) and is multilineal (i.e., bilateral) in descent. Parsons associates kinship solidarity with unilineal descent, that is, with a "structural bias in favor of solidarity with the ascendant and descendant families in any one line of descent" (1954, p. 184). The absence of such bias in the American descent system, Parsons suggests, is in large measure responsible for "the structural isolation of the individual conjugal family" (i.e., its autonomy).

The importance Parsons attributes to unilinearity as a factor in facilitating strong dependence upon kin ties is exemplified by his highlighting two exceptions to the structural isolation of the conjugal family in America—the upper-class elements, whose status depends on the continuity of their patrilineages' solidarity, and the lower-class elements, in which there is "a strong tendency to instability of marriage and a 'mother-centered' type of family structure" (Parsons 1954, p. 185). However, Parsons regards the urban middle class as characterizing "the focal American type of kinship." Since in the middle class the residence of the conjugal family typically is neolocal, and the conjugal family is economically independent of "the family of orientation of either spouse," the role of the conjugal family in U.S. society can be, for theoretical purposes, understood as master of its own destiny, rid of the impediments of extended-family ties.

In reaction to those sociologists who see modernity as inimical to bonds of kinship, other social scientists (e.g., Adams 1968; Firth et al. 1969; Litwak 1985; Mogey 1976; Shanas et al. 1968; Sussman 1959) turn their attention to the attenuated functions of kinship in contemporary society. Just as Goode (1963) notes a "fit" between the needs of modern capitalist society for a socially and geographically highly mobile population and the flexibility of the isolated conjugal family system, the revisionists indicate a similar fit between the existence of a highly mobile population and the presence of kin who give emergency aid and social support to relatives. The revisionists shift our attention away from constraints imposed by kinship loyalties and obligations and direct it instead to sources of services, goods, and emotional support that cannot readily be supplied by bureaucracies, markets, or other agencies. In his typology, Litwak (1960a, 1960b) distinguishes the isolated nuclear family (without kiship resources) from the traditional extended family (implying a hierarchy of authority), on the one hand, and from the modified extended family (which consists of a network of related but autonomous nuclear families), on the other. Although the revisionists have not destroyed the foundation of the bipolar family typologies, they do focus on a previously neglected area of analysis.

Three-Stage Typologies. Some modernization typologies introduce a third, transitional stage between traditional and modern kinship and family structures. These typologies accept the position that initially there is an emancipation from traditional kinship constraints and obligations, but they also propose that at some point new values of modernity emerge to fill the vacuum left by the dissipation of the old kinship constraints. For example, building on the work of LePlay, Zimmerman and Frampton (1966) offer a scheme of transformation in which families change from a patriarchal form to a stem-family structure and thence to an unstable family type. Zimmerman and Frampton begin with the premise that each social organization derives its "essential character" from a triad of "imperishable institutions"—family, religion, and property. However, in their view, "familism is necessary in all complete social organization to a degree more imperative than the need for property" (1966, p. 14; 1947). Zimmerman and Frampton regard the patriarchal family as the most familistic form. The patriarchal type is rooted in idealistic religious values and is characterized by a common household of a patriarch and his married sons and their families, wherein the property is held in the name of the "house," with the father as trustee. They identify the patriarchal form as having been prevalent among agriculturists in the Orient, in rural Russia, and among Slavonic peasants.

With urbanization and industrialization, however, the unstable family becomes predominant. Zimmerman and Frampton associate the unstable family with materialism and individualism and the resulting atomization of social life. Individuals are "freed from all obligations toward their parents and relatives" (1966, p. 15), and the identity of each conjugal family as a social unit ends with the death of the parents and the dispersal of the children.

The stem family represents a transitional state between the patriarchal and unstable forms. The stem family extends branches into urban centers while retaining its roots in the ancestral lands. As a result, the stem family provides a balance between the security of the traditional influences and resources of the "house" and the freedom and resources of the cities. (However, historical researchers yield less idyllic descriptions of the stem family than the Zimmerman and Frampton portrait. See Berkner 1972.)

A less romantic depiction of a transitional family type is drawn by Lawrence Stone (1975) in his typology of the English family's movement from feudalism to modernity. Stone posits the existence of a dual historical process. He places the decline of the importance of kin ties in the context of the emergence of a powerful, centralized state, and he then regards the rise of the modern family as an ideological emergence accompanying the development of capitalism.

According to Stone's typology, feudal England emphasized (1) kin-group responsibility for crimes and treasonable acts of members and (2) the institution of cousinship with its broad obligations. As political and economic power moved away from the traditional, landed elite to the state and the entrepreneurial class, the common law of the courts no longer recognized criminal and civil deviance as a kin-group responsibility, and cousinship lost its effectiveness. To fill the vacuum left by the decline of kinship as a factor in one's destiny, the relatively denuded conjugal family had to take over the task of guiding the destiny for its members. Consequently, by the sixteenth century, as an intermediate step toward the modern family, there was a trend toward authoritarianism in husband–wife interaction, and governance in the conjugal family took the form of patriarchy.

Stone (1975, p. 15) suggests that it was not until the eighteenth century that the spread of individualism and utilitarianism gave rise to a more companionate and egalitarian family structure. This last family form has been designated by Alan Macfarlane (1986) as the Malthusian marriage system, in which (1) marriage is seen as ultimately the bride's and groom's concern rather than that of the kin group; (2) marital interaction is supposed to be primarily companionate; and (3) love is supposed to be a precursor of marriage. Functionally, the Malthusian system yields relatively fewer children—by choice—than earlier family forms.

The Problem of Structure in Modernity Typologies. Typologies depicting historical transformations in family and kinship place much emphasis on the "fit" between the needs of modern industrial society and the presence of the conjugal family type (Litwak 1960a, 1960b; Parsons 1954). Despite this conjecture, Parsons (1954, p. 184) suggests that in Western society an "essentially open system" of kinship, with its "primary stress upon the conjugal family" and its lack of larger kin structures, has existed for centuries, long before the modern period. Like Macfarlane (1986), Parsons dates its establishment in late medieval times "when the kinship terminology of the European languages took shape." Moreover, Goode's (1963) analysis of family trends in eleven societies indicates that acceptance of modern, conjugal family ideology may precede economic and industrial development rather than come as a subsequent adaptation. Such findings cast doubt on the validity of the dichotomy between traditional societies and modernity as providing a theoretical basis for the typologies discussed above.

Parsons argues that (1) there is an incompatibility between corporate kinship and multilineal systems, and (2) in large measure, this incompatibility accounts for the prevalence of highly adaptable, structurally independent conjugal households in modern societies. However, findings by Davenport (1959), Mitchell (1963), Pehrson (1957), Peranio (1961), and others that corporate structures of kinship (such as clans) do exist in some multilineal kinship systems undercut Parsons's argument that such structures are to be found only in unilineal systems. Nevertheless, if multilateral kinship systems can accommodate corporate structures, then they can also include other kinship elements that sustain loyalties to descent groups and facilitate segmentation of the society.

The Problem of Connecting Kinship and Family in Modernity Typologies. Revisionists of the isolated conjugal family position have presented considerable evidence of residual elements of kinship ties in contemporary society. However, they do not adequately explain the connections between types of kinship systems and variation in performance of family functions in different parts of the social structure. Their main concern is with changes in kinship and family, changes that are consistent with the general loosening of tradition in modern society. But their focus on emancipation from tradition diverts their attention from (1) the influence of emerging ethnic, religious, or class interests upon patterns of integration of family networks in the larger social structure and (2) the temporal dimensions of kinship, which go beyond living kin to departed ancestors and generations yet to come.

Additionally, given the fact that the family–kinship typologies described above have their roots in the distinction between tradition and modernity, they overlook those nonindustrial, primarily nonurban societies in which families approach the companionship model as well as those ethnic and religious segments of industrial, primarily urban societies where strong familistic tendencies persist. Except for Stone (1975) and Zimmerman and Frampton (1966), these typologies are based on the concept of emancipation from tradition, and they do not deal explicitly with the emergence of new family values (other than flexibility and freedom). Most of all, their emphasis on emancipation from the constraints of tradition precludes their explaining why cohesive forces of family and kinship may remain strong (or increase in strength) in the face of an economic and social environment that is hostile to stable family life. (Exceptions are Sennett 1970 and Harris and Rosser 1983.)

Critical Commentary on Historical Typologies. Family typologies describing historical trends from one period of history to another are vulnerable to criticism of their teleological assumptions. Criticisms often involve (1) the definition of polar concepts and (2) the problem of inevitability.

(1) Definition of polar concepts. The definition of polar concepts depends upon the value commitments of the analyst. For example, those analysts who view trends in kinship and family as movement toward liberation from traditional constraints and from obstacles to personal independence define the original state as confining and generally unjust and the future state as enabling emancipation from these obsolete social structures.

Family-theorist Ernest Burgess and associates (1963) view the evolution of family structure as going "from institution to companionship"—from external community constraints upon family relations to voluntaristic unity that derives from affection, domestic peace, and common goals. Similarly, Marxists define the transition as being away from family structures required to sustain an economic system based on unearned rewards of the dominant class and suppression of the laboring class. Their claim is that following the rise of future true communism, the dissolution of economic classes would liberate family life from the constraints and suffering imposed by economic position; for Frederick Engels ([1885] 1942), under true communism, family life would be liberated from economic demands, and, founded on personal bonds, families would endure only as long as these bonds lasted.

By way of contrast, analysts favoring traditional values define the trend in family life as a steady decay of family structure. Pitirim Sorokin (1937, vol. 4, p. 776), upon whose work Zimmerman and Frampton base their typology, notes that "the family as a sacred union of husband and wife, of parents and children, will continue to disintegrate . . . . [T]he home will become a mere overnight parking place mainly for sex-relationship." From another perspective, the behaviorist John Watson (1927) predicted that "in fifty years [1977], unless there is some change, the tribal custom of marriage will no longer exist. Family standards have broken down . . . The mystery and beauty of marriage and the rearing of children has pretty well broken down." In the Aldous Huxley's science fiction novel *Brave New World* (1955), all functions now performed by families would be community undertakings, and the word "mother" would be regarded as obscene.

The distinction between typologies focusing on personal liberation and those portraying decay highlights the fact that each approach deals with partial realities. Liberation typologies tend to slight disruptive activities of emerging family structure (e.g., spouse abuse, child abuse, splitting into factions, isolation from resources of kin and family). Instead, they tend to associate these activities with traditional family structures. In the Soviet Union, family problems were generally attributed to survivals of the traditional pre-Revolution family forms. Decay typologies do the opposite. They tend to underestimate unifying elements and personal satisfactions associated with the emerging family types and to overestimate the chaos associated with these types.

(2) Problem of inevitability. Some typologies posit a straight-line progression from a beginning

state to an end state, while others at least imply a degree of indeterminacy in movement. For any particular typology, the degree of indeterminacy depends on the analyst's conception of history. For example, the Burgess institution-to-companionship family typology assumes there to be a major historical evolution from fairly isolated rural communities to societies with a high degree of industrialization; the family and kinship institutions evolve through a long series of adaptations to keep up with the industrialization of societies and a movement from a rural to an urban way of life. Similar typologies—like Toennies's *Gemeinschaft* to *Gesellschaft* ([1887] 1957) and Redfield's folk society to civilization (1947)—are based on comparable assumptions deriving from the dictum of Henry Maine, namely, that, as an overarching historical trend, the basis for social relations has been evolving from status to contract.

Despite the inevitability of trends implicit in the definition of polarities of family and kin structure in typologies of liberation (or decay), with the passage of time, definitions of polarities change. For example, analysts have redefined the concept of companionship as an end-state. In the 1940s, Burgess (1948; Burgess et al. 1963) regarded the future end-state as one in which the husband and wife (1) would be married without interference from family and community constraints, (2) would remain united through affection and common interests, (3) would maintain an equality in decision making and other aspects of family status, and (4) would orient their parenthood toward producing children with healthy personalities. But variations in family life included under the "companionship family" definition have been broadly expanded over time. By the end of the twentieth century, the end-state of the companionship family (as well as the unstable-family concept) has been redefined to include a diversity of household arrangements, such as (1) couples living together without formal marriage, (2) same-sex couples and their children (by adoption or by birth from previous or supplementary liaisons), and (3) voluntary single-parent households. Given these modifications in the concept of the companionship family, the very nature of the typology has been transformed. As a result, it is difficult to determine what family and kinship theorists will consider to be the evolutionary outcome twenty-five years from the present.

According to Murdoch's (1949) depiction of main sequence theory (described earlier), the changing pattern of employment has facilitated the widespread movement of women into broad sectors of occupations. This change has affected the composition of residences and, subsequently, will affect the descent structure and eventually kinship terminology. Evidence of this development can readily be seen. Around 1960, in an offhand comment during a lecture, Murdoch predicted that the control over wealth in America (1) would flow increasingly into the hands of women, (2) would at some point create shifts in household patterns, and (3) in the long run would produce a kinship structure dominated by women. Regardless of the accuracy of Murdoch's prediction, changes in practices pertaining to kinship are appearing in various ways: (1) Newspapers obituaries have routinely begun to include "life companions" (of either gender) in the list of related survivors; (2) public policy pertaining to health insurance coverage has been modified in some communities to include unmarried domestic partners; (3) in some countries (e.g., Russia, Israel), intestacy laws have been amended to include unrelated household residents; (4) the issue of legally recognizing same-sex marriages (or domestic partners) as a valid arrangement has emerged in a wide range of communities.

Unlike the theoretical inevitability of collectively rational adaptations assumed by evolutionary theorists, the typologies formulated by cyclical theorists lead away from regarding their end-states as inevitable. In their portrayal of historical processes, the cyclical theorists have the burden of explaining conditions for triggering reversals in historical cycles. These reversals imply that critical periods arise through cultural innovations and conflicts. The effects of novelty and conflict in these critical periods introduce an indeterminancy into the historical process. This indeterminacy brings to the foreground the problem of the inhibition of change: What introduces a new cycle, and what brings the cycle to a halt? For example, as discussed earlier, Zimmerman and Frampton (1947) see the history of the family as a series of repetitive cycles: a decay from corporate family forms (based on idealistic values) to unstable, chaotic families (based on materialistic values and individualism), followed by a regeneration of familism. Their scheme of analysis explains the oscillations between various degrees of familism and individualism in terms of a conflict between maintaining an enduring, traditional social structure and attending to persistent personal yearnings. The idealism of religious or ascetic values facilitates social stability in corporate family settings. However, the stifling of personal aims and desires, without idealism, encourages the adoption of materialistic values and sensuality associated with the unstable family. Hence, there is no guarantee that an old cycle will end or that new ideals supporting familism will again emerge.

A TRANSHISTORICAL TYPOLOGY OF KINSHIP AND FAMILY SYSTEMS

For well over a millennium, church intellectuals have been aware of variations in marital selection and their implications for family structure and kinship ties as well as for social structure. Early in the fifth century, in his *De Civitate Dei* (*City of God*), Saint Augustine of Hippo (1984, pp. 623–625) noted that in early biblical times demographic insufficiencies made it necessary for Jews to practice kinship endogamy. However, he proposed that marrying close relatives, and thereby creating multiple family ties with the same people, restricted the potential expanse of social circles that could be tied into a coherent community. Kinship endogamy tends to divide societies into segments. On the other hand, marrying persons from previously unrelated families would "serve to weld social life securely" by binding diverse peoples into an extensive web of relationships. Later, in the twelfth century, Gratian suggested that God commanded the Hebrews to select relatives as mates "because the salvation of man was realized in the pure Jewish race" but that the Christian faith, which could be readily spread through teaching, made kinship endogamy obsolete (Chodorow 1972, p. 74).

Gratian's argument suggests that the differences between Judaic and Christian marriage systems have broad implications for contemporaneous functions of kinship as well as for temporal functions, connecting past and future generations. The discussion that follows presents a kinship and family typology derived ultimately from Augustine's and Gratian's depictions of marriage systems as well as from issues pertaining to descent.

This typology involves theoretical concerns drawn from sociology and anthropology.

Contemporaneous and Temporal Functions of Kinship Systems. Both marriage systems and descent rules affect the character of links between contemporaneous networks of families. A major controversy that at one time occupied many social anthropologists was whether marriage systems (i.e., marital alliances between groups) are more fundamental in generating forms of social organization than are descent rules or vice versa. At stake in the controversy was the issue of whether the social solidarity undergirding descent rules is more fundamental than the ideas of reciprocity and exchange involved in marriage systems. In the end, Africanists favored descent rules, while Asianists leaned toward marital alliances. In their assessment of the controversy, Buchler and Selby (1968) found evidence for the validity of both views.

However, despite the chicken-and-egg character of the controversy, the alliance–descent issue highlights the contradictory nature of kinship structure. This contradiction is depicted in the opposing views of structuralists such as Claude Levi-Strauss (1963), who supports the alliance position, and functionalists such as Meyer Fortes (1969), who argues for the descent position.

Alliance theories of kinship systems identify the primary function of kinship as the integration of networks of related families into the contemporaneous social fabric. Alliance adherents begin with marriage as the central element in structuring the way kinship operates. To alliance theorists, the significance of marriage lies in the idea that marriage is essentially a mode of exchange whose primary reason for existence is to inhibit conflict in society. In their view, kin groups exist as organized entities to effect marital exchanges. According to Levi-Strauss, the leading figure in alliance theory, "exchange in human society is a universal means of ensuring the interlocking of its constituent parts" (1963, p. 2). In unilineal systems, women are exchanged for equivalent valuable property, services, or both; in bilateral systems (which by their nature become multilateral in the long run), commitments to each other's relatives are exchanged. In bilateral kinship, bride and groom are of presumably equivalent value. Thus, in general, alliance theorists regard descent groupings primarily as a necessary ingredient for sustaining the marriage exchange system over the generations.

The descent theory of kinship systems rests on the assumption that the continued welfare of kindred over the generations is the primary function of kinship. In particular, Fortes regards "filiation"—being ascribed the status of a child of one's parents, with all the lifetime rights and obligations attached to that status (1969, p. 108)—as the "crucial relationships of intergenerational continuity and social reproduction" (pp. 255–256). He proposes that, as a concomitant of filiation, "the model relationship of kinship amity is fraternity, that is sibling unity, equality, and solidarity" (p. 241), and he provides a biblical example of the tie between David and Jonathan. But he also notes that "the Euro-American kinship institutions and values of Anglo-Saxon origin are imbued with the same notion of binding force of kinship amity" (p. 242), and he cites the mother–daughter relationship in England (in research findings by Young and Willmott 1957) as exemplifying that same moral code of diffuse but demanding reciprocal obligations.

On the one hand, alliance theory postulates that the basic drive in kinship organization is derived externally, from the kind of alliances appropriate to the structure of power in the community. Collectively, marital alliances create between families a network of links that integrate them in reference to overarching religious, economic, and political institutions. On the other hand, descent theory ascribes the bases of organization to internal demands, structural factors in the persistence of the kindred: rules governing residential location, division of labor and authority among members, and the various economic and political functions to be performed by the kinship system (Buchler and Selby 1968, p. 129).

Given the contradiction in the impulse for kinship organization, there is an apparent "impasse between the alliance and filiation point of view" (Buchler and Selby 1968, p. 141). What appears to be at issue is the depiction of the kinds of reciprocity norms that define the character of kinship. Descent theory presumes that an axiom of amity (i.e., prescriptive altruism or general reciprocity) is basic to the coherence of kin groups; alliance theory holds that balanced reciprocity (i.e., the rightness of exchanges for overt self-interest, opportunistic individualism, or noumenal norms) is in the final analysis the glue that integrates families and kin groups into a coherent whole.

The contradiction is apparent in many ways. For example, in biblical references and religious writings, the Ten Commandments enjoin one to honor parents and, conversely, to "cleave" to one's spouse and maintain peace in the household. In terms of kinds of reciprocity, one commandment involves unconditional giving or honoring, while the other concerns maintaining domestic peace (implying fair give-and-take).

Similarly, contemporary writers on marriage generally find the concept of balanced reciprocity appropriate in describing the quality of husband–wife ties. For example, Walster and Walster (1978) report that marriages work best when both husband and wife (as well as lovers) believe that each is receiving a fair exchange for what he or she offers in the relationship. Moreover, in their review of research on the quality of marriage, Lewis and Spanier (1982) note the importance of the symmetry of exchange in establishing and maintaining strong marital ties. However, in the socialization of children and in the allocation of resources, the rule of amity (or prescriptive altruism) is supposed to prevail. For example, parents are ordinarily expected to make "sacrifices" for their children when necessary; to do otherwise is to be a "bad" parent. In the American court system, the general rule for the disposition of children in cases of divorce, child neglect or abuse, or adoption is that the court should base its decision on the welfare of the child rather than on the interests of the parents or other parties.

To some extent, the descent–marriage contradiction can be obscured by compartmentalizing marital, parental, and filial conduct and by dividing responsibilities of husband and wife. However, conflicts in norms for dealing with family members and kindred may occur for several reasons, but they occur principally because of scarcities of time and resources required to carry out duties and obligations in the face of a wide range of simultaneous and conflicting demands. Since the resulting dilemmas are widespread in the society, there is a need for a general rule. Because contradictory alliance and descent impulses are operative, each group is pushed to establish a coherent kinship scheme that gives priority to one impulse over the other or at least establishes some form of compromise between them.

There is evidence that rules governing marital functions conflict with those pertaining to descent functions, paralleling the alliance–descent controversy in kinship systems. Where descent functions are given precedence in family organization, marital functions are subordinated (and vice versa). Examples of this inverse relationship are (1) if husband–wife unity is central, then the unity between siblings is peripheral (and the reverse), and (2) if marriage between close affines is forbidden, first-cousin marriage is permitted (and vice versa). These examples are discussed in the sections that follow.

Marital Unity Versus Unity of the Sibling Group. Comparisons between societies indicate that ties between siblings have an inverse relationship to husband–wife ties. Where descent is valued over alliance or marriage in kinship relations, brother–sister bonds are particularly close (Parsons 1954), while the husband–wife relationship is relatively distant. In such family systems (whether or not its therapeutic implications are true), parents are expected to remain together for the sake of the children, and this expectation expresses the priority of descent over marital ties. Conversely, in family systems where the marriage function is more valued, the husband–wife relationship is intense (e.g., the importance of the give-and-take of love and of companionship for marriage) and the brother–sister relationship is competitive, distant, or both and the incest taboo justifies their apartness (see Lopata 1973 on widows and their brothers). In societies where priority is given to marital bonds over descent ties, the presence of children is of less importance in dissolving an unhappy marriage, and there is greater ambiguity about what is best for the children. The mere fact that the strength of brother–sister ties and that of marital ties vary inversely in different societies lends support to the proposition that there is a contradiction in the family system between its marital functions and its descent functions.

Affines and Cousins in American Marriage Law. The opposition between marital and descent functions in the family is also illustrated by the inverse relationship in American law of marriages considered to be incestuous: As a general tendency, states that forbid second marriages between a person and certain affines (such as that person's parents-in-law and sons- or daughters-in-law) allow first cousins to marry, while those that permit marriage between close affines forbid first-cousin marriage (Farber 1968). If the preferred function of marriage is to reinforce close consanguineous kinship ties, then this pattern of marital prohibitions signals a subordination of affinal bonds to those of consanguinity. Marrying into the family of the former spouse will not reinforce any of the other existing bonds of consanguinity. Consequently, although first-cousin marriage is to be permitted in order to reinforce intimate kinship ties, marriage with close affines should be avoided. However, if marriage is considered to be primarily a mechanism for creating new bonds between previously unrelated families, then a second marriage into the same family merely serves to maintain the affinal bonds initiated in the first marriage.

Social Structure and Kinship Systems. The presence of contradictory impulses in organizing kinship ties produces a predicament in establishing priorities between them. This contradiction evokes a question: Which circumstances lead some societies (and ethnic and religious subgroups) to give priority to descent and others to favor alliance assumptions in their kinship and family organization (Farber 1975)? In their analyses of the relationship between kinship organization and social structure, both Paige (1974) and Swanson (1969) distinguish between societies that feature the legitimacy of special interests—factionalism—in organizing social life and those that feature the importance of common interests—communalism—as an organizing theme.

Factions are a means for gathering forces and mobilizing members for conflict or competition with other factions. They emerge as a reaction to perceived danger to their well-being from other groups (cf. Douglas 1966). Factions emerge where either (1) special interest groups vie for superiority over other groups for access to power, wealth, or some other property, or (2) groups sense a danger to their continued autonomous existence as an ethnic or religious entity.

In kinship organization, the continual mobilization of family and kin results in the generation of norms that are centripetal in nature, that is, they facilitate the pulling inward of human, symbolic, and material resources. This centripetal tendency permits each kin group to separate itself from competing groups in order to endure. As a result, centripetal kin groups favor norms strengthening descent relationships over norms facilitating new alliances with other groups through marriage. Insofar as descent-group norms are rooted in the axiom of amity, one would expect centripetal kinship organization to feature the norm of prescriptive altruism over balanced reciprocities in kinship and family relations (see Farber 1975).

Jewish family norms provide some insight into the relationship between centripetal kinship systems and the application of the axiom of amity. In its basic ideology and in the code of laws supporting that ideology, Judaism assigns a major significance to the concept of nurturance (Farber 1984). Since nurturance is a central feature of maternal giving, it can be regarded as a metaphor for the axiom of amity. *The Code of Jewish Law* (*Shulkhan Arukh*) offers numerous instances that signify the place of nurturance in Judaism (Ganzfried 1963). For example, the code sublimates feeding and eating into sacred, ritualistic acts. The act of eating is invested with holiness, to be enjoyed in abundance, particularly on feast days and the Sabbath. A connection is made in the code between providing food and giving gifts and charity. It proposes that festive occasions are also times for charity to the needy and for sending gifts. In addition to drawing a connection between food and charity, the code applies the metaphor of the parent–child relationship to charity giving and assigns a priority to family in its general concept of nurturance: First parents, then offspring, and "other kinsmen take precedence over strangers" (Ganzfried 1963, chap. 34). The injunction to nurture children involves an emphasis not only on food but on other aspects as well (for example, an exaggerated emphasis on elaborated linguistic codes for use in child rearing). Zena Smith Blau (1974) writes that "whatever Jewish mothers did for their children—and they did a great deal—was accompanied by a flow of language, consisting of rich, colorful expressive words and phrases" (p. 175). The aim of socialization is presumably to turn the child into a *Mensch*— to transform the child from a receiver of nurture to a giver of nurture (Zborowski and Herzog 1952). Hence, in traditional Judaism, the concept of

nurturance seems to tie together the kinship emphasis on descent and the axiom of amity in organizing family relationships.

If nurturing the next generation is a form of prescriptive altruism, this nurturing can also occur in symbolic form. Like the transmission of physical wealth and nurturing, the parents can also transmit a "symbolic estate" to the next generation. In a real sense, along with material resources, people inherit a collection of living and dead relatives connected to them by birth and/or marriage. These relatives constitute a trove of heroes and villains whose personal qualities, exploits, and ideas are remembered in socializing succeeding generations. This "symbolic estate" defines for individuals (1) a sense of belonging to an identifiable "family," (2) role models to emulate (or disown), (3) a legitimation of one's place in community and society (Farber 1971). Craig (1979) sees the symbolic estate as a vehicle for achieving personal and familial immortality. Implicitly, it is one's duty in centripetally-oriented kinship systems to contribute to the symbolic estate by living an exemplary life (however this way of life is defined in particular historical circumstances).

To be operative as memorials (or reminders), the content of symbolic estates must have some bearing upon the personal identities (or destinies) of family members. In Judaism, historically this meant assessing the "quality" of one's ancestry (*yachas*), however defined; this assessment was particularly important in eras of arranged marriages. However, Yerushalmi (1982) notes the general importance of collective memory for the endurance of Judaism. Its centrality is suggested by the appearance of the verb *zakhar* (to remember) "in the [Hebrew] Bible no less than one hundred sixty-nine times" (Yerushalmi 1982, p. 5). Moreover, numerous memorials have been incorporated into holy day observances (e.g., the retelling of the story of the Exodus annually at the family *seder* at Passover). Especially significant for sustaining symbolic estates among Jews is the ritualizing of the remembrance of dead relatives through (1) memorial prayer services (*yizkor*) on four major holy days, and (2) partly as a means to continue to honor one's parents after their death, the recitation of the prayer for the dead (*kaddish*) on anniversaries of the death of each family members.

The concept of symbolic estates connects collective family memories—such as legends, myths, and moral ideas—to the continuity of "family" from one generation to the next. In her study of Genesis, Steinmetz (1991) applies the concept of "symbolic estates" to the succession from father to son of the obligation to ensure the realization of God's command to found and then maintain a Jewish nation. She regards the entire structure of Genesis as resting upon the transfer of this ideal to worthy heirs in the family line. Her emphasis upon the transmission of "symbolic estates" is echoed in an investigation by Bendor (1996) of the social structure of ancient Israel. Bendor concludes that Israeli social stratification is derived to a large extent from the kinship ideology of familial perpetuity—rather than from the influence of economic factors upon kinship and family life. The findings on ancient Israel by Steinmetz and Bendor bear upon historical and contemporary studies of kinship and family. Examples are the research reports by Pina-Cabal (1997) on family legends in urban Portugal, Attias-Donfut (1997) on home-sharing in France, Hastrup (1982) on establishing Icelander ethnicity, and Weigert and Hastings (1977) on maintaining family archives of photographs, old records, letters, and other memorials. The focus in these studies is upon symbolic mechanisms for sustaining family continuity. (The discussion of centrifugal kinship systems in the next section will describe obstacles to the perpetuation of "symbolic estates.")

As opposed to factionalism, communalism implies a situation in which special interests are subordinated to common concerns of diverse groups. In stateless societies, these common concerns may well emerge from economic interdependence or the presence of a common enemy. In societies with a centralized government, the state presumably symbolizes a concern for the common welfare of the populace. Other unifying concerns may exist as well, for example, the presence of a universal church (as opposed to competing sects and denominations), nationalism (as opposed to ethnic self-determination), a centralized bureaucracy or market (as opposed to regional competition for dominance), and so on. The common concerns would best be served if members of kin groups were to be dispersed by marriage to previously unrelated people living throughout the society. This dispersal would maximize the number of diverse kin groups with which any family is connected, and it would thereby scatter kinship loyalties, obligations, and property as widely as possible. Consequently, this kind of kinship system, associated with communalism, can be identified as applying an outward pressure upon its constituents; it is centrifugal in nature.

In contrast to the centripetal system, the centrifugal system subordinates kinship ties to conjugal family ties and extends marital prohibitions widely in order to inhibit marriages that would merely reinforce existing consanguineous ties. According to the theory outlined above, in centrifugal kinship systems, in which marriage functions are given priority over descent functions, the appropriate norm for defining family interaction is balanced reciprocity—exchange rather than the axiom of amity.

In the United States, although the centrifugal kinship system appears in a wide range of socioeconomic, religious, and ethnic groups, it is found disproportionately at lower socioeconomic levels, where families seek improved integration into the larger society (Farber 1981).

The application of balanced exchange as a norm in family and kinship is exemplified in a study of poor families by Stack (1974). She describes the prevalence of "swapping" as a named, bartering norm governing both ties between kin and between family members in their struggle for survival. Stack notes that "reciprocal obligations last as long as both participants are mutually satisfied" and that they continue such exchange relationships as long as they can "draw upon the credit they accumulate with others through swapping" (p. 41). Indeed, according to Stack, "those actively involved in domestic networks swap goods and services on a daily, practically an hourly, basis" (p. 35). But this exchange does not constitute a playing out of the axiom of amity since "the obligation to repay carries kin and community sanctions" (p. 34) and it extends beyond family and kin to friends. Although swapping may involve some element of trust, it exists to ensure exchanges in the lean times that predictably recur in domestic networks that are too marginal in resources to be magnanimous. It pays to create numerous bartering arrangements rather than to accumulate obligations within a very small network of intimate kin. Thus, in its own way, swapping mimics the proliferation of networks of previously unrelated families characteristic of centrifugal kinship systems.

In contrast to the importance of "symbolic estates" for facilitating the "immortality" of families in centripetal kinship systems, families in centrifugal systems are often characterized by a "legacy of silence." This silence may signify the existence of shameful or immoral acts of relatives, or it may simply reflect an emphasis upon individualism in these families. In Germany after World War II, this "legacy of silence" functioned to erase the collective memory of parental activities and ideas they held during the Nazi era (Larney 1994, pp. 146–162). For victims of torture and displacement under the Nazi regime, the legacy of silence enabled them to wipe their degradation from memory (Bar-On 1989). In either case, whereas symbolic estates provide a vehicle for family continuity, the legacy of silence established a discontinuity.

The German experience may result in a single break in family continuity—to permit starting afresh. However, the institutionalization of the legacy of silence in centrifugal kinship systems perpetuates this discontinuity between generations of nuclear families. This legacy has been found to be prevalent in low socioeconomic-level families populating urban slums (Farber 1971). Families tend to exchange little information about one another; in fact what is hidden may permit closer ties between kin than the revelation of illicit or immoral acts. Then too, in families where welfare agencies and police intrude, silence serves to maintain the privacy of the household.

The tacit norm of collective forgetting in these centrifugal kinship systems places the onus for kinship unity upon mutual assistance, friendship, and availability of kin. Yet, in her study of kinship among poor racial and ethnic minorities, Roschelle (1997) found that degree of mutual assistance between families and extent of interaction among relatives depend largely upon availability of kin. Migrant families frequently are isolated in time of need and the legacy of silence may thereby be enhanced.

In a society marked by much internal migration and social mobility, there are many opportunities for a proliferation of centrifugal tendencies in kinship. Whether centrifugal systems actually emerge through mobility may depend upon a variety of factors. Gullestad (1997) notes a shift in the meaning of kinship in urban Norway. She describes a social transformation from norms regarding "being of use" and social solidarity to self-realization and "finding oneself" (or "being oneself"), that is, from norms sustaining family continuity to norms fostering separation and discontinuity. She attributes this shift to "transformed modernity" involving "fundamental restructurings of home and neighborhood because women and children are not present in the same way or to the same extent as before" (Gullestad 1997, p. 210). Transformed modernity, as well as advances in reproductive technology, is identified also as a factor in the proliferation of diverse forms of kinship structure in contemporary society (Strathern 1992).

One can interpret the emergence of feminist movements as both stimulating and stimulated by the "transformed modernity" cited by Gullestad. For some forms of feminism, post-modern thought provides a rationale for denigrating traditional symbolic estates. Post-modern writings propose that the framing of "factual" and theoretical statements have an exclusionary element—that is, they mark a population segment for exclusion from free participation. These "factual" statements justify this exclusion. As "factual" statements, posing as objective discourses, these statements have a hidden core. This core reflects the special interests of those with the power to define "truth" for the society. (See Foucault [1971] 1996.) Certain feminists claim that the hidden core of meaning in statements justifying exclusion of women from full participation in society is to promote male dominance in social structure (Barnard 1993). The symbolic estates that facilitate the endurance of existing lines of descent are thus seen as supporting patriarchy. Consequently, they are regarded as an obstacle to the full participation of women in society. Yet, as women's participation in economic and political spheres continues to expand, it is likely that symbolic estates will eventually be infused with a marked increase in content pertaining to exploits and interests of women.

Kinship-Map Typology. Although mapping of kinship ties cannot express all aspects of kinship relations, it can generate models expressing general orientations implicit in various patterns of kinship structure. Basically, genealogical maps of consanguineal ("blood") relationships merely locate positions in an ideal web of biological connections. Variations in mapping come into play when these maps are used to describe how one's obligations and proscriptions vary in different kinship structures. Such obligations and proscriptions pertain to marriage, remarriage, birth and adoption, inheritance, relations between generations and genders, and so on.

One advantage of models of genealogical mapping is that these models express the logical connections between functions of kinship in a particular society and priorities assigned to different kin statuses. For instance, a kinship type with a prohibition to marry a first cousin generally has a different function in society as compared to one permitting such marriage. This pattern of marital prohibitions will likely be related to priorities in inheritance. For instance, in American state laws, permitting first-cousin marriage would be associated with giving a niece or nephew precedence over a grandparent in intestate inheritance (i.e., when there is no written will). The opposite will likely be true where first-cousin marriage is forbidden.

The relationship between genealogical mapping and functions of kinship has a long history in Western civilization. Atkins (1974) has explored a wide range of formulae for generating different patterns of priorities in mapping genealogical relationships. Implied in genealogical mapping is the principle that the smaller the number of links (by birth or marriage) between relatives, other things being equal, the greater is the degree of obligation between them. Thus, in such matters as succession to estates, when a choice is to be made among kin, genealogically close relatives are presumed to be given priority over more distantly related kin. However, since the various formulae differ in the patterns of priority among kin generated, choice of an appropriate pattern of mapping depends on the role of kinship in the particular society.

In general, three patterns of priority for mapping kin have been applied in the Western world (mainly in laws of intestacy and marriage). However, in practice, each society makes modifications in these patterns to fit its needs. Examples of these patterns occur in (1) Catholic canon law and the state of Georgia, (2) the civil code of the Twelve Tables of the Roman Republic and more recently in Napoleonic Code and Louisiana law, and (3) the

parentela orders in the Hebrew Bible and in abbreviated form in Israel, Germany, and various states (e.g., Arizona) (Farber 1981).

At one pole, the canon law of the Catholic Church stipulates that a function of the church is to create a unity that ties together diverse segments of its constituency in a web of extensive relationships (including family bonds). This aim implies that collateral ties between families are equal in importance to ties between ascendants and descendants (i.e., between generations). Under such conditions, ties between are extended outward in a centrifugal fashion. In laws governing marital prohibitions, marriage is discouraged within the second degree of distance of collateral kin (i.e., first cousins). In earlier generations, marital prohibitions in Canon Law were even more inclusive; for example, in thirteenth century, consanguineous marriages were prohibited within the fourth degree of relatedness.

In assigning distances from Ego in the canon law genealogical model (e.g., for priorities in inheritance), (1) all consanguineal members of Ego's nuclear family (parents, siblings, and children) are one degree of distance from Ego, (2) relatives just outside the nuclear family are two degrees of distance (grandparents, aunts and uncles, first cousins, nieces and nephews, and grandchildren), and so on. The canon law model thereby expresses the general principle that neither line of descent nor collateral distance is given special emphasis—only degree of distance from one's nuclear family is significant.

At the opposite pole, the parentela orders genealogical model places much emphasis upon line of descent (and among collateral relatives, the closeness of line of descent). Like the sociobiological ideal, the parentela orders model is oriented toward the survival of any given line of descent (or failing that, the next closest line of descent). This model expresses centripetal tendencies in kinship structure. In marriage law, collateral prohibitions are minimal, and marrying someone in the closest line of descent (first cousin) is preferred.

As the parentela orders model is applied to intestacy law, the centripetal principle is expressed in the Hebrew Bible in Numbers 27:8–11 and 36:7–9. In this model, priorities among relatives are allocated by line of descent: (1) Direct descendants of Ego are given first priority (children, grandchildren, etc.); (2) if there are no direct descendants, those of Ego's parents are given next priority (siblings, nieces and nephews, etc.); (3) next in priority are descendants of Ego's grandparents (aunts and uncles, first cousins, etc.)—and so on. In theory, Ego's estate will be passed on to the closest survivor in the closest line of descent to Ego's.

Between the extremes of centrifugality of the canon law model and the centripetality of the parentela orders model stands the civil law model. This model gives somewhat more weight in assigning closeness in kinship distance to direct-line ascendants and descendants than to collateral relatives (i.e., those related to Ego through a common ancestor). In computing kinship distance from Ego, the civil law model counts generations between Ego and the common ancestor as well as generations between the other relative and the common ancestor; for direct-line relatives, only those generations between Ego and the other relative need be counted. Obviously, the nearer the common ancestor is to Ego, the closer is the collateral relative in genealogical distance (and vice versa). Thus, Ego's grandparent is closer genealogically than a niece or nephew; the reverse is true for parentela orders priorities, and both are equidistant from Ego in the canon law model.

Several social surveys have been undertaken to test empirically the above propositions about ways in which people's conceptions about priorities assigned to different relatives in kinship mapping are actually reflected in their lives—religious affiliation, socioeconomic status, minority status, and so on. In these surveys, the respondents were asked to choose priorities among kin (for which the kinship-map models differ) if they were to write a law to govern intestacy (i.e., where there is no written will). For ten pairs of relatives for whom the kinship models differed in assigning a priority, within each pair, the respondents were to select the relative they thought should have precedence (as a general rule). (Equal priority was one alternative.) Respondents were then classified according to the kinship model to which a majority of their choices conformed.

The first surveys were undertaken in the United States (Farber 1977, 1979). The results indicate that Jewish respondents do indeed tend to view priorities from the perspective of the parentela orders model, while Catholics tend to be overrepresented in the canon law category. Of course, these are tendencies and not blanket findings covering all Jews or Catholics. For example, the degree to which a religious grouping adheres to scripture and/or ritual practices seems important in influencing kinship mapping. When religious branch was taken into account, responses of Jews who identified themselves as Conservative (a fairly traditional branch) tended to conform to the parentela orders model and none conformed to the canon law model, while those in the Reform category more often conformed to the canon law model than to than to the parentela orders model. Similarly, among Mormons whose marriage was sealed in the Temple, their responses were like those of the Conservative Jews, whereas those whose marriage was not sealed for time and eternity responded like Reform Jews. Moreover, neofundamentalist Protestants were the only other religious grouping overrepresented in the parentela orders category (Farber 1981, pp. 73–75).

Taken together, the above findings suggest that the parentela orders model tends to be prevalent in groupings where endurance of the particular religious community into the distant future may be problematic. The community would then be motivated to intensify its inward pull—its centripetal incentive—to keep succeeding generations within the fold.

In the course of one investigation (Farber 1981), a reanalysis of findings yielded a fourth kinship model. This model, whose computation is the reverse of the parentela orders model, emphasizes obligations to ancestors who have been responsible for preparing the groundwork for Ego's place in society. In the serendipitous model, Ego's direct ancestors are given priority over any descendants—first priority is given to parents, grandparents, and so on; the next set of priorities consists of Ego's children, then Ego's brothers and sisters, aunts and uncles, great-uncles and great-aunts, and so on; following these, Ego's grandchildren, nieces and nephews, first cousins, and on and on (Farber 1981, p. 50).

The serendipitous model was disproportionately prevalent in several sectors of respondents—nonminority Protestants, those in professional and managerial occupations and at higher income levels, and those persons with U.S.-born fathers. In addition, persons who conformed to this model tended to come from smaller families (Farber 1981, p. 217) and expected to have fewer offspring than did other respondents (Farber 1981, p. 147). Since almost half the sample studied conformed to this model, it seemed appropriate to name it the Standard American model. The U.S. findings on the standard American model are consistent with Alexis de Tocqueville's observation made almost two centuries ago in *Democracy in America* ([1850] 1945), namely, that compared with Continental Europeans, Americans live in the present and show little interest in the perpetuation of family lines.

European data on the genealogical models throw further light on differences in the conception of kinship priorities between U.S. and Continental populations. An investigation in central Europe (Vienna, Bremen, and Cologne) shows parentela orders to be by far the most prevalent kinship model, especially among those families at upper socioeconomic levels (Baker 1991). By way of contrast, Baker's (1991) data from Dublin, Ireland, tend to be similar to the American findings: Jews display a strong tendency to conform to the parentela orders model, while Protestants and Catholics favor the standard American model (called by Baker the intercultural bourgeois model). Despite all the changes that have occurred over the generations, traditional perceptions of priorities in kinship claims still persist.

The typology of kinship maps (or collaterality models) is a heuristic for understanding an implicit theory of the workings of kinship structure. In itself, the typology is too simplistic to denote the complexity of norms and values and the operation of mechanisms involved. But these criticisms about the heuristic character of the types of collaterality models can be applied to all typologies used in kinship analysis. They are merely methodological tools for gaining insight into what is going on. To gain this insight, one forgoes the many nuances that give color to understanding the functioning of kinship.

Related Transhistorical Typologies. Variations on issues pertinent to the structural contradiction typology have been developed in other transhistorical schemes associated with the role of marriage and descent systems in organizing family and kinship

systems. For instance, Guichard (1977) distinguishes between Eastern/Islamic and Western/Christian kinship systems. According to his typology, in the Eastern system, (1) descent is patrilineal; (2) marital ties are weak, and polygyny and easy divorce are permitted; (3) close ties exist between kin related through male lineage groups; (4) strong preference is given to endogamy within patrilineages; and (5) the sexes are segregated and women are relatively secluded within the home. In contrast, in the Western system, (1) kinship is bilineal or bilateral/multilateral, with ties to the maternal family considered important and with an emphasis on affinal connections as well; (2) marital bonds are the dominant unifying feature in family and kinship, with monogamy as prescribed and with extended kin ties as weak; (3) kin ties are defined according to individual connections rather than by lineage groups, with an emphasis on the ascending line rather than the descending line and with little importance attached to lineal continuity or solidarity; (4) kinship exogamy is prescribed, with endogamy permitted primarily for economic reasons; and (5) interaction between the sexes occurs in a wide range of circumstances.

In his reaction to Guichard, Goody (1983) revives the anthropological controversy between alliance theory and descent theory. Goody criticizes Guichard for basing his typology on marital norms (i.e., the endogamy–exogamy distinction) and suggests that by not starting with descent factors (i.e., inheritance practices), Guichard has overlooked a more fundamental distinction—that between kinship systems in which property is passed from one generation to the next through both sexes (by means of inheritance and dowry) and those systems in which property is transmitted unisexually (usually through males). Goody contends that passing property down unisexually encourages the development of corporate kinship groups (e.g., African systems). However, the use of bilateral devolution discourages such corporate structures, and Goody places both Eastern and Western systems in Guichard's dichotomy in the bilateral category. He faults Guichard for overstating the existence of corporate structures in Eastern kinship and proposes that Guichard's Western type represents merely a later historical development away from its roots in the Eastern system. Goody sees the primary problem of explaining the character of family and kinship in Western society as one of discerning how European societies shifted from preferred kinship endogamy (e.g., first-cousin marriage) to prescribed exogamy.

In his analysis of European kinship, Goody considers the changes introduced by the Christian (i.e., Roman Catholic) church from its beginnings to the late medieval period. He interprets the shift from kinship endogamy to exogamy mainly as a strategic move by the church to gain control over the lives of its members. As part of this effort, it had to wrest access to resources (especially productive land) from enduring control by family and kin. As a result, church laws evolved favoring those norms that might enhance allegiance to the church and weaken competition from the family and the state. In consequence, the church favored (1) the use of testation permitting bequests to the church; (2) the prescription of kinship exogamy as a means for inhibiting both the reinforcement of close kin ties and the passing down of resources exclusively within lineages; (3) the requirement of the consent of both bride and groom in marriage; (4) late marriage as a means for weakening family control over mate selection; (5) prohibition of divorce even for childless couples; and so on.

Goody seems to overstate his case in trying to interpret the shifts in kinship in ways that are consistent with his basic typology. For example, in giving primacy to inheritance patterns, Goody asserts that the ban on divorce in Roman Catholicism was devised primarily to encourage bequeathing estates to the church in case of childlessness. But, in fact, when there were no children, bequests usually were made "to brothers and sisters and to nieces and nephews" (Sheehan 1963, p. 75). Moreover, Goody's explanation of the ban ignores the widespread practice of bequeathing a portion of one's estate to the church even when one left a widow, children, or both. Sheehan (1963) reports that these bequests were made for the good of the soul: "Among the Anglo-Saxons, bequests to the palish church became so general that they were eventually required by law" (p. 292). This practice was not restricted to England. According to Sheehan, "Christians in the Mediterranean basin had developed the practice of bequeathing part of their estate in alms" (p. 303). Thus, church heirship in medieval Christian Europe was tied to repentance regardless of the existence of familial beneficiaries. Since church acquisition did not have to depend on bequests from childless couples, it is unlikely that the ban on divorce derives primarily from the desire of the church for additional benefices.

In addition, Goody dismisses the intermittent presence of kinship endogamy in medieval Europe as opportunistic deviations from the moral injunctions of the church. Yet, as Duby (1977) indicates, in medieval Europe the ebb and flow in kinship endogamy was tied to the amount of emphasis given to strengthening lines of descent. For example, Duby notes that in northern France, from before the tenth century to about the middle of the eleventh century, there was little utilization of the concept of lineage and only vague awareness of genealogy and knowledge about ancestors. Prior to that time, even members of the aristocracy considered their family to consist of "a horizontal grouping" of neighbors and kin "whose bonds were as much the result of marriage alliances as of blood" (Duby 1977, p. 147). Then, beginning in the tenth century, there was a change in ideas and norms regarding kinship—a conscious strengthening of lineage by controlling marriage, which frequently took place between close relatives despite impediments in canon law (Canon Law Society 1983). To summarize, Goody's argument is that medieval deviation from canon law consisted of opportunistic economic decisions and did not derive from a different set of norms. But Duby describes the coordination of kinship endogamy with the emerging notion of the legitimacy of lineage—a complex of ideas that requires a consensus among the kin in order to be effective. Hence, it appears that the change in marriage rules and the significance of lineage signaled more that ad hoc departures from church law.

There is still another reason for questioning Goody's conclusions: Goody makes the point that through bequests the Catholic church became the largest landowner in Europe. In his focus on the growth of exogamy as a consequence of the devolution of estates to both sexes, he has overlooked the church's own involvement as a major heir in the inheritance system. Particularly in the light of the church's view that ties through faith are equivalent to blood ties, the church is identified with spiritual kinship (Goody 1983, pp. 194ff). However, if it is legitimate to consider the church as an heir on a par with familial heirs, the system becomes one of *trilateral* devolution—sons, daughters, *and* the church. In that case, the European system differs markedly from the Eastern kinship system described by Guichard. Indeed, in contrast to Judaism and Islam, Christianity, at least until the end of the medieval period, saw family and kinship ties as *competitive* with church interests, and the strategies the church applied to weaken these ties altered both the marriage and the inheritance systems. The data imply that, despite their contradictory implications, the marriage, the alliance component, and the descent component should be addressed as equal factors in organizing family life. A task that remains is to integrate typologies of the emergence of modern kinship systems with transhistorical, structural typologies.

(SEE ALSO: *Alternative Life Styles; American Families; Family and Household Structure; Family Roles*)

REFERENCES

Adams, Bert N. 1968 *Kinship in an Urban Setting*. Chicago: Markham.

Atkins, John R. 1974 "On the Fundamental Consanguineal Numbers and Their Structural Basis" *American Ethnologist* 1:1–31.

Attias-Donfut, Claudine 1997 "Home-Sharing and the Transmission of Inheritance in France." In M. Gullestad and M. Segalen, eds., *Family and Kinship in Europe*. London: Pinter.

Augustine, Saint 1966 *The City of God Against the Pagans*. New York: Penguin Books.

Baker, David J. 1991 *Conceptions of Collaterality in Modern Europe: Kinship Ideologies from Companionship to Trusteeship*. Unpublished doctoral dissertation, University of Illinois, Urbana–Champaign.

Barnard, Malcolm 1993 "Economy and Strategy: The Possibility of Feminism." In Chris Jenks, ed., *Cultural Reproduction*. New York: Routledge.

Bar-On, Dan 1989 *The Legacy of Silence: Encounters with Children of the Third Reich*. Cambridge, Mass.: Harvard University Press.

Bendor, S. 1996 *The Social Structure of Ancient Israel*. Jerusalem: Simor.

Berkner, Lutz 1972 "The Stem Family and the Developmental Cycle of a Peasant Household: An Eighteenth-Century Example." *American Historical Review* 77:398–418.

Blau, Zena Smith 1974 "The Strategy of the Jewish Mother." In Marshall Sklare, ed., *The Jew in American Society*. New York: Behrman House.

Buchler, Ira R., and Henry A. Selby 1968 *Kinship and Social Organization*. New York: Macmillan.

Burgess, Ernest W. 1948 "The Family in a Changing Society." *American Journal of Sociology* 53:417–422.

——, Harvey J. Locke, and Mary Margaret Thomes 1963 *The Family: From Institution to Companionship*. New York: American Book Company.

Canon Law Society of Great Britain and Ireland 1983 *The Code of Canon Law*. London: Collins Liturgical Publications.

Chodorow, Stanley 1972 *Christian Political Theory and Church Politics in the Mid-Twelfth Century*. Berkeley: University of California Press.

Craig, Daniel 1979 "Immortality through Kinship: The Vertical Transmission of Substance and Symbolic Estate." *American Anthropologist* 81:94–96.

Davenport, W. 1959 "Nonunilinear Descent and Descent Groups." *American Anthropologist* 61:557–572.

Douglas, Mary 1966 *Purity and Danger*. London: Routledge and Kegan Paul.

Duby, Georges 1977 *The Chivalrous Society*. London: Edward Arnold.

Engels, Frederick (1885) 1942 *The Origin of Family, Private Property, and the State*. New York: International Publishers.

Farber, Bernard 1968 *Comparative Kinship Systems*. New York: Wiley.

—— 1971 *Kinship and Class: A Midwestern Study*. New York: Basic Books.

—— 1975 "Bilateral Kinship: Centripetal and Centrifugal Types of Organization." *Journal of Marriage and the Family* 37:871–888.

—— 1977 "Social Context, Kinship Mapping, and Family Norms." *Journal of Marriage and the Family* 39:227–240.

—— 1979 "Kinship Mapping Among Jews in a Midwestern City." *Social Forces* 57:1107–1123.

—— 1981 *Conceptions of Kinship*. New York: Elsevier.

—— 1984 "Anatomy of Nurturance: A Structural Analysis of the Contemporary Jewish Family." Paper presented at Workshop on Theory Construction and Research Methodology, National Council on Family Relations, San Francisco, October.

Firth, Raymond, Jane Hubert, and Anthony Forge 1969 *Families and Their Relatives*. New York: Humanities Press.

Fortes, Meyer 1969 *Kinship and Social Order*. Chicago: Aldine.

Foucault, Michel (1971) 1996 "The Discourse on Language." In R. Kearney and M. Rainwater, eds., *The Continental Philosophy Reader*. New York: Routledge.

Ganzfried, Solomon 1963 *Code of Jewish Law (Kitzur Shulkhan Aruhh)*, rev., annot. ed. New York: Hebrew Publishing Company.

Goode, William J. 1963 *World Revolution and Family Patterns*. New York: Free Press.

Goody, Jack 1983 *The Development of the Family and Marriage in Europe*. New York: Cambridge University Press.

Guichard, P. 1977 *Structures sociales 'Orientales' et 'occidentales' dans l'Espagne musulmane*. Paris: Mouton.

Gullestad, Marianne 1997 "From 'Being of Use' to 'Finding Oneself:' Dilemmas of Value Transmission between Generations in Norway." In M. Gullestad and M. Segalen, eds., *Family and Kinship in Europe*. London: Pinter.

Harris, C. C., and Colin Rosser 1983 *The Family and Social Change*. Boston: Routledge and Kegan Paul.

Hastrup, Kirsten 1982 "Establishing an Ethnicity: The Emergence of the 'Icelanders' in the Early Middle Ages." In David Parkin, ed., *Semantic Anthropology*. New York: Academic Press.

Huxley, Aldous 1955 *Brave New World*. New York: Bantam.

Larney, Barbara Elden 1994 Children of World War II in Germany: A life course analysis. Unpublished doctoral diss.

Levi-Strauss, Claude 1963 *Structural Anthropology*. New York: Basic Books.

—— 1969 *The Elementary Structures of Kinship*. Boston: Beacon Press.

Lewis, Robert A., and Graham B. Spanier 1982 "Marital Quality, Marital Stability and Social Exchange." In F. Ivan Nye, ed., *Family Relationships: Rewards and Costs*. Beverly Hills, Calif.: Sage.

Litwak, Eugene 1960a "Occupational Mobility and Extended Family Cohesion." *American Sociological Review* 25:9–21.

—— 1960b "Geographical Mobility and Extended Family Cohesion." *American Sociological Review* 25:385–394.

—— 1985 *Helping the Elderly: The Complementary Roles of Informal Networks and Formal Systems*. New York: Guilford Press.

Lopata, Helena Znaniecki 1973 *Widowhood in an American City*. Cambridge, Mass.: General Learning Press.

Macfarlane, Alan 1986 *Marriage and Love in England: Modes of Reproduction 1300–1840* New York: Basil Blackwell.

Maine, Henry S. (1861) 1963 *Ancient Law*. Boston: Beacon Press.

Mitchell, William E. 1963 "Theoretical Problems in the Concept of the Kindred." *American Anthropologist* 65:343–354.

Mogey, John 1976 "Content of Relations with Relatives." In J. Caisenier, ed., *The Family Life Cycle in European Societies*. Paris: Mouton.

Murdock, George Peter 1949 *Social Structure*. New York: Macmillan.

Naroll, Rauol 1970 "What Have We Learned from Cross-Cultural Surveys?" *American Anthropologist* 75:1227–1288.

Paige, Jeffery M. 1974 "Kinship and Polity in Stateless Societies." *American Journal of Sociology* 80:301–320.

Parsons, Talcott 1954 "The Kinship System of the Contemporary United States." In Talcott Parsons, ed., *Essays in Sociological Theory*. New York: Free Press.

Pehrson, R. N. 1957 *The Bilateral Network of Social Relations in Konkama Lapp District*. Bloomington: Indiana University Research Center in Anthropology, Folklore, and Linguistics.

Peranio, R. 1961 "Descent, Descent Line, and Descent Group in Cognatic Social Systems." In V. E. Garfield, ed., *Proceedings of the Annual Meeting of the American Ethnological Association*. Seattle: University of Washington Press.

Pina-Cabral, Joao de 1997 "Houses and Legends: Family as a Community of Practice in Urban Portugal." In Marianne Gullestad and Martine Segalen, eds., *Family and Kinship in Europe*. London: Pinter.

Redfield, Robert 1947 "The Folk Society." *American Journal of Sociology* 52:293–308.

Roschelle, Anne R. 1997 *No More Kin: Exploring Race, Class, and Gender in Family Networks*. Thousand Oaks, Calif.: Sage Publications.

Sennett, Richard 1970 *Families Against the City: Middle Class Homes of Industrial Chicago, 1872–1890*. Cambridge, Mass.: Harvard University Press.

Shanas, Ethel, Peter Townsend, Dorothy Wedderburn, Henning Friis, Paul Milhoj, and Jan Stehouwer 1968 *Old People in Three Industrial Countries*. New York: Atherton Press.

Sheehan, Michael M. 1963 *The Will in Medieval England: From the Conversion of the Anglo-Saxons to the End of the Thirteenth Century*. Toronto: Pontifical Institute of Medieval Studies.

Sorokin, Pitirim 1937 *Social and Cultural Dynamics*. Four Volumes. New York: Harper.

Stack, Carol B. 1974 *All Our Kin*. New York: Harper Colophon Books.

Steinmetz, Devora 1991 *From Father to Son: Kinship, Conflict, and Continuity in Genesis.* Louisville, KY: Westminster/John Knox Press.

Stone, Lawrence 1975 "Rise of the Nuclear Family in Early Modern England: The Patriarchal Stage." In Charles E. Rosenberg, ed., *The Family in History.* Philadelphia: University of Pennsylvania Press.

Strathern, Marilyn 1992 *After Nature: English Kinship in the Late Twentieth Century.* New York: Cambridge University Press.

Sussman, Marvin 1959 "The Isolated Nuclear Family: Fact or Fiction?" *Social Problems* 6:333–340.

Swanson, Guy E. 1969 *Rules of Descents: Studies in the Sociology of Parentage.* Anthropological Papers, no. 39. Ann Arbor: Museum of Anthropology, University of Michigan.

Tocqueville, Alexis de (1850) 1945 *Democracy in America.* New York: Knopf.

Toennies, Ferdinand (1887) 1957 *Community and Society.* East Lansing: Michigan State University Press.

Walster, Elaine, and G. William Walster 1978 *A New Look at Love.* Reading, Mass.: Addison-Wesley.

Watson, John 1927 *Chicago Tribune.* March 6, p. 1.

Weigert, Andrew J., and Ross Hastings 1977 "Identity Loss, Family, and Social Change." *American Journal of Sociology* 82:1171–1185.

Wirth, Louis 1956 *Community Life and Social Policy.* Chicago: University of Chicago Press.

Yerushalmi, Yosef Hayim 1982 *Zakhor: Jewish History and Jewish Memory.* Seattle: University of Washington Press.

Young, Michael, and Peter Willmott 1957 *Family and Kinship in East London.* London: Routledge and Kegan Paul.

Zborowski, Mark, and Elizabeth Herzog 1952 *Life Is with People: The Culture of the Stetl.* New York: Shocken Books.

Zimmerman, Carle C., and Merle E. Frampton 1947 *Family and Civilization.* New York: Harper.

—— 1966 "Theories of Frederic LePlay." In Bernard Farber, ed., *Kinship and Family Organization.* New York: Wiley.

BERNARD FARBER

L

LABELING THEORY

See Deviance Theories.

LABOR FORCE

Although labor-force concepts were originally designed to study economic activity and guide government policies, economic activities are a form of *social* behavior with numerous social determinants and consequences. Hence labor-force behavior has been the subject of a substantial body of sociological research.

MEASUREMENT

The U.S. Bureau of the Census developed the labor-force concept to measure the number of working-age people who were economically active during a particular time period—the calendar week preceding the sample interview (Cain 1979; U.S. Bureau of Labor Statistics 1982). It has two components: (1) *The employed*: those who, during the reference week, did any work at all as paid employees, were self-employed, or worked as unpaid family workers at least fifteen hours in a family-operated enterprise; included also are those who were employed but on vacation, home sick, etc. (2) *The unemployed*: those who were not employed during the reference week but who were available for work and had actively sought employment sometime within the preceding four-week period. All those who are neither employed nor unemployed are defined as being out of the labor force and primarily include students, housewives, the retired, and the disabled. Since the size of the population affects the number of people who work, labor-force measures are usually expressed in ratio form. The *labor-force participation rate* is the percentage of the total working-age *population* that is in the labor force, while the *unemployment rate* is the percentage of the *labor force* that is unemployed. In order to compare particular subgroups in the population, analysts compute group-specific measures such as the percentage of all women versus men who are in the labor force or the percentage of black versus white labor-force members who are unemployed.

The Census Bureau developed the labor-force concepts during the Great Depression of the 1930s in response to the government's difficulty in charting the severity of unemployment during that crisis. Prior to 1940, measures of economic activity were collected only at the time of the decennial censuses, making it impossible to track business-cycle fluctuations in unemployment; for example, most of the Great Depression came between the 1930 and the 1940 censuses. Hence, in order to provide ongoing unemployment data, the Census Bureau initiated the monthly Current Population Survey in the 1940s.

A second problem was the ambiguity of the previously used measure of economic activity—the "gainful worker concept"—which was designed to ascertain individuals' *usual* occupation, if they had one, rather than whether they were actually working at any given time (Hauser 1949). In fact, census enumerators were often specifically instructed to record an occupation, even if the individual was currently unemployed, thus *over*stating the number employed. On the other hand, some kinds of employment were often *under*estimated because people who considered their market work to be secondary to their other activities, such as taking care of the home and children or going to school, were less likely to report themselves as employed in response to a question on their usual occupation. Misreporting of this type is unlikely with the labor-force measure since most people will remember whether they had worked at all the previous week or, if not, whether they had been looking for a job. Information on occupation and on other important characteristics of their employment, such as hours worked, was then obtained separately in response to additional questions.

While labor-force concepts are relatively unambiguous measures of current economic activity, they too exhibit problems. One general concern is the adequacy of the unemployment measure. The extent of unemployment may be understated if persistently unemployed persons eventually give up trying and drop out of the labor force. The Census Bureau has therefore included additional questions to try to ascertain the number of such "discouraged workers" as well as to measure additional aspects of unemployment or underemployment (Cain 1979; Bregger and Haugen 1995). Clifford Clogg and Teresa Sullivan have extended this approach to address the larger question of "*under*employment" (Sullivan 1978; Clogg and Sullivan 1983). They have developed and applied a variety of indicators of underemployment in order to achieve a more extensive assessment of the problem. In addition to the usual unemployment rate and estimates of discouraged workers, they use three other indicators—a measure of involuntary part-time work (due to economic factors); low work-related income relative to the poverty level, and a measure of the proportion of workers who are "overeducated" ("mismatched") for the jobs they hold. The "adequately employed" are all those who are not underemployed in any one of these five categories. Their results indicate that underemployment is more common among the young and the old, and appears to have increased in recent years. While several of the indexes, particularly the mismatch measure, are somewhat

controversial (Keyfitz 1981), the work of Sullivan and Clogg represents an important innovation in the multidimensional measurement of underemployment.

A major characteristic of the labor-force concept is that it is a measure of *market*-oriented economic activities. People are considered employed only if they work for pay (or in the production of goods or services for sale). Yet there is a considerable amount of economic production for *home* consumption. Hence, labor-force status per se is an imperfect indicator of whether an individual is economically productive; for example, full-time homemakers are never counted as employed although they usually put in long hours producing goods and services for their families. However, if the market-oriented nature of the measure is kept in mind, this limitation is not too serious in a modern industrial society. Increases in married women's labor-force participation can then be interpreted as indicating their growing participation in the *market* sector of the economy, usually in addition to their *home* productive activities, although working wives do less housework than nonworking wives (Vanek 1974; Berardo et al. 1987).

More serious problems arise in comparing societies at different levels of economic development (Moore 1953). Preindustrial subsistence economies produce few goods or services for a market. As societies develop economically, an increasing proportion of labor is sold in the marketplace, and the goods and services families consume are also increasingly purchased rather than home-produced. It is often difficult to undertake a meaningful comparison of labor force or unemployment rates among such different economies. The measurement of agricultural employment, especially that of women and youth, can be particularly problematic in countries with a large subsistence sector, and measurement inconsistencies are common (Dixon 1982). Moreover, *unemployment*, especially in rural areas, is often manifested as *under*employment, and its extensiveness is difficult to determine.

Although best suited for examining whether people are currently economically active, labor force and employment status measures have also been invaluable in the analysis of more complex sociological and economic concepts because of the ready availability of these data in time series. However, here it is important to recognize the ambiguities and limitations of such measures at the same time we exploit their utility. One example of this problem has to do with charting the extensiveness of changes in married women's economic role in the family; another concerns the measurement of life-course transitions such as the transition to work or to retirement. In the first case, the frequently reported time series of the changes in the average proportion of married women who were in the labor force in any given week each year, or even of the proportion who had worked at some time during a year, are valuable but also imperfect indicators of how extensively women's economic role has changed over time. For example, the proportion of married women with children under age 18 who were employed at some point during the year rose from 51 to 73 percent between 1970 and 1990. However, although the proportion who worked full-time, year-round had also increased considerably, it had only reached 34 percent by 1990; of women with children under age 6, only 28 percent had worked full-time year-round in 1990 (Bianchi 1995, p. 117). Hence, the commonly used time series of married women's labor-force status during as short a time period as a week will exaggerate the magnitude of the changes in wives' economic role in the family. And neither annual labor-force participation rates nor the weeks and hours worked during a whole year provide longitudinal data on the extensiveness of individual women's labor-market involvement over their adult life courses. Yet it is this sort of information that we would really like to have in assessing the changing nature of women's economic roles.

Although commonly used for this purpose, labor-force or employment status data also have their limitations as indicators of the timing of life-course transitions. The problem is that life-course transitions are not as clear-cut as the data make them appear (Oppenheimer and Kalmijn 1995; Oppenheimer et al. 1997). Students are increasingly likely to be working, at least part time, and young people go in and out of the labor force before they are able—or willing—to make a regular commitment to year-round full-time employment. Hence, the proportion of young people employed in any given week overstates whether they have completed the transition to work. Changes

in the proportion of *older* persons who are currently employed is also an ambiguous indicator because of a fair amount of labor-market turnover among this age group as well. Hence, some studies of retirement use information on when individuals start to receive pensions. However, older persons may be receiving private pensions and/or Social Security but still be working, if only part time; moreover, the retirement these pensions signify may not be entirely voluntary, complicating our interpretation of the phenomenon. So the goal of measuring when "permanent" withdrawal from work occurs can be quite elusive (Guillemard and Rein 1993; Henretta 1992).

DETERMINANTS AND CONSEQUENCES OF LABOR-FORCE CHANGES

The size and rate of growth of the labor force are dependent on three factors:

1. *The size and rate of population growth.* A large and/or rapidly growing population will produce a large and/or growing labor force.

2. *The propensity of the population to enter the labor force and how this varies among population subgroups.* Age and sex, and what these signify biologically and socially, are the major reasons for varying propensities. Infants and young children do not work, but, generally starting in adolescence, labor-force participation increases with age, peaking for those in their late thirties and early forties and starting an accelerating decline thereafter. Married women, particularly mothers of young children, have historically had lower labor-force participation rates than adult males, although this is much less so now than in the past (U.S. Bureau of the Census 1998, pp. 408–409).

3. *The composition of the population*: Since different population segments have different work propensities, the composition of the population will affect the overall proportions who are in the labor force. Sharp *short*-run fluctuations in the U.S. birthrate have led to corresponding variations in the relative size of the working-age population. Baby booms greatly increase

the number of new labor-force entrants after 16–18 years, while baby busts reduce this number. However, the overall *long*-run declines in U.S. fertility, combined with declines in mortality among the elderly, have increased the relative number of elderly in the population, an age group with low work propensities. On the other hand, foreign migration to the United States somewhat counteracts the effects of an aging population, since it has historically been disproportionately composed of young working-age adults, drawn to the United States by job opportunities.

One important long-term trend in labor-force participation in the United States has been the decline in the employment rate of young men, on the one hand, and of older men, on the other. In part, the decline for *younger* males has been due to more extended schooling, although this was somewhat offset by a rise in student employment (U.S. Bureau of Labor Statistics 1988). However, an additionally significant factor has been a decrease in the employment of moderately to less educated males, itself just one aspect of a trend in rising labor market inequality, encompassing declines in earnings as well as levels of employment (Burtless 1990; Levy 1998).

Another important long-term shift is the decline in the labor-force participation of older males, primarily due to the institution and spread of the social security system combined with the greater availability of disability benefits and private pensions. However, these declines have been observed not only for men aged 65 and older but also for men in their fifties and early sixties, although not to the same extent. Thus the labor-force participation rates for men aged 65–69 decreased from 64 percent in 1950 to 26 percent in 1990, but during these years the rates of men 60–64 and 55–59 also substantially declined, from 83 to 56 and from 90 to 80 percent, respectively (Gendell and Siegel 1992, p. 24). The increasing coverage of Social Security benefits for men retiring at age 65 and the institution of early retirement, at age 62, under the Social Security Act of 1962 has played the major role in the decreasing rates for those in their sixties. However, the declines for men in their fifties must be for other reasons. One important factor seems to be the growth of private pension

plans and employers' utilization of early retirement provisions to help downsize and restructure their firms (Guillemard and Rein 1993; Henretta 1992).

An important question is: How will the rapid raise in the older population affect the labor-force participation of older people? There is by no means an obvious answer to this question. For one thing, given the sensitivity of older persons' employment behavior to when Social Security is available, future changes in how old individuals must be in order to qualify for Social Security benefits will play an important role. Already the 1983 amendments to the Social Security Act have set in motion a rise in the age of entitlement to a full pension—from age 65 to 66 by 2009, and to 67 by 2027—and a higher rate of reduction will gradually be applied to pensions for those who retire earlier than 65. These changes in the law should operate to increase labor-force participation among the elderly. Other factors may also increase the employment of men in their fifties and sixties. Traditionally, the decline in employment over time has been disproportionately concentrated among the less educated who have fewer marketable skills and for whom the Social Security pension is relatively more attractive. However, with the rising educational attainment of the population, older adults in the twenty-first century might be expected to remain employed longer (Besl and Kale 1996). On the other hand, the state and structure of the economy is an important factor in the extent to which employers use private pension plans to encourage earlier retirement in periods of downturns or rapid structural change.

Probably the most substantial postwar change in employment behavior has been the enormous increase in married women's labor-force participation. While paid employment used to be generally limited to the period between school and marriage, since the 1940s married women's employment has become so prevalent that by 1997 between 66 and 76 percent of those in the 20–44 age groups were in the labor force. Moreover, 64 percent of married mothers of children under age 6 were also in the labor force (Oppenheimer 1970; U.S. Bureau of the Census 1998).

There are several reasons for this rapid rise in women's employment. One is that the bureaucratization of government and industry has raised the demand for clerical workers; population growth, prosperity, and rising living standards have greatly expanded the consumption of services. This, in turn, raises the demand for sales workers and for those in the "helping" professions, such as teachers and social workers, as well as nurses and others in health-related occupations. All these are occupations that have been dominated by women workers for over a century. However, because the great majority of young, single, out-of-school women have worked throughout the twentieth century, the result of this increasing demand in the postwar period has been a strong and continuing demand for a previously underutilized source of female labor—married women (Oppenheimer 1970).

Married women have often had several major reasons for wanting to work—the need, early in marriage, to help set up a new household and perhaps to save money for a down payment on a house; the increasing importance of saving for children's schooling; the couple's aspiration to achieve a high level of living; and the desire for greater personal economic security and autonomy. Periodic rises in the cost of living and the stagnating or even declining economic position of many men since the 1970s have also increased the importance of having two earners in a family (Levy 1998).

The effects of changing labor-force behavior are not just limited to the economic realm; a number of sociologists (as well as economists) have argued that this behavior has also had an important impact on marriage and the family. Since the late 1960s the average age at marriage has risen substantially, after having first declined through most of the twentieth century; nonmarital cohabitation has become increasingly prevalent; and marital instability has accelerated its long-term upward trend after a sharp reversal in the early post–World War II period. However, the divorce rate appears to have stabilized recently. Two competing employment-related explanations for these trends are currently under debate. In one, the argument is that married women's rapidly rising labor-force participation has increased their economic independence of males (Becker 1981; Espenshade 1985; Goldscheider and Waite 1986; Farley 1988; McLanahan and Casper 1995). The result, it is argued, is a decreasing desire on the part of women to remain in an unhappy marriage or even to marry at all. In addition, since women's

traditional time- and energy-consuming familial roles of childbearing and childrearing compete with the pursuit of individual career goals, more women are either forgoing childbearing entirely or settling for one or two children at most.

While the women's "independence" hypothesis appears plausible and the juxtaposition of time series data on marriage and family behavior with that of women's labor-force participation appears to support it, this is largely because the time series utilized have typically been limited to the postwar period, the period during which married women's employment was rising rapidly. The problem with these comparisons is that they use the family behavior of the early 1950s as the model of "traditional" family behavior against which to compare subsequent trends. However, the marriage and fertility behavior of the 1950s was by no means traditional (Cherlin 1992; Oppenheimer 1994). This was the baby boom era when, after a 150-year decline, the total fertility rate reversed itself and rose so much that, by the 1950s, it was back up to the level of 1900. Moreover, age at marriage had been decreasing throughout the twentieth century, at the same time that women's employment was rising, so that the early postwar age at marriage was much younger than what was "traditional" before married women's employment began its historic climb (Cherlin 1992; Oppenheimer 1994). In sum, the changes since the 1960s are more of a return to traditional patterns than a major departure from them. The independence hypothesis has also not held up to more recent micro-level empirical analyses using longitudinal data. For example, as summarized by Oppenheimer (1997), the evidence from several studies indicates that single women's labor-market position tends to have little effect on marriage formation, but that what effect it does have is positive.

A characteristic of the women's independence explanation of recent trends in family behavior is that it ignores the possible role of *men's* changing economic position in these changes. Yet it is well known that marriage and family behavior are related to men's employment characteristics (Cherlin 1979; Goldscheider and Waite 1986; Ross and Sawhill 1975; Teachman et al. 1987). Furthermore, there is a long demographic tradition, dating back to Malthus, which argues that changes in men's economic position has an effect on marriage and fertility behavior. Supporting the view that these changes might also be an important factor in the rise in both men's and women's age at marriage since the early 1970s is the well-documented finding that there has been a large absolute and relative decline in the labor-market position of young men with a high school education or less. In addition, there has been an increase in economic inequality within each educational group, including those with a college education (Levy 1998; Juhn et al. 1993). The reasons for these trends appear to be quite complex, and, to date, no general consensus has yet been reached regarding the relative importance of several proposed explanations. A variety of factors appear to be making a contribution. The globalization of manufacturing and the resulting competition from cheap semiskilled labor in developing countries may be decreasing the demand for less skilled American workers, workers who previously were able to command relatively high wages in manufacturing; moreover, this same globalization has weakened the position of unions and hence their ability to protect such workers from an erosion in their job security and wages. All this has fostered the continued decline in the proportion of workers in manufacturing and the rapid rise in the proportion in service industries. However, the growth of service industries per se cannot be driving these changes because the growth in some service industries has increased the demand for more highly skilled labor while the expansion of other service industries has only resulted in a rising demand for low-wage unskilled labor, leaving the semiskilled in an increasingly poor position. Moreover, it does not appear that industrial restructuring alone can satisfactorily account for all or perhaps even most of these changes because, *within* industries, there is evidence of a sharp rise in the demand for more skilled labor pointing to an important role for technological change in both the manufacturing process and the production of services (Levy 1998; Meisenheimer 1998).

Whatever the reasons for the declining economic position of young, less educated males, recent research provides evidence that men in a poorer labor-market position do tend to delay marriage (Mare and Winship 1991; Lloyd and South 1996; Oppenheimer et al. 1997). Oppenheimer's work, in particular, has indicated that substantial inequalities in the length and difficulty of the career-entry process exist both within

and between race-schooling groups and lead to substantial differences in the marriage timing of young men.

This article has reviewed the history of labor-force measures as well as several important current issues in labor-force analysis. First, the study of the labor force reveals the changing significance of work in the lives of different segments of the population. Second, since economic behavior impacts on other social systems, such as the family and stratification systems, labor-force analysis will continue to be an essential field for sociological analysis.

REFERENCES

Becker, Gary S. 1981 *A Treatise on the Family*. Cambridge, Mass.: Harvard University Press.

Berardo, Donna Hodgkins, Constance L. Shehan, and Gerald R. Leslie 1987 "A Residue of Tradition: Jobs, Careers, and Spouses' Time in Housework." *Journal of Marriage and the Family* 49:381–390.

Besl, John R., and Balkrishna D. Kale 1996 "Older Workers in the 21st Century: Active and Educated, a Case Study." *Monthly Labor Review* 119:18–28.

Bianchi, Suzanne 1995 "Changing Economic Roles of Women and Men." Pp. 107–154 in Reynolds Farley ed., *State of the Union: America in the 1990s*, Vol. 1. New York: Russell Sage.

Bregger, John E., and Steven E. Haugen. 1995. "BLS Introduces New Range of Alternative Unemployment Measures." *Monthly Labor Review* 118:19–26.

Burtless, Gary, ed. 1990 *A Future of Lousy Jobs?* Washington: Brookings Institution.

Cain, Glenn C. 1979 "Labor Force Concepts and Definitions in View of Their Purposes." *Concepts and Data Needs–Appendix*, vol. 1. Washington: National Commission on Employment and Unemployment Statistics.

Cherlin, Andrew J. 1979 "Work Life and Marital Dissolution." Chapter 9 in George Levinger and Oliver C. Moles, eds., *Divorce and Separation: Contexts, Causes and Consequences*. New York: Basic Books.

—— 1992 *Marriage, Divorce, and Remarriage*. Cambridge, Mass.: Harvard University Press.

Clogg, Clifford C., and Teresa A. Sullivan 1983 "Labor Force Composition and Underemployment Trends, 1969–1980." *Social Indicators Research* 12:117–152.

Dixon, Ruth B. 1982. "Women in Agriculture: Counting the Labor Force in Developing Countries." *Population and Development Review* 8:539–561.

Espenshade, Thomas J. 1985 "Marriage Trends in America: Estimates, Implications, and Underlying Causes." *Population and Development Review* 11:193–245.

Farley, Reynolds 1988 "After the Starting Line: Blacks and Women in an Uphill Race." *Demography* 25:477–495.

Gendell, Murray, and Jacob S. Siegel. 1992. "Trends in Retirement Age by Sex, 1950–2005." *Monthly Labor Review* 115:22–29.

Goldscheider, Frances Kobrin, and Linda J. Waite 1986 "Sex Differences in the Entry into Marriage." *American Journal of Sociology* 92:91–109.

Guillemard, Anne-Marie, and Martin Rein 1993 "Comparative Patterns of Retirement: Recent Trends in Developed Societies." *Annual Review of Sociology* 19:469–503.

Hauser, Philip M. 1949 "The Labor Force and Gainful Workers—Concept, Measurement and Comparability." *American Journal of Sociology* 54:338–355.

Henretta, John C. 1992 "Uniformity and Diversity: Life Course Institutionalization and Late-Life Work Exit." *The Sociological Quarterly* 33:265–279.

Juhn, Chinhui, Kevin Murphy, and Brooks Pierce 1993 "Wage Inequality and the Rise in Returns to Skills." *Journal of Political Economy* 101:410–442.

Keyfitz, Nathan 1981 "Review of *Measuring Underemployment*, by C. C. Clogg." *American Journal of Sociology* 86:1163–1165.

Levy, Frank 1998 *New Dollars and Dreams*. New York: Russell Sage.

Lloyd, Kim M., and Scott J. South 1996 "Contextual Influences on Young Men's Transition to First Marriage." *Social Forces* 74:1096–1119.

Mare, Robert D., and Christopher Winship 1991 "Socioeconomic Change and the Decline of Marriage for Blacks and Whites." Pp. 175–202 in Christopher Jencks and Paul E. Peterson, eds., *The Urban Underclass*. Washington: Brookings Institution.

McLanahan, Sara, and Lynne Casper 1995 "Growing Diversity and Inequality in the American Family. In Reynolds Farley, ed., *State of the Union: America in the 1900s*, vol 1. New York: Russell Sage Foundation.

Meisenheimer, Joseph R., II 1998 "The Services Industry in the 'Good' versus 'Bad' Jobs Debate," *Monthly Labor Review* 121:22–47.

Moore, Wilbert E. 1953 "The Exportability of the Labor Force Concept." *American Sociological Review* 18:68–72.

Oppenheimer, Valerie Kincade 1970 *The Female Labor Force in the United States: Demographic and Economic Factors Governing Its Growth and Changing Composition*. Population Monograph Series, no. 5. Institute of International Studies, University of California, Berkeley.

—— 1994 "Women's Rising Employment and the Future of the Family in Industrial Societies." *Population and Development Review* 20:293–342.

—— 1997 "Women's Employment and the Gain to Marriage: The Specialization and Tradition Model." *Annual Review of Sociology* 23:431–453.

——, and Matthijs Kalmijn 1995 "Life-Cycle Jobs." *Research in Social Stratification and Mobility* 14:1–38.

——, Matthijs Kalmijn, and Nelson Lim 1997 "Men's Career Development and Marriage Timing during a Period of Rising Inequality." *Demography* 34:311–330.

Ross, Heather L., and Isabel V. Sawhill. 1975. *Time of Transition: The Growth of Families Headed by Women*. Washington,: Urban Institute.

Sullivan, Teresa A. 1978 *Marginal Workers, Marginal Jobs: The Underutilization of American Workers*. Austin: University of Texas Press.

Teachman, Jay D., Karen A. Polonko, and Geoffrey K. Leigh 1987 "Marital Timing: Race and Sex Comparisons." *Social Forces* 66:239–268.

U.S. Bureau of Labor Statistics 1982 *BLS Handbook of Methods*, vol 1. Washington: Government Printing Office.

—— 1988 *Labor Force Statistics Derived from the Current Population Survey*, Bulletin 2307. Washington: Government Printing Office.

U.S. Bureau of the Census 1998 *Statistical Abstract of the United States: 1998*. Washington: Government Printing Office.

Vanek, Joan 1974 "Time Spent in Housework." *Scientific American* 231:116–120.

VALERIE KINCADE OPPENHEIMER

LABOR MOVEMENTS AND UNIONS

Labor movements are collective activities by wage and salaried workers in market societies to improve their economic, social, and political status. The main manifestations of such movements are labor unions and political parties, but sometimes they include producer and consumer cooperatives; credit unions; newspapers; and educational, welfare, cultural, and recreational organizations. Labor movements and unions need sociological analysis because they are integral parts of two major and related institutions of society, the economy and polity. Apart from bringing about changes in these institutions, they are the main vehicles for mobilizing the class interests of wage and salaried employees. No other social science discipline offers such a broad perspective of study.

Yet, in the United States since the inception of sociology, labor movements have received surprisingly little attention. From their founding up to 1999, three main journals—*The American Journal of Sociology, The American Sociological Review*, and *Social Forces*—together representing 219 years of publication, published only sixty-three articles whose titles mention labor movements, unions, or strikes. American sociological research on the topic has fluctuated with labor's fortunes. As union membership grew from 1940 to 1960, research expanded and then lagged, with falling membership in the 1970s. The more rapid decline of labor since 1980 has recently stimulated research on the causes.

The bulk of American labor research has been done by historians and labor economists. To be sure, sociologists have made contributions while working on other topics such as social stratification (e.g., working-class formation, income inequality), organizations (leadership turnover), race and gender (discrimination in unions), political sociology (party preferences of union members), case studies of industry (shop-floor life, the labor process), and social movements (Jenkins 1985). Combining these contributions with those of labor economists and historians, a sizable literature is now available (see the bibliography in Stern and Cornfield 1996). In Europe, the bulk of labor research has been done by sociologists and historians.

ORIGIN OF THE LABOR MOVEMENT

Labor movements and unions emerged with the rise of capitalism, the Industrial Revolution, and free labor markets in eighteenth-century Europe. Historians agree that labor unions did not evolve from medieval guilds, which were status groups of master-owners whose monopoly of skills was protected by public authorities. Journeymen, apprentices, and laborers had fewer or no privileges (Pirenne 1932; Lederer 1932). In early capitalism, factory workers created ad hoc organizations to withhold their labor from employers, to control production and job training, and to protect

wages and working conditions. Re-created with recurring crises, the organizations eventually became permanent (Jackson 1984). As product markets grew and spread, unions were forced to organize new locals in those markets to prevent wage competition among communities. The labor movement became larger, more institutionalized, and more diversified as it organized workers in different occupations, industries, and regions (Sturmthal 1974).

This fragmented response to threats forced labor leaders to press for a more united and centralized organization to respond to threats wherever and whenever they appeared. Invariably, some unions were reluctant to commit their resources for the welfare of a vague "movement." Failure to consider this persistent resistance has led many scholars to equate labor movement growth with the formation of the working class and with working-class politics. Although the two are related, their linkage varies enormously in different times and places. Where labor movements first emerged, they were not class movements, but efforts by a minority of skilled workers to protect their traditional privileges (Calhoun 1982). Even when unions expanded to include most workers, internal factions remained, based on skill, industry, status, and influence (Form 1985, p. 96). The emergence of class movements, on the other hand, involved complex processes of linking labor movements to other special interest groups and political parties (Katznelson and Zolberg 1986).

The character and strength of labor movements must be explained in the context of the societies in which they emerge, especially the ways they relate to distinctive traditions, economies, and political and governmental systems. Autonomous labor movements survive best in capitalist democratic industrial societies. To sustain free collective bargaining, labor, management, and government must exhibit considerable independence but not exert overwhelming power in the tripartite relationship. Where union membership is compulsory and universal, where unions are completely dominated by government and/or enterprise managers, unions lack the autonomy and strength to advance the special interests of workers. Paradoxically, where labor has total control over government and the economy, it lacks opposition and the attributes of free labor movements (Sturmthal 1968).

TYPES OF LABOR MOVEMENTS

Labor movements vary in structure and behavior according to their relationships to government and other institutions. Movements fall into roughly five types. In the independent type, as in the United States, labor is independent of all major institutions, especially parties, government, and religion. Although labor seeks political influence, it participates in a shifting multiclass coalition of a particular party. Corporate labor movements, as exhibited in Britain, Scandinavia, Germany, Italy, and France, are often formally incorporated into the political system, sometimes playing a dominant role in labor, religious, socialist, or social democratic parties. When such parties win electoral victories, labor participates in governmental bodies—cabinets, legislatures, and government agencies. In the third or party-dominant movement, sometimes found in developing societies with mixed economies, labor is part of a permanent ruling coalition—for instance, the Institutional Revolutionary Party of Mexico. Here labor loses some freedom to push for the special interests of workers because it is rarely strong enough to resist decisions of the coalition. In totalitarian fascist and communist regimes, labor movements are totally subordinate to the ruling party and exhibit the least independence. Finally, in enterprise labor movements, labor functions primarily in a consultative capacity at the enterprise level. Nationally, labor belongs to a loose federation of unions with weak links to major parties, organizations, and institutions.

In independent movements, labor seeks economic gains primarily by bargaining with management. In the political realm, it seeks governmental protection for the right to organize and bargain as well as protective legislation such as unemployment, old age, and medical insurance. In the corporate type, apart from bargaining with employers, labor makes gains through legislation that forces management to deal with labor in arriving at enterprise policies regarding job rights, the organization of work, investment and other decisions, as in codetermination in Germany and Scandinavia (Nutzinger and Backhaus 1980). Public ownership of certain industries (often mines, public utilities, and transportation) is also an option. Labor strength is highest in this type of movement. In the party-dominant movement, labor at best makes gains for a minority of organized workers,

stratifying the working class. Under totalitarian regimes, labor may be given certain functions, such as assigning housing or supervising cooperatives, but its ability to bargain with government and enterprise management is severely limited (Lane and O'Dell 1978). In enterprise unionism, organized workers may gain employment security and career rewards in exchange for loyalty to the enterprise. The unorganized are exposed to the vicissitudes of the market (Okochi et al. 1974).

AMERICAN EXCEPTIONALISM

Scholars have long tried to explain why the American labor movement has not developed into the sort of corporatist socialist movement found in other advanced industrial democracies (Sombart 1906). Most scholars agree that European societies, compared to the United States, have had longer and stronger links to past institutions. When landed aristocrats, business, military, and religious elites resisted worker participation in the political system, class-oriented parties appeared. In such class environments, labor unions developed or joined other parties to obtain voting rights for workers, government protection of unions, benefits unavailable through collective bargaining, and eventual public ownership of industries. In addition to supporting class parties, labor movements developed structures attuned to their interests— for example, an intellectual elite, cooperatives, newspapers, banks, schools, and recreational clubs. In response to socialist and communist movements, Catholics not only launched their own labor movements and parties, but also organized schools, hospitals, newspapers, and clubs to embrace workers in a harmonious class-inclusive environment (Knapp 1976). Rejecting "captured" socialist, communist, and religious labor movements, liberals sought to organize free or neutral unions and parties that appealed to some workers and middle-class adherents (Sturmthal 1968).

The labor movement in the United States faced a different environment. The absence of an agricultural aristocracy and traditional governmental, military, and religious elites dampened class sentiments. Early extension of suffrage to all adult males removed that objective as a rallying cry for labor parties. The rapid expansion of industry into new cities, high rates of internal migration and immigration, the separation of ethnic groups in neighborhoods, and religious diversity slowed the formation of multiple working-class bonds. Moreover, an aggressive capitalist class, not bound by traditional obligations toward subordinates, fashioned laws and courts to protect property rights and suppress unions as conspiratorial monopolies (Dougherty 1941, pp. 635–677).

Even so, trade assemblies and craft unions emerged in several cities in the decade after the Civil War. In the 1880s, the Knights of Labor tried to organize unions that included all workers, even the white-collar and small businesses. This attempt lasted roughly a decade. Beginning in 1905, the militant International Workers of the World (IWW) organized workers of all skills to join unions and engage in political action to destroy capitalism (Dougherty 1941, pp. 317–349). The IWW too lasted a decade. For a few years, splintered socialist parties tried to support class-oriented unions. These efforts failed largely because the American political system places structural limitations on the development of third parties. The presidential system, decentralized state structures, constitutional barriers to the federal government making national economic policy, and the electoral college system favor a multiclass two-party system (Lipset 1977).

Weaknesses of class-oriented unions favored the American Federation of Labor (AFL), which successfully began to organize the skilled trades in 1891. The AFL concentrated on the skilled, because skilled workers dominated their trades and were capable of the sustained solidarity needed to win strikes. As an elite minority of the working class, the Federation focused largely on wage gains, better working conditions, and remained "neutral" in party politics. Yet, without legislative protection, union gains were periodically eroded by market downturns and antiunion employer drives. Thus, as a percentage of the labor force, the AFL experienced robust growth in the prosperous years before and during World War I. Membership declined rapidly in the depressions following the war; rose dramatically along with the formation of the Committee on Industrial Organizations just before and during World War II; declined slowly after the war for two decades; and then declined more rapidly in the economic recessions of the 1970s and 1980s, from which it has not recovered. That the decline was not more precipitous after World War II was due to the legislative protection that labor received in the late 1930s under the Democratic administration's New Deal.

POSSIBLE CONVERGENCE OF LABOR MOVEMENTS

A combination of events has tilted the American labor movement toward the European social democratic model and the latter toward the American. During the Great Depression in the United States, the Democratic Party came to power with the backing of urban-industrial and middle-class voters. The party quickly enacted legislation to increase labor's purchasing power, reduce price competition in industry, protect union organizing, and restore economic order. The National Labor Relations Act (1935) gave unions legal protection to organize, and labor conducted a militant drive for members. The recruitment of many semiskilled workers into new unions organized by the Committee on Industrial Organization (CIO) of the AFL threatened the dominance of the skilled trades in the Federation, leading to a withdrawal of the CIO from the Federation. Yet, eager to protect and extend recent gains, the divided labor movement began to abandon its traditional nonpartisan political stand. After World War II, both labor movements created electoral organizations to support Democratic candidates and mobilize their members to vote. The two labor movements merged in 1955, as did their electoral arms, to form the Committee on Political Education (COPE), formally independent of the Democratic party, but essentially functioning as part of it.

This labor-party rapprochement, committed to a social security program and a welfare state, led some scholars to conclude that the American labor movement was no longer exceptional, because it had helped create a welfare state similar to that forged by the social democratic parties in Europe (Greenstone 1977). The claim is strained because neither American labor nor the major parties ever embraced a socialist framework (Marks 1989, Chap. 6). More important, American labor has never been formally incorporated into the party and government, nor has government passed laws giving labor consultative rights in work plant operations, both central features of European corporatist labor movements.

In Europe, experiments by labor-dominated governments to nationalize industries have met with limited success (Panitch 1976), and some parties have abandoned or severely curtailed nationalization programs. The matter has been and remains an issue within parties, with some unions strongly opposing it (Currie 1979). To obtain power or maintain it by democratic means, the parties found it necessary to obtain the support of middle-class employees who want the social security guarantees of a welfare state, but not nationalization of industry. To maintain a vigorous economy, social democratic parties have enacted pro-business policies, not unlike those of the Democratic Party in the United States. For example, pro-business legislation by the Clinton administration or free trade with Latin America opposed by labor. In short, conservative forces both in and outside social democratic parties have pushed European political economies toward the American model.

Where labor is part of a coalition of a permanent ruling party as in the Mexico or the former Yugoslavia, labor has sometimes shown independence and initiated strikes despite government opposition (Bronstein 1995). And even in Japan, some enterprise unions have abandoned traditional consensus policies and challenged management and government with strikes and political turmoil (Okochi et al. 1974; Kuruvilla et al. 1990). Korea has moved even farther in this direction (Deyo 1997).

If present trends continue, perhaps a slow convergence of labor movement structures will take place. Sufficient research is not available to uncover all the causes of this plausible trend, but several play a role. In totalitarian or enterprise labor movements, when governments or managements create organizations that resemble labor movements (unions, elections, bargaining sessions, and consultation), appearances may become realities during leadership crises, especially in face of turbulent external events. Thus, in Poland, during authority crises of the ruling party and the state in the late 1980s, unions began to assert control over working conditions, wage determination, and political choice (Martin 1997). With the help of clergy, intellectuals, farmers, and others, unions defied central authority and instigated a movement to bring about a democratic party and state.

These authority crises in the party-dominant, totalitarian, and enterprise labor movements often result from changes in their external environments. Top labor officials become acquainted with the independent and corporate types of movements while participating in international agencies like the International Labor Office of the United Nations. The ability of independent and corporate movements to gain visible economic and political rewards for their members has not escaped the notice of labor leaders of other types of movements. Thus, when they confront authority crises, they have a vision of the kind of changes that would help them.

More important, rising global trade and economic interdependence fosters convergence. For example, in the 1970s, Japanese and Korean auto manufacturers began to enlarge their share of the automobile markets of the United States and western Europe increasing their unemployment. While management and unions both called for tariff protection, Japanese and Korean and labor demanded and received pay increases (Deyo 1989). On making a partial recovery, American and European corporations, in pursuit of higher profits, began to outsource production in countries with lower wage rates—for example, Mexico and Brazil. Then, with limited success, American labor leaders pressed government to place tariffs on auto imports and urged labor leaders in the exporting countries to demand higher wages. However, international labor cooperation remains puny compared to growth of world trade.

TRENDS IN LABOR MOVEMENTS

In the advanced industrial capitalist democracies since the 1970s, the proportion of union members has declined in manufacturing and risen in the services and government. Some movements have shrunk rapidly, while others have remained relatively stable. Unions that had earlier won legal rights in the conduct of enterprise (codetermination, administering unemployment insurance, production planning, national bargaining) lost fewer members, for instance, corporate types of labor movements as found in Scandinavia and Germany rather than the independent type as in the United States.

In a study of eighteen advanced capitalist countries from 1970 to 1990, Western (1995) found increasing dispersion in the rates of union decline, with the highest declines in countries with the lowest initial union density—such as the United States, Britain, and France. By 1990, the declines, wherever they occurred, were traced to unfavorable global economic conditions, decentralization of collective bargaining institutions, and electoral weakening of labor-oriented parties.

In the United States, the percentage of the labor force that was unionized shrank from 37 percent in 1945 to 14 percent in 1999. Union density in the private sector declined to one-tenth of the labor force, while public sector union density grew to over two-fifths. As unions were forced into a defensive position, strike rates declined precipitously. The causes of labor's decline are complex. The most common explanation, the shift from a manufacturing to a service economy, is inadequate. In a study of eleven capitalist democracies, Lipset (1986) found that union decline did not vary with manufacturing decline. Goldfield's study (1987) showed that after eliminating changes in the economy, industries, and occupations as possible causes, employer antiunion drives under Republican administrations tilted decisions of the National Labor Relations Board (NLRB) against organized labor. But Freeman and Medoff (1984) emphasized that white-collar unions grew rapidly despite employer resistance. Finally, some of the union decline is traced to labor's spending less money on organizing drives.

Undoubtedly, other factors were also involved in the decline, notably the outsourcing of manufacturing to other countries and the national conservative trend attending Republican electoral victories and consequent antilabor policies. Moreover, several new constituencies in the Democratic Party (blacks, women, educators, business) competed for party influence. Despite some Democratic electoral victories since 1992 and greater organizing efforts by the new AFL-CIO leadership, labor's slow downward trend has continued.

Labor movements trends in other parts of the world defy easy generalization. The best descriptions of their recent experiences appear in the *International Labour Review*. Clearly, free labor movements did not automatically emerge with the demise of totalitarian regimes in former soviet states. For example, in Poland, where the union-sponsored Solidarity Party gained governmental control, unions almost ceased behaving like unions at the plant level, failing to bargain with management in support of the government's anti-inflation policy. In contrast, unions in the Czech Republic, by not participating in the Civic Forum which gained control of the government, bargained with government to win codetermination rights in industry and reduce unemployment (Ost 1997). In Romania, miners have episodically threatened violence against the government to win back-pay and wage increases. In other ex-soviet countries, especially Russia, the collapse of the economy virtually stalled the formation of a free labor movement.

In east Asia, union density has been declining recently not only in the industrializing tigers of Taiwan, Korea, Hong Kong, and Singapore but also in the more recent industrializing countries of Thailand, Indonesia, Malaysia, China, and Vietnam (Deyo 1997). Where unions and the working class have improved their positions, labor-market shortages, favorable government policies, and paternalism have been primarily responsible, rather than strong unions. Patriarchal and patrimoninal regimes have excluded unions from decision making at the enterprise level or have weakened them when they appeared. Only in Korea, where industrial workers are rather homogeneous, are residentially concentrated, and have developed autonomous organization, have unions intermittently exhibited strong independence (Deyo 1989).

In Latin America, recent declines in autocratic regimes have encouraged the rise of autonomous labor movements. Yet, three factors that vary enormously by country are union autonomy from the state; the amount of collective bargaining; and dialogue among unions, the state, and management. Although some progress toward free-trade unionism has appeared in Argentina, Brazil, Mexico, and Chile, government pressure to achieve economic stability in the face of inflation, unemployment, poverty, and the legacy of autocratic military regimes has slowed basic changes in the tripartite relations of labor, state, and management (Bronstein 1995).

DEMOCRACY OR OLIGARCHY IN THE LABOR MOVEMENT

Even labor movements that are large, strong, and autonomous face constant problems. Unlike most institutions, all labor movements claim to be democratic in ideology, structure, and behavior. Union officers are supposed to be leaders, not bosses, and, their primary task is to improve the well-being of membership. Sociologists have long pondered whether large and complex democratic organizations can escape becoming oligarchies with self-serving officers. The most famous proponent of this proposition was Roberto Michels (1911), who studied the history of the Socialist Party in pre–World War I Germany. He found that its officers had become a self-perpetuating elite who controlled communication with the membership, appointed their staff and successors, and pursued their self-interests, often oblivious of member needs and concerns.

Several case studies of unions have challenged Michels's thesis. Lipset, Trow, and Coleman (1956) found that the unique party system of the International Typographical Union fostered electoral competition, officer turnover, and membership involvement in union affairs. Edelstein and Warner's (1979) study of fifty-one international unions revealed that officer turnover varied with constitutional provisions, such as frequency of elections, percentages of officers elected, and frequency of conventions. Cornfield (1989) found that substantial ethnic turnover among officers of the United Furniture Workers resulted from changes in the economy, the regional dispersal of the industry, political disputes among officers, ethnic tolerance of the membership, and a tradition of membership involvement in union affairs.

While most case studies of turnover among union leaders have focused on relatively small unions whose members exhibit rather homogeneous skills and earnings, the studies do not reveal the extent to which these conditions apply to the universe of unions. Marcus's study (1964) of all major unions in the country revealed that the larger and more heterogeneous the union, the slower the leadership turnover, the less frequently conventions were held, and the more decision making was concentrated in the officers.

Other dimensions of stratification within unions persist over their life histories. In a rare study, Bauman (1972) demonstrated that cleavages along skill lines persisted during the entire history of the British labor movement. At the beginning of the Industrial Revolution, skilled workers formed their own societies. From 1850 to 1890, they formed craft unions that gained recognition. Between 1890 and 1924, they became an elite sector of the labor movement and maintained their status and influence in the large industrial unions. With the development of the Liberal and Labour parties, trade union leaders became subordinated to university-trained, middle-class intellectuals who dominated the parties, seats in Parliament, and high government positions. Herman Benson (1986) argued that this pattern also applies to the American labor movement, and Alain Touraine (1986) argued it is universal. In short, the rising size and organizational complexity of the labor movement are accompanied by increasing internal stratification and a less responsive bureaucracy, confirming Michels's original argument.

CONCLUSIONS

Although the future of the American labor movement is difficult to predict, the movement will surely survive and change. Michels argued that as movements become institutions, they lose the loyalty and commitment of the founding generations. Although economic gains always remain paramount goals of unions, money is not uppermost in the minds of members while they are working. Whatever changes take place in the economy or polity, workers live where they work. The historic union goal to improve working conditions erodes with the bureaucratization of enterprises and the labor movement. Therefore, improving the quality of work life must become a renewed priority of labor leaders, so as to invigorate member loyalty and commitment. This involves greater worker participation in the control of work organization, a challenge that management will surely resist, but union leaders must relentlessly pursue.

When labor was a larger constituency of the American Democratic Party, it had more influence in party affairs despite COPE's weak electoral organization. Form (1995) has shown that especially at the grass-roots level, COPE is severely fragmented along occupational and industrial lines; more important, union members are hardly aware of labor's political goals and electoral efforts. Understandably, Democratic Party elites have responded more to other, better-organized constituencies. Unless labor makes common cause with some of them in the workplace as well as in the political arena, labor's party influence will continue to decline. Paradoxically, the more selflessly labor supports other constituencies, the more politically influential it will become. Labor's natural allies are African Americans, Hispanics, educators, women's movements, and environmentalists. The challenge of labor leaders is to convince their members to support this strategy.

Finally, like business, labor must become a worldwide movement. Self-interest requires labor movements in advanced capitalist economies to assist foreign labor movements in making economic, social, and political gains. This surely is the toughest assignment, but unless progress is made on this front, labor may continue to decline.

(SEE ALSO: *Labor Force, Social Movements*)

REFERENCES

Bauman, Zymunt 1972 *Between Class and Elites*. Manchester, England: Manchester University Press.

Benson, Herman 1986 "The Fight for Union Democracy," in Seymour Martin Lipset, ed., *Unions in Transition*. San Francisco: Institute for Contemporary Studies.

Bronstein, Arturo S. 1995 "Societal Change and Industrial Relations in Latin America: Trends and Prospects." *International Labour Review* 139:163–186.

Calhoun, Craig 1982 *The Question of Class Struggle*. Chicago: University of Chicago Press.

Cornfield, Daniel B. 1989 *Becoming a Mighty Voice: Conflict and Change in the United Furniture Workers of America*. New York: Russell Sage Foundation.

Currie, Robert 1979 *Industrial Politics*. Oxford: Clarendon.

Deyo, Frederic C. 1989 *Beneath the Miracle: Labor Subordination in the New Asian Industrialism*. Berkeley: University of California Press.

—— 1997 "Labor and Post-Fordist Industrial Restructuring in East and Southeast Asia." *Work and Occupations* 24:97–118.

Dougherty, Carroll R. 1941 *Labor Problems in American Industry*. Boston, Mass.: Houghton Mifflin.

Edelstein, J. David, and Malcolm Warner 1979 *Comparative Union Democracy*. New Brunswick, N.J.: Transaction Press.

Form, William 1985 *Divided We Stand: Working-Class Stratification in the United States*. Urbana: University of Illinois Press.

—— 1995 *Segmented Work, Fractured Labor: Labor Politics in American Life*. New York: Plenum.

Freeman, Richard B., and James I. Medoff 1984 *What Do Unions Do?* New York: Basic Books.

Goldfield, Michael 1987 *The Decline of Organized Labor in the United States*. Chicago: University of Chicago Press.

Greenstone, J. David 1977 *Labor in American Politics*. Chicago: University of Chicago Press.

Jackson, Kenneth Robert 1984 *The Formation of Craft Markets*. New York: Columbia University Press.

Jenkins, J. Craig 1985 *The Politics of Insurgency: The Farm Workers' Movement in the 1960s*. New York: Columbia University.

Katznelson, Ira, and Aristride R. Zolberg (eds.) 1986 *Working-Class Formation: Nineteenth Century Patterns in Europe and the United States*. Princeton, N.J.: Princeton University Press.

Knapp, Vincent J. 1976 *Europe in the Era of Social Transformation: 1700–Present*. Englewood Cliffs, N.J.: Prentice-Hall.

Kuruvilla, Sarush, Daniel G. Gallagher, Jack Fiorito, and Mitusuru Wakabayushi 1990 "Union Participation in Japan: Do Western Theories Apply?" *Industrial and Labor Relations Review* 43:366–373.

Lane, David, and Felicity O'Dell 1978 *The Soviet Worker*. New York: St. Martin's Press.

Lederer, Emil 1932 "Labor" *Encyclopedia of the Social Sciences*. New York: Macmillan.

Lipset, Seymour Martin 1977 "Why No Socialism in the United States?" In Seweryn Bialer and Sophis Suzlar, eds., *Sources of Contemporary Radicalism*. Boulder, Colo.: Westview.

—— 1986 "North American Labor Movements." In Seymour Martin Lipset, ed., *Unions in Transition: Entering the Second Century*. San Francisco: Institute of Contemporary Studies.

——, Martin A. Trow, and James A. Coleman 1956 *Union Democracy*. New York: Free Press.

Marcus, Philip H. 1964 "Organizational Change: The Case of American Trade Unions." In George Zollschan and Walter Hirsch, eds., *Explorations in Social Change*. Boston: Houghton Mifflin.

Marks, Gary 1989 *Unions in Politics: Britain, Germany, and the United States in the 19th and Early 20th Centuries*. Princeton, N.J.: Princeton University Press.

Martin, Brian D. 1997 Institutional change and strike mobilization in pre- and post-transition Poland. Ph.D. Diss., Ohio State University, Columbus.

Michels, Robert (1911) 1959 *Political Parties*. New York: Dover.

Nutzinger, Hans G., and Jurgen Backhaus 1980 *Co-Determination*. Berlin: Springer-Verlag.

Okochi, Kazuo, Bernard Karsh, and Solomon B. Levine (eds.) 1974 *Workers and Employers in Japan: The Japanese Employment Relations System*. Princeton, N.J.: Princeton University Press.

Ost, David 1997 "Can Unions Survive Communism?" *Dissent* Winter: 21–27.

Panitch, Leo 1976 *Social Democracy and Industrial Militancy*. New York: Cambridge University Press.

Pirenne, Henri 1932 "Guilds, European." *Encyclopedia of the Social Sciences*. New York: Macmillan.

Seidman, Jack, J. London, B. Karsh, and Daisy L. Tagliacozzo 1958 *The Worker Views His Union*. Chicago: University of Chicago Press.

Sombart, Werner 1906 *Warum gibt es in den Vereingten Staaten keinen Socializmus?* Tubingen: Mohr.

Stern, Robert N., and Daniel Cornfield 1996 *The U.S. Labor Movement: References and Resources*. New York: G. K. Hall.

Sturmthal, Adolf F. 1968 "Labor Unions: Labor Movements and Collective Bargaining in Europe." *International Encyclopedia of the Social Science*. New York: Macmillan and Free Press.

—— 1974 "Trade Unionism." *Encyclopedia Britanica*. Chicago: William Benton.

Touraine, Alain 1986 "Unionism as a Social Movement." In Seymour Martin Lipset, ed., *Unions in Transition*. San Francisco: Institute for Comparative Studies.

Western, Bruce 1995 "A Comparative Study of Working-Class Disorganization: Union Decline in Eighteen Advanced Capitalist Countries." *American Sociological Review* 60:179–201.

WILLIAM FORM

LABOR THEORY OF VALUE

See Marxist Sociology.

LATIN AMERICAN STUDIES

Sociological research on Latin American societies has focused on the understanding of the causes and consequences of different patterns of development. In the past decades, this research has been guided by the counterpoint between two different theoretical approaches and the findings generated with their help. In the 1950s and 1960s, the field was dominated by what came to be known as the modernization approach. In the 1970s and 1980s, dependency and world-system theories became prevalent (Klaren and Bossert 1986; Valenzuela and Valenzuela 1978). Each of these paradigms spawned useful lines of research, but eventually they became unsatisfactory, either because some of their assumptions were inconsistent with the facts, or because they were incapable of encompassing important areas of social reality. The field is now ripe for a new conceptual framework, which could incorporate useful aspects of the previous ones. In the past few years, there has been a shift toward a state-centered approach, but it is still unclear whether it will develop into a synthetic paradigm.

THE REGION

The study of Latin American societies is complicated by the heterogeneous nature of the region. The nations that compose Latin America share some common traits, but they also have important differences.

Countries vary in terms of their economy and social structure, their ethnic composition, and their political institutions. The economic differentials are very substantial. The region includes Argentina and Uruguay, whose per capita gross national products (GNPs) are $8,570 and $6,020, respectively, higher than those of the Czech Republic and Hungary but lower than those of Portugal and Greece, the poorer countries in the European Union. At the other extreme, there are countries like Haiti and Honduras, with per capita gross national products (GNPs) of $330 and $700, respectively, which are comparable to those of the Central African Republic and the Congo, respectively (World Bank 1999). Social structures vary accordingly: About 90 percent of the Argentine and Uruguayan population is urban, but the percentages in Haiti and Guatemala are 35 percent and 44 percent (PNUD 1997); manufacturing accounts for about 20 to 25 percent of the GDP of Argentina, Brazil, and Mexico (about the same as in France, Germany, and Italy), but the proportion is only 3 percent in Bolivia and 9 percent in Panama, whose levels of industrialization are comparable to those of Cambodia and Bangladesh, respectively. Enrollment ratios in post-secondary education vary from about 40 to 50 percent of the 20 to 24-year-olds in Argentina and Uruguay to about 8 to 9 percent in Honduras or Paraguay (World Bank 1992).

Latin American societies differ widely in their ethnic composition. The three basic components, Iberian settlers and other European immigrants, Indians, and blacks, are found in different proportions and mixes in different societies. Some are relatively homogeneous: most of the Argentine and Uruguayan populations are of European origin (the greater part are the product of transatlantic immigration at the turn of the century), and the population of Haiti is basically African. Other societies, like Mexico, Peru, and Guatemala, have maintained the colonial pattern of ethnic stratification, with mostly "white" elites ruling over largely Indian citizenries. Most of the population in Chile, Colombia, Venezuela, the Dominican Republic, El Salvador, and Honduras is the product of miscegenation. Brazil has a very heterogeneous population, with large contingents of all the ethnic groups and their different mixes (Ribeiro 1971; Lambert 1967).

With respect to their political institutions, countries in the region vary as well. Some, like Costa Rica, Chile, and Uruguay, have had long histories of constitutional rule (punctuated, by authoritarian episodes), while others, like Argentina, Brazil, and Peru, have wavered between instability and authoritarianism for much of the postwar period. All over the region, military dictatorships gave way to constitutional governments in the 1980s (O'Donnell and Schmitter 1986), and the 1990s has been the decade of democratic consolidation (Huntington 1991; Linz and Stepan 1996). The legitimacy and overall potential for institutionalization of these new governments vary according to the strength of liberal democratic traditions, the subordination of the state apparatus to the government, the vitality of the party system, and the dynamism of the economy. Authoritarian rule and state corporatism are still being dismantled in Mexico, and guerrillas operate in Colombia and Peru. Finally, Cuba is one of the few remaining state socialist polities in the world.

Nevertheless, there are economic, social, and political commonalities, besides the obvious cultural and religious ones. As far as the economy is concerned, and in spite of the variability noted above, Latin American countries share four important traits. First, all these societies belong, in terms of their per capita product, to the low or lower-middle ranks in the world system. Second, all Latin American nations have basically been, and most still are, in spite of the considerable industrialization that took place in the most advanced countries, exporters of commodities and importers of manufacturing products. Third, industrialization, from the Depression of the 1930s up to the recent past, has been based on import-substitution policies. These policies have led to low growth rates, and even outright stagnation, once the domestic markets were saturated, a stage that the most advanced countries in the region reached in the 1970s and 1980s. Fourth, Latin American societies are highly dependent, in most instances because large segments of their economies are under the control of external actors (multinational corporations in particular), and in practically all cases because of their high levels of indebtedness to the advanced industrial countries.

There are many differences among Latin American social structures and political institutions, but all these societies except Haiti originated as Spanish and Portuguese colonies. The pillars of the original institutional matrix were the organization of the economy around the large agrarian property, a highly centralized political system in which representative features were weak, and a cultural system centered in the church, and in which the toleration of pluralism was extremely low (Lambert 1967; Veliz 1980). This institutional core disintegrated as a consequence of the economic and social changes of the nineteenth and twentieth centuries: New social actors were formed, and old ones were transformed by urbanization, industrialization, and the expansion of education, and also by the irruption of external economic, political, and cultural forces. Further, in some societies there were substantial changes in the composition of the population. However, the common origins still account for important similarities in the historical trajectories of the countries of the region.

In the realm of politics, commonalities are also evident in the post-independence period, especially after the Great Depression of the 1930s. At that time, liberal-democratic regimes, most of which had not integrated the lower classes into the political system, collapsed throughout the region.

In the following decades, most Latin American countries wavered between unstable democracy and nondemocratic forms of rule. South America has been especially prone to two of these: populist-corporatist regimes and bureaucratic military dictatorships (Malloy 1977; Pike and Stritch 1974; Stepan 1978; O'Donnell 1973, 1988). Many South American polities evolved cyclically in that period: populist-corporatist regimes (such as those headed by Juan Peron in Argentina and Getulio Vargas in Brazil) were frequent from World War II to the 1960s; military regimes and their coercive counter parts in society, guerrilla warfare and terrorism, predominated in the 1960s and 1970s (in Argentina, Brazil, Chile, Uruguay, and Peru); and democratization has swept the area in the 1980s.

MODERNIZATION THEORY

Modernization perspectives shared two core assumptions that distinguished them from dependency and world-system theories. The first was that the central variables for understanding the development of a society are internal to the society; the second, that development is an evolutionary process, whose main characteristics are common to all societies. These commonalities underlie different approaches, which can be classified in terms of the variables they have considered central for the analysis of development, because of their primary causal weight, and in terms of the nature of the evolutionary process societies were supposed to undergo.

A first approach, sometimes of Parsonian or anthropological inspiration, privileged the value system, or culture, as the basic part of society, in the sense that values were expected to determine the basic traits of the economy or the polity. Change in values or culture appeared then as a key dimension in the process of transition from "traditionality" to "modernity." Examples of this perspective are Seymour Martin Lipset's analysis of entrepreneurship in Latin America (1967) and Howard Wiarda's argument about the influence of the corporatist Iberian tradition on the political evolution of Latin American societies (1973).

The second approach was structural, in the sense that it viewed the social or economic structures as the determining part of society, and that it saw changes in these structures as the central aspect of the process of development. The most elaborate versions of this perspective were inspired in Durkheim and in the most structural version of Parsonian theory: They regarded the degree of integration of society as the key characteristic of the social order and focused on the processes of differentiation and integration as the keys for the understanding of development, still conceptualized in terms of the "traditionality-modernity" continuum. Gino Germani's model of Latin American modernization in terms of the counterpoint between mobilization and integration is a good example of this perspective (1962, 1981; see also Kahl 1976). The typology of stages of economic development made popular by the influential Economic Commission for Latin America (ECLA) of the United Nations (Rodriguez 1980), shared these presuppositions.

These approaches spawned important types of sociological research in the 1950s and 1960s, but reality showed that the assumptions behind the evolutionary paradigm were problematic. Toward the end of the 1960s, it became clear that the predictions derived from the model of the traditionality-modernity continuum in relation to the social structure and the political system were inconsistent with the facts. In the social structure, the expansion of capitalist agriculture and the development of industry in societies with large peasantries did not lead to the dissolution of "traditional," or precapitalist, rural social relations. Its survival (Stavenhagen 1970; Cotler 1970) and the emergence of what came to be known as "dualistic," or structurally heterogeneous, societies meant that the patterns of social development of Latin America were not replicating those of the western European countries that were considered as the universally valid models of modernization.

Political processes in the 1960s and early 1970s were also paradoxical in relation to this theory: Lipset's thesis that liberal democracy was a correlate of development (as measured by variables such as income, urbanization, industrialization, and education) ([1960] 1981, pp. 27–63) seemed to be contradicted by the fact that it was precisely the most "modern" countries (Argentina, Uruguay, and Chile) that were the most prone to instability and authoritarianism. On the basis of this propensity, Guillermo O'Donnell (1973) argued that, in the peculiar situation of Latin American industrialization, countries of this type were the most likely candidates for bureaucratic authoritarianism. This proposition was itself questioned from different perspectives (see Collier 1979), but the lack of correlation between development and democracy seemed nevertheless obvious at that time. Later, the wave of democratization that swept Latin America in the 1980s and the revolutions of 1989–1990 in eastern Europe would indicate that the relationship proposed by Lipset does exist, even though it does not seem to be linear.

DEPENDENCY AND WORLD-SYSTEM THEORIES

Approaches based on dependency and world-system theories were the contemporary elaboration of themes found in Marxism, the theory of imperialism in particular (Lenin 1968; Luxemburg 1968). They were based on two propositions that sharply contradicted the assumptions of modernization theory. The first was that internal characteristics of a society, such as its level of development or the nature of its political system, are determined by the society's position in the international system. The second assumption was a corollary of the first: Since the main causes of development are external, there is no reason to expect that all societies will follow the same evolutionary trajectory. On the contrary: The world system is organized into a more dynamic, developed, and powerful core, and a more passive, backward, and dependent periphery. Beyond these commonalities, there were differences between the dependency and world-system approaches.

Dependency theory, which in itself was a Latin American product, emphasized the radical distinction between core and periphery, and it took dependent societies as its unit of analysis. Its focus was on the mechanisms it claimed were responsible for the preservation of underdevelopment, the transfer of economic surplus to the center via trade and investment in particular (Cardoso and Faletto 1979; Frank 1969, 1972). Wallerstein's world-system approach (1974), on the other hand, singled out the world economy as the unit of analysis, and it explored the functions of different types of society (core, semiperiphery, and periphery) in that system.

These theories have generated, since the late 1960s, important pieces of research. Fernando H. Cardoso and Enzo Faletto's comparative analysis of Latin American societies (1979) showed how different positions in the world economy generated different class structures and different patterns of development (see also Kahl 1976). Peter Evans (1979), in a study of Brazil, showed how the peculiarities of the country's development were shaped by the interaction among the state, foreign capital, and the domestic bourgeoisie. Gary Gereffi (1983) explored the consequences of dependency in a key industry. From a world-system perspective, Alejandro Portes and his colleagues (1981, 1985, 1989) conducted important studies of the labor flows in the world economy, and of the articulation between the formal and informal economies.

These approaches improved our understanding of Latin American development in two ways. First, by focusing on the effects of external factors and processes (those in the economy in particular, but the political and cultural ones as well), dependency and world-system perspectives corrected the assumption characteristic of modernization theory that societies could be studied in relative isolation. Second, since these theories constructed models of the world economy that were either pericentric (Doyle 1986), as in dependency theory; or that emphasized the analysis of peripheral and semiperipheral social structures alongside that of the core, as in world-system theory, they balanced the emphasis on core structures and processes characteristic of most preexisting studies of imperialism, which tended to ignore the institutions and dynamism of the periphery.

However, the basic tenets of dependency and world-system theories have also led in some cases (but not in the best research spawned by these perspectives) to simplistic assumptions, in particular to a tendency to consider internal structures and processes, especially the political and cultural ones, as transmission belts for external economic and political forces. The pendulum swung to the other extreme: from the neglect of external economic and political determinants of social change, characteristic of modernization theory, to a disregard for internal factors.

TOWARD A NEW PARADIGM

In the late 1980s the basic assumptions of dependency and world-system theories also became problematic. In the first place, research on the role of the state in the development process led to its reconceptualization as an autonomous actor (see Evans et al. 1985; Evans 1995; and Waisman 1987 for a Latin American case). This challenged the conceptions characteristic of most approaches close to the Marxist tradition—dependency and world-system theories included—which tended to see the state, claims of "relative autonomy" notwithstanding, as basically an instrument of either domestic ruling classes or foreign forces. Second, there was a rediscovery of social movements in the region (a consequence that the redemocratization processes of the 1980s could not fail to produce). More often than in the past, agency came to be seen as relatively independent in relation to its structural and institutional context (see the essays in Eckstein [1989], for instance), a conceptualization that differs sharply from the structuralist assumption inherent in dependency and world-system perspectives. Finally, the proposition according to which the central determinants of the development of Latin American countries are external has also been challenged (Waisman 1987; Zeitlin 1984). In the 1990s there is a growing consensus, as there was in the 1970s, that existing paradigms do not encompass our current understanding of Latin American development.

A new theoretical synthesis should integrate the valid components of the modernization, dependency, and world-system approaches, and should also allow for the autonomy of the state and the role of agency. A point of departure should be the recognition of three facts. First, the division of the world into core, periphery, and semiperiphery is not sufficient to encompass the diversity of developmental situations and trajectories relevant for the study of the countries of Latin America. It is necessary to construct a typology of more specific kinds of peripheral societies (and of core societies as well: the core-periphery distinction is still too abstract), and to describe more systematically the structural "tracks" that have crystallized in the region at different stages of development of the world economy.

Second, the different developmental paths followed by Latin American societies have been determined by empirically variable constellations of external and internal processes, and of economic, political, and ideological-cognitive ones. Few propositions that privilege the causal role of specific factors are likely to be generally valid. Rather than seeking propositions of this type, as modernization, dependency, and world-system approaches have tried to do, it would be more productive to map the specific bundles of factors that have influenced developmental outcomes in critical situations. Third, development is a discontinuous process (an instance of punctuated equilibrium, in Stephen D. Krasner's [1984] words), but we lack a theory of the transition points, that is, of the crossroads where acceleration, stagnation, retrogression, and changes of developmental tracks have taken place. The Latin American experience indicates that these are the points in which major changes in the world system, such as depressions, wars, important technological developments, organizational changes in production or trade, and restructuring of the economic or military balance of power, have interacted with domestic processes economic, political, and cultural processes.

LATIN AMERICA IN THE PAST DECADE: THE DOUBLE TRANSFORMATION

In the past two decades, Latin America has been undergoing two simultaneous transformations: economic liberalization and democratization (Waisman 1998). The pervasive nature of these transitions is indicated by the fact that they have been independent of level of development and of political regime. Most countries in the region, from relatively underdeveloped Bolivia and Paraguay to relatively industrialized Brazil and Argentina, have moved from military rule to liberal democracy in the past decade. As for economic liberalization, it took place in authoritarian Argentina and also in democratic Argentina, in authoritarian Chile and also in democratic Chile, in state-corporatist Mexico, in social-democratic Venezuela and also in social-Christian Venezuela. Like the depressions of the 1870s or the 1930s, this is a critical juncture, a reshaping of domestic economic and political institutions, the regional manifestation of the processes of economic globalization and reconstitution of the world order following the collapse of communism.

Economic liberalization was the result of a constellation of internal and external determinants. In most cases, the former seem to be central, but in any case exogenous factors constituted a powerful set of incentives and constraints pushing countries toward the liberalization road. These external causes can be classified into economic, political, and cultural.

The debt crisis of the 1980s was, for many Latin American countries, the central economic constraint (Felix 1990; Kahler 1986; Nelson 1990; Stallings and Kaufman 1989; Wesson 1988; Wionczek 1987). This crisis forced highly indebted countries to increase and diversify exports, which presupposed a higher rate of investment, and to reduce government spending. These objectives could have been sought with variable mixes of industrial policy ("picking the winners") and trade liberalization, but the policies of creditors and international lending agencies produced strong incentives for privatization, deregulation, and the opening up of the economy. Saying that the debt crisis has been in the 1980s both a powerful constraint and a substantial incentive for economic liberalization does not mean, of course, that the relationship between crisis and reform was necessary or sufficient. In fact, liberalization had begun in the 1960s and 1970s, as a consequence of perceived export opportunities, of export-oriented foreign investment, or of deliberate attempts by governments to overcome stagnating tendencies in the economy. The difference is that what had been a developmental option in previous decades had now become an imperious necessity.

As for political factors, the end of the Cold War facilitated not only political liberalization, which is more or less obvious, but also large-scale economic reform, especially in democratic settings. First, the collapse of communism led to the organizational and ideological disarmament of the radical left, and this rendered armed subversion less likely. Second, and more important, in the new international conditions the fear, be it realistic or paranoid, of exogenously induced revolution either weakened or disappeared. This fear, often unrealistic, was not only a central determinant of the exclusionary policies carried out by local elites and a reason for American and European support for authoritarian regimes, but it was also a constraint on elite behavior. During the Cold War, important segments of the state and political elites in many countries espoused the view that populist and protectionist economic policies were an antidote to communism, and many believed that the drastic social consequences of

the dismantling of autarkic capitalism would be a breeding ground for revolution (Waisman 1987).

Finally, the international demonstration effects received by the segments of Latin American societies most open to outside influences (economic and political elites, middle classes, and the intelligentsia) have favored, since the early 1980s, both economic and political liberalization. The economic success of capitalist economies and the crisis in the socialist ones, as well as the eastern European revolutions, have conferred an aura of empirical validity on two propositions: first, that capitalism and liberal democracy are both efficacious, while socialism as both an economic and a political formula is not; and second, that a capitalist economy and a democratic polity presuppose each other.

These external factors interacted with endogenous determinants. The most important of these was the realization, by state and political elites, but also by economic and intellectual ones, that autarkic capitalism had run its course, and caused in many countries stagnation or retrogression in the economy and instability and illegitimacy in the polity. It was simply no longer viable as an institutional model.

Autarkic capitalism was carried to its extreme in the countries of the Southern Cone: Argentina, Chile, and Uruguay. The long-term effects of radical import-substituting industrialization could only be stagnation, or at least stagnating tendencies, because industrialization was based on the transfer of resources from the internationally competitive export sector to a manufacturing sector shielded from the world by extraordinarily high levels of protection, both tariff and nontariff (outright prohibitions to import included). Advanced autarkic industrialization led to a situation in which most of the capital and labor in the society was committed to this captive domestic market. The outcome of this massive misallocation of resources could only be, in the long run, stagnation, and even retrogression.

Instability and illegitimacy were the long-term outcome of autarkic industrialization because this pattern of growth eventually produced an explosive combination: a stagnated economy and a society made up of highly mobilized and organized social forces, labor and the intelligentsia in particular. Stagnation led to the mobilization of large segments of the lower classes and the intelligentsia. In some countries, such as those of the Southern Cone in the 1960s and 1970s, truly revolutionary situations, in the Leninist sense of the term, appeared. Eventually, they triggered, or justified, the establishment of authoritarian regimes.

The demise of autarkic capitalism was the result, as was the case with communism, of a revolution from above. In both situations, it was the elites who dismantled the existing regimes, after having reached the conclusion that the stagnation and illegitimacy experienced by their societies were the consequence of existing institutions, and that there was no solution to the economic and political crises within these institutions. In some cases, such as Argentina and Chile, this realization took place when radical import substitution had approached its limits, and produced not only stagnation but also a revolutionary regime in Chile, and guerrillas and food riots in Argentina. In other cases, such as Brazil, the switch is taking place before these consequences appear, largely as a consequence of the demonstration effects of other Latin American countries.

THE CONTRADICTORY LOGICS OF ECONOMIC AND POLITICAL TRANSFORMATION

There are three possible sequences between economic and political liberalization (Bresser Pereira et al. 1993; Haggard and Kaufman 1995; Lijphart and Waisman 1997). To give them Latin American names, they would be the Chilean model, in which privatization, deregulation, and the opening up of the economy preceded democratization; the Venezuelan pattern, in which the liberalization of the economy takes place in the context of political institutions that have been in place for several decades; and finally the Argentine sequence, in which economic liberalization and the consolidation of democracy take place more or less at the same time. The three are fraught with dangers, but the third is the least favorable. The reason is that economic liberalization and the consolidation of democracy are governed by opposing social logics (Liphart and Waisman 1997; Waisman 1998).

Privatization, deregulation, and the opening up of the economy are governed by the logic of differentiation. Their first impact on the society is the increase of social differentiation in both the vertical and the horizontal senses: Polarization between rich and poor as a whole intensifies, and so does polarization between "winners" and "losers" within each social class, and also between sectors of the economy and regions of the country.

On the other hand, the consolidation of democracy is governed by the logic of mobilization. The political context of a new democracy renders the mobilization of those affected by economic liberalization more likely, due to the lowering of the costs of political action in relation to what was the case in the predemocratic period. Moreover, new democracies create incentives for political entrepreneurship, for in the new political conditions political and labor activists must secure and organize social and political bases. Economic liberalization presents them with an inventory of grievances that easily translates into a political agenda. Thus, both from below and from above, institutional factors are conducive to the articulation of movements of resistance to economic liberalization.

These two logics have the potential for inhibiting each other, and consequently for blocking or derailing economic liberalization, or the consolidation of democracy, or both. And yet, economic liberalization and the consolidation of democracy are occurring simultaneously in many Latin American countries, and so far no serious blockage or derailing has occurred as a consequence of the interaction between these processes. In several countries, there is an impressive consensus, involving state and economic elites, and even labor and some of the parties in the left and center that had supported state socialism or economic nationalism in the past.

The reason that, so far, the two opposing logics discussed above have not clashed lies in the operation of three "cushions" or moderating factors, which inhibit political mobilization. These can be classified into structural, institutional, and cognitive-ideological.

The structural cushion consists simply in the fact that economic liberalization itself weakens and destroys the power bases of the coalitions supporting the old regime (rent-seeking entrepreneurs and unions, and in some cases managers and workers in the public sector) and in general of those hurt by trade liberalization, privatization, and deregulation. On the one hand, these processes of economic transformation generate insecurity and economic deprivation, and thus discontent. On the other, impoverishment and marginalization also reduce social groups' capacity for organization and mobilization in defense of their interests.

Business elites, both private and public, face the choice between recycling into competitive capitalists and dropping out from the elites. This group is usually differentiated, and its most entrepreneurial elements, and/or those endowed with large amounts of economic and social capital, usually join, or become, the elite in the open economy. Labor is also dualized: Workers in the competitive sectors of the economy, or in sectors insulated from foreign competition (e.g., those producing nontradeable goods) are likely to join the train of economic conversion, and to engage in bargaining-oriented unionism. Sectors weakened by deindustrialization, by the increase of unemployment, and in general by the growth of poverty, on the other hand, are more likely to develop confrontational forms of political action, but in the end their impact is likely to be modest, because of the factors discussed above. In many countries, the weakening of labor actually began before economic liberalization, for impoverishment and the growth of the labor reserve were manifestations of the crisis of the old regime itself.

In the second place, the clash between the two opposing logics discussed above has been inhibited by institutional change. The design or redesign of some of the basic economic and political institutions is in many cases a necessary component and in general an important contributing factor to successful transitions.

Finally, cognitive-ideological factors have both external and internal sources. As I argued above, economic nationalists as well as leftists have been affected by the collapse of communism (and also by the apparent success of the Thatcher-Reagan economic policies), and by a process of political learning, triggered by the experience of the economic and political consequences of the old regime. The cumulative effect of these cognitive processes has been not only the abandonment of autarkic capitalism, but also the acceptance of the liberal model, either under the form of active support, or because of ideological surrender produced by the exhaustion of alternatives.

Given this quasi-consensus, the negative consequences of the economic transformation are not conceptualized by large segments of economic, political, and intellectual elites as necessary or permanent attributes of the emerging institutional model, but to a large extent as the product of the failure of autarkic capitalism. And the new course is not perceived as a leap in the dark, but as a transition, whose undesirable side effects are in any case the inevitable and temporary cost of the only process that can ensure, in the long run, affluence and even a higher measure of equality of opportunity in the society. The most significant leftist and radical arguments, on the other hand, focus on the espousal of social democracy in opposition to the most radical forms of the market economy, often characterized as "Darwinian" or "savage" capitalism.

Both the strengthening of civil society and the enhancement of state capacity are necessary conditions not only for the consolidation of democracy but also for the success of the economic transformation.

The typical situation in the countries that are undergoing the double transformation is that the state is shrinking while its effectiveness remains questionable in many areas. At the same time, the corporatist apparatus that was characteristic of autarkic capitalism is being dismantled. Civil society has been weakened by the authoritarian experience, and by the increased social differentiation that follows economic liberalization. The consensus supporting the new course could erode unless the new model is institutionalized, something that cannot happen without a more effective state and a stronger civil society.

This is, thus, an inflection point in the relationship between state and society, a conjuncture that could be conceptualized both a danger and an opportunity. The danger resides in the fact that, in these conditions, the structural, institutional, and cognitive "cushions" discussed above could gradually lose their effectiveness. The social dislocation produced by economic liberalization would either increase the atomization of the society, and lead to mass anomie; or facilitate "praetorian" mobilization. The first outcome would entail a deterioration of the already modest quality of the new democracies, while the second would lead to disturbances. In both cases, the legitimacy of the policies of economic transformation would fall precipitously. But this situation also represents and opportunity for social and political agency, whose goal would be the strengthening of civil society and the enhancement of state capacity.

REFERENCES

Bresser Pereira, Luis C., Jose M. Maravall, and Adam Przeworski 1993 *Economic Reforms in New Democracies: A Social-Democratic Approach*. New York: Cambridge University Press.

Cardoso, Fernando H., and Enzo Faletto 1979 *Dependency and Development in Latin America*. Berkeley: University of California Press.

Collier, David (ed.) 1979 *The New Authoritarianism in Latin America*. Princeton, N.J.: Princeton University Press.

Costin, Harry, and Hector Vanolli (eds.) 1998 *Economic Reform in Latin America*. Fort Worth, Tex.: Hartcourt Brace.

Cotler, Julio 1970 "The Mechanisms of Internal Domination and Social Change in Peru." In Irving L. Horowitz, ed., *Masses in Latin America*. New York: Oxford University Press.

Doyle, Michael W. 1986 *Empires*. Ithaca, N.Y.: Cornell University Press.

Eckstein, Susan 1989 *Power and Popular Protest: The Latin American Social Movements*. Berkeley: University of California Press.

Evans, Peter B. 1979 *Dependent Development: The Alliance of Multinational, State, and Local Capital in Brazil*. Princeton, N.J.: Princeton University Press.

—— 1995 *Embedded Autonomy: States and Industrial Transformation*. Princeton, N.J.: Princeton University Press.

——, Dietrich Rueschemeyer, and Theda Skocpol (eds.) 1985 *Bringing the State Back In*. Cambridge, England: Cambridge University Press.

Felix, David (ed.) 1990. *Debt and Transfiguration: Prospects for Latin America's Economic Revival*. Armonk, N.Y.: M. E. Sharpe.

Frank, Andre G. 1969 *Capitalism and Underdevelopment in Latin America*. New York: Monthly Review.

—— 1972 *Lumpenbourgeoisie–Lumpendevelopment*. New York: Monthly Review.

Gereffi, Gary 1983 *The Pharmaceutical Industry and Dependency in the Third World*. Princeton, N.J.: Princeton University Press.

Germani, Gino 1962 *Politica y sociedad en una epoca de transicion (Politics and Society in an Epoch of Transition)*. Buenos Aires: Paidos.

—— 1981 *The Sociology of Modernization: Studies of Its Historical and Theoretical Aspects with Special Regard to the Latin American Case*. New Brunswick, N.J.: Transaction.

Haggard, Stephan, and Robert R. Kaufman 1995 *The Political Economy of Democratic Transitions*. Princeton, N.J.: Princeton University Press.

Horowitz, Irving L. (ed.) 1970 *Masses in Latin America*. New York: Oxford University Press.

Huntington, Samuel P. 1991 *The Third Wave: Democratization in the Late Twentieth Century*. Norman: University of Oklahoma Press.

Kahl, J. A. 1976 *Modernization, Exploitation, and Dependency in Latin America*. New Brunswick, N.J.: Transaction.

Kahler, Miles (ed.) 1986 *The Politics of International Debt*. Ithaca, N.Y.: Cornell University Press.

Klaren, Peter F., and Thomas J. Bossert (eds.) 1986 *Promise of Development*. Boulder, Col.: Westview.

Krasner, Stephen D. 1984 "Approaches to the State: Alternative Conceptions and Historical Dynamics." *Comparative Politics* 16(2):223–246.

Lambert, Jacques 1967 *Latin America: Social Structures and Political Institutions*. Berkeley: University of California Press.

Lenin, V. I. 1968 *Imperialism: The Highest Stage of Capitalism*. Moscow: Progress.

Linz, Juan J., and Alfred Stepan 1996 *Problems of Democratic Transition and Consolidation: Southern Europe, South America, and Post-Communist Europe*. Baltimore, Md.: Johns Hopkins University Press.

Lijphart, Arend, and Carlos H. Waisman (eds.)1997 *Institutional Design in New Democracies*. Boulder, Colo.: Westview.

Lipset, Seymour M. 1967 "Values, Education, and Entrepreneurship." In Seymour M. Lipset and Aldo Solari, eds., *Elites in Latin America*. New York: Oxford University Press.

—— (1960) 1981 *Political Man: The Social Bases of Politics*. Baltimore, Md.: Johns Hopkins University Press.

Luxemburg, Rosa 1968 *The Accumulation of Capital*. New York: Monthly Review.

Malloy, James M. (ed.) 1977 *Authoritarianism and Corporatism in Latin America*. Pittsburgh: University of Pittsburgh Press.

Nelson, Joan (ed.) 1990 *Economic Crisis and Policy Choice: The Politics of Adjustment in the Third World.* Princeton, N.J.: Princeton University Press.

O'Donnell, Guillermo A. 1973 *Modernization and Bureaucratic-Authoritarianism: Studies in South American Politics.* Berkeley, Calif.: Institute of International Studies.

—— 1988 *Bureaucratic Authoritarianism: Argentina, 1966–73 in Comparative Perspective.* Berkeley: University of California Press.

——, and Phillippe C. Schmitter 1986 *Transitions from Authoritarian Rule: Tentative Conclusions about Uncertain Democracies.* Baltimore, Md.: Johns Hopkins University Press.

Pike, Frederick B., and Thomas Stritch (eds.) 1974 *The New Corporatism.* Notre Dame: University of Notre Dame Press.

PNUD (Programa de las Naciones Unidas para el Desarrollo) 1997 *Informe sobre el desarrollo humano (Human Development Report)* Madrid: Mundi-Prensa.

Portes, Alejandro, and John Walton 1981 *Labor, Class, and the International System.* New York: Academic Press.

Portes, Alejandro, and Robert L. Bach 1985 *Latin Journey: Cuban and Mexican Immigrants in the United States.* Berkeley: University of California Press.

Portes, Alejandro, Manuel Castells, and Lauren A. Benton (eds.) 1989 *The Informal Economy: Studies in Advanced and Less Developed Countries.* Baltimore, Md.: Johns Hopkins University Press.

Ribeiro, Darcy 1971 *The Americas and Civilization.* New York: E. P. Dutton.

Rodriguez, Octavio 1980 *La teoria del subdesarrollo de la CEPAL (The ECLA Development Theory)* Mexico City: Siglo XXI.

Stallings, Barbara, and Robert R. Kaufman (eds.) 1989 *Debt and Democracy in Latin America.* Boulder, Colo.: Westview.

Stepan, Alfred 1978 *The State and Society: Peru in a Comparative Perspective.* Princeton, N.J.: Princeton University Press.

Stavenhagen, Rodolfo 1970 "Classes, Colonialism, and Acculturation." In Irving L. Horowitz, ed., *Masses in Latin America.* New York: Oxford University Press.

Valenzuela, J. Samuel, and Arturo Valenzuela 1978 "Modernization and Dependency: Alternative Approaches in the Study of Latin American Underdevelopment." *Comparative Politics* 10(2):535–557.

Veliz, Claudio 1980 *The Centralist Tradition in Latin America.* Princeton, N.J.: Princeton University Press.

Waisman, Carlos H. 1987 *Reversal of Development in Argentina.* Princeton, N.J.: Princeton University Press.

—— 1998 "The Political Dynamics of Economic Reform in Latin America." In Harry Costin and Hector Vanolli, eds., *Economic Reform in Latin America.* Fort Worth, Tex.: Harcourt Brace.

Wallerstein, Immanuel 1974 *The Modern World System: Capitalist Agriculture and the Origins of the European World-Economy in the Sixteenth Century.* New York: Academic.

Wesson, Robert G. (ed.) 1988 *Coping with the Latin American Debt.* New York: Praeger.

Wiarda, Howard J. (ed.) 1973 "Towards a Framework for the Study of Political Change in the Iberic-Latin Tradition: The Corporative Model." *World Politics* 25:206–235.

Wionczek, Miguel S. 1987 *La crisis de la deuda externa en America Latina (The Latin American External Debt Crisis).* Mexico: Fondo de Cultura Economica.

World Bank 1992 *World Development Report 1998/99.* New York: Oxford University Press.

—— 1999 *World Development Report 1998/99.* New York: Oxford University Press.

Zeitlin, Maurice 1984 *The Civil Wars in Chile.* Princeton, N.J.: Princeton University Press.

CARLOS H. WAISMAN

LAW AND LEGAL SYSTEMS

The term *law* is surprisingly difficult to define. Perhaps the best-known definition within the sociology of law community is that of Max Weber: "An order will be called *law* if it is externally guaranteed by the probability that coercion (physical or psychological), to bring about conformity or avenge violation, will be applied by a *staff* of people holding themselves specially ready for that purpose" (1954, p. 5). Similar definitions include Donald Black's terse statement: "Law is governmental social control" (1976, p. 2). While these types of definitions have sometimes been attacked as employing a Westernized conception, appropriate for developed states but inappropriate for other societies, Hoebel advances a similar definition of law in all societies: "The really fundamental *sine qua non* of law in any society—primitive or civilized—is the legitimate use of physical coercion by a socially authorized agent" (1954, p. 26).

Definitions such as these are more interesting for what they exclude than for what they include. Weber and Hoebel each attempt to draw a line where the boundary between law and something else is fuzziest. By including the term *legitimate*, Hoebel's definition is intended to distinguish law from the brute exercise of force. The leader of a criminal gang who forces people to give him money may be doing many things, but he is not enforcing the law. He is not a socially authorized agent, and his use of force is not legitimate. Legitimacy itself is a slippery concept, and disagreements about when it is present give rise to questions such as whether the Nazis governed under the rule of law.

The inclusion of coercion and specialized agents of enforcement in both Weber's and Hoebel's definitions is meant to distinguish law from customs or norms, the breach of which either is not sanctioned or is sanctioned only by members of the group against which the breach occurred. The internal rules (norms and customs) governing a family's life or an organization's life are not law unless they are reinstitutionalized, that is, unless they are "restated in such a way that they can be applied by an institution designed (or at very least, utilized) specifically for that purpose" (Bohannan 1965, p. 36). Some have rejected such definitions and argued that law consists of the regularized conduct and patterns of behavior in a community or society (Ehrlich 1936: Malinowski 1926). They fear that if the study of law is restricted to legal rules enforced by specialized legal staffs, it will exclude much of what legal anthropologists and legal sociologists may find interesting. Regularized conduct definitions in turn suffer from their inability to offer a clear boundary between legal norms and other norms in the society. However, they do capture the idea that there is law-stuff everywhere. Families and organizations do generate rules and do coerce or induce compliance. These groups constitute what Moore (1973) calls "semi-autonomous fields." Not only are the rules of these organizations interesting in their own right, the interaction of these rules and the state rules we call law helps to shape the fundamental choice between avoidance and compliance that is faced by all to whom rules are addressed.

The boundary maintenance functions of definitions such as those of Weber, Hoebel, and Bohannan undoubtedly have their place, but law's empire is so large that the border skirmishes occurring out on its frontiers have limited influence on our shared understanding of the words *law* and *legal system*. Wherever it occurs, law is a body of rules that speak to how people should behave in society (substantive law) and how the legal system itself should proceed (adjective law). The volume and complexity of rules may be expected to parallel the size and complexity of the society of which they are a part. But broad categories of substantive law—tort law, property law, criminal law—apparently exist in all legal orders, as do the fundamentals of adjective law—procedure and evidence. The various definitions of "law" exist in an uneasy tension (Tamanaha 1997). This tension can serve us well if we follow Griffiths's advice (1984) and view "legalness" as a variable rather than thinking of "law" as a special, definable phenomenon. The complex body of substantive and adjective rules at different levels comprise a legal system.

LEGAL SYSTEMS

The comparative study of law might trace its roots to Aristotle's comparison of Greek city-state constitutions. A more recent example is Montesquieu, who, in *The Spirit of the Laws* ([1748] 1962), attempted to explain legal diversity in terms of various factors in the social setting. Interspersed between these efforts were comparisons of canon law with Roman law in Europe and with the common law in England. Despite these precursors, the modern study of comparative legal systems has become a topic of sustained academic interest only during the last 100 to 150 years.

The history of comparative law is set forth in a number of works, including Zweigert and Kotz (1987) and David and Brierley (1985). The present essay discusses a small part of this history, focusing on what Zweigert and Kotz call scientific or theoretical comparative law rather than legislative comparative law, in which foreign laws are examined and invoked in the process of drafting new nation-state laws.

Early theoretical efforts, exemplified by Maine's *Ancient Law* ([1861] 1963), adopted evolutionary theories of legal development. In Maine's famous formulation, legal systems, following changes in social arrangements, move from *status*, wherein one's rights and duties are determined by one's social niche (the law of feudalism), to *contract*, wherein ones rights and duties are determined by

LAW AND LEGAL SYSTEMS

oneself and the contracts one enters into (eventually the law of capitalism).

A second well-known developmental theory of changes in legal systems is that of Durkheim ([1893] 1964). A societal movement from mechanical to organic solidarity is accompanied by a movement from repressive law (law that punishes those who violate a shared moral understanding) to restitutive law (law that attempts to facilitate cooperation and to return people to a *status quo ante* when rule violations occur).

From the sociological point of view, perhaps the most important contributor to the early development of comparative law was that preeminent lawyer-social scientist, Max Weber. Weber's contribution was in three parts. First, he developed the device of an ideal type, a stylized construct that represents the perfect example of a phenomenon. The ideal type acts as a yardstick against which we might measure actual legal systems. Second, using ideal types, he provided a typology of legal systems classified by the formality and the rationality of their decision-making processes. Ideally, legal systems could be thought of as formal or substantive, rational or irrational. A legal system is formal to the extent that the norms it applies are intrinsic to the system itself. Substantive law, as the term was used earlier, should not be confused with the substantive dimension of Weber's typology. A legal system is substantive in Weber's sense to the extent that the source of the norms it applies is extrinsic to the legal system. For example, a legal system would be substantive if a court resolved disputes by reference to a religious rather than a legal code.

A legal system is rational if it yields results that are predictable from the facts of cases; that is, if case outcomes are determined by the reasoned analysis of action in light of a given set of norms. A legal system is irrational when outcomes are not predictable in this way. Basically, a legal system is rational to the extent that similar cases are decided similarly.

A formally irrational system exists when the legal order produces results unconstrained by reason. Classic examples are judgments following consultation with an oracle or trial by ordeal. Substantive irrationality exists when lawmakers and finders do not resort to some dominant general norms but, instead, act arbitrarily or decide upon the basis of an emotional evaluation of a particular case. Weber apparently had in mind the justice dispensed by the Khadi, a Moslem judge who, at least as Weber saw him, sat in the marketplace and rendered judgment by making a free and idiosyncratic evaluation of the particular merits of each case.

A substantively rational legal system exists when lawmakers and finders follow a consistent set of principles derived from some source other than the legal system itself. Again, Weber thought that Moslem law tended toward this type insofar as it tried to implement the thoughts and commands of the Prophet.

Western legal systems, especially those of civil law countries such as France and Germany, most nearly approximate the formally rational ideal, a legal system where the generality of legal rules is high and where the legal rules are highly differentiated from other social norms.

The relationship between formal and substantive law is obviously more complex than can be reflected in these four Weberian types. For example, legal systems may be procedurally quite formal while incorporating substantive norms rooted in nonlegal institutions. Moreover, rational systems may incorporate potentially irrational components, as when the final judgment in a case is left to a lay jury. Nevertheless, as ideal types Weber's categories help to locate idealized Western law in a wider universe of possible legal systems.

The importance of Weber's categories, like those of Maine, resides in large part in his efforts to link types of rationality with different types of societies and different ways of organizing legal systems. Weber associated an irrational legal order with domination by a charismatic leader. Formal rationality, on the other hand, accompanies the rise of the bureaucratic style of organization. Weber regarded logically formal rationality as the most "advanced" kind of legal ordering and as particularly hospitable to the growth of the capitalist state.

Weber's third contribution to comparative legal studies was his insight that the nature of a society's legal system is shaped by the kinds of individuals who dominate it. On the European continent, in the absence of a powerful central court, domination fell into the hands of the university law faculties who strove, through the promulgation and interpretation of authoritative texts, to create and understand the legal system as a general and autonomous set of rules. The common law in England, on the other hand, grew under the tutelage of a small elite judiciary and an accompanying centralized bar, more concerned with pronouncing rules for the settlement of disputes than with developing generalized rules of law (Weber 1954). In time, the differences in the legal systems created by these different sets of legal actors helped to spur interest in comparative legal systems.

Overall, Weber's contribution was part of a general movement away from comparing the legal codes of various societies and toward a comparison of the legal solutions that "are given to the same actual problems by the legal systems of different countries seen as a complete whole" (Zweigert and Kotz 1987, p. 60, quoting Ernst Rabel). From this perspective, legal systems confront similar problems, and if we examine the whole system we will uncover fundamental differences and similarities in their various solutions. The effort to uncover these similarities and differences has taken several different paths.

Macrocomparisons. One path has involved attempts to develop macrocomparisons of entire legal systems. This effort has resulted in a number of taxonomies of legal systems in which the laws of nations are grouped by what are commonly called "legal families." The criteria for classification and the ultimate categories of family types have varied from scholar to scholar. Among the factors that have been used are historical tradition, the sources of law, the conceptual structure of law, and the social objectives of law. Socialist writers have traditionally focused on the relationship of law to underlying economic relations and a society's history of class conflict (Szabo and Peteri 1977; Eorsi 1979), although more recent efforts paint a more complex picture that threatens some of the presumed differences between socialist and "capitalist" law (Sypnowich 1990). David (1950) and David and Brier ley (1985) base their classification on ideology (resulting from philosophical, political, and economic factors) and legal technique. Zweigert and Kotz (1987, p. 69) base their classification on a multiple set of criteria they call the "style" of law. Legal style includes: historical background and

development, predominant modes of thought in legal matters (contrasting the use of abstract legal norms in civil law versus the narrow, reasoning by analogy typical of the common law), distinctive concepts (such as the trust in the common law and the abuse of right in civil law), the source of law (statutory or case law), and ideology (e.g., the ideology of socialist and Western legal families).

Given the wide variety of criteria used by various scholars, perhaps it is surprising that the resulting "families" tend to be quite similar. To provide but one example, Zweigert and Kotz (1987) divide the world into the following eight families: (1) Romanistic family (e.g., France); (2) Germanic family (e.g., Germany); (3) Nordic family (e.g., Sweden); (4) common law family (e.g., England); (5) socialist family (e.g., Soviet Union); (6) Far Eastern family (e.g., China); (7) Islamic systems; and (8) Hindu law. While some taxonomies may have fewer civil law divisions, this set of categories shares with many others a Eurocentric emphasis and a resulting inability to fit non-European legal systems easily into the taxonomy (see Ehrmann 1976; David and Brierley 1985), although the rise of non-Western societies such as Japan should help to redress this imbalance in time (see Institute of Comparative Law, Waseda University 1988).

The Eurocentric and Western emphasis is not simply a matter of greater particularity in describing differences between the legal traditions of Europe. It is also reflected in the concepts used to make distinctions. The categories of the various typologies are based primarily on a comparison of private law rather than on public or constitutional law and on substantive law rather than on adjective law. A different focus may lead to different family configurations. For example, American and German constitutional law are in some ways more similar to each other than to French or English constitutional law. The focus on private substantive law has the additional result that it overemphasizes legal doctrine while underemphasizing the degree to which legal systems are a product of the surrounding society. The consequence is to understate similarities in Western legal arrangements that may be captured by the idea of a legal culture.

One alternative designed to avoid this tendency is found in Merryman's concept of legal traditions (1969). Legal traditions are:

a set of deeply rooted, historically conditioned attitudes about the nature of law, about the role of law in the society and the polity, about the proper organization and operation of a legal system, and about the way law is or should be made, applied, studied, perfected, and taught. The legal tradition relates the legal system to the culture of which it is a partial expression. (Merryman 1969, p. 2)

From this perspective the Western legal tradition may be usefully compared to and contrasted with legal systems in other cultures (Barton et al. 1983).

A second alternative to the "legal families" approach is taxonomies that are not based on differences in substantive law. One recent example, closer to the Weberian heritage, is that of Damaska (1986). Like Weber, Damaska uses two dimensions to develop ideal-typical legal orders. The first dimension divides legal orders into activist and reactive systems of justice. Activist states attempt to use law to manage society, whereas reactive states attempt only to provide a legal framework for social interaction. At the heart of the image of law of the activist state is the state decree, spelling out programs, assigning tasks, and distributing welfare to citizens. At the heart of the reactive state are devices facilitating agreement, contracts, and pacts. While it might be thought that this dimension is designed primarily to distinguish capitalist and socialist legal orders, Damaska observes that not all types of socialist models follow the state socialism that has dominated the Soviet Union and eastern Europe. Yugoslavian self-management concepts speak to this reactive tradition in socialism. Likewise, capitalist societies exhibit considerable differences in their commitment to an activist state.

Damaska's second dimension divides legal orders into hierarchical and coordinate systems of judicial organization. In the hierarchical ideal officials are professionals who are arranged in a strict hierarchy and who employ special, technical standards of decision making. The coordinate ideal describes a more amorphous machine in which legal functionaries are amateurs who are arranged in relationships of relatively equal authority and who do justice based on prevailing ethical, political, or religious norms. Weber's vision of the Moslem Khadi applying substantive (religious) law would appear to describe this type of legal order.

There are other strong parallels between Damaska's and Weber's ideal types. Their categories are less obviously Eurocentric and, more important, employ a set of concepts that facilitate an understanding of ways in which the relationship between the state and society is mediated through law. Both analyses are inclined toward a functional approach. Rather than beginning with individual legal histories and doctrines and grouping them into families, this approach begins with a set of problems—how to mediate the relationship of the state and society and how to organize the structure of legal actors—and arranges legal systems according to how they address these problems.

Damaska's distinction between the hierarchical and coordinate ideal and Weber's distinction between formal and substantive rationality direct our attention to a central issue concerning law—the degree to which different legal systems are autonomous. Formalist theories of law posit a self-contained enterprise separate from the rest of society (Kelsen 1967), while most Marxist theories view law solely as an instrument of domination (Spitzer 1983).

More recent theoretical discussions of autonomy include those of the Critical Legal Studies Movement, Niklas Luhmann (1985), and Pierre Bourdieu (1987). Critical Legal Studies focuses on law's indeterminacy and on the role of social forces and power relations as the actual determinants of legal outcomes (Kelman 1987). Luhmann's theory, to the contrary, views the legal system as autopoietic. An *autopoietic system*, like a living organism, produces and reproduces its own elements by the interaction of its elements (Teubner 1988). Bourdieu offers a complex view of the autonomy of the "juridical field." Legal system autonomy is the result of the constant resistance of the law to other forms of social practice. One way this is accomplished is by requiring those who wish to have their disputes resolved in court to surrender their ordinary understandings and experiences. Actions and actors brought into the legal system are dealt with only after they and their dispute are translated into a set of legal categories (e.g., debtor—unsecured creditor; lessor—lessee;). Western courts tend to treat as irrelevant and inappropriate those accounts that attempt to introduce the details of litigants' social lives (Conley and O'Barr 1990).

Interest in the question of legal autonomy has been reinvigorated by the collapse of socialist regimes in central and eastern Europe. The legal systems in the formerly communist societies of central and eastern Europe enjoyed relatively less autonomy than their Western counterparts. For example, judges were sometimes told how to decide politically sensitive cases. Because the directive usually came via telephone, the practice acquired the pithy name "telephone law." In the last decade much attention has been devoted to the question of how to establish the rule of law—that is, greater legal system autonomy—in Russia and eastern Europe (Hendley 1996). One would be wrong, however, to conclude that legal systems in capitalist societies enjoy complete autonomy. The intrusion of politics into the legal systems of these societies is more subtle but nevertheless substantial (Jacob et al. 1996). What is different is the way judicial field is structured: for example, the relative independence of the judiciary and the organization of the legal profession. These structures, as Bourdieu notes, make it easier for the legal system to resist penetration. Indeed, intrusion is not a one-way street. The "centrality of law" thesis argues that the legal system increasingly penetrates into other areas of modern society (Hunt 1993). Modern states have "more" law, larger state bureaucratic legal institutions, and growing numbers of legal professionals. Moreover, legal forms are exported to other spheres of life, as when the workplace becomes infused with due process requirements.

It should be clear by now that legal autonomy is a multifaceted phenomenon. Systems differ in their degree of judicial independence and judicial formalism, the extent to which their laws are status neutral, and whether those forced into the legal arena enjoy equal legal competence (Lempert 1987). One of the strengths of Weber's and Damaska's typologies is that they suggest dimensions along which legal system autonomy may vary. For example, systems that reflect Damaska's hierarchical ideal will be more likely to exhibit some of the features of greater autonomy.

Microcomparisons. Microcomparisons of legal systems are concerned with the details of specific legal rules and institutions rather than with entire legal systems (Rheinstein 1968). The functional approach is even more pronounced at this level. Scholars often begin with a specific social problem and seek to discover the various ways in which legal systems solve it, or they begin with a specific legal institution and examine how it operates in various systems. For example, Shapiro (1981) makes a comparative analysis of the court as an institution in common law, civil law, imperial Chinese, and Islamic legal systems.

The most valuable work done at this level has been that of legal anthropologists. By examining the dispute-processing activities of African, Latin American, and Asian legal tribunals, they have provided new insights into the connection between a society's social relationships and the way in which it processes disputes. Ethnographies by Gluckman (1967), Gulliver (1963), Nader (1969), and others exposed a general pattern wherein tribunals confronted with disputes among individuals who are in multiplex and enduring relationships are more likely to widen the range of relevant evidence and to search for outcomes that allow flexibility, compromise, and integration. Tribunals confronted with disputes among individuals who are in one-dimensional and episodic relationships are more likely to narrow the range of relevant evidence and to provide binary outcomes in which one side clearly wins and the other loses.

Legal ethnographies have also supported the earlier observation based on macrocomparisons that the organization of courts and judges plays a role in determining styles of dispute processing. Fallers (1969), for instance, found that the Soga, a society in many ways very similar to the Barotse studied by Gluckman, tended to craft decisions that were narrower and that resulted in "legalistic" rulings. His explanation was that the "judiciary" in the two societies differed in at least one key respect. The Soga courts were more purely "judicial" bodies without administrative and executive functions. A specialized legal staff was more likely to issue narrower opinions. Moreover, because binary outcomes result in a judgment to be enforced against a losing party, the availability of a coercive judicial apparatus may facilitate this type of dispute resolution (Lempert and Sanders 1986).

Perhaps because of the seminal work by Llewellyn and Hoebel (1941) on the Cheyenne, the work of legal anthropologists, more than most macro approaches to the study of legal systems, builds on the sociological jurisprudence and the legal realist traditions (Pound 1911–1912; Oliphant 1928; Llewellyn 1930; Arnold 1935). It is concerned with the law in action, with the actual experience of the legal staff and the disputants (Merry 1990). As a consequence, legal anthropology has had a substantial influence on the sociological study of disputing and what has come to be called alternative dispute resolution in Western societies (Greenhouse 1986; Abel 1981). Postmodern legal anthropology has grown increasingly preoccupied with the problem that confronts all comparativist work—understanding the effect of the observers' own backgrounds on the ways in which we distinguish legal systems (Comaroff and Comaroff 1992). Undoubtedly, however, the ethnographic tradition has provided rich detail to our understanding of the differences among legal systems.

Recently, anthropologists have come to appreciate the degree to which African and other consensual legal systems are themselves partly the outgrowth of colonial experience and of the distribution of power in society (Starr and Collier 1989). This observation underlines a more general point that has been noted by macro and micro scholars alike. Nearly all existing legal systems are, to a greater or lesser extent, externally imposed, and therefore all legal systems are layered (Watson 1974). In many societies layering occurs because of the existence of a federal system creating an internal hierarchy of rules, some of which are imposed from above. Layered legal systems also occur when nations such as Turkey (the Swiss code) or Japan (the German code) shop abroad and adopt the laws of another nation as the basic framework for substantial parts of their own legal system. In some situations the imposition is done wholesale and involuntarily, as when colonial powers impose a legal system. The result can be considerable social dislocation (Burman and Harrell-Bond 1979). In time, multiple layers may exist, as in Japan, where indigenous law has been overlaid by both the adopted German code and American constitutional law concepts imposed after World War II (Haley 1991).

In each of these situations a society's legal system is unlikely to fit easily within any of the legal families. For instance, a society may borrow another's substantive and adjective law for commercial law purposes but retain the existing law of domestic relations. Frequently, such societies are said to have a "dual legal system." However, to the degree that this phrase describes a situation in which two equal systems stand side by side and rarely interact, it fails to capture the rich variety of hierarchical structures in layered systems. An important task for the students of legal systems is to understand the process by which individuals and groups use law at different levels and in so doing transform both.

At the uppermost layer of legal systems are legal arrangements that are multinational or transnational in scope. Within the European Economic Community, following the Treaty of Rome in 1957 and the Single European Act in 1987, the adoption or imposition of a multinational regime is proceeding rapidly. The process requires the harmonization of a large body of law including corporate, intellectual property, environmental, tax, products liability, banking, transportation, product regulation (e.g., food and pharmaceuticals), and antitrust law. Member states must conform their national laws to comply with community directives, inevitably leading to the homogenization of European law. This process, along with the substantial alterations in property and contract law accompanying the economic changes in the Soviet Union and eastern Europe, suggests that the differences among legal systems of European origin will diminish over the next few decades, especially differences among laws governing commercial and economic transactions.

Indeed, the existence of a global economic order promotes some similarities in all laws governing economic transactions. Islamic law has been compelled to create a number of legal devices and fictions designed to avoid direct confrontation will several teachings of the Koran, such as the prohibition against charging interest that would make participation in a modern economic order difficult (David and Brierley 1985, p. 469). The emerging global economy has also created a new layer if transnational legal actors who at once attempt to export their nationalist version of law and to create a set of transnational institutional arrangements that sometimes complement and sometimes are in opposition to national legal structures. For example, Dezalay and Garth (1996) describe the emergence of a cadre of international commercial arbitrators and their creation of a international legal field with its own networks, hierachical relationships, expertise, and rules.

A number of additional global issues also create pressures toward the creation of transnational legal arrangements. These include transnational crime; ethnic and racial conflict; world population and migration patterns; labor flows; and, perhaps most significant, environmental regulation. Common legal structures created to address these issues and demands that nation-state legal systems enact and enforce appropriate compliance mechanisms may lead to the rebirth of the ideal of international legal unification that was popular at the beginning of the century. As can be seen in the European example, such unification inevitably involves some imposition of law.

Because pressures to build a more complex body of transnational law coincide with the diminution of differences in Western legal systems, over the next few decades one of the most interesting issues in the study of legal systems will involve movements toward and resistance to a transnational legal order premised on the hegemony of Western legal systems and Western legal concepts. The ongoing task of comparative law is to understand the processes of borrowing, imposition, and resistance, both among nations and between levels of legal systems.

(SEE ALSO: *Court Systems and Law; Law and Society; Social Control; Sociology of Law*)

REFERENCES

Abel, Richard 1981 *The Politics of Informal Justice*, 2 vols. New York: Academic.

Arnold, Thurman 1935 *The Symbols of Government*. New Haven, Conn.: Yale University Press.

Barton, John, James Gibbs, Victor Li, and John Merryman 1983 *Law in Radically Different Cultures*. St. Paul, Minn.: West Publishing.

Black, Donald 1976 *The Behavior of Law*. New York: Academic.

Bohannan, Paul 1965 "The Differing Realms of the Law." *American Anthropologist* 67 (6, point 2):133–142.

Bourdieu, Pierre 1987 "The Force of Law: Toward a Sociology of the Juridical Field." (Richard Terdiman, trans.) *Hastings Law Journal* 38: 805–853.

Burman, Sandra, and Barbara Harrell-Bond, eds. 1979 *The Imposition of Law*. New York: Academic.

Comaroff, John, and Jean Comaroff 1992 *Ethnography and the Historical Imagination*. Boulder, Col.: Westview.

Conley, John M., and William M. O'Barr 1990 *Rules versus Relationships: The Ethnography of Legal Discourse*. Chicago: University of Chicago Press.

Damaska, Mirjan 1986 *The Faces of Justice and State Authority: A Comparative Approach to the Legal Process*. New Haven, Conn.: Yale University Press.

David, René 1950 *Traité élémentaire de droit civil comparé*. (Introduction to the Principles of Comparative Civil Law.) Paris: Librairie Generale de Droit et de Juris prudence.

———, and John Brierley 1985 *Major Legal Systems in the World Today*. London: Stevens.

Dezalay, Yves, and Bryant G. Garth 1996 *Dealing in Virtue: International Commercial Arbitration and the Construction of a Transnational Legal Order*. Chicago: University of Chicago Press.

Durkheim, Emile (1893) 1964 *The Division of Labor in Society*. New York: Free Press.

Ehrlich, Eugen 1936 *Fundamental Principles of the Sociology of Law*. Cambridge, Mass.: Harvard University Press.

Ehrmann, Henry 1976 *Comparative Legal Cultures*. Englewood Cliffs, N.J.: Prentice-Hall.

Eorsi, Gy 1979 *Comparative Civil Law*. Budapest: Akademiai Kiado.

Fallers, Lloyd 1969 *Law without Precedent: Legal Ideas in Action in the Courts of Colonial Busoga*. Chicago: University of Chicago Press.

Gluckman, Max 1967 *The Judicial Process among the Barotse of Northern Rhodesia*. Manchester, England: Manchester University Press.

Greenhouse, Carol 1986 *Praying for Justice*. Ithaca, N.Y.: Cornell University Press.

Griffiths, John 1984 "The Division of Labor in Social Control." In Donald Black, ed., *Toward a General Theory of Social Control*. New York: Academic.

Gulliver, P. M. 1963 *Social Control in an African Society: A Study of the Arusha*. London: Routledge and Kegan Paul.

Haley, John 1991 *Authority without Law: Law and the Japanese Paradox*. New York: Oxford University Press.

Hendley, Kathryn 1996 *Trying to Make Law Matter: Legal Reform and Labor Law in the Soviet Union*. Ann Arbor: University of Michigan Press.

Hoebel, E. Adamson 1954 *The Law of Primitive Man*. Cambridge, Mass.: Harvard University Press.

Hunt, Alan 1993 *Explorations in Law and Society*. New York: Routledge and Kegan Paul.

Institute of Comparative Law, Waseda University, ed. 1988 *Law in East and West*. Tokyo: Waseda University Press.

Jacob, Herbert, Erhard Blankenburg, Herbert Kritzer, Doris Marie Provine and Joseph Sanders. 1996 *Courts, Law and Politics in Comparative* Perspective. New Haven, Conn.: Yale University Press.

Kelman, Mark 1987 *A Guide to Critical Legal Studies*. Cambridge, Mass.: Harvard University Press.

Kelsen, Hans 1967 *The Pure Theory of Law*. Berkeley: University of California Press.

Lempert, Richard 1987 "The Autonomy of Law: Two Visions Compared." In Gunther Teubner, ed., *Autopoietic Law: A New Approach to Law and Society*. New York: Walter de Gruyter.

——, and Joseph Sanders 1986 *An Invitation to Law and Social Science*. Philadelphia: University of Pennsylvania Press.

Llewellyn, Karl 1930 "A Realistic Jurisprudence: The Next Step." *Columbia Law Review* 30:431–465.

——, and E. Adamson Hoebel 1941 *The Cheyenne Way: Conflict and Case Law in Primitive Society*. Norman: University of Oklahoma Press.

Luhmann, Niklas 1985 *A Sociological Theory of Law*. London: Routledge and Kegan Paul.

Maine, Henry (1861) 1963 *Ancient Law: Its Connection with the Early History of Society and Its Relation to Modern Ideas*. Boston: Beacon.

Malinowski, Bronislaw 1926 *Crime and Custom in Savage Society*. New York: Harcourt, Brace.

Merry, Sally Engle 1990 *Getting Justice and Getting Even: Legal Consciousness among Working-Class Americans*. Chicago: University of Chicago Press.

Merryman, John Henry 1969 *The Civil Law Tradition: An Introduction to the Legal Systems of Western Europe and Latin America*. Stanford, Calif.: Stanford University Press.

Montesquieu (1748) 1962 *The Spirit of the Laws*, 2 vols. New York: Hafner.

Moore, Sally Falk 1973 "Law and Social Change: The Semi-Autonomous Social Field as an Appropriate Subject of Study." *Law and Society Review* 7:719–746.

Nader, Laura 1969 "Styles of Court Procedure: To Make the Balance." In Laura Nader, ed., *Law in Culture and Society*. Chicago: Aldine.

Oliphant, Herman 1928 "A Return to *Stare Decisis*." *American Bar Association Journal* 14:71, 159.

Pound, Roscoe 1911–1912 "The Scope and Purpose of Sociological Jurisprudence," Parts 1, 2, and 3. *Harvard Law Review* 24:591–619; 25:140–168; 25:489–516.

Rheinstein, Max 1968 "Legal Systems." Pp. 204–210 in David L. Sills, ed., *International Encyclopedia of the Social Sciences*, vol. 9. New York: Macmillan.

Shapiro, Martin 1981 *Courts: A Comparative and Political Analysis*. Chicago: University of Chicago Press.

Spitzer, Stephan 1983 "Marxist Perspectives in the Sociology of Law." *Annual Review of Sociology* 9:103.

Starr, June, and Jane Collier, eds. 1989 *History and Power in the Study of Law: New Directions in Legal Anthropology*. Ithaca, N.Y.: Cornell University Press.

Sypnowich, Christine 1990 *The Concept of Socialist Law*. Oxford: Clarendon Press.

Szabo, I., and Z. Peteri, eds. 1977 *A Socialist Approach to Comparative Law*. Leyden, The Netherlands: A. W. Sijthoff.

Tamanaha, Brian Z. 1997 *Realistic Socio-Legal Theory: Pragmatism and A Social Theory of Law*. Oxford, England: Clarendon.

Teubner, Gunther, ed. 1988 *Autopoietic Law: A New Approach to Law and Society*. Berlin: Walter de Gruyter.

Watson, Alan 1974 *Legal Transplants: An Approach to Comparative Law*. Charlottesville, Va.: University Press of Virginia.

Weber, Max 1954 *On Law in Economy and Society*. New York: Simon and Schuster.

Zweigert, Konrad, and Hein Kotz 1987 *Introduction to Comparative Law*, vol. 1, *The Framework*. Oxford, England: Clarendon.

JOSEPH SANDERS

LAW AND SOCIETY

NOTE: *Although the following article has not been revised for this edition of the Encyclopedia, the substantive coverage is currently appropriate. The editors have provided a list of recent works at the end of the article to facilitate research and exploration of the topic.*

The concepts of *law* and *society* refer to macrostructural phenomena. Is there a macro-oriented theory of law and society or a macro sociolegal theory to guide this field? As an interdisciplinary endeavor, the sociology of law relies upon, or is influenced by, the intellectual assumptions and propositions of general sociology and legal theory. This article will therefore consider the relationship of this field to both parent disciplines.

RELATIONSHIP TO GENERAL SOCIOLOGY

It is no exaggeration to state that the field of sociology lacks a systematically developed and precise theory of society. Although interest in macro-sociological theory building has been in evidence for the past two decades, particularly among those concerned with comparative sociology (Eisenstadt and Curelaru 1977), no such theory has yet been developed in sufficient detail and precision to guide empirical research. This is not to deny the fact that such macrotheorists as Marx, Durkheim, Weber, and Parsons have exerted a pervasive influence on various specialties within sociology, including the relationship between law and society.

Marx. Marx conceived of law as a component of the "superstructure" of a capitalist society. As an epiphenomenon of the superstructure, it provides a rationale or ideology for preserving the existing class relations in a capitalist economy. Concepts of property and contract, for example, become instrumentalities for maintaining and reproducing class hegemony. In other words, legal concepts and doctrines reinforce the position of the ruling class and, at the same time, become the constituents of the "false consciousness" from which the working class suffers. Implicit in this theory of law as a weapon wielded by the state in a capitalist society against the working class is the assumption that if private property were abolished and a classless socialist society were ushered in, the state would "wither away" and, with it, law would "wither away" as well.

As usually formulated, the Marxian theory of law and society is not empirically verifiable. It does not follow, however, that this theory is devoid of any empirical implications. Questions can be raised—and have been raised—concerning class bias in the adjudication of civil and criminal cases, in the emergence of significant legal norms—for example, those regarding inheritance—and in the recurrent failure of agrarian reform laws. Likewise, it is possible to investigate a proposition counter to the Marxian thesis, namely, that the passage of laws in a capitalist state can potentially diminish the power of the ruling class vis-à-vis the working class. A case in point is the enactment of the National Labor Relations Act of 1935 in the United States, which institutionalized the rights of employees to unionize and to engage in collective bargaining with employers. Research questions such as those cited above would test the validity of some propositions derivable from the Marxian theory of law and society.

Durkheim. Turning to Durkheim's contribution to this field, one of necessity reverts to his *Division of Labor in Society* (1933), in which he argued that in societies characterized by "mechanical solidarity" there is a predominance of repressive laws, whereas in societies characterized by "organic solidarity" there is a predominance of restitutive laws. A number of social scientists have subjected Durkheim's thesis to empirical tests and have found it wanting (Schwartz and Miller 1964). It is a testament, however, to the intriguing character of Durkheim's thesis that it continues to evoke the interest of researchers (Baxi 1974; Schwartz 1974; Sheleff 1975). A more general formulation of Durkheim's thesis would be that societies differing along various dimensions of societal development—of which the division of labor is but one—will exhibit systematic differences in their legal systems (Evan 1968).

In the course of developing his thesis that the division of labor is the principal source of social solidarity, Durkheim formulated his seminal idea of an "index" (Durkheim 1933, pp. 64–65). Apart from his fame as the "father of modern sociology," Durkheim is the originator of the concept of an "index", that is, an indirect and "external" measure of a complex dimension of social structure such as social solidarity. That he developed the concept of an index in connection with "juridical rules" and types of laws is of particular interest to sociologists of law and legal scholars. Under the circumstances, it is indeed surprising that to date, with few exceptions (Evan 1965, 1968, 1980; Merryman, Clark, and Friedman 1979; Lidz 1979), this facet of Durkheim's work has been neglected. The concept of a "legal index" or a "legal indicator" merits systematic attention if we are to become more precise in our understanding of the role of law in social change.

Weber. In comparison with the work of Durkheim and Marx, Weber's contributions to the sociology of law are appreciably more diverse and complex. Embedded in an intricate mosaic of ideal types and comparative and historical data on the emergence of legal rationality in Western civilization and on the role of law in the origins of capitalism (Weber 1950; Rheinstein 1954; Trubek

1972; Collins 1980), Weber's welter of legal conceptualizations poses a difficult challenge to the empirically oriented researcher. For example, his famous typology of lawmaking and lawfinding suggests possible research leads for comparative and historical analysis. Rheinstein, who edited and translated Weber's work on the sociology of law, lucidly summarizes his typology in the following manner:

1. *irrational, i.e., not guided by general rules*

   a. *formal: guided by means which are beyond the control of reason (ordeal, oracle, etc.)*

   b. *substantive: guided by reaction to the individual case*

2. *rational, i.e., guided by general rules*

   a. *substantive: guided by the principles of an ideological system other than that of the law itself (ethics, religion, power, politics, etc.)*

   b. *formal:*

   (1) *extrinsically, i.e., ascribing significance to external acts observable by the senses*

   (2) *logically, i.e., expressing its rules by the use of abstract concepts created by legal thought itself and conceived of as constituting a complete system.*

(Rheinstein 1954, p. 1)

Assuming that the meaning of each of these ideal type categories can be clarified and that legal indicators can be developed for each of the types, a comparative study could be undertaken to explore differences in lawmaking and in lawfinding of such major legal systems as common law, civil law, socialist law, and Moslem law. Equally challenging would be a study of long-term trends within each of these legal systems. The findings of such an inquiry would shed light on the occurrence of the evolutionary stages postulated by Weber.

The general development of law and procedure may be viewed as passing through the following stages: first, charismatic legal revelation through "law prophets"; second, empirical creation and finding of law by legal honoratiores; . . . third, imposition of law by secular or theocratic powers; fourth and finally, systematic elaboration of law and professionalized administration of justice by persons who have received their legal training

in a learned and formally logical manner. (Rheinstein 1954, p. 303)

Another significant thesis in Weber's corpus of writings on law is the innovative role he attributes to "legal honoratiores" or "legal notables" (Bendix 1960). Is Weber's thesis more valid for civil law systems, with its heavy immersion in Roman law, than it is for common law, let alone for socialist law or Moslem law? Once again it would be necessary to develop appropriate legal indicators to measure the degree to which legal notables—lawyers, judges, and high-level civil servants—introduce new rules and new interpretations of existing legal norms in the course of administering justice.

Parsons. For decades, Parsons was the leading macrosociological theorist in the United States, making singular contributions to structural functionalism and to a general theory of action. Focusing on the action of social systems, Parsons developed a "four-function paradigm." According to Parsons, every society faces four subsystem problems: adaptation, goal attainment, integration, and pattern maintenance or latency (AGIL). The societal subsystems associated with these four functional problems are, respectively, the economy, the polity, law, and religion and education.

Following Weber, Parsons treats law as a rational-legal system consisting of a set of prescriptions, proscriptions, and permissions. The legal system, especially in highly differentiated modern societies, performs the functions of a "generalized mechanism of social control" (Parsons 1962). This function is performed vis-à-vis the economy, the polity, and pattern maintenance or latency. The net effect of the pervasive normative regulation is the integration of society. As Parsons puts it: "The legal system . . . broadly constitutes what is probably the single most important institutional key to understanding . . . problems of societal integration" (Parsons 1978, p. 52).

With his four-function paradigm, Parsons addresses the nexus between law and society with the aid of "generalized media of interchange." The economy in a developed and differentiated society uses the medium of money for transactions. Functionally analogous media of exchange operate in each of the other subsystems—power in the polity, value commitment in pattern maintenance, and influence in law.

Suggestive as Parsons's framework is for understanding interinstitutional relations, the generalized media of interchange have not, as yet, been operationalized so as to explain how the legal system interacts with other societal subsystems. In other words, since Parsons has not explicated specific linkages between the legal and nonlegal subsystems, it is difficult to discern what hypotheses can be tested against any body of data. Hence, a reasonable conclusion is that Parsons's macrosociological theory, in its present form, is actually a metatheory.

The foregoing review of some sociological theories of law and society raises two common themes: (1) each of the theorists endeavored to comprehend the macrostructural relationships between law and other institutional systems of a society, and (2) if the hypotheses implicit in these theories are to be empirically tested, systematic attention would have to be devoted to the development of a body of legal indicators. The current generation of sociologists of law has yet to face up to the problems engendered by both of these themes.

RELATIONSHIP TO LEGAL THEORY

Is the relationship between the sociology of law and the field of legal theory any less problematic than it is with general sociology? On its face, the question should be answered in the affirmative because the sociologist of law must take some of the legal scholars' subjects as objects of inquiry. In actuality, because of the traditions of legal scholarship, legal scholars do not generally provide an analytical basis for sociological research. Legal scholarship tends to be preoccupied with legal rules, legal principles, and their application to a multitude of specific conflict situations. As a consequence, the scholarly literature—apart from being intellectually insular—is almost entirely verbal and idiographic, with virtually no interest in a *nomothetic*, let alone *quantitative*, analysis of legal phenomena. Furthermore, there is a high degree of specialization within legal scholarship such that most scholars tend to devote their entire careers to a particular body of law, be it labor law, criminal law, contract law, family law, and so forth, in their own country. Those scholars specializing in comparative law are inclined to study a particular specialty, for example, family law, by comparing case studies from two or more countries (Glendon

1975). Relatively few legal scholars seek to study the legal system of an entire society, such as the work of Hazard (1977) and Berman (1963) on the Soviet legal system. And fewer still have had the temerity to undertake systematic comparisons of total legal systems or families of legal systems, as exemplified in the work of David and Brierly (1968) and Wigmore (1928); and those who make no effort tolerate characteristics of total legal systems to the social-structural attributes of the societies in which they are embedded.

Surveying current legal theory, three distinct theoretical perspectives can be discerned: the theory of legal autonomy, critical legal studies, and autopoietic law. Each of these perspectives will be briefly reviewed and appraised for their implications for a theory of law and society.

Legal Autonomy. Traditional conceptions of the legal order and "sources of law" are based on two assumptions, the first being that the law is a "seamless web," a relatively "closed system." Whatever processes of change occur in the law are generated from within the legal system, not from without. In other words, processes of change are immanent or endogenous and are not externally induced. The second assumption is that the legal system is, by definition, autonomous from other systems or institutions of a society. Therefore, it is unnecessary to inquire into how the legal system interacts with other subsystems of a society or into what degree of autonomy a given legal system actually has from other societal subsystems.

Perhaps the most quintessential articulation of the theory of legal autonomy in recent years can be found in the work of Watson, a renowned legal historian and comparative law scholar. Watson has repeated his thesis of legal autonomy in a number of monographs and articles (Watson 1974, 1978, 1981, 1983, 1985, 1987). He contends that the growth and evolution of the law is determined largely by an autonomous legal tradition, which exists and operates outside the sphere of societal needs.

> To a large extent law possesses a life and vitality of its own; that is, no extremely close, natural or inevitable relationship exists between law, legal structures, institutions and rules on the one hand and the needs and desires and political economy of the ruling elite

or of the members of the particular society on the other hand. If there was such a close relationship, legal rules, institutions and structures would transplant only with great difficulty, and their power of survival would be severely limited. (Watson 1978, pp. 314–315)

Law is largely autonomous and not shaped by societal needs; though legal institutions will not exist without corresponding social institutions, law evolves from the legal tradition. (Watson 1985, p. 119).

Unlike the Marxist view of law, Watson's is that the law does not advance the interests of the ruling class; instead, it reflects the "culture" of the legal elite. He bolsters his provocative thesis with a study of legal borrowing, which he refers to as "legal transplants" (1974). The fact that the individual statutes, legal doctrines, and entire codes have been borrowed by countries differing in cultural, political, economic, and other respects provides evidence, according to Watson, in support of his thesis of legal autonomy.

The concept of "legal transplant" has a naturalistic ring to it as though it occurs independent of any human agency. In point of fact, however, elites—legal and nonlegal—often act as "culture carriers" or intermediaries between societies involved in a legal transplant. Legal scholars who are associated with political elites may be instrumental in effecting a legal transplant. Moreover, many instances of legal borrowing involve the "imposition" of a foreign body of law by a colonial power (Burman and Harrell-Bond 1979). Hence, it is a mistake to describe and analyze the diffusion of law as if it were devoid of human agency. If human volition is involved, it is indeed questionable whether the borrowed legal elements do not perform a societal function—at the very least on behalf of the legal elite.

Critical Legal Studies. Unlike Watson's internalist focus on the legal system and its autonomous development, the critical legal studies (CLS) movement appears to pursue a dual strategy: externalist as well as internalist. CLS is externalist in its critique of the social order and of the values dominating judicial decision making. It is internalist in its fundamental critique of traditional jurisprudence and legal reasoning.

The CLS movement emerged in the late 1970s in American law schools. It brought together a diverse group of scholars with a left-of-center ideology concerned about inequality and injustice in American society. Although lacking any consensus regarding societal transformation, CLS scholars sought to identify the impact of society's dominant interests on the legal process and the impact of social and political values on legal decision making.

In his introduction to a volume of essays by CLS authors, David Kairys discusses the "basic elements" of the legal theory of this movement. Three of these elements are externalist in nature:

We place fundamental importance on democracy, by which we mean popular participation in the decisions that shape our society and affect our lives . . . We reject the common characterization of the law and the state as neutral, value-free arbiters, independent of and unaffected by social and economic relations, political forces, and cultural phenomena. The law's ultimate mechanism for control and enforcement is institutional violence, but it protects the dominant system of social and power relations against political and ideological as well as physical challenges. (Kairys 1982, pp. 3–5)

These three externalist principles of the CLS movement have a familiar ring to them; namely, they are reminiscent of criticisms leveled by Marxists and neo-Marxists against the legal order of capitalist societies.

By far the most distinctive contribution of the CLS movement has been its elaborate internalist critique of legal reasoning and legal process. As Kairys puts it:

We reject . . . the notion that a distinctly legal mode of reasoning or analysis characterizes the legal process or even exists . . . There is no legal reasoning in the sense of a legal methodology or process for reaching particular, correct results. There is a distinctly legal and quite elaborate system of discourse and body of knowledge, replete with its own language and conventions of argumentation, logic, and even manners. In some ways these aspects of the law are so distinct and all-embracing as to amount to a separate culture; and for many lawyers the courthouse, the law firm, the language, the style, become a way of life. But in terms of a method or process for decision making–for determining correct rules, facts, or results–the law provides only a wide and conflicting variety of stylized rationalizations from which courts pick and choose. Social and political judgments about the substance, parties, and context of a case guide such choices, even when they are not the explicit or conscious basis of decision. (Kairys 1982, p. 3)

Not only do critical legal scholars reject the notion of legal reasoning, they also reject other idealized components constituting a "legal system," in particular, that law is a body of doctrine, that the doctrine reflects a coherent view of relations between persons and the nature of society, and that social behavior reflects norms generated by the legal system (Trubek 1984, p. 577).

The general conclusion CLS writers draw from "unmasking" the legal system, "trashing" mainstream jurisprudence, and "deconstructing" legal scholarship (Barkan 1987) is that "law is simply politics by other means" (Kairys 1982, p. 17). Such a conclusion, on its face, does not hold out any promise for developing a new, let alone heuristic, approach to a theory of law and society. On the contrary, its antipositivism combined with its search for a transformative political agenda has prompted CLS writers to view with increasing skepticism the sociology of law and research into the relationship between law and society (Trubek and Esser 1989).

Autopoietic Law. Similar in some respects to Watson's theory of legal autonomy, but fundamentally different from the theory of the CLS movement, autopoietic law claims to be a challenging new theory of law and society (Teubner 1988a). For the past few years several continental social theorists, who are also legal scholars, have enthusiastically developed and propagated the theory of autopoietic law. A complex cluster of ideas, this theory is derived from the work of two biologists, Maturana and Varela (Varela 1979; Maturana and Varela 1980).

In the course of their biological research, Maturana and Varela arrived at some methodological realizations that led them to generalize about the nature of living systems. Maturana coined the term *autopoiesis* to capture this new "scientific epistemology" (Maturana and Varela 1980, p. xvii).

"This was a word without a history, a word that could directly mean what takes place in the dynamics of the autonomy proper to living systems." Conceptualizing living systems as machines, Maturana and Varela present the following rather complex and abstract definition:

Autopoietic machines are homeostatic machines. Their peculiarity, however, does not lie in this but in the fundamental variable which they maintain constant . . . an autopoietic machine continuously generates and specifies its own organization through its operation as a system of production of its own components, and does this in an endless turnover of components under conditions of continuous perturbations and compensation of perturbations. (Maturana and Varela 1980, pp. 78–79)

Another definition of autopoiesis is presented by Zeleny, one of the early advocates of this new theory:

An autopoietic system *is a distinguishable complex of component-producing processes and their resulting components, bounded as an autonomous unity within its environment, and characterized by a particular kind of relation among its components, and component-producing processes: the components, through their interaction, recursively generate, maintain, and recover the same complex of processes which produced them.* (Zeleny 1980, p. 4)

Clearly, these definitions and postulates are rather obscure and high-level generalizations that, from a general systems theory perspective (Bertalanffy 1968), are questionable. Especially suspect is the assertion that autopoietic systems do not have inputs and outputs. The authors introduce further complexity by postulating second- and third-order autopoietic systems, which occur when autopoietic systems interact with one another and, in turn, generate a new autopoeitic system (Maturana and Varela 1980, pp. 107–111). Toward the end of their provocative monograph, Maturana and Varela raise the question of whether the dynamics of human societies are determined by the autopoiesis of its components. Failing to agree on the answer to this question, the authors postpone further discussion (Maturana and Varela 1980, p. 118). Zeleny, however, hastens to answer this question and introduces the notion of "social autopoiesis" to convey that human societies are autopoietic (Zeleny 1980, p. 3).

Luhmann, an outstanding German theorist and jurist, has also gravitated to the theory of autopoiesis. According to Luhmann, "social systems can be regarded as special kinds of autopoietic systems" (1988b, p. 15). Influenced in part by Parsons and general systems theory, Luhmann applied some systems concepts in analyzing social structures (1982). In the conclusion to the second edition of his book *A Sociological Theory of Law* (1985), Luhmann briefly refers to new developments in general systems theory that warrant the application of autopoiesis to the legal system. Instead of maintaining the dichotomy between closed and open systems theory, articulated by Bertalanffy, Boulding, and Rapoport (Buckley 1968), Luhmann seeks to integrate the open and closed system perspectives. In the process he conceptualizes the legal system as self-referential, self-reproducing, "normatively closed," and "cognitively open"—a theme he has pursued in a number of essays (1985, 1986, 1988c).

This formulation is, to say the least, ambiguous. Given normative closure, how does the learning of the system's environmental changes, expectations, or demands get transmitted to the legal system? Further complicating the problem is Luhmann's theory of a functionally differentiated modern society in which all subsystems—including the legal system—tend to be differentiated as self-referential systems, thereby reaching high levels of autonomy (Luhmann 1982). Although Luhmann has explicitly addressed the issue of integrating the closed and open system perspectives of general systems theory, it is by no means evident from his many publications how this is achieved.

Another prominent contributor to autopoietic law is the jurist and sociologist of law Gunther Teubner. In numerous publications, Teubner discusses the theory of autopoiesis and its implications for reflexive law, legal autonomy, and evolutionary theory (Teubner 1983a, 1983b, 1988a, 1988b). One essay, "Evolution of Autopoietic Law" (1988a), raises two general issues: the pre-requisites of autopoietic closure of a legal system, and legal evolution after a legal system achieves autopoietic

closure. With respect to the first issue, Teubner applies the concept of *hypercycle*, which he has borrowed from others but which he does not explicitly define. Another of his essays (Teubner 1988b) reveals how Teubner is using this concept. For Teubner, all self-referential systems involve, by definition, "circularity" or "recursivity" (1988b, p. 57). Legal systems are preeminently self-referential in the course of producing legal acts or legal decisions. However, if they are to achieve autopoietic autonomy their cyclically constituted system components must become interlinked in a "hypercycle," "i.e., the additional cyclical linkage of cyclically constituted units" (Teubner 1988b, p. 55). The legal system components—as conceptualized by Teubner, "element, structure, process, identity boundary, environment, performance, function" (1988b, p. 55)—are general terms not readily susceptible to the construction of legal indicators.

The second question Teubner addresses, legal evolution after a legal system has attained autopoietic closure, poses a similar problem. The universal evolutionary functions of variation, selection, and retention manifest themselves in the form of legal mechanisms.

In the legal system, normative structures take over variation, institutional structures (especially procedures) take over selection and doctrinal structures take over retention. (Teubner 1988a, p. 228)

Since Teubner subscribes to Luhmann's theory of a functionally differentiated social system, with each subsystem undergoing autopoietic development, he confronts the problem of intersubsystem relations as regards evolution. This leads him to introduce the intriguing concept of *co-evolution*.

The environmental reference in evolution however is produced not in the direct, causal production of legal developments, but in processes of co-evolution. The thesis is as follows: In co-evolutionary processes it is not only the autopoiesis of the legal system which has a selective effect on the development of its own structures; the autopoiesis of other subsystems and that of society also affects—in any case in a much more mediatory and indirect way—the selection of legal changes. (Teubner 1988a, pp. 235–236)

Given the postulate of "autopoietic closure," it is not clear by what mechanisms nonlegal subsystems of a society affect the evolution of the legal system and how they "co-evolve." Once again, we confront the unsolved problem in the theory of autopoiesis of integrating the closed and open systems perspectives. Nevertheless, Teubner, with the help of the concept of co-evolution, has drawn our attention to a critical problem even if one remains skeptical of his proposition that "the historical relationship of 'law and society' must, in my view, be defined as a co-evolution of structurally coupled autopoietic systems" (Teubner 1988a, p. 218).

At least three additional questions about autopoietic law can be raised. Luhmann's theory of a functionally differentiated society in which all subsystems are autopoietic raises anew Durkheim's problem of social integration. The centrifugal forces in such a society would very likely threaten its viability. Such a societal theory implies a highly decentralized social system with a weak state and a passive legal system. Does Luhmann really think any modern society approximates his model of a functionally differentiated society?

A related problem is the implicit ethnocentrism of social scientists writing against the background of highly developed Western societies where law enjoys a substantial level of functional autonomy, which, however, is by no means equivalent to autopoietic closure. In developing societies and in socialist countries, many of which are developing societies as well, this is hardly the case. In these types of societies legal systems tend to be subordinated to political, economic, or military institutions. In other words, the legal systems are decidedly *allopoietic*. To characterize the subsystems of such societies as *autopoietic* is to distort social reality.

A third problem with the theory of autopoietic law is its reliance on the "positivity" of law. This fails to consider a secular legal trend of great import for the future of humankind, namely, the faltering efforts—initiated by Grotius in the seventeenth century—to develop a body of international law. By what mechanisms can autopoietic legal systems incorporate international legal norms? Because of the focus on "positivized" law untainted by political, religious, and other institutional values, autopoietic legal systems would have a

difficult time accommodating themselves to the growing corpus of international law.

Stimulating as is the development of the theory of legal autopoiesis, it does not appear to fulfill the requirements for a fruitful theory of law and society (Blankenburg 1983). In its present formulation, autopoietic law is a provocative metatheory. If any of its adherents succeed in deriving empirical propositions from this metatheory (Blankenburg 1983), subject them to an empirical test, and confirm them, they will be instrumental in bringing about a paradigm shift in the sociology of law.

The classical and contemporary theories of law and society, reviewed above, all fall short in providing precise and operational guidelines for uncovering the linkages over time between legal and nonlegal institutions in different societies. Thus, the search for a scientific macro sociolegal theory will continue. To further the search for such a theory, a social-structural model will now be outlined.

A SOCIAL-STRUCTURAL MODEL

A social-structural model begins with a theoretical amalgam of concepts from systems theory with Parsons' four structural components of social systems: values, norms, roles, and collectivities (Parsons 1961, pp. 41–44; Evan 1975, pp. 387–388). Any subsystem or institution of a societal system, whether it be a legal system, a family system, an economic system, a religious system, or any other system, can be decomposed into four structural elements: values, norms, roles, and organizations. The first two elements relate to a cultural or normative level of analysis and the last two to a social-structural level of analysis. Interactions between two or more subsystems of a society are mediated by cultural as well as by social-structural elements. As Parsons has observed, law is a generalized mechanism for regulating behavior in the several subsystems of a society (Parsons 1962, p. 57). At the normative level of analysis, law entails a "double institutionalization" of the values and norms embedded in other subsystems of a society (Bohannan 1968). In performing this reinforcement function, law develops "cultural linkages" with other subsystems, thus contributing to the degree of normative integration that exists in a society. As disputes are adjudicated and new legal norms are enacted, a value from one or more of the nonlegal subsystems is tapped. These values provide an implicit or explicit justification for legal decision making.

Parsons's constituents of social structure (values, norms, roles, and organizations) are nested elements, as in a Chinese box, with values incorporated in norms, both of these elements contained in roles, and all three elements constituting organizations. When values, norms, roles, and organizations are aggregated we have a new formulation, different from Parsons's AGIL paradigm, of the sociological concept of an institution. An institution of a society is composed of a configuration of values, norms, roles, and organizations. This definition is applicable to all social institutions, whether economic, political, religious, familial, educational, scientific, technological, or legal. In turn, the social structure of a society is a composite of these and other institutions.

Of fundamental importance to the field of the sociology of law is the question of how the legal institution is related to each of the nonlegal institutions. A preliminary answer to this question will be set forth in a model diagramming eight types of interactions or linkages between legal and nonlegal institutions (see Figure 1).

On the left-hand side of the diagram are a set of six nonlegal institutions, each of which is composed of values, norms, roles, and organizations. If the norms comprising the nonlegal institutions are sufficiently institutionalized, they can have a direct regulatory impact on legal personnel as well on the citizenry (interaction 4, "Single institutionalization"). On the other hand, according to Bohannan (1968), if the norms of the nonlegal institutions are not sufficiently strong to regulate the behavior of the citizenry, a process of "double institutionalization" (interaction 1) occurs whereby the legal system converts nonlegal institutional norms into legal norms. This effect can be seen in the rise in the Colonial period of "blue laws," which were needed to give legal reinforcement to the religious norms that held the Sabbath to be sacred (Evan 1980, pp. 517–518, 530–532). In addition, the legal system can introduce a norm that is not a component of any of the nonlegal institutions. In other words, the legal system can introduce an innovative norm (interaction 2) that does not have a counterpart in any of the nonlegal institutions (Bohannan 1968). An example of such an innovation is "no-fault" divorce (Weitzman 1985; Jacob 1988).

The legal system's regulatory impact (interaction 3) may succeed or fail with legal personnel, with the citizenry, or with both. Depending on whether legal personnel faithfully implement the law, and the citizenry faithfully complies with the law, the effect on the legal system can be reinforcing (interaction 7) or subversive (interaction 5), and the effect on nonlegal institutions can be stabilizing (interaction 9) or destabilizing (interaction 6).

In systems-theoretic terms, the values of a society may be viewed as goal parameters in comparison with which the performance of a legal system may be objectively assessed. The inability of a legal system to develop "feedback loops" and "closed loop systems" to monitor and assess the efficacy of its outputs makes the legal system vulnerable to various types of failures. Instead of generating "negative feedback," that is, self-corrective measures, when legal personnel or rank-and-file citizens fail to comply with the law, the system generates detrimental "positive feedback" (Laszlo, Levine, and Milsum 1974).

CONCLUSION

What are some implications of this social-structural model? In the first place, the legal system is not viewed as only an immanently developing set of legal rules, principles, or doctrines insulated from other subsystems of society, as expressed by Watson and to some extent by Luhmann and Teubner. Second, the personnel of the legal system, whether judges, lawyers, prosecutors, or administrative agency officials, activate legal rules, principles, or doctrines in the course of performing their roles within the legal system. Third, formally organized collectivities, be they courts, legislatures, law-enforcement organizations, or administrative agencies, perform the various functions of a legal system. Fourth, in performing these functions, the formally organized collectivities comprising a legal system interact with individuals and organizations representing interests embedded in the nonlegal subsystems of a society. In other words, each of the society's institutions or subsystems—legal and nonlegal—has the same structural elements: values, norms, roles, and organizations.

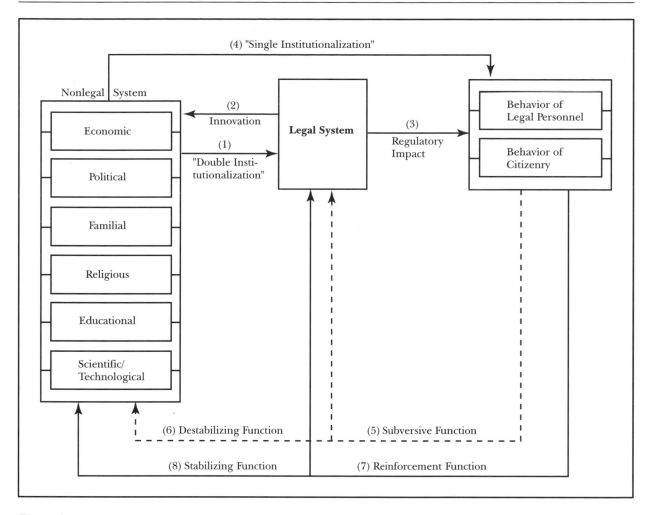

Figure 1

NOTE: A Social-Structural Model of the Interactions of Legal and Nonlegal Institutions

Interinstitutional interactions involve an effort at coupling these structural elements across institutional boundaries. A major challenge to the sociologists of law is to discover the diverse coupling or linkages—cultural and social-structural—between the legal system and the nonlegal systems in terms of the four constituent structural elements. Another challenge is to ascertain the impact of these linkages on the behavior of legal personnel and on the behavior of the citizenry, on the one hand, and to measure the impact of "double institutionalization" on societal goals, on the other.

A serendipitous outcome of this model is that it suggests a definition of law and society or the sociology of law, that is, that the sociology of law deals primarily with at least eight interactions or linkages identified in Figure 1. Whether researchers accept this definition will be determined by its heuristic value, namely, whether it generates empirical research concerning the eight linkages.

(SEE ALSO: *Law and Legal Systems; Social Control; Sociology of Law*)

REFERENCES

Abraham, David 1994 "Persistent Facts and Compelling Norms: Liberal Capitalism, Democratic Socialism, and the Law." *Law and Society Review* 28:939–946

Barkan, Steven M. 1987 "Deconstructing Legal Research: A Law Librarian's Commentary on Critical Legal Studies." *Law, Library Journal* 79:617–637.

Barnett, Larry D. 1993. *Legal Construct, Social Concept: a Macrosociological Perspective On Law*. Hawthorne, N.Y.: Aldine De Gruyter.

Baxi, U. 1974 "Comment—Durkheim and Legal Evolution: Some Problems of Disproof." *Law and Society Review* 8:645–651.

Bendix, Reinhard 1960 *Max Weber: An Intellectual Portrait*. New York: Doubleday.

Berman, Harold J. 1963 *Justice in the U.S.S.R: An Interpretation of the Soviet Law*. Cambridge, Mass.: Harvard University Press.

Bertalanffy, Ludwig von 1968 *General System Theory*. New York: G. Braziller.

Blankenburg, Erhard 1983 "The Poverty of Evolutionism: A Critique of Teubner's Case for 'Reflexive Law.'" *Law and Society Review* 18:273–289.

Bohannan, Paul 1968 "Law and Legal Institutions." In David L. Sills, ed., *International Encyclopedia of the Social Sciences*. New York: Macmillan and Free Press.

Buckley, Walter (ed.) 1968 *Modern Systems Research for the Behavioral Scientist*. Chicago: Aldine.

Burman, Sandra, and Barbara E. Harrell-Bond (eds.) 1979 *The Imposition of Law*. New York: Academic Press.

Chambliss, William J., and S. Zatz Marjorie 1993 *Making Law: The State, the Law, and Structural Contradictions*. Bloomington: Indiana University Press.

Collins, Randall 1980 "Weber's Last Theory of Capitalism: A Systemization" *American Sociological Review* 45:925–942.

Cooney, Mark 1995 "Legal Sociology and the New Institutionalism." *Studies in Law Politics, and Society* 15:85–101.

Cotterell, Roger 1997 *Law's Community: Legal Theory In Sociological Perspective*. New York: Oxford University Press.

—— 1988 "Why Must Legal Ideas Be Interpreted Sociologically?" *Journal of Law and Society 25:171–192*.

David, Rene, and John E. C. Brierley 1968 *Major Legal Systems in the World Today*. London: Free Press and Collier-Macmillan.

Durkheim, Emile 1933 *The Division of Labor in Society*. New York: Free Press.

Eisenstadt, S. N., and M. Curelaru 1977 "Macro-Sociology: Theory, Analysis and Comparative Studies." *Current Sociology* 25:1–112.

Evan, William M. 1965 "Toward A Sociological Almanac of Legal Systems." *International Social Science Journal* 17:335–338.

—— 1968 "A Data Archive of Legal Systems: A Cross-National Analysis of Sample Data." *European Journal of Sociology* 9:113–125.

—— 1975 "The International Sociological Association and the Internationalization of Sociology." *International Social Science Journal* 27:385–393.

—— 1980 *The Sociology of Law*. New York: Free Press.

—— 1990 *Social Structure and Law: Theoretical and Empirical Perspectives*. Thousand Oaks, Calif.: Sage Publications.

Glendon, Mary Ann 1975 "Power and Authority in the Family: New Legal Patterns as Reflections of Changing Ideologies." *American Journal of Comparative Law* 23:1–33.

Habermans, Jurgen, and William Regh 1996. *Between Facts and Norms: Contributions to a Discourse Theory of Law and Democracy*. Cambridge: MIT Press.

Hazard, John N. 1977 *Soviet Legal System: Fundamental Principles and Historical Commentary*, 3rd ed. Dobbs Ferry, N.Y.: Oceana Press.

Jacob, Herbert 1988 *Silent Revolution: The Transformation of Divorce Law in the United States*. Chicago: University of Chicago Press.

Kairys, David (ed.) 1982 *The Politics of Law*. New York: Pantheon.

Laszlo, C. A., M. D. Levine, and J. H. Milsum 1974 "A General Systems Framework for Social Systems." *Behavioral Science* 19:79–92.

Lidz, Victor 1979 "The Law as Index, Phenomenon, and Element: Conceptual Steps Towards a General Sociology of Law." *Sociological Inquiry* 49:5–25.

Luhmann, Niklas 1982 *The Differentiation of Society*. New York: Columbia University Press.

—— 1985 *A Sociological Theory of Law*. trans. Elizabeth King and Martin Albrow. London: Routledge and Kegan Paul.

—— 1986 "The Self-Reproduction of Law and Its Limits." In Gunther Teubner, ed., *Dilemmas of Law in the Welfare State*. Berlin: Walter de Gruyter.

—— 1988a "The Sociological, Observation of the Theory and Practice of Law." In Alberto Febrajo, ed., *European Yearbook in the Sociology of Law*. Milan: Giuffre Publisher.

—— 1988b "The Unity of Legal Systems." In Gunther Teubner, ed., *Autopoietic Law: A New Approach to Law and Society*. Berlin: Walter de Gruyter.

—— 1988c "Closure and Openness: On Reality in the World of Law." In Gunther Teubner, ed., *Autopoietic Law: A New Approach to Law and Society*. Berlin: Walter de Gruyter.

McIntyre, Lisa J. 1994 *Law in the Sociological Enterprise: a Reconstruction*. Boulder, Colo.: Westview Press.

Maturana, Humberto R., and Francisco J. Varela 1980 *Autopoiesis and Cognition*. Dordrecht, The Netherlands: D. Reidel Publishing.

Merryman, John Henry, David S. Clark, and Lawrence M. Friedman 1979 *Law and Social Change in Mediterranean Europe and Latin America*. Stanford, Calif.: Stanford Law School.

Parsons, Talcott 1961 "An Outline of the Social System." In Talcott Parsons, Edward Shils, Kasper D. Naegele, and Jesse R. Pitts, eds., *Theories of Society*. New York: Free Press.

—— 1962 "The Law and Social Control." In William M. Evan, ed., *Law and Sociology*. New York: Free Press.

—— 1978 "Law as an Intellectual Stepchild." In Harry M. Johnson, ed., *Social System and Legal Process*. San Francisco: Jossey-Bass.

Rheinstein, Max (ed.) 1954 *Max Weber on Law in Economy and Society*. Cambridge, Mass.: Harvard University Press.

Schwartz, R. D. 1974 "Legal Evolution and the Durkheim Hypothesis: A Reply to Professor Baxi." *Law and Society Review* 8:653–668.

——, and J. C. Miller 1964 "Legal Evolution and Social Complexity." *American Journal of Sociology* 70:159–169.

Sheleff, L. S. 1975 "From Restitutive Law to Repressive Law: Durkheim's *The Division of Labor in Society* Revisited." *European Journal of Sociology* 16:16–45.

Tamanaha, Brian Z. 1996 "The Internal/External Distinction and the Notion of a "Practice" in Legal Theory and Sociolegal Studies." *Law and Society Review* 30:163–204.

—— 1999 *Realistic Socio-Legal Theory: Pragmatism and A Social Theory of Law*. New York: Oxford University Press.

Teubner, Gunther 1983a "Substantive and Reflexive Elements in Modern Law." *Law and Society Review* 17:239–285.

—— 1983b "Autopoiesis in Law and Society: A Rejoinder to Blankenburg." *Law and Society Review* 18:291–301.

—— 1988a *Autopoietic Law: A New Approach to Law and Society*. Berlin: Walter de Gruyter.

—— 1988b "Hypercycle in Law and Organization: The Relationship Between Self-Observation, Self-Constitution, and Autopoiesis." In Alberto Febrajo, ed., *European Yearbook in the Sociology of Law*. Milan: Giuffre Publisher.

—— 1997 "The King's Many Bodies: The Self-Deconstruction of Law's Hierarchy." *Law and Society Review* 31:763–787.

Travers, Max 1993 "Putting Sociology Back into the Sociology of Law." *Journal of Law and Society* 20:438–451.

Trubek, David M. 1972 "Max Weber on Law and the Rise of Capitalism." *Wisconsin Law Review* 730:720–753.

—— 1984 "Where the Action Is: Critical Legal Studies of Empiricism." *Stanford Law Review* 36:575.

——, and John Esser 1989 "'Critical Empiricism' in American Legal Studies: Paradox, Program, or Pandora's Box?" *Law and Social Inquiry* 14:3–52.

Varela, Francisco J. 1979 *The Principle of Autonomy*. New York: North-Holland.

Watson, Alan 1974 *Legal Transplants: An Approach to Comparative Law*. Charlottesville: University of Virginia Press.

—— 1978 "Comparative Law and Legal Change." *Cambridge Law Journal* 37:313–336.

—— 1981 *The Making of the Civil Law*. Cambridge, Mass.: Harvard University Press.

—— 1983 "Legal Change, Sources of Law, and Legal Culture." *University of Pennsylvania Law Review* 131:1,121–1,157.

—— 1985 *The Evolution of Law*. Baltimore, Md.: Johns Hopkins University Press.

—— 1987 "Legal Evolution and Legislation." *Brigham Young University Law Review* 1987:353–379.

Weber, Max 1950 *General Economic History*. New York: Free Press.

Weitzman, Lenore J. 1985 *The Divorce Revolution: The Unexpected Social and Economic Consequences for Women and Children in America*. New York: Free Press.

Wigmore, John Henry 1928 *A Panorama of the World's Legal Systems*. 3 vols. St. Paul, Minn.: West Publishing.

Zeleny, Milan 1980 *Autopoiesis, Dissipative Structures, and Spontaneous Social Orders*. Boulder, Colo.: Westview Press.

WILLIAM M. EVAN

LAW ENFORCEMENT

See Criminology; Penology; Police.

LEADERSHIP

The concept of leadership has been the focus of research and discussion of scholars in a variety of disciplines. Literary authors and philosophers provided the initial descriptions and guidance for leaders of their time. With the evolution of social sciences, scholars of political science, anthropology, sociology, psychology, and business have all explored the nature of leaders and the process of leadership. Although each of these various approaches did add a different perspective through the decades, there seem to be some who perceive a merging of disciplines in understanding leadership as we approach the close of the twentieth century. However, there are others who still maintain that leaders in different settings are fundamentally different.

As leadership is a vast field of research, only the most prevalent and unique approaches will be acknowledged in the following sections. Readers can find a more thorough review of leadership research and theories in texts such as Bass (1990), Chemers (1997), Chemers and Ayman (1993), and Dansereau and Yammarino (1998).

HISTORICAL REVIEW

The definition of leadership has varied across time and cultures. In ancient times, the focus was on kings and rulers, who received guidance from philosophers. In many civilizations around the world, authors have written essays on good and bad leadership. For example, Confucius and Mencius wrote essays on leaders' proper behavior during the end of the fourth century and the beginning of the fifth century B.C. in China. Aristotle's book, *The Politics*, describes the characteristics of the kings and kingship in ancient Greece (fourth century B.C.). In eleventh-century Iran, Unsuru'l-Ma'ali wrote *Qabus-Nameh* and Nezam Mulk Tussi wrote *Siyassat Nameh*, advising the kings of the time in effective governance. Machiavelli wrote *The Prince*, in Florence, Italy, during the sixteenth century, guiding European rulers in politics. Ibn-e-khaldun from Tunisia provided his observations and guidance to the ruling groups of North Africa in his famous book *Muqiddimah* in the fourteenth century.

From the end of the eighteenth century to the beginning of the twentieth century, during the evolution of industrialization, the concept of "leader" also came to include leaders of industry. Only a hundred and fifty years ago the first chief executive officer (CEO) appeared (Smoler 1999). Smoler stated that the increased volume of economic activity required the increased efficiency and administrative coordination that gave rise to this kind of leadership. The twentieth century saw steep growth in the numbers of CEOs and of top executive management positions.

At the close of the twentieth century there is a debate on differentiating between leaders and managers, and between leadership and management (Kotter 1988). The saying that some leaders and managers both lead and manage, but most leaders do not manage and most managers do not lead, may make this distinction. A popular phrase that clarifies the relation between leader and managers is, "Good managers do things right and good leaders do the right thing."

At the beginning of the twentieth century, two schools of thought on leadership evolved (Ayman 1993; Bass 1990). In Britain, Thomas Carlyle (1907) presented the "great-man theory," and in Germany, Karl Marx (1906) explained leadership from a zeitgeist approach (i.e., as being in the spirit of the time). The great-man approach focuses on the unique characteristics of the individual as the basis for being a leader. In this approach there is a strong belief that some people have leadership qualities and some do not; thus the born-leader concept. In the zeitgeist approach, the assumption is that the situation provides the opportunity for the individual to become a leader. Thus, it is not the person but the circumstances or the waves of time that puts people in leadership positions. These two approaches have been the foundation of leadership research throughout the twentieth century.

As the end of the century is approaching, the fascination with leaders seems to be at an all-time high, based on the number of publications about and for leaders (Ayman 1997). Many of these publications are inspirational and guiding. The scholars of leadership maintain a steady effort to refine the conceptualization of leadership and enhance the methodologies used in the study of leadership.

The twentieth century was the beginning of scientific and systematic study of leadership. Many disciplines have contributed to this endeavor, such as political science, anthropology, sociology, social psychology, and, most recently, industrial and organizational psychology. Each discipline has explored this phenomenon uniquely, guided by its own perspective and orientation. The psychologists' focus was initially influenced by the "great-man theory," whereas the sociologists and social psychologists were more interested in the situational perspective. As the investigations proceeded and the disciplincs evolved, the interplay of these approaches and the complexity of leadership became apparent. The following sections will briefly review various approaches: the trait and behavior approaches, which evolved from the great-man theory; the situational approach, which evolved from the zeitgeist approach; and, finally, the contingency approach, which combined the two approaches. At the end of this article, some challenges facing leadership practice and research are delineated.

TRAIT APPROACH

The initial work on leadership was influenced by the *great-man theory*, which focuses on the characteristics of individuals in leadership situations. The primary focus of this approach is to compare the characteristics of those who are leaders and those who are not. The majority of trait research began in the early part of the twentieth century and declined somewhat in the late 1940s. In a majority of these studies, there seemed to be a search for one trait that best differentiated leaders from nonleaders. Stogdill (1948) reviewed studies in various settings and identified a list of traits that were most commonly studied to identify leaders. The traits that differentiated leaders from nonleaders included "sociability, initiative, persistence, knowing how to get things done, self-confidence, alertness to and insight into situations, cooperativeness, popularity, adaptability, verbal facility" (Bass 1990, p. 75). However, Stogdill (1948) concluded that research on leader's traits is inconclusive and that, depending on the situation, one trait may be more important than another.

Early industrial psychologists interested in selection maintained their focus on the trait approach. Therefore, primary pursuit of trait approach was by practitioners who were interested in selection and succession planning of managers in work settings. Later, Lord and colleagues (1986), with the assistance of meta-analytical techniques, reanalyzed past research by Stogdill (1948) and Mann (1959) and, across studies, identified certain characteristics more associated with leaders than with nonleaders. The result of these studies was to identify intelligence, masculinity, and dominance as strongly related to leadership, whereas adaptability, introversion/extroversion, and conservatism had a weaker relationship. The adjustment and flexibility competency has received attention in recent years. In various studies, adaptability, as operationalized by the self-monitoring scale (Snyder 1979), has also been used to predict leader emergence and effectiveness with some degree of success (Zaccaro et al. 1991; Ayman and Chemers 1991). Hogan and colleagues (1994) revived interest in the trait approach by introducing a multitrait approach to the study of leaders. The traits included in the profile are known as the "big five" and consist of extroversion, emotional stability, openness, intellect, and surgency. In addition to the big five, there are also other measures (e.g., Myers Briggs) that are used to identify leader's profiles. However, results for predicting effective leaders from these traits are inconclusive. Overall, most of the trait research has focused on differentiating the characteristics of leaders from nonleaders, and on measuring leadership potential.

BEHAVIORAL APPROACH

The first known study focusing on leader behavior examined the differing effects of democratic, autocratic, and laissez-faire leadership behaviors (Lewin et al. 1939; Lippitt and White 1943). These studies were conducted with groups of Boy Scouts led by trained graduate students. The results of these studies showed that groups with democratic leaders had the best-satisfied members. Those with autocratic leaders demonstrated the highest level of task activity, but only when the leader was present. Starting in the 1950s, the interest of the U.S. scholar gravitated toward understanding the leader's behaviors and the relationship between these behaviors and effectiveness. Three main research centers concurrently studied leader behavior in small teams at Ohio State University, led by Stogdill and his associates; at the University of Michigan, led by Likert and his colleagues; and at Harvard, led by Bales and his collaborators. Although these studies were conducted in different work settings such as the military, education, insurance companies, car manufacturing, and laboratory settings, they all found the same results.

These results led to two categories of leader behavior. One category dealt with behaviors that establish and maintain relationships, commonly referred to as considerate, people-oriented, or socio-emotional behaviors. The second category focused on behaviors that get the task accomplished, commonly referred to as initiating-structure, production-oriented, or task-focused behaviors. Although many measures were designed to assess the leader's behaviors, the most prominent are three Ohio State measures: the Leader Behavior Description Questionnaire (LBDQ), the Subordinate Behavior Description, and the Leader Opinion Questionnaire (Cook et al. 1985).

The leadership behavior researchers in other countries identified two similar categories of structure and consideration, but also found some additional categories. Unlike the findings in the United States, the two behaviors in Iran were found to be intertwined, resulting in the concept of "benevolent paternalism," or the "father figure" leader (Ayman and Chemers 1983). In India, Sinha (1984) identified "nuturant-task" behavior as an addition to the two main behavioral categories. In Japan, Misumi (1985) introduced a measure that had behavioral categories similar to those in the U.S. findings, but the behaviors were assessed in context. He referred to this model as maintenance-production (MP) behaviors.

In the 1960s and 1970s, researchers investigated the relationship between these two categories of behaviors and various indexes of effectiveness (e.g., team satisfaction, performance, turnover, and grievance) in different work settings. Fisher and Edward's meta-analysis (1988) is among the studies that supported the overall effects of these two behaviors (cited in Bass 1990).

Since the middle of the 1980s, a paradigm shift in the study of leadership behavior emerged, which moved scholars from focusing on consideration and initiating structure behaviors, often referred to as "transactional leadership," to what is referred to as "transformational leadership" behavior. This movement started with the work of McGregor Burns (1978) and House (1977), and was further developed by two groups of scholars, Bass and Avolio (see Bass 1985); Avolio and Bass (1988) in the United States, and Conger and Kanungo (1987) in Canada. In this new approach,

the leader provided guidance to ensure that the work was done properly and that subordinates were happy, and also was responsible for developing a relationship with employees based on mutual trust. It was proposed that transformational leadership not only changes the subordinate, but is also evolutionary for the leader and the task. A recent meta-analysis has provided a promising review of the effects of transformational leadership behavior in a variety of settings (Lowe et al. 1996). Also, it was through these approaches that the emphasis on empowerment in leadership evolved (Conger and Kanungo 1988b). Empowering, coaching, and facilitating are behaviors that were not noted extensively in leadership literature until the middle of the 1980s. During this period many inspirational and guiding documents were presented by various authors (e.g., Kouzes and Posner 1987).

Three main categories of criticism have been directed at the behavioral approaches. The first, advanced by Korman (1966) and by Kerr and colleagues (1974), argued that situational factors moderate the relationship between leader's behavior and outcomes. In addition, Fisher and Edwards (1988) more recently reviewed the studies using LBDQ and outcome variables, and acknowledged that there is a need for studying moderators.

The second criticism is based on the fact that almost all leader behavior measures are based on perception of self or the perception of others (Ayman 1993). In the 1980s, a series of studies demonstrated that perceived behavior is contaminated with various factors that are not necessarily related to the leader's behavior (Lord and Maher 1991). In these studies it was demonstrated that people's memory of the behaviors that occurred can be affected by what they think of the leader (e.g., Larson 1982; Philips and Lord 1982). The implication of this criticism is critical in exploration of diversity and cross-cultural leadership, topics that will be discussed later.

The third criticism focused on the level of conceptualization and analysis. This criticism is based on the premise that leaders may treat different people differently. That is to say, is leadership a group-level phenomenon, dyadic, or is it in the eyes of the beholder? Recently, a multilevel approach has been investigated in relation to various leader behavior paradigms (see Dansereau and Yammarino 1998).

SITUATION AND LEADERSHIP

In the 1950s, parallel to the development of leader behavioral studies, many scholars examined situational factors that gave rise to the identification of a leader without examining their characteristics. Some examined seating arrangement, or distance of the individuals (e.g., Bass et al. 1953; Howells and Becker 1962). The results of these studies demonstrated that individuals at the head of the table and who commanded more space were more often identified as the leader. Other studies examined communication patterns (Leavitt 1951) in the work team. The results demonstrated that those who have access to most of the information and are the center of the information flow are most often identified as leaders. The frequency of contribution to the team's goal achievement and verbal visibility was another contributor to the emergence of the leader (Bavelas et al. 1965). The position in the organization and assigned roles were also demonstrated to predict how a new leader behaved (Shartle 1951). That is, the best predictor of leadership behavior was the behavior of the leader's boss or predecessor. By the 1960s, there was some evidence that different tasks elicited different behaviors from the leaders (e.g., Morris and Hackman 1969).

In the 1980s, substitutes for leadership theory (Kerr and Jermier 1978; Howell et al. 1986) diverted the attention of leadership researchers again to the situation and provided a taxonomy for the role of the situation in leadership. This new approach categorized situations as neutralizers, enhancers, supplements, and substitutes (Schriesheim 1997). This approach has received mixed results, but the contribution of its taxonomy and methodological clarification has clarified the role of the situation in leadership research (Howell 1997).

In conclusion, the situational studies demonstrated that regardless of the leader's values, traits, or other characteristics, situational factors can influence the emergence of the leader and the behavior of the leader. Visibility and control of information are some of the necessary situational factors that assisted an individual being recognized as a leader. The more recent work on the situation has further extended the role of the situation in leadership effectiveness.

LEADERSHIP EMERGENCE

Early situational research and trait approaches focused on leadership emergence. Most studies on leader behavior attended to the effectiveness of leaders and teams. Hollander's concept of idiosyncrasy credit (1958) examined the exchange that occurs in the work team and leader emergence process. This concept gave rise to a series of studies (e.g., Hollander 1978; Hollander and Julian 1970) that demonstrated that, in a team, the members who contribute to the team's goal achievement and are loyal to the values held by the team establish credibility or idiosyncrasy credits. These studies demonstrated that idiosyncrasy credits then could be spent as the individual took risks to lead the group. Hollander's work may be seen as the first work that brought leadership and the management of innovation and change close together.

Hollander's work also demonstrated that the exchange process in teams resulted in the emergence of the member with the highest credits as the team leader. Later, the work of Graen (1976) further expanded the nature of this exchange in the vertical-dyad linkage (VDL) model. In the VDL model, the leader and the subordinates establish their relationship by negotiating their roles. Therefore, in work groups, there are some members who form the core group and are closer to the leader. Also, there may be other members who stay on the periphery of the work group.

The results of the initial studies were criticized, and unfortunately this line of research was abandoned due to methodological limitations (Dansereau et al. 1975). However, the notion of exchange between the leader and his or her subordinates is still a fertile area of research, known as leader-member exchange theory (e.g., Graen and Uhl-bien 1995).

CONTINGENCY APPROACHES

Korman (1966) and Stogdill (1948) criticized past research on leader behavior and traits, and called for the study of leadership to be situation-based. In the early 1970s, two main categories of contingency approaches emerged, one based on the leader's trait and the other based on the leader's behavior.

The first scholar who operationalized the contingency approach to leadership and presented a trait-based model in this paradigm was Fred Fiedler. Several narrative reviews of the model have been written (see Ayman et al. 1998; Fiedler 1978). This model has been an impetus for many studies and some have criticized it over the years. However, several meta-analyses have provided some validating support on the thirty years of research (e.g., Strube and Garcia 1981; Peters et al. 1985).

The model is composed of three elements: one is the leader's motivational orientation, as measured by the "Least Preferred Coworker" scale; the second is the degree of leader's control and influence in a situation; and the third is the match between the situation and the leader's trait. In this model, three aspects of the situation were examined: leader-members relationship, task structure, and position power. The model's assumption is that leaders who are more focused on getting their job done than their relationship with people, do better than their counterparts in situations of high and low control and they are known to be in-match. Similarly, in situations of moderate control, those leaders with more focus on relationships will be more effective and are known as being in-match. When task oriented leaders are in moderate control condition and relationship oriented leaders are in high or low situational control conditions, they are referred to as being out-of-match (Ayman et al. 1995 and Ayman et al. 1998).

The strength of this model has been primarily in predicting team performance. More recently, subordinates' satisfaction and leader's experience of stress have also been included as outcomes examined by the model. Another strength of the model is that the information about the dependent variables and the independent variables are gathered from different sources. Leaders usually provide their motivational orientation by completing a quasi-projective test of Least Preferred Coworker. Sometimes the leader and other times the experimenter assessed the situation. A third party primarily has provided the assessments of the performance.

One area of potential improvement for the model is to include more than one trait. Recently, additional traits have been incorporated into the contingency model research. In 1993, Fiedler proposed the cognitive resource theory. This theory included the leader's intelligence and experience and proposed that their contribution to the team's success may have contradictory effects depending on the stressfulness of the situation. Also, Ayman and Chemers (1991) included the leader's self-monitoring capability in their study, which was conducted with Mexican managers. Results showed that subordinates' work satisfaction was higher for out-of-match leaders who are high self-monitors than for those who were lower self-monitors. This may indicate that self-monitoring trait compensate for leaders who are out of match based on the contingency model of leadership effectiveness. However, the subordinates of in-match, high, self-monitoring leaders were not as satisfied with their work as the low self-monitoring in-match leaders. Therefore, self-monitoring seemed to only work for those who find themselves in situations that are not conducive to their internal state. As this is only one study, future work on these or other traits is warranted.

The contingency models of leader behavior examined the moderators that influence the relationship between leaders' behaviors and the outcome variables. As there are multiple leader behaviors and multiple ways that the situation can be conceptualized, many models have emerged. Two models have received substantial empirical attention (i.e., path goal theory [House 1971]) and the normative model of decision making [Vroom and Yetton 1973; Vroom and Jago 1974]). However, other models have made conceptual contributions, such as the multiple-influence model of leadership (Hunt 1991) and the multiple linkage model (Yukle 1989). These models' contributions have been in the development of taxonomy for situational factors and managerial behavior (see Chemers 1998). The behavior domains studied in this category of contingency models are managerial, supervisory, and decision-making behavior. However, most managers and leaders are also involved with managing interpersonal conflict, and this behavior domain has not received much attention by leadership researchers. In this section we will primarily review path goal theory and the decision-making model, and will acknowledge the relevance of conflict management to leadership.

Path goal theory (House 1971) was based on Vroom's expectancy model of motivation. Its proposition was that the leader as a supervisor needed to help the subordinates by clearing their path to goal attainment. Therefore, the model predicted that the leader's behavior would be dependent on the situation, which was determined by the characteristics of the subordinates and the nature of their work. Therefore it predicted that subordinates with high ability were more satisfied and less stressed when their leaders were perceived as behaving considerately. Subordinates with complex tasks were more satisfied with leaders who were perceived as more directive. The model acknowledged four behavioral choices for the leaders: participative, supportive, directive, and achievement-focused. However, the majority of the research used Ohio State's measure of LBDQ-XII to define the leader's behavior as either considerate or structuring. In most of the studies, the descriptions of the situation, the subordinates' behavior, and the leader's behavior were assessed according to the subordinates' perceptions. Research on path goal theory received mixed results. In the majority of the studies either the subordinates' characteristics or their tasks were investigated. Also, the studies were primarily supportive, predicting subordinates' satisfaction but not their performance.

The decision-making model (Vroom and Yetton 1973; Vroom and Jago 1974) was mostly assessed from the leader's perspective. It provided the leader with choices of team decision-making strategies (e.g., very participative, partially participative, and very autocratic). The success of these choices depended on the situations. The model provided strategic questions that would help a leader determine the extent to which he or she should be participative or autocratic based on eight different criteria. These questions assessed the leader's knowledge and the subordinates' supportiveness in a given situation. The key finding was that subordinates who were part of the decision-making process were more satisfied, compared to those who were not part of this process.

Studies that have examined conflict management strategies of leaders are limited. The most commonly used measures are those by Rahim (1985) and by K. W. Thomas (1992). The two approaches identify five conflict management styles (competitive, withdrawing, accommodating, compromising, and collaborating) that represent the degree to which leaders are focused on themselves or the task, or the extent to which they are concerned about the subordinates' welfare.

In the same vein, the subordinates' choice of action with the leader was also examined. The situational factors studied so far have been the status of the actor in relationship to the target and the presence of an interpersonal conflict. The evidence seems to show that leaders have been perceived as using competitive and withdrawal strategies and subordinates tend to use more accommodating and compromising strategies. This line of research is new and requires more development. There is little evidence connecting choices of conflict management strategies to outcomes such as subordinate satisfaction or leader's influence or team performance.

Overall, the strength of behavioral approaches lies in their focus on the leader's behavior, which is assumed to present an aspect of the leadership process. These approaches are also sensitive to the moderating factor of situational elements; that is, they assume that not all successful or effective leaders behave the same way across situations. The behavioral approach provided some clarity in leadership process that allowed trainers to design training and development programs guiding leaders in how to behave.

These models have also faced challenges. First, the assessment of leader behavior and the situation in these models were dependent on the perception of the leader or the subordinates, thus susceptible to social cognitive influences, which will be briefly discussed in the next section. Second, most of these studies were based on a single source of information, that is, the same person who provided the predictors (e.g., the leader's behavior descriptions and the situation) also provided the assessment of the outcome and the moderator (i.e., situational factors). Finally, these models initially examined leadership only at a team level; thus assumed leaders treated everyone similarly. However, the criticism is that leader behavior may vary with each individual.

NEW TOPICS AND FUTURE DIRECTIONS

After a century of empirical research, there are theoretical and methodological issues that have drawn the attention of the leadership researchers, theorists, and practitioners alike. Theoretically, three issues that need to be explored are: (1) the role of social cognition in leadership, (2) the role of diversity and multiculturalism in leadership, and (3) moving toward an integrative theory. From a methodological perspective, four issues need to be considered: single sources variance, level of conceptualization and analyses, a systematic conceptualization and measurement of the situation, and measurement of leadership effectiveness.

Many scholars have recognized the role of social cognition in leadership studies (e.g., Calder 1977; Martinko and Gardner 1987). Some have argued that leadership is a product of our imaginations (Miendl 1990), whereas others have respected the role of perception in the study of leadership (Ayman 1993; Lord and Maher 1991). From these discussions and the studies that have transpired, it has been substantiated that people have an image of a leader in "their mind's eye." This schema or the mental map does affect their perception and evaluation of leaders they meet (Larson 1982; Lord et al. 1978).

Research on diversity and multiculturalism in leadership has gained momentum in the later part of the century. Initially many studies in the United States focused on gender. This may have been partially due to sample availability. Studies have demonstrated that overall, in the United States and other cultures, across age and gender, the image of a leader is more similar to the image of a man than a woman (e.g., Ayman-Nolley et al. 1993; Schein et al. 1989, 1996). Although many meta-analyses have reflected that, across studies, men and women leaders' behavior differences are not very noticeable (Eagly and Johnson 1990), and that the differences that were found were mostly on task behaviors. However, the authors identified various moderators in determining a leader's gender and behavior relationship, such as self/subordinate rating, male-dominated setting, and role congenial position (Eagly and Johnson 1990). In measuring leader effectiveness across indexes such as overall satisfaction and performance, no gender difference was found. However, women leaders were favored more than men were when subordinates' satisfaction was measured, and men did better than women when performance was measured. In addition, the moderator of the gender role congeniality of the job was identified as a major predictor of this relationship. Therefore, it is possible that the dominant masculine image of a leader (i.e., more prevalent in traditional male-dominated roles) has been the major challenge of

women in breaking the glass ceiling (Morrison and Van Glinow 1990).

As leadership process is dependent on perception and social judgement, the saliency of the stimuli's characteristics is important in this process. Although most of the diversity studies on leadership have been on gender differences, other diversity indexes also need to be examined. In studying leaders who are diverse, it is critical that the superficial diversity elements (i.e., those that can be seen, such as sex and color) and the deep diversity elements (i.e., those that cannot be seen, such as traits and education) be considered separately (Harrison et al. 1998). For example, Korabik (1997) has presented evidence that women may perceive themselves differently based on their sex-role orientation. But observers perceive women mostly based on the feminine stereotypes.

In addition, the process of social interaction between leaders and subordinates involves the leader as the actor and others as observers who judge this leader. In this case, both the leader's characteristics and the characteristics of subordinates need to be considered. In gender studies already reviewed, the gender composition of the group has been shown to affect the selection of a man or a woman as the leader (Eagly and Karau 1991) and to impact on men and women leaders' evaluation (Eagly et al. 1995). Research has demonstrated that in mixed-gender teams, men are more often favored than women. So, in studying leaders of other cultures or ethnic groups, it is not sufficient to study their behavior or expectations with their own culture; rather, it is critical to examine their interaction with people from other cultures (Ayman 1997). For example, Thomas and Ravlin (1995) found that American autoworkers rated more negatively on the dimension of trust when Japanese managers behaved like American leaders, but perceived these Japanese managers as more similar and effective.

Recently, several researchers and scholars have conducted cross-paradigm studies and provided integrated models of leadership. In the last five years there have been studies that examined the relationship between traits and leader behavior, such as Myers-Briggs and transformational behavior (Roush and Atwater 1992) and Bem's sex-role inventory and transformational leadership (Hackman et al. 1992). There are also studies connecting leader member exchange with transformational leadership (Basu and Green 1997). More efforts to connecting various leadership research approaches are warranted. Chemers (1997) has presented an integrative model of leadership enabling researchers to approach leadership research with a more comprehensive understanding in the future. That is, although each study may be limited in scope, using a model like that of Chemers can help place it in the universe of leadership research. Doing cross-theory studies of leadership will enhance the understanding of this complex phenomenon.

The methodological challenge facing leadership research may be categorized in three topics (i.e., single-source variance, level issues, and measurement of the situation and the effectiveness of the leader). Many models reviewed in this article were validated on a single source of information. In other words, the same person who provided the predictor (e.g., the leader's behavior description) also provided the criterion (e.g., satisfaction or performance). This can artificially inflate the relationships under investigation (Yukle and Van Fleet 1992). One solution that some have used is that one subordinate describes the leader's behavior and another provides the effectiveness measure (Avolio et al. 1991). Although this is a step in the right direction, still both the leader and the subordinates have a vested interest in the relationship and thus may provide a biased perception.

Level of conceptualization and analysis is another methodological challenge that recently became the focus of leadership researchers' attention (Dansereau et al. 1995). These authors propose that the level of variables used in leadership studies needs to consider whether it is assessing the phenomenon at an individual, a dyadic, a group, or an organizational level. Also, it is important to consider the level issues in design and analysis of a study. In some studies the measures and the analyses may stay in the same level or go across levels to examine a meso-level relationship. The gravity of this issue and the methodologies involved in this procedure are reflected in a two-volume book edited by Dansereau and Yammarino (1998). In these volumes, many leadership approaches and theories are examined with the multilevel question in mind. It is not necessary for all models to be validated at all levels. However, it is valuable to understand the parameters of the various models in relation to the level issue.

The third challenge is the assessment of leadership situation and leadership effectiveness. Although in situational studies and in contingency models some element of the situation is operationalized, a more systematic, cohesive model for evaluating these variables across theories would assist the field's evolution. Fiedler and Chemers (Ayman and Romano 1998) have identified three elements in the situation that affect the leaders' perceived control (leader-member relation, task structure, and position power). These aspects of situational control parallel French and Raven's sources of power (Ayman et al. 1998). The relative degree of importance of these aspects of situation has been substantiated both in contingency model research (Fiedler 1978) and in sources-of-power research (Podsakoff and Schriesheim 1985). Also, Hunt (1991) identified different levels within the organization as another situational factor affecting leadership. What is important to remember is that the prominent models of leadership reviewed here were validated in various work settings and industries. These models have been able to explain leadership regardless of whether the person is a political leader, a hospital administrator, a factory manager, a retail manager, a school principal, or a military leader. Consequently, future work is needed on a framework for identifying elements and dimensions that are important to consider in leadership situations. For example, one dimension that has been identified is the leader's power base. What are others?

Leadership effectiveness (e.g., group performance, leader's performance, group cohesion, subordinate satisfaction, organizational commitment, employee turnover rate) has been measured by various indexes and by various sources such as self report, superiors, and subordinates. Some models were more effective in predicting leaders emergence than effectiveness. Others have been more successful in predicting the well-being and cohesion of the group, such as subordinate satisfaction, turnover in the group, and subordinates stress. Several have predicted group performance measures by subordinates' evaluation or a superiors' assessment, or have used performance criteria such as financial indexes, sales, or goals met (e.g., sport teams' scores). It is important to consider the parameter of models and the measures used to assess leadership. Some models may be better in predicting one criterion than another.

In conclusion, some have said, "Leadership is paradoxical; popular thinking . . . emphasizes the importance of . . . leadership establishing excellent organizations, but many academic publications assert that leadership is consequential" (Day and Lord, in Hunt 1991, p. 1). However, as Fiedler said in a personal comment to the author: "This is a pretzel shape universe that requires a pretzel shape model." The complexity of the world and the challenges it presents may call for a different form of leadership from the one-person-focused leadership. Since the team approach is being used in many organizations, it may be that the future of leadership will also be a team leadership approach. Compared to many fields of science, study of leadership is very young. Although challenges are present and the phenomenon is nebulous, leaders would attest that there are some things going on that make things work, but they are hard to explain. Future researchers are charged to systematically overcome the challenges and to collectively gain control of understanding of leadership in a global dynamic environment.

REFERENCES

Avolio, B., and B. M. Bass 1988 "Transformational Leadership, Charisma and Beyond." In J. G. Hunt, B. R. Balaga, H. P. Dachler, and C. Schriesheim, eds., *Emerging Leadership Vistas*. Elmsford, N.Y.: Pergamon.

Avolio, B. J., F. J. Yammarion, and B. M. Bass 1991 "Identifying Common Methods Variance with Data Collected from a Single Source: An Unresolved Sticky Issue." *Journal of Management* 17:571–587.

Ayman, R. 1993 "Leadership Perception: The Role of Gender and Culture." In M. M. Chemers and R. Ayman, eds., *Leadership Theory and Research: Perspectives and Directions*. New York: Academic.

—— 1997 "Organizational Leadership." In S. W. Sadava and D. R. McCreary, eds., *Applied Social Psychology*. Upper Saddle River, N.J.: Prentice Hall.

——, and M. M. Chemers 1983 "Relationship of Supervisory Behavior Ratings to Work Group Effectiveness and Subordinate Satisfaction." *Journal of Applied Psychology* 68:338–341.

—— 1991 "The Effect of Leadership Match on Subordinate Satisfaction in Mexican Organizations: Some Moderating Influence of Self-Monitoring." *Applied Psychology: An International Review* 40:299–314.

——, and F. Fiedler 1998 "The Contingency Model of Leadership Effectiveness: Its Levels of Analysis." In F. Dansereau and F. J. Yammarino, eds., *Leadership: The Multiple-Level Approaches–Classical and New Wave*. Stamford, Conn.: JAI.

——, and R. Romano 1998 "Appendix: Measures and Assessments for the Contingency Model of Leadership Effectiveness." In F. Dansereau and F. J. Yammarino, eds., *Leadership: The Multiple-Level Approaches–Classical and New Wave*. Stamford, Conn.: JAI.

Ayman-Nolley, S., R. Ayman, and J. Becker 1993 "Gender Affects Children's Drawings of a Leader." Paper Presented At The Annual Convention Of American Psychological Society, Chicago (June).

Bass, B. M. 1985 *Leadership and Performance beyond Expectations*. New York: Free Press.

—— 1990 *Bass and Stogdill's Handbook of Leadership: Theory, Research, and Managerial Applications*, 3rd ed. New York: Free Press.

——, S. Kulbeck, and C. R. Wurster 1953 "Factors Influencing the Reliability and Validity of Leaderless Group Discussion Assessment." *Journal of Applied Psychology* 37:26–30.

Basu, R., and S. G. Green 1997 "Leader-Member Exchange and Transformational Leadership: An Empirical Examination of Innovative Behaviors in Leader-Member Dyads." *Journal of Applied Social Psychology* 27:477–499.

Bavelas, A., A. H. Hastorf, A. E. Gross, and W. R. Kite 1965 "Experiments on the Alteration of Group Structure." *Journal of Experimental Social Psychology* 1:310–320.

Burns, J. M. 1978 *Leadership*. New York: Harper and Row.

Calder, B. J. 1977 "Attribution Theory of Leadership." In B. M. Staw and G. R. Salanick, eds., *New Directions in Organizational Behavior*. Chicago: St. Clair.

Carlyle, T. (1841) 1907 *Heroes and Hero Worship*. Boston: Adams.

Chemers, M. M. 1997 *An Integrative Theory of Leadership*. Mahwah, N.J.: Lawrence Erlbaum.

——, and R. Ayman 1993 *Leadership Theory and Research: Perspectives and Directions*. New York: Academic.

Conger, J. A., and R. A. Kanungo 1987 "Towards a Behavioral Theory of Charismatic Leadership in Organizational Settings." *Academy of Management Review* 12:637–647.

—— 1988 "The Empowerment Process: Integrating Theory and Practice." *Academy of Management Review* 13:471–482.

Cook, J. D., S. J. Hepworth, T. D. Wall, and P. B. Warr 1985 *The Experience of Work: A Compendium and Review of 249 Measures and Their Use*. New York: Academic.

Dansereau, F., G. Graen, and W. J. Haga 1975 "A Vertical Dyad Linkage Approach to Leadership in Formal Organizations." *Organizational Behavior and Human Performance* 13:46–78.

——, and F. J. Yammarino (eds.) 1998 "Leadership: The Multiple-Level Approaches," vols. I and II. Stamford, Conn.: JAI.

Dansereau, F., F. J. Yammarino, and S. E. Markham 1995 "Leadership: The Multiple-Level Approaches." *Leadership Quarterly* 6:97–110.

Eagly, A. H., and B. T. Johnson 1990 "Gender and Leadership Style: A Meta-Analysis." *Psychological Bulletin* 108:233–256.

——, and S. J. Karau 1991 "Gender and the Emergence of Leaders: A Meta-Analysis." *Journal of Personality and Social Psychology* 60:685–710.

——, and M. G. Makhijani 1995 "Gender and the Effectiveness of Leaders: A Meta-Analysis." *Psychological Bulletin* 117(1):125–145.

Fiedler, F. E. 1978 "The Contingency Model and the Dynamics of the Leadership Process." In L. Berkowitz, ed., *Advances in Experimental Social Psychology*, vol. 11. New York: Academic.

—— 1993 "The Leadership Situation and the Black Box in Contingency Theories." In M. M. Chemers and R. Ayman, eds., *Leadership Theory and Research: Perspectives and Directions*. New York: Academic.

—— 1995 "Cognitive Resource and Leadership." *Applied Psychology: An International Review* 44:5–28.

——, and M. M. Chemers 1984 *Improving Leadership Effectiveness: The Leader Match Concept*, 2nd ed. New York: John Wiley.

Fisher, B. M., and J. E. Edwards 1988 "Consideration and Initiating Structure and Their Relationships with Leader Effectiveness: A Meta Analysis." In *Best Papers Proceedings, Academy of Management*. Anaheim, Calif.: Academy of Management.

Graen, G. 1976 "Role Making Processes within Complex Organizations." In M. D. Dunnette, ed., *Handbook of Industrial and Organizational Psychology*. Chicago: Rand McNally.

Graen, G. B., and Uhl-Bien 1995 "Relationship-Based Approach to Leadership: Development of Leader-Member Exchange (LMX) Theory of Leadership over 25 Years: Applying a Multi-Level Multi-Domain Perspective." *The Leadership Quarterly* 6:219–247.

Hackman, M. Z., A. H. Furniss, M. J. Hills, and T. J. Paterson 1992 "Perceptions of Gender-Role Characteristics and Transformational and Transactional Leadership Behaviors." *Perceptual and Motor Skills* 75:311–319.

Harrison, D. A., K. H. Price, and M. P. Bell 1998 "Beyond Relational Demography: Time and the Effects of Surface- and Deep-Level Diversity on Work Group Cohesion." *Academy of Management Journal* 41:96–107.

Hogan, R., G. J. Curphy, and J. Hogan 1994 "What We Know about Leadership: Effectiveness and Personality." *American Psychologist* 49(6):493–504.

Hollander, E. P. 1958 "Conformity, Status, and Idiosyncrasy Credit." *Psychological Review* 65:117–127.

—— 1978 *Leadership Dynamics: A Practical Guide to Effective Relationships*. New York: Free Press.

——, and J. W. Julian 1970 "Studies in Leader Legitimacy, Influence, and Innovation." In L. Berkowitx, ed., *Advances in Experimental Social Psychology*, vol. 5. New York: Academic.

House, R. J. 1971 "A Path Goal Theory of Leader Effectiveness." *Administrative Science Quarterly* 16:321–338.

—— 1977 "A 1976 Theory of Charismatic Leadership." In J. G. Hunt and L. L. Larson, eds., *Leadership: The Cutting Edge*. Carbondale, Ill.: Southern Illinois University Press.

Howell, J. P. 1997 "Substitutes for Leadership: "Their Meaning And Measurement"—An Historical Assessment." *Leadership Quarterly* 8:113–116.

——, P. W. Dorfman, and S. Kerr 1986 "Moderator Variables in Leadership Research." *Academy of Management Review* 11:88–102.

Howells, L. T., and S. W. Becker 1962 "Seating Arrangement and Leadership Emergence." *Journal of Abnormal and Social Psychology* 64:148–150.

Hunt, J. G. 1991 *Leadership: A New Synthesis*. Newbury Park, Calif.: Sage.

Kerr, S., and J. M. Jermier 1978 "Substitutes for Leadership: Their Meaning and Measurement." *Organizational Behavior and Human Performance* 22:374–403.

Kerr, S. C., C. J. Schriesheim, C. J. Murphy, and R. M. Stogdill 1974 "Towards a Contingency Theory of Leadership Based upon the Consideration and Initiating Structure Literature." *Organizational Behavior and Human Performance* 12:62–82.

Korabik, K. 1997 "Applied Gender Issues." In S. W. Sadava and D. R. McCreary, eds., *Applied Social Psychology*. Upper Saddle River, N.J.: Prentice Hall.

Korman, A. K. 1966 "Consideration, Initiating Structure, and Organizational Criteria—A Review." *Personnel Psychology* 19:349–361.

Kotter, J. P. 1988 *The Leadership Factor*. New York: Free Press.

Kouzes, J. M., and B. Z. Posner 1987 *The Leadership Challenge: How To Get Extraordinary Things Done in Organizations*. San Francisco: Jossey-Bass.

Larson, J. R., Jr. 1982 "Cognitive Mechanisms Mediating the Impact of Implicit Theories of Leader Behavior on Leader Behavior Rating." *Organizational Behavior and Human Performance* 29:129–140.

Leavitt, H. J. 1951 "Some Effects of Certain Communication Patterns on Group Performance." *Journal of Abnormal and Social Psychology* 46:38–50.

Lewin, K., R. Lippitt, and R. K. White 1939 "Patterns of Aggressive Behavior in Experimentally Created Social Climates." *Journal of Social Psychology* 10:271–301.

Lippitt, R., and R. K. White 1943 "The Social Climate of Children's Groups." In R. G. Baker, J. S. Kounin, and H. F. Wright, eds., *Child Behavior and Development*. San Francisco: Freeman.

Lord, R. G., J. F. Binning, M. C. Rush, and J. C. Thomas 1978 "The Effect of Performance Cues and Leader Behavior on Questionnaire Rating of Leadership Behavior." *Organizational Behavior and Human Performance* 21:27–39.

Lord, R. G., C. L. Devader, and G. M. Alliger 1986 "A Meta-Analysis of the Relation between Personality Traits and Leadership Perceptions: An Application of Validity Generalization Procedures." *Journal of Applied Psychology* 71:402–410.

Lord, R. G., and K. J. Maher 1991 *Leadership and Information Processing: Linking Perceptions and Performance*. Boston: Harper Collins.

Lowe, K. B., K. G. Kroeck, and C. A Campo 1996 "Effectiveness Correlates of Transformational and Transactional Leadership: A Meta-Analytic Review of the MLQ Literature." *The Leadership Quarterly* 7:385–426.

Mann, R. D. 1959 "A Review of the Relationship between Personality and Performance in Small Groups." *Psychological Bulletin* 56:241–270.

Martinko, M. J., and W. L. Gardner 1987 "The Leader/ Member Attribution Process." *Academy of Management Review* 12:235–249.

Marx, K. 1906 *Capital*. Chicago: Charles H. Kerr.

Miendl, J. R. 1990 "On Leadership: An Alternative to the Conventional Wisdom." In B. A. Staw, ed., *Research in Organizational Behavior*, vol. 12. New York: JAI.

Misumi, J. 1985 *The Behavior Science of Leadership: An Interdisciplinary Japanese Research Program*. Ann Arbor: University Of Michigan Press.

Morris, C. G., and J. R. Hackman 1969 "Behavorial Correlates of Perceived Leadership." *Journal of Personality and Social Psychology* 13:350–361.

Morrison, A. M., and M. A. Von Glinow 1990 "Women and Minority in Management." *American Psychologist* 45:200–208.

Peters, L. H., D. D. Hartke, and J. F. Pohlmann 1985 "Fielder's Contingency Theory of Leadership: An Application of the Meta-Analysis Procedures of Schmitt and Hunter." *Psychological Bulletin* 97:274–285.

Philips, J. S., and R. G. Lord 1982 "Schematic Information Processing and Perception of Leadership in Problem-Solving Groups." *Journal of Applied Psychology* 67:486–492.

Podsakoff, P. M., and C. A. Schriesheim 1985 "Field Studies of French and Raven's Bases of Power. Critique, Reanalysis, and Suggestions for Future Research." *Psychological Bulletin* 97:387–411.

Rahim, M. A. 1985 "Referent Role and Styles of Handling Interpersonal Conflict." *The Journal of Social Psychology* 126:79–86.

Roush, P. E., and L. Atwater 1992 "Using the MBTI to Understand Transformational Leadership and Self-Perception Accuracy." *Military Psychology* 4:17–34.

Schein, V. E., R. Mueller, and C. Jacobson 1989 "The Relationship Between Sex-Role Stereotypes and Requisite Management Characteristics among College Students." *Sex Role* 20:103–110.

Schein, V. E., R. Mueller, T. Lituchy, and J. Liu 1996 "Think Manager—Think Male: A Global Phenomenon?" *Journal of Organizational Behavior* 17:33–41.

Schriesheim, C. A. 1997 "Substitute for Leadership Theory: Development and Basic Concepts." *Leadership Quarterly* 8:103–108.

Shartle, C. L. 1951 "Studies in Naval Leadership." In H. Guetzkow, ed., *Groups, Leadership, and Men*. Pittsburgh: Carnegie.

Sinha, J. B. P. 1984 "A Model of Effective Leadership Styles in India." *International Studies of Management and Organization* 14:86–98.

Smoler, F. 1999 "The History of the CEO." *Worth* 5:150–154.

Snyder, M. 1979 "Self-Monitoring Process." In L. Berkowitz, ed., *Advances in Experimental Social Psychology*, vol. 12. New York: Academic.

Stogdill, R. M. 1948 "Personal Factors Associated with Leadership: A Survey of the Literature." *Journal of Psychology* 25:35–71.

Strube, M. J., and J. E. Garcia 1981 "A Meta-Analysis Investigation of Fiedler's Contingency Model of Leadership Effectiveness." *Psychological Bulletin* 90:307–321.

Thomas, D. C., and E. C. Ravlin 1995 "Responses of Employees to Cultural Adaptation by a Foreign Manager." *Journal of Applied Psychology* 80:133–147.

Thomas, K. W. 1992 "Conflict and Negotiation Processes in Organizations." In M. D. Dunnette and L. M. Hough, eds., *Handbook of Industrial and Organizational Psychology*, 2nd ed., vol. 3. Palo Alto. Calif.: Consulting Psychologists.

Vroom V. H., and A. G. Jago 1974 "Decision-Making as a Social Process: Normative and Descriptive Models of Leader Behavior." *Decision Sciences* 5:743–769.

Vroom V.H., and P. W. Yetton 1973 *Leadership and Decision-Making*. Pittsburgh: University Of Pittsburgh Press.

Yukle, G. 1989 *Leadership in Organizations*, 2nd ed. Englewood Cliffs, N.J.: Prentice Hall.

——, and D. D. Van Fleet 1992 "Theory and Research on Leadership in Organizations." In M. D. Dunnette and L. M. Hough, eds., *Handbook of Industrial and Organizational Psychology*, 2nd ed., vol. 3. Palo Alto. Calif.: Consulting Psychologists.

Zaccaro, S. J., R. J. Foti, and D. A. Kenny 1991 "Self-Monitoring and Trait-Based Variance in Leadership: An Investigation of Leader Flexibility across Multiple Group Situations." *Journal of Applied Psychology* 76:179–185.

ROYA AYMAN, PH.D.

LEARNING THEORIES

See Behaviorism; Socialization; Social Psychology.

LEGISLATION OF MORALITY

In *The Division of Labor in Society* ([1893] 1984), Emile Durkheim advanced the idea that the distinctive sociological feature of crime is society's reaction to it. Durkheim was writing at a time when Lombroso's view on the heritability of criminality dominated scientific and popular opinion. Science sought the etiology of crime in the biology of the criminal, in *atavism*—crime viewed as a reversion to primitive, ancestral characteristics.

From this perspective, the harmfulness of criminality was taken for granted. Given his more comparative and anthropological outlook, Durkheim rejected the idea that crime was condemned by society because of its harmful consequences or because the deviant act was in itself evil. For Durkheim, many things that attracted the severest reprimands of society were objectively quite harmless, such as the neglect of the food taboos or the neglect of religious observance. In his view, the major issue was the integrative function of law, not the individual sources of deviance. Indeed, in *Suicide* ([1897] 1951) he characterized individual acts of despair as expressions of social structural pathologies. He also noted that the integrative function of law extracted far more from the condemnation of the lower class thief than from the middle-class embezzler—even though the latter's financial gain was greater and the social consequences of his acts much more adverse. From these observations Durkheim concluded that the societal reactions to crime and deviance were not based on rational models of the incapacitation or deterrence of the offender. In contrast to such utilitarian thinking, the societal reaction to crime was marked by an impassioned moral condemnation. This common feeling of moral outrage was a mark of the collective consciousness of society, particularly in highly cohesive, simple, or "tribal" societies. The condemnation of crime exercised the collective outlook, and it reinforced the group's collective beliefs and values. In short, the criminal was a scapegoat, and if he did not exist in fact, given his functional importance, he could be invented.

With the advance of more competitive and technologically sophisticated societies, the division of labor resulted in a partitioning of the collective consciousness across various elements of society and resulted in the rise of legal codes with less appetite for vengeance and with a greater investment in the reconciliation of competing interests. Hence, for Durkheim, punitive criminal law was the hallmark of primitive societies, which enjoyed a "mechanical" division of labor (i.e., a homogeneity of work functions), while reconciliatory civil law characterized advanced societies with an "organic" division of labor (i.e., a diverse but mutually dependent specialization of tasks). The former societies were characterized by brutal executions, the latter by written contracts.

Other nineteenth-century authorities tackled the role of law in society. Marx and Engels shared Durkheim's insight that the thing that needed explaining was not why people break laws—the problem of criminology—but why people make laws—the problem of the sociology of law (Cain and Hunt 1979). In their view, law was primarily an instrument of control and a source of both mystification and legitimation. As the urban merchant classes expanded their private estates into the countryside, these classes employed laws to transform the existing common rights of the rural peasants to the harvest of the forest—to deer, fish, pasture, firewood, and so forth—into crimes of theft from private property (Thompson 1975). In addition, the rise of capitalist agriculture, which was associated with the international trade in wool, cleared the British and European common lands of subsistent peasant farmers. Under contract law, the disenfranchised peasants became independent juridical subjects, able to engage in agreements to sell their labor for wages in the cities, although the urban working classes, having been displaced from subsistence on rural estates, had little choice, aside from starvation, but to work in factories.

Durkheim's position on law as an expression of the collective consciousness and Marx and Engel's views on law as an instrument of control continue to exert influence on contemporary thinking about law and morality. Where Durkheim treated the law as an expression of general social consciousness, Marx and Engels viewed it as an expression of a class consciousness, although, to be fair, Durkheim's model of collective consciousness held for a sort of mythic primitive society—akin to Hobbes on the "natural" state of man confronting the war of all against all or akin to Veblen or Freud's primal horde. In each case, the ideal type was an imaginative, indeed a fictional, reconstruction of human origins. The division of consciousness by class would have been possible for Durkheim in advanced societies—even if it constituted a state that he classified in *The Division of Labor in Society* as "abnormal" and even if it was the sort of awareness he wanted to overcome through the "corporations" that cut across class divisions and that Durkheim speculated might form the political nucleus of a future society.

In North America, sociological theories about the legislation of morality took a distinctive turn with investigations of "moral panics," "victimless crimes," and "moral entrepreneurs"—all of which figured importantly in the labeling theories of the 1960s. The studies investigated distinctively morally charged issues and stressed the influence of both social movements and the mass media in the construction of the criminal law. By way of example, Sutherland (1950) examined the role of "moral crusaders" in the context of the sexual psychopathy laws that were enacted in 1937 and thereafter in eleven northern states, California, and the District of Columbia. These laws provided for indefinite incarceration in hospitals for the criminally insane for anyone pronounced by a psychiatrist to be a sexual psychopath. Retrospectively, this diagnosis is not based on a discernible medical disease. In fact, many psychiatric categories are only labels for things we do not like. Nonetheless, a wide series of jurisdictions, with one eye to reforming sexual deviants, enacted laws based on this "disease."

There was a threefold process underlying the creation of these laws. First, the laws were enacted after a state of fear and hysteria followed newspaper accounts of several sex crimes committed coincidentally in quick succession. In these states there was a rush to buy guns, guard dogs, and locks and chains, reflecting widespread evidence of public fears. Second, these fears were fueled by news coverage of related sex crimes in other areas and other times in history and of sex-related behaviors and morality (including questions regarding striptease) and by letters to newspaper editors and statements made by public figures. The third phase was the creation of committees to study "the facts" of the sex crimes and "the facts" of sexual psychopathology. These committees, though initially struck on the basis of collective terror, persisted long after the fear and news stories subsided. They resulted in a presentation of briefs to legislative bodies, particularly by a new class of medical experts—psychiatrists. The community hysteria was legitimated by the identification of the crimes as a form of disease by the psychiatric professionals. The legislatures responded to public fears by passing laws to control the offending parties, in this instance by making sexual psychopaths subject to incarceration under psychiatric supervision.

A second important illustration is the history of the American prohibition movement, reported in the classic sociological study by Joseph Gusfield—*Symbolic Crusade* (1963). From 1919 to 1933 an amendment to the American Constitution outlawed the manufacture and sale of alcoholic beverages. The law was passed after decades of lobbying by members of the numerous "temperance movements," who originated predominantly from fundamentalist Protestant stock, largely from rural areas, and initially from middle-class backgrounds. They were the upholders of the Protestant ethic and valued hard work, self-reliance, and sobriety.

Gusfield argues that as America industrialized during the nineteenth century, the traditional rural settlers experienced a loss of social status compared to the new urban classes and experienced a challenge to their traditional values as urban development introduced increasingly nontraditional immigrants. The temperance movements were a form of status politics designed to reaffirm the prestige of a lifestyle. In the early period (1825–1875) the temperance movements pursued their objective through education, persuasion, and the reform of social conditions that caused excessive drinking. With increasing urbanization and greater European immigration, however, the tactics changed from a policy of socialization to one of coercive reform. The temperance movement became a prohibition movement. And when conservative forces came to dominate the political scene in America following World War I, the value of sobriety was to be achieved coercively—by outlawing booze. In Canada prohibition was approved in a national plebiscite in 1898 and enabled by federal law in 1916. The federal law allowed provinces to implement their own legislation, and all but Quebec outlawed booze, although booze continued to be manufactured for export—usually illicitly to the United States—and was available in Canada by prescription in pharmacies. The Canadian experiment in forced temperance ended in the mid-1920s, and the United States repealed Prohibition in 1933.

Gusfield's work is important for several reasons. It stressed the idea that legislation was "symbolic"—that it reflected the values of distinctive social groups and that such groups struggled to have their views insinuated into state legislation. Unlike Marx, who viewed political struggle as class politics, Gusfield stressed "status" politics—the advancement of group respectability or status by seeking to have the group values enshrined in law. Gusfield further implied that laws, particularly in the field of "victimless crimes," were symbolic in another sense. Instrumentally, prohibition was a terrible failure. It created huge markets for organized crime, and liquor consumption appears to have proceeded in spite of the law. Hence, the condemnation of insobriety was merely ritualistic (i.e., symbolic) because it did not extirpate drunkenness nor seriously inhibit liquor consumption. Similar arguments have been raised regarding the criminalization of narcotics, prostitution, and pornography—classical "victimless crimes," the markets for which thrive on a demand that seems little impeded by legal proscription.

The labeling theories of the 1960s developed the Durkheimian emphasis on the importance of societal reaction to crime (Kitsuse 1962; Lemert 1967) and identified some of the processes by which conduct was successfully labeled as criminal or how it successfully evaded such a label (Becker 1963). Theorists explored the self-fulfilling prophecies of deviant labels and the role of stigma in stabilizing rejected identities (Goffman 1961, 1963). The role of moral entrepreneurs was identified; these Weberian charismatics personified the struggle against evil and expedited legal change by campaigning in the media on the dire consequences of everything from dance halls to crime comics to television violence and marijuana use. Research on societal reaction proliferated. Studies focused on the manufacture of mental illness (Scheff 1999; Szasz 1961, 1970), the creation of witchcraft as a form of labeling (Erikson 1966; Currie 1968), the selective policing and the resulting social construction of delinquents (Cicourel 1968), the political hysteria that underlay political show trials (O'Connor 1972), the role of hysterical stereotypes in the criminalization of narcotics (Cook 1969; Lindesmith 1965), and the mythification of the Hell's Angels in the popular press (Thompson 1966).

The studies of this period had an insurgent flavor and a barely concealed contempt for legal structures and institutions that drew the line between conformity and deviance in an arbitrary fashion. This was particularly true in the context of legislation outlawing "victimless crimes." John Stuart Mill had established the ideological pedigree of this critique when he suggested that the democratic state's sole justification for limiting the freedom of an individual was that the person's behavior was harmful to others. Legal critics in the 1960s and 1970s objected to the extension of the law to cover vices and immoral activities since the participants in these acts, it was argued, were autonomous beings who had chosen them voluntarily and so were mischaracterized as either criminals or victims. The argument was that participants were not criminals since their behavior was not harmful to others, and they were not victims since their fates were chosen voluntarily (Schur 1965). Since these activities flowed from free choice in democratic states, how could they have been made unlawful? The answer lay in the fact that conservative forces led by moral entrepreneurs had stampeded democratic governments through wild allegations that the activities in question were so harmful that they struck at the very fabric of society and that however voluntary or self-inflicted the corruption, its control and eradication was justified for the sake of society itself. More recent studies have taken a different turn. Studies of the law-and-order campaigns associated with the resurgency of political conservatism have led sociologists to ask different sorts of questions.

Where Gusfield stressed that legislation might take on a symbolic aspect that reflects the interests of discrete social groups, recent work suggests that laws may *mystify* the social conditions that give rise to them and consequently may result in social control that is sought for altogether different reasons than the ones identified in the legislation. Taylor (1982) argues that many crime waves, moral panics, and anticrime campaigns are orchestrated in response to basic social conflicts and shifting economic realities and that they function to misdirect our attention away from social contradictions. Three noted British investigations lend support to this view. Hall and colleagues (1978) argue that the moral panic in British papers over street mugging in the early 1970s that resulted in calls for tougher jail sentences and more law and order in England mystified a basic structural shift in employment patterns that occurred during attempts to dismantle the British welfare state. In the late 1960s and early 1970s there was a conservative political movement in both America and Great Britain to curb state investments in public welfare—to "downsize" governments and to privatize public institutions. There was a certain amount of conscious political resistance in the labor movement and in socialist political quarters. However, the control culture succeeded in redefining the political resistance into an issue of individual lawlessness that required tougher policing, particularly of those persons who experienced the greatest amount of

social dislocation as a result of fiscal restraint— poor youth, minority groups, and immigrants. The reports of street "muggings" imparted to England the imagery of lawlessness from the American ghetto, creating the impression that there were dramatic increases in street crime, that the crimes were disturbingly "un-British," and that they were symptomatic of a wider threat to Great Britain's collective security as witnessed by violence in industrial disputes (fights at picket lines) and misconduct among soccer fans.

Having defined the problem as individual lawlessness, the conservative solution of more law and order, greater investment in policing, longer jail sentences, and so forth, occluded the problem of youthful unemployment that *resulted* from conservative fiscal policies and that contributed to theft and other petty rackets in the first place. In this interpretation, moral panics have a material foundation in everyday experience, but where the earlier labeling theorists viewed the panics as *causes* of legal change, the British theorists suggest that panic was the *result* of social change. Sensationalism over crime in the popular media legitimates the introduction of coercive legislation that frequently suspends normal democratic liberties and replaces parsimonious forms of control with more punitive measures. In the case reported by Hall and colleagues (1978), penalties for petty street crimes increased dramatically as the public, the judiciary, and the politicians were treated to hysterical excesses in the popular press of violent youth running amok.

A similar structural argument is advanced by Stanley Cohen in *Folk Devils and Moral Panics* (1972). This study examines the role of the media in the re-creation of the "mods" and "rockers." There have been a series of distinct trends in youth culture in both America and Great Britain over the last four or five decades—the zoot suiters, the Teddy Boys, the beats, the skin heads and punks, the soccer hooligans, and the motorcycle rebels— all of whom expressed antiauthoritarianism and youthful rebellion. What seems to have set off the postwar youth cultures was society's relative affluence, which created conditions for distinctive consumption patterns supporting unique fashion styles, musical tastes, and recreational opportunities. The mods and rockers were motorcycle-riding youth groups who appeared in the British seaside resorts in the middle 1960s. As Hunter Thompson discovered in his study (1966) of the California Hell's Angels, the British newspapers made a feast of the mods' antics, typically exaggerating and reporting spuriously on their activities. Cohen (1972) stresses that the function of the news hysteria was to create a kind of rogue's gallery of folk devils—vivid, even fearsome images that registered collective fears about the youth, their mobility, and their independence, which served as collective reminders of what youth should not be.

In this approach, moral panics are an ongoing, recurrent, and predictable aspect of the popular culture. From this perspective, they are not considered the handiwork of individual moralists who may or may not decide for personal reasons to pursue a moral campaign. Moral panics are orchestrated when individuals feel compelled by their sense of the collective consciousness to repair a breach in the ideological fabric of society. Typically, either such persons are affiliated with institutions that have a longstanding investment in moral control—church organizations, community groups, political parties, and so forth—or they occupy roles as self-appointed arbiters in democratic societies—academic experts, professional journalists, and publishers.

Also, moral panics and the legislative changes they engender track important shifts in social structure fairly closely. This is the conclusion of Pearson's *Hooligan: A History of Respectable Fears* (1983). Pearson reports that the current "public" appetite for law and order, for stiffer justice, and for a return to the past are recurrent themes in Western history. The historical perspective suggests that the feelings that, from the perspective of crime and delinquency, things are at an unprecedented nadir, that the present conduct of society compares poorly with the way things were in a previous golden age, that the family is falling apart, and that the popular entertainments of the lower classes are criminogenic, are recurrent in every major period of British history from the 1750s to the present. Over time, the rhetoric of decline has an uncanny similarity. Pearson's point is that crime fears or moral panics occur when the legitimacy of state control over the working class is somehow challenged or brought into question. In the nineteenth century the British working class was only partially integrated into the political process. Consequently, their consent to government—which was dominated by the propertied classes—was usually testy. In the 1840s in particular, there is an apprehension in philanthropical writings about the working-class "dodgers," bold, independent delinquents viewed as potential revolutionaries who might fuel the Chartist movement and overthrow the private ownership of property. In this context, philanthropists prescribed education and policing to create internal restraints in the interest of protecting property.

From this perspective, class tensions were misinterpreted in the public press and by middle-class politicians as "rising crime and delinquency," and the middle-class solutions were recurrently more "law and order" on the one hand and education on the other—that is, more police repression and control, a return to birching, a removal of the un-British elements of the population, a repudiation of meretricious American culture, and a return to the tranquility of the golden age when people knew their place.

It is difficult to give an overall assessment of how the processes of legislating morality discovered in the labeling period in America can be integrated with the class conflict approaches stressed in the recent British studies. Certainly, there is no reason to believe that the class antagonisms that characterize British society are as developed in North America, nor that these would be a monolithic source of legal change. On the other hand, there is also no reason that the search for systematic sources of moral panics as effects of social change could not be undertaken in North American studies. Since the early 1980s it has become clear that the preoccupation with abortion, pornography, the funding of acquired immunodeficiency syndrome (AIDS) research, gay bashing, and the Equal Rights Amendment in U.S. public discourses is related to important trends in family composition and female labor force participation. For the tradition minded, the suppression of access to abortion, pornography, and the Equal Rights Amendment (ERA) as well as lethargy in dealing with AIDS, all seem to be an attempt to turn the clock back toward patriarchal families. For more progressive feminists, access to abortion on demand, suppression of degrading pornography, and the confrontation of the epidemics of sexual and physical violence against women and children are essential ideological matters for the insurance of greater female social and economic advancement. In both cases, the public imagery of epidemics of fetal massacres on the one hand, and epidemics of incest and female abuse on the other, are not the products of idiosyncratic moral campaigns but arise in the context of profound social structural transformations—suggesting the need to develop a convergence of theories of symbolic interests and structural shifts that have developed independently to date.

As we enter the new millennium in American politics, it is clear that the contemporary issues in moral discourse are distinct from the earlier focus on the criminalization of things such as drugs and alcohol. Political observers have coined the term "culture war" to characterize the attempt of the "Moral Majority" of Christian right-wing politicians to topple "the moral decline of the nation" and to substitute "moral sanity" in the form of widespread laws consistent with their religious beliefs (Scatamburlo 1998). Despite the dominance in the U.S. House of Representatives and the Senate by leading proponents of "born-again" politics over the past decade (Shupe and Stacey 1982), the New Right has effectively capitulated and virtually despaired of incorporating its views into American public and personal life (CBS 1999). Its proponents have failed repeatedly to achieve significant change. Specifically, they have failed to reintroduce prayer into the public school system—at the very time when American schools were racked by senseless shootings by disgruntled students. They have failed to curb the use of abortion as a method of birth control, failed to oust a philandering president despite a relentless investigation by a special prosecutor, and failed to curb the spread of sexual explicitness and capricious violence in everything from video games to Hollywood movies in spite of the fear that a great deal of youthful violence appears to be copied from mass media images. Further, they have failed to protect the hegemonic status of the traditional, heterosexual family and its access to spousal benefits from incursions by lesbian and gay lobbyists. They have made headway in downsizing the welfare state, but this has been achieved to varying degrees throughout the Western democracies without the same moral agenda.

The other side of the culture war has been associated with the rise of "identity politics"—a growth in social movements among *racial minorities*, women, and sexual minorities during the past two decades. In an attempt to recenter knowledge and power on the basis of experiences overlooked by male, Eurocentric, and heterosexual perspectives, claims have sometimes been made that gynocentric, Afrocentric, and gay voices have epistemological and moral standpoints that are superior to those which have traditionally overshadowed them (Seidman 1994, p. 234). Though such claims are extravagant, they signal cultural conflicts over basic moral and social questions and foster power politics resulting from the emancipation of racial minorities, women, and gays and lesbians This explains in part the Moral Majority's sense of crisis, its backlash against political correctness, and its desire to return to the previous equilibrium. Schlesinger argues that the crisis is further fueled by the feeling that the common presuppositions that are required for democracy are imperiled by the spread of "strident multiculturalism," radical ethnocentrism, and the undermining of the very possibility of a common American identity (Schlesinger 1998). The matter is only intensified by the shifting racial composition of America. Maharidge's *The Coming White Minority* (1996) documents the apprehension among white Californians about becoming a minority group in their "own" state, a trend true of America as a whole in the larger global perspective. The social processes are not unlike those identified by Gusfield in the analysis of the temperance movement, suggesting that the social forces explaining the cultural conflicts are not unfamiliar to students of moral panic. What is less well acknowledged, and what might be important to keep in mind for resolution of what is regrettably labeled the "culture war" is the following. From the start, the Moral Majority campaign tended to be exclusionary and fundamentalist (Snowball 1991). Democracy requires coalitions and a broad basis of mutual support. When politicians in a democracy take their policies from religion, moral condemnation overshadows political dialogue. Political decisions are not arrived at through compromise and mutual dependence but through faith. Given these tendencies, "average citizens" have failed to assent to the moral absolutes required by politics based on religious righteousness, and the movement appears to have run its course (Weyrich 1999). Whether the culture war is amenable to an alternative, more inclusive, multicultural resolution remains to be seen.

(SEE ALSO: *Deviance; Social Control*)

REFERENCES

Becker, Howard S. 1963 *Outsiders*. New York: Free Press.

Cain, M., and A. Hunt 1979 *Marx and Engels on Law*. New York: Academic.

Cicourel, Aaron 1968 *The Social Organization of Juvenile Justice*. London: Heinemann.

Cohen, Stanley 1972 *Folk Devils and Moral Panics*. Oxford: Basil Blackwell.

Cook, S. 1969 "Canadian Narcotics Legislation 1908–1923: A Conflict Approach." *Canadian Review of Sociology and Anthropology* 6:36–46.

Columbia Broadcasting System (CBS) 1999 "The Moral Minority." *60 Minutes*, report by Leslie Stahl, May 16.

Currie, Elliott P. 1968 "Crimes without Criminals: Witchcraft and Its Control in Renaissance Europe." *Law and Society Review* 3(1):7–132.

Durkhcim, Emile (1897) 1951 *Suicide*. New York: Free Press.

—— (1893) 1984 *The Division of Labor in Society*. New York: Free Press.

Erikson, Kai T. 1966 *Wayward Puritans*. New York: John Wiley.

Goffman, Erving 1961 *Asylums*. New York: Doubleday/Anchor.

—— 1963 *Stigma*. Englewood Cliffs, N.J.: Prentice-Hall.

Gusfield, Joseph R. 1963 *Symbolic Crusade: Status Politics and the American Temperance Movement*. Urbana: University of Illinois Press.

Hall, S., C. Critcher, T. Jefferson, J. Clarke, and B. Roberts 1978 *Policing the Crisis: Mugging, the State, and Law and Order*. London: Macmillan.

Kitsuse, John I. 1962 "Societal Response to Deviance: Social Problems of Theory and Method." *Social Problems* 9:247–256.

Lemert, Edwin 1967 "The Concept of Secondary Deviation." In E. Lemert, ed., *Human Deviance, Social Problems, and Social Control*. Englewood Cliffs, N.J.: Prentice-Hall.

Lindesmith, A. 1965 *The Addict and the Law*. Bloomington: Indiana University Press.

Maharidge, Dale 1996 *The Coming White Minority: California's Eruptions and the Nation's Future*. New York: Times Books/Random House.

O'Connor, Walter D. 1972 "The Manufacture of Deviance: The Case of the Soviet Purge, 1936–1938." *American Sociological Review* 37:403–413.

Pearson, Geoffrey 1983 *Hooligan: A History of Respectable Fears*. London: Macmillan.

Scatamburlo, Valerie 1998 *Soldiers of Misfortune: The New Right's Culture War and the Politics of Political Correctness*. New York: Peter Lang.

Scheff, Thomas 1999 *Being Mentally Ill*. New York: Aldine.

Schlesinger, Arthur M. 1998 *The Disuniting of America: Reflections on a Multicultural Society*, rev. ed. New York: Norton.

Schur, Edwin 1965 *Crimes without Victims*. Englewood Cliffs, N.J.: Prentice-Hall.

Seidman, Steven 1994 *Contested Knowledge: Social Theory in the Postmodern Era*, Cambridge, Mass.: Blackwell.

Shupe, Anson, and William S. Stacey 1982 *Born Again Politics and the Moral Majority: What Social Surveys Really Show*. New York: Edwin Mellen.

Snowball, David 1991 *Continuity and Change in the Rhetoric of the Moral Majority*. New York: Praeger.

Sutherland, Edwin 1950 "The Diffusion of Sexual Psychopath Laws." *American Journal of Sociology* 56:142–148.

Szasz, Thomas 1961 *The Myth of Mental Illness*. New York: Heuber-Harper.

—— 1970 *The Manufacture of Madness*. New York: Harper and Row.

Taylor, Ian 1982 "Moral Enterprise, Moral Panic, and Law-and-Order Campaigns." In M. M. Rosenberg, R. A. Stebbins, and A. Turowitz, eds., *The Sociology of Deviance*. New York: St. Martin's.

Thompson, E. P. 1975 *Whigs and Hunters*. Harmondsworth, England: Penguin.

Thompson, Hunter S. 1966 *Hell's Angels*. New York: Random House.

Weyrich, Paul 1999 "A Conservative Throws in the Towel." *FrontPage Magazine*, February 16. http://www.frontpagemag.com/archives/politics/weyrich2-17-99.htm.

AUGUSTINE BRANNIGAN

LEGITIMACY

See Interpersonal Power; Organizational Structure.

LEISURE

Since 1930 the sociology of leisure in North America and Europe has not developed in a linear or cumulative fashion. Rather, research agendas, the accepted premises for research and theory, and the "common wisdom" of the field have been revised and challenged. Change did not come in one great overturning, but in a sequence of revisions. A dialectical model seems to be most appropriate to follow the sequence. Through the 1950s, there was an accepted consensus as to both issues and premises. This common wisdom was eroded as well as challenged by new research. The "revised consensus" expanded agendas for both research and theory without completely overturning earlier developments.

Since 1985, a more critical antithesis with multiple sources has emerged to subject the second consensus to a more thoroughgoing revision. The sources of this antithesis have included conflict or neo-Marxist theory, gender-focused critiques, non-Western perspectives, and various poststructural analytical approaches. Critiques are associated with concepts such as hegemony and power, commodification, cultural and social fragmentation, gender and patriarchical structures, imperialism, world views, symbol systems, ideologies, and existential action. Now a central question concerns the kind of synthesis that will be developed in the ongoing process.

The dialectical sequence provides a dynamic framework for a review of central areas in the study of leisure. Although many issues and lines of research can be identified, four have consistently been most salient. In a highly abbreviated form, we will summarize the dialectics of theory and research in relation to (1) work and time, (2) family and community, (3) aging and the life course, and (4) the nature of leisure.

WORK AND TIME

Leisure and Work Domains. When sociologists turned their attention to leisure in the 1960s, three perspectives were adopted. The first, based on earlier community studies, approached leisure as a dimension of the social organization of the community (Lundberg, Komarovsky, and McInerney 1934; Dumazedier 1967). The second, exemplified by David Riesman and initiated at the University of Chicago, viewed leisure as social action that created its own worlds of meaning. The third, the one that came to shape domain assumption and research agendas, emerged from the sociology of work. Its fundamental premise was that economic

institutions are central to the society and economic roles the primary determinants of other roles. Especially leisure was assumed to be secondary and derivative. As a consequence, various models of determination by work were proposed that modeled leisure as similar to work ("spillover" or identity), contrasting (compensation), or separate (Wilensky 1960; Parker 1971). The bias, however, was clearly toward some kind of determination rather than segmentation.

As research proceeded, the "long arm of the job" was found to be both shorter and less powerful than expected as only limited, modest, and sometimes inconsistent relationships were found between leisure styles and occupational level and type (Wilson 1980). In a fuller perspective, on the other hand, it was evident that economic roles are determinative of the social context of adult lives—schedules, control of resources, autonomy, and other basic conditions (Blauner 1964). Leisure is part of the reward structure of a social system with differential access to resources based largely on socioeconomic position.

A second revision of the common wisdom concerned time available for leisure. The long-term reduction in the average workweek from as high as eighty hours in the early days of the industrial revolution to about forty hours in the post–World War II period along with the five-day workweek and paid vacations for many workers had led to an unquestioned assurance that more and more leisure time would be the product of increased economic productivity. In the 1970s, however, the declining rate of the decrease moving toward stability produced a revised consensus suggesting segmented time scarcity and a variety of social timetables. Most recently, analysis of labor statistics indicates that workers in high-pressure occupations and some services may have average workweeks much longer than forty hours (Schor 1991) even though time-diary research identifies a small overall increase in time for leisure (Robinson and Godbey 1997). Considerable attention has also been given to those impacted by the time scarcities of those, mostly women, with multiple work, household, and caregiving roles.

A next challenge to the early common wisdom was a recognition of leisure as a dimension of life with its own meaning and integrity. Leisure is more than leftover and derivative. It has its own place in the rhythm and flow of life. First, leisure came to be defined more as activity than as empty time. Among the themes emerging were relative freedom of choice, distinction from the obligations of other roles, and the variety of meanings and aims that might be sought in such activity. Just as important as the revised definition, however, was the identification of leisure as something more than a derivation of work. Social life could not be divided into a work versus leisure dichotomy, but consisted of multiple sets of intersecting roles. Leisure, although it has a particular relationship with the bonding of family and other immediate communities (Cheek and Burch 1976), had multiple contexts, connections, and meanings (Kelly 1981).

The Challenge of Critical Theory. The domain assumptions of functional sociology have been challenged by critical analyses with roots in neo-Marxist cultural studies (Clarke and Critcher 1986; Rojek 1985), historical study that focuses on power and the struggles of the working class, and social construction approaches that take into account the interpretive symbolic activity of social actors (Rojek 1995).

The central theme of the critical challenge is social control by ruling elites. Leisure is seen as a critical element in the hegemony of ruling elites in a capitalist society. In order to assure compliance in the routinized "Fordist" workplace, the political arena, and the marketplace, leisure has emerged as central to the capitalist reward and control system. Leisure is, from this critical perspective, a market-mediated instrument that binds workers to the production process and to roles that support the reproduction of the capital-dominated social system. Leisure is defined as a commodity that must be earned and is indissolubly connected to what can be purchased and possessed.

A number of themes are gathered in this critique. The power to enforce compliance is masked behind an ideology in which "freedom" comes to be defined as purchasing power in the marketplace of leisure. Such "commodity fetishism" (Marx 1970) of attachment to things defines life and leisure in terms of possessions. Leisure, then, becomes "commodified" as the consumption of marketed goods and services, entertainment in contrast with commitment to involving,

challenging, and developmental activity (Kelly and Freysinger 1999). Social status is symbolized by leisure display (Veblen 1899). Absorption in mass media, especially low-cost and easy-access television (Robinson and Godbey 1997), legitimates consumption-oriented values and worldviews (Habermas 1975). What appear to be varying styles of leisure reflect the profoundly different conditions of work, family, and leisure assigned by class, gender, and race (Clarke and Critcher 1986).

A Prospective Synthesis. The fundamental presupposition of any sociology of leisure is that leisure is a thoroughly social phenomenon. It is a part of the culture and a product of the social system. Leisure is not separate and secondary, but embedded in the institutional structures, social times, and power allocations of the society. In a complex social system, both individual self-determination and institutional control differ by economic and social position. Leisure is not segmented, but woven into the system. Out of the current dialectic between the consensus and the critique, a number of issues call for attention.

The first agenda is to move beyond ideologies to examine the lived conditions of poor, excluded, and disinherited children, women, and men. Their struggles for life in the present, and their struggles for a future, are reflected in what they do to express themselves, create community, fill ordinary hours and days, and seek new possibilities.

The second issue is to identify the ways in which economic roles provide contexts, resources, limitations, and orientations for the rest of life—family and community as well as leisure. In a "post-Fordist" global economy with a loss of linear work careers and fragmented cultural schemes, the question is not the simple determination of life and leisure by work, but how determinative definitions of both the self and society are learned in a power-differentiated social context.

The third issue is meanings. Purchasing is not necessarily commodification and owning is not fetishism. What are the commitments, symbols, meanings, self-definitions, and worldviews that are the cognitive context of decisions and actions? What are the meanings and outcomes of leisure-related spending, media use, packaged entertainment and travel, and images of pleasure? Possession may be a way of life or an instrument of activity. Does leisure reflect a culture of possession? Or is there a deep paradox between alienation and creation that permeates the entire society?

The fourth issue revolves around time. It is necessary to discard misleading models about average workweeks and the "more or less leisure" argument. Rather, what are the actual patterns and varieties of time structure and allocation? How do these patterns and possibilities vary by economic role, gender, life course, family conditions, ethnicity and race, location, and other placement factors? Time remains a basic resource for leisure action, one that not only varies widely but is one index of the possibility of self-determination.

FAMILY AND COMMUNITY

Leisure as a Context for Family Bonding. If leisure is not just activity determined by and complementary to work, then is there some other critical relationship to the social system? The evident connection is to family and other immediate communities (Roberts 1970). Most leisure is in or around the home. The most common leisure companions are family and other close friends and intimates.

The basis of the first common wisdom was the series of community studies beginning in the 1930s (Lundberg, Komarovsky, and McInerny 1934; Lynd and Lynd 1956). Leisure was found to be a web of ordinary activity, mostly social interaction and tied to the institutions of the community from the family outward to status-based organizations. From this perspective, the later work of Cheek and Burch (1976) argued that the primary function of leisure is to provide a context for social bonding, especially that of family and ethnic community.

An anomaly in family leisure began a revision to the first consensus. The family context was reaffirmed and the centrality of the family to leisure supported (Kelly 1983). Despite the traditional focus on freedom as the primary defining theme of leisure, activity with major components of obligation was found to be most important to most adults. The major theme was that leisure was closely tied to central roles, not separate from them.

Leisure, then, is bound to both the roles and the developmental requirements of life (Rapoport and Rapoport 1976). In fact, from this perspective it may be quite central to life, not residual or

secondary at all. It is a primary setting for social bonding and expression as well as for human development. The implied issue, on the other hand, is the consequences for the nature of freedom and choice in leisure. No activity embedded in primary role relationships can ever be free of accompanying obligations and responsibilities (Kelly 1987a, chap. 6). Leisure might be more central but is also less pure and simple.

Power and Self-determination in Leisure Roles. First, there is the challenge posed by changing family patterns now that an unbroken marriage and family through the life course has become a minority probability. The most radical response and antithesis, however, begins with the suggestion that leisure, like other areas of life, has roles. That is, the expectations and power differentials that characterize family, work, and community roles are found in leisure as well. Currently the most salient source of this challenging antithesis is the focus on gender, especially from a feminist perspective (Henderson et al. 1996).

The critique calls for sociologists to go beneath the leisure rhetoric of freedom and self-expression to the realities of lives with limited power of self-determination. From this perspective, the history of the culture is characterized by male domination of women in profound and multifaceted ways that permeate every aspect of life (Deem 1986). Women have been repressed in where they are permitted to go and what they are allowed to do in leisure. Men have had the power to sexualize social contexts to objectify women and their bodies. Physical power and even violence have rendered many leisure times and places unsafe for women.

Even in the home, women's leisure is fundamentally different from that of men. It is usually women who are expected to do the work that makes "family leisure" possible. It is the "hidden work" of women that offers relative freedom to much of the leisure of men and children. Women both enable men's leisure and are leisure for men.

What, then, is the meaning of freedom and self-determination for any subordinate population segment? What about the poor, the racially and ethnically excluded, those cut off from opportunity in abandoned urban areas, and even many of the old? Again, many potential leisure venues in the inner city are unsafe, especially for children and the old. The resources of time, money, access, and autonomy are evidently unevenly distributed in any society.

In this antithesis, the connections of leisure to nonwork roles and resources, especially family and community, and the positive evaluation of how leisure contributes to development through the life course are brought up against a critical model of society. Leisure may indeed be indissolubly tied to family and community, but in ways that reflect social divisions and dominations as well as expressive action.

Leisure's Immediate Context: a New Agenda. Leisure takes place in its small worlds, but also in the larger scale of the society. Further, its actualization is in the midst of real life. Research may be based on premises of systemic integration and the benefits of leisure as well as challenged by critiques reflecting ideologies of subjugation and alienation. A new agenda for research, however informed, should be directed toward the actual lived conditions of decisions and actions, relationships and roles. In such an agenda related to community and family, several themes are highlighted by critiques of the common wisdom:

First, the realities of leisure as a struggle for action and self-determination in the midst of acute differences in power and access to resources will receive more attention. Especially gender, race, and poverty will reconstitute research strategies and frames past the easy assumptions that leisure is equally free and beneficial for all. The realities of family instability and crisis as well as of community divisions and conflicts will be taken into account as the immediate communities of leisure are reformulated.

Second, underlying the new agenda is the theme of differential power, not only power to command resources but to determine the course of one's life and what is required of others. In the action of leisure, there is both a relative openness for action and modes of repression that stimulate submission and resistance.

Third, the pervasiveness of sexuality, gender roles, and sexual orientation throughout life in society will gain greater prominence in leisure sociology. One set of issues revolves around sexuality and related emotions to leisure. Simple models of explanation based solely on rational action will be recognized as inadequate. Also, gender will be seen as negotiated identity and power of self-determination rather than a simple dichotomized category.

Fourth, the danger of leisure's becoming increasingly privatized, bound only to immediate communities and the small worlds of personal life construction, is a perspective that runs counter to the functional view of leisure as a context for social bonding. There may be a negative side to a focus on the family basis of leisure activity and meanings. As technologies increasingly make the home a center of varied entertainment, leisure could become more and more cut off from larger communities.

In general, leisure is surely not peripheral to the central concerns and relationships of life. That, however, does not lead simply to bonding without domination, to development without alienation, or to intimacy without conflict.

AGING AND THE LIFE COURSE

Continuity and Change in the Life Course. The earliest common wisdom was simply that age indexed many kinds of leisure engagement. In a simple model, age was even referred to as a cause of decreased rates of participation. It was assumed that something decremental happened to people as they aged. The rates of decline varied according to activity: rapid for sports, especially team sports; more gradual for travel and community involvement. Attention given to those in their later years, generally their sixties and seventies but sometimes their fifties as well, suggested that such "disengagement" might even be functional. Perhaps older people needed to consolidate their activity and recognize their limitations.

The revised common wisdom began by recasting age as an index of multiple related changes rather than an independent variable. Further, the revised framework became the life course rather than linear age (Neugarten 1968). A number of themes emerged:

First, in the Kansas City study of adult life, normative disengagement was replaced with activity (Havighurst 1961). Instead of making a necessary or desirable withdrawal from activity, older people were found to revise their patterns and commitments in ways that fit their later life roles and opportunities. Leisure was conceptualized as multidimensional in meaning as well as in forms. More recently, this approach has led to a discovery of the "active old," those before and in retirement who adopt lifestyles of engagement in a variety of leisure activities and relationships. Further, such engagement has been consistently found to be a major factor in life satisfaction (Cutler and Hendricks 1990).

Second, the model of inevitable decrement was challenged by research that failed to measure high correlations between age and functional ability. Rather, a model of aging that stressed *continuity* rather than loss and change was applied to leisure as well as other aspects of life (Atchley 1989). A return to earlier socialization studies provided a base for a revised model that identified lines of commitment rather than age-graded discontinuity. Especially the "core" of daily accessible activity and interaction remains central to time allocation through the life course (Kelly 1983).

Third, the life course also provided a perspective in which intersecting work, leisure, and family roles and opportunities were related to developmental changes (Rapoport and Rapoport 1976). Leisure is not a list of activities dwindling with age, but a social environment in which many critical issues of life may be worked out. Developing sexual identity for teens, expressing intimacy for those exploring and consolidating family commitments, reconstituting social contexts after midlife disruptions, and ensuring social integration in later years are all central requirements of the life course that are developed in leisure. Not only interests, but also significant identities are often found in leisure as well as in family and work (Gordon, Gaitz, and Scott 1976).

In the revised consensus, then, the life course with its interwoven work, family, and community roles was accepted as a valuable framework for analyzing both the continuities and the changes of leisure. Leisure was seen as tied not only to role sequences but also to developmental preoccupations. The life course was found to incorporate revisions and reorientations rather than being simply an inevitable downhill slide measured by participation rates in selected recreation pursuits.

An Integrated View of Life . . . and Leisure. The regular and predictable transitions of the life-course model, however, seem to gloss over many of the realities of contemporary life. A majority of adults in their middle or later years have experienced at least one disrupting trauma in health, work, or the family that has required a fundamental reconstituting of roles and orientations (Kelly 1987b). Further, conditions are not the same for all persons in a social system. Race, gender, class, and ethnicity designate different life chances.

In this perspective of continuity and change in a metaphor of life as journey, a number of issues call for attention. First, salient differences in life conditions are more than variations in starting points for the journey. Rather, deprivation and denial are cumulative in ways that affect every dimension of life. Second, individuals come to define themselves in the actual circumstances of life, not in an abstracted concept. Identities, the concepts of the self that are central to what we believe is possible and probable in our lives, are developed in the realities of the life course. Third, the structures of the society, including access to institutional power, provide forceful contexts of opportunity and denial that shape both direction and resources for the journey.

In this revised life-course approach, leisure remains as a significant dimension, tied to family, work, education, community, and other elements of life. Changes in one may affect all the others. Leisure, then, is distinct from the product orientation of work and the intimate bonding of the family, and yet is connected to both.

Leisure and the Life Course: New Agendas. From the perspective of the life course, research focusing on leisure now requires several revised issues. Among the most significant are:

First, leisure is woven through the life course. It is existential in a developmental sense. That is, leisure is action that involves *becoming*, action in which the actor becomes something more than before. For example, leisure is central to changing early socialization in the increased activity scheduling, electronic entertainment and interaction, and professional supervision of upper- and middle-class children. It is the main context for exploring sexuality and romance for teens and young adults.

Second, the developmental orientation of some leisure is highlighted by this perspective that recognizes lines of action as well as singular events and episodes. What has been termed "serious leisure" by Robert Stebbins (1979) is activity in which there is considerable personal investment in skills and often in equipment and organization. Such investment places serious leisure in a central position in identity formation and expression. Leisure identities may provide continuity through the transitions and traumas of the life course. Yet, how women and men define themselves and take action toward redefinition has been a subject of speculation more than research.

Third, what is the place of leisure in the schema of life investments and commitments? Further, how do those investments differ according to the life conditions of men and women as they make their way through the shifting expectations and possibilities of the life course? Xavier Gallier (1988) presents a model of the life course that emphasizes disruptions rather than linear progress. In an irregular life journey, work, family, and leisure may rise and fall both in salience and in the "chunks" of time they are allocated. He proposes that education, production, and leisure become themes woven through life rather than discrete sequential periods.

THE NATURE OF LEISURE

As already suggested, perspectives on the nature of leisure have changed in the modern period of scholarly attention from the 1930s to now. The change is not self-contained, but reflects shifts in theoretical paradigms as well as drawing from other disciplines, especially social psychology.

Leisure as Free Time and Meaning. Despite repeated references to Greek roots and especially Aristotle, the first accepted operational definition of leisure was that of time. Leisure did not require that all other role obligations be completed, but that the use of the time be more by choice than by requirement. How choice was to be measured was seldom addressed. Concurrently, international "time-budget" research quantified leisure as one type of activity that could be identified by its form (Szalai 1974). Leisure was assumed to be clearly distinguished from work, required maintenance, and family responsibilities.

The first consensus, although persisting in many research designs, did not endure long without amendment. To begin with, it was obvious that any activity might be required, an extension of work or other roles. Further, even such simple terms as "choice" and "discretionary" implied that the actor's definition of the situation might be crucial.

In the 1970s, the field claimed more attention from psychologists, who focused on attitudes rather than activities. Leisure was said to be defined by attitudes or a "state of mind" that included elements such as perceived freedom, intrinsic motivation, and a concentration on the experience rather than external ends (Neulinger 1974). Attention was directed toward meanings, but wholly in the actor rather than in definitions of the social context. Such psychological approaches were one salient influence on sociologists, who added at least three dimensions to the earlier time- and activity-known to common definitions.

First, in the 1950s, the Kansas City research (Havighurst 1961) along with the community studies tied leisure to social roles. The satisfactions anticipated in an activity involved meanings and relationships brought to the action context as well as what occurred in the time frame.

Second, the immediate experience might be the critical focus for leisure, but it occurs in particular environments that involve social learning, acquired skills and orientations (Csikszentmihalvi 1981), and interaction with components imported from other role relationships (Cheek and Burch 1976). Freedom is perceived, or not, in actual circumstances.

Third, although the dimension of freedom recurs in the literature, studies of experiences and activity engagements found that leisure seldom is monodimensional. The meanings, outcomes, motivations, and experiences themselves are multifaceted (Havighurst 1961; Kelly 1981).

Leisure, then, in the revised approaches is a more complex phenomenon than either the earlier sociologists or the psychologists proposed. In fact, the consensus broke down under the weight of multiple approaches that ranged from individualistic psychology to functional sociology, from presumably self-evident quantities of time to interpretive self-definitions and lines of action, and from discrete self-presentations (Goffman 1967) to actions embedded in life-course role sequences (Rapoport and Rapoport 1976).

Revolt against the Abstract. Antithetical themes came from several directions.

First, which is fundamental to accounting for life in society, the interpretive acts of the individual or the social context in which the action takes place (Giddens 1979)? Further, since the forms and symbols by which action is directed are learned and reinforced in the society, can action be prior to the context? The nature of leisure, then, is neither an acontextual nor a determined social role. Rather, it is actualized in processual action. And this process has continuities that extend beyond the immediate to personal development and the creation of significant communities (Kelly 1981).

Second, a number of critical analysts have raised questions about the positive cast usually given to leisure. Such positive approaches seem to presuppose resources, options, perspectives, and self-determination that are in fact unequally distributed in societies (Clarke and Critcher 1986). Do the unemployed and the poor have enough resources for discretion and choice to be meaningful concepts? Do histories of subjugation and life-defining limits for women in male-dominated societies make assumptions of self-determining action a sham? Such opportunity differences are most substantive in a market system of buying, renting, or otherwise acquiring resources. The real contexts of leisure are not voids of time and space, but are extensions of the structures of the society and ideologies of the culture. There is clearly an "other side" to leisure that includes many kinds of activity with destructive potential such as gambling, substance use, and sexual exploitation. There are also negative elements in other activities such as physical violence and racial stereotyping in sport, sexual violence in socializing, and even turning driving into a contest endangering others. All social forms of exploitation and exclusion are found in leisure (Rojek 1995; Kelly and Freysinger 1999).

Third, a consequence of this distorted and constricted context of leisure is alienation. Leisure is not entirely free, creative, authentic, and community-building activity. It may also be, perhaps at the same time, stultifying and alienating. It may separate rather than unite, narrow rather than expand, and entrap rather than free. It may, in short, be negative as well as positive. It is not a rarified ideal or a perfect experience. It is real life, often struggle and conflict as well as development and expression.

The dialectic between expression and oppression that characterizes the rest of life in society is the reality of leisure as well. Being role-based in a stratified society means being limited, directed, and excluded. The contexts of any experience, however free and exhilarating, are the real culture and social system. The multiple meanings of leisure include separation as well as community, determination as well as creation, and routine as well as expression. The former simplicity of leisure as essentially a "good thing" becomes alloyed by situating it in the real society with all its forces, pressures, and conflicts.

Leisure as a Dimension of Life. The question, then, is what does such extension and critique do to any conceptualization of the nature of leisure? Leisure encompasses both the existential and the social. It has myriad forms, locales, social settings, and outcomes. Leisure is neither separated from social roles nor wholly determined by them. Leisure has developed amid conflict as well as social development, in division as well as integration, with control as well as freedom. It may involve acquiescence as well as resistance, alienation as well as authenticity, and preoccupation with self as well as commitment to community. Leisure, then, is multidimensional and cannot be characterized by any single or simple element.

A further issue is whether leisure is really a domain of life at all. Is leisure clearly distinguished from work, family, community, church, and school: or is it a dimension of action and interaction within them all? In the Preparation period, leisure is a social space for the exploration and development of sexual identities as well as working out the issues of peer identification and independence from parents and the past. It also stresses the theme of expression that is central to developing a sense of selfhood, of personal identity among emerging social roles. In the Establishment period, leisure adds the dimension of bonding to intimate others, especially in the formation and consolidation of the family. In the Third Age, leisure has meanings tied to both integration with significant other persons and maintenance of a sense of ability when some work and community roles are lost (Kelly 1987b). Leisure, then, might be conceptualized as being woven into the intersecting role sequences of the life course rather than being a segregated realm of activity. Productivity is not limited to work, nor bonding to the family, nor learning and development to education, nor expression to leisure. Production, bonding and community, learning and development, and relative freedom and self-authenticating experience may all be found in any domain of life.

Yet there must also be distinguishing elements of leisure or it disappears into the ongoing round of life. Further, those elements should be significant in relation to central issues of life such as production and work, love and community, sexuality and gender, learning and development, emotion and involvement. Leisure should connect with the lived conditions of ordinary life rather than being an esoteric and precious idea to be actualized only in rare and elite conditions.

Leisure, then, may be more a dimension than a domain, more a theme than an identifiable realm (Kelly 1987a). That dimension is characterized by three elements: First, it is action in the inclusive sense of doing something, of being an intentioned and deliberate act. Such action is existential in producing an outcome with meaning to the actor. Second, this action is focused on the experience more than on the result. It is done primarily because of what occurs in the defined time and space. Third, leisure as a dimension of life is characterized by freedom more than by necessity. It is not required by any role, coercive power, or repressive ideology. Leisure is not detached from its social and cultural contexts, but is a dimension of relatively self-determined action within such contexts. Its meaning is not in its products as much as in the experience, not in its forms as much as in its expression.

The Sociology of Leisure in the Future. Leisure sociology, then, is not a closed book or a finalized product. Rather, central issues are currently being raised that promise to reform the field in its premises as well as conclusions. No common wisdom will go unchallenged, no consensus remain unchanged, and no theoretical formulation be above conflict. Yet, every challenge, every conflict, and every developing synthesis provides a new basis for at least one conclusion: Leisure is a significant dimension of life that calls for both disciplined and innovative attention. From this perspective, a number of issues are likely to receive greater attention in the new century (Kelly and Freysinger 1999):

The first issue is the ascendancy of the market sector as the primary leisure resource provider, with an estimated 97 percent of total spending. In a global economy, leisure including tourism is attracting more investment capital with a significant bias toward upscale markets, big-ticket toys, sport as business and spectacle, and entertainment with multiple entrance fees. This bias combined with media images of a commodified "good life" may underlie trends away from skill-based physical activity and "serious" leisure with high time costs. Is there a fundamental conflict between developmental and consumptive leisure?

The second issue is the emergence of a global culture. The dominant direction of the dispersal is currently from the West through the mass media. However, as communication links and business and cultural contacts become more common, both the concepts and the practices of leisure in the West will become more affected by other cultures.

Third, a focus on gender is leading away from male-oriented "reasoned action" modes of leisure decisions and toward the significance of emotions and especially sexuality. Since all social interaction is gendered and most has deep dimensions of sexuality, leisure will be understood more as a multidimensional process rather than a singular choice. Leisure, then, is both contextual and contested.

Fourth, leisure becomes more a part of "ordinary life" rather than segregated activities with special designations. In a more fragmented social milieu, elements of leisure may be located in almost any social context. Further, if work itself loses familiar continuities, then leisure may become more central to identities and persistent lines of meaning as individuals seek to make sense of their lives.

Fifth, there will likely be concerns over many negative aspects of leisure. Will easy entertainment lessen personal investments in challenging leisure? Will available and affordable electronics damage the social fabric of associations and intimate relationships? Will leisure increasingly become privatized at the cost of community exploitative of the poor and powerless? Will leisure become spectacular rather than engaging, violent rather than sharing, destructive of natural environments, and divisive rather than integrating?

The basic questions, of course, are those of the kind of society that is emerging and the kind of people who will live in it. It is clear, whatever is ahead, that leisure will be a significant dimension in a variety of forms and contexts.

(SEE ALSO: *Life Course, Gender, Social Class, Social Identity*)

REFERENCES

Atchley, Robert 1989 "A Continuity Theory of Normal Aging." *The Gerontologist* 29:183–190.

Blauner, Robert 1964 *Alienation and Freedom: The Factory Worker and His Industry*. Chicago: University of Chicago Press.

Cheek, Neil, and William Burch 1976 *The Social Organization of Leisure in Human Society*. New York: Harper and Row.

Clarke, John and Chas Critcher 1986 *The Devil Makes Work: Leisure in Capitalist Britain*. Champaign: University of Illinois Press.

Csikszentmihalyi, Mihaly 1981 "Leisure and Socialization." *Social Forces* 60:332–340.

Cutler, Stephen, and Jon Hendricks 1990 "Leisure and Time Use across the Life Course." In R. Binstock and L. George, eds., *Handbook of Aging and the Social Sciences*, 3rd ed. New York: Academic Press.

Deem, Rosemary 1986 *All Work and No Play: The Sociology of Women and Leisure*. Milton Keynes, United Kingdom: Open University Press.

Dumazedier, Joffre 1967 *Toward a Society of Leisure*. New York: Free Press.

Gallier, Xavier 1988 *La Deuxieme Carriere: Ages, Emplois, Retraite*. Paris: Editions du Seuil.

Giddens, Anthony 1979 *Central Problems in Social Theory: Action, Structure, and Contradiction in Social Analysis*. Berkeley: University of California Press.

Goffman, Erving 1967 *Interaction Ritual*. New York: Anchor Books.

Gordon, Chad, C. Gaitz, and J. Scott 1976 "Leisure and Lives: Personal Expressivity across the Life Span." In R. Binstock and E. Shanas, eds., *Handbook of Aging and the Social Sciences*. New York: Van Nostrand Reinhold.

Habermas, Jurgen 1975 *Legitimation Crisis*. Boston: Beacon Press.

Havighurst, Robert 1961 "The Nature and Values of Meaningful Free-time Activity." In R. Kleemeier, ed., *Aging and Leisure*. New York: Oxford University Press.

Henderson, Karla, M. Deborah Bialeschki, Susan Shaw, and Valeria Freysinger 1996 *Both Gains and Gaps: Feminist Perspectives on Women's Leisure*. State College, Pa.: Venture Publishing.

Kelly, John R. 1981 "Leisure Interaction and the Social Dialectic." *Social Forces* 60:304–22.

—— 1983 *Leisure Identities and Interactions*. London: Allen and Umwin.

—— 1987a *Freedom to Be: a New Sociology of Leisure*. New York: Macmillan.

—— 1987b *Peoria Winter: Styles and Resources in Later Life*. Lexington. Mass.: Lexington Books.

Kelly, John R., and Valeria Freysinger 1999. *21st Century Leisure: Current Issues*. Boston: Allyn and Bacon.

Lundberg, George, Mirra Komarovsky, and M. McInerney 1934. *Leisure: A Suburban Study*. New York: Columbia University Press.

Lynd, Helen, and Robert Lynd 1956 *Middletown*. New York: Harcourt Brace.

Marx, Karl 1970 *The Economic and Philosophical Manuscripts of 1844*. London: Lawrence and Wishart.

Neugarten, Bernice 1968 *Middle Age and Aging*. Chicago: University of Chicago Press.

Neulinger, John 1974 *The Psychology of Leisure*. Springfield, Ill.: C. C. Thomas.

Parker, Stanley 1971 *The Future of Work and Leisure*. New York: Praeger.

Rapoport, Rhona, and Robert Rapoport 1976 *Leisure and the Family Life Cycle*. London: Routledge.

Roberts, Kenneth 1970 *Leisure*. London: Longmans.

Robinson, John, and Geoffrey Godbey 1997 *Time for Life: The Surprising Ways Americans Use Their Time*. University Park: Pennsylvania University Press.

Rojek, Chris 1985 *Capitalism and Leisure Theory*. London: Tavistock.

—— 1995 *Decentring Leisure*. London and Thousand Oaks, Calif.: Sage.

Schor, Juliet 1991 *The Overworked American*. New York: Basic Books.

Stebbins, Robert 1979 *Amateurs: On the Margin between Work and Leisure*. Beverly Hills, Calif.: Sage.

Szalai, Alexander 1974 *The Use of Time: Daily Activities of Urban and Suburban Populations in Twelve Countries*. The Hague: Mouton.

Veblen, Thorstein (1899) 1953 *The Theory of the Leisure Class*. New York: New American Library.

Wilensky, Harold 1960 "Work, Careers, and Social Integration." *International Social Science Journal* 12:543–560.

Wilson, John 1980 "Sociology of Leisure." *Annual Review of Sociology* 6:21–40.

JOHN R. KELLY

LESBIANISM

See Alternative Life Styles; Sexual Orientation.

LEVELS OF ANALYSIS

Determining the level of analysis is usually straightforward, but whether to, or how to, draw inferences from one level of analysis to another is a difficult problem for which there is no general solution. The cases used as the units in an analysis determine the level of analysis. These cases may be quite varied, for example, countries, political parties, advertisements, families, or individuals. Thus, analysis may occur at the individual level, family level, advertisement level, and so forth.

The types of variables used at any one level of analysis, however, may be quite different. As an example, in studying the determinants of individuals' attitudes toward public education, the individuals (the units of analysis) may be described in terms of their sex and race (measures of individual properties), whether they attended a public or private college, and the region of the country in which they reside (measures of the collectives to which they belong). The analysis in this example is at the individual level because the cases used are individuals who are described in terms of individual properties and the properties of the collectives to which they belong.

This article focuses on (1) the types of variables used to describe the properties of collectives and members and the use of these variables at different levels of analysis; (2) problems that arise when using relationships at one level of analysis to make inferences about relationships at another level of analysis; (3) a brief discussion of a statistical model that explicates these problems; (4) some useful data analytic techniques to use when data at two or more levels of analysis are available, and (5) proposed solutions or partial solutions to the problem of cross level inference when data at only a single level of analysis are available.

TYPES OF VARIABLES USED TO DESCRIBE COLLECTIVES AND MEMBERS

Lazarsfeld and Menzel (1969) propose a typology of the kinds of properties (variables) that describe "collectives" and "members." For example, in discussing the properties of collectives, Lazarsfeld and Menzel distinguish between analytical, structural, and global properties.

Analytical properties are obtained by performing some mathematical operation upon some property of each *single* member. These properties are typically referred to as aggregate variables. Examples are the percentage of blacks in cities, the sex ratio for different counties, and the Gini Index as a measure of inequality of incomes in organizations.

Structural properties of collectives are obtained by performing some operation on data about the relations of each member to some or all of the others. Such measures are common in network analysis. Friendship density, for example, could be defined as the relative number of pairs of members of a collective who are directly connected by friendship ties. Since the total number of potential ties in a group with N members is $N(N-1)/2$, one measure of density is the total number of ties divided by this number.

Global properties of collectives do not use information about the properties of individual members either singly or in relationship to one another. Having a democratic or nondemocratic form of government is a global property of collectives. Being a private rather than a public school is a global property of a school. The proportion of gross national product (GNP) spent on education is a global property of countries.

Thus, variables that describe collectives can be based on summary data concerning single members of those collectives, the relationships of members to other members, or some global characteristic of the collective itself. Turning to variables that describe the properties of members of collectives, there are four major types: absolute, relational, comparative, and contextual.

Absolute properties are obtained without making use either of information about the characteristics of the collective or of information about the relationships of the member being described to other members. Thus, sex, level of education, and income are absolute properties of individuals.

Relational properties of members are computed from information about the substantive relationships between them and other members. For example, the number of friends an individual has at school or the number of family members is a property of the individual based on other members in the collective.

Comparative properties characterize a member by a comparison between his or her value on some (absolute or relational) property and the distribution of this property over the entire collective to which the person belongs. A person's class rank and birth order are comparative properties.

Contextual properties describe members by a property of the collective to which they belong. For example, being from a densely populated census tract or a school with a certain percentage of nonwhite students is a contextual property describing the context in which the member acts. Contextual properties are characteristics of collectives that are applied to members.

Contextual variables remind us that the level of analysis is determined by the cases used as the units of analysis, not by the level of the phenomena described by a particular variable. Thus, all the variables that describe a collective may be used at the individual level of analysis as well as those that describe individual properties; for example, a person's attitude may be predicted on the basis of the percentage of blacks in the person's school (contextual/analytic), whether or not the school is private or public (contextual/global), the density of friendships at the school (contextual/structural), the person's sex (absolute), his or her class standing (comparative), and the number of friendship choices he or she receives (relational).

INFERENCES FROM ONE LEVEL TO ANOTHER

The section above describes abstractly two different levels of analysis, the collective (or aggregate) and the member (or individual). Sociologists typically distinguish levels concretely depending on

the units of analysis; for example, the units may be schools, advertisements, children's stories, or riots. To make inferences from relationships discovered at one level of analysis to relationships at another level is not logically valid, and sociologists have labeled such inferences "fallacies." Still, at times one may be able to argue for the reasonableness of such inferences. These arguments may be based on statistical considerations (Achen and Shively 1995; Duncan and Davis 1953; Goodman 1953, 1959; King 1997) or on rationales that closely tie relationships at one level with those at another (Durkheim [1897] 1966; Dornbusch and Hickman 1959).

Disaggregative fallacies (often called ecological fallacies) are the classic case of cross level fallacies. Robinson (1950) brought them to the attention of sociologists. He cites two cases of cross level inferences, both of which involve making inferences about relationships at the individual level based on relationships discovered at the aggregate level. Robinson noted that the Pearson product moment correlation between the percent black and the percent illiterate in 1930 for the Census Bureau's nine geographical divisions was 0.95 and for states it was 0.77, while the correlation (measured by phi) on the individual level between being illiterate or not and being black or not was only 0.20. The relationship between percent illiterate and percent foreign-born was negative for regions and states (-0.62 and -0.53, respectively), while the relationship between being illiterate and being foreign-born at the individual level was positive (0.12).

Robinson demonstrated that relationships at one level of analysis do not have to be the same as those at another level. To assume that they must be the same or even that they must be quite similar is a logical fallacy.

Aggregative fallacies occur in the opposite direction, that is, when one assumes that relationships existing at the individual level must exist at the aggregate level. Robinson's results show that the positive relationship between being foreign born and being illiterate at the individual level may not be mirrored at the state level.

Universal fallacies (Alker 1969) occur when researchers assume that relationships based on the total population must be true for subsamples of the whole. It may be true, for example, that the relationship between population density and the crime rates of cities for all cities in the United States is not the same for southern cities or for cities with a population of over one million. Here, the fallacy is to assume that a relationship based on the total population must hold for selected subpopulations.

Similarly, one might commit a *selective fallacy* (Alker 1969) by assuming that relationships based on a particular sample of cities must hold for all cities. If the selected cities are a random sample of cities, this is a problem of statistical inference, but if they are selected on some other basis (e.g., size), then making inferences to all cities is a selective fallacy.

Cross-modality fallacies occur when the inference is from one distinct type of unit to another distinct type of unit. A cross-modality fallacy occurrs when trends in advertisement content are used to make inferences about trends in the attitudes of individuals, or designs on pottery are used to infer the level of need for achievement in different cultures. (Aggregative and disaggregative fallacies are cross-modality fallacies because groups and individuals are distinct units. But these fallacies have traditionally been classified separately.)

Cross-sectional fallacies occur when one makes inferences from cross-sectional relationships (relationships based on units of analysis from a single point in time) to longitudinal relationships. For example, if unemployment rates and crime rates are positively related at the city level, this fallacy is committed by inferring that increases over time in the unemployment rate are related to increases in the crime rate over time.

Longitudinal fallacies occur when one makes inferences from longitudinal relationships (relationships based on units of analysis across time units) to cross-sectional ones, that is inferring from a relationship between unemployment rates and crime rates over time to the relationship between these rates over units such as cities, counties, or states at a given point in time.

In all of their varied manifestations, cross-level inferences are not logically valid inferences (Skyrms 1975). That is, relationships on one level of analysis are not necessarily the same as those on another level. They may not even be similar. In the final section of this article, however, we note that data at one level of analysis may serve as evidence for relationships at another level of analysis even if they do not strictly imply such a relationship.

STATISTICAL ANALYSIS OF DISAGGREGATIVE AND AGGREGATIVE INFERENCES

This section presents the results of a mathematical demonstration of why disaggregative and aggregative inferences are fallacies, that is, why results at the aggregate level are not necessarily mirrored at the individual level. The derivation of this model is not shown here but may be found in several sources (Duncan et al. 1961; Alker 1969; Hannan 1971; and Robinson 1950). Readers who prefer can skip to the next section without loss of continuity.

The individual level or total correlation (r^t_{xy}) between two variables (X and Y) can be written as a function of the correlation between group means (the aggregate level correlation: r^b_{xy}), the correlation of individual scores within groups (a weighted average of the correlations within each of the groups: r^w_{xy}), and the correlation ratios for the two variables, X and Y. The correlation ratio is the ratio of the variance between groups (the variance of the group means: V^b_x) to the total variance (variance of the individual scores: V^t_x). Thus, the individual level or total correlation can be written

$$r^t_{xy} = r^w_{xy} \sqrt{1 - \left(\frac{V^b_x}{V^t_x}\right)^2} \sqrt{1 - \left(\frac{V^b_y}{V^t_y}\right)^2}$$
$$+ r^b_{xy} \left(\frac{V^b_x}{V^t_x}\right)\left(\frac{V^b_y}{V^t_y}\right) \quad (1)$$

Similarly, the individual level regression coefficient can be written as a function of the within-group regression coefficient, the group level (between group) regression coefficient, and the correlation ratio for variable X (equation 2):

$$b^t_{yx} = b^w_{yx} + \left(\frac{V^b_x}{V^t_x}\right)^2 (b^b_{yx} - b^w_{yx}) \quad (2)$$

It is a simple algebraic exercise to derive formulas for r^b_{xy} and b^b_{yx} (the aggregate level correlation and regression coefficients) in terms of correlation ratios, and correlation and regression coefficients at other levels.

These formulas clearly demonstrate why one cannot use the ecological or group level correlation or regression coefficients to estimate individual level relationships: The individual level relationships are a function of group level relationships, within-group level relationships, and correlation ratios. This approach can be extended to include other levels of analysis, for example, individuals on one level, counties on another, states on another, and time as yet another level (see, e.g., Alker 1969; Duncan et al. 1961).

SEPARATING AGGREGATE LEVEL AND INDIVIDUAL LEVEL EFFECTS

Obtaining data at the different levels of analysis solves the problem of inferring relationships from one level to another. Researchers in this situation know the relationship at both levels for their data. Such data also provide additional information about the relationships at different levels of analysis.

O'Brien (1998) shows that when individual level data are aggregated to create summary measures at the aggregate level (e.g., means or rates for aggregates), then it is possible to estimate the reliability of the aggregate level measures. Further, when two or more of the aggregate level measures are based on samples of the same respondents within each aggregate, correlated errors between aggregate level measures are likely to occur. This correlated error can be measured and the aggregate level relationships can be corrected for this spurious correlation as well as for unreliability in the aggregate level measures.

In some situations one may want to argue that the best measures of individual level "effects" (in a causal sense) are provided by analyses at the individual level that include as predictors relevant individual properties and the properties of the collective to which the individuals belong (contextual variables). Estimates of these individual level relationships are then "controlled" for group level effects (Alwin and Otto 1977).

Since the relationship between group level means may reflect nothing more than the relationship between variables at the individual level, it has been suggested that the best estimate of group level "effects" compares the regression coefficient for the group means and for the individual scores. Lincoln and Zeitz (1980) show how this may be done in a single regression equation while at the same time controlling for other relevant variables. For both of these techniques to work, some stringent assumptions must be met, including assumptions of no measurement error in the independent variables and of a common within-group regression coefficient. Most importantly, these techniques depend upon having data from different levels of analysis.

The introduction of Hierarchical Linear Models (HLM) provides a flexible method for examining the relationship of individual level variables to group level variables (Bryk and Raudenbush 1992). These models allow for the relationships between individual level variables to vary within different groups and for differences between these relationships to be predicted by group level characteristics. It might be the case, for example, that the relationship between socioeconomic standing and student achievement differs depending upon class size and whether the school is private or public. These models allow for the prediction of different relationships for different individuals based on group level characteristics. These models may be extended to several levels of analysis in which members are nested within collectives.

SOLUTIONS TO THE PROBLEM OF INFERENCES FROM ONE LEVEL TO ANOTHER

Even when data at only one level of analysis are available, cross level inferences can be and often are made by sociologists. There is no absolute stricture against making such inferences, but when researchers make them, they need to do so with some awareness of their limitations.

While both Duncan and Davis (1953) and Goodman (1953, 1959) maintain that it is generally inappropriate to use aggregate level (ecological) relationships to make inferences about individual level relationships, they each propose strategies that set bounds on the possible relationships that could exist at one level of analysis given relationships that exist at the other. The bounds are designed for use with aggregated data (analytic measures), and in some circumstances these techniques are useful.

Goodman (1953, 1959) suggested a technique called "ecological regression," which became the most widely used method for making inferences from aggregate level data to individual level relationships when group level variables are "analytical properties of collectives." Goodman's method has been extended by a number of authors and summarized in the work of Achen and Shively (1995). King (1997) has proposed a statistical "solution to the problem of ecological inference," but the success of that solution is controversial (Freedman et al. 1998).

"Theory" may also allow one to make cross level inferences. For example, Dornbusch and Hickman (1959) tested Riesman et al.'s contention (1950) that other-directedness in individuals declined in the United States during the first half of the twentieth century. They obviously could not interview individuals throughout the first half of the century, so they turned to advertisements in a women's magazine (*Ladies Home Journal*, 1890–1956) to examine whether these ads increasingly used themes of other-directedness. Their units of analysis were advertisements, but they explicitly stated that they wanted to make inferences about changes in the other-directedness of individuals. Is this justified? The answer is no, on strictly logical grounds, and this constitutes a cross-modality fallacy. Certainly changes in the contents of advertisements do not demonstrate changes in individuals' personalities. But Dornbusch and Hickman (1959) convincingly argue that advertisements (in this case) are likely to reflect aspects of other-directedness in the targets of the advertisements (individuals). They recognize the need for other tests of this hypothesis, using other types of data.

Perhaps the classic case in sociology of an analysis built on the ecological fallacy is Emile Durkheim's analysis of suicide ([1897] 1966). One factor that Durkheim sees as "protecting" individuals from suicide is social integration. When individuals are married, have children, are members of a church that provides a high degree of social integration (e.g., Catholic rather than Protestant), or live at a time when their countries are in crisis (e.g., a war or electoral crisis), they are seen as more integrated into social, religious, and political society and less likely to commit suicide. Much of the data available to Durkheim did not allow an analysis on the individual level. There was no "suicide registry" with detailed data on the sex, religion, family status, and so forth of those committing suicide. There were, however, census data

on the proportion of Catholics, the proportion married, and the average family size in different regions. Other sources could be used to ascertain the rate of suicide for different regions. Using these data, Durkheim showed that Catholic countries had lower suicide rates than Protestant countries, and that, France and Germany, Catholic cantons exhibited lower suicide rates than Protestant cantons. Further, departments in France with larger average family sizes had lower suicide rates, and the suicide rate was lower during the months of electoral crises in France than during comparable months of the previous or following year. He combined this evidence with other evidence dealing with individuals (e.g., suicide rates for married versus unmarried men), and it was all consistent with his theory of suicide and social integration.

One could dismiss these aggregate level relationships by arguing that perhaps in Protestant countries those of other religions kill themselves at such a high rate that the suicide rates are higher in Protestant countries than in Catholic countries (and similarly in Protestant cantons in France and Germany). Isn't it possible that in departments with relatively small average family sizes there is a tendency for those in large-size families to kill themselves relatively more often? This would create a relationship at the aggregate level (department level) in which smaller average family size is associated with higher rates of suicide. It is possible, because relationships at one level of analysis are not necessarily mirrored at another level of analysis. But Durkheim's results are not easily dismissed.

Strict logic does not justify cross level inferences. But strict logic is not the only rational way to justify inferences. If a series of diverse relationships that are predicted to hold at the individual level are found at the aggregate level, they do not prove that the same relationships would be found at the individual level, but they are not irrelevant. It is incumbent on the critic of a study such as Durkheim's to give a series of alternative explanations explaining why the relationships at the aggregate level should differ from those at the individual level. If the alternative explanations are not very convincing or parsimonious, researchers are likely to find Durkheim's evidence persuasive. To the extent that social scientists are convinced that a set of advertisements is designed to appeal to motivations in their target population, that the target population of the magazine in which the advertisements appears represents the population of interest, and so on, they will find Dornbusch and Hickman's cross level inference persuasive. That a relationship at one level of analysis does not imply a relationship at another level of analysis does not mean that it cannot be used, along with other evidence, to help infer a relationship at another level of analysis.

Persuasion is a matter of degree and is subject to change. Sociologists would want to examine additional studies based on, for instance, other populations, modalities, and periods. These data might strengthen cross level inferences.

REFERENCES

Achen, Christopher H., and W. Phillips Shively 1995 *Cross-Level Inference*. Chicago: University of Chicago Press.

Alker, Hayward R. 1969 "A Typology of Ecological Fallacies." In Mattei Dogan and Stein Rokkan, eds., *Quantitative Ecological Analysis in the Social Sciences*. Cambridge, Mass.: MIT Press.

Alwin, Duane F., and Luther B. Otto 1977 "High School Context Effects on Aspirations." *Sociology of Education* 50:259–272.

Bryk, Anthony S., and Stephen W. Raudenbush 1992 *Hierarchical Linear Models: Applications and Data Analysis Methods*. Newbury Park, Calif.: Sage Publications.

Dornbusch, Sanford M., and Lauren C. Hickman 1959 "Other-Directedness in Consumer-Goods Advertising: A Test of Riesman's Historical Theory." *Social Forces* 38:99–102.

Duncan, Otis D., Ray P. Cuzzort, and Beverly Duncan 1961 *Statistical Geography: Problems in Analyzing Areal Data*. Glencoe, Ill.: Free Press.

Duncan, Otis D., and Beverly Davis 1953 "An Alternative to Ecological Correlation." *American Sociological Review* 18:665–666.

Durkheim, Emile (1897) 1966 *Suicide*. New York: Free Press.

Freedman, D. A., S. P. Klein, M. Ostland, and M. R. Roberts 1998 "A Solution to the Ecological Inference Problem (Book Review)." *Journal of the American Statistical Association* 93:1518–1522.

Goodman, Leo A. 1953 "Ecological Regression and Behavior of Individuals." *American Sociological Review* 18:663–664.

—— 1959 "Some Alternatives to Ecological Correlation." *American Journal of Sociology* 64:610–625.

Hannan, Michael T. 1971 *Aggregation and Disaggregation in Sociology*. Lexington, Mass.: Lexington Books.

——, and Leigh Burstein 1974 "Estimation from Grouped Observations." *American Sociological Review* 39:374–392.

King, Gary 1997 *A Solution to the Ecological Inference Problem*. Princeton, N.J.: Princeton University Press.

Lazarsfeld, Paul F., and Herbert Menzel 1969 "On the Relation Between Individual and Collective Properties." In Amitai Etzioni, ed., *A Sociological Reader on Complex Organizations*. New York: Holt, Rinehart, and Winston.

Lincoln, James R., and Gerald Zeitz 1980 "Organizational Properties from Aggregate Data: Separating Individual and Structural Effects." *American Sociological Review* 45:391–408.

O'Brien, Robert M. 1998. "Correcting Measures of Relationship Between Aggregate-Level Variables for Both Unreliability and Correlated Errors: An Empirical Example." *Social Science Research* 27:218–234.

Reisman, David, Nathan Glazer, and Reuel Denney 1950 *The Lonely Crowd*. New Haven, Conn.: Yale University Press.

Robinson, William S. 1950 "Ecological Correlations and the Behavior of Individuals." *American Sociological Review* 15:351–357.

Skyrms, Brian 1975 *Choice and Chance*. Encino, Calif.: Dickenson.

ROBERT M. O'BRIEN

LIBERALISM/CONSERVATISM

NOTE: *Although the following article has not been revised for this edition of the Encyclopedia, the substantive coverage is currently appropriate. The editors have provided a list of recent works at the end of the article to facilitate research and exploration of the topic.*

"Is (or was) Blank a liberal?" The precise reply to this question inevitably begins with a throat-clearing preface such as, "It all depends on the period you have in mind—and the place. Are you speaking of someone in nineteenth-century England, the United States during the Franklin Roosevelt New Deal days, contemporary Great Britain, continental Europe, or contemporary U.S.A.?"

For Americans nurtured on the "liberal" tradition of Franklin Delano Roosevelt and the Democratic party, the significance of the *L* word was quite clear. The private business establishment, left to its own devices, had brought about the economic collapse of 1929. "Rugged individualism" had demonstrated its inadequacies even for many rugged individualists themselves. Almost two-thirds of a century after that collapse, the Great American Depression still retains the power to evoke terrifying memories of mass unemployment, bank failures, small business bankruptcies, soup kitchens, and popular ditties like "Brother can you spare a dime?" These were all nostalgic but chilling reminiscences of the desolation to which "nonliberal," or "conservative," social, economic, and political policies had led. There seems to persist an enormous reluctance to release this era and its memories to the historians as just another noteworthy episode in American history like the War of 1812 or the Panic of 1873.

For other Americans, some of whom matured perhaps too rapidly during the late 1960s and whose memories were filled with visions of the war in Vietnam, the battles for Civil Rights, and the turmoil in urban ghettos, things were much less clear. Stalwarts of liberalism like Hubert Humphrey (senator, vice president, and unsuccessful Democratic candidate for President) seemed to become part of the very establishment toward which hostility was directed. Government, instead of representing a liberating force, increasingly was seen as the source of existing difficulties. Liberalism, for many, was no longer the solution; it had become part of the problem.

Liberalism has often been identified with the struggle to free individuals from the confining embraces of other persons, institutions, or even habitual ways of behaving. It is seen by its advocates as a liberating orientation. Thoughts that, in various times and places, have been called liberal, all seem to have as their common denominator this fundamental notion of freedom for individual human beings.

It was during the period between the Reformation and the French Revolution that a new social class emerged. Political control by a landowning aristocracy was challenged by this new class whose power lay only in the control of movable capital. It consisted of such people as bankers, traders, and manufacturers. Science began to replace religion as the source of ultimate authority; contract replaced status as the legal foundation of society. The ideas of individual initiative and individual control became the basis for a new philosophy: liberalism (Laski 1962, p. 11).

Liberalism began as the champion of freedom and the foe of privilege derived from inherited class position. But freedom was not fought for on behalf of everyone in society. The constituency of liberalism consisted of those who had property to defend. Its supporters sought to limit the range of political authority and tried to develop a system of fundamental rights not subject to invasion by the state (Laski 1962, p. 13). Most of the population (e.g., factory and agricultural workers) were not initially included in the concerns of liberalism. But redefinitions of governmental concerns and authority inevitably had consequences for all members of society. Thoughtful economists and others soon realized this.

Thus, from the perspective of the closing years of twentieth-century America, it is easy to forget that classical economists like Adam Smith and David Ricardo, far from being simply reflex ideologists for the business establishment, were deeply concerned about liberty for individuals and saw their classical economic doctrines as the best way to insure it. In this sense, many contemporary Americans could legitimately view them as representatives of the liberal, rather than the conservative, genre. The *free enterprise* game was originally a liberal game.

For many participants in this great game of free enterprise, it became increasingly more obvious that the game was "fixed," that somehow participants did not emerge with either their liberty or their pocketbooks intact. To insure even a modicum of freedom and liberty for individuals, it became necessary to provide them with a helping hand from a source outside the marketplace. This source, a powerful and beneficent outsider, the national government, could help monitor the rules and to some extent the play of the economic game. It *could* provide, for heavy losers or potential losers, social benefits in the form of such consolations as unemployment insurance, old age pensions, insured bank accounts, and coordinated measures to combat environmental pollution. It *could* help protect consumers from the harmful effects of adulterated food and drug products; it *could* protect workers from the hazards of unregulated workplaces. In short, the liberal ethos in twentieth-century America incorporated as one of its tenets reliance on government action to protect the liberty of individuals.

The conservative ethos, on the other hand, during the same period has been characterized by a hands-off posture with respect to many aspects of government policy. This constitutes a fascinating reversal of traditional conservatism. The shades of Edmund Burke and other historical conservative spirits might well cringe at the characterization of their philosophy as "less government."

For some observers, this liberal-conservative contrast seems to be based on different psychological sets, or frames, of mind. Thus, we have been told that liberals are more hospitable to change, more willing to reexamine institutions and established practices in the light of new problems and needs. From this perspective, conservatives are those who appeal to the experience of the past but do not learn from it. Liberals are presented as being less reverent of the status quo, more venturesome in the realm of ideas, and much more optimistic about the possibilities available through exploration and discovery (Girvetz 1966).

Willingness to change becomes meaningful only when viewed against the nature of the status quo. When "liberal" governments adopt measures to provide for persons who are aged, ill, unemployed, or handicapped (as they have in some Scandinavian countries), to be "liberal" may mean to *retain* the status quo. To eliminate the measures —to engage in change—may be precisely what Western conservatives might demand.

For many observers of the dramatic events occurring at the end of the 1980s and in the early 1990s in Eastern Europe, members of communist parties who struggled to maintain their power in government were labeled "conservatives." Those fighting for *free enterprise* and other capitalist-like changes were called "liberal reformers." Communists for many years had been viewed by Western conservatives as the ultimate enemy; liberals were characteristically referred to by many of these conservatives as thinly disguised "Reds." In a dramatic and even comic reversal, dedicated Stalinists were now described as "conservatives."

At one time or another a wide variety of ideas have been called conservative. There have been efforts, however, to reduce the essence of these ideas to a limited number of more or less well defined notions. Clinton Rossiter and Russell Kirk, two ardent defenders of the conservative faith, once prepared a summary that received widespread approval. Although not all conservatives would necessarily agree with everything appearing in their summary, "it would be exceedingly difficult to find a conservative who did not agree with a good deal of what Professors Kirk and Rossiter impute to their tradition" (Witonski 1971, pp. 34–35).

The imputation begins with an assumption about the more or less immutable character of human nature. Behind the curtain of civilized behavior there exists, in human beings, wickedness, unreason, and an urge to engage in violence. In addition, a great deal of emphasis is placed upon the conviction that people are not naturally equal in most qualities of mind, body, and spirit. Liberty is more important than social equality. This leads to the conclusion that society must always have its classes. It is futile to level or eliminate them. Accordingly, societies will always require ruling aristocracies; efforts to have majority rule will lead to errors and potential tyranny.

Human beings, this conservative ethos insists, are not born with rights. These are earned as a result of duties performed. Service, effort, obedience, cultivation of virtue and self-restraint are the price of rights. Of primary importance to liberty, order, and progress, is the institution of private property. Inherited institutions, values, symbols, and rituals are indispensable and even sacred. Human reason is subject to error and severely limited; the surest guide to wisdom and virtue is historical experience.

Beyond this, fundamental to conservatism is the belief that all political problems are fundamentally religious in nature. Narrow rationality cannot, in itself, satisfy human needs. Both society and conscience are ruled by divine intent. Conservatives, it is asserted, have an affection for the traditional life; others (presumably liberals) favor narrow uniformity, egalitarianism, and pursuit of utilitarian goals. The only true equality is moral equality; civilized society requires orders and classes. Property and freedom are inseparable. If property is separated from private possession, liberty disappears.

This basic conservative creed goes on to say that human beings have anarchic impulses and are governed more by emotion than by reason. It therefore becomes necessary to place controls on human appetite. The correct method of accomplishing this is through tradition and sound "prejudice."

Finally, the proper instrument for social change is Providence. Some change is necessary from time to time to conserve society. It is like the perpetual renewal of the human body. But this change must always be accomplished slowly and with an awareness of the direction in which Providence is moving social forces (Witonski 1971, pp. 32–34).

Undergirding the entire structure of this conservative doctrine is a more or less explicit version of the *chain of being*. This metaphor is designed to express the enormous extent, variety, order, and unity of "God's Creation." The chain stretches from the foot of God's throne to the meanest of inanimate objects. Every speck of creation is a link in this chain, and every link except those at the two extremities is simultaneously bigger and smaller than another; there can be no gap (Tillyard 1959). The classic examination of the history of this idea was written by Arthur S. Lovejoy (1960).

Every category of things excels at *something*. Plants are higher than stones, but stones are stronger and more durable. Animals ("Beasts") are above plants, but plants can assimilate nourishment better. Human beings are above beasts but inferior to them in physical energy and desires.

All this suggests a sort of interdependency among all objects and living creatures. Central to the idea of the chain is the concept that every object, animal or person, is part of an all-encompassing whole. Basic to the metaphor is an implicit, if not always explicit, view of the universe as an organism (strong traces of this continue to be found in some formulations of contemporary systems theory).

Pushed to its logical conclusion, this suggests that all creatures and objects are equally important. Every existing part of the cosmic organism might well be seen as necessary (perhaps in some unknown way) for the survival of the whole. This, in turn implies that, although they do different things, all human beings, for example, are equally necessary. This logic could lead to dangerous subversive doctrines about social equality. Another feature was required to make the chain-of-being notion acceptable to those searching for reasons to justify existing inequalities in human societies. This was found in the *primacy doctrine*, the idea that, within each category of objects and creatures, there is one above the others, a *primate*. The eagle is first among birds; the whale or dolphin, among "fishes"; the rose, among flowers; the fire, among elements; the lion or elephant, among beasts; and, naturally, the emperor, among men (Tillyard 1959, pp. 29–30).

More recently, the distinguished conservative sociologist Robert Nisbet has insisted that conservatism is simply one of three major political ideologies of the eighteenth and nineteenth centuries. The other two are *liberalism* and *socialism*. Interestingly, an ideology for him, in addition to having a "reasonably" coherent body of ideas, has a *power base* that makes possible a victory for the body of ideas. It extends over a period of time and has "major" advocates or spokespersons as well as a "respectable" degree of institutionalization and charismatic figures. For conservatism, these figures would include people like Edmund Burke, Benjamin Disraeli, and Winston Churchill. Liberals have their own counterparts to these. The philosophical substance of conservatism dates from 1790 with the publication of Edmund Burke's *Reflections on the Revolution in France* (Nisbet 1986; Burke 1855).

There is a fascinating contradiction to be found in conservative doctrine. Methodologically, Nisbet offers it as a champion of historical method. This he approves of as an alternative to the liberal utilitarianism of Jeremy Bentham that is "soulless," "mechanical," and even "inhuman." Bentham's doctrine idolizes pure reason, but human beings require a different mode of thought, one based on feelings, emotions, and long experience, as well as on pure logic.

In attacking liberal utilitarianism, Nisbet is attacking a doctrine essentially abandoned by twentieth-century American liberals. Sociologist L. T. Hobhouse must be credited with having made the most serious effort to reformulate liberal doctrine.

Utilitarianism, as fashioned by Jeremy Bentham and his followers, was the visible core of nineteenth-century liberalism. It has been defined as "nothing but an attempt to apply the principles of Newton to the affairs of politics and morals" (Halevy 1972, p. 6). The principle of utility, the notion that every possible action of human beings is either taken or not depending upon whether it is seen as resulting in either pleasure or pain, was the basis for an "objective science" of behavior modeled on the physical sciences. As such, in common with other alleged sciences, it was perhaps congenitally soulless, somewhat mechanical, and potentially inhuman. Using a "rational" (but not empirically derived) model, it announced that, by pursuing his or her own pleasure and avoiding pain, each person would maximize happiness for everyone. Society was simply a collection of separate individuals operating in their individual self-interests. Government action, or "interference," constituted a disservice to these individuals and should be rejected on "scientific" grounds.

Hobhouse took issue with this view but modestly presented John Stuart Mill as the transition figure between the old and new liberalisms. Mill, reared on Benthamite doctrine, continually brought it into contact with fresh experience and new trains of thought. As a result, Mill is, "the easiest person in the world to convict of inconsistency, incompleteness, and lack of rounded system. Hence also his work will survive the death of many consistent, complete, and perfectly rounded systems" (Hobhouse 1964, p. 58).

Hobhouse noted that, although the life of society is, ultimately, the life of individuals as they act upon each other, the lives of individuals would be quite different if they were separated from society. He stressed the fact that collective social action does not necessarily involve coercion or restraint. The state is simply one of many forms of human association, a form to which individuals owe much more of their personal security and freedom than most people recognize. "The value of a site in London," he pointed out, "is something due essentially to London, not to the landlord. More accurately, a part of it is due to London, a part to the British empire, a part, perhaps we should say, to Western civilization" (Hobhouse 1964, p. 100). "Democracy," he tells us, "is not founded merely on the right or the private interest of the individual. . . It is founded equally on the function of the individual as a member of the community" (Hobhouse 1964, p. 116).

In sum, Hobhouse helped provide a theoretic basis for a twentieth-century liberalism severed from the constricted framework of its origins and aimed at the liberation of *all* members of society. It continues to be very much concerned with feelings, emotions, and historical experience. Twentieth-century *conservatism* assumed the mantle of rigid utilitarianism shorn of its humanistic aspirations.

The contradictions in conservative doctrine become even more apparent when the matter of prejudice is considered. As Nisbet explains it, prejudice has its own intrinsic wisdom anterior to intellect. It can be readily applied in emergencies and does not leave one indecisive at the moment of decision. It sums up in an individual mind tradition's authority and wisdom (Nisbet 1986, p. 29).

This seems to epitomize the "mechanical" thought attributed to utilitarian or enlightenment liberals. Prejudice, in these terms, is, in effect, a mode of preprogrammed decision making. It insists upon shackling the human mind when confronted with new or unforeseen situations. It demands that such situations be dealt with through the use of what may well be outdated modes of thought, with strategies that were perhaps once useful but have lost their relevance. It denies a role for human creativity.

It is but a step from this doctrine to the prejudice castigated by civil rights activists and others. We meet a man whose skin is black or yellow; we meet a woman whose features tell us she is Jewish. We have preprogrammed responses to each of these, based on the "wisdom" of tradition, informing us that they, in various ways, are inferior creatures who must be dealt with accordingly.

The feudal origins of conservative doctrine are seen most clearly in its adamant stand on the issue of inheritance and property. Not only does it fight all efforts to loosen property from family groups by means of taxation, it fights all other efforts to redistribute wealth, ranging from special entitlements to affirmative action programs. It insists upon the indestructability of existing hierarchical structures in society, seeing all efforts to modify them as attacks on cultural and psychological diversity.

Further complicating the distinction between liberalism and conservatism has been what some might refer to as a fringe movement within conservatism, called *neoconservatism*.

One explanation for the emergence of this phenomenon begins by noting that in the mid-1960s American universities, as well as literature and art in general, had become increasingly radicalized. Some cold war liberals, others who were uncomfortable with black power politics, and some critics of the counterculture disengaged themselves from liberalism. Prominent names in this group include Irving Kristol, Norman Podhoretz, and sociologists Seymour Martin Lipset, Nathan Glazer, Daniel Bell, and James Coleman. Some of these continue to reject the label but "it is as though by some invisible hand their writings and lectures gave help to the conservative cause when it was needed" (Nisbet 1986, p. 101).

Periodicals most strongly identified with neoconservatism are *The Public Interest* and *Commentary*. Neoconservatives have had close ties with the Scaife, Smith Richardson, John M. Olin, and other foundations. They have appeared as resident scholars and trustees of think tanks like the Hoover Institution, The Heritage Foundation, and the American Enterprise Institute (Gottfried and Fleming 1988, p. 73).

Unlike more traditional conservatives, neoconservatives are not irrevocably opposed to some possible versions of a welfare state. They do not depend upon historical methodology; on the contrary, they seem to show a marked preference for quantification.

Thus, the difference between contemporary liberalism and conservatism is apparently not to be found in issues of methodology, personality, or individual items of public policy. Yet there seems to remain an ineradicable core of difference. Ultimately this must be sought in the structure of material interests on the one hand and values on the other.

Historically, conservative doctrine was formulated as an intellectual defense of feudal property rights against the onslaughts of an emerging, business-oriented, industrializing bourgeoisie. Liberalism, with its early defense of individualism, championed the enemies of conservative doctrine and properly (from its perspective) fought against dominance by a central governing authority. Subsequently (as in the case of New Deal liberalism), it discovered that the logic of unhampered individualism led to serious economic difficulties for large numbers of the population. Experiments with varieties of the welfare state since the days of Bismarck probably can all be traced in considerable measure to the fear of more drastic consequences that might follow any effort to persist in an uncontrolled laissez-faire economy.

In the contemporary world complexity has become compounded. It has probably always been the case that some people refuse to act in accordance with their own more or less self-evident material interests. These days, however, the arts of propaganda and advertising have been raised to a level of effective applied science. It is difficult for many to recognize exactly where their own self-interest lies. Beyond this, numerous techniques have been developed with the practical effect of inducing many to adopt positions in marked contrast to their own existing material interests. Government-sponsored lotteries hold out the hope of dramatic changes in class position. Tales of fabulous profits to be made in real estate or the stock market induce many to identify with the interests toward which they aspire rather than with those they hold and are likely to retain.

This is not the only source of confusion. Although many intellectuals, as well as others, having "made it," subsequently become concerned with the maintenance of an order that has been good to them (Coser 1977), there are many others who, despite coming from very well-to-do backgrounds, maintain values consistent with economic deprivation. There are indeed generous souls as well as villains to be found among adherents of both liberalism and conservatism.

The shape of values is by no means always coterminous with the shape of existing material interests. Labels like liberalism and conservatism are uncertain predictors of specific actions, as are existing material interests. A variety of social forms, or structures, can be used to serve either selfish or communally oriented values. It is these values that are ultimately more reliable auguries.

In recent years there have been efforts to develop more useful theoretical frameworks for conceptualizing value configurations and more empirically based social policy alternatives. For example, Amitai Etzioni has elaborated an "I-We" paradigm as a substitute for both "unfettered" individualism and organismic views of society (Etzioni 1988). S. M. Miller and his colleagues eschew the *liberal* label in favor of *progressive*, a term less saddled with conflicting conceptual baggage. They have provided an agenda for social policy issues requiring considerable rethinking by those unwilling to accept either contemporary conservative and neoconservative doctrine or traditional socialist formulations (Ansara and Miller 1986).

It is clear that serious linguistic difficulties serve to exacerbate the problem of distinguishing clearly between liberalism and conservatism. Each term tends to represent a generic symbol for a range of widely diversified issues, values, and interests. Surrogate expressions are used extensively in popular speech to convey either finer shades of meaning or degrees of opprobrium.

For conservatives these expressions may include "right-wing crazies," "extreme right," "right-wing," "supply-siders," "libertarians," "filthy rich," "Republicans," and others. In contemporary America, portions of the conservative spectrum voice strong opinions not only on economic issues but also on such "social" issues as pornography, abortion, and affirmative action, although opinion on these issues is by no means unanimous. Traditional conservatism would, of course, back state-supported cultural standards in speech, art, literature, and entertainment. Nineteenth-century liberalism would oppose these in the name of individual "rights." Is abortion a woman's "right" or is it an "offense" against society? Many conservatives might define it as an offense; others might well define it as a right—a traditional liberal position.

Among liberals, surrogate expressions in use include "Red," "parlor-pink," "left-liberal," "bleeding heart," "tax and spender," "Democrat," and "Progressive." The liberal spectrum tends to support rights of women to have abortions or, more generally, to maintain control over their own bodies. It opposes abrogation of rights of self-expression through pornography legislation, censorship, or other efforts to monitor art, literature, theatre, and other communication vehicles. On the other hand, American liberals favor limitations on the asserted "rights" of corporations or individual business persons to discriminate in employment, housing, and other areas on the basis of skin color, age, religion, or physical disability—property rights that many conservatives insist are inviolable.

As one might expect, survey researchers have made and continue to make strong efforts to detect empirical differences between persons who are called or who call themselves liberal or conservative. Data from a variety of survey research studies indicate that, despite the existence of important philosophical differences between liberals and conservatives, changing social and economic conditions have at times compelled them to alter their positions on certain economic, social, and political issues without altering their underlying philosophies (McCloskey and Zaller 1984, p. 191). In general, these studies seem to confirm stereotypical images of both liberals and conservatives.

Liberals show a marked preference for social progress and human betterment, especially for the poor and powerless. Some believe personal happiness and success depend heavily upon institutional arrangements. Most liberals are "inveterate reformers"; they continually look for ways to improve the human condition by remodeling social, economic, and political institutions. Underlying this pursuit of change, social reform, and benevolence is faith in the potential perfectability of human beings and their capacity to manage their own affairs in a responsible and reasoned fashion.

Conservatives have a different notion of what constitutes the good society and how it can be achieved. Survey research data show that they have a more pessimistic view of human nature and its perfectability. They feel that people need strong leaders, firm laws and institutions, and strict moral codes to keep their appetites under control. Firm adherence to conventional norms and practices is essential for human well-being. They believe that those who fail in life must bear primary responsibility for its consequences. They are far less likely than liberals to support movements that have as their objectives the eradication of poverty, the better treatment of oppressed minorities, or the alleviation of social distress generally. They maintain that these movements, by disrupting existing institutions, do more harm than good (McCloskey and Zaller 1984, pp. 190–191).

Conventional public opinion polling techniques encounter increasing difficulties in this area. Thus, one study examined a hypothesized inverse relationship between socioeconomic status and conservatism on a wide range of so-called social issues.

(Many observers felt that, during the 1970s and 1980s, as well as during the late 1960s, the main support for liberal and left political parties in the United States and other Western industrialized countries came from youthful members of the upper or middle strata.) It found that, in practice, many issues defied a neat separation of interests and values or of economic versus social arenas. Many social issues such as environmental protection, nuclear power, defense spending, and race or gender problems have an economic dimension, to the extent that they influence opportunities for jobs or profits. Conversely, government domestic spending, a classic economic issue, may have a social dimension if it is seen as involving welfare or aid to minorities. No consistent relationship between socioeconomic status and conservatism was found, with one exception. Liberalism on social issues tends to increase with education, but even here the relationship varies considerably from issue to issue. The authors suggest that lack of a consistent relationship reflects both the diversity of social issues and the fuzziness of the social/economic distinction (Himmelstein and McCrae 1988).

Another study examined what appeared to be an anomaly in this area. It postulated that high socioeconomic status remains one of the best predictors of Republican party support and conservative attitudes in the United States, that Republicans are wealthier, more educated, and hold higher status jobs than Democrats and independents. Jewish liberalism, however, confounds this general relationship. American Jews are generally wealthier, better educated, and hold higher status jobs than average Americans but continue to be the most liberal white ethnic group in the United States (Lerner, Nagai, and Rothman 1989, p. 330).

The emergence of a small cadre of Jewish neoconservative intellectuals has raised questions about Jewish liberalism. A sample of Jewish elites was compared with their Gentile counterparts. The study found that Jewish elites continue to be more liberal. Despite a plethora of competing explanations, the study concludes that Jewish liberalism is a product of a family tradition of liberalism that developed in response to European conditions. Specifically, the authors suggest that the Jewish elites inherited a tradition of responding in particular ways to felt marginality. This raises the question as to whether a realignment might occur when this cohort of American Jews loses its prominence and is replaced by a cohort with different patterns of socialization. In a concluding footnote, the authors raise the open question of whether events in the Middle East and the emergence in the Democratic party of an increasingly powerful African-American presence less supportive of Israel can transform the liberalism of American Jews (Lerner, Nagai, and Rothman 1989).

A study of public opinion on nuclear power concludes that assessing public opinion through responses to survey questions with fixed categories presents serious difficulties. It compares these difficulties with those arising from the effort to "impose elite dichotomies such as 'liberal' and 'conservative' on a mass public whose beliefs are not organized by such dimensions" (Gamson and Modligani 1989, p. 36).

Perhaps the more general difficulty is not to be found solely in the insufficiency of measuring instruments but in the increasingly more truncated vistas of the "mass publics." Fundamental philosophical positions and value orientations seem to have become increasingly more obscured by the exigencies of short-range decision making.

In societies where immediate job opportunities, social pressures, and short-range profits have serious implications not only for the quality of life but also for existence itself, it is scarcely surprising to find that many public issues and even individual values are filtered through the prisms of short-run individual economic concerns and ethnic identification. Manipulating perceptions of vital interests through sophisticated media technology does much to resolve the recurrent riddle, "Is Blank a liberal—or a conservative?"

(SEE ALSO: *Attitudes; Individualism; Public Opinion; Value Theory and Research; Voting Behavior*)

REFERENCES

Ansara, Michael, and S. M. Miller 1986 "Opening Up of Progressive Thought." *Social Policy* 17:3–10.

Bell, Daniel A. 1997 "Liberal Neutrality and Its Role in American Political Life." *Responsive Community* 7:61–68.

Burke, Edmund 1855 "Reflections on the Revolution in France." In *Works*, Vol. 1. New York: Harper.

Cohen, Mitchell 1997 "Why I'm Still 'Left'." *Dissent* 2:43–50.

Cohen, Steven M., and Charles S. Liebman 1997 "American Jewish Liberalism: Unraveling the Strands." *Public Opinion Quarterly* 61:405–430.

Coser, Lewis A. "Introduction." In Coser, Lewis A., and Irving Howe, eds., 1977 *The New Conservatives: A Critique from the Left.* New York: Meridian.

Etzioni, Amatai 1988 *The Moral Dimension: Toward a New Economics.* New York: Free Press.

Favela, Alejandro, and Miriam Calvillo 1996 "Liberalism and Postmodernity; Liberalismo y posmodernidad." *Estudios Politicos* 13:55–69.

Gamson, William A., and Andre Modigliani 1989 "Media Discourse and Public Opinion on Nuclear Power: A Constructionist Approach." *American Journal of Sociology* 95:1–37.

Girvetz, Harry K. 1966 *The Evolution of Liberalism.* New York: Collier.

Gottfried, Paul, and Thomas Fleming 1988 *The Conservative Movement.* Boston: Twayne.

Halevy, Elie (1928) 1972 *The Growth of Philosophic Radicalism,* trans. Mary Morris. London: Faber and Faber.

Himmelstein, Jerome L., and James A. McRae, Jr. 1988 "Social Issues and Socioeconomic status." *Public Opinion Quarterly* 52:492–512.

Hobhouse, L. T. (1911) 1964 *Liberalism.* New York: Oxford University Press.

Laski, Harold J. (1936) 1962 *The Rise of European Liberalism.* New York: Barnes & Noble.

—— 1997 *The Rise of European Liberalism* (*New Edition*). New Brunswick, N.J.: Transaction.

Lerner, Robert, Althea K. Nagai, and Stanley Rothman 1989 "Marginality and Liberalism Among Jewish Elites." *Public Opinion Quarterly* 53:330–352.

Lovejoy, Arthur 1960 *The Great Chain of Being: A Study of the History of an Idea.* New York: Meridian.

McCloskey, Herbert, and John Zaller 1984 *The American Ethos: Public Attitudes Toward Capitalism and Democracy.* (A Twentieth Century Fund Report) Cambridge, Mass.: Harvard University Press.

Miller, Alan S., and Takashi Nakamura 1997 "Trends in American Public Opinion: A Cohort Analysis of Shifting Attitudes from 1972–1990." *Behaviormetrika* 24:179–191.

Nisbet, Robert 1986 *Conservatism.* Minneapolis: University of Minnesota Press.

Sandel, Michael J. 1996 *Democracy's Discontent: America in Search of a Public Philosophy.* Cambridge, Mass.: Belknap Press of Harvard University Press.

Stone, Brad Lowell 1997 "Classical Liberalism and Sociology." *Sociological Forum* 12:497–512.

Tillyard, E. M. W. 1959 *The Elizabethan World Picture.* New York: Vintage.

Witonski, Peter (ed.) 1971 *The Wisdom of Conservatives,* vol. 1. New York: Arlington.

ROBERT BOGUSLAW

LIBRARY RESOURCES AND SERVICES FOR SOCIOLOGY

INTRODUCTION

Libraries have a long history of providing access to the resources sociologists and other social scientists have needed and used, and to the literature they produce. In addition, libraries have established a strong tradition of providing reference and instructional services. Although the recent and pervasive growth in information technology has led to major changes in the way these resources and services are provided, libraries will continue to serve an important function to the discipline. Knowing how libraries are organized and how they work, what research tools and services are available, and how to use these tools and services effectively can help researchers at various levels to be more efficient and productive.

AN OVERVIEW OF ACADEMIC LIBRARIES

Many of the thousands of academic libraries in the United States and other parts of the world support sociological course work and research, and researchers near major urban centers can also obtain important materials and substantial research help from some of the larger nonacademic public and research libraries. However, each library's ability to provide these kinds of support is affected greatly by the size of its budget, collections, and staff.

At the larger end of the size continuum, libraries can be quite complex organizationally, although most users will be aware of only the parts and functions of direct relevance to them. In the United States, libraries are organized so that users can use them effectively on their own, identifying what is needed through a public catalog and an open "stacks" area. Almost all users have contact with staff members at a circulation desk, who check out books and sometimes periodicals to them. These staff members also help users locate items they may not be able to find on their own and help make resources available by enforcing loan periods, recalling books from other users, setting up reserve reading rooms for heavily used materials assigned for course readings, and so on. Academic libraries also typically organize their journals into periodical reading rooms or stack areas, and may provide related support services there. Interlibrary loan departments provide access to resources owned by other libraries.

Almost all libraries provide reference service in a variety of ways, and often in different settings. The role of the reference librarian typically extends far beyond the answering of informational questions, and may include providing individualized help in using electronic or complex print resources, or organizing a literature search, as well as speaking to classes about major disciplinary research tools and strategies. Reference librarians often have special areas of subject expertise and may perform liaison or collection development work with academic departments for book and journal purchasing. Where this is the case, graduate students may find it helpful to get to know the librarian responsible for sociology. College and university libraries will generally also have special sections or departments for government publications. Because these resources can be quite specialized, and access to them complex, staff help can be especially important.

Regardless of size, most academic libraries must deal with a variety of interrelated budgetary and technological pressures. For the last several years and for a variety of reasons, the costs of providing periodicals and other serials have been rising more rapidly than other indicators of inflation. (Ketcham–Van Orsdel and Born 1998). This trend has resulted both in a larger share of budgets being devoted to serials and in an ongoing need to evaluate and sometimes cancel subscriptions to journals. At the same time, there has been very rapid growth in book title production in the United States (Bosch 1998), with the result that libraries typically buy a decreasing share of the domestic books published in most disciplines. Economic pressures and increased book production abroad have also made it more difficult for research libraries to buy as large a share of foreign language books and journals as in the past. Accordingly, libraries rely increasingly on cooperative buying and resource sharing. Paradoxically, library users may now actually have better access to some resources than in the past when locally owned resources were relied on more exclusively.

Key developments in information technology such as the CD-ROM and the World Wide Web, have also introduced new options for delivering information. On-line catalogs with sophisticated search features and other functionality have quickly replaced card catalogs. In addition, many periodical indexes and abstracts and the text of key journals are also now available online. These services make it possible for researchers to locate information quickly and easily—even from their homes or offices—but they almost always cost substantially more to purchase and support than do comparable print resources. Together, these factors make for a complex, rapidly changing environment for academic libraries and their users.

LIBRARIES AND THE LITERATURE OF SOCIOLOGY

Because of sociology's great topical and methodological diversity, it is difficult to characterize its literature. This diversity is well represented in the hundreds of articles in this encyclopedia, and in recent discussions of sociology's most influential books (Clawson and Zussman 1998; Gans 1998; Marwell 1998; Sullivan 1994). Sociologists rely on and use a range of publications and information sources for their research, including books, journals, statistical publications and data sets, and governmental and other specialized reports (Zabel 1996; Shapiro 1985). Of these, the most important outlets for sociological writings have been books and scholarly journals, which appear to assume somewhat greater or lesser importance for different research communities. Some have suggested, for example, that there are two fairly distinct research cultures in sociology—one a "book sociology" that relies on, values, and publishes primarily in books, and the other an "article sociology" that relies on and publishes in scholarly journals. To some extent article sociology may be more characteristic of the scientific end of the discipline, and book sociology more characteristic of its humanistic, historical, ethnographic, and theoretical emphases and traditions (Sullivan 1994).

The sociological journal literature is quite extensive. Of the 5965 items judged significant enough to be included in the 1996 volume of the *International Bibliography of Sociology*, roughly three-quarters were periodical articles, and even more articles are indexed annually in *Sociological Abstracts*. According to the 1998–1999 *Ulrich's International Periodicals Directory*, several hundred periodicals relevant to the field are published worldwide, although this count includes newsletters and other less substantial publications. Hargens (1991) estimated that roughly 250 of these might be characterized as research journals publishing original reports of relevant research findings. Lists of the more prominent or important titles have ranged in size from a couple of dozen (Sociology Writing Group 1998) to sixty or so (Katz and Katz 1997; Aby 1997), to well over a hundred (Bart and Frankel 1986). As in many other disciplines, a handful of journals (primarily the *American Journal of Sociology*, *American Sociological Review*, and *Social Forces*) are widely regarded as the most prestigious and/or influential. However, it appears that publication of important research is less likely to be concentrated in these few journals than in some other disciplines, and use of and reliance on review serials like the *Annual Review of Sociology* is relatively low (Hargens 1991). As in other disciplines, articles submitted to journals in sociology are typically refereed, or subjected to critical evaluation by peers who thus serve an important gatekeeping function (Mullins 1977; Osburn 1984; Simon 1994).

Many journals are now available electronically as part of larger full-text services to which libraries subscribe, and archives of the journals published by the American Sociological Association are now available electronically via the World Wide Web through the innovative JSTOR program (Guthrie and Lougee 1997; see also http://www.jstor.org/). In addition, a few sociological journals are available exclusively via the Web, and there has been much recent speculation that journal publishing may soon undergo fundamental change in response to the Web's interactive possibilities. As in the field of physics, for example, articles in other disciplines may commonly circulate on the Web prior to formal publication. The statistical data on which an article is based may also be linked to the Web version of the article for further analysis—which may have special significance for sociology.

As noted earlier, books are also important to the discipline and annual production numbers at least in the thousands. The 1996 volume of the *International Bibliography of Sociology*, mentioned earlier, listed about 1,300 titles from around the world, but this number did not include textbooks or popular titles. A broader count of relevant titles published or distributed in the United States that same year put the figure at 4,186 (Bosch 1998), up more than 50 percent from 1989. As with journals, hardly any library can build a comprehensive book collection, and libraries select on the basis of relevance to local emphases, user requests, judgments of quality, cost, and other factors. Often book vendor "approval programs," which match published books with formalized interest profiles, are relied on, since they can supply new books quickly and efficiently. Standard book review publications like *Choice* (aimed at undergraduate libraries) and *Contemporary Sociology* (a publication mainly for sociologists) may also be systematically utilized for selection, but they lack the space to be comprehensive. (During 1997, for example, *Choice* reviewed only 216 of the available titles, and *Contemporary Sociology* roughly 500.) At this writing relatively few newly published books or monographs are being made available electronically, but this seems likely to change in the near future.

There are a variety of other outlets for sociological research in addition to books and journal articles, and sociologists use many other sources of information in their research. For example, those sociologists who work for government agencies often write formal reports, which may be published by the agency. Statistical reports of various kinds that are of interest to sociologists (the U.S. Census being a prime example) are often also published in printed form by government agencies and distributed to academic libraries. These data are also increasingly being made available via the Web. A few academic libraries also pay for and coordinate their institutions' memberships in the Interuniversity Consortium for Political and Social Research (ICPSR), and make the associated survey data and codebooks available, although it is more typical for other campus agencies to do so.

And, of course, the dissertations written by doctoral students are typically acquired and cataloged by their institution's libraries, and sold through Bell and Howell Information and Learning in Ann Arbor, Michigan.

The published literature in sociology can also be seen as part of a broader professional communication system which includes less formal interchanges like presentation of papers at regional and national conferences (Osburn 1984). Developments in information technology have fostered the growth of such "invisible colleges"—especially in sociology, where computers have long been important tools. Sociologists have, for many years, made use of data analysis packages the Statistical Package for the Social Sciences (SPSS) and now quite commonly have their own personal computers with word processing software and connections to the Internet. As a result, formerly disparate activities like data analysis, writing, and publishing have begun to merge (Anderson 1998). E-mail listserv discussion groups, and the ease with which writings can be posted to the World Wide Web have fostered efficient communication among sociologists sharing research interests, and seem to hold considerable promise for the discipline (Bainbridge 1995). Libraries participate in and help foster these developments in a variety of ways. For example, many libraries participate in the JSTOR program, subscribe to full text services, and provide their users with on-line access to journal indexes like *Sociological Abstracts* and the *Social Sciences Citation Index*. Many also support the development of exclusively electronic journals by directing users to them through their on-line catalogs and Web pages.

GENERAL STRATEGIES FOR LITERATURE SEARCHING IN SOCIOLOGY

It is difficult to provide good general strategies for location information in sociology for a variety of reasons. As noted, any number of topics and approaches may be pursued, and a large number of journals and other sources may contain important articles or other information. In addition, a doctoral student "terrorized by the literature" in anticipation of preliminary exam questions (Becker 1986) will need to use different research strategies than will an undergraduate student writing the

typical library term paper. Rapid changes in information technology make it even harder to suggest tactics that will be valid five years from now. It is also useful to remember that, although librarians tend to view literature searching as something of a structured and rationalized activity, it can and should often take place in a more open, informal, serendipitous, or even mysterious way—especially in the early stages of a research project. Nevertheless, being alert to the following issues and suggestions can help make literature searching more effective and more efficient. Users are urged to consult their local library staff for additional advice and guidance, and for current information on local resources.

1. *Overview or summarizing tools*. Although sociologists tend not to use or rely on review serials like the *Annual Review of Sociology*, these can often prove helpful by summarizing and evaluating the main themes of recent research and setting them in a broader context. A similar function is played by subject encyclopedias like this one, by disciplinary handbooks (such as Smelser 1988; Smelser and Swedberg 1994; Gilbert et al. 1998), and to some extent by sociology textbooks. Some summarizing sources like these can be found in general and specialized reference books and guides (Aby 1997; Balay 1996; Wertheimer 1986; Zabel 1996). In addition, searches of electronic databases can sometimes be limited to "review articles."

2. *Differences in indexing terminology*. Periodical indexes and library catalogs quite often use a defined list of subject terms, which may vary from those commonly used in an area of literature, by a community of scholars, or by an individual student trying to describe a topic. Successful use of these tools often requires matching an idea to indexing terminology. This can save time by helping to eliminate irrelevant citations.

3. *Techniques for searching electronic resources*. The scholarly communication system in all disciplines seems destined to be tied increasingly to developments in information technology, and researchers will need to understand how to interact with and

use electronic tools effectively. Although most users now know that rough "keyword" searching can give them relevant citations, it is also important to know how to use "Boolean operators," such as AND, OR, and NOT to combine and manipulate terms (Sociology Writing Group 1998) and to incorporate subject indexing terms into a search strategy.

4. *Evaluation of sources.* The gatekeeping role played by peer reviewers of journal articles helps guarantee that an article has passed a test of quality or adherence to accepted research norms. This is less apt to be the case with other information sources—especially those found on Web pages or via Web search engines. It is consequently useful to develop a generally skeptical outlook on information sources, and to evaluate such sources on the basis of such things as credibility of origin, scope and coverage, currency, and reputation (Sociology Writing Group 1998).

5. *Library collections as a linked system.* Since it seems unlikely that the financial constraints facing academic libraries will ease in the foreseeable future, libraries will continue their efforts to share resources efficiently. As a result, library users should assume that the collections available to them extend far beyond what their local libraries own. Graduate students and faculty, especially, will need to be aware of how their libraries are making these broader resources available and how long it will take to obtain publications from elsewhere.

LOCATING PERIODICAL LITERATURE

The most important tools for locating relevant periodical articles are known by librarians as abstracting and indexing services, because they abstract (or summarize) articles and index them (apply subject terms to them) according to a vocabulary developed for the purpose. These tools are frequently available in both printed and electronic form, and the electronic versions offer powerful searching capabilities and other features such as links to the full text of articles. The most important for researchers in sociology are the *Social*

Sciences Index (and some competing products), *Sociological Abstracts,* and *Social Sciences Citation Index.*

The *Social Sciences Index* and several competing products are important because they provide students with relatively easy access to a more manageable subset of the available literature than do the other two main tools. Because even smaller academic libraries will tend to subscribe to the majority of periodicals indexed in them, they are especially helpful for beginning students. For many years the printed *Social Sciences Index* was the primary general tool for social science researchers. It has gradually grown in coverage and now indexes roughly four hundred important social science journals, including about fifty titles in sociology, and is available in a few different electronic versions with abstracts and the full text of some of the indexed articles. Articles are carefully indexed according to subject, with "see" and "see also" references pointing users to other relevant subjects.

Within the last several years a few companies like EBSCO, the Gale Group, and Bell and Howell have offered some other, more general periodical indexes aimed at the college or undergraduate library market which cover largely the same range of social science literature. Although the sociology journals indexed are fairly similar, these products do differ in their indexing and abstracting practices, how far back their indexing and full text coverage extends, which titles are provided in full text, and in their search capabilities and limitations.

In contrast to these general sources, *Sociological Abstracts* covers the sociological literature much more comprehensively. Since this source is so fundamental to literature searching in sociology, it is worth quoting the publisher's description at length:

> *Sociological Abstracts* provides access to the world's literature in sociology and related disciplines, both theoretical and applied. The database includes abstracts of journal articles selected from over 2,500 journals, abstracts of conference papers presented at various sociological association meetings, relevant dissertation listings from *Dissertation Abstracts International,* enhanced bibliographic citations of book reviews, and abstracts of selected sociology books published in *Sociological Abstracts* (SA) and *Social*

Planning/Policy and Development Abstracts (SOPODA) since 1974.

Approximately 2,500 journals in thirty different languages from about fifty-five countries are scanned for inclusion, covering sociological topics in fields such as anthropology, economics, education, medicine, community development, philosophy, demography, political science, and social psychology. Journals published by sociological associations, groups, faculties, and institutes, and periodicals containing the term "sociology" in their titles, are abstracted fully, irrespective of language or country of publication. Noncore journals are screened for articles by sociologists and/or articles of immediate interest or relevance to sociologists.

The abstracts provided are typically lengthy and detailed, and articles are indexed by author and a sufficient number of indexing terms from the *Thesaurus of Sociological Index Terms* to describe their content. The *Thesaurus* has been developed over time with sociological concepts and terminology in mind, and this tool—which may be integrated into an electronic version of the publication—is a key to making searching more efficient and effective. As shown by the following sample entry for the term "Satisfaction," the *Thesaurus* indicates what subject terms are available for searching, and what relationships they have with one another.

Satisfaction
DC D740400
SN A context-dependent term for an individual's positive assessment of self or circumstances. Select a more specific entry or coordinate with other terms.
HN Formerly (1963–1985) DC 403350
UF Fulfillment (1969–1985)
BT Attitudes
NT Community Satisfaction
Job Satisfaction
Life Satisfaction
Marital Satisfaction
RT Discontent
Emotions
Happiness
Improvement

Needs
Quality
Self Esteem

The most important codes shown in this example are as follows. **SN** stands for a "scope note," or definition of the term. **BT** indicates that the "broader term" of "Attitudes" can be used. **NT** stands for "narrower" or more specific terms, and **RT** for "related terms." **UF** means that "Satisfaction" is "used for" Fulfillment (in other words, fulfillment is not used as a subject term). (For a complete discussion of the codes and their meaning and use, consult the *Thesaurus*.)

Users of both the printed and electronic versions of *Sociological Abstracts* would be able to find abstract entries using these terms. The printed index refers users to an abstract number, which is then looked up in another part of the volume to actually locate the abstract, whereas the electronic version would provide a set of abstracts that could be reviewed and printed out. The following example was found on line by searching for "Life Satisfaction" as a subject term using a version of Sociological Abstracts produced by Silver Platter Information in Norwood, Massachusetts.

TI: Marital Status, Gender, and Perception of Well-Being
AU: Mookherjee,-Harsha-N.
IN: Dept Sociology Tennessee Technological U, Cookeville 38505
SO: Journal-of-Social-Psychology; 1997, 137, 1, Feb, 95–105.
IS: 0022–4545
CO: JSPSAG
DT: aja Abstract-of-Journal-Article
LA: English
CP: United-States
PY: 1997
AB: Draws on data from the combined 1982–1991 National Opinion Research Center's General Social Surveys (total N = 12,168 adults) to reexamine relationships among marital status, gender, & perception of well-being. ANOVA revealed that marriage significantly enhances perception of well-being for both men & women, though in general, women express more satisfaction than men. Well-being perceptions were significantly affected by

race & financial status, regardless of marital status. 3 Tables, 44 References. Adapted from the source document

DEM: *Marital-Status (D491150); *Well-Being (D916500); *Sex-Differences (D758100); *Single-Persons (D771900); *Life-Satisfaction (D463800)

DES: United-States-of-America (D890700)

SH: social psychology; personality & social roles (individual traits, social identity, adjustment, conformism, & deviance) (0312)

The "DEM" label in this entry stands for "major descriptors", and indicates that the main topics of this article are Marital Status, Well-Being, Sex-Differences, Single-Persons, and Life-Satisfaction. The "DES" label stands for "minor descriptors," and shows that although the article has been indexed under "United-States-of-America," this is not an important focus.

As noted earlier, a key technique in using this and other electronic indexes is combining terms using Boolean operators to make searching more precise and to limit the amount of material that must be reviewed. In this case, this article and other entries could have been found by searching for the subject terms "Life Satisfaction" AND "Sex Differences." A slightly more complex search strategy or statement might have been to search for "Life Satisfaction OR Well-Being" AND "Marital Status OR Single Persons." This kind of search statement can be made as elaborate as necessary to the situation. It is also possible to limit search results by date, language, journal, and type of publication (such as book review, journal article, or conference paper), and to search on virtually any combination of words found in the article title and abstract entry. It is, of course, impossible or impractical to do so with the printed publication. Because of its comprehensiveness, many users of *Sociological Abstracts* will need to adjust their search strategies to exclude conference papers and dissertations (which are often difficult to obtain) and foreign language publications.

The *Social Sciences Citation Index* (*SSCI*) does not cover journals in sociology quite as extensively as *Sociological Abstracts*, but it covers journals in other social science disciplines more completely than the latter, and much more comprehensively than does the *Social Sciences Index*. In 1997, for example, the *SSCI* indexed 1,725 journals "completely," including 92 titles in sociology, and indexed another 1,371 on a selective basis. During that year, 72,665 articles and another 39,412 book reviews in all social science disciplines were indexed. Unlike *Sociological Abstracts*, abstracts have only recently begun to be provided in *SSCI* (in the electronic versions only), and articles are not indexed according to a fixed indexing vocabulary. Instead, heavy reliance is made in the print version on words from the titles of articles. Articles are also indexed by author, of course, although the publisher uses only authors' first and middle initials, rather than their full names, which can occasionally cause confusion.

What is uniquely valuable about this source is that it enables users to search "by citation," or to locate articles that have cited an earlier author or article. Eugene Garfield, the founder of the Institute for Scientific Information, which publishes *SSCI*, described the idea behind citation indexes as follows:

> The concept of citation indexing is simple. Almost all the papers, notes, reviews, corrections, and correspondence published in scientific journals contain citations. These cite—generally by title, author, and where and when published—documents that support, provide precedent for, illustrate or elaborate on what the author has to say. Citations are the formal, explicit linkages between papers that have particular points in common. A citation index is built around these linkages. It lists publications that have been cited and identifies the sources of the citations. Anyone conducting a literature search can find from one to dozens of additional papers on a subject just by knowing one that has been cited. And every paper that is found provides a list of new citations with which to continue the search. (Garfield 1979, p. 1)

Books as well as journal articles in sociology can be, and often are, cited by the journal articles indexed in *SSCI* (Sullivan 1994) and the ability to search on cited references may provide a large number of additional "access points" for locating an article. The article on marital status that was used as the sample record from *Sociological Abstracts*, for example, cited forty-four earlier articles and studies. Users of *SSCI* could search on any of those citations and locate the article that way.

One difficulty with performing citation searches lies in knowing when it will be useful do so. In sociology, although it is possible to perform citation searches on the handful of authors in the recognized pantheon (i.e., Marx, Durkheim, Weber, and some others), such an approach will often result in far too many references with only tenuous subject relationships to one another. It may consequently be necessary to combine a result set from a citation search with some other group of search terms. Where citation searching seems most useful in sociology is when tracing a methodological article, or in other somewhat narrow circumstances. To do a citation search for a journal article—using either the printed SSCI or its electronic counterpart—requires that a researcher know the author's name and initials, and preferably the volume, volume number, year, and page of the publication. For example. Clifford Clogg and Gerhard Arminger's 1993 article titled "On Strategy for Methodological Analysis" from the publication *Sociological Methodology* (vol. 23, pp. 57–74) is listed in SSCI as:

CLOGG CC SOCIOL
METHODOL 23 57 1993

By searching the printed or electronic versions of SSCI under this entry, it would be possible to find other articles which cited this article. It would also be possible to look at the list of sources cited by Clogg and Arminger and find other articles which have cited them. As with *Sociological Abstracts*, the electronic version of *SSCI* makes for far more efficient searching—especially of citations. Another interesting use to which citation searching is often put is comparing faculty members' research productivity—especially for promotion and tenure consideration. This procedure is controversial for a variety of reasons—especially when comparing faculty members from different disciplines, which may not share the same publication and citation patterns.

Depending on the particular topic being researched, and the depth with which the search must be carried out, a number of other tools in neighboring or related fields may prove useful, including *Anthropological Literature, EconLit, Popline, Psychological Abstracts/PsycInfo*, and *Social Work Abstracts*. In addition, researchers may be able to avail themselves of journal article "alerting" services, such as *Uncover Reveal*, which automatically sends the tables of contents of specified journals and article citations containing specified keywords to users via e-mail. Although some of the electronic versions of the indexes discussed also provide linkages to a local library's journal holdings information or to on-line full text, accurately determining which articles are available locally still typically requires a separate step.

LOCATING BOOKS, JOURNALS, AND OTHER RESOURCES IN LIBRARIES

As noted earlier, most libraries now provide on-line versions of their catalogs. Unlike card catalogs, on-line catalogs can be searched via keyword, and with Boolean operators or combinations. They may also provide direct links to electronic resources on the World Wide Web, as well as the circulation status of a book. In addition, many now permit users to view lists of the books they have checked out and to reserve items checked out to other users. Despite these and other less visible changes, books are catalogued in much the same way they have been for years: by author, title, and subject. Few college students will be unaware that books can be searched by author and title, but they may also mistakenly assume that a journal article can be found by its author or title in a library catalog. Instead, the title of the journal must be searched, and then the specific volume and page located on the shelf within that journal.

Although many students will also realize that books can be located by subject, few will understand how the subject heading system works. The system used for this in most academic libraries was developed at the Library of Congress in Washington, D.C., and the headings themselves are called Library of Congress Subject Headings (LCSH). These headings are published in multivolume sets by the same name, which now closely resemble database thesauri like the *Thesaurus of Sociological Index Terms*. They can be used in the same way to find relevant subject headings for searching. For example, the entry for "Satisfaction" in the 1997 edition of LCSH looks like this:

Satisfaction
BT   Self
RT   Self-realization
NT   Consumer satisfaction

Contentment
Housing—Resident satisfaction
Job satisfaction
Libraries—User satisfaction
Office buildings—Tenant satisfaction
Patient satisfaction
Public housing—Resident satisfaction
Rental housing—Resident satisfaction
— **Religious aspects**
— — **Buddhism, [Christianity, etc.]**

Like the entry from the *Thesaurus*, this shows the availability of Broader (BT), Related (RT), and Narrower (NT) terms. Unlike terms from the *Thesaurus*, though, *LCSH* lists a large number of terms that are subdivisions of more general terms. In other words, if a researcher were to look under "Libraries" as a subject term, she or he might find books listed under many subdivisions, including "User satisfaction." This is also true of subject headings that are more directly related to sociology. For example, the term "Sociology" can be subdivided by a country or other geographic term, or by such terms as "—Methodology", "—Philosophy," or "—Statistical methods." Subject headings can also be modified by adding a comma and an adjective to a term. For instance, "Sociology, Islamic" would be used instead of "Islamic Sociology." Although it is not necessary to thoroughly understand this system, it is useful to realize that it exists, and that some help from library staff in identifying useful subject headings may be needed. As with other databases, noticing what subject headings have been applied to relevant, known books may be a good start, and may lead to the finding of other important books.

Most academic libraries now also physically organize their book and journal collections using another system developed at the Library of Congress: its call number scheme. Unlike the Dewey Decimal system that is commonly used in school and public libraries, Library of Congress call numbers start with one or two letters. For example, sociology and economics have both been assigned the letter H, to which a second letter is added for a further breakdown. For sociology, the primary classes are:

SOCIOLOGY
7HM   General Works, Theory
HN   Social History and Conditions;
            Social Problems, Social Reform

HQ-HT	Social Groups
HQ	Family, Marriage, Woman
HS	Societies: Secret, Benevolent, etc., Clubs
HT	Communities, Classes, Races
HV	Social Pathology. Social and Public Welfare; Criminology

Numbers make these breakdowns more specific. For example, before extensive changes were introduced recently, the numbers between HM 1 and HM 299 were used for topics in sociology. Under the revised scheme, HM numbers 401 and higher will be used instead, which will allow a finer topical breakdown and arrangement. For example, under the old scheme the numbers from HM 251 to HM 299 were assigned to various topics in Social Psychology, such as:

HM	251	General
	255	Instinct in social psychology
	261	Public Opinion
	263	Publicity. Propaganda.

A particular book in general social psychology would have been assigned the subject call number HM 251, to which additional combinations of letters, numbers and possibly dates designating the author or work would be applied. For example, the 1998 edition of the *Handbook of Social Psychology* was assigned the number HM 251 H224 1998, where H224 represents the title, and 1998 the edition. Under the revised system, books in social psychology will receive numbers HM 1000 and above, and the same *Handbook* cataloged under it might have the call number HM 1033 H34 1998. This will obviously and unfortunately cause books on similar topics but classed under the older and newer systems to be separated on library shelves. Again, it is not necessary to fully understand the call number system, but having a general sense of how it works can make locating books a little easier.

Many researchers will also need to develop an understanding of the kinds of materials that may be available in a given library but not listed in its catalog. The single largest category of such material, in most cases, consists of government publications or documents—especially those things published by the U.S. federal government, but also by state and local governments, the governments of other countries, and the United Nations or other international agencies. Because there are so many of these publications and documents, very few libraries can provide thorough and complete coverage of them. As a result, other indexes and similar sources are often necessary. For the federal government publications of the United States, the primary tool is the *Monthly Catalog of United States Government Publications*, although there are a number of other supplementary sources available. For example, the *American Statistics Index* provides very detailed indexing coverage of federal statistical publications. Both of these tools were originally published in paper, but are now available both in electronic versions. Access to publications of U.S. state governments and those of other countries are also unlikely to be catalogued, and other tools may be needed.

REFERENCES

Aby, Steven 1997 *Sociology: A Guide to Reference and Information Resources*, 2nd ed. Englewood, Col.: Libraries Unlimited.

American Statistics Index. 1974– Washington, D.C.: Congressional Information Service.

Anderson, Ronald E. 1998 "Computing in Sociology." Pp. 52–65 in *Encyclopedia of Library and Information Science*, vol. 63, sup. 26. New York: Marcel Dekker.

Annual Review of Sociology 1975– Palo Alto, Calif., Annual Reviews.

Bainbridge, William Sims 1995 "Sociology on the World-Wide Web." *Social Science Computer Review* 13:508–523.

Balay, Robert 1996 *Guide to Reference Books*, 11th ed. Chicago: American Library Association.

Bart, Pauline, and Linda Frankel 1986 *The Student Sociologist's Handbook*, 4th ed. New York: Random House.

Becker, Howard S. 1986 *Writing for Social Scientists: How to Start and Finish Your Thesis, Book, or Article*. Chicago: University of Chicago Press.

Bosch, Steven 1998 "Prices of U.S. and Foreign Published Materials." Pp. 495–520 in *The Bowker Annual of Library and Book Trade Information, 1998*. New York: R. R. Bowker.

Choice 1964– Chicago: American Library Association.

Clawson, Dan, and Robert Zussman 1998 "Canon and Anti-Canon for a Fragmented Discipline." Pp. 3–17 in Dan Clawson, ed., *Required Reading: Sociology's Most Influential Books*. Amherst: University of Massachusetts Press.

Contemporary Sociology 1972– Washington, D.C.: American Sociological Association.

Dissertation Abstracts. 1952– Ann Arbor, Mich.: University Microfilms.

Gans, Herbert J. 1998 "Best-Sellers by American Sociologists: An Exploratory Study." Pp. 19–27 in Dan Clawson, ed., *Required Reading: Sociology's Most Influential Books*. Amherst: University of Massachusetts Press.

Garfield, Eugene 1979 *Citation Indexing–Its Theory and Application in Science, Technology, and the Humanities*. New York: Wiley.

Gilbert, Daniel T., Susan T. Fiske, and Gardner Lindzey 1998 *The Handbook of Social Psychology*, 4th ed. Boston: McGraw-Hill.

Guthrie, Kevin M., and Wendy P. Lougee 1997 "The JSTOR Solution: Accessing and Preserving the Past." *Library Journal* 122 (February 1): 42–44.

Halstead, Kent 1998 "Price Indexes for Public and Academic Libraries." Pp. 440–456 in *The Bowker Annual of Library and Book Trade Information, 1998*. New York: R. R. Bowker.

Hargens, Lowell L. 1991 "Impressions and Misimpressions about Sociology Journals." *Contemporary Sociology* 20 (May): 343–349.

International Bibliography of Sociology 1955– London: Tavistock Publications; Chicago: Beresford.

Katz, William, and Linda Sternberg Katz 1997 *Magazines for Libraries*, 9th ed. New Providence, N.J.: R. R. Bowker.

Ketchum–Van Orsdel, Lee, and Kathleen Born 1998 "E-Journals Come of Age: LJ's 38th Annual Periodical Price Survey," *Library Journal* (April):40–45.

Library of Congress 1997 *Library of Congress Subject Headings*, 20th ed., vol. 1–4. Washington, D.C.: Library of Congress.

Marwell, Gerald 1998 "Sociological Politics and *Contemporary Sociology*'s Ten Most Influential Books." Pp. 189–195 in Dan Clawson, ed., *Required Reading: Sociology's Most Influential Books*. Amherst: University of Massachusetts Press.

Monthly Catalog of United States Government Publications. 1951– Washington, D.C.: Cataloging Branch, Library Division, Library Programs Service, Superintendent of Documents, Government Printing Office.

Mullins, Carolyn J. 1977 *A Guide to Writing and Publishing in the Social and Behavioral Sciences*. New York: Wiley

Osburn, Charles B. 1984 "The Place of the Scholarly Journal in the Scholarly Communications System." *Library Resources and Technical Services* 28 (October): 315–324.

Shapiro, Beth J. 1985 "Sociology." Pp. 188–198 in Patricia A. McClung, ed., *Selection of Library Materials in the*

Humanities, Social Sciences, and Sciences. Chicago: American Library Association.

Simon, Rita J. 1994 "An Effective Journal Editor: Insights Gained from Editing the *American Sociological Review*." Pp. 33–44 in Rita J. Simon and James J. Fyfe, eds., *Editors as Gatekeepers: Getting Published in the Social Sciences*. Lanham, Md.: Rowman and Littlefield.

Smelser, Neil J. 1988 *Handbook of Sociology*. Newbury Park, Calif.: Sage.

——, and Richard Swedberg 1994 *The Handbook of Economic Sociology*. Princeton, N.J.: Princeton University Press.

Social Science Index 1974 ff. New York: H.W. Wilson Co.

Social Sciences Citation Index 1956– Philadelphia, Pa.: Institute for Scientific Information.

Social Sciences Citation Index Guide and Lists of Source Publications, 1997 1998 Philadelphia, Pa.: Institute for Scientific Information.

Sociological Abstracts 1953– Bethesda, Md.: Cambridge Scientific Abstracts.

Sociology Writing Group 1998 *A Guide to Writing Sociology Papers*, 4th ed. New York: St. Martin's.

Sullivan, Teresa A. 1994 "Genre in Sociology: The Case for the Monograph." Pp. 159–175 in Rita J. Simon and James J. Fyfe, eds., *Editors as Gatekeepers: Getting Published in the Social Sciences*. Lanham, Md.: Rowman and Littlefield.

Thesaurus of Sociological Indexing Terms, 4th ed. 1996 San Diego, Calif.: Sociological Abstracts.

Ulrich's International Periodicals Directory, 37th ed. 1999 New Providence, N.J.: R. R. Bowker.

Wertheimer, Marilyn L. 1986 "Sociology." Pp. 275–331 in William H. Webb, ed., *Sources of Information in the Social Sciences: A Guide to the Literature*. Chicago: American Library Association.

Zabel, Diane 1996 "Sociology." In Nancy L. Herron, ed. *The Social Sciences: A Cross-Disciplinary Guide to Selected Sources*, 2nd ed., Englewood, Colo.: Libraries Unlimited.

TIMOTHY D. JEWELL

LIFE COURSE, THE

INTRODUCTION

The study of lives represents an enduring interest of sociology and the social sciences, reflecting important societal changes and their human consequences. Most notably, developments after World War II called for new ways of thinking about people, society, and their connection. In the United States, pioneering longitudinal studies of children born in the 1920s became studies of adults as the children grew up, thereby raising questions about the course they followed to the adult years and beyond. The changing age composition of society assigned greater significance to problems of aging and their relation to people's lives. Insights regarding old age directed inquiry to earlier phases of life and to the process by which life patterns are shaped by a changing society.

This essay presents the life course as a theoretical orientation for the study of individual lives, human development, and aging. In concept, the life course refers to a pattern of age-graded events and social roles that is embedded in social structures and subject to historical change. These structures vary from family relations and friendships at the micro level to age-graded work organizations and government policies at the macro level. Life-course theory defines a common domain of inquiry with a framework that guides research in terms of problem identification and formulation, variable selection and rationales, and strategies of design and analysis. Beginning in the 1960s, this theoretical orientation has diffused across substantive domains and disciplinary boundaries in the social and behavioral science.

It has uniquely forged a conceptual bridge between developmental processes, the life course, and ongoing changes in society, one based on the premise that age places people in the social structure and in particular birth cohorts. To understand this conceptual bridge, it is useful to distinguish among three levels of the life course and their interplay over a person's life: (1) *institutionalized pathways* in society, as established by state policies, education, the workplace, and so on; (2) the *individual life course* that is formed by the individual's choices and constraints, frequently in terms of a career or trajectory; and (3) the *developmental or aging trajectory of the individual*, defined, for example, by intellectual functioning or self-confidence.

Each of these levels are illustrated by Spilerman (1977) in terms of work. He used the concept of "career line" to refer to pathways that are defined by the aggregated work histories of individuals. Career lines are patterned by industry structures and the labor market. A person's work life is one part of the individual life course, and it varies by the career requirements of firm and marketplace. At the psychological level, changes in work life have consequences for personal feelings of efficacy (Bandura 1997).

In this essay, I first take up concepts that have been used interchangeably—the life course, life cycle, life history, and life span. Then I turn to the emergence of life-course theory since the 1960s and its paradigmatic principles.

CLARIFICATION OF CONCEPTS

A number of concepts have been applied interchangeably to lives (life course, life cycle, life history, and life span), but each makes a distinctive contribution that deserves notice in mapping this domain (Elder 1998). The *concept of life course* is defined by trajectories that extend across the life span, such as family or work; and by short-term changes or transitions, such as entering and leaving school, acquiring a full-time job, and the first marriage. Each life-course transition is embedded in a trajectory that gives it specific form and meaning. Thus, work transitions are core elements of a work-life trajectory; and births are key markers along a parental trajectory. Multiple marriages and divorces are elements of a marital trajectory.

Multiple roles of this kind become interlocking trajectories over time. These linked trajectories may define the life course of a parent and her child. Goode (1960) argues that an individual's set of relationships at any point in time is both "unique and overdemanding," requiring strategies that minimize demands by rescheduling transitions (such as entry into work, the birth of a second child), where possible. The synchronization of role demands may entail a spreading out of commitments or obligations, as in the transition to adulthood or in the family formation years. Among dual-earner couples, the timing of retirement has become a synchronization issue in working out an appropriate action for each partner and their relationship (O'Rand et al. 1991). The synchronization of lives is central to life-course planning in families.

Major transitions in the life course typically involve multiple life changes, from entry into the diverse roles of adulthood (Modell 1989) to later-life changes in work, residence, and family (Hareven 1978; Kohli 1986). These transitions may also

entail a sequence of phases or choice points. The transition to unwed motherhood thus involves premarital sexual experience followed by decisions not to have an abortion, not to give the child up for adoption, and not to marry the father. Causal influences vary across choice points. Early transitions can have developmental consequences by affecting subsequent transitions, even after many years and decades have passed. They do so through behavioral consequences that set in motion cumulative disadvantages or advantages, with radiating implications for other aspects of life (Furstenberg et al. 1987). For example, early teenage childbearing may curtail education and work-life prospects.

The social meanings of age give structure to the life course through age norms, sanctions, and age-graded relationships. In theory, a normative concept of social time specifies an appropriate time or age for marriage, childbearing, and retirement (Neugarten and Datan 1973). This concept also provides a guideline on the meaning of career advancement, whether accelerated or lagging relative to one's age. Empirical findings are beginning to cumulate on event timing, sequences, and durations, although the knowledge base is thin on causal mechanisms (Shanahan in press). Beyond these social distinctions, age has historical significance for the life course as it locates people in historical context according to birth cohorts.

Family connections invariably place the life course in a broader matrix of kinship relationships, one that extends beyond the boundaries of the immediate family to in-laws, grandparents, uncles, aunts, and cousins (Rossi and Rossi 1990). Within the life course of each generation, unexpected and involuntary events occur through life changes in related generations. Thus, a thirty-year old woman becomes a grandmother when her adolescent daughter has a first baby. People lose their status as grandchildren when their grandparents pass away, and their roles as sons or daughters when their parents die. They become the oldest generation in the family. Ties to family members are part of the normative regulation of life-course decisions.

The *life-cycle concept* is frequently used to describe a sequence of life events from birth to death, though its more precise meaning refers to an intergenerational sequence of parenthood stages over the life course, from the birth of the children to their own departure from home and childbearing (O'Rand and Krecker 1990). This sequence, it should be noted, refers to a reproductive process in human populations. Within a life cycle of generational succession, newborns are socialized to maturity, give birth to the next generation, grow old, and die. The cycle is repeated from one generation to the next, though only within the framework of a population. Some people do not have children and consequently are not part of an intergenerational life cycle.

The life cycle is commonly known in terms of a family cycle, a set of ordered stages of parenthood defined primarily by variations in family composition and size (Hill 1970). Major transition points include marriage, birth of the first and the last child, the children's transitions in school, departure of the eldest and the youngest child from the home, and marital dissolution through death of one spouse. The stages are not defined in terms of age, as a rule, and typically follow a preferred script of a marriage that bears children and survives to old age, an increasingly rare specimen in view of the divorce rate. The life-cycle concept tells us about the sequence of family events, but it does not indicate how closely spaced the events are or when the sequence began in a woman's life, whether in adolescence or in the late thirties. A rapid sequence of births produces a different family process from that of widely dispersed births. The life stage of the mother also has relevance to the meaning of a birth sequence. Moreover, some woman do not bear children.

Life history commonly refers to a lifetime chronology of events and activities that typically and variably combines data records on education, work life, family, and residence. A life history may also include information on physical health, social identity change, and emotional well-being. These records may be generated by obtaining information from archival materials or from interviews with a respondent. Some interviews are prospective and focus on the present; others are retrospective and enable the investigator to obtain information that was not collected in the past (Giele and Elder 1998). The accuracy of these reports of the past depends on the type of information requested. Subjective states in the past cannot be recovered accurately in retrospective reports. They are interpreted in terms of the present.

A retrospective life history or calendar is based on an age-event matrix (Freedman et al. 1988; Caspi et al. 1996). It records the age (year and month) at which transitions occur in each activity domain, and thus depicts an unfolding life course in ways uniquely suited to event-history analyses (Mayer and Tuma 1990) and to the assessment of time-varying causal influences. The advantages and disadvantages of retrospective life histories and prospective reports are discussed by Scott and Alwin (1998). In developing societies especially, retrospective life calendars are typically the only sources of information on prior life experience.

The term "life history" also refers to a self-reported narration of life, as in Thomas and Znaniecki's famous life history of Wladek, a Polish peasant, in *The Polish Peasant in Europe and America* (1918–1920). Narrative accounts are frequently recorded on tape and then transcribed. Another common approach assigns the interviewer a more active editorial role in actually putting together a life history. In *American Lives* (1993), Clausen interviewed six adults in their later years and prepared life histories, which the respondents later reviewed for accuracy. He has written about this method in two essays (1995, 1998) that discuss the difference between life stories and life histories.

This qualitative approach to life histories is increasingly considered one part of a multimethod approach to the study of lives. In their pathbreaking longitudinal study of juvenile delinquents, Laub and Sampson (1998) show how the qualitative life histories provide critical insight, when combined with quantitative data, on events that turned men's lives around toward productive work and good citizenship. Events that are turning points change the direction of lives, they are often "course corrections." Examples include marriage, military service, and higher education.

Life span specifies the temporal scope of inquiry and specialization, as in life-span psychology or sociology. A life-span study extends across a substantial period of life and generally links behavior in two or more life stages. Instead of limiting research to social and developmental processes within a specific life stage, such as adolescence or the middle years, a life-span design favors studies of antecedents and consequences. Sociologists tend to focus on the social life course, in which "life stage" refers to either socially defined positions, such as the age of young adulthood, or to analytically defined positions, such as the career stage of men or women at age forty (i.e., where they are in their career at this age). Thus, men who differ in age when they encounter work-life misfortune occupy different life stages at the time.

Developmental stages and trajectories are the focus of life-span developmental psychology. Examples of a stage theory include Erik Erikson's (1963) psychosocial stages, such as the stage of generativity in the later years. Life-span developmental psychology gained coherence and visibility through a series of conferences at the University of West Virginia beginning in the late 1960s (Baltes and Reese 1984). The approach is defined by a concern with the description and explanation of age-related biological and behavioral changes from birth to death.

All the above concepts have a place in studies of the life course. Contemporary inquiry extends across the life span and frequently draws upon the life records and life cycles of successive generations. The life course takes the form of a multidimensional and intergenerational concept: a dynamic life pattern of interlocking trajectories and transitions, such as work, marriage, and being parents. Within this context, misfortune and opportunities are intergenerational as well as personal life events. Failed marriages and work lives can lead adult offspring back to the parental household and alter the parents's life plans for their later years (Goldscheider and Goldscheider 1993). Conversely, parents' economic setbacks and marital dissolution may impede their children's transition to adulthood by postponing higher education and marriage. Each generation is bound to fateful decisions and events in the other's life course.

THE EMERGENCE OF LIFE-COURSE THEORY

When pioneering investigators followed children born before 1930 into their adult years, they encountered major limitations in conventional approaches to human development, including those associated with a child-based model. Three such limitations and their challenges, in particular, played a major role in the genesis of life course theory and appropriate methods (Elder 1998):

1. To formulate concepts that apply to development and aging across the life span as a replacement for child-based, growth-oriented accounts.

2. To conceptualize how human lives are socially organized and evolve over time.

3. To relate lives to an ever-changing society, with emphasis on the linking processes and mechanisms and the developmental effects of changing circumstances.

Responses to the first challenge in the 1970s led to the formulation of more life-span concepts of development and aging (Baltes and Baltes, 1990; Baltes et al. 1998), especially with the field of life-span developmental psychology. Life-span development is conceived as a life-long adaptational process. Some processes are discontinuous and innovative, while others are continuous and cumulative. Biological resources tend to decline over the life span, whereas cultural resources may increase, as in the growth of wisdom. Theorists stress the lifelong interaction of person and social context, the relative plasticity and agency of the aging organism, and the multidirectionality of life-span development (Lerner 1991). Psychologist Paul Baltes at the Berlin Max Planck Institute is a leading figure in the programmatic effort to study development and aging across the life span.

This emergence of life-span thinking on human development and aging occurred with little attention to a well-established "relationship" view of human lives. Dating back to the nineteenth century, social scientists have viewed the individual's life pattern in terms of multiple role sequences and their transitions (Cain 1964; Kertzer and Keith 1984). Changes in social roles, such as from dependency to marriage and parenthood, represent changes in social stage across the life cycle. Commitments to a line of action arise from obligations to significant others. Stable relationships ensure a measure of personal stability, just as entry into such relationships can stabilize a person's life and minimize involvement in unconventional and illegal activities (Robins 1966). A change in relationships may produce a turning point, a redirection of the life course.

Life-cycle theory helped to contextualize people's lives by emphasizing the social dynamic of "linked lives." These connections extend across the generations and across people's lives through convoys of friends and relatives—others who remain part of their social network as they age (Kahn and Antonucci 1980). One of the earliest proponents of a life-cycle view of lives was sociologist William I. Thomas. With Florian Znaniecki, he used life-record data to study the emigration of Polish peasants to European and American cities around the turn of the century (1918–1920). The societies they left and entered presented contrasting "lines of genesis" or role sequences for individual lives.

For many decades, the life cycle perspective offered a valuable way of thinking about the social patterning of lives, though insensitive to age, time, and historical context. During the 1960s, the life-cycle approach began to converge with new understandings of age to draw upon the virtues of each tradition; of *linked lives* across the life span and generations, and of *temporality* through an age-graded sequence of events and social roles, embedded in a changing world. The emerging theory of the life course was informed as well by life-span concepts of human development.

Three discoveries of variation in lives were based on this new understanding of age, and together they gave rise to life-course thinking. First, studies in the 1960s began to identify substantial *variation in age patterns* across lives: Contrary to established views (Eisenstadt 1956), people of the same age varied in the pace and sequencing of transitions in their lives. During the late 1950s and early 1960s, Bernice Neugarten (1968) developed a research program that featured normative timetables and individual deviations from such expectations. Ever since this pioneering work and the growth of social demography, the study of differential timing and order among events has been one of the most active domains in life-course study. However, we still know little about age expectations in large populations.

Second, *social relations and kinship* especially emerged as a primary source of variation and regulation of life trajectories. Lives are lived interdependently among members of family and kin. The most significant integration of age and relationship distinctions is found in *Of Human Bonding* (Rossi and Rossi 1990). Using a three-generation sample in the Boston region, the study investigates the interlocking nature of the life course within family systems, with particular focus on the relationship beween individual aging and kin-defined relationships across the life span.

Third, the new work on aging made visible the role of *historical variation* as a source of life variations. Studies of social change and life patterns had been conducted up to the 1960s as if they had little in common, an assumption effectively challenged by Norman Ryder's concept of the interaction of individual lives and history (1965). Ryder proposed the term "cohort" as a concept for studying the life course—the age at which the person enters the system. With its life-stage principle, Ryder's essay provided a useful point of departure for understanding the interaction between social change and the life patterns of birth cohorts. The impact of a historical event on the life course reflects the life or career stage at which the change was experienced. The publication of *Aging and Society* (Riley et al. 1972) strengthened this sensitivity to the historical setting of lives through membership in a particular birth cohort.

The three streams of life-course theory (social relations–life cycle, age, and life-span concepts of development) came together in a study of children who were born in the early 1920s, grew up in the Great Depression, and then entered service roles in World War II. In *Children of the Great Depression* (Elder, [1974] 1999), the study began with ideas from the relationship tradition, such as generation and social roles, and soon turned to the analytic meanings of age for ways of linking family and individual experience to historical change, and for identifying trajectories across the life course. The study tested Ryder's life-stage principle by comparing the effects of drastic income loss during the Great Depression on the family and individual experience of the Oakland study members with that of a younger cohort born toward the end of the 1920s (Elder et al. 1984). Consistent with the life-stage hypothesis, the younger boys in particular were more adversely influenced by family hardship, when compared to the older boys. But similar effects were not observed among the girls.

By the 1990s, the life course had become a general theoretical framework for the study of lives, human development, and aging in a changing society. This advance is coupled with the continued growth of longitudinal studies and the emergence of new methodologies for the collection and analysis of life history data (Giele and Elder 1998; Mayer and Tuma 1990).

PARADIGMATIC PRINCIPLES

Life course theory is organized around paradigmatic principles that guide inquiry on issues of problem identification, model formulation, and research design. Four principles are primary: 1) the interplay of human lives and development with changing times and places; 2) the social timing of lives; 3) the interdependence of lives; and 4) human agency in choice-making and actions (Elder 1998).

1. *The life course of individuals is embedded in and shaped by the historical times and places they experience over their lifetime.*

    When societies are undergoing rapid change, different birth years expose individuals to historical worlds with different opportunity systems, cultures, and structural constraints. Historical influences on life trajectories take the form of a cohort effect when social change differentiates the life course of successive cohorts, such as older and younger men before the World War II. History also takes the form of a period effect when the impact of social change is relatively uniform across successive birth cohorts. Birth year and cohort membership locate people in relation to historical change, such as the economic recession of 1982–83, but they do not indicate actual exposure to the change or the process by which historical influences are expressed. Direct study of such change and its influences is essential for identifying explanatory mechanisms.

    Life stage informs such mechanisms; people of unlike age and those who occupy different roles are differentially exposed to and influenced by particular types of social change. Four other components of an explanatory mechanism (for linking social change to lives) are worth noting (Elder 1998, pp. 959–61). One linking factor is defined by *social imperatives*, the behavioral demands or requirements of new situations. The more demanding the situation, the more individual behavior is constrained to meet role expectations. Studies of worklives by Kohn and Schooler (1983) suggest that the establishment of a new set of occupational and workplace imperatives can alter how workers think and function. A second factor involves the dynamics of a *control cycle*. A loss of personal control occurs when people enter a new world and this sets in motion efforts to regain this control. These efforts may entail new choices that construct a different direction in life, a different life course. Historical influences are often expressed through a network of relationships. *Interdependent lives* are thus a linking factor in the explanatory analysis. The last factor involves *accentuation*. When a social transition heightens a prominent attribute that people bring to the new role or situation, the process accentuates the effect of the change. Our understanding of such change is enhanced by the *principle of timing in lives*.

2. *The developmental impact of a life transition or event is contingent on when it occurs in a person's life.*

    This principle subsumes the concept of life stage; social change affects the individual according to when the exposure occurred over the life course. Recruitment into the military illustrates this point (Sampson and Laub 1996). Mobilization immediately after high school occurs before marriage and worklife obligations, and during World War II, entry into the service at this time was less disruptive than it was for males who entered in their late twenties or thirties. Studies of veterans from World War II indicate that late entry into the armed forces significantly increased the risk of divorce, worklife disruption, and an accelerated pattern of physical health decline (Elder and Chan 1999). By comparison, early entry provided access to educational and job opportunities without the costs of life disruption.

    Across the life course, Neugarten's (1996) emphasis on the consequences of timing variations has been followed by extensive research on differential timing patterns, from marriage and births to retirement (Shanahan in press). The impact of a life event, such as a personal loss, depends in part on when the event occurs. But to fully assess this impact, we must consider also the *principle of linked lives.*

3. *Lives are lived interdependently and social and historical influences are expressed through this network of shared relationships.*

Social relationships represent a vehicle for transmitting and amplifying the effects of stressful change, as in families under economic stress. For example, Depression hardship tended to increase the explosiveness of fathers who were inclined toward irritability before the crisis (Elder et al. 1986). And the more explosive they became under stress, the more adversely it affected the quality of marriage and effectiveness as a parent. Unstable family relations (marital, parent-child) became mutually reinforcing dynamics across the life course and generations. These dynamics tended to persist from one generation to the next through a process of individual continuity and intergenerational transmission.

Linked lives tend to transmit the life course implications of an ill-timed event in a person's life. One of the clearest examples of this phenomenon comes from a study of female lineages in Los Angeles (Burton and Bengtson 1985). The birth of a child to the teenage daughter of a young mother created a large disparity between age and kinship status, between being young and facing the prospects of grandparental obligations. Four out of five mothers of young mothers actually refused to accept these new child-care obligations, shifting the burden up the generational ladder to the great-grandmother, who in many cases was carrying a heavy load. By comparison, the women who became grandmothers in their late forties or so were eager for the new role; in this lineage, a daughter's timely transition to motherhood set in motion her mother's timely transition to grandmotherhood. In

both cases, the *principle of human agency* addresses the process by which lives and life courses are socially constructed.

4. *Individuals construct their own life course through the choices and actions they have taken within the constraints and opportunities of history and social circumstances.*

Human agency has been a central theme in the study of biographies. Lives are influenced by social structures and cultures, but human agency can shape lives through the choices that are made under such conditions. In Clausen's *American Lives* (1993), the central question is not how social systems made a difference in the life course, but why people made certain choices and thereby constructed their own life course. Clausen focused on the primary role of planful competence in late adolescence, that competent young people who think about the future with a sense of efficacy are more effective in making sound choices and in implementing them. This study found substantial support for this hypothesis in the lives of men in particular from adolescence to the retirement age of 65. However, longitudinal research (Shanahan et al. 1997) shows that planful competence makes a difference only when opportunities are available. Planful competence was not expressed in education or occupational career among men who entered the labor market in the depressed 1930s.

The emergence of life course theory and methods can be viewed as a response to pressing questions in the 1960s. The rapidly developing field of human development and aging needed a conceptual framework for thinking about the patterning of human lives in changing societies and its consequences. As life course theory addressed issue of this kind, it gained prominence as a theoretical orientation among fields of gerontology, criminology, social history, medical studies, developmental science, education, and social stratification. Noting such developments, Colby (Giele and Elder 1998, pp. x), refers to this approach as "one of the most important achievements of social science in the second half of the 20th century." Only time will tell about the accuracy of this appraisal. In the meantime, the field of life course studies continues to flourish.

REFERENCES

Baltes, Paul B., and Margaret M. Baltes, eds. 1990 *Successful Aging: Perspectives from the Behavioral Sciences*. New York: Cambridge University Press.

——, and Hayne W. Reese 1984 "The Life-Span Perspective in Developmental Psychology." In Marc H. Bornstein and Michael E. Lamb, eds., *Developmental Psychology: An Advanced Textbook*. Hillsdale, N.J.: Earlbaum.

——, Ulman Lindenberger, and Ursula M. Staudinger 1998 "Life Span Theory in Developmental Psychology." In William Damon, general ed., and Richard M. Lerner, volume ed., *Handbook of Child Psychology, Volume 1: Theoretical Models of Human Development*, 5th ed. New York: Wiley

Bandura, Albert 1997 *Self-Efficacy: The Exercise of Control*. New York: W. H. Freeman.

Burton, Linda M., and Vern L. Bengtson 1985 "Black Grandmothers: Issues of Timing and Continuity of Roles." In Vern L. Bengtson and Joan F. Robertson, eds., *Grandparenthood*. Beverly Hills, Calif.: Sage.

Cain, Leonard 1964 "Life Course and Social Structure." In Robert E. L. Faris, ed., *Handbook of Modern Sociology*. Chicago: Rand McNally.

Caspi, Avshalom, Terrie E. Moffitt, Arland Thornton, Deborah Freedman, James W. Amell, Honalee Harrington, Judith Smeijers, and Phil A. Silva 1996 "The Life History Calendar: A Research and Clinical Assessment Method for Collecting Retrospective Event-History Data." *International Journal of Methods in Psychiatric Research* 6:101–114

Clausen, John A. 1993 *American Lives: Looking Back at the Children of the Great Depression*. New York: Free Press.

——. 1995. "Gender, Contexts, and Turning Points in Adults' Lives." In Phyllis Moen, Glen H. Elder, Jr., and Kurt Lüscher, eds., *Examining Lives in Context: Perspectives on the Ecology of Human Development*. Washington: APA Press.

——, 1998. Life Reviews and Life Stories." In Janet Z. Giele and Glen H. Elder, Jr., eds., *Methods of Life Course Research: Qualitative and Quantitative Approaches*, Thousand Oaks, Calif.: Sage.

Colby, Anne 1998 "Forward: Crafting Life Course Studies." In Janet Z. Giele and Glen H. Elder, Jr., eds., *Methods of Life Course Research: Qualitative and Quantitative Approaches*. Thousand Oaks, Calif.: Sage.

Eisenstadt, Shmuel N. 1956 *From Generation to Generation: Age Groups and Social Structure*. Glencoe, Ill.: Free Press.

Elder, Glen H., Jr. 1974 *Children of the Great Depression: Social Change in Life Experience*. Chicago: University of Chicago Press. (25th Anniversary Edition, enlarged, 1999, Boulder, Col.: Westview.)

—— 1998 "The Life Course and Human Development." In William Damon, general ed., and Richard M. Lerner, volume ed., *Handbook of Child Psychology, Volume 1: Theoretical Models of Human Development*, 5th ed. New York: Wiley.

——, Avshalom Caspi, and Geraldine Downey 1986 "Problem Behavior and Family Relationships: Life Course and Intergenerational Themes." In Aage B. Sørensen, Franz E. Weinert, and Lonnie R. Sherrod, eds., *Human Development and the Life Course: Multidisciplinary Perspectives*. Hillsdale, N.J.: Erlbaum.

——, and Christopher Chan (1999) "Wars Legacy in Men's Lives." In Phyllis Moen and Donna Dempster-McClain, eds., *A Nation Divided: Diversity, Inequality and Community in American Society*. Ithaca, N.Y.: Cornell University Press.

——, Jeffrey K. Liker, and Catherine E. Cross 1984 "Parent-Child Behavior in the Great Depression: Life Course and Intergenerational Influences." In Paul B. Baltes and Orville G. Brim, Jr., eds., *Life-Span Development and Behavior*, vol. 6 New York: Academic Press.

Erikson, Erik H. 1963 *Childhood and Society*, 2nd ed. New York: Norton.

Freedman, Deborah, Arland Thornton, Donald Camburn, Duane Alwin, and Linda Young-DeMarco 1988 "The Life History Calendar: A Technique for Collecting Retrospective Data." *Sociological Methodology* 18:37–68.

Furstenberg, Frank F., Jr., Jeanne Brooks-Gunn, and S. P. Morgan 1987 *Adolescent Mothers in Later Life*, New York: Cambridge University Press.

Giele, Janet A., and Glen H. Elder, Jr., eds. 1998 *Methods of Life Course Research: Qualitative and Quantitative Approaches*. Thousand Oaks, Calif.: Sage.

Goldscheider, Frances K., and Calvin Goldscheider 1993 *Leaving Home before Marriage: Ethnicity, Familism, and Generational Relationships*. Madison: University of Wisconsin Press.

Goode, William J. 1960 "A Theory of Role Strain." *American Sociological Review* 25(4):483–496.

Hagestad, Gunhild O. 1990 "Social Perspectives on the Life Course." In Robert H. Binstock and Linda K. George, eds., *Handbook of Aging and the Social Sciences*, 3rd ed. New York: Academic Press.

Hareven, Tamara K. 1978 *Transitions: The Family and the Life Course in Historical Perspective*. New York: Academic.

Hill, Reuben 1970 *Family Development in Three Generations*. Cambridge, Mass.: Schenkman.

Kahn, Robert L,. and Toni C. Antonucci 1980 "Convoys Over the Life Course: Attachment, Roles, and Social Support." In Paul B. Baltes and Orville G. Brim, Jr., eds, *Life-Span Development and Behavior: Volume 3.* New York: Academic Press.

Kertzer, David I., and Jennie Keith, eds. 1984 *Age and Anthropological Theory*. Ithaca, N.Y.: Cornell University Press.

Kohli, Martin 1986 *The World We Forgot: A Historical Review of the Life Course.* In Victor W. Marshall, ed., *Later Life: The Social Psychology of Aging*. Beverly Hills, Calif.: Sage.

Kohn, Melvin L., and Carmi Schooler 1983 *Work and Personality: An Inquiry into the Impact of Social Stratification*. Norwood, N.J.: Ablex.

Laub, John H., and Robert J. Sampson 1998 "Integrating Quantitative and Qualitative Data." In Janet Z Giele and Glen H. Elder, Jr., eds, *Methods of Life Course Research: Qualitative and Quantitative Approaches*. Thousand Oaks, CA: Sage.

Lerner, Richard M. 1991 "Changing Organism-Context Relations as the Basic Process of Development: A Developmental Contextual Perspective." *Developmental Psychology* 27(1):27–32.

Mayer, Karl U., and Nancy B. Tuma (eds.) 1990 *Event History Analysis in Life Course Research*. Madison, Wisc.: University of Wisconsin Press.

Merton, Robert K. 1968 *Social Theory and Social Structure*. New York: Free Press.

Modell, John 1989 *Into One's Own: From Youth to Adulthood in the United States 1920–1975*. Berkeley: University of California Press.

Neugarten, Bernice L. 1968 *Middle Age and Aging: A Reader in Social Psychology*. Chicago: University of Chicago Press.

——, and Nancy Datan 1973 "Sociological Perspectives on the Life Cycle." In Paul B. Baltes and K. W. Schaie, eds., *Life-Span Developmental Psychology: Personality and Socializaton*, New York: Academic Press.

—— 1996 *The Meanings of Age: Selected Papers of Bernice L. Neugarten*, edited, and with a foreword by Dail A. Neugarten. Chicago: University of Chicago Press.

O'Rand, Angela M., and Margaret L. Krecker 1990 "Concepts of the Life Cycle: Their History, Meanings and Uses in the Social Sciences." *Annual Review of Sociology* 16:241–262.

O'Rand, Angela M., John C. Henretta, and Margaret L. Krecker 1991 "Family Pathways to Retirement: Early and Late Life Family Effects on Couples' Work Exit Patterns." In Maximiliane Szinovacz, D. Ekerdt, and Barbara H. Vinick, eds., *Families and Retirement: Conceptual and Methodological Issues*. Newbury Park, CA: Sage.

Riley, Matilda W., Marilyn E. Johnson, and Anne Foner, eds. 1972 *Aging and Society: A Sociology of Age Stratification*, vol. 3. New York: Russell Sage Foundation.

Robins, Lee. 1966. *Deviant Children Grown Up*. Baltimore, Md.: Williams and Wilkins.

Rossi, Alice S., and Peter H. Rossi 1990 *Of Human Bonding: Parent-Child Relations across the Life Course*. New York: Aldine.

Ryder, Norman B. 1965 "The Cohort as a Concept in the Study of Social Change." *American Sociological Review* 30(6):843–861.

Sampson, Robert J., and John H. Laub 1996 "Socioeconomic Achievement in the Life Course of Disadvantaged Men: Military Service as a Turning Pont, Circa 1940–1965." *American Sociological Review* 61(3):347–367.

Scott, Jacqueline, and Duane Alwin 1998 "Retrospective versus Prospective Measurement of Life Histories in Longitudinal Research." In Janet Z. Giele and Glen H. Elder, Jr., eds., *Methods of Life Course Research: Qualitative and Quantitative Approaches*. Thousand Oaks, Calif.: Sage.

Shanahan, Michael J. (In press) "Pathways to Adulthood in Changing Societies; Variability and Mechanisms in Life Course Perspective." *Annual Review of Sociology*.

Shanahan, Michael J., Glen H. Elder, Jr., and Richard A. Miech 1997 "History and Agency in Men's Lives: Pathways to Achievement in Cohort Perspective." *Sociology of Education* 70(1):54–67.

Spilerman, Seymour 1977 "Careers, Labor Market Structure, and Socioeconomic Achievement." *American Journal of Sociology* 83(3):551–593.

Thomas, William I., and Florian Znaniecki 1918–1920 *The Polish Peasant in Europe and America*, vol. 1–2. Urbana: University of Illinois Press.

GLEN H. ELDER, JR.

LIFE CYCLE

The *life cycle* is the socially defined, age-related sequence of stages individuals pass through beginning with birth and ending with death. Underlying the life cycle is the recognition that humans are biological organisms that are born, mature, and die. As with other biological organisms, reproduction is a key feature of human maturation, ensuring the persistence of the species.

FORMS OF THE LIFE CYCLE

In very simple societies, the life cycle may consist simply of two stages—infant and adult. Once infant survivorship is reasonably certain (typically by about age 6) young persons participate in adult work life, doing jobs that are suitable to their physical strength or as apprentices learning more complex skills. Work continues until death. But such a simple definition of the life cycle rarely endures the complexities attendant on reproduction. Among women, physical maturation separates childhood from the age when childbearing is possible. For men, marriage entails responsibility for supporting a family and guaranteeing their safety, something that typically must await completion of puberty and the achievement of economic viability. Even in societies with a low life expectancy, some adults survive to the point at which they are no longer able to work.

These examples illustrate how individual *social roles* (such as work or having a child) define a human life cycle that is more complex than the biological minimum. These roles are almost always defined as age related, and typically are also different for men and women. The concept of age-appropriate roles enables societies to regulate or prohibit behavior that is occurring "too early." These societies also use the concept of age appropriateness to move individuals along in their maturation process, urging the adoption of a social role before it is "too late."

Age. In most societies, chronological age is a handy proxy for maturity, with particular age groups assigned certain responsibilities and rights. In some societies (such as in postwar Japan) the age appropriateness of the sequence of social roles is rigorously defined by cultural values and enforced by social institutions (such as schools or labor markets) which impose strict age rules on entry, promotion, and exit. In African age-set societies the system is even more rigid: Groups of persons born during contiguous years are defined as members of a particular age group (age set). These age sets experience together the transition from one life cycle stage to the next, under community traditions that specify the formal requirements and ceremonies necessary to move from one set of social roles to another. Typically this process is one of considerable dispute—the moving up of one age set causes all members of the society to move to the next life-cycle stage so that one group will have to give up preferred adult roles for old age.

Age Stratification and Cohort Succession. Individual childbearing and the aging of individuals ready to assume new age-appropriate roles drive the societal process of age stratification and cohort succession (Riley 1985). The more complex the society, the more social roles that need to be filled. Most such roles in the society are gender linked and age stratified (defined as age appropriate and differing markedly from age to age). The use of chronological age rather than maturational capacity to construct the age-stratification system mandates that individuals as they age will move from one age stratum to the next, with an implicit societal mandate of assuming new roles. The birth of persons in contiguous years (what demographers call a "birth cohort") reinforces the dynamic of the age-stratification system by producing new role entrants who can only be accommodated by the movement of all age strata to the next life-cycle stage. In the United States we can see this system at work in age-graded schooling: When one group achieves high school graduation, the remaining students are promoted from one grade to the next. This opens entry-level spaces for a new cohort to begin school. Universities develop a variety of incentives to get elderly faculty to retire so that newly trained and presumably more innovative faculty can be hired.

The Life Cycle in Social Science. To summarize, the lives of humans from birth to death are organized as socially defined, age-related sequence of stages individuals pass through over their lifetime. These stages are inherently age related, with individuals maturing from one life-cycle stage to the next. Reproduction is a key feature of human maturation, distinguishing the roles of men and women and linked to the age-related biological capacity to bear children. An ongoing flow of new births ensures the persistence of human populations. Accommodating these new members of society also drives the dynamic of life-cycle change by necessitating the movement of earlier cohorts to more mature positions in the age-stratification system. This process of cohort succession is, in turn, a major source of societal innovation and change, as new cohorts take a fresh look at the content and form of the age strata they have just reached. In this way, the life-cycle concept links individual aging, the organization of roles in society, reproduction, and societal innovation and change.

CONTRIBUTIONS OF THE LIFE CYCLE

The life cycle has proved to be a powerful and flexible tool for the analysis and explanation of human lives, used by researchers from a number of different disciplines. Anthropologists have focused on the process of socialization by which one age stratum is taught to succeed the next over the life cycle, linking social roles to the cultural system of beliefs and values. Age-set societies have been intensively described because of the very visible structure of age stratification and the explicit group-level patterns of life-cycle stages. Rites of passage are the symbolic counterparts of age-set transitions from one age stratum to the next, marking the personal change and announcing it to the entire community.

Developmental psychologists have used the life cycle as an organizing principle for specifying the steps in human development. The process of aging drives this principle, which is defined and structured by social organizations and individual roles. A prominent example is Erikson's eight stages of life (1968). In this model, psychosocial stages are identified, consisting of times in which opportunities for success and the risk of failure are present. For example, the young adult stage is marked by the capacity for intimacy versus isolation, and integration, while a choice between wisdom and despair marks old age. The passage from one of the eight life stages to the next is regarded as a *turning point* that is fraught with vulnerability and heightened potential.

The life cycle forced gerontologists to recognize that the study of old age in isolation from the prior life cycle is not viable. The economic resources, health, knowledge, and family situations of the elderly result from the cumulating of life-cycle experiences. These same factors influence the chronological age at which people take on characteristics of the aged. Gerontology as a field has expanded to encompass the dynamics of life-cycle transitions. Immediately noteworthy when one adopts this aging approach is the fact that persons currently reaching old age have prior life-cycle experiences that may better prepare them for becoming old than did prior cohorts. The sociological interest in aging motivates gerontologists to attend to both the lifelong process of aging and potentially dramatic intercohort changes in successive cohorts of the aged.

Life Cycle Squeeze. Economists have relied on the life cycle and the gendered division of labor to study household and family economics. Wages follow a curvilinear pattern over the life cycle: Young workers receive the lowest wages; wages increase over the life cycle, peaking at midlife; while workers older than 55 tend to experience stability or even a decline in earnings. Women's earnings show much less of an age profile, both because young women frequently interrupt or reduce labor-force involvement when children are born, and because women's jobs are less likely to take the form of careers in which progression upward from one job to the next occurs.

This life-cycle pattern of earnings does not always match family income needs. Early in the life cycle, children are net consumers of income. As societies require a more educated population, youth and adolescents also become net income consumers. While this has long-term payoff for the society and for new cohorts of workers, it increases the costs and reduces the economic value of children to families. These costs most often occur when workers are at the low point in their earnings. Later in the life cycle, earnings are higher but the cost of a college education and assisting children in getting started also may be high. At the same time, elderly parents may become a social and financial obligation for children, leading to the powerful concept of the "life-cycle squeeze."

Cohorts facing this new mix of obligations with the traditional earnings profile have acted to reduce desynchronies in the stages of the life cycle.

Credit mechanisms (for example, long-term mortgages, home equity loans to pay for college education) smooth income and costs over the lifetime. The intercohort upgrading of the situations of the elderly in the United States means that parents become dependent on their adult children at an older age. The government has intervened to bear much of the cost of the elderly. Life-cycle pressures have also resulted in intercohort changes in the content of the life cycle of men and women—delays in marriage and first birth, a reduction in family size, the shift to two-earner families, and increases in divorce.

Sociologists have devoted considerable attention to the cohort-level study of life-cycle transitions. Turning points imply inevitability and potential crisis. Sociologists study the form of the transition (for example, cohabitation or marriage), whether or not a transition occurs (for example, parenthood), and the average age and variability in age of a transition across individuals of the same cohort. This approach recognizes (building on the idea of an age-stratification system) that a variety of transitions are crosscutting (for example, work and marriage, birth of a first child and marriage).

The Life Cycle in Demographic Models. It is the educational, labor-force, and family outcomes that interest demographers. The study of family life has proceeded with the measurement of marriage and then the progression to first birth, second birth, and so forth (taking into account both the number and the timing of births). A special tool called *parity progression analysis* has enabled demographers to identify turning points in fertility decisions, and how these have changed across cohorts. This approach to the study of demographic life-cycle stages, along with the recognition that fertility is inherently a biological process, has led demographers to develop population models of fertility that take into account marriage patterns, the level of marital fertility, and birth limitation. The life-cycle model also has informed research on age patterns of migration, and its regularities across time and place.

The life-cycle perspective has produced a variety of unexpected results. The American baby boom of the late 1940s and the 1950s was largely due to the temporal coincidence of childbearing by successive cohorts, rather than to a dramatic increase in family size. During the baby boom, women 35 and older made up childbearing that had been delayed by the Great Depression and World War II. Women reaching adulthood during the baby boom years responded to favorable economic conditions for young families by having their first child at a younger age and having subsequent children more quickly.

Family Life Cycle. Family sociologists made a great leap in developing the family life cycle as a variant form of the life cycle (Glick 1965). The family life cycle is unusual in that it focuses on family formation and childbearing, ignoring such linked transitions as completion of schooling and work. The family life cycle stretched the life-cycle model to incorporate role changes associated with the transitions of other individuals. (For example, a husband makes the transition to marriage at the same time as the wife. Only when all children grow up and leave the home does the family experience an "empty nest.") The family life cycle became a predominant research paradigm in family studies.

The family life cycle can be a useful analytic tool for understanding the succession of family roles in populations in which families predominate over individual interests. The family life-cycle model works only for those populations in which marriage precedes childbearing, the ages of each are specified within a narrow time band, and marriages do not end (by widowhood or divorce) before the last child leaves home.

None of these assumptions are even approximately satisfied for the United States. First births often precede marriage (among blacks this is the typical pattern). Many couples postpone childbearing within marriage, and as many as one-fifth remain voluntarily childless. Over half of all first marriages end within twenty years. Remarriage often follows. This degree of inconstancy in household membership begs the question of how to define the family whose life cycle is being described, and followed over time. The family life cycle is now widely regarded as a useless conceptual tool because it utterly fails to capture the realities of contemporary family life.

LIFE CYCLE AND LIFE COURSE

The life cycle defines pathways for individuals as they age from birth to death, specifying usual expectations about the sequence and timing of roles (for example, a first birth when married and at age 18 or older). Empirical research that uses the life cycle to analyze the lives of population *cohorts* typically find that these life-cycle stages, as socially defined and demarcated, follow expected patterns.

Research on the transitions of *individuals* over their lifetime has demonstrated the essential incorrectness of this supposition. For many individuals, childbearing precedes marriage, parenthood occurs when the parents are not yet economically self-sufficient, and adult children return to their parental household after they have assumed (and sometimes failed at) adult family and economic roles. This has caused researchers to consider whether new life-cycle patterns are emerging, or whether a group of individuals is somehow "deviant" from the established life cycle.

Clearly there have been marked intercohort changes in the life cycle, reflecting the varying opportunity structures of time periods and cultural change. For example, the availability of the GI Bill for college education and interruptions in education associated with wartime military service allowed many men to marry and have children before they finished school and became economically established. In recent cohorts of young women there is a decreasing emphasis on the necessity of marrying before having a child, and, on the part of all adults, a greater readiness to assist rather than condemn single mothers.

An even greater source of departure from the population life-cycle model is the large number of persons in each cohort who never make a transition to a given life-cycle stage (e.g., those not marrying or not becoming parents), who retreat from a given life-cycle stage to an earlier stage (e.g., fathers who divorce and abandon their families, and retired persons who return to work), and who are not part of the typical life cycle (e.g., the severely disabled, persons who die before reaching old age). These features of the life cycle vary by such primary sociological variables as social class origin, education, race and ethnic group, and place of residence.

Among Americans the seeming conformity of cohorts to the life-cycle patterns masks the overwhelming number and frequency of individual departures. In this situation the life cycle seems to be a far less useful analytic device. Social scientists

have adopted in its place the more sophisticated and flexible "life-course" perspective. The life course sees individual lives as a series of trajectories (such as family or career) that are socially recognized and defined. Age is significant in the life-course approach because it is an indicator of biological aging and locates individuals in historical context through birth cohorts. The social meaning of age helps define life-course pathways (recognized routes of trajectories) through age norms and sanctions, and social timetables for the occurrence and order of events. Transitions (leaving home, getting a job, marrying) define trajectories. Interlocking transitions and their trajectories lead to multiple roles that define the individual life course from birth to death.

Because of the emphasis on variations in trajectories across individuals, every individual life course has the potential to be unique. Much of the population-level research with the life-course model has focused on transitions—the proportion of cohorts making a transition, average age at transitions, and the range of ages at which cohorts typically make these transitions. The life cycle gives analytic meaning to these life-course transitions by providing a standard against which to measure how transitions vary across cohorts and differ among key population groups within cohorts.

Causal analyses of the life course are usually done at the individual level, typically with a class of statistical methods called "event history" or "hazards" models. These statistical methods enable investigators to examine empirical data on individual transitions, modeling the age-graded pattern of transitions from one social role to another and identifying "heterogeneity" (sources of variation in transitions at the individual level).

The Necessity for Life Cycle in Studies of the Life Course. This points to a dilemma for social scientists—the very life-cycle model that the life-course approach undermines provides the essential theoretical framework that gives meaning to individual behaviors. Because social scientists are part of the societies they study, they also carry in their own heads models of the life cycle—what should be done when it should be done, and what denotes success or failure. The life-course perspective on pathways that define typical trajectories and the social meanings of age capture the essence of a life-cycle model. The apparent tension between the life-cycle and life-course conceptualizations is perhaps overdrawn.

The life-cycle model retains many valuable features that are typically missing from life-course studies. Life-course transitions focus on individuals at particular times during their lives (adolescents becoming adults, older workers becoming disabled or retired). While past experiences and current opportunities are often included in life-course models, the life-course perspective has not lent itself well to viewing transitions at particular ages in the context of the lifelong process of aging, an idea that is innate in the life-cycle approach. Economic research, which is theoretically driven and uses a life-cycle model, has been most successful at integrating findings from transitions at a given age into the lifetimes of individuals.

With such an approach it is also possible to simulate the effects of changes in transition rates (resulting from heterogeneity in rates and changes in population composition) on cohort-life cycle behaviors. The life-course perspective typically views cohorts as proxies for age-specific experiences with the social structure; the life-cycle model brings a necessary emphasis on intercohort change as a method of social innovation.

The life-course approach emphasizes variability in transitions and trajectories to such an extent that many social scientists have neglected regularities and consistencies in behaviors, and the advantages they may entail. There is a great deal of research on adolescent mothers but relatively little research on why married women have children. There is more interest in unemployment and poverty than in the advantages of paid employment and career lines. While children of welfare mothers disproportionately go on to become welfare mothers themselves (the subject of much research), the overwhelming majority grow up to be free of welfare dependence (a subject about which we know very little). Nor do we have a strong explanation of the reasons persons marry. The life-cycle approach draws attention to these questions of social organization, and the matching of individual behaviors to necessary social roles.

FUTURE OF LIFE CYCLE

The life cycle thus remains a viable and valuable conceptual tool for studying human lives. In much of the developing world, transitions and trajectories are sufficiently universal and age regulated that the life-cycle model remains a highly useful tool for social science. In societies where such regularities are no longer the norm, the life-course approach is the more appropriate. To be meaningful, the life course must be interpreted in light of the life cycle—the underlying beliefs about the shape and timing of the life stages to understand the social meanings of age, identify alternative pathways for life trajectories, draw attention to the strong regularities in transition behaviors and linkages, and direct attention to intercohort stability and change. The concept of the life cycle thus will continue to be a valuable and necessary tool for the social sciences.

(SEE ALSO: *Life Course*)

Further Readings

Erikson, Erik H. 1968 "Life Cycle." Pp. 286–292 in David L. Sills, ed., *International Encyclopaedia of the Social Sciences*, vol. 9. New York: Mcmillan Free Press.

Glick, Paul C. and Robert Parke, Jr. 1965 "New Approaches in Studying the Life Cycle of the Family." *Demography* 2:187–202.

Greenwood, M. J. 1997 "Internal Migration in Developed Countries." Pp. 647–720 in Mark R. Rosenzweig and Oded Stark, eds., *Handbook of Population and Family Economics*, vol. 1B. Amsterdam: Elsevier.

Hotz, V. J., J. A. Klerman, and R. J. Willis 1997 "The Economics of Fertility in Developed Countries: A Survey." Pp. 275–347 in Mark R. Rosenzweig and Oded Stark, eds., *Handbook of Population and Family Economics*, vol. 1A. Amsterdam: Elsevier.

O'Rand, Angela M. and Margaret L. Krecker 1990 "Concepts of the Life Cycle: Their History, Meanings, and Uses in the Social Sciences. *Annual Review of Sociology* 16:241–262.

Riley, Matilda White 1985 "Age Strata in Social Systems." Pp. 369–411 in Robert H. Binstock and Ethel Shanas, eds., *Handbook of Aging and the Social Sciences*, 2nd ed. New York: Van Nostrand Reinhold.

DENNIS P. HOGAN

LIFE EXPECTANCY

Life expectancy (or the expectation of life) is the average length of life remaining to be lived by a population at a given age. It is computed in the process of building a life table and can be computed for any age in the life table. Life expectancy at birth is the most commonly presented value because this measure provides a succinct indicator of mortality that reflects mortality conditions across the age range and is unaffected by the age structure of the actual population and thus can be compared across populations. The symbol used to represent life expectancy is $\mathring{e}_x$ where x represents an exact age.

LIFE EXPECTANCY IN THE UNITED STATES

In 1996, life expectancy at birth, $\mathring{e}_0$, in the United States was 76.1 years; at age 65, $\mathring{e}_{65}$ was 17.5 years; and at age 85, $\mathring{e}_{85}$ was 6.1 years (Anderson 1998). These figures can be interpreted to mean that if a baby born in 1996 were exposed to the mortality conditions existing at each age of the life span in 1996, the baby with an average length life would live 76.1 years.

PERIOD AND COHORT VALUES OF LIFE EXPECTANCY

The 1996 U.S. life table is a period life table, based on cross-sectional data collected over a year; thus, this life table indicates the mortality experience of a hypothetical cohort. No actual cohort ever experiences the mortality in a period or cross-sectional life table; rather, the table indicates mortality conditions if the mortality levels of each age group at the period of time used as a reference were experienced by the hypothetical cohort. Because mortality has been falling over time, period life tables for a cohort's year of birth have indicated an average expected length of life that is lower than that actually achieved by the cohort. For instance, in 1900 the cross-sectional life table for the United States showed life expectations of 46 for males and 49 for females. On the basis of their actual experience up through the age of 80, the 1900 birth cohort had an average length of life of 52 years for males and 58 years for females (Faber and Wade 1983).

Generation or cohort life tables, like the one mentioned above, based on the experience of an actual cohort are sometimes constructed. These indicate the average length of life actually lived after specific ages for a real cohort. The major difficulty faced in building cohort life tables is obtaining population and death data for a cohort from birth until the last survivors have died—over a 100-year period.

A mistaken notion held by many people is that life expectancy at birth is a good indicator of the age at which an older individual will die. This notion has undoubtedly led to some poor planning for old age because a person who has already reached older adulthood on average will die at an age that exceeds life expectancy at birth by a significant amount. As mentioned above, expectation of life in 1996 was 17.5 years for 65-year-olds, 11.1 for 75-year-olds, and 6.1 for 85-year-olds. With this number of years remaining to be lived on average, 65-year-olds should expect to live to 83 on average. Those who live to 75 should expect to live to 86, and those who live to 85 can expect to live to 91 on average. While expectation of life decreases as age increases, the expected age at death increases for those who survive.

CHANGES IN LIFE EXPECTANCY OVER TIME

As noted above, life expectancy has been increasing over time. This has probably been going on since some time in the last half of the nineteenth century, although reliable data for large sections of the country are not available to track the increase before 1900. In 1900, life expectancy at birth for both sexes was 47.3 years (U.S. Bureau of the Census 1975). This indicates an increase in life expectancy between 1900 and 1996 of 28.8 years. Most of this increase in life expectancy since 1900 is due to declines in mortality among infants and children. These mortality declines were primarily due to the diminishing force of infectious and parasitic diseases which were the most important causes of death among children.

Because life expectancy was low in the past, people often hold the mistaken notion that very few people ever reached old age under high mortality conditions. Yin and Shine (1985) have demonstrated that this mistaken notion was so prevalent that it was commonly incorporated into gerontology textbooks. The fact is that even under conditions of low life expectancy, once childhood is survived, the chances of living to old age are quite high. This is indicated by the fact that life expectancy at the older years has not increased over time nearly as much as life expectancy at birth. For instance, while life expectancy at birth for white males has increased almost 26 years since 1900, from 48.2 to 73.9 years, life expectancy for white males at age 40 has increased almost 9 years between 1900 and 1996, from 27.7 years to 36.4 years; at age 70, the increase for males has been just over 3 1/2 years, from 9.0 to 12.6 (Anderson 1998).

It should be noted, however, that in the past three decades the pace of improvement in life expectancy at the oldest ages has increased. In 1970 expectation of life for white males at age 70 was 10.5 years, indicating an improvement of 1.5 years in the 70 years between 1900 and 1970. Between 1970 and 1998, the increase was 2 years—significantly greater than the improvement during the first seven decades of the century. This reflects the new era of mortality decline in which decreases in mortality are due to decreased mortality from chronic conditions and are concentrated among the old.

A number of authors have studied the relationships between changes in age-specific mortality and life expectancy. Vaupel (1986) concludes that a reduction in the force of mortality of 1 percent at all ages would not produce as much gain in life expectancy today as it did in 1900. This is because we have already made so much progress in lowering infant and child mortality, the ages that have the greatest effect on life expectancy. Vaupel also shows that as mortality moves to lower levels, more progress is made in increasing life expectancy from mortality declines at older ages rather than at younger ages. At the level of mortality now experienced in the United States, much of the future increase in life expectancy will come from mortality declines occurring at ages over 65. This is true because of the prior success in reducing mortality at earlier ages to such low levels.

CALCULATION OF LIFE EXPECTANCY WITHIN THE LIFE TABLE

These observations about changes in life expectancy should make clear that life expectancy at birth is heavily weighted by mortality conditions at the youngest ages. A brief explanation of the life table and how life expectancy is calculated demonstrates why this is the case.

The life table is a statistical model that provides a comprehensive description of the mortality level of a population. Life table measures are particularly valuable because they are succinct indicators of mortality that reflect mortality conditions across the age range, are unaffected by the age structure of the actual population, and thus can be compared across populations. Life table measures can also be used to describe the characteristics of the stationary population that would result from an unchanging schedule of age-specific mortality rates in a closed population with a constant number of births.

There are a number of functions that appear in most life tables and for which conventional notation is widely recognized: q_x, l_x, d_x, L_x, T_x, and $\mathring{e}_x$. Each of these measures provides information useful in describing some aspect of the mortality conditions and/or characteristics of the stationary population. The definitions and interpretations of the life table functions follow below. In order to clarify the interpretation of the abridged life table functions, the life table for the U.S. population for 1996 is used as an example (Table 1).

$_nq_x$ is the probability of dying between exact age x and $x + n$. As shown in Table 1, the probability of dying in the first year of life is 0.00732. This is higher than at subsequent ages until age 60 to 65, when the probability of death is 0.06649.

l_x is the number of survivors reaching exact age x out of the original life table population. The size of the original life table population, the radix or l_o, is usually assumed to be 100,000; however, this is a convention and other values can be used. Mortality conditions in 1996 were such that out of 100,000 births, 99,268 would reach age 1. This column of the life table can be used to compute how many people who reach a given age will survive to a later age. For instance, among the 80,870 people who reach age 65, 33,629 people or 42 percent will reach age 85 with mortality conditions as shown in Table 1.

$_nd_x$ is the number of deaths in the life table population between exact age x and $x + n$.

Abridged Life Table: United States, 1996

Age Interval	Proportion Dying	Of 100,000 Born Alive		Stationary Population		Average Remaining Lifetime
Period of Life between Two Exact Ages Stated in Years	Proportion of Persons Alive at Beginning of Age Interval Dying during Interval	Number Living at Beginning of Age Interval	Number Dying during Age Interval	In the Age Interval	In This and All Subsequent Age Intervals	Average Number of Years of Life Remaining at Beginning of Age Interval
(1) X to $X+n$	(2) $_nq_x$	(3) l_x	(4) $_nd_x$	(5) $_nL_x$	(6) T_x	(7) $\overset{\circ}{e}_x$
Total						
0–1	0.00732	100,000	732	99,370	7,611,825	76.1
1–5	0.00151	99,268	150	396,721	7,512,455	75.7
5–10	0.00097	99,118	96	495,329	7,115,734	71.8
10–15	0.00118	99,022	117	494,883	6,620,405	66.9
15–20	0.00390	98,905	386	493,650	6,125,522	61.9
20–25	0.00506	98,519	499	491,372	5,631,872	57.2
25–30	0.00544	98,020	533	488,766	5,140,500	52.4
30–35	0.00710	97,487	692	485,746	4,651,734	47.7
35–40	0.00944	96,795	914	481,820	4,165,988	43.0
40–45	0.01283	95,881	1,230	478,549	3,684,168	38.4
45–50	0.01801	94,651	1,705	469,305	3,207,619	33.9
50–55	0.02733	92,946	2,540	458,779	2,738,314	29.5
55–60	0.04177	90,406	3,776	443,132	2,279,535	25.2
60–65	0.06649	86,630	5,760	419,530	1,836,403	21.2
65–70	0.09663	80,870	7,814	385,659	1,416,873	17.5
70–75	0.14556	73,056	10,634	339,620	1,031,214	14.1
75–80	0.21060	62,422	13,146	280,047	691,594	11.1
80–85	0.31754	49,276	15,647	207,474	411,547	8.4
85 and over	1.00000	33,629	33,629	204,073	204,073	6.1

Table 1

SOURCE: R. N. Anderson 1988 *United States Abridged Life Tables, 1996. National Vital Statistics Reports: From the Centers for Disease Control and Prevention, National Center for Health Statistics, National Vital Statistics System* 47(13):5. Hyattsville, Md.: National Center for Health Statistics.

In the sample life table, 732 of the 100,000 births would die between ages 0 and 1 and 7,814 would die between ages 65 and 70.

$_nL_x$ is the total number of years lived by the life table population between exact age x and $x + n$. Between birth and age 1, the life table population represented in Table 1 would live 99,370 years. This column also can be interpreted as the number of people in the stationary population at each year of age.

T_x is the total number of years lived after exact age x by the life table population surviving to age x, or the number of people in the stationary population age x and older. The 100,000 entrants to the life table in Table 1 would live a total of 7,611,825 years, and the 80,870 who reach age 65 would live a total of 1,416,873 more years.

$\overset{\circ}{e}_x$ is the expectation of life at exact age x or the average length of life remaining to be lived for the life table population which survives to exact age x. $\overset{\circ}{e}_x$ is computed from the T_x and l_x columns of the life table: $\overset{\circ}{e}_x = T_x/l_x$. As indicated earlier, at birth, the life table population in Table 1 has a life expectancy of 76.1 years.

DIFFERENTIALS IN LIFE EXPECTANCY

There are large differentials in life expectancy among demographic and socioeconomic groups in the United States. Males have lower life expectancies than females throughout the age range. Males' lower chances for a longer life are thought to result from a combination of biological differences and lifestyle factors. In 1996, $\mathring{e}_0$ was 73.1 for males and 79.1 for females (Anderson 1998). By age 50, the difference is narrowed to 4.3 years, with a life expectancy of 27.2 for men and 31.5 for women. At age 85, men can expect to live another 5.4 years, while women can expect to live 6.4 years.

There is also a significant difference in life expectancy between whites and African Americans in the United States. This is assumed to result primarily from the difference in socioeconomic status and accompanying life circumstances that exist between African Americans and whites in the United States. In 1996, life expectancy at birth was 76.8 for whites and only 70.2 for blacks. At age 65, white life expectancy was 17.6 years; while for blacks of that age, it was 15.8 years. At the oldest ages, a crossover in mortality rates by race has been observed in the past. After the age of crossover, African-American mortality rates are lower than white mortality rates. In 1987 this was true at ages above 83. In the past, this crossover has shown up repeatedly in comparisons of African-American and white mortality in the United States and has been attributed to the "survival of the fittest" among the black population (Manton and Stallard 1981). Recently, however, doubt has been raised as to whether the crossover is real or is a statistical artifact resulting from age misstatement by older African Americans in both the census and vital records of deaths (Coale and Kisker 1986; Elo and Preston 1994; Preston et al. 1996). Interestingly, Hispanics appear to have life expectancy values that are higher than non-Hispanic whites (Anderson et al. 1997).

INTERNATIONAL DIFFERENCES

In general, the life expectancy of a country is related to its level of socioeconomic development. Most countries that are classified as "more developed" have higher levels of life expectancy at birth than most of the countries classified as "developing"; however, within each of these groups of countries there is quite a bit of variability in life expectancy. While the United States has a high level of life expectancy compared to that of the developing countries of the world, the United States ranks quite low in life expectancy among

developed countries and relative to its income level. A recent United Nations listing of the developed countries by level of life expectancy at birth ranks U.S. males as nineteenth and U.S. females as fourteenth (United Nations 1997). The countries with higher life expectancy for women include Japan and the Scandinavian countries. For men, most European countries including some in southern Europe have higher life expectancies at birth than the United States. The low ranking of the United States is attributed, in part, to the inequities in mortality among subgroups of the population, especially the high level among African Americans, and also to the high level of violent deaths. In recent years Japan has become the world leader in life expectancy at birth with values of $\mathring{e}_0$ of 76.4 for men and 82.9 for women in 1995 (Ministry of Health and Welfare, Japan 1999). These values exceed 1996 U.S. values by 3.3 years for men and 3.8 years for women. The success of the Japanese in raising their levels of life expectancy has been due to large declines in mortality from cerebrovascular disease and maintenance of low levels of heart disease relative to other developed countries (Yanagishita and Guralnik 1988).

RELATED CONCEPTS

There are some other concepts that are related to life expectancy and are sometimes confused with life expectancy. One is "life span." The *life span* of a species is the age to which the longest-lived members survive. The life span of humans is thought to be approximately 115 years; however, Madame Jeanne Calment, whose age was well documented, died in 1997 at the age of 122. Current thinking is that while life expectancy has increased dramatically over the last century, the life span of humans has not changed over time; however, this does not mean it will never change. If discoveries are made in the future that enable us to retard the aging process, it may be possible to lengthen the human life span in the future.

"Life endurancy" is a related concept that, like life expectancy, is computed from the life table. This is the age at which a specified proportion of the life table entry cohort is still alive. For instance, in 1990 the age at which 0.1, or 10 percent, of the life table population remained alive was 90 years for men and 96 years for women. Life endurancy has been increasing over time and is expected to continue to change with changes in survival rates. In 1900 the 10 percent survival age was 81 and 82 for men and women, respectively (Faber and Wade 1983).

Finally, "healthy or active life expectancy" is a subset of total life expectancy. Total life expectancy at any age is the sum of two parts: healthy life expectancy and unhealthy life expectancy. While the concept of health life expectancy was introduced in the 1960s (Sanders 1964) and developed in the 1970s (Sullivan 1971a, 1971b), it has only become widely adapted by governments and international organizations in the 1990s.

Interest in healthy life expectancy has grown recently as people have recognized that gains in total life expectancy today may not mean the same thing as in the past. Past gains in life expectancy came about largely because fewer people died of infectious diseases, either because they did not get the diseases or they received treatment that prevented death. People thus saved from death were generally free of the disease. Under these circumstances gains in life expectancy were accompanied by better health in the population surviving. Now, with gains in life expectancy being made because of declining death rates from chronic diseases especially among the old, it is not clear that the surviving population is a healthier population. This is because generally there is no cure for the chronic diseases, and for many their onset has not yet been prevented. People may be saved from death but they live with disease. This is the basis for questioning whether the additions to life expectancy are healthy or unhealthy years.

Crimmins and colleagues (1997) estimated that healthy life expectancy or disability-free life expectancy at birth in the United States in 1990 was 58.8 years for men and 63.9 years for women. The difference between blacks and whites in disability-free life expectancy at birth was even greater than the difference in total life expectancy. In 1990 black disability-free life expectancy for males at age 20 was 37.9 years while that for whites was 45.8 years (Hayward and Heron 1999). Studies that addressed the issue of changes in healthy life expectancy for the 1970 and 1980 period generally found that when *healthy life* was defined as nondisabled life, active life expectancy had not increased (Wilkins and Adams 1983; Crimmins et al. 1989). More recent studies have found increases in active

life expectancy (Crimmins et al. 1997; Robine and Mormiche 1994).

Healthy life expectancy can be defined in many ways. Examples include average length of life free from a disability that causes a person to alter his or her normal activity; average length of life free of dependency on others for the performance of basic activities necessary to living, such as eating, bathing, and getting in and out of bed; and average length of life without disease (Bebbington 1988; Colvez et al. 1986; Crimmins et al. 1997; Crimmins et al. 1994; Rogers et al. 1989). Some measures of healthy life combine multiple indicators of health using weights; for instance, the U.S. National Center for Health Statistics measure combines self-assessed health and disability in its indicator of healthy life (Erickson et al. 1995).

There are multiple methodological approaches to estimating health expectancy. Most can be described under one of two headings: the Sullivan method or the multistate method (Sullivan 1971a; Schoen 1988). Microsimulation techniques have also been employed recently (Laditka and Wolf 1998).

REFERENCES

Anderson, R.N. 1998 *United States Abridged Life Tables, 1996. National Vital Statistics Reports: from the Centers for Disease Control and Prevention, National Center for Health Statistics, National Vital Statistics System*, 47(13). Hyattsville, Md.: National Center for Health Statistics.

——, K. D. Kochanek, and S. L. Murphy 1997 *Report of Final Mortality Statistics, 1995. Monthly Vital Statistics Report*, 45(11), suppl. 2. Hyattsville, Md.: National Center for Health Statistics.

Bebbington, A. C. 1988 "The Expectation of Life without Disability in England and Wales." *Social Science and Medicine* 27:321–326.

Coale, A. J., and E. E. Kisker 1986 "Mortality Crossovers: Reality or Bad Data?" *Population Studies* 40:389–401.

Colvez, A., J. M. Robine, D. Bucquet, F. Hatton, B. Morel, and S. Lelaidier 1986 "L'espérance de Vie Sans Incapacité en France en 1982." (Expectation of Life without Disability in France in 1982.) *Population* 41:1025–1042.

Crimmins, E. M., M. D. Hayward, and Y. Saito 1994 "Changing Mortality and Morbidity Rates and the Health Status and Life Expectancy of the Older Population." *Demography* 31:159–175.

Crimmins, E. M., Y. Saito, and D. Ingegneri 1989 "Changes in Life Expectancy and Disability-Free Life

Expectancy in the United States." *Population and Development Review* 15:235–267.

——— 1997 "Trends in Disability-Free Life Expectancy in the United States, 1970–1990." *Population and Development Review* 23:555–572.

Elo, I. T., and S. H. Preston 1994 "Estimating African-American Mortality from Inaccurate Data." *Demography* 31:427–458.

Erickson, P., R. Wilson, and I. Shannon 1995 "Years of Healthy Life." *Healthy People 2000: Statistical Notes* 7:1–15.

Faber, J., and A. Wade 1983 *Life Tables for the United States: 1900–2050*. Actuarial Study No. 89. Washington: U.S. Department of Health and Human Services, Social Security Administration, Office of the Actuary.

Hayward, M. D., and M. Heron 1999 "Racial Inequality in Active Life among Adult Americans." *Demography* 36:77–91.

Laditka, S. B., and D. A. Wolf 1998 "New Methods for Modeling and Calculation Active Life Expectancy." *Journal of Aging and Health* 10:214–241.

Manton, K. G., and E. Stallard 1981 "Methods for Evaluating the Heterogeneity of Aging Processes in Human Populations Using Vital Statistics Data: Explaining the Black/White Mortality Crossover by a Model of Mortality Selection." *Human Biology* 53:47–67.

Ministry of Health and Welfare, Japan 1999 "Abridged Life Tables for Japan, 1995." http://www.mhw.go.jp/english/database/lifetbl/part6.html.

Preston, S. H., I. T. Elo, I. Rosenwaike, and M. Hill 1996 "African-American Mortality at Older Ages: Results of a Matching Study." *Demography* 33:193–209.

Robine, J. M., and P. Mormiche 1994 "Estimation de la Valeur de l'Espérance de Vie Sans Incapacité en France en 1991." (Estimation of Expectation of Life without Disability in France in 1991.) *Les Français et Leur Santé* 1:17–36.

Rogers, R., A. Rogers, and A. Belanger 1989 "Active Life among the Elderly in the United States: Multistate Life Table Estimates and Population Projections." *Milbank Quarterly* 67:370–411.

Sanders, B. 1964 "Measuring Community Health Level." *American Journal of Public Health* 54:1063–1070.

Schoen, R. 1988 *Modeling Multigroup Population* New York: Plenum.

Sullivan, D. F. 1971a "A Single Index of Mortality and Morbidity." *HSMHA Health Reports* 86:347–354.

——— 1971b *Disability Components for an Index of Health. Vital and Health Statistics* 2 (42). Rockville, Md.: National Center for Health Statistics.

United Nations 1997 "Life Expectancy and Infant Mortality Rate, 1995–2000: Developed Regions." http://www.un.org/Depts/unsd/gender/3-1dev.htm.

U.S. Bureau of the Census 1975 *Historical Statistics of the U.S., Colonial Times to 1970. Bicentennial Edition. Part 2.* Washington, D.C.: U.S. Government Printing Office.

Vaupel, J. 1986 "How Change in Age-Specific Mortality Affects Life Expectancy." *Population Studies* 40:147–157.

Wilkins, R., and O. B. Adams 1983 "Health Expectancy in Canada, Late 1970s: Demographic, Regional, and Social Dimensions." *American Journal of Public Health* 73:1073–1080.

Yanagishita, M., and J. Guralnik 1988 "Changing Mortality Patterns that Led Life Expectancy in Japan to Surpass Sweden's: 1972–1982." *Demography* 25:611–624.

Yin, P., and M. Shine 1985 "Misinterpretations of Increases in Life Expectancy in Gerontology Textbooks." *Gerontologist* 25:78–82.

EILEEN M. CRIMMINS

LIFE HISTORIES AND NARRATIVES

The life history approach to social research and theory subsumes several methodological techniques and types of data. These include case studies, interviews, use of documents (letters, diaries, archival records), oral histories, and various kinds of narratives. The popularity of this approach has waxed and waned since the early 1900s. It was used extensively in the 1920s and 1930s and was identified with the Chicago sociology of W. I. Thomas, Robert Park, Clifford Shaw, and others. The succeeding generation of sociology witnessed the solidification of quantitative measurement techniques coupled with survey data collection, and the increased use of those approaches paralleled a relative decline in life history research. In the 1970s, however, there began a resurgence of interest in life history research not only in the United States but in Europe. The work of some sociologists, such as Howard S. Becker and Anselm Strauss, has maintained the early Chicago tradition, while newer generations of scholars—such as Norman Denzin and Michal McCall (United States), Ken Plummer (England), Daniel Bertaux (France), and Fritz Schütze (Germany)—have augmented life history research. This resurgence has been accompanied by the creation of Research Committee 38 (Biography and Society) of the International Sociological

Association in the late 1970s and has included a broadened interdisciplinary base through the incorporation of narrative theory and methods from other disciplines. In this broadened use there has been a transition from using the approach as purely a methodological device to using it as method, theory, and substance. It is this transition that frames this article.

The main assumptions of this approach are that the actions of individuals and groups are simultaneously emergent and structured and that individual and group perspectives must be included in the data used for analysis. Accordingly, any materials that reveal those perspectives can and should be regarded as essential to the empirical study of human social life. Life history materials, as described above (see Denzin 1989b, chap. 8; Plummer 1983, chap. 2; Gottschalk et al. 1945), contain first-, second-, and third-order accounts of past actions, as well as plans and expectations regarding future actions. Those materials will reveal significant information concerning the author's (writer and speaker) meanings. Invariably, these materials pertain also to the processual character of social life, and thus there is a major emphasis on temporal properties such as sequence, duration, and tempo. These assumptions and emphases have been characteristic of the vast majority of life history studies.

The first major empirical study in American sociology that systematically combined explicit theory and method was Thomas and Znaniecki's *The Polish Peasant in Europe and America* (1918–1920). The purpose of these researchers was to investigate Polish immigrants in America, especially their problems in adjusting to American urban life. The researchers used their famous attitude-value scheme as an explanatory framework. In this scheme, *attitudes* referred to individual subjective meanings and *values* to objective societal conditions. Thomas and Znaniecki proposed a set of causal explanations based on how the relations of attitudes and values were interpreted by individuals and groups. In their five-volume, 2,200-page work, they presented almost 800 pages of life history data in support of their conclusions and generalizations. The data included newspaper articles, letters to family members, records from courts and social work agencies, and a 300-page biography of one person that was presented as a representative case (Blumer 1939).

This research, which the Social Science Research Council in 1938 voted as the most outstanding in sociology to that date, depended solely on life history data. Because of its systematic incorporation of theory and method, it stimulated and became an exemplar for a long series of similar studies. These included research on race relations, delinquency, housing, mass media, migration, occupations, and other issues centered primarily in the areas of ethnic and urban studies (Bulmer 1984). The emphasis during this period was on the contributions of life history methods to sociology as an empirical and scientific discipline. Accordingly, researchers using this approach focused on methodological problems such as reliability, validity, hypothesis formation, and the making of generalizations, although comparatively less concern was given to sampling (Gottschalk et al. 1945). Reflecting the major issue of pre–World War II sociological work, the focus was on the adequacy of this approach for discovering lawlike behavior or empirically valid generalizations. The emphasis, in short, was on the approach as a research tool.

The developments in this approach since the early 1970s, perhaps stimulated in part by increased interest in historical sociology and in part by the articulation of insoluble problems in statistical approaches, have been more interdisciplinary, international, and sophisticated than the early works (McCall and Wittner 1990; Jones 1983; Roth 1987). It is increasingly recognized that all social science data, whether represented in discursive or numeric form, are interpretations (Denzin 1989a; Gephart 1988). This recognition is one of the central tenets of the narrative approach to social research (Fisher 1987; Reed 1989; Richardson 1990; Maines 1993), which makes the ontological claim that human beings are inherently storytellers. This shift in emphasis concerning the subject matter of sociology, in which human behavior is conceptualized as significantly communicative and narrative in nature, is precisely what has reframed the utility and potential of the life history approach.

Current uses of life history research display considerable variation as well as more precise conceptual distinctions. Terms such as *life story, biography, discourse, history, oral history, personal experience narratives, collective narratives,* and *sagas* are now distinguished from one another (Denzin 1989b, pp. 184–187), and frameworks for linking types of verbal accounts to types of generalizations have been developed (Sperber 1985, pp. 9–34). Moreover, these developments have occurred within and across different theoretical approaches and disciplines.

It is now common to regard life histories as a legitimate form of data in which currency is established through the propositions contained in narrative theory. Some of the uses found in contemporary work include the following. Schütze (1983) has developed what he calls the narrative interview. This approach focuses on establishing event sequences across the life course on the basis of interview data. These sequences are derived from detailed analyses of biographical materials, with special attention to the structural factors that have shaped the person's life. Analytical summaries are developed and, through analytical inductive procedures, are compared to subsequently developed summaries. The goal is to produce theoretical interpretations centering on various analytical interests such as life course transitions, career models, or natural histories. Riemann and Schütze (1991) provide a substantive application of this method in the area of chronic illness.

Bertaux (1981; Bertaux and Kohli 1984) has long been an advocate of life history research and was the primary organizer of the Biography and Society Section of the International Sociological Association. He has conducted a number of projects that have goals similar to those of Schütze. His collaborative research on social movements (1990), for example, used life history data from members of students movements in the United States, England, Ireland, Italy, West Germany, and France. There he shows the application of the method in large-scale comparative research projects. The epistemological approach was not to gather data on lived, biographical experiences of the activists but to analyze those data in collective, generic terms. That is, his strategy was to focus on similarities rather than differences across nations and to ground empirically theoretical statements about, for example, processes of commitment to social-movement ideologies. The contention of this research is that biographical and life history data from ordinary people will reveal those similarities and thus make contributions to cross-national research.

Dolby-Stahl (1989), a folklorist, has developed a variation of the life history approach. She calls it *literary folkloristics*, and it focuses on personal narrative data. She uses reader response theory to develop an interpretive method for studying the interdependence of personal narratives (stories) and collective narratives (e.g., ethnic group folklore). Her procedures entail locating the respondent (storyteller) in large collectivities (e.g., single parents), identifying salient themes (e.g., day care), and connecting personal to collective narratives (e.g., the respondent's accounts of day care and media or community accounts). The assumption of this approach is that personal and collective narratives are inherently connected, and thus a personal story is always in some way a collective story. Further, the assumption that the researcher in varying ways is part of the collective story requires facing the interpretive nature of data collection. In this respect, the researcher draws on her own shared cultural experiences to analyze the life history or narrative data provided by the respondent. These procedures locate the life history approach squarely in interpretive social theory, in which credible interpretation is the goal as opposed to, say, producing explanations justified by measures of reliability and validity.

Similarly, Denzin (1989a) has developed an interpretive approach that draws conceptually from postmodernism and phenomenology, and methodologically from Clifford Geertz's advocacy of thick description. He calls his method *interpretive biography*, and it is designed to study the turning points of problematic situations in which people find themselves during transition periods. Data include documents, obituaries, life histories, and personal experience stories, with the emphasis on how such information is read and used. The basic question he asks concerns how people live and give meaning to their lives, and how meaning is represented in written, narrative, and oral forms. His approach thus addresses an enduring problem in sociology, which C. Wright Mills located at the intersection of biography and history, as well as the newer problem articulated by interpretive theories regarding the interpretations of texts, cultural forms, and personal acts.

Most of the developments in the 1990s continue to be flamed largely under the rubric of narrative inquiry, signified by the 1991 inception of the *Journal of Narrative and Life History*. These recent lines of work can be organized loosely into four categories. First, there have been a considerable increase in substantive studies. Ezzy (1998) joins a rather large number of scholars (e.g., Angrosino 1995) studying narrative identity, which Orbuch (1997) moves more generically into the arena of accounts. Gubrium (1993) uses narrative data in his examination of quality of life among nursing home residents. Plummer (1995) uses similar data to study sexuality. Maines and Bridger (1992) studied the narrative character of land-use decisions. Randall (1999) has studied the narrative aspects of intelligence. Eheart and Power (1995) assess processes of success and failure in families with adopted children. Maines (1999) has provided data about how racial attitudes about justice are embedded in larger narrative structures. TenHouten (1999) has used life history interviews in a comparative analysis of temporality among Austrialian aborignies and Europeans.

These substantive topics overlap with the second line of work pertaining to historical sociology. Barry Schwartz (1996, 1997) has rekindled sociological interest in collective memory to show how historical processes contribute to changing cultural representations (see also Wertsch and O'Conner 1994). Another strand of work has pertained to causal analysis. Abbott (1992) articulated his version as *narrative positivism* which focuses on the properties of events and sequence to move quantitative sociology from the study of variables to the study of actual events. Griffin (1993) uses data on lynchings to propose a similar approach, utilizing computer-assisted event structure analysis that focuses directly on temporality. Gotham and Staples (1996) follow these studies with a theoretical analysis of narrative in the relations of agency and social structure, as does Berger (1995) in his analysis of Jewish Holocaust survivors. Mahoney (1999) addresses nominal, ordinal, and narrative dimensions of causal analysis, noting that "narrative analysis has the obvious strength of allowing the analyst to show sensitivity to detail, process, conjuncture, and causal complexity" (p. 1168).

The third area concerns methods of data collection and analysis. Holstein and Gubrium (1995) treat the interview as a social encounter that itself constructs the data gathered. In these encounters, respondents are regarded as narrators who tell the story of their "own past attitudes, feelings, and behaviors" (p. 32). McMahan and Rogers (1994) likewise present oral history interviewing as an interactive, negotiated process. They synthesize a large amount of materials about potential biases, and make concrete suggestions for developing skills to deal with them. On the other hand, Lieblich and associates (1998) present a model for analyzing life story data. Their model is composed of two continua: holistic versus categorical (whether a life story is taken as a whole or dissected into parts or categories) and content versus form (analysis of the substance or structure of life story accounts). This model is suggested as useful for guiding analyses for varying purposes. Mishler (1995) also addresses the diversity of narrative inquiry, and proposes a typology of narrative analyses. These include modes of analysis that focus on (1) the correspondence between temporal sequences of actual events and their textual representation, (2) how types of stories acquire structure and coherence, and (3) the content and function of stories. This typology organizes a large literature on narrative, and serves as a heuristic for discerning similarities and differences in analytical approaches and purposes. Finally, Atkinson (1998) describes procedures for the life story interview, whose "product is entirely a first-person narrative, with the researcher removed as much as possible from the text" (p. 2). These procedures would encourage respondents to see and tell their lives as a whole, and Atkinson has developed a growing archival data base of over 300 documents suitable for various analytical purposes.

The life story interview merges with the fourth line of work, which focuses on biographies and authbiographies. Smith (1994) provides an excellent overview of biographical methods. He begins with Charles Darwin's biography and brings the reader to contemporary issues that cut across various disciplines in the human sciences. In doing so, he emphasizes that biographical analysis remains an unfinished project that is filled with both conflict and creativity. Inside that space of conflict and creativity rests the new genre of *auto-ethnography*, or literally the study of oneself. Bochner and Ellis (1992) provide one of the more interesting instances of this approach. Each author was involved in the same first-time event. Wanting to fully explore the meaning of that event, they first wrote extensive personal accounts of it. Second, they shared those accounts with one another and with friends; and third, they wrote a joint account from the standpoint of their relationship. Through these procedures, they were able to preserve their own biographical perspectives on the event as well as depicting its intersubjective, consensual meanings.

The auto-ethnography stimulates attention to writing as a way of knowing, which is an issue widely discussed in the last decade among narrative scholars. Richardson (1994) discusses an array of issues pertaining to writing as inquiry, and then provides a detailed autobiographical account of how context affects writing (Richardson 1997). Her account includes her family, academic departments, networks of colleagues, and students, and shows how her relationships and experiences with these people were part and parcel of how and what she wrote as a professional sociologist. Her writing, she shows, was intimately tied to constructions of knowledge.

While Richardson and others illustrate what Polkinghorne (1988) has termed "narrative knowing" Diane Bjorklund (1998) treats autobiographies as sociological subject matter. She analyzed a sample of the 11,000 American autobiographies written from 1800 to 1980 to provide a historical analysis of representations of the self. She shows how social conventions and vocabularies for describing oneself have changed through four discernible eras of American history. By taking autobiographies seriously, this analysis powerfully locates the "texts" of personhood in cultural and social structural contexts.

Scholars working in the area of life history research accept that all social science data are made up of human interpretations and that nearly all such data are reconstructions or representations of past events and experiences. Because of its development of techniques for gathering, coding, and analyzing explicitly reconstructive data, the life history approach is suitable for studying not only the subjective phases of social life but the historical and structural aspects as well. It can be used for a wide variety of topics and purposes, ranging from research on the trajectories of personal biographies to organizational functioning to migration patterns. It invariably leads to development of theories emphasizing social processes. Recent scholarship on narrative has shown three dominant and related trends. The first, which represents an extension of the life history research of the 1920s, pertains to the linking of collective and personal narratives. The second, a departure from the earlier work, recognizes scholars as active narrators themselves and thus creators of narrative knowing. The third trend is the broad appeal of this area of work. It is found in all disciplines of the human sciences, it uses a wide variety of theoretical approaches, and it incorporates the array of analytical methods typical of sociological work found among American and European scholars.

(SEE ALSO: *Case Studies; Qualitative Methods*)

REFERENCES

Abbott, Andrew 1992 "From Causes to Events: Notes on Narrative Positivism." *Sociological Methods and Research* 20:428–455.

Angrosino, Michael 1995 "Metaphors of Ethnic Identity: Projective Life History Narratives of Trinidadians of Indian Descent." *Journal of Narrative and Life History* 5:125–146.

Atkinson, Robert 1998 *The Life Story Interview*. Thousand Oaks, Calif.: Sage.

Berger, Ronald 1995 "Agency, Structure, and Jewish Survival of the Holocaust: A Life History Study." *Sociological Quarterly* 36:15–36.

Bertaux, Daniel 1990 "Oral History Approaches to an International Social Movement." In Else Oyen, ed., *Comparative Methodology: Theory and Practice in International Social Research*. London: Sage.

——, ed. 1981 *Biography and Society: The Life-History Approach in the Social Sciences*. London: Sage.

——, and Martin Kohli 1984 "The Life-Story Approach: A Continental View." *Annual Review of Sociology* 10:149–167.

Bjorklund, Diane 1998 *Interpreting the Self: Two Hundred Years of American Autobiography*. Chicago: University of Chicago Press.

Blumer, Herbert 1939 *An Appraisal of Thomas and Znaniecki's "The Polish Peasant in Europe and America."* New York: Social Science Research Council.

Bochner, Arthur, and Carolyn Ellis 1992 "Personal Narrative as an Approach to Interpersonal Communication." *Communication Theory* 2:165–172.

Bulmer, Martin 1984 *The Chicago School of Sociology*. Chicago: University of Chicago Press.

Denzin, Norman 1989a *Interpretive Biography*. Newbury Park, Calif.: Sage.

—— 1989b *The Research Act*. Englewood Cliffs, N.J.: Prentice-Hall.

Dolby-Stahl, Sandra 1989 *Literary Folkloristics and the Personal Narrative*. Bloomington: Indiana University Press.

Eheart, Brenda Krause, and Martha Bauman Power 1995 "Adoption: Understanding the Past Present, and Future through Stories." *Sociological Quarterly* 36:197–216.

Ezzy, Douglas 1998 "Theorizing Narrative Identity: Symbolic Interactionism and Hermeneutics." *Sociological Quarterly* 39:239–252.

Fisher, Walter 1987 *Human Communication as Narrative.* Columbia: University of South Carolina Press.

Gephart, Robert 1988 *Ethnostatistics: Qualitative Foundations for Quantitative Research.* Newbury Park, Calif.: Sage.

Gotham, Kevin Fox, and William Staples 1996 "Narrative Analysis and the New Historical Sociology." *Sociological Quarterly* 37:481–501.

Gottschalk, Louis, Clyde Kluckhohn, and Robert Angell 1945 *The Use of Personal Documents in History, Anthropology, and Sociology.* New York: Social Science Research Council.

Griffin, Larry 1993 "Narrative, Event Structure, and Causal interpretation in Historical Sociology." *American Journal of Sociology* 98:403–427.

Gubrium, Jaber 1993 *Speaking of Life: Horizons of Meaning for Nursing Home Residents.* Hawthorne, N.Y.: Aldine de Gruyter.

Holstein, James, and Jaber Gubrium 1995 *The Active Interview.* Thousand Oaks, Calif.: Sage.

Jones, Gareth 1983 "Life History Methodology." In Gareth Morgan, ed., *Beyond Method: Strategies for Social Research.* Beverly Hills, Calif.: Sage.

Lieblich, Amia, Rivka Tuval-Mashiach, and Tamar Zilber 1998 *Narrative Research.* Thousand Oaks, Calif.: Sage

McCall, Michal, and Judith Wittner 1990 "The Good News about Life History." In Howard S. Becker and Michal McCall, eds., *Symbolic Interaction and Cultural Studies.* Chicago: University of Chicago Press.

McMahan, Eva, and Kim Lacy Rogers 1994 *Interactive Oral History Interviewing.* Hillsdale, N.J.: Lawrence Erlbaum.

Mahoney, James 1999 "Nominal, Ordinal, and Narrative Appraisal in Macrocausal Analysis." *American Journal of Sociology* 104:1154–1196.

Maines, David 1993 "Narrative's Moment and Sociology's Phenomena: Toward a Narrative Sociology." *Sociological Quarterly* 34:17–38.

—— 1999 "Information Pools and Racialized Narrative Structures." *Sociological Quarterly* 40:317–326.

——, and Jeffery Bridger 1992 "Narrative, Community, and Land Use Decisions." *Social Science Journal* 29:363–380

Mishler, Elliot 1995 "Models of Narrative Analysis: A Typology." *Journal of Narrative and Life History* 5:87–124.

Orbuch, Terri 1997 "People's Accounts Count: The Sociology of Accounts." *Annual Review of Sociology* 23:455–478.

Plummer, Ken 1983 *Documents of Life.* London: Allen and Unwin.

—— 1995 *Telling Sexual Stories: Power, Change, and Social Worlds.* London: Routledge

Polkinghorne, Donald 1988 *Narrative Knowing and the Human Sciences.* Albany: State University of New York Press.

Randall, William Lowell 1999 "Narrative Intelligence and the Novelty of Our Lives." *Journal of Aging Studies* 13:11–28.

Reed, John Sheldon 1989 "On Narrative and Sociology." *Social Forces* 68:1–14.

Richardson, Laurel 1990 "Narrative and Sociology." *Journal of Contemporary Ethnography* 19:116–135.

—— 1994 "Writing: A Method of Inquiry." In Norman Denzin and Yvonna Lincoln, eds., *Handbook of Qualitative Research.* Thousand Oaks, Calif.: Sage.

—— 1997 *Fields of Play: Constructing an Academic Life.* New Brunswick, N.J.: Rutgers University Press.

Riemann, Gerhard, and Fritz Schütze 1991 "Trajectory as a Basic Theoretical Concept for Analyzing Suffering and Disorderly Social Processes." In David R. Maines, ed., *Social Organization and Social Processes: Essays in Honor of Anselm Strauss.* Hawthorne, N.Y.: Aldine de Gruyter.

Roth, Paul 1987 *Meaning and Method in the Social Sciences.* Ithaca, N.Y.: Cornell University Press.

Schütze, Fritz 1983 "Biographieforschung und narratives Interview." *Neue Praxis* 3:283–293.

Schwartz, Barry 1996 "Memory as a Cultural System: Abraham Lincoln in World War II." *American Sociological Review* 61:908–927.

—— 1997 "Collective Memory and History: How Abraham Lincoln Became a Symbol of Racial Equality." *Sociological Quarterly* 38:469–496.

Smith, Louis 1994 "Biographical Method." In Norman Denzin and Yvonna Lincoln, eds., *Handbook of Qualitative Research.* Thousand Oaks, Calif.: Sage.

Sperber, Dan 1985 *On Anthropological Knowledge.* Cambridge, England: Cambridge University Press.

TenHouten, Warren 1999 "Text and Temporality: Patterned-Cyclical and Ordinary-Linear Forms of Time-Consciousness, Inferred from a Corpus of Australian

Aboriginal and Euro-Australian Life-Historical Interviews." *Symbolic Interaction* 22:121–137.

Thomas, W. I., and Florian Znaniecki 1918–1920 *The Polish Peasant in Europe and America*, 5 vols. Chicago: University of Chicago Press.

Wertsch, James, and Kevin O'Conner 1994 "Multivoicedness in Historical Representation: American College Students' Accounts of the Origin of the United States." *Journal of Narrative and Life History* 4:295–309.

DAVID R. MAINES

LIFE TABLES

See Demography; Life Expectancy.

LIFESTYLES AND HEALTH

Lifestyles are a major determinant of who shall live and who shall die (Fuchs 1974; McKinlay and Marceau 1999). Mechanic (1978, p. 164) argues that the concept of lifestyles refers to a diverse set of variables, including nutrition, housing, health attitudes and beliefs, risk-taking behavior, health behavior and habits, and preventive health behavior.

CONFIRMING THE LINK BETWEEN LIFESTYLES AND HEALTH

Establishing the causal linkage between lifestyles and health is not a simple task. Variables included in lifestyles interact with each other (Mechanic 1978), making it difficult to adjust for confounding variables such as race and ethnicity, gender, social class, and psychological distress.

In addition, there are problems in specifying the nature of the etiological relationship between lifestyles and disease. Not every person who engages in an unhealthy lifestyle will die prematurely. For example, some heavy smokers do not develop lung cancer. Genetic predisposition, comorbidities, other health habits, and access to adequate medical care are factors that may intervene in the relationship between host and disease. For certain conditions, it may be complicated to determine the precise role of risky lifestyle behaviors in the development of disease.

The most convincing models of the relationship between lifestyles and health are those built on triangulated evidence from animal, clinical, and epidemiological studies. As an example, consider the link between tobacco use and cancer. In controlled randomized trials using animal subjects that are genetically the same, the experimental group of animals is exposed to tobacco smoke while the control group is not. If the experimental group has a higher incidence of cancer than the control group, the study provides evidence to link tobacco smoke to cancer. Another strategy to link lifestyle behavior to health involves clinical studies with human subjects. Lung tissue of smokers is compared with lung tissue of nonsmokers. If more smokers than nonsmokers have cancerous cells in the lung tissue, this provides additional data to confirm that smoking causes lung cancer. A final strategy uses epidemiological methods. In prospective studies, separate groups of smokers and nonsmokers are followed over time to ascertain the risk of developing cancer within each group. All else being equal, if smokers develop more cases of cancer, the causal relationship between smoking and cancer is confirmed.

With these methodological issues in mind, four selected behaviors are used below to illustrate how lifestyles impact on health: tobacco use, alcohol consumption, diet, and sexual behavior and injection-related practices that increase the risk of acquiring the human immunodeficiency virus (HIV). For each behavior, extensive animal, clinical, and epidemiological data exist to support the causal relationship between each agent and disease. Gender differences in these behaviors are used to illustrate how lifestyles vary across social groups. Men are more likely to engage in these risky behaviors compared to women; this helps explain why women live longer than men do (Crose 1997). Finally, examples of successful efforts to change risky life-style behaviors are provided.

TOBACCO USE

Tobacco use has been defined as the most important single preventable cause of death and disease in society. Smoking causes an average of 430,700 deaths per year in the United States. One in every five deaths is smoking related (Centers for Disease Control and Prevention 1997a).

Careful epidemiological studies have determined that tobacco use increases the risks for heart disease, lung cancer, emphysema, and other lung diseases. Smoking during pregnancy increases the risk for premature births, complications of pregnancy, low-birthweight infants, stillbirths, and infant mortality. Fetuses exposed to smoke in utero and young infants exposed to secondhand smoke are at increased risk for sudden infant death syndrome, poor lung development, asthma, and respiratory infections (Centers for Disease Control and Prevention 1997b; Environmental Protection Agency 1992; Floyd et al. 1993). Secondhand smoke is also associated with adult illnesses (Centers for Disease Control and Prevention 1997a). Increased risks for lung cancer and heart disease are reported for nonsmokers who live with smokers.

Age-adjusted rates indicate that 27 percent of men smoked in 1995, compared to 23 percent of women (National Center for Health Statistics 1998). The gender gap used to be wider. In 1965, men were 1.5 times more likely to smoke than women were. Today, the gender difference is only 17 percent. The decline in cigarette smoking has been greater among men. While the prevalence of smoking among men dropped by almost half from 1965 to 1995, the rate for women dropped by only one-third. Traditionally, smoking by women was not condoned, but over time these attitudes have changed. As a result, the smoking rates for men and women are nearly the same. This translates into a 400 percent increase in deaths from lung cancer among women between 1960 and 1990 (Centers for Disease Control and Prevention 1997a).

Various prevention efforts have reduced the prevalence of smoking in the United States. Smokefree workplaces are the norm rather than the exception. Warning labels appear on cigarette packages, and billboards advertising cigarettes are banned. Community-based public education campaigns and worksite programs have been successful in smoking reduction (COMMIT Research Group 1995).

ALCOHOL

The National Institute on Alcohol Abuse and Alcoholism (NIAAA 1997) estimates that alcohol use is responsible for 100,000 deaths in year in this country. About 44 percent of the motor vehicle fatalities in 1994 were alcohol related (National Highway Traffic Safety Administration 1994). Alcohol use is frequently implicated in accidental injuries and deaths from falls, drowning, interpersonal and family violence, occupational hazards, and fires (NIAAA 1997).

From 10 to 20 percent of heavy drinkers develop cirrhosis of the liver, which was the tenth leading cause of death in the United States in 1996 (DeBakey et al. 1995; National Center for Health Statistics 1998). The liver is the primary site of alcohol metabolism, and drinkers are at risk for other forms of liver disease, including alcoholic hepatitis and cancer.

Heavy alcohol use causes loss in heart muscle contractile function, arrhythmias, degenerative disease of the heart muscle, and heart enlargement, and also increases the risk for hypertension and stroke. Alcohol is implicated in esophageal, breast, and colorectal cancer, and it may increase the risk for other types of cancer as well. NIAAA concludes, "The range of medical consequences of alcohol abuse is both immense and complex—virtually no part of the body is spared the effects of excessive alcohol consumption" (1990, p. 127).

Alcohol also functions as a teratogen, producing defects in the human fetus in utero. The possible effects of alcohol on the fetus include gross morphological defects as well as cognitive and behavioral dysfunctions. Alcohol ingestion during pregnancy causes a variety of birth defects, including fetal alcohol syndrome, alcohol-related birth defects, and alcohol-related neurodevelopmental disorder. Fetal alcohol syndrome is the most severe consequence of the mother's heavy drinking during pregnancy and is characterized by craniofacial anomalies, mental retardation, central nervous system dysfunction, and growth retardation. Fetal alcohol syndrome is one of the leading causes of preventable birth defects (Stratton et al. 1996).

Men are more likely to drink alcohol than women are. Twenty-two percent of men are lifetime abstainers from alcohol, versus 45 percent of women. About 56 percent of men are current drinkers, compared to 34 percent of women. Heavy drinking is gender related. Almost 12 percent of men average more than fourteen alcoholic drinks per week, compared to less than 4 percent of women (NIAAA 1998).

Various prevention efforts are directed toward decreasing alcohol consumption. The alcohol beverage warning label, implemented in 1989, warns drinkers about birth defects, drunk driving, operating machinery, and health problems; however, its impact has been modest. Other alcohol prevention programs have been implemented, including dram shop liability (servers are legally responsible for damage or injury caused by drunk patrons), training servers of alcohol to avoid selling to intoxicated persons and to minors, lowering the allowable blood alcohol concentration levels for drivers, changing the availability of alcohol, enforcing impaired driving laws, and designating one person in a car as the nondrinking driver. These community intervention programs have reduced alcohol-related traffic deaths significantly (NIAAA 1997).

DIET

Dietary factors have been linked to mortality from cardiovascular disease (heart disease and stroke) and cancer; these diseases are the leading causes of death in the United States. Diet affects four of the major risk factors for cardiovascular disease: hypertension, obesity, diabetes, and high cholesterol. Obesity, as well as diets high in saturated fats, trans fatty acids, and cholesterol, raise blood cholesterol concentration and blood pressure, thus increasing the risk for coronary heart disease and stroke. Diets low in saturated fats but high in fiber and some omega-3 fatty acids (found in walnuts, certain oils [fish, canola, soybean], and green leafy vegetables) lower the risk for heart disease (Hu et al. 1997; Ascherio et al. 1996).

Diet also affects cancer risk. While the link between dietary intake and breast cancer is controversial, there is evidence that a diet high in saturated fat plays an etiological role (Kolonel 1997; Hankin 1993). High fat intake increases the risk for prostate cancer, lung cancer, and colorectal cancer (Kolonel 1997). On the other hand, diets high in fruits, vegetables, and fiber lower the probability of developing various types of cancer, including breast, colorectal, stomach, and lung (Ziegler 1991; Hankin 1993).

Gender differences in diet and obesity exist. For example, women are more likely to be overweight compared to men (39 percent versus 36 percent). Among the poor, the gender gap is larger: 46 percent of poor women versus 31 percent of poor men suffer from obesity (National Center for Health Statistics 1998). Despite this increased risk for obesity, women consume healthier food than men do. While men consume more meat, saturated fat, and high-calorie foods, women eat more fruits, vegetables, whole grains, and lower-calorie foods (Crose 1997). Successful programs have been developed to encourage healthier eating habits for men and women, including interventions in worksites and families (Sorensen et al. 1999). The public has responded to these efforts, as evidenced by a 4 percent drop in blood cholesterol levels from 1978 to 1990 (National Heart, Lung, and Blood Institute 1996).

SEXUAL AND INJECTION-RELATED PRACTICES

The human immunodeficiency virus (HIV) causes acquired immune deficiency syndrome (AIDS), the eighth leading cause of death in the United States in 1996 (Peters et al. 1998). HIV is transmitted through blood products, bodily fluids, and breast milk. Transmission of HIV can be prevented by the use of safe sexual practices and sterile needles.

There are clear gender differences in the way AIDS is contracted, and the infection rate among women has been rising. Forty-eight percent of AIDS patients acquire the disease through male homosexual contact. Another 10 percent of AIDS cases appear in men who have sexual relations with a male or female partner and also use intravenous drugs. Almost 26 percent become ill solely through infected needles, and 6 percent through heterosexual contact that was not related to intravenous drug use. Among women, the most common route of infection is intravenous drug use (by herself or her partner), 60 percent or unprotected sex with an infected partner, 22 percent (Centers for Disease Control and Prevention 1998a).

While some HIV prevention programs promote abstention from sex and cessation of drug injecting, most programs define harm reduction as the goal (Kelly 1999). This policy promotes using condoms correctly on a consistent basis, having sex with uninfected partners, and cleaning needles with bleach or exchanging contaminated syringes for sterile ones.

Programs designed to decrease (1) the rate of unprotected anal sex among men who have sex with men and (2) the proportion of men having unprotected sex with multiple male partners contributed to the reduction in AIDS cases among homosexuals during the 1980s and early 1990s. However, 1997 data suggest that unprotected anal sex among gay men and unprotected sex with multiple partners is increasing, especially among younger gay men (Centers for Disease Control and Prevention 1999).

The second major mode of HIV transmission, especially among women, is by infected needles. Syringe exchange programs or the use of bleach to clean syringes prevent the spread of HIV among injecting-drug users. The number of syringe exchange programs has grown rapidly; 17.5 million needles were exchanged in 100 programs in 1997 (Centers for Disease Control and Prevention 1998b). Other communities have distributed bleach kits that reduce the spread of HIV (CDC AIDS Community Demonstration Projects Research Group 1999).

DISCUSSION

Four examples were selected to illustrate the role of lifestyles and health. There are other lifestyles that are related to health, which are beyond the scope of this article. For example, stressful lifestyles have been linked to mental illness, gastrointestinal illness, and heart disease. Regular use of seatbelts reduces the likelihood of death or injury in automobile accidents. Proper dental hygiene decreases the rate of dental caries. Childhood immunizations prevent measles, mumps, and polio.

When discussing lifestyles and health, several unresolved issues remain. First, the role of lifestyles in health is still evolving. As Becker (1993) argues, what is said to be bad for us one day may be determined to be good for us the next (and vice versa). For example, while researchers have documented the deleterious effects of alcohol on health, there is some recent evidence that red wine consumption may lower cholesterol levels (NIAAA 1997).

Second, there is continuing debate about the pros and cons of changing an individual's lifestyle versus changing the social milieu (Kelly 1999). Should we invest in programs designed to encourage an individual to stop smoking? Is it better to develop strategies that change societal norms about the acceptability of smoking? Should we do both?

Third, policy makers note that healthy lifestyle programs must be tailored to the individual, the subgroup (gender, age, race or ethnicity, and social class) and the particular community at risk (Kelly 1999). Thus, designing successful interventions to alter lifestyles is challenging.

Finally, it must be emphasized that that while a healthy lifestyle may be a necessary condition for longevity; it is not a sufficient condition. Many variables interact with lifestyles to protect against disease and death. For example, evidence is mounting that genetic predispositions are very important in the etiology of certain diseases. Thus, the models predicting who shall live and who shall die involve complicated interactions of lifestyles, preventive health behavior, genetic risk, sociodemographic characteristics, and so on. Nonetheless, individuals who abstain from smoking and injecting drugs, drink alcohol in moderation, reduce the intake of saturated fat and cholesterol, and use safe sex practices have a better chance of survival than those who eat and drink excessively and do not follow recommended safe sex practices.

REFERENCES

Ascherio, Alberto, Eric B. Rimm, Edward L. Giovannuccci, Donna Spiegelman, Meir Stampfer, and Walter C. Willett 1996 "Dietary Fat and Risk of Coronary Heart Disease in Men: Cohort Follow Up Study in the United States." *British Medical Journal* 313:84–90.

Becker, Marshall 1993 "A Medical Sociologist Looks at Health Promotion." *Journal of Health and Social Behavior* 34:1–6.

Centers for Disease Control AIDS Community Demonstration Projects Research Group 1999. "Community-Level HIV Intervention in 5 Cities: Final Outcome Data from Demonstration Projects." *American Journal of Public Health* 89:336–345.

Centers for Disease Control and Prevention 1997a *Facts about Cigarette Mortality.* Atlanta, Ga.: CDC, May 23.

—— 1997b *Fact Sheet, Smoking and Pregnancy*, Atlanta, Ga.: CDC, November 7.

—— 1998a *HIV/AIDS Surveillance Report*, No. 10. Atlanta, Ga.: CDC.

—— 1998b "Update: Syringe Exchange Programs—United States, 1997." *Morbidity and Mortality Weekly Report* 47:652–655.

—— 1999 "Increases in Unsafe Sex and Rectal Gonorrhea among Men Who Have Sex with Men—San Francisco, California, 1994–1997." *Morbidity and Mortality Weekly Report* 48:45–48.

COMMIT Research Group 1995 "Community Intervention Trial for Smoking Cessation (COMMIT): I. Cohort Results from a Four Year Community Intervention." *American Journal of Public Health* 85:183–192.

Crose, Royda 1997 *Why Women Live Longer than Men . . . and What Men Can Learn from Them*. San Francisco: Jossey-Bass.

DeBakey, S. F., F. S. Stinson, B. F. Grant, and M. C. Dufour 1995 *Liver Cirrhosis Mortality in the US 1970–1992*, Surveillance Report No. 37. Rockville, Md.: NIAAA Division of Biometry and Epidemiology.

Environmental Protection Agency, Office of Research and Development 1992 *Respiratory Health Effects of Passive Smoking*, EPA/600/6-90/006F. Washington, D.C.: EPA.

Floyd, R. L., B. K. Rimer, G. A. Giovano, P. D. Mullen, and S. E. Sullivan 1993 "A Review of Smoking in Pregnancy: Effects on Pregnancy Outcomes and Cessation Efforts." *Annual Review of Public Health* 14:379–411.

Fuchs, Victor 1974 *Who Shall Live? Health Economics and Social Change*. New York: Basic Books.

Hankin, Jean H. 1993 "Role of Nutrition in Women's Health: Diet and Breast Cancer." *Journal of the American Dietetic Association* 93:994–999.

Hu, Frank B., Meir J. Stampfer, JoAnn E. Manson, Eric Rimm, Graham A. Colditz, Bernard A. Rosner, Charles H. Hennekens, and Walter C. Willett 1997 "Dietary Fat Intake and the Risk of Coronary Heart Disease in Women." *New England Journal of Medicine* 337:1491–1499.

Kelly, Jeffrey A. 1999 "Community-Level Interventions Are Needed to Prevent New HIV Infections." *American Journal of Public Health* 89:299–301.

Kolonel, Laurence N. 1997 "Fat and Cancer: The Epidemiologic Evidence in Perspective." Pp. 1–19 in American Institute for Cancer Research, ed., *Dietary Fat and Cancer*. New York: Plenum.

McKinlay, John B., and Lisa D. Marceau 1999 "A Tale of 3 Tails." *American Journal of Public Health* 89:295–298.

Mechanic, David 1978 *Medical Sociology*, 2nd ed. New York: Free Press.

National Center for Health Statistics 1998 *Health, United States, 1998 with Socioeconomic Status and Health*, DHHS Pub. No. 98-1232. Hyattsville, Md.: Centers for Disease Control and Prevention.

National Heart, Lung, and Blood Institute 1996 *Facts about Blood Cholesterol*, NIH Pub. No. 94-2696. Bethesda, Md.: U.S. Department of Health and Human Services.

National Highway Safety Administration 1994 *Traffic Safety Facts 1994: A Compilation of Motor Vehicle Crash Data from the Fatal Accident Reporting System and the General Estimates System*. DOT HS 808 169. Washington, D.C.: Department of Transportation National Center for Statistics and Analysis.

National Institute on Alcohol Abuse and Alcoholism 1990 *Seventh Special Report to the U.S. Congress on Alcohol and Health*, DHHS Pub. No. (ADM) 90-1656. Rockville, Md.: U.S. Department of Health and Human Services.

—— 1997 *Ninth Special Report to the U.S. Congress on Alcohol and Health*. DHHS Pub. No. (ADM) 97-4017. Rockville, Md.: U.S. Department of Health and Human Services.

—— 1998 *Drinking in the United States: Main Findings from the 1992 National Longitudinal Alcohol Epidemiologic Survey*. DHHS Pub. No. 99-3519. Bethesda, Md.: U.S. Department of Health and Human Services.

Peters, Kimberley D., Kenneth D. Kochanek, and Sherry L. Murphy 1998 *Deaths: Final Data for 1996; National Vital Statistics Report*, vol. 47, no. 9. Atlanta, Ga.: U.S. Department of Health and Human Services, Centers for Disease Control and Prevention, National Center for Health Statistics.

Sorensen, Glorian, Anne Stoddard, Karen Peterson, Nancy Cohen, Mary Kay Hunt, Evelyn Stein, Ruth Palombo, and Ruth Lederson 1999 "Increasing Fruit and Vegetable Consumption through Worksites and Families in the Treatwell 5-A-Day Study." *American Journal of Public Health* 89:54–60.

Stratton, Kathleen, Cynthia Howe, and Frederick Battaglia, eds. 1996 *Fetal Alcohol Syndrome: Diagnosis, Epidemiology, Prevention, and Treatment*. Washington, D.C.: National Academy Press.

Ziegler, Regina G. 1991 "Vegetables, Fruit, and Carotenoids and the Risk of Cancer." *American Journal of Clinical Nutrition* 53:251S–295S.

JANET HANKIN

LINGUISTICS

See Sociolinguistics.

LITERATURE AND SOCIETY

Interest in the relationship between literature and society is hardly a new phenomenon. We still read and refer to the ancient Greeks in this regard. In *The Republic*, for example, Plato presages both Mme. de Staël's treatise of 1800, which was the first to discuss cross-national differences in literature, and later notions of literary reflection with his idea of imitation. What is new, however, is the relative legitimacy of the study of literature within the discipline of sociology. This is due both to the increasing interest in culture in sociology after years of marginalization (Calhoun 1989) and to the increasing influence of cultural studies on sociology and throughout the academy.

A broader interest in and acceptance of cultural sociology has meant that the types of research questions and methods common to sociological studies of literature are now more widely accepted within the field. Sociology has extended its methodological boundaries in response to both attacks on the dominance of positivism and the rising power of alternative stances suggested by postmodernism. At the same time, changes in the goals, and sometimes the methods, of studying literature sociologically have moved the area closer to what is still the mainstream of the discipline. Thus the sociology of literature has benefited from a twofold movement in which (1) sociology as a discipline has become more interested in and accepting of research questions pertaining to meaning (cf. Wuthnow 1987, however, for a particularly strong attack on meaning from within the culture camp) and employing qualitative methods; and (2) the sociology of literature has evolved in the direction of more mainstream sociological areas through the merging of quantitative with qualitative methods and of empirical with hermeneutic research questions.

TRADITIONAL APPROACHES

As recently as 1993, Wendy Griswold maintained that the sociology of literature was a "nonfield" and "like an amoeba . . . lack[ing] firm structure" (1993, p. 455). Certainly the sociology of literature has been a marginal area in the discipline of sociology. As such, it has generally failed to attract the kind of career-long commitments common to

more central areas of the discipline. Many scholars writing on the sociology of literature see the area as a sideline and produce only a single book or article on the subject. This has exacerbated the lack of structure in the development of the field. Even so, it is surprising just how much sociological research has been done on literature and on literature's relationship to social patterns and processes.

Reflection Theory. Traditionally, the central perspective for sociologists studying literature has been the use of literature as information about society. To a much lesser degree, traditional work has focused on the effect of literature in shaping and creating social action. The former approach, the idea that literature can be "read" as information about social behavior and values, is generally referred to as *reflection theory*. Literary texts have been variously described as reflecting the "economics, family relationships, climate and landscapes, attitudes, morals, races, social classes, political events, wars, [and] religion" of the society that produced the texts (Albrecht 1954, p. 426). Most people are familiar with an at least implicit reflection perspective from journalistic social commentary. For instance, when *Time* magazine put the star of the television show *Ally McBeal* on its cover, asking "Is Feminism Dead?" (1998), it assumed that a television show could be read as information on Americans' values and understanding of feminism.

Unfortunately, "reflection" is a metaphor, not a theory. The basic idea behind reflection, that the social context of a cultural work affects the cultural work, is obvious and fundamental to a sociological study of literature. But the metaphor of reflection is misleading. Reflection assumes a simple mimetic theory of literature in which literary works transparently and unproblematically document the social world for the reader. In fact, however, literature is a construct of language; its experience is symbolic and mediating rather than direct. Literary realism in particular "effaces its own status as a sign" (Eagleton 1983, p. 136; see also Candido [1995, p. 149] on the "liberty" of even naturalist authors). Literature draws on the social world, but it does so selectively, magnifying some aspects of reality, misspecifying others, and ignoring most (Desan et al. 1989). The reflection metaphor assumes a single and stable meaning for literary texts. Anyone who has ever argued about what a book "really" meant knows what researchers have worked hard to demonstrate—textual meaning is contingent, created by active readers with their own expectations and life experiences that act in concert with inherent textual features to produce variable meanings (Jauss 1982; Radway 1984; Griswold 1987).

Despite repeated demonstrations of reflection's myriad failings (e.g., Noble 1976; Griswold 1994; Corse 1997), the idea of literature as a mirror of society still seems a fundamental way of thinking about why sociologists—and indeed many other people as well—are interested in literature. A relatively crude reflection approach remains common for teaching sociology department courses on literature, and also in certain types of journal articles whose main interest is not the sociology of literature per se, but the illumination of some sociological theory or observation through literary "evidence" (e.g., Corbett's article [1994] advocating the use of novels featuring probation officers to teach courses on the sociology of occupations, or the continuing stream of articles examining gender portrayals in children's literature [e.g., Grauerholz and Pescosolido 1989]). Convincing research arguing for literary evidence of social patterns now requires the careful specification of how and why certain social patterns are incorporated in literature while others are not (e.g., Lamont 1995), thorough attention to comparative data across either place or time (e.g., Long 1985), and a detailed consideration of the processes that transform the social into the literary (e.g., Corse 1997).

Structural Reflection. A more sophisticated but still problematic type of reflection argues that it is the form or structure of literary works rather than their content that incorporates the social: "successful works . . . are those in which the form exemplifies the nature of the social phenomenon that furnishes the matter of the fiction" (Candido 1995, p. xiii). The "humanist" Marxist Georg Lukács is perhaps the seminal figure in the development of a Marxist literary sociology. Marxism is the only one of the three major strands of classical theory to have generated a significant body of work on literature. Lukács (1971) argued that it is not the content of literary works but the categories of thought within them that reflect the author's social world.

Goldmann (1964, 1970), Lukács's most prominent student and the one most influential for American sociology, proposed the concept of a homologous relationship between the inherent structure of literary works and the key structures of the social context of the author. Goldmann justified his focus on the canonical works he studied by arguing that lesser works fail to achieve the necessary clarity of structure that allows the sociologist to see the homologies present in works by, for example, Racine and Pascal (1964). In the 1960s Louis Althusser challenged the preeminence of Lukács's tradition through, in part, his emphasis on the autonomy of literature. Thus Goldmann's work, though it was influential at the time of its publication, has been eclipsed as newer theories have made more problematic the notion that literature embodies a single meaning that is reducible to an expression of class consciousness.

The High Culture/Popular Culture Divide. Traditionally in the United States sociologists have left the study of high culture to specialists in literature, art, and music. This attitude was partially a product of sociologists' discomfort with aesthetic evaluation. Popular culture, on the other hand, was seen as simply unworthy of attention or study. To the extent that sociologists did consider literature, they tended to focus on high-culture literature, in part because of the largely Marxist orientation of many early sociologists of literature. Marxist thought defines literature as part of the ideological superstructure within which the literatures of elites are the ruling ideas since culture serves to legitimate the interests of the ruling class.

The tendency to concentrate on high-culture literature was intensified by the Frankfurt School, which understood "mass" culture as a destructive force, imposed on a passive audience by the machinery of a capitalist culture "industry" (e.g., Horkheimer and Adorno 1972). Lowenthal's ([1961] 1968) analysis of popular magazine biography, for example, stressed the increasing focus on leisure-time consumption over production and on personality over business and political achievement, as the private lives of movie stars and sports figures came to dominate magazine biographies. This approach highlighted the passivity and docility of audiences, tying mass culture to the increasing apathy of the public. Thus this work saw literature both as a reflection of changing social patterns and as a force shaping those patterns. Although researchers now rarely use the term "mass" culture, the Frankfurt School's critique continues to inform much of current cultural sociology, although often it does so on an implicit level as researchers react either positively or negatively to this understanding of popular culture.

One response to the critique of mass culture was articulated by the scholars of the Birmingham School. This line of research shared earlier understandings of culture as a resource for the powerful, but focused in large part on the potential for active participation on the part of cultural receivers. Work in the Birmingham School tradition drew heavily on feminist approaches and demonstrated how "mass" audiences of popular cultural forms might engage in resistance, undermining earlier arguments of cultural hegemony and of passive cultural "dopes" (e.g., Hall et al. 1980; Hebdige 1979). This interest in resistance and the meaning-making activity of readers remains an important line of research, particularly for studies of popular culture (e.g., Radway 1984). The continued relevance of the distinction between high and popular culture, however, is now under debate, as some charge that the hierarchical dichotomy is no longer the most powerful conceptualization of cultural differences (e.g., Crane 1992; DiMaggio 1987).

Sociology through Literature. A final type of traditional sociological interest in literature also stems from an implicit reflectionist approach. This type of work sees literature as exemplary of sociological concepts and theories or uses literature simply as a type of data like any other. While Coser's (1972) anthology exemplifies the former tradition, the recent ASA publication *Teaching Sociology with Fiction* demonstrates the persistence of the genre. Examples of the latter are altogether too numerous, including, for example, an article testing recent Afrocentric and feminist claims of differing epistemological stances across genders and races by coding differences in the grounding of knowledge in novels for adolescent readers (Clark and Morris 1995). Such work ignores ignoring the mediated nature of literary "reality." These discussions, although common, are not properly part of the sociology of literature.

SOCIOLOGICAL ADVANCES

The 1980s saw the institutionalization of sociological studies of cultural objects and processes as most prominently indicated by the establishment of the Culture Section of the American Sociological Association (ASA)—now one of the largest sections of the ASA with over one thousand members. This groundswell of interest in culture did not produce an equally large increase in interest in the sociology of literature, but it certainly created a more favorable climate for such work, as well as reenergizing research within the field.

Wendy Griswold is the key figure in the contemporary sociological study of literature in the United States. Her early research (1981, 1983, 1987) set the stage for a new synthesis that both takes seriously the issue of literary meaning and recognizes the importance of extratextual variables, while deploying the empirical data demanded by much of the discipline. By balancing these often-competing claims, Griswold allows for a study of literature that is sociological in the deepest sense of the word. Her concern for what she has called a "provisional, provincial positivism" (1990, p. 1580) has legitimated the sociology of literature to other sociologists and has articulated to nonsociologists the unique power of literary sociology. By publishing repeatedly in *American Journal of Sociology* and in *American Sociological Review*, Griswold made the sociology of literature visible to an extent previously unknown.

Griswold's work (1981) began with a critique of reflection theory's exclusive focus on "deep" meaning, demonstrating the importance of production variables such as copyright legislation for explaining the diversity of books available in a market. A second project (1983, 1986) investigated the determinants of cultural revival, arguing that Elizabethan plays are revived most frequently when the social conditions of the day resonate with those the plays originally addressed. In 1987, Griswold published the results of a third project centrally located in the new reception of culture approach. This innovative work used published reviews as data on reception, thus allowing Griswold (1987) to address reception across time and across three very diverse audiences—an impossible strategy in the first instance and a prohibitively expensive strategy in the second when using interviews to gather data on audience interpretation. The 1990s saw Griswold (1992) beginning a large-scale project on the literary world of Nigeria, a project that returned Griswold to her initial interest in nationalism and literature among other concerns.

Griswold's impact on the sociology of literature has been powerful because she has systematically developed a methodological approach to studying literature and other cultural products and because her substantive research integrates a concern for meaning and the unique properties inherent in literary texts with an equal interest in social context, in the actors, institutions, and social behaviors surrounding texts.

Griswold's concern for the integration of literary content with social context is shared by many. Janet Wolff, although she works primarily in visual arts rather than literature, has repeatedly challenged sociological students of culture to take content and aesthetics seriously, allying these concerns with their traditional specialty in social context and history (e.g., 1992; see also Becker in Candido 1995, p. xi). Priscilla Parkhurst Clark/ Ferguson (e.g., 1987) has written extensively on the literary culture of France, combining a study of specific works and authors with detailed analyses of literary institutions and social processes, in addition to her normative writings on improving the sociology of literature (1982). Corse (1995, 1997) combines a detailed reading of three types of American and Canadian novels with a historical consideration of the two nations' canon development and a survey of the respective publishing industries to create a full picture of cross-national literary patterns and the explanation thereof. These works draw upon several important new approaches developed in the last twenty years.

The Production of Culture. The production of culture approach was the earliest of the new paradigms reinvigorating the study of culture in sociology. It stemmed from the growing interest of several prominent organizational sociologists in the sociology of culture (e.g., Hirsch 1972; Peterson 1976). These scholars made the now obvious insight that cultural objects are produced and distributed within a particular set of organizational and institutional arrangements, and that these arrangements mediate between author and audience and influence both the range of cultural products available and their content. Such arguments stand in stark contrast to earlier nonsociological conceptions of artistic production that featured artists as romantic loners and inspired geniuses with few ties to the social world. Art, in this view, is the product of a single artist and the content of

artistic works and the range of works available are explained by individual artistic vision. Becker's influential *Art Worlds* (1982) effectively refuted such individualistic conceptions of cultural producers, at least in sociological research. Researchers in the production of culture tradition have showed conclusively that even the most antisocial artistic hermits work within an art world that provides the artistic conventions that allow readers to decode the work. Artists are free to modify or even reject these conventions, but the conventions are a crucial component of the work's context. Art worlds also provide the materials, support personnel, and payment systems artists rely upon to create their works.

The social organization of the literary world and the publishing industry became obvious focuses for sociological investigations, from the production-of-culture approach. Walter W. Powell initiated a major research project with his dissertation, which was followed by his work on *Books: The Culture and Commerce of Publishing* (Coser et al. 1982) and *Getting into Print* (Powell 1985). This stream of research demonstrates how production variables, such as the degree of competition in the publishing industry, the web of social interactions underlying decisions about publication, and the fundamental embeddedness of publishing in particular historical and social circumstances, affect the diversity of books available to the public.

Peterson (1985) outlines six production factors constraining the publishing industry. Berezin (1991) demonstrates how the Italian facist regime under Mussolini shaped the theatre through bureaucratic production. Long (1986) situates the concern with economic concentration in the publishing industry in a historical perspective, and argues that a simple relationship between concentration and "massification" is insufficient for understanding contemporary publishing. Similarly, although as part of larger projects, Radway (1984), Long (1985), and Corse (1997) analyze the publishing industry and its changes as a backdrop for an understanding of particular literary characteristics. Radway traces the rise of mass-market paperbacks and the marketing of formulaic fiction to help explain the success of the romance genre (1984; chapter 1). Long (1985; chapter 2) acknowledges the importance of post World War II changes in the publishing houses and authorial demographics in her analysis of the changing visions of success enshrined in best-selling novels, although she grants primary explanatory power to changes in the broader social context. Corse (1997, chapter 6) provides a cross-national study of Canada and the United States, arguing that the publishing industry in the latter dominates the former because of market size and population density. Canada's publishing industry has become largely a distributive arm of the American publishing industry, despite governmental subsidies and other attempts to bolster Canadian publishing. The result is that American novels dominate the Canadian market (Corse 1997, pp. 145–154).

One important focus of production approaches is gender. Tuchman (1989) analyzes the movement of male authors into the previously female-dominated field of British novel publishing during the late 1800s as the field became increasingly remunerative. Rogers (1991), in her ambitious attempt at establishing a phenomenology of literary sociology, notes the gendered construction of both writers and readers. Rosengren's (1983) network analysis of authorial references in book reviewing demonstrates, among other suggestive findings, the persistence of the literary system's underrepresentation of female authors.

Reception Theory and the Focus on Audience. A second fundamental shift in the sociology of literature occurred as sociologists became familiar with the work of German reception theorists. Reception theory, and several other strains of similar work, shifted scholarly attention to the interaction of text and reader. The central figures in Germany in the late 1960s and 1970s were Hans Robert Jauss and Wolfgang Iser. In *Toward an Aesthetic of Reception* (1982) Jauss presents his main argument: that literature can be understood only as a dialectical process of production and reception in which equal weight is given to the text and the reader. Iser's (1978) central focus is the act of reading itself.

Janice Radway's (1984) seminal *Reading the Romance* introduced reception theory with its central interest in audience interpretation to many American sociologists, as well as to many scholars in related fields. To those already familiar with the work of reception theorists, Radway's work powerfully demonstrated the potential of reception approaches for the sociology of literature. Radway's

interviews with "ordinary" readers of genre romance novels (1984) uncovered multiple interpretations, instances of resistance, and fundamental insights into literary use and gender in a genre previously scorned as unworthy of serious scholarly attention.

Reception theory has generated a fruitful line of research in the sociology of literature. Long (1987) has examined women's reading groups and their acceptance or rejection of traditional cultural authority in the selection and interpretation of book choices. Howard and Allen (1990) compare the interpretations made by male and female readers of two short stories in an attempt to understand how gender affects reception. Although they find few interpretive differences based solely on gender, they find numerous differences based on "life experience" and argue that gender affects interpretation indirectly through the "pervasive gender-markings of social context" (1990, p. 549). DeVault (1990) compares professional readings to her own reading of a Nadine Gordimer novel to demonstrate both the collective and the gendered nature of reception. Lichterman (1992) interviewed readers of self-help books to understand how such books are used as what he describes as a "thin culture" that helps readers with their personal lives without requiring any deep personal commitment to the book's advice.

Griswold (1987) innovatively applied the reception perspective to a study of the cross-national range of published reviews of a single author, generating another fruitful line of research. Bayma and Fine (1996) analyze 1950s reviews of Vladimir Nabokav's *Lolita* to demonstrate how cultural stereotypes of the time constructed reviewers' understandings of the novel's protagonist. Corse and Griffin (1997) analyze the history of reception of Zora Neale Hurston's *Their Eyes Were Watching God*, analyzing the different positionings of the novel over time and detailing how various "interpretive strategies" available to critics construct the novel as more or less powerful.

Stratification. One final area of growth centers on the relationship between cultural products and stratification systems. Perhaps the central figure is Pierre Bourdieu (1984, 1993), whose analyses of class-based differences in taste, concepts of cultural capital and habitus, and examination of the distinction between the fields of "restricted" and "large-scale" production have profoundly affected sociological thinking. Bourdieu (1984) has demonstrated how constructed differences in capacities for aesthetic judgment help reproduce the class structure. This fundamentally affects the conditions under which types of culture are produced, interpreted, and evaluated (1993). Bourdieu's theoretical insights have inspired many researchers, although few work in literary sociology directly. For example, Corse (1997) examined the use of high-culture literature in elite programs of nation building, Halle (1992) investigated class variations in the display of artistic genres in the home, and DiMaggio and Mohr (1985) correlated cultural capital and marital selection. Cultural consumption and use are also stratified across categories other than class, for example, gender, race, and ethnicity. These categories have received even less attention than class in the sociology of literature, although some work has been done in gender (e.g., Simonds and Rothman 1992; Wolff 1990; Radway 1984).

Bourdieu, among others, has also highlighted the need for sociological understanding of aesthetic evaluation as a social process and for a recognition of the contested nature of the cultural authority manifested in aesthetic judgments (e.g., DiMaggio 1991). Although this is not a new point (e.g., Noble 1976), sociology is finally coming to terms with literary evaluations and the codified hierarchy of value as objects of sociological attention (Lamont 1987; Corse and Griffin 1997; Corse 1997).

International Approaches. Obviously much of the material discussed so far is international, primarily European, in origin. European social theory has always been part of American sociology—the "fathers" of sociology are, after all, European—but there are cycles of more and less cross-fertilization. Historically, European sociologists certainly evinced greater interest in the sociology of literature than did their American counterparts; an example is the ongoing series of articles in *The British Journal of Sociology* debating the state of literary sociology (e.g., Noble 1976). The reasons for European sociology's greater interest in the sociology of literature are several: the relatively greater influence of Marxist and neo-Marxist traditions; methodological differences that legitimate

qualitative and hermeneutic traditions; and the tighter link between sociology and the humanities compared to the "science-envy" and concomitant embrace of positivism characterizing much of American sociology.

These historical differences have at least residual remains. Marxist and hermeneutic approaches and methods more reminiscent of the humanities are still more prevalent in Europe. For example, there is greater acceptance of work looking at a single novel, an approach rarely seen in American sociology (e.g., Wahlforss's 1989 discussion of the success of a best-selling Finnish love story). Differences have decreased, however, primarily from the American embrace of European theories and methods rather than from the opposite movement.

One important group in the sociology of literature also proves a major exception to the historic differences in method between American and European sociologies of literature. The Marketing and Sociology of Books Group at Tilburg University in the Netherlands specializes in an institutional approach to understanding "the functioning of literary and cultural institutions . . . [and] the various aspects of consumer behavior towards books and literary magazines" (Verdaasdonk and van Rees 1991, p. 421; see also, for example, Janssen 1997). The group includes Cees van Rees, editor of the journal *Poetics*, which lives up to its subtitle— *Journal of Empirical Research on Literature, the Media and the Arts*. The International Association for the Empirical Study of Literature (IGEL) sponsors an annual conference concentrating on such work (see Ibsch et al. 1995).

BROADER IMPLICATIONS

The sociology of literature has implications for wider social issues. In the debate over the opening of the canon—the question of what should be considered "great literature" and therefore required in school—people on both sides assume that reading X is different in some important way than reading Y. If not, it wouldn't matter what was taught. Sociology of literature illuminates the process of canon formation helping to explain why certain books are canonized rather than others (Corse 1997; Corse and Griffin 1997); it sheds analytic light on processes of cultural authority detailing who gets cultural power and how (DiMaggio 1991); and it elucidates the meaning-making activities of readers, showing what different audiences draw from particular texts (Griswold 1987). Sociological studies can help explain why people read, what they make of their reading, and how reading affects their lives. The relevance of literary sociology to the canon debates and its foundational arguments regarding the importance of extraliterary processes and structures can be seen in the increasing interest scholars outside sociology are showing in sociological variables and studies of literature (e.g., Tompkins 1985; Lauter 1991).

Similarly, many of the same questions of interest to sociologists of literature inform debates on media effects, debates such as whether watching cartoon violence causes children to act violently. This debate—and similar ones about the danger of rap music lyrics or the value of reading William Bennett's *Book of Virtues* rather than cyberpunk or social fears about Internet chat rooms—centers on the core question of what effect art and culture have on their audiences. Radway (1984), for example, asks whether reading romance novels teaches women to expect fulfillment only through patriachal marriage—and demonstrates that the answer is a qualified yes. Corse (1997) argues that reading canonical novels is used to help construct national identities and feelings of solidarity among disparate readers. Griswold (1992) shows how the "village novel" establishes a powerful yet historically suspect sense of Nigerian identity. The question of the effect of reading—and the related question of literary use—is central to a complete sociology of literature. Although recent developments have moved us closer to answers, these are the key questions the sociology of literature needs to answer in the future.

REFERENCES

Albrecht, Milton C. 1954 "The Relationship of Literature and Society." *American Journal of Sociology* 59:425–36.

Bayma, Todd, and Gary Alan Fine 1996 "Fictional Figures and Imaginary Relations." *Studies in Symbolic Interaction* 20:165–78.

Becker, Howard S. 1982 *Art Worlds*. Berkeley: University of California Press.

Berezin, Mabel 1991 "The Organization of Political Ideology." *American Sociological Review* 56:639–51.

Bourdieu, Pierre 1984 *Distinction*, transl. Richard Nice. Cambridge, Mass.: Harvard University Press.

—— 1993 *The Field of Cultural Production*. New York: Columbia University Press.

Calhoun, Craig 1989 "Social Issues in the Study of Culture." *Comparative Social Research* 11:1–29.

Candido, Antonio 1995 *Antonio Candido: On Literature and Society*, translated, edited and with an introduction by Howard S. Becker. Princeton, N.J.: Princeton, University Press.

Clark Priscilla Parkhurst 1982 "Literature and Sociology." In Jean-Pierre Barricelli and Joseph Gibaldi, eds., *Interrelations of Literature*. New York: Modern Language Association.

—— 1987 *Literary France: The Making of a Culture*. Berkeley: University of California Press.

Clark, Roger, and Leanna Morris 1995 "Themes of Knowing and Learning in Recent Novels for Young Adults." *International Review of Modern Sociology* 25(1):105–123.

Corbett, Ronald P., Jr. 1994 "'Novel' Perspectives on Probation: Fiction as Sociology." *Sociological Forum* 9:307–114.

Corse, Sarah M. 1995 "Nations and Novels: Cultural Politics and Literary Use." *Social Forces* 73:1279–1308.

—— 1997 *Nationalism and Literature: The Politics of Culture in Canada and the United States*. Cambridge, Eng.: Cambridge University Press.

——, and Monica D. Griffin 1997 "Reception, Evaluation, and African-American Literary History: Re-Constructing the Canon." *Sociological Forum* 12:173–203.

Coser, Lewis 1972 *Sociology through Literature*, 2nd ed. Englewood Cliffs, N.J.: Prentice Hall.

——, Charles Kadushin, and Walter W. Powell 1982 *Books: The Culture and Commerce of Publishing*. New York: Basic Books.

Crane, Diana 1992 "High Culture versus Popular Culture Revisited." In Michèle Lamont and Marcel Fournier, eds., *Cultivating Differences*. Chicago: University of Chicago Press.

de Staël, Madame (Anne-Louise-Germaine) [1800], 1998, *De la littérature considérée dans ses rapports avec les institutions sociales*. Paris: Infomédia Communication.

Desan, Philippe, Priscilla Parkhurst Ferguson, and Wendy Griswold, eds. 1989 *Literature and Social Practice*. Chicago: University of Chicago Press.

DeVault, Marjorie L. 1990 "Novel Readings." *American Journal of Sociology* 95:887–921.

DiMaggio, Paul 1987 "Classification in Art." *American Sociological Review* 52:440–455.

—— 1991 "Social Structure, Institutions, and Cultural Goods." In Pierre Bourdieu and James S. Coleman, eds., *Social Theory for a Changing Society*. Boulder, Col.: Westview.

——, and John Mohr 1985 "Cultural Capital, Educational Attainment, and Marital Selection." *American Journal of Sociology* 90:1231–1261.

Eagleton, Terry 1983 *Literary Theory*. New York: Basil Blackwell.

Goldmann, Lucien 1964 *The Hidden God*. London: Routledge and Kegan Paul.

—— 1970 "The Sociology of Literature." In Milton Albrecht, James H. Barnett, and Mason Griff, eds., *The Sociology of Literature*. New York: Praeger.

Grauerholz, Elizabeth, and Bernice A. Pescosolido 1989 "Gender Representation in Children's Literature." *Gender and Society* 3:113–125.

Griswold, Wendy 1981 "American Character and the American Novel." *American Journal of Sociology* 86:740–765.

—— 1983 "The Devil's Techniques." *American Sociological Review* 48:668–680.

—— 1986 *Renaissance Revivals*. Chicago: University of Chicago Press.

—— 1987 "The Fabrication of Meaning." *American Journal of Sociology* 92:1077–1117.

—— 1990 "A Provisional, Provincial Positivism: Reply to Denzin." *American Journal of Sociology* 95:1580–1583.

—— 1992 "The Writing on the Mud Wall: Nigerian Novels and the Imaginary Village." *American Sociological Review* 57:709–724.

—— 1993 "Recent Moves in the Sociology of Literature." *Annual Review of Sociology* 19:455–467.

—— 1994 *Cultures and Societies in a Changing World*. Thousand Oaks, Calif.: Pine Forge.

Hall, Stuart, D. Hobson, A. Lowe, and Paul Willis 1980 *Culture, Media, Language: Working Papers in Cultural Studies*. London: Hutchinson with the Centre for Contemporary Culture Studies, University of Birmingham.

Halle, David 1992 "The Audience for Abstract Art." In Michèle Lamont and Marcel Fournier, eds., *Cultivating Differences*. Chicago: University of Chicago Press.

Hebdige, Richard 1979 *Subculture: The Meaning of Style*. London: Methuen.

Hirsch, Paul 1972 "Processing Fads and Fashions." *American Journal of Sociology* 77:639–659.

Horkheimer, Max, and Theodor W. Adorno 1972 "The Culture Industry." In *Dialectic of Enlightenment*. New York: Herder and Herder.

Howard, Judith A., and Carolyn Allen 1990 "The Gendered Context of Reading." *Gender and Society* 4:534–552.

Ibsch, Elrud, Dick Schram, and Gerard Steen, eds. 1995 *Empirical Studies of Literature: Proceedings of the Second IGEL Conference, Amsterdam 1989*. Amsterdam: Rodopi.

Iser, Wolfgang 1978 *The Act of Reading*. Baltimore, Md.: John Hopkins University Press.

Janssen, Susanne 1997 "Reviewing as Social Practice." *Poetics* 24(5):275–297.

Jauss, Hans Robert 1982 *Toward an Aesthetic of Reception*, transl. Timothy Bahti. Minneapolis: University of Minnesota Press.

Lamont, Michèle 1987 "How to Become a Dominant French Philosopher." *American Journal of Sociology* 93:584–622.

—— 1995 "National Identity and National Boundary Patterns in France and the United States." *French Historical Studies* 19:349–365.

Lauter, Paul 1991 *Canons and Contexts*. Chicago: University of Chicago Press.

Lichterman, Paul 1992 "Self-Help Reading as Thin Culture." *Media, Culture, and Society* 14:421–447.

Long, Elizabeth 1985 *The American Dream and the Popular Novel*. Boston: Routledge and Kegan Paul.

—— 1986 "The Cultural Meaning of Concentration in Publishing." *Book Research Quarterly* 1:3–27.

—— 1987 "Reading Groups and the Postmodern Crisis of Cultural Authority." *Cultural Studies* 1:306–327.

Lowenthal, Leo (1961) 1968 "The Triumph of Mass Idols." In *Literature, Popular Culture, and Society*. Palo Alto, Calif.: Pacific Books.

Lukács, Georg 1971 *History and Class Consciousness*. London: Merlin Press.

Noble, Trevor 1976 "Sociology and Literature." *British Journal of Sociology* 27:211–224.

Peterson, Richard A., ed. 1976 *The Production of Culture*. Beverly Hills, Calif.: Sage.

—— 1985 "Six Constraints on the Production of Literary Works." *Poetics* 14:45–67

Powell, Walter W. 1985 *Getting into Print: The Decision-Making Process in Scholarly Publishing*. Chicago: University of Chicago Press.

Radway, Janice 1984 *Reading the Romance*. Chapel Hill: University of North Carolina Press.

Rogers, Mary F. 1991 *Novels, Novelists, and Readers.* Albany, N.Y.: State University of New York Press.

Rosengren, K. E. 1983 *The Climate of Literature.* Report No. 5 of *Cultural Indicators: The Swedish Symbol System.* Lund: Studentlitteratur.

Simonds, Wendy, and Barbara Katz Rothman 1992 *Centuries of Solace: Expressions of Maternal Grief in Popular Literature.* Philadelphia: Temple University Press.

Time 1998. Cover (June 29).

Tompkins, Jane 1985 *Sensational Designs.* New York: Oxford University Press.

Tuchman, Gaye (with Nina E. Fortin) 1989 *Edging Women Out: Victorian Novelists, Publishers, and Social Change.* New Haven, Conn.: Yale University Press.

Verdaasdonk, H., and C. J. van Rees 1991 "The Dynamics of Choice Behavior towards Books." *Poetics* 20:421–437.

Wahlforss, Jaana 1989 "*Soita minuelle, Helena!*—An Interpretation of the Content and Reception of a Popular Novel." *Sosiologia* 26(4):277–285.

Wolff, Janet 1990 *Feminine Sentences.* Berkeley: University of Calfornia Press.

—— 1992 "Excess and Inhibition: Interdisciplinarity in the Study of Art." In Lawrence Grossberg, Cary Nelson, and Paula A. Treichler, eds., *Cultural Studies.* New York: Routledge.

Wuthnow, Robert 1987 *Meaning and Moral Order: Explorations in Cultural Analysis.* Berkeley: University of California Press.

SARAH M. CORSE

LONG-TERM CARE

Long-term care (LTC) includes the full range of health, personal care, and social services provided at home and in the community for a continuing period to adults who lack or have lost the capacity to care fully for themselves and remain independent (Dearborn Financial Publishing 1997). A narrower but fairly common view is that LTC encompasses principally *residential* and institutional accommodation for older persons with special care needs. However, "long-term care" is a broad term, variously defined and interpreted in different countries and even within individual health and social care systems. As distinct from acute care, LTC is not primarily curative but aims to maintain people either in the community or in residential (institutional) settings of various sorts.

Much discussion of LTC has focused, for demographic reasons, on care for elderly people. They are the main user groups in LTC, although long-term care users also include adults with special needs because of physical disability and mental illness or handicap. There are policy, finance, and practice issues inevitably raised by the mixed clientele of LTC (Binstock et al. 1996). A popular image is that LTC comprises mainly formal facilities and qualified personnel or trained volunteers delivering services in institutions and the community. However, probably the most common form of LTC worldwide and especially in developing countries is that provided by informal caregivers, particularly the families of those needing care. This can be a source of both pride and frustration for many families. There is increasing recognition of the burden and strain on informal family caregivers. In many cultures, the tradition of family care is ensconced in the notion of filial piety. While this is a particularly Chinese and East Asian concept of (reciprocal) duty of care between parents and their children, the realities of family responsibility and interactions in care are readily recognizable in all cultures.

The numbers and proportions of people, elderly persons in particular, living in formal LTC *institutions* vary considerably from one country to another. The size of the population group in question is not generally a very good indicator of the need for LTC, or its likely provision, in any given country. More important are the evolution and philosophy of health and welfare of provision. Epidemiologically and demographically, the gender balance in any given population is also important, as patterns of disability and service use tend to differ considerably between males and females. However, data on LTC are notoriously difficult to compare internationally. There are considerable differences in both definition and provision of the various types of residential facilities, nursing homes, and hostels, as well as of duration of stay. In Europe, for example, the percentages of people aged 65 and over living in an institution in the early 1990s ranged from 1.8 percent in Greece, 2.4 percent in Spain, 5.1 percent in France and the United Kingdom, and 5.4 percent in Denmark and

Germany to 9.1 percent in the Netherlands. The percentages of those living with their children showed an even greater range, from 7 percent in Denmark, and 18 percent in Britain and France to 35 percent in Greece and 48 percent in Spain. In the United States, on any one day, it has been estimated that 5 percent of the older population lives in a nursing home. However, between 25 percent and 43 percent of 65-year-olds (depending on estimates) can expect to use a nursing home at some time in their lives. Indeed, the older the person, the greater the chance of living in a nursing home. A person aged 85 or over in the United States in 1985 had almost a twenty times greater chance than someone aged 65–74 of living in a nursing home (Novak 1997).

ASSESSING NEED FOR LTC

An individual adult's *need* for LTC typically arises when physical or cognitive abilities impair the ability at any age to perform basic activities of daily living (ADL) such as bathing, dressing and toileting and, increasingly, the ability to conduct instrumental ADL such as shopping and house cleaning. To help assess need for and provision of LTC, various forms of ADL scales have been developed. Two of the best known are by Katz et al. (1963) and Mahoney and Barthel (1965). Other important instruments include the Functional Independence Measure (FIM); the principal component of the Uniform Data Set (UDS); and the Minimum Data Set (MDS), a component of the Residential Assessment Instrument (RAI). The nursing home RAI includes a set of core assessment items (the MDS) for assessment and care screening for nursing home residents on, say, admission and periodically thereafter. This enables the identification of any significant change in status and the development of individualized restorative plans of care and it has been successfully applied in the United States and many other countries, for a range of specific purposes in LTC. Another relevant scale is the SF-36 for health-related quality of life, although it is not primarily designed for use in LTC settings.

Aggregate need for LTC is influenced by a wide range of factors. Aging of populations is an important factor, but the health status of populations is perhaps even more important. Expectation of life at birth is increasing almost everywhere, and, more important, expectation of life at age 60 and over is also increasing. The significance for LTC can be in at least two directions, depending on whether the expansion of morbidity or compression of morbidity hypotheses hold true. The "expansion" hypothesis suggests that further reductions in old-age mortality will expose the remaining population to a longer duration in which the nonfatal diseases of senescence are likely to emerge. The disabled portion of elderly life span will increase faster than the healthy and active portion. If this hypothesis holds true, with growing proportions of the "older-old" in the populations of most countries, there will be a steadily growing demand for community and institutional LTC provision. (See Table 1.)

Alternatively, the compression of morbidity hypothesis holds that mortality and morbidity will be simultaneously compressed and that lifestyle changes will reduce the risk of death from fatal and nonfatal diseases of senescence. A compression of morbidity is likely to have crucial implications for LTC need and provision, but precise details are difficult to assess. It implies that fewer people will need to live for long periods in institutions; conversely, there will probably be an increased need for social and community LTC for increasingly elderly population. Many of these people will be single and may not be very well provided for financially. This is especially true for single (usually widowed) elderly women, among whom many aspects of poverty are concentrated in many societies. They may disproportionately require low-cost or publicly funded community-based LTC. However, while there is some evidence, it is still early to state categorically that compression of morbidity will occur uniformly or continuously. Rather, there is increasing evidence of health *variations* both within and between populations and subgroups.

SERVICES AND PROVIDERS IN LTC

Nursing and Residential Homes. These are the institutions many people associate with long-term care. Definitions of nursing homes vary internationally, but, we will consider a home to be in this category (rather than as a retirement home, as old people's home, a board-and-care home, or the like) if it provides a specified amount of actual nursing and personal care and attention. Internationally, a nursing home has been defined as "an

Factors That May Affect the Demand for Long-Term Care

Demographic: Increase in the number of very old people; increased morbidity with increasing age; in particular, increase in numbers of older people suffering from dementing illnesses.

Social: Changes in the pattern of family structures and responsibilities at work and at home; increased tendency for some families to live at a distance from each other.

Economic and consumer: Improved financial position of many older people; older people making a positive choice about long-term care.

Service: Increased pressure on long-stay hospital beds; more effective use of acute hospital beds; closure of psychiatric hospitals.

Political: Initial stimulation through public funding of private and voluntary provision via supplementary benefit; community care legislation; attack on residential provision. Transfer of state funding to cash-limited local authority budgets since April 1993.

Ideological: Increasing popular support for a pluralist approach to welfare during the 1980s. Increasing reliance during the late 1980s and the 1990s on the market within health and social welfare services.

Table 1

SOURCE: Peace et al. (1997, p. 23)

institution providing nursing care 24 hours a day, assistance with ADL and mobility, psychosocial and personal care, paramedical care, such as physiotherapy and occupational therapy, as well as room and board" (Ribbe et al. 1997, p. 4). In general, nursing homes provide the highest level of nursing cum medical care outside acute hospitals. In many countries, especially in the developed world, they are licensed and inspected and subject to a variety of rules and standards. Some nursing homes have a medical or nursing teaching affiliation. Although the majority of long-term care is home-based and provided by informal caregivers (see below), nursing homes still epitomize the popular view of LTC, especially among those responsible for financing and legislating in this area. Indeed, this view of institutional care as the dominant form of LTC is rather difficult to change and represents a challenge to social scientists.

International Variations in Nursing Home Provision The proportions of people living in nursing homes and the per capita provision manifestly vary internationally, compounded by differences in definitions of nursing and residential homes. (See Table 2.) However, relative preponderance can be illustrated from a multicountry study of provision and structure of LTC systems. The countries studied are developed nations with high life expectancies; they include Sweden (with the oldest population in the study), Iceland (with the youngest), and Japan (forecast to have the highest aging rates in the coming three decades). Between 2 and

5 percent of elderly people were found to live in nursing homes, with variable percentages in residential homes (although the definitions also varied). Iceland, with the youngest age structure, actually showed the highest rates of institutionalization and nursing home residence, while Sweden, with the oldest, had a relatively lower percentage. This study found little correlation between the aging status of a country and the number of nursing home beds. Institutionalization rates differ as much according to population age structure and need as to differences in organization and financing of LTC services, the responsibility assumed for the care of elderly people by various sectors and the availability of LTC beds. Cultural factors and traditions of family care also influence strongly these levels of provision and uptake in any given country.

Residential Homes. Residential homes offer lower levels of care compared with nursing homes and they, rather than nursing homes per se, often provide the bulk of serviced accommodation for elderly people and adults with moderate disabilities. The terminology, scale, standards, registration, and licensing of "residential homes" vary considerably internationally. This category can include old people's homes, old-age homes, homes for the elderly, residential homes, board-and-care homes, boarding homes, and elderly hostels, among others. Many are small-scale, board-and-lodging establishments with few residents, no specialist staff, and very few facilities. Others are specialized

Percentage of People Over 65 Years of Age Living at Home and in Institutions (prevalence data; different years in the early 1990s)

Place of Residence	U.S.	Japan	Iceland[a]	Sweden	Denmark	Netherlands	U.K.	France	Italy
					Country				
Own home, independently or with informal and/or formal care (including domestic help and home nursing)	–	94.0	87.0	94.0	85.0	90.0	93.0	94.0	96.0
Residential homes, home for the aged, old people's homes (low levels of care)	1.5[b]	0.5	5.0	3.0	10.5[c]	6.5	3.5[d]	4.0	1.0
Nursing homes (high levels of care)	5.0	1.5	8.0	2.0	4.0	2.5	2.0	–[e]	<2.0
Hospitals (intensive medical care)	–	4.0	–	<1.0	<1.0	<1.0	1.5	–	1.0

Table 2

NOTE: [a]Including only elderly of ≥67 years.

[b]Including only residential care homes and not group facilities such as board and care homes.

[c]Including some sheltered housing and other special dwellings for elderly.

[d]Including some young disabled.

[e]No facilities described as nursing homes; 2 percent of elderly reside in nursing-home-like facilities.

SOURCE: Ribbe et al. (1997, p.6)

and provide high-standard, often high-cost, residential care with full meal service, facilities, grounds, and services. In some systems, most are licensed and inspected (above a certain size); in other systems, regulations are far more relaxed.

Admission to a residential setting often stems from an inability to manage at home because of difficulties with activities of daily living (ADL). In some residential homes, assistance is given with basic activities of daily living. In others, admission may be for social reasons of company or a lack of wish to maintain a home. However, while most residents will be basically ambulatory, in many aging nations there is a growing overlap among residents in residential homes and those in nursing homes. Indeed, increasing age and deteriorating health status can alter the case mix of some residential homes so that they sometimes resemble nursing homes but lack specialized facilities and staff. This can present a serious problem to the delivery of appropriate and quality care.

Sheltered Housing. Sheltered housing is generally purpose-built accommodation in which residents live in their own unit, with their own front door, but in a group development, with a system of linkages or alarms and served (usually full time) by a supervisor or warden. A range of services such as cleaning, shopping and entertainment, and common facilities may be provided on site, but these vary a great deal among sheltered housing schemes. Some schemes are small scale and involve only a handful of houses and residents. At the extreme, retirement villages established for older adults, increasingly common in North America and Australia, may be regarded as a type of sheltered housing. In many countries, various types of congregate housing are central to LTC.

Sheltered housing may be publicly provided, but it can be individually owned and provide a means for elderly people to remain in owner-occupancy. Increasingly, in countries such as the United Kingdom, a distinction is emerging between "ordinary" sheltered housing and "very sheltered" accommodation. In sheltered accommodation, residents generally require little more than suitable housing with the moral support of an alarm system to call emergency assistance. Very sheltered accommodation provides a greater intensity of services more akin to those in residential care settings. Many people feel that sheltered or very sheltered housing is an ideal form of accommodation for LTC delivery, and it certainly does have many positive aspects when the designs are appropriate and residents able largely to live independently. However, the question of what happens when tenants become older and more frail is difficult, as are the potential for ghettoization of elderly people (Tinker 1992, 1997). In a high-density accommodation society such as Hong Kong, sheltered housing has been adapted to accommodate unrelated single elderly people for whom the provision of totally independent homes has proved difficult. Since the late 1980s, under the Housing for Senior Citizens scheme, public housing apartments have been provided. Usually three elderly people share an apartment. Each has an individual bedroom, and they share a communal living room and kitchen. Alarm systems and a warden provide continuity of contact, and certain communal activities are arranged for residents.

Care for Younger Adults: Psychiatric and Group Homes. Younger adults are often in need of LTC because of physical or mental incapacity. Sometimes, specialist care and accommodation is required because of, for example, spinal cord injuries. Younger LTC residents often also have different needs and perspectives from older recipients: a goal might be to find ways to assist younger people get out and about, commute to work, enjoy a full range of activities, and be contributing members of society. Home- and community-based services are as important for the younger as for the older persons in need of LTC (Binstock et al. 1996). However, some younger adults, for example, with severe mental or physical problems, might remain in LTC psychiatric accommodation or community-based group homes or hostels for a very long period of time, while receiving various forms of adult day care or respite care (see below).

Home and Community Care. Community and home-based services have the main aim of enabling people to continue living in their own homes or in the community for as long as possible. They involve a wide range of types of services and facilities provided by the formal and informal sectors. Home health care programs deliver health care and related services to people's homes; they have been called "hospitals without walls." Again, as in LTC generally, definitions of "home care" vary among countries. A recent study of fifteen countries in Europe found considerable variation and defined *home care* as care provided at home by professional home nursing organizations and home help services. Other professionals—such as general practitioners (family doctors), occupational therapists, and physiotherapists—were excluded, although it is recognized that they do have a clear function in delivering care and often enable people to continue living at home (Hutten and Kerkstra 1996). *Home nursing services* include rehabilitative, promotive, preventive, and technical nursing care, with an emphasis mainly on the nursing of sick people at home. *Home help services* can provide a wide range of care, including shopping, cooking, cleaning, and laundering. They sometimes help with dressing and washing, and they often help care recipients to do administrative paperwork, pay bills, collect pensions, and the like. Many studies show that a home helper is also valued for providing company and someone to talk to. Clients are generally elderly (for example, in Britain, almost 90 percent). In some countries, the growing frailty of clients has led to the development of more intensive home care schemes that provide personal care in addition to doing simple cleaning and other tasks.

Several factors have raised the importance of home-based care: *increasing demand* from aging populations; *policies of substitution* of home care for institutional care (hospital care for the sick and residential care for elderly people) because of health care costs; and the *changing nature of home care* itself, with its increasing ability to deliver innovative services at home. However, while home is becoming the venue for delivery of care for many people of all ages, it is not necessarily a cheaper option than institutional care, especially for those requiring twenty-four-hour care. In addition, its future is not necessarily troublefree. The increasing numbers of older-old mean that complex home and family settings may evolve. For example, there will be increasing numbers of adult children in their sixties caring for parents in their eighties or nineties; likewise, there is an increasing number of elderly parents caring for adult disabled children at home. This is likely to require a very complex mix of support services to be delivered in the community and to people's homes.

Community-Based Care Facilities. These are also very varied and can provide care or more informal meeting, contact, and social support. *Adult day care*, variously titled, is a community-based provision that provides health, social, and related support services in a protective setting but for less than 24 hours on a daily or less frequent basis. Such facilities are becoming increasingly important in the spectrum of LTC services. Adult day care may follow the medical model or the social model or some combination of both. Day care is sometimes provided in a clinic or hospital, where it may have a specific clinical or rehabilitation aim; it may also be provided in a residential home, a day center, or a club. Purpose-built and converted day centers or clubs often provide social contact, recreation, and education. Some offer meal service, and they may act as a base for home delivery of services such as meals on wheels. Many adult day care centers provide transportation, and some have medically trained staff members. Day care is often helpful in relieving relatives from the care of an elderly person or a disabled adult for a few hours a day; recent innovative services provide care in the evenings or at night. An extension of this is respite services (see below) which may be based in the community or in an institution.

Family and Informal Caregivers. The majority of informal caregivers are family members, of closer or more distant relationship, but some are friends and neighbors. While increasing attention is paid to the professionalization of community-based LTC in most developed-world countries, informal caregivers undoubtedly provide the major portion of care at all levels of need at home. Ironically, ideological shifts from hospital to community in the process of deinstitutionalization have, as a by-product, increased the importance of informal and family caregivers, but often in the absence of full-fledged community care systems. In some societies, especially in the developing world, the family is popularly and sometimes officially regarded as the main and only source of long-term care. Considerable shame and disapprobation can descend on the family that neglects the care of its elderly members, in more traditional societies. Indeed, even in highly developed societies, there is often popular pressure or at least an assumed expectation that the family will take responsibility for LTC of its immediate members, even if this is provided with paid assistants. This can hold true even when the individual is resident in formal LTC settings and family members have visiting or care-providing roles.

Informal caregivers in LTC are predominantly female. American studies show that family caregivers are wives (23 percent), daughters (29 percent), other females (20 percent), husbands (13 percent), sons (8 percent), and other males (7 percent). This pattern holds true in many cultures. In China, for example, it provides an underpinning for the strong belief in the importance of having a son: Once a daughter marries, she traditionally lives with her husband and his parents, thus depriving her own parents of her potential future LTC help and domestic or financial assistance. Research in the United Kingdom and elsewhere indicates that family care is central to the lives of a substantial proportion of older people. In many countries, however, social change—including smaller families; women increasingly in the workforce; greater longevity; and social factors such as divorce, remarriage, and migration—all render the caring potential of the family more difficult. In developing countries, there is often very strong rural-to-urban migration of young working-age people. This can often render rural elders bereft of children who would provide day-to-day help, especially in the absence of formal LTC provision.

The reciprocal nature of family care is increasingly recognized—care flowing from parents to children, grandparents to grandchildren, and in reverse. This is often intricately bound up with exchange relationships, duties, and inheritance patterns. Elderly people themselves also have key roles as caregivers and, as noted above, among retired couples, the principal LTC provider is generally a spouse, often as old as or older than the recipient. Elderly parents often shoulder great responsibility for the LTC of their adult children with developmental disabilities. Indeed, the aging of children with mental retardation and severe physical disabilities has become an acknowledged research and policy issue only over the last two decades, with the shift from an emphasis on early childhood concerns to those of life-span issues. The progressive aging of almost all societies has increased the average age of caregivers of both elderly people and disabled adults. This necessitates important shifts in policy toward, for example, rendering housing more amenable and providing aging generations with greater frequency and variety of support, including respite care (see below).

In spite also of the strong emotional preference for being cared for by family members, many older people and their families, as well as the families of disabled younger adults, increasingly favor the support of professional caregivers when there are extensive care needs. This can be a recognition of *caregiver burden*—the stresses placed on family members by their caring responsibilities—but it is also a practical recognition of the limitations of families and informal caregivers. Researchers are increasingly focusing on the problems of family caregivers, especially those coping with physical and mental illness and especially those associated with disorders such as dementia. The impacts of providing LTC on family life, privacy, and on other members of the family besides the primary caregiver are also increasingly being recognized.

Respite Care. Respite care is temporary, short-duration, usually residential care with supervision and/or nursing provided for dependent adults, who typically cannot be left alone to live. The purpose is to provide caregivers (usually family members but often formal live-in caregivers) with temporary relief or respite from their caring roles. This clearly recognizes the family context within which much LTC is provided and acknowledges the burden that can be placed on caregivers. It is also a pragmatic recognition that, given appropriate breaks and holidays, family members may be able to continue to provide LTC support that would otherwise not be possible.

Respite care has the explicit aim of relieving the primary caregivers of impaired elderly persons, and its use has been extended to other caregivers of handicapped nonelderly adults. Many caregivers report that the main service they would like is to be given "a break" from caring duties and the chance for a holiday or participation in social activities. While this is undoubtedly the case, evidence is not conclusive that these services significantly reduce caregiver stress. In addition, a range of other services, such as meals on wheels, transport services, befrienders, and home help services might provide some of the functions of short-term respite care, yet they are not classed as such and are not really in this category. The major problem with respite care is that it is only as a rule available on a local basis; it has not generally received high funding priority, and caregivers therefore often feel they cannot rely on it to be available if and when they require it. In addition, there is evidence that, for various reasons, respite care places are often not fully occupied, a feature which renders the service vulnerable when budget reviews are undertaken.

FUNDING OF LTC

Sources of financial support for and cost of LTC vary considerably internationally and are likely to become even more variable as many countries undertake health sector reform and reassess public expenditure on welfare. Classically, LTC falls between health and social care; by its very nature, it lies at the interface between the two. Many public or insurance schemes have been able or willing to pay only for eligible clients who are in the residential or nursing home medical end of the LTC spectrum. By contrast, community-based LTC services for individuals and client groups have emerged piecemeal and have often been excluded from private insurance or public welfare payments. They can be very much a patchwork, dependent on local historical provision and the evolution of national programs. Care by the family, neighbors, and volunteers have also been of extreme importance for LTC recipients in the community, so individual resources and funding remain critical in many systems. At least five public policy options (other than total private reliance) exist for funding LTC. These include means-tested public funding; private insurance; public-private partnerships; social insurance; and funding from general taxation. Increasingly, there is an international focus not purely on value for money or efficiency and quality of LTC (as these are notoriously difficult to define) but on the concept of "best value."

Funding of LTC is fraught with emotion among the public and politicians in many countries, and the moral panic (excess concern about future numbers of elderly people, in particular, and escalation of costs) has frequently made rational debate difficult. The issue is of major concern in the United States, where policies and, by implication, funding, are under considerable debate (O'Brien and Flannery 1997). Welfare states such as the United

Kingdom have in the past been based on a combination of free National Health Service provision for health care aspects and social welfare payments for the social care aspects. Increasingly until the early 1990s, there was assistance from local authorities and from generous publicly underpinned funding of private sector homes for elderly people. Private LTC homes flourished during the 1980s. Much of this has changed in the mid-1990s since an extensive review of the nature and funding mechanisms of community care and the retrenchment of more or less automatic public sector support for residents of private old people's homes. A new approach to privatization has resulted in more stringent assessment of residents in private homes who are to receive public support to target the most needy with care packages. Many private old people's homes have subsequently gained vacancies following this policy shift (Bartlett and Phillips 1996).

Comparative analysis of international systems of LTC can be valuable. A study of the evolution of the United Kingdom's LTC policies and those of Israel, which are based on a system of national insurance, attempts to draw some lessons for the United States (Cox 1997). Israel's 1988 Community Long Term Care Insurance Law sought to ensure that all of the state organizations involved in LTC of elderly people would be integrated into one system. Israel attempted to calculate of costs of alternatives to institutionalization. It was estimated that some 60 percent of disabled elderly people on waiting lists for institutional care could, through a basket of services, home care, day care, and personal care to relieve the burden on families, be cared for in their homes at substantially lower costs than those of the institutions. This is a thorny issue, rarely adequately addressed. Modeling exercises have suggested that, in the case of the United States, for example, efficient allocation of home care services can produce some net LTC cost savings. Greene et al. (1998) estimated that reducing nursing home use and using an optimal allocation of home care services could achieve savings of around 10 percent in the overall LTC costs for an identified frail elderly population. However, this involved targeting and a more medically oriented mix of services than has been implemented to date. It appears that the expansion of personal care services may not be significantly justified in terms of cost containment or potential to reduce nursing home use.

Some countries have addressed the philosophy and financing of LTC systematically. The United Kingdom appointed a Royal Commission to review the long and short-term options for a sustainable system of funding LTC for older persons, both in their homes and other settings (Royal Commission on LTC 1999). They recommended coverage by "risk pooling," rather than private insurance, and services underwritten by general taxation. The report of the Commission provides useful sources of costs and means of delivery. *Japan*, for example, likely in the next two decades to become proportionately the most elderly country in the world, demonstrates the social, economic, and political importance of LTC. Japan has experienced increased lengthening and seriousness of LTC, with one out of every two bedridden persons being bedridden for two years or more. More than half the care attendants are themselves aged 60 or older. The percentage of elderly people living with their children has fallen to just over one-half, and the proportion of women working is increasing. The Japanese Ministry of Health and Welfare estimates that the percentage of people aged 65 and over who need care will rise from 11.8 percent in 1993 to 14 percent in 2010 and even 16 percent in 2025.

As a result of these pressures, in December 1997, legislation was passed for a new public LTC insurance scheme—Kaigo Hoken—to be fully operational from 2000. This makes Japan only the third country, after Holland and Germany (see below), to provide such insurance. These proposals are very significant because they depart radically from the Japanese tradition that families are primarily responsible for long-term care. Eligibility criteria will no longer take into account the extent of informal care available to patients; and ultimate responsibility for care will lie with the state rather than with families. The scheme separates LTC services from medical care insurance and will pay for institutional and home-based care not only for those aged 65 or more, but also for people over 40 years old with "age-related" diseases such as dementia. Each municipal government is deemed a provider, and levels of services are decided by the patients' impairment. Half the funding is from monthly premiums levied on people over 40, with a 10 percent co-payment at the point of service; rates are altered for those on low income. The rest of the funding comes from general taxation.

The scheme has two potential drawbacks. First, health and social services professionals in each municipal government will have to assess eligibility and decide on care plans, skills that have long been neglected in Japan. Second, the mechanism of quality assurance has not been clearly defined. The scheme nevertheless is a major departure in Japanese social policy (Arai 1997). It aims to underpin the development of a more diverse system in which users have more choice and may use the services they wish. It also hopes to promote the change from the excessive reliance on geriatric hospitals to sanatorium-type wards with suitable environments for long-term recuperation.

Germany introduced a new LTC insurance program in 1995. This required a considerable shift in focus from traditional rights to curative medical procedures toward long-term residential and home care, which previously had to be paid privately or from means-tested social assistance. There was political agreement that LTC costs threatened ordinary citizens with impoverishment in later life, a contrast with high levels of social expenditure available for health and pensions. After extensive public debate, a public insurance system was chosen, which requires equal contributions from all employers and employees; pensioners also contribute. Benefits from the LTC insurance may be taken in kind or in cash for home care and in kind for institutional care. Benefit payment levels are graded according to fairly narrow dependency definitions: dependent, seriously dependent (in need of extensive care), and very seriously dependent (needing extensive twenty-four-hour care) (Evers 1998). The cash alternative for home care is designed to allow private family-based arrangements to be made. Various additional benefits include short-term respite care to allow family caregivers four weeks' holiday, subsidized housing improvements, and contributions to the social security system. The new scheme, ostensibly a simple extension of the German insurance-based welfare approach, does create reliable rights for everyone in serious need of care as opposed to means testing. However, there have been discussions about the appropriateness of linking care costs to employer and employee payments. In addition, the LTC fixed-sum payments are likely to meet only part of the total costs of care. Residents of nursing homes in particular still have to spend individual resources, albeit at a slower rate. Due to the high proportion of recipients of home care initially opting for cheaper cash reimbursements, the system went into early profit and has amassed a surplus. This preference for cash has been taken to indicate the importance of the family in Germany's LTC, but some higher-cost medical care services can still be reimbursed from health insurance.

By contrast, even in some countries with advanced approaches to welfare, full-fledged support for long-term care remains highly dependent on local variations. In *Canada*, for example, what is regarded as continuing care has been called a "patchwork quilt" of long-term care, mainly institutional, and home or community care, mainly noninstitutional. The institutional components are widely provided across the country, with public and private funding. The noninstitutional components are developing, unevenly provided and also funded publicly and privately. While access to acute care is guaranteed, this is not the case for continuing care. The amalgam of services that compose continuing care involve the community-based and residential LTC services outlined above. Funding varies by province in Canada, with decreasing federal support, and is typically still complicated by the situation of LTC at the interface of health and social welfare. Various types of continuing care are cost-shared between province and municipality of residence. Ownership of facilities nationally falls under three categories, and the relative balance varies considerably between provinces: public (49 percent), private for-profit (26 percent), and private nonprofit (25 percent) ownership. For illustration, Quebec has 78 percent and Nova Scotia 36 percent publicly owned facilities on average, but 100 percent of care facilities for advanced chronic mental and physical conditions are publicly owned in Nova Scotia. While funding comes from a variety of sources, there is a move toward universal rather than means-tested benefits, and cost sharing with users is the norm. In most provinces, people are not required to spend down their assets to receive public support, though they will usually have to co-pay daily rates for lower levels of care. Community-based nursing services are virtually universally supplied in Canada, although home care and support vary considerably. The picture is evolving, with increasing emphasis on noninstitutional care and budget reallocation to this sector.

QUALITY ISSUES

Quality of provision in LTC is of increasing international interest and revolves around standard setting, regulation, inspection, and ethics. It can require legislation and a mature and sensitive appreciation of care needs on the part of LTC providers and the many professions involved. Service quality in LTC residential settings has at least five dimensions (Duffy et al. 1997): tangibles (physical facilities, equipment); reliability (ability to perform promised services); responsiveness (willingness and promptness); assurance (conveyance of confidence and trust by personnel); empathy (caring, individualized attention provided by the facility). There is also an important economic aspect to quality related to costs of services delivered: value and satisfaction.

In addition to broader quality issues, specific features such as the use of restraints also give indications of the quality and respect for individuals in a LTC system. In this and other respects, international standards vary. For example, an eight-country study of use of restraints in nursing homes (Denmark, France, Iceland, Italy, Japan, Spain, Sweden, and the United States) found considerable variation. Total use of restraints was less than 9 percent in Denmark, Iceland, and Japan; between 15 and 17 percent in France, Italy, Sweden, and the United States; but almost 40 percent in Spain. The intensity of use of restraints and the types applied varied. In all countries, there was a constant increase in the use of restraints with increasing ADL difficulties and cognitive dysfunction (Ljunggren et al. 1997). It is clear that financial factors concerned with staffing levels, staff culture and training, the balance between better and less well trained staff, and the physical nature of facilities influence levels of use of restraints. Cultural variations and the thresholds for applying restraints also vary greatly internationally. The same is undoubtedly true of many other facets of LTC.

LTC–ISSUES OF POLICY AND PRACTICE

LTC systems have generally emerged as a series of incremental responses to a growing problem or set of problems, over a number of political eras and in many jurisdictions. The result is often a medley of noncomplementary and even conflicting programs for people with chronic disability, which are typically ineffective and inefficient. In many countries, especially in the developing world, there is still enormous emotional and even official attachment to care by the family. At the extreme, placing one's parents or relative into an LTC residential facility can be anathema. Even in countries such as the United States, with expensive health care systems and an established range of community-based programs, LTC does not work well.

It is doubtful whether a universal blueprint for LTC can be devised. The development and financing of long-term care services in many countries has been at best haphazard. Until the Japanese and German experiences, and perhaps those in Australia and the United Kingdom at present, elsewhere it has rarely been asked what the ultimate LTC system should look like. Most systems have evolved piecemeal and have suffered from being at the interface of technically expanding and expensive health care and lower-technology, but fragmented, social care.

Basic policy issues and questions arise. What should LTC encompass? How can the role of housing policy in LTC be recognized? Is LTC an individual, a family, an employer, or a state responsibility, or is it (increasingly) some complex combination of all of these? What is the role of the family, and how can it be supported? Should LTC be provided to various disability groups and ages? If so, how? What is the ideal balance and relationship between LTC and the acute health care sector? What should be the balance between the various residential, social care, nursing, ancillary services, and informal care? What resources should be devoted to home care, assisted living, and other options? Underpinning many of these questions is the basic philosophy within specific countries regarding collective and individual responsibility for vulnerable citizens.

Housing is clearly crucial to the success of LTC. The internal home environment and its interaction with the local external environment adds to the challenge of life for many people with chronic disabilities, and their ADL are compounded by their environment. Initiatives have appeared such as sheltered housing (assisted daily living), with wardening and support services, residential homes, and various schemes to assist adaptation of existing dwellings, but, in most countries, there has been little coherent policy development in this area. Ironically, many initiatives to build specialist housing for elderly or handicapped people have come from private sector developers, who have identified a new and underserved market segment for specialist housing. Aging in place and care in the community can often be enabled by relatively minor housing improvements. These may be administrative; for example, in public housing, there may be provision for flexibility enabling residents to exchange current units for more appropriate, often smaller ones. Many academic disciplines, including sociology, gerontology, planning, geography, environmental psychology, and architecture, can contribute to this important aspect of policy development.

What will future LTC look like? It can be provided in a number of different settings, by a range of personnel, and to people with varying types and levels of disability. Nevertheless, in many systems, institutional care such as nursing homes still represent the majority of expenditure on LTC. Residential and nursing homes do indeed often represent an important care option, but they would be unlikely to occupy such an important position in a newly designed LTC system. As many systems have gradually emerged piecemeal from a range of initiatives, they do not meet the needs of the recipients or providers of LTC today, nor the needs of those who pay for care. Internationally, there is little agreement about potential policy solutions. In many countries, thoroughgoing debate and reappraisal need to be initiated.

REFERENCES

Arai, Yumiko 1997 "Insurance for Long-term Care Planned in Japan." *The Lancet* 350(9094):1831.

Bartlett, Helen, and David R. Phillips 1996 "Policy Issues in the Private Health Sector: Examples from Long-Term Care in the U.K." *Social Science and Medicine* 43(5):731–737.

Binstock, Robert H., Leighton E. Cluff, and Otto von Mering 1996 *The Future of Long-Term Care: Social and Policy Issues*. Baltimore, Md.: Johns Hopkins University Press.

Cox, Carole 1997 "Long-Term Care: A Comparison of Policies and Services in Israel and the United Kingdom and Implications for the United States." *Journal of Aging and Social Policy* 9(2):81–99.

Dearborn Financial Publishing 1997 *Long-Term Care*, 2nd ed. Chicago: Dearborn Financial Publishing.

Duffy, Jo Ann, Michael Duffy, and William Kilbourne 1997 "Cross National Study of Perceived Service Quality in Long-Term Care Facilities." *Journal of Aging Studies* 11(4):327–336.

Evers, Adalbert 1998 "The New Long-Term Care Insurance Program in Germany." *Journal of Aging and Social Policy* 10(1):77–98.

Greene, Vernon L., Jan Ondrich, and Sarah Laditka 1998 "Can Home Care Services Achieve Cost Savings in Long-Term Care for Older People?" *Journal of Gerontology: Social Sciences* 55B(4):S228–238.

Hutten, Jack, and Ada Kerkstra (eds.) 1996 *Home Care in Europe: A Country-Specific Guide to its Organization and Financing*. Aldershot, England: Arena Publications.

Katz, S., A. B. Ford, R. W. Moskowitz, B. A. Jackson, and M. W. Jaffe 1963 "Studies of Illness in the Aged: The Index of ADL: A Standardized Measure of Biological and Psychosocial Function." *Journal of the American Medical Association* 185:914–919.

Ljunggren, Gunnar, Charles D. Phillips, and Antonio Sgadari 1997 "Comparison of Restraint Use in Nursing Homes in Eight Countries." *Age and Ageing* 26(S2):43–47.

Mahoney, F. I., and D. W. Barthel 1965 "Functional Evaluation: The Barthel Index." *Maryland State Medical Journal* 14:61–65.

Novak, Mark 1997 *Issues in Aging: An Introduction to Gerontology*. New York: Addison Wesley Longman.

O'Brien, Raymond C., and Michael T. Flannery 1997 *Long-Term Care: Federal, State and Private Options for the Future*. New York: Haworth Press.

Peace, Sheila, Leonie Kellaher, and Dianne Willcocks 1997 *Re-evaluating Residential Care*. Buckingham, England: Open University Press.

Ribbe, Miel W., Gunnar Ljunggren, Knight Steel, Eva Topinkova, Catherine Hawes, Naoki Ikegami, Jean-Claude Henrard, and Palmi V. Jonnson 1997 "Nursing Homes in 10 Nations: A Comparison Between Countries and Settings." *Age and Aging* 26 (S2):3–12.

Royal Commission on Long Term Care 1999 *With Respect to Old Age: Long Term Care–Rights and*

Responsibilites. Report by the Royal Commission on LTC. London: The Stationery Office.

Tinker, Anthea 1992, 1997 *Elderly People in Modern Society*. London: Longman.

DAVID R. PHILLIPS

LONG-TERM CARE FACILITIES

THE SPECTRUM OF LONG-TERM CARE

While the nursing home remains the most prevalent option for elderly persons requiring long-term care, in recent years there has been a great upsurge in alternative options. Changes in the spectrum of long-term care services provided have come about primarily based on changes in the demographic profile of long-term care users, in health care financing, and in policies impacting the provision of long-term care.

Nursing homes reflect the major long-term care option that has been available in the United States under Medicare and Medicaid financing. However, recent trends reflect new developments targeting self-financed long-term care, particularly in the form of assisted living, continuing care retirement communities, and special need facilities focusing on dementia or hospice care. In addition, discharge policies of acute care hospitals have resulted in the development of subacute care and rehabilitation facilities sponsored by hospitals or nursing homes. There has also been an increase in the provision of home care services to frail older adults who can forestall entry to sheltered living arrangements, including nursing homes, through the use of these services. Growing recognition of the diversity of elders requiring long-term care is leading to the diversification of settings to meet these needs, and to a blurring of boundaries between home care and residential care (R. A. Kane, 1995–1996).

In spite of the proliferation of new residential options for frail and old-old adults, those requiring extensive assistance or supervision continue to rely on nursing homes as the only viable publicly financed alternative. Consequently, this essay will only briefly touch on some of the more recent options in the spectrum of long-term care, such as assisted living facilities and continuing care retirement communities. Rehabilitative or subacute care units in nursing homes will not be addressed because they reflect mechanisms for providing short-term care. Nor will we discuss senior housing sites or retirement communities, which serve as residential options to well elders. After considering assisted living facilities and continuing care retirement communities, the major focus of our discussion will be on the nursing home.

ASSISTED LIVING FACILITIES

Assisted living facilities (ALFs) have taken over some of the original functions of nursing homes, providing services to moderately frail elders in the context of a homelike residential setting that includes less surveillance and regimentation, and more privacy and autonomy for residents than the traditional nursing home (R. A. Kane 1995). ALFs combine housing with personal support services such as meals, laundry, housekeeping, and maintenance services. Board and care homes and personal care homes may also be included under the ALF designation. Generally, residents in ALFs pay on a month-to-month basis, although financing of home health services may occur under Medicare (Pearce 1998). Assisted living facilities are an outgrowth of the group home tradition, generally reflecting small business operations. In recent years, however, assisted living facilities have increasingly been sponsored and built by hospitals, nursing homes, and large publicly traded companies (Meyer 1998).

Consistently with the model of social care (R. A. Kane and Wilson 1993), ALF services are geared toward meeting resident preferences and wishes, and consider residents to be consumers rather than patients or clients to be taken care of according to staff-based directives. Assisted living arises from a commercial model of fees for services, and its consumer-driven orientation differs from nursing home care, which generally reflects third-party payment dynamics. While these advantages make assisted living a highly attractive long-term option for frail elders with some means, potential problems include lack of regulation and inaccessibility of this type of care to the poor. Furthermore, assisted living facilities can serve only the needs of older adults with limited disabilities (R. A. Kane 1995–1996).

CONTINUING CARE RETIREMENT COMMUNITIES

Continuing care retirement communities (CCRCs) may also be termed "life care communities," and they typically offer a continuum of services from independent living to assisted living and nursing care. These facilities are appealing to well old-old persons who are still able to live independently but want to have the security of planning for increasing service needs as they arise. These older adults want to know that their changing personal and health care needs can be met within an organizational framework, which they select. Most elderly persons initially enter independent living units of CCRCs. Between 50 percent and 70 percent of entering residents eventually utilize assisted living and/or nursing home components of the CCRC (Newcomer et al. 1995).

CCRCs vary greatly in both the types and the range of services offered and in sponsorship and management. The fees may be structured as a refundable entry fee along with a monthly service fee, or it can be based on an endowment, a rental, or a condominium purchase (Pearce 1998). While fee structures differ, arrangements for these services have generally moved from exclusive reliance on entrance fees to requiring monthly maintenance fees along with fees paid at the time of initiation. With the rapid growth of CCRCs around the country, states have enacted legislation to protect older adults, particularly against bankruptcy of the organizations sponsoring the CCRC (Netting and Wilson 1994). These facilities are generally considered and regulated as insurance programs, and there has been great inconsistency in ways of implementing their regulation across different states.

CCRCs represent not only an emerging comprehensive long-term care alternative, but may constitute a new paradigm for long-term care (Vladeck 1995). Managed care CCRCs can offer flexibility and a more community-responsive paradigm for delivering long-term care. This form of care draws on the know-how of diverse industries, including housing, hospitality, insurance, and health care. This allows for a cross-fertilization of different value orientations regarding care, and different approaches to financing and management.

Large-scale national research on CCRCs finds (Sherwood et al. 1997) that such facilities tend to be utilized by well-educated, middle-class, white, elderly persons aged 75 and over, with women being overrepresented among the users. More than 85 percent had been white-collar workers (Sherwood et al. 1997). When compared with community residents, CCRC-dwelling elderly were found to be in comparable or better health and to have comparable social supports, although community-dwelling elders interact more frequently with their family members. Social research on assisted living and CCRC communities has not been extensive, and generally considers administrative and organizational dimensions of care, rather than aspects of social life and social interactions. Studies comparing CCRC residents and elderly people living in the community have noted that the former are more likely to utilize nursing units after acute hospital stays and outpatient surgery. At the same time, CCRC residents have lower rates of hospital admissions than do community-dwelling elders (Newcomer et al. 1995).

NURSING HOMES

Nursing homes are of interest to sociologists on both the macro and the micro levels. On the macro level they reflect society's orientation to financing, regulating, and delivering long-term care services to its frail citizens who are no longer capable of fully autonomous community living. Sociologists have been particularly interested in those factors affecting long-term care delivery that reflect social construction of the reality of the lives of marginal individuals such as aged persons.

On a micro level, nursing homes represent formal organizations that regulate and control the daily lives of frail elders, while providing them with medical and social care. The tension between expectations for rehabilitative or prosthetic services and actual delivery of palliative care or of dependency-inducing treatment, with iatrogenic consequences, has been a particular source of fascination and concern to gerontologists (Baltes 1996; E. Kahana, Kahana, and Riley 1989; Kane 1995–1996). Complementing this interest has been the search for understanding person-environment interactions and interpersonal and intergroup relationships involving residents, staff, and families within the institutional context (Diamond 1992; Gubrium 1975, 1993; E. Kahana, Liang, and Felton, 1980).

The following discussion about nursing homes includes an introductory section outlining models of nursing home care, followed by a discussion of demographic profiles of residents and an analysis of nursing home characteristics and financing. Efforts to ensure high quality of care are discussed in terms of both regulatory efforts and formal interventions. We next consider the effects of institutionalization on the social lives of residents, and their adaptation to the nursing home. Discussion then turns to new initiatives in formal program development and effects of interventions on resident life in the nursing home. The article concludes with a discussion of emerging trends in nursing home care and the future of long-term care facilities in the United States.

Even as we aim to review sociological contributions to the understanding of nursing homes, it is important to note that information about this subject has been obtained through the research efforts of diverse disciplines, with epidemiologists, political scientists, social workers, psychologists, nurses, and physicians all contributing to the literature. In fact, medical sociologists have focused their investigation primarily on acute health care delivery in general hospitals, and many of the theoretical constructs they have developed are more applicable to acute illness than to chronic disability (Cockerham 1998; Charmaz and Paterniti 1999). Consequently, this discussion of the nursing home draws upon multidisciplinary sources.

MODELS OF CARE IN NURSING HOMES

Those requiring institutional care represent a highly select group of the most vulnerable aged persons (Hing 1987), particularly since there are now many options which can keep frail elders in the community. Any therapeutic efforts to enhance the functioning of the very frail older adults living in nursing homes thus represent a regimen of limited objectives (E. Kahana, B. Kahana, and Chirayath 1999). Nevertheless, nursing home settings can serve important therapeutic and rehabilitative functions and can enhance the quality of life of frail elders by ensuring comfort and even some measure of autonomy (Agich 1993). Moving away from an exclusive focus on poor quality of care in nursing homes, recent research has begun to consider criteria for high quality of care and even

excellence in nursing home settings (Andersen 1987; Brittis 1996; Groger 1994; Looman et al. 1997).

Conceptualizations of models of care typically reflect the philosophies and traditions of the disciplines from which they originate. Sociology, medicine, nursing, the allied health professions, psychology, and social work—each has a distinct set of traditions that influence its respective conceptualizations of long-term care. Interventions arising from these diverse traditions may include therapeutic interventions (psychology), programs that enhance function (nursing or medicine), and interventions that empower patients (sociology and social work).

The *medical model* of care considers nursing homes as health care institutions designed to deliver high-quality chronic care to patients. As such, nursing homes are expected to provide competent and well-trained personnel to meet health care needs of patients (R. L. Kane et al. 1994). In principle, the criterion for successful care is improved health or at least minimal health decline of the patient. In practice, quality of care is generally approached by the organization through adherence to certain standards of care delivery, such as adequate staff recruitment and training, and high staff-patient ratios (Nyman and Geyer 1989; L. Z. Rubenstein and Wieland 1993).

The organizational climate of managed care has brought with it a new emphasis on *management-centered* interventions and care. Management-oriented approaches often treat patients as objects of intervention who must be manipulated to achieve desired objectives. One such approach, continuous quality improvement (CQI), is an organizational management framework based on older business models such as total quality management (TQM) (Schnelle et al. 1997). The goal of CQI is to make systematic improvements by employing multiple short cycles of designing, evaluating, and implementing interventions. These cycles of continuous intervention and assessment drive long-range systematic change. Attempts at CQI in nursing homes have included interventions in incontinence and physical restraints, but have been hindered by a lack of information technology and by care standards legislated by the Omnibus Budget Reconciliation Act (OBRA) of 1987 (Schnelle et al. 1997).

The *social model* (R. L. Kane and R. A. Kane 1978; R. A. Kane et al. 1998) considers the ideal model of long-term care to be a sheltered housing arrangement for older adults who can no longer function independently in the community. The goal of such sheltered living arrangements is ensuring a good quality of life for residents through encouragement of maximum autonomy in a homelike setting. The criterion for successful care is defined in terms of sustained psychosocial well-being, self-esteem, and life satisfaction of residents.

While medical definitions of care dictate provision of diagnostic and treatment activities, social definitions suggest emphasis on comfort, choice, and adaptation. Advocates of quality-of-life approaches have often argued for major redirection in the way long-term care is handled. They seek greater support for the home-based rather than the institution-based model of care (Leutz et al. 1992). The growing popularity of assisted living options in long-term care reflects this orientation. Empowering older clients to act as consumers provides a major mechanism for the social care model (Burger et al. 1996; Cox and Parsons 1994). Since residents living in nursing homes are typically too frail and powerless to demand active consumer involvement in their care, there is little evidence of actual empowerment-based approaches in nursing home settings (E. Kahana 1999).

The *Patient-Responsive Care Model* (Kahana, Kahana, Kercher, and Chirayath 1999) has been developed to recognize social, psychological, and physical needs of frail patients who are not able to function in residential settings and who require nursing home care. The Patient-Responsive Care Model is an ecological model guided by communitarian principles of sociologists (Bellah 1996; Etzioni 1993). It calls for a systematic and empathetic discernment by staff of resident perspectives and preferences. This approach is based on earlier work on person-environment fit as a determinant of resident well-being in nursing homes (E. Kahana 1973; E. Kahana 1982). Environments may be matched to resident needs by altering the physical or social environment and by enhancing staff responsiveness in an effort to improve residents' quality of life (E. Kahana, B. Kahana, and Riley 1989). This model is also consistent with recently proposed "cultural" models of nursing home care proposed by Scandinavian scholars who advocate individualized care based on "knowing the patient" (Evans 1996).

The major requisite of patient-responsive care is an understanding and an empathetic appreciation of nursing home life from the patient's perspective. Four major areas of need, loosely based on Maslow's hierarchy of needs (1970), are to be met by staff: reducing physical distress, meeting basic physiological needs, meeting emotional needs, and meeting social needs. Since cognitively impaired and frail elders are limited in their ability to articulate their needs, a major challenge of patient-responsive care is to elicit expressions of resident needs and preferences. This model is predicated on empathetic listening to the patient's lived experience (Gubrium 1993; Savishinsky 1991) as a basis for developing Patient-Responsive Care, and does not rely on need assessments based on objective test data.

Staff behaviors along dimensions of responsiveness can range from total lack of involvement (ignoring or dismissing a problem) to hearing and validating patient concerns. Staff who are responsive to patients provide reassurance and, whenever possible, take constructive actions toward resolving problems. Eliciting information about patient needs and validating those needs are proposed as concrete requisites of providing patient-responsive care. Action components of responsive care also involve communicating with family members and with other staff in advocating on the patient's behalf. Responsiveness involves three central actions by staff: eliciting the patient's definition of need, validating the need, and acting or advocating on the patient's behalf. The pattern of responsiveness thus involves observing, questioning, listening, and responding. Exemplifying this approach, aides who care for the elderly may be trained to redefine their jobs from providing custodial care to providing therapeutic measures. For example, personnel delivering meals could easily be trained to engage in conversation with residents during meals, explaining what the resident is eating and contributing to the enjoyment of the meal. Staff providing responsive care may be empowered through this very initiative. Providing responsive care can serve to enhance staff's self-efficacy and sense of competence (E. Kahana et al. 1999).

While none of the models described above fully fit, the complex realities of frail older persons living in institutional settings within the constraints of managed care, each helps us appreciate the multifaceted nature of efforts to meet resident needs in the framework of long-term care.

PROFILE OF NURSING HOME RESIDENTS

In 1995, about 1.4 million American elderly persons over the age of 65 were residing in 16,700 nursing homes. While 4.5 percent of the elderly are in nursing homes at any given time, 30 percent of older adults can expect to spend some time during their lives in a nursing home. The majority of residents enter a nursing home immediately after discharge from an acute care hospital (Lewis et al. 1985). Most of these patients need ongoing medical care and some may require rehospitalization (Densen 1987). Others enter a nursing home directly from the community, due to multiple risk factors including physical and cognitive frailty and nonavailability of caregivers. Additionally, during the era of deinstitutionalization of the mentally ill, some elderly were transferred to nursing homes from mental hospitals. Among social risk factors for institutionalization, studies have identified that those elderly persons who were never married, those who are widowed, and those who do not have children nearby are overrepresented (R. A. Kane 1995–1996).

A demographic profile of nursing home residents has been provided by the U.S. Bureau of the Census (1998) based on a 1995 survey of residents in U.S. nursing homes (National Center for Health Statistics 1997). According to the report, 24.7 percent of nursing home residents are men and 75.3 percent are women.

Older women are three times as likely as older men to reside in nursing homes, both because of their longevity and because they are more likely to be widowed, and moreover without caregivers.

Nursing home placements are generally due to a combination of functional impairments, mental infirmity and unavailability of caregivers (R. L. Kane et al. 1998; Rovner and Katz 1993).

Of those elderly living in a nursing home, 8 percent were between ages 65 and 74; another 42 percent were between ages 75 and 84, and 40 percent were over age 85. Although the vast majority of nursing home residents are elderly, about 10 percent are younger than age 65 (U.S. Bureau of the Census 1998).

Although representation of minorities in long-term care facilities has been increasing over time, such groups continue to be underrepresented (Bonifazi 1998). Racial composition of nursing home residents is: 89.5 percent white, as compared to 8.5 percent black and 2.3 percent Hispanic (R. L. Kane et al. 1998; U.S. Bureau of the Census 1998). Both the greater willingness of black and Hispanic families to care for elders and barriers to the utilization of nursing home by minorities have been cited as possible reasons for these racial differences (Mui and Burnette 1994; Wallace et al. 1998).

Based on the 1995 National Nursing Home Surveys, the majority of elderly persons residing in nursing homes need significant assistance with both activities of daily living (ADLs) and instrumental activities of daily living (IADLs) (National Center for Health Statistics 1997). The study reports that 96 percent of residents in a nursing home need help with showering, 87 percent need help with dressing, 45 percent need help with eating, 24 percent need help with transferring, and 58 percent need help with toileting. Limitations were also found in IADL function, with 78 percent of respondents needing assistance with care of personal possessions and 69 percent needing help with managing money. High levels of physical impairment in this group are also reflected in extensive use of assistive devices. Thus, 64 percent of all elderly in nursing homes utilize a wheelchair, 25 percent use a walker, and 78 percent occupy a hospital bed. Sensory and communicative impairments are also prevalent among nursing home residents, with 51 percent of residents having moderate to severe hearing loss (Garahan et al. 1992) and 24 percent exhibiting visual problems (National Center for Health Statistics 1997).

There is increasing recognition that the prevalence of diagnosable neuropsychiatric disorders in nursing homes is high, with estimates ranging up to 80 percent or greater (Kim and Rovner 1996; Rovner and Katz 1993). Elders with schizophrenia or other psychoses compose only a very small proportion of the nursing home population. The most prevalent neuropsychiatric disorders include dementia (primarily Alzheimer's disease) and depression.

Over 50 percent of elderly persons admitted to nursing homes will live out their lives in a nursing facility, with about 10 percent dying during the first year of their nursing home stay. The average length of stay of long-term care residents is two to three years. In any given year, 25 percent of residents return to the community from a nursing home (Cohen-Mansfield et al. 1999). The majority of those returning to the community have spent time in short-term, rehabilitative units of nursing homes.

CHARACTERISTICS AND DISTRIBUTION OF NURSING HOMES

The number of nursing homes in the United States has decreased from 19,100 in 1985 to 16,700 in 1995. This represents a decline of 2,400 homes over the past decade. The number of nursing home residents has increased only slightly over the same decade from 1.49 million residents in 1985 to 1.55 million residents in 1995 (U.S. Bureau of the Census 1998). In 1995, there were about 1.77 million nursing home beds. The average number of beds per nursing home increased from 85 in 1985, to an average of 106 beds per nursing home by 1995. These changes parallel organizational shifts toward the entrance of large nursing home chains into the market. At the most recent 1995 survey, 66 percent of nursing homes were proprietary, 26 percent were nonprofit, and 8 percent were sponsored by the government (U.S. Bureau of the Census 1998). Fifty-five percent of nursing homes were run by commercial organizations operating chains of facilities. Of the total nursing homes, 66 percent were certified by both Medicare and Medicaid, 20 percent by Medicaid only, 6 percent by Medicare only, and 4 percent were not certified by either Medicare or Medicaid (U.S. Bureau of the Census 1998). Nursing homes generally have high occupancy rates (87 percent) in part based on newly proliferating special units such as respite care, rehabilitative services, hospice, dementia units, and acquired immune deficiency syndrome (AIDS) special care units (U.S. Bureau of the Census 1998). Nevertheless, there are some indications that frail older adults are not entering nursing homes at the same rate they previously did. The increase in assisted living settings and other residential options is likely to contribute to this trend (Strahan 1997).

There are regional differences in both distribution and utilization of nursing homes. Older adults in the Midwest and the South have the largest number of nursing homes available to them, each with 33 percent of the total number of nursing homes in the United States. The Northeast, containing 17 percent of the country's total number of nursing homes, has the highest occupancy rate compared to the Midwest, South, and West. The West, in contrast, has a small proportion of nursing homes and has the lowest occupancy rates (U.S. Bureau of the Census 1998). Migration patterns may influence nursing home occupancy rates. Many older adults, upon retiring, move to warmer Sunbelt states seeking to improve their quality of life. This group is likely to enter nursing homes as they become frail in old-old age, thus contributing a high demand for nursing homes in the South (Longino 1998). At the same time, when they require more extensive care, significant numbers of older adults may return from the Sunbelt to the states from which they originally migrated. These countermoves may also affect the utilization rates of nursing homes in certain regions. Rural-urban comparisons of nursing home distribution reveal that metropolitan areas have a larger supply of nursing home beds per capita than do rural areas (62 versus 45 certified beds per 100 elders, respectively) (Shaughnessy 1994).

FINANCING OF LONG-TERM CARE

It has been argued that, in the United States, funding mechanisms have been largely responsible for shaping the delivery of health care in general and the delivery of long-term care in particular (R. A. Kane et al. 1998). In 1995, nursing home expenses totaled $77.9 billion, sharply up from $36 billion in 1985 (Levit et al. 1996). Medicare, a universal age-based health care program, has traditionally covered the acute and rehabilitative health care needs of older adults and reimburses only a very limited number of nursing home expenses. Medicaid, a need-based, state-administered program, on the other hand, covers nursing home expenses for older adults after their financial resources are depleted. Thus, while Medicare paid 9 percent of nursing home expenses in

1995, Medicaid paid 47 percent of the expenditures. Thirty-seven percent of nursing home expenses were paid out of pocket, whereas private insurance paid only 3 percent of nursing home expenses (Levit et al. 1996).

While private nursing home insurance is increasingly advocated as an important protection for older adults, only very few adults are currently benefiting from such coverage. This limited role played by private insurance may be attributable to high cost, limited coverage afforded by such policies, and lack of information about the availability of insurance (Cohen 1998). Most elderly individuals start their nursing home stays as privately paying patients. Nursing home care, in fact, represents the major portion (82.5 percent) of out-of-pocket health care expenses of the elderly (Rice 1989). After personal resources are depleted (usually in less than a year), patients become eligible for Medicaid financing (Lusky and Ingman 1994).

There is continuing pressure for cost containment to reduce burdens of nursing home costs. The major response to these needs has been the proliferation of assisted living facilities, CCRC facilities, and home health care. In 1995, the average annual cost of a nursing home stay was over $38,000, while out-of-pocket costs for home health care averaged $370 a month, or $4,440 annually (Cohen 1998). There have also been reductions in reimbursable nursing home services by Medicare and Medicaid. Efforts directed at cost containment through reduced payments for care pose a serious threat to the provision of high-quality services. In addition, the profit motive inherent in proprietary health care may be seen as posing a conflict of interest with the provision of high-quality care.

ENSURING STANDARDS OF NURSING HOME CARE

Ensuring high quality of care and standards for services has posed a major challenge to the nursing home industry (Vladeck 1980; R. A. Kane 1995–1996). Problems have been encountered in terms of poor staff training (R. A. Kane 1995–1996), high staff turnover rates (Banazac-Holl and Hines 1996), and limited physician involvement (Fortinsky and Raff 1995–1996). Nurses' aides, the

staff members with the most limited training and education and at the lowest end of the pay scale, provide the majority of patient care in nursing homes (IOM 1996). Higher ratios of registered nurses (RNs) to patients are associated with higher patient survival rates, increased functional status, and increased numbers of patients discharged from the nursing home (IOM 1996). Nevertheless, pay differentials between hospitals and nursing homes have contributed to a paucity of RNs working in nursing homes and an overrepresentation of nurses with limited educational backgrounds working in long-term care facilities (IOM 1996). It is noteworthy that nursing assistants employed in nursing homes are also less well paid than their counterparts working in hospitals (BLS 1995). Nursing assistants have limited education, with 46 percent having high school diplomas, while nearly 18 percent have not graduated from high school (IOM 1996). In addition to morale problems resulting from low-status jobs with poor pay, many nursing assistants also face personal problems exacerbated by their low socioeconomic status (Coons and Mace 1996). These factors are related to very high turnover rates among nursing assistants, resulting in poorer quality of care (Schnelle et al. 1993).

Generally speaking, assessing quality of care involves an inquiry into three key ingredients of health care quality: structure, process, and outcomes. Structural measures gauge the presence of certain provider characteristics that are thought to produce good-quality outcomes. Process measures compare the actual care delivered to standards or norms of practice. Outcome measures serve to indicate the results of the care received (e.g., death, functional change). Reliable measures of appropriate outcomes of care are sought by quality-assurance programs in long-term care (R. A. Kane, R. L. Kane, and Ladd 1998). In the context of improvement in care quality, outcome assessments may be used to allocate resources to those areas that require remediation.

Although diverse quality assurance and enhancement programs have been advocated, regulation continues to serve as the major approach to insuring high quality of care. Until Medicare and Medicaid were enacted in 1965, nursing home regulation was each state's responsibility. Once federal programs began paying for nursing home services, the federal government became more involved in regulating nursing homes. It has been argued that Medicare and Medicaid had a major influence on delivery of care in nursing homes due to the regulations placed on facilities and the standards established for certification and for eligibility for payments (R. A. Kane, R. L. Kane, and Ladd 1998; Lusky and Ingman 1994). Lack of uniformity from state to state in care delivery arises as states decide who is eligible for Medicaid. They also impose their own diverse standards for quality care and regulation of such care through inspections.

Alternative approaches to ensuring standards for services have been advanced through regulation or free market economy (Nyman and Geyer 1989). Regulation seeks to enforce high quality of care through staffing standards, care plans, and result audits. In general, regulation aims to ensure the most basic aspects of quality of care, such as appropriate medical care, sanitary living conditions, sufficient exercise, adequate diet, and at least limited privacy for residents. Regulatory efforts are widely employed and have had at least limited success in defining and monitoring quality of health care. However, regulation is seen by many as a costly and often ineffective approach that is dependent on enforcement of a limited set of universally agreed-upon standards (Nyman and Geyer 1989).

In free market competition, consumers do the work of raising quality by making informed choices and purchasing high-quality services. Ensuring standards through the use of the free market economy rests on the assumption that the consumer can identify good-quality care and has furthermore researched the market and will choose to reside in a facility that provides the best care. However, third-party payment systems limit the effectiveness of consumers in exercising market choices. Severely impaired nursing home patients (who may also lack family or advocates) are limited in their ability to exercise sufficient rational market choice to ensure nursing home quality.

Alternative approaches to improving quality of care have been noted in addition to those of regulation or competition. For example, increased involvement by volunteers, family members, and other representatives of the community may enhance care by increasing public awareness and accountability. Community advocacy programs that encourage local citizens to press for patient rights and for improved care delivery have been found to be useful (Williams 1986). In addition, there has been increasing education of the public to have patients and families serve as their own advocates in choosing high-quality nursing homes and in seeking high-quality care through awareness of nursing home residents' rights (Burger et al. 1996). There has also been evidence of the useful roles played by nursing home ombudsmen in helping to resolve disputes involving residents (J. Kahana 1994).

In a 1986 report, the Institute of Medicine called for improvements in the quality of care in nursing homes. A landmark development following this report was the Omnibus Budget Reconciliation Act (OBRA) of 1987 setting forth guidelines by the Health Care Financing Administration for nursing home care. This act aimed to protect resident rights and improve residents' quality of life through a broad set of regulations. These included training and certification of nursing assistants, establishment of quality assurance committees, mandated resident assessments to allow for individualized care planning, reduction of physical and chemical restraints and preadmission screening for mental illness (Hamme 1991). OBRA also enforces a regulation that sets standards of care by increasing financial sanctions for noncompliance. Accordingly, noncompliant homes could be subject to fines and have Medicaid and Medicare payments withheld (Hamme 1991).

The enactment of OBRA raised high hopes about ensuring a high quality of care in nursing homes, and its implementation has resulted in improvements in quality of care. There is evidence of reduced use and overuse of drugs, in particular psychotropic medications (Borson and Doane 1997; Lantz et al. 1996), as well as a reduction in the use of physical restraints in nursing homes since the implementation of OBRA (Dunbar et al. 1996; Siegler et al. 1997). Research has also documented improvements in the accuracy of information in residents' medical records and in comprehensiveness of care plans (Hawes et al. 1997). There has also been an increase in positive programs such as presence of advanced directives and participation in activities by residents (Hawes et al. 1997). As an outgrowth of OBRA legislation, psychiatric assessments and screening programs have resulted in some improvement in matching residents to appropriate mental health services (Borson and Doane 1997). Nevertheless, many problems and challenges have remained in the wake of OBRA. Thus, for example, the OBRA-mandated freedom of residents to select their own physicians can seldom be implemented, because most physicians will not follow their patients to the nursing home to deliver care. Lack of funding for inspections allows violations to go undetected (Day 1996). There have also been only limited advances made in the treatment of the depressed elderly (Snowden and Roy-Byrne 1998).

RECENT TRENDS IN PROGRAMS AND CARE DELIVERY IN NURSING HOMES

In addition to mandated programs to enhance nursing home quality, there have also been notable developments in recent years to introduce innovative or at least new approaches to caring for older adults in nursing homes and other long-term care facilities. We will review two major approaches to such developments: special units and formal intervention programs to improve quality of care and of residential life.

Special Units. Special units within nursing homes are based on homogeneous groupings of people with special needs. The assumption underlying this movement is that specially trained staff may best meet the unique needs of specific patient groups. Segregating populations of residents with stigmatized or disruptive characteristics may also be seen as benefiting other residents by limiting their exposure to these populations.

Special programs can be targeted to unique groups such as dementia patients and patients in the final stages of life. Each of these will be discussed below. Although there is increasing recognition of the role of nursing homes in meeting the special needs of populations such as patients with AIDS (Zablosky and Ory 1995) or patients with brain injuries (Parsons 1997), programs for such individuals have been sporadic and limited. Often these special needs groups include higher proportions of younger patients and models of nursing home care geared to the elderly are poorly matched to their needs. Furthermore, research evaluating such programs is generally lacking.

Dementia Care Units Special care units in nursing homes have been proliferating for dementia patients. About 20 percent of nursing homes had dementia-specific special care units in the mid-1990s (Aronson 1994). These units are based on presumed benefits of functionally homogeneous resident groupings and generally target programs for confused but ambulatory residents.

It has been argued that dementia patients need "high-touch" rather than "high-tech" interventions (Aronson 1994). Many programs targeting dementia patients, are not reimbursable under skilled care guidelines. Special units for dementia care have been in the forefront of the development of certain innovative programs and particularly in integrating family members in patient care (Gaston 1994). Family members' prior knowledge of the older adult when he or she was functioning well can enable expressions of emotional support, which in turn facilitates maintenance of the dignity and self-worth of these elders. Effective formal programs in dementia units that involve families in the care of elders range from family stories workshops (Hepburn et al. 1997) to the inclusion of families in staff-initiated treatment programs (Grower et al. 1994).

Hospice Units As greater numbers of older adults are dying in nursing home settings, the provision of hospice care is becoming a more central function of nursing homes. Between 1992 and 1995, the number of nursing homes with hospice units increased 100 percent, although the development of such units is constrained by market forces such as Medicaid reimbursement (Castle 1998). The value of the hospice as a useful model for end-of-life care has been increasingly recognized. This approach to care emphasizes holistic patient care aimed at diminishing pain and enhancing comfort and meaning. This orientation brings both dignity and autonomy to the process of dying for the elderly resident (Hayslip and Leon 1992).

The hospice model also points the way to recognition that the nursing home often serves as the context where older adults prepare for dying. Accordingly, a much-needed and often-absent function of nursing homes is helping residents come to terms with awareness and acceptance of their finitude (Johnson and Barer 1997).

Formal Interventions to Improve Quality of Life in Nursing Homes. While sociologists have generally focused on the specification of broad social features of nursing homes that impact on the life and welfare of the resident, psychologists, nurses, and social workers have been more involved in implementing specific and circumscribed intervention efforts in nursing homes. Direct interventions to improve resident functioning and/or the quality of resident life in nursing homes have been limited by the absence of systematic theories, on the one hand, and lack of resources, on the other. Diverse efforts to improve care have generally yielded some success, suggesting that almost any type of intervention can improve the quality of life or functioning of residents (E. Kahana, B. Kahana, and Chirayath 1999). Interventions may be broadly classified into two types: those aiming to improve the physical or social environment of the setting, and those aiming to improve the coping strategies, psychosocial well-being, or cognitive functioning of residents. Interventions may alternatively be directed at the resident, the environment, family, or staff.

Interventions to improve health and physical functioning of nursing home residents typically include programs that attempt to reduce impairment and disability (e.g. nutritional problems, urinary incontinence) or the risk of falling. Some interventions aimed at improving health and physical functioning expand their scope by attempting to improve overall quality of life for the resident. Such interventions include programs which grant residents greater autonomy and locus of control (Wagner et al. 1994), and those that incorporate self-image enhancements (Plautz and Timen 1992). Intergenerational programs that promote interaction between nursing home residents and children or young adults have been found to be successful in enhancing quality of life for nursing home patients as well as young children (Gaston 1994; Newman 1985). Such programs have generally been found to improve the activities and social interactions of the elderly.

Interventions targeting cognitively impaired residents include divergent approaches. Montessori methods have also shown success in improving the cognitive functioning of demented elders (Camp and Mattern 1999). Cueing and reality orientation have been therapeutic strategies aimed at reinforcing orientation to time, place, and person among cognitively impaired elderly (Aronson 1994; Whanger 1980). Fantasy validation therapy takes a divergent view, providing staff acceptance of nursing home patients through expressing empathy in response to unrealistic beliefs or behaviors (Feil 1982).

Behavioristic approaches to the treatment of psychiatric problems in nursing homes include reinforcement of appropriate behaviors through token economies or habit training (Whanger 1980). Educational opportunities to enhance competent coping strategies have also been advocated (E. Kahana and B. Kahana 1983). Regarding the physical environment of the nursing home, prosthetically designed environments have been found to retard decline among mentally impaired elderly (Lawton et al. 1984). Milieu therapy is a systematic approach to enhancing all aspects of the social and physical environment in order to encourage social interactions among residents (Soth 1997).

As illustrated in the above discussion of systematic interventions in nursing homes, much of the empirical work relevant to person-environment transactions focuses on only one of the two related influences: the patient or the milieu. Thus, while conceptual frameworks recognize the dynamic nature of person-institution transactions, these complex interactions have not yet been incorporated in therapeutic interventions.

Focus on the Life of the Nursing Home Resident: Effects of Institutionalization. We will now consider those aspects of institutionalization that impact on the experiences, lifestyles, and well-being of the individuals who enter even the best of nursing homes. It is primarily this area of inquiry, relating social processes to the life experiences of the individual patient, to which sociologists have addressed their research on nursing homes. Considering the individual resident in the context of the physical and social milieu of a given institution, we can appreciate both the factors that induce negative reactions and those resources which facilitate positive responses to institutionalization. On this level of analysis, the sociologist moves away from considering the patient as a mere object of care and notes the interactive nature of the encounter between the institutionalized person and diverse elements within the nursing home environment.

The problems brought about by institutionalization go beyond problems of quality health care and in fact, may be inherent in the very nature of congregate care. Accordingly, sociologists have recognized that the nursing home, by its very nature, represents a unique social context with homogenizing qualities, and that there are alterations in the normal patterns of interaction and social exchange, even in facilities providing high-quality care (Linz et al. 1993). Holistic analyses of life in the nursing home have been conducted primarily in a qualitative tradition. They range from firsthand accounts to in-depth interviews and participant observations of the nursing home (Diamond 1992; Gubrium 1993; Henderson and Vesperi 1995; Laird 1979; Savishinsky 1991; Shield 1988). There have been few, if any, quantitative research projects to address the complex fabric of residents' experiences of nursing home life in the past two decades. Conceptual developments have also been limited, highlighting the seminal nature of Goffman's original conceptualizations of the total institution as the most comprehensive and best model in our field.

Goffmann's classical depiction of the total institution (1961) still serves as a standard for understanding the problems of institutional living. The *total institution* is described as a place where inmates are brought together under a common authority, are stripped of their normal identities, and are expected to engage in activities of daily living according to formal rules and a rational plan that regiments them. Activities of work, play, and sleep overlap and are typically conducted in the presence of others. The institution (which is often located at a distance from friends and from the previous community of the resident) also effectively cuts residents off from social ties in the outside world. It has been suggested that, among nursing home residents, isolation from society and loss of control over one's life lead to learned helplessness (Coons and Mace 1996; Baltes 1996; Baltes and Baltes 1986).

Frail older persons who typically enter nursing homes are particularly vulnerable because of physical and mental infirmities, sensory impairments, and loss of social supports that have created the need for such placement (Resnick et al. 1997; E. Kahana, B. Kahana, and Kinney 1990). Such vulnerable individuals are particularly sensitive to environmental change, and adverse living conditions (Lawton 1980). Elderly persons living in the community generally fear institutional placement and seldom plan for a move to an institution (E. Kahana, B. Kahana, and Young 1985; Schoenberg and Coward 1997). The transition to living in a nursing home is typically involuntary, with patients seldom playing major roles in the relocation decision or choice of facility (Reinardy 1992). Furthermore, the new institutional setting is unfamiliar to the resident in terms of both physical features and social expectations. Fewer than half of family members visit facilities prior to placement of an elder (Lieberman and Kramer 1991). Unpredictability and uncontrollability are major risk factors accounting for the negative outcomes of institutional relocation (Schultz and Brenner 1977). Lack of involvement in decision making has also been associated with adjustment problems (Rubenstein et al. 1992). Alternatively, positive adjustment can be facilitated where older adults participate in decision-making about relocation (Armer 1993).

It is difficult to establish conclusively which elements of institutionalization are responsible for negative outcomes among residents because the effects of morbidity, relocation, and institutionalization occur concurrently and are difficult to separate (Lieberman and Kramer 1991). Yet the negative personal consequences of life in nursing homes have been documented. Institutionalization has been described in terms of dismantling one's home with its comforts, memories, and freedoms (Savishinsky 1991). Institutionalized elders have shown loss of self-esteem and identity (Tobin 1991), and often manifest withdrawal, apathy, and depression (Gubrium 1975, 1993; R. A. Kane 1995–1996; Vladeck 1980).

Gubrium (1993) conducted qualitative interviews with nursing home residents and found great disjunctures in meaning between the workings of the nursing home as an organization and the textured realities of the "lived experience" of residents. Residents live in a rich world of subjective meaning, which is seldom recognized and validated by the nursing home. In fact, nursing homes may actively resist responding to subjective realities of residents, in an effort to introduce an organizational rationality (Diamond 1992). It has been documented that institutional environments providing limited control over the daily lives of residents result in negative resident outcomes, including diminished life satisfaction (R. L. Kane et al. 1990; Timko et al. 1993).

In spite of the evidence of adverse effects of institutionalization, there is a growing body of research and clinical observation that documents positive features and potential benefits of residential life in nursing homes (Patchner and Balgopal 1993; Pynoos and Regnier 1991). For isolated older persons who can no longer care for themselves, the nursing home can offer protection, improved living conditions, and even homelike qualities (Groger 1994). Advantages of living in a nursing home can also include behavioral expectations that are well matched to the competencies of the frail resident (Baltes and Werner 1992; Werner et al. 1994; Lawton 1980).

Nutritious meals, regular medical care, and supervised administration of medications may maximize health for frail elders living in nursing homes. Proximity to other residents may allow for social needs to be met, and organized activities can lead to meaningful social participation (Bitzan and Kruzich 1990). Indeed, there is some evidence that resident satisfaction subsequent to institutionalization exceeds expectations (E. Kahana, B. Kahana, and Young 1985). Some early studies have noted improved morale (Spasoff et al. 1978) and enhanced family relationships subsequent to institutionalization of elders (Smith and Bengtson 1979).

There are indications that elderly nursing home residents find their lives to be meaningful and that their sources of meaning do not differ significantly from those of community-living older adults (DePaola and Ebersole 1995). Well-being among residents subsequent to institutionalization may reflect not so much the positive influences of institutional life as the resilience and survival skills of residents. Accordingly, Lieberman and Tobin (1983) demonstrated that even in the face of major involuntary environmental changes such as institutionalization, many elderly persons continue to preserve a coherent and consistent self-image.

Adaptation in Institutions. There is growing evidence supporting the view that residents are active agents who attach meaning to and impact actively on their environment, continuing to take personal initiatives to remain socially engaged in the face of personal and environmental obstacles for doing so (E. Kahana, B. Kahana, and Chirayath 1999; Mor et al. 1995; Gubrium 1993).

Goffman (1961) described a range of adaptive responses among inmates of total institutions. *Withdrawal* refers to the resident's efforts to curtail interaction with others and to withhold emotional investment in his or her surroundings. *Intransigence* is a response that challenges institutional authority through noncooperation. These two modes of responding are likely to result in further alienation and to invite negative responses from staff and other residents. *Colonization* represents a strategy of maximizing satisfactions within the confines of the institution by accepting the rules and norms of institutional life. *Conversion* represents an identification with both the outward characteristics and the values of staff. Patients who opt for conversion submerge their identities into their patient roles. Although Goffman's conceptualization and description provide the earliest and possibly the richest sociological efforts to understand resident adaptation in nursing homes, there has been little follow-up research to confirm the typologies that he proposed.

Research has documented that there are active efforts even among frail institutionalized elderly to adapt to demands and stresses of institutional living and to remain socially engaged even while living in an institution (Mor et. al 1995). Instrumental coping strategies have been associated with maintenance of psychological well-being subsequent to institutionalization, whereas affective modes of coping have been related to decline in morale (E. Kahana, B. Kahana, and Young 1987).

Appraisals of life in a nursing home may contribute greatly to perceptions of stress, to coping responses, and ultimately to adaptive outcomes. In fact, an understanding of the interpretive meaning of institutional life may help integrate conflicting findings about effects of selection, relocation, and institutionalization on psychosocial well-being of elders residing in nursing homes (Gubrium 1993).

Aspects of physical frailty that create a need for institutional placement, along with perceived or real abandonment by family, require major reappraisals of both one's worldview and one's self-concept. Given a vulnerable self and loss of intimacy with significant others, the safety of one's physical and social milieu becomes a critical concern. To the extent that new residents of nursing homes can appraise their physical and social environment as safe, they will feel protected. To the extent that they feel that other residents who compose their new reference group are helpful, social integration may be possible, and depersonalization may be avoided. There is evidence that residents in assisted living facilities engage in reciprocal helping social interaction and derive satisfaction from being providers of assistance to others (Litwin 1998). This research supports earlier work (E. Kahana, B. Kahana, Sterin, Fedirko, and Brittis 1990) which demonstrated that perceptions of even minor acts of helpfulness by other residents help the institutionalized elderly reinterpret their surroundings as benign. Formation of social ties with other patients represents an important mode of positive adaptation for nursing home residents (Mor et al. 1995).

Personal backgrounds of residents as well as environmental influences affect the nature of adaptations that residents make in institutions. Lack of mental impairment and few mobility limitations and sensory deficits are associated with maintenance of close social ties within the nursing home (Bitzan and Kruzich 1990). Personality and cognitive traits such as impulse control have been found to be associated with psychosocial well-being subsequent to institutionalization (B. Kahana and E. Kahana 1976).

In order to better understand and operationalize person-environment transactions in nursing homes, several conceptual models have been articulated that take into account both personal and environmental features. Lawton's ecological model (1980) focuses on the importance of matching environmental elements to personal competencies of frail elders. E. Kahana's person-environment congruence model (1982) emphasizes the role of individual differences in needs and environmental preferences, and specifies alternative formulations for expected outcomes based on oversupply, undersupply, or congruence of environmental characteristics, such as stimulation or homogeneity, in relation to personal preferences. It is notable that there has been very limited attention to advancing conceptual models in this arena during the past two decades.

Interactionist perspectives lead to a better understanding of social influences in nursing homes by calling attention to the importance of both personal reactions and environmental presses. Environmental design and intervention approaches

in nursing homes have focused on improving adjustment of residents to nursing homes by providing environments that benefit residents in general, or interventions that improve fit between the environment and personal needs of residents. Research has demonstrated that resident characteristics interact with environmental features of the nursing home to predict outcomes (Baltes et al. 1991; Timko et al. 1993). Accordingly, supportive physical features and assistive services were found to benefit impaired residents while policies permitting resident control were most likely to benefit independent residents. Furthermore, specification of salient dimensions of the institutional milieu has been one important area of progress toward designing better nursing home environments. Moos and Lemke (1996) have conducted pioneering work in providing reliable and valid indicators of social dimensions of the institutional environment.

Specific components of the institutional environment determine the demands, constraints, and benefits of institutional life for residents. They include the administrative structure, the physical environment, and the social environment. The social environment may be further subdivided into staff environment; patient environment; and community representatives such as volunteers, or friends and family, who visit the resident in the institution. There is growing evidence that the perspectives of residents, staff, and families diverge with regard to quality of life in nursing homes (Brennan et al. 1988). Research on administrative structure has focused primarily on size, financing, and type of ownership. Although it has been argued that proprietary ownership may result in poorer quality of care, the link between type of ownership and level of care has not been conclusively established. Similarly, suggested links between size of home or proportion of Medicaid patients and quality of care have not been fully documented (Shapiro and Tate 1995).

Similarities in ethnic, cultural, and social backgrounds of staff and residents appear to facilitate positive interactions, whereas discrepancies in cultural values have been found to hamper communication and mutual understanding (E. Kahana, B. Kahana, Sterin, Fedirko, and Taylor 1993; Harel 1987). Institutional norms as well as formal policies have been found to shape the impact of institutions on residents (Kiyak et al. 1978). Research also suggested that perceived social support from family not only deters institutional placement but also relates to higher self-esteem and diminished depression among elderly nursing home residents (McFall and Miller 1992).

Resident-to-Resident Interactions There has been very little research focusing on the social milieu of nursing homes in terms of resident-to-resident interactions. It is indeed noteworthy that, in one study of nursing home residents, nearly 50 percent of all residents were found never to talk to their roommates, typically because of barriers to communication such as hearing or speech problems (Kovach and Robinson 1996). Nevertheless, among those residents able to talk to their roommates, rapport with the roommate was found to be a significant predictor of life satisfaction. It is notable that communication rules about talking often inhibit communication and contribute to living in silence among nursing home residents (Kaakinen 1992).

The salience of friends appears to be limited for nursing home residents, as there are many barriers to elderly friends maintaining contact with their noninstitutionalized friends. Accordingly, perceived social support from friends did not significantly relate to positive outcomes of nursing home residents (Commerford and Reznikoff 1996).

Family-Resident Interactions Interactions with family also play an important role in social integration of residents. Research has underscored that the majority of institutionalized elderly maintain meaningful ties and interactions with family members (Schwartz and Vogel 1990; High and Rowles 1995; Smith and Bengtson 1979). Ties to children who visit most frequently appear to be closest, followed by ties to other family members and friends (Bitzan and Kruzich 1990). Proximity of family members and previous history of extensive social interactions facilitate continued contact between residents and kin (York and Calsyn 1977). In turn, visitation by families and friends has been associated with enhanced residential functioning and well-being (Greene and Monahan 1982).

Broader roles for family members for being involved in the support and direct care of patients have been discussed, particularly in the social work literature (LaBrake 1996). However, systematic investigations of the efficacy of such efforts are sparse. Some family support group activities as well as family counseling programs have reported success in bringing family and staff closer together (Campbell and Linc 1996). There have also been some educational efforts directed at assisting family members in coming to terms with psychological issues that they face regarding institutionalization of the elder relative (Drysdale et al. 1993).

Even while there is limited indication of systematic and welcoming programs initiated by the nursing home for the involvement of families in the care of residents, there are indications about naturally occurring involvement by family members in the lives and care of institutionalized older adults. Thus, for example, studies indicate that families are highly involved in assisting their relatives with decision making, and in actually making decisions when needed (High and Rowles 1995). Although researchers had expected to find less participation in decision making by families over time (since it was assumed that they would gradually defer to staff in making decisions), it was found that families do remain highly involved in their relatives' lives and well-being, even after four years. Families reported involvement in a broad range of decisions, ranging from those made during crises to those concerning the physical environment and treatment decisions.

There is also evidence, from surveys of family perspectives on nursing home care, that family members are typically sensitive and understanding about the constraints under which nursing home staff work and the difficulties posed by caring for frail elders, and particularly those with dementia (Looman et al. 1997). This research found that families also appreciate positive interpersonal ties between nursing assistants and residents.

The potential of constructive family involvement for improving resident life in nursing homes is yet to be recognized. It could have a major positive influence on helping break down barriers between the outside world and those of the institutions, addressing Goffman's classic challenge to the total institution (1961).

Future Prospects for Policy and Long-Term Care Delivery. It has been argued that, in the future, home care may evolve into a model of personal assistance services, and thus could blur the boundaries between institutional (nursing home) and community-based care (R. A. Kane 1995). To the extent that personal care and housing-related services in nursing homes could be separated, residents and families could gain greater control of their lives. With the support of flexible home care options, many frail older persons could remain in innovative community residential options, such as assisted living arrangements, for the remainder of their lives. Such potential developments are attractive, but assume major changes in the financing of long-term care and the building of private accommodations, which include baths and kitchenettes, in housing for nursing home residents. Such new trends in financing and delivery of care would have to be based on dramatic expansion of personal long-term care insurance and/or availability of savings to finance long-term care. Alternatively, they could be implemented based on major new universal services furnished through social insurance programs (Kingson 1996). However, there are no clear indications that any of these financing options is likely to materialize in the near future. Furthermore it is likely that in the future most new and even existing long-term care services will be implemented by individual states. Increasing involvement in delivery of long-term care by states is likely to lead to increasing variability in the quality of care delivered (R. L. Kane et al. 1998).

In spite of expected increases in alternative long-term care facilities, the population of old-old adults residing in nursing homes is expected to increase dramatically, due largely to the ever-increasing age structure of the U.S. population. It is notable in this regard that research projecting future nursing home use demonstrates that better health in future cohorts of the old-old will only slightly decrease the proportion of time older adults will spend in nursing homes, or the proportion of this cohort who will enter nursing homes (Laditka 1998). Thus the nursing home as an organization is here to stay for the foreseeable future.

Furthermore, it is important to recognize that all the numerous alternatives proposed to address the shortcomings in the current system involve potential problems and tradeoffs (R. A. Kane et al. 1998). Ultimately, the planning, financing, delivery, and oversight of long-term care challenges our values and ingenuity as a society. Accordingly, sociologists, who have generally opted out of the study of long-term care, are very much needed to get involved in this area, if we are to gain deeper understandings and develop systematic research based guidelines for improving services in this field.

CONCLUSION

The foregoing discussion has highlighted a series of counterpoints in consideration of nursing home care on the macro and micro levels. On the macro level, distinctions between medical and social models of care, quality-of-care, and quality-of-life issues have been discussed. Societal needs for cost containment have been juxtaposed with the need to invest greater resources in long-term care to ensure provision of high-quality care. Regulation and free market competition have been presented as alternative strategies to improve standards of care. Uncertainty about service models, along with a great concern about costs of care, have resulted in a stalemate in the field of long-term care (Vladeck 1995).

On the micro level, we have noted evidence for depersonalizing aspects of institutional living, along with data about protective features and benefits of long-term care environments. Furthermore, residents of nursing homes have been described as frail and vulnerable on the one hand, and as adaptable and resilient on the other. The ultimate well-being of nursing home residents is seen as a function of the environment, of the person, or of transactions between the two. These dualities are useful to propel dialogue and to permit a thorough examination of nursing home care. At the same time they hold the danger of oversimplification of issues that may be approached from a unidimensional framework as proponents advocate one pole of the duality or the other. In fact, a sociological understanding of nursing homes underscores the complexity and multidimensionality of the social context and the social world of the nursing home. Thus, there is great benefit in attempting to integrate insights gained from both poles of the dualities discussed.

The nursing home resident of the future is likely to be ever more frail, especially if we succeed in developing more home-based alternatives to care. Hence, we cannot reject the medical model in favor of a social model of care, or focus exclusively on quality of life rather than on quality of care. Instead, we need to complement concerns of high-quality health care with those of high standards for social care. Similarly, just as proprietary care is likely to remain a part of health care in the United States, so regulation is here to stay. Although prospective nursing home residents are likely to be ever more frail, they are also likely to be more highly educated and more conscious of their rights as consumers. Financing mechanisms that enhance the ability of the consumers of long-term care to exercise control over their lives can complement regulatory efforts to upgrade quality of care in nursing home settings. On the broadest societal level, decisions about both commitment of resources and development of creative alternatives to institution-based, long-term care are likely to shape the parameters and qualities of nursing homes of the future.

The experience of a given individual in being cared for in a nursing home must ultimately be understood in the context of the complex matrix of influences posed by institutional living. Accordingly, it is not fruitful to focus exclusively on either the ill effects or the benefits of institutionalization. Reviews of nursing homes continue to focus on normative understandings, generally highlighting poor quality of care in such facilities. As we have noted in this essay, empirical support for such negative conclusions is generally derived from qualitative research. Quantitative studies generally provide less support for expectations of decline and adverse patient reactions. In an effort to understand conflicting conclusions of different genres of research in this area, it is useful to focus on personal as well as environmental and situational influences that moderate the effects of institutional living. More carefully designed nursing home–based research, utilizing quantitative as well as qualitative approaches, is needed to specify conditions of both person and environment that maximize the well-being of the individual requiring institutional care.

Newer health care options, such as CCRCs, assisted living, and special care units, have been touted as more patient-responsive solutions to care than traditional nursing homes. Nevertheless, true consumer control and resident outcomes are still largely contingent on the resident's power to demand and advocate for appropriate care options. If an older adult becomes physically frail or mentally impaired, such options are likely to diminish, or even evaporate. Consumers are once again at the mercy of bureaucratic decision making about their best interests.

Even advocates of alternative forms of long-term care acknowledge that nursing home care will continue to be needed and utilized by the increasing segment of old-old citizens. Sanctions, incentives, and intervention programs have all been shown to be beneficial, at least to a limited extent, in improving the quality of care and the quality of life in nursing homes.

Enhancing the quality of nursing home care creates a challenge for society to commit greater resources generated by currently productive citizens to the care of those who have made previous contributions. The resources society devotes to long-term care ultimately mirror the value placed by society on its frail or dependent citizens. Thus, a devaluing of older people is likely to result in a devaluing of institutions that care for them, along with a devaluing of the providers of their care. Conversely, more positive societal attitudes toward frail elders are likely to be translated into increasing involvement by high-caliber, trained professionals in the care of the institutionalized elderly. In addition, positive societal attitudes should bring family members and community representatives into closer contact with institutions, and should help to break down barriers between the nursing home and community living.

REFERENCES

Agich, G. J. 1993 *Autonomy and Long-Term Care.* New York: Oxford University Press.

Andersen, B. R. 1987 "What Makes Excellent Nursing Homes Different from Ordinary Nursing Homes?" *Danish Medical Bulletin, Special Supplement Series* 5:7–11.

Armer, J. M. 1993 "Relocation and Adjustment in the PGC Morale Scale and the IRA." *Clinical Gerontologist* 13(3):77–81.

Aronson, M. K. (ed.) 1994 *Reshaping Dementia Care: Practice and Policy in Long-Term Care.* Thousand Oaks, Calif.: Sage.

Baltes, M. M. 1996 *Many Faces of Dependency in Old Age.* Cambridge, Eng. Cambridge University Press.

——, and P. B. Baltes 1986 *Psychology of Control and Aging.* Hillsdale, N.J.: Lawrence Erlbaum.

Baltes, M. M., and W. H. Werner 1992 "Behavior System of Dependency in the Elderly: Interaction with the Social Environment." In M. G. Ory, R. P. Ables, and P. D. Lipman, eds., *Aging, Health, and Behavior.* Newbury Park, Calif.: Sage.

——, and R. Monika 1991 "Successful Aging in Long-Term Care Institutions." In S. K. Warner and M. P. Lawton, eds., *Annual Review of Gerontology and Geriatrics.* New York: Springer.

Banaszak-Holl, J., and M. A. Hines 1996 "Factors Associated with Nursing Home Staff Turnover." *The Gerontologist* 36(4):512–517.

Bellah, R. N. 1996 *Habits of the Heart: Individualism and Commitment in American Life: Updated Edition with a New Introduction.* Berkeley: University of California Press.

Bitzan, J. E., and J. M. Kruzich 1990 "Interpersonal Relationships of Nursing Home Residents." *The Gerontologist* 30(3):385–390.

Bonifazi, W. L. 1998 "Changing Population." *Contemporary Long-Term Care* 21(12):54–58.

Borson, S., and K. Doane 1997 "The Impact of OBRA-87 on Psychotropic Drug Prescribing in Skilled Nursing Facilities." *Psychiatric Services* 48(10):1289–1296.

Brennan, P. L., R. H. Moos, and S. Lemke 1988 "Preferences of Older Adults and Experts for Physical and Architectural Features of Group Living Facilities." *Gerontologist* 28:84–90.

Brittis, S. 1996 "Sharing Destinies: Staff and Residents' Perspectives on Excellence in High Quality Nursing Homes in London, England and New York City, U.S.A." Unpublished doctoral dissertation, Case Western Reserve University.

Bureau of Labor Statistics (BLS) 1995 *Special Tabulations Prepared for the Institute of Medicine Committee on the Adequacy of Nurse Staffing in Hospitals and Nursing Homes.* Washington, D.C.: U.S. Department of Labor.

Burger, S. G., V. Fraser, S. Hunt, and B. Frank 1996 *Nursing Homes: Getting Good Care There.* San Louis Obispo, Calif.: Impact.

Camp, C., and J. Mattern 1999 "Innovations in Managing Alzheimer's Disease." In *Innovations in Practice and Service Delivery Across the Lifespan.* New York: Oxford University Press.

Campbell, J., and L. Linc 1996 "Support Groups for Visitors of Residents in Nursing Homes." *Journal of Gerontological Nursing* 22(2):30–35.

Castle, N. G. 1998 "Innovations in Dying in the Nursing Home: The Impact of Market Characteristics." *Omega* 36(3):227–240.

Charmaz, K., and D. A. Paterniti 1999 *Health, Illness, and Healing: Society, Social Context, and Self.* Los Angeles: Roxbury.

Cockerham, W. C. 1998 *Medical Sociology,* 7th ed. Englewood Cliffs, N.J.: Prentice-Hall.

Cohen, M. A. 1998 "Emerging Trends in the Finance and Delivery of Long-Term Care: Public and Private Opportunities and Challenges." *Gerontologist* 38(1):80–89.

Cohen-Mansfield, J., M. S. Marx, S. Lipson, and P. Werner 1999 "Predictors of Mortality in Nursing Home Residents." *Journal of Clinical Epidemiology* 52(4):273–280.

Commerford, M. C., and M. Reznikoff 1996 "Relationship of Religion and Perceived Social Support to Self-Esteem and Depression in Nursing Home Residents." *Journal of Psychology* 130(1):35–50.

Coons, D., and N. Mace 1996 *Quality of Life in Long-Term Care.* New York: Hayworth.

Cox, E. O., and R. J. Parsons 1994 *Empowerment-Oriented Social Work Practice with the Elderly.* Pacific Grove, Calif.: Brooks/Cole.

Day, W. V. 1996 "There 'Oughta Be a Law' to Eliminate so Many Laws." *Nursing Homes Long-Term Care Management* 45(10):16–18.

Densen, P. M. 1987 "The Elderly and the Health Care System: Another Perspective." *Milbank Memorial Fund Quarterly* 65:614–638.

DePaola, S. J., and P. Ebersole 1995 "Meaning in Life Categories of Elderly Nursing Home Residents." *International Journal of Aging and Human Development* 40(3):227–236.

Diamond, T. 1992 *Making Grey Gold: Narratives of Nursing Home Care.* Chicago: University of Chicago Press.

Drysdale, A. E., C. F. Nelson, and N. M. Wineman 1993 "Families Need Help Too: Group Treatment for Families of Nursing Home Residents." *Clinical Nurse Specialist* 7(3):130–134.

Dunbar, J. M., R. R. Neufield, H. C. White, and L. S. Libow 1996 "Retrain, Don't Restrain: The Educational Intervention of the National Nursing Home Restraint Removal Project." *Gerontologist* 36(4):539–542.

Etzioni, A. 1993 *The Spirit of Community.* New York: Touchstone.

Evans, L. K. 1996 "Knowing the Patient: The Route to Individualized Care." *Journal of Gerontological Nursing* 3:13–19.

Feil, N. 1982 *V/F Validation, the Feil Method: How to Help Disoriented Old-Old.* Cleveland, Ohio: Edward Feil.

Fortinsky, R. H., and L. Raff 1995–1996 "Changing Role of Physicians in Nursing Homes." *Generations* 19(4):30–35.

Garahan, M. B., J. A. Waller, M. Houghton, W. A. Tisdale, and C. F. Runge 1992 "Hearing Loss Prevalence and Management in Nursing Home Residents." *Journal of the American Geriatrics Society* 40:130–134.

Gaston, P. 1994 "Families as an Integral Part of Dementia Care." In M. K. Aronson, ed., *Reshaping Dementia Care: Practice and Policy in Long-Term Care*. Thousand Oaks, Calif.: Sage.

Goffman, E. 1961 *Asylums: Essays on the Social Situation of Mental Patients*. New York: Anchor.

Greene, V. L., and D. Monahan 1982 "The Impact of Visitation on Patient Well-Being in Nursing Homes." *Gerontologist* 22(4):418–423.

Groger, L. 1994 "Decision as Process: A Conceptual Model of Black Elders' Nursing Home Placement." *Journal of Aging Studies* 8(1):77–94.

Grower, R., C. Wallace, G. Weinstein, K. Lazar, S. Leventer, and T. Martico-Greenfield 1994 "Approaches to Social Programming." In M. K. Aronson, ed., *Reshaping Dementia Care: Practice and Policy in Long-Term Care*. Thousand Oaks, Calif.: Sage.

Gubrium, J. 1975 *Living and Dying at Murray Manor*. New York: St. Martin's Press.

—— 1993 *Speaking of Life: Horizons of Meaning for Nursing Home Residents*. Hawthorne, N.Y.: Aldine de Gruyter.

Hamme, J. M. 1991 "Federal Nursing Home Reform: An Overview." In *The Long-term Care Handbook: Legal, Operational, and Financial Guideposts*. Washington: National Health Lawyers Association.

Harel, Z. 1987 "Ethnicity and Aging: Implications for Service Organizations." In C. H. Hayes, R. A. Kalish, and D. Guttman, eds., *European-American Elderly*. New York: Springer.

Hawes, C., V. Mor, C. D. Phillips, E. Fries-Brant, J. N. Morris, E. Steel-Friedlob, A. M. Greene, and M. Nennstiel 1997 "OBRA-87 Nursing Home Regulations and Implementation of the Resident Assessment Instrument: Effects on Process Quality." *Journal of the American Geriatrics Society* 45(8):977–985.

Hayslip, B., and J. Leon 1992 *Hospice Care*. Newbury Park, Calif.: Sage.

Henderson, J. N., and M. D. Vesperi 1995 *The Culture of Long-Term Care: Nursing Home Ethnography*. Westport, Conn.: Bergin and Garvey.

Hepburn, K. W., W. Caron, M. Luptak, S. Ostwald, L. Grant, and J. M. Keenan 1997 "The Family Stories Workshop: Stories for Those Who Cannot Remember." *Gerontologist* 37(6):827–832.

High, D. M., and G. D. Rowles 1995 "Nursing Home Residents, Families, and Decision Making: Toward an Understanding of Progressive Surrogacy." *Journal of Aging Studies* 9(2):101–117.

Hing, E. 1987 "Use of Nursing Homes by the Elderly: Preliminary Data from the 1985 National Nursing Home Survey." *NCHS Advancedata* 135:1–11.

Institute of Medicine (IOM) 1986 *Improving the Quality of Care in Nursing Homes*. Washington, D.C.: National Academy Press.

—— 1996 *Nursing Staff in Hospitals and Nursing Homes: Is it Adequate?* In G. S. Wunderlich, F. A. Sloan, and C. K. Davis, eds., Washington, D.C.: National Academy Press.

Johnson, C. L., and B. M. Barer 1997 *Life Beyond 85 Years: The Aura of Survivorship*. New York: Springer.

Kaakinen, J. W. 1992 "Living with Silence." *Gerontologist* 32(2):258–264.

Kahana, B., and E. Kahana 1976 "The Relationship of Impulse Control to Cognition and Adjustment Among Institutionalized Aged Women." *Journal of Gerontology* 30(6):679–687.

Kahana, E. 1973 "The Humane Treatment of Old People in Institutions." *Gerontologist* 13:282–289.

——, J. Liang, and B. Felton 1980 "Alternative Models of Person-Environment Fit: Prediction of Morale in Three Homes for the Aged." *Journal of Gerontology* 35:584–595.

—— 1982 "A Congruence Model of Person-Environment Interactions." In M. P. Lawton, P. G. Windley, and T. O. Byerts, eds., *Aging and the Environment: Theoretical Approaches*. New York: Springer.

Kahana, E., and B. Kahana 1983 "Environmental Continuity, Discontinuity, and Futurity, and Adaptation of the Aged." In G. Rowles and R. Ohta, eds., *Aging and Milieu: Environmental Perspectives on Growing Old*. New York: Academic.

——, and H. Chirayath 1999 "Innovations in Institutional Care from a Patient-Responsive Perspective." In D. E. Biegel and A. Blum, eds., *Innovations in Practice and Service Delivery across the Lifespan*. New York: Oxford University Press.

Kahana, E., B. Kahana, K. Kercher, and H. Chirayath 1999 "A Patient-Responsive Model of Hospital Care." In J. J. Kronenfeld, ed., *Research in the Sociology of Health Care* 16:31–54.

Kahana, E., B. Kahana, and J. M. Kinney 1990 "Coping among Vulnerable Elders." In Z. Harel, P. Ehrlich, and R. Hubbard, eds., *Understanding and Servicing Vulnerable Aged*. New York: Springer.

Kahana, E., B. Kahana, and K. Riley 1989 "Person-Environment Transactions Relevant to Control and Helplessness in Institutional Settings." In P. S. Fry, ed., *Psychological Perspectives of Helplessness*. Alberta, Canada: Elsevier Science.

Kahana, E., B. Kahana, G. Sterin, T. Fedirko, and S. Brittis 1990 "Patterns of Mutual Assistance and Well-Being among Ethnic Nursing Home Residents." Paper presented at the meeting of the Society for Traumatic Stress, New Orleans.

Kahana, E., B. Kahana, G. Sterin, T. Fedirko, and R. Taylor 1993 "Adaptation to Institutional Life among Polish, Jewish, and Western European Elderly." In C. Barresi and D. Stull, eds., *Ethnicity and Long-Term Care*. New York: Springer.

Kahana, E., B. Kahana, and R. Young 1985 "Social Factors in Institutional Living." In W. Peterson and J. Quadagno, eds., *Social Bonds in Later Life: Aging and Interdependence*. Beverly Hills, Calif.: Sage.

—— 1987 "Strategies of Coping and Post-Institutional Outcomes." *Research on Aging* 9:182–199.

Kahana, J. 1994 "Reevaluating the Nursing Home Ombudsman's Role with a View toward Expanding the Concept of Dispute Resolution." *Journal of Dispute Resolution* 94:217–233.

Kane, R. A. 1995 "Expanding the Home Care Concept: Blurring Distinctions among Home Care, Institutional Care, and Other Long-Term Care Services." *Milbank Quarterly* 73(2):161–186.

—— 1995–1996 "Transforming Care Institutions for the Frail Elderly: Out of One Shall Be Many." *Generations* 4:62–68.

——, R. L. Kane, and R. C. Ladd 1998 *The Heart of Long-Term Care*. New York: Oxford University Press.

——, and K. B. Wilson 1993 *Assisted Living in the United States: A New Paradigm for Residential Care for Frail Older Persons?* Washington, D.C.: American Association for Retired Persons.

Kane, R. L., J. G. Evans, and MacFadyen 1990 *Improving the Health of Older People: A World View*. Oxford, England: Oxford University Press.

——, and R. A. Kane 1978 "Care of the Aged: Old Problems in Need of New Solutions." *Science* 200(26):913–919.

——, ——, and R. C. Ladd, W. N. Veazie 1998 "Variation in State Spending for Long-Term Care: Factors Associated with More Balanced Systems." *Journal of Health Politics, Policy, and Law* 23(2):363–390.

——, J. G. Ouslander, and I. B. Abrass 1994 *Essentials of Clinical Geriatrics*, 3rd ed. New York: McGraw-Hill.

Kim, E., and B. Rovner 1996 "Psychiatric Care in the Nursing Home." In W. E. Reichman, and P. R. Katz, eds., *The Nursing Home as a Psychiatric Hospital*. New York: Oxford University Press.

Kingson, E. R. 1996 "Ways of Thinking about the Long-Term Care of the Baby-Boom Cohorts." *Journal of Aging and Social Policy* 7(3–4):3–23.

Kiyak, A., E. Kahana, and N. Lev 1978 "The Role of Informal Norms in Determining Institutional Totality in Homes for the Aged." *Long-Term Care and Health Administration Quarterly* 2(4):102–110.

Kovach, S. S., and J. D. Robinson 1996 "The Roommate Relationship for the Elderly Nursing Home Resident." *Journal of Social and Personal Relationships* 13(4):627–634.

LaBrake, T. 1996 *How to Get Families More Involved in the Nursing Home: Four Programs That Work and Why*. New York: Haworth.

Laditka, S. B. 1998 "Modeling Lifetime Nursing Home Use under Assumptions of Better Health." *Journal of Gerontology: Social Sciences* 53B(4):S177–S187.

Laird, C. 1979 *Limbo: A Memoir about Life in a Nursing Home by a Survivor*. Novato, Calif.: Chandler and Sharp.

Lantz, M. S., V. Giambanco, and E. N. Buchalter 1996 "A Ten-Year Review of the Effect of OBRA-87 on Psychotropic Prescribing Practices in an Academic Nursing Home." *Psychiatric Services* 47(9):951–955.

Lawton, M. P. 1980 *Environment and Aging*. Monterey, Calif.: Brooks/Cole.

——, M. Fulcomer, and M. H. Kleban 1984 "Architecture for the Mentally Impaired Elderly." *Environment and Behavior* 16(6):730–757.

Leutz, W. N., J. A. Capitman, M. Macadam, and R. Abrahams 1992 *Care for Frail Elders: Developing Community Solutions*. Westport, Conn.: Greenwood.

Levit, K. R., H. C. Lazenby, B. R. Braden, C. A. Cowan, P. A. McDonnell, L. Sivarajan, J. M. Stiller, D. K. Won, C. S. Donham, A. M. Long, and M. W. Stewart 1996 "National Health Expenditures, 1995." *Health Care Financing Review* 18(1):175–214.

Lewis, M. A., S. Cretin, and R. L. Cane 1985 "The Natural History of Nursing Home Patients." *Gerontologist* 25(4):382–388.

Linz, C. W., L. Fischer, and R. M. Arnold 1993 *The Erosion of Autonomy in Long-Term Care*. New York: Oxford University Press.

Lieberman, M. A., and J. H. Kramer 1991 "Factors Affecting Decisions to Institutionalize Demented Elderly." *Gerontologist* 31(3):371–374.

Lieberman, M. A., and S. S. Tobin 1983 *The Experience of Old Age: Stress, Coping and Survival.* New York: Basic Books.

Litwin, H. 1998 "The Provision of Informal Support by Elderly People Residing in Assisted Living Facilities." *Gerontologist* 38(2):239–246.

Longino, C. F. 1998 "Geographic Mobility and the Baby Boom." *Generations* 22(1):60–64.

Looman, W. J., L. S. Noelker, D. Schur, C. J. Whitlatch, and K. Ejaz-Farida 1997 "Nursing Assistants Caring for Dementia Residents in Nursing Homes: The Family's Perspective on the High Quality of Care." *American Journal of Alzheimer's Disease* 12(5):221–226.

Lusky, R. A., and S. R. Ingman 1994 "Medical Care in Residential Settings: The Nursing Home in Transition." In W. E. Folts and D. E. Yeatts, eds., *Housing and the Aging Population: Options for the New Century.* New York: Garland.

Maslow, A. H. 1970 *Motivation and Personality.* New York: Harper and Row.

McFall, S., and B. Miller 1992 "Caregiver Burden and the Continuum of Care: A Longitudinal Perspective." *Research on Aging* 14(3):376–398.

Meyer, H. 1998 "The Bottom Line on Assisted Living." *Hospitals and Health Networks* (July 20).

Moos, R. H., and S. Lemke 1996 *Evaluating Residential Facilities: The Multifacet Environmental Assessment Procedure.* Thousand Oaks, Calif.: Sage.

Mor, V., Kenneth Branco, J. Fleishman, and C. Hawes 1995 "The Structure of Social Engagement among Nursing Home Residents." *Journals of Gerontology: Series B: Psychological Sciences and Social Sciences* 50B(3):P1–P8.

Mui, A. C., and D. Burnette 1994 "Long-Term Care Service Use by Frail Elders: Is Ethnicity a Factor?" *Gerontologist* 34(2):190–198.

National Center for Health Statistics (NCHS) 1997 "An Overview of Nursing Homes and their Current Residents: Data from the 1995 National Nursing Home Survey." *Advance Data from Vital and Health Statistics,* no. 280. Bethesda, Md.: NCHS.

Netting, F. E., and C. C. Wilson 1994 "CCRC Oversight: Implications for Public Regulations and Private Accreditation." *Journal of Applied Gerontology* 13:250–266.

Newcomer, R., S. Preston, and S. S. Roderick 1995 "Assisted Living and Nursing Unit Use among Continuing Care Retirement Community Residents." *Research on Aging* 17(2):149–167.

Newman, S. J. 1985 "Housing and Long-Term Care: The Suitability of the Elderly's Housing to the Provision of In-Home Services." *Gerontologist* 25(1):35–40.

Nyman, J. A., and C. R. Geyer 1989 "Promoting the Quality of Life in Nursing Homes: Can Regulations Succeed?" *Journal of Health Politics, Policy and Law* 14(4):797–816.

Parsons, Y. 1997 "No Shades of Gray." *Contemporary Long-Term Care* 20(9):42–47.

Patchner, M. A., and P. R. Balgopal 1993 *Excellence in Nursing Homes.* New York: Springer.

Pearce, B. W. 1998 *Senior Living Communities: Operations Management and Marketing for Assisted Living, Congregate, and Continuing Care Retirement Communities.* Baltimore, Md.: Johns Hopkins University Press.

Plautz, R., and B. Timen 1992 "Positioning Can Make the Difference." *Nursing Homes* 41(1):30–33.

Pynoos, J., and V. Regnier 1991 "Improving Residential Living Environments for the Frail Elderly: Bridging the Gaps between Theory and Application." In J. E. Birren, J. E. Lubber, J. C. Rowe, and D. E. Deutchman, eds., *The Concept and Measurement of Quality of Life in the Frail Elderly.* New York: Academic.

Reinardy, J. R. 1992 "Decisional Control in Moving to a Nursing Home: Post-Admission Adjustment and Well-Being." *Gerontologist* 32(1):96–103.

Resnick, H. E., B. E. Fries, and L. M. Verbrugge 1997 "Windows to Their World: The Effect of Sensory Impairments on Social Engagement and Activity Time in Nursing Home Residents." *Journals of Gerontology: Series B: Psychological Sciences and Social Sciences* 52B(3):S135–S144.

Rice, T. 1989 "The Use, Cost, and Economic Burden of Nursing-Home Care in 1985." *Medical Care* 27(12):1133–1147.

Rovner, B. W., and I. R. Katz 1993 "Psychiatric Disorders in the Nursing Home: A Selective Review of Studies Related to Clinical Care." *International Journal of Geriatric Psychiatry* 8:75–87.

Rubenstein, R. L., J. C. Kilbride, and S. Nagy 1992 *Elders Living Alone: Frailty and the Perception of Choice.* New York: Aldine.

Rubenstein, L. Z., and D. Wieland 1993 *Improving Care in the Nursing Home: Comprehensive Reviews of Clinical Research.* Newbury Park, Calif.: Sage.

Savishinsky, J. S. 1991 *The Ends of Time: Life and Work in a Nursing Home.* New York: Bergin and Garvey.

Schnelle, J. F., M. P. McNees, S. F. Simmons, M. E. Agnew, and V. C. Crooks 1993 "Managing Nurse Aides to Promote Quality of Care in the Nursing Home." In L. Z. Rubenstein and D. Wieland, eds., *Improving Care in the Nursing Home: Comprehensive Reviews of Clinical Research.* Newbury Park, Calif.: Sage.

Schnelle, J. F., J. G. Ouslander, and P. A. Cruise 1997 "Policy Without Technology: A Barrier to Improving Nursing Home Care." *Gerontologist* 37(4):527–532.

Schoenberg, N. E., and R. T. Coward 1997 "Attitudes about Entering a Nursing Home: Comparisons of Older Rural and Urban African-American Women." *Journal of Aging Studies* 11(1):27–47.

Schultz, R., and G. Brenner 1977 "Relocation of the Aged: A Review and Theoretical Analysis." *Journal of Gerontology* 32:323–333.

Schwartz, A. N., and M. E. Vogel 1990 "Nursing Home Staff and Resident's Families Role Expectations." *Gerontologist* 30(1):49–53.

Shapiro, E., and R. B. Tate 1995 "Monitoring the Outcomes of Quality of Care in Nursing Homes Using Administrative Data." *Canadian Journal on Aging* 14(4):755–768.

Shaughnessy, P. W. 1994 "Changing Institutional Long-Term Care to Improve Rural Health Care." In R. T. Coward, C. N. Bull, G. Kukulka, and J. M. Galliher, eds., *Services for Rural Elders*. New York: Springer.

Sherwood, S., H. S. Ruchlin, C. C. Sherwood, and S. A. Morris 1997 *Continuing Care Retirements Communities*. Baltimore, Md.: Johns Hopkins University Press.

Shield, R. R. 1988 *Uneasy Endings: Daily Life in an American Nursing Home*. Ithaca, N.Y.: Cornell University Press.

Siegler, E. L., E. Capezuti, G. Maislin, M. Baumgarten, L. Evans, and N. Strumpf 1997 "Effects of a Restraint Reduction Intervention and OBRA '87 Regulations on Psychoactive Drug Use in Nursing Homes." *Journal of the American Geriatrics Society* 45(7):791–796.

Smith, K., and V. Bengston 1979 "Positive Consequences of Institutionalizations: Solidarity between Elderly Parents and Their Middle-Aged Children." *Gerontologist* 19(5):438–447.

Snowden, M., and P. Roy-Byrne 1998 "Mental Illness and Nursing Home Reform: OBRA-87 Ten Years Later." *Psychiatric Services* 49(2):229–233.

Soth, N. B. 1997 *Informed Treatment: Milieu Management in Psychiatric Hospitals and Residential Treatment Centers*. Lanham, Md.: Medical Library Association/ Scarecrow.

Spasoff, R. A., A. S. Kraus, E. J. Beattie, D. E. Holden, and J. S. Lawson 1978 "A Longitudinal Study of Elderly Residents of Long-Stay Institutions." *Gerontologist* 18(3):281–291.

Strahan, G. W. 1997 "An Overview of Nursing Homes and Their Current Residents: Data from the 1995 National Nursing Home Survey." *Advance Data from National Center for Health Statistics, Number 280*. Atlanta: Centers for Disease Control and Prevention.

Timko, C., A. T. Q. Nguyen, W. Williford, and R. H. Moos 1993 "Quality of Care and Outcomes of Chronic Mentally Ill Patients in Hospitals and Nursing Homes." *Hospital and Community Psychiatry* 44(3):241–246.

Tobin, S. S. 1991 *Personhood in Advanced Old Age: Implications for Practice*. New York: Springer.

U.S. Bureau of the Census 1998 *Statistical Abstract of the United States*, 118th ed. Washington, D.C.: National Technical Information Services.

Vladeck, B. C. 1980 *Unloving Care–The Nursing Home Tragedy*. New York: Basic.

—— 1995 "Long-Term Care: The View from the Health Care Financing Administration." In J. M. Wiener, S. B. Clauser, and D. L. Kennell, eds., *Persons with Disabilities: Issues in Health Care Financing and Service Delivery*. Washington, D.C.: Brookings Institution.

Wagner, L., V. Wahlberg, and A. M. Worning 1994 "Drug Consumption among Elderly–A Four-Year Study." *Scandinavian Journal of Caring Sciences* 8(2):113–117.

Wallace, S. P., L. Levy-Storms, R. Kington, and R. M. Andersen 1998 "The Persistence of Race and Ethnicity in the Use of Long-Term Care." *Journal of Gerontology: Social Sciences* 53B(2):S104–S112.

Werner, P., V. Koroknay, J. Braun, and J. Cohen-Mansfield 1994 "Individualized Care Alternatives Used in the Process of Removing Physical Restraints in the Nursing Home." *Journal of American Geriatrics Society* 42:3.

Whanger, A. D. 1980 "Treatment within the Institutions." In *Handbook of Geriatric Psychiatry*. New York: Van Nostrand Reinhold.

Williams, C. 1986 "Improving Care in Nursing Homes Using Community Advocacy." *Social Science and Medicine* 23(12):1297–1303.

York, J., and R. Calsyn 1977 "Family Involvement in Nursing Homes." *Gerontologist* 17(6):500–505.

Zablotsky, D. L., and M. G. Ory 1995 "Fulfilling the Potential: Modifying the Current Long-Term Care System to Meet the Needs of Persons with AIDS." *Research in the Sociology of Health Care* 12:313–328.

EVA KAHANA

LONGITUDINAL RESEARCH

NOTE: *Although the following article has not been revised for this edition of the Encyclopedia, the substantive coverage is currently appropriate. The editors have provided a list of recent works at the end of the article to facilitate research and exploration of the topic.*

According to Heckman and Singer, "Longitudinal data are widely and uncritically regarded as a panacea . . . The conventional wisdom in social science equates 'longitudinal' with 'good' and discussion of the issue rarely rises above that level" (1985, p. ix).

There is probably no methodological maxim in sociology more often repeated than the call for longitudinal data. From the work of David Hume more than 250 years ago, to the exhortations for a "radical reformation" in the work of Stanley Lieberson (1985, p. xiii), the importance of longitudinal data has been emphasized and reemphasized. Yet it is doubtful that there is an area of sociological method in which more disagreement exists both as to rationale and as to method. Until relatively recently, it has been possible to ignore the problem because longitudinal data have been relatively rare, and methods for their analysis quite sparse. Since 1965, however, there has been a virtual flood of new longitudinal data and a concomitant increase in sophisticated methods of analysis. In large part the computer has made both developments possible, permitting the management of data sets of enormous complexity along with analyses undreamed of only a short while ago.

At the micro level, numerous longitudinal studies have tracked individuals over a good share of their lifetimes. For example, some participants in the Oakland and Berkeley studies of growth and development have been sporadically studied from birth until well into their seventies (Elder, this volume). On a more systematic basis, the Panel Study of Income Dynamics (PSID) has interviewed a panel based on an original sample of five thousand families (households) on an annual basis since the mid 1960s, supplementing the sample with new households formed as split-offs from the original families (Duncan and Morgan 1985). Many other large-scale panel studies, some extending over periods of thirty years and longer, are in progress (Migdal et al. 1981).

At the macro level, extended time series on various social and economic indicators such as GNP, fertility, mortality, and education are gradually becoming available in machine-readable form from virtually all industrialized societies and from many that are less developed. In some cases, data series, particularly for vital statistics, go back for decades. In other cases, such as China and the Soviet Union, modern-era data are gradually being accumulated and linked to earlier series. Descriptions of many such data sets can be found in the annual guide published by the Inter-University Consortium for Political and Social Research (ICPSR 1991).

Perhaps the most exciting developments are at the nexus of macro- and micro-level analysis. In the United States, for example, the General Social Survey (GSS) has obtained data on repeated cross-sectional samples of the population (that is, the population is followed longitudinally but specific individuals are not) on an annual basis (with two exceptions) since 1972. More recently, annual surveys modeled on the GSS have been started in a number of other countries (Smith 1986). Because of the careful replication, these surveys permit one to track aggregate responses of the changing population on a wide variety of issues (such as on attitudes toward abortion or capital punishment) over time. As the time series becomes ever longer, it is possible to carry out a multilevel analysis, linking micro and macro variables. For example, using the GSS, DiPrete and Grusky (1990) attempt to link short-term changes in rates of social mobility to macro-level changes in the U.S. economy.

Although the size and complexity of the longitudinal data base has expanded rapidly, so have the statistical tools with which to analyze it. Perhaps the most exciting development is in the area of "event history models," which permit one to relate an underlying rate of transition in continuous time to a set of "covariates" or independent variables. However, event models are by no means the only development. New and powerful approaches to the analysis of means over time, to structural equation models, and to various forms of categorical data analysis have given the researchers unprecedented power. Standard computer packages now make routine what was impossible in the 1980s.

THE RATIONALE FOR LONGITUDINAL RESEARCH

Longitudinal studies are carried out in virtually every area of the social sciences. Although studies of infant development and national development share certain similarities, it is not likely that a single rationale, design, or approach to analysis will simultaneously apply to every area in which longitudinal data might be collected. At the most abstract level, there are three basic reasons for conducting a longitudinal study.

First, in any area in which development and change over time are at issue, there is, almost by definition, a necessity to obtain time-ordered data. Questions pertaining to rate and sequence of change, and to variability in rates and sequences are at the heart of longitudinal research. At one level, these questions are essentially descriptive, and getting an adequate descriptive handle on time-ordered data is an essential first step in coming to any understanding of change.

A second reason involves the role of temporal priority in causal analysis. There are few things on which philosophers of science agree when it comes to causation (see Marini and Singer 1988 for a superb review), but one is that A must precede B in time if A is to be taken as a cause of B. It is natural to assume that observing A before B means that A precedes B. Unfortunately, designs that actually allow one to establish temporal, let alone causal, priority are not as easily arrived at as one might think.

Related to the issue of temporal priority is the cross-sectional fallacy. Lieberson (1985, pp. 179–183) argues that assertions of causality based on cross-sectional data must necessarily imply a longitudinal relationship. To show that city size "leads to crime" based on cross-sectional data implies a dynamic relationship that may or may not be true. The problem is particularly acute in cross-sectional age comparisons that are necessarily confounded with cohort differences. All cross-sectional attempts to ascertain the "effect" of age on income confound cohort differences in average income with age differences.

A third reason, particularly relevant to sociologists, is the necessity to distinguish gross change from net change. A census taken at two points in time shows changes in the distribution of a variable, say occupation, at the macro level. We might find that the proportion of the population in service-oriented occupations increases over the period of a decade. That indicator of net change conceals myriad patterns of gross change at the individual level. The count of persons in service occupations at two points in time consists of persons who were occupationally stable over the interval and persons who changed in various ways. Of course the population itself changed over the interval due to age-related changes in the labor

force, migration, and differing levels of labor-force participation. All of this is masked by repeated cross-sectional samples.

Finally, although not really a "rationale" for longitudinal research, observation plans with repeated measures on the same individuals can offer certain statistical advantages. Cook and Ware (1983) discuss these in detail.

TYPES OF LONGITUDINAL DATA

For many sociologists, the term *longitudinal* connotes a particular design, usually referred to as a panel study, in which individual subjects are measured repeatedly over time. A more general definition is desirable. Longitudinal data consist of information that can be ordered in time. Such data can be obtained in a variety of ways: by measuring the subject prospectively at repeated intervals, by obtaining a retrospective history in one or more interviews, from institutional records, or various combinations of these approaches. "Strong" longitudinal data preserve exact time intervals, while "weak" data provide sequence and order but lose interval. The distinction is parallel to that between interval and ordinal measurement.

As Featherman (1977) notes, under some circumstances, retrospective data collection may have substantial advantages of time and cost. Most surveys collect retrospective data of one kind or another, such as educational attainment, family background, and marital histories. Using structured interviewing methods in which the respondent is provided with a time-oriented matrix, it is possible to collect quite accurate information on many aspects of the life course. For example, as part of an ongoing panel, Freedman et al. (1988) obtained retrospective reports of family structure and other demographic variables that had previously been measured contemporaneously. The results are highly encouraging; when retrospective questions of this kind are asked carefully and interviewers are well trained, respondents can provide accurate and detailed information.

Of course not all variables can be measured retrospectively. Most researchers would argue that any attempt to measure past psychological states is invalid on its face. Reporting of the timing and frequency of events, even those which are quite salient, such as hospitalization, appears to suffer from serious recall problems. Subjects tend to forget them or to telescope them in time. Reports of exact earnings, hours worked, and other economic variables may suffer from similar problems. The truth is that we don't have much information on what can and cannot be measured retrospectively. A systematic research program on these issues is becoming more and more necessary as new methods of data analysis that depend on the exact timing of events continue to evolve.

Another serious weakness of the retrospective design is that it represents the population that survives to the point of data collection and not the original population. In some situations this kind of selection bias can be quite serious—for example, in intervention studies that are subject to high levels of attrition.

Prospective studies in which a subject is measured at some baseline and then at repeated intervals are usually referred to as panel studies. Panel designs have a number of strengths along with several significant weaknesses. The primary strength, at least in principle, is accuracy of measurement and correct temporal referents. Depending on the exact design of data collection, subjects are measured at a point close enough in time to the event or status in question to permit reliable and valid assessment. Under certain circumstances temporal priority may be more firmly established.

Second, the prospective design provides greater leverage on attrition. Besides measuring a population defined at baseline, preattrition information can be used to determine the extent to which attrition is "random" and perhaps can be used to correct estimates for selection bias. There is a trade-off, however. Frequent measurement has two potentially undesirable side effects. First, subjects may tire of repeated requests for cooperation and drop out of the study. Second, "panel conditioning" may result in stereotypic responses to repeated questions. Thus, relative to the retrospective design, there may actually be a net *decrease* in data quality.

On the surface, prospective designs that extend in time are far more costly than retrospective designs. There is a clear cost/quality trade-off, however, that cannot be easily evaluated without consideration of the purposes of the survey. In obtaining population estimates over time, the panel may actually be less expensive to maintain than resampling the population repeatedly. On the other hand, using a panel for this purpose brings problems of its own in the form of attrition and panel conditioning.

QUASI-EXPERIMENTAL AND DESCRIPTIVE APPROACHES

The large-scale, multiwave surveys so common now have rather diffuse origins. Paul Lazarsfeld introduced the panel design (Lazarsfeld and Fiske 1938). In his hands, the panel study was basically a *quasi-experimental design*. A panel of subjects was recruited and measured repeatedly, with the foreknowledge that a particular event would occur at a particular time. The most famous application is to election campaigns. As such, the design is a simple example of an interrupted time series.

A second source of current designs is the child development tradition. Baltes and Nesselroade (1979) cite examples going back to the late eighteenth century, but systematic studies date to the 1920s (Wall and Williams 1970). The best of these studies emphasized cohort-based sampling of newborns and systematic assessment of development at carefully determined intervals. In the tradition of experimental psychology, investigators paid attention to careful control of the measurement process, including the physical environment, the raters and observers, and the measurement instruments. The development of age-specific norms in the form of averages and variation about them was seen as a primary goal of the study. Unanticipated events, such as an illness of either mother or child or factors affecting the family, were seen as undesirable threats to the validity of measurement rather than as opportunities to assess quasi-experimental effects.

Large-scale multiwave panel studies of the kind described above combine aspects of both traditions, often in somewhat inchoate and potentially conflicting ways. On the one hand, investigators are interested in describing a population as it evolves. Often basic descriptive information on rates, variability, and sequence is unknown, calling for frequent measurement at fixed intervals. On the other hand, there is also interest in evaluating the impact of specific transitions and events, such as childbearing, retirement, and loss of spouse. Meeting these two objectives within the constraints of a single design is often difficult.

DESIGN ISSUES

Although it might be argued that the ideal longitudinal study should take a huge sample of the population without age restriction, measure it constantly, and follow it in perpetuity with systematic supplements to the original sample, cost and logistics intervene. Although there is an infinite range of potential designs, longitudinal studies can be classified on various dimensions including (a) the consistency of the sample over time, (b) population coverage, particularly with regard to age, and (c) measurement protocols, including not only choice of variables but also timing, interval, and frequency. These factors will influence the extent to which the study can be used for descriptive purposes, relating information to a well-defined population, and/or drawing causal inferences on temporal and quasi-experimental aspects of the design.

Consistency of the Sample. The following classification is based on Duncan and Kalton (1987) and on Menard (1991).

1. *Repeated Cross-Sectional Surveys.* A new sample is drawn at each measurement point. The GSS, described above, is an example. This is a longitudinal study at the macro level. It describes a dynamic population.

2. *Fixed-Sample Panel.* A sample is drawn at baseline and measured repeatedly over time. No new subjects enter the sample after baseline. Several examples are described above. The sample refers only to the cohorts from which it was drawn. It may continue to represent them adequately if panel attrition is completely at random.

3. *Dynamic Sample Panel.* After baseline, subjects are added to the panel in an attempt to compensate for panel attrition and represent changes in the underlying population. The PSID is a major example.

4. *Rotating Panels.* A sample is drawn and interviewed for a fixed number of waves and then dropped. At each measurement point a new sample is also drawn so that samples enter and leave on a staggered basis. The best-known example is the Current Population Survey carried out by the U.S. Bureau of the Census. At any given time, the sample consists of subjects who have been in the panel from one to four months.

5. *Split Panels.* In addition to a basic panel survey, a coordinated cross-sectional survey is drawn at each measurement point. In effect, this is a quasi-experimental design in which comparisons between samples permit tests of panel conditioning, among other things. This design is rare.

Population Definition. The broader the population sampled, the wider the potential generalization. On the other hand, homogeneity provides greater leverage for some kinds of causal inference. The following rough classification is useful. See Campbell (1988) for elaboration.

1. *Unrestricted Age Range.* A sample of the entire (adult) population is selected and followed.

2. *Restricted Age Range.* A sample of persons in a narrow age band, such as adolescents in developing nations, is selected, with resulting homogeneity of developmental process.

3. *Event-Based.* A sample is selected on the basis of a particular event. Birth is the prime example; others are motherhood, school completion, business start-up, and administrative reorganization. Subjects can be members of a cohort experiencing the event at a fixed time or can be drawn on a floating baseline, as is the case when each new patient in a given clinic is followed prospectively.

4. *Population at Risk.* A sample is selected on the likelihood (but not the certainty) that it will experience a particular event. Although similar to an event-based sample, it is less controlled. Age-restricted samples are usually at risk for certain events, which is one reason for restricting age in the first place. An interesting example at the macro level is a sample of cities likely to experience a disaster such as an earthquake or a hurricane.

Measurement Protocols. What variables should one measure with what frequency at what time intervals? Answering such a question requires a clear appreciation of the linkage between the substantive purpose of an investigation and the mode of data analysis. For example, if one's intent is to study labor-force participation using event history models, then frequency of measurement would be dictated primarily by (a) the frequency of change of labor-force status among subjects, (b) the amount of variability in individual rates of change, (c) the necessity to obtain exact dates of transitions for the analysis, and (d) the maximum time interval at which subjects can provide reliable and valid recall data. If the investigators have explanatory models in mind, then the measurement protocol will have to deal with similar issues for the regressors.

If one is, however, interested in the effects of widowhood, which might be studied either descriptively or as a quasi-experiment using an interrupted time series approach, very different measurement strategies would be optimal. At the very least, one would try to schedule measurements at fixed intervals *preceding and following* the event. If economic effects were the primary focus, annual measurement might be sufficient; but if the grief process was the focus, more frequent measurement would be required.

The more undifferentiated the sample, and the more multipurpose the study, the more difficult it is to achieve an effective measurement strategy. Many of the large-scale longitudinal studies carried out since the 1960s have one or more of the following characteristics that tend to interfere with analysis:

1. Multiple substantive foci that result in attempts to measure scores, if not hundreds, of variables.

2. Nonoptimal measurement intervals because of conflicting demands of different kinds of variables and topics. A secondary problem is that intervals are often determined by administrative and funding criteria rather than by substantive intent.

3. Measurement strategies that are chosen without regard to statistical analysis. The problem is acute for event history models that require dated transitions rather than reports of status at fixed intervals. Other examples are failure to acquire multiple indicators of constructs for LISREL models and intersubject variation in measurement intervals that interferes with growth curve estimation.

4. Weak identification of temporal sequence. This problem is most often a result of a "snapshot" orientation to measurement in which the subject's status is ascertained at a sequence of fixed measurement points. Knowing that at time 1 someone is married and prosperous and that at time 2 that person is single and poverty-stricken doesn't tell us much about causal order or effect.

CAUSAL INFERENCE AND LONGITUDINAL DESIGN

As noted, the extent to which longitudinal studies allow one to establish causal effects is the subject of some controversy. Indeed, the whole issue of causal inference from nonexperimental data is extremely controversial (Berk 1988; Freedman 1991), with some taking the position that it is impossible in any circumstance other than a randomized design involving an experimentally manipulated stimulus. Although that may be an extreme position, the assumption that one can use time-ordered observational data to establish causal order is difficult to defend.

Cross-sectional analyses and retrospective designs suffer from the fact that variables which are supposed to have time-ordered causal effects are measured simultaneously. As a result, various competing explanations of observed associations, particularly contaminated measurement, cannot be ruled out. Asking about educational aspirations after completion of schooling is an example. Panel designs at least have the advantage of measuring presumed causes prior to their effects. Even in that case, establishing temporal order is not as easy as it might appear. This is particularly true when one attempts to relate intentions, attitudes, and similar cognitive variables to behaviors. Marini and Singer (1988) give an example based on education and marriage. Consider two women who leave school and get married. One may have decided to terminate her education in light of a planned marriage, and the other may have decided to marry following a decision to terminate education. The observed sequence of events tells us nothing. They note:

> Because human beings can anticipate and plan for the future, much human behavior follows from goals, intentions and motives, i.e., it is teleologically determined. As a result, causal priority is established in the mind in a way that is not reflected in the temporal sequences of behavior or even in the temporal sequence of the formation of behavioral intentions. (Marini and Singer 1988, p. 377)

Because of the many varieties of longitudinal research design and the many controversies in the field, it is difficult to give hard-and-fast rules about when causal inference may be justified. Dwyer (1991), writing for epidemiologists, provides a useful way to approach the problem based on whether there is variance in presumed causes and effects at baseline.

Variation in Independent Variable

		NO	YES
Variation in Dependent Variable	NO	I	II
	YES	III	IV

Examples include the following:

I. Follow crime-free baseline sample through possible arrest, incarceration, and later recidivism.
II. Relate aspirations of eighth graders to eventual level of educational attainment.
III. Carry out an experimental intervention, such as a job training program, that attempts to increase existing skill levels.
IV. Relate organizational characteristics at baseline to later levels of productivity.

Cases I and III can be observational or (quasi-)experimental. Cases II and IV are strictly observational. In each case, although variation may not exist in the variable of direct interest, there may be variation in closely related variables. In the experimental case, this corresponds to lack of randomization and, thus, uncontrolled variation in potential causal variables. The same is true in purely observational studies. In case II, although there is no variation in the direct outcome of interest, there is often variation in related variables at baseline. In the example given, although there is no variation in educational attainment in terms of years of schooling completed, aspirations are certainly based in part on the child's prior academic success in the grade school environment. Case IV presents the most difficult situation because it picks up data in the middle of an ongoing causal sequence. This is precisely the situation where many researchers believe that panel data can untangle causal sequence, but neither temporal-sequenced observations nor complex analysis is likely to do so.

To reiterate an important point about design, in large-scale longitudinal research each of these four cases is typically embedded in a complex design, and the degree of causal inference depends on many factors ranging from the timing of measurement to attrition processes.

COMMON PROBLEMS IN LONGITUDINAL DATA ANALYSIS

Those who collect and analyze longitudinal data face certain generic problems. Virtually any researcher will face some or all of the following difficulties.

Conceptualizing Change. James Coleman notes that the concept of change is "a second order abstraction . . . based on a comparison, or difference, between two sense impressions, and, simultaneously, a comparison of the times at which the impressions occurred" (1968, pp. 428–429). It is particularly difficult to think about the *causes* of change, and this difficulty has been reflected in arguments about how to model it. In particular, there has been a running debate about the use of change scores, computed as a simple difference ($\Delta Y = Y_2 - Y_1$) versus a regression approach in which the time 2 variable is regressed on time 1 plus other variables. In an influential paper, Bohrnstedt (1970) showed that simple gain scores tended to have very low reliability relative to either variable composing them. In light of that and other problems, Cronbach and Furby (1969) argued that the best way to model change was to treat "residualized gain scores" as dependent variables in regression analysis. The basic equation is

$$Y_2 = a + \beta_1 Y_1 + \beta_2 X_1 \cdots + \beta_k X_k + \varepsilon$$

where Y_1 is the baseline measure and the X's are any set of independent variables. Hence the effect of X is net of the baseline score. This method has become standard in many fields of inquiry.

More recently, a number of papers have appeared that question the use of residualized gain scores. Liker, Augustyniak, and Duncan (1985) argue that equations in which one takes differences on both sides of the model ($\Delta_y = \alpha + \beta(\Delta X) + \varepsilon$) have strong advantages, particularly when one wants to "difference out" unchanging characteristics of subjects. Allison (1990) argues that in some cases the difference score as a dependent variable is not only acceptable but necessary. The issue is not purely statistical; it depends in large part on exactly what process one is attempting to model. Suffice it to say here that an issue which was once thought to be resolved has been reopened for serious examination.

Related to the issue of change scores and their reliability is the problem of regression toward the mean. Whenever a variable is positively correlated over time, subjects with high scores at time 1 will tend to have somewhat lower scores at time 2, while those with lower time 1 scores will tend to have higher scores at time 2. As a result, gain scores will be negatively correlated with initial values. This problem is exacerbated by random measurement error and was a primary reason for the predominance of residualized gain models in the past. Again, however, the issue is one of the underlying model. There are cases where feedback processes do indeed result in regression to the mean (Dwyer 1991) and the regression is by no means an "artifact." There is no question that one

always needs to correct for measurement error, but regression to the mean should not necessarily be treated as an annoyance to be gotten rid of by statistical manipulation.

Lack of Independence. A standard assumption in elementary statistical models such as least squares regression is that errors are independent across observations. In the equation we typically assume $\text{cov}(\varepsilon_i \varepsilon_j) = 0$. If the same subject is observed at two or more points in time, the independence assumption is almost certain to be violated due to omitted variables, correlated errors of measurement, or other problems. This difficulty permeates virtually all statistical approaches to longitudinal data and requires complex methods of estimation.

Articulating Analysis with Observation Plan. Ideally, one should have in mind a model for how the underlying process of change in a variable articulates with the observation plan. In part, this requires some knowledge of causal lag or how long it takes for changes in X to result in changes in Y. The data analysis method chosen should be congruent with both the underlying process of change and the observation plan. Observation plans may obtain exact dates of transitions (when did you quit your job?), locate the subject's state at time t (are you currently working?), or obtain retrospective information relative to some other time point (were you working as of June 30?). Studies that have multiple goals are difficult to optimize in this respect.

Construct Validity. In long-term longitudinal studies, the validity of constructs may degrade over time, sometimes through changes in the subjects themselves, sometimes through measurement problems such as conditioning, and sometimes through changes in the environment. For example, the meaning of terms used in political research such as *liberal* may change with time, or references to specific issues such as abortion may become more or less salient. In growth studies, subjects may "age out" of certain variables. This issue is quite understudied, at least by sociologists.

Measurement Error. Measurement error is a serious problem for statistical analysis, particularly regression, because it results in biased estimates.

The problem is particularly acute when independent variables are subject to error. In the longitudinal case, errors of measurement tend to be correlated across subjects over time, causing even greater difficulty. A major reason for the popularity of structural equation packages like LISREL (Jöreskog and Sörbom 1988; Bollen 1989) is that they permit one to model correlated error structures. This is not to say that LISREL is an all-purpose solution; indeed, its error-handling capabilities probably lead to its use in situations where other approaches would be better.

Time-varying Independent Variables. In a typical situation one is faced with a set of fixed independent variables such as age, sex, and race, and a set of variables whose values may change over the course of a study. In studies of income, for example, educational levels and family structure may change between observations. Although work on this problem has been going on in economics for some years (Hsiao 1986), sociologists have been slow to respond. The problem always leads to great statistical and computational complexity.

Missing Data, Attrition, Censoring, and Selection Bias. Attrition in panel studies is inevitable. In rare cases attrition is completely random, but more commonly it is associated with other variables. Standard listwise and pairwise missing data "solutions" are rarely appropriate in this situation. Three types of solutions are available. First, one can develop weights to correct for attrition. Second, one can model the attrition process directly, using "selection bias" models (Heckman 1979; Berk 1983). Finally, one can impute estimates of missing data (Little and Rubin 1987). This entire area is controversial and under rapid development. A special case of attrition occurs when observations are *censored* in such a way that measurement stops before a transition of interest, such as ending a panel study of fertility before all subjects have completed childbearing.

APPROACHES TO DATA ANALYSIS

The period since 1975 or 1980 has seen enormous increases in the power and sophistication of longitudinal data analysis. Singer (1985) is a useful overview; Dwyer and Feinleib (1991), especially chapter 1, provides a comprehensive review, as does Von Eye (1990). This material is much too complex to cover in this brief review. A more reasonable goal is to provide a few examples of the kinds of substantive questions that one can ask with longitudinal data and appropriate methods for answering them.

Outcomes at Fixed Points in Time. Example: "predicting" a person's savings at age sixty five. This is the simplest longitudinal question; indeed, in one sense it is not longitudinal at all. The dependent variable involves change over time very indirectly, and the independent variables usually involve life cycle variables like the nature of labor-force participation. These data can often be collected retrospectively, and the only advantage of a *repeated measures* approach is control over measurement error.

It is not uncommon to see models for fixed outcomes at arbitrary time points—for example, level of education attainment as of the last available wave of an ongoing panel study. This is a particular problem when the sample consists of subjects who vary in age or is not defined on the basis of some reasonable baseline. When the outcome is a discrete transition, such as marriage, censoring is often a problem.

Means over Time. Example: Comparison of aspiration levels of boys and girls over the middle school years. With a sequence of independent samples, this is a straightforward analysis-of-variance problem. If the same individuals are measured repeatedly, a number of problems arise. First, the observations are not independent over time; we have to assume that the usual statistical assumption of independence in the error terms will be violated. Within the ANOVA tradition, this problem can be approached via multivariate analysis of variance or as a classic univariate design. Hertzog and Rovine (1985) compare the two approaches. Sociologists have tended to ignore mean comparisons, preferring to work with structural equations; however, analyses of means are often far more direct and informative. See Fox (1984) for an interesting application to an interrupted time series.

Classic ANOVA ignores individual-level heterogeneity. Over the course of five observation points, students vary about the group means. The description of change at the individual level rather than at the group level may be of some interest. A simple approach is to use "blocking variables" such as race to account for additional heterogeneity. Adding covariates to the model is another. A more sophisticated approach is to model the individual-level growth curve directly. Conceptually, analysis begins by estimating an equation to describe each respondent's score with respect to time, often using a polynomial model. The coefficients of these equations are then treated as dependent variables in a second-stage analysis. There are a number of different statistical approaches to this kind of analysis. Rogosa (1988) has argued forcefully in favor of approaching longitudinal analysis in this way. Dwyer (1991) provides an interesting example. McCardle and Aber (1990) deal with such models in a LISREL context.

Structural Equation Systems. Figure 1, based on Blau and Duncan's classic path model of occupational mobility, is a longitudinal analysis, although it is not often thought of in those terms. For our purposes, the important point is that the exact timing of variables was not assumed to be of great import, although the sequence was. Education was taken to intervene between measures of family background and occupational attainment, and its timing was not specified. The latter variable was assumed to reach some plateau relatively early in the occupational career; again, timing was not important. Models of this kind, with rather vague time referents and in which it is assumed that the order of events does not vary across subjects, have played an important role in sociology for some time, adding great clarity to the notion of intervening variables. It is natural to assume that structural equation models are a natural way to analyze multiwave panel data.

Kessler and Greenberg (1981) deal at length with the application of structural equation models to panel data, particularly to cross-lagged structures where both variables vary at baseline. They show that attempting to estimate relative causal effects must be handled in the context of a formal

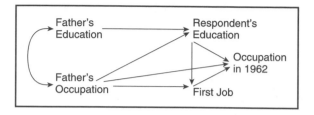

Figure 1

NOTE: A Basic Model of Attainment (Adapted from Blau and Duncan 1967)

model rather than by comparing cross-lagged partial correlations. Figure 2, based on Campbell and Mutran (1982), is a multiwave panel model with intervening variables. Here, a number of statistical and conceptual difficulties become obvious. First, what is the lag time for the effect of health on income satisfaction and vice versa? Second, how does one deal with the potentially complex error structure of observed variables? Third, if illnesses intervene (as measured by times in hospital), how does the timing of events relative to the timing of observations affect the results? Fourth, how does one deal with discrete intervening variables that fail to meet standard distributional assumptions? Finally, how does one handle correlated errors in equations over time? These are by no means the only questions that could be raised, and it is not clear that models of this kind are the most effective way to approach multiwave panel data.

Event History Models. This class of models treats the underlying rate of change in a discrete variable as the dependent variable in a regression-like framework. Typically, the dependent variable is conceived of as the instantaneous risk of transition at time t conditional on prior history. The formulation is dynamic rather than static, and time enters the analysis explicitly. Allison (this volume) discusses a number of such models in detail. At first glance, the model may seem mathematically esoteric, but the basic ideas are straightforward. The underlying concepts are closely related to the life table and to Markov models. The Markov model, as applied in the classic labor-force studies of Blumen, Kogen, and McCarthy (1955), assumes a transition process that is constant over time and invariant across subjects. Event history

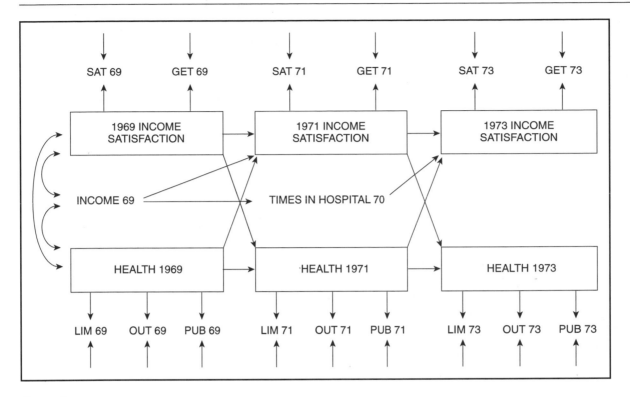

Figure 2

NOTE: A Model for Health and Income Satisfaction (Adapted from Campbell and Mutron 1982)

models allow one to relax both assumptions, specifying a time-dependent rate of change and a set of individual-level "covariates" that allow transition processes to vary with characteristics of the subjects. Covariates can be allowed to change with time as well, at the cost of substantial computational complexity.

In one of the first applications in sociology, Tuma, Hannon, and Groeneveld (1979) showed that the rate of marital dissolution among subjects in an income-maintenance experiment depended on the treatment condition, thus demonstrating that event models could be used for causal analysis. Event models are inherently dynamic and take the timing of transitions explicitly into account. They are having enormous impact not only on how sociologists analyze data but also on how they conceptualize problems and design data collection.

Differential Equation Models. Coleman (1964, 1968, 1981), among others, has argued that the appropriate way to study change in continuous variables is via differential equation models. A simple differential equation relating Y to its own level and to an exogenous variable takes the form

$$\frac{dY}{dt} = a + b_1 Y + b_2 X_1$$

where dY/dt is the rate of change in Y with respect to time, that is, the derivative. The rate of change is not directly observed, of course; and to estimate the coefficients of the model, it is necessary to integrate the equation. Coleman (1968) shows that for this particular model, it is possible to obtain estimates of a, b_1, and b_2 by first estimating a regression equation of the form

$$Y_t = a^* + b_1^* Y_{(t-1)} + b_2^* X_1$$

using ordinary regression and then transforming the regression coefficients to obtain the coefficients of the differential equation model. In this particular case the coefficients of the differential equation model are

$$a = \frac{a^* C^*}{\Delta t}$$

$$b_1 = \frac{\ln b_1^*}{\Delta t}$$

$$b_2 = \frac{b_2^* C^*}{\Delta t}$$

where

$$C^* = \frac{\ln b_1^*}{(b_1^* - 1)}$$

The resulting coefficients describe the time path of Y as a function of its initial value and the value of X. Note that this model assumes that X is not changing over time. One implication of this model is that if one wishes to assume that Y at time t does not depend on its initial value, then residualized gain score models of the kind described above are inappropriate.

Applications of differential equation models in sociology have been relatively rare, although they would seem to be a natural way to approach the analysis of change. Many of the seemingly endless arguments about the representation of change in regression models stems from the application of static methods to dynamic processes. The difficulty is that it is not easy or always possible to transform the differential equations in such a way that they can be estimated by simple regression. Doing so requires considerable mathematical sophistication on the part of the researcher. Tuma and Hannon (1984) discuss these and related models at length. Arminger (1986) provides an example of how to recast a standard three-wave LISREL-based panel analysis into a differential equation model.

CONCLUSION

It is no accident that words like *controversial* and *under discussion* recur frequently in this review. Many important issues regarding the collection, analysis, and interpretation of longitudinal data remain to be resolved. Frequently, what are in fact conceptual issues are argued in statistical terms. The literature is technical and mathematically demanding. But important progress is being made

and will continue as new methods of research continue to emerge.

(SEE ALSO: *Causal Inference Models; Cohort Analysis; Event History Analysis; Time Series Analysis; Quasi-Experimental Research Designs*)

REFERENCES

Allison, Paul D. 1984 *Event History Analysis: Regression for Longitudinal Event Data.* Newbury Park, Calif.: Sage.

—— 1990 "Change Scores as Dependent Variables in Regression Analysis." In Clifford C. Clogg, ed., *Sociological Methodology*, Vol. 20. London: Basil Blackwell.

—— 1996 "Fixed-Effects Partial Likelihood for Repeated Events." *Sociological Methods and Research* 25:207–222.

Anderson, Edward R. 1993 "Analyzing Change in Short-Term Longitudinal Research Using Cohort-Sequential Designs." *Journal of Consulting and Clinical Psychology* 61:929–940.

Arminger, Gerhard 1986 "Linear Stochastic Differential Equation Models for Panel Data with Unobserved Variables." In Nancy B. Tuma, ed., *Sociological Methodology*, Vol. 16. Washington, D.C.: American Sociological Association.

Baltes, Paul B., and John R. Nesselroade 1977 "History and Rationale of Longitudinal Research." In John R. Nesselroade and Paul B. Baltes, eds., *Longitudinal Research in the Study of Behavior and Development.* New York: Academic Press.

Barton, Thomas R., Vijayan K. Pillai, and Tracy J. Dietz 1996 "Program Evaluation Using Event History Analysis." *Evaluation Practice* 17:7–17.

Berk, Richard A. 1983 "An Introduction to Sample Selection Bias in Sociological Research." *American Sociological Review* 48:386–398.

—— 1988 "Causal Inference in Social Science." In Neil J. Smelser, ed., *Handbook of Sociology.* Newbury Park, Calif.: Sage.

Bijleveld, Catrien C. J. H. et al. 1998 *Longitudinal Data Analysis: Designs, Models and Methods.* London: Sage Publications.

Blau, Peter M., and Otis Dudley Duncan 1967 *The American Occupational Structure.* New York: Wiley.

Blossfeld, Hans-Peter, Goetz Rohwer, and Gotz Rohwer 1995 *Techniques of Event History Modeling: New Approaches to Causal Analysis*, vol. 31. Mahwah, N.J.: Lawrence Erlbaum Associates.

Blumen, Isadore, M. Kogan, and P. J. McCarthy 1955 *The Industrial Mobility of Labor as a Probability Process.* Ithaca, N.Y.: Cornell University Press.

Bohrnstedt, George W. 1969 "Observations on the Measurement of Change." In Edgar F. Borgatta, ed., *Sociological Methodology*, Vol. 2. San Francisco: Jossey-Bass.

Bollen, Kenneth A. 1989 *Structural Equations with Latent Variables.* New York: Wiley.

Campbell, Richard T. 1988 "Integrating Conceptualization, Design, and Analysis in Panel Studies of the Life Course." In K. W. Schaie, R. T. Campbell, W. Meredith, and S. C. Rawlings, eds., *Methodological Issues in Aging Research.* New York: Springer.

——, and Elizabeth Mutran 1982 "Analyzing Panel Data in Studies of Aging." *Research on Aging* 4:3–41.

Coleman, James S. 1964 *Introduction to Mathematical Sociology.* New York: Free Press.

—— 1968 "The Mathematical Study of Change." In Hubert M. Blalock, Jr., and Ann B. Blalock, eds., *Methodology in Social Research.* New York: McGraw Hill.

—— 1981 *Longitudinal Data Analysis.* New York: Basic Books.

Collins, Linda M. 1996 "Measurement of Change in Research on Aging: Old and New Issues From an Individual Growth Perspective." In J. E. Birren and K. W. Schaie, eds., *Handbook of the Psychology Aging.* San Diego: Academic Press.

Cook, Nancy R., and James H. Ware 1983 "Design and Analysis Methods for Longitudinal Research." *Annual Review of Public Health* 4:1–23.

Cronbach, Lee J., and Leta Furby 1970 "How We Should Measure Change—Or Should We?" *Psychological Bulletin* 74:32–49.

DeShon, Richard P., Robert E. Ployhart, and Joshua M. Sacco 1998 "The Estimation of Reliability in Longitudinal Models." *International Journal of Behavioral Development* 22:493–515.

DiPrete, Thomas A., and David B. Grusky 1990 "Structure and Trend in the Process of Stratification for *American Men and Women.*" *American Journal of Sociology* 96:107–143.

Duncan, Greg J., and Graham Kalton 1987 "Issues of Design and Analysis of Surveys Across Time." *International Statistical Review* 55:97–117.

Duncan, Greg J., and James Morgan 1985 "The Panel Study of Income Dynamics." In Glen H. Elder, ed., *Life Course Dynamics: Trajectories and Transitions*, 1968–1980. Cambridge: Cambridge University Press.

Duncan, Terry E. et al. 1999 *An Introduction to Latent Variable Growth Curve Modeling: Concepts Issues, and Applications.* Mahwah, N.J.: Lawrence Erlbaum Associates.

Dwyer, James 1991 "Overview of Models for Longitudinal Data." In James Dwyer and Manning Feinleib, eds., *Statistical Models for Longitudinal Studies of Health.* Oxford: Oxford University Press.

——, and Manning Feinleib (eds.) 1991 *Statistical Models for Longitudinal Studies of Health.* Oxford: Oxford University Press.

Featherman, David L. 1977 "Retrospective Longitudinal Research: Methodological Considerations." *Journal of Economics and Business* 32:152–169.

Fox, John 1984 "Detecting Change in Level and Slope in Repeated Measures Analysis." *Sociological Methods and Research* 12:263–278.

Freedman, David A. 1991 "Statistical Models and Shoe Leather." In Peter V. Marsden, ed., *Sociological Methodology.* Oxford: Basil Blackwell.

Freedman, Deborah, Arland Thornton, Donald Camburn, Duane Alwin, and Linda Young-DeMarco 1988 "The Life History Calendar: A Technique for Collection of Retrospective Data." In Clifford C. Clogg, ed., *Sociological Methodology*, Vol. 18. Washington D.C.: American Sociological Association.

Goodman, Jodi S., and Terry C. Blum 1996 "Assessing the Non-Random Sampling Effects of Subject Attrition in Longitudinal Research." *Journal of Management* 22:627–652.

Gottman, John-Mordechai 1995 *The Analysis of Change.* Mahwah, N.J.: Lawrence Erlbaum Associates.

Heckman, James J. 1979 "Sample Selection Bias as a Specification Error." *Econometrica* 47:153–161.

——, and Burton Singer 1985 *Longitudinal Analysis of Labor Market Data.* Cambridge: Cambridge University Press.

Hertzog, Christopher, and Michael Rovine 1985 "Repeated-Measures Analysis of Variance in Developmental Research: Selected Issues." *Child Development* 56:787–809.

Hsiao, Cheng 1986 *Analysis of Panel Data.* Cambridge: Cambridge University Press.

Inter-University Consortium for Political and Social Research 1991 *Guide to Resources and Services.* Ann Arbor, Mich.: Institute for Social Research.

Jöreskog, Karl G., and Dag Sörbom 1988 *LISREL 7: A Guide to the Program and Applications.* Chicago: SPSS.

Kessler, Ronald C., and David F. Greenberg 1981 *Linear Panel Analysis: Models of Quantitative Change.* New York: Academic Press.

Lazarsfeld, Paul R., and M. Fiske 1938 "The 'Panel' as a New Tool for Measuring Opinion." *Public Opinion Quarterly* 2:596–612.

Lieberson, Stanley 1985 *Making It Count*. Berkeley: University of California Press.

Liker, Jeffrey, Susan Augustyniak, and Greg J. Duncan 1985 "Panel Data and Models of Change: A Comparison of First Order Difference and Conventional Two-Wave Models." *Social Science Research* 14:80–101.

Little, Roderick J. A., and Donald B. Rubin 1987 *Statistical Analysis with Missing Data*. New York: Wiley.

Magnusson, David et al. 1994 *Problems and Methods in Longitudinal Research: Stability and Change*. Cambridge: Cambridge University Press.

Marini, Margaret M., and Burton F. Singer 1988 "Causality in the Social Sciences." In Clifford C. Clogg, ed., *Sociological Methodology*, Vol. 18. Washington, D.C.: American Sociological Association.

Maxwell, Scott E. 1998 "Longitudinal Designs in Randomized Group Comparisons: When will Intermediate Observations Increase Statistical Power?" *Psychological Methods* 3:275–290.

McArdle, John J. 1998 "Modeling Longitudinal Data by Latent Growth Curve methods." In G. A. Marcoulides, ed., *Modern Methods for Business Research. Methodology for Business and Management*. Mahwah, N.J.: Lawrence Erlbaum Associates.

——, and Mark S. Aber 1990 "Patterns of Change within Latent Variable Structural Equation Models." In Alexander von Eye, ed., *Statistical Methods in Longitudinal Research*, Vol 1. San Diego, Calif.: Academic Press.

McPhee, Robert D. 1998 "Alternate Approaches to Integrating Longitudinal Case Studies." In George P. Huber and Andrew H. Van de Ven, eds., *Longitudinal Field Research Methods: Studying Processes of Organizational Change*. Thousand Oaks, Calif.: Sage.

Menard, Scott 1991 *Longitudinal Research*. Newbury Park, Calif.: Sage.

Migdal, Susan, Ronald P. Abeles, and Lonnie R. Sherrod 1981 *An Inventory of Longitudinal Studies of Middle and Old Age*. New York: Social Science Research Council.

Nielson, Francois, and Rachel A. Rosenfeld 1981 "Substantive Interpretations of Differential Equation Models." *American Sociological Review* 46:159–174.

Petersen, Trond 1993 "Recent Advances in Longitudinal Methodology." *Annual Review of Sociology* 19:425–454.

Pitts, Steven C., Stephen G. West, and Tein Jenn-Yun 1996 "Longitudinal Measurement Models in Evaluation Research: Examining Stability and Change." *Evaluation and Program Planning* 19:333–350.

Raykov, Tenko 1993 "On Estimating True Change Interrelationships with Other Variables." *Quality and Quantity* 27:353–370.

Rogosa, David 1988 "Myths About Longitudinal Research." In K. W. Schaie, R. T. Campbell, W. Meredith, and S. C. Rawlings, eds., *Methodological Issues in Aging Research*. New York: Springer.

——, and Hilary Saner 1995 "Longitudinal Data Analysis Examples with Random Coefficient Models." *Journal of Educational and Behavioral Statistics* 20:149–170.

Rovine, Michael J, and Pete C. M. Molenaar 1998 "A Nonstandard Method for Estimating a Linear Growth Model in LISREL." *International Journal of Behavioral Development* 22:453–473.

Singer, Burton 1988 "Longitudinal Data Analysis." In Samuel Kotz and Norman Johnson, eds., *Encyclopedia of Statistical Sciences*, Vol. 5. New York: Wiley.

Smith, Tom W. 1986 "The International Social Survey Program." *Journal of Official Statistics* 2:337–338.

Speer, David C., and Paul E. Greenbaum 1995 "Five Methods for Computing Significant Individual Client Change and Improvement Rates: Support for an Individual Growth Curve Approach." *Journal of Consulting and Clinical Psychology* 63:1044–1048.

Thornberry, Terence P., Beth Bjerregaard, and William Miles 1993 "The Consequences of Respondent Attrition in Panel Studies: A Simulation Based on the Rochester Youth Development Study." *Journal of Quantitative Criminology* 9:127–158.

Tuma, Nancy Brandon, and Michael T. Hannan 1984 *Social Dynamics: Methods and Models*. Orlando, Fla.: Academic Press.

Vermunt, Jeroen K. 1997 *Log-linear Models for Event Histories*. Thousand Oaks, Calif.: Sage.

von Eye, Alexander 1990 *Statistical Methods in Longitudinal Research*. San Diego: Academic Press.

Wall, W. D., and H. L. Williams 1970 *Longitudinal Studies and the Social Sciences*. London: Heinemann.

RICHARD T. CAMPBELL

LOVE

Sociologists agree that love is one of the most complex and elusive concepts to deal with from a scientific point of view. Indeed, they often point out that poets, novelists, and musical composers are much more adept at producing eloquent expressions about this pervasive sentiment. Dictionary definitions are of limited use in categorizing the essential ingredients of love, except to connote its many variations as an attitude, an emotion, or a behavior. No one definition can capture all the dimensions of love, which can involve a wide range of elements such as romantic obsession, sexuality, caring, even irrationality. Indeed, some have argues: "There is no single, subjective meaning of love that everyone experiences in the same way" (Hendrick and Hendrick, 1992). Part of the difficulty is that individuals and their cultures define love very differently, depending on particular relationships and circumstances.

HISTORICAL CONCEPTIONS OF LOVE

Conceptions of love have varied not only from one culture to another, but also from one historical era to another (Murstein 1974; Hunt 1959). Prominent among these are courtly love, Romanticism, and Victorian-era love (Hendrick and Hendrick 1992), as well as the modern era of love (Seidman 1991). Various forms of courtly love appeared in the twelfth century. This marked the beginning of the transformation of love from a philosophical or theological ideal to a practical way of relating between men and women. Sexual desire and expression were seen as one of the goals of love, and the love relationship was seen as intense and passionate. This bond was not limited to one's spouse, however. Marriage was seen as a more mundane and practical relationship. In contrast, courtly love was impractical, as the time commitment necessary to follow its elaborate rules and customs limited involvement to the wealthier or aristocratic classes. It often found its expression—sometimes sexual, but often not—in the idealized devotion of a knight or nobleman to a lady of nobility, who symbolized the perfect partner. Men and women did not relate in the day-to-day interaction associated with more recent intimate relationships.

In the late eighteenth to early nineteenth centuries, Romanticism replaced courtly love. In Romanticism it is possible to recognize the origins of some of our modern ideas about love: concern with similarities between partners, equality in the relationship, and the experience of the emotional side of love. This form furthered the courtly love ideal of sexual expression between partners as a worthy goal, with the added recognition that this fusion of emotion and sexuality could (and ideally should) occur with one's spouse.

The Victorian era (approximately 1830–1900) brought great changes to the idea of romantic love. This is hardly surprising, as people of this time were also adjusting to the changes in work and community life brought about by the Industrial Revolution. In the shift from the home economy to paid labor, the status of women declined, and new myths and ideas about love and its expression emerged. The partnership-oriented focus of Romanticism all but disappeared. Women in the Victorian era were seen as weaker and less intelligent than men. Within marriage, this assumption defined women as mothers and helpers, not individuals who might have complementary interests and a rightful concern for equality within a relationship. Women were also seen as childlike and asexual during this time, and were thought to need their husband's protection. This is an abrupt departure from earlier modes of loving, which acknowledged sexuality as an important aspect of the experience of love. In the Victorian era, sexual matters were not discussed between spouses.

In the modern era (1890–1960), the literature on love and marriage once again recognized the importance of an intimate bond between partners. Marital advice from this time shows a preoccupation with couples' happiness and the security of the marital bond. During this period, romantic love and sexual compatibility were inseparable, and this sexualization of love (Seidman 1991) brought the perception of sexual expression in romantic relationships full circle. Sexual expression was no longer seen as a component of love (whether an idealized or neglected one) but the very basis of love itself.

Sexual impulses and romantic love are often directed at the same person, but they are not the same. People are known to pursue sexual encounters in the absence of any romantic feelings. Sexual impulses are derived from our biological heritage, and romantic love is a learned cultural pattern. The two bear a relationship to one another, however, in that romance often encompasses sexually motivated behavior plus a cluster of cultural expectations (Hatfield and Rapson 1993)

CULTURAL DIFFERENCES

The range of psychological and social meanings attached to love would, therefore, appear to be limitless. However, we experience and express love mostly according to the culture and subcultures in which we have formed our sentiments. The formation of these sentiments begins very early and evolves through the physical and emotional attachments that characterize the parent-child relationship. While idiosyncratic patterns exist, love scripts by and large reflect the influence of social conditioning. In short, love is largely a learned response.

Despite cultural differences, several aspects of love seem to be universal (Sternberg 1998). Everywhere love involves four ideals: the suitable partner, the emotional experience of loving, the mental experience or thought process of loving, and the actions deemed acceptable and expected between the lover and his or her partner. Although these components seem to be found in all societies, how they are defined is culturally specific. The suitable partner may be of the opposite or the same sex, younger or older than oneself (or the same age), and tall and thin or short and heavy. Similarly, thoughts about love may be pragmatic or passionate, and emotions may range from deeply affectionate to reserved and respectful. The potential combinations that add up to "love" vary widely, and might be unrecognizable to a person from another culture. For example, in some tribes in Africa there is a traditional system known as "sweethearting" in which young people choose partners based on emotional and physical attraction (Goode, 1963). Even within this system there is variation. Some tribes allow sweethearting to lead to marriage, while others permit their young people to take lovers by choice but maintain the practice of arranging marriages for girls when they are still children. In the Arab world, love may also take secondary importance to familial concerns in taking a spouse. Many unmarried adults in Arab countries report that love is their ideal basis for marriage. However, married adults report varying levels of emotional closeness with their spouse prior to marriage, including love, acquaintance, and kinship ties without either love or acquaintance.

Cultural norms are internalized and program us to fall in love with specific types of people, within certain social contexts, to the exclusion of others. However, love is not necessarily related to marriage. There is a saying, for example, that in the West one falls in love and then gets married, whereas in the East one marries and then falls in love. In some societies, arranged marriages were and still are contracted. The emotional intensity a couple feel toward each other is given little or no consideration. Instead, emphasis is given to the sociopolitical implications of the marital alliance for the families and kinship groups involved.

In the United States, on the other hand, love is viewed as an important condition to marriage. We are generally suspicious of anyone who would marry for any other reason. We are not comfortable with the idea that in some cultures a man marries his mother's brother's daughter because that is the prescribed pattern. Even among our upper classes, where concern about protecting family resources leads to a greater emphasis on practical considerations in mate selection, couples are expected to espouse mutual love as the basis for their marriage, or else their motives become suspect. Revelation of marital alliances designed to preserve or enhance family wealth often receive a cynical response from the public at large.

Families recognize that courtship and mate selection merge not only two individuals but also two different kinship lines, which in turn may affect their socioeconomic and political stature. Consequently, families invest considerable energy and resources to control love (Goode 1959). Several mechanisms to accomplish this have been identified, including the direct control provided by (1) child marriages, in which betrothal may occur before puberty or even before the child is born; (2) defining the pool of eligibles, that is, delineating whom one can and cannot marry; (3) physical or social isolation to limit the probabilities of contact; and (4) various indirect controls such as moving to preferred residential neighborhoods, enrolling children in appropriate schools, joining select organizations, or attending certain churches. The latter mechanism is most characteristic of Western societies.

THE ROMANTIC LOVE COMPLEX

In American society a *romantic love complex* exists, and this complex posits love as a central prerequisite to marriage. The basic components of this complex are assimilated through the mass media—through romantic stories in novels, magazines, television, and movies. In this way we are psychologically prepared to fall in love. The major characteristics of romantic love include *romantic democracy*; that is, cultural differences between couples are minimized or ignored because "love and love alone" is sufficient. Indeed, it involves the notion that romantic love thrives on such differences. Romantic love also includes *romantic intensity*; that is, people are expected to fall in love instantly (to experience love at first sight) and deeply, with great emotional attachment. Finally, romantic love includes *romantic monopoly* in that once the "bolt from the blue" strikes, the couple presume exclusive emotional and social rights to each other, in perpetuity (Merrill 1959). A person experiencing the full thrust of this complex is, supposedly, consumed by constant thoughts about the beloved, a longing to spend all one's time with that person, a sad pining in the beloved's absence, and a feeling that life would not be worth living without him or her (Tennov 1980).

There is disagreement about the extent to which people adhere to the tenets of the romantic love complex and whether it actually influences mate selection. Sociologists have generally viewed it as a poor basis for the establishment of permanent unions, inasmuch as it involves an element of capricious choice based upon an unpredictable emotion. Moreover, romantic love is not completely rational. Part of its credo is that there is one and only one true love or ideal mate. Yet we know that people fall in and out of love several times in a lifetime.

People caught up in the romantic complex often idealize their partners. Some argue that this process of *idealization*, in which a distorted positive picture of the love partner is constructed, results from the blockage of sexual impulses by cultural prohibitions. If this were true, then one would expect a liberalization of our sexual mores to be accompanied by a decline in romanticism. However, this does not appear to have happened, at least in Western societies. What does happen is that the elements of the romantic love complex, including the idealized picture of the partner, are modified to fit the reality of that person that emerges through close and intimate interaction over time. Couples unable to make this accommodation are apt to suffer disillusionment, and their marriages may encounter persistent difficulties. For marriage to succeed, the overly romanticized notions and idealizations of romantic love must eventually be replaced by *conjugal love*, which is based upon habits, common interests, mutual acceptance, and mature companionship derived from a shared history.

THE MASS MEDIA AND LOVE

The mass media undoubtedly encourages many romantic myths about love. This can be problematic for several reasons (Ellis 1985). Fictional lovers, whether in the movies or in novels, can magically go about their romantic business without the mundane everyday constraints faced by real people. Fictional portrayals of romantic love also tend to idealize the partners as beautiful, perfect people who are in the earliest passionate stages of love. It is assumed that this stage of love will last forever for the couple. In reality, few of us are unencumbered by family expectations or blessed with perfect beauty. Perhaps more damaging, the passionate stage of love shown on the silver screen tends to mature and deepen in real life into a more companionate form of love—which may then be taken as not being "real" love by those who subscribe to the romanticized media ideal.

Media portrayals of love and family life may also set up a template for behavior that is difficult or impossible for a couple to enact and sustain, while at the same time making them feel wrong somehow for failing to meet this expectation (Coontz 1992). Many intimate partners do not choose to follow the homemaker-breadwinner pattern in their relating. For some others who would like to be able to do so, this may be a financial impossibility. To make matters even more complicated, mass media presents other images of lifestyles that are at odds with the nuclear family image. Messages of consumerism and mass consumption in television shows and commercials encourage individuals to keep their choices open and to accept only the best. This message of individualism makes intimacy and commitment between romantic partners more difficult, as some may shy away from choosing a partner out of fear that something better may come along. Our kinship system does not provide a protective mechanism against this individualism. Because we trace kinship bilaterally through both the mother and the father, lineage concerns do not keep couples together (Farber 1964). As a result, marital status and presumed romantic exclusivity do not prevent partners from being available as a potential mates to others.

GENDER AND LOVE

There appear to be gender differences with respect to love and loving. It is generally assumed that such differences reflect culturally defined sex roles. Women have been stereotypically portrayed as starry-eyed romantics, while men are viewed as exploitative realists. However, research shows that men fall in love more quickly than women do and with less deliberation, score higher on scales of romanticism, express stronger romantic attitudes, and suffer greater emotional stress when relationships are terminated. Compared to men, women are more apt to exhibit a companionate rather a passionate approach to love. The difference between the two centers around the element of emotional intensity. Companionate love "is a calm, steady, relaxed state; passionate love is an emotional roller coaster, with intense highs and lows" (Fehr 1995). Because women may have potentially more to lose from a social and an economic standpoint, they tend to be more prudent or discriminating in establishing and maintaining love relationships (Hochschild 1983). They are more apt to take into account practical considerations regarding mate selection. Hence, in comparison to men, women are more likely to terminate relationships and are able to disengage emotionally more easily when they break up (Rubin 1973).

Men and women also have different expectations of love (Cancian 1987). The common denominator among many of these differences seems to be communication styles and preferences. Women have an advantage in communicating emotionally, because traditional gender norms have allotted the jobs of nurturing and relationship maintenance to them. They also tend to have more emotionally close (but not sexually intimate) relationships than do men. This suggests that women have less difficulty with emotional vulnerability and communication. Women tend to want more intimacy through verbal communication from their partners. This can cause a host of problems, as men tend to express feelings of love actively rather than verbally.

Love is also experienced differently by men and women partly because of varying levels of dependency. Although a large proportion of women now hold paid employment, economic dependence on men is still a factor in many wives' and mothers' experience. They are more likely to put their careers on hold to raise children than are men, to earn less than their spouses, and to relocate due to a spouse's career needs. The critical link between gendered experience of love and financial concerns can be seen in socioeconomic class differences. Working- and middle-class men are less likely to identify strongly with their work than are men in the upper middle class. As a result, it is in the upper middle class that conflict between wives' needs for intimacy and husbands' desires for self-fulfillment and career achievement may be felt most acutely.

The gendered differences inimical to romantic love are found in communication as well (Gray 1992). Men and women have vastly different communication styles, and problems arising from miscommunication may lead to difficulties within a relationship. For a man to feel truly loved he must feel that he is needed. For a woman to feel loved she must feel understood and appreciated as well. These requirements stem from men's desire to feel competent and women's desire to feel socially and emotionally connected to others. When partners relate, however, they tend to speak to one another in ways that they would like to be spoken to themselves because they do not recognize these differing bases for feeling loved. Women tend to air their problems and difficulties with their partners in order to feel validated and understood. In response, men tend to offer solutions to women's problems or to minimize these problems—offering the vote of confidence in their partners' competency that they would want in similar circumstances. These differences can potentially undermine feelings of love experienced by the partners (Gray 1993). A woman is left feeling that her partner does not truly listen or understand her when he offers solutions to her grievances, and she feels abandoned when he withdraws to consider his own problems in privacy. A man can feel blamed by his partner's complaints and stunned by her negative reaction to his proposed solutions, and tends to feel hounded if she attempts to penetrate the silence he needs to work issues out for himself.

Social scientists have explored the sequences through which the dimensions of love relationships develop and have constructed numerous theories, models, and typologies of love (Fehr 1995). They have also detected and described a number of styles of loving (Kemper 1988; Lee, 1988; Hendrick and Hendrick, 1986; Lasswell and Lasswell 1980). Love is said to begin typically with physical symptoms—palpitations of the heart, rapid breathing, sweating, and so on. At this stage the symptoms are essentially similar to those associated with other emotions such as fear. Next the person proceeds to label his arousal as a love response. This labeling process gains impetus from social pressures and cultural dictates, which prod one to define the experience as love and to follow its ritualistic patterns.

The optimum conditions for love to flourish require that the couple be equally involved in and committed to each other and the relationship. Where there is unequal involvement, the person with the strongest commitment may be vulnerable to exploitation. This is known as the *principle of least interest*, in which the partner with the least interest has the most control. Few relationships that are based on this principle can endure.

(SEE ALSO: *Courtship; Interpersonal Attraction; Mate Selection, Theories*)

REFERENCES

Cancian, Francesca M. 1987 *Love in America: Gender and Self-Development.* Cambridge and New York: Cambridge University Press.

Coontz, Stephanie 1992 *The Way We Never Were: American Families and the Nostalgia Trap.* New York: Basic Books–HarperCollins.

Ellis, Albert 1985 "Romantic Love." In John F. Crosby, ed., *Reply to Myth: Perspectives on Intimacy.* New York: Wiley. pp. 218–227.

Farber, Bernard 1964 *Family: Organization and Interaction.* San Francisco: Chandler.

Fehr, Beverley 1995 "Love." In David Levinson, ed., *Encyclopedia of Marriage and the Family,* vol. 2. New York: Simon and Schuster–Macmillan.

Goode, William J. 1959 "The Theoretical Importance of Love." *American Sociological Review* 24:38–47.

—— 1963 *World Revolution and Family Patterns.* New York: Free Press.

Gray, John 1992 *Men Are from Mars, Women Are from Venus.* New York: HarperCollins.

—— 1993 *Men, Women and Relationships,* rev. 2nd ed. Hillsboro, Oreg.: Beyond Words Publishing.

Hatfield, E., and Rapson, R. L. 1993 *Love, Sex, and Intimacy: Their Psychology, Biology, and History.* New York: HarperCollins.

Hendrick, Clyde, and Susan S. Hendrick 1986 "A Theory and Method of Love." *Journal of Personality and Social Psychology.* 50:392–402.

Hendrick, Susan S. and Clyde Hendrick 1992 *Romantic Love.* Newbury Park, Calif.: Sage.

Hochschild, Arlie R. 1983 *The Managed Heart.* Berkeley: University of California Press.

Hunt, Morton 1959 *The Natural History of Love.* New York: Knopf.

Kemper, Theodore 1988 "Love and Like and Love and Love." In David Franks, ed., *The Sociology of Emotions.* Greenwich, Conn.: JAI Press.

Lasswell, Marcia, and Norman M. Lasswell 1980 *Styles of Loving.* New York: Doubleday.

Lee, J. A. 1988 "Love Styles." In R. J. Sternberg and M. L. Barnes, eds., *The Psychology of Love.* New Haven, Conn.: Yale University Press.

Merrill, Francis E. 1959 *Courtship and Marriage.* New York: Holt-Dryden.

Murstein, Bernard 1. 1974 *Love, Sex, and Marriage through the Ages.* New York: Springer.

Rubin, Zick 1973 *Loving and Liking.* New York: Holt, Rinehart and Winston.

Schwartz, Gary, Don Mertem, Fran Beham, and Allyne Rosenthal 1980 *Love and Commitment.* Beverly Hills, Calif.: Sage.

Seidman, Steven 1991 *Romantic Longings: Love in America, 1830–1980.* New York and London: Routledge.

Sternberg, Robert J. 1998 *Cupid's Arrow: The Course of Love through Time.* Cambridge and New York: Cambridge University Press.

Tennov, Dorothy 1980 *Love and Limerence: The Experience of Being in Love.* New York: Stein and Day.

FELIX M. BERARDO
ERICA OWENS

M

MACROSOCIOLOGY

The term "macro" denotes "large"; thus *macrosociology* refers to the study of large-scale social phenomena. This covers a very broad range of topics that includes groups and collectivities of varying sizes, the major organizations and institutions of one or more societies, cross-sectional or historical studies of a single society, and both comparative and historical analyses of multiple societies. At the grandest level it may cover all human society and history.

Sociologists distinguish macrosociology from microsociology, which focuses on the social activities of individuals and small groups. The micro-macro distinction forms one of the central dualisms characterizing divergent sociological perspectives. Seemingly polar opposites such as conflict-consensus, stability-change, structure-agency, subjective-objective, and materialist-idealist, as well as micro-macro, provide a shorthand method for denoting differences in central assumptions, subjects, and models. As with many other oppositional concepts, however, the boundary between microsociology and macrosociology is not clearly distinguished, and at the margins there is much room for overlap.

Typically, micro-level studies examine individual thought, action, and interaction, often coinciding with social-psychological theories and models, whereas macro-level investigations target social structures and those forces that organize as well as divide individuals into political, social or religious organizations, ethnic populations, communities, and nation-states. Nevertheless, in defining these terms there is major conceptual ambiguity that can be formulated as a question: Should the distinction be based on substantive criteria (specialty and subdisciplinary areas within sociology such as social change and development), theoretical criteria (e.g., functionalist, Marxist), metatheoretical criteria (type of paradigm, epistemology), or methodological criteria (type of research design and analysis techniques)? Since sociologists often use the terms "micro" and "macro" quite casually as convenient devices for categorizing broad areas of theory and research, each of these criteria can be found in the literature, and quite often they are seriously confounded.

A useful means of distinguishing between the two approaches is based on the concept of "units of analysis." Macrosociology uses as its subjects structural-level units of analysis or cases that are larger than observations of individual action and interaction. Even here, however, there is ambiguity, since it is quite possible to make observations on smaller units (e.g., individuals) with the intention of analyzing (making inferences about) larger entities (e.g., groups, classes). Also, the issue of where to draw the line remains. Rather than attempting to draw any hard-and-fast line delineating macro-level from micro-level phenomena, it is helpful to conceptualize a continuum of the subject matter of sociology with "micro" and "macro" defining two end points and with societal-level phenomena clearly placed at the macro pole. George Ritzer, for example, describes one "level of social reality" as a micro-macro continuum moving from individual thought and action through interaction, groups, organizations, and societies to culminate in world systems (Ritzer 1988, pp. 512–518).

Since the macro end of the continuum focuses on social structure, it is important to clarify the use of this term. In a review essay, Neil Smelser (1988, pp. 103–129) describes structure as patterned relationships that emerge from the interaction of individuals or groups over time and space. Institutions and identifiable collectivities are the outcomes of systematically related structures of activities. Structure is dually defined as located in collective actors and in their interaction. Thus social class is an example of social structure, as are the relationships between classes whose locus is the economy. The study of social class and the study of the economy are examples of macrosociology.

Other examples emerge from the macrosociological focus on large-scale structural arrangements and activities of a great number of individuals in large-scale geographical space over long periods of time. Thus macroscopic questions in sociology conventionally revolve around the largest social, spatial, and temporal processes, such as the rise and decline of civilizations; the origins and development of modern nation-states, social movements, and revolutions; and the origins and consequences of social, political, economic, and cultural transformations. Examples include the rise and spread of secular ideologies and religious belief systems, democratic transitions, and the nature and effects of large-scale institutions and organizations. Macro-level analysis is usually embedded in structural and conflict theories, and in studies of societal dynamics and epochal transformations of cultures and social structures. Topics are located within numerous subfields of sociology, including but not limited to stratification and inequality, resource mobilization, political and economic sociology, world systems, human evolution, and ecology. They are equally likely to cross or link disciplinary boundaries to incorporate history, geography, political economy, and anthropology.

HISTORICAL BACKGROUND

The concern with macro-level phenomena is as old as the discipline of sociology and arguably is the primary motivation for the creation of classical sociological theory and research. The men generally accorded honored places in the pantheon of sociology's founders, such as Auguste Comte, Herbert Spencer, Karl Marx, Emile Durkheim, and Max Weber (and additional historical figures such as Alexis de Tocqueville), all included macro-level phenomena among their dominant concerns. The traditions they established retain their definitive role for the central issues of sociology in general and macrosociology in particular.

The themes pursued by these and other classical theorists are found in subsequent theory and research. For example, the evolutionary perspectives on the development of human society advanced by early theorists have been modified, revised, and developed by contemporary evolutionary theorists such as Lenski (Lenski et al. 1995) and in the modern functionalist and neo-functionalist theories of Talcott Parsons (1966), Niklas Luhmann (1982), and Jeffrey Alexander (1998). Marx's historical materialist explanation of the unfolding of capitalism has spawned numerous offspring, including dependency and world system theories (Amin 1976; Frank 1967; Wallerstein 1974), and studies of the rise of the modern state and class conflict by Moore (1966). Similarly, Weber's comparative and historical studies of social stratification and the development of modern states are reflected in the works of Reinhard Bendix (1977; 1978), Theda Skocpol (1979) and Michael Mann (1986; 1993) Emile Durkheim's analysis of the division of labor in modern societies as well as the sources of societal integration underlie all modernization theory and functional perspectives on race and ethnic relations, as well as most contemporary studies of occupational structures. Alexis de Tocqueville's comparative study of democracy has remained an inspirational source for contemporary theories of democracy and social change. In short, the macrosociological problems defined early in the history of sociology remain major focuses of current sociological research.

Also located in these early works but often overlooked in subsequent interpretations is an issue that is the current central project of many social theorists: the links between macro- and micro-level phenomena. At least in the writings of Marx, Weber, and Durkheim, to a greater or lesser degree, efforts are made to connect individual and structural level activities in some coherent fashion. For example, Marx is often considered the quintessential macrosociologist, providing the foundation for much current macrosociology. Yet as

Bertell Ollman (1976) and others point out, there is a distinct social psychology anchored in Marx's concept of alienation that in turn motivates and is motivated by his macro-level modes of productive relations and class conflict. This concern with linkage has often been ignored or forgotten in the distinctive development of different schools of sociological thought. After years of separate development and sometimes acrimonious debate, efforts to conduct research and develop social theories that include both ends of the micro-macro continuum now constitute a major agenda for many sociologists.

THEMES IN MACROSOCIOLOGICAL THEORY AND RESEARCH

Macrosociogical studies vary in both subject and theoretical orientation, but the two are closely related. For example, large-scale studies of single total societies or particular societal institutions often operate from a functionalist or systems perspective in which the effort is to understand how component parts fit together and serve larger social goals. On the other hand, studies of social change, either within a single society or across cultures, more often use one of the many variants of conflict—Marxist, neo-Marxist, and Weberian perspectives. They do so because such theories are better equipped to explain conflict and change than the relatively static models promoted by functionalism, and because functionalism no longer dominates sociology. These are broad generalizations, however, which invite counterexample.

Given the sweeping scope of macrosociology, it is not possible to provide comprehensive coverage of all the topics and theories subsumed under this approach. The next section will illustrate key concerns of macrosociologists by describing exemplary theory and research in some major areas of macrosociology.

Societal Evolutionary Change. The numerous approaches to the study of societal change illustrate the diversity of sociological perspectives. At the most sweeping level, evolutionary theories take all human history and society as their subject, but there are numerous variants to this approach. For example, evolutionary theory has gone hand in hand with functionalism, as in the later work of

Talcott Parsons on human societies (1966), which features the basic assumptions of evolutionary theory in terms of holism (the whole unit rather than its parts), universalism (natural and perpetual change), and unidirectionality (progressive and cumulative change). An idealist version of an evolutionary perspective can be found in Jurgen Habermas (1979), who uses an evolutionary model to explain the development of normative structures and forms of rationality. Alternatively, it has also taken a materialist form, as developed by anthropologists (Harris 1977) and a few sociologists (Lenski, 1966, Lenski et al. 1995), to explain inequality and uneven distribution of social resources. Another version of societal evolutionary change that deviates somewhat from the mainstream of progressive evolution are the cyclical dynamics of societal and cultural change proposed in works of Pitirim Sorokin (1962). Evolutionary analysis also was once popular in the fields of human ecology (Hawley 1971), modernization (Smelser 1964), and structural and cultural assimilation of different racial groups in modern society (Gordon 1964).

Currently, there are relatively few sociologists who operate on this scale or who find it useful for analyzing more confined periods of historical change. Nevertheless, contemporary theories of human evolution have been influential in providing comparative evidence for the material and normative bases of different forms of social organization and for describing the broadest patterns of societal change. These include the distribution of societal goods and services, enduring forms of inequality (e.g., patriarchy), and normative systems.

Modernization and Development. Sociologists often limit their study of change to the emergence of modern industrial society, either to trace the paths taken by mature industrialized societies to reach their current state of development or to investigate the problems of developing nations. Here, too, different approaches emerge from different theoretical perspectives.

Modernization theory, which until the 1960s dominated accounts of development and change, grew out of functionalism and evolutionary perspectives. In the version articulated by economist W. W. Rostow (1960), nonindustrial societies, through diffusion and a natural developmental sequence, were expected to follow a series of stages previously traversed by fully industrialized nations to attain the significant characteristics of modern societies considered prerequisites for development. This process required breaking from traditional social norms and values to build institutions based on "modern" values such as universalism, rationalization, and achievement orientation.

Although today largely abandoned in favor of more historically and materially grounded theories, modernization theory was highly influential among both scholars and policy makers of the post–World War II era. In fact, it can be argued that the influence of modernization theory in part explains its repudiation, since students of and from emerging developing nations viewed it as an instrument of continued colonial domination and capitalist exploitation. Their search for tools to provide a better explanation for their disadvantaged and subordinate position in the international arena led to the adoption of Marxist-based models of dependency, underdevelopment, and world systems to replace modernization as the dominant approach to change and development within the modern era. As summarized by Peter Evans and John Stephens (1988, p. 740), these "approaches turned the modernization theorists' emphasis on diffusion . . . on its head, arguing instead that ties to 'core' countries were a principal impediment to development."

In an influential early formulation, dependency theorist Andre Gunder Frank (1967) maintained that the experience of most nonindustrial nations is explained by the "development of underdevelopment." In other words, the exploitation of peripheral Third World nations by capital in the core, developed world increased the economic, social, and political misery experienced by the majority populations of those Third World countries. Alliances between local and international elites actively worked to defend the status quo distribution of power and privilege at the expense of peasant- and working-class majorities. Later versions refined the models of class conflict and competition or, as in the writings of Samir Amin (1976), elaborated the model of the relationships between center and periphery economies to show how underdevelopment grows out of the exploitive links between the two types of systems.

All versions contribute to a refutation of the trajectory of development described by modernization theory.

A more global approach to development issues was formulated by Immanuel Wallerstein (1974, 1980, 1988) and his followers. World system theory elaborates the Marxist model of economic domination into a system in which exploitation occurs worldwide. Wallerstein broadens the focus on class relations among and across nations to examine the development of an international division of labor in the capitalist world economy where core industrial nations exploit peripheral regions as sources of raw materials and labor. This approach has been both enormously influential and controversial, generating massive amounts of research on the model itself, particular spatial and historical portions of the world system, and particular subsectors and groups. A helpful overview that charts the intricacies of this perspective can be found in a text by Thomas Shannon (1989).

The emphasis on First World as well as Third World development found in world-system theory provides a bridge to a slightly different tradition that focuses on the emergence of the core industrial nations and their political systems. Much of this literature is concerned with development of modern political as well as economic systems. For example, while Barrington Moore's study (1966) of the transformation of agrarian societies into modern industrial states remains firmly anchored in a Marxist emphasis on class relations and productive systems, it is also concerned with the political roles played by antagonistic classes and the political outcomes of their confrontation. Numerous other studies pursue a similar comparative perspective on the upheavals that accompanied the emergence of modern Western industrial nations (cf. Tilly et al. 1975).

One other type of study in this tradition deserves mention. These are studies of social and political change that occur within a particular society at various stages in the industrialization process. John Walton (1987) provides a convenient typology based on cross-classifying epochs and processes of industrialization. The resulting types range from protoindustrialization through deindustrialzation. Studies from early periods focus on the emergence of particular classes, on class conflict, and on the influence of classes on the historical development of modern nations, as in E. P. Thompson's and John Foster's influential accounts of English class formation (Thompson 1963; Foster 1974), Ron Aminzade's analysis of nineteenth-century France (1984), and Herbert Gutman's studies of American class culture and conflict (1966). Influential studies of transitions in later periods of industrial development examine the consolidation of control of the labor process (Burawoy 1979; Edwards 1979), deindustrialization (Bluestone and Harrison 1982), informalization of labor markets (Portes et al. 1989), and post-Fordist production systems (Mingione 1991).

Finally, while beyond the scope of this review, there are also other important traditions that have strong links to one or the other approaches described above. One of these is found in a vast literature on social movements that has many points of intersection with the work on comparative and historical social and political change discussed here. Another is work that applies the theories of dependency and uneven development to regional development problems internal to particular societies. Finally, there are structural and poststructural approaches to the development of major social institutions and forms of repression, as found in the complex but influential work of Michel Foucault (1979, 1980, 1985). While this last example could as easily be classified under studies of social institutions and processes, it is included here because of its focus on changes in historical times that have produced modern social forms.

State Formation and State Breakdown. The study of state formation and state breakdown has always been a central focus of macrosocial inquiry, especially in the area of comparative historical sociology. Studies of state formation examine the nature of state power and the processes by which it develops. While some sociologists have seen the state as emerging from internal dynamics of society, largely in terms of the interests and struggles of social classes, others have turned their attention to the external dynamics of society along with the market forces of the capitalist system. Tilly (1975, 1990) demonstrates that the modern states were created in the process of capital concentration and consolidated under the pressure of increased international military competition (war and preparation for war).

Michael Mann (1986, 1993) examines the nature of power in human societies by focusing on the interrelations of four principal sources of social power—economic, ideological, military, and political resources—and relates them to the rise of city-states, militaristic empires, modern nation-states, and nationalism. Another important theory on the relations between the state and society is Robert Wuthnow's (1989) analysis of how conflicts between the state, elites, and cultural entrepreneurs caused the great ideological movements to challenge the status quo in the development of modern society.

Contemporary theory of revolution and state breakdown starts with Barrington Moore (1966) who proposed a model of agrarian class politics. Drawing upon both Marxian and Weberian theoretical perspectives, Skocpol's (1979) breakthrough analysis introduced the state-centered theoretical paradigm of revolution in her case study of French, Russian, and Chinese revolutions. Treating the state as an "autonomous entity," Skocpol argues that the state has its own military and fiscal interests, and that under certain circumstances, state interests necessarily are in deep conflict with the interests of social classes. State breakdown occurs when the state experiences high levels of fiscal crisis induced by strain on resources from both internal elite conflicts and external military pressure. In Skocpol's theory, the state thus becomes the central actor and the location of crisis in revolutionary situations.

This state-centered theme developed by Skocpol has been further expanded by Goldstone (1991), who uses a structural-demographic approach to indicate that the early modern boom in population led to strain on state resources associated with the taxation system and economic development. Goldstone argues that in a system tied to agricultural output, the agrarian state depends mainly on land taxes for revenue. As growing population places pressure on the agricultural economy, rising grain prices result in inflation that erodes state revenues, leads to higher taxes, and exacerbates elite conflict. Rising prices generate profits for some elites who are quick to take advantage of commercial opportunities, but hurts other elites who are slow to adjust and lag behind in social mobility. Revolution is the ultimate outcome of the state's failure to meet its obligations.

While Skocpol's and Goldstone's models emphasize either structural or demographic sources of strain on the state, interest in geopolitical principles and strains became increasingly prominent during the 1980s, inspired by Paul Kennedy's analysis (1987) of the rise and fall of great powers. Randall Collins's geopolitical theory (1986, 1995) offers another route to state breakdown. Bringing in the Weberian principle that legitimacy of the governing apparatus at home depends on the state's power and prestige abroad, Collins's analysis, given validation by his prediction of the collapse of the Soviet Union, demonstrates that a state's geopolitical position has a crucial effect on its ability to mobilize critical resources and manage internal politics. In Collins's model, geopolitical strains result in inability to maintain fiscal health. A state that suffers the geopolitical disadvantage of being surrounded by multiple enemy states experiences logistical overextension and fiscal crisis, and thus tends to decline and disintegrate to the point of revolution and state fragmentation.

Social Structures, Processes, and Institutions. The research described above incorporates investigation of many of the major social structures, processes, and institutions that form the core subject matter of sociology. Studying change in economic and political systems requires scrutiny of economies, polities, and other social institutions and their major organizational manifestations and constituencies. However, other theoretical and substantive approaches subsumed under macrosociology either have fallen outside the scope of these large-scale studies of social change and development or are at their periphery. Theoretical perspectives include relatively recent developments such as structural, poststructural, postmodern, and feminist theories. Important substantive areas are defined by cumulating empirical bases of knowledge about power structures; work structures; social stratification and mobility; labor markets; household and family arrangements; and the intersections of race, class, gender, and nationality.

While it is impossible to survey each of these areas, the explosive growth of feminist theories to investigate both gender stratification and economic change and development provides a prime example of new influences on macrosociology. Feminist theorists argue that gender analysis must be integrated with class, race, ethnicity, nationality, and other sources of social cleavage, and that analyses that ignore the system of gender relations embedded in society are incomplete. Feminist theories have contributed to macrosociology by demonstrating how theories of social reproduction must be joined to theories of economic production to understand social life fully, thus delineating the ways patriarchy coexists with particular economic and political systems to explain the position of women in society.

For example, the subordination of women is predicated on the allocation of tasks that exist outside formal labor markets such as household and reproductive labor and consumption activities as well as labor market work. Heidi Hartmann's early, influential, socialist feminist analysis of the intersection of capitalism and patriarchy (1981) explains women's disadvantaged status in both the labor market and the household in late capitalism as the outcome of an uneasy alliance between the two systems. With increasing demand for women's labor in the second half of the twentieth century, the intersection of the two systems has taken the form of the double and even the triple day—that is, women burdened by responsibility for formal labor market activity; household work; and, frequently, informal work as well.

Similar insights from feminist perspectives have informed studies of developing nations and processes of industrialization and globalization. For example, Ester Boserup's critique of conventional development theories (1970) demonstrates the pitfalls for development projects resulting from ignoring women, as well as the ways women have been marginalized by development scholars and practitioners. Numerous feminist scholars have built on this and related work, combining it with other theoretical perspectives such as world systems and globalization theories, to expand knowledge of the gendered social consequences of core nation exploitation of the periphery (Ward 1990) and the general pattern of ignoring women in large-scale societal accounting schemes (Beneria 1981). Postcolonial theories and "Third World feminism" further explore the intersections of race, class, and gender as they influence different populations in the global economy (Alexander and Mohanty 1997) Finally, the historical research of Louise Tilly and Joan Scott (1978), among others, has been important in an understanding of how the shift from household economies to wage labor affected working-class women and their families. Unfortunately, much of this work remains underutilized and unincorporated in the kind of macro-level analyses reviewed in previous sections, representing parallel developments rather than integrated studies of macrosocial processes.

RESEARCH METHODOLOGY OF MACROSOCIAL INQUIRY

In the past decades, research methodology in macrosociology has been widely discussed among sociologists. Both quantitative and qualitative methods are used extensively, often in the same larger study. Virtually any methodological tool available to social science is found in macrosocial analysis, ranging from survey research to hermeneutic inquiry.

Quantitative approaches include quantification of documentary and archival data, such as analysis of the lists of grievances, or *cahiers de doleances* (Markoff 1996); analysis of official socioeconomic, demographic, and political data aggregated for larger geopolitical units such as counties, states, or nations; time series of such data for a single state or nation; and standard survey research techniques interpreted to represent structural and contextual process (Coleman et al. 1970). Trend analysis using survey data is one method frequently used by sociologists to establish long-term patterns of change by examining historical change in statistical data. Quantitative methods that use longitudinal designs of panel and cohort analyses to conduct observations at two or more points in time have been extensively employed in the assessment of social change and development at the local, national, and global levels.

Historical and comparative methods are featured prominently in macrosociological analysis and have been consistently used by the most prominent classical and contemporary sociologists. This approach develops ideal-typical case studies of large-scale organizations, nations, and civilizations across time and space. Thus, social and cultural differences manifest in temporal processes and contexts are the focal point of macrohistorical studies that, as Skocpol (1984, p. 1) summarizes:

(1) "address processes over time, and take temporal sequences seriously in accounting for outcomes," (2) "attend to the interplay of meaningful actions and structural contexts in order to make sense of the unfolding of unintended as well as intended outcomes in individual lives and social transformations," and (3) "highlight the particular and varying features of specific kinds of social structures and patterns of change."

In the existing literature on macrosociological research, historical and comparative methods, with their focus on case studies devoted to understanding the nature and effects of large-scale structures and fundamental processes of change, have proven to be an effective approach to macrosociological explanations of macrosocial phenomena. While most historical and comparative research still involves qualitative analyses using available documents and records, more and more research attempts to employ both qualitative and quantitative approaches.

In advocating "moving beyond qualitative and quantitative strategies" Charles Ragin (1987) points out that, in macrosociological analysis, there are two basic strategies: the case-oriented strategy and the variable-oriented strategy. The former is very much evidence oriented, while the latter is theory centered. The goals of case-oriented investigation, with its extensive use of ideal types, often are both historically interpretive and causally analytic. "Investigators who used case-oriented strategies often want to understand or interpret specific cases because of their intrinsic values" (Ragin 1987, p. 35). Work by Bendix (1977, 1978) exemplifies this approach.

Unlike the case-oriented strategy, the variable-oriented strategy tests hypotheses derived from theory, often using quantitative techniques such as multivariate statistical analysis. In macrosocial analysis, a typical variable-oriented study "examines relationships between general features of social structures conceived as variables. Social units, such as nation-states, have structural features which interact in the sense that changes in some features produce changes in other features, which in turn may produce changes in others" (Ragin 1987, p. 55). For example, a cross-national study of modernization by Delacroix and Ragin (1978) is a typical example of variable-oriented research, and this approach has remained quite popular in the study of development issues as well as in macro-level studies of organizations.

Each of these two strategies has its strengths and weaknesses. The case-oriented research enables investigators to comprehend diversity and address complexity by examining causal processes more directly in historical and comparative context. In variable-oriented research, by contrast, generality is given precedence over complexity when investigators are able to digest large numbers of cases. In some macrosociological studies, scholars combine the two approaches, as in Jeffrey Paige's *Agrarian Revolution* (1975).

THE FUTURE OF MACROSOCIOLOGY

Macroscopic analysis of human society stands as a foundational area of research in sociology, and it is safe to predict that it will continue to grow and expand its scope of inquiry. In an increasingly global economy, marked by shifting boundaries and allegiances, and linked by rapidly advancing communications and information technology, there will be pressing need for explanation and analysis of the major historical and contemporary social movements and upheavals. Events of state formation, transition, and breakdown; revolution and devolution; conflicts based on gender, race, ethnicity, religion, region, and class; global movements of populations; and numerous other large-scale processes that increasingly mark the post–cold war era will provide the raw materials for scholarly and policy relevant analysis.

At the same time, in the interests of advancing social theory, sociologists will continue to seek ways to link macroprocesses to microprocesses. One of the perennial debates that surfaces among sociologists is whether macroprocesses or microprocesses have primacy in explaining social life. A variant revolves around the issue of whether microprocesses can be derived from macroprocesses or vice versa. Those who believe that the macro has causal priority risk being labeled structural determinists. Those who think that macrophenomena can be derived from microprocesses are dismissed as reductionists. Quite often an uneasy truce prevails in which practitioners of the two types of sociology go their own ways, with little interaction or mutual influence.

Despite pendulum swings that alternately emphasize one approach over the other, there are ongoing efforts to construct theory and conduct research built on genuine principles of micro-macro linkage. These have come form a variety of theoretical traditions and perspectives, including those with both macro and micro foundations. While many of these efforts ultimately result in de facto claims for theoretical primacy of one or the other approach, they nonetheless represent an interesting effort to create uniform and widely applicable sociological theory (Huber 1991).

Ultimately, most of the efforts to integrate micro and macro levels reflect the initial concerns of the theorist. For example, Randall Collins's efforts (1998) begin with a microfocus on interaction to derive macrophenomena, while neofunctionalist Jeffrey Alexander (1985) gives primacy to subjective forms of macrophenomena. Perhaps the most highly developed integrative effort is found in Anthony Giddens's theory of structuration (1984) in which social structure is defined as both constraining and enabling human activity, as well as being both internal and external to the actor.

The efforts to link microphenomena and macrophenomena are mirrored in a growing body of empirical research. Such work appears to follow Giddens's view of the constraining and enabling nature of social structure for human activity and the need to link structure and action. It appears safe to say that, while macrosociology will always remain a central component of sociological theory and research, increasing effort will be devoted to creating workable models that link it with its micro counterpart.

REFERENCES

Alexander, M. Jacqui, and Chandra Talpade Mohanty, eds. 1997 *Feminist Genealogies, Colonial Legacies, Democratic Futures*. New York and London: Routledge.

Alexander, Jeffrey (ed.) 1985. *Neofunctionalism*. Beverly Hills, Calif.: Sage.

—— 1998 *Neofunctionalism and After*. Malden, Mass.: Blackwell.

Amin, Samir 1976 *Unequal Development: An Essay on the Social Formations of Peripheral Capitalism*. New York: Monthly Review Press.

Aminzade, Ron 1984 "Capitalism Industrialization and Patterns of Industrial Protest: A Comparative Urban Study of Nineteenth-Century France." *American Sociological Review* 49:437–453.

Beneria, Lourdes 1981 "Conceptualizing the Labour Force: The Underestimation of Women's Economic Activities." *Journal of Development* 17:10–28.

Bendix, Reinhard 1977 *Nation-Building and Citizenship: Studies of Our Changing Social Order.* Berkeley: University of California Press.

—— 1978 *Kings or People: Power and the Mandate to Rule.* Berkeley: University of California Press.

Bluestone, Barry, and Bennet Harrison 1982 *The Deindustrialization of America: Plant Closings, Community Abandonment, and the Dismantling of Basic Industry.* New York: Basic Books.

Boserup, Easter 1970 *Women's Role in Economic Development.* New York: St. Martin's Press.

Burawoy, Michael 1979 *Manufacturing Consent: Changes in the Labor Process under Monopoly Capital.* Chicago: University of Chicago Press.

Coleman, James S., Amitai Etzioni, and John Porter 1970 *Macrosociology: Research and Theory.* Boston: Allyn and Bacon.

Collins, Randall 1986 "Future Decline of the Russian Empire." In Randall Collins, ed., *Weberian Sociological Theory.* New York: Cambridge University Press.

—— 1995 "Prediction in Macrosociological Theory: The Case of the Soviet Collapse." *American Journal of Sociology* 100: 1552–1593.

—— 1988 "The Micro Contribution to Macro Sociology." *Sociological Theory* 6:242–253.

Delacroix, Jacques, and Charles Ragin 1978 "Modernizing Institutions, Mobilization, and Third World Development: A Cross-National Study." *American Journal of Sociology* 84:123–150.

Edwards, Richard 1979 *Contested Terrain: The Transformation of the Workplace in the Twentieth Century.* New York: Basic Books.

Evans, Peter, and John Stephens 1988 "Development and the World Economy." In Neil Smelser, ed., *Handbook of Sociology.* Newbury Park, Calif.: Sage.

Foster, John 1974 *Class Struggle and the Industrial Revolution: Early Industrial Capitalism in Three English Towns.* London: Weidenfeld and Nicholson.

Foucault, Michel 1979 *Discipline and Punish: The Birth of the Prison.* New York: Vintage.

—— 1980 *The History of Sexuality, Volume 1: An Introduction.* New York: Vintage.

—— 1985 *The History of Sexuality, Volume 2: The Uses of Pleasure.* New York: Pantheon.

Frank, Andre Gunder 1967 *Capitalism and Underdevelopment in Latin America.* New York: Monthly Review Press.

Giddens, Anthony 1984 *The Constitution of Society: Outline of the Theory of Structuration.* Berkeley: University of California Press.

Goldstone, Jack A. 1991 *Revolution and Rebellion in the Early Modern World.* Berkeley: University of California Press.

Gordon, Milton 1964 *Assimilation in American Life: The Role of Race, Religion, and National Origins.* New York: Oxford University Press.

Gutman, Herbert G. (1966) 1977 *Work, Culture, and Society in Industrializing America.* New York: Vintage Books.

Habermas, Jurgen 1979 *Communication and the Evolution of Society.* Boston: Beacon Press.

Harris, Marvin 1977 *Cannibals and Kings: The Origins of Cultures.* New York: Random House.

Hartmann, Heidi 1981 "The Family as the Locus of Gender, Class, and Political Struggle: The Example of Housework." *Signs* 6:366–394.

Hawley, Amos H. 1971 *Urban Society: An Ecological Approach.* New York: Wiley.

Huber, Joan (ed.) 1991 *Macro-Micro Linkages in Sociology.* Newbury Park, Calif.: Sage.

Kennedy, Paul 1987 *The Rise and Fall of the Great Powers: Economic Change and Military Conflict from 1500 to 2000.* New York: Random House.

Lenski, Gerhard 1966 *Power and Privilege.* New York: McGraw-Hill.

Lenski, Gerhard, Patrick Nolan, and Jean Lenski 1995 *Human Societies,* 7th ed. New York: McGraw-Hill.

Mann, Michael 1986 *The Sources of Social Power, Vol. 1: A History of Power from the Beginning to A.D. 1760.* New York: Cambridge University Press.

—— 1993 *The Sources of Social Power, Vol. 2: The Rise of Classes and Nation-States, 1760–1914.* Cambridge: Cambridge University Press.

Luhmann, Niklas 1982 *The Differentiation of Society* (trans. S. Holmes and C. Larmore). New York: Columbia University Press.

Markoff, John 1996 *The Abolition of Feudalism: Peasants, Lords and Legislators in the French Revolution.* University Park: Pennsylvania State University.

Mingione, Enzo 1991 *Fragmented Societies: A Sociology of Economic Life beyond the Market Paradigm* (trans. Paul Goodrick). Oxford: Basil Blackwell.

Moore, Barrington, Jr. 1966 *Social Origins of Dictatorship and Democracy: Lord and Peasant in the Making of the Modern World*. Boston: Beacon Press.

Ollman, Bertell 1976 *Alienation*, 2nd ed. Cambridge: Cambridge University Press.

Paige, Jeffrey 1975 *Agrarian Revolution: Social Movements and Export Agriculture in the Underdeveloped World*. New York: Free Press.

Parsons, Talcott 1966 *Societies: Evolutionary and Comparative Perspectives*. Englewood Cliffs, N.J.: Prentice-Hall.

Portes, Alejandro, Manuel Castells, and Lauren Benton, eds. 1989 *The Informal Economy: Studies in Advanced and Less Developed Countries*. Baltimore, Md.: Johns Hopkins University Press.

Ragin, Charles C. 1987 *The Comparative Method: Moving beyond Qualitative and Quantitative Strategies*. Berkeley: University of California Press.

Ritzer, George 1988 *Sociological Theory*, 2nd ed. New York: Knopf.

Rostow, W. W. 1960 *The Stages of Economic Growth*. Cambridge: Cambridge University Press.

Shannon, Thomas Richard 1989 *An Introduction to the World System Perspective*. Boulder, Col.: Westview Press.

Skocpol, Theda 1979 *States and Social Revolutions*. Cambridge: Cambridge University Press.

—— (ed.) 1984 *Vision and Method in Historical Sociology*. New York: Cambridge University Press.

Smelser, Neil 1964 "Toward a Theory of Modernization." Pp. 268–284 in Amitai Etzioni and Eva Etzioni, eds., *Social Change*. New York: Basic Books.

—— 1988 "Social Structure." In Neil Smelser, ed., *Handbook of Sociology*. Newbury Park, Calif.: Sage.

Sorokin, Pitirim 1962 *Social and Cultural Dynamics*. New York: Bedminster Press.

Thompson, E. P. 1963 *The Making of the English Working Class*. New York: Vintage.

Tilly, Charles 1975 *The Formation of National States in Western Europe*. Princeton, N.J.: Princeton University Press.

—— 1990 *Coercion, Capital, and the Rise of European States A.D. 990–1990*. Cambridge, Mass.: Blackwell.

——, Louise Tilly, and Richard Tilly 1975 *The Rebellious Century, 1830–1930*. Cambridge, Mass.: Harvard University Press.

Tilly, Louise, and Joan Scott 1978 *Women, Work, and Family*. New York: Holt, Rinehart, and Winston.

Wallerstein, Immanuel 1974 *The Modern World-System: Capitalist Agriculture and the Origins of the European World-Economy in the Sixteenth Century*. New York: Academic Press.

—— 1980 *The Modern World-System II: Mercantilism and the Consolidation of the European World-Economy, 1600–1750*. New York: Academic Press.

—— 1988 *The Modern World-System III: The Second Era of Great Expansion of the Capitalist World-Economy, 1730–1840*. San Diego, Calif.: Academic Press.

Walton, John 1987 "Theory and Research on Industrialization." *Annual Review of Sociology* 13:89–108.

Ward, Kathryn, ed. 1990 *Women Workers and Global Restructuring*. Ithaca, N.Y.: Industrial and Labor Relations Press.

Wuthnow, Robert 1989 *Communities of Discourse: Ideology and Social Structure in the Reformation, the Enlightenment, and European Socialism*. Cambridge, Mass.: Harvard University Press.

ANN R. TICKAMYER AND JIELI LI

MAJOR PERSONALITY THEORIES

Problems of definition arise with the terms *personality* and *personality theories*. Personality is understood by some people to mean self-concept; by others, the consensus of other people's opinions about one's character, and by others, one's true character. Some personality theories have elaborate coordinated concepts discussing how personality originates and develops from conception to senescence, taking up cognitive, conative, and affective aspects of the mind as well as free will, holism, philosophy, and other issues. On the other hand, there are relatively simple, one-dimensional theories of personality that pay little attention to what seems important to other theorists.

This topic is complicated not only by its complexity and variations but also by intellectual belligerence among those who favor one theory over another and those who differ about the same theory. The analogy to religions is inescapable.

In view of this situation, personality theories will be handled in an unusual way. Sentences in italics are reprinted from *Personality Theories, Research, and Assessment* (Corsini and Marsella 1983).

Some Personality Theories and Their Originators

Abelson, R.P.	Least effort	Lowen, Alexander	Bio-energetics
Allport, Gordon W.	Personalism	Maltz, Albert	Psychocybernetics
Angyll, Andreas	Organismic theory	Maslow, Abraham	Self-actualizations
Assiogoli, Roberto	Psychosynthesis	May, Rollo	Existentialism
Berne, Eric	Transactional analysis	Mead, G.H.	Social interaction
Binwangers, Ludwig	Daseinanalysis	Miller, Neal	Learning theory
Branden, Nathaniel	Biocentrism	Meyer, Adolf	Psychobiological theory
Burrow, Trigant	Phyloanalysis	Moreno, J.L.	Sociometry
Bühler, Charlotte	Humanistic psychology	Mowrer, O.H.	Two-factor theory
Bühler, Karl	Funktionlust	Murphy, Gardner	Biosocial theory
Boss, Medard	Daseinanalysis	Murray, H.A.	Need-press theory
Cattell, Raymond	Multivariate theory	Osgood, Charles	Congruity theory
Combs, Arthur	Phenomenology	Perls, Frederick	Gestalt theory
Ellis, Albert	Rational-emotive theory	Piaget, Jean	Developmental theory
Erikson, Erik	Developmental theory	Rank, Otto	Will theory
Eysenck, Hans	Developmental theory	Reich, Wihelm	Character analysis
Frankl, Victor	Logotherapy	Rolf, Ida	Structural integration
Fromm, Erich	Humanistic psychoanalysis	Rotter, Julian	Social learning
Heider, Fritz	Balance theory	Sarbin, Theodore	Role theory
Horney, Karen	Sociopsychological theory	Sheldon, William	Morphological theory
Jackson, Don	Systems theory	Sulivan, H.S.	Interpersonal theory
Kelly, Charles	Neo-Reichian theory	Van Kaam, Adrian	Transpersonal psychology
Korsybski, Alfred	General semantics	Werner, Heinz	Developmental theory
Lecky, Philip	Self-consistency	Wolpe, Joseph	Behavior theory
Lewin, Kurt	Topological psychology		

Table 1

NOTE: Some Personality Theories and Their Originators

They contain quotes of selected assertions about the various theories written by authorities of nine major systems. Additional sources presenting comparative information on personality theories include: Burger 1993; Cloninger 1993; Corsini and Wedding 1995; Drapela 1995; Engler 1999; Ewen 1997; Schultz and Schultz 1994.

Table 1 is a list of a number of other important personality theories.

PSYCHOANALYSIS (SIGMUND FREUD, 1856–1939)

Psychoanalysis is both a theory of personality and a form of psychotherapy (see Freud 1952–1974). Highly controversial throughout Freud's lifetime, it continues to be so.

Freud saw personality as a dynamic conflict within the mind between opposing instinctual and social forces. *The topographical hypothesis views the mind in terms of three systems.* They are: the unconscious, the preconscious, and the conscious. *The mind is composed of the id, ego, and superego.* The id consists of primitive instinctual demands, the superego represents society's influence restricting the id's demands, and the ego is dynamically in between the two. *Fundamental motives are instinctual.* Instincts are the basic forces (drives) of the psyche. The aim of drives is their satisfaction. *All instincts are basically sexual.* Freud's concept of sexuality was equivalent to physical pleasures. *There is a series of built-in stages of sexual development.* Freud postulated that people went through three sexual stages: An oral stage following the primary infantile narcissistic stage, then an anal phase, and finally a phallic phase. *Children develop libidinal attitudes towards parents.* This notion of the Oedipus and Electra complex of children having sexual attractions to parents of the opposite sex has especially generated controversy.

The psyche develops a number of defenses. To survive, the human being's ego develops a number of processes intended to repress awareness of conflicts. Repression is the main mental mechanism, but others defenses are related to it, including rationalization, displacement, identification and conversion. *Dreams have meaning and purpose.* According to Freud, dreams are disguised desires permitting people to sleep by permitting expressions of illicit desires disguised by various symbolisms.

INDIVIDUAL PSYCHOLOGY (ALFRED ADLER, 1870–1937)

Alfred Adler's personality theory is distinguished by its common sense and simple language (see Adler 1956). In contrast to Freud and Jung, Adler's views demonstrate social concern.

Man, like all forms of life, is a unified organism. This basic holistic notion contradicts Freud's classifications and opposing theses and antitheses. Adler viewed the individual as an indivisible totality that could not be analyzed or considered in sections. *Life is movement, directed towards growth and expansion.* Adler took a dynamic and teleological attitude toward life, that people were always striving toward goals of personal self-improvement and enhancement. *Man is endowed with creativity and within limits is self-determined.* Instead of taking the usual position that only biology and society were to be considered in the formation of personality, Adler posited a third element: personal creativity or individual responsibility, akin to the concept of free will. Adler accepted that we all have certain biological and social givens and what is made of them is the responsibility of individuals.

Man lives inextricably in a social world. Adler had a social personality theory. *Individuale* in German does not have the same denotation as *individual* in English but rather denotes indivisibility or unity. Adler did not see humans apart from society. *The important life problems–human relations, sex, occupation–are social problems.* Adler believed that to be successful in life all humans had to complete the life tasks of socialization, family, and work.

Social interest is an aptitude that must be consciously developed. Social interest is the criterion of mental health. Social interest is operationally defined as social usefulness. This trio of related statements is an explicit philosophy unique for personality theories. Adler believed that psychological normality

depended on *Gemeinschaftsgefühl*—social interest. He saw all human failures, such as criminals, the insane, and neurotics, as lacking this element.

ANALYTICAL PSYCHOLOGY (CARL G. JUNG, 1875–1961)

Jung's analytical psychology stresses unconscious mental processes and features elements in personality that derive from mankind's past (Jung 1953–1972).

Personality is influenced by potential activation of a collective transpersonal unconscious. Jung believed that individuals upon conception came with something from the past that directed their personalities, a concept somewhat like Lamarckism relative to physical heredity. *Complexes are structured and energized around an archetypical image.* This is an extension of the first assertion. Complexes refer to important bipolar aspects of personality, such as introversion–extraversion. Complexes, directed by archetypes, are seen as innate and universal capacities of the mind to organize human experiences. Archetypes are considered innate potentials of the mind derived from the experiences of ancestors, a kind of directing blueprint of one's character.

The ego mediates between the unconscious and the outside world. According to Jung, a strong, well-integrated ego is the ideal state for a person. *Unconscious psychic reality is as important as the outside world.* Jung stressed the importance of phenomenology in contrast to overt behavior. He explored people's inner realms with great diligence. He even exceeded Freud in concentrating on the importance of the unconscious. *Personality growth occurs throughout the life cycle.* Jung saw individuals in constant growth and development with imperceptible stages that sometimes, as in the case of adolescence and midlife crises, became evident. *The psyche spontaneously strives towards wholeness, integration, and self-realization.* This last statement is echoed in many different ways by a number of other theorists, including the two just considered, and is made a central point by some theorists such as Carl Rogers and Kurt Goldstein.

PERSON-CENTERED THEORY (CARL ROGERS 1902–1987)

Carl Rogers developed his theory as part of his system of client-centered or nondirective therapy (see Rogers 1951). He had a lifelong abiding faith in the potentials of people to correct the errors of their past if a therapeutic environment could be created in which the client felt understood and accepted by a neutral nonevaluative therapist. His system emerges from one central theme, the first assertion below.

Each person has an inherent tendency to actualize unique potential. Rogers viewed each person as having a built-in tendency to develop all his or her capacities in ways that serve to maintain or enhance the organism. *Each person has an inherent bodily wisdom which enables differentiation between experiences that actualize and those that do not actualize potential.* Rogers's trust in people is indicated here: There is a wisdom of the body in that everyone knows what is best for one's self in terms of the ultimate goal of self-realization.

It is crucially important to be fully open to all experiences. Experiencing becomes more than bodily sensing as one grows older. Through complex interactions with our body and with other persons we develop a concept of self. These three assertions belong together, and in them Rogers is taking up the nature-nurture, heredity-environment controversy. Essentially, his position is that personality is a function of bodily wisdom and the effect of others (primarily parents).

One can sacrifice the wisdom of one's own experiences to gain another's love. Rogers as a therapist came to the conclusion that a great deal of human suffering is due to the tendency of people to sacrifice their own body wisdom to gain positive regard from others. Children, in order to gain acceptance by their parents, will too often agree with them, accept their premises, and maintain them throughout life, generating problems thereby if the premises are incorrect. His therapeutic system was intended to get people to understand their historical processes and to be able to revise the history of their life. *A rift can develop between what is actually experienced and the concept of self.* The same theme is here elaborated. A person may deny reality to gain approval from others, and this bifurcation can generate a host of problems. *When the rift between experiencing and self is too great, anxiety or disorganized behavior can result.* Once again, the same theme is emphasized. We all want to be loved and accepted, but the continued pursuit of acceptance may separate us from reality. *Validating experiencing in terms of others can never be completed. All maladjustments come about through denial of experiences discrepant with the self-concept.* And so, one must depend on one's self for reality and not on others. Adler believed that maladjusted people lacked social interest, while Rogers stated that maladjustment essentially came from people listening to others rather than to their own bodily wisdom.

PERSONAL CONSTRUCTS THEORY (GEORGE A. KELLY, 1905–1967)

Kelly was a highly original thinker. He developed a unique cognitive system that called for the use of idiosyncratic language (see Kelly 1955). While his personal constructs theory covers all of psychology from the ideographic point of view, he bypassed usual terms and concepts such as *learning* and *emotions* and paid no attention to the environment or heredity.

All our interpretations of the universe are subject to revision. Kelly starts with a skepticism about beliefs and takes the position that there is no absolute reality. He took the position of constructive alternativism to indicate that people with differences of opinions could not necessarily be divided in terms of right and wrong. Two people can view the same situation in quite different ways and both can be right, both can be wrong, or one or the other may be right. *No person needs to be a victim of his own biography.* Here we have a statement of the freewill concept in a different form.

A person's processes are psychologically channelized by the ways in which he anticipates events. This is Kelly's fundamental postulate. Essentially, this viewpoint states that what is important is how events are interpreted rather than the events themselves. This assertion leads naturally to Kelly's major contribution to personality theory, a series of other personal constructs, relative to how people view reality. We need not attempt to cover all of his constructs, but a few of them will give the reader a sense of Kelly's thinking: *A person anticipates events by construing their replication.* (The construction corollary.) *Persons differ from one another in their construction of events.* (The individuality corollary.) *A person may successively employ a variety of construction subsystems which are inferentially incompatible with each other.* (The fragmentation corollary.) This last corollary relates directly to Carl Rogers's theme that maladjustment comes from divergent forces: from within and from without.

Many of the important processes of personality and behavior arise as a person attempts to change or is threatened with forced change in his construct system. Kelly's point here is echoed by many other theorists, that one establishes some sort of life pattern or life-style, but changes in thinking about one's self and others will disrupt the individual.

Kelly's system is the purest cognitive system of any discussed here, solely dependent on perceptions and interpretations.

OPERANT REINFORCEMENT THEORY (B.F. SKINNER 1904–1990)

Skinner has denied that his operant reinforcement is a personality theory, but rather that it covers all aspects of overt human behavior (Skinner 1938). In contrast to those theorists who view personality as essentially phenomenological, Skinner decries the term mind and concerns himself solely with overt behavior. As a radical behaviorist, Skinner does not deny internal processes but considers them not relevant to psychology as an objective science of behavior.

Personality is acquired and maintained through the use of positive and negative reinforcers. Skinner applies operant reinforcement to all aspects of human behavior. We tend to repeat what works and to give up what does not work, to continue behavior that leads to pleasant consequences and

to discontinue behavior that leads to unpleasant consequences. *Behavior may be altered or weakened by the withholding of reinforcers.* If other people change their ways of operating towards an individual, this in turn will affect that person's behavior and consequently his personality.

Personality develops through a process of discrimination. In life, we experience all kinds of consequences, and we have to make decisions about our future behavior to these consequences. *Personality becomes shaped or differentiated.* Over time, our personalities are shaped by generalizations about ways that lead to the achievement of goals.

SOCIAL LEARNING THEORY (ALBERT BANDURA, 1925–)

Bandura, like Skinner, came to his opinions about personality mostly through research (Bandura and Walters 1963). His system is of the cognitive-learning type stressing the capacity of individuals to generalize in terms of symbols.

The causes of human behavior are the reciprocal interaction of behavioral, cognitive, and environmental influences. Bandura believes personality is a function of how we think and act and our responses of the environment's reactions to our behavior. In terms of the three elements of biology, society, and creativity, Bandura stresses the latter two. Heredity is discounted as a major determiner in personality development: How a person thinks and acts and how the environment responds to a person's behavior determines one's personality. *Behavior can be self-governed by means of self-produced consequences (self-reinforcement).* This assertion also emphasizes the importance of reciprocity: life is interaction: the individual versus the world, with the individual changing the world and the world changing the individual.

Individuals may be influenced by symbols which act as models. Reality to people need not only be direct stimuli, such as a smile or a slap, but reality can also be via symbols, such as pictures or words. Bandura's major research studies called for children to watch the behavior of others. He found that if a person considered to be a model acted in an aggressive manner and got what he wanted, that observers were likely to imitate the model. Consequently, not only direct stimuli and responses (as per Skinner) but symbolic experiences also determine personality. *Reinforcements (and punishment) can operate in a vicarious manner.* This is more of the above. Various kinds of behavior can be changed by seeing what happens to others. We learn not only by doing and getting responses but also by observing.

EXISTENTIAL PERSONALITY THEORY

Existential psychology is a loosely organized and ill-defined set of concepts mostly based on the work of philosophers and theologians (see Blackham 1959; Grimsley 1955). Essentially, existentialists see individuals as being in search of meaning. People are also seen as striving to achieve authenticity.

Personality is primarily constructed through attribution of meaning. Essentially, this point of view is similar to Kelly's concept of constructs. *Persons are characterized by symbolization, imagination, and judgment.* These are seen as attempts to find meaning. The human being is always trying to make sense out of existence, others, and self and uses mental processes in interaction with self and the world.

Life is best understood as a series of decisions. The human individual not only has to make evident decisions such as what to eat, but more subtle and important ones, such as who he or she really is. One has to decide what the world is like, what is real, what is important, and how to participate in the world. *Personality is a synthesis of facticity and possibility.* Facticity means the givens of heredity and environment and possibility becomes the creative aspect of personality. The facts of reality limit behavior variations.

A person is always faced with the choice of the future, which provokes anxiety, and the choice of the past, which provokes guilt. The human condition is such that people looking backwards in time can find reasons to be guilty and looking forward can find reasons to be afraid. Existentialists see anxiety and guilt as essential elements of the human being.

Ideal development is facilitated by encouraging individuality. Here we find traces of Carl Rogers's concept of the importance of listening to one's own body or Adler's and Kelly's requirement for personal courage. A human problem is to escape the effects of one's early environment, especially the effects of one's family.

CONSTITUTIONAL THEORIES

The oldest theories of personality formation are the constitutional that state that personality is a function of the nature of one's corporeal body. Aristotle (1910) in his *Physiognomica*, for example, stated that the "ancients" had a variety of theories to explain differences in human character. The Greek physician Galen took Hippocrates's physiological explanation of bodily health as a function of the balance between certain bodily fluids and stated that various personality types were a function of excesses of these fluids. Gall and Spurzheim (1809) extolled phrenology (the shape of the human head) in establishing personality. Kretschmer (1922) declared that people with certain kinds of body types tended to have particular types of mental conditions. Lombroso (1911) declared that criminal types were distinguished by a number of physiological anomalies. The list goes on and on. At present there are a variety of constitutional personality theories, some of which will be discussed below.

Structural Approach. William Sheldon (see Sheldon and Stevens 1942) classified individuals in terms of body shapes claiming that there was a positive correlation between various structural variations and personality types. He spent many years in doing basic research to find evidence for his theory. He found strong evidence to support the validity of his views. Other investigators also found supporting evidence but not to any useful degree.

The somatotype provides a universal frame of reference for growth and development that is independent of culture. This statement by implication discounts society and creativity. Born with a particular body type and you will have a specific personality type. *Three polar extremes called endomorphy, mesomorphy, and ectomorphy identify the essential components of the somatotype.* Sheldon had a somewhat complex classificatory system with three main body types:

mesomorphs had an excess of muscle, endomorphs an excess of fat, and ectomorphs were relatively thin. For example, mesomorphs were considered to be bold, endomorphs to be extraverted and ectomorphs to be introverted.

Experiential Approach. This particular constitutional position is championed by Schilder (1950) and Fisher (1970) among others. It is a combined learning/physiological approach, referring to the nature of the experiences that a person has via contact during life, between the inner viscera, the skin, and the environment's effect on the body.

Body sensations provide the primary basis for initial differentiation of self from environment. The basic notion is that an unborn infant is only aware of internal sensations, but following birth, now becomes aware of stimuli from the outside world. Thus, the body surface becomes the locus of separation of self from the environment and the child now becomes able to identify the self and the outer world. *The development of the body image proceeds through stages, each of which has a lasting effect upon the body image as a whole.* This assertion has elements of the Freudian sexual stages and of Skinner's behaviorism in that contact with the outside world not only establishes the world but also the individual's personality.

Holistic Approach. Kurt Goldstein, who worked primarily with brain-injured patients, is primarily identified with this viewpoint (see Goldstein 1939). In working with various cases of physical pathology, such as stroke victims, he came to the realization of the importance of a human's attempt to maximize and organize potentials to survive and to enhance one's situation.

The normal human organism is equipped to maximize self-actualization, provided environmental forces do not interfere. This statement is accepted in a variety of ways by a number of other personality theorists, but Goldstein made this his central point. Of those theorists already discussed, Adler, Jung, and Rogers would have agreed completely. *Self-actualization is manifested by maximum differentiation and by the highest possible level of complexity of an integrated system.* This statement follows from the prior one and gives emphasis to the concept of the wisdom of the body. *The key to effective behavior is adequate functioning of part-whole relations.* Goldstein used Gestalt concepts of figure and ground to give evidence of the importance of understanding behavior as a totality, and consequently he can be considered an holistic theorist.

SUMMARY

At present there are a considerable number of personality theories, each working as it were completely independently of one another. There is lack of a common vocabulary that in turn leads to different people saying the same thing in different words. A complete eclectic theory would consider all elements mentioned, taking up the issue of personality in terms of the issues of heredity, environment and creativity, self and the environment.

(SEE ALSO: *Personality and Social Structure; Social Psychology*).

REFERENCES

Adler, A. 1956 *The Individual Psychology of Alfred Adler.* H. L. Ansbacher and R. Ansbacher, eds., New York: Basic Books.

Aristotle 1910 *Physiognomica.* Oxford: Oxford University Press.

Bandura, A., and R. Walters 1963 *Social Learning Theory and Personality Development.* Englewood Cliffs, N.J.: Prentice-Hall.

Blackham, G. W. 1959 *Six Existential Thinkers.* New York: Harper and Row.

Burger, Jerry M. 1993 *Personality.* Pacific Grove, Calif. Brooks/Cole Publishing

Cloninger, Susan C. 1993 *Theories of Personality: Understanding Persons.* Englewood Cliffs, N.J.: Prentice-Hall

Corsini, R. J., and A. J. Marsella 1983 *Personality Theories, Research, and Assessment.* Itasca, Ill.: Peacock.

Corsini, Raymond J. and Danny Wedding 1995 *Current Psychotherapies*, 5th ed. Itasca, Ill.: Peacock.

Drapela, Victor J. 1995 *A Review of Personality Theories*, 2nd ed. Springfield Il.: Charles C. Thomas

Ewen, Robert B. 1997 *An Introduction to Theories of Personality*, 5th ed. Hillsdale, N.J.: Erlbaum Associates.

Fisher, S. 1970 *Body Experience in Fantasy and Behavior*. New York: Appleton-Century-Crofts.

Freud, S. 1952–1974 *The Complete Psychological Works of Sigmund Freud*. London: Hogarth Press (24 volumes).

Gall, F. J., and J. C. Spurzheim 1809 *Recherches sur la système nerveux*. Paris: Schoell.

Goldstein, K. 1939 *The Organism*. New York: American Book Co.

Grimsley, R. 1955 *Existentialist Thought*. Cardiff: University of Wales Press.

Jung, C. G. 1953–1972 *The Collected Works of C. G. Jung*. Princeton, N.J.: Princeton University Press.

Kelly, G. A. 1955 *The Psychology of Personal Constructs*. New York: W. W. Norton.

Kretschmer, E. 1922 *Physique and Character*. London: Paul, Trench Trubner.

Lombroso, C. 1911 *The Criminal Man*. Boston: Little, Brown.

Monte, Christopher F. 1995 *Beneath the Mask: An Introduction to Theories of Personality*, 5th ed. Ft. Worth, TX: Harcourt Brace.

Rogers, C. R. 1951 *Client-Centered Therapy*. Boston: Houghton Mifflin.

Schilder, P. 1950 *The Image and Appearance of the Human Body*. New York: International Universities Press.

Schultz, Duane P. and Sydney Ellen Schultz 1994 *Theories of Personality* 5th ed. Pacific Grove, Calif.: Brooks/Cole Publishing.

Sheldon, W. H., and S. S. Stevens 1942 *Varieties of Human Temperament*. New York: Harper and Row.

Skinner, B. F. 1938 *The Behavior of Organisms*. New York: Appleton-Century-Crofts.

RAYMOND J. CORSINI

MALTHUSIAN THEORY

See Demographic Transition; Human Ecology and Environmental Analysis.

MARGINAL EMPLOYMENT

INTRODUCTION

In industrialized countries the principal way in which adults and their families make ends meet economically is through employment in the formal labor force. In the United States, earnings in the form of wages and salaries account for 71 percent of household income, on average. Even among individuals in poor families, half (49 percent) of all household income comes from earnings—their single most important source of income (Current Population Survey 1998). The centrality of work for economic well-being also is reflected in the close connection between finding gainful employment and exiting poverty on the one hand, and losing employment and sliding into poverty on the other. While formal employment is a necessary condition for economic well-being among almost all nonwealthy, able-bodied adults and their families, it is not a sufficient condition. Not all jobs pay well, many come without health and other benefits that workers must either pay for through their wages or do without, some are merely part-time, and some jobs are highly unstable and offer little long-term security. *Marginal employment can be conceptually defined as the circumstance in which the formal employment of adults (or groups of adults within families) fails to generate the earnings needed to achieve a minimally acceptable standard of living, either because they work too few hours (insufficient labor supply), and/or because their wages are too low.*

Two trends motivate increasing concern over marginal employment. The first is a shift in social welfare systems which, as in the United States, have come to place greater emphasis on formal employment as the route out of poverty and reliance on the state. In recent years industrialized nations have reoriented their social welfare programs to encourage employment and work preparedness (Cornea and Danziger 1997). In the United States, the Personal Responsibility and Work Opportunity Reconciliation Act of 1996 has placed strict time limits on Public Assistance receipt. The image of thrusting people off the welfare rolls to fend for themselves in the open labor market has generated deep concern over their employment prospects. Second, in recent decades the structure of employment opportunities has changed in ways detrimental to low-skilled workers. Whether due to changing technology (e.g., computerization), which is displacing labor; to the globalization of production and trade, which is leading to outsourcing of low-skilled work; to competition through increased immigration; or to changes in wage-setting institutions (e.g., declines in unionization or real minimum wages), low-skilled workers have slipped further behind their better-skilled counterparts in terms of wages and total compensation (Freeman and Gottschalk 1998). The point is, just when many governments are foisting more responsibility for the economic well-being of citizens on the labor market and workers themselves, questions are being raised about the implications of macroeconomic changes for the quality of jobs available, especially for low-skilled groups. As such, marginal employment—its severity, causes, and consequences—has become an important concern for sociologists and policy makers alike.

MARGINAL EMPLOYMENT AS UNDEREMPLOYMENT

Marginal employment per se is not as yet a conventional concept in sociology and thus there are no standard empirical definitions of this term. As noted, we conceptualize it as consisting of both the degree of attachment to the labor force and the quality of jobs. A composite measure that incorporates both these dimensions is *underemployment*. Drawing on the Labor Utilization Framework of Phillip Hauser (1974), Clifford Clogg (1979) developed a measure of underemployment that consists of the following categories. The *working poor* are those people who are working full-time, full-year, but whose labor market earnings are less than 125 percent of the poverty threshold for single individuals. *Involuntary part-time workers* include those who are working fewer than full-time hours (thirty-five-hours per week) only because they are unable to find full-time work. The *unemployed* are those who are not currently working and are either actively looking for work or on layoff. (The unemployment rate—a standard aggregate measure of the health of the economy—is simply calculated as the number unemployed divided by the number in the labor force, where the latter is the sum of those employed and those unemployed.) Finally, *discouraged workers* (sometimes referred to as the *subunemployed*) are neither working nor looking for work, but would nonetheless like to be working if they could find a job. All other adults, those who are not working and do not want to be, are considered *not in the labor force* and are excluded from analyses of underemployment. It is important to recognize that this operationalization of underemployment is an imperfect empirical measure of marginal employment as conceptually defined above. Discouraged or involuntary part-time workers, for example, could be in families that are otherwise well off economically. While this caveat needs to be borne in mind, the statistical patterns described below suggest underemployment is a reasonable measure of marginal employment.

Table 1 shows the distribution of underemployment and its types for the U.S. population as a whole, and for important demographic groups. The data are from the March 1998 Current Population Survey, a nationally representative survey of 64,659 U.S. households and a key source of official employment data (Current Population Survey 1998). In 1998, of all U.S. adults aged 18–64 who either were working or would like to have been working, 18.0 percent were underemployed. We stress that by this definition, over one in six U.S. workers or would-be workers are marginally employed. Of these, 4.7 percent were unemployed, 6.3 percent were working part-time but wanted full-time work, 6.1 percent were working full-time but for near- or below-poverty wages, and 0.8 percent had given up in the search for work, despite wanting a job.

Underemployment is not distributed equally across demographic groups, but parallels well-known correlates of economic well-being generally. At over one-third, the young (those aged 18–24) are far more likely to be underemployed than older adults. A more refined age breakdown for all adult age groups (not shown) suggests a curvilinear pattern, with young adults and elderly Americans at greater risk of underemployment than those in their prime working ages. Women have long been disadvantaged in the U.S. labor market with respect to wages and occupational prestige, so it is little surprise that there also is gender inequality in underemployment. In relative terms,

Percentage distribution of underemployment by selected characteristics

			Underemployed			Adequately Employed
	Total	Low income	Low hours	Unemployed	Discouraged	
Total	18.0%	6.1%	6.3%	4.7%	0.8%	82.0%
Age						
18-24	33.8	1.34	9.0	9.5	1.9	66.2
25-34	17.7	5.5	6.6	5.0	0.6	82.3
45-54	15.5	5.0	5.9	3.9	0.6	84.5
55-64	14.4	5.4	5.4	5.3	3.0	85.6
Gender						
Mon	16.9	4.9	6.4	5.0	0.6	83.1
Women	19.2	7.5	6.2	4.5	1.0	80.8
Race/ethnicity						
Non-Hispanic white	15.2	5.4	5.6	3.7	0.6	84.8
Non-Hispanic black	25.3	7.1	7.5	8.8	1.9	74.7
Hispanic	28.3	10.2	10.0	7.1	1.1	71.7
Asian	17.5	6.5	6.2	3.9	1.0	82.5
Native American	19.4	9.1	8.8	9.8	1.7	70.6
Marital status						
Married	13.2	4.6	5.1	3.1	0.5	86.8
Divorced/separated	19.7	5.7	7.8	5.3	0.9	80.3
Widowed	23.1	8.4	9.3	4.1	1.3	76.9
Never married	17.1	9.6	8.1	8.0	1.5	72.9
Immigrant status						
Third (or higher) generation	17.0	5.7	6.0	4.6	0.8	83.0
Second generation	18.1	5.9	5.9	5.2	1.0	81.9
First generation	24.6	9.2	8.8	5.6	1.0	75.4
Education						
Less than high school	36.3%	12.2%	11.5%	10.5%	2.2%	63.7%
High school or GED	20.8	7.0	7.4	5.5	0.9	79.2
Some college	16.5	6.1	5.8	4.0	0.7	83.5
College degree or more	7.5	2.4	3.1	1.8	0.2	92.5
Residence						
Nonmetropolitan	21.6	8.2	7.4	5.3	0.8	78.4
Metropolitan	17.2	5.7	6.1	4.6	0.8	82.8
Central city	20.5	6.7	6.8	5.7	1.2	79.5
Non-central city	15.0	5.0	5.5	3.9	0.6	85.0
Not identified	18.3	5.9	6.8	5.0	0.6	81.7

Table 1

NOTE: Percentage Distribution of Underemployment by Selected Characteristics.

SOURCE: Original calculations from the March 1998 Current Population Survey.

women are 14 percent (2.3 percentage points) more likely than mcn to be underemployed, a difference that is due primarily to their greater risk of being working poor. Blacks, Hispanics and, to a lesser degree, Native Americans, are distinctly disadvantaged with respect to non-Hispanic whites. Indeed, about one-fifth of Native Americans, and over one-quarter of blacks and Hispanics, are underemployed, which compares to only 15 percent of non-Hispanic whites. Being married carries an advantage, while being divorced, separated, or widowed increases the risk of underemployment.

With respect to immigrant status, first-generation adults (immigrants themselves), are far more likely than the native-born to be underemployed, and among natives, those with a foreign-born parent (the second generation), are slightly disadvantaged compared to those with native-born parents (the third and higher generations). (This pattern should not be taken as direct evidence of economic assimilation, however, given immigrant-cohort differences in factors that determine the risk of underemployment.) The rising wage inequality of the 1980s and 1990s is due largely to deteriorating conditions among low-skilled workers (Freeman and Gottschalk 1998). Indeed, as shown in Table 1, education is strongly associated with underemployment. Whereas 36.3 percent of those with less than a high school education are underemployed, only 7.5 percent of college graduates are similarly situated. Finally, the risk of underemployment is not distributed evenly across space. Despite legitimate and well-chronicled concern over declining employment opportunities in the inner city (Wilson 1996), at 21.6 percent the prevalence of underemployment is higher in nonmetropolitan (nonmetro) counties of the United States, than in metropolitan areas. Indeed, the nonmetro risk is even higher than that for those living in central cities of metro areas (20.5 percent). Thus, marginal employment is both an inner city and a rural problem.

THE DYNAMICS OF MARGINAL EMPLOYMENT

Underemployment and its component parts are countercyclical. They rise in prevalence when the state of the wider economy declines, and they fall as the economy heats up. For example, above we noted the underemployment rate in 1998—a relatively good year economically—was 18.0 percent. In 1968, another good year, it stood at 15.2 percent. Amid recession in 1983, by comparison, 24.3 percent were underemployed. The rise and fall in the prevalence of marginal employment over time reflects the dynamic nature of labor markets. In large numbers individuals are constantly moving into and out of the labor force, between part-time and full-time work, and between good jobs and bad jobs.

While cross-sectional studies are useful for describing the broad contours of marginal employment and identifying sociodemographic groups that are more vulnerable, sociologists have begun to turn their attention to the nature and determinants of the movement between labor-force states. In an analysis of data from the Current Population Surveys of 1968 through 1993, Jensen and colleagues (1999) explored the determinants of transitions between adequate employment and underemployment. They found that adequately employed adults are more likely to slide into underemployment from one year to the next if they are black or Hispanic, female, less well educated, or young, or

if they live in a nonmetropolitan area. The risk of becoming underemployed also was higher amid a souring economy, and lower when the economy was strengthening. Once underemployed, these same groups were found to be disadvantaged with respect to their likelihood of finding adequate employment. Similarly, using data from the Survey of Income and Program Participation, Hsueh and Tienda (1996) explored transitions between being employed, unemployed, and out of the labor force altogether. They document greater labor-force instability among women, blacks and Hispanics, young adults, those with only a high school degree or less, and those who are not married.

That minorities and women, particularly those who are less well educated, have greater labor-force instability is important for understanding persisting gender and racial or ethnic inequality in society. The checkered work history that comes from frequent transitions into and out of the labor force means less opportunity to gain valuable work experience, and may signal to prospective employers a questionable commitment to work (Tienda and Stier 1996). The negative implications of work instability can accumulate over time, darkening future labor market outcomes and increasing the likelihood of marginal employment (Clogg et al. 1990).

JOB DISPLACEMENT

Even a stable work history is no guarantee against future employment hardship. An important determinant of labor-force instability is job displacement. Displaced workers are often technically defined as "persons 20 years and older who lost or left a job [which they had held for three or more years] because their plant or company closed or moved, there was insufficient work for them to do, or their positions or shifts were abolished" (Hipple 1997, p. 38). Sometimes referred to as "structurally unemployed" (because their unemployment is due to structural rather than cyclical shifts in the economy), displaced workers have little prospect of getting their old jobs back: Their job loss is permanent. To get a sense of the magnitude of the problem, consider that between 1993 and 1995, 15 percent of U.S. workers experienced job displacement (Kletzer 1998). The underlying causes of displacement are not well documented, but are likely rooted in technological change, rising foreign competition, and declining productivity within industries (Kletzer 1998). More is known about differences across sociodemographic groups in the risk of displacement. Recent evidence indicates that those who are black, less well educated, and employed in production occupations (as craftsmen, operatives, or laborers) and in manufacturing industries have higher rates of displacement (Kletzer 1998). Once displaced, there also is inequality in the prospects of finding new work after displacement. Here it helps to be white, male, and better educated.

CONTINGENT AND TEMPORARY WORKERS

Also contributing to volatility of labor-force attachment is the emergence of contingent labor and temporary workers. In the 1970s, international competition had begun to challenge U.S. industries, marking an end to two decades of economic expansion and growing corporate profits. In response U.S. firms began to restructure in order to maintain their competitive edge. By the mid-1980s, terms such as "mergers," "acquisitions," "deindustrialization," and "downsizing" had become commonplace (Harrison and Bluestone 1988). In the process, the traditional relationship between employer and employee began to change. Today, for a growing percentage of U.S. workers the postwar model of relatively stable and secure full-time employment with fringe benefits, steady wages, and the opportunity, if not expectation, of internal advancement within a firm, is no longer a reality (Henson 1996). Instead an increasing proportion of the American workforce is now engaged in *contingent work*.

To date there is no conventional definition of contingent work. The term has been used broadly in the literature to refer to a range of nonstandard employment practices including "part-time work, work performed by independent contractors and on-call workers, and work done by temporary workers, hired either directly for limited-duration projects or through temporary help firms" (Blank 1998, p. 258). In 1989, the Bureau of Labor Statistics (BLS) developed the following definition: "Contingent work is any job in which an individual does not have an explicit or implicit contract for long-term employment"(Polivka 1996, p. 3). In sum, despite disagreements over specifics, contingent work usually refers to nonstandard employment relationships that are associated with temporary or insecure employment duration, inadequate wages and benefits, and a conditional relationship that limits the attachment between employer and employee. Compared to permanent employees, contingent workers earn less and are less likely to be covered by employer health insurance or pension plans (Cohany et al. 1998; Hipple 1996). Depending upon the definition used, contingent workers composed between 2.2 and 16 percent of the labor force in 1995 (Barker and Christensen 1998).

The use of contingent workers has grown rapidly in recent decades. This growth has been driven primarily by a combination of employee desires (supply-side explanations) and employer strategies (demand-side explanations). On the supply side, contingent work often has features that some workers prefer, such as limited and flexible hours, independence, and variety. And some workers use contingent work as a way to shop around for good jobs and employers, in the hopes of obtaining more permanent work (Blank 1998). However, the idea that the rise in contingent work is being driven by worker preferences should not go too far since, by one estimate, two-thirds of contingent workers would prefer permanent work (Cohany et al. 1998). Demand-side factors include fluctuations in product demand which give rise to the need for flexibility in hiring and firing, reduced labor costs, and the ability to screen employees for permanent, full-time work (Blank 1998). Thus, in response to the growth of global competition and increasingly volatile consumer demand, employers have used contingent workers to shift the risk of market uncertainties from the firm to the worker. By reducing the obligation of the employer to the employee, firms are able to be more flexible in adjusting labor inputs and reducing labor costs. One of the primary reasons that firms have been able to cut costs at the expense of labor is the transition in the balance of power between labor and management in recent decades (Golden and Applebaum 1992). As labor unions have gradually lost bargaining power, management has increasingly been able to exercise cost cutting strategies at the expense of workers.

A subgroup of contingent workers that appear to be particularly marginalized are temporary help workers or "temps." Temps are typically employees of temporary help supply (THS) firms, which provide workers to other businesses on a contractual basis (Ofstead 1998). In most cases, THS firms remain the worker's legal employer while the worker provides services to another establishment. THS firms emerged as labor market actors in the 1940s, but have seen tremendous growth in recent decades. Research by the Bureau of Labor Statistics shows that the number of temporary jobs filled daily by THS firms has increased more than two and a half times since 1982 (Golden and Applebaum 1992). Further, research has found that over 90 percent of employers use temporary workers and that more than five million workers seek employment through THS firms in a given year (Golden and Applebaum 1992). THS firms typically specialize in worker placement in one of four occupational areas: office, industrial, medical, or engineering and technical, with office workers comprising over half of all temporary workers (Carey and Hazelbaker 1986).

Temporary workers are subject to an earnings penalty in comparison to permanent workers. Research has shown that temporary workers typically earn between 80 and 52 percent of the wage earned by their permanent counterparts (Barker and Christensen 1998). Further, research shows that the temporary workforce is disproportionately composed of individuals that face disadvantage in the labor force in general: women, minorities, and the young (Barker and Christensen 1998; Howe 1986). The predominance of women and the young among temporary workers is likely due in part to the flexibility allowed by the employment relationship. However, limited alternative employment opportunities and employer perceptions of what types of workers prove to be risky investments as permanent employees, also may be at play.

As it continues, the growth of contingent labor and proliferation of temporary workers will likely contribute significantly to the segmentation and bifurcation of the labor force. Permanent workers are able to realize higher wages, receive fringe benefits, receive on-the-job training, and have opportunities to climb the occupational ladder. On the other hand, contingent workers earn lower wages; receive few, if any, benefits; and enjoy little opportunity for advancement. In the case of those who engage in contingent employment because of personal preference, this may not present a problem. However, that many of those engaged in contingent work do so involuntarily is of concern. There is potential for the expansion of a fringe class of workers disenfranchised and marginalized from the mainstream labor force. At the very least, the growing use of contingent workers represents a fundamental shift in the relationship between employer and employee.

To summarize, marginal employment is a concept of increasing importance for sociologists. Structural economic shifts that are giving rise to job displacement and deterioration in the employment circumstances of low-skilled workers, combined with the increasing tendency for industrialized countries to link government help with work and/or work preparedness, have thrown a spotlight of concern on those most vulnerable to employment hardship. In addition to simply documenting the nature and trends in marginal employment, sociologists have begun to adopt more dynamic empirical approaches to model the movement of workers into and out of various states of marginal employment. All this work points to significant and persisting difficulties faced by women, racial and ethnic minorities, immigrants, young adults and elders, those with low achieved human capital, those who are unmarried, and rural or inner-city residents. Sociologists have also begun to explore the institutional changes that have contributed to the persistence of marginal employment and its unequal distribution across sociodemographic groups. Key among these is the rise in contingent work which is characterized by part-time and temporary employment arrangements, often at lower wages and lacking in the fringe benefits enjoyed by permanent workers.

REFERENCES

Barker, Kathleen, and Kathleen Christensen 1998 *Contingent Work: American Employment Relations in Transition*. Ithaca, N.Y.: Cornell University Press.

Blank, Rebecca M. 1998 "Contingent Work in a Changing Labor Market." In Richard B. Freeman and Peter Gottschalk, eds., *Generating Jobs: How to Increase Demand for Less-Skilled Workers*. New York: Russell Sage Foundation.

Carey, Max L., and Kim L. Hazelbaker 1986 "Employment Growth in the Temporary Help Industry." *Monthly Labor Review* 109(4):37–43.

Clogg, C. C. 1979 *Measuring Underemployment: Demographic Indicators for the United States*. New York: Academic.

——, Scott R. Eliason, and Robert Wahl 1990 "Labor Market Experiences and Labor Force Outcomes." *American Journal of Sociology* 95:1536–1576.

Cohany, Sharon R., Steven F. Hipple, Thomas J. Nardone, Anne E. Polivka, and Jay C. Stewart 1998 "Counting the Workers: Results of a First Survey." In Kathleen Barker and Kathleen Christensen, eds., *Contingent Work: American Employment Relations in Transition*. Ithaca, N.Y.: Cornell University Press.

Cornea, Andrea Giovanni, and Sheldon Danziger 1997 *Child Poverty and Deprivation in the Industrialized Countries*, 1945–1995. Oxford: Clarendon.

Current Population Survey 1998 Conducted by the Bureau of the Census for the Bureau of Labor Statistics. Washington, D.C.: U.S. Bureau of the Census, March, 1998. (Machine-readable data file.)

Freeman, Richard B., and Peter Gottschalk 1998 *Generating Jobs: How to Increase Demand for Less-Skilled Workers*. New York: Russell Sage Foundation.

Golden, Lonnie, and Eileen Applebaum 1992 "What Was Driving the 1982–99 Boom in Temporary Employment?" *American Journal of Economics and Sociology* 51(4):473–493.

Harrison, Bennett, and Barry Bluestone 1988 *The Great U-Turn: Corporate Restructuring and the Polarizing of America*. New York: Basic.

Hauser, Philip M. 1974 "The Measurement of Labor Utilization." *Malayan Economic Review* 19:1–17.

Henson, Kevin D. 1996 *Just a Temp*. Philadelphia: Temple University Press.

Hipple, Steven F. 1996 "Earnings and Benefits of Contingent and Noncontingent Workers." *Monthly Labor Review* 119(10):22–30.

—— 1997 "Worker Displacement in an Expanding Economy." *Monthly Labor Review* (December):26–39.

Howe, Wayne J. 1986 "Temporary Help Workers: Who They Are, What Jobs They Hold." *Monthly Labor Review* 109(11):45–47.

Hsueh, Sheri, and Marta Tienda 1996 "Gender, Ethnicity, and Labor Force Instability." *Social Science Research* 25:73–94.

Jensen, Leif, Jill L. Findeis, Wan-Ling Hsu, and Jason P. Schachter 1999 "Slipping Into and Out of Underemployment: Another Disadvantage for Nonmetro Workers?" *Rural Sociology* 64(3):417–438.

Kletzer, Lori G. 1998 "Job Displacement." *Journal of Economic Perspectives* 12(1):115–136.

Ofstead, Cynthia 1998 *Temporary Help Firms and the Job Matching Process*. Unpublished doctoral dissertation. Department of Sociology, University of Wisconsin, Madison.

Polivka, Anne E. 1996 "Contingent and Alternative Work Arrangements Defined." *Monthly Labor Review* 119(10):3–9.

Tienda, Marta, and Haya Stier 1996 "Generating Labor Market Inequality: Employment Opportunities and the Accumulation of Disadvantage." *Social Problems* 43(2):147–165.

Wilson, William J. 1996 *When Work Disappears: The World of the New Urban Poor*. New York: Knopf.

LEIF JENSEN
TIM SLACK

MARITAL ADJUSTMENT

Marital adjustment has long been a popular topic in studies of the family, probably because the concept is believed to be closely related to the stability of a given marriage. Well-adjusted marriages are expected to last for a long time, while poorly adjusted ones end in divorce. Simple as it seems, the notion of marital adjustment is difficult to conceptualize and difficult to measure through empirical research. After more than half a century of conceptualization about and research on marital adjustment, the best that can be said may be that there is disagreement among scholars about the concept, the term, and its value. In fact, several scientists have proposed abandoning entirely the concept of marital adjustment and its etymological relatives (Lively 1969; Donohue and Ryder 1982; Trost 1985).

CONCEPTUAL ISSUES

Scientists have long been interested in understanding which factors contribute to success in marriage and which to failure. As early as the 1920s, Gilbert Hamilton (1929) conducted research on marital satisfaction by using thirteen clusters of questions. In 1939, Ernest Burgess and Leonard Cottrell published *Predicting Success or Failure in Marriage*, in which they systematically discussed marital adjustment. They defined *adjustment* as "the integration of the couple in a union in which the two personalities are not merely merged, or submerged, but interact to complement each other for mutual satisfaction and the achievement of common objectives" (p. 10).

Researchers have not agreed upon the use of any one term. To describe the seemingly same phenomenon, some have used the terms "marital quality," "marital satisfaction," and "marital happiness." Robert Lewis and Graham Spanier have defined *marital quality* as "a subjective evaluation of a married couple's relationship" (1979, p. 269)—a concept similar to that of "marital adjustment." There have been numerous definitions of "marital adjustment" and "marital quality" (Spanier and Cole 1976), and it may not be fruitful to attempt to define the concept in a sentence or two. Rather, the following description of the factors that constitute marital adjustment or quality may prove more meaningful.

Since Burgess and Cottrell's formulation, scientists have examined extensively the factors constituting marital adjustment. Although there has been no consensus among researchers, factors constituting marital adjustment include agreement, cohesion, satisfaction, affection, and tension. Agreement between spouses on important matters is critical to a well-adjusted marriage. Though minor differences may broaden their perspectives, major differences between the spouses in matters such as philosophy of life, political orientations, and attitudes toward gender roles are detrimental to marital adjustment. In addition, agreement on specific decisions about family matters must be reached in good accord. *Marital cohesion* refers to both spouses' commitment to the marriage and the companionship experienced in it. In a well adjusted marriage, both spouses try to make sure that their marriage will be successful. They also share common interests and joint activities. In a well-adjusted marriage, both spouses must be satisfied and happy with the marriage. Unhappy but long-lasting marriages are not well-adjusted ones. Spouses in well-adjusted marriages share affection, and it is demonstrated as affectionate behavior. Finally, the degree of tension in a well-adjusted marriage is minimal, and when tension arises it is resolved amicably, probably in discussion, and the level of tension and anxiety is usually low.

The core component of marital adjustment is marital satisfaction, and it has been extensively studied as a stand-alone concept. As such, it deserves separate consideration. *Marital satisfaction* has been defined as:

> *The subjective feelings of happiness, satisfaction, and pleasure experienced by a spouse when considering all current aspects of his marriage. This variable is conceived as a continuum running from much satisfaction to much dissatisfaction. Marital satisfaction is clearly an attitudinal variable and, thus, is a property of individual spouses. (Hawkins 1968, p. 648).*

Again, scientists disagree about the definition. Some scholars conceptualize satisfaction rather as "the amount of congruence between the expectations a person has and the rewards the person actually receives" (Burr et al. 1979, p. 67). Because marital satisfaction is influenced not only by the congruence between expectations and rewards but also by other factors, the former definition is broader than the latter and thus is adopted here.

Although Hawkins's definition of marital satisfaction subsumes happiness, marital happiness is usually considered a distinct variable. According to Campbell et al. (1976), happiness is similar to satisfaction, but these two qualities do differ in one important aspect:

> [A] term like "happiness" seems to evoke chiefly an absolute emotional state, whereas "satisfaction" implies a more cognitive judgment of a current situation laid against external standards of comparison such as "other people I know" or more private levels of aspiration. (p. 31)

Since happiness (and marital happiness) denotes an emotional state, it has been known to be affected by the mood swing of the respondent. For that reason, this article does not specifically use the concept "marital happiness." Since marital happiness, marital satisfaction, marital quality, and marital adjustment are highly related to each other, interchangeable use of these terms is relatively common.

Although many scientists treat marital satisfaction as a factor of marital adjustment, there exist possibly major differences between these two concepts about the unit of analysis. Because satisfaction is a subjective property of an actor, there are two kinds of marital satisfaction in a marriage, the husband's and the wife's, and they are conceptually distinct. As Jessie Bernard (1972) stated, there are always two marriages in a family; the husband's marriage and the wife's marriage. Then, do these two marital satisfactions go hand in hand, or are they independent of each other? Research has produced mixed findings. In general, the more satisfied one spouse is with the marriage, the more satisfied is the other, but the correlation between the husband's and the wife's marital satisfactions is far from perfect (Spanier and Cole 1976). Marital adjustment or quality, on the other hand, can be either an individual or a dyadic property. When we say "a well-adjusted marriage," we refer to the dyad, while when we say, "She is well adjusted to

her marriage," we refer to the individual. No one has proposed valid measurement techniques for examining marital adjustment as a dyadic property, although some observational methods might be considered.

Another difference between marital satisfaction and marital adjustment is that while the former is a static product, the latter can be a dynamic process. In fact, marital adjustment is sometimes defined as a dynamic process, and marital satisfaction is listed as one of the outcomes of the adjustment process (Spanier and Cole 1976, pp. 127–128). It has also been proposed that marital adjustment be defined as a dynamic process and yet be measured as a state at a given point in time, a "snapshot" conception (Spanier and Cole 1976). Nevertheless, this connotation of dynamic process in the term "adjustment" has been criticized (Trost 1985) as a confusion of its meaning, because no measure of "adjustment" involves dynamic change, such as negotiation between the spouses.

Without agreeing on either which term to use or on the definition of such a term, researchers have tried for decades to measure marital adjustment, quality, or satisfaction. Burgess and Cottrell (1939) created one of the first measures of marital adjustment from twenty-seven questions pertaining to five subareas (agreement; common interests and joint activities; affection and mutual confidences; complaints; and feelings of being lonely, miserable, and irritable). Along with numerous attempts at measuring marital adjustment, Locke and Wallace (1959) modified Burgess and Cottrell's measure and called it the Marital Adjustment Test. Based on factor analysis, the test consists of fifteen questions ranging from the respondent's overall happiness in the marriage, the degree of agreement between the spouses in various matters, how they resolve conflicts, and the number of shared activities, to the fulfillment of their expectations about the marriage.

This measure was widely used until a new measure, the Dyadic Adjustment Scale, was proposed (Spanier 1976). It is composed of thirty-two questions and four subscales. The dyadic satisfaction subscale is composed of ten questions such as

"How often do you and your partner quarrel?" and "How often do you discuss or have you considered divorce, separation, or terminating your relationship?" The dyadic cohesion subscale is made up of five questions, "Do you and your mate engage in outside interests together?" and "How often would you say the following events occur between you and your mate?—have a stimulating exchange of ideas, laugh together, calmly discuss something, or work together on a project." The dyadic consensus subscale is based on thirteen questions on "the extent of agreement or disagreement between you and your partner." Items range from handling family finances, religious matters, and philosophy of life, to household tasks. Finally, the affectional expression subscale is composed of four questions related to affection and sex, two of which are agreement questions on demonstration of affection and sex relations.

All the above measures have been criticized as lacking a criterion against which the individual items are validated (Norton 1983; Fincham and Bradburn 1987). Some scholars have argued that only global and evaluative items, rather than content-specific and descriptive ones, should be included in marital adjustment or quality measures, because the conceptual domain of the latter is not clear. What constitutes a well-adjusted marriage may differ from one couple to another as well as cross-culturally and historically. Whether or not spouses kiss each other every day, for example, may be an indicator of a well-adjusted marriage in the contemporary United States but not in some other countries. Thus, marital adjustment or quality should be measured by the spouses' evaluation of the marriage as a whole rather than by its specific components. Instead of "How often do you and your husband (wife) agree on religious matters?" (a content-specific description), it is argued that such questions as "All things considered, how satisfied are you with your marriage?" and "How satisfied are you with your husband (wife) as a spouse?" (a global evaluation) should be used. By the same reasoning, the Kansas Marital Satisfaction (KMS) scale has been proposed. This test includes only three questions: "How satisfied are you with your (a) marriage: (b) husband (wife)

as a spouse: and (c) relationship with your husband (wife)?" (Schumm et al. 1986).

Traditional indexes also have been criticized for their lack of theoretical basis and the imposition of what constitutes a "successful marriage." On the basis of exchange theory, Ronald Sabatelli (1984) developed the Marital Comparison Level Index (MCLI), which measures marital satisfaction by the degree to which respondents feel that the outcomes derived from their marriages compare with their expectations. Thirty-six items pertaining to such aspects of marriage as affection, commitment, fairness, and agreement were originally included, and thirty-two items were retained in the final measure. Because this measure is embedded in the tradition of exchange theory, it has strength in its validity.

PREDICTING MARITAL ADJUSTMENT

How is the marital adjustment of a given couple predicted? According to Lewis and Spanier's (1979) comprehensive work, three major factors predict marital quality; social and personal resources, satisfaction with lifestyle, and rewards from spousal interaction.

In general, the more social and personal resources a husband and wife have, the better adjusted their marriage is. Material and nonmaterial properties of the spouses enhance their marital adjustment. Examples include emotional and physical health, socioeconomic resources such as education and social class, personal resources such as interpersonal skills and positive self-concepts, and knowledge they had of each other before getting married. It was also found that good relationships with and support from parents, friends, and significant others contribute to a well-adjusted marriage. Findings that spouses with similar racial, religious, or socioeconomic backgrounds are better adjusted to their marriages are synthesized by this general proposition.

The second major factor in predicting marital adjustment is satisfaction with lifestyle. It has been found that material resources such as family income positively affect both spouses' marital adjustment. Both the husband's and the wife's satisfaction with their jobs enhances better-adjusted marriages. Furthermore, the husband's satisfaction with his wife's work status also affects marital adjustment. The wife's employment itself has been found both instrumental and detrimental to the husbands' marital satisfaction (Fendrich 1984). This is because the effect of the wife's employment is mediated by both spouses' attitudes toward her employment. When the wife is in the labor force, and her husband supports it, marital adjustment can be enhanced. On the other hand, if the wife is unwilling to be employed, or is employed against her husband's wishes, this can negatively affect their marital adjustment. Marital adjustment is also affected by the spouses' satisfaction with their household composition, by how well the couple is embedded in the community, and the respondent's health (Booth and Johnson 1994).

Parents' marital satisfaction was found to be a function of the presence, density, and ages of children (Rollins and Galligan 1978). Spouses (particularly wives) who had children were less satisfied with their marriages, particularly when many children were born soon after marriage at short intervals. The generally negative effects of children on marital satisfaction and marital adjustment could be synthesized under this more general proposition about satisfaction with lifestyle.

It has been consistently found that marital satisfaction plotted against the couple's family life-cycle stages forms a U-shaped curve (Rollins and Cannon 1974; Vaillant and Vaillant 1993). Both spouses' marital satisfaction is quite high right after they marry, hits the lowest point when they have school-age children, and gradually bounces back after all children leave home. To illustrate this pattern, publicly available data from the National Survey of Families and Households (collected in 1987 and 1988) are analyzed here. Figure 1 shows the result. While husbands' average marital satisfaction hit the lowest point when their oldest child was between 3 and 5 years old, wives satisfaction was lowest when their oldest child was between 6 and 12 years old.

This pattern has been interpreted as a result of role strain or role conflict between the spousal, parental, and work roles of the spouses. Unlike

right after the marriage and the empty-nest stages, having children at home imposes the demand of being a parent in addition to being a husband or wife and a worker. When limited time and energy cause these roles to conflict with each other, the spouses feel strain, which results in poor marital adjustment (Lavee et al. 1996). Along this line of reasoning, Wesley Burr et al. (1979) proposed that marital satisfaction is influenced by the qualities of the individual's role enactment as a spouse and of the spouse's role enactment. They argue further, from the symbolic-interactionist perspective, that the relationship between marital role enactment and marital satisfaction is mediated by the importance placed on spousal role expectations.

As seen above, the concept of family life cycle seems to have some explanatory power for marital adjustment. Researchers and theorists have found, however, that family life cycle is multidimensional and conceptually unclear. Once a relationship between a particular stage in the family life cycle and marital adjustment is identified, further variables must be added to explain that relationship—variables such as the wife's employment status, disposable income, and role strain between spousal and parental roles (Crohan 1996; Schumm and Bugaighis 1986). Furthermore, the proportion of variance in marital adjustment "explained" by the family's position in its life cycle is small, typically less than 10 percent (Rollins and Cannon 1974). In the case of our analysis above, it is only 3 percent for both husbands and wives. Thus, some scholars conclude that family life cycle has no more explanatory value than does marriage or age cohort (Spanier and Lewis 1980).

The last major factor in predicting marital adjustment is the reward obtained from spousal interaction. On the basis of exchange theory, Lewis and Spanier summarize past findings that "the greater the rewards from spousal interaction, the greater the marital quality" (Lewis and Spanier 1979, p. 282). Rewards from spousal interaction include value consensus; a positive evaluation of oneself by the spouse; and one's positive regard for things such as the physical, mental, and sexual attractiveness of the spouse. Other rewards from spousal interaction include such aspects of emotional gratification as the expression of affection;

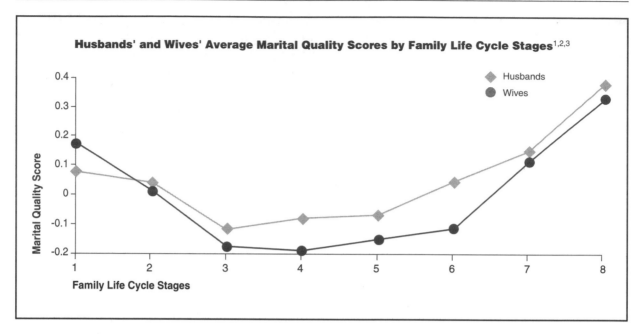

Figure 1. Husbands' and Wives' Average Marital Quality Scores by Family Life Cycle Stages[1,2,3]

NOTE: 1. See Sweet, Bumpass, and Call (1988) for the structure and data of the survey. Included in this figure are first-time married couples with at least one child or no child but married for less than 10 years.

2. Family life cycles stages are defined as follows (see Duvall 1977):

Stage 1 (Married Couples): Married for less than 10 years with no children

Stage 2 (Childbearing Families): The oldest child younger than 30 months

Stage 3 (Families with Preschool Children): The oldest child younger than 6

Stage 4 (Families with School Children): The oldest child younger than 13

Stage 5 (Families with Teenagers): The oldest child younger than 20

Stage 6 (Families Launching Young Adults): The oldest child 20 or older

Stage 7 (Middle-Aged Parents): The youngest child 20 or older

Stage 8 (Aging Families): The youngest child 20 or older and one of the spouses is 60 or older

3. Marital quality is measured by three questions: "Taking things all together, how would you describe your marriage? Very happy (7) to Very unhappy (1)." "Do you feel that your marriage might be in trouble right now? Yes (2) or No (1)." "What do you think the chances are that you and your husband/wife will eventually separate or divorce? Very low (5) to Very high (1)." The last two items are rescaled in such a way that the three items are given the same weight and the mean is set to 0. The final score is the average of these three scores.

respect and encouragement between the spouses; love and sexual gratification; and egalitarian relationships. Married couples with effective communication, expressed in self-disclosure, frequent successful communication, and understanding and empathy, are better adjusted to their marriages (Erickson 1993). Complementarity in the spouses' roles and needs, similarity in personality traits, and sexual compatibility all enhance marital adjustment. Finally, frequent interaction between the spouses leads to a well-adjusted marriage. The lack of spousal conflict or tensions should be added to the list of rewards from spousal interactions.

In this context, it is interesting to compare the average marital quality between men and women (Figure 1). The husbands' average marital quality is higher than the wives' *except* before they have their first child. The wife's marital quality is initially higher than the husband's, but it decreases after the arrival of her first baby. After that, it tends to be lower than that of her husband during the entire span of their marriage. Given that women perform most of the child care and household work, the steep decline in the average marital quality for women from Stage 1 to Stage 3 can be interpreted as a result of this burden of household work and child care. Women's rewards from marriage are lower than those of men, on the average, and this differential appears as a gender difference in marital adjustment over the family life-cycle stages.

Symbolic interactionists also argue that relative deprivation of the spouses affects their marital satisfaction: If, after considering all aspects of the marriage, spouses believe themselves to be as well off as their reference group, they will be satisfied with their marriages. If they think they are better off or worse off than others who are married, they will be more or less satisfied with their marriages, respectively (Burr et al. 1979).

CONSEQUENCES OF MARITAL ADJUSTMENT: PERSONAL ADJUSTMENT AND MARITAL STABILITY

It has been widely shown that married persons tend to be better adjusted in their lives than either never-married, separated, divorced, or widowed persons. This seems true not only in the area of psychological adjustments such as depression and general life satisfaction, but also in the area of physical health. Married people are more likely to be healthy and to live longer. Two factors should be considered to account for this relationship. First, psychologically and physically well-adjusted persons are more likely to get married and stay married. Second, the favorable socioeconomic status of married persons may explain some of this relationship. Nevertheless, scholars generally agree that marriage has a positive effect on personal adjustment, in both psychological and physical aspects.

If marriages in general affect personal adjustment in a positive fashion, it is likely that well-adjusted marriages lead to well-adjusted lives. Past research shows just this, though the findings should be cautiously interpreted. Some people tend to favorably answer "adjustment" questions, whether the questions are about their marriages, their personal lives in general, or their subjective health. The apparent positive relationship may be spurious. Nevertheless, if the psychological adjustment

is a composite of the adjustments in various aspects of life (i.e., marriage, family, work, health, friendship, etc.), high marital adjustment should lead to high psychological adjustment. In addition, positive effects of well-adjusted marriages on physical health may be accounted for, in part, by psychosomatic aspects of physical health.

This relationship provides an important policy implication of marital adjustment. Well-adjusted marriages may reduce health service costs, involving both mental and physical health. This is in addition to the more obvious reduction in social service costs derived from unstable and/or unhappy marriages. Children of divorce who need special care and domestic violence are just two examples through which poorly adjusted marriages become problematic and incur social services expenses.

Does marital adjustment affect the stability of a marriage? Does a better-adjusted marriage last longer than a poorly adjusted one? The answer is generally yes, but this is not always the case. Some well-adjusted marriages end in divorce, and many poorly adjusted marriages endure. As for the latter, John Cuber and Peggy Harroff conducted research on people whose marriages "lasted ten years or more and who said that they have never seriously considered divorce or separation" (1968, p. 43). They claim that not all the spouses in these marriages are happy and that there are five types of long-lasting marriages. In a "conflict-habituated marriage," the husband and the wife always quarrel. In a "passive-congenial marriage," the husband and the wife take each other for granted without zest, while "devitalized marriages" started as loving but have degenerated to passive-congenial marriages. In a "vital marriage," spouses enjoy together such things as hobbies, careers, or community services, while in a "total marriage," spouses do almost everything together. It should be noted that even conflict-habituated or devitalized marriages can last as long as vital or total marriages. For people in passive-congenial marriages, the conception and the reality of marriage are devoid of romance and are different from other people's.

What then determines the stability of marriage and how the marital adjustment affects it? It is proposed that although marital adjustment leads to marital stability, two factors intervene; alternative attractions and external pressures to remain married (Lewis and Spanier 1979). People who have both real and perceived alternatives to poorly adjusted marriages—other romantic relationships or successful careers—may choose divorce. A person in a poorly adjusted marriage may remain in it if there is no viable alternative, if a divorce is unaffordable or would bring an intolerable stigma, or if the person is exceptionally tolerant of conflict and disharmony in the marriage. Nevertheless, it should be emphasized that even though marital stability is affected by alternative attractions and external pressures, marital adjustment is the single most important factor in predicting marital stability. Lack of large-scale longitudinal data and adequate statistical technique have hampered scholars' efforts to establish this link between marital adjustment and stability. Given recent availability of longitudinal and technological development, this area of research holds a high promise.

(SEE ALSO: *Divorce*; *Family Roles*; *Interpersonal Attraction*; *Marriage*)

REFERENCES

Bernard, Jessie 1972 *The Future of Marriage*. New York: World Publishing.

Booth, Alan, and David R. Johnson 1994 "Declining Health and Marital Quality." *Journal of Marriage and the Family* 56:218–223.

Burgess, Ernest W., and Leonard Cottrell, Jr. 1939 *Predicting Success or Failure in Marriage*. New York: Prentice-Hall.

Burr, Wesley R., Geoffrey K. Leigh, Randall D. Day, and John Constantine 1979 "Symbolic Interaction and the Family." In W. Burr, R. Hill, F. I. Nye, and I. Reiss, eds., *Contemporary Theories about the Family*. New York: Free Press.

Campbell, Angus, Philip E. Converse, and Willard L. Rodgers 1976 *The Quality of American Life: Perceptions, Evaluations, and Satisfactions*. New York: Russell Sage Foundation.

Crohan, Susan E. 1996 "Marital Quality and Conflict Across the Transition to Parenthood in African American and White Couples." *Journal of Marriage and the Family* 58:933–944.

Cuber, John F., and Peggy B. Harroff 1968 *The Significant Americans: A Study of Sexual Behavior among the Affluent*. Baltimore: Penguin Books.

Donohue, Kevin C., and Robert G. Ryder 1982 "A Methodological Note on Marital Satisfaction and Social Variables." *Journal of Marriage and the Family* 44:743–747.

Duvall, Evelyn M. 1977 *Marriage and Family Development*, 5th ed. Philadelphia: Lippincott.

Erickson, Rebecca J. 1993 "Reconceptualizing Family Work: The Effect of Emotion Work on Perception of Marital Quality." *Journal of Marriage and the Family* 55:888–900.

Fendrich, Michael 1984 "Wives' Employment and Husbands' Distress: A Meta-Analysis and a Replication." *Journal of Marriage and the Family* 46:871–879.

Fincham, Frank D., and Thomas N. Bradbury 1987 "The Assessment of Marital Quality: A Reevaluation." *Journal of Marriage and the Family* 49:797–809.

Hamilton, Gilbert V. 1929 *A Research in Marriage*. New York: A. and C. Boni.

Hawkins, James L. 1968 "Associations Between Companionship, Hostility, and Marital Satisfaction." *Journal of Marriage and the Family* 30:647–650.

Lavee, Yoav, Shlomo Sharlin, and Ruth Katz 1996 "The Effect of Parenting Stress on Marital Quality: An Integrated Mother-Father Model." *Journal of Family Issues* 17:114–135.

Lewis, Robert A., and Graham B. Spanier 1979 "Theorizing about the Quality and Stability of Marriage." In W. Burr, R. Hill, F. I. Nye, and I. Reiss, eds., *Contemporary Theories About the Family*. New York: Free Press.

Lively, Edwin L. 1969 "Toward Concept Clarification: The Case of Marital Interaction." *Journal of Marriage and the Family* 31:108–114.

Locke, Harvey J., and Karl M. Wallace 1959 "Short Marital-Adjustment and Prediction Tests: Their Reliability and Validity." *Marriage and Family Living* 21:251–255.

Norton, Robert 1983 "Measuring Marital Quality: A Critical Look at the Dependent Variable." *Journal of Marriage and the Family* 45:141–151.

Rollins, Boyd C., and Kenneth L. Cannon 1974 "Marital Satisfaction over the Family Life Cycle: A Reevaluation." *Journal of Marriage and the Family* 36:271–282.

——, and Richard Galligan 1978 "The Developing Child and Marital Satisfaction of Parents." In R. M.

Lerner and G. B. Spanier, eds., *Child Influences on Marital and Family Interaction.* New York: Academic Press.

Sabatelli, Ronald M. 1984 "The Marital Comparison Level Index: A Measure for Assessing Outcomes Relative to Expectations." *Journal of Marriage and the Family* 46:651–662.

Schumm, Walter R., and Margaret A. Bugaighis 1986 "Marital Quality over the Marital Career: Alternative Explanations." *Journal of Marriage and the Family* 48:165–168.

Schumm, Walter R., Lois A. Paff-Bergen, Ruth C. Hatch, Felix C. Obiorah, Janette M. Copeland, Lori D. Meens, and Margaret A. Bugaighis 1986 "Concurrent and Discriminant Validity of the Kansas Marital Satisfaction Scale." *Journal of Marriage and the Family* 48:381–387.

Spanier, Graham B. 1976 "Measuring Dyadic Adjustment: New Scales for Assessing the Quality of Marriage and Similar Dyads." *Journal of Marriage and the Family* 38:15–28.

——, and Charles L. Cole 1976 "Toward Clarification and Investigation of Marital Adjustment." *International Journal of Sociology and the Family* 6:121–146.

Spanier, Graham B., and Robert A. Lewis 1980 "Marital Quality: A Review of the Seventies." *Journal of Marriage and the Family* 42:825–839.

Sweet, James A., Larry L. Bumpass, and Vaughn R. A. Call 1988 *A National Survey of Families and Households.* Madison: Center for Demography and Ecology, University of Wisconsin.

Trost, Jan E. 1985 "Abandon Adjustment!" *Journal of Marriage and the Family* 47:1072–1073.

Vaillant, Caroline O., and George E. Vaillant 1993 "Is the U-Curve of Marital Satisfaction an Illusion? A 40-Year Study of Marriage." *Journal of Marriage and the Family* 55:230–239.

YOSHINORI KAMO

MARRIAGE

The current low rates of marriage and remarriage and the high incidence of divorce in the United States are the bases of deep concern about the future of marriage and the family. Some have used these data to argue the demise of the family in American Society (Popenoe 1993). Others see such changes as normal shifts and adjustments to societal changes (Barich and Bielby 1996). Whatever the forecast, there is no question that the institution of marriage is currently less stable than it has been in previous generations. This article explores the nature of modern marriage and considers some of the reasons for its vulnerability.

Marriage can be conceptualized in three ways: as an institution (a set of patterned, repeated, expected behaviors and relationships that are organized and endure over time); as rite or ritual (whereby the married status is achieved); and as a process (a phenomenon marked by gradual changes that lead to ultimate dissolution through separation, divorce, or death). In the discussion that follows we examine each of these conceptualizations of marriage, giving the greatest attention to marriage as a process.

MARRIAGE AS INSTITUTION

From a societal level of analysis the institution of marriage represents all the behaviors, norms, roles, expectations, and values that are associated with the legal union of a man and woman. It is the institution in society in which a man and woman are joined in a special kind of social and legal dependence to found and maintain a family. For most people, getting married and having children are the principal life events that mark the passage into mature adulthood. Marriage is considered to represent a lifelong commitment by two people to each other and is signified by a contract sanctioned by the state (and for many people, by God). It thus involves legal rights, responsibilities, and duties that are enforced by both secular and sacred laws. As a legal contract ratified by the state, marriage can be dissolved only with state permission.

Marriage is at the center of the kinship system. New spouses are tied inextricably to members of the kin network. The nature of these ties or obligations differs in different cultures. In many societies almost all social relationships are based on or mediated by kin, who may also serve as allies in times of danger, may be responsible for the transference of property, or may be turned to in times of economic hardship (Lee 1982). In the United States, kin responsibilities rarely extend beyond the nuclear family (parents and children). There is the possible exception of caring for elderly parents, where norms seem to be developing (Eggebeen and Davey 1998). There are no normative obligations an individual is expected to fulfill for sisters or brothers, not to mention uncles, aunts, and cousins. Associated with few obligations and responsibilities is greater autonomy and independence from one's kin.

In most societies the distribution of power in marriage is given through tradition and law to the male—that is, patriarchy is the rule as well as the practice. For many contemporary Americans the ideal is to develop an egalitarian power structure, but a number of underlying conditions discourage attaining this goal. These deterrents include the tendency for males to have greater income; higher-status jobs; and, until recently, higher educational levels than women. In addition, the tradition that women have primary responsibility for child rearing tends to increase their dependency on males.

Historically, the institution of marriage has fulfilled several unique functions for the larger society. It has served as an economic alliance between two families, as the means for legitimizing sexual relations, and as the basis for legitimizing parenthood and offspring. In present-day America the primary functions of marriage appear to be limited to the legitimization of parenthood (Davis 1949; Reiss and Lee 1988) and the nurturance of family members (Lasch 1977). Recently, standards have changed and sexual relationships outside marriage have become increasingly accepted for unmarried people. Most services that were once performed by members of a family for other members can now be purchased in the marketplace, and other social institutions have taken over roles that once were assigned primarily to the family. Even illegitimacy is not as negatively sanctioned as in the past. The fact that marriage no longer serves all the unique functions it once did is one reason some scholars have questioned the vitality of the institution.

MARRIAGE AS RITE OR RITUAL

Not a great deal of sociological attention has been given to the study of marriage as a rite or ritual that transfers status. Philip Slater, in a seminal piece published in 1963, discussed the significance of the marriage ceremony as a social mechanism that underscores the dependency of the married couple and links the new spouses to the larger social group. Slater claims that various elements associated with the wedding (e.g., bridal shower, bachelor party) help create the impression that the couple is indebted to their peers and family members who organize these events. He writes,

[F]amily and friends [are] vying with one another in claiming responsibility for having "brought them together" in the first place. This impression of societal initiative is augmented by the fact that the bride's father "gives the bride away." The retention of this ancient custom in modern times serves explicitly to deny the possibility that the couple might unite quite on their own. In other words, the marriage ritual is designed to make it appear as if somehow the idea of the dyadic union sprang from the community, and not from the dyad itself. (p. 355)

Slater describes the ways in which rite and ceremony focus attention on loyalties and obligations owed others: "The ceremony has the effect of concentrating the attention of both individuals on every OTHER affectional tie either one has ever contracted" (Slater 1963, p. 354). The intrusion of the community into the couple's relationship at the moment of unity serves to inhibit husband and wife from withdrawing completely into an intimate unit isolated from (and hence not contributing to) the larger social group.

Martin Whyte (1990) noted the lack of information on marriage rituals and conducted a study to help fill this gap. He found that, since 1925, wedding rituals (bridal shower, bachelor party, honeymoon, wedding reception, church wedding) have not only persisted but also increased in terms of the number of people who incorporate them into their wedding plans. Weddings also are larger in scale in terms of cost, number of guests, whether a reception is held, and so on. Like Slater, Whyte links marriage rituals to the larger social fabric and argues that an elaborate wedding serves several functions. It *serves notice that the couple is entering into a new set of roles and obligations associated with marriage, it mobilizes community support behind their new status, it enables the families involved to display their status to the surrounding community, and it makes it easier for newly marrying couples to establish an independent household. (p. 63)*

MARRIAGE AS PROCESS

Of the three ways in which marriage is conceptualized—institution, rite or ritual, and process—most scholarly attention has focused on process. Here the emphasis is on the interpersonal relationship. Changes in this relationship over the course of a marriage have attracted the interest of most investigators. Key issues studied by researchers include the establishment of communication, affection, power, and decision-making patterns; development of a marital division of labor; and learning spousal roles. The conditions under which these develop and change (e.g., social class level, age at marriage, presence of children) and the outcomes of being married that derive from them (e.g., degree of satisfaction with the relationship) are also studied. For illustrative purposes, the remainder of this article will highlight one of these components, marital communication, and one outcome variable, marital quality. We also address different experiences of marriage based on sex of spouse: "his" and "her" marriage.

The Process of Communication. The perception of a "failure to communicate" is a problem that prompts many spouses to seek marital counseling. The ability to share feelings, thoughts, and information is a measure of the degree of intimacy between two people, and frustration follows from an inability or an unwillingness to talk and listen (Okun 1991). However, when the quality of communication is high, marital satisfaction and happiness also are high (Holman and Brock 1986; Burleson and Denton 1997; Gottman 1994).

The role of communication in fostering a satisfactory marital relationship is more important now than in earlier times, because the expectation and demands of marriage have changed. As noted above, marriage in America is less dependent on and affected by an extended kin network than on the spousal relationship. One of the principal functions of contemporary marriage is the nurturance of family members. Perhaps because this function and the therapeutic and leisure roles that help fulfill it in marriage are preeminent, "greater demands are placed on each spouse's ability to communicate" (Fitzpatrick 1988, p. 2). The communication of positive affect and its converse, emotional withdrawal, may well be the essence and the antithesis, respectively, of nurturance. Bloom and colleagues (1985) suggest that one important characteristic of marital dissatisfaction is the expectation that marriage is a "source of interpersonal nurturance and individual gratification and growth" (p. 371), an expectation that is very hard to fulfill.

In the 1990s many studies focused on the relationship between communication and marital satisfaction (Burleson and Denton 1997). The findings from this body of research suggest that there are clear communication differences between spouses in happy and in unhappy marriages. Patricia Noller and Mary Anne Fitzpatrick (1990) reviewed this literature, and their findings can be summarized as follows: Couples in distressed marriages report less satisfaction with the social-emotional aspects of marriage, develop more destructive communication patterns (i.e., a greater expression of negative feelings, including anger, contempt, sadness, fear, and disgust), and seek to avoid conflict more often than nondistressed couples. Nevertheless, couples in distressed marriages report more frequent conflict and spend more time in conflict. In addition, gender differences in communication are intensified in distressed marriages. For example, husbands have a more difficult time interpreting wives' messages. Wives in general express both negative and positive feelings more directly, and are more critical. Spouses in unhappy marriages appear to be unaware that they misunderstand one another. Generally, happily married couples are more likely to engage in positive communication behaviors (agreement, approval, assent, and the use of humor and laughter), while unhappy couples command, disagree, criticize, put down, and excuse more. Recently, Burleson and Denton (1997) explored the complexity of the communication–marital satisfaction relationship and found a variety of moderating factors: skills in communicating (realizing the communication goal, producing and receiving messages, social perception), the context or setting in which communication takes place, and the cognitive complexity of each spouse. They suggest that communication problems are best viewed as a symptom of marital difficulties and should not be seen merely as a diagnostic tool for distressed relationships.

Communication patterns may be class linked. It has long been found that working-class wives in particular complain that their husbands are emotionally withdrawn and inexpressive (Komarovsky 1962; Rubin 1976). Olsen and his colleagues (1979) assign communication a strategic role in marital and family adaptability. In their conceptualization of marital and family functioning, communication is the process that moves couples along the dimensions of cohesion and adaptability. In another study the absence of good communication skills is associated with conjugal violence (Infante 1989).

Differences between the sexes have been reported in most studies that examine marital communication. The general emphasis of these findings is that males appear less able to communicate verbally and to discuss emotional issues. However, communication is not the only aspect of marriage for which sex differences have been reported. Other components of marriage also are experienced differently, depending on the sex of spouse. The following paragraphs report some of these.

Sex Differences. In her now classic book, *The Future of Marriage* (1972), Jessie Bernard pointed out that marriage does not hold the same meanings for wives as for husbands, nor do wives hold the same expectations for marriage as do husbands. These sex differences (originally noted but not fully developed by Emile Durkheim in 1897 in *Le Suicide*) have been observed and examined by many others since Bernard's publication (Larson 1988; Thompson and Walker 1989; Kitson 1992). For example, researchers have reported differences between husbands and wives in perceptions of marital problems, reasons for divorce, and differences in perceived marital quality; wives consistently experience and perceive lower marital quality than do husbands.

Sex differences in marriage are socially defined and prescribed (Lee 1982; Blaisure and Allen 1995). One consequence of these social definitions is that sex differences get built into marital roles and the division of labor within marriage. For example, it has been observed that wives do more housework and child care than husbands (Thompson and Walker 1989; Presser 1994). Even wives who work in the paid labor force spend twice as many hours per week in family work as husbands (Benin and Agostinelli 1988; Coltran and Ishii-Kuntz 1992; Demo and Acock 1993). Wives are assigned or tend to assume the role of family kin keeper and caregiver (Montgomery 1992). To the extent that husbands and wives experience different marriages, wives are thought to be disadvantaged by their greater dependence, their secondary status, and the uneven distribution of family responsibilities between spouses (Baca Zinn and Eitzen 1990).

All these factors are assumed to affect the quality of marriage—one of the most studied aspects of marriage (Adams 1988; Berardo 1990). It will be the subject of our final discussion.

Marital Quality. Marital quality may be the "weather vane" by which spouses gauge the success of their relationship. The reader should be sure to differentiate the concept of marital quality from two other closely related concepts: family quality and the quality of life in general, called "global life satisfaction" in the literature. Studies show that people clearly differentiate among these three dimensions of well-being (Ishii-Kuntz and Ihinger-Tallman 1991).

Marriage begins with a commitment, a promise to maintain an intimate relationship over a lifetime. Few couples clearly understand the difficulties involved in adhering to this commitment or the problems they may encounter over the course of their lives together. More people seek psychological help for marital difficulties than for any other type of problem (Veroff et al. 1981). For a large number of spouses, the problems become so severe that they renege on their commitment and dissolve the marriage.

A review of the determinants of divorce lists the following problems as major factors that lead to the dissolution of marriage: "alcoholism and drug abuse, infidelity, incompatibility, physical and emotional abuse, disagreements about gender roles, sexual incompatibility, and financial problems" (White 1990, p. 908). Underlying these behaviors appears to be the general problem of communication. In their study of divorce, Gay Kitson and Marvin Sussman (1982) report lack of communication or understanding to be the most common reason given by both husbands and wives concerning why their marriage broke up. The types of problems responsible for divorce have not changed much over time. Earlier studies also list nonsupport, financial problems, adultery, cruelty, drinking, physical and verbal abuse, neglect, lack of love, in-laws, and sexual incompatibility as reasons for divorce (Goode 1956; Levinger 1966).

Not all unhappy marriages end in divorce. Many factors bar couples from dissolving their marriages, even under conditions of extreme dissatisfaction. Some factors that act as barriers to marital dissolution are strong religious beliefs, pressure from family or friends to remain together, irretrievable investments, and the lack of perceived attractive alternatives to the marriage (Johnson et al. 1999).

One empirical finding that continues to be reaffirmed in studies of marital quality is that the quality of marriage declines over time, beginning with the birth of the first child (Glenn and McLanahan 1982; Glenn 1991; White et al. 1986). Consequently the transition to parenthood and its effect on the marital relationship has generated a great deal of research attention (Cowen and Cowen 1989; McLanahan and Adams 1989). The general finding is that marital quality decreases after the birth of a child, and this change is more pronounced for mothers than for fathers. Two reasons generally proposed to account for this decline are that the amount of time couples have to spend together decreases after the birth of a child, and that sex

role patterns become more traditional (McHale and Huston 1985).

In an attempt to disentangle the duration of marriage and parenthood dimensions, White and Booth (1985) compared couples who became new parents with nonparent couples over a period of several years and found a decline in marital quality regardless of whether the couple had a child. A longitudinal study conducted by Belsky and Rovine (1990) confirmed the significant declines in marital quality over time reported in so many other studies. They also found the reported gender differences. However, their analysis also focused on change scores for individual couples. They reported that while marital quality declined for some couples, this was not true for all couples: It improved or remained unchanged for others. Thus, rather than assume that quality decline is an inevitable consequence of marriage, there is a need to examine why and how some couples successfully avoid this deterioration process. The authors called for the investigation of individual differences among couples rather than continuing to examine the generally well-established finding that marital quality declines after children enter the family and remains low during the child-rearing stages of the family life cycle.

Finally, the overall level of marital satisfaction is related to the frequency with which couples have sex (Call et al. 1995). The argument states that happy couples have sex more frequently, leading to more satisfying marriage, and that satisfaction in marriage leads to a greater desire for sex and the creation of more opportunities for sex.

Many students of the family have found it useful to consider marital development over the years as analogous to a career that progresses through stages of the family life cycle (Duvall and Hill 1948; Aldous 1996). This allows for consideration of changes in the marital relationship that occur because of spouses' aging, the duration of marriage, and the aging of children. In addition to changes in marital quality, other factors have been examined, such as differences in the course of a marriage, when age at first marriage varies (e.g., marriage entered into at age 19 as opposed to in the mid-30s), varied duration of childbearing (few versus many years), varied number of children (small family versus large), and the ways in which consumer decisions change over the course of marriage (Aldous 1990).

CONCLUSION

If the vitality of marriage is measured by the extent to which men and women enter marriage, then some pessimism about its future is warranted. Marriage rates are currently lower than during the early depression year 1931 (*Statistical Abstracts* 1998, 1938)—which was the lowest in our nation's recent history (Sweet and Bumpass 1987). One conclusion that might be drawn from reading the accumulated literature on marriage, especially the writings that discuss the inequities of men and women within marriage, the increasing incidence of marital dissolution, cohabitation as a substitute for marriage, and the postponement of marriage, is that the institution is in serious trouble. These changes have been interpreted as occurring as part of a larger societal shift in values and orientations (Glick 1989) that leans toward valuing adults over children and individualism over familism (Glenn 1987; White 1987; see also the entire December 1987 issue of *Journal of Family Issues*, which is devoted to the state of the American family). Supporting this perspective are the data on increased marital happiness among childless couples and lower birth rates among married couples.

Yet every era has had those who wrote of the vulnerability of marriage and the family. For example, earlier in this century Edward Alsworth Ross wrote, "we find the family now less stable than it has been at any time since the beginning of the Christian era" (1920, p. 586). Is every era judged to be worse than previous ones when social institutions are scrutinized? More optimistic scholars look at the declining first-marriage rate and interpret it as a "deferral syndrome" rather than an outright rejection of the institution (Glick 1989). This is because, in spite of declines in the overall rate, the historical 8 percent to 10 percent of never-married people in the population has remained constant: Almost 90 percent of all women in the United States eventually marry at least once in their lifetimes. Also, projections that about two-thirds of all first marriages in the United States will end in divorce (Martin and Bumpass 1989) do not deter people from marrying. In spite of the high divorce rate, an increased tolerance for singleness as a way of life, and a growing acceptance of cohabitation, the majority of Americans continue to marry. Marriage is still seen as a source of personal happiness (Kilbourne et al. 1990).

More fundamentally, marriage rates and the dynamics of marital relationships tend to reflect conditions in the larger society. What appears clear, at least for Americans, is that they turn to marriage as a source of sustenance and support in a society where, collectively, citizens seem to have abrogated responsibility for the care and nurturance of each other. Perhaps it is not surprising that divorce rates are high, given the demands and expectations placed on modern marriages.

(SEE ALSO: *Alternative Life-Styles*; *Courtship*; *Family Roles*; *Heterosexual Behavior Patterns*; *Intermarriage*; *Marital Adjustment*; *Remarriage*; *Sexual Behavior and Marriage*)

REFERENCES

Adams, Bert N. 1988 "Fifty Years of Family Research: What Does It Mean?" *Journal of Marriage and the Family* 50:5–17.

Aldous, Joan 1990 "Family Development and the Life Course: Two Perspectives on Family Change." *Journal of Marriage and the Family* 52:571–583.

—— 1996 *Family Careers: A Rethinking*. Thousand Oaks, Calif.: Sage.

Baca Zinn, Maxine, and D. Stanley Eitzen 1990 *Diversity in Families*, 2nd ed. New York: Harper & Row.

Barich, Rachel Roseman, and Denise D. Bielby 1996 "Rethinking Marriage: Change and Stability in Expectations, 1967–1994." *Journal of Family Issues* 17:139–169.

Barry, W. A. 1970 "Marriage Research and Conflict: An Integrative Review." *Psychological Bulletin* 73:41–54.

Belsky, Jay, and Michael Rovine 1990 "Patterns of Marital Change across the Transition to Parenthood: Pregnancy to Three Years Postpartum." *Journal of Marriage and the Family* 52:5–19.

Benin, Mary H., and Joan Agostinelli 1988 "Husbands' and Wives' Satisfaction with the Division of Labor." *Journal of Marriage and the Family* 50:349–361.

Berardo, Felix M. 1990 "Trends and Directions in Family Research in the 1980s." *Journal of Marriage and the Family* 52:809–817.

Bernard, Jessie 1972 *The Future of Marriage*. New York: Bantam.

—— 1982 *The Future of Marriage*. New Haven, Conn.: Yale University Press.

Blaisure, Karen, and Katherine R. Allen 1995 "Feminists and the Ideology and Practice of Marital Equality." *Journal of Marriage and the Family* 57:5–19.

Bloom, Bernard L., Robert L. Niles, and Anna M. Tatacher 1985 "Sources of Marital Dissatisfaction among Newly Separated Persons." *Journal of Family Issues* 6:359–373.

Burleson, Brant R., and Wayne H. Denton 1997 "The Relationship between Communication Skills and Marital Satisfaction: Some Moderating Effects." *Journal of Marriage and the Family* 59:884–902.

Call, Vaughn, Susan Sprecher, and Pepper Schwartz 1995 "The Incidence and Frequency of Marital Sex in a National Sample." *Journal of Marriage and the Family* 57:639–652.

Coltrane, Scott, and Masako Ishii-Kuntz 1992 "Men's Housework: A Life Course Perspective." *Journal of Marriage and Family* 54:43–57.

Cowen, Phillip, and C. Cowen 1989 "Changes in Marriage during the Transition to Parenthood: Must We Blame the Baby?" In G. Michaels and W. Goldberg, eds., *The Transition to Parenthood: Current Theory and Research*. New York: Cambridge University Press.

Davis, Kingsley 1949 *Human Society*. New York: Macmillan.

Demo, David H., and Alan C. Acock 1993 "Family Diversity and the Division of Domestic Labor: How Much Have Things Really Changed?" *Family Relations* 42:323–331.

Durkheim, Emile 1897 *Le Suicide*. Paris: F. Alcan.

Duvall, Evelyn M., and Reuben Hill 1948 "Report of the Committee on the Dynamics of Family Interaction." Paper delivered at the National Conference on Family Life, Washington.

Eggebeen, David J., and Adam Davey 1998 "Do Safety Nets Work? The Role of Anticipated Help in Times of Need." *Journal of Marriage and the Family* 60:939–950.

Fincham, Frank D., and Thomas N. Bradbury 1987 "The Assessment of Marital Quality: A Reevaluation." *Journal of Marriage and the Family* 49:797–809.

Fitzpatrick, Mary Anne 1988 "Approaches to Marital Interaction." In P. Noller and M. A. Fitzpatrick, eds., *Perspectives on Marital Interaction*. Clevedon, England: Multilingual Matters.

Glenn, Norval D. 1987 "Tentatively Concerned View of American Marriage." *Journal of Family Issues* 8:350–354.

—— 1991 "Qualitative Research on Marital Quality in the 1980s: A Critical Review." In A. Booth, ed., *Contemporary Families: Looking Forward, Looking Back*. Minneapolis, Minn.: National Council on Family Relations.

——, and Sara McLanahan 1982 "Children and Marital Unhappiness: A Further Specification of the Relationship." *Journal of Marriage and the Family* 44:63–72.

Glick, Paul C. 1989 "The Family Life Cycle and Social Change." *Family Relations* 38:123–129.

Goode, William J. 1956 *After Divorce*. New York: Free Press.

Gottman, John Mordechai 1994 *What Predicts Divorce? The Relationship between Marital Processes and Marital Outcomes*. Hillsdale, N.J.: Lawrence Erlbaum.

Holman, Thomas B., and Gregory W. Brock 1986 "Implications for Therapy in the Study of Communication and Marital Quality." *Family Perspectives* 20:85–94.

Infante, D. A. 1989 "Test of an Argumentative Skill Deficiency Model of Interpersonal Violence." *Communication Monographs* 56:163–177.

Ishii-Kuntz, Masako, and Marilyn Ihinger-Tallman 1991 "The Subjective Well-Being of Parents." *Journal of Family Issues* 12:58–68.

Ishii-Kuntz, Masako, and Scott Coltrane 1992 "Remarriage, Stepparenting, and Household Labor." *Journal of Family Issues* 13:215–233.

Johnson, Michael P., John P. Caughlin, and Ted L. Huston 1999 "The Tripartite Nature of Marital Commitment: Personal, Moral, and Structural Reasons to Stay Married." *Journal of Marriage and the Family* 61:160–177.

Kilbourne, Barbara S., Frank Howell, and Paula England 1990 "Measurement Model for Subjective Marital Solidarity: Invariance across Time, Gender and Life Cycle Stage." *Social Science Research* 19:62–81.

Kitson, Gay C. 1992 *Portrait of Divorce: Adjustment to Marital Breakdown*. New York: Guilford Press.

——, and Marvin B. Sussman 1982 "Marital Complaints, Demographic Characteristics and Symptoms of Mental Distress in Divorce." *Journal of Marriage and the Family* 44:87–102.

Komarovsky, Mirra 1962 *Blue Collar Marriage*. New York: Vintage.

Larson, Jeffrey H. 1988 "The Marriage Quiz: College Students' Beliefs in Selected Myths about Marriage." *Family Relations* 37:3–11.

Lasch, Christopher 1977 *Haven in a Heartless World*. New York: Basic.

Lee, Gary 1982 *Family Structure and Interaction: A Comparative Analysis*, 2nd ed., rev. Minneapolis: University of Minnesota Press.

Levinger, George 1996 "Sources of Marital Dissatisfaction among Applicants for Divorce." *American Journal of Orthopsychiatry* 36:803–807.

Martin, Teresa C., and Larry L. Bumpass 1989 "Recent Trends in Marital Disruption." *Demography* 26:37–51.

McHale, Susan M., and Ted L. Huston 1985 "Men and Women as Parents: Sex Role Orientations, Employment, and Parental Roles." *Child Development* 55:1349–1361.

McLanahan, Sara, and J. Adams 1989 "The Effects of Children on Adults' Psychological Well-Being. *Social Forces* 68:124–146.

Montgomery, Rhonda J. 1992 "Gender Differences in Patterns of Child-Parent Caregiving Relationships." In J. W. Dwyer and R. T. Coward, eds., *Gender, Families, and Elder Care*. Newbury Park, Calif.: Sage.

Noller, Patricia, and Mary Anne Fitzpatrick 1990 "Marital Communication in the Eighties." *Journal of Marriage and the Family* 52:832–843.

O'Donohue, William, and Julie L. Crouch 1996 "Marital Therapy and Gender-Linked Factors in Communication." *Journal of Marital and Family Therapy* 22:87–101.

Okun, B. F. 1991 *Effective Helping, Interviewing, and Counseling Techniques*, 13th ed. Monterey, Calif.: Brooks/Cole.

Olsen, David H., D. Sprenkle, and C. Russell 1979 "Circumplex Model of Marital and Family Systems I: Cohesion and Adaptability Dimensions, Family Types and Clinical Applications." *Family Process* 18:3–28.

Popenoe, David 1993 "American Family Decline, 1960–1990: A Review and Appraisal." *Journal of Marriage and the Family* 55:527–555.

Presser, H. B. 1994 "Employment Schedules among Dual-Earner Spouses and the Division of Household Labor by Gender." *American Sociological Review* 59:348–364.

Reiss, Ira L., and Gary Lee 1988 *Family Systems in America*. New York: Holt, Rinehart, and Winston.

Rosenthal, Carolyn 1985 "Kinkeeping in the Familial Division of Labor." *Journal of Marriage and the Family* 47:965–974.

Ross, Edward Alsworth 1920 *The Principles of Sociology*. New York: Century.

Rubin, Lillian 1976 *Worlds of Pain: Life in the Working Class Family*. New York: Basic.

Ruble, Diane, A. Fleming, L. Hackel, and C. Stangor 1988 "Changes in the Marital Relationship during the Transition to First-Time Motherhood: Effects of Violated Expectations Concerning the Division of Labor." *Journal of Personality and Social Psychology* 55:78–87.

Slater, Philip 1963 "On Social Regression." *American Sociological Review* 28:339–364.

Statistical Abstracts of the United States 1939 Washington: Bureau of the Census, Department of Commerce.

—— 1998 Washington: Bureau of the Census, Department of Commerce.

Sweet, James A., and Larry L. Bumpass 1987 *American Families and Households*. New York: Russell Sage Foundation.

Thompson, Linda, and Alexis J. Walker 1989 "Gender in Families: Women and Men in Marriage, Work, and Parenthood." *Journal of Marriage and the Family* 51:845–871.

Veroff, Joseph, Richard Kulka, and Elizabeth Douvan 1981 *Mental Health in America: Patterns of Help-Seeking from 1957 to 1976*. New York: Basic.

White, Lynn K. 1987 "Freedom versus Constraint: The New Synthesis." *Journal of Family Issues* 8:468–470.

—— 1990 "Determinants of Divorce: Review of Research in the Eighties." *Journal of Marriage and the Family* 52:904–912.

——, and Alan Booth 1985 "The Transition to Parenthood and Marital Quality." *Journal of Family Issues* 6:435–449.

——, and John N. Edwards 1986 "Children and Marital Happiness: Why the Negative Correlation?" *Journal of Family Issues* 7:131–147.

Whyte, Martin K. 1990 *Dating, Mating, and Marriage*. New York: Aldine de Gruyter.

MARILYN IHINGER-TALLMAN

MARRIAGE AND DIVORCE RATES

Marriage and divorce rates are measures of the propensity for the population of a given area to become married or divorced during a given year. Some of the rates are quite simple, and others are progressively more refined. The simple ones are called *crude rates* and are expressed in terms of the number of marriages or divorces per 1,000 persons of all ages in the area at the middle of the year. These are the only marriage and divorce rates available for every state in the United States. They have the weakness of including in the base not only young children but also elderly persons, who are unlikely to marry or become divorced. But the wide fluctuations in crude rates over time are obviously associated with changes in the economic, political, and social climate.

More refined rates will be discussed below, but the following illustrative crude rates of marriage for the United States will demonstrate the readily identifiable consequences of recent historical turning points or periods (NCHS 1990a, 1990b, 1998).

Between 1940 and 1946 the crude marriage rate for the United States went up sharply, from 12.1 per 1,000 to 16.4 per 1,000, or by 36 percent, showing the effects of depressed economic conditions before, and disarmament after, World War II.

Between 1946 and 1956 the rate went down rapidly to 9.5 per 1,000, or by 42 percent, as the baby boom peaked. The unprecedented increase in the number of young children was included in the base of the rate, and this helped to lower the rate.

Between 1956 and 1964 the rate declined farther to 9.0 per 1,000, or by 5 percent, as the baby boom ended and the Vietnam War had begun. Between 1964 and 1972 the rate went up moderately to a peak of 10.9 per 1,000, or by 21 percent, as the Vietnam War ended and many returning war veterans married.

Between 1972 and 1990 the crude marriage rate declined irregularly to 9.8 per 1,000 persons of all ages and on down to 8.9 in 1997. The factors involved are discussed below.

At the time of this writing, vital statistics annual reports present only *crude* marriage and device rates for the United States and individual states (NCHS 1998). More *refined* rates were last published for 1987 on some subjects and for 1990 on other subjects.

Refined marriage rates show the propensity to marry for adults who are eligible to marry. They exclude from the base all persons who are too young to marry and may also limit the base to an age range within which most marriages occur. The conventional practice of basing these rates on the number of women rather than all adults has the advantage of making the level of the rates correspond approximately to the number of couples who are marrying. Moreover, the patterns of changes in rates over time are generally the same for men and women.

Changes over time in the tendency for adults to marry are more meaningful and may fluctuate more widely if they are reported in refined rather than crude rates. To illustrate, the crude marriage rate declined between 1972 and 1980 from 10.9 per 1,000 population to 10.6, or by only 3 percent, while the refined rate (marriages per 1,000 women 15 to 44 years old) declined from 141.3 to 102.6, or by 27 percent. A change that appeared to be small when measured crudely turned out to be large when based on a more relevant segment of the population. Persons who want to have others believe that the change was small may cite the crude rates, and persons who want to demonstrate that the marital situation was deteriorating rapidly may cite the refined rates. But persons interested in making a balanced presentation may choose to cite both types of results and explain the differences between them.

Still greater refinement can be achieved by computing marriage rates according to such key variables as age groups and previous marital status. Examples appear in Table 1 and Figures 1 and 3 for the United States from 1971 to 1990. Table 1 and Figure 1 show first marriage rates by age for the only marital status category of eligible persons, namely, never-married adults (women) 15 years old and over. Figure 2 shows divorce rates by age for married women, and Figure 3 shows remarriage rates by age for divorced women. The low remarriage rates for widows are not shown here but are treated briefly elsewhere in the article. Rates of separation because of marital discord are also not presented here: Separated adults are still legally married and are therefore included in the base of divorce rates.

First Marriage Rates per 1,000 Never-Married Women, Divorce Rates per 1,000 Married Women, and Remarriage Rates per 1,000 Divorced Women, by Age: United States, 1970–1990

AGE (YEARS)	1970a	1975	1980b	1983	1985	1987	1990
				First Marriage Rate			
15 or over	93	76	68	64	62	59	58
15 to 17	36	29	22	16	13	12	11
18 to 19	150	115	92	73	67	58	53
20 to 24	198	144	122	107	102	98	93
25 to 29	131	115	104	105	104	105	109
30 to 34	75	62	60	61	66	69	71
35 to 39	48	36	33	38	37	42	47
40 to 44	27	26	22	22	24	22	20
45 to 64	10	9	8	8	11	10	NA
65 or over	1	1	1	1	1	1	1
				Divorce Rate			
15 or over	14	NA	20	19	19	19	19
15 to 19	27	NA	42	48	48	50	49
20 to 24	33	NA	47	43	47	46	46
25 to 29	26	NA	38	36	36	34	37
30 to 34	19	NA	29	28	29	27	28
35 to 44	11	NA	24	25	22	22	NA
45 to 54	5	NA	10	11	11	11	NA
55 to 64	3	NA	4	4	4	4	NA
				Remarriage Rate			
15 or over	133	117	104	92	82	81	76
20 to 24	420	301	301	240	264	248	252
25 to 29	277	235	209	204	184	183	200
30 to 34	196	173	146	145	128	137	138
35 to 39	147	117	108	99	97	92	93
40 to 44	98	91	69	67	63	69	69
45 to 64	47	40	35	31	36	37	NA
65 or over	9	9	7	5	5	5	5

Table 1

NOTE: aFirst marriage and remarriage rates for 1971.

bFirst marriage and remarriage rates for 1979.

SOURCE: National Center for Health Statistics 1990b, 1990c, 1995a, 1995b.

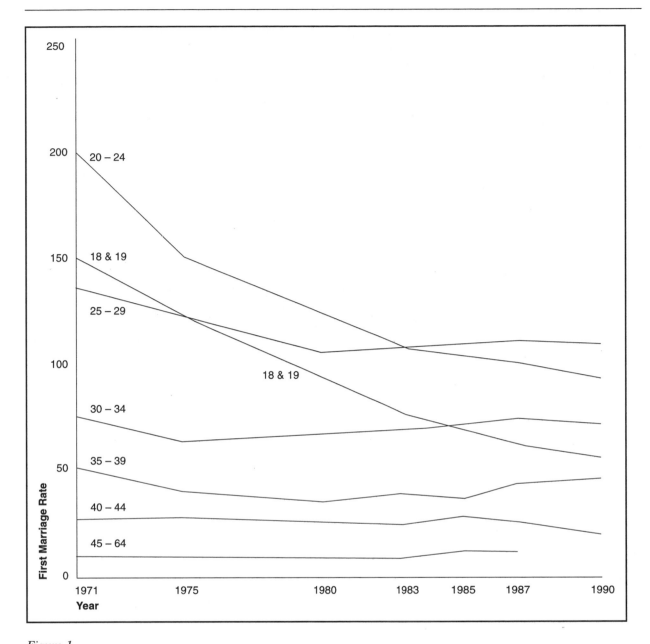

Figure 1

NOTE: First marriage rate per 1,000 never-married women, by age: United States, 1971–1990.

The marriage and divorce rates in Table 1 were based on data from reports published by the National Center for Health Statistics (NCHS). These reports contain information, obtained from central offices, of vital statistics in the states that are in the Marriage Registration Area (MRA) and the Divorce Registration Area (DRA). In 1990 the District of Columbia and all but eight states were in the MRA, while the District of Columbia and only thirty-one states were in the DRA. Funding for the central offices is determined by each state's legislature. But for states not in the MRA or DRA, the NCHS requests the numbers of marriages and divorces from local offices where marriage and divorce certificates are issued. The reports on divorce include the small number of annulments and dissolutions of marriage. Bases for the marriage and divorce rates in Table 1 were obtained from special tabulations made by the U.S. Bureau of the Census from Current Population Survey data. These are tabulations of adults in MRA and DRA states and classified by marital status, age, and sex. Because not all the population of the United States is included in the MRA and DRA, the detailed marriage and divorce statistics published by the NCHS constitute approximations of the marital situation in the country as a whole. This article contains much numerical information that was published in one or more of the NCHS reports listed in References.

FIRST MARRIAGE RATES BY AGE

Illustrations of first marriage rates appear in table 1. For the United States, the first marriage rates per 1,000 never-married women 15 years old and over were 93 in 1971 and 58 in 1990. In effect, 9.3 percent of the never-married women in 1971 and 5.8 percent in 1990, became married for the first time. For men the corresponding rates were 68 in 1971 and 47 in 1990.

First marriage rates tend to decline with age, and the rates for most of the age groups shown in Table 1 were declining over time. The rates for the age groups under 20 years of age were among the highest, but they dropped so sharply that they were only about one-third as high in 1990 as they had been in 1971. At the oldest ages, the change appears to have been slight. Obviously, the propensity to marry was falling far more abruptly among the young than among the older singles, probably in reaction to the suddenly changing cultural climate.

The generally downward trend in the marriage rate for each young age group was especially rapid during the early 1970s. By 1975, the veterans of the Vietnam War had already entered delayed marriages, and the upsurge in cohabitation outside marriage was only beginning to depress the first marriage rate. During the 1980s the slight upturn in the first marriage rate for women over 30 years of age probably reflected an increase in marriages among women who had delayed marrying for the purposes of obtaining a higher education and becoming established in the workplace.

Research has produced evidence that women who marry for the first time after they reach their thirties are more likely to have stable marriages than those who marry in their twenties (Norton and Moorman 1987). Although first marriage rates among adults in their forties are relatively low, they are by no means negligible.

As first marriage rates declined between the mid-1960s and the late 1980s, the median age at first marriage rose at an unprecedented pace over this short period of time. According to vital statistics, the median age at first marriage for women went up from 20.3 years in 1963 to 24.0 in 1990, for men it went up from 22.5 years to 25.9 years. As age at first marriage increased, the distribution of ages at first marriage also increased (Wilson and London 1987).

One of the consequences of the great delay of first marriage has been a very sharp rise in premarital pregnancy. Only 5 percent of births in 1960 occurred to unmarried mothers, but this increased to 24 percent in 1987 and to 32 percent in 1996. Research by Bumpass and McLanahan (1989) showed that one-half of nonmarital births during the late 1980s were first births, and about one-third occurred to teenagers. Moreover, about one-tenth of brides were pregnant at first marriage. Thus, about one-third of the first births during the late 1980s were conceived before marriage.

As the first marriage rate declined, the proportion of all marriages that were primary marriages (first for bride and groom) also declined. In 1970, two-thirds (68 percent) were primary marriages, but by 1987 the proportion was barely over one-half (54 percent). Meantime, marriages of divorced brides to divorced grooms nearly doubled, from 11 percent to 19 percent, while marriages of widows to widowers went down from 2 percent to 1 percent.

Men and women, regardless of previous marital status, tend to marry someone whose age is similar to their own. But men who enter first marriage when they are older than the average age of men at marriage have a reasonable likelihood of marrying a woman who has been divorced.

Procedures have been developed for projecting the proportion of adults of a certain age who

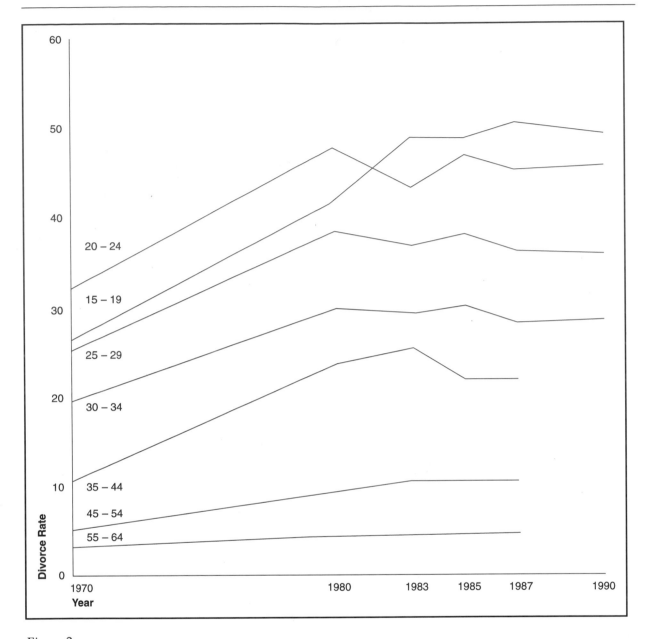

Figure 2

NOTE: Divorce rate per 1,000 married women, by age: United States, 1970–1990.

are likely to enter first marriage sometime during their lives. This measure is, in effect, "a lifetime first marriage rate." One of these procedures was used by Schoen and colleagues (1985) to find that about 94 percent of men who were born in the years 1948 to 1950 and who survived to age 15 were expected to marry eventually; for women, it was 95 percent. Their projections for those born in 1980 were significantly lower, 89 percent for men

and 91 percent for women. Despite the implied decline, a level of nine-tenths of the young adults deciding to marry at least once is still high by world standards.

DIVORCE RATES BY AGE

As indicated above, *crude* divorce rates are the only rates available annually for the United States and

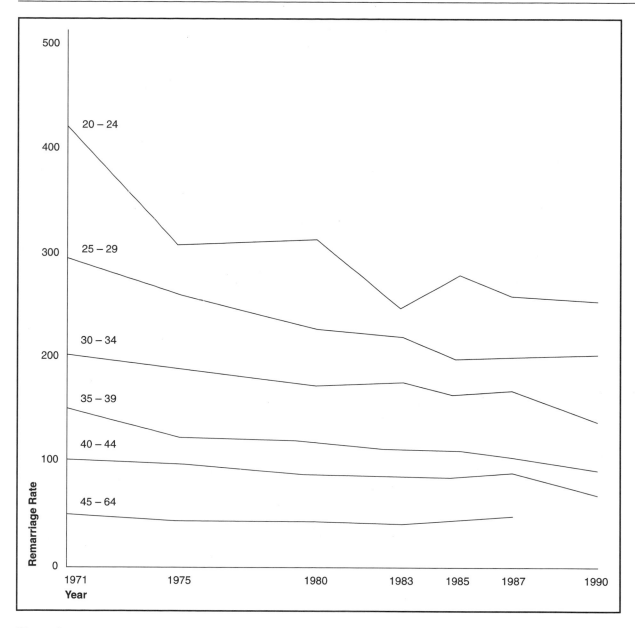

Figure 3

NOTE: Remarriage rate per 1,000 divorced women, by age: United States, 1971–1990.

individual states. As recently as 1965, the rate was only 2.5 divorces per 1,000 persons in the United States, but by 1979 the rate reached a peak more than twice that high, 5.3. Then the rate declined gradually until 1997, when it was down to 4.3, the lowest rate since 1973.

The most recent *refined* divorce rates available include those by age and sex in Table 1 for 1990. The report for that year also presented other refined divorce statistics on the number of divorces occurring among persons in their first marriage, their second marriage, and their third or subsequent marriage (NCHS 1995b). But the required bases for computing first divorce rates and redivorce rates are not available. During the 1980s, about three-fourths of the divorces were obtained by adults in their first marriage, about one-fifth by

those in their second marriage, and one-twentieth by those who had been married at least three times.

The divorce rates in Table 1 provide illustrations of the magnitude of the rates for the period 1970 to 1990. The divorce rate per 1,000 married women was 14 in 1970 and 19 in 1990. Corresponding rates for men were the same. The rate reached a peak of 20 in 1980, nearly half again as high as in 1970, and declined slightly to 19 in 1987, a level still well above that in 1970.

The divorce rate for married women rose dramatically in every age group during the 1970s and changed relatively little from then through the 1980s. In January 1973 the Vietnam War ended, and at that time the norms regarding the sanctity of marriage were being revised. The advantages of a permanent marriage were being weighed against the alternatives, including freedom from a seriously unsatisfactory marital bond and the prospect of experimenting with cohabitation outside marriage or living alone without any marital entanglements.

By 1994, one-fourth of divorced persons were cohabiting outside marriage, one-third were living alone, and most of the rest were in single-parent families (U.S. Bureau of the Census 1996).

Married women under 25 years of age have consistently high divorce rates resulting largely from adjustment difficulties associated with early first marriage. Noteworthy in this context is the finding that 30 percent of the women entering a first marriage in 1980 were in their teens, while 40 percent of those obtaining a divorce had entered their marriage while teenagers.

More divorces during the 1980s were occurring to married adults 25 to 34 years of age than to those in any other ten-year age group. A related study by Norton and Moorman (1987) concluded that women in their late thirties in 1985 were likely to have higher lifetime divorce rates (55 percent) than those either ten years older or ten years younger. This cohort was born during the vanguard of the baby boom and became the trend setter for higher divorce rates. The lower rate for those ten years younger may reflect their concern caused by the adjustment problems of their older divorced siblings or friends.

Married women over 45 years of age have quite low divorce rates. Most of their marriages must still be reasonably satisfactory, or not sufficiently unsatisfactory to persuade them to face the disadvantages that are often associated with becoming divorced. Yet, the forces that raised the divorce rate for younger women greatly after 1970 also made the small rate for the older women increase by one-fourth during the 1970s and remain at about the same level through the 1980s.

The median duration of marriage before divorce has been seven years for several decades. This finding is not proof of a seven-year itch. In fact, the median varies widely according to previous marital status from eight years for first marriages to six years for second marriages and four years for third and subsequent marriages. The number of divorces reaches a peak during the third year of marriage and declines during each succeeding year of marriage.

Among separating couples, the wife usually files the petition for divorce. However, between 1975 and 1987, the proportion of husband petitioners increased from 29.4 percent to 32.7 percent, and the small proportion of divorces in which both the husband and the wife were petitioners more than doubled, from 2.8 percent to 6.5 percent. These changes occurred while the feminist movement was becoming increasingly diffused and the birthrate was declining, with the consequence that only about one-half (52 percent) of the divorces in 1987 involved children under 18 years of age and one-fourth (29 percent) involved only one child. It is not surprising that nine-tenths of children under 18 living with a divorced parent live with their mother, far more often in families with smaller average incomes than those living with divorced fathers.

Although only about one-tenth of the adults in the United States in 1988 were divorced (7.4 percent) or separated (2.4 percent), the lifetime experience of married persons with these types of marital disruption is far greater. Based on adjustments for underreporting of divorce data from the Current Population Survey and for underrepresentation of divorce from vital statistics in the MRA, Martin and Bumpass (1989) have concluded that two-thirds of current marriages are likely to end in separation or divorce.

REMARRIAGE RATES BY AGE

Remarriage rates published by NCHS include separate rates for remarriages after divorce and after widowhood as well as for all remarriages. In this article attention is concentrated on remarriages after divorce, which constitute about nine-tenths of all remarriages. As mentioned above, the remarriage rate after divorce is a measure of the number of divorced women who marry in a given year per 1,000 divorced women at the middle of the year. For example, Table 1 shows that the remarriage rate after divorce for the United States was 133 in 1970 and 76 in 1990. Therefore, about 13 percent of the divorced women in 1970 became remarried in that year, as compared with 8 percent in 1990, only three-fifths as much as in 1970.

Divorced men have far higher remarriage rates than divorced women (in 1990, 106 versus 76). This situation and women's greater longevity largely account for the number of divorced women 45 years old and over in 1994 being one and one-half times the number of divorced men of that age (U.S. Bureau of the Census 1996).

Like first marriage rates, remarriage rates tend to decline with age, and the rate for each age group declined after 1970. The especially sharp drop during the first half of the 1970s for women under 40 years of age resulted from the compounding effect of a rapid increase in divorce and a rapid decline in remarriage during that period.

A large majority of divorced persons eventually remarry. In 1980, among persons 65 to 74 years old, 84 percent of the men and 77 percent of the women who had been divorced had remarried (U.S. Bureau of the Census 1989). But because of the declining remarriage rates, a projection based on information from the National Survey of Families and Households conducted in 1987 and 1988 shows that 72 percent of the recently separated persons are likely eventually to remarry (Bumpass, et al. 1989). About 6 percent of those who become separated never become divorced and therefore are not eligible for remarriage. Two-thirds of the remarriages in recent years occurred to women who entered first marriages as teenagers, according to the same study. Moreover, the rate of remarriage declines as the number of young children increases. Among married parents of young children with one or both parents remarried, about one-third of the children were born after the remarriage, and the others are stepchildren with the usually accompanying adjustment problems (Glick and Lin 1987).

In a given year about two of every three adults who marry are marrying for the first time, but this includes those marrying after widowhood as well as divorce. Among those who remarry after divorce, about three-fourths have been married only once, one-fifth have been married twice, and one-twentieth three or more times. Some couples who remarry had been married to each other previously. According to unpublished data from the National Survey of Families and Households, this occurred in about 3.3 percent of all marriages and closer to 5 percent for those in the age range when most remarriages after divorce occur.

Men are older than women, on the average, when they marry for the first time or when they remarry. Moreover, the gap is considerably wider at remarriage than at first marriage, but it narrowed somewhat between 1970 and 1987. Thus, successive marriages have been happening at older ages but with shorter intervals between them. In this context, the wider gap at remarriage than at first marriage may be less socially significant than an identical gap would have been at first marriage.

A woman in her second marriage is likely to be married to a man who is about ten years older than her first husband when she married him. Therefore, her second husband was probably more advanced in his occupation than her first husband was when she married him. But research has established that her first husband was probably about as far advanced ten years after her first marriage as her second husband was when she married him (Jacobs and Furstenberger 1986).

OTHER MARRIAGE AND DIVORCE RATES

Another rate that differs from the rates shown in Table 1 is the *total marriage rate*. This rate is intended to show the number of marriages that group of 1,000 men and women would have if they experienced in their lives the age-sex marriage rates observed in a given year (NCHS 1990b). It is therefore a hypothetical rate analogous to a total fertility rate. Both first marriage rates and remarriage rates have as the base the total population of the

United States without regard to previous marital status.

The total first marriage rate for the United States in 1987 implied that only 69 percent of men and 70 percent of women would eventually marry. The corresponding remarriage rates were 45 percent for men and 41 percent for women. Because both rates are based on the population regardless of marital status, they are additive. Therefore, the (combined) total marriage rate for 1987 implied that men are likely to have 1.14 marriages during their lifetime and women 1.11. These results may seem low because of the assumptions involved. For instance, if currently about 90 percent of every 100 adults marry, if one-half of the first marriages end in divorce, and if 70 percent of the divorced persons remarry, this would mean that 100 young adults in the 1990s are likely to have 90 first marriages and 32 second marriages after divorce (.90 + .90 x .50 x .70). In addition, many will redivorce and remarry again, and others will become widowed and remarry. Thus, realistically, the average young adult in the 1990s who marries is likely to have more than 1.1 marriages.

Remarriage among widowed adults is not featured in this article. However, the remarriage rate per 1,000 widows declined from 7 to 5 in 1990, while the rate for widowers declined from 32 to 24. The remarriage rate for widowers is much higher than the rate for widows because about one-half of them marry widows, who outnumber them five to one (U.S. Bureau of the Census 1989). Of all men and women who married in 1987, 68 percent had never previously married, 29 percent were divorced, and only 3 percent were widowed.

Divorce rates per 1,000 involving children under 18 published by NCHS shows that in 1987, the rate was 17, implying that 1.7 percent of the children under 18 years of age in the United States were involved in parental divorces in that year. This finding implies further that, if the same rate continued for eighteen years, 30.6 percent of the children would likely experience parental divorce before they reached 18 years of age. Data from the U.S. Bureau of Census used by Norton and Glick (1986) put the estimate at 40 percent. They also estimated that about an additional 20 percent of children become members of one-parent families because of premarital birth, parental separation

that does not end in divorce, or death of a parent. Therefore, about 60 percent of the children born in the 1990's and later may expect to spend a significant amount of time in a one-parent family before they become 18 years of age.

Marriage rates vary among countries as a reflection of dissimilar social, demographic, and economic conditions. An analysis of marriage rates in fifteen developed countries revealed that between 1965 and 1980 the rate per 1,000 unmarried women declined in all but two of the countries (Glick 1989). The marriage rates in English-speaking countries and Israel were above the average for the entire group, but the rates were below the average in the Germanic, French, and Scandinavian countries. A special reason for the differences was the extent to which cohabitation had been accepted as at least a temporary alternative to marriage. The generally downward trend among the marriage rates shows that the changing social conditions related to the propensity toward marriage have become widely diffused.

Divorce rates per 1,000 married women in almost all of the fifteen countries went up between 1965 and 1980 and doubled in the majority of them. Most of the countries with divorce rates above the overall average were English speaking. High divorce rates tended to be associated with high marriage rates because remarriages after divorce make an important contribution to the level of the marriage rates per 1,000 unmarried women.

Remarriage rates have been falling in most of the fifteen countries. In Canada a part of the decline between 1965 and 1980 was attributed to a change in the divorce laws and an increase in the delay of remarriage. The remarriage rate in New Zealand actually rose slightly in the context of a baby boom and an increase in immigration of young adults with subsequent high divorce rates. Countries with the highest remarriage rates were English speaking, and those with the lowest were Scandinavian countries, France and certain other European countries where cohabitation outside marriage had risen sharply.

Variation in the level of marriage and divorce rates among the American regions and states can be documented only by the use of crude rates. The Northeast and Midwest had consistently lower marriage rates than the South and West. The general pattern is similar for divorce rates. Some of the variations in the rates by states result from differences in the strictness of residence requirements for obtaining a marriage or divorce license. About seven of every eight marriages occur in the state where both the bride and the groom have their usual residence.

SELECTED VARIABLES RELATED TO MARRIAGE AND DIVORCE

Marriage and divorce rates are not presented in the NCHS reports by education and race of those involved. However, some reports do show distributions of first marriages and remarriages by several categories of education and race. The 1987 report documents that those marrying for the first time had more education, on the average, than those who were remarrying. Information from the 1980 census showed that women 25 to 34 years of age who had exactly four years of college training had distinctly the largest proportion of intact first marriages; those with graduate school training had a somewhat smaller proportion; and those with an incomplete college education had a smaller proportion than those in any other education category (U.S. Bureau of Census 1985).

The 1990 report on marriage provided evidence that white adults tend to marry at a younger age than black adults. The difference was two years for both brides and grooms at first marriage and two years at remarriage after divorce. Information for 1988 from the U.S. Bureau of the Census (1989) indicated that 18 percent of black adults had not married by the time they were 40 years old, as compared to 8 percent for white adults of the same age. The pressure to marry and to remain married evidently tends to be less for black adults than for white adults.

Interracial marriage occurs between a small but socially significant proportion of those who marry. In 1987, 2 percent of black brides married white grooms, and 6 percent of black grooms married white brides. Also, nearly 2 percent of black women obtaining divorces were married to white men, and more than 4 percent of black men obtaining divorces were married to white women. Thus, among those who intermarried, the marriages of black men to white women tend to be more stable than marriages of white men to black women.

Cohabitation outside marriage increased dramatically from only one-half million heterosexual couples in 1970 to 3.5 million in 1993, with about one million of their households maintained by the woman. This numerical growth occurred primarily among adults below middle age and has contributed importantly to the decline in marriage rates as well as to the increase in the number of separated persons. According to the 1987–1988 National Survey of Families and Households, "almost half of the persons in their early thirties and half of the recently married have cohabited" (Bumpass and Sweet 1989, p. 615). In order to provide some balance on the issue, Thornton has concluded that "even though cohabitation will be experienced by many, most people will continue to spend substantially more time in marital unions than in cohabiting unions" (1985, p. 497).

The health of adults is related to marital selection and marital stability, but NCHS does not provide marriage and divorce rates by the health status of those involved. The center does, however, publish current information on several indicators of the health condition of adults by marital status. Nearly all the indicators confirm that people with more signs of good health are likely to marry and remain married or to remarry after marital dissolution (Wilson and Schoenborn 1989). Parental divorce tends to be related to health problems of children but largely through the custodial parents' loss of income and time to spend with the children after divorce (Mauldon 1988). And stress prior to an event such as divorce or premarital breakup may actually reduce the impact of the life transition (Wheaton 1990).

Current trends in marriage and divorce rates do not necessarily indicate whether the rates will tend to stabilize at or near their 1990 levels, to resume their movement in historical directions, or to continue fluctuating in response to future social developments. A few more decades of observing the impact of past changes in marriage and divorce rates on the persons involved may be necessary before a definitive evaluation can be made concerning the longtime effect of these changes on family and child welfare.

(SEE ALSO: *Divorce; Marriage; Remarriage*)

REFERENCES

Bumpass, Larry, and Sara McLanahan 1989 "Unmarried Motherhood: Recent Trends, Composition, and Black-White Differences." *Demography* 26:279–286.

Bumpass, Larry, and James A. Sweet 1989 "National Estimates of Cohabitation." *Demography* 26:615–625.

Bumpass, Larry, James A. Sweet, and Teresa Castro Martin 1989 "Changing Patterns of Remarriage." Working Paper 89–02. Madison: Center for Demography and Ecology, University of Wisconsin.

Glick, Paul C. 1989 "The Family of Today and Tomorrow." In K. Ishwaran, ed., *Family and Marriage: Cross-Cultural Perspectives*. Toronto: Wall and Thompson.

Glick, Paul C., and Sung-Ling Lin 1987 "Remarriage after Divorce: Recent Changes and Demographic Variations." *Sociological Perspectives* 30:162–179.

Jacobs, Jerry A., and Frank F. Furstenberg, Jr. 1986 "Changing Place: Conjugal Careers and Women's Marital Stability." *Social Forces* 63:714–732.

Lin, Sung-Ling 1987 "Marital Selection and Child-Bearing and Companionship Functions of Marriage and Remarriage." Ph.D. dissertation, Arizona State University, Tempe.

Martin, Teresa Castro, and Larry L. Bumpass 1989 "Recent Trends in Marital Disruption." *Demography* 26:37–51.

Mauldon, Jane 1988 "The Effect of Marital Disruption on Children's Health." Paper presented at the Population Association of America meeting, New Orleans. National Center for Health Statistics (NCHS) 1990a "Births, Marriages, Divorces, and Deaths for 1989." *Monthly Vital Statistics Report* 38, no. 12.

—— 1990b "Advance Report of Final Marriage Statistics, 1987." *Monthly Vital Statistics Report* 38, no. 12, Supplement.

—— 1990c "Advance Report of Final Divorce Statistics, 1987." *Monthly Vital Statistics Report* 38, no. 12, Supplement 2.

—— 1995a "Advance Report on Final Divorce Statistics, 1989 and 1990." *Monthly Vital Statistics Report* 43, No. 9, Supplement.

—— 1995b "Advance Report on Final Marriage Statistics, 1989 and 1990." *Monthly Vital Statistics Report* 43, No. 12, Supplement.

—— 1998 "Births, Marriages, Divorces, and Deaths for 1997." *Monthly Vital Statistics Report* 46, No. 12.

Norton, Arthur J., and Paul C. Glick 1988 "One-Parent Families: A Social and Economic Profile." *Family Relations* 35:9–17.

Norton, Arthur J., and Jeanne E. Moorman 1987 "Current Trends in Marriage and Divorce among American Women." *Journal of Marriage and the Family* 49:3–14.

Schoen, Robert, William Urton, Karen Woodrow, and John Baj 1985 "Marriage and Divorce in Twentieth-Century American Cohorts." *Demography* 22:101–114.

Thornton, Arland 1988 "Cohabitation and Marriage in the 1980s." *Demography* 25:492–508.

U.S. Bureau of the Census 1985 *1980 Census of Population: Marital Characteristics*. Washington: U.S. Government Printing Office.

—— 1996 "Marital Status and Living Arrangements: March 1994" *Current Population Reports* P-20, no. 484 Washington: U.S. Government Printing Office.

Wheaton, Blair 1990 "Life Transitions, Role Histories, and Mental Health." *American Sociological Review* 55:209–223.

Wilson, Barbara F., and Kathryn A. London 1987 "Going to the Chapel." *American Demographics* 9:26–31.

——, and Charlotte Schoenborn 1989 "A Healthy Marriage." *American Demographics* 11:40–43.

PAUL C. GLICK

MARXIST SOCIOLOGY

The concept of a Marxist sociology does not refer to a clearly defined approach to social research; indeed, it is "now employed so widely that it has begun to lose all meaning" (Abercrombie et al. 1988, p. 148). The ambiguity of the term stems from the multiplicity of interpretations of the work of Karl Marx and Friedrich Engels, whose approach to social theory is usually termed *historical materialism*. The most well-known version is that of Soviet communism (Marxism-Leninism) and is identified with the worldview of *dialectical materialism* (a term never used by Marx and Engels), which has served largely the interests of Soviet ideology. The influence of historical materialism in modern sociology, however, stems primarily from the lesser-known independent tradition of European "Western Marxism" and the resulting forms of Marxist sociology (Agger 1979).

Contemporary usage of the term *Marxist sociology* varies considerably. In the United States, for example, the term *Marxist* is often used rather loosely, to designate virtually any type of radical or critical approach influenced by Marxian concepts (e.g., Ollman and Vernoff 1982; Flacks 1982). In societies with more strongly developed social democratic labor movements, as in Europe, the term is more closely identified with communist parties. Given the inherent ambiguity of the term, it is therefore useful to define Marxist sociology rather narrowly and concretely as a specific form of conflict theory associated with Western Marxism's objective of developing a positive (empirical) science of capitalist society as part of the mobilization of a revolutionary working class.

It is also useful to distinguish three basic types of relations between sociologists and Marxist sociology: those who work directly within the Marxist tradition (Marxist sociology proper) but "incorporate sociological insights, findings, and methodologies"; those who are Marxist-influenced in the sense of being stimulated by its historical approach and the "big questions" Marxists have posed but remain indifferent to "whether the best explanatory answers turn out to be Marxist" (Burawoy and Skocpol 1982, p. vii); and those identifying with highly revisionist critical theories (sometimes still in the name of Marxism) that seek to preserve the emancipatory vision of the Marxist tradition despite abandonment of the conventional notion of working-class revolution (Held 1980; Kellner 1989). It should also be stressed that Marxist sociology in this first sense refers to a historically identifiable—but widely contested—interpretation of the sociological implications of Marx's approach. As the most well-known British Marxist sociologist has concluded with particular reference to the German Frankfurt tradition of critical theory: "The tasks of a Marxist sociology, as I conceive it, are therefore very different from those of a neo-critical theory of society" (Bottomore 1984, p. 81). Marxist sociology in this strict sense thus tends in its most rigid form to resist any eclectic appropriation of sociological concepts: "Marxism has been courted by virtually every conceivable non-Marxist ideology: by existentialism, phenomenology, critical academic sociology, and by several variants of theology. To raise the question of a Marxism of Marxism is to take a resolute standagainst all attempts to capture and exploit Marx for non-Marxist purposes; and to adopt as a guiding principle . . . the claim that Marx himself made for his work: that Marxism is a specific science, related to the working class as a guide to socialist revolution" (Therborn 1976, p. 40).

The distinction between Marxism as "science" and as "critique" provides another way of describing the aspirations of Marxist sociology, which most commonly seeks to develop an objective, political economic science of society rather than a critical philosophy of praxis (Bottomore 1975; Gouldner 1980). Such a project is inherently interdisciplinary and often referred to under the heading of *political economy*, a term designating Marxist-oriented research that may be carried out in various disciplines: economics, political science, and history, as well as sociology (Attewell 1984). Though those identifying with neo-Weberian conflict or critical theories accept many of the empirical findings of neo-Marxist sociology and political economy, they tend to disagree about their broader interpretation and relation to political practice and social change.

ORIGINS

All forms of Marxist sociology trace themselves to the general theoretical approach of historical materialism as developed by Marx and Engels (Marx and Engels 1978; Bottomore and Goode 1983; Bottomore et al. 1983). Standard accounts of Marx's theoretical program stress that it does not constitute a unified system so much as diverse, though interrelated, modes of theorizing.

- Early writings that outline a theory of philosophical critique, an analysis of alienated labor, and a normative vision of human emancipation;

- A general sociology in the form of historical materialism (i.e., a theory of modes of production) as an approach to historical evolution;

- A specific account of capitalism and its economic contradictions deriving from this general theory; and

- A political philosophy and theory of praxis concerned with translating objective crisis tendencies in capitalism into a revolutionary transformation that would bring about a new form of "socialist" and eventually "communist" society (Giddens 1971, pp. 1–64; Bottomore 1975).

The precise relationship among these areas remains controversial. Though each level of theorizing has sociological implications, Marxist sociology has drawn primarily from the general sociology suggested by historical materialism and the more historically specific analysis of capitalist development that is the empirical focus of Marx's social theory and historical sociology. The key concept of a mode of production serves as the comparative framework for analyzing different social formations in terms of the contradictory relationship between their forces of production (primarily technology) and relations of production (forms of work organization and exploitation). The resulting mode of production directly shapes the specific structures of the class system and the manner in which the economic base determines the cultural superstructure composed of the state and various ideological institutions such as the mass media, education, law, religion, political ideologies, and so forth. In capitalist societies the contradiction deriving from the unresolvable polarization between labor and capital becomes the basis for revolutionary change under conditions of economic crisis.

As a positive science of society, Marxist sociology emerged in the period following Marx's death in 1883 through World War I. Strongly influenced by Engels's conception of "scientific socialism" as elaborated by Karl Kautsky in Germany, it was institutionalized in German Social Democracy and the Second International. Particular stress was placed upon how this approach provided an account of the historical "laws" that explained the causes of changes in modes of production and class formation and struggle. According to these laws a transition to socialism could be deduced from the "necessary" breakdown of capitalism. Extensive further development of such a scientific socialism was carried out by the Austro-Marxists, who deepened the logical analysis of Marxism as a form of causal explanation by drawing upon contemporary debates in the philosophy of science; as well, they extended Marx's theory to new phenomena such as the analysis of nationalism and the ethical foundations of Marxist sociology (Bottomore 1975, 1978; Bottomore and Goode 1978).

These two traditions of scientific socialism, however, did not develop much beyond the level codified in Bukharin's textbook of 1921 (*Historical Materialism: A System of Sociology*, translated in 1925). The primary reason was that there was considerable resistance to Marxism in the academy (related in part to identification of Marxism with the Soviet Union), ignorance of the richness of the suppressed tradition of Western Marxism, and a broad post–World War II institutionalization of sociology that virtually excluded Marxist sociology, despite some marginal influences of research in social stratification and change (e.g., Ralf Dahrhendorf in West Germany and C. Wright Mills in the United States). For all practical purposes the resurgence of Marxist sociology (often identified as "political economy" as opposed to "critical theory") coincides with the parallel emergence of radical and critical theories in the late 1960s, along with the recovery of the deeper foundations of Marxian theory with the proliferation of translations of Western Marxist texts in the 1970s.

It is customary to distinguish two basic starting points of a Marxist sociology based on different interpretations of the base–superstructure metaphor that underlies the concept of a mode of production: economistic or instrumental approaches as opposed to structuralist reproduction models. Economistic interpretations—sometimes associated with the idea of orthodox or "vulgar" Marxism—are based on a more or less reductionistic, causal account of the effects of the economic base or infrastructure upon the cultural superstructure, especially as causally derived from the assumed objective consequences of class interests.

Structuralist theories of social and cultural reproduction, in contrast, argue that the base–superstructure relation is more complex, involving functional relations that ensure the relative (if variable) autonomy of cultural factors, even if the economic is determinant in the last instance. Such structuralist interpretations derive primarily from the concept of the social reproduction of labor power developed in Marx's later works, the theory of cultural hegemony developed by the Italian Marxist leader and theorist Antonio Gramsci (1971) in the 1930s, and the reinterpretation of both Marx and Gramsci by the French philosopher Louis Althusser in the 1960s (Althusser 1971; Althusser and Balibar [1968] 1979).

CONTEMPORARY THEMES IN MARXIST SOCIOLOGY

The most convenient way to speak of contemporary themes in Marxist sociology—thus differentiating it from conflict or critical theory generally—is to restrict the concept to research that continues to adhere to the basic principles of neo-Marxist theory. Such a Marxist sociology would sometimes include adherence to the labor theory of value (which holds that labor is the only source of profit) but more essentially the primacy of economic and class factors, the priority of objective structures over subjectivity and consciousness, and the privileged role of the working class in a transition to socialism as defined by direct state ownership of the means of production (Anderson 1984; Wood 1986; Archibald 1978).

With respect to more recent developments in Marxist sociology, the immense literature and wide national variations make it appropriate to focus primarily—if not exclusively—on the remarkable resurgence of Marxism in American sociology. This phenomenon stems from the 1970s and has been traced to four key influences: the broadened audience of the journal *Monthly Review*, which was founded in 1949 and pioneered the application of Marxist economic theory for an analysis of the United States and its "imperial" role in world politics; Marxist historians who developed a critique of American liberalism and proposed a class-based reinterpretation of American history; the Hegelian Marxism and Critical Theory of the Frankfurt School tradition; and, finally, structuralist Marxism of largely French inspiration that sought to reestablish the credentials of Marx's theory as a science of society (Burawoy 1982, pp. 4–6). To illustrate the concerns of recent Marxist sociology, it is instructive to review some of the most representative examples of research in four key areas: work and the division of labor, class structure, the state and crisis theory, and culture and ideology. Research on the political economy of the world system and dependency theory have also been important but will not be discussed here (see, however, So 1990).

The Labor Process and the New International Division of Labor.

Until the late 1960s, Marxist theory was associated primarily with either communist ideologies or economic theory (Sweezy [1942] 1968). Not surprisingly, the pioneering, technically sophisticated Marxist research in the United States was concerned with an economic analysis of the new form of "monopoly capitalism" (Baran and Sweezy 1966). Drawing out the sociological implications of such, political economy is most closely associated with subsequent pathbreaking work involving the rediscovery of the labor process (i.e., Braverman 1974; Burawoy 1979) that gave work the central place that had been lost with the sense of consensus in postwar labor relations (Thompson 1983; Attewell 1984, pp. 93–141). Particular attention was given to the logic of capital's need to cheapen labor costs in ways that degrade and divide workers. More recent work has attempted to emphasize the incorporation of a subjective dimension to the labor process; further, it has developed a comparative perspective through the analysis of factory regimes in different types of economic systems and in relation to the new international division of labor (e.g., Burawoy 1985).

Class. Class analysis of course remains the key aspect of any Marxist sociology, but the focus contrasts sharply with conventional sociological approaches, even those (e.g., Max Weber) that acknowledge the importance of class conflict. Marxist sociology strongly insists on the primacy of the relations of production over the market processes stressed by neo-Weberians (Grabb 1990). The most influential empirical research in this area has stressed the importance of contradictory class locations and of reconnecting the objective and subjective dimensions of class with a theory of exploitation (Grabb 1990, pp. 152–163; Wright 1978, 1985).

Recent Marxist class analysis has been confronted by a number of challenges that pose serious problems for orthodox approaches; for example, the problem of the urban question, the role of ethnicity or race and especially gender as independent sources of domination (Shaw 1985), the emergence of the middle strata and the decline of the traditional "working class" (Walker 1978), the failure of class consciousness and actions to develop in the ways required for revolutionary transition, and other issues. The relation between Marxist and feminist theory has proved most controversial. More orthodox Marxist sociologists have attempted to incorporate gender into the theory of class and modes of production through the concept of unpaid "domestic labor" that contributes to the overall process of social reproduction (Fox

1980). But many feminists have abandoned Marxist sociology precisely because of its insistence on the primacy of class at the expense of gender (and other sources of domination).

The State and Crisis Theory. The contributions of Marxist sociology to the theory of the state have been wide-ranging and influential (Carnoy 1984; Jessop 1982; Holloway and Picciotto 1978). As well, they illustrate most clearly the issues involved in the debate between instrumental and structuralist interpretations of the base–superstructure model. In the context of theories of the state, this issue takes the form of whether the dominant class controls the state directly through its elite connections or indirectly through the functional economic and political imperatives that constrain public policy, regardless of who happens to hold power in a democratic regime. For example, the so-called Miliband-Poulantzas debate sharply defined the different empirical consequences of these two approaches. Miliband ([1969] 1973) stressed the actual empirical link between economic elites and political power of the dominant class, hence the role of the state as an instrument of class rule. Poulantzas ([1968] 1978), on the other hand, analyzed the state as a factor of cohesion that requires relative autonomy in order indirectly to serve the process of social reproduction in the long run.

Another central theme of Marxist sociology has been the relationship between economic crisis tendencies and the state in advanced capitalism (Attewell 1984, pp. 142–206). Research has focused especially on the concept of the "fiscal crisis of the state" (O'Connor 1973). It has been argued that the state is caught between the contradictory pressures of ensuring capital accumulation and legitimating the negative effects of the economy with the safety nets of the welfare state and that these conflicts become the potential basis for the emergence of new class-based oppositional movements.

Culture and Ideology. The most recent flourishing area of research has been in Marxist-influenced analyses of cultural phenomena as manifestations of ideology. The central focus has been on how cultural hegemony (or domination) is formed and the types of resistance that oppressed groups may develop against it. The stress of economistic Marxism has been upon the way in which the cultural superstructure of society "reflects" or "mirrors" economic processes and class relations. This approach often resulted in crude, reductionistic political and class analyses that were often unsatisfactory to those intimately acquainted with both high and popular culture. With the emergence of more sophisticated structuralist models of cultural reproduction, however, the relative autonomy of cultural forms could be acknowledged without obscuring their origins in "material" social relations. In the more extreme form represented by structuralist Marxism, it has been more generally held that all of the cultural institutions of society (e.g., the media, family, law, arts, etc.) functioned in the last instance as "ideological state apparatuses" that served the long-term interests of capital (Althusser 1971). Research based on both instrumentalist and structuralist approaches has been applied to the range of cultural activities (e.g., art, literature, law, sport, etc.), but education and the mass media figure most prominently, and they can serve as illustrations.

In the case of the Marxist sociology of education the result was a shift from an instrumentalist perspective (i.e., the role of capitalist ideology in directly using the educational system to shape consciousness in its interests) to one based on the idea of social reproduction as an indirect form of social control. Initially, structuralist approaches put particular stress upon the formal "correspondence" between the economic base and the hegemonic superstructure, despite the autonomy of the latter. Hence, structuralist research on education attempted to demonstrate the way in which the hidden curriculum of the school "corresponded" to the type of labor required by capital (Bowles and Gintis 1977; Cole 1988). Research on the political economy of the media was more strongly represented by instrumentalist perspectives that stressed the role of the media as instruments of "mind control" on the part of the dominant class and the broader dominance of the American media globally (Schiller 1971; 1973); others argued from a more structuralist perspective that the primary function of the media is the "selling of audiences," irrespective of the specific ideological content of programming (Smythe 1981).

THE CRISIS OF MARXIST SOCIOLOGY

As a specific theoretical approach that seeks to discover the role of economic and class factors in social change, Western Marxist sociology will certainly endure, though its significance will vary with the type of social formation and topic examined. As a philosophy of history or general theory of modes of production, and more especially as part of a particular theory of working-class revolution, orthodox Marxist sociology has been seriously called into question, especially in advanced capitalism. It has already collapsed in Eastern bloc countries, where a completely new tradition of social science is in the process of formation. This is not to say that economic and class factors or Marx become irrelevant, though the broader crisis of historical materialism suggests their significance and relation to social, political, and cultural processes will have to be interpreted in more self-critical, flexible, and historically specific ways (Aronowitz 1981). The complex outcome of the crisis of Marxist sociology in advanced capitalism is suggestively anticipated in the response of three contemporary countertendencies.

So-called analytical Marxism is defined more by its methodological stance than its substantive content. It thus differentiates itself from traditional Marxism in its commitment to abstract theorizing (as opposed to more concrete historical analysis), a search for rethinking the foundations by asking heretical questions, and "using state-of-the-art methods of analytical philosophy and 'positivist' social science" (Roemer 1986, pp. 1–2). Though these developments will undoubtedly have some impact on social theory, they are clearly too heterogeneous and revisionist to fall under the heading of Marxist sociology in the sense used here.

A second, opposing "poststructuralist" strategy is evident in the work of some former Marxists who have retreated from orthodox class concepts, arguing that a "post-Marxism" is required that involves eliminating the notion of the working class as a "universal class" and resurrecting a new conception of socialist democracy (Laclau and Mouffe 1985). Not surprisingly, this (partial) "retreat from class" has been treated with hostility by many neo-Marxists (Wood 1986), but it has provoked important debates about the role of new social movements and democratic processes in any defendable conception of socialist transformation.

A third tendency has been loosely referred to as "cultural Marxism." Such critics of the functionalist

tendencies of structuralist Marxism put particular stress upon the contested and uneven character of cultural reproduction in capitalist societies. In particular, various researchers have pointed to how dominated groups resist cultural domination in ways that often become the basis of counterhegemonic social movements. Further, it is argued that a crucial feature of contemporary "postmodern" societies is the distinctive role of the "cultural." The result has been a flowering of cultural research often identified, especially in the British context, with the notion of "cultural studies" (e.g., the work of Raymond Williams, Richard Johnson, Stuart Hall, et al.; see Brantlinger 1990). A related tendency has been the cultural Marxist historiography of E. P. Thompson (Kaye and McClelland 1990) that has influenced a major reinterpretation of Marx as a historical sociologist (Sayer 1983; Corrigan and Sayer 1985). A distinctive aspect of the cultural Marxist tradition, an aspect that has led it away from Marxist sociology in its more restrictive sense, has been its ability actively to engage in debate with and appropriate concepts from a wide variety of non-Marxist approaches. Much of the recent work carried out in the name of cultural Marxism thus increasingly blends with poststructuralist and critical theories of culture, reflecting the circumstance that "Marxism is no longer a single coherent discursive and political practice" (Nelson and Grossberg 1988, p. 11). One consequence is that it is no longer "possible to talk unproblematically of a 'Marxist' sociology, since Marxism has become a major contributor to sociology in general, while Marxist-influenced sociologists increasingly identify with their discipline (Shaw 1985, p. 16).

THE 1990S: THE DECLINE OF MARXIST SOCIOLOGY AND RECONSTRUCTIONS OF MARXIAN CRITICAL THEORY

By the end of the 1990s, several key shifts had redefined the fate of Marxist theory in the social sciences: (1) the collapse of the Soviet bloc; (2) a proliferation of metatheoretical debates—loosely grouped as postmodernist—that called into question the capacity of theory generally, and Marxist theory in particular, to provide general explanations or ethical critiques of social life; (3) a blurring of disciplinary boundaries that contributed to the flow of Marxist-related concepts into the humanities, especially under the heading of cultural studies; and (4) a substantive focus on globalization as a framework for rethinking the Marxian theory of society and change. The outcome of these tendencies was a decline of Marxist sociology as a clearly identifiable research orientation. Yet these developments also reinforced the three tendencies previously visible in the 1980s: (1) the continuing development of analytical Marxism (Jacobs 1996); (2) the proliferation of poststructuralist critiques of class essentialism that attempted to include standpoints such as race and gender in Marxist theory; and above all, (3) the continuing development of cultural Marxism, especially in the humanities. Many of those who continued to develop such questions had strayed so far from classical Marxist positions that they more often identified with an expanded notion of "critical theory" than with "Marxism" in the strict sense; rather than referring primarily to the Frankfurt School tradition, such an ecumenical reference to critical theory reflected a shared aspiration for a fundamental rethinking of the Marxian tradition.

The disintegration of the Soviet bloc culminating in 1989 marked the end of the failed experiment of "actually existing socialism." Though Western Marxists had generally rejected the Soviet model as an expression of Marx's utopian vision, its sudden demise came as a shock and unleashed a complex theoretical debate (Magnus and Cullenberg 1995). Western Marxists greeted this momentous historical transformation with mixed emotions. On the one hand, they were relieved to see the end of this tragic example of state socialism. On the other hand, they were perturbed by the uncritical embracing of the market model of development as the only alternative and the triumphalist heralding of these changes as the "end of Marxism." Within the ex-Soviet bloc the disillusionment with Marx was so intense that the very idea of Marxist sociology was generally repudiated; partly as a consequence the "Marxist" interpretation of these events (e.g. the important work of Michael Burawoy) has been undertaken, paradoxically, by Western Marxists (Kennedy and Galtz 1996). In Latin America, though Marx remained in influential intellectual force, political debate shifted from revolutionary rhetoric toward pragmatic questions of "democratic transition" (Castañeda 1993). Though many Marxist social scientists moved toward variants of

post-Marxist critical theory in response to these events, others insisted that the collapse of these regimes did not constitute "proofs of the bankruptcy of Marxism as a tradition of social scientific practice," though conceding that "it must be reconstructed in various ways" (Wright 1996, pp. 121–122). Though Marxist sociology declined precipitously as a specific orientation in the 1990s—hence its absence from leading social theory anthologies, discussion of Marxist theory continued to flourish in a few journals, most notably the *New Left Review* in Britain and *Rethinking Marxism* in the United States. Despite sporadic attempts to defend Marxism as a science (Burawoy 1990) or "test" classic Marxist claims (e.g., Boswell and Dixon 1993; Cockshott et al. 1995; Smith 1994), the revitalization of empirical Marxist research appeared increasingly dependent upon working out the implications of major theoretical reconstructions (e.g., Postone 1993; Wright et al. 1992). Such efforts have also been influenced by "Weberian Marxism," despite the resistance of more orthodox Marxists (Gubbay 1997; Lowy 1996).

A second major shift that has contributed to the decline of Marxist sociology in the 1990s can be identified with the elusive concept of "postmodernism" and related poststructuralist tendencies. The Marxist tradition was a specific target of epistemological postmodernism which called into question all "meta-narratives" or grand theories of society and history, whether as explanations or as the basis of universalistic ethical claims. Related poststructuralist critiques of essentialism challenged Marxist theories of the working class and called for a decentered conception of the subject that acknowledged the diversity of subject positions, a theme especially central to feminist, gender, and racial research. Some Marxists simply defended classical Marxist theory against these developments, but many felt compelled to revise their positions in the direction of an "emancipatory postmodernism," a "postmodern Marxism," or a "poststructuralist materialism." In this context, various efforts were made to reconcile selective poststructuralist and postmodernist arguments with a reconstructed neo-Marxist, critical theory (e.g., Best and Kellner 1997). On the one hand, such postmodernist-influenced approaches acknowledged that the fundamental cultural shifts linked to the mass media and new information technologies have profound implications for a "postmodern" society that was not foreseen by Marx. On the other, they also conceded that classic Marxist theory (though not necessarily Marx himself) relied on an inadequate, teleological philosophy of history, economic reductionism, and an essentialist conception of the working-class subject.

A third tendency that has become more clearly defined over the past decade has been the partial erosion of disciplinary boundaries and the diverse impact of Marxist theorizing on the humanities, especially under the heading of cultural studies and poststructuralist textual theories. Paradoxically, though the influence of Marxist theory declined within sociology in the 1990s, it had a continuing renaissance and diffuse effect in other disciplines, especially literary studies. Much of this work has in turn influenced cultural Marxism, as well as sociologists of culture and the media. In its most ambitious form, such neo-Marxist cultural theory has culminated in an account of postmodernity as an historical epoch (Jameson 1991). Another outcome was an expansion and revision of the canons of classical Marxian theory. Though his status as a "Marxist" has been disputed, the Soviet scholar Mikhail Bakhtin (1895–1975) was rehabilitated as a major theorist of culture whose dialogical theory of language anticipated many of the later developments in poststructuralist critiques of Marxism (Bell and Gardiner 1998). Similarly, Antonio Gramsci's cultural and linguistic writings have been reinterpreted in terms of his poststructuralist anticipations (Holub 1992).

Finally, the most sustained empirical development in the 1990s was the emergence of the problematic of globalization (and aspects of postcolonial theory) as a reference point for an historical materialist account of social change (Hoogvelt 1997; Larrain 1994). From this perspective, "postmodernism" could be read as a symptom of processes better understood from the perspective of a political economy of globalization. Hence it was argued that Marx was the pioneer of globalization theory, given his account of the ceaseless worldwide expansion of markets, a theme elaborated in Wallerstein's world-system theory. But many other Marxists have joined critical theorists in emphasizing the distinctiveness of more recent developments since World War II, especially the transformation of production processes (e.g., the shift from "Fordism" to "post-Fordism") and the impact of information technologies, resulting in changed relations between space and time (Harvey 1989). Unlike those who uncritically celebrated the advent of an "information society" and globalization as the inevitable outcomes of capitalism, such Marxists and critical theorists have pointed to the selective characteristics of this "modernization" and its inadequate vision of the alternatives (Webster 1995). The most elaborate empirical effort to describe this new "informational mode of production" in Marxist-influenced but also innovative sociological terms can be found in Manuel Castells' three-volume *The Information Age* (Castells 1996–1998). As against various postmodernist currents, neo-Marxist conceptions of globalization (and related variants of critical theory) are united by their political opposition to neoliberalism (or what is often referred to as neoconservatism in the United States) and an empirical concern with analyzing capitalist globalization in terms of its grave implications for marginalized groups and societies, as well as nature itself. For the most part, such researchers no longer appeal to the classic conception of working-class revolution, though they hold out hope for new social movements as the basis of constructive forms of resistance and democratic renewal. As a consequence, Marxist sociologists have increasingly moved toward positions previously staked out by the Frankfurt tradition of critical theory and related poststructuralist French developments (Morrow 1994), though often without consistently acknowledging the full implications for the "death of Marxism" as an oppositional political discourse (Fraser 1998).

(SEE ALSO: *Critical Theory; Macrosociology; Materialism; Socialism*)

REFERENCES

Abercrombie, Nicholas, Stephen Hill, and Bryan S. Turner 1988 *The Penguin Dictionary of Sociology*, 2nd ed. Harmondsworth, England: Penguin.

Agger, Ben 1979 *Western Marxism: An Introduction– Classical and Contemporary Sources*. Santa Monica, Calif.: Goodyear.

Althusser, Louis 1974 "Ideology and Ideological State Apparatuses." In *Lenin and Philosophy and Other Essays*, Ben Brewster, trans. New York: Monthly Review.

——, and Etienne Balibar (1968) 1979 *Reading Capital*. Ben Brewster, trans. London: Verso.

Anderson, Perry 1984 *In the Tracks of Historical Materialism*. London: Verso.

Archibald, W. Peter 1978 *Social Psychology as Political Economy*. Toronto: McGraw-Hill.

Aronowitz, Stanley 1981 *The Crisis of Historical Materialism: Class, Politics, and Culture in Marxist Theory*. New York: Praeger/J. F. Bergin.

Attewell, Paul A. 1984 *Radical Political Economy since the Sixties: A Sociology of Knowledge Analysis*. New Brunswick, N.J.: Rutgers University Press.

Baran, Paul A., and Paul M. Sweezy 1966 *Monopoly Capital: An Essay on the American Economic Order*. New York: Monthly Review.

Bell, Michael Mayerfeld, and Michael Gardiner, eds. 1998 *Bakhtin and the Human Sciences: No Last Words*. London: Sage.

Best, Steve, and Douglas Kellner 1997 *The Postmodern Turn*. New York Guilford.

Boswell, Terry, and William J. Dixon 1993 "Marx's Theory of Rebellion: A Cross-National Analysis of Class Exploitation, Economic Development, and Violent Revolt." *American Sociological Review* 58 (October:681–702).

Bottomore, Tom 1975 *Marxist Sociology*. London: Macmillan.

——, 1978 "Marxism and Sociology." In Tom Bottomore and Robert Nisbet, eds., *A History of Sociological Analysis*. New York: Basic.

—— 1984 *The Frankfurt School*. New York: Ellis Horwood/Tavistock.

——, and Patrick Goode, eds. 1978 *Austro-Marxism*, T. Bottomore and P. Goode, trans. Oxford: Clarendon.

—— 1983 *Readings in Marxist Sociology*. Oxford, England: Oxford University Press.

Bottomore, Tom, et al., eds. 1983 *A Dictionary of Marxist Thought*. Cambridge, Mass.: Harvard University Press/ Basil Blackwell.

Bowles, Samuel, and Herbert Gintis 1977 *Schooling in Capitalist America: Educational Reform and the Contradictions of Economic Life*. New York: Basic.

Brantlinger, Patrick 1990 *Crusoe's Footprints: Cultural Studies in Britain and America*. New York: Routledge.

Braverman, Harry 1974 *Labor and Monopoly Capital: The Degradation of Work in the Twentieth Century*. New York: Monthly Review.

Burawoy, Michael 1979 *Manufacturing Consent: Changes in the Labor Process under Monopoly Capitalism*. Chicago: University of Chicago Press.

—— 1982 "Introduction: The Resurgence of Marxism in American Sociology." In Michael Burawoy and Theda Skocpol, eds., *Marxist Inquiries: Studies of Labor, Class, and States*. Chicago: University of Chicago Press.

—— 1985 *The Politics of Production*. London: Verso.

—— 1990 "Marxism as Science: Historical Challenges and Theoretical Growth." *American Sociological Review* 55:775–793.

——, and Theda Skocpol, eds. 1982 *Marxist Inquiries: Studies of Labor, Class, and States*. Chicago: University of Chicago Press.

Castañeda, Jorge G. 1993 *Utopia Unarmed: The Latin American Left after the Cold War*. New York: Knopf.

Castells, Manuel 1996–1998. *The Information Age: Economy, Society and Culture*, 3 vols. Oxford, England: Basil Blackwell.

Cockshott, Paul, Allin Cottrell, and Greg Michaelson 1995 "Testing Marx: Some New Results from UK Data." *Capital and Class* 55:103–129.

Cole, Mike, ed. 1988 *Bowles and Gintis Revisited: Correspondence and Contradiction in Educational Theory*. New York: Falmer.

Corrigan, Philip, and Derek Sayer 1985 *The Great Arch: English State Formation as Cultural Revolution*. Oxford, England: Basil Blackwell.

Flacks, Richard 1982 "Marxism and Sociology." In Bertell Ollman and Edward Vernoff, eds., *The Left Academy: Marxist Scholarship on American Campuses*. New York: McGraw-Hill.

Fox, Bonnie, ed. 1980 *Hidden in the Household: Women's Domestic Labour under Capitalism*. Toronto: Women's Press.

Fraser, Nancy 1998 "A Future for Marxism." *New Politics (New Series)* 6 (Winter):95–98.

Giddens, Anthony 1971 *Capitalism and Modern Social Theory*. Cambridge, England: Cambridge University Press.

Gouldner, Alvin W. 1980 *The Two Marxisms: Contradictions and Anomalies in the Development of Theory*. New York: Seabury.

Grabb, Edward G. 1990 *Theories of Social Inequality: Classical and Contemporary Perspectives*, 2nd ed. Toronto: Holt, Rinehart and Winston.

Gramsci, Antonio 1971 *Selections from the Prison Notebooks*, Quintin Hoare and Geoffrey Nowell Smith, eds. and trans. New York: International.

Gubbay, Jon 1997 "A Marxist Critique of Weberian Class Analyses." *Sociology* 31:73–89.

Harvey, David 1989 *The Condition of Postmodernity*. Oxford, England: Basil Blackwell.

Held, David 1980 *Introduction to Critical Theory: Horkheimer to Habermas*. Berkeley: University of California Press.

Holloway, John, and Sol Picciotto, eds. 1978 *State and Capital: A Marxist Debate*. London: Edward Arnold.

Holub, Renate 1992 *Antonio Gramsci: Beyond Marxism and Postmodernism*. New York: Routledge.

Hoogvelt, Ankie 1997 *Globalization and the Postcolonial World: The New Political Economy of Development*. Baltimore, Md.: Johns Hopkins University Press.

Jacobs, Lesley A. 1996 "The Second Wave of Analytical Marxism." *Philosophy of the Social Sciences* 26:279–292.

Jameson, Fredric 1991 *Postmodernism, or, The Cultural Logic of Late Capitalism*. Durham, N.C.: Duke University Press.

Jessop, Bob 1982 *The Capitalist State: Marxist Theories and Methods*. Oxford: Martin Robertson.

Kaye, Harvey J., and Keith McClelland, eds. 1990 *E. P. Thompson: Critical Perspectives*. Philadelphia: Temple University Press.

Kellner, Douglas 1989 *Critical Theory, Marxism, and Modernity*. Baltimore, Md.: Johns Hopkins University Press.

Kennedy, Michael D, and Naomi Galtz 1996 "From Marxism to Postcommunism: Socialist Desires and East European Rejections." *Annual Review of Sociology* 22:437–458.

Laclau, Ernest, and Chantal Mouffe 1985 *Hegemony and Socialist Strategy: Towards a Radical Democratic Politics*, Winston Moore and Paul Cammack. trans. London: Verso.

Larrain, Jorge 1994 *Ideology and Cultural Identity: Modernity and the Third World Presence*. Cambridge: Polity.

Lowy, Michael 1996 "Figures of Weberian Marxism." *Theory and Society* 25 (June):431–446.

Magnus, Bernd, and Stephen Cullenberg 1995 *Whither Marxism? Global Crises in International Perspective*. New York: Routledge.

Marx, Karl, and Friedrich Engels 1978 *The Marx-Engels Reader*, 2nd ed. Robert C. Tucker, ed. New York: Norton.

Miliband, Ralph (1969) 1973 *The State in Capitalist Society: The Analysis of the Western System of Power*. London: Quartet.

Morrow, Raymond A. 1994 *Critical Theory and Methodology*. Newbury Park, Calif.: Sage.

Nelson, Cary, and Lawrence Grossberg, eds. 1988 *Marxism and the Interpretation of Culture*. Urbana, Ill.: University of Illinois Press.

O'Connor, James 1973 *The Fiscal Crisis of the State*. New York: St. Martin's.

Ollman, Bertell, and Edward Vernoff, eds. 1982 *The Left Academy: Marxist Scholarship on American Campuses*. New York: McGraw-Hill.

Postone, Moishe 1993 *Time, Labor, and Social Domination: A Reinterpretation of Marx's Critical Theory*. New York: Cambridge University Press.

Poulantzas, Nicos (1968) 1978 *Political Power and Social Classes*. Timothy O'Hagan, trans. London: Verso.

Roemer, John, ed. 1986 *Analytical Marxism*. Cambridge, England: Cambridge University Press.

Sayer, Derek 1983 *Marx's Method: Ideology, Science, and Critique in "Capital."* Atlantic Highlands, N.J.: Harvester/Humanities.

Schiller, Herbert I. 1971 *Mass Communications and the American Empire*. Boston: Beacon.

—— 1973 *The Mind Managers*. Boston: Beacon.

Shaw, Martin, ed. 1985 *Marxist Sociology Revisited: Critical Assessments*. London: Macmillan.

Smith, Murray E.G. 1994 *Invisible Leviathan: The Marxist Critique of Market Despotism beyond Postmodernism*. Buffalo, N.Y.: University of Toronto Press.

Smythe, Dallas W. 1981 *Dependency Road: Communications, Capitalism, Consciousness, and Canada*. Norwood, N.J.: Ablex.

So, Alvin Y. 1990 *Social Change and Development: Modernization, Dependency, and World-System Theories*. Newbury Park, Calif.: Sage.

Sweezy, Paul M. (1942) 1968 *The Theory of Capitalist Development: Principles of Marxian Political Economy*. New York: Monthly Review.

Therborn, Göran 1976 *Science, Class, and Society: On the Formation of Sociology and Historical Materialism*. London: New Left.

Thompson, Paul 1983 *The Nature of Work: An Introduction to Debates on the Labour Process*. London: Macmillan.

Walker, Pat, ed. 1978 *Between Labor and Capital*. Montreal: Black Rose.

Webster, Frank 1995 *Theories of the Information Society*. New York: Routledge.

Wood, Ellen Meiksins 1986 *The Retreat from Class: A New "True" Socialism*. London: Verso.

Wright, Erik Ohlin 1978 *Class, Crisis, and the State*. London: Verso.

—— 1985 *Classes*. London: Verso.

—— 1996 "Marxism after Communism." Pp. 121–145 in S. P. Turner, ed., *Social Theory and Sociology*. Cambridge, Mass.: Blackwell.

——, Andrew Levine, and Elliott Sober 1992 *Reconstructing Marxism*. London: Verso.

RAYMOND A. MORROW

MASCULINITY

See Femininity/Masculinity.

MASS MEDIA RESEARCH

The interest of sociologists in mass communication was stimulated by developments in technology allowing the reproduction and speedy transmission of messages. It began with the rise of the popular press, followed by the invention of film, sound broadcasting (or radio), and the audiovisual, including television and cable television. In the past decade, this interest has grown to embrace computer-influenced adaptations of these traditional mass media, the latest being the World Wide Web (www), which is part of the Internet, or the Information Superhighway.

All of us live in a world of media-constructed images that, presumably, significantly influence what we think and how we partition our attention, time, and other scarce resources. So pervasive has been the media presence that issues relating to these influences have also drawn the attention of researchers from disciplines other than sociology.

It is to Harold Lasswell (1947), an empirically oriented political scientist, that the social science community owes a succinct formula that lays out the major elements within the field of communication research: *Who* says *what* in which *channel* to *whom* and with what *effects*? Only some channels lend themselves to *mass* communication, which can be defined, in the terms of the above formula, as the transmission by professional communicators (who) of a continuous flow of a uniform content (what) by means of a complex apparatus (channel, or how) to a large, heterogeneous, and geographically dispersed audience (to whom), the members of which are usually anonymous to the communicator and to each other.

Not included in this definition of mass communication are its effects or, more broadly speaking, its consequences, toward which most of the sociological research effort has been directed. The physical or electronic transmission of message content does not in itself suffice for communication. Communication is indisputably social, in that it consists of a meeting of minds between communicator and audience, in the sense of mutual accommodation. Yet the nature and extent of effects have been, over the years, the central problem of sociological interest in media research.

Effects, however, do not stand alone as a separate and independent dimension for research. More accurately, scholars have investigated the effects of each element in Lasswell's formula. For example, there has been analysis of what effects the different kinds of communicator controls may have, whether the *who* be defined by demographic characteristics and professional values of the communicator (Weaver and Wilhoit 1996; Weaver with Wu 1998) or as the growing big-business controls over mass media through concentration of ownership by not more than ten corporations (Bagdikian 1997). In other research, the effects of different kinds and amounts of media content have been analyzed to determine what was likely to have influenced particular audience behavior, as has been what difference it makes whether news is obtained from radio, television, or newspapers.

Media effects have been studied on three levels: the atomistic, the aggregate, and the societal. Effects on the atomistic level involve the cognitive processes and behavioral responses of *individuals* who make up the various mass audiences. By contrast, aggregate measures take into account only *distributions* that produce changes in averages usually expressed as net effects. Consequences for society have more to do with the political, cultural, and other *institutional* changes that represent cumulative adaptations over time to the dominance of a particular mass medium. Inferences based on the observation of effects on one level when ascribed to effects on a different level have often turned out to be invalid.

THE ATOMISTIC LEVEL

Much of the media research effort has been a response to the operational needs of communicators and propagandists, or of those who wished to defend the public against what was perceived as the pernicious influence of the media. The basic problem has been that of precisely pinpointing effects: What were the characteristics of the potential audience? Who among them was susceptible? What were the determinants of their reactions?

To answer these and similar questions, audience research has typically focused on the situations in which mass communications are received and on the habits and cognitive processes that underlie the responses of individuals either to specific media messages or to some significant part of the media fare. The responses under scrutiny have ranged from the arousal of interest, gains in knowledge, the recognition of dangers, changes of opinion, and other attitudinal measures to such behavioral indicators as consumer purchases, electoral decisions, and the "elevation" of cultural taste.

Precisely because of its focus on the individual, this line of research tends to stress the diversity of ways in which individuals relate to media content. First of all, audiences are found to be stratified by education, interest, taste, habits, gender, and age. Taken together, education and age tend to account for considerable variance in media use. The observation that some content had only minimal audience penetration helped explain why some information campaigns failed. Consistent patterns of exposure to different kinds of content further suggested that members of the mass audience, by and large, found what suited their needs and interests.

Second, even common exposure turns out to be a less strong predictor of response than expected. Not everyone understands or understands fully, and reactions are affected by the preconceptions with which people approach the content, by preconceptions rooted in past socialization experience but also reflecting the perspective of groups with which they are associated or identify themselves. Audiences are obstinate and people have options in how they orient themselves to any particular set of messages. They can ignore, misunderstand, accept, find fault with, or be entertained by the same content. In other words, there is no assurance that anyone other than those, for whatever reason, already so disposed will accept the facts, adopt the opinion, or carry out the actions suggested by the mass communicator (Schramm 1973).

This downplaying of the importance of content elements by a methodical partitioning of the mass audience received systematic formulation in the "minimal effects" theorem, derived from Joseph Klapper's review (1960) of certain empirical research findings of studies conducted mostly during the 1940s and 1950s. He generalized that certain factors, such as audience characteristics and a pluralistic media structure, which mediated between content and response, worked primarily in the service of reinforcement of prior attitudes. Changes triggered by exposure were pretty much limited to people whose situations already impelled them to move in that direction. Klapper did, however, acknowledge the power of mass communication to move people on matters with which they were unfamiliar and concerning which they had no distinct views of ingrained habits.

Strong evidence in favor of not-so-minimal effects has come from observations made in the laboratory, especially through the series of experimental studies on children, reported in *Television and Social Behavior*, conducted under the auspices of the U.S. Surgeon General (Murray and Rubinstein 1972). After exposure to programs that included "violent" behavior, subjects often engaged in similar behavior during their play, and were more likely than subjects not so exposed to commit other violent acts.

Such experiments generally have been set up to maximize the possibility of demonstrating direct effects. Thus, in this instance, children, especially young children, would be inclined to model their own behavior on what they see. Moreover, such findings of short-term effects observed in a play situation have to be considered within the context of the whole socialization experience over many years. Longitudinal studies and experimental studies of older children in a more natural setting have yielded results that are more ambiguous (Milavsky et al. 1973). Laboratories do not fully replicate communication situations of real life (Milgram 1973).

Over years of study, conflicting evidence emerged about the relation between mass media (largely televised) violence and its influence on aggressive behavior. Operational definitions of key variables, research designs, and support for research having come from the television industry or not, all have been viewed as possible influences on the research results themselves.

The media-violence effects issue is one in which research results have played an important role in public policy debates involving the broadcast industry often pitted against public interests. Decades of debate eventually led to passage of the Telecommunications Act of 1996, authorizing an electronic device called the V-chip, that would allow blocking programs with violent programing from television viewing (Rowland 1997).

In recent years, concern over the media-violence effects issue has been "exported" to the rest of the world through the multiple means of transmission and aggressive marketing by multinational corporate media interests. Public opinion surveys in all corners of the globe indicate disturbance by the ubiquitousness of television violence (Maherzi 1997).

The challenges posed by experimental studies have to be faced. Casual but repeated exposure to televised messages results in incidental learning. For example, content of advertising appeals gradually intrude into our consciousness until we associate a product with a particular brand name, or issues dominating the news become the criteria by which we measure the effectiveness of a political leadership. Insofar as the various mass media sources transmit similar content and play on similar themes, such limited effects, if they are cumulative, can produce shifts of significant proportions.

AGGREGATE EFFECTS

Because the responses of persons are so diverse, the effect of communication en masse has to be conveyed in some kind of summary measure—as an average, a trend, a general movement. From this perspective, the magnitude of the shift in the responses of individuals, or whether this represents reinforcement or a reversal, matters less than the general picture, taken over time.

How differently effects can appear when viewed from different perspectives, and at different periods of time, may be illustrated by reference to studies of the diffusion of innovations (Rogers 1995). Detailed documentation in the more than fifty-year tradition of diffusion studies has spanned many disciplines and many nations, bringing revision and fine-tuning to the original concepts. The early diffusion model was applied to post–World War II development programs in agriculture, family planning, public health, and nutrition. Today, the model is being applied to areas as diverse as acquired immunodeficiency syndrome (AIDS) and the Internet.

The process by which innovations are adopted and spread suggests that early adopters, also called "influentials" or "opinion leaders," depending on context, are more cosmopolitan in their orientation and hence more attuned to certain media messages. They select from the total stream the messages that best meet their needs and interests. Others will adopt an innovation only after its success has been demonstrated or, if that is precluded—as it would be in most political decisions—out of trust in the expertise of the pacesetters. One can account for the different behavior of leaders and followers in such situations—that is, why one person moves ahead and another is content to wait—in terms of personal characteristics and social relationships. Aggregate effects, on the other hand, have to do with whether or not there has been a general movement toward acceptance or rejection of the innovation.

The most direct measures of aggregate effects are to be found in two-variable relationships designed to show cause and effect, with one variable functioning as an indicator of media presence and the other representing the response. Many such combinations are possible. One can use media penetration (e.g., newspaper circulation, or the proportion of homes with a television set) or content characteristics (e.g., the number of violent acts in children's programs, editorial endorsements, or issues emphasized in the news). This rules out media behavior, which is voluntary for individuals in the audience, and may bring into question the influence of still other, often unmeasured, variables that also account for the presumed effect.

As the age of television dawned, opportunities for "controlled" observation—comparing two matched areas, one receiving television and the other not yet within reach of the broadcast signal—were never fully exploited. Rarely did findings about the advent of television go beyond documenting the rather obvious fact that television viewing cut into the use of some other media, especially radio and to a lesser degree movie attendance and children's comic book reading. Nor were the consequences of this reallocation of time at all clear.

A study of children in "Teletown" and "Radiotown," the latter community still without television but comparable in other respects, concluded that before television, many children (had gone) through the same type of change as today from fantasy-seeking media behavior toward reality-seeking media behavior (Schramm et al. 1961).

For another natural experiment, a researcher was able to identify a Canadian town that was to get television within a year, after being unable to obtain reception because of geographic location. Comparisons were made with two other communities, one that would receive a second television channel and one that remained the same that year, with four channels. Results showed that the arrival of television did make a difference in children's reading skills, aggression levels, sex role stereotyping, and attendance at social events outside the home (Williams 1986).

Any such cause-effect evidence from natural experiments is lacking on matters relating to citizen participation among adults in national elections. Systematic comparisons between the turnout and overall responsiveness to "party" issues during the 1952 presidential election in counties with high TV penetration and low TV penetration revealed no consistent differences, probably because other media were already saturated enough with campaign material to have produced a high level of interest. Situations subject to such "ceiling" effects prevent further research in response to the presence of a new medium.

Variations in content, when they occur, have offered far more opportunities for controlled observations, many of which have challenged the conventional wisdom. That voters on the west coast of the United States would be dissuaded from voting in the presidential election once television, based on early returns, had declared a winner seemed only logical. Yet studies showed that westerners continued to cast ballots in roughly the same proportions as their compatriots in states where polls had already closed. In voting, they were evidently moved by considerations other than practical utility and by other competing media messages. Whatever the effects of such broadcast returns on the decision to vote or not to vote, they have been too small for detecting with present techniques of measurements (Lang and Lang 1984, ch. 5). As regards editorial endorsements, where the range of variations is greater, research has shown that such support gives candidates for minor offices, many of whom are only names on a ballot, an incremental but nevertheless

distinct advantage over other minor candidates on the same slate.

Correlations that pair media use variables with some measure of response always imply change over time. The alternative is to conduct before-and-after studies in response to events as they are being communicated via the mass media: a televised speech by a political leader, the announcement of an unexpected reversal of government policy, news of foreign crisis, or simply the flow of information about economic conditions and problems facing the country.

Polls before and after an appropriately timed speech have documented the power of a head of state to move opinion through appeals directed to the public. Speeches can create greater awareness. They are designed to focus attention on those issues and actions from which the politician stands to benefit. The effectiveness of such media events is apt to be greatest when an issue is just surfacing. Leaders also have the ability to make news. Even without an undisputed success, their public appearances, diligently reported by the news media, are used to dramatize their own role in promoting solutions to matters believed to be of general concern, thereby conferring status on themselves, as well as on the matters they seek to promote.

Careful analysis of the impact of many such events over the years again challenges the conventional wisdom. Neither speeches nor foreign travel by American presidents over the many administrations have, by themselves or in combination, *uniformly* shored up public support. Public response to these events has been highly dependent on the political context—that is, on whether they coincided with other events that tended to enhance the president's standing or whether his administration was plagued by intractable problems, such as public concern about a declining economy, an indignation over American hostages whose release it could not effect, or revelations of governmental wrongdoing such as those that surfaced during Watergate and led to the resignation of Richard Nixon as chronicled by Lang and Lang (1983).

What stands out in a long line of studies is the general correspondence over time between the overall amount of attention a topic, an issue, or a personality enjoys in the media and the audience's awareness, interest in, and concern about these. Mass communication influences not so much *what* people think (opinion) but what they think *about* (recognition). Insofar as there is enough common emphasis, the media perform an "agenda-setting" function (McCombs and Shaw 1972, 1976; Iyengar and Kinder 1987). Collectively, the media and the audience define the terms of public debate. Media attention also confers status on some of the many voices clamoring to be recognized.

Agenda-setting research requires at least two steps; that is, content analysis is conducted to define the media agenda, and surveys are used to identify the public or audience agenda. This simple formulation, which has been a central focus of effects research in political communication for some years, attributes to the media at one and the same time too much and too little influence. On the one hand, the media do not, all on their own, dictate or control the political agenda. Neither public awareness nor recognition of a problem is sufficient to stir a controversy on which people take sides. On the other hand, access to the media is a major resource for the advocates of particular policies. Concerns become issues through discussion in which political leaders, government officials, news and commentary in the press, and the voices of citizens reciprocally influence one another in a process more aptly characterized as "agenda building" (Lang and Lang 1984). In fact, three agendas—those of the media, the public, and the policy makers—all influence each other in a rather interactive political process (Rogers and Dearing 1988).

THE SYSTEMIC PERSPECTIVE

The dissemination of content via the mass communication system occurs in a highly selective fashion. Some information is privileged; other information is available only to those with the interest and resources to pay for it, thereby stratifying societies into the "haves" and have-nots," or into the information rich and the information poor. The upshot of all the efforts to direct communication flow is a repertoire of images of events and ongoing social activities. Media organizations are themselves producers of content. The mass communications through which the world is brought into focus are, in the broadest sense, cultural creations that incorporate the perspectives of the producers and of others whose views have to be taken into account. This influence of the communications system on content, intended or not, is a source of bias often unrecognized by those responsible for it.

One has to differentiate between two sources of bias: technological and social. Technological bias stems from the physical characteristics of the medium. Harold Innis (1951), the Canadian institutional economist, distinguished between bias toward space and bias toward time. Paper, he averred, because of its light weight, was easily transported but also perishable, and so supported the development of centralized administration. The uniformity thus imposed over a given area (space) was usually at the expense of continuity (time). A more flexible medium could adapt to an oral tradition that favored spontaneous cooperation among autonomous units. Indeed, signs continue to point in the direction that cheaper and smaller electronic devices may be radically increasing the control individuals have over the information available to them and what to do with it (Beniger 1986). Information is central to the control individuals have over the social events of the world in which they live.

Applied mechanistically, without regard to who is in control, these categories lead to a simpleminded media determinism. Social bias has to do with how the capabilities intrinsic to the dominant medium are exploited. Television, in and of itself, may not have had a demonstrable effect on voter turnout but nevertheless contributed indirectly. Thus, a nonpartisan political coverage, designed not to offend but with an insatiable appetite for scandal, was implicit in the economic logic of aiming at the largest possible audience while the American regulatory system opened the way for a well-financed candidate could buy nearly unlimited time to air well-targeted, and often negative, political messages. Both trends fed into an already existing distrust of government. Meanwhile, campaign strategies adapted to the medium of television helped undermine the power of party machines to deliver votes. The nominating conventions in which political bosses once traded votes have been transformed into showpieces, played for a national audience as the curtain raiser for the U.S. presidential election campaign.

More generally, its penetration into the spheres of other institutions—political, cultural, educational, and so on—is what makes mass communication a potentially powerful influence on the societal level. It hardly matters whether the media are viewed as a resource or as a threat. The publicity generated through mass communication brings the norms of the larger society to bear on actions that once might have been considered privileged or at least shielded from public scrutiny. Conversely, the competition for visibility is an inducement for elite institutions to adopt at least some of the conventions of the media culture.

There remains the question of who sets these norms and standards. Some scholars have argued that repeated exposure to a sanitized media culture results in "mainstreaming" (Gerbner et al. 1986), or what has been commonly referred to as homogenizing consequences. Accordingly, all but a few of the diverse currents that feed into the kaleidoscope of minority United States cultures, including women and racial and ethnic minorities, receive comparatively little or no recognition. Lacking an effective institutional representation, they are more readily marginalized. Content analyses of character portrayal and the values espoused by heroes and villains, victims and perpetrators of violence in the popular entertainment fare, as well as by surveys of adults, adolescents, and children in the United States, have lent some support to the charge of "mainstreaming." Such cultivation analysis in cross-cultural settings also is finding support for these kinds of media effects (Signorielli and Morgan 1990). Despite the premium on novelty, most media organizations are inclined not to stray too far from what is popularly accepted but will be likely to eagerly imitate any demonstrated success.

The representation of political views is similarly constrained. Despite the independence of the press and a few celebrated instances where a small number of persistent journalists initiated an inquiry, as when the Woodward and Bernstein team pursued the Watergate story, the more typical pattern is to wait until political actors have highlighted a problem. Usually, it is they, rather than the press, who define the terms of controversies over policy, as was the case in the much-studied limited role of the media, largely American and mostly Cable News Network (CNN), in the 1991 Persian Gulf conflict (Dennis et al. 1991; *Media*

Development, 1991). To paraphrase W. Lance Bennett (1988), when the institutional voices speaking in protest are stilled, all but the more radical media are inclined to drop the issue as well. Discussion and diversity exist but usually within self-imposed limits.

It should be clear that major media organizations, though important players, are less than fully separate from other establishments. Their influence on events is greatest when they act in conjunction with other agencies.

INTERNATIONAL, OR GLOBAL, RESEARCH

Into the 1950s, mass communication research was very much a product of the United States: U.S. media programming and news events, U.S. media practices and policies, with necessary consideration of U.S. politics and society. There was a tendency for mass media research to concentrate on one aspect of the communication process originally outlined by Lasswell, namely effects. Later, research refocused some attention on other elements of the communication process—on what was produced and how it was produced.

Research also began exploring dimensions of mass media influence outside the United States. Some studies were international extensions of research already being conducted in the United States, as with the media-violence issue, diffusion of innovations, and cultivation analysis. For other research, the international perspective was the question under investigation: What should be considered when news, television entertainment programming, and other media products cross geopolitical boundaries?

In the 1950s, the identification of four theoretical perspectives of the press—authoritarian, communist, libertarian, and social responsibility—focused attention on the social, political, cultural, and philosophical underpinnings that determine how and why the mass media of various parts of the world are different (Siebert et al. 1956). Here, the press was defined as all available mass media responsible for dissemination of news. Some country-specific case studies have helped to elucidate these differences (Mickiewicz 1988; Alot 1982; Howkins 1982).

The post–World War II era was concerned with reconstruction and development of the so-called Third World and spawned a developmental perspective of the mass media (Schramm 1964; Lerner and Schramm 1967). A fifth concept of the press focused on revolutionary goals of the mass media, with China's transitions over the past century and the recent emergence of terrorism as examples of present-day extensions of this perspective (Chu 1977; Lull 1991; Nacos 1994).

Debate over international communication issues has been strongly influenced by the political and economic imbalances among the nations of the world. So-called North-South debates juxtapose the concerns of the politically independent, industrialized, and developed part of the world against those of the newly independent countries, which have been trying to shed their colonial pasts and, because they have missed out on the Industrial Revolution, are still developing. Other debates between the East and the West have been reflections the cold-war conflicts between the former Soviet Union and the United States, in which an emergent group of nonaligned countries, largely in the developing world, have refused to take sides.

In the 1970s, the United Nations Educational, Scientific and Cultural Organization (UNESCO) became an outspoken supporter of efforts by this developing Third World to create a New World Information and Communication Order (NWICO) as the counterpart to calls for a less well known New World Economic Order. UNESCO formed an advisory commission of international scholars, diplomats, and specialists, headed by Irishman Sean MacBride, to study the world's communications problems, and to address Third World protests against the domination of news flow from industrialized countries of the West to the rest of the world. It was also concerned with issues as diverse as governmental controls, censorship, cultural dominance or imperialism, concentration of media ownership and powerful control of transnational corporations, freedom and responsibility of the press, commercialization of mass media, protection of journalists when they are at work in countries other than their home, access to technology and infrastructure development, and rights to communication (International Commission for the Study of Communication Problems 1980).

Studies proliferated in relation to the various issues posited by the UNESCO report. "Cultural imperialism" that reflected political imperialism of older models from historical colonialism was the theoretical perspective from which empirical studies documented imbalances in the world's media infrastructures and contents. The "media imperialist" was decidedly Western, and largely American. UNESCO together with professional organizations of scholars and practitioners supported large multicountry studies of international news flow (Sreberny-Mohammadi 1984; Kirat and Weaver 1985). These studies analyzed images, distortion in content, and the role of news agencies, and also explored factors that determine what becomes news (Galtung and Ruge 1965).

This research showed that certain factors do influence news production, such as economic considerations in distribution of news-gathering resources and ease of reporting; importance to the country producing the news in terms of trade, social and cultural ties, geographic proximity, and relative standing or status of nations in the eyes of others. Such findings have influenced shifts in mass media structures and output, such as the increase in national and regional news through agencies like the New China News Agency, also known as Xinhua, and the Caribbean News Agency (CANA).

In these nearly twenty years, the UNESCO debate over NWICO has faded and resurfaced more than once, and UNESCO-sponsored round table discussions continue on a regional basis to provide a forum for discussion of research on global communication issues. A recent UNESCO report on the status of the world's mass media and how they are handling the challenges of new technologies claims that the problems identified by the MacBride Commission "still remain a burning issue" and are likely to continue to be the focus of research efforts at national, regional, and international levels (Maherzi 1997).

One issue highlighted in the original UNESCO report that has received considerable national and multinational research attention is the inequality of women and girls in societies around the globe, their disproportionate representation in media-related employment, and their stereotyped images in news and entertainment media portrayals. More than a decade behind the U.S. civil rights and women's movements that triggered considerable mass media research with implications for local media practices, programming decisions and U.S. policy, this UNESCO report was to become pivotal in pitching these issues to the rest of the world for research and analysis.

The United Nations Fourth World Conference on Women, held in Beijing in 1995, included women and media among the thirteen major substantive areas for consideration. There were reports on country-specific surveys of media practices, characteristics and attitudes of those holding jobs in the media, and program content (All-China Journalists Association and Institute of Journalism, Chinese Academy of Social Sciences 1996) and studies that involved the coordination of data collection in many countries. For example, the Global Media Monitoring Project gathered data from news media—radio, television and newspapers—in seventy-one countries for representation and portrayal of women at one point in time: January 18, 1995. Based on the data, an overall report and separate regional reports were produced. The study provides a large database with policy implications for UNESCO and for media systems in many countries. A benchmark for measuring future change, the Media Monitoring Project's study remains the most extensive survey of portrayals of women in the world's news media that has been undertaken to date (Media Watch 1995).

On balance, however, it remains unclear from available research whether women and men working in the mass media take different approaches on issues or events, even if women and men have a different range of interests they select for media attention. Though there has been an increase in the number of women working in the media in the past few years, surveys also show that the world of media remains strongly male (Maherzi 1997).

Most recently, research questions emerging in international communications are centering on the concept of globalization of mass media producers and their products. The concentration and control of media industries into fewer and fewer transnational corporations has long been a concern in research that points to the negative effects of increasing global "homogenization." It is not without some irony that, on the one hand, the results of mass media investigations have brought about international pressure for diversifying media products with voices of women and minorities of all kinds, while on the other hand, ownership of the world's media is concentrated in the hands of a few corporate giants.

NEW MEDIA TECHNOLOGIES

One of these corporate giants in the media world is Time Warner. Years ago, Warner Brothers produced films and Time produced a news magazine. Together, they are now also involved with other aspects of the media environment, including newspapers, magazines, television, cable television, radio, video games, telephones, and computers in the United States and around the world. Understanding why such a corporate giant was created is key to understanding the impacts of new media technologies: "Convergence" of technical infrastructures is leading to consolidation of media products and services.

The Internet, or the Information Superhighway, with the World Wide Web (www), is the most recent development, which has the potential to offer any or all of the aforementioned media products and services through on-line information networks. Current Internet services are transmitted via computer-telephone connections, but explorations of other methods of transmissions are under way, such as cable television and direct satellite links. Obviously, the corporate giants wish to be positioned to take their share of any new media offerings and to provide new delivery systems. What technology will deliver news and entertainment, as well as other information and services, in the future remains an open question.

Regardless of how the infrastructure question is decided, will the definition of "news" remain the same? Because of the vast storage capacity of computers, the role of editors and gatekeepers may change. With the ability of computers to allow more personalized reception of news offerings, will the "newspaper" still be considered a *mass* medium?

Internet-related services and e-mail already are providing new possibilities for on-line public opinion polls. But so far, such surveys are similar to volunteer call-in or write-in polls and are limited to Internet users. While the number of new Internet users grows daily, by the year 2000 the numbers of

U.S. adults on-line is expected to reach only 60 million (Pew Research Center 1996). Increasingly, on-line users are "decidedly mainstream," according to a nationwide telephone survey, and for now, television is losing in their allocations of time (Pew Research Center 1998).

At the atomistic level, researchers have conducted ethnographic and clinical observation on how people relate to computers and how they may be reconstructing their basic sense of identity (Turkle 1995).

How will the traditional mass communication conceptualizations of diffusion of innovations, agenda-setting and agenda-building, cultivation, and mainstreaming help us to understand the new media environment?

Is our new world more global or more local (Sreberny-Mohammadi et al. 1997)? Are we moving into Marshall McLuhan's long-promised "global village"? Or is it a global megalopolis? Are we moving from UNESCO's "many voices, one world" to many worlds, one voice?

These are some of the many questions that will occupy media researchers in the near future.

REFERENCES

All-China Journalists Association, and Institute of Journalism, Chinese Academy of Social Sciences 1996 "Survey on the Current Status and Development of Chinese Women Journalists." Beijing.

Alot, Magaga 1982 *People and Communication in Kenya*. Nairobi: Kenya Literature Bureau.

Bagdikian, Ben H. (1983) 1997 *The Media Monopoly*, 5th ed. Boston: Beacon Press.

Beniger, James R. 1986 *The Control Revolution: Technological and Economic Origins of the Information Society*. Cambridge, Mass.: Harvard University Press.

Bennett, W. Lance 1988 *News: The Politics of Illusion*. New York: Longman.

Chu, Godwin C. 1977 *Radical Change through Communication in Mao's China*. Honolulu: East-West Center/University Press of Hawaii.

Dennis, Everette E., ed. 1991 *The Media at War: The Press and the Persian Gulf Crisis*. New York: Gannett Foundation Media Center.

Galtung, Johan, and Mari Holmboe Ruge 1965 "The Structure of Foreign News," *Journal of Peace Research* 2:64–91.

Gerbner, George, Larry Gross, Michael Morgan, and Nancy Signorielli 1986 "Living with Television: The Dynamics of the Cultivation Process." In J. Bryant and D. Zillmann, eds., *Perspectives on Media Effects*. Hillsdale, N.J.: Lawrence Erlbaum.

Howkins, John 1982 *Mass Communication in China*. New York: Longman.

Innis, Harold A. 1951 *The Bias of Communication*. Toronto: University of Toronto Press.

International Commission for the Study of Communication Problems 1980 *Many Voices, One World: Communication and Society, Today and Tomorrow*. New York: Unipub.

Iyengar, Shanto, and Donald R. Kinder 1987 *News That Matters: Television and Public Opinion*. Chicago: University of Chicago Press.

Kirat, Mohamed, and David Weaver 1985 "Foreign News Coverage in Three Wire Services: A Study of AP, UPI and the Nonaligned News Agencies Pool," *Gazette* 35:31–47.

Klapper, Joseph T. 1960 *The Effects of Mass Communication*. New York: Free Press.

Lang, Gladys Engel, and Kurt Lang 1984 *Politics and Television Re-Viewed*. Beverly Hills, Calif.: Sage.

——, and —— 1983 *Battle for Public Opinion: The President, the Media, and the Polls During Watergate*. New York: Columbia University Press.

Lasswell, Harold D. 1947 "The Structure and Function of Communication in Society." In L. Bryson, ed., *The Communication of Ideas*. New York: Harper.

Lerner, Daniel, and Wilbur Schramm 1967 *Communication and Change in the Developing Countries*. Honolulu: East-West Center Press.

Lull, James 1991 *China Turned On: Television, Reform and Resistance*. New York: Routledge.

McCombs, Malcom E., and Donald L. Shaw 1972 "The Agenda-Setting Function of Mass Media." *Public Opinion Quarterly* 36:176–187.

—— 1976 "Structuring the 'Unseen Environment.'" *Journal of Communication* (Spring):18–22.

Maherzi, Lotfi 1997 *World Communication Report: The Media and the Challenge of New Technologies*. Paris: UNESCO.

Media Development 1991 "Reporting the Gulf War," Special Issue, October. London: World Association for Christian Communication.

Media Watch 1995 *Global Media Monitoring Project: Women's Participation in the News*. Toronto and Ontario: National Watch on Images of Women in the Media (Media Watch) Inc.

Mickiewicz, Ellen 1988 *Split Signals: Television and Politics in the Soviet Union.* New York: Oxford University Press.

Milavsky, J. Ronald, Horst Stipp, Ronald C. Kessler, and William S. Rubens 1982 *Television and Aggression: A Panel Study.* New York: Academic.

Milgram, Stanley 1973 *Television and Anti-Social Behavior: A Field Experiment.* New York: Academic.

Murray, John P., and Eli A. Rubinstein 1972 *Television and Social Behavior: Reports and Papers*, 5 vols. Washington, D.C.: National Institute for Mental Health.

Nacos, Brigitte L. 1994 *Terrorism and the Media: From the Iran Hostage Crisis to the World Trade Center Bombing.* New York: Columbia University Press.

Pew Research Center for the People and the Press 1996 "One in Ten Voters Online for Campaign." September. http://www.people-press.org.

—— 1998 "Online Newcomers More Middle-Brow, Less Work-Oriented: The Internet News Audience Goes Ordinary." October-December. http://www.people-press.org.

Rogers, Everett M. (1962) 1995 *Diffusion of Innovations*, 4th ed. New York: Free Press.

——, and James W. Dearing 1988 "Agenda-Setting Research: Where Has It Been, Where Is It Going?" In J. Anderson, ed., *Communication Yearbook 11.* Newbury Park, Calif.: Sage.

Rowland, Willard D., Jr. 1997 "Television Violence Redux: The Continuing Mythology of Effects." In M. Baker and J. Petley, eds., *Ill Effects: The Media/Violence Debate.* New York: Routledge.

Schramm, Wilbur 1964 *Mass Media and National Development.* Stanford, Calif.: Stanford University Press.

—— 1973 *Men, Women, Messages and Media.* New York: Harper and Row.

——, Jack Lyle, and Edwin B. Parker 1961 *Television in the Lives of Our Children.* Stanford, Calif.: Stanford University Press.

Siebert, Fred, Theodore Peterson, and Wilbur Schramm 1956 *Four Theories of the Press.* Urbana: University of Illinois Press.

Signorielli, Nancy, and Michael Morgan, eds. 1990 *Cultivation Analysis: New Directions in Media Effects Research.* Newbury Park, Calif.: Sage.

Sreberny-Mohammadi, Annabelle 1984 "The 'World of the News.'" *Journal of Communication* (Winter):121–134.

——, Dwayne Winseck, Jim McKenna, and Oliver Boyd-Barrett, eds. 1997 *Media in Global Context: A Reader.* New York: Arnold/Hodder Headline Group.

Turkle, Sherry 1995 *Life on the Screen: Identity in the Age of the Internet.* New York: Simon and Schuster.

Weaver, David H., and G. Cleveland Wilhoit 1996 *The American Journalist in the 1990s: U.S. News People at the End of an Era.* Mahwah, N.J.: Lawrence Erlbaum Associates.

——, with Wei Wu 1998 *The Global Journalist: News People Around the World.* Cresskill, N.J.: Hampton Press.

Williams, Tannis, ed. 1986 *The Impact of Television.* New York: Academic Press.

JANICE M. ENGSBERG
KURT LANG
GLADYS ENGEL LANG

MASS SOCIETY

The mass society theory, in all its diverse formulations, is based on a sweeping general claim about "the modern world," one announcing a "breakdown of community." The leading nineteenth-century proponents of this position were Louis de Bonald, Joseph de Maistre, and, from a different perspective, Gustave Le Bon. These formulations argue the collapse of the stable, cohesive, and supportive communities found in the days of yore. In modern times, as a consequence, one finds rootlessness, fragmentation, breakdown, individuation, isolation, powerlessness, and widespread anxiety (Giner 1976; Halebsky 1976).

The original formulations of this position, those of the nineteenth century, were put forth by conservatives, by persons identified with or defending the old regime. These were critiques of the liberal theory or, more precisely, of liberal practice. The basic aim of the liberals was to free individuals from the restraints of traditional institutions. That aim was to be accomplished by the dismantling of the "irrational" arrangements of the old regime. Liberals, understandably, were enthusiastic about the achievement: Free men could do things, achieve things, create things that were impossible under the old arrangement. The collective benefits, they argued, were (or would be) enormous. The conservative critics agreed about some aspects of the history. They agreed about the general process of individuation. They, however, called it fragmentation or a decline of community. More important, they provided very different assessments of the consequences. At its simplest, the liberals argued an immense range of benefits coming with the transformation, a conclusion signaled, for example, in Adam Smith's title, *The Wealth of Nations*. The mass society theorists agreed with the basic diagnosis but drew strikingly opposite conclusions pointing to a wide, and alarming, range of personal and social costs.

The modern world begins, supposedly, with an enormous uprooting of populations. Ever greater numbers are forced from the small and stable communities into the large cities. In place of the strong, intimate, personal supports found in the small community, the large cities were characterized by fleeting, impersonal contacts. The family was now smaller. The isolated nuclear family—father, mother, and dependent children—was now the rule, replacing the extended family of farm and village. The urban neighborhoods were and are less personal. The frequent moves required in urban locales make deep, long-lasting friendships difficult if not impossible. As opposed to the support and solidarity of the village, instrumental and competitive relationships are typical in the large cities and this too makes sustained social ties problematic. In the mass society people are "atomized." The human condition is one of isolation and loneliness. The claims put forth in this tradition are typically unidirectional—the prediction is "more and more." There is ever more uprooting, more mobility, more societal breakdown, more isolation, and more anxiety.

The nineteenth-century versions of this theory focused on the insidious role of demagogues. In those accounts, traditional rulers, monarchs, aristocracy, and the upper classes did their best to govern fundamentally unstable societies. But from time to time, demagogues arose out of "the masses," men who played on the fears and anxieties of an uneducated, poorly informed, and gullible populace. The plans or programs offered by the demagogues were said to involve "easy solutions." But those, basically, were unrealistic or manipulative usages, ones providing no solutions at all. The demagogues brought revolution, which was followed by disorder, destruction, and death. The traditional patterns of rule were disrupted; the experienced and well-meaning leaders were displaced, either killed or driven into exile. The efforts of the demagogues made an already-desperate situation worse.

Conservative commentators pointed to the French Revolution as the archetypical case with Robespierre and his associates as the irresponsible demagogues. Mass society theorists also pointed to the experience of ancient Greece and Rome. There too the demagogues had done their worst, overthrowing the Athenian democracy and bringing an end to the Roman republic. The republic was succeeded by a series of emperors and praetorians, men who, with rare exceptions, showed various combinations of incompetence, irresponsibility, and viciousness.

The lesson of the mass society theory, in brief, was that if the masses overthrew the traditional leaders, things would be much worse. The "successes" of liberalism, the destruction of traditional social structures, the elimination of stable communities, and the resulting individualism (also called "egoism") could only worsen an already precarious situation. The theory, accordingly, counseled acceptance or acquiescence.

It is easy to see such claims as ideological, as pretense, as justifications for old-regime privilege. Such claims were (and are) given short shrift in the opposite liberal dramaturgy and, still later, in the dramaturgy of the left. In those opposite accounts, the old regime is portrayed as powerful. The rulers, after all, had vast wealth and influence; they controlled the police and the ultimate force, the army.

In private accounts, however, the leaders of the old regime reported a sense of powerlessness. Their "hold" on power, they felt, was tenuous; they stood on the edge of the abyss. Chateaubriand, the French ambassador, congratulated Lord Liverpool on the stability of British institutions. Liverpool pointed to the metropolis outside his windows and replied: "What can be stable with these enormous cities? One insurrection in London and all is lost." The French Revolution itself proved the flimsiness of "established" rule. In 1830, the restored monarchy in France collapsed after only a week of fighting in the capital. In 1848, Louis Philippe's regime fell after only two days of struggle. A month later, the Prussian king and queen, effectively prisoners of the revolution, were forced to do obeisance to the fallen insurgents. The queen's comment—"Only the guillotine is missing." More than a century later, the historian J. R. Jones declared that "during long periods of this time, many conservatives felt that they were irretrievably on the defensive, faced not with just electoral defeat but also doomed to become a permanent and shrinking minority, exercising a dwindling influence on the mind and life of the nation."

Early in the twentieth century, sociologists in Europe and North America developed an extensive literature that also argued a loss-of-community thesis. Among the Europeans, we have Ferdinand Tönnies, Georg Simmel, and, with a difference, Emile Durkheim. Simmel's essay, "The Metropolis and Mental Life," had considerable influence in North America, especially in the development of sociology at the University of Chicago. The Chicago "school" was founded by Robert Ezra Park who had studied under Simmel. Park's essay, "The City: Suggestions for Investigation of Human Behavior in the Urban Environment," provided the agenda for generations of sociologists. Another central work in the Chicago tradition was Louis Wirth's 1938 article, "Urbanism as a Way of Life." The city, Wirth wrote, is "characterized by secondary rather than primary contacts. The contacts of the city may indeed be face to face, but they are nevertheless impersonal, superficial, transitory, and segmental . . . . Whereas the individual gains, on the one hand, a certain degree of emancipation or freedom from the personal and emotional controls of intimate groups, he loses, on the other hand, the spontaneous self-expression, the morale, and the sense of participation that comes with living in an integrated society. This constitutes essentially the state of *anomie*, or the social void, to which Durkheim alludes" (p. 153).

Writing almost a half-century after Wirth, sociologist Barrett A. Lee and his coworkers—in an important challenge to those claims—commented on this tradition as follows: "Few themes in the literature of the social sciences have commanded more sustained attention than that of the decline of community . . . . In its basic version, the thesis exhibits a decidedly antiurban bias, stressing the invidious contrast between the integrated small-town resident and the disaffiliated city dweller" (pp. 1161–1162). Those sociologists do not appear to have had any clear political direction. Their work was value-neutral. It was pointing to what they took as a basic fact about modern societies without proposing any specific remedies.

Later in the twentieth century, a new version of the mass society theory made its appearance. This may be termed the *left variant*. All three versions of the theory, right, neutral, and left, agree on "the basics," on the underlying root causes of the modern condition, all agreeing on the "decline of community." But the right and left differ sharply in their portraits of the rulers, of the elites, the upper classes, or the bourgeoisie. In the rightist version, the rulers face a serious threat from below, from the demagogues and their mass followings. Their control is said to be very tenuous. In the left version, the rulers are portrayed as skillful controllers of the society. The key to their successful domination is to be found in their adept use of the mass media.

The bourgeoisie, the ruling class, or its executive agency, the "power elite," is said to control the mass media of communication, the press, magazines, motion pictures, radio, and television, using them for their purposes. News and commentary, much of it, is said to be self-serving. It is essentially ideological, material designed to justify and defend "the status quo." The entertainment provided is diversionary in character, intended to distract people from their real problems. Advertising in the media serves the same purposes—distraction, creation of artificial needs, and provision of false solutions. The bourgeoisie, it is said, owns and controls "the media." With their vast resources, they are able to hire specialists of all kinds, market researchers, psychologists, and so forth, to aid in this manipulative effort. The near-helpless audience (as ever, atomized, powerless, and anxious) is psychologically disposed to accept the "nostrums" provided.

Elements of this position appeared in the writings of the Italian Marxist, Antonio Gramsci, with his concept of ideological hegemony. Some writers in the "Frankfurt school," most notably Herbert Marcuse, also argued this position. It appeared also in the work of C. Wright Mills, in his influential book, *The Power Elite*. Many others have offered variants of this position.

The left mass society theory provided a third "revision" of the Marxist framework, that is, after those of Bernstein and Lenin. It is the third major attempt to explain the absence of the proletarian revolution. Marx and Engels assigned no great importance to the mass media. They occasionally referred to items in the "bourgeois" press, adding sardonic comments about its "paid lackeys." But newspaper reports were treated as of little importance. They could not stop or reverse the "wheel of history." But in this third revision, "the bourgeoisie" had found the means to halt the "inevitable" course. The controllers of the media were able to penetrate the minds of "the masses" and could determine the content of their outlooks. The masses were said to be drugged or, to use a favored term, they were "narcotized."

In the 1950s, in the Eisenhower era, the mass media were unambiguously affirmative about "society" and its major institutions. Families were portrayed as wholesome and happy; the nation's leaders, at all levels, were honorable and upstanding. It was this "affirmative" content that gave rise to the argument of the media as manipulative, as distracting. In the late 1960s, media content changed dramatically. Programs now adopted elements of the mass society portrait, dwelling on themes of social dissolution. Families, neighborhoods, and cities were now "falling apart." Many exposés, in books, magazines, motion pictures, and television, in the news and in "investigative reports," told tales of cunning manipulation. Unlike the right and left versions of the mass society theory, these critics do not appear to have any clear political program. They appear, rather, to be driven by an interest in "exposure." No evident plan, directive, or call for action seems to be involved. Studies indicate that most of the participants are modern-day liberals, not socialists or Marxists.

The mass society theory has had a peculiar episodic history, a coming-and-going in popularity. It had a wave of popularity in the 1940s when Karl Mannheim, Emil Lederer, Hannah Arendt, and Sigmund Neumann, all German exile-scholars, attempted to explain the major events of the age. A sociologist, William Kornhauser presented an empirically based synthesis in 1959, but this effort, on balance, had little impact. In the 1960s, the wave of "left" mass society theorizing appeared, beginning with the influential work of Herbert Marcuse. In 1970, Charles Reich's *The Greening of America* appeared, a book destined to have, for several years, an enormous influence. It provided a depiction of the nation that was entirely within the mass society framework: "America is

one vast, terrifying anti-community. The great organizations to which most people give their working day, and the apartments and suburbs to which they return at night are equally places of loneliness and isolation. Modern living has obliterated place, locality, and neighborhood" (p. 7).

Few research-oriented social scientists have given the mass society theory much credence in the last couple of decades, this for a very good reason: virtually all the major claims of the theory have been controverted by an overwhelming body of evidence (Campbell et al. 1976; Campbell 1981; Fischer 1981; Fischer 1984; Hamilton and Wright 1986).

The mass society portrait is mistaken on all key points. Most migration is collective; it is serial, chain migration, in which people move with or follow other people, family and friends, from their home communities. Most migration involves short-distance moves; most migrants are never very far from their "roots." Cities do grow through the addition of migrants; but they also grow through annexation, a process that does not disturb established social ties. The typical mass society account, moreover, is truncated, providing an incomplete narrative. The "lonely and isolated" migrants to the city supposedly remain that way for the rest of their lives. Those lonely people presumably have no capacity for friendship; they are unable to get together with others to overcome their powerlessness, and so forth.

Many academics in other fields, however, continue to give the theory considerable credence. It is a favorite of specialists in the literary sciences, of those in the humanities. The theory, as noted, is also a favorite of journalists, of social affairs commentators, of writers, dramatists, and poets.

This paradoxical result requires some explanation. The literature dealing with "the human condition" has a distinctive bifurcated character. The work produced by research-oriented scholars ordinarily has a very limited audience, most of it appearing in limited-circulation journals for small groups of specialists. Those specialists rarely attempt to bring their findings to the attention of larger audiences. Attempts to correct misinformation conveyed by the mass media are also infrequent. The producers of mass media content show an opposite neglect: they rarely contact academic specialists to inquire about the lessons found in the latest research.

Those who argue and defend mass society claims, on the whole, have an enormous audience. Writing in 1956, Daniel Bell, the noted sociologist, stated that apart from Marxism, the mass society theory was probably the most influential social theory in the Western world. Four decades years later, the conclusion is still valid. The intellectual productions based on this theory reach millions of susceptible members of the upper and upper-middle classes, most especially those referred to as the "intelligentsia."

The mass society theory proves well-nigh indestructible. It continues to have wide and enthusiastic support in some circles regardless of any and all countering evidence. Some people know the relevant evidence but engage in various "theory-saving" efforts, essentially ad hoc dismissals of fact. Some people, of course, simply do not know the available evidence, because of the compartmentalization of academia. Some academics do not make the effort required to find out what is happening elsewhere. Some others appear to be indifferent to evidence.

REFERENCES

Bell, Daniel 1961 "America as a Mass Society: A Critique." *End of Ideology: On the Exhaustion of Political Ideas in the Fifties.* New York: Collier.

Campbell, Angus, Philip E. Converse, and Willard L. Rodgers 1976 *The Quality of American Life: Perceptions, Evaluations, and Satisfactions.* New York: Russell Sage Foundation.

—— 1981 *The Sense of Well-Being in America: Recent Patterns and Trends.* New York: McGraw-Hill.

Fischer, Claude S. 1981 *To Dwell Among Friends: Personal Networks in Town and City.* Chicago: University of Chicago Press.

—— 1984 *The Urban Experience,* 2nd ed. San Diego, Calif.: Harcourt Brace Jovanovich.

Giner, Salvador 1976 *Mass Society.* London: Martin Robertson.

Halebsky, Sandor 1976 *Mass Society and Political Conflict: Toward a Reconstruction of Theory.* Cambridge, England: Cambridge University Press.

Hamilton, Richard F. forthcoming "Mass Society, Pluralism, Bureaucracy: Explication, Critique, and Assessment." Westport, Conn.: Praeger.

——, and James D. Wright 1986 *The State of the Masses.* New York: Aldine.

Jones, J. R. 1966 "England." In Hans Rogger and Eugen Weber, eds., *The European Right: A Historical Profile.* Berkeley, Calif.: University of California Press.

Kornhauser, William 1959 *The Politics of Mass Society.* Glencoe: Free Press.

Lee, Barrett A., R. S. Oropesa, Barbara J. Metch, and Avery M. Guest 1984 "Testing the Decline-of-Community Thesis: Neighborhood Organizations in Seattle, 1929 and 1979." *American Journal of Sociology* 89:1161–1188.

Nisbet, Robert A. (1953) 1962 *The Quest for Community: A Study in the Ethics of Order and Freedom,* New York: Oxford University Press. Reissued as *Community and Power.* New York: Oxford University Press.

Reich, Charles 1970 *The Greening of America.* New York: Random House.

Sennett, Richard, ed. 1969 *Classic Essays on the Culture of Cities.* New York: Appleton-Century-Crofts.

RICHARD F. HAMILTON

MATE SELECTION THEORIES

Social scientists who study the family have long been interested in the question "Who marries whom?" On one level, the study of mate selection is conducted from the perspective of family as a social institution. Emphasis is placed on the customs that regulate choice of mates. A counterperspective views the family as an association. This perspective centers instead on the couple and attempts to understand the process of marital dyad formation. Both of these perspectives generate an abundance of knowledge concerning mate selection. Beginning primarily in the 1920s, theoretical and empirical work in the area of mate selection has made great advances in answering the fundamental question "Who marries whom?"

INSTITUTIONAL PERSPECTIVES ON MATE SELECTION

The purview of anthropologists has centered on kinship structures as they relate to mate selection in arranged marriage systems. Sociological inquiry that sees the family as a social institution in the context of the larger society focuses instead on the evolution of courtship systems as societies modernize. In this respect, it is important to note the contributions of scholars such as Bernard Murstein (1974, 1976) who have pointed out the importance of cultural and historical effects on courtship systems that lead to marriage.

Historical evidence suggests that, as a society modernizes, changes in the courtship system reflect a movement toward autonomous courtship systems. Thus, parentally arranged marriages diminish in industrialized cultures, since arranged marriages are found in societies in which strong extended kinship ties exist or in which the marriage has great significance for the family and community in terms of resources or status allocation. As societies modernize, arranged marriages are supplanted by an autonomous courtship system in which free choice of mate is the preferred form. These autonomous courtship systems are also referred to as "love" marriages, since the prerequisite for selection of a mate has shifted from the need to consolidate economic resources to that of individual choice based on love. Of course, family sociologists are quick to point out that the term "love marriage" is somewhat of a misnomer, since many other factors operate in the mate selection process.

Family social scientists have tried to understand the human mate selection process by using a variety of data sources and theoretical perspectives. The most global or macro approaches have made use of vital statistics such as census data or marriage license applications to study the factors that predict mate selection. Attention has been placed on social and cultural background characteristics such as age, social class, race, religion, and educational level.

THEORY BEHIND THE MARRIAGE MARKET

Before considering individual background characteristics and interpersonal dynamics of the mate selection process, it is important to note the increasing attention given to the marriage market and the marriage squeeze. The term "marriage market" refers to the underlying assumption that we make choices about dating and marriage partners in a kind of free-market situation. Bargaining and exchange take place in contemporary selection processes, and these exchanges are based on common cultural understandings about the value of the units of exchange. The basis for partner selection plays out in a market situation that is influenced by common cultural values regarding individual resources, such as socioeconomic status, physical attractiveness, and earning potential. Numerous studies have concluded that gender roles play a significant part in the marriage market exchange process, with men trading their status and economic power for women's attractiveness and domestic skills. But changes in contemporary gender roles suggest that as women gain an economic viability of their own, they are less likely to seek marriage partners (Waite and Spitze 1981). Thus, the marriage market and the units of exchange are not constant but subject to substantial variation in terms of structure and selection criteria.

The premise that marital partners are selected in a rational choice process is further extended in the study of the effects of the marriage squeeze. The "marriage squeeze" refers to the gender imbalance that is reflected in the ratio of unmarried, available women to men. In theory, when a shortage of women occurs in society, marriage and monogamy are valued. But when there are greater numbers of women, marriage as an institution and monogamy itself take on lesser importance. Similarly, when women outnumber men, their gender roles are thought to be less traditional in form (Guttentag and Secord 1983).

The marriage squeeze has important effects for theoretical consideration, especially in studying the lower rates of marriage among African-American women in today's society. Due to a shortage of African-American men, coupled with greater expectations on the part of African-American women of finding mates with economic resources (Bulcroft and Bulcroft 1993), the interplay between the marriage squeeze and motivational factors to marry suggest that future research needs to disentangle the individual and structural antecedents in mate selection. These studies also point to the complexity of mate selection processes as they take place within both the social structure and cultural gender role ideologies.

The marriage squeeze is further exacerbated by the marriage gradient, which is the tendency for women to marry men of higher status. In general, the trend has been for people to marry within the same socioeconomic status and cultural background. But men have tended to marry women slightly below them in age and education (Bernard 1982). The marriage gradient puts high-status women at a disadvantage in the marriage market by limiting the number of potential partners. Recent changes in the educational status of women, however, suggest that these norms of mate selection are shifting. As this shift occurs, one can speculate that the importance of individual characteristics such as physical attractiveness, romantic love, and interpersonal communication will increasingly come to play important roles in the mate selection process in postmodern society (Beck and Beck-Gersheim 1995; Schoen and Wooldredge 1989).

Norms of endogamy require that people marry those belonging to the same group. Concomitantly, exogamous marriages are unions that take place outside certain groups. Again, changes in social structures, ethnic affiliations, and mobility patterns have dramatically affected the modern marriage market. More specifically, exogamy takes place when marriage occurs outside the family unit or across the genders. Taboos and laws regulating within-family marriage (i.e., marriages considered to be incestuous that occur between brother and sister, mother and son, etc.) and marriage to same-sex partners are examples of the principle of endogamy. Recent attempts have been made to legally recognize same-sex marriages, thus suggesting that norms of endogamy are tractable and subject to changes in the overall values structure of a society or social group.

In addition to endogamy and exogamy, the marriage market is further defined by norms of homogamy and heterogamy. Mate selection is considered to be homogenous when a partner is selected with similar individual or group characteristics. When these characteristics differ, heterogamy is evidenced. The norm of homogamy continues to be strong in American society today, but considerable evidence suggests we are in a period of change regarding social attitudes and behaviors with regard to interracial and interfaith unions.

Recent data suggest that the number of interracial marriages for African-Americans has increased from 2.6 percent in 1970 to 12.1 percent in 1993 (Besharov and Sullivan 1996). But African-American mate selection operates along lines of endogamy to a larger degree than do the mate selection processes of Asian-American, Native American, or other nonwhite groups. Nearly one-half of all Asian-Americans marry non-Asians (Takagi 1994) and over half of all Native-Americans marry non–Native Americans (Yellowbird and Snipp 1994).

Similarly, rates of interfaith marriage have increased. For example, only 6 percent of Jews chose to marry non-Jewish partners in the 1960s. Today nearly 40 percent of Jews marry non-Jewish partners (Mindel et al. 1988).

The background characteristics of age and socioeconomic status also demonstrate norms of endogamy. The Cinderella story is more of a fantasy than a reality, and self-help books with titles such as *How to Marry a Rich Man (Woman)* have little basis for success.

The conditions of postmodern society are shaping mate selection patterns as they relate to endogamy and homogamy. The likelihood of marrying across social class, ethnic, and religious boundaries is strongly affected by how homogeneous (similar) the population is (Blau et al. 1982). In large cities, where the opportunity structures are more heterogeneous (diverse), rates of intermarriage are higher, while in small rural communities that demonstrate homogeneous populations, the norm of endogamy is even more pronounced.

Again, the complex interplay between the marriage market and individual motives and preferences is highlighted. The extent to which marriage outside one's social group is the result of changing preferences and attitudes or largely the result of shifting opportunity structures, known as marriage market conditions, is not clear at this time (Surra 1990).

The factors that operate in the selection process of a mate also function in conjunction with opportunity structures that affect the potential for social interaction. The evidence suggests that propinquity is an important factor in determining who marries whom. Thus, those who live geographically proximate to each other are more likely to meet and marry. Early work by James Bossard (1932) shows that at the time of the marriage license application, about 25 percent of all couples live within two city blocks of each other.

Bossard's Law, derived from his empirical findings, states "the proportion of marriages decreases steadily and markedly as the distance between the consenting parties increases." Or, put more simply, "Cupid's wings are best suited for short flights." Of course, current American society has changed since the time Bossard studied mate selection patterns in Philadelphia, and there is a tendency to think that as society becomes more mobile propinquity plays less of a role in the choice of a mate. Propinquitous mate selection does not mean nonmobility, however. It is simply the case that the influence of propinquity shifts as the individual geographically shifts. Thus, one is likely to marry someone who is currently near than someone previously propinquitous. The overriding effect of propinquity is that people of similar backgrounds will meet and marry, since residential homogamy remains a dominant feature of American society. However, changing marriage patterns, such as delaying age of first marriage, will impact the strength of propinquity in the mate selection process by expanding the opportunity structures and breaking down homogenous marriage markets.

One interesting area of research that often goes overlooked in discussions of the correlates of mate selection concerns homogamy of physical attractiveness. Based on the equity theory of physical attractiveness, one would expect that persons who are similar in physical attractiveness levels would marry. Many experimental designs have been conducted to test the effects of physical attractiveness on attraction to a potential dating partner. In general, the experimental conditions have yielded the findings that the more highly attractive individuals are the most desired as dating partners. But studies of couples actually involved in selecting a mate or who are already married support the notion that individuals who are similar in attractiveness marry on their own level. Thus, while attractiveness is a socially valued characteristic in choice of a mate, the norms of social exchange dictate that we select a partner who is similar in attractiveness and is thus attainable. It is only when other highly valued factors such as wealth, wit, or intelligence compensate for deficits in attractiveness that inequity of physical attractiveness in mate selection might occur.

In review, theories of mate selection are more often applied to the study of personality characteristics or process orientations than to marriage market conditions. It is important to note, however, that the basic assumption is that the marriage market operates in a social exchange framework. Men and women make selections under relative conditions of supply and demand with units of exchange. The market is further shaped by cultural norms such as endogamy and homogamy that can further restrict or expand the pool of eligibles.

NEED COMPLEMENTARITY

While earlier work on the correlates of mate selection focused on homogamy of background characteristics, the work of Robert Winch (1958) set the stage for further investigation into the hypothesis that "opposites attract." That is, persons of dissimilar values or personality traits would marry. While value theorists speculated that similarity of values and personality would lead to great affiliation and propensity to marry, Winch posited that persons select mates whose personality traits are complementary (opposite) to their own. Inherent in Winch's theoretical work is the notion that certain specific trait combinations will be gratifying to the individuals involved. For example, a submissive person would find it gratifying or reciprocal to interact with a mate who had a dominant personality. Winch developed twelve such paired complementary personality traits, such as dominant-submissive and nurturant-receptive, for empirical testing using a very small sample of recently married couples. In Winch's work, as well as the work of others, the notion that complementarity of traits was the basis for marriage was not supported by the data.

Although empirical support for need complementarity is lacking, the concept remains viable in the study of mate selection. The appeal of the concept rests in its psychological origins, as work prior to Winch's focused primarily on structural and normative influences in mate selection. The work of Winch set the stage for research commencing in the 1960s that began to examine the processes of mate selection on the dyadic level.

PROCESS THEORIES OF MATE SELECTION

The process of selecting a mate received considerable attention beginning in the 1970s. The basic form these theories take follows the "filter theory"

of Alan Kerckoff and Keith Davis (1962). Kerckoff and Davis found empirical support that individuals, having met through the channels of propinquity and endogamy, proceed through a series of stages or steps in the development of the relationship. According to their theory, social status variables such as social class and race operate early on in the relationship to bring people together. The next stage involved the consensus of values, during which time the couple determines the degree of similarity in their value orientations. Couples who share similar values are likely to continue to the third stage, need complementarity. However, the data collected by Kerckoff and Davis offered only weak support for need complementarity as part of the process of mate selection.

Development of process theories of mate selection continued into the 1970s and is exemplified in the work of Ira Reiss (1960), Bernard Murstein (1970), Robert Lewis (1973), and R. Centers (1975). While these theoretical perspectives differ in terms of the order and nature of the stages, they have much in common. Melding these theories of mate selection, the following assumptions can be made concerning the stages of dyad formation that lead to marriage:

1. There are predictable trajectories or stages of dyadic interaction that lead to marriage.

2. The social and cultural background of a couple provides the context for the interpersonal processes.

3. Value similarity leads to rapport in communication, self-disclosure, and the development of trust.

4. Attraction and interaction depend on the exchange value of the assets and liabilities that the individuals bring to the relationship.

5. Conditional factors such as age, gender, or marital history may influence the order or duration of the stages, or the probability that the relationship will end in marriage.

All the studies of the mate selection process have struggled with methodological difficulties. Most studies have relied on small, volunteer samples of couples. Most have used college-age, never-married couples. Finally, most studies have made extensive use of retrospection in assessing the process of dyad formation rather than collecting longitudinal data. These methodological difficulties may, in part, account for the recent decline in the number of studies examining the process of mate selection.

Furthermore, these stages may or may not result in marriage, but the primary focus of the research is on relationships that endure or terminate in marriage. Therefore, relatively little is known about the mate selection process as it pertains to rejection of a potential mate or how such terminations of relationships affect subsequent mate selection processes.

More current research has begun to shift away from antecedents that lead to legal marriage and turn instead to disentangling the trajectory of relationship development over the life course. More attention will turn to the formation and development of interpersonal relationships that may move through stages of romance, cohabitation, friendship, marriage, divorce, and so forth. Emphasis on relationship quality and durability, gender role negotiations, commitment processes, and romantic love have recently taken on increased importance in social science studies of mate selection (Surra and Hughes 1997; Houts et al. 1996; Surra 1990).

Many of the theories have also overlooked the influence of peer groups and family members in the mate selection process. The theoretical and empirical inquiry that has paid attention to peer and kin influences is restricted to studies of dating. Unfortunately, studies of dating and studies of mate selection have not been sufficiently integrated to provide the field with adequate data concerning the interrelationships between dating and mate selection processes.

Yet another area of research that has the potential for contribution to further understanding of the mate selection process is studies of romantic love. Process theories of mate selection seldom examine love as the basis, or even as a stage, in the development of a heterosexual relationship. While there is a large body of empirical and theoretical work on romantic love, conceptually the studies of love have been treated as quite distinct from the research on mate selection. Contrary to popular opinion, the relationship between love and marriage is not well understood.

FUTURE DIRECTIONS

As the family system changes in American society, so too the direction of research on mate selection shifts. As more couples delay first marriage, examination of courtship cohabitation becomes more salient. Future studies of courtship cohabitation will most likely examine the association between increasing rates of cohabitation and decreasing rates of marriage. On the individual level, the effects of the cohabitation experience on the decision to marry also warrant attention.

Research is just beginning on the mate selection process of remarriage (Bulcroft et al. 1989; Rodgers and Conrad 1986; Spanier and Glick 1980). While some factors that predict first marriage may remain constant in remarriage, such as endogamy and propinquity, other factors may come into play in remarriage. For example, age homogeneity may be less of a factor in remarriage since the pool of eligible mates is impacted by sex ratio imbalance. The exchange relationship in the mate selection process also differs in remarriage, since presence of children, prior marital history, and the economic liabilities of child support and alimony bring new dimensions to considerations of remarriage. Of particular interest are barriers to remarriage in the middle and later years of the life cycle, such that cohabitation or serious dating may offer more long-term rewards to the couple than legal marriage might provide. Thus, the strong profamilial norms that encourage the younger members of society to marry dissipate at mid and later life. Low rates of remarriage for individuals over the age of 50, in part, indicate that societal pressure to marry is greatly reduced.

Last, it has generally been assumed that homogamy of background characteristics leads to similarity of values, shared marital role expectations, rapport, and intimacy in the process of mate selection. But due to changing gender role expectations, this assumption may no longer be valid. As a result, more attention needs to be given to the process of role negotiation as part of the mate selection process.

In summary, studies of mate selection began with understanding the correlates of mate selection. Social scientists began by studying demographic data on homogamy in religion, social class, age, and other factors as these variables related to who married whom. For a brief period in the 1960s through the early 1980s, attention was turned to theories and data that examined the process of mate selection. Current research in the 1990s has not abandoned the study of the correlates and theories of mate selection, but as the nature of the family system changes, researchers have begun to consider that the generalizability of theories and findings may be limited when a researcher is trying to explain mate selection at a point later than young adulthood. Recent studies on the courtship processes of divorced (O'Flaherty and Workman 1988) and later life mate selection (Veevers 1988) point to the future focus of theories and research on mate selection processes.

REFERENCES

Beck, Ulrich, and Elisabeth Beck-Gernsheim 1995 *The Normal Chaos of Love*. Cambridge, Mass.: Blackwell.

Bernard, Jessie 1982 *The Future of Marriage*. New York: Columbia University Press.

Besharov, D., and T. Sullivan 1996 "Welfare-Reform and Marriage." *Public Interest* 125:81–94.

Blau, Peter, Terry Blum, and Joseph Schwartz 1982 "Heterogeneity and Intermarriage." *American Sociological Review* 47:45–62.

Bossard, James 1932 "Residential Propinquity as a Factor in Marriage Selection." *American Journal of Sociology* 38:219–224.

Bulcroft, Kris, Richard Bulcroft, Laurie Hatch, and Edgar F. Borgatta 1989 "Antecedents and Consequences of Remarriage in Later Life." *Research on Aging* 11:82–106.

Bulcroft, Richard, and Kris Bulcroft 1993 "Race Differences in Attitudinal and Motivational Factors in the Decision to Marry." *Journal of Marriage and the Family* 55:338–355.

Centers, Richard 1975 *Sexual Attraction and Love: An Instrumental Theory*. Springfield, Ill.: C. C. Thomas.

Guttentag, M., and P. Secord 1983 *Too Many Women?* Thousand Oaks, Calif.: Sage.

Houts, Renate, Elliot Robins, and Ted Houston 1996 "Compatibility and Development of Premarital Relationships." *Journal of Marriage and the Family* 58:7–20.

Kerckoff, Alan, and Keith Davis 1962 "Value Consensus and Need Complementarity in Mate Selection." *American Sociological Review* 27:295–303.

Lewis, Robert 1973 "A Longitudinal Test of a Developmental Framework for Premarital Dyadic Formation." *Journal of Marriage and the Family* 35:16–27.

Mindel, Charles, Robert Haberstein, and Roosevelt Wright 1988 *Ethnic Families in America: Patterns and Variations*. 3rd ed., New York: Elsevier North Holland.

Murstein, Bernard 1974 *Love, Sex, and Marriage through the Ages*. New York: Springer.

—— 1976 *Who Will Marry Whom? Theories and Research in Marital Choice*. New York: Springer.

O'Flaherty, Kathleen, and Laura E. Workman 1988 "Courtship Behavior of the Remarried." *Journal of Marriage and the Family* 50:499–506.

Reiss, Ira 1960 "Toward a Sociology of the Heterosexual Love Relationship." *Marriage and Family Living* 22:139–145.

Rodgers, Roy, and Linda Conrad 1986 "Courtship for Remarriage: Influences on Family Reorganization after Divorce." *Journal of Marriage and the Family* 48:767–775.

Schoen, Robert, and John Wooldredge 1989 "Marriage Choices in North Carolina and Virginia 1969–71 and 1979–81." *Journal of Marriage and the Family* 51:465–481.

Spanier, Graham, and Paul Glick 1980 "Paths to Remarriage." *Journal of Divorce* 3:283–298.

Surra, Catherine 1990 "Research and Theory on Mate Selection and Premarital Relationships in the 1980s." *Journal of Marriage and the Family* 52:844–856.

——, and Debra Hughes 1997 "Commitment Processes in Accounts of the Development of Premarital Relationships." *Journal of Marriage and the Family* 59:5–21.

Takagi, Diana 1994 "Japanese American Families." In R. L. Taylor, ed., *Minority Families in the United States: A Multicultural Perspective*. Engelwood Cliffs, N.J.: Prentice Hall.

U.S. Bureau of the Census 1986 *Statistical Abstract of the United States*. Washington, D.C.: Government Printing Office.

Veevers, Jean 1988 "The 'Real' Marriage Squeeze: Mate Selection Mortality and the Marriage Gradient." *Sociological Perspectives* 31:169–189.

Waite, L., and G. Spitze 1981 "Young Women's Transition to Marriage." *Demography* 18:681–694.

Winch, Robert 1958 *Mate Selection: A Study of Complementary Needs*. New York: Harper and Row.

Yellowbird, Michael, and C. Matthew Snipp 1994 "American Indian Families." In R. L. Taylor, ed., *Minority Families in the United States: A Multicultural Perspective*. Engelwood Cliffs, N.J.: Prentice Hall.

KRIS BULCROFT

MATERIALISM

Materialism posits the epistemological primacy of matter over ideas, mind, values, spirit, and other incorporeal phenomena. Philosophical perspectives stressing the fundamental importance of physical conditions and needs have grown more elaborate with the increasing differentiation and autonomy of secular knowledge from religion. Materialists oppose magical, religious, and metaphysical explanations of worldly affairs, criticizing their role as mystifications and socioeconomic or political legitimations. The enduring debate over materialism and idealism (which gives primacy to ideas) centers on the two approaches' relative effectiveness as guides to scientific, technical, and sociopolitical practices. In social science, materialism refers to often tacit metatheories, or heuristic devices, which frame distinctive types of research problems, hypotheses, concepts, and theories stressing the causal force of physical realities on sociocultural matters.

Two contrasting threads of the materialist tradition have divergent consequences for the behavioral and social sciences. *Reductionists* posit that phenomena are determined strictly by physical causes. Their view that existential knowledge is a reflection of corporeal conditions denies the autonomy of psychological and sociocultural factors and, thus, suggests that the behavioral and social sciences have no distinct content. *Nonreductionists* hold that psychological and sociocultural phenomena arise from and are dependent upon physical substrata. They also accord "primacy" to physical realities and corporeal impulses, motives, values, representations, and interests, seeing them as basic constraints that "determine," or channel, the direction of human practices. By contrast to reductionists, however, they treat the sociocultural realm as an "emergent," "sui generis," "relatively autonomous" domain having distinct properties, processes, and laws and exerting reciprocal causality with the material realm. Implying interpenetrating sociocultural and material spheres, they include socially constituted entities and processes (e.g., technology and labor) as prime "material" determinants.

Modern materialism is rooted in ancient Greek conceptions of elementary bodies. Atomistic philosophers held that all existing things are composed of indivisible, ultimate objects of the same material in perpetual motion in empty space. They argued that perceptible objects derive from atoms of various sizes and shapes colliding, getting entangled, and forming different combinations, and that sensations arise from atoms passing through the sense organs and impacting on the soul (also composed of atoms). From the start, materialists considered knowledge to be a "subjective" manifestation of "objective" reality, holding that physical realities ultimately determine individual experiences and sociocultural constructions. However, claims about the scope of this determination varied widely with the degree to which the thinker adhered to reductionist or nonreductionist presuppositions.

Atomistic materialism reemerged as a major cultural force during the Renaissance science revolution. Galileo and Newton again portrayed physical reality as ultimate particles moving in empty space, but their distinction between precisely measurable, primary sensory qualities (i.e., length, width, weight, figure) and nonmathematizable secondary qualities (e.g., color, smell, taste, texture) established a sharp boundary between objective and subjective experience and decisive methodological standard for distinguishing science from metaphysical, aesthetic, or sociocultural thought. The capacity of diverse observers, employing the same experimental techniques, to arrive at similar findings supported materialist claims about the primacy of the physical world and certainty of objective knowledge.

The extraordinary success of Newtonian science contributed greatly to an extensive secularization of knowledge that reduced barriers to materialist approaches in human affairs. For example, Hobbes argued that social actions are also effects of matter in motion; material primacy is manifested in the dominant drive for self-preservation, all-pervasive power struggles, and subsequent need for absolute monarchy. Locke's Newtonian theory of mind held that primary sense qualities reflect external objects and that complex ideas merely combine the simple ones received directly from sense experience. However, Descartes' dualistic vision of a materialist physical world and an autonomous mind blessed with innate ideas of divine origin exemplifies the seventeenth century tendency to provide separate grounds for science, which avert direct subversion of religion. The power of the Roman Catholic Church and its censors, who saw materialism as a subversive force, was already inscribed powerfully in the earlier trial and conviction of Galileo and in his concession to dualism. Even Hobbes left space for spiritual realities. The strong subjectivist currents and subject-object dualism in Western philosophy derived from its earlier religious roots and its lack of autonomy in relation to the Church.

Enlightenment thinkers fashioned a new cultural space for free inquiry and autonomous science, subverting the power of religion and paving the way for modern materialism. La Mettrie, D'Holbach, and Diderot held that all experience has material causes. Idealizing Newtonian mechanics, the philosophes believed that naturalistic explanation of all phenomena would demystify religious and metaphysical superstition, limit the rule of the Church and nobility, and animate scientifically guided social reform. Revolutionary advances in eighteenth-century medicine, chemistry, and biology upheld their faith in materially based rationality, disenchantment, and progress. The later social revolutions against the ancien régime, secularization of political power, and gradual rise of liberal democracy favored the spread of materialist thinking in new social domains.

Manifesting Enlightenment culture, Karl Marx set the agenda for modern materialism. Even today's debates about the topic center on different interpretations of his work. Following Feuerbach, Marx charged that religion and its secular, idealist substitutes (e.g., Hegelian philosophy) are "inverted," or "alienated," projections of human capacities and potentialities. As "natural beings," he argued, people must satisfy their needs by appropriating and shaping physical objects. Although he attacked Hegel's speculative history of "spirit," Marx retained his view that people create themselves and their societies through their labor. Young Marx called for a "true" materialism, or a new science of humanity focusing on "social relationships." He wanted to illuminate ideologically obscured forms of socially structured production and exploitation, which, in his view, constitute the "real history" of "corporeal" human beings.

Divergent strains of Marxian materialism—"dialectical materialism" and "historical materialism"—are rooted ultimately in tensions between the political and scientific sides of Marx's and

Engels' works. The terms were coined after Marx's death and codified into a variety of schematic orthodoxies. *Dialectical materialism* is a philosophy of nature developed first by Engels, elaborated by Plekhanov and Lenin, and fashioned by Marxist-Leninists into an eschatology of the communist movement. Serving primarily as a political ideology and metalanguage that justified communist states and insurgencies, it did not have much impact on social science outside the communist regimes and movements. By contrast, *historical materialism*, Marx's main metatheory of social development, has much relevance for sociology. Yet even this approach was stated variously by him, and gave rise to conflicting interpretations. The elder Engels ([1890–1894] 1959, pp. 395–400), who earlier helped Marx frame his theories, berated first-generation "Marxists" for using materialism "as an excuse for *not* studying history," or as a dogmatic Hegelian "lever for construction," instead of as "a guide to study." Accepting partial responsibility for the later vulgar interpretations, he admitted that Marx and he, in the heat of political battle, often spoke with too much certainty. However, he insisted that Marx and he opposed the idea of all-encompassing, mechanistic causality by narrowly conceived economic factors and that their materialism meant nothing more than that "the production and reproduction of real life" is "the *ultimately* determining element in history."

Engels implied a problematic split in Marx's thought. On the one hand, Marx sometimes implied, in Hegelian fashion, progressively unfolding stages of history, animated by relentless technological advance and ever more unified classes rationally taking account of material factors, controlling them, and speeding history to an "inevitable" emancipatory conclusion. Such points were warranties for his political program. On the other hand, the scientific side of Marx's work breaks from teleological thinking. His *historical* materialism stresses empirical inquiry about specific material conditions and practices and their sociocultural consequences among particular groups in finite space and time, and calls for reconstruction of theory and practice in light of the findings. This approach has more affinity for the empirical and secular thrust of the Darwinian revolution than for earlier Enlightenment ideas of progress and science, which implied a new faith or civil religion. After the failed revolutions of 1848 and the rise of the new Napoleonic dictatorship in France, Marx qualified his formerly highly optimistic views about "making history," holding that we do not make it in accord with circumstances or outcomes that we freely choose. This insight was precursory to his mature work on capitalism, which, although retaining certain Hegelian taints, manifested clearly his historical materialism.

Following Adam Smith, Marx held that a specialized division of labor enhances productive powers geometrically. However, by contrast to Smith, he specified that capitalism's exceptional productivity derives expressly from its historically specific forms of complex cooperation, which end the relative isolation of peasants and other independent producers. Marx charged that economists mystify this process by obscuring the fundamental role of labor and portraying capitalist growth as if it were animated by a "fantastic . . . relation between things," rather than by a specific type of "social relation" (Marx [1887] 1967, pp. 71–83). He saw the unequal relationship between capitalists and workers as the "secret" of capitalist accumulation. Treating associated labor and related forms of social organization, extraction, and domination as the decisive "material" forces in human affairs, Marx averted the reductionist physicalism of the early atomists, awkward dualism of the Renaissance thinkers, and mechanistic determinism of the dialectical materialists.

Marx and Engels ([1845–1846] 1964, pp. 31–32) said that the "first premise of all human history" is the production of "the means of subsistence" and a characteristic "*mode of life*." As productive forces are refined, they held, growing surpluses offer provision beyond subsistence and allow certain individuals and strata to be freed from direct production for other activities, including the creation of fresh technical knowledge and new productive forces. Marx and Engels contended that incremental advances in production generate increasingly elaborate socio-cultural differentiation, class structure, and domination and more universal "class struggles" over the productive forces. In their view, material determination in the "last instance" means that socially structured patterns of production, extraction, and disposition of surplus shape social development. A materialist sociology focuses on these processes and their consequences.

The central tenet of historical materialism is that the "base," or "mode of production," determines "superstructure," or "the forms of intercourse." The base is composed of "productive forces," which contribute directly to production for material needs (i.e., natural resources, tools, technical knowledge, labor power, and modes of cooperation), and "property relations," which provide certain "classes" effective control over production and relegate others to direct labor. "Superstructure" is composed of nonproductive types of social intercourse (i.e., noneconomic forms of public organization, private association, and thought), which are determined by and, in turn, maintain, or reproduce, the base.

There is a core technological root to Marx's materialism, but he also implied reciprocal causality between the physical and sociocultural realms. Thus, he was not a reductionist. Although granting productive forces ultimate theoretical primacy, his historical analyses dwelled more on property relations and class dynamics. Moreover, he did not hold that material determination operated with the same intensity throughout society. Rather, he emphasized that its strongest force is exerted in institutions that play a direct role in reproducing the mode of production and that the rest of society and culture has much more autonomy. For example, under capitalism, mainstream public discourses about property rights or free trade are central to ideology, but most music and fiction, as well as Marx's critical writings, bear only the broad imprint of the level and form of productive development. Marx envisioned society as composed of interdependent social structures and cultural forms, implying that each element has a distinct impact on the whole. Yet he still saw the base as the most decisive factor shaping overall society and its internal relations. He treated the productive activities of subordinate producers and surplus extraction by superordinate classes as the most central and obscured processes in social life and the root of the most major institutions, conflicts, and transitions.

In a much-debated argument about the capitalist mode of production, Marx held that the rate of profit would fall under highly mechanized production. He believed that the trend toward automation in heavy industry reduces the proportion of direct laborers to fixed capital, diminishing the ultimate source of capitalist profit and requiring hyperexploitation of remaining workers to pay for vastly increased technical investment. Marx argued that the classes would be compressed into a tiny monopoly stratum of owners and a huge impoverished mass of de-skilled workers and permanently unemployed people. However, he also held that science and technology, having replaced direct labor as the leading productive force, would provide the material basis for proletarian revolution and an emancipated, postcapitalist order (i.e., scientific production and administration, greatly reduced work and material necessity, and uncoerced cooperation). This hopeful scenario about collective agency and planning as replacing blind history, and material determinism as becoming truly "in the last instance," went beyond the scientific thrust of historical materialism and reflected the Hegelian residue in his thought.

By the early twentieth century, pathbreaking ideas about electromagnetic fields, relativity theory, and quantum mechanics relativized space and time, eroded the borders between energy and mass, and fashioned a new relational cosmology that undermined Newtonianism. Similarly, Nietzsche, James, Dewey, Heidegger, and Wittgenstein subverted the foundations of modern Western philosophy. Major social changes accompanied the intellectual shifts. A more complex system of classes and subclasses, new types of workplaces, indirect forms of ownership and control, and state intervention altered the structure of capitalism and blurred the line between base and superstructure. Stalinism; fascism; resurgent irrationalism; and persistent racial, ethnic, gender, and religious splits also cried out for new types of theory. In this climate, Marxists tended to drift toward new types of cultural theory or to embrace dialectical materialism, which remained the official ideology of global communism.

In the 1930s, when sociology was being transformed into a professionally specialized discipline in the United States, Talcott Parsons relegated Marx to the status of a footnote in the history of social theory and gave a strong primacy to values and ideas that turned Marx on his head. Parsons's leading role in post–World War II sociology helped harden mainstream opposition to materialism. Claiming that class was no longer a prime basis of association, a determinant of political and cultural beliefs, or a source of major social conflicts, numerous North American sociologists and many thinkers from other liberal democracies argued that materialism did not come to terms with the nascent "postindustrial society." Although certain critics dissented, most mainstream sociologists dismissed materialism as a crude ideology, or simply ignored the approach.

Materialist themes appeared much more prominently in later 1960s social theory, animated, in part, by New Left attacks on functionalism and positivism. Very influential among European theorists, Lewis Althusser's "structuralist" interpretation of Marx radically revised materialism. However, G. A. Cohen's *Karl Marx's Theory of History* (1978) helped stimulate wider efforts to reconstruct historical materialism (e.g., Anderson 1974a, 1974b; Shaw 1978; McMurtry 1978; Roemer 1982; Bhaskar 1989). Dispensing with overt political facets and overcoming conceptual gaps, the new works were more systematic versions of the original approach. However, they did not have much impact on mainstream sociology.

Materialist theory fell on hard times in a climate where "post-materialist" identity politics were ascendent over labor-centered or class politics, and failed communism and resurgent neoliberalism seemed to doom the socialist "alternative" (Anderson 1983; Antonio 1990). In this climate, a new "cultural sociology" blossomed as part of a broader interdisciplinary turn to "representation" and "discourse." Postmodern arguments about the primacy of culture were often pitched directly against Marxian materialism, which they declared moribund. These new cultural theories tended to shift the focus among "critical sociologists" from "structural determinants" (i.e., production and labor) to "cultural surfaces," especially mass entertainment and other signifiers of mass consumption. Many of these theorists argued that a defining feature of postmodern culture is its increased, or, even, total autonomy from material underpinnings.

Although materialist theory has declined in recent years, historical-comparative and empirical work, manifesting tacit materialism and clear connections to nondoctrinaire forms of Marxism, was well established in North American sociology by the 1980s. It still flourishes among significant subgroups in the discipline. These thinkers do not directly employ the base-superstructure model (which is now associated with dialectical materialism and dogmatic Marxism), but they share historical materialist presuppositions, albeit often fused with other traditions. Recent historical changes are intensifying interest in materialist themes. First, neoliberal globalization and restructuring stimulate heated debates over multinational firms, international finance, socioeconomic dislocations, and related public policy initiatives. Second, the collapse of eastern European communism and global decline of communism raise major questions about socioeconomic reconstruction in postcommunist society and detach materialism from communist politics. Third, new materialist critiques counter claims about the primacy of culture and representation in interdisciplinary theory circles. Historical materialism is a heuristic device that poses problems and hypotheses, and is perhaps best judged on this account. Consider the current "materialist" issues below.

MATERIALIST ANALYSES OF THE NEW PHASE OF CAPITALISM

As in Marx's time, today's materialism arises in a climate of perceived rupture, or the end of the post–World War II socioeconomic system and its distinctive patterns of growth, regulation, and geopolitics. Materialists focus on the shifts in the system of production and their impacts on other aspects of social life, especially on inequality, conflict, and politics.

Globalization and Restructuring. Recent materialist work focuses on the new "flexible" forms of production, network firms, international division of labor, and multinational economic blocs—for example, the North American Free Trade Association (NAFTA) and the European Union (EU). The core debates among these analysts concern the shape, permanence, and consequences of the new global economy and the degree to which it departs from postwar capitalism (i.e., they ask whether a new multinational, or "post-Fordist," phase of capitalism has replaced "Fordism," or simply modified it.) (e.g., Harvey 1989; Harrison 1994; Gordon 1996).

Income and Wealth Inequality. Neoliberal deregulation, free trade, and recommodification of public goods have increased global disparities of wealth, income, jobs, and life chances (Braun 1997; Davis 1992). Inequality is most extreme between the richest and the poorest nations, but it has also grown considerably within societies, including wealthy ones, such as the United States. Materialists debate the scope of economic inequality, its relation to global restructuring, and its consequences.

Class, Labor, and Politics. Materialists also focus on the impact of restructuring and polarizing labor markets on organized labor. For example, they ask: Are new types of unions arising among formerly unorganized low-wage service workers and professional groups? Will transnational labor organizations arise in the emergent economic blocs? Are new fusions of class politics and cultural politics arising?

The State. Materialists raise questions about the impact of capital mobility and new forms of international financial and labor markets on the state's capacity to protect and regulate its various environments and maintain public goods (e.g., health, education, welfare, retirement). They also study the role of the state's police and military arms in the global political economy.

Environmental Issues and Sustainability. Increasing threats of resource depletion, global warming, hazardous waste, and overall environmental destruction, the need for alternative forms of energy and technologies, and the communist regimes' dismal environmental records have stimulated sharp criticism of earlier materialism's "productivism" and inattention to the costs, risks, and limits of growth. They pose questions about sustainable growth and material limits to political aspirations.

Communication and Information Technologies. These industries play a major role in globalization and restructuring and, thus, are a central focus in fresh materialist inquiries.

FOUNDATIONAL ISSUES IN
MATERIALIST THEORY

Although certain thinkers (e.g., Wallerstein 1991; Postone 1993; Wood 1995; Wright 1997) have begun reframing materialism in light of the recent historical changes, more fundamental rethinking

of the tradition is likely, especially in the two broad areas discussed below.

The Role of Technology. This area has long been a central focus of materialism. In the late nineteenth century, Marx held that science and technical knowledge were already becoming the primary productive force, altering fundamentally the capitalist mode of production and materialist dynamics of all preceding epochs. Certain contemporary theorists argue that information and communication technologies are giving rise to an "informational society" (e.g., Poster 1990; Castells 1996). These thinkers raise basic questions about previous ideas of production, property, labor, organization, and other aspects of earlier materialism, which could lead to a new generation of theories framed around a knowledge-driven logic of material development.

Materialism and Politics. The effort to unify theory and practice, and the consequent fusion of science and politics, generate distinct resources (i.e., they provide a "critical" thrust) as well as major sources of tension (i.e., between science and ideology) in Marxian materialism. As "critical theorists," materialists focus on the contradictions between democratic ideology's claims about freedom, equality, abundance, and participation, on the one hand, and actual conditions of capitalist and state socialist societies, on the other. They claim to illuminate the determinate, historical possibilities for progressive social change (i.e., "emancipatory" structural factors, cultural conditions, and social movements), which favor reconstructing modern societies according to revised versions of their own democratic ideals. However, the failure of proletarian revolution and communism have blurred materialist political aims. Some materialists abandon critical theory completely, fashioning a strictly empirical sociology, while others substitute highly generalized ideals of "discursive" or "radical" democracy and cultural politics for socialism. It is hard to predict the fate of critical theory, but increasing inequalities in wealth, polarizing labor markets, and declining social benefits raise major questions about unmet needs and the material bases of inclusive democratic citizenship. The bankruptcy of soviet-style regimes and the erosion of social democracies make materialist political goals an open question, but the consequent loss of certainty undercuts the tradition's dogmatic side and increases chances for theoretical reconstruction and restored vitality.

REFERENCES

Anderson, Perry 1974b *Lineages of the Absolutist State.* London: New Left Books.

—— 1974a *Passages from Antiquity to Feudalism.* London: New Left Books.

—— 1983 *In the Tracks of Historical Materialism.* London: New Left Books.

Antonio, Robert 1990 "The Decline of the Grand Narrative of Emancipatory Modernity: Crisis or Renewal in Neo-Marxian Theory?" In George Ritzer, ed., *Frontiers of Social Theory: The New Syntheses.* New York: Columbia University Press.

Bhaskar, Roy 1989 *Reclaiming Reality.* London: New Left Books.

Braun, Denny 1997 *The Rich Get Richer: The Rise of Income Inequality in the United States and the World,* 2nd ed. Chicago: Nelson-Hall Publishers.

Castells, Manuel 1996 *The Information Age: Economy, Society and Culture: Vol. 1: The Rise of Network Society.* Malden, Mass.: Blackwell.

Cohen, G. A. 1978 *Karl Marx's Theory of History: A Defence.* Princeton, N.J.: Princeton University Press.

Davis, Mike 1992 *City of Quartz: Excavating the Future in Los Angeles.* New York: Vintage Books.

Engels, Friedrich (1890–1894) 1959 "Letters on Historical Materialism." Pp. 395–412 in Lewis S. Feuer, ed., *Karl Marx and Friedrich Engels: Basic Writings on Politics and Philosophy.* Garden City, N.Y.: Anchor Books.

Gordon, David M. 1996 *Fat and Mean: The Corporate Squeeze of Working Americans and the Myth of Managerial "Downsizing."* New York: Free Press.

Harrison, Bennett 1994 *Lean and Mean: The Changing Landscape of Corporate Power in the Age of Flexibility.* New York: Basic Books.

Harvey, David 1989 *The Condition of Postmodernity: An Inquiry into the Origins of Cultural Change.* Cambridge, Mass.: Blackwell.

McMurtry, John 1978 *The Structure of Marx's World-View.* Princeton, N.J.: Princeton University Press.

Marx, Karl (1887) 1967 *Capital: A Critique of Political Economy,* vol. 1. New York: International Publishers.

——, and Frederick Engels (1845–1846) 1964 *The German Ideology.* Moscow: Progress Publishers.

Poster, Mark 1990 *The Mode of Information: Poststructuralism and Social Context.* Chicago: University of Chicago Press.

Postone, Moishe 1993 *Time, Labor, and Social Domination: A Reinterpretation of Marx's Critical Theory.* New York: Cambridge University Press.

Roemer, John E. 1982 *A General Theory of Exploitation and Class.* Cambridge, Mass.: Harvard University Press.

Shaw, William H. 1978 *Marx's Theory of History.* Stanford, Calif.: Stanford University Press.

Wallerstein, Immanuel 1991 *Unthinking Social Science: The Limits of Nineteenth-Century Paradigms.* Cambridge, U.K.: Polity.

Wood, Ellen Meiksins 1995 *Democracy Against Capitalism: Renewing Historical Materialism.* New York: Cambridge University Press.

Wright, Erik Olin 1997 *Class Counts: Comparative Studies in Class Analysis.* New York: Cambridge University Press.

ROBERT J. ANTONIO

MATHEMATICAL SOCIOLOGY

Mathematical sociology means the use of mathematics for formulating sociological theory more precisely than can be done by less formal methods. The term thus refers to an approach to theory construction rather than to a substantive field of research or a methodology of data collection or analysis; it is also not the same as statistical methods, although it is closely related. Mathematical sociology uses a variety of mathematical techniques and applies to a variety of different substantive research fields, both micro and macro.

Theory involves abstraction from and codification of reality; formulation of general principles describing what has been abstracted; and deduction of consequences of those formulations for the sake of understanding, predicting, and possibly controlling that reality. When social phenomena can be described in mathematical terms, the deductive power of mathematics enables more precise and more detailed derivations and predictions based on original premises.

Mathematical expression also enables sociologists to discover that the same abstract forms and processes sometimes describe what seem to be diverse social phenomena. If the same type of formulation describes both the spread of a disease and the adoption of an innovation, then a common type of process is involved and the theorist can search further for what generates that commonality. Ideally, therefore, mathematics provides the basis for very general and powerful integrative theory.

The vigor of mathematical sociology varies widely over the different subfields of sociology. Precise formulation requires precise observations and careful induction of general patterns from those observations. Some sociologists have rejected any attempts to quantify human behavior, either on the grounds that what is important is in principle not subject to precise measurement or from a philosophical unwillingness to consider human behavior to be in any way deterministic. That issue will not be addressed here, but clearly it is much easier to obtain precise information in some areas of inquiry than in others. For example, census data provide reasonably precise counts of many sociological interesting facts, with the consequence that mathematical demography has long flourished.

Mathematics can be thought of as an elegant logic machine. Application of mathematics to any substantive discipline involves careful translation of the substantive ideas into mathematical form, deriving the mathematical consequences, and translating the results back into a substantive interpretation. There are three key aspects to the process: (1) finding a satisfactory way of expressing the substantive ideas in mathematical terms, (2) being able to solve the mathematical puzzle, and (3) eventually being able to compare derivations from the model with data from the substantive application.

The mathematical expression of a substantive theory is called a *model*. Often, models are created with primary emphasis on their being tractable, or readily solved. Some types of models appear frequently in substantive literature because they are widely known, are relatively simple mathematically, and have easy solutions. Basic models and applications can be found in Coleman (1964), Fararo (1973), and Leik and Meeker (1975). Mathematics and sociological theory are discussed in Fararo (1984). A wealth of more complex models can be found in specialized volumes and in periodicals such as the *Journal of Mathematical Sociology*.

Simple models have the advantage of presenting an uncluttered view of the world, although derivations from such models often do not fit observed data very well. When the goal is heuristic, a simple model might be preferable to one that matches more closely the reality being modeled. However, when the goal is accurate prediction and possible control, then more complex models are typically needed.

There are two general questions to be raised in deciding whether developing a mathematical model has been useful. One is whether the mathematics of the model lead to new ideas about how the system being modeled operates. This is purely a theoretical question, concerned with understanding reality better by creating an abstraction of it that enables us to think more clearly about it. The second question concerns how well the model fits that reality, and is a statistical question.

Statistical models are concerned solely with fitting an underlying mathematical model to data from a sample of real-world cases. The underlying model may be complex or simple, but the statistical concerns are whether the sample can be assumed to represent adequately the population from which it was selected and whether the parameter (equation constant) estimates based on that sample can be considered accurate reflections of how the variables of the underlying model are related in that population.

A HISTORY OF RECENT APPROACHES TO FORMAL THEORY

During much of this century, there has been concern in sociology over the relationship between theory and research. Whereas theory was abstract and typically discursive, research increasingly employed statistical methods. The gulf between verbal statements about theoretical relationships and statistical tests of empirical patterns was great. Beginning in midcentury, some sociologists suggested that one way to bridge this gulf is to translate theoretical ideas into mathematics. Proposals for ways that theoretical ideas could be represented mathematically included those by Simon (1957) and several summarized by Berger et al. (1962).

Another approach to more formal presentation of theories that seemed to offer a bridge over the chasm between verbal statements and statistical tests was Zetterberg's concept of axiomatic theory (1965). The popularized result was *axioms* in the form of monotonic propositions ("The greater the X, the greater the Y") and hypotheses derived solely from concatenating (multiplying) the signs of the relationships. For example, the axioms "As A increases, B increases" and "As B increases, C decreases" lead to the hypothesis that "As A increases, C decreases." Standard statistical tests of the deduced hypotheses were presumed to be proper tests of the theory that generated the axioms. The approach was quick, convenient, and readily understood, and did not require expertise in mathematics or statistics. Consequently, it quickly became popular.

Numerous inadequacies with such theories soon became apparent, however (see for example critiques in Hage 1994), and interest turned to *path models* based on earlier work by Wright (1934). Path models assume that empirical measurements coincide exactly with theoretical concepts; that all variables are continuous (or reasonably close to continuous); that all relationships (paths) are bivariate, linear, and causal; that there is no feedback in the system (the recursive assumption); and that all relevant variables have been included in the model (the "closed-system" assumption). The underlying theoretical model is therefore very simplistic but does allow for the introduction of assumptions about multiple causal paths, and for different types of causal relationships including intervening, spurious, modifying, and counteracting.

If the assumptions are reasonable, then the causal effects, or path coefficients, are equal to ordinary multiple regression coefficients. That is, the underlying mathematical model feeds directly into a well-known statistical model, and the tie between theory and research seems well established. Are the assumptions reasonable?

The closed-system assumption, for example, implies that there is no correlation between the prediction errors across the various equations. If error correlations appear, then path coefficient estimates based on the statistical model will be in error, or biased, so the theory will not be tested properly by the statistics. Only two solutions are possible: (1) add more variables or paths to the model or (2) develop a statistical model that can accommodate correlated errors.

The assumption that measurement equals concept poses a different problem whenever various scales or multiple indicators are used to represent a theoretical concept not readily assessed in a simple measure. Traditionally, the statistical model called *factor analysis* has been used to handle this measurement-concept problem, but factor analysis was not traditionally linked to the analysis of theoretical systems.

Recent years have seen very extensive development and elaboration of statistical models for linear systems, and these models address both the correlated error and the measurement-concept problems while allowing departure from recursiveness. They are called *linear structural models* (Joreskog 1970; Hayduk 1987). The underlying mathematical model still said that all variables are continuous and all relationships bivariate, linear, and causal. This development focused entirely on technical statistical questions about bias in parameter estimates. Furthermore, although the theory generally supposed that one variable affects another over time, the data are normally from only one or a very few points of time. From a general theory point of view, the underlying linear model's assumptions, which were imposed for tractability, are highly restrictive.

MOVING BEYOND LINEAR MODELS

Consider the assumption of linearity. If a dynamic process is being modeled, linear relationships will almost always prove faulty. How change in some causal factor induces change in some consequent system property is typically constrained by system limits and is likely to be altered over time through feedback from other system factors.

As a disease like acquired immune deficiency syndrome (AIDS) spreads, for example, the rate at which it spreads depends on how many people are already infected, how many have yet to be infected, and what conditions allow interaction between the not-yet-infecteds and the infecteds. With very few infected the rate of spread is very small because so few cannot quickly infect a very large number of others. As the number of infecteds grows, so does the rate of spread of the disease, because there are more to spread it. On the other hand, if nearly everyone had already been infected, the rate of spread would be small because there would be few left to spread it to. To complicate theoretical matters further, as the disease has generated widespread concern, norms governing sexual contact have begun to change, influencing the probabilities of transmission of the virus. In mathematical terms, the implication is that the rate of change of the proportion infected (i.e., the rate of spread of the disease) is not constant over time, nor is it a constant proportion of change in any variable in the system. In short, the process in inherently nonlinear.

Nonlinear models in mathematics take many forms. If the variables are conceived as continuous over time, and the primary theoretical focus is on how variables change as a consequence of changes in other variables, then the most likely mathematical form is differential equations. The substantive theory is translated into statements about rates of change (Doreian and Hummon 1976). Most diffusion and epidemiology models, like the AIDS problem just noted, use differential equations. So do a number of demography models. Recently some of the numerous differential equations models dealing with topics such as conflict and arms control have been applied to theoretical questions of cooperation and competition in social interaction (e. g., Meeker and Leik 1997).

For relatively simple differential equations models, once the model is developed it is possible to determine the trajectory over time of any of the properties of the system to ascertain under what conditions the covariation of system properties will shift or remain stable, and to ask whether that system will tend toward equilibrium or some other theoretical limit, oscillate in regular patterns, or even "explode."

None of these questions could be asked of a linear model because the mathematics of the linear model leaves nothing about the model itself to be deduced. Only statistical questions can be asked: estimates of the regression coefficients that fit the model to the data and the closeness of that fit. To the extent that sociology addresses questions of process, appropriate theory requires nonlinear models.

What about the assumption of continuous variables? For cross-sectional data, or data from only two or three time points, new techniques of statistical analysis suitable for categorical data have been developed. However, these focus once again on technical statistical problems of bias in estimation of parameters and generally rely on assumptions of linearity. Within mathematical sociology, other approaches exist. If time or time-related variables were to be treated in discrete units, there are at least three different approaches available. For handling dynamic systems without the calculus of differential equations, difference equations are the appropriate form. Huckfeldt and colleagues (1982) provide a convenient overview of this approach.

For extensive time series with relatively few variables, there are Box-Jenkins and related types of models, although these have seen relatively little use in sociology. Because they are closer to statistical models than general theoretical models, they are only mentioned in passing.

Many theories treat systems as represented by discrete states. For example, over a lifetime, an individual is likely to move into and out of several different occupational statuses. Are certain status transitions more likely than others? In simplest form, the implied theoretical model involves a matrix algebra formulation that specifies the probability of moving from each of the states (occupational statuses for this example) to each of the other states. Then the mathematics of matrix algebra allows deduction of a number of system consequences from this "transition matrix." Such a treatment is called a *Markov chain*. An early application by Blumen and colleagues (1955) demonstrated that certain modifications of a Markov chain were needed for the theory to fit the data they had available on occupational transitions. Their work was the initial inspiration for a distinguished string of mathematical models of social mobility. Another classic is by White (1970), who conceptualized mobility of vacant positions as well as of individuals into and out of positions.

Another type of substantive problem that deals with discrete data is the analysis of social networks such as friendship structures. These can be modeled using the mathematics of *graph theory*, the basic concepts of which include *nodes* (or *points*) and *relationships between pairs of nodes* (or *lines*). One of the most vigorous modeling areas in sociology, network analysis has produced a rich and elaborate literature addressing a wealth of substantive issues. Typically, network data consists of whether or not any two cases (nodes in the network) are linked in one or more ways. The resulting data set, then, usually consists of presence or absence of a link of a given type over all pairs of nodes.

Early network analyses concerned friendships, cliques, and rudimentary concepts of structurally based social power. With the introduction of directed graph theory (Harary et al. 1965), random or probabilistic net theory, and block modeling, powerful tools have been developed to approach social structure and its consequences from a network point of view. As those tools emerged, the range of questions addressed via network analysis has greatly expanded. Over the past twenty years, numerous articles in the *Journal of Mathematical Sociology* have dealt with networks. The journal *Social Networks* also publishes work in this area. Overviews and examples can be found in Burt and Minor (1983), and in Wellman and Berkowitz (1988).

Graph theory may be applied to other theoretical issues; for example, a graph-theoretic model developed by Berger and colleagues (1977) helps explain the processes by which people combine information about the various characteristics of themselves and others to form expectations for task performance.

Small group processes have also generated a variety of mathematical formulations. Because observations of groups often generate counts of various types of acts (for example amount of talking by members of a discussion group) that display remarkable empirical regularity, these processes have intrigued model builders since the early 1950's. Recent developments, combining network analyses with Markov chains, include Robinson and Balkwell (1995) and Skvoretz and Fararo (1996).

At the most micro level of sociology, the analysis of individual behavior in social contexts has a long tradition of mathematical models of individual decision making. Recent developments include the satisfaction-balance decision-making models of Gray and Tallman (Gray et al. 1998).

An exciting aspect of these different levels of development is that, increasingly, inquiries into microdynamics based on social exchange theory are working toward formulations compatible with the more general network structural analyses. These joint developments, therefore, promise a much more powerful linking of micro-system dynamics with macro-system structural modeling (Cook 1987; Willer 1987). Recent work on power as a function of the linkages that define the exchange system is an example. The use of mathematics to express formal definitions has enabled researchers to pinpoint where there are theoretical differences, leading to productive debate (Markovsky et al. 1988; Cook and Yamagishi 1992; Friedkin 1993; Bonacich 1998).

There are other examples of work in mathematical sociology involving attempts to develop appropriate mathematical functions to describe a theoretically important concept. One is Jasso's innovative work on models of distributive justice (e.g., 1999). Similarly, affect control theory (e.g., Smith-Lovin and Heise 1988) represents mathematical formulation in an area (symbolic interaction and sociology of emotions) typically considered not subject to such treatment.

One other area of vigorous development deserves attention; the treatment of strings of events that constitute the history of a particular case, process, or situation (Allison 1984; Tuma and Hannan 1984; Heise 1989). Event history analysis has some of its origins in traditional demographers' life tables, but methods and models have experienced a great deal of attention and growth in recent years. If one had lifetime data on job placements, advancements, demotions, and firings (i.e., employment event histories) for a sample of individuals, then event history methods could be used for examining what contributes to differential risks of one of those events occurring, how long someone is likely to be in a given situation ("waiting time" between events), and so forth.

An important recent development is the use of complex computer simulations for developing and exploring mathematically expressed theories. We have noted above the tension between simple models that are mathematically tractable and more complex models that may be more realistic as for example including feedback loops and random processes. Computer simulation is a way of showing what can be derived from the assumptions of a model without an analytic mathematical solution; examples include Macy and Skvoretz (1998), Carley (1997), and Hanneman (1995).

Like many other areas of social and behavioral science, mathematical sociology has been influenced by developments in game theory, from early work by Rapoport (1960) to the more recent idea of evolutionary games introduced by Axelrod (1984) and extensive interest in problems of collective action (Marwell and Oliver 1993). These consider how actions of individuals may produce unintended outcomes because of the logic of their interdependence with actions of others. The related theoretical area of rational choice theory also has a strong mathematical component (Coleman 1990); see also recent issues of the journal *Rationality and Society*.

A notable feature of current work in mathematical sociology is that the development, testing, and refinement of mathematical models is located within substantive research programs. Mathematical formulations appear in mainstream sociology journals and are becoming accepted as one component of continuing programs of research along with development and refinement of theory and collection and analysis of empirical data (several examples can be found in Berger and Zelditch 1993).

One indication of continuing interest in mathematical sociology is the recent formation of the Mathematical Sociology Section of the American Sociological Association. There is also a large amount of work internationally, including in Japan (Kosaka 1995) and in England and Europe (Hegselmann et al. 1996). Mathematical work in sociology is alive and vigorous. It truly does promise a higher level of theoretical precision and integration across the discipline.

(SEE ALSO: *Paradigms and Models*; *Scientific Explanation*)

REFERENCES

Allison, Paul D. 1984 *Event History Analysis: Regression for Longitudinal Event Data*. Beverly Hills, Calif: Sage.

Axelrod, Robert M. 1984 *The Evolution of Cooperation*. New York: Basic Books.

Berger, Joseph, Bernard P. Cohen, J. Laurie Snell, and Morris Zelditch, Jr. 1962 *Types of Formalization in Small Group Research*. Boston: Houghton Mifflin.

——, M. Hamit Fisek, Robert Z. Norman, and Morris Zelditch, Jr. 1977 *Status Characteristics and Social Interaction: An Expectation-States Approach*. New York: Elsevier.

——, and Morris Zelditch, Jr., eds. 1993 *Theoretical Research Programs: Studies in the Growth of Theory*. Stanford, Calif: Stanford University Press.

Blumen, Isadore, Marvin Kogan, and Philip H. McCarthy 1955 *The Industrial Mobility of Labor as a Probability Process*. Ithaca, N.Y.: Cornell University Press.

Bonacich, Phillip 1998 "A Behavioral Foundation for a Structural Theory of Power in Exchange Networks." *Social Psychology Quarterly* 61:185–198.

Burt, Ronald S., and Michael J. Minor 1983 *Applied Network Analysis*. Beverly Hills, Calif.: Sage.

Carley, Kathleen, ed. 1997 *Computational Organizational Theory*. New York: Gordon and Breach (special issue of the *Journal of Mathematical Sociology*).

Coleman, James S. 1964 *Introduction to Mathematical Sociology*. New York: Free Press.

—— 1990 *Foundations of Social Theory*. Cambridge, Mass.: Harvard University Press.

Cook, Karen S., ed. 1987 *Social Exchange Theory*. Newbury Park, Calif.: Sage.

——, and Toshio Yamagishi 1992 "Power in Exchange Networks: a Power-Dependence Formulation." *Social Networks* 14:245–266.

Doreian, Patrick, and Norman P. Hummon 1976 *Modeling Social Processes*. New York: Elsevier.

Fararo, Thomas J. 1973 *Mathematical Sociology*. New York: Wiley.

——, ed. 1984 *Mathematical Ideas and Sociological Theory*. New York: Gordon and Breach (special issue of the *Journal of Mathematical Sociology*).

Friedkin, Noah E. 1993 "An Expected Value Model of Social Exchange Outcomes." Pp. 163–193 in E. J. Lawler, B. Markovsky, K. Heimer, and J. O'Brien, eds., *Advances in Group Processes*, vol. 10. Greenwich, Conn.: JAI Press.

Gray, Louis N., Irving Tallman, Dean H. Judson, and Candan Duran-Aydintug 1998 "Cost-Equalization Applications to Asymmetric Influence Processes." *Social Psychology Quarterly* 61:259–269.

Hage, Jerald, ed. 1994 *Formal Theory in Sociology: Opportunity or Pitfall?* Albany: State University of New York Press.

Hanneman, Robert A., ed. 1995 *Computer Simulations and Sociological Theory*. Greenwich Conn.: JAI (special issue of *Sociological Perspectives*).

Harary, Frank, Robert Z. Norman, and Dorwin Cartwright 1965 *Structural Models*. New York: Wiley.

Hayduk, Leslie A. 1987 *Structural Equation Modeling with LISREL*. Baltimore, Md.: Johns Hopkins University Press.

Hegselmann, Rainer, Ulrich Meuller, and Klaus G. Troitzsch 1996 *Modelling and Simulation in the Social Sciences from the Philosophy of Science Point of View* Dordrecht, The Netherlands: Kluwer Academic.

Heise, David R. 1989 "Modeling Event Structures." *Journal of Mathematical Sociology* 14:139–169.

Huckfeldt, Robert R., C. W. Kohfeld, and Thomas W. Likens 1982 *Dynamic Modeling: An Introduction.* Beverly Hills, Calif.: Sage.

Jasso, Guillermina 1999 "How Much Injustice Is There in the World? Two New Justice Indexes." *American Sociological Review* 64:133–167.

Joreskog, Karl G. 1970 "A General Method for Analysis of Covariance Structures." *Biometrika* 57:239–232.

Kosaka, Kenji, ed. 1995 *Mathematical Sociology in Japan.* New York: Gordon and Breach (special issue of the *Journal of Mathematical Sociology*).

Leik, Robert K., and Barbara F. Meeker 1975 *Mathematical Sociology.* Englewood Cliffs, N.J.: Prentice-Hall.

Macy, Michael W., and John Skvoretz 1998 "The Evolution of Trust and Cooperation between Strangers: A Computational Model." *American Sociological Review* 63:638–660.

Markovsky, Barry, David Willer, and Travis Patton 1988 "Power Relations in Exchange Networks." *American Sociological Review* 53:220–236.

Marwell, Gerald, and Pamela Oliver 1993 *The Critical Mass in Collective Action: A Micro-Social Theory.* Cambridge, England: Cambridge University Press.

Meeker, Barbara F., and Robert K. Leik 1997 "Computer Simulation: an Evolving Component of Theoretical Research Programs." Pp. 47–70 in J. Szmatka, J. Skvoretz, and J. Berger, eds., *Status, Network and Structure: Theory Construction and Theory Development.* Palo Alto, Calif.: Stanford University Press.

Rapoport, Anatol 1960 *Fights, Games, and Debates.* Ann Arbor: University of Michigan Press.

Robinson, Dawn T., and James W. Balkwell 1995 "Density, Transitivity, and Diffuse Status in Task-Oriented Groups." *Social Psychology Quarterly* 58:241–254.

Simon, Herbert A. 1957 *Models of Man: Social and Rational.* New York: Wiley.

Skvoretz, John, and Thomas J. Fararo 1996 "Status and Participation in Task Groups: a Dynamic Network Model." *American Journal of Sociology* 101:1355–1414.

Smith-Lovin, Lynn, and David R. Heise 1988 *Affect Control Theory: Research Advances.* New York: Academic.

Tuma, Nancy B., and Michael T. Hannan 1984 *Social Dynamics: Models and Methods.* New York: Academic.

Wellman, Barry, and S. D. Berkowitz, eds. 1988 *Social Structures: A Network Approach.* New York: Gordon and Breach.

White, Harrison C. 1970 *Chains of Opportunity; System Models of Mobility in Organizations.* Cambridge, Mass.: Harvard University Press.

Willer, David 1987 *Theory and the Experimental Investigation of Social Structures.* New York: Gordon and Breach.

Wright, Sewell 1934 "The Method of Path Coefficients." *Annals of Mathematical Statistics* 5:161–215.

Zetterberg, Hans 1965 *On Theory and Verification in Sociology.* Totowa, N.J.: Bedminster.

BARBARA F. MEEKER
ROBERT K. LEIK

MEASUREMENT

There are many standards that can be used to evaluate the status of a science, and one of the most important is how well variables are measured. The idea of measurement is relatively simple. It is associating numbers with aspects of objects, events, or other entities according to rules, and so measurement has existed for as long as there have been numbers, counting, and concepts of magnitude. In daily living, measurement is encountered in myriad ways. For example, measurement is used in considering time, temperature, distance, and weight. It happens that these concepts and quite a few others are basic to many sciences. The notion of measurement as expressing magnitudes is fundamental, and the observation that *if something exists, it must exist in some quantity* is probably too old to attribute to the proper authority. This notion of quantification is associated with a common dictionary definition of *measurement*: "The extent, capacity, or amount ascertained by measuring."

A concept such as distance may be considered to explore the meaning of measurement. To measure distance, one may turn to a simple example of a straight line drawn between two points on a sheet of paper. There is an origin or beginning point and an end point, and an infinite number of points between the beginning and the end. To measure in a standard way, a unit of distance has to be arbitrarily defined, such as an inch. Then the distance of any straight line can be observed in inches or fractions of inches. For convenience, arbitrary rules can be established for designating number of inches, such as feet, yards, and miles. If another standard is used—say, meters—the relationship between inches and meters is one in which no information is lost in going from one to the other. So, in summary, in the concept of measurement as considered thus far, there are several properties, two of which should be noted particularly: the use of arbitrary standardized units and the assumption of continuous possible points between any two given points. The case would be similar if time, temperature, or weight were used as an example.

There is another property mentioned above, a beginning point, and the notion of the beginning point has to be examined more carefully. In distance, if one measures 1 inch from a beginning point on a straight line, and then measures to a second point 2 inches, one may say that the distance from the beginning point of the second point is twice that of the first point. With temperature, however, there is a problem. If one measures temperature from the point of freezing using the Celsius scale, which sets 0 degrees at the freezing point of water under specified conditions, then one can observe temperatures of 10 degrees and of 20 degrees. It is now proper to say that the second measurement is twice as many degrees from the origin as the first measure, but one cannot say that it is twice the temperature. The reason for this is that the origin that has been chosen is not the origin that is required to make that kind of mathematical statement. For temperature, the origin is a value known as absolute zero, the absence of any heat, a value that is known only theoretically but has been approximated.

This problem is usually understood easily, but it can be made more simple to understand by illustrating how it operates in measuring distance. Suppose a surveyor is measuring distance along a road from A to B to C to D. A is a long distance from B. Arriving at B, the surveyor measures the distance from B to C and finds it is 10 miles, and then the distance from B to D is found to be 20 miles. The surveyor can say that the distance is twice as many miles from B to D as from B to C, but he cannot say that the distance from A to D is twice the distance from A to C, which is the error one

would make if one used the Celsius temperature scale improperly. Measuring from the absolute origin for the purpose of carrying out mathematical operations has become known as *ratio level measurement*.

The idea of "levels of measurement" has been popularized following the formulation by the psychologist S. S. Stevens (1966). Stevens first identifies scales of measurement much as measurement is defined above, and then notes that the type of scale achieved depends upon the basic empirical operations performed. The operations performed are limited by the concrete procedures and by the "peculiarities of the thing being scaled." This leads to the types of scales—nominal, ordinal, interval, and ratio—which are characterized "by the kinds of transformations that leave the 'structure' of the scale undistorted." This "sets limits to the kinds of statistical manipulation that can legitimately be applied to the scaled data."

Nominal scales can be of a type like numbering individuals for identification, which creates a class for each individual. Or there can be classes for placement on the basis of equality within each class with regard to some characteristic of the object. *Ordinal* scales arise from the operation of rank ordering. Stevens expressed the opinion that most of the scales used by psychologists are ordinal, which means that there is a determination of whether objects are greater than or less than each other on characteristics of the object, and thus there is an ordering from smallest to largest. This is a crucial point that is examined below. *Interval* scales (equal-interval scales) are of the type discussed above, like temperature and these are subject to linear transformation with invariance. There are some limitations on the mathematical operations that can be carried out, but in general these limitations do not impede use of most statistical and other operations carried out in science. As noted, when the equal-interval scales have an absolute zero, they are called *ratio* scales. A lucid presentation of the issue of invariance of transformations and the limitations of use of mathematical operations (such as addition, subtraction, multiplication, and division) on interval scales is readily available in Nunnally (1978).

What is important to emphasize is that how the scales are constructed, *as well as how the scales are used*, determines the level of measurement. With regard to ordinal scales, Nunnally makes a concise and precise statement that should be read carefully: "With ordinal scales, none of the fundamental operations of algebra may be applied. In the use of descriptive statistics, it makes no sense to add, subtract, divide, or multiply ranks. Since an ordinal scale is defined entirely in terms of inequalities, only the algebra of inequalities can be used to analyze measures made on such scales" (1978, p. 22). What this means is that if one carries out a set of operations that are described as making an ordinal scale, the moment one adds, subtracts, divides, or multiplies the ranks, one has treated the scale as a particular type of interval scale. Most commonly, the type of scale that is de facto created when ordinal data are subject to ordinary procedures like addition, subtraction, division, and/or multiplication is through the assumption that the difference between ranks are equal, leading to sets like 1, 2, 3, 4, 5, 6, and thus to the treatment for ties such as 1, 2, 4, 4, 4, 6. This is sometimes called a flat distribution with an interval of one unit between each pair of ordered cases. Effectively, this is the same kind of distribution in principle as the use of ordered categories, such as quartiles, deciles, or percentiles, but it is a more restrictively defined distribution of one case per category. To repeat, for emphasis: The use of addition, subtraction, division, and/or multiplication with ordinal data automatically requires assumptions of intervals, and one is no longer at the level of ordinal analysis. *Thus, virtually all statistical procedures based on collected ordered or rank data actually assume a special form of interval data.*

ISSUES ON LEVEL OF MEASUREMENT

A number of issues are associated with the notion of levels of measurement. For example, are all types of measurement included in the concepts of nominal, ordinal, interval, and ratio? What is the impact of using particular statistical procedures when data are not in the form of well-measured interval scales? What kind of measurement appears (epistemologically) appropriate for the social and behavioral sciences?

The last question should probably be examined first. For example, are measures made about attributes of persons nominal, ordinal, or interval?

In general, we cannot think of meaningful variables unless they *at least* imply order, but is order all that one thinks of when one thinks about characteristics of persons? For example, if one thinks of heights, say of all males of a given age, such as 25, does measurement imply ordering them on an interval scale? We know that height is a measure of distance, so we assume the way one should measure this is by using a standard. For purposes of the example here, an interval scale is proposed, and the construction is as follows. The shortest, 25 year-old male (the category defined as 25 years and 0 days to 25 years and 365 days of age) and the tallest are identified. The two persons are placed back to back, front to front, and every other possible way, and the distance between the height of the shortest and the tallest is estimated on a stick. Many estimates are made on the stick, until the spots where agreement begins to show discretely are evident; and so, with whatever error occurs in the process, the locations of beginning and end are indicated on the stick. Now the distance between the beginning and the end is divided into equal intervals, and thus an interval scale has been created. On this scale it is possible to measure every other male who is 25 years old, and the measure can be stated in terms of the number of intervals taller than the shortest person. Note that all possible values can be anticipated, and this is a continuous distribution.

Now if a million persons were so measured, how would they be distributed? Here the answer is on the basis of naive experience, as follows. First, there would be very few people who would be nearly as short as the shortest or as tall as the tallest. Where would one expect to find most persons? In the middle of the distance, or at some place not too far from it. Where would the next greatest number of persons be found? Close to the biggest. With questions of this sort one ends up describing a well-distributed curve, possibly a normal curve or something near it.

It is proper now to make a small diversion before going on with answering the questions about the issues associated with level of measurement. In particular, it should be noted that there are many sources of error in the measurement that has just been described. First, of course, the age variable is specified with limited accuracy. At the limits, it may be difficult to determine exact age because of the way data are recorded. There are differences implied by the fact that where one is born makes a difference in time, and so on. This may seem facetious, but it illustrates how easily sources of error are bypassed without examination. Then it was noted that there were different estimates of the right location for the point of the shortest and the tallest person as marked on the stick. This is an error of observation and recording, and clearly the points selected are taken as mean values. Who are the persons doing the measuring? Does it make a difference if the person measuring is short or tall? These kinds of errors will exist for all persons measured. Further, it was not specified under what conditions the measurements taken or were to be taken. Are the persons barefoot? How are they asked to stand? Are they asked to relax to a normal position or to try to stretch upward? What time of day is used, since the amount of time after getting up from sleep may have an influence? Is the measurement before or after a meal? And so forth.

The point is that there are many sources of error in taking measures, even direct measures of this sort, and one must be alert to the consequences of these errors on what one does with the data collected. Errors of observation are common, and one aspect of this is the limit of the discriminations an observer can make. One type of error that is usually built into the measurement is rounding error, which is based on the estimated need for accuracy. So, for example, heights are rarely measured more accurately than to the half-inch or centimeter, depending on the standard used. There is still the error of classification up or down, by whatever rule is used for rounding, at the decision point between the intervals used for rounding. Rounding usually follows a consistent arbitrary rule, such as "half adjusting," which means keeping the digit value if the next value in the number is 0 to 4 (e.g., 24.456 = 24) or increasing the value of a digit by 1 if the next value is 5 to 9 (e.g., 24.789 = 25). Another common rounding rule is simply to drop numbers (e.g., 24.456 = 24 and 24.789 = 24). It is important to be aware of which rounding rule is being used and what impact it may have on conclusions drawn when the data collected are used.

The use of distribution-free statistics (often called nonparametric statistics) was popularized beginning in the mid-1950s, and quickly came to be erroneously associated with the notion that most of the measurement in the social and behavioral sciences is of an ordinal nature. Actually, the use of the distribution-free statistics was given impetus because some tests, such as the sign test, did not require use of all the information available to do a statistical test of significance of differences. Thus, instead of using a test of differences of means, one could quickly convert the data to plus and minus scores, using some arbitrary rule, and do a "quick-and-dirty" sign test. Then, if one found significant differences, the more refined test could be carried out at one's leisure. Some of the orientation was related to computing time available, which meant time at a mechanical calculator. Similarly, it was well known that if one used a Spearman rank correlation with larger samples, and if one were interested in measuring statistical significance, one would have to make the same assumptions as for the Pearson product moment correlation, but with less efficiency.

However, this early observation about distribution-free statistics suggests that measures can be thought of in another way. Namely, one can think of measures in terms of how much they are degraded (or imperfect) interval measures. This leads to two questions that are proper to consider. First, what kind of measure is implied as appropriate by the concept? And second, how much error is there in how the measure is constructed if one wants to use procedures that imply interval measurement, including addition, subtraction, multiplication, and division?

What kind of measure is implied by the concept? One way of answering this is to go through the following procedure. As an example, consider a personal attribute, such as aggressiveness. Is it possible to conceive of the existence of a least aggressive person and a most aggressive person? Obviously, whether or not such persons can be located, they can be conceived of. Then, is there any reason to think that persons cannot have any and all possible quantities of aggressiveness between the least and the most aggressive persons? Of course not. Thus, what has been described is a continuous distribution, and with the application of a standard unit, it is appropriately an interval scale. *It is improper to think of this variable as intrinsically one that is ordinal because it is continuous. In fact, it is difficult to think of even plausible examples of variables that are intrinsically ordinal.* As Kendall puts it, "the essence of ranking is that the objects shall be orderable, and the totality of values of a continuous variate cannot be ordered in this sense. They can be regarded as constituting a range of values, but between any two different values there is always another value, so that we cannot number them as would be required for ranking purposes" (1948, p. 105). While a few comments were published that attempted to clarify these issues of measurement in the 1960s (Borgatta 1968), most methodologists accepted the mystique of ordinal measurement uncritically.

Often measures of a concept tend to be simple questions with ordered response categories. These do not correspond to ordinal measures in the sense of ordering persons or objects into ranks, but the responses to such questions have been asserted to be ordinal level measurement because of the lack of information about the intervals. So, for example, suppose one is attempting to measure aggressiveness using a question such as "When you are in a group, how much of the time do you try to get your way about what kinds of activities the group should do next?" Answer categories are "never," "rarely," "sometimes," "often," "very often," and "always." Why don't these categories form an interval scale? The incorrect answer usually given is "because if one assumes an interval scale, one doesn't know where the answer categories intersect the interval scale." However, this *does not* create an ordinal scale. It creates an interval scale with unknown error with regard to the spacing of the intervals created by the categories.

Thus, attention is now focused on the second question: How much error is involved in creating interval scales? This question can be answered in several ways. A positive way of answering is by asking how much difference it makes to distort an interval scale. For example, if normally distributed variables (which are assumed as the basis for statistical inference) are transformed to flat distributions, such as percentiles, how much impact does this have on statistical operations that are carried out? The answer is "very little." This property of not affecting results of statistical operations has been called robustness. Suppose a more gross set of transformations is carried out, such as deciles. How much impact does this have on statistical operations? The answer is "not much." However,

when the transformations are to even grosser categories, such as quintiles, quartiles, thirds, or halves, the answer is that because one is throwing away even more information by grouping into fewer categories, the impact is progressively greater. What has been suggested in this example has involved two aspects: the transformation of the shape of the distribution, and the loss of discrimination (or information) by use of progressively fewer categories.

CONSEQUENCES OF USING LESS THAN NORMALLY DISTRIBUTED VARIABLES

If one has normally distributed variables, the distribution can be divided into categories. The interval units usually of interest with normally distributed variables are technically identified as standard deviation units, but other units can be used. When normally distributed variables are reduced to a small number of (gross) categories, substantial loss of discrimination or information occurs. This can be illustrated by doing a systematic exercise, the results of which are reported in Table 1. The data that are used for the exercise are generated from theoretical distributions of random normal variables with a mean of 0 and a standard deviation of 1. In the exercise, one aspect is examining the relationship among normally distributed variables, but the major part of the exercise involves the data in ordered categorical form, much as it is encountered in "real" data. The exercise permits reviewing several aspects associated with knowledge about one's measurement.

As noted, the exercise is based on unit normal variables (mean = 0, standard deviation = 1) that are sampled and thus are subject to the errors of random sampling that one encounters with "real" data. The theoretical underlying model is one that is recommended in practice, specified as follows: (1) A criterion variable is to be predicted, that is, the relationships of some independent (predictor) variables are to be assessed with regard to the criterion variable.

(2.) For each sample in which the relationship of the independent variables is assessed, the theoretical underlying relationship of the independent variables is specified, and thus for the purposes of the exercise is known. For the exercise, four levels of underlying theoretical relationship are product

Median Correlation of Scores with Criterion Variable, Range of 9 Samples (N=150) of Unit Normal Deviates, Additive Scores Based on Four Items with Theoretical Correlations of .8, .6, .4, and .2 with the Criterion Variable in the Population

	XO	XOR	XOA	XOAR	XOB	XOBR	XO^2	XOA^2	XOB^2
SumX.8	.94	.93–.96	.75	.69–.78	.66	.52–.73	.88	.56	.44
SumA.8	.92	.90–.94	.76	.74–.80	.62	.56–.67	.85	.58	.38
SumB.8	.89	.87–.92	.68	.63–.74	.62	.58–.68	.78	.46	.38
SumC.8	.85	.81–.86	.78	.69–.84	.51	.46–.59	.72	.61	.36
SumDL.8	.72	.64–.74	.54	.48–.60	.72	.64–.77	.52	.29	.52
SumDR.8	.71	.64–.76	.55	.49–.58	.26	.23–.30	.50	.30	.07
SumX.6	.84	.78–.88	.65	.56–.75	.57	.49–.71	.71	.42	.32
SumA.6	.82	.77–.85	.66	.60–.71	.58	.48–.62	.67	.44	.34
SumB.6	.79	.70–.81	.62	.55–.65	.51	.43–.60	.62	.38	.26
SumC.6	.74	.70–.79	.65	.56–.70	.48	.40–.54	.55	.42	.23
SumDL.6	.62	.56–.69	.53	.45–.58	.56	.45–.67	.38	.28	.31
SumDR.6	.62	.57–.67	.52	.45–.56	.32	.23–.36	.38	.27	.10
SumX.4	.65	.59–.71	.53	.44–.57	.48	.31–.54	.42	.28	.23
SumA.4	.66	.51–.72	.52	.47–.60	.42	.27–.55	.44	.27	.18
SumB.4	.61	.48–.67	.47	.37–.55	.41	.33–.46	.37	.22	.17
SumC.4	.59	.49–.66	.48	.39–.58	.38	.27–.43	.35	.23	.14
SumDL.4	.45	.32–.52	.39	.30–.47	.33	.15–.51	.20	.15	.11
SumDR.4	.50	.45–.59	.43	.38–.49	.26	.22–.27	.25	.18	.07
SumX.2	.39	.25–.51	.31	.20–.41	.25	.12–.45	.15	.10	.06
SumA.2	.31	.26–.42	.23	.16–.34	.27	.22–.31	.10	.05	.07
SumB.2	.32	.20–.49	.29	.12–.29	.23	.10–.29	.10	.08	.05
SumC.2	.28	.23–.42	.22	.15–.40	.17	.10–.24	.08	.05	.03
SumDL.2	.29	.17–.35	.16	.12–.24	.22	.16–.35	.08	.03	.05
SumDR.2	.24	.19–.37	.20	.04–.31	.17	.07–.30	.06	.04	.03

Table 1

moment correlation coefficients of .8, .6, .4, and .2, between the predictor variables and the criterion variable. This represents different levels of relationship corresponding to magnitudes commonly encountered with "real" social and behavioral data.

(3.) For each sample that is used in the exercise, totally independent distributions are drawn from the theoretical distributions. That is, each sample in the exercise is created independently of all other samples, and in each case the criterion and independent predictor variables are drawn independently within the definition of the theoretical distributions.

(4.) Corresponding to a common model of prediction, assume that the independent variables are of a type that can be used to create scores. Here we will follow a common rule of thumb and use four independent variables to create a *simple additive score*; that is, the values of the four independent variables are simply added together. There are many ways to create scores, but this procedure has

many virtues, including simplicity, and it permits examining some of the consequences of using scores to measure a concept.

(5.) The independent variables are modified to correspond to grouped or categorical data. This is done before adding the variables together to create scores, as this would be the way variables encountered in research with "real" data are usually defined and used. The grouped or categorical independent variables are modified in the following ways:

A. Four groups or categories are created by using three dividing points in the theoretical distribution, −1 standard deviation, the mean of 0, and +1 standard deviation. The values for four variables, now grouped or categorical data, are added to give the score used in the correlation with the criterion variable. Thus, looking at Table 1, the row SumA.8 involves samples in which four independent variables based on data having four categories as defined above, and having an underlying theoretical correlation coefficient for each independent variable to the criterion variable of .8, have been used to create a score. The variables defined by these cutting points correspond to a notion of variables with response categories, say, such as "agree," "probably agree," "probably disagree," and "disagree," and as it happens the responses theoretically are well distributed, roughly 16 percent, 34 percent, 34 percent, and 16 percent.

B. Three groups or categories are created by using two dividing points in the theoretical distribution, -1 and +1, corresponding to a notion of variables with response categories, say, such as "agree," "don't know or neutral," and "disagree," and these are again theoretically well distributed, but in this case the center category is large (about 68 percent of responses). The scores for these samples are identified as SumB.8 for the case of the underlying theoretical distribution of the independent variables having a correlation coefficient with the criterion variable of .8.

C. Two groups or categories are created by using one dividing point at the mean of the theoretical distribution, and this corresponds to variables with response categories such as "agree" and "disagree," or "yes" and "no." Division of a variable at the midpoint of the distribution is usually considered statistically to be the most efficient for dichotomous response categories.

DL. Two groups or categories may be created that are not symmetrical, unlike the case of C above. Here we create two sets of samples, one identified by Sum DL with the cutting point at -1 standard deviation, or the left side of the distribution as it is usually represented. Presumably, when variables are not well distributed, more information is lost in the data collection if the skew is due to the way the question is formulated.

DR. Two groups or categories are created with the skew on the right side of the distribution at +1 standard deviation. SumDR scores are created in parallel to the SumDL scores.

Finally, the rows of SumX are those where scores are computed and no conversion of the variables has been carried out, so the independent variables are drawn from the theoretically formulated unit normal distributions at the level of correlation coefficient between the independent variables and the criterion variable.

In summary, for each sample the predictor score is an additive score based on four variables, each related to the criterion variable in a theoretical distribution at a given level, with the examples in the exercise the levels chosen as product moment correlation coefficients of .8, .6, .4, and .2.

The rationale for the choice of four variables in each score is drawn arbitrarily from the theoretical distribution of reliability coefficients, which, for variables of equal reliability, is a curve of diminishing return with each increment of the number of variables. At four variables a score is usually considered to be at an efficient point, balancing such things as time and effort needed to collect data, independence of variable definitions, and the amount of improvement of reliability expected. Using more variables in the "real" world usually involves using less "good" items progressively from the point of view of content, as well as the diminishing efficiency even if they were equally as good as the first four.

With regard to the criterion variable, the dependent variable to be predicted, we have generated three as follows: First, the variable is drawn from a theoretical unit normal distribution without modification, and this involves correlation coefficients reported in column XO. Second, the dependent variable is drawn from the theoretical distribution dichotomized at the mean of 0, creating a symmetric dichotomous variable (two categories), and this involves correlation coefficients reported in column XOA. Third, the variable is drawn from the theoretical distribution dichotomized at -1 standard deviation, creating an asymmetrical dichotomous variable and this involves correlation coefficients reported in column XOB.

As noted above, we are dealing with generated data from theoretical distributions, so all that is done is subject to sampling error, which permits in a limited way for variation of results to be shown. This is useful in illustrating the variation that occurs simply by random processes in the study of variables. For the exercise there were 648 samples of 150 cases each. The choice of 150 cases was selected for several reasons, convenience in the data set generated being one, but also because 150 cases was, as a rule of thumb, a reasonable number of cases proposed for doing research at an earlier time in the discipline when a Guttman scale was anticipated, and too much "shrinkage" in the subsequent use of the Guttman scale was to be avoided. Shrinkage referred to the experience of finding out that the scale in a subsequent use did not have the same characteristics as in the first (generating) use. The samples are grouped in the six procedures, as noted above, of the full normal data and of five created sets of categories, each with nine repetitions (i.e., samples) carried out to permit examination of distribution of results for each theoretical level of correlation coefficient and for each of the three criterion variable definitions.

A sense of the stability of the relationships involved is provided by using many samples, and *the values that are in columns XO, XOA, and XOB are the median product moment correlation coefficients between a Sum score and a criterion variable.* In the table there are two other sets of columns. XOR, XOAR, and XOBR are the actual range of values for the product moment correlation coefficients between a Sum score and the criterion variable for nine independently drawn samples of 150 cases each. The additional (last three columns) at the right of the table are the squared values of XO, XOA, and XOB, and these values represent the amount of variance that is accounted for by the correlation coefficient.

The table is somewhat complex because it includes a great deal of information. Here we will only review a number of relatively obvious points, but with emphasis. First, note the relationship between SumX.8 and XO, which is .94. Recall that the theoretical correlation coefficient between each independent predictor variable and the criterion variable was defined as .8 in the exercise. Thus, we illustrate rather dramatically the importance of building scores rather than depending on a single predictor variable. The actual improvement in prediction is from a theoretical value of 64 percent of the variance being accounted for by a single predictor variable to the median value of 88 percent of the variance in the median sample of the exercise, an extremely impressive improvement! Examining the correlation coefficient between SumX.6, SumX.4, and SumX.2, it is seen that the

advantage of using scores rather than single items is actually even more dramatic when the relationship between the criterion and the predictor variables is weaker.

Now, examine the relationships between all the Sum variables and XO. It is noted that having the SumA.8 as a well distributed categorical variable lowers the correlation to XO somewhat (.92) compared to the full normal SumX.8 (.94), and, indeed, with SumB.8 and SumC.8 the correlation coefficients are still lower. This illustrates that the more information that is available in the categorical data, the more variance can be predicted for a criterion variable. Note further, that for SumDL.8 and SumDR.8, which are based on dichotomous but skewed variables, the correlation coefficients are still lower. Note that the results for the weaker variables SumX.6 to SumDR.6, for SumX.4 to SumDR.4, and for SumX.2 to SumDR.2 are in general roughly parallel to the results noted, but some irregularity is noted when the relationship between the criterion and the predictor variables is weaker.

The results we have been examining are the median values of nine samples in each case. It is appropriate to look at column XOR and to note that there is quite a bit of variation in the correlation coefficients based on the nine samples of size 150 cases each.

One additional finding needs to be pointed out and emphasized. Compare the correlation coefficients of SumDT.8 and XOB, and of SumDR.8 and XOB. In the former case, the criterion variable and predictor variables are both asymmetric but matched (at the same cutting point), and the median correlation coefficient value is .72. In the latter case they are asymmetric but unmatched, and the median correlation coefficient is .26. This indicates the need to know how cutting points (difficulty levels) of variables can affect the values of correlation coefficients that are encountered.

The reader is urged to examine this table in detail, and it may be useful to keep the table as a guideline for interpreting results. How? If the researcher finds as a result a correlation coefficient of a given size, where does it fit on this table, taking into consideration the characteristics of the criterion variable and the scores based on the predictor variables? Doing this type of examination should help the researcher understand the meaning of a finding. However, this is but one approach to the issues of measurement. The articles in this encyclopedia that are vital for researchers to consider are those on *Reliability*, *Validity*, and *Quasi-Experimental Research Design*. Additionally, measurement issues are discussed in a variety of types of texts, ranging from specialized texts to books on research methods to general statistics books, such as the following: Agresti and Finaly 1997; Babbie 1995; De Vellis 1991; Knoke and Bohrnstedt 1994; Lewis-Beck 1994; Neuman, 1997; and Traub 1994.

OTHER MEASURES

The consideration of measurement thus far has concentrated on interval measurement, with some emphasis on how it can be degraded. There are many other issues that are appropriately considered, including the fact that the concepts advanced by Stevens do not include all types of measures. As the discussion proceeds to some of these, attention should also be given to the notion of nominal scales. Nominal scales can be constructed in many ways, and only a few will be noted here. By way of example, it is possible to create a classification of something being present for objects that is then given a label A. Sometimes a second category is not defined, and then the second category is the default, the thing not being present. Or two categories can be defined, such as male and female. Note that the latter example can also be defined as male and not male, or as female and not female. More complex classifications are illustrated by geographical regions, such as north, west, east, and south, which are arbitrary and follow the pattern of compass directions. Such classifications, to be more meaningful, are quickly refined to reflect more homogeneity in the categories, and sets of categories develop such as Northeast, Middle Atlantic, South, North Central, Southwest, Mountain, Northwest, and Pacific, presumably with the intention of being inclusive (exhaustive) of the total area. These are complex categories that differ with regard to many variables, and so they are not easily ordered.

However, each such set of categories for a nominal scale can be reduced to dichotomies, such as South versus "not South"; these variables are commonly called "dummy variables." This permits analysis of the dummy variable as though it represented a well-distributed variable. In this case, for example, one could think of the arbitrary underlying variable as being "southernness," or whatever underlies the conceptualization of the "South" as being different from the rest of the regions. Similarly, returning to the male versus female variable, the researcher has to consider interpretatively what the variable is supposed to represent. Is it distinctly supposed to be a measure of the two biological categories, or is it supposed to represent the social and cultural distinction that underlies them?

Many, if not most, of the variables that are of interest to social and behavioral science are drawn from the common language, and when these are used analytically, many problems or ambiguities become evident. For example, the use of counts is common in demography, and many of the measures that are familiar are accepted with ease. However, as common a concept as city size is not without problems. A city is a legal definition, and so what is a city in one case may be quite different from a city in another case. For example, some cities are only central locations surrounded by many satellite urban centers and suburbs that are also defined as cities, while other cities may be made up of a major central location and many other satellite urban centers and suburbs. To clarify such circumstances, the demographers may develop other concepts, like Standard Metropolitan Areas (SMAs), but this does not solve the problem completely; some SMAs may be isolated, and others may be contiguous. And when is a city a city? Is the definition one that begins with the smallest city with a population of 2,500 (not even a geographical characteristic), or 10,000 population, or 25,000 population? Is city size really a concept that is to be measured by population numbers or area, or by some concept of degree of urban centralization? Is New York City really one city or several? Or is New York City only part of one city that includes the urban complexes around it? The point that is critical is that definitions have to be fixed in arbitrary ways when concepts are drawn practically from the common language, and social concepts are not necessarily parsimoniously defined by some ideal rules of formulating scientific theory. Pragmatic considerations frequently intervene in how data are collected and what data become available for use.

An additional point is appropriate here: that in demography and in other substantive areas, important measures include *counts* of discrete entities, and these types of measures do not easily fit the Stevens classification of levels of measurement. A discussion of several technical proposals for more exhaustive classifications of types of measures is considered by Duncan (1984).

CONSTRUCTING MEASURES

There are obviously many ways that measures can be constructed. Some have been formalized and diffused, such as Louis Guttman's cumulative scale analysis, so popular that it has come to be known universally as Guttman scaling, a methodological contribution that was associated with a sociologist and had an appeal for many. An early comprehensive coverage of Guttman scaling can be found in Riley and colleagues (1954). The essence of Guttman scaling is that if a series of dichotomous items is assumed to be drawn from the same universe of content, and if they differ in difficulty, then they can be ordered so that they define scale types. For example, if one examines height, questions could be the following: (1) Are you at least five feet tall? (2) Are you at least five and a half feet tall? (3) Are you at least six feet tall? (4) Are you at least six and a half feet tall? Responses to these would logically fall into the following types: a + to indicate yes and a - to indicate a no:

1	2	3	4
+	+	+	+
+	+	+	−
+	+	−	−
+	−	−	−
−	−	−	−

The types represent "perfect" types, that is, responses made without a logical error. The assumption is that within types, people are equivalent. In the actual application of the procedure, some problems are evident, possibly the most obvious being that there are errors because in applying the procedure in studies, content is not as well specified as being in a "universe" as is the example of height; thus there are errors, and

therefore error types. The error types were considered of two kinds: unambiguous, such as - + + +, which in the example above would simply be illogical, a mistake, and could logically be classed as + + + + with "minimum error." The second kind is ambiguous, such as + + - +, which with one (minimum) error could be placed in either type + + - - or type + + + +.

Experience with Guttman scaling revealed a number of problems. First, few scales that appeared "good" could be constructed with more than four or five items because the amount of error with more items would be large. Second, the error would tend to be concentrated in the ambiguous error type. Third, scales constructed on a particular study, especially with common sample sizes of about one hundred cases, would not be as "good" in other studies. There was "shrinkage," or more error, particularly for the more extreme items. The issue of what to do with the placement of ambiguous items was suggested by an alternative analysis (Borgatta and Hays 1952): that the type + + - + was not best placed by minimum error, but should be included with the type + + + - between the two minimum error locations. The reason for this may be grasped intuitively by noting that when two items are close to each other in proportion of positive responses, they are effectively interchangeable, and they are involved in the creation of the ambiguous error type. The common error is for respondents who are at the threshold of decision as to whether to answer positively or negatively, and they are most likely to make errors that create the ambiguous error types.

These observations about Guttman scaling lead to some obvious conclusions. First, the scaling model is actually contrary to common experience, as people are not classed in ordered types in general but presumably are infinitely differentiated even within a type. Second, the model is not productive of highly discriminating classes. Third, and this is possibly the pragmatic reason for doubting the utility of Guttman scaling, if the most appropriate place for locating nonscale or error types of the common ambiguous type is not by minimum error but between the two minimum error types, this is effectively the same as adding the number of positive responses, essentially reducing the procedure to a simple additive score. The remaining virtue of Guttman scaling in the logical placement of unambiguous errors must be balanced against other limitations, such as the requirement that items must be dichotomous, when much more information can be gotten with more detailed categories of response, usually with trivial additional cost in data collection time.

In contrast with Guttman scaling, simple addition of items into sum scores, carried out with an understanding of what is required for good measurement, is probably the most defensible and useful tool. For example, if something is to be measured, and there appear to be a number of relatively independent questions that can be used to ascertain the content, then those questions should be used to develop reliable measures. *Reliability* is measured in many ways, but consistency is the meaning usually intended, particularly internal consistency of the component items, that is, high intercorrelation among the items in a measure. Items can ask for dichotomous answers, but people can make more refined discriminations than simple yeses and nos, so use of multiple (ordered) categories of response increases the efficiency of items.

The question of whether the language as used has sufficient consistency to make refined quantitative discriminations does not appear to have been studied extensively, so a small data collection was carried out to provide the following example. People were asked to evaluate a set of categories with the question "How often does this happen?" The instructions stated: "Put a vertical intersection where you think each category fits on the continuum, and then place the number under it. Categories 1 and 11 are fixed at the extremes for this example. If two categories have the same place, put the numbers one on top of the other. If the categories are out of order, put them in the order you think correct." A continuum was then provided with sixty-six spaces and the external positions of the first and the last indicated as the positions of (1) always and (11) never. The respondents were asked to locate the following remaining nine categories: (2) almost always (3) very often; (4) often; (5) somewhat often; (6) sometimes; (7) seldom; (8) very seldom; (9) hardly ever; and (10) almost never. It is not surprising that average responses on the continuum are well distributed, with percent locations respectively as 9, 15, 27, 36, 48, 65, 75, 86, and 93; the largest standard deviation for placement location is about 11 percent. Exercises with alternative quantitatively oriented

questions and use of a series of six categories from "definitely agree" to "definitely disagree" provide similar evidence of consistency of meaning. In research, fewer than the eleven categories illustrated here usually used, making the task of discrimination easier and faster for respondents. The point of emphasis is that questions can be designed to efficiently provide more information than simple dichotomous answers and thus facilitate construction of reliable scores.

MEASUREMENT IN THE REAL WORLD

Many variations exist on how to collect information in order to build effective measurement instruments. Similarly, there are alternatives on how to build the measuring instruments. Often practical considerations must be taken into account, such as the amount of time available for interviews, restraints placed on what kinds of content can be requested, lack of privacy when collecting the information, and other circumstances.

With the progressive technology of computers and word processors, the reduced dependence of researchers on assistants, clerks, and secretaries has greatly facilitated research data handling and analysis. Some changes, like Computer Assisted Telephone Interviewing (CATI) may be seen as assisting data collection, but in general the data collection aspects of research are still those that require most careful attention and supervision. The design of research, however, still is often an ad hoc procedure with regard to the definition of variables. Variables are often created under the primitive assumption that all one needs to do is say, "The way I am going to measure XXX is by responses to the following question." This is a procedure of dubious worth, since building knowledge about the measurement characteristics of the variables to be used should be in advance of the research, and is essential to the interpretation of findings.

A comment that is commonly encountered is that attempting to be "scientific" and developing a strict design for research with well-developed measures forecloses the possibility of getting a broad picture of what is being observed. The argument is then advanced that attempting to observe and accumulate data in systematic research is not as revealing as observing more informally (qualitatively) and "getting a feel" for what is going on.

Further, when systematic research is carried out, so goes the argument, only limited variables can be assessed instead of "getting the complete picture." This, of course, is the ultimate self-delusion and can be answered directly. If positive findings for the theory do not result from more rigorous, well-designed research, then the speculative generalizations of more casual observation are never going to be any more than that, and giving them worth may be equivalent to creating fictions to substitute for reality. *The fact that attempted systematic empirical research has not produced useful findings does not mean that more intuitive or qualitative approaches are more appropriate.* What it means is that the theory may not be appropriate, or the design of the research may be less than adequate.

Further, this does not mean that there is anything wrong with informal or qualitative research. What it does mean is that there is a priority order in the accumulation of knowledge that says that the informal and qualitative stages may be appropriate to produce theory, which is defined as speculation, about what is being observed, and this may then be tested in more rigorous research. This is the common order of things in the accumulation of scientific knowledge.

If a sociological theory has developed, then it must be stated with a clear specification of the variables involved. One cannot produce a volume on the concept of anomie, for example, and then use the word "anomie" to mean twenty different things. The concept on which one focuses *must* be stated with a clear specification of one meaning, and there are two elements that go into such a definition. The first is to indicate how the concept is to be measured. The second is more commonly neglected, and that is to specify how the concept is differentiated from other concepts, particularly those that are closely related to it in meaning.

The development of well-measured variables in sociology and the social sciences is essential to the advancement of knowledge. Knowledge about how good measurement can be carried out has advanced, particularly in the post–World War II period, but it has not diffused and become sufficiently commonplace in the social science disciplines.

It is difficult to comprehend how substituting no measurement or poor measurement for the best measurement that sociologists can devise can produce better or more accurate knowledge. Examples of the untenable position have possibly decreased over time, but they still occur. Note for example: "Focus on quantitative methods rewards *reliable* (i.e., repeatable) methods. Reliability is a valuable asset, but it is only one facet of the value of the study. In most studies, reliability is purchased at the price of lessened attention to theory, validity, relevance. etc." (Scheff 1991). Quite the contrary, concern with measurement and quantification is concern with theory, validity, and relevance!

Finally, it is worth emphasizing two rules of thumb for sociologists concerned with research, whether they are at the point of designing research or interpreting the findings of a research that has been reported. First, check on how the variables are specified and ask whether they are measured well. This requires that specific questions be answered: Are the variables reliable? How does one know they are reliable? Second, are the variables valid? That is, do they measure what they are supposed to measure? How does one know they do? If these questions are not answered satisfactorily, then one is dealing with research and knowledge of dubious value.

(SEE ALSO: *Levels of Analysis: Nonparametric Statistics; Reliability, Validity; Quasi-Experimental Research Design*)

REFERENCES

Agresti, Alan, and Barbara Finaly 1997 *Statistical Methods for Social Sciences.* Englewood Cliffs, N. J.: Prentice Hall.

Babbie, Earl 1995 *The Practice of Social Research.* Belmont, Calif.: Wadsworth.

Borgatta, Edgar F. 1968 "My Student, the Purist: A Lament." *Sociological Quarterly* 9:29–34.

——, and David G. Hays 1952 "Some Limitations on the Arbitrary Classifications of Non-Scale Response Patterns in a Guttman Scale." *Public Opinion Quarterly* 16:273–291.

De Vellis, Robert F. 1991 *Scale Development.* Newbury Park, Calif.: Sage.

Duncan, Otis Dudley 1984 *Notes of Social Measurement.* New York: Russell Sage Foundation.

Herzog, Thomas 1997 *Research Methods and Data Analysis in the Social Sciences.* Englewood Cliffs, N.J.: Prentice Hall.

Kendall, Maurice G. 1948 *Rank Correlation Methods.* London: Griffin.

Knoke, David, and George W. Bohrnstedt 1994. *Statistics for Social Data Analysis.* Itasca, Ill.: Peacock.

Lewis-Beck, Michael, ed. 1994 *Basic Measurement.* Beverly Hills, Calif.: Sage.

Neuman, Lawrence W. 1997 *Social Research Methods: Qualitative and Quantitative Approaches.* Boston: Allyn and Bacon.

Nunnally, Jum C. 1978 *Psychometric Theory.* New York: McGraw-Hill.

Riley, Matilda White, John W. Riley, Jr., and Jackson Toby 1954 *Sociological Studies in Scale Analysis.* New Brunswick, N.J.: Rutgers University Press.

Scheff, Thomas J. 1991 "Is There a Bias in *ASR* Article Selection." *Footnotes* 19(2, February):5.

Stevens, S. S., ed. 1966 *Handbook of Experimental Psychology.* New York: John Wiley.

Traub, Ross E. 1994 *Reliability for the Social Sciences.* Beverly Hills, Calif.: Sage.

EDGAR F. BORGATTA
YOSHINORI KAMO

MEASUREMENT INSTRUMENTS

See Factor Analysis; Measurement; Quasi-Experimental Research Designs; Reliability; Survey Research; Validity.

MEASURES OF ASSOCIATION

Long before there were statisticians, folk knowledge was commonly based on statistical associations. When an association was recognized between stomach distress and eating a certain type of berry, that berry was labeled as poisonous and avoided. For millennia, farmers the world over have observed an association between drought and a diminished crop yield. The association between pregnancy and sexual intercourse apparently was not immediately obvious, not simply because of the lag between the two events, but also because the association is far from perfect—that is, pregnancy does not always follow intercourse. Folk knowledge has also been laced with superstitions, commonly based on erroneously believed statistical associations. For example, people have believed that there is an association between breaking a mirror and a long stretch of bad luck, and in many cultures people have believed that there is an association between certain ritual incantations and benevolent intervention by the gods.

Scholarly discussions sometimes focus on whether a given association is actually true or erroneously believed to be true. Is there an association between gender and mathematical ability? Between harsh punishment and a low incidence of crime? Between the size of an organization and the tendency of its employees to experience alienation? In contemporary discussions, questions and conclusions may be expressed in terms of "risk factors." For example, one might seek to find the risk factors associated with dropping out of school, with teen suicide, or with lung cancer. "Risk factors" are features that are associated with these outcomes but that can be discerned prior to the outcome itself. Although a reference to "risk" suggests that the outcome is undesirable, researchers may, of course, explore factors that are associated with positive as well as negative outcomes. For example, one could examine factors associated with appearance in *Who's Who*, with the success of a treatment regimen, or with a positive balance of international trade.

Referring to a "risk factor" entails no claim that the associated factor has an effect on the outcome, whereas a statistical association is sometimes erroneously interpreted as indicating that one variable has an effect on the other. To be sure, an interest in the association between two variables may derive from some hypothesis about an effect. Thus, if it is assumed that retirement has the effect of reducing the likelihood of voting, the implication is that retirement and non-voting should be statistically associated. But the reverse does not hold; that is, the fact that two variables are statistically associated does not, by itself, imply that one of those variables has an effect on the other. For example, if it is true that low attachment to parents encourages involvement in delinquency, it should be true that low attachment and delinquency are statistically associated. But a statistical association between low attachment and delinquency involvement might arise for other reasons as well. If both variables are influenced by a common cause, or if both are manifestations of the same underlying tendency, those variables will be statistically associated with each other, even if there is no effect of one on the other. Finding a statistical association between two variables, even a strong association, does not, in itself, tell the reason for that association. It may result from an effect of one variable on another, or from the influence of a common cause on both variables, or because both variables reflect the same underlying tendency. Furthermore, if the association is transitory, it may appear simply because of an accident or coincidence. Discovering the reason for a statistical association always entails inquiry beyond simply demonstrating that the association is there.

WHY MEASURE ASSOCIATION?

The focus here is on measures of association for categorical variables, with brief attention to measures appropriate for ordered categories. Quantitative variables, exemplified by age and income, describe each case by an amount; that is, they locate each case along a scale that varies from low to high. In contrast, categorical variables, exemplified by gender and religious denomination, entail describing each case by a category; that is, they indicate which of a set of categories best describes the case in question. Such categories need not be ordered. For example, there is no inherent ordering for the categories that represent region. But if the categories (e.g., low, medium, and high income) are ordered, it may be desirable to incorporate order into the analysis. Some measures of association have been designed specifically for ordered categories.

The degree of association between categorical variables may be of interest for a variety of reasons. First, if a weak association is found, we may suspect that it is just a sampling fluke—a peculiarity of the sample in hand that may not be found when other samples are examined. The strength of association provides only a crude indication of whether an association is likely to be found in other samples, and techniques of statistical inference developed specifically for that purpose are preferred, provided the relevant assumptions are met.

Second, a measure of the degree of association may be a useful descriptive device. For example, if the statistical association between region and college attendance is strong, that suggests differential access to higher education by region. Furthermore, historical changes in the degree of association may suggest trends of sociological significance, and a difference in the degree of association across populations may suggest socially important differences between communities or societies. For example, if the occupations of fathers and sons are more closely associated in Italy than in the United States, that suggests higher generational social mobility in the latter than in the former. Considerable caution should be exercised in comparing measures of association for different times or different populations, because such measures may be influenced by a change in the marginal frequencies as well as by a change in the linkage between the variables in question. (See Reynolds 1977)

Third, if a statistical association between two variables arises because of the effect of one variable on the other, the degree of association indicates the relative strength of this one influence as compared to the many other variables that also have such an effect. Unsophisticated observers may assume that a strong association indicates a causal linkage, while a weak association suggests some kind of noncausal linkage. But that would be naïve. The strength of association does not indicate the reason for the association. But *if* an association appears because of a causal link between two variables, the strength of that association provides a rough but useful clue to the relative importance of that particular cause relative to the totality of other causes. For example, income probably influences the tendency to vote Democratic or Republican in the United States, but income is not the only variable affecting the political party favored with a vote. Among other things, voting for one party rather than another is undoubtedly influenced by general political philosophy, by recent legislative actions attributed to the parties, by specific local representatives of the parties, and by the party preferences of friends and neighbors. Such multiple influences on an outcome are typical, and the degree of association between the outcome and just one of the factors that influence it will reflect the relative "weight" of that one factor in comparison to the total effect of many.

Fourth, if a statistical association between two variables arises because both are influenced by a common cause, or because both are manifestations of the same underlying tendency, the degree of association will indicate the relative strength of the common cause or the common tendency, in comparison to the many other factors that influence each of the two variables. Assume, for example, that participation in a rebellious youth subculture influences adolescents to use both alcohol and marijuana. If the resulting association between the two types of substance use is high, this suggests that the common influence of the rebellious youth subculture (and perhaps other common causes) is a relatively strong factor in both. On the other hand, if this association is weak, it suggests that while the rebellious youth subculture may be a common cause, each type of substance use is also heavily influenced by other factors that are not common to both types.

Fifth, the degree of association indicates the utility of associated factors ("risk factors") as predictors, and hence the utility of such factors in focusing social action. Assume, for example, that living in a one-parent home is statistically associated with dropping out of high school. If the association between these two variables is weak, knowing which students live in a one-parent home would not be very useful in locating cases on which prevention efforts should be concentrated for maximum effectiveness. On the other hand, if this association is strong, that predictor would be especially helpful in locating cases for special attention and assistance.

In summary, we may be interested in the degree of statistical association between variables because a weak association suggests the possibility that the association is a fluke that will not be replicated, because changes in the degree of association may help discern and describe important social trends or differences between populations, because the degree of association may help determine the relative importance of one variable that influences an outcome in comparison to all other influences, because the degree of association may reflect the degree to which two variables have a common cause, and because the degree of association will indicate the utility of associated factors in predicting an outcome of interest.

MEASURING THE DEGREE OF ASSOCIATION

The degree of statistical association between two variables is most readily assessed if, for a suitable set of cases, the relevant information is tallied in a cross-classification table. Table 1 displays such a

College Attendence by Race in a Sample of 20-Year-Olds in Centerville, 1998 (Hypothetical Data)

ATTENDING COLLEGE?	WHITE	BLACK	ASIAN-AMERICAN	TOTAL
Yes	400	60	80	540
No	300	140	20	460
Total	700	200	100	1,000

Table 1

table. For a contrived sample of young adults, this table shows the number who are and who are not attending college in each of three racial groupings. Hence the two variables represented in this table are (1) race (white, black, Asian-American) and (2) attending college (or not) at a given time. The frequencies in the cells indicate how the cases are jointly distributed over the categories of these two variables. The totals for each row and column (the "marginal frequencies" or simply the "marginals") indicate how the cases are distributed over these two variables separately.

If young adults in all racial groupings were equally likely to be attending college, then there would be no association between these two variables. Indeed, the simplest of all measures of association is just a percentage difference. For example, blacks in this set of cases were unlikely to be attending college (i.e., 30 percent were enrolled), while Asian-Americans were very likely to be attending (80 percent). Hence we may say that the percentage attending college in the three racial groupings represented in this table ranges from 30 percent to 80 percent, a difference of 50 percentage points. In this table, with three columns, more than one percentage difference could be cited, and the one alluded to above is simply the most extreme of the three comparisons that could be made between racial groupings. Generally speaking, a percentage difference provides a good description of the degree of association only in a table with exactly two rows and two columns. Even so, citing a percentage difference is a common way of describing the degree of statistical association.

Leaving aside the difference between percentages, most measures of association follow one of two master formulas, and a third way of assessing association provides the basis for analyzing several variables simultaneously. The oldest of these master formulas is based on the amount of departure from statistical independence, normed so that the measure will range from 0 (when the two variables are statistically independent and hence not associated at all) to 1.0 or something approaching 1.0 (when the cross-classification table exhibits the maximum possible departure from statistical independence). The several measures based on this master formula differ from each other primarily in the way the departure from statistical independence is normed to yield a range from 0 to 1.

The second master formula is based on the *improvement* in predictive accuracy that can be achieved by a "prediction rule" that uses one variable to predict the other, as compared to the predictive accuracy achieved from knowledge of the marginal distribution alone. The several measures based on this master formula differ from each other in the nature of the "prediction rule" and also in what is predicted (e.g., the category of each case, or which of a pair of cases will be higher). When such a measure is 0 there is no improvement in predictive accuracy when one variable is predicted from another. As the improvement in predictive accuracy increases, these measures of association will increase in absolute value up to a maximum of 1, which indicates prediction with no errors at all.

A third important way of assessing association, used primarily when multiple variables are analyzed, is based on the difference in *odds*. In Table 1, the odds that an Asian-American is attending college are "4 to 1"; that is, 80 are in college and 20 are not. If such odds were identical for each column, there would be no association, and the ratio of the odds in one column to the odds in another would be 1.0. If such ratios differ from 1.0 (in either direction), there is some association. An analysis of association based on *odds ratios* (and more specifically on the logarithm of odds ratios) is now commonly referred to as a *loglinear analysis*. This mode of analysis is not discussed in detail here.

Departure from Statistical Independence. The traditional definition of statistical independence is expressed in terms of the probability of events; that is, events A and B are statistically independent if, and only if:

$$P(A/B) = P(A) \qquad (1)$$

"$P(A)$" may be read as the probability that event A occurs. This probability is usually estimated empirically by looking at the proportion of all relevant events (A plus not-A) that are A. Referring to Table 1, if event A means attending college, then the probability of event A is estimated by the proportion of all relevant cases that are attending college. In Table 1, this is .54 (i.e., 540 were attending out of the table total of 1,000).

"$P(A|B)$" may be read as the conditional probability that event A occurs, given that event B occurs, or, more briefly "the probability of A given B." This conditional probability is usually estimated in a manner parallel to the estimation of $P(A)$ described above, except that the relevant cases are limited to those in which event B occurs. Referring to Table 1 again, if event A means attending college and event B refers to being classified as Asian-American, then $P(A|B)$ = .80 (i.e., 80 are attending college among the 100 who are Asian-American).

As indicated above, the traditional language of probability refers to "events," whereas the traditional language of association refers to "variables." But it should be evident that if "events" vary in being A or not-A, then we have a "variable." The difference between the language used in referring to the probability of "events" and the language used in referring to a statistical association between "variables" need not be a source of confusion, since one language can be translated into the other.

If we take as given the "marginal frequencies" in a cross-classification table (i.e., the totals for each row and each column), then we can readily determine the probability of any event represented by a category in the table; that is, we can determine $P(A)$. Since $P(A|B)$ = $P(A)$ if statistical independence holds, we can say what $P(A|B)$ *would be* for any A and B in the table if statistical independence held. Otherwise stated, if the marginal frequencies remain fixed, we can say what frequency would be *expected* in each cell if statistical independence held. Referring again to Table 1 and assuming the marginal frequencies remain fixed as shown, if statistical independence held in the table, then 54 percent of those in each racial grouping would be attending college. This is because, if statistical independence holds, then $P(A)$ (i.e., .54) must equal $P(A|B)$ for all B (i.e., the proportion enrolled in each of the columns). Hence, if statistical independence held, we would have 378 whites in college (i.e., 54 percent of the 700 whites in the table), 108 blacks in college (i.e., 54 percent of the 200 blacks in the table), and 54 Asian-Americans in college (i.e., 54 percent of the 100 Asian-Americans in the table.) Evidently, the number *not* enrolled in each racial grouping could be obtained in a similar way (i.e., 46 percent of each column total), or by subtraction (e.g., 700 whites minus 378 whites enrolled leaves 322 whites not attending college). Hence, the frequencies that would be "expected" for each cell if statistical independence held can be calculated, not just for Table 1 but for any cross-classification table.

If the "expected" frequencies for each cell are very similar to the "observed" frequencies, then the departure from statistical independence is slight. But if the "expected" frequencies differ greatly from the corresponding "observed" frequencies, then the table displays a large departure from statistical independence. When the departure from statistical independence reaches its maximum, an ideally normed measure of association should then indicate an association of 1.0.

A quantity called *chi square* is conventionally used to reflect the degree of departure from statistical independence in a cross-classification table. Chi square was originally devised as a statistic to be used in tests against the null hypothesis; it was not designed to serve as a measure of association for a cross-classification table and hence it does not range between 0 and 1.0. Furthermore, it is not well suited to serve as a measure of association because it is heavily influenced by the total number of cases and by the number of rows and columns in the cross-classification table. Even so, calculating chi square constitutes the first step in calculating measures of association based on departure from statistical independence. For a cross-classification table, this statistic will be zero when the observed frequencies are identical to the frequencies that would be expected if statistical independence held, and chi square will be progressively larger as the discrepancy between observed and expected frequencies increases. As indicated below, in the calculation of chi square, the differences between the frequencies observed and the

frequencies expected if statistical independence held are squared and weighted by the reciprocal of the expected frequency. This means, for example, that a discrepancy of 3 will be more heavily weighted when the expected frequency is 5 than when the expected frequency is 50. These operations are succinctly represented in the following formula for chi square:

$$\chi^2 = \Sum \frac{(Oi - E_i)^2}{E_i} \qquad (2)$$

where χ^2 = chi square

Σ is the instruction to sum the quantity that follows over all cells

O_i = the frequency observed in the ith cell

E_i = the frequency expected in the ith cell if statistical independence holds

To illustrate equation (2), consider Table 2, which shows (1) the observed frequency (O) for each cell as previously shown in Table 1; (2) the frequency expected (E) for each cell if statistical independence held (*in italics*), and, (3) for each cell, the squared difference between observed and expected frequencies, divided by the expected frequency (in bold type). When the quantities in bold type are summed over the six cells—in accord with the instruction in equation 2—we obtain a chi square of 76.3. There are various ways to norm chi square to create a measure of association, although no way of norming chi square is ideal since the maximum possible value will not be 1.0 under some commonly occurring conditions.

The first measure of association based on chi square was Pearson's *Coefficient of Contingency* (C), which is defined as follows:

$$C = \sqrt{\frac{\chi^2}{\chi^2 + N}} \qquad (3)$$

This measure can never reach 1.0, although its maximum possible value approaches 1.0 as the number of rows and columns in the table increases. For Table 1, $C = .27$.

An alternative measure of association based on chi square is Cramer's V, which was developed in an attempt to achieve a more appropriately normed measure of association. V is defined as follows:

$$V = \sqrt{\frac{\chi^2}{(N)[\text{Min}\,(r-1,\,c-1]}} \qquad (4)$$

The instruction in the denominator is to multiply the table total (N) by whichever is smaller: the number of rows minus 1 or the number of columns minus 1 (i.e., the "Min," or minimum, of the two quantities in parentheses). In Table 1, the minimum of the two quantities is $r - 1 = 1$, and the denominator thus becomes N. Hence, for Table 1, $V = .28$.

While this measure *can* reach an upper limit of 1.0 under certain conditions, it cannot be 1.0 in some tables. In Table 1, for example, if *all* of the 540 persons attending college were white, and all blacks and Asian-Americans were not in college, chi square would reach a value of approximately 503 (and no other distribution that preserves the marginals would yield a larger chi square). This maximum possible departure from statistical independence (given the marginal frequencies) yields a V of .71.

In the special case of a cross-classification table with two rows and two columns (a "2 × 2 table") V becomes phi (Φ), where

$$\Phi = \sqrt{\frac{\chi^2}{N}} \qquad (5)$$

The maximum possible value of phi in a given table is 1.0 if and only if the distribution over the two row categories is identical to the distribution over the two column categories. For example, if the cases in the two row categories are divided, with 70 percent in one and 30 percent in the other, the maximum value of phi will be 1.0 if and only if the cases in the two column categories are also divided, with 70 percent in one and 30 percent in

College Attendance by Race: Observed Frequencies (from Table 1), Expected Frequencies Assuming Statistical Independence (in Italic), and $(O-E)^2/E$ for Each Cell (in Bold Type)

ATTENDING COLLEGE?	WHITE	BLACK	ASIAN-AMERICAN	TOTAL
Yes	400	60	80	540
	378	*108*	*54*	
	1.3	**21.3**	**12.5**	
No	300	140	20	460
	322	*92*	*46*	
	1.5	**25.0**	**14.7**	
Total	700	200	100	1,000

$\chi^2 = 1.3 + 21.3 + 12.5 + 1.5 + 25.0 + 14.7 + 76.3$

$C = 0.27$

$V = 0.28$

Table 2

the other. Some consider measures of association based on chi square to be flawed because commonly encountered marginals may imply that the association cannot possibly reach 1.0, even if the observed frequencies display the maximum possible departure from statistical independence, given the marginal frequencies. But one may also consider this feature appropriate because, if the degree of statistical association in a cross-classification table were perfect, the marginal distributions would not be disparate in a way that would limit the maximum value of the measure.

A more nagging concern about measures of association based on the departure from statistical independence is the ambiguity of their meaning. One can, of course, use such measures to say that one association is very weak (i.e., close to zero) and that another is relatively strong (i.e., far from zero and perhaps close to the maximum possible value, given the marginals), but "weak" and "strong" are relatively crude descriptors. The measures of association based on chi square may also be used in making comparisons. Thus, if a researcher wished to compare the degree of association in two populations, C or V could be compared for the two populations to determine whether the association was approximately the same in both and, if not, in which population the association was stronger. But there is no clear interpretation that can be attached to a coefficient of contingency of precisely .32, or a Cramer's *V* of exactly .47.

Relative Reduction in Prediction Error. We shift now to measures of association that reflect the relative reduction in prediction error. Since such measures indicate the proportion by which prediction errors are reduced by shifting from one prediction rule to another, we follow common practice and refer to them as *proportional reduction in error* (PRE) measures. Every PRE measure has a precise interpretation, and sometimes it is not only precise but also clear and straightforward. On the other hand, the PRE interpretation of some measures may seem strained and rather far removed from the common sense way of thinking about the prediction of one variable from another.

The basic elements of a PRE measure of association are:

1. a specification of what is to be predicted, and a corresponding definition of prediction error. For example, we might say that what is to be predicted is the row category into which each case falls, and a corresponding definition of prediction error would be that a case falls in a row category other than that predicted. Referring again to Table 1, if we are predicting whether a given case is attending college or not, a corresponding definition of prediction error would be that our predicted category (attending or not) is not the same as the observed category for that case.

2. a rule for predicting either the row variable or the column variable in a cross-classification table from knowledge of the marginal distribution of that variable alone. We will refer to the prediction error when applying this rule as E_1. For example, if what is to be predicted is as specified above (i.e., the row category into which each case falls), the rule for predicting the row variable from knowledge of its marginal distribution might be to predict the modal category for every case. This is not the only possible prediction rule but it is a reasonable one (and there is no rule based only on the marginals that would have higher predictive accuracy). Applying this rule to Table

1, we would predict "attending college" (the modal category) for every case. We would then be wrong in 460 cases out of the 1,000 cases in the table, that is, each of the 460 cases not attending college would be a prediction error, since we predicted attending college for every case. Hence, in this illustration $E_1 = 460$.

3. A rule for predicting the same variable as in step (2) from knowledge of the joint distribution of both variables. We will refer to the prediction error when applying this rule as E_2. For example, continuing with the specifications in steps (1) and (2) above, we specify that we will predict the row category for each case by taking the modal category for each column. Thus, in Table 1, we would predict "attending college" for all whites (the modal category for whites), "not attending college" for all blacks (the modal category for blacks), and "attending college" for Asian-Americans. The prediction errors are then 300 for whites (i.e., the 300 not attending college, since we predicted attending for all whites), 60 for blacks (i.e., the 60 attending college, since we predicted nonattending for all blacks), and 20 for Asian-Americans, for a total of 380 prediction errors. Thus, in this illustration $E_2 = 380$.

4. The calculation of the proportion by which prediction errors are reduced by shifting from the rule in step (2) to the rule in step (3), that is, the calculation of the proportional reduction in error. This is calculated by:

$$\text{PRE} = \frac{E_1 - E_2}{E_1} \tag{6}$$

The numerator in this calculation is the amount by which error is reduced. Dividing this amount by the starting error indicates what proportion of the possible reduction in prediction error has actually been achieved. Utilizing the error calculations above, we can compute the proportional reduction in error.

(7)

$$\text{PRE} = \frac{460 - 380}{460} = \frac{80}{460} = .174$$

This calculation indicates that we achieve a 17.4 percent reduction in prediction error by shifting from predicting the row category that is the marginal mode for all cases to predicting the column-specific modal category for all cases in a given column.

The PRE measure of association with prediction rules based on modal categories (illustrated above) is undoubtedly the simplest of the many PRE measures that have been devised. This measure is called lambda (λ), and for a given cross-classification table there are two lambdas. One of these focuses on predicting the row variable (λ_r), and the other focuses on predicting the variable that is represented in columns (λ_c). In the illustration above, we computed λ_r; that is, we were predicting college attendance, which is represented in rows. Shifting to λ_c (i.e., making the column variable the predicted variable), we find that the proportional reduction in error is 0. This outcome is evident from the fact that the modal column for the table ("White") is also the modal column for each row. Thus, the prediction errors based on the marginals sum to 300 (i.e., the total who are not "white") and the prediction errors based on row-specific modal categories also sum to 300, indicating no reduction in prediction error. Thus, the proportional reduction in prediction error (as measured by lambda) is not necessarily the same for predicting the row variable as for predicting the column variable.

An alternative PRE measure for a cross-classification table is provided by Goodman and Kruskal's tau measures (τ_r and τ_c) (1954). These measures are based on prediction rules that entail distributing predictions so as to recreate the observed distributions instead of concentrating all predictions in the modal category. In doing so, there is an expected number of misclassified cases (prediction errors), and these expected numbers are used in calculating the proportional reduction in error. In Table 1, $\tau_r = .25$ and $\tau_c = .05$. Although λ_c was found to be zero for Table 1 because the modal column is the same in all rows, τ_c is not zero because the percentage distributions within rows are not identical.

Other PRE measures of association have been developed, and some have been designed specifically for a cross classification of ordered categories (ordinal variables). For example, if people were classified by the highest level of education completed (e.g., into the categories pre–high school, high school graduation, bachelor's degree, higher degree) we would have cases classified into a set of ordered categories and hence an ordinal variable. If the same cases were also classified into three levels of income (high, medium, and low) the result would be a cross classification of two ordinal variables. Although several measures of association for ordinal variables have been devised, the one now most commonly used is probably Goodman and Kruskal's gamma (γ). Gamma is a PRE measure, with a focus on the prediction of order within pairs of cases, with order on one variable being predicted with and without knowledge of the order on the other variable, disregarding pairs in which there is a tie on either variable.

These and other PRE measures of association for cross-classification tables are described and discussed in several statistics texts (See, for example, Blalock 1979; Knoke and Bohrnstedt 1991; Loether and McTavish 1980; Mueller et al. 1977). In some instances, the prediction rules specified for a given PRE measure may closely match the specific application for which a measure of association is sought. More commonly, however, the application will not dictate a specific kind of prediction rule. The preferred measure should then be the one that seems likely to be most sensitive to the issues at stake in the research problem. For example, in seeking to identify "risk factors" associated with a relatively rare outcome, or with a very common outcome, one of the tau measures would be more appropriate than one of the lambda measures, because the modal category may be so dominant that lambda is zero in spite of distributional differences that may be of interest.

MEASURES OF ASSOCIATION IN APPLICATION

When the initial measures of association were devised at the beginning of the twentieth century, some regarded them as part of a new mode of inquiry that would replace speculative reasoning and improve research into the linkages between events. At the end of the twentieth century, we now recognize that finding a statistical association between two variables raises more questions than it answers. We now want to know more than the degree to which two variables are statistically associated; we want also to know why they are associated: that is, what processes, what conditions, and what additional variables are entailed in generating the association?

To a limited degree, the measures of association discussed above can be adapted to incorporate more than two variables. For example, the association between two variables can be explored separately for cases that fall within each category of a third variable, a procedure commonly referred to as "elaboration." Alternatively, a new variable consisting of all possible combinations of two predictors can be cross-classified with an outcome variable. But the traditional measures of association are not ideally suited for the task of exploring the reasons for association. Additional variables (e.g., potential sources of spuriousness, variables that mediate the effect of one variable on another, variables that represent the conditions under which an association is weak or strong) need to be incorporated into the analysis to yield an improved understanding of the meaning of an observed association—not just one at a time but several simultaneously. Additional modes of analysis (e.g., loglinear analysis; see Goodman 1970; Knoke and Burke 1980) have been developed to allow an investigator to explore the "interactions" between multiple categorical variables in a way that is roughly analogous to multiple regression analysis for quantitative variables. Computer technology has made such modes of analysis feasible.

The same technology has generated a new use for relatively simple measures of association in exploratory data analysis. It is now possible to describe the association between hundreds or thousands of pairs of variables at very little cost, whereas at an earlier time such exhaustive coverage of possible associations would have been prohibitively expensive. Measures of association provide a quick clue to which of the many associations explored may identify useful "risk factors" or which associations suggest unsuspected linkages worthy of further exploration.

REFERENCES

Blalock, Hubert M., Jr. 1979 *Social Statistics*, 2nd ed. New York: McGraw-Hill.

Bohrnstedt, George W., and David Knoke 1988 *Statistics for Social Data Analysis*, 2nd ed. Itasca, Ill.: F. E. Peacock Publishers.

Costner, Herbert L. 1965 "Criteria for Measures of Association." *American Sociological Review* 30:341–353.

Fienberg, S. E. 1980 *The Analysis of Cross-Classified Categorical Data*. Cambridge, Mass.: MIT Press.

Goodman, Leo A. 1970 "The Multivariate Analysis of Qualitative Data: Interactions among Multiple Classifications." *Journal of the American Statistical Association* 65:226–257.

—— 1984 *The Analysis of Cross-Classified Data Having Ordered Categories*. Cambridge, Mass.: Harvard University Press.

Goodman, Leo A., and William H. Kruskal 1954 "Measures of Association for Cross Classifications." *Journal of the American Statistical Association* 49:732–764.

—— 1959 "Measures of Association for Cross Classifications: II. Further Discussion and References." *Journal of the American Statistical Association* 54:123–163.

—— 1963 "Measures of Association for Cross Classifications: III. Approximate Sampling Theory." *Journal of the American Statistical Association* 58:310–364.

—— 1972 "Measures of Association for Cross Classifications: IV. Simplification of Asymptotic Variances." *Journal of the American Statistical Association* 67:415–421.

Kim, Jae-on 1984 "PRU Measures of Association for Contingency Table Analysis." *Sociological Methods and Research* 13:3–44.

Knoke, David, and George W. Bohrnstedt 1991 *Basic Social Statistics*. Itasca, Ill.: F. E. Peacock Publishers.

Knoke, David, and Peter Burke 1980 *Loglinear Models*. Beverly Hills, Calif.: Sage.

Loether, Herman J., and Donald G. McTavish 1980 *Descriptive Statistics for Sociologists: An Introduction*. Boston: Allyn and Bacon.

Mueller, John H., Karl F. Schuessler, and Herbert L. Costner 1977 *Statistical Reasoning in Sociology*. Boston: Houghton Mifflin.

Reynolds, H. T. 1977 *Analysis of Nominal Data*. Beverly Hills, Calif.: Sage.

HERBERT L. COSTNER

MEDIA

See American Society; Mass Media Research; Popular Culture.

MEDICAL SOCIOLOGY

Over the past several decades medical sociology has become a major subdiscipline of sociology, at the same time assuming an increasingly conspicuous role in health care disciplines such as public health, health care management, nursing, and clinical medicine. The name *medical sociology* garners immediate recognition and legitimacy and, thus, continues to be widely used—for instance, to designate the Medical Sociology Section of the American Sociological Association—even though most scholars in the area concede that the term is narrow and misleading. Many courses and texts, rather than using the term "sociology of medicine," refer instead to the sociology of health, health and health care, health and illness, health and medicine, or health and healing. The study of medicine is only part of the sociological study of health and health care, a broad field ranging from (1) *social epidemiology*, the study of socioeconomic, demographic, and behavioral factors in the etiology of disease and mortality; to (2) studies of the *development and organizational dynamics* of health occupations and professions, hospitals, health maintenance and long-term care organizations, including interorganizational relationships as well as interpersonal behavior, for example, between physician and patient; to (3) the *reactions of societies* to illness, including cultural meanings and normative expectations and, reciprocally, the reactions of individuals in interpreting, negotiating, managing, and socially constructing illness experience; to (4) the *social policies, social movements, politics, and economic conditions* that shape and are shaped by health and disease within single countries, as well as in a comparative, international context.

The rise of contemporary medical sociology can be traced back to the immediate post-World War II period, when science and medicine were dominant cultural forces, fueling a modern optimism that many of society's ills could be eliminated. Several key contributions during the 1950s gave credibility and spurred scholarly interest in the newly developing subfield. Koos's *The Health of Regionville* (1954) and Hollingshead and Redlich's

Social Class and Mental Illness (1958) addressed the connections between social circumstances and health status, and were instrumental in establishing a strong tradition of sociological research focusing on the social determinants of health. The finding that individuals in the lower socioeconomic levels of society experience greater morbidity and mortality has turned out to be one of the most consistent of these patterns. Also during this time, a number of sociology's most prominent theorists turned their attention to health and health care. They approached the topic not because their primary interest was in health care or medicine, but out of a generic interest in authority and the maintenance of social order. Robert Merton, Everett Hughes, and Anselm Strauss all studied professional organizations and socialization during the 1950s, focusing primarily on physicians and the process of medical education (Merton et al. 1957; Becker et al. 1961).

The theoretical work of the 1950s most influential for medical sociology was undoubtedly Talcott Parsons's *The Social System* (1951). In it, Parsons recognized illness as a major threat to the stability and productivity of societies and introduced the "sick role" concept to describe the social regulation of sickness and explain the mechanism through which individuals are induced to return to productive activity. Parsons argued that because sick persons were unable to perform their expected social roles, they were subject to being negatively sanctioned. On the other hand, if they had not intended to become ill and were motivated to get well, then, according to Parsons's analysis, they could claim and be granted temporary exemption without blame from normally expected role responsibilities. Rather than being held accountable for failure to perform, they would be excused as sick. Parsons's work generated enormous sociological interest because of its analysis of illness and medical care in terms of their broad social consequences and because of its focus on the structure and functions of social roles. His work also expanded the theoretical foundations of medical sociology by provoking equally compelling work from contrasting perspectives. Elliot Freidson in *Profession of Medicine* (1970) analyzed the dominance of the medical profession, suggesting that power relations in health care were fundamentally contentious. He saw physicians as rising to dominate health care through a process of struggle with competitors in which they prevailed largely because they gained the support of political institutions, limiting the role of competing occupations. In contrast to the fixed roles in structural-functional theory, Freidson argued that illness definitions and illness behavior were socially constructed through a process of negotiation. The debate over structure and agency represented in these early contributions laid theoretical pathways for subsequent scholarship and solidified medical sociology's ties to some of the central issues of the discipline.

Medical sociology became established in only a few sociology departments during its early years, typically in elite universities. It was not until the 1970s that most graduate departments of sociology began to offer medical sociology. Today, sociology courses on health and medicine can be found in nearly every graduate program in the United States as well as in many other nations, notably the United Kingdom and Germany (Bloom 1986). Research funding to support the growth of medical sociology in many countries has come from government sources. In the 1960s and 1970s, U.S. medical sociology expanded in part because social science research was held in favor by the federal government as well as by influential private foundations. Major funding sources at that time included the National Institute of Mental Health (NIMH) and, later, the National Center for Health Services Research (NCHSR).

It has been argued that the fortunes of medical sociology have shifted in relation to the social-medical environment (Pescosolido and Kronenfeld 1995). Until the 1980s, medical sociology experienced relatively fertile conditions due in part to the fact that the health care system was dominated by professional medicine. Access to health care was the primary health policy concern, while research funding priorities focused on the biomedical and psychosocial aspects of disease, disease prevention, and patient care. This environment encouraged medical sociologists to pursue quantitative research, including surveys, national-level studies, and multivariate statistical models that predicted utilization of health services and the effects of risk factors and other variables. Two particular lines of medical sociology research gained prominence as a result of this focus. The first involved researchers studying utilization patterns for health services. There were two groups, each

using a somewhat different explanatory model. Marshall Becker and his colleagues employed the Health Belief Model, a cognitive framework originated by Rosenstock (1966) and eventually applied in research, to explain a wide variety of preventive and health-related behaviors (Becker and Maiman 1975). Ronald Andersen developed the somewhat broader sociobehavioral model (1995), which included health beliefs but also emphasized economic factors and health needs. The second line of research concerned quantitative studies of social stress. David Mechanic, one of the founders of medical sociology, pioneered sociological research on stress and mental health as early as the 1960s (Mechanic and Volkart 1961). The "stress process" group that emerged in the late 1970s, however, was closer to an interface of psychology and sociology. Using multivariate analyses, they examined the relationships among stress (Aneshensel 1992), social support (Turner and Marino 1994), and coping (Pearlin and Schooler 1978). Much of this research was published in the American Sociological Association's *Journal of Health and Social Behavior*, beginning in the late 1970s and continuing into the present (Thoits 1995).

The social-medical environment in the United States changed dramatically in the 1980s, threatening the autonomy and authority of physicians (Starr 1982). The federal government's increasing role in financing health care (through the Medicare and Medicaid programs) combined with rapidly escalating health care costs and the concern expressed by business, leading to a major federal policy shift. Rather than inequality in access and social factors in illness, public policy attention was now placed on cost control and the cost effectiveness of care. NIMH support for medical sociology was weakened, and soon afterward, the NCHSR became the Agency for Health Care Policy and Research with an agenda of research focused on managed care and evidence-based medicine. Research funding priorities gravitated from the behavioral and social sciences to economics and clinical medicine and epidemiology. No doubt these changes contributed to critical claims in the late 1980s and the 1990s, that medical sociology research had become fragmented.

The significance of health system changes for the profession of medicine became a hotly debated topic among medical sociologists during the

1980s. The controversy was sparked in 1985 with the publication of McKinley and Arch's "Toward the Proletarianization of Physicians," in which the authors argued that historical processes of bureaucratic rationalization were finally reaching medicine, irreversibly eroding the functional autonomy of physicians. This directly challenged Freidson's medical dominance perspective (1970). Also part of the debate was the hypothesis, introduced by Marie Haug (1976), that physicians had lost authority due to the increasing knowledge and medical sophistication of patients. A plethora of articles appeared, identifying and discussing at length various hypothesized changes in medical dominance and authority and culminating, though by no means ending, with a special issue of the *Milbank Quarterly* in 1988.

Much of the early growth of medical sociology can be attributed to scholars located outside sociology departments in medical schools, nursing schools, schools of public health, and health administration programs. These individuals addressed research concerns and questions that were of paramount importance in their respective settings, such as the reasons people engage in health-promoting behavior, define themselves as sick, use health services, and comply with medical treatment. They contributed to medical and health care disciplines by bringing attention to the significance of culture and human interaction in producing the *meaning* of illness and shaping illness-related behavior (Zola 1966; Mechanic 1995). They dispelled the image of the physician as a purely rational scientist. Sociologists also contributed to the development of social epidemiology, mapping the social patterns of disease, and adding social factors to the causal understanding of mortality and chronic diseases (Berkman and Syme 1979). A third group studied hospitals and health care organizations, bringing an organizational sociology perspective into the field of health services research (Flood and Fennell 1995).

Robert Straus, a medical school sociologist, introduced in 1957 what became for many years a popular way of dividing the subfield. Sociologists such as those described above were designated "sociologists *in* medicine" in contrast to sociologists *of* medicine who were typically based in sociology departments. According to Straus, sociologists *of* medicine used medical settings to address

questions of sociology while sociologists *in* medicine used sociological knowledge to address questions of medicine. Today, the boundaries between those working in health care settings and those in academic departments of sociology are blurred; sociologists in both venues conduct applied research as well as research that contributes to basic sociological theorizing. In fact, it is quite common for medical sociologists to have multiple academic appointments. On the other hand, the distinction remains valid in the pressure to conduct research that reflects the priorities of the dominant group. Medical sociologists in medicine often engage in research shaped by medical issues and a biomedical approach, whereas those in sociology have an easier time posing sociological questions grounded in sociological theory. In its early years, medical sociology was sometimes dismissed by other academic sociologists as "applied" sociology, based on the rather elitist assumption that its research did not contribute to the basic body of knowledge of the discipline and that it lacked a theoretical body of its own. Today, there is greater understanding of the links between basic sociological theory and medical sociology (Gerhardt 1989). Medical sociology concepts such as "medicalization" have added to the broader understanding of social order and social control (Conrad 1992). Medicine and the other health care disciplines recognize sociology as a valuable discipline that can contribute much to the understanding and application of health care. Academic sociology has come to regard the sociology of medicine as a fruitful area of specialization.

It is in their role of social critic that medical sociologists encounter the greatest resistance from mainstream medicine and health care. Critical medical sociology emerged from both Marxist and social constructionist traditions within the discipline (Waitzkin 1989; Brown 1995). Symbolic interactionists and labeling theorists in the 1960s saw that, despite the Parsonian notion of the sick role, many types of illness and disability were responded to socially as forms of deviance. Goffman's concept of stigma (1963) explored the relationship between labeling and identity as a process of managing spoiled identity. One of the most powerful explanatory concepts in medical sociology, stigma has been used for decades to capture the experience of mental illness, alcoholism, physical disability, and many types of chronic illness. Goffman

(1961) and Zola (1972), among others, turned the standard notion of medical care as a service on its head by arguing that medicine functions as an institution of social control. Despite strong microsociological interest in the social construction and social consequences of medical labels (i.e., diagnoses), the professional power of physicians made it exceedingly difficult for sociologists to study these processes until the 1980s. What could be studied, however, using the broader, cultural meaning of social construction, were processes of medicalization. Building on the social control perspective of Zola and others, a number of studies examined the processes through which nonmedical phenomena—such as childbirth, excessive drinking, children's active behavior, and menstrual distress—became medical phenomena, with diagnostic criteria and specific medical treatments.

Bias in medicine and social inequality in health care have been concerns of critical medical sociology as well as of corresponding social movements initiated to improve health care. Gender analyses, especially those from a feminist perspective, offered a critical, alternative perspective on the medical profession (Lorber 1984) and the health care system (Zimmerman and Hill 1999), as did research on the women's health movement (Ruzek 1978; Weisman 1998). This work examined the relationship between cultural ideas about gender, medical knowledge, and gender stratification systems; pointed out that the division of labor in medicine is also a gendered division of labor; and observed that the factors that often make women sick are linked to their social roles and disadvantaged social circumstances. Other critical perspectives were offered by disability researchers (Zola 1982) and by researchers focusing on the health and health care of racial and ethnic minorities (Hill 1992; Williams and Collins 1995).

The critical perspective in medical sociology was fortified by Mishler's (1981) critique of the biomedical model, in which he argued that medicine was itself a culture, based as much on customs, social norms, and values as on scientific fact. Mishler's view of medicine as socially constructed led to a concern with medical discourse analysis (1984) and, for some researchers, to the study of illness narratives. Departing from the political and critical concerns of the 1980s and 1990s, these

scholars have conducted in-depth, qualitative studies of illness experience, incorporating aspects ignored by their predecessors, such as emotions and the body (Charmaz 1991; Weitz 1991). The "postmodern turn" that swept over academic humanities and social science departments in the latter decades of the twentieth century influenced a number of symbolic interactionist and social constructionist medical sociologists. Working at the interface of constructionism and postmodernism, these scholars created new ways to explore the relationship between illness and identity (Frank 1995; Hall 1998).

Reviewing the literature of medical sociology reveals an unusually broad range of topics, theoretical perspectives, and research methodologies. Beyond the contributions reviewed above, medical sociologists are also active in international comparative research studying health systems or specific health care sectors within them. They are involved in health policy research both at the federal and at the local community level; they are studying alternative health care providers and their clients as well as various forms of folk medicine and lay care; and they are doing research on informal caregivers and the process of care work. Even these additions do not exhaust the parameters of the field. Medical sociology has enriched and continues to enrich the discipline of sociology, as well as making unique and valuable contributions to important policy issues and to the needs of health care professionals, managers, and patients.

REFERENCES

Andersen, Ronald 1995 "Revisiting the Behavioral Model and Access to Care: Does It Matter?" *Journal of Health and Social Behavior* 36:1–10.

Aneshensel, Carol S. 1992 "Social Stress: Theory and Research." *Annual Review of Sociology* 18:15–38.

Avison, William R., and R. Jay Turner 1988 "Stressful Life Events and Depressive Symptoms: Disaggregating the Effects of Acute Stressors and Chronic Strains." *Journal of Health and Social Behavior* 29:253–264.

Becker, Howard S., Blanche Geer, Everett C. Hughes, and Anselm Strauss 1961 *Boys in White: Student Culture in Medical School.* Chicago: University of Chicago Press.

Becker, Marshall, and Lois Maiman 1975 "Sociobehavioral Determinants of Compliance with Health and Medical Care Recommendations." *Medical Care* 13:10–24.

Berkman, Lisa, and Leonard Syme 1979 "Social Network, Host Resistance and Mortality: A Nine Year Follow-up Study of Alameda County Residents." *American Journal of Epidemiology* 190:186–204.

Bloom, Samuel W. 1986 "Institutional Trends in Medical Sociology." *Journal of Health and Social Behavior* 27:265–276.

Brown, Phil 1995 "Naming and Framing: The Social Construction of Diagnosis and Illness." *Journal of Health and Social Behavior* (Extra Issue):34–52.

Charmaz, Kathy 1991 *Good Days, Bad Days: The Self in Chronic Illness and Time*. New Brunswick, N.J.: Rutgers University Press.

Conrad, Peter 1992 "Medicalization and Social Control." *Annual Review of Sociology* 18:137–162.

Flood, Ann Barry, and Mary L. Fennell 1995 "Through the Lenses of Organizational Sociology: The Role of Organizational Theory and Research in Conceptualizing and Examining Our Health Care System." *Journal of Health and Social Behavior* (Extra Issue):154–169.

Frank, Arthur 1995 *The Wounded Storyteller: Body, Illness and Ethics*. Chicago: University of Chicago Press.

Freidson, Elliot 1970 *Profession of Medicine*. New York: Dodd, Mead.

Gerhardt, Uta 1989 *Ideas about Illness: An Intellectual and Political History of Medical Sociology*. New York: New York University Press.

Goffman, Erving 1961 *Asylums*. New York: Doubleday.

—— 1963 *Stigma: Notes on the Management of Spoiled Identity*. Englewood Cliffs, N.J.: Prentice Hall.

Hall, Lisa Cox 1998 "Illness, Identity and Survivorship: Modern and Postmodern Breast Cancer Narratives." *Illness, Crisis and Loss* 6:255–274.

Haug, Marie 1976 "The Erosion of Professional Authority: A Cross-Cultural Inquiry in the Case of the Physician." *Milbank Memorial Fund Quarterly* 54:83–106.

Hill, Shirley A. 1992 *Managing Sickle Cell Disease in Low Income Families*. Philadelphia: Temple University Press.

Hollingshead, August B., and Frederick Redlich 1958 *Social Class and Mental Illness*. New York: John Wiley.

Koos, Earl L. 1954 *The Health of Regionville*. New York: Columbia University Press.

Lorber, Judith 1984 *Women Physicians: Careers, Status and Power*. New York: Tavistock.

McKinley, John, and Joan Arches 1985 "Toward the Proletarianization of Physicians." *International Journal of Health Services* 15:161–195.

Mechanic, David 1995 "Sociological Dimensions of Illness Behavior." *Social Science and Medicine* 41:1207–1216.

——, and E. H. Volkart 1961 "Stress, Illness Behavior and The Sick Role." *American Sociological Review* 26:51.

Merton, Robert K., G. G. Reeder, and Patricia Kendall 1957 *The Student Physician*. Cambridge Mass.: Harvard University Press.

Mishler, Elliot G. 1981 "Critical Perspectives on the Biomedical Model." In E. G. Mishler, Lorna R. Amara Singham, Stuart T. Hauser, Ramsay Liem, Samuel D. Osherson, ans Nancy E. Waxler, eds., *Social Contexts of Health, Illness, and Patient Care*. New York: Cambridge University Press.

—— 1984 *The Discourse of Medicine: Dialectics of Medical Interviews*. Norwood, N.J.: Ablex.

Parsons, Talcott 1951 *The Social System*. New York: Free Press.

Pearlin, Leonard I., and Carmi Schooler 1978 "The Structure of Coping." *Journal of Health and Social Behavior* 19:2–21.

Pescosolido, Bernice A., and Jennie J. Kronenfeld 1995 "Health, Illness, and Healing in an Uncertain Era: Challenges from and for Medical Sociology." *Journal of Health and Social Behavior* (Extra Issue):5–33.

Rosenstock, Irwin M. 1966 "Why People Use Health Services." *Milbank Memorial Fund Quarterly* 44:94–106.

Ruzek, Sheryl Burt 1978 *The Women's Health Movement: Feminist Alternatives to Medical Control*. New York: Praeger.

Starr, Paul 1982 *The Social Transformation of American Medicine*. New York: Basic Books.

Strauss, Robert 1957 "The Nature and Status of Medical Sociology." *American Sociological Review* 2:200–204.

Thoits, Peggy A. 1995 "Stress, Coping and Social Support Processes: Where Are We? What Next?" *Journal of Health and Social Behavior* (Extra Issue):53–79.

Turner, J. Jay, and Franco Marino 1994 "Social Support and Social Structure: A Descriptive Epidemiology." *Journal of Health and Social Behavior* 35:193–212.

Waitzkin, Howard 1989 "A Critical Theory of Medical Discourse: Ideology, Social Control, and the Processing of Social Context in Medical Encounters." *Journal of Health and Social Behavior*. 30:220–239.

Weisman, Carol S. 1998 *Women's Health Care: Activist Traditions and Institutional Change*. Baltimore, Md.: Johns Hopkins University Press.

Williams, David R., and Chiquita Collins 1995 "U.S. Socioeconomic and Racial Differences in Health: Patterns and Explanations." *Annual Review of Sociology* 21:349–386.

Weitz, Rose 1991 *Life with AIDS*. New Brunswick, N.J.: Rutgers University Press.

Zimmerman, Mary K., and Shirley A. Hill 1999 "Health Care as a Gendered System." In J. S. Chafetz, ed., *Handbook of the Sociology of Gender*. New York: Plenum.

Zola, Irving K. 1966 "Culture and Symptoms: An Analysis of Patients' Presenting Complaints." *American Sociological Review* 31:615–630.

—— 1972 "Medicine as an Institution of Social Control." *Sociological Review* 20:487–504.

—— 1982 *Missing Pieces: A Chronicle of Living with a Disability*. Philadelphia, Pa.: Temple University Press.

MARY K. ZIMMERMAN

MEDICAL-INDUSTRIAL COMPLEX

The concept of the medical-industrial complex was first introduced in the 1971 book, *The American Health Empire* (Ehrenreich and Ehrenreich 1971) by Health-PAC. The medical-industrial complex (MIC) refers to the health industry, which is composed of the multibillion-dollar congeries of enterprises including doctors, hospitals, nursing homes, insurance companies, drug manufacturers, hospital supply and equipment companies, real estate and construction businesses, health systems consulting and accounting firms, and banks. As employed by the Ehrenreichs, the concept conveys the idea that an important (if not the primary) function of the health care system in the United States is business (that is, to make profits) with two other secondary functions, research and education.

Since that time, a number of authors have examined the medical-industrial complex: Navarro (1976, pp. 76, 80), Relman (1980), Estes and colleagues (1984), Wohl (1984), and McKinlay and Stoeckle (1994). Himmelstein and Woolhandler (1990) argue that health care facilitates profit making by (1) improving the productivity (health) of workers, (2) ideologically ensuring the social stability needed to support production and profit, and (3) providing major opportunities for investment and profit (p. 16). The last function, profit, is now "the driving force," as health care has fully "come into the age of capitalist production" (p. 17).

Arnold Relman (1980), Harvard medical professor and editor of the *New England Journal of Medicine*, was the first mainstream physician to write about the medical-industrial complex, observing that the corporatization of medicine is a challenge to physician authority, autonomy, and even legitimacy for the doctors who become health care industry owners. Ginzberg (1988) and others (Andrews 1995; Estes et al. 1984; Himmelstein and Woolhandler 1990) have written about the monetarization, corporatization, and proprietarization of "health" care. By the mid-1980s, the author of a book appearing with the title *The Medical Industrial Complex* (Wohl 1984) did not see the need to define it but, rather, began with "the story of the explosive growth of . . . corporate medicine" and focused on "medical moguls," monopoly, and a prescription for profit.

While the health care industry has certainly contributed to improvements in the health status of the population, it has also strengthened and preserved the private sector and protected a plurality of vested interests. In U.S. society, the medical-industrial complex functions economically as a source of growth, profit accumulation, investment opportunity, and employment (Estes et al. 1984, pp. 56–70). It also contributes to the human capital needed for productivity and profit by preserving an able-bodied workforce whose work is not sapped by illness (Rodberg and Stevenson 1977), although another interpretation suggests that private capital's stability is built upon the appropriation of the working-class population's health (see Navarro 1976, 1982, 1995).

STRUCTURE OF THE HEALTH CARE INDUSTRY

Industry Components Today's medical-industrial complex consists of more than a dozen major components: hospitals; nursing homes; physicians (salaried and fee-for-service); home health agencies; supply and equipment manufacturers; drug companies; insurance companies; managed care organizations (HMOs, PPOs, IPAs); specialized centers (urgi, surgi, dialysis); hospices; nurses and all other health care workers; administrators, marketers, lawyers, and planners; and research organizations. In addition to these entities, thousands of other organizations are springing up in long-term care (e.g., case management, respite care, homemaker/chore, independent living center) and other services for the disabled and aging, including social services that have incorporated health care components such as senior centers.

Changes in the Structure of the Industry. There were a number of significant changes in the structure of the health care industry between the 1970s and 1990s, including (1) rapid growth and consolidation of the industry into larger organizations; (2) horizontal integration; (5) vertical integration; (4) change in ownership from government to private, nonprofit, and for-profit organizations; and (5) diversification and corporate restructuring (Starr 1982; McKinlay and Stoeckle 1994). These changes occurred across the different sectors, which are dominated by large hospital, insurance, and managed care organizations.

Rapid Growth and Consolidation Health care has long been moved from its cottage industry stage with small individual hospitals and solo physician practitioners to large corporate enterprises. Health care corporations are diverse and growing in terms of size and complexity. Hospitals are the largest sector of the health care industry, and while the growth rate in hospital expenditures was increasing rapidly, the number of community hospitals actually declined from 5,830 in 1980 to 5,194 in 1995 (a decrease of 11 percent) (American Hospital Association 1996) (see Table 1). The number of community hospital beds also began to decline going down to 988,000 in 1980 and continuing so that by 1995 there were only 873,000 (a decrease from 12 percent) (AHA 1996).

Nursing homes grew rapidly in numbers of facilities and beds after the passage of Medicaid and Medicare legislation. In 1996, there were 17,806 licensed nursing facilities with 1.82 million beds (Harrington et al. 1998). The number of facilities increased by 25 percent and the number of beds increased by 37 percent between 1978 and 1996. More recently, their overall growth has leveled off, so that growth is not keeping pace with the aging of the population (Harrington et al. 1998).

Relatively new and influential corporate forces in the health industry are the managed-care organizations such as health maintenance organizations (HMOs), preferred provider organizations (PPOs), and independent practice associations (IPAs). There has been a large growth in HMOs, which provide health care services on the basis of fixed monthly charges per enrollee. In 1984, there

were only 337 HMOs with 17 million enrollees. By 1988, there were 31 million members enrolled in 643 HMOs (InterStudy 1989). Managed-care enrollees grew to more than 50 million in 1996 and are expected to reach 100 million by the year 2002. Nearly 75 percent of U.S. workers with health insurance now receive that coverage through an HMO, a PPO, or a point of service plan (PSP) (McNamee 1997). There have been numerous rounds of mergers and acquisitions among HMOs, and some nonprofit HMO corporations have established profit-making operations (Gallagher 1999).

PPOs are modified HMOs that provide health care for lower costs when the enrollee uses participating providers who are paid on the basis of negotiated or discount rates (U.S. DOC 1990). In 1988 there were about 620 PPOs with about 36 million members.

Private health insurance companies constitute another large sector of the health industry. In 1988, the United States had over 1,000 for-profit, commercial health insurers and 85 Blue Cross/Blue Shield plans (Feldstein 1988). These private insurance organizations, along with HMOs, PPOs, and other third-party payers, paid for 32 percent ($348 billion out of $1,092 billion) of the total expenditures in 1997 (Srinivasan et al. 1998).

Physician practice patterns changed rapidly between the 1970s and 1990s, moving toward larger partnerships and group practices. Eighteen percent of physicians were in group practices (with three or more physicians) in 1969, compared to 28 percent in 1984 (Andersen and Mullner 1989). It is estimated that about 75 percent of all practicing physicians are part of at least one qualified health management organization (U.S. DOC 1990). Thus, physicians are moving toward larger and more complex forms of group practice. In addition, physicians are actively involved in the ownership and operation of many of the newer forms of HMOs, PPOs, IPAs, and other types of corporate health care activities (Relman 1980; Iglehart 1989).

Horizontal Integration The major changes in corporate arrangements have been the development of multiorganizational systems through horizontal integration. The formation of multihospital systems has grown tremendously within the industry. Ermann and Gable (1984) estimated there

Community Hospitals and Beds by Ownership, 1980, 1990, and 1995

Type of Ownership	1980		1990		1995	
	Hospitals	Beds	Hospitals	Beds	Hospitals	Beds
Nonprofit	3,322 (57%)	692 (70%)	3,191 (60%)	657 (71%)	3,092 (60%)	610 (70%)
Investor	730 (13%)	87 (9%)	749 (14%)	101 (11%)	752 (14%)	106 (12%)
State and local government	1,778 (30%)	209 (21%)	1,444 (27%)	169 (18%)	1,350 (26%)	157 (18%)
Total	5,830	988	5,384	927	5,194	873

Table 1

NOTE: : Excludes federal psychiatric, tuberculosis, and other hospitals.

SOURCE: Adapted from American Hospital Association. *Hospital Statistics, 1989–1990 and 1996–1997 Editions.* Chicago: AHA, 1989, 1996.

were 202 multihospital systems controlling 1,405 hospitals and 293,000 beds in 1975 (or 24 percent of the hospitals and 31 percent of all beds). In 1997, there were 280 multihospital systems controlling 1,514 hospitals, and 543,588 beds (Table 2). This represents a 39 percent increase in the number of multihospital systems, a small (7 percent) increase in the number of hospitals, and an 86 percent increase in the number of beds between 1975 and 1997.

Multihospital corporations are becoming consolidated, with large companies controlling the largest share of the overall hospital market. Most of the recent increase in these systems has been the result of purchases or leases of existing facilities and mergers of organizations, rather than of construction of new facilities.

Vertical Integration Vertical integration involves the development of organizations with different levels and types of organizations and services. One such type of integration has involved the linkage of hospitals and health maintenance organizations and/or insurance companies. For example, National Medical Enterprises owned hospitals, nursing homes, psychiatric hospitals, recovery centers, and rehabilitation hospitals (Federation of American Health Systems 1990). There has also been an increase in the number of academic medical center hospitals that have relationships with proprietary hospital firms (Howard S. Berliner and Burlage 1990, p. 97). Many of the major investor-owned

health care corporations are diversified, with many different types of health care operations.

Changes in Ownership Between the 1970s and the 1990s the organizational side of health care witnessed a surge in the growth of both for-profit and not-for-profit health care delivery corporations, initially in hospitals and later extending to other types of health organizations. The ownership of hospitals shifted from public to nonprofit and for-profit organizations (see Table 1). The percentage of government-owned community hospitals dropped from 30 percent of the total community hospitals in 1980 to 26 percent in 1995, and the percentage of total beds declined from 21 percent to 18 percent during the same period (AHA 1996). In contrast, the percentage of proprietary facilities increased from 13 percent to 14 percent, and the percentage of proprietary beds increased from 9 percent to 12 percent, of the total during the 1980–1995 period. The percentage of total U.S. hospitals owned by nonprofit corporations increased from 57 percent to 60 percent during the period, while the percentage of beds remained at 70 percent (AHA 1996). Of the total 280 multihospital systems in 1997 (down from 303 systems in 1988), investor-owned systems controlled 40 percent of the hospitals and 27 percent of the beds, compared to nonprofit facilities (AHA 1997). The federal government controlled 9.8 percent of hospitals and 13 percent of beds, while nonprofit organizations controlled 50 percent of hospitals and 59 percent of beds (AHA 1997). We note that this represents a 3 percent decrease in the number

Hospitals and Beds in Multihospital Health Care Systems, by Type of Ownership and Control, 1997

Type of Ownership	TOTAL NOT-FOR-PROFIT		INVESTOR-OWNED		ALL SYSTEMS	
	Hospitals	Beds	Hospitals	Beds	Hospitals	Beds
Owned, leased, or sponsored	1,343 (53%)	309,216 (62%)	887 (35%)	119,466 (24%)	2,525 (100%)	501,724 (100%)
Contract-managed	171 (36%)	12,901 (31%)	301 (64%)	28,963 (69%)	472 (100%)	41,864 (100%)
Total	1,514 (50%)	322,117 (59%)	1,188 (40%)	148,429 (27%)	2,997 (100%)	543,588 (100%)

Table 2

SOURCE: Adapted from American Hospital Association. *Guide to the Health Care Field. 1997–1998 Edition.* Chicago: AHA, 1997, Table B3.

of hospitals and a 6 percent decrease in the number of beds in multihospital systems controlled by investor-owned systems since 1988.

Nursing homes have the largest share of proprietary ownership in the health field (except for the drug and medical supply industries). In 1997, some 65 percent of all nursing homes were profit-making, 28 percent were nonprofit, and 7 percent were government-run (Harrington et al. 1999). By 1997, chains owned 54 percent of the total nursing home facilities.

For-profit companies dominate the health maintenance organization (HMO) market. Between 1981 and 1997, for-profit HMOs grew from representing 12 percent to 62 percent of total HMO enrollees and from 18 percent to 75 percent of health plans (Srinivasan et al. 1998). Investor-owned corporations have also established themselves in many other areas of health care, ranging from primary-care clinics to specialized referral centers and home health care. The number of proprietary home health corporations is increasing rapidly, while the number of traditional visiting nurse associations is declining (Estes et al. 1992). In 1982 it was estimated that 14 percent of the Medicare home health charges were by proprietary agencies, 26 percent by nonprofit organizations, 32 percent by visiting nurse associations, 15 percent by facility-based agencies, and 14 percent by other agencies (U.S. Department of Health and Human Services 1989). By 1996, proprietary agencies accounted for 44 percent of total Medicare agencies, nonprofit care for 37 percent, and government and others for 19 percent (U.S. DHHS 1997).

Forty-four percent of home health agencies were part of a multifacility chain. This represents a dramatic shift in ownership structure within a six-year period. The changes brought about by the for-profit chains are more extensive than their proportionate representation among health care providers might suggest (Bergthold et al. 1990; Estes and Swan 1994). By force of example and direct competition, for-profit chains have encouraged many nonprofit hospitals and other health entities to combine into chains and convert to for-profit status (Dube 1999).

Diversification, Restructuring, and Growth. Diversification of health care corporations is continuing to occur. Some large hospital corporations have developed ambulatory care centers (such as Humana, which later sold its centers), while others have developed their own HMOs or insurance. By the mid-1980s, many experts expected America's health care system to be dominated by the four largest for-profit hospital chains: Hospital Corporations of America (HCA), Humana, National Medical Enterprises, and American Medical International. By the late 1990s, only Humana and HCA were left standing, and HCA had already merged with Columbia. Eventually HCA Columbia almost collapsed as the result of a scandal over fraud during the late 1990s (*Multinational Monitor* 1998). Economic problems in the late 1980s resulted in some industry restructuring, by scaling down operations and spinning off substantial segments (Ginzberg 1988).

In the 1990s, this cycle repeated itself, as the frenzy of mergers and acquisitions has produced ever-greater desires for cost cutting and restructuring. One report states that much of this drive for cost containment stemmed from drug companies' raising prices and from an increase in patient visits to doctors (utilization costs) (Hayes 1997). High stock values and the desire to improve market share have catalyzed many health care firms to seek growth through mergers and acquisitions. The number of mergers among health services (483) and HMO companies (33) peaked in 1996. These mergers were valued at $27 billion and $13.3 billion, respectively (Hayes 1997).

As HMOs grow, it has become clear that their primary goals are market control, profit making, and cost containment (through capitation and other mechanisms). For example, the merger of Aetna and U.S. Health care in 1996 put a "corporate giant in control of the care of 1 in 12 people in the United States" (Slaughter 1997, p. 22). In the years 1994–1999 a dozen companies were merged or acquired by six of the biggest firms: Aetna, Cigna, United HealthCare, Foundation Health Systems, Pacificare, and Wellpoint Health Networks.

As managed-care organizations became the dominant player in the health care industry in the 1990s, both doctors and patients began to voice complaints about the system. Many patients felt that they were no longer able to receive the quality time and personal care of a primary physician, because the physicians had to provide hurried treatment to patients in order to maintain efficiencies demanded by HMOs (Managed Care Improvement Task Force 1998). For their part, many doctors argued that capitation and other structures introduced by HMOs limited their freedom to make treatment decisions.

Many doctors and patients argued that these trends were producing lower-quality care (Dao 1999, p. A1). Additionally, registered nurses were increasingly being used in place of doctors to lower labor costs. Registered nurses, in turn, were also being replaced with less skilled and lower-paid personnel. In response, both doctors and nurses have begun a fervent effort to unionize (Slaughter 1997). While some critics argue that the impacts of this growth at all costs by both for-profit and nonprofit organizations are often devastating to communities (Bond and Weissman 1997; Kassirer 1997), others find few negative effects (Fubini and Limb 1997).

Financial Status and Profits. The private health care sector was marked by great volatility and growth in the 1990s. *Forbes*'s annual report on investor-owned health corporations shows that the median five-year average return-on-equity for health corporations was 14.6 percent, well above the 10.5 percent for all U.S. industries (Condon 1998) (see Table 3). Median health industry sales for investor-owned companies grew 8.8 percent for 1997 and at a 11.1 percent rate for the five-year average. Earnings per share were 15.5 percent in the most recent twelve months, compared with 8.6 percent for the five-year average. The earnings per share were higher than the 14.9 percent earnings for all U.S. industries in the most recent twelve months in 1997 (Condon 1998).

The *Forbes* financial reports for the largest health corporations are shown in Table 3 for three different sectors of the industry: health care services, drugs, and medical supply companies (Condon 1998; Hayes 1998). The most profitable health care service corporation in 1989 was Humana, which owns both hospitals and insurance companies. In 1989 its group health insurance division had almost 1 million members and a $4 billion operating profit (Fritz 1990). The most profitable health care service corporation in 1997 was HBO and Company, while Oxford Health Plans had the strongest five-year average.

While large investor-owned HMOs are growing each year, the 1990s were tumultuous financially. As *Forbes* Annual Report on American Industry put it, "Health care providers are supposed to make people well, but many of these companies are very sick themselves" (Hayes 1998, p. 180). Although Oxford Health Plans had the higher five-year average, between July 1997 and January 1998 its stock lost over 80 percent of its value. Similarly, the number two–ranked company, Mid Atlantic Medical Services, saw its stock drop by more than 50 percent of its value in a year's time. Rapid growth, through mergers, acquisitions, and internal sales, "eventually outstripped management's ability to run these companies" (Hayes 1998, p. 180).

Earnings per share of drug companies were at 15.8 percent in 1997, which was up from the five-year average of 11.9 percent (Condon 1998). Return on equity reported for drug companies was at 11.7 percent in 1997, significantly less than the 14.3 percent on average over the previous five

Selected U.S. Health-Care Investor Corporations, 1998

	RETURN ON CAPITAL		PROFITABILITY GROWTH SALES		EARNINGS PER SHARE		NET INCOME
Company	5-Year Average (%)	Latest 12 Months (%)	5-Year Average (%)	Latest 12 Months (%)	5-Year Average (%)	Latest 12 Months (%)	Latest 12 Months $ million
Health Care Services:							
Oxford Health Plans	36.5	4.2	116.0	46.2	74.7	−72.0	25
Mid Atlantic	34.4	2.7	21.7	2.9	NM	−67.6	5
Health Management	20.8	22.3	25.0	25.4	33.2	27.6	108
WellPoint Health	19.8	15.0	15.1	43.0	6.0	17.2	203
Sun Healthcare	18.9*	7.4	89.9	28.2	NM	D–P	49
PacifiCare Health	18.3	18.2	33.7	69.5	8.9	37.0	124
United HealthCare	17.4	10.0	62.2	19.0	24.2	64.1	436
HBO & Co	17.0	23.6	35.8	43.0	NM	63.6	145
Quorum Health	14.5	11.3	50.3	28.4	32.1	20.0	88
Humana	12.3	11.0	22.2	15.3	32.7	270.8	147
Medians	**10.4**	**7.4**	**24.9**	**22.3**	**6.0**	**23.5**	**52**
Drugs:							
Schering-Plough	49.6	58.1	8.9	15.9	15.1	17.5	1,378
Abbott Labs	38.1	35.2	9.5	10.8	13.3	12.8	2,038
Amgen	35.4	29.6	25.1	10.6	37.4	0.9	643
Bristol-Myers Squibb	34.9	41.8	6.4	10.2	3.6	57.4	3,119
Warner-Lambert	32.1	19.7	7.6	6.2	32.5	8.6	805
Medians	**14.3**	**11.7**	**14.7**	**10.7**	**11.9**	**15.8**	**198**
Medical Supplies:							
Medtronic	28.1	31.5	16.5	8.7	27.2	15.5	564
Johnson & Johnson	26.5	26.2	11.5	7.3	14.6	14.7	3,229
Patterson Dental	24.4	20.4	18.9	19.9	30.6	24.3	37
Stryker	20.1	16.2	20.7	8.8	24.2	21.0	119
Perkin-Elmer	19.7	26.9	5.4	10.5	13.6	271.9	107
Medians	**14.6**	**13.4**	**8.7**	**5.9**	**4.7**	**15.5**	**79**
Industry Medians	14.6	12.7	11.1	8.8	8.6	15.5	107
All Industry Medians	10.5	10.3	8.9	7.9	6.7	14.9	96

Table 3

NOTE: : D-P: Deficit to profit. NM: Not meaningful. *Four-year average.

SOURCE: Adapted from *Forbes*, January 12, 1998, pp. 176–182.

years (Condon 1997). On the other hand, earnings per share of medical supply companies were doing well at 15.5 percent in 1997, far better than their five-year median earnings of 4.7 percent. In 1989 a number of large drug company mergers occurred, particularly between U.S. firms and foreign corporations such as Genentech, Inc., and Roche Holding, Ltd., of Switzerland (Southwick 1990). These international mergers continued into the 1990s.

Although the biotechnology industry did not show overall profits in 1989, the sales growth rates were strong, and some companies had high profit rates, such as Diagnostic Products, with a 22.3 percent earnings per share and 23.6 percent return on equity in 1989 over the previous year (Clements 1990, p. 182). Biotechnology saw an upsurge of economic growth and media coverage when several new developments emerged in the 1990s. The first was the introduction of "gene therapies" whereby scientists could modify a person's genetic makeup to fight against otherwise deadly or incurable diseases such as cancer and Alzheimer's. The second was the launching of the Human Genome Project, a massive effort by scientists in government and industry to "map" the structure of the human genetic code. The third, was the announcement, by a Scottish scientist in 1997, that he had successfully cloned a sheep from another sheep's DNA.

While all these developments signaled the importance of biotechnology in the future of health care research and policy, some observers were critical of these technological "advances." First, the cloning of animals like sheep leaves open the distinct possibility that human beings might soon be cloned. The prospect of this event raised dire concerns among bio-ethicists, politicians, scientists, and religious leaders during 1997, and President Bill Clinton issued a worldwide call asking scientists to voluntarily refrain from any such activities. Second, some critics have noted that the Human Genome Project has been associated with efforts to "locate" genes believed not only to be the cause of certain diseases like breast cancer, but also those genes believed to be associated with certain types of deviant, or criminal, behavior. Focusing on the genetic "causes" of certain diseases and social behaviors raises many problematic scenarios for public policy (for example, defining breast cancer as genetically based, rather than

being rooted in social structures and the production of toxins by industry). Third, some biotechnology companies have been associated with efforts to patent life forms around the globe, including parts of the human body—prompting some critics to label this practice "biopiracy" or "biocolonization" (Kimbrell 1996). Taken together, these charges suggest that, through biotech, the medical-industrial complex is charting revolutionary territory that has allowed private interests to define, claim ownership over, and even create life on this planet. Despite these criticisms, biotechnology stocks continue to rise. As noted, the pharmaceutical industry alone traded upward of $110 billion globally in 1997, while the overall health expenditures topped $1 trillion by the end of the 1990s. Some analysts project health costs to more than double by 2015 to $2.3 trillion, of which the government share will be between 25 and 50 percent (Pardes et al. 1999).

In summary, the 1970s, 1980s, and 1990s were decades of enormous growth in health care spending and the rationalization of health care service delivery, with the formation of large, complex, bureaucratically interconnected units and arrangements that reached well beyond the hospital and permeated virtually all sectors of the health care industry. At the same time, new sectors emerged (e.g., genetic research and subacute care), bringing additional industry developments. This vertical and horizontal integration of medical organizations and industries, combined with the revival of market ideologies and government policies promoting competition and deregulation, have profoundly altered the shape of U.S. health care delivery. As we enter the new millennium, these changes continue to signal a fundamental transformation of American medicine and a rationalization of the system under private control that was described by Paul Starr (1982).

The Need for Regulation. The federal government has been playing and continues to play a crucial role in the development of the medical-industrial complex. After World War II, the federal role expanded as Congress enacted legislation and authorized money for research, education, training, and the financing of health services. The passage of Medicare and Medicaid in 1965 was pivotal in expanding the medical-industrial complex, as government became the third-party payer for health care services (Estes et al. 1984). As a consequence, public demand for health care among the aged, blind, disabled, and poor (all previously limited in access) was secure. Medicare and Medicaid provided the major sources of long-term capital financing for hospitals and contributed to the marked increase in service volume and technology, as well as to the continued oversupply of physicians (McKinlay and Stoeckle 1994). Thus, federal financing of health care has performed the very important functions of sustaining aggregate demand through health insurance programs, protecting against financial risks, subsidizing research and guaranteeing substantial financial returns, supporting the system's infrastructure through training subsidies and capital expansion, and regulating competition through licensure and accreditation (LeRoy 1979).

In addition to government spending, third-party insurance offered by Blue Cross/Blue Shield and private commercial companies covered most of the remaining inpatient hospital expenditures and a significant proportion of physician costs. The cost-based service reimbursement by private insurers, Blue Cross, and Medicare created and sustained strong cash flows in the hospital industry (Ginzberg 1988). With public and private sector third-party payments covering 90 percent of all inpatient hospital expenditures, the hospital business had become virtually riskfree.

In the 1980s and 1990s, two other forces were responsible for the dramatic changes in the medical-industrial complex: a change in the ideological climate with the election of President Ronald Reagan, President George Bush, and later President Bill Clinton, and changes in state policies to promote privatization, rationalization, and competition in health care (Estes 1990). These changes contributed to increases in the proportion of services provided by proprietary institutions (Schlesinger et al. 1987).

While policies of the 1960s and 1970s encouraged a form of privatization built on the voluntary sector (Estes and Bergthold 1988), President Reagan, President Bush, and President Clinton shifted the direction and accelerated privatization. In the 1980s and 1990s, the form of privatization was government subsidy of a growing proportion of for-profit (rather than nonprofit) enterprises (Bergthold et al. 1990). There was also privatization in the form of a transfer of work from the formal sector of the hospital to the informal sector of

home and family with ambulatory surgery and shortened lengths of hospital stays (Binney et al. 1993). Regulatory and legislative devices were important in stimulating and accelerating privatization in the health and social services. The Omnibus Reconciliation Act of 1980 and the Omnibus Budget Reconciliation Act of 1981 contributed to competition and deregulation, private contracting, and growth of for-profits in service areas that were traditionally dominated by nonprofit or public providers (e.g, home health care).

President Clinton introduced a health care reform plan in 1993 that ultimately failed, giving way to a private sector–driven market reform managed care, promoting a system that many contend benefits investors over patients, doctors, and community hospitals (Andrews 1995). Given the long-term historical role of the private, nonprofit sector in U.S. health and social services since the earliest days of the republic and the rapid organizational changes of the 1980s and 1990s, vertical and horizontal integration have blurred boundaries between the nonprofit and for-profit health care sectors. For-profit entities have nonprofit subsidiaries, and vice versa, and conceptual and structural complexities have multiplied, rendering impossible the simple differentiation of public from private. It is noteworthy that government-initiated privatization strategies did not reduce public sector costs (see the section entitled "Financial Status and Profits").

The distinction between for-profit and nonprofit is less meaningful when both organizational forms appear to be pursuing greater revenues through cost cutting and mergers. Eight of the ten largest health care systems (by net patient revenues) in 1997 were nonprofits; that same year, four out of the ten largest health care systems (by number of hospitals owned) were also nonprofits (Bellandi and Jaspen 1998, p. 36). Whether not-for-profits are still oriented toward the needs of the community is unclear, as many of these organizations (both insurance plans and hospitals) are undergoing "conversions" to for-profit status (Marsteller et al. 1998).

The concern that many communities have is that these conversions may mean less attention to the health needs of local residents. The increase in conversions has "heightened the need for accountability regarding the accurate determination and disposition of assets developed with the assistance of tax subsidies for nonprofit medical entities such as Blue Cross" (Estes and Linkins 1997, p. 436). Federal and state laws require that their assets remain in the charitable sector and continue to be used for the community's benefit. Twenty-three states now have conversion laws clarifying the authority of attorneys general to regulate these conversions. Conversion laws mandate varying degrees of public participation and public disclosure, but often are best implemented when there is an active community-based activist presence to monitor the organization's practices.

From social movements to the federal government, institutions across the nation are recognizing the increasing need for monitoring and regulation of the myriad branches of the medical-industrial complex. As noted earlier, physicians are advocating new legislation and even beginning to unionize against HMOs. Unfortunately, often when regulation exists, it is easily circumvented. For example, the Health Insurance Portability and Accountability Act of 1996 was intended to protect Americans who change or lose their jobs by assuring portability of plans across groups and into the individual market. It was also intended to protect people against denial of coverage for preexisting conditions. However, many insurers have skirted this law by denying commissions to their agents who sell insurance to people with medical problems (Pear 1997).

In other cases, there is little to no regulation of purchasers, such as large employers who self-insure under the Employment Retirement Income Security Act (ERISA) of 1974. These employers are exempt from state insurance laws and are bound by no federal regulation in this area. More than 125 million Americans who have HMO coverage cannot sue their providers for punitive damages. As *Time* magazine recently reported, this represents a "clear subordination to corporate interests" (Howe 1999, p. 46). Furthermore, the continuing rapid pace of mergers and acquisitions in the health care industry has created a consolidation of markets that raise questions about the need for antitrust policies directed at this sector.

At the federal level, the President's Advisory Commission on Consumer Protection and Quality in the Health Care Industry has called for a "consumer bill of rights," while others clamor for "patient's bill of rights." These proposals would provide, for example, the right to sue HMOs for damages, prohibitions against negative financial incentives, and external reviews of patient complaints. Whether this proposal will ever become national legislation is unclear. But as, under the "New Federalism," previously federal responsibilities are "devolved" to the states, it is certain that fifty separate governments will have great difficulty coherently regulating a health care system for the entire nation. This is especially troublesome because of the growing numbers of the uninsured and those in need of long-term care (Estes and Linkins 1997).

Long-term care (LTC) is an area of health policy in need of greater attention as the age distribution of the population changes, so that the number of persons over 65 and over 85 is increasing rapidly. Medicare, Social Security and other entitlement programs affecting the elderly have been the focus of the "devolution revolution" (Estes and Linkins 1997) and raise serious questions about the quality and accessibility of LTC under managed care. There are profits to be made in this sector of the industry as well. One publication referred to 1997 as the "year of assisted living" because seven of the top ten health care provider organizations were assisted-living companies and half of them posted returns of 50 percent or greater (*SeniorCare Investor* 1998). LTC will have to meet the "bottom line" criterion of "cost-saving" or "profit generation," and this is likely to produce problems for those in need of these services. Indeed the needs of all less powerful groups—the elderly, the poor, the working and middle classes, women, and people of color—are increasingly being confronted by these business directives as well. Regulation of health care institutions in the interests of these marginalized groups is especially difficult when the American Medical Association is second to none in money spent on lobbying the Congress and state legislatures (Jaspen 1999).

The U.S. Medical-Industrial Complex in a Global Context. The U.S. health and health care systems rank near the bottom of all industrialized nations on a number of key dimensions. By comparison, the health of U.S. citizens is poorer and the number of underinsured and uninsured individuals is greater than in any other industrialized nation. Among the top 24 industrialized nations, the United States ranks sixteenth in life expectancy for women, seventeenth for men, and twenty-first in infant mortality (Andrews 1995, p. 38). A Harris poll indicated that the citizens of Canada, western Europe, the United Kingdom, and Japan report much higher satisfaction with their health care systems than do Americans (Isaacson 1993). Additionally, compared with other nations, doctors in the United States receive much higher incomes relative to the average worker. For example, in 1987 the income ratio of doctors to the average worker in the United States was 5.4, while in Canada it was 3.7 and in Japan and the United Kingdom it was 2.4 (Isaacson 1993). This poor performance of the United States on health indicators is ironic, given that the United States spends more money on its health care system than any other nation in the world.

Multinational health enterprises are an increasingly important part of the medical-industrial complex, with investor-owned and investor-operated companies active not only in the United States but also in many foreign countries. In 1990 a report showed 97 companies reporting ownership or operation of 1,492 hospitals with 182,644 beds in the United States and 100 hospitals with 11,974 beds in foreign countries (FAHS 1990, pp 16–17). The four largest for-profit chains owned two-thirds of the foreign hospitals (Berliner and Regan 1990). Pharmaceutical firms have also become major global corporate players. In 1990, foreign control over pharmaceutical production was 72 percent in Australia, 61 percent in the United Kingdom, 57 percent in Italy, and 30 percent in the United States (Tarabusi and Vickery 1998). The total value of global pharmaceutical exports and imports is estimated to be in excess of $110 billion (Tarabusi and Vickery 1998). The effects of these developments in foreign countries and the profit potential of these operations are not clearly understood (Berliner and Began 1990).

Because of the pluralistically financed health care system in the United States, administrative costs are much higher than those of the national and publicly financed health care systems of virtually all other Western industrialized nations, with the exception of South Africa. U.S. health care expenditures were increasing at an alarming rate until around 1993, when the rate of growth in expenditures began to slow. However, this trend is expected to reverse itself, and one study projects that "health spending is expected to rise as a share of gross domestic product (GDP) beginning in 1988, climbing from 13.6 percent in 1996 to an estimated 16.6 percent by 2007" (Smith et al. 1998, p. 128).

Examining the U.S. medical-industrial complex in a comparative context provides an understanding of the role of the welfare state and government vis-à-vis civil society and private capital. What has become clear is that the unique problems the U.S. medical-industrial complex has created are rooted in the subordination of the state and civil society to corporate interests. Other nations whose health care systems are much more effective are marked by the state's taking an active role to restrict the profit motive in health insurance, "or they simply never let a commercial market develop" (Andrews 1995, p. 36). This is because voluntary insurance in many other countries historically preceded public legislation, and these insurance funds were linked to labor unions, political groups, and religious groups—not to private companies and health care providers, as in the United States. In these cases, government policy was, and remains, heavily influenced by nongovernmental organizations (NGOs), namely religious and labor groups. The medical-industrial complex in particular and corporate-civil society relations in general in the United States are much less democratic largely because of the lower levels of mobilization by trade unions and other NGOs. Government agencies in the United States can learn from other nations and begin to implement policies that leverage the power of the state and NGOs in ways that bring a greater balance among the stakeholders in the medical-industrial complex.

Issues Raised by the Medical-Industrial Complex Commodification. Commercialization, proprietarization, and *monetarization* are terms used to describe an increasingly salient dynamic in the medical-industrial complex: the potentially distorting effects of money, profit, and market rationality as a (if not *the*) central determining force in health care. After three decades devoted to market rhetoric, cost containment, and stunning organizational rationalization, the net result is the complete failure of any of these efforts to stem the swelling tide of problems of access and cost. For example, while national health care expenditures make up around 15 percent of the GDP, the number of uninsured

Americans was fully 43.4 million, or 16.1 percent of the population in 1997—the highest level in a decade (Kuttner 1999). Moreover, there are alarming increases in the uninsured population among African-Americans, Latinos, and the middle class (Carrasquillo et al. 1999). Of those Americans who do have insurance, a recent study found that the number of persons insured by the private sector is much less than previously believed. While many studies had estimated that 61 percent of the insured received coverage through the private sector, Carrasquillo and colleagues (1999) found that the public sector subsidizes much of this coverage so that, in fact, only 43 percent of the population receives insurance through the private sector. Thus, not only is the burden on the state greater than previously thought because of this subsidy to the private sector, but the general decline in private insurance coverage will also produce further strains on the government's budget.

The rapidly growing health care industry is creating strains on the economic system while it also is creating a financial burden on government, business, and individuals through their payments for health services. These strains are occurring simultaneously when, in 1999, a huge federal deficit has been turned into a surplus, an event of historic significance. The budget surplus has produced a combination of euphoria and vigorous debate over what the government should do with it. This surplus emerged against the backdrop of an unusually high economic growth rate and strong general U.S. economy as we enter the new millennium. Responses to these deficit strains and fluctuations have included cutbacks in services and reimbursements; cost shifts onto consumers; and alterations in the structure of the health care system itself to accord better with a competitive, for-profit model. The competition model as a prescription for the nation's health-care woes has restricted access to health care and raised questions of quality of care (Bond and Weissman 1997; Harrington 1996; Kassirer 1997). Cost shifting to consumers is increasingly limiting access to needed services for those with less ability to pay. Managed care has not delivered the cost savings it promised, and the Health Care Financing Administration acknowledges that Medicare does not benefit from cost reductions from HMO enrollment of elders due to continuing adverse risk selection (DePearl 1999).

The juxtaposition of the commercial ethos familiar in fast-food chains with health care collides with traditional images of medicine as the embodiment of humane service. Investor-owned health care enterprises have elicited a number of specific criticisms. It has been argued that commercial considerations can undermine the responsibility of doctors toward their patients; can lead to unnecessary tests and procedures; and, given other financial incentives, can lead to inadequate treatment. The interrelationships among physicians and the private health care sector, particularly for-profit corporations, raises many issues about the effects on quality of care and health care utilization and expenditures. Many have argued that the potential for abuse, exploitation, unethical practices, and disregard of fiduciary responsibilities to patients is pervasive (Iglehart 1989). Legislation has even been introduced in Congress that would prohibit physicians from referring patients to entities in which they hold a financial interest and from receiving compensation from entities to which they refer patients (Iglehart 1989). In the late 1990s several versions of a "patient's bill of rights" were considered at the state and federal levels of government.

Critics of for-profits argue that such ownership drives up the cost of health care, reduces quality, neglects teaching and research, and excludes those who cannot pay for treatment. Opponents of the market model for health care reflect diverse interests, including members of the medical profession seeking to preserve their professional autonomy, advocates for access to health care for the poor and uninsured, those concerned about the impact of profit seeking on quality of care, and many others. As government and business attempt to restrain health care spending, cutting into profits and forcing cost reductions, these concerns intensify.

The medical-industrial complex is an inherently fascinating topic for sociological analysis because it underscores many of the less obvious dimensions of health care. Profits, power, and market control are not terms that have traditionally come to mind when the average person in the United States talked about their health care provider (although this is changing as we observe the managed-care "backlash"). Yet, these are some of the primary goals of those organizations administering our medical care. Sociology itself arose as an effort to wrestle with the myriad social impacts of nineteenth century industrialization (Durkheim [1893] 1984; Marx [1867] 1976). Early sociologists were especially concerned about how changes in communities were created by industrial production. Over the last century, sociologists have maintained a particular interest in the connection between advanced capitalism and the emergence of specific types of work, formal organizations, political systems, families, and cultural beliefs. An examination of the medical-industrial complex is therefore one of the more recent attempts to refocus core sociological questions about community, power, stratification, and social change.

Underlying this early sociological research on the impact of industrialization was an interest in power. How does power get accumulated and applied in a market-based society? How does it get distributed unevenly to social groups? To what ends do empowered social groups apply their power? One school of thought has been that industrial production skews power to an elite class (Domhoff 1998; Gramsci [1933] 1971). Max Weber's theory of bureaucracy, for example, suggested that this was an organizational form that pervades all social institutions. Its emphases on rationality, efficiency, predictability, calculability, and control (Weber [1921] 1961) were in part seen as a social advance over arbitrary religious, charismatic, and personalized forms of authority. Later analysts of bureaucracy, in contrast, saw this formalization of organizations as a dehumanizing and antisocial mechanism.

Issues for sociological investigation include the systematic identification of the ways in which the new commercial practices and organization of health care affect health care delivery. Organizational studies are needed to disentangle the effects of organizational characteristics (e.g., tax status and system affiliation) on the outcomes of equity, access, utilization, cost, and quality of care. The effects on provider-patient interactions of these structural and normative changes in health care require investigation as well. A general sociological theory of the professions will emerge from understanding the ways in which the dominant medical profession responds to the ongoing restructuring of health care and accompanying challenges to its ability to control the substance of its own work, erosions in its monopoly over medical knowledge, diminishing authority over patients

resulting from health policy changes, major technological and economic developments, and changes in the medical-industrial complex. Finally, sociologists must confront the coming biotechnological revolution and its impacts on society, human health, and the environment. The corporatization of health care and health-related research and the medical industrial complex are topics of great interest to scholars studying social movements, organization behavior, stratification, health and illness, and science and technology.

(SEE ALSO: *Health Care Financing*; *Health Policy Analysis*; *Health Services Utilization*; *Medical Sociology*)

REFERENCES

American Hospital Association 1989 *Hospital Statistics, 1989–90*. Chicago: AHA.

—— 1996 *Hospital Statistics, 1996–97*. Chicago: AHA.

—— 1997 *AHA Guide to the Health Care Field 1997–1998*. Chicago: AHA.

Andersen, Ronald M., and Ross M. Mullner 1989 "Trends in the Organization of Health Services." Pp. 144–165 in H. E. Freeman and S. Levine, eds., *Handbook of Medical Sociology*, 4th ed. Englewood Cliffs, N.J.: Prentice Hall.

Andrews, Charles 1995 *Profit Fever: The Drive to Corporatize Health Care and How to Stop it*. Monroe, Me.: Common Courage.

Bellandi, Deanna, and Bruce Jaspen 1998 "While You Weren't Sleeping." *Modern Healthcare* (May 25): 35–42.

Bergthold, Linda A. 1990 "Business and the Pushcart Vendors in an Age of Supermarkets." In J. W. Salmon, ed., *The Corporate Transformation of Health Care: Issues and Directions*. Amityville, N.Y.: Baywood.

——, Carroll L. Estes, and A. Villanueva 1990 "Public Light and Private Dark: The Privatization of Home Health Services for the Elderly in the United States." *Home Health Services Quarterly* 11:7–33.

Berliner, Howard S., and R. K. Burlage 1990 "Proprietary Hospital Chains and Academic Medical Centers." In J. W. Salmon, ed., *The Corporate Transformation of Health Care: Issues Acid Directions*. Amityville, N.Y.: Baywood.

Berliner, Howard W., and C. Regan 1990 "Multi-National Operations of U.S. For Profit Hospital Chains: Trends and Implications." In J. W. Salmon, ed., *The Corporate Transformation of Health Care Issues and Directions*. Amityville, N.Y.: Baywood.

Binney, Elizabeth A., Carroll L. Estes, and Susan E. Humphers 1993 "Informalization and Community Care for the Elderly." Pp. 155–170 in Carroll L. Estes, James Swan, and Associates, eds., *The Long Term Care Crisis*. Newbury Park, Calif.: Sage.

Bond, Patrick, and Robert Weissman 1997 "The Costs of Mergers and Acquisitions in the U.S. Health Care Sector." *International Journal of Health Services* 27:77–87.

Carrasquillo, Olveen, David Himmelstein, Steffie Woolhandler, and David Bor 1999 "Going Bare: Trends in Health Insurance Coverage, 1989–1996." *American Journal of Public Health* 89:36–42.

Clements, J. 1990 "Insurance." *Forbes* (January 8):184–186.

Condon, Bernard 1998 "Annual Report on American Industry: Health Care Products." *Forbes* (January 12):176–178.

Dao, James 1999 "Concern Rising about Mergers in Health Plans." *New York Times* (January): A1.

DePearl, Nancy Aun Min 1999 "The Future of Medicare," presentation at the Commonwealth Fund Conference on the Future of Medicare, Washington, D.C., February.

Domhoff, G. William 1998 *Who Rules America? Power and Politics in the Year 2000*. Mountain View, Calif.: Mayfield.

Dube, Monte 1999 "Lighten Your Load: In the Race to Compete, Public Hospitals Shed Excess Baggage." *Trustee* (January):17–19.

Durkheim, Emile (1893) 1984 *The Division of Labor in Society*. New York: Free Press.

Ehrenreich, Barbara, and John Ehrenreich 1971 *The American Health Empire: Power, Profits and Politics*. New York: Vintage.

Ermann, Dan, and Jon Gabel 1984 "Multihospital Systems: Issues and Empirical Findings." *Health Affairs* 3:50–64.

Estes, Carroll L. 1990 "The Reagan Legacy: Privatization, the Welfare State and Aging." In J. Quadagno and J. Myles, eds., *Aging and the Welfare State*. Philadelphia: Temple University Press.

——, and Linda A. Bergthold 1988 "The Unravelling of the Nonprofit Service Sector in the U.S." In J. I. Nelson, ed., *The Service Economy* (special issue of *International Journal of Sociology and Social Policy*) 9:18–33.

——, Lenore E. Gerard, Jane Sprague Zones, and James H. Swan 1984 *Political Economy, Health, and Aging*. Boston: Little, Brown.

——, and Karen Linkins 1997 "Devolution and Aging Policy: Racing to the Bottom in Long-Term Care."

International Journal of Health Services Research 27:427–442.

——, and J. H. Swan 1994 "Privatization and Access to Home Health Care." *Milbank Quarterly* 72:277–298.

——, ——, and associates 1993 *The Long Term Care Crisis*. Newbury Park, Calif.: Sage.

——, ——, L.A. Bergthold, and P. Hanes-Spohn 1992 "Running as Fast as They Can: Organizational Changes in Home Health Care." *Home Health Care Services Quarterly* 13:35–69.

Federation of American Health Systems 1990 *1990 Directory*. Little Rock, Ark.: FAHS.

Feldstein, Paul J. 1988 *Health Care Economics*. New York: John Wiley.

Fritz, M. 1990 "Health." *Forbes* (January 8):180–182.

Fubini, Sylvia, and Stephanie Limb 1997 "The Ties that Bind." *Health Systems Review* (September/October):44–47.

Gallagher, Leigh 1999 "The Big Money is in Small Towns." *Forbes* (January 11):182–183.

Ginzberg, Eli 1988 "For Profit Medicine: A Reassessment." *New England Journal of Medicine* 319:757–761.

Gramsci, Antonio (1933) 1971 *Selections from the Prison Notebooks*. New York: International.

Harrington, Charlene 1996 "The Nursing Home Industry: Public Policy in the 1990s." In Phil Brown, ed., *Perspectives in Medical Sociology*, 2nd ed. Prospect Heights, Ill.: Waveland.

——, Helen Carrillo, Susan Thollaug, and Peter Summers 1999 *Nursing Facilities, Staffing, Residents, and Facility Deficiencies, 1991–1997*. San Francisco: University of California Press.

——, J. Swan, Carrie Griffin, et al. 1998 *1996 State Data Book on Long Term Care Programs and Market Characteristics*. San Francisco: University of California Press.

Hayes, John 1997 "Annual Report on American Industry." *Forbes* (January 13):166–168.

——, 1998 "Annual Report on American Industry." *Forbes* (January 12):176–182.

Himmelstein, David U., and Steffie Woolhandler 1986 "Cost without Benefit: Administrative Waste in the U.S." *New England Journal of Medicine* 314:440–441.

——, 1990 "The Corporate Compromise: A Marxist View of Health Policy." *Monthly Review* (May):14–29.

Howe, Robert 1999 "The People vs. HMOs." *Time* (February 6):46–47.

Iglehart, John K. 1989 "The Debate over Physician Ownership of Health Care Facilities." *New England Journal of Medicine* 321:198–204.

—— 1999 "The American Health Care System: Expenditures." *New England Journal of Medicine* 340:70–76.

InterStudy 1989 "Findings on Open-Ended HMOs Reports by InterStudy." *InterStudy Press Release*, March 7. Excelsior, Md.: InterStudy.

Isaacson, Elisa 1993 "Prescription for Change." *San Francisco Bay Guardian* (April 14).

Jaspen, Bruce 1999 "AMA Firing Impolitic—or Just Politics?" *Chicago Tribune* 5 (January 31):1.

Kassirer, Jerome 1997 "Mergers and Acquisitions—Who Benefits? Who Loses?" *New England Journal of Medicine* 334:722–723.

Kimbrell, Andrew 1996 "Biocolonization: The Patenting of Life and the Global Market in Body Parts." In Jerry Mander and Edward Goldsmith, eds., *The Case against the Global Economy and for a Turn Toward the Local*. San Francisco: Sierra Club.

Kuttner, Robert 1999 "The American Health Care System: Health Insurance Coverage." *New England Journal of Medicine* 340:163–168.

LeRoy, Lauren 1979 "The Political Economy of U.S. Federal Health Policy: A Closer Look at Medicare," unpublished manuscript. University of California, San Francisco.

McKinlay, John B., and John D. Stoeckle 1994 "Corporatization and the Social Transformation of Doctoring." In Peter Conrad and Rochelle Kern, eds., *The Sociology of Health and Illness: Critical Perspectives*. New York: St. Martin's.

McNamee, Mike 1997 "Health-Care Inflation: It's Baaack!" *Business Week* (March 17):28–30.

Managed Health Care Improvement Task Force 1998 "Public Perceptions and Experiences with Managed Care: Background Paper." (January).

Marsteller, Jill, Randall Bovbjerg, and Len Nichols 1998 "Nonprofit Conversion: Theory, Evidence, and State Policy Options." *Health Services Research* 33:5.

Marx, Karl (1867) 1976 *Capital: A Critique of Political Economy*, vol 1. Middlesex, England: Penguin.

Multinational Monitor 1998 "Blowing the Whistle on Columbia/HCA: An Interview with Marc Gardner." *Multinational Monitor* (April):17–20.

Navarro, Vicente 1976 *Medicine under Capitalism*. New York: Prodist.

—— 1982 "The Labor Process and Health: A Historical Materialist Interpretation." *International Journal of Health Services* 12:5–29.

—— 1995 "Why Congress Did Not Enact Health Care Reform." *Journal of Health Politics, Policy and Law* 20:455–461.

Pardes, Herbert, Kenneth G. Manton, Eric S. Lander, H. Dennis Tolley, Arthus D. Ullian, and Hans Palmer 1999 "Effects of Medical Research on Health Care and the Economy." *Science* (January):36–37.

Pear, Robert 1997 "Health Insurers Skirting New Law, Officials Report." *New York Times* (October 5, 1997):A1.

Relman, Arnold S. 1980 "The New Medical-Industrial Complex." *New England Journal of Medicine* 303:963–970.

Rodberg, L., and G. Stevenson 1977 "The Health Care Industry in Advanced Capitalism." *Review of Radical Political Economics* 9:104–115.

Schlesinger, Mark, Theodore R. Marmor, and Richard Smithey 1987 "Nonprofit and For-Profit Medical Care: Shifting Roles and Implications for Health Policy." *Journal of Health Politics, Policy and Law* 12(3):427–457.

SeniorCare Investor 1998 "The Public Market." 10:1.

Shadle, M., and M. M. Hunter 1988 *National HMO Firms 1988*. Excelsior, Minn.: InterStudy.

Slaughter, Jane 1997 "Doctors Unite: Corporate Medicine and the Surprising Trend of Doctor Unionization." *Multinational Monitor* (November):22–24.

Smith, Sheila, Mark Freeland, Stephen Heffler, David McKusick, and the Health Expenditures Projection Team 1998 "The Next Ten Years of Health Spending: What Does the Future Hold?" *Health Affairs* 17:5.

Southwick, Karen 1990 "More Merger Mania among Drugmakers." *Healthweek* 4:1–51.

Srinivasan, Srija, Larry Levitt, and Janet Lundy 1998 "Wall Street's Love Affair with Health Care." *Health Affairs*. 17:4.

Starr, Paul 1982 *The Social Transformation of American Medicine*. New York: Basic Books.

Sussman, David 1990 "HMOs Are Still Riding a Wave of Profitability." *Healthweek* 4:12.

Tarabusi, Claudio Casadio, and Graham Vickery 1998 "Globalization of the Pharmaceutical Industry, Parts I and II." *International Journal of Health Services* 28:67–105, 281–303.

U.S. Department of Commerce, International Trade Administration 1990 "Health and Medical Services." *U.S. Industrial Outlook 1990*. Washington, D.C.: U.S. DOC.

U.S. Department of Health and Human Services 1989 *Health United States, 1989*, DHHS 90-1232. Hyattsville, Md.: U.S. DHHS.

—— 1997 *Home Health Agencies*. Health Care Financing Administration, unpublished data. Baltimore, Md.: U.S. DHHS.

U.S. National Center for Health Statistics [U.S.. NCHS], E. Hing, E. Sekscenski, and G. Strahan 1989 "National Nursing Home Survey: 1985 Summary for the United States." *Vital and Health Statistics Series 18*. Hyattsville, Md.: Public Health Service.

U.S. Office of National Cost Estimates (U.S. ONCE) 1990 "National Health Expenditures, 1988." *Health Care Financing Review* 11:1–41.

Weber, Max (1921) 1961 *General Economic History*. New York: Collier.

Wohl, Stanley 1984 *The Medical Industrial Complex*. New York: Harmony.

CARROLL L. ESTES
CHARLENE HARRINGTON
DAVID N. PELLOW

MENTAL HEALTH

See Positive Mental Health.

MENTAL ILLNESS AND MENTAL DISORDERS

After years of empirical research and theoretical activity, social scientists still do not agree about what mental illness actually is, let alone about what its primary causes are or about the efficacy of various treatments. Sociologists disagree about whether or not mental disorder is truly a disease that some people have and other people do not have, thus fitting a medical model of health and illness. They disagree about the relative importance of genetics, biochemical abnormalities, personality characteristics, and stress in the onset and course of psychiatric impairment. Most sociologists do, however, agree that definitions of mental illness are shaped by the historical, cultural, and interpersonal contexts within which they occur. They argue that the significance of any particular set of psychological or behavioral symptoms to a diagnosis of mental disorder lies in part with the actor and in part with the audience. Given this understanding of mental illness, sociologists are often as interested in understanding the consequences of being labeled mentally ill as they are in understanding the causes. Sociologists do, indeed,

study the social distribution and determinants of mental disorder. However, they also study social reactions to mental illness and the mentally ill and investigate ways in which mental health professionals and institutions can come to serve as agents of social control.

CLASSIFICATION AND DIAGNOSIS

Although psychiatrists themselves have difficulty defining mental illness, the official system for classifying and diagnosing mental disorder in the United States is produced by the American Psychiatric Association (APA). It is known as the *Diagnostic and Statistical Manual of Mental Disorder* (DSM) and was first published in 1952. In its earliest form, DSM-I included a list of 60 separate mental illnesses. By the second edition in 1968, psychiatric definitions of mental illness had changed so markedly that 145 different types of mental disorder were included. Despite the attempt in DSM-II to define the parameters of mental illness more precisely, critics from inside and outside psychiatry pointed out that diagnoses of mental disorder were extremely unreliable. When different psychiatrists independently used DSM-II to diagnose the same patients, they did so with substantially different results. Studies conducted during the 1960s and 1970s indicated that there was poor agreement about what disease classification was appropriate for any given patient; studies also found that clinicians had difficulty in differentiating normal persons from mental patients and that they frequently disagreed about prognosis and the clinical significance of particular symptom patterns (Loring and Powell 1988).

After years of debate, some of which was quite heated, the APA published a third edition of DSM in 1980. *Mental disorder* was defined in DSM-III as "a clinically significant behavioral or psychological syndrome or pattern that occurs in an individual and that is associated with either a painful symptom (distress) or impairment in one or more areas of functioning (disability)" (APA 1980, p. 6); deviant behaviors and conflicts between individuals and society were specifically excluded from this definition *unless* they were symptoms of another diagnosable disorder. DSM-III took a purely descriptive approach to diagnosis, outlining the essential and associated features of each disorder but making no attempt to explain the etiology of either symptoms or illnesses. At the time of the most recent revision (DSM-IV) in 1994, there was considerable debate about whether or not to actually retain the phrase "mental disorder" in the title of the DSM. The argument was that doing so implied a false distinction between mind and body, and between mental disorders and physical or general medical conditions. For lack of a better term, however, DSM-IV retained the same terminology and definition of mental disorder that had been used in DSM-III. DSM-IV contains hundreds of mental diagnoses, including such disorders as caffeine intoxication, circadian rhythm sleep disorder, and hypoactive sexual desire disorder. It also contains a section on "other conditions that may be a focus of clinical attention" but that are not mental disorders themselves. Included here are such conditions as relational problems connected with a family member's mental disorder, noncompliance with treatment, religious or spiritual, academic, occupational, acculturative, and phase-of-life problems.

The use of DSM-III and DSM-IV criteria has vastly improved the overall reliability of psychiatric diagnoses, thereby enabling psychiatry to meet one of the major criticisms of the medical model of mental disorder. The inclusion of more and more categories of illness in each succeeding version of DSM has led to more precise and consequently more reliable diagnoses. However, some scholars have argued that this expansion of mental diagnoses has less to do with problems of disease classification than with "problems" of third-party reimbursement (Kirk and Kutchins 1992; Mirowsky and Ross 1989). Each increase in the number of disorders listed in DSM has increased the scope of psychiatric practice. As the number of patients with recognized illnesses increases, so too does the amount of compensation that psychiatrists receive from insurance companies.

Even the firmest supporters of DSM-IV recognize that the classification of mental disorder is influenced by nonmedical considerations. In fact, DSM-IV itself includes a discussion of specific culture, age, and gender features which should be taken into account for each diagnosis. Pressures from outside psychiatry also influence diagnostic classifications. In order to reduce their payment liabilities, insurance companies have lobbied the APA to reduce the number of diagnoses. Changes in public attitudes toward sexual preference issues

led, in 1974, to dropping homosexuality from the list of mental disorders, and veterans' groups successfully pressed for the inclusion of posttraumatic stress syndrome (Scott 1990). The storm of controversy that surrounds the issue of whether premenstrual syndrome is a medical or a psychological condition, or whether it is socially unacceptable behavior, is another example of the intersection of political, social, economic, and diagnostic concerns (Figert 1994); at the insistence of feminists inside and outside psychiatry, premenstrual dysphoric disorder has been relegated to an appendix of DSM-IV on the basis that there is currently little scholarly evidence to support such a diagnosis and that its social implications dangerously feed "the prejudice that women's hormones are a cause of mental illness" (Tavris 1993, p. 172). In sum, there is a less than perfect correspondence between some disease-producing entity or syndrome and the diagnosis of mental disorder; psychiatric diagnosis is based partly in the reality of disordered behavior and emotional pain, and partly in the evaluations that society makes of that behavior and pain. Thus, questions about the validity of psychiatric diagnosis are as troubling for DSM-IV as they were for DSM-I. As one observer has noted, "We have learned how to make reliable diagnoses, but we still have no adequate criterion of their validity" (Kendell 1988, p. 374). Given the problems scholars have in defining "mental disorder" and given the validity problems that ensue, it is not surprising that epidemiologists have used a number of different strategies to estimate rates of psychiatric impairment. These different research methodologies often have led to quite different interpretations of the role of social factors in the etiology of mental illness.

MEASUREMENT

The earliest sociological research on mental disorder relied on data from individuals receiving psychiatric care. In a classic epidemiological study, Faris and Dunham (1939) reviewed the records of all patients admitted to Chicago's public and private mental hospitals between 1922 and 1934. They found that admission rates for psychosis were highest among individuals living in the inner city. Several years later, researchers used a similar design to study the social class distribution of mental disorder in New Haven. In contrast to the

Chicago study, which focused only on individuals who had been hospitalized, Hollingshead and Redlich (1958) included individuals receiving outpatient care from private psychiatrists in their study. Results from the New Haven study confirmed the earlier findings; the lower the social class, the higher the rate of mental disorder. More recent studies have also used information on treated populations. Studies of patient populations provide useful information to be sure; findings shed light on the social factors that influence the course of mental health treatment. Individuals receiving treatment for mental disorder, however, are not a random subset of the population of individuals experiencing psychological distress. Everybody who has potentially diagnosable mental disorder does not receive treatment. Furthermore, pathways to mental health care may be systematically different for individuals with different social characteristics. Consequently, research based on treated rates of mental disorder seriously underestimates the true rate of mental illness in a population. (In 1994 the Institute of Medicine Committee on the Prevention of Mental Disorders estimated, for instance, that only 10–30 percent of those with a mental disorder receive any treatment.) Furthermore, such research may confuse the effects of variables such as social class, gender, place of residence, and age on psychiatric treatment with the impact of those same variables on the development of psychiatric impairment.

An alternative strategy for studying the epidemiology of mental disorder is the community survey. Early studies such as the Midtown Manhattan study (Srole et al. 1962) used symptom checklists with large random samples to estimate the amount of psychiatric impairment in the general population. Although such studies provided less biased estimates of the prevalence of psychological distress than did research on patient populations, they were subject to a different set of criticisms. The most serious limitation of the early community studies was that they used impairment scales that measured global mental health. Not only did the scales fail to distinguish different types of disorders, they confounded symptoms of physical and psychological disorder (Crandall and Dohrenwend 1967), measured relatively minor forms of psychiatric impairment, and frequently failed to identify the most serious forms of mental illness (Dohrenwend and Crandall 1970). Since it

was not clear what relationship psychological symptom scales bore to cases of actual psychiatric disorder, it was also not clear how results from those studies contributed to an understanding of the social causes of mental illness.

Since the early 1980s, symptom scales that measure specific forms of impairment have largely replaced the early global scales with the consequence that the reliability and validity of community survey research has been vastly improved. The CES-D, for instance, is a twenty-item depression scale that can accurately distinguish clinical from normal populations and depression from other psychiatric diagnoses (Weissman et al. 1977). Consistently with the overall improvement in diagnostic reliability that has accompanied the development of DSM-III and DSM-IV, methods have been developed that provide reliable psychiatric diagnoses of many disorders among community residents. The most widely used diagnostic instrument of this sort was developed by a team of researchers at Washington University as part of the National Institute of Mental Health (NIMH) Division of Biometry and Epidemiology's Catchment Area Program. Called the Diagnostic Interview Schedule (DIS), the instrument can be administered by nonpsychiatrists doing interviews with the general population. Using DSM-IV criteria, it provides both current and lifetime diagnoses for many adult psychiatric disorders (Eaton et al. 1985). Enormous amounts of time and money have been devoted to the development of the DIS, and research that makes use of it promises to provide a vital link between studies of clinical and community populations. Nevertheless, even instruments like the DIS have shortcomings.

Mirowsky and Ross (1989) have challenged the DIS and the DSM upon which it is based on the grounds that psychiatric diagnosis is a weak form of measurement and that it is of questionable validity. These authors claim that psychiatric disorders are dimensional, not categoric. By collapsing a pattern of symptoms into a single diagnostic case, valuable information is lost about the nature of the disorder. As a result, the causes of mental, emotional, and behavioral problems are obscured. Mirowsky and Ross go on to suggest that the reliance on diagnosis does not give a true, that is, a valid, picture of psychiatric distress. Instead, psychiatrists use diagnosis because it allows them to receive payment from insurance companies who will pay only for cases and because it establishes mental distress as a problem that can be treated only by a physician. Although their criticisms are harsh, these authors reestablish the important distinction between the social construction of psychiatric diagnoses and the social causes of psychological pain. It is the latter issue, however, that most sociological research has addressed.

THE EPIDEMIOLOGY OF MENTAL DISORDER

Socioeconomic Status. The inverse relationship between socioeconomic status and mental disorder is now so well established that it has almost acquired the status of a sociological law. The relationship is surprisingly robust; it holds for most forms of mental disorder, no matter how socioeconomic status is measured, and for both patient populations and community samples. The relationship is strongest and most consistent for schizophrenia, personality disorders, and medically based syndromes. Findings for the major affective disorders are somewhat less consistent. Studies tend to report weak to moderate inverse relationships between social class and the incidence of major affective disorders such as anxiety and depression (Kessler et al. 1994). However, studies sometimes report no relationship (Weissman et al. 1991) or a positive class gradient (Weissman and Myers 1978). Evidence on the class distribution of minor depression is more clear-cut, with studies almost universally showing higher levels of depressive symptomatology among the lower strata. Similarly, research consistently shows that the highest levels of general distress are also found among those with the lowest income, education, or occupational status.

There are two general qualifications to the pattern outlined above. First, even though socioeconomic status is negatively associated with most types of mental disorder, the relationship is probably not linear. Extremely high rates of disorder are typically found in the lowest stratum. Higher strata do have progressively lower rates, but variation is considerably less between them than between the lowest and next-to-lowest tier. Some scholars have claimed, therefore, that serious mental illness is primarily an underclass phenomenon. Second, the inverse relationship between social class and mental disorder may be stronger in urban than in rural areas and is probably stronger in the United States than in other societies. (For a comprehensive review of this literature, see Ortega and Corzine 1990.)

Most, if not all, of the major sociological theories of mental illness begin with the empirical observation that psychological disorder is most prevalent among those individuals with the fewest resources and the least social power. Until recently, researchers focused almost exclusively on one dimension of inequality—social class. Indeed, the dominant paradigms in the sociology of mental health have derived primarily from the attempt to explain this relationship; hypotheses regarding the effects of gender, age, or marital status on psychological distress are often simple elaborations of models derived from the study of social class and mental disorder. Three general models of the relationship between social resources and mental illness have been suggested. These are (1) the "social causation" hypothesis; (2) the "social selection" or "drift" hypothesis; and (3) the "labeling" or "societal reaction" approach.

Social Causation. *Social causation* is a general term used to encompass a number of specific theories about the class-linked causes of mental disorder. Perhaps the most common version of social causation explains the higher rates of mental disorder among the lowest socioeconomic strata in terms of greater exposure to stress. According to this perspective, members of the lower class experience more stressful life events and more chronic strains (Turner et al. 1995). In addition, they are more likely to experience physical hazards in the environment, blocked aspirations, and status frustration (Cockerham 1996). Taken together, these stresses produce elevated rates of psychiatric impairment. In another version of social causation, scholars have argued that class differences in coping resources and coping styles are at least as important in the etiology of mental disorder as are class differences in exposure to stress (Pearlin and Schooler 1978). In this view, poverty increases the likelihood of mental illness because it (1) disrupts precisely those social networks that might effectively buffer the effects of stressful events and (2) inhibits the development of an active, flexible approach to dealing with problems. For both social and psychological reasons, then, the lower classes make use of less effective coping strategies. Finally, part of the class difference in mental disorder, especially rates of treated disorder, may stem from class differences in attitudes toward mental illness and psychiatric care. Because of more negative attitudes toward mental illness and because of inadequate access to appropriate psychiatric care, the lower classes may be more seriously ill when they first come in contact with the mental health care system, and thus they may be more likely to be hospitalized (Rushing and Ortega 1979).

Social Selection and Drift. This perspective implies that, rather than causing mental disorder, low socioeconomic status is a result of psychological impairment. Two mobility processes can be involved. According to the drift hypothesis, the onset of mental disorder adversely affects an individual's ability to hold a job and generate income. As a result of psychological disorder, then, individuals experience downward intragenerational mobility and physical relocation to less socially desirable neighborhoods (Eaton 1980). Social selection, on the other hand, occurs when premorbid characteristics of the mentally disordered individual prevent him or her attaining as high a social status as would be expected of similar individuals in the general population. Here, the focus is on intergenerational mobility (Kendler et al. 1995).

Labeling or Societal Reaction. Based on the work of Thomas Scheff (1966), this approach holds that much of the class difference in mental disorder stems not from any real difference in mental illness but rather from a tendency to diagnose or label a disproportionate number of lower-class individuals as psychologically impaired. According to Scheff, the process works as follows. Psychiatric symptoms have many different causes and many people experience them. Only a few individuals, however, are ever labeled as mentally ill. People who are so labeled are drawn from the ranks of those least able to resist the imputation of deviance. Once an individual is identified as mentally ill, a number of forces work to reinforce and solidify a mentally ill self-identity. Once labeled, individuals are encouraged by family and mental health professionals to acknowledge their illness. They are rewarded for behaving as "good" patients should, a task made easier by virtue of the fact that individuals learn the stereotypes of mental illness in early childhood. When individuals are

discharged from the mental hospital, or when they otherwise terminate treatment, they may be rejected by others. This rejection has psychological consequences that simply reinforce a mentally ill identity. The process is self-fulfilling, leading Scheff to conclude that attachment of the mentally ill label is the single most important factor in the development of chronic mental disorder.

An Assessment. After two decades or more of acrimonious debate, the search for unitary explanations of the relationship between mental disorder and social class has largely been abandoned. Sociologists seldom claim that mental illness is derived only from medical factors, is caused only by features of the social environment, or stems purely from societal reaction. Most scholars now believe that different types of disorders require different types of explanations. Genetic and other biomedical factors are clearly involved in schizophrenia, and certain forms of depression. However, genetics, brain chemistry, and other medical factors do not provide the entire answer since, even among identical twins, concordance rates for mental illness fall only in the range of 30 to 50 percent. Thus, the causes of mental disorder must also be sought in the social environment. Research does suggest a modest relationship between the social stressors attendant to lower-class status and the onset of some forms of mental disorder. The evidence is clearest, however, for anxiety, substance abuse, and relatively minor forms of depression or psychological distress. For the more severe forms of mental illness and for conduct disorders, the drift and selection hypothesis appears to have the most empirical support. (See Miech et al. 1999 for a comprehensive review and data bearing on these points.) Although labeling is not the only cause of chronic mental illness, it is clear that the mental illness label does have negative consequences. In what has come to be called modified labeling theory, researchers have demonstrated that the status of ex-mental patient and the discrimination that follows from it, coupled with the ex-patient's expectation of rejection by others, adversely affects earnings, work status, and subsequent mental health (Link 1987; Markowitz 1998). Thus, labeling is one of the processes through which drift occurs. As researchers continue to refine the definitions and measurement of various mental disorders and as they more clearly delineate the processes of social causation, drift, and labeling, it is likely that further theoretical convergences will be identified.

Gender. It is not yet clear whether there are significant gender differences in overall rates of mental illness. There is little doubt, however, that certain types of disorders occur more frequently among women than among men. Research clearly shows that women are more likely to suffer from major and minor depression and anxiety than are men (Kessler et al. 1994); men, however, are usually found to have higher rates of antisocial personality disorders and the various forms of substance abuse and dependence (Aneshensel et al. 1991). The sex ratio for some forms of mental disorder may be age dependent; males have higher rates of schizophrenia prior to adolescence and females have higher rates in later adulthood (Loring and Powell 1988). Studies also find that male-female differences in levels of depression are most pronounced among young adults (Dean and Ensel 1983). Furthermore, gender effects appear to interact with those of marital, occupational, and parental roles.

Scholars continue to disagree about the precise form of the interaction effects of gender and marital status on mental illness. Virtually all studies report that gender differences are most pronounced among married persons; married women consistently show higher levels of depression and anxiety than married men. Evidence on the unmarried, however, is mixed. Research based on treated populations often finds higher rates of disorder among single men. Studies based on community samples more frequently report higher distress levels among unmarried women. The interaction between gender and marital status is further complicated by the presence of children, work outside the home, or both.

Some research on married persons finds that gender differences are reduced when both husbands and wives are employed. Studies comparing groups of women often find that employment has modest, positive effects on mental health. However, other studies report no difference between employed women and housewives (Carr 1997) and a few report that married, full-time homemakers with children have fewer worries and more life satisfaction (Veroff et al. 1981). These apparently contradictory findings stem, in part, from the different measures of mental health and illness used. It is possible, for instance, that small children can simultaneously increase their mothers' life satisfaction and their overall levels of anxiety and distress. However, two substantive factors also appear to be involved. First, it is the demands created by children and employment, rather than by parental or employment status per se, that cause elevated levels of distress among married women (Rosenfeld 1989). The level of demands varies, of course, depending upon the level of male responsibility for child care and housework. Second, employment decreases gender differences in distress only when it is consistent with both the husband's and the wife's desires. Married men's distress levels may, in fact, surpass married women's when wives work but their husbands prefer them not to (Ross et al. 1983).

As is true for social class, explanations for gender differences in mental disorder fall into three broad classes: social causation, social selection, and labeling. Because of the consistency of gender effects (at least for depression and anxiety) and improvements in the reliability of psychiatric diagnoses, most recent work has focused on the ways in which the social and psychological correlates of male and female roles cause variation in rates of mental disorder. Some have argued that differences in sex-role socialization make females more likely to direct frustration inward, toward themselves, rather than towards others, as males might. Thus, women are more likely to develop intropunitive disorders, whereas men are more likely to behave in antisocial ways (Loring and Powell 1988). Others have argued that women are more attached to others and are more sensitive to others' needs than are men. As a result, not only is women's mental health influenced by their own experiences but, also in contrast to men, they are more psychologically vulnerable to the stresses or losses of loved ones (Kessler and McLeod 1984). Although the empirical literature is far from clear on this point (cf. Umberson et al. 1996), according to this perspective, women experience more stressful events and are more psychologically reactive to them than are men. Other explanations—for both direct and interactive effects—of gender on mental illness have focused on male-female differences in power, resources, demands, and personal control. Insofar as employment increases women's power and resources, it is likely to have positive effects on mental health. Well-educated employed women have fewer mental symptoms than nonworking women; among working-class and lower-class women, however, employment may actually increase anxiety and depression because it elevates demands at the same time that it produces only marginal increases in resources (Sales and Hanson Frieze 1984). Since employed women generally retain full responsibility for children, the demands of caring for children, particularly those under the age of 6, exacerbate work-related stress. Thus, male-female differences in power and resources produce differences in ability to control demands. Gender differences in control, in turn, shape perceptions of personal mastery; personal mastery is the psychological mechanism that connects gender differences in resources and demands to gender differences in mental illness (Rosenfield 1989).

The social selection perspective is valid only for explaining male-female differences in the relationship between marital status and mental disorder. The argument is that mental illness is more likely to select men out of marriage than women. (See Rushing 1979 for a related discussion.) According to this perspective, male forms of mental disorder—psychosis and antisocial personality, for example—prevent impaired men from satisfactorily discharging the traditional male obligation to be good economic providers, making them ineligible as marriage partners. In contrast, female forms of psychiatric impairment may go undetected for long periods of time and may not seriously interfere with a woman's ability to fulfill the traditional housekeeping role. Thus, the higher rates of female disorder among the married may be a partial artifact of the differing probabilities of marriage for mentally disordered men and women.

The labeling explanation for male-female differences in psychiatric impairment begins by challenging the notion that women actually experience more symptoms and disorders than men do. Labeling theorists argue that women are overdiagnosed and overmedicated because of biases on the part of predominantly male psychiatrists and because of the male biases inherent in psychiatric nomenclature. Coupled with the greater willingness of females to admit their problems and to seek help for them, these biases simply produce the illusion that women are more likely to be disordered than men. Scholars using the labeling–societal reaction–critical perspective argue that the effects of gender biases are not benign and that they have consequences at two levels. First, individual women are unlikely to receive appropriate services for their real mental health problems. Second, and at a societal level, critics argue that psychiatry simply legitimates traditional gender roles, thereby buttressing the status quo (Chesler 1973).

A Theoretical Assessment. With the development of DSM-IV and with increases in the number of female mental health professionals, concern over the issues raised by labeling theorists has diminished somewhat. Trusting that the most blatant instances of sexism have been eliminated, researchers have turned their attention toward specifying the social psychological dynamics of the gender–mental health equation; considerable progress has been made in elucidating the circumstances under which women are most likely to experience symptoms of mental disorder. Nevertheless, it may be premature to close the question of gender bias in psychiatric disorders. In one study, male clinicians appeared to overestimate the prevalence of depressive disorders among women, a tendency that is certainly consistent with gender stereotypes. In the same study, black males were most likely to be diagnosed as paranoid schizophrenics, a view consistent with both gender and racial stereotypes (Loring and Powell 1988). In yet another study, male and female psychiatrists made similar diagnoses of male and female patients presenting severe Axis I conditions but made significantly different diagnoses for male and female patients with Axis II conditions, such as personality disorders (Dixon et al. 1995). Thus, advances of DSM-III (and IV) notwithstanding, the authors of these studies conclude that sex and race of client and psychiatrist continue to influence diagnosis even when psychiatric criteria appear to be clear-cut.

Age. Among adults, and with the exception of some types of dementia and other syndromes due to general medical conditions, rates of mental illness decrease with age. Rates of schizophrenia, manic disorder, drug addiction, and antisocial personality all peak between the ages of 25 and 44 (Robins et al. 1984). Furthermore, an older person with a serious mental disorder is likely to have had a first psychiatric episode in young or middle adulthood. At least 90 percent of older schizophrenics experienced the onset of the disorder in earlier life. Similarly, about two-thirds of older alcoholics have a long history of alcohol abuse or dependence (Hinrichsen 1990). Depression is the disorder most likely to occur among the elderly, and a substantial proportion of older community residents do report some of its symptoms. In general, the relationship between age and depression appears to be curvilinear, with depression lowest among the middle aged, higher among younger and older adults, and highest among the oldest (Mirowsky and Ross 1992). Nevertheless, relatively few of these older individuals meet criteria for clinical depression (Blazer et al. 1987), and rates of major depression are lower among older adults than in younger age groups. Some older persons, however, are more vulnerable to depression than others. As is true throughout the life cycle, women, individuals with health problems, the unmarried, and those with lower socioeconomic status are at greater risk of depression in late life than their peers. Estimating the true prevalence of depression among the elderly is especially problematic because its symptoms are frequently confused with Alzheimer's disease or other forms of dementia.

According to some estimates, two to four million older Americans suffer some form of mental disorder due to a general medical condition. Of these, roughly half are diagnosed with Alzheimer's, a disease that involves an irreversible, progressive deterioration of the brain. Approximately half of all nursing home residents are estimated to suffer from some form of dementia. Because there is no known treatment for most of these disorders, older mental patients receive little psychiatric care. Critics suggest, however, that many older persons are improperly diagnosed as having disorders of general medical origin. A sizable minority may actually be depressed; others may have treatable forms of dementia caused by medications, infection, metabolic disturbances, alcohol, or brain tumors. In some instances, then, the stereotype that senility is a concomitant of the aging process prevents appropriate diagnosis, intervention, and treatment.

Most explanations of the age–mental health relationship have focused on specific age groups.

Clinicians suggest, for instance, that anxiety and depression in middle age are a consequence of hormonal change or of changes in family and occupational roles. The personality disorders of young adulthood are often explained in terms of the stresses produced by the transition from adolescence to full adult roles. Among the elderly, explanations have focused on either organic or environmental factors. The dementias have recognized organic causes. Although neither is a normal part of the aging process, the two major causes of these disorders are (1) the deterioration of the brain tissue that is associated with Alzheimer's disease and (2) cerebral arteriosclerosis. However, environmental factors also contribute to the onset of the dementias. They do so, in part, by increasing the likelihood of stroke or heart attack. In contrast, primary mental disorders, such as depression, personality disorders, and anxiety, depend more directly upon environmental factors. Some types of depression appear to have a genetic component, but the genetic link appears to be stronger in early- than in late-onset cases. Individuals who have their first episode of clinical depression prior to the age of 50, for instance, are more likely to have relatives with depression than those who become depressed in later years (Hinrichsen 1990). Consequently, losses typical of late life—losses of health, occupation, income, and loved ones—appear to be the primary causes of mental health problems among older adults.

Clearly, no single theory can adequately explain the etiology of mental disorder; at each stage of the life cycle, variables that are relevant to the onset of one type of disorder may be insignificant in the onset of other illnesses. Similarly, no single variable or set of variables is likely to explain age differences in overall rates of mental disorder. Nevertheless, efforts are under way to systematically explain the inverse relationship between age and primary psychiatric impairment. Gove and his associates have suggested that psychological distress decreases with age because individuals are able, over time, to find and settle into an appropriate social niche; as individuals move through life, they become less emotional and less self-absorbed, function more effectively in their selected roles, and generally become more content with themselves and with others. As a result, rates of mental disorder decrease from late adolescence through late life (Gove 1985; Gove et al. 1989).

Place of Residence. Sociologists have commonly assumed that rates of mental disorder are higher in urban than in rural areas. However, this assumption is based more on the antiurban bias of much sociological theory than it is on empirical research. In a thoughtful and systematic review, Wagenfeld (1990) has argued that there is little evidence in the mental health literature to suggest the superiority of rural life. In several of the rural community studies Wagenfeld cites, researchers report a "probable" case rate of depression and anxiety of 12 to 20 percent. Studies that explicitly compare rural and urban communities generally find that rates of psychosis are higher in rural communities and that rates of depression are somewhat higher in urban areas. Residents of metropolitan communities also appear more likely to have multiple diagnoses than do rural residents, leading Kessler et al. (1994) to conclude that urban-rural differences in the prevalence of mental disorder probably reflect differences in comorbidity rather than differences in rates of individuals having a psychiatric condition. Differences in case definition and diagnosis, differences in how "rural place of residence" is defined and measured, and differences in the time period during which studies were conducted make it difficult, overall, to assess whether rural communities have significantly higher overall rates of pathology than urban areas. Results are sufficient, however, to suggest that rural life is not as blissful as it is often claimed to be. Recent declines in the rural economy, the out-migration of the young and upwardly mobile, and the relative paucity of mental health services are likely to be major contributing factors in the etiology of rural mental health problems.

Other factors. Epidemiologists have also explored the relationships between the incidence or prevalence of mental disorder and such variables as race and ethnicity, migration, social mobility, and marital status. In each case, results generally support the view that individuals with the fewest resources—both economic and social—are most likely to experience psychiatric impairment. However, most research has adopted a rather static view; few studies have assessed the extent to which relationships between each of these variables and mental disorder have changed over time. Given the significant changes in diagnostic practices and in the mental health professions over the last decades, this is a striking omission.

AN AGENDA FOR FUTURE RESEARCH

Since the early 1960s, psychiatric sociology has undergone enormous changes. During the 1960s and 1970s, much of the literature was sharply critical of psychiatry and of medical models of madness. Although sociologists were divided about the relative importance of labeling processes in the etiology of mental illness, most agreed that psychiatric diagnoses were unreliable and were influenced by social status and social resources, that long-term institutionalization had detrimental effects, and that at least some patients were hospitalized inappropriately. Such criticisms provided one impetus for the substantial change that took place in psychiatric care during the same period; laws were changed to make involuntary commitment more difficult; steps were taken to deinstitutionalize many mental patients; and a major effort was made to improve the reliability of mental diagnoses. By the time DSM-III was published in 1980, the most flagrant abuses and the sharpest criticism of psychiatry seemed to have disappeared. Consequently, many sociologists shifted their attention from concerns about the lives of people with serious mental disorder to the social correlates of psychological distress among the general population (Cook and Wright 1995). Using what is basically a medical model of impairment, researchers have focused on delineating the relationship between social variables (such as gender, age, race, social class, place of residence, life events, and stress) and specific diagnoses (most often depressive symptoms, anxiety, and substance abuse). Indeed, the psychiatric view of mental disorder is so well established in sociology that the growing literature on homelessness has generally accepted the assertion of mental health professionals that most of the homeless are simply individuals who have fallen through the cracks of the mental health care system. (For notable exceptions, see Bogard et al. 1999; Snow, Baker, and Anderson 1986.) It is surprising that sociologists have been so uncritical in their acceptance of this position; it is also surprising that in the decade of the 1990s, declared by the National Institute of Mental Health to be the "Decade of the Brain," they have been so ready to accept the view that mental illness is primarily a problem of genetics or brain chemistry and that it can be treated just like any other disease. It is certainly true that enormous strides have been made in the diagnosis and psychopharmacological

treatment of mental disorder. It is also certainly true that biomedical factors are causally involved in some types of mental illness. Sociologists must, therefore, continue their efforts to develop a model of mental disorder that integrates medical, psychological, and social factors.

As some critics point out, however, the current emphasis on diagnoses, cases, and the medical model of mental illness has limitations. Acceptance of the psychiatric view of mental disorder leads to the acceptance of policy recommendations that are not yet firmly grounded in empirical research. It is far from clear, for instance, that deinstitutionalization of the mentally ill is the primary cause of homelessness in America. As Bogard et al. (1999) point out, conventional wisdom notwithstanding, very few homeless mothers are mentally ill; it can be reasonably argued, then, that the enormous resources that have been directed toward providing them with mental health care might more appropriately and effectively be used to provide safe, affordable housing. In a similar vein, Link and Phelan (1995) note that current attention to individual risk factors in disease gives rise to "personal policy" recommendations that leave totally unaddressed the fundamental social conditions that cause differential exposure to risk.

Furthermore, few studies have assessed the extent to which changes in psychiatric diagnosis or changes in the civil rights guarantees of mental patients have affected the delivery and quality of mental health services. Consumers and families have voiced concern that the powerful new psychopharmacological drugs are being inappropriately used as forms of social control and chemical restraint at the same time that research continues to show that it is racial and ethnic minority consumers who are most likely to be so restrained (Cook and Wright 1995). Aside from the field trials used in their formulation, few studies have assessed the reliability and validity of DSM-IV diagnoses. However, results from several studies show that nonclinical factors such as gender, race, the availability of viable community housing and the presence of reliable caretakers significantly affect not only diagnosis but treatment protocols and outcomes. (See Cook and Wright [1995] for a review of these studies and these concerns.) It is far from clear, then, that lower-class women are any more likely to receive appropriate care in 1999 than they were in 1950 or 1970. It is unclear whether urban-rural differences in rates of mental disorder have changed over time and, if so, to what extent changes in diagnostic systems or service availability are implicated. Evidence that rural residents may actually experience mental illness at approximately the same rates as urban residents coupled with an acute shortage of rural mental health providers suggest the importance of understanding the diagnostic practices of primary-care physicians and of providing appropriate training to them.

Research in the next century must adopt a more dynamic or process view of mental health issues. The consequences of changes in psychiatric diagnosis, of the increased reliance on drug therapies, of changes in mental health law and policy, and in the availability of mental health services must be assessed. Changes in the mental health system must be linked to changes in the composition of the pool of "potential clients" and to issues regarding the development of gender, age, class, and culturally appropriate systems of care.

REFERENCES

American Psychiatric Association 1980 *Diagnostic and Statistical Manual of Mental Disorders III*. Washington: APA.

—— 1994 *Diagnostic and Statistical Manual of Mental Disorders IV*. Washington: APA.

Aneshensel, Carol S., Carolyn M. Rutter, and Peter A. Lachenbruch 1991 "Social Structure, Stress, and Mental Health." *American Sociological Review* 56:166–178.

Blazer, Dan, Dana C. Hughes, and Linda K. George 1987 "The Epidemiology of Depression in an Elderly Community Population." *Gerontologist* 27:281–287.

Bogard, Cynthia J., J. Jeff McConnell, Naomi Gerstel, and Michael Schwartz 1999 "Homeless Mothers and Depression: Misdirected Policy." *Journal of Health and Social Behavior* 40:46–62.

Carr, Deborah 1997 "The Fulfillment of Career Dreams at Midlife: Does It Matter for Women's Mental Health?" *Journal of Health and Social Behavior* 38:331–344.

Chesler, Phyllis 1973 *Women and Madness*. New York: Avon.

Cockerham, William 1996 *Sociology of Mental Disorder*, 4th ed. Upper Saddle River, N.J.: Prentice Hall.

Cook, Judith A., and Eric R. Wright 1995 "Medical Sociology and the Study of Severe Mental Illness:

Reflections on Past Accomplishments and Directions for Future Research." *Journal of Health and Social Behavior* (Extra Issue):95–114.

Crandall, D. L., and B. P. Dohrenwend 1967 "Some Relations among Psychiatric Symptoms, Organic Illness, and Social Class." *American Journal of Psychiatry* 1527–1538.

Dean, Alfred, and Walter M. Ensel 1983 "Socially Structured Depression in Men and Women." In James Greenley, ed., *Research in Community Mental Health*, vol. 3. Greenwich, Conn.: JAI.

Dixon, Jo, C. Gordon, and T. Khomusi 1995 "Sexual Symmetry in Psychiatric Diagnosis." *Social Problems* 42:429–448.

Dohrenwend, Bruce P., and D. L. Crandall 1970 "Psychiatric Symptoms in Community, Clinic, and Mental Hospital Groups." *American Journal of Psychiatry* 126:1611–1621.

Eaton, William W. 1980 *The Sociology of Mental Disorder*. New York: Praeger.

——, M. M. Weissman, J. Anthony, L. Robins, D. Blazer, and M. Karno 1985 "Problems in the Definition and Measurement of Prevalence and Incidence of Psychiatric Disorder." In W. Eaton and R. Kessler, eds., *Epidemiologic Field Methods in Psychiatry: The NIMH Epidemiologic Catchment Area Program*. Orlando, Fla.: Academic.

Faris, Robert E., and H. Warren Dunham 1939 *Mental Disorders in Urban Areas*. Chicago: University of Chicago Press.

Figert, Anne 1994 *Women and the Ownership of PMS: The Structuring of a Psychiatric Diagnosis*. Hawthorne, N.Y.: Aldine de Gruyter.

Gove, Walter R. 1985 "The Effect of Age and Gender on Daviant Behavior: A Biopsychosocial Perspective." In Alice Rossi, ed., *Gender and the Life Course*. New York: Aldine de Gruyter.

——, Suzanne T. Ortega, and Carolyn Briggs Style 1989 "The Maturational and Role Perspectives on Aging and Self Through the Adult Years: An Empirical Evaluation." *American Journal of Sociology* 94:1117–1145.

Hinrichsen, Gregory A. 1990 *Mental Health Problems and Older Adults*. Santa Barbara, Calif.: ABC-CLIO.

Hollingshead, A. B., and F. C. Redlich 1958 *Social Class and Mental Illness*. New York: John Wiley.

Institute of Medicine, Committee on Prevention of Mental Disorders, Division of Biobehavioral Sciences and Mental Disorders 1994 *Reducing Risks for Mental Disorders: Frontiers for Preventive Intervention Research*. Washington: National Academy Press.

Kendell, R. E. 1988 "What is a Case? Food for Thought for Epidemiologists." *Archives of General Psychiatry* 45:374–376.

Kendler, Kenneth S., Ellen E. Walters, Michael C. Neale, Ronald C. Kessler, Andrew C. Health, and Lindon J. Eaves 1995 "The Structure of the Genetic and Environmental Risk Factors for Six Major Psychiatric Disorders in Women: Phobia, Generalized Anxiety Disorder, Panic Disorder, Bulimia, Major Depression, and Alcoholism." *Archives of General Psychiatry* 52:374–383.

Kessler, Ronald C., Katherine A. McGonagle, Shanyang Zhao, Christopher B. Nelson, Michael Hughes, Suzanne Eshleman, Hans-Ulrich Wittchen, and Kenneth S, Kendler 1994 "Lifetime and 12-Month Prevalence of DSM-III-R Psychiatric Disorders in the United States: Results from the National Comorbidity Study." *Archives of General Psychiatry* 51:8–19.

——, and Jane McLeod 1984 "Sex Differences in Vulnerability to Undesirable Life Events." *American Sociological Review* 49:620–631.

Kirk, Stuart A., and Herb Kutchins 1992 *The Selling of DSM*. Hawthorne, N.Y.: Aldine de Gruyter.

Link, Bruce 1987 "Understanding Labeling Effects in the Area of Mental Disorders: An Assessment of Expectations of Rejection." *American Sociological Review* 52:96–112.

——, and Jo Phelan 1995 "Social Conditions as Fundamental Causes of Disease." *Journal of Health and Social Behavior* (Extra Issue):80–94.

Loring, Marti, and Brian Powell 1988 "Gender, Race, and DSM-III: A Study of the Objectivity of Psychiatric Behavior." *Journal of Health and Social Behavior* 29:1–22.

Markowitz, Fred E. 1998 "The Effects of Stigma on the Psychological Well-Being and Life Satisfaction of Persons with Mental Illness." *Journal of Health and Social Behavior* 39:335–347.

Miech, Richard A., Avshalom Caspi, Terrie E. Moffitt, Bradley R. Entner Wright, and Phil A. Silva 1999 "Low Socioeconomic Status and Mental Disorders: A Longitudinal Study of Selection and Causation during Young Adulthood." *American Journal of Sociology* 104:1096–1131.

Mirowsky, John, and Catherine E. Ross 1992 "Age and Depression." *Journal of Health and Social Behavior* 33:187–205.

——, and Catherine E. Ross 1989 "Psychiatric Diagnosis as Reified Measurement." *Journal of Health and Social Behavior* 30:11–25.

Ortega, Suzanne T., and Jay Corzine 1990 "Socioeconomic Status and Mental Disorders." In James

Greenley, ed., *Research in Community and Mental Health*, vol. 6. Greenwich, Conn.: JAI.

Pearlin, Leonard, and Carmi Schooler 1978 "The Structure of Coping." *Journal of Health and Social Behavior* 19:2–21.

Robins, Lee N., J. E. Helzer, M. M. Weissman, H. Orvaschel, E. Gruenberg, J. D. Burke, Jr., and D. A. Regier 1984 "Lifetime Prevalence of Specific Disorders in Three Sites." *Archives of General Psychiatry* 41:949–958.

Rosenfield, Sarah 1989 "The Effects of Women's Employment: Personal Control and Sex Differences in Mental Health." *Journal of Health and Social Behavior* 30:77–91.

Ross, Catherine E., John Mirowsky, and Joan Huber 1983 "Dividing Work, Sharing Work, and In-Between: Marriage Patterns and Depression." *American Sociological Review* 48:809–823.

Rushing, William A. 1979 "The Functional Importance of Sex Roles and Sex-Related Behavior in Societal Reactions to Residual Deviants." *Journal of Health and Social Behavior* 20:208–217.

——, and Suzanne T. Ortega 1979 "Socioeconomic Status and Mental Disorder: New Evidence and a Sociomedical Formulation." *American Journal of Sociology* 84:1175–1200.

Sales, Esther, and Irene Hanson Frieze 1984 "Women and Work: Implications for Mental Health." In L. E. Walker, ed., *Women and Mental Health Policy*. Beverly Hills, Calif.: Sage.

Scheff, Thomas J. 1966 *Being Mentally Ill: A Sociological Theory*. Chicago: Aldine de Gruyter.

Scott, Wilbur J. 1990 "PTSD in DSM-III: A Case in the Politics of Diagnosis and Disease." *Social Problems* 37:294–310.

Snow, David, Susan Baker, and Leon Anderson 1986 "The Myth of Pervasive Mental Illness among the Homeless." *Social Problems* 33:407–423.

Srole, L., T. S. Langner, S. T. Michel, M. D. Opler, and T. C. Rennie 1962 *Mental Health in the Metropolis: The Midtown Manhattan Study*. New York: McGraw-Hill.

Tavris, Carol 1993 "Do You Menstruate? If So, Psychiatrists Think You May Be Nuts." *Glamour* (November):172.

Townsend, John M. 1980 "Psychiatry versus Societal Reaction: A Critical Analysis." *Journal of Health and Social Behavior* 21:268–278.

Turner, R. Jay, Blair Wheaton, and Donald A. Lloyd 1995 "The Epidemiology of Social Stress." *American Sociological Review* 60:104–125.

Umberson, Debra, Meichu D. Chen, James S. House, Kristine Hopkins, and Ellen Slaten 1996 "The Effect of Social Relationships on Psychological Well-Being: Are Men and Women Really So Different?" *American Sociological Review* 61:837–857.

Veroff, Joseph, Elizabeth Douvan, and Richard A. Kulka 1981 *The Inner American*. New York: Basic.

Wagenfeld, Morton O. 1990 "Mental Health and Rural America: A Decade Review." *Journal of Rural Health* 6:507–522.

Weissman, Myrna M., Martha L. Bruce, Phillip J. Leaf, Louis P. Florio, and Charles E. Holzer 1991 "Affective Disorders." In Lee N. Robins and Darrel A. Regier, eds., *Psychiatric Disorders in America: The Epidemiological Catchment Area Study*. New York: Free Press.

——, and Jerome K. Myers 1978 "Affective Disorders in a U.S. Urban Community." *Archives of General Psychiatry* 35:1304–1311.

——, D. Scholomskas, M. Pottenger, B. Prusoff, and B. Locke 1977 "Assessing Depressive Symptoms in Five Psychiatric Populations: A Validation Study." *American Journal of Epidemiology* 106:203–214.

Suzanne T. Ortega
Sharon L. Larson

MERITOCRACY

See Affirmative Action; Equality of Opportunity.

META-ANALYSIS

Meta-analysis is the practice of statistically summarizing empirical findings from different studies, reaching generalizations about the obtained results. Thus, "meta-analysis" literally refers to analysis of analyses. Meta-analysis, a term coined by Glass (1976), is also known as *research synthesis* and *quantitative reviewing*. Because progress within any scientific field has always hinged on cumulating empirical evidence about phenomena in an orderly and accurate fashion, reviews of studies have historically proved extremely influential (e.g., Mazela and Malin 1977). With the exponential growth in the numbers of studies available on a given social scientific topic, the need for these reviews has increased proportionally, meaning that reviews are potentially even more important each day. The empirical evidence, consisting of multiple studies examining a phenomenon, exists as a literature on the topic. Although new studies rarely replicate earlier studies without changing or adding new features, many studies can be described as conceptual replications that use different stimulus materials and dependent measures to test the same hypothesis, and still others might contain exact replications embedded within a larger design that adds new experimental conditions. In other instances, repeated tests of a relation accrue in a less systematic manner because researchers sometimes include in their studies tests of particular hypotheses in auxiliary or subsidiary analyses.

In order to reach conclusions about empirical support for a phenomenon, it is necessary to compare and contrast the findings of relevant studies. Therefore, accurate comparisons of study outcomes—reviews of research—are at the very heart of the scientific enterprise. Until recently these comparisons were nearly always made using informal methods that are now known as *narrative reviewing*, a practice by which scholars drew overall conclusions from their impressions of the overall trend of the studies' findings, sometimes guided by a count of the number of studies that had either produced or failed to produce statistically significant findings in the hypothesized direction. Narrative reviews have appeared in many different contexts and still serve a useful purpose in writing that does not have a comprehensive literature review as its goal (e.g., textbook summaries, introductions to journal articles reporting primary research). Although narrative reviewing has often proved useful, the method has often proved to be inadequate for reaching definitive conclusions about the degree of empirical support for a phenomenon or for a theory about the phenomenon. One indication of this inadequacy is that independent narrative reviews of the same literature often have reached differing conclusions.

COMMON PROBLEMS WITH NARRATIVE REVIEWS

Critics of the narrative reviewing strategy (e.g., Glass et al. 1981; Rosenthal 1991) have pointed to four general faults that frequently occur in narrative reviewing: (1) Narrative reviewing generally involves the use of a convenience sample of studies, perhaps consisting of only those studies that the reviewer happens to know. Because the parameters of the reviewed literature are typically not explicit, it is difficult to evaluate the adequacy of the definition of the literature or the thoroughness of the search for studies. If the sample of studies was biased, the conclusions reached may also be biased. (2) Narrative reviewers generally do not publicly state the procedures they used for either cataloging studies' characteristics or evaluating the quality of the studies' methods. Therefore, the review's claims about the characteristics of the studies and the quality of their methods are difficult to judge for their accuracy. (3) In cases in which study findings differed, narrative reviewing has difficulty in reaching clear conclusions about whether differences in study methods explain differences in results. Because narrative reviewers usually do not systematically code studies' methods, these reviewing procedures are not well suited to accounting for inconsistencies in findings. (4) Narrative reviewing typically relies much more heavily on statistical significance to judge studies' findings than on the *magnitude* of the findings. Statistical significance is a poor basis for comparing studies that have different sample sizes, because effects of identical magnitude can differ widely in statistical significance. Because of this problem, narrative reviewers often reach erroneous conclusions about a pattern in a series of studies, even in literatures as small as ten studies (Cooper and Rosenthal 1980).

As the number of available studies cumulates, the conclusions reached in narrative reviews become increasingly unreliable because of the informality of the methods they use to draw these conclusions. Indeed, some historical scholars have attributed crises of confidence in central social scientific principles to apparent failures to replicate findings across studies (e.g., Johnson and Nichols 1998). Clearly, there will be practical limitations on the abilities of scholars to understand the vagaries of a literature containing dozens if not hundreds of studies (e.g., by 1978, there were at least 345 studies examining interpersonal expectancy effects, according to Rosenthal and Rubin 1978; and by 1983, there were over 1,000 studies evaluating whether birth order is related to personality, as reported by Ernst and Angst 1983). From this perspective, the social sciences might be considered victims of their own success: Although social scientists have been able to collect a myriad of data about a myriad of phenomena, they were forced to rely on their intuition when it came to assessing the state of the knowledge about popular topics. Since the 1980s, however, as scholars have gained increasing expertise in reviewing research literatures, literatures that once appeared haphazard at best and fragile at worst now frequently are shown to have substantial regularities (Johnson and Nichols 1998). For example, although scholars working in the 1950s and on through the 1970s frequently reached conflicting conclusions about whether men or women (or neither) are more easily influenced by others, reviewers using meta-analytic techniques have found highly reliable tendencies in this same literature. For example, Eagly and Carli's meta-analysis (1981) showed that men are more influenced than women when the communication topic is feminine (e.g., sewing), and that women are more influenced than men when the topic is masculine (e.g., automobiles). Moreover, contemporary meta-analysts now almost routinely move beyond relatively simple questions of whether one variable relates to another to the more sophisticated question of *when* the relation is larger, smaller, or reverses in sign. Thus, there is, indeed, a great deal of replicability across a wide array of topics, and inconsistencies among study findings can often be explained on the basis of methodological differences among the studies.

META-ANALYTIC REVIEWS OF EVIDENCE

Because of the importance of comparing study findings accurately, scholars have dedicated considerable effort to making the review process as reliable and valid as possible and thereby circumventing the criticisms listed above. These efforts highlight the proposition that research synthesis is a scientific endeavor—there are identifiable and replicable methods involved in producing reliable and valid reviews (Cooper and Hedges 1994). Although scientists have cumulated empirical data from independent studies since the early 1800s (see Stigler 1986), relatively sophisticated techniques for synthesizing study findings emerged only after the development of such standardized indexes as *r*-, *d*-, and *p*-values, around the turn of the twentieth century (see Olkin 1990). Reflecting the field's maturation, Hedges and Olkin (1985) presented a sophisticated version of the statistical bases of meta-analysis, and standards for meta-analysis have grown increasingly rigorous. Meta-analysis is now quite common and well accepted because scholars realize that careful application of

these techniques often will yield the clearest conclusions about a research literature (Cooper and Hedges 1994; Hunt 1997).

Conducting a meta-analysis generally involves seven steps: (1) determining the theoretical domain of the literature under consideration, (2) setting boundaries for the sample of studies, (3) locating relevant studies, (4) coding studies for their distinctive characteristics, (5) estimating standardized effect sizes for each study, (6) analyzing the database, and (7) interpreting and presenting the results. The first conceptual step is to specify with great clarity the phenomenon under review by defining the variables whose relation is the focus of the review. Ordinarily a synthesis evaluates evidence relevant to a single hypothesis; the analyst studies the history of the research problem and of typical studies in the literature. Typically, the research problem will be defined as a relation between two variables, such as the influence of an independent variable on a dependent variable (e.g., the influence of silicon breast implants on connective tissure disease, as reported by Perkins et al. 1995). Moreover, a synthesis must take study quality into account at an early point to determine the kinds of operations that constitute acceptable operationalizations of these conceptual variables. Because studies testing a particular hypothesis typically differ in the operations used to establish the variables, it is no surprise that these different operations were often associated with variability in studies' findings. If the differences in studies' operations can be appropriately judged or categorized, it is likely that an analyst can explain some of this variability in effect size magnitude.

The most common way to test competing explanations is to examine how findings pattern across studies. Specifically, a theory might imply that a third variable should influence the relation between the independent and dependent variables: The relation should be larger or smaller with a higher level of this third variable. Treating this third variable as a potential moderator of the effect, the analyst would code the studies for their status on the moderator. This meta-analytic strategy, known as the moderator variable approach, tests whether the moderator affects the examined relation across the studies included in the sample. This moderator variable approach, advancing beyond the simple question of *whether* the independent variable is related to the dependent variable, addresses the question of *when* the magnitude or sign of the relationship varies. In addition to this moderator variable approach to synthesizing studies' findings, other strategies have proved to be useful. In particular, a theory might suggest that a third variable serves as a mediator of the critical relation because it conveys the causal impact of the independent variable on the dependent variable. If at least some of the primary studies within a literature have evaluated this mediating process, mediator relations can be tested within a meta-analytic framework by performing correlational analyses that are an extension of path analysis with primary-level data (Shadish 1996).

Clearly, only some studies will be relevant to the conceptual relation that is the focus of the meta-analysis, so analysts must define boundaries for the sample of studies, the second step in conducting a meta-analysis. Decisions about the inclusion of studies are important because the inferential power of any meta-analysis is limited by the methods of the studies that are integrated. To the extent that all (or most) of the reviewed studies share a particular methodological limitation, any synthesis of these studies would be limited in this respect. As a general rule, research syntheses profit by focusing on the studies that used stronger methods to test the meta-analytic hypotheses. Nonetheless, it is important to note that studies that have some strengths (e.g., manipulated independent variables) may have other weaknesses (e.g., deficiencies in ecological validity). In deciding whether some studies may lack sufficient rigor to include in the meta-analysis, it is important to adhere to methodological standards within the area reviewed. Although a large number of potential threats to methodological rigor have been identified (Campbell and Stanley 1963; Cook and Campbell 1979), there are few absolute standards of study quality that can be applied uniformly in every meta-analysis. As a case in point, although published studies are often thought to be of higher quality than unpublished studies, there is little basis for this generalization: Many unpublished studies (e.g., dissertations) have high quality, and many studies published in reputable sources do not. It is incumbent on the analyst to define the features of a high-quality study and to apply this definition to all studies in the literature, regardless of such considerations as the reputation of the journal.

Analysts often set the boundaries of the synthesis so that the methods of included studies differ dramatically only on critical moderator dimensions. If other, extraneous dimensions are thereby held relatively constant across the reviewed studies, moderator variable analyses can be more clearly interpreted. Nonetheless, an analyst should include in the sample all studies or portions of studies that satisfy the selection criteria, or, if an exhaustive sampling is not possible, a representative sample of those studies. Following this principle yields results that can be generalized to the universe of studies on the topic.

Because including a large number of studies generally increases the value of a quantitative synthesis, it is important to locate as many studies as possible that might be suitable for inclusion, the third step of a meta-analysis. To ensure that a sufficient sample of studies is located, reviewers are well advised to err in the direction of being extremely inclusive in their searching procedures. As described elsewhere (e.g., Cooper 1998; White 1994), there are many ways to find relevant studies; ordinarily, analysts should use all these techniques. Because computer searches of publication databases seldom locate all the available studies, it is important to supplement them by (1) examining the reference lists of existing reviews and of studies in the targeted literature, (2) obtaining published sources that have cited seminal articles within the literature, (3) contacting the extant network of researchers who work on a given topic to ask for new studies or unpublished studies, and (4) manually searching important journals to find some reports that might have been overlooked by other techniques.

Once the sample of studies is retrieved, analysts code them for their methodological characteristics, the fourth step in the process. The most important of these characteristics are potential moderator variables, which the analyst expects on an a priori basis to account for variation among the studies' effect sizes, or which can provide useful descriptive information about the usual context of studies in the literature. In some cases, reviewers recruit outside judges to provide ratings of methods used in studies. Because accurate coding is crucial to the results of a meta-analysis, the coding of study characteristics should be carried out by two or more coders, and an appropriate index of interrater reliability should be calculated.

To be included in a meta-analysis, a study must contain some report of a quantitative test of the hypothesis that is under scrutiny in order to convert summary statistics into effect sizes, the fifth step of the process. Most studies report the examined relation by one or more inferential statistics (e.g., *t*-tests, *F*-tests, *r*-values), which can be converted into an effect size (see Cooper and Hedges 1994b; Glass et al. 1981; Johnson 1993; Rosenthal 1991). The most commonly used effect size indexes in meta-analysis are the standardized difference and the correlation coefficient (see Rosenthal 1991, 1994). The standardized difference, which expresses the finding in standard deviation units, was first proposed by Cohen (1969) in the following form:

$$g = \frac{M_A - M_B}{SD} \qquad (1)$$

where M_A; and M_B; are the sample means of two compared groups, and *SD* is the standard deviation, pooled from the two observations. Because this formula overestimates population effect sizes to the extent that sample sizes are small, Hedges (1981) provided a correction for this bias; with the bias corrected, this effect estimate is conventionally known as *d*. Another common effect size is the correlation coefficient, *r*, which gauges the association between two variables. Because the sampling distribution of a sample correlation coefficient tends to be skewed to the extent that the population correlation is large, it is conventional in meta-analysis to use a logarithmic transform of each correlation in statistical operations (Fisher 1921). The positive or negative sign of the effect sizes computed in a meta-analysis is defined so that studies with opposite outcomes have opposing signs. When a study examines the relation of interest within levels of another variable, effect sizes may be calculated within the levels of this variable as well as for the study as a whole. In addition to correcting the raw *g* and *r* because they are biased estimators of the population effect size, analysts sometimes correct for many other biases that accrue from the methods used in each study (e.g., unreliability of a measure; see Hunter and Schmidt 1990). Although it is unrealistic for analysts to take into account all potential sources of bias in a meta-analysis, they should remain aware of biases that may be important within the context of their research literature.

Once the effect sizes are calculated, they are analyzed, the sixth step of the process, using either fixed- or random-effects models. Fixed-effects models, which are the most common analysis used, assume that there is one underlying, but unknown, effect size and that study estimates of this effect size vary only in sampling error. Random-effects models assume that each effect size is unique and that the study is drawn at random from a universe of related but separate effects (see Hedges and Vivea 1998 for a discussion). The general steps involved in the analysis of effect sizes usually are: (1) to aggregate effect sizes across the studies to determine the overall strength of the relation between the examined variables; (2) to analyze the consistency of the effect sizes across the studies; (3) to diagnose outliers among the effect sizes; and (4) to perform tests of whether study attributes moderate the magnitude of the effect sizes. Although several frameworks for modeling effect sizes have been developed (for reviews, see Johnson et al. 1995; Sánchez-Meca and Marín-Martínez 1997), the Hedges and Olkin fixed-effect approach (1985) appears to be the most popular and therefore will be assumed in the remainder of this discourse. These statistics were designed to take advantage of the fact that studies have differing variances by calculating the nonsystematic variance of the effect sizes analytically (Hedges and Olkin 1985). Because this nonsystematic variance of an effect size is inversely proportional to the sample size of the study and because sample sizes typically vary widely across the studies, the error variances of the effect sizes are ordinarily quite heterogeneous. These meta-analytic statistics also permit an analysis of the consistency (or homogeneity) of the effect sizes across the studies, a highly informative analysis not produced by conventional, primary-level statistics. As the homogeneity calculation illustrates, analyzing effect sizes with specialized meta-analytic statistics rather than the ordinary inferential statistics used in primary research allows a reviewer to use a greater amount of the information available from the studies (Rosenthal 1991, 1995).

As a first step in a quantitative synthesis, the study outcomes are combined by averaging the effect sizes with each weighted by its sample size. This procedure gives greater weight to the more reliably estimated study outcomes, which are in general those with the larger sample sizes (see

Hedges et al. 1992; Johnson et al. 1995). As a test for significance of this weighted mean effect size, a confidence interval is typically computed around this mean, based on its standard deviation, $d_+ \pm 1.96 \sqrt{v_+}$, where 1.96 is the unit-normal value for a 95 percent confidence interval (CI) (assuming a nondirectional hypothesis). If the CI includes zero (0.00), the value indicating exactly no difference, it may be concluded that aggregated across all studies there is no significant association between the independent and dependent variables (X and Y). For example, Perkins and colleagues (1995) found no evidence across thirteen studies that silicone breast implants increased risk of connective tissue disease. In a different literature, He and colleagues (1999) found that, across eighteen studies, nonsmokers exposed to passive smoke had a higher relative risk of coronary heart disease than nonsmokers not exposed to smoke.

Once a meta-analysis has derived a weighted mean effect size, it, and other meta-analytic statistics, must be interpreted and presented, which is the seventh step of conducting a meta-analysis. If the mean effect is nonsignificant and the homogeneity statistic is small and nonsignificant, an analyst might conclude that there is no relation between the variables under consideration. However, in such cases, it is wise to consider the amount of statistical power that was available: If the total number of research participants in the studies integrated was small, it is possible that additional data would support the existence of the effect. Even if the mean effect is significant and the homogeneity statistic is small and nonsignificant, concerns about its magnitude arise. To address this issue, Cohen (1969, 1988) proposed some guidelines for judging effect magnitude, based on his informal analysis of the magnitude of effects commonly yielded by psychological research. Cohen intended "that medium represent an effect of a size likely to be visible to the naked eye of a careful observer" (1992, p. 156). He intended that small effect sizes be "noticeably smaller yet not trivial" (p. 156) and that large effect sizes "be the same distance above medium as small is below it" (p. 156). As Table 1 shows, a "medium" effect turned out to be about $d = 0.50$ and $r = .30$, equivalent to the difference in intelligence scores between clerical and semiskilled workers. A "small" effect size was about $d = 0.20$ and $r = .10$, equivalent

Cohen's (1969) Guidelines for Magnitude of d and r

Size	Effect size metric		
	d	r	r^2
Small	0.20	.10	.01
Medium	0.50	.30	.09
Large	0.80	.50	.25

Table 1

to the difference in height between 15- and 16-year-old girls. Finally, a large effect was about $d = 0.80$ and $r = .50$, equivalent to the difference in intelligence scores between college professors and college freshmen.

Another popular way to interpret mean effect sizes is to derive the equivalent r and square it. This procedure shows how much variability would be explained by an effect of the magnitude of the mean effect size. Thus, a mean d of 0.50 produces an R^2 of .09. However, this value must be interpreted carefully because R^2, or variance explained, is a directionless effect size. Therefore, if the individual effect sizes that produced the mean effect size varied in their signs (i.e., if the effect sizes were not all negative or all positive), the variance in Y explained by the predictor X, calculated for each study and averaged, would be larger than this simple transformation of the mean effect size. Thus, another possible procedure consists of computing R^2 for each individual study and averaging these values.

When the weighted mean effect size and the CI are computed, the homogeneity of the d's is statistically examined, in order to determine whether the studies can be adequately described by a single effect size (Hedges and Olkin 1985). If the effect sizes can be so described, then they would differ only by unsystematic sampling error. If there is a significant fit statistic, the weighted mean effect size may not adequately describe the outcomes of the set of studies because it is likely that quite different mean effects exist in different groups of studies. Further explanatory work would be merited, even when the composite effect size is significant. The magnitude of individual study outcomes would differ systematically, and these differences may include differences in the direction (or sign) of the relation. In some studies, the independent variable might have had a large positive effect on the dependant variable, and in other studies, it might have had a smaller positive effect or even a negative effect. Even if the homogeneity test is nonsignificant, significant moderators could be present, especially when the fit statistic is relatively large (for further discussions, see Johnson and Turco 1992; Rosenthal 1995). Nonetheless, in a meta-analysis that attempts to determine the relation of one variable to another, rejecting the hypothesis of homogeneity could be troublesome, because it implies that the association between these two variables likely is complicated by the presence of interacting conditions. However, because analysts usually anticipate the presence of one or more moderators of effect size magnitude, establishing that effect sizes are not homogeneous is ordinarily neither surprising nor troublesome.

To determine the relation between study characteristics and the magnitude of the effect sizes, both categorical models and continuous models can be tested. In *categorical models*, analyses may show that weighted mean effect sizes differ in magnitude between the subgroups established by dividing studies into classes based on study characteristics. In such cases, it is as though the meta-analysis is broken into sub-meta-analyses based on their methodological features. For example, He and colleagues (1999) found that risk of coronary heart disease was greater for women than for men nonsmokers who were exposed to passive smoke. If effect sizes that were found to be heterogeneous become homogeneous within the classes of a categorical model, the relevant study characteristic has accounted for the systematic variability between the effect sizes. Similarly, *continuous models*, which are analogous to regression models, examine whether study characteristics that are assessed on a continuous scale are related to the effect sizes. As with categorical models, some continuous models may be completely specified in the sense that the systematic variability in the effect sizes is explained by the study characteristic that is used as a predictor. Continuous models are least squares regressions, calculated with each effect size weighted by the reciprocal of its variance (sample size). For example, He and colleagues (1999) found that risk of coronary heart disease was greater to the extent that nonsmokers had greater exposure to passive

smoke. Goodness-of-fit statistics enable analysts to determine the extent to which categorical or continuous models, or mixtures of these models provide correct depictions of study outcomes.

As an alternative analysis to predicting effect sizes using categorical and continuous models, an analyst can attain homogeneity by identifying outlying values among the effect sizes and sequentially removing those effect sizes that reduce the homogeneity statistic by the largest amount (e.g., Hedges 1987). Studies yielding effect sizes identified as outliers can then be examined to determine whether they appear to differ methodologically from the other studies. Also, inspection of the percentage of effect sizes removed to attain homogeneity allows one to determine whether the effect sizes are homogeneous aside from the presence of relatively few aberrant values. Under such circumstances, the mean attained after removal of such outliers may better represent the distribution of effect sizes than the mean based on all the effect sizes. In general, the diagnosis of outliers should occur prior to calculating moderator analyses; this diagnosis may locate a value or two that are so discrepant from the other effect sizes that they would dramatically alter any models fitted to effect sizes. Under such circumstances, these outliers should be removed from subsequent phases of the data analysis. Alternatively, outliers can be examined following categorical or continuous models (e.g., finding those that deviate the most from the values predicted by the models).

TRENDS IN THE PRACTICE OF META-ANALYSIS

Although the quality of meta-analyses has been quite variable, it is possible to state the features that compose a high-quality meta-analysis, including success in locating studies, explicitness of criteria for selecting studies, thoroughness and accuracy in coding moderators variables and other study characteristics, accuracy in effect size computations, and adherence to the assumptions of meta-analytic statistics. When meta-analyses meet such standards, it is difficult to disagree with Rosenthal's conclusion (1994) that it is "hardly justified to review a quantitative literature in the pre-meta-analytic, prequantitative manner" (p. 131). Yet merely meeting these high standards does not necessarily make a meta-analysis an important scientific contribution. One factor affecting scientific contribution is that the conclusions that a research synthesis is able to reach are limited by the quality of the data that are synthesized. Serious methodological faults that are endemic in a research literature may well handicap a synthesis, unless it is designed to shed light on the influence of these faults. Also, to be regarded as important, the review must address an interesting question. Moreover, unless the paper reporting a meta-analysis "tells a good story," its full value may go unappreciated by readers. Although there are many paths to a good story, Sternberg's recommendations to authors of reviews (1991) are instructive: Pick interesting questions, challenge conventional understandings if at all possible, take a unified perspective on the phenomenon, offer a clear take-home message, and write well. Thus, the practice of meta-analysis should not preclude incorporating aspects of narrative reviewing, but instead should strive to incorporate and document the richness of the literature.

One reason that the quality of published syntheses has been quite variable is that it is a relatively new tool among scholars who practice it. Yet, as the methods of quantitative synthesis have become more sophisticated and widely disseminated, typical published meta-analyses have improved. At their best, meta-analyses advance knowledge about a phenomenon by explicating its typical patterns and showing when it is larger or smaller, negative or positive, and by testing theories about the phenomenon (see Miller and Pollock 1994). Meta-analysis should foster a healthy interaction between primary research and research synthesis, at once summarizing old research and suggesting promising directions for new research. One misperception that scholars sometimes express is that a meta-analysis represents a dead end for a literature, a point beyond which nothing more needs to be known. In contrast, carefully conducted meta-analyses can often be the best medicine for a literature, by documenting the robustness with which certain associations are attained, resulting in a sturdier foundation on which future theories may rest. In addition, meta-analyses can show where knowledge is at its thinnest, to help plan additional, primary-level research (see Eagly and Wood 1994). As a consequence of a carefully conducted meta-analysis, primary-level studies can

be designed with the complete literature in mind and will therefore have a better chance of contributing new knowledge. In this fashion, scientific resources can be directed most efficiently toward gains in knowledge. As time passes and new studies continue to accrue rapidly, it is likely that social scientists will rely more on quantitative syntheses to inform them about the knowledge that has accumulated in their research. Although it is possible that meta-analysis will become the purview of an elite class of researchers who specialize in research integration, as Schmidt (1992) argued, it seems more likely that meta-analysis will become a routine part of graduate training in many fields, enabling students to develop the skills necessary to ply the art and science of meta-analysis and to integrate findings across studies as a normal and routine part of their research activities.

REFERENCES

Bond, R., and P. B. Smith 1996 "Culture and Conformity: A Meta-Analysis of Studies Using Asch's (1952b, 1956) Line Judgment Task." *Psychological Bulletin* 119:111–137.

Campbell, D. T., and J. T. Stanley 1963 *Experimental and Quasi-Experimental Designs for Research*. Chicago: Rand-McNally.

Cohen, J. 1969 *Statistical Power Analysis for the Behavioral Sciences*. New York: Academic.

—— 1988 *Statistical Power Analysis for the Behavioral Sciences*, 2nd ed. Hillsdale, N.J.: Erlbaum.

—— 1992 "A Power Prime." *Psychological Bulletin* 112:155–159.

Cook, T. D., and D. T. Campbell 1979 *Quasi-Experimentation: Design and Analysis Issues for Field Settings*. Boston: Houghton Mifflin.

Cooper, H. 1998 *Integrative Research: A Guide for Literature Reviews*, 3rd ed. Newbury Park, Calif.: Sage.

——, and L. V. Hedges 1994a. "Research Synthesis as a Scientific Enterprise." Pp. 3–14 in H. Cooper and L. V. Hedges, eds., *The Handbook of Research Synthesis*. New York: Russell Sage.

——, and L.V. Hedges, (eds.) 1994b *The Handbook of Research Synthesis*. New York: Russell Sage.

——, and Rosenthal, R. (1980). "Statistical versus Traditional Procedures for Summarizing Research Findings." *Psychological Bulletin* 87:442–449.

Eagly, A. H., and L. Carli 1981 "Sex of Researchers and Sex-Typed Communications as Determinants of Sex

Differences in Influenceability: A Meta-Analysis of Social Influence Studies." *Psychological Bulletin* 90:1–20.

——, and W. Wood 1994 "Using Research Syntheses to Plan Future Research." Pp. 485–500 in H. Cooper and L. V. Hedges, eds., *The Handbook of Research Synthesis.* New York: Russell Sage.

Ernst, C., and J. Angst 1983 *Birth Order: Its Influence on Personality.* New York: Springer-Verlag.

Fisher, R. A. 1921 "On the "Probable Error" of a Coefficient of Correlation Deduced from a Small Sample." *Metron* 1:1–32.

Glass, G. V. 1976 "Primary, Secondary, and Meta-Analysis of Research. *Educational Researcher* 5:3–8.

——, B. McGraw, and M. L. Smith 1981 *Meta-Analysis in Social Research.* Beverly Hills, Calif.: Sage.

He, J., S. Vupputuri, K. Allen, M. R. Prerost, J. Hughes, and P. K. Whelton 1999 "Passive Smoking and the Risk of Coronary Heart Disease—A Meta-Analysis of Epidemiologic Studies." *New England Journal of Medicine* 340:920–926.

L. V. Hedges 1981 "Distribution Theory for Glass's Estimator of Effect Size and Related Estimators." *Journal of Educational Statistics* 6:107–128.

—— 1987 "How Hard Is Hard Science, How Soft Is Soft Science? The Empirical Cumulativeness of Research." *American Psychologist* 42:443–455.

—— 1994 "Statistical Considerations." Pp. 29–38 in H. Cooper and L. V. Hedges, eds., *The Handbook of Research Synthesis.* New York: Russell Sage.

——, H. Cooper, and B. J. Bushman 1992 "Testing the Null Hypothesis in Meta-Analysis: A Comparison of Combined Probability and Confidence Interval Procedures." *Psychological Bulletin* 111:188–194.

——, and I. Olkin 1985 *Statistical Methods for Meta-Analysis.* Orlando, Fla.: Academic.

——, and J. L. Vevea 1998 "Fixed- and Random-Effects Models in Meta-Analysis." *Psychological Methods* 3:486–504.

Hunt, M. 1997 *How Science Takes Stock: The Story of Meta-Analysis.* New York: Russell Sage.

Hunter, J. E., and F. L. Schmidt 1990 *Methods of Meta-Analysis: Correcting Error and Bias in Research Findings.* Newbury Park, Calif.: Sage.

Johnson, B. T. 1993 *DSTAT 1.10: Software for the Meta-Analytic Review of Research Literatures.* Hillsdale, N.J.: Erlbaum.

——, B. Mullen, and E. Salas 1995 "Comparison of Three Major Meta-Analytic Approaches." *Journal of Applied Psychology* 80:94–106.

——, and D. R. Nichols 1998 "Social Psychologists' Expertise in the Public Interest: Civilian Morale Research during World War II." *Journal of Social Issues* 54:53–77.

——, and R. Turco 1992 "The Value of Goodness-of-Fit Indices in Meta-Analysis: A Comment on Hall and Rosenthal." *Communication Monographs* 59:388–396.

Mazela, A., and M. Malin 1977 *A bibliometric Study of the Review Literature.* Philadelphia: Institute for Scientific Information.

Miller, N., and V. E. Pollock 1994 "Meta-Analysis and Some Science-Compromising Problems of Social Psychology" Pp. 230–261 in W. R. Shadish and S. Fuller, eds., *The Social Psychology of Science.* New York: Guilford.

Olkin, I. 1990 "History and Goals." In K. W. Wachter and M. L. Straf, eds., *The Future of Meta-Analysis.* New York: Russell Sage.

Perkins, L. L., B. D. Clark, P. J. Klein, and R. R. Cook 1995 "A Meta-Analysis of Breast Implants and Connective Tissue Disease." *Annals of Plastic Surgery* 35:561–570.

Rosenthal, R. 1990 "How Are We Doing in Soft Psychology?" *American Psychologist* 45:775–777.

—— 1991 *Meta-Analytic Procedures for Social Research,* rev. ed. Beverly Hills, Calif.: Sage.

—— 1994 "Parametric Measures of Effect Size." Pp. 231–244 in H. Cooper and L. V. Hedges, eds., *The Handbook of Research Synthesis.* New York: Russell Sage.

—— 1995 "Writing Meta-Analytic Reviews." *Psychological Bulletin* 118:183–192.

——, and D. Rubin 1978 "Interpersonal Expectancy Effects: The First 345 Studies." *Behavioral and Brain Sciences* 3:377–415.

Sánchez-Meca, J., and Marín-Martínez, F. 1997 "Homogeneity Tests in Meta-Analysis: A Monte-Carlo Comparison of Statistical Power and Type I Error." *Quality & Quantity* 31:385–399.

Schmidt, F. L. 1992 "What Do Data Really Mean? Research Findings, Meta-Analysis, and Cumulative Knowledge in Psychology." *American Psychologist* 47:1173–1181.

Shadish, W. R. 1996 "Meta-Analysis and the Exploration of Causal Mediating Processes: A Primer of Examples, Methods, and Issues." *Psychological Methods* 1:47–65.

Sternberg, R. J. 1991 Editorial. *Psychological Bulletin* 109:3–4.

Stigler, S. M. 1986 *History of Statistics: The Measurement of Uncertainty before 1900.* Cambridge, Mass.: Harvard University Press.

White, H. D. 1994 "Scientific Communication and Literature Retrieval." In H. Cooper and L. V. Hedges eds., *The Handbook of Research Synthesis*, pp. 41–55. New York: Russell Sage.

B. T. JOHNSON

METATHEORY

Metatheory in sociology is a relatively new specialty that aims to describe existing sociological theory systematically, and also, to some degree, to prescribe what future sociological theories ought to be like. It leaves to other specialties—most notably the sociology and history of sociology and the logic of theory construction—the problems of explaining and predicting how such theories have been, and can be, formulated.

There are two broad varieties of metatheory. One variety, *synthetic*, classifies whole theories according to some overarching typology; the other variety, *analytic*, first dissects theories into their underlying constituents and then classifies these constituents into types.

Some typologies encountered in synthetic metatheory refer to the time periods when the theories were originated, for example, forerunner, classical, and contemporary (Timasheff and Theodorson 1976 and Eisenstadt 1976 provide examples). Some refer to the places where the theories were originated, for example, France, Germany, Italy, and the United States (Bottomore and Nisbet 1978 and Gurvitch and Moore 1945 provide examples). Some refer to the substantive themes of the theories, for example, structural-functional, evolutionist, conflict, and symbolic interactionist (Turner 1986 and Collins 1988 provide examples). Some refer to the ideologies supported by the theories, for example, pro-establishment and anti-establishment (Martindale 1979 provides an example). Some refer to various combinations of all the above differences (Wiley 1979 and Ritzer 1983 provide examples).

Analytic metatheory is divisible into two broad classes: one in which the constituents of theories are required to have empirical referents, either directly or indirectly, and another in which these constituents are required or permitted to have nonempirical referents. Thus, one sociologist claims our theory should be brought "closer to nonempirical standards of objectivity" (Alexander 1982), while another claims "sense-based inter-subjective verification is indispensable [to sociology]" (Wallace 1983). (This difference in kind of analytic metatheory reflects an applicability of the synthetic-analytic distinction to meta*method* in sociology: In the synthetic variety of metamethod, whole methods are characterized as *empirical* or *nonempirical*, *positivistic* or *hermeneutical*, *experimental* or *participant-observational*, and so on. In the analytic variety, such methods are dissected into their underlying constituents, which are then classified as *measurement, interpretation, speculation, comparison, test, generalization, specification, deduction, induction*, and so on.)

Some types of underlying constituents encountered in empirical analytic metatheory are "control" (Gibbs 1989); "individual actors," "corporate actors," "interests," and "rights" (Coleman 1990); "rational action," "nonrational action," "individualist order," and "collectivist order" (Alexander 1982); "social and cultural structures," "spatial and temporal regularities," "instinct," "enculture," "physiology," "nurture," "demography," "psychical contagion," "ecology," and "artifacts" (Wallace 1983, 1988); and general causal images like "convergence," "amplification," "fusion," "fission," "tension," "cross-pressure," "dialectic," and "cybernetic" (Wallace 1983, 1988). Some types of underlying constituents encountered in nonempirical analytic metatheory have been called (so far, without further explication or specification), "moral implication," "moral commitments," and "moral preferences" (Alexander 1982).

Metatheory in general has been sweepingly condemned as a dead end leading only to the study of "the grounds of other people's arguments rather than substantive problems" (Skocpol 1987), and as holding "little prospect for further developments and new insights" (Collins 1986). Against such characterizations, however, certain unique and indispensable contributions of both synthetic and analytic metatheory to sociology should not be overlooked.

Synthetic metatheory plays obviously central roles in descriptive classifications of sociological theory (e.g., textbooks and course outlines), but they are no less central to the sociology and history of sociology, where efforts to account for the rise and fall of schools, or perspectives, in sociological analysis require systematic conceptualization of such groupings. The contributions of nonempirical analytic metatheory remain unclear (as mentioned, the kinds of ideological commitment and moral foundation to which it refers, and their consequences for sociological theory, have yet to be specified) and, therefore, will not be examined here. The contributions of empirical analytic metatheory will occupy the rest of this article.

THREE CONTRIBUTIONS OF EMPIRICAL ANALYTIC METATHEORY

Empirical analytic metatheory can aid (1) systematic cumulation of the *end product* of sociological investigation (namely, collectively validated empirical knowledge about social phenomena); (2) systematic construction of new versions of the principal *means* employed in generating that end product (namely, collectively shared theory and method); and (3) a sense of discipline-wide *solidarity* among sociologists of all theoretical traditions, all specializations and, eventually one hopes, among all social scientists.

Cumulation of Sociological Knowledge Knowledge can only cumulate when new knowledge of a given phenomenon is added to old knowledge of that same phenomenon (or, rather, insofar as no phenomenon is ever repeated exactly, that same *type* of phenomenon). The key to holding such objects of investigation constant is, of course, communication. That is to say, only the communication to investigator B of the identity of the exact phenomenon investigator A has examined, together with the exact results of that examination, can enable investigator B systematically to add new knowledge to A's knowledge.

Disciplinary Communication Now it may be imagined that we already possess such communication in sociology, but we do not. Consider the terms *social structure* and *culture*. One can hardly doubt that, by denoting the substantive heart of our discipline, they indicate what the entire sociological enterprise is about. By virtually all accounts, however, each term signifies very different kinds of phenomena to different sociologists.

Thus, *social structure* has been authoritatively said, at various times for over two decades, to be "so fundamental to social science as to render its uncontested definition virtually impossible" (Udy 1968); to attract "little agreement on its empirical

referents" (Warriner 1981); and to possess a meaning that "remains unclear" (Turner 1986). "Few words," it has been said, "do sociologists use more often than 'structure,' especially in the phrase 'social structure.' Yet we seldom ask what we mean by the word" (Homans 1975). In a more detailed statement, one analyst asserts that

> *The concept of social structure is used widely in sociology, often broadly, and with a variety of meanings. It may refer to social differentiation, relations of production, forms of association, value integration, functional interdependence, statuses and roles, institutions, or combinations of these and other factors.*
> *(Blau 1975)*

Indeed, we can still read that "sociologists use the term ['social structure'] in diverse ways, each of which is either so vague as to preclude empirical application or so broad as to include virtually all collective features of human behavior" (Gibbs 1989). As recent evidence of this diversity, it is noteworthy that, where one sociologist claims that "for sociologists, the units of social structure are conceived of . . . as *relational* characteristics" (Smelser 1988), another refers, without explanation, to a type of "social structure" in which the participants "have *no relations*" (Coleman 1990).

The situation is no different with the term *culture*. Some years ago it was said that "by now just about everything has been thrown into 'culture' but the kitchen sink," and the author of this remark then reflected that "The kitchen sink has been thrown in too" as part of "material culture" (Schneider 1973). Years later, it has again been pointed out that "Theorists of culture remain sorely divided on how best to define culture" (Wuthnow et al. 1984) and "values, orientations, customs, language, norms, [and religion]" have been referred to as though they were all somehow different from "culture" (Coleman 1990). No wonder at least one sociologist has simply given up: "*[A]ny* definition" of culture, he claims, "will be (1) inclusive to the point of being meaningless, (2) arbitrary in the extreme, or (3) so vague as to promise only negligible empirical applicability" (Gibbs 1990).

More recently still, Gilmore affirms that "there is no current, widely accepted, composite resolution of the definition of culture," and claims that as a result "the contemporary concept of culture in sociology does not exclude any particular forms of [collective] activity." This difficulty notwithstanding, there has arisen, Gilmore says, "a new appreciation of the salience of culture as an explanatory perspective in contemporary sociological research" (1992). To the extent that these judgments are true, one can only wonder what contribution an explanatory perspective that lacks even a rudimentary and tentative definition of its own central variable (and which expresses a kitchen-sink inclusiveness that "does not exclude any particular empirical forms of activity") can possibly make to social science.

Regarding social structure, Rytina asserts his conviction that "Social structure is a general term for any collective social circumstance that is unalterable and given for the individual" and that such social structure "is the same for all and is beyond the capacity for alteration by any individual will" (1992). Apart from noticing, again, the kitchen-sink inclusiveness of this claim ("*any* collective social circumstance"), one wonders what good can come of conceptualizing social structure in a way that rules out the possibility of variable individual *power* (i.e., "the probability that one actor within a social relationship will be in a position to carry out his own will" [Weber 1978]). See, however, Sewell (1992) for explicit inclusion of "power" in structure"—although Sewell lumps "resources" and "schemas" (i.e., what others would distinguish as components of social structure and culture, respectively) together into a single undifferentiated "structure" concept.

Some other discussions of the ongoing social structure versus culture problem may be found in Emirbayer and Goodwin (1994), Hays (1994), Holmwood and Stewart (1994), Wallace (1986), and Whitmeyer (1994). It will also be noticed that in addition to "social structure" and "culture" the concept "agency" appears in some of these discussions, and a brief comment on it may be useful. Human "agency" is said, by Sewell, to refer to "the efficacy of human action," and to arise from the actor's "ability to apply [known schemas] to new contexts" and to act "creatively" (1992, pp. 2, 20). It is not easy to understand, however, why a special anthropocentric term is needed for such a phenomenon inasmuch as *all* action, by *whatever* agent, is (by any physical definition of "action") efficacious, and *all* "applications," by definition, occur in "new" contexts and are thus "creative."

In response to such expressions of disciplinary decline (and acknowledging their strong evidential basis), empirical analytic metatheory falls back on Durkheim's argument that insofar as "Every scientific investigation concerns a specific group of phenomena which are subsumed under the same definition," it follows that "[the] sociologist's first step must . . . be to define the things he treats so that we may know—he as well—exactly what his subject matter is. This is the prime and absolutely indispensable condition of any proof or verification" (1982).

Empirical analytic metatheory, then, seeks a common disciplinary language for sociologists everywhere, regardless of their specializations. Its proponents believe that only with the adoption of some such language can our discipline begin solving its central problems, namely, systematic knowledge cumulation, theory innovation, and solidarity enhancement.

(SEE ALSO: *Epistemology; Scientific Explanation*)

REFERENCES

Alexander, Jeffrey C. 1982 *Positivism, Presuppositions, and Current Controversies.* Berkeley: University of California Press.

Blau, Peter M. 1975 "Parameters of Social Structure." In Peter M. Blau, ed., *Approaches to the Study of Social Structure.* New York: Free Press.

Bottomore, Tom, and Robert Nisbet 1978 *A History of Sociological Analysis.* New York: Basic.

Brinkerhoff, David B., and Lynn K. White 1985 *Sociology.* St. Paul Minn.: West.

Broom, Leonard, Philip Selznick, and Dorothy Broom Darroch 1981 *Sociology.* New York: Harper and Row.

Coleman, James S. 1990 *Foundations of Social Theory.* Cambridge, Mass.: Harvard University Press.

Collins, Randall 1986 "Is 1980s Sociology in the Doldrums?" *American Journal of Sociology* 91:1336–1355.

—— 1988 *Theoretical Sociology.* San Diego: Harcourt Brace Jovanovich.

Durkheim, Emile 1982 *The Rules of Sociological Method.* New York: Free Press.

Eisenstadt, S. N., with M. Curelaru 1976 *The Form of Sociology: Paradigms and Crises.* New York: Wiley.

Emirbayer, Mustafa, and Jeff Goodwin 1994 "Network Analysis, Culture, and the Problem of Agency." *American Journal of Sociology* 99(6)1411–1454.

Gibbs, Jack P. 1989 *Control, Sociology's Central Notion*. Urbana: University of Illinois Press.

Gilmore, Samuel 1992 "Culture." In Edgar F. Borgatta and Marie L. Borgatta, eds., *Encyclopedia of Sociology*, 1st ed. New York: Macmillan.

Gurvitch, Georges, and Wilbert E. Moore 1945 *Twentieth Century Sociology*. New York: Philosophical Library.

Hays, Sharon 1994 "Structure and Agency and the Sticky Problem of Culture." *Sociological Theory* 12(1):57–72.

Holmwood, John, and Alexander Stewart 1994 "Synthesis and Fragmentation in Social Theory: A Progressive Solution," *Sociological Theory* 12(1):83–100.

Homans, George C. 1975 "What Do We Mean by 'Social Structure'?" In Peter M. Blau, ed., *Approaches to the Study of Social Structure*. New York: Free Press.

Martindale, Don 1979 "Ideologies, Paradigms, and Theories." In William E. Snizek, Ellsworth R. Fuhrman, and Michael K. Miller, eds., *Contemporary Issues in Theory and Research*. Westport, Conn.: Greenwood.

Orenstein, David Michael 1985 *The Sociological Quest: Principles of Sociology*. St. Paul, Minn.: West.

Ritzer, George 1983 *Contemporary Sociological Theory*. New York: Knopf.

Rytina, Steven L. 1992 "Social Structure." In Edgar F. Borgatta and Marie L. Borgatta, eds., *Encyclopedia of Sociology*, 1st ed. New York: Macmillan.

Schneider, Louis 1973 "The Idea of Culture in the Social Sciences: Critical and Supplementary Observations." In Louis Schneider and Charles M. Bonjean, eds., *The Idea of Culture in the Social Sciences*. Cambridge, England: Cambridge University Press.

Sewell, William H., Jr. 1992 "A Theory of Structure: Duality, Agency and Transformation." *American Journal of Sociology* 98(1):1–29.

Skocpol, Theda 1987 "The Dead End of Metatheory." *Contemporary Sociology* 16:10–12.

Smelser, Neil J. 1988 "Social Structure." In Neil H. Smelser, ed., *Handbook of Sociology*. Newbury Park, Calif.: Sage.

—— 1989 "Reviewing the Field of Sociology: A Response." *Contemporary Sociology* 18:851–855.

Timasheff, Nicholas S., and George A. Theodorson 1976 *Sociological Theory*, 4th ed. New York: Random House.

Tumin, Melvin M. 1973 *Patterns of Society*. Boston: Little, Brown.

Turner, Jonathan 1986 *The Structure of Sociological Theory*. Chicago: Dorsey.

—— 1989 "The Disintegration of American Sociology." *Sociological Perspectives* 32:419–433.

Udy, Stanley H., Jr. 1968 "Social Structure: Social Structural Analysis." In David L. Sills, ed., *International Encyclopedia of the Social Sciences*, vol. 14. New York: Free Press.

Wallace, Walter L. 1983 *Principles of Scientific Sociology*. Hawthorne, N.Y.: Aldine.

Wallace, Walter L. 1986 "Social Structural and Cultural Structural Variables in Sociology." *Sociological Focus* 19(April):125–138

—— 1988 "Toward a Disciplinary Matrix in Sociology." In Neil J. Smelser, ed., *Handbook of Sociology*. Newbury Park, Calif.: Sage.

Warriner, Charles K. 1981 "Levels in the Study of Social Structure." In Peter M. Blau and Robert K. Merton, eds., *Continuities in Structural Inquiry*. Beverly Hills, Calif.: Sage.

Weber, Max 1978 *Economy and Society*. Berkeley: University of California Press.

Whitmeyer, Joseph M. 1994 "Why Actor Models Are Integral to Structural Analysis." *Sociological Theory* 12(2):153–165.

Wiley, Norbert 1979 "The Rise and Fall of Dominating Theories in American Sociology." In William E. Snizek, Ellsworth R. Fuhrman, and Michael K. Miller, eds., *Contemporary Issues in Theory and Research*. Westport, Conn.: Greenwood.

Wuthnow, Robert, James Davison Hunter, Albert Bergesen, and Edith Kurzweil 1984 Introduction." In Robert Wuthnow et al., eds., *Cultural Analysis*. Boston: Routledge and Kegan Paul.

WALTER L. WALLACE

MEXICAN STUDIES

Mexican history since the country achieved its independence from Spain in 1821 is marked by a set of dramatic events that created the context for fundamental social and economic changes. These events shaped contemporary Mexican society and established much of the current agenda of Mexican social and political studies. Three issues in particular have long historical antecedents. These are the ethnic question, the role of the state in development, and relations with the United States. Despite these continuities, social trends and preoccupations in Mexico have also differed according to historical period. In order to handle both continuity and change, we will organize the discussion in terms of four main periods, each initiated by major events, and will consider the dominant trends and intellectual orientations of each period. The time between Mexican independence and the Mexican-American War, the first period is marked by economic stagnation and political fragmentation. The second period lasts from the aftermath of the Mexican-American War until the Mexican Revolution of 1910. Rapid but uneven economic development and political unification distinguish the second period. The third period begins with the consolidation of the Mexican Revolution and goes through the 1920s and on into the debt crises of the early 1980s. Nationalism, political centralization, and high rates of urbanization and industrialization characterize this period. Finally, we consider the two last decades of the twentieth century, shaped by the external opening of the economy with its accompanying economic and political liberalization.

This historical context and the unevenness of Mexico's development make U.S.-Mexican relations different, in significant respects, from relations between other neighboring countries. The U.S.-Mexican border is the only international frontier that divides a developing country and a highly developed country. The contradictory trends of Mexico's development shape U.S.-Mexican relations (Weintraub 1990). The two populations have been brought closer to each other in terms of trade, tourism, labor migration, and consumer aspirations. This increasing proximity can also create social distance as each population develops opposing images of the other. These are often based on the misunderstandings that result from wide disparities in income, standards of living, and political and family culture (Pastor and Castañeda 1988). For many Mexicans, the history of conflictive relations with the United States continues to negatively color perceptions of U.S. political and economic intentions toward Mexico.

Independence from Spain left Mexico an impoverished and fragmented nation. The main sources of external revenue—mining and specialized plantation agriculture—declined substantially. Internal markets were not strongly developed and were mainly concentrated in a few major cities. Thus, neither internal nor external trade provided enough stimuli to expand local agricultural or industrial production. The economy was organized on a local and regional basis rather than on a national one. Within this context, politics was dominated by a decentralized system of *caudillos* (regional leaders, often military) and *caciques* (local bosses and power brokers). The formal government alternated between a centralist and a federalist republic, after the short-lived Empire of Iturbide. The proponents of a centralist republic tended to be conservatives, supporting the maintenance of corporatist institutions such as the church, the army, the guilds, and the indigenous communities. In a sociological account of the processes shaping the Independence movement, the intellectual leader of the conservatives, Lucas Alamán ([1847] 1942), advocated a strong central power, economic protectionism, the remedying of class inequality, and populating the empty spaces to the north through European Catholic colonization. In contrast, the federalists tended to be economically and politically liberal, arguing for individual property rights, free markets, and individual civil and political equality. The radical liberal parliamentarian, José María Luis Mora, went so far as to argue for the complete incorporation of the indigenous population into the market as a means to remedy backwardness and poverty (Lira Gonzalez 1984). A leading liberal politician and intellectual, Lorenzo de Zavala, admired the United States and considered it a model to emulate. He also viewed favorably the colonization of the northern territories by Protestant colonists from the United States (Lira Gonzalez 1984). Later, Zavala became the first vice president of the independent Republic of Texas. In order to govern, both the federalists and centralists relied on the *caudillo-cacíque* power structure. Thus, the paradigmatic *caudillo* of this period, Santa Anna, was president several times, under both centralist and federalist banners.

The loss of half of the national territory, first in the Texas War of Independence of 1835–1836 and then in the Mexican-American War of 1846–1848, demonstrated dramatically the costs of Mexico's political and economic fragmentation. The conservatives entrenched themselves further in their corporate and hierarchical beliefs, leading finally to the ill-fated, conservative-backed empire of Maximillian of Hapsburg (1864–1867). The aftermath of the Mexican-American war was perhaps more traumatic for the liberals. They saw themselves as betrayed by the United States, which they had regarded as a friend and an ally in modernizing Mexico. Thereafter, particularly with the experiences of the French intervention, Mexican liberals, while supporting market and individual freedoms and the abolition of corporations, were to become the main proponents of a strong state and of nationalism in Mexico.

Beginning with Beníto Juarez (president, 1861–1863 and 1867–1872), liberals were to dominate the politics of Mexico until the Mexican Revolution, even in the paradoxical guise of the dictator, Porfirio Díaz (president, 1877–1880, 1884–1911). In face of the difficulties of achieving spontaneous economic and social progress, liberalism was modified, however, in an authoritarian and positivist direction. A disciple of Comte, Gabino Barreda, reorganized the educational system of the country to ensure a uniform and centralized system (Zea 1974). Justo Sierra (1969 [1901–1903]), one of Díaz's ministers, wrote a new version of Mexican history as a political evolution that needed a period in which political rights would be limited. He saw economic progress as depending on civic education, as well as individualizing property rights in agriculture, industrial modernization, foreign investment, and trade. Though corporate rights to land had been abolished under Juarez, Díaz made this effective, particularly for the indigenous communities. Railways were built and roads improved. Political control was centralized through a bureaucratic system of patronage that gave the central government a more effective control of state and local governments. For the first time in fifty years, Mexico experienced a long period of peace and stability.

The Díaz period was one of considerable economic expansion in Mexico, but the style of development resulted in a series of social and economic dislocations that were to contribute to the Mexican Revolution of 1910. Commercial haciendas expanded, depriving many peasants of access to land. The new economic opportunities and improvements in communication affected communities throughout Mexico, encouraging villagers to give up traditional livelihoods for wage labor in mines, plantations, or as sharecroppers. As dependence on the market grew, so too national and regional economic downturns caused increasing discontent and hardship. Advocates of progress, such as Andrés Molina Enríquez ([1909] 1978), one of the intellectual leaders of the Mexican

Revolution, denounced the economic inequities produced by land concentration. Instead, he placed his hopes on the emerging *mestízo* middle class of medium-scale farmers, merchants, manufacturers, and professionals. With Molina Enriquez, there is a clear statement of the ethnic basis of social change. Both the European-origin upper class and the indigenous peasantry are seen as incapable of progress. He sees the *mestízo* as the crucial Mexican identity capable of achieving economic development and social equity. By the time of the Mexican Revolution, the indigenous population, defined in census terms by "race" and non–Spanish-language use, constituted nearly half the Mexican population.

In spite of political centralization, the economy remained regionalized during the Díaz regime. The Mexican Revolution was essentially a set of regional movements and leaders, that responded to the particular economic problems and possibilities that the Porfirian expansion brought to local economies. These regional contexts included the sugar economy of Morelos; the *henequen* economy of Yucatan; the sharecropping, ranching, and mining economy of Chihuahua and Coahuila; and the emerging commercial farming economy of Sonora (Knight 1986).

The years from after the Mexican Revolution until approximately 1980 transformed Mexico from a society in which three-quarters of the population was agricultural and lived in small villages, to one in which less than a quarter of the population worked in agriculture and most people lived in large cities. This transformation was shaped by two outcomes of the revolution. One was an agrarian reform that destroyed the *hacienda* system, replacing it with small and medium-scale commercial farming and a system of social property (the *ejido*) that reinstated and, at times, extended the rights to land of peasant communities. In the first thirty years after the Revolution, Mexican peasant agriculture was sufficiently strong to feed the growing urban population and help the country's industrialization.

The second major legacy of the revolution was the consolidation of a centralized, modern political system around the official party of the revolution, known as the PRI (*Partido Revolucionario Institucional*) since 1948. The PRI based its control on corporate affiliations by industrial and peasant unions. Also, the massive extension of state employment in education, health, social and administrative services modernized the country and served to create an extensive web of government patronage (Eckstein 1977). Part of the program of social incorporation was the movement known as *Indígenismo*, which was founded by the anthropologist Manuel Gamio ([1935] 1987). Though the movement sought to protect the indigenous population, its final objective was to incorporate them into the dominant *mestízo* culture through education, health campaigns, and local development programs sponsored by specialized government agencies. By 1940, the indigenous population, defined in terms of those who speak an Indian language, had declined according to the census of that year to just over 14 percent of the population. In general, the indigenous population remained poorer than the *mestízo* peasant population.

Economically, the PRI was nationalist, protecting local industries and restricting foreign investment. The state intervened in the economy, managing industries in sectors which were considered vital to the national interest, such as the oil industry, railroads, certain branches of transport, and telephones. However, it tolerated and, at times, promoted private ownership in many industrial sectors, by including entrepreneurs in the corporate alliances through which the PRI governed. For Mexico, the 1940–1970 decades were the "golden years" of development, when annual rates of gross domestic product (GDP) growth of 6 percent and more were common (Leopoldo Solis, 1970). It was also a period in which a strong political nationalism accompanied economic nationalism. Under various presidents, Mexico made clear its independence from U.S. political and economic influence, as in the nationalization of oil and as in its continuing relations with Castro's Cuba.

The understanding of these processes was aided by the development of social sciences in Mexico, stimulated by an interest in issues of national identity and culture in face of rapid modernization. Anthropology developed under the auspices of official nationalism in the National Institute of Anthropology and History and the National Indigenist Institute, promoting the restoration and preservation of the pre-Hispanic archeological patrimony as symbols of Mexican nationaiity (Vazquez 1995). Gamio's ([1931] 1969) interest in national identity led him to document the living and working conditions of Mexican labor migrants in the United States. He and the American anthropologist Paul Taylor (1928–1934) demonstrated that the experiences of these migrants would often reinforce Mexican nationalism through ill treatment, prejudice, and summary deportations.

Within Mexico, anthropologists undertook empirical studies of acculturation and cultural integration, viewed as irreversible trnds (Aguirre Beltrán 1957). By the 1970s, sociologists and political scientists working at the National University and at El Colegio de México were questioning the Mexican style of development, focusing on issues of class and ethnic inequality (Stavenhagen 1969; Instituto de Investigaciones Sociales 1970–1973; Benítez Zenteno 1977). Some openly questioned the institutional authoritarianism of the political system and the vertical control that the government exercised over the peasantry and industrial workers through the PRI's corporatist structure (González Casanova, 1972). The critical tone of Mexican social science increased after the student movements of 1968 and their repression by the government.

The anthropologists and economists who concentrated on the rural sector showed that, despite the propeasant rhetoric of the Mexican Revolution and of its successor governments, the lot of the small, subsistence-oriented farmer—the peasant farmer—did not significantly improve (Bartra 1974; Esteva 1983; Warman 1980; Hewitt de Alcantara 1976). Mexican and foreign social scientists demonstrated that agrarian reform had only limited success in creating employment opportunities in agriculture, in diversifying the rural economy, and in stimulating development of rural market and service centers. The expense of producing efficiently for high-risk markets deterred many members of the *ejido* from continuing in agriculture (de la Peña 1981). The deterrence increased with the advent of new technological packages that offered substantially improved yields, but which indebted the small producer and created dependence on state bureaucracy or on private sector agro-industries (Barkin 1990). Agricultural modernization in Mexico meant the displacement of the peasant farmer and the increasing importance of commercial cultivation, often linked to agro-industry (Arroyo 1989; Sanderson 1986).

One major factor that changed the pattern of political incorporation was the extension of government bureaucracy from the 1960s onward (Grindle 1977). In agriculture, this resulted in a considerable increase in government personnel administering various programs of rural development, credit, and technical advice. Direct contacts with government officials enabled peasants to bypass local power brokers, thus weakening the broker's position; but it created a new issue, the interface between bureaucracy and the peasant. Bureaucratic officials implemented central government policy but pursued their own career goals, and both objectives often came into conflict with the strategies of peasant farmers.

Demographic factors also conditioned the processes of social change, geographical mobility, and concentration of wealth. The Mexican population has had high rates of growth as a result of significant declines in mortality without offsetting declines in fertility (Alba and Potter 1982). High rates of population growth combined with the lack of economic opportunities in the countryside result in substantial rural-urban and international migration (Massey et al. 1987; Arroyo 1986). The urban growth rate of Mexico between 1940 and 1980 averaged 4.7 percent a year, with approximately a third of urban growth due to migration from rural areas. This rapid increase and the high urban primacy that resulted in Mexico City having a population six times larger than the next-largest city, Guadalajara, attracted the attention of many researchers, often in collaboration with U.S. or European social scientists. Led by Luis Unikel (1977), researchers at the Colegio de Mexico focused on the "urban bias' of Mexican development policies in which subsidies encouraged urban concentration. Garza (1985) showed that without these subsidies the profitability of Mexico City enterprises would have been less than that of enterprises in smaller cities. Other researchers focused on rural-urban migration showing the high social mobility of rural migrants in the urban labor markets, despite the importance of the informal economy (Balán et al. 1973; Muñoz et al. 1977; Escobar 1986). However, other studies looked at the social and political implications of this rapid urban growth in the spread of squatter settlements, the aggravation of poverty, and the beginnings of urban social movements in demand for basic services (Montaño 1976; Lomnitz 1977; Alonso 1980; Cornelius 1985; Ward 1998).

The last period is that following the debt crises of the early 1980s. These crises reflected the exhaustion of the import-substituting model of development in Mexico. The national industries were not competitive internationally and Mexico desperately needed foreign investment to continue its modernization. From the mid-1980s onward, under strong pressure from international agencies and the United States, the Mexican government adopted a free market approach to development, marked by its accession to the General Agreement on Tariffs and Trade (GATT) in 1985 and its joining with the United States and Canada in the North American Free Trade Agreement (NAFTA) in 1993. Commercial interests in Mexico saw *ejídal* property rights as discouraging foreign and national investment in agriculture and in the cities where *ejídal* land hemmed in city boundaries. In 1992, laws were passed that permitted the private sale of *ejídal* land, thus effectively dismantling the agrarian reform system (de Janvry et al. 1997).

Accompanying these economic policies was a political liberalization, which included electoral reform and a greater role for opposition parties. The regime's new economic policies undermined much of its corporate political support. The abolition of the *ejido* effectively weakened the power of PRI's National Peasant Confederation in the countryside. Deregulation, particularly of labor markets, weakened the main industrial unions. The political challenge to the PRI became greater in this period because economic liberalization also created economic instability (Otero 1996). Income inequality grew and employment became unstable, as indicated by the growth of the urban informal economy.

The growth of the urban population continued, but less rapidly than earlier as a result of declines in fertility and in a diminishing pool of rural migrants (Demos 1997). According to the population count of 1995, 63 percent of Mexico's 91 million inhabitants live in places of more than 10,000 people. The fastest growing cities in the period 1990–1995 (3.1 percent growth annually) were the ones that began the period with between 100,000 and 1 million inhabitants (Solís 1997). An important component of the new population dynamic is a gradual change in the pattern of internal migration in Mexico. From a predominantly rural-urban migration focusing mainly on Mexico City, Mexican migration patterns have become increasingly interurban, with a movement of population from the center and south of the country toward the cities of the north (Lozano et al. 1997).

The changes in migration patterns reflect the changing economic geography of Mexico resulting from the development of export-oriented manufacturing mainly in the north of the country along or close to the U.S. border. By 1999, the in bond industry (*maquiladora*) sector generated over a million jobs, mainly in the cities of the north. In contrast, in the 1980s manufacturing lost jobs in the old industrial regions of the center of the country, although industrial restructuring in the Federal District of Mexico in the 1990s has reasserted Mexico City's importance in industrial production. The industrial transformation is a complex one. There are assembly-line operations that use cheap, mainly female labor (Fernández-Kelly 1983; Young and Fort 1994). There are also plants with high levels of technology that require workers with high levels of qualification and that are prepared to offer attractive conditions of work. The Mexican car industry has shifted to northern Mexico as part of an integrated North American production system, with Mexico shipping cars as well as parts to the U.S. market (Carrillo 1989). These processes are creating a distinct border region straddling the frontier, neither fully Mexican nor fully American (Bustamante 1981; Tamayo and Fernandez 1983).

The Mexican economy is not only highly regionalized and predominantly urban, but is increasingly based on service employment (García 1988). By 1995, the majority of employment (53 percent) was in services and commerce, with manufacturing and construction contributing 21 percent and agriculture 25 percent (Pacheco 1997). The same source shows that these shifts in sectoral employment have also been accompanied by increasing rates of female economic participation, growing from 21.5 percent in 1979 to 34.5 percent in 1995. Also, after 1979, the employment categories associated with the urban informal economy—self-employed and unpaid family workers—increase from 33.7 percent to 38.3 percent of employment, whereas employees decline from 62.9 percent to 57.2 percent (Pacheko 1997).

New intellectual tendencies are emerging in face of these realities. There is now less emphasis on rural studies than in the past, although there is a growing focus on the consequences for rural areas of economic integration with the United States, including international migration (Cornelius and Myhre 1998). Mexican and U.S. scholars are studying the impact of the U.S. market on production and commercialization in Mexico with respect to crops such as avocados, mangos, and tomatoes (González Chávez 1991). Particular focuses are the difficulties faced by small-scale farmers, given the capital and technology needed to compete in the U.S. market. Also, there is a greater concern with environmental issues than in the past as market development puts greater competitive pressures on local agriculture or creates incentives to develop ecologically fragile areas for tourism (Tudela 1989; Moreno 1992; Toledo 1994).

Studies of international migration have become increasingly numerous, showing how migration to the United States has become the major means by which poor rural households complement inadequate incomes, attracting even the skilled and better educated (Massey et al. 1994). The existence of large Mexican-origin communities in cities throughout the United States, but particularly in Los Angeles and other cities of the Southwest, provides bridgeheads facilitating immigration. The importance of the U.S. migration experience has led scholars to document extensively the life histories of migrants, sometimes explicitly comparing their experiences with those recorded by Gamio and Taylor in the 1930s (Durand 1996). Mexican and U.S. researchers have also focused on the significance for U.S.-Mexico relations of transnational migrant communities where migrants settled in the U.S. maintain active links with their Mexican communities of origin, even to the extent of participating in local politics and development projects (Roberts et al. 1999).

In the realm of urban research, there is now considerable attention given to studies of family, gender and female economic participation (Benería and Roldán 1987; García and Oliveira 1997). These studies began with an emphasis on household coping strategies in face of poverty, particularly the pooling of resources and placing more members in the labor market (González de la Rocha

1994; Chant 1991; de la Peña et al. 1990; Selby et al. 1990; Roberts 1989). They have increasingly taken up issues of the changing role of women within the household as they gain a certain economic independence. The researchers question assumptions about the strength of the Mexican family and its ability to cope on its own with the fragmenting pressures coming from economic adjustment and migration. Domestic violence has become an important topic of research. In contrast with these demythifying visions of the Mexican family, other studies that focus on elites and entrepreneurial groups show that family cooperation and hierarchy are crucial for upper-class social mobility and business success, particularly among foreign immigrants and innovators willing to take risks (Lomnitz and Pérez Lizaur 1987; Ramírez 1994; Padilla Dieste 1997).

There has also been considerable research on the impact of international economic integration and "neoliberal" policies on two phenomena: poverty and political participation. The new faces of poverty and inequality have been examined through the analysis of representative surveys and case studies, but also from the perspective of the state's retreat from welfare and social services (González de la Rocha and Escobar 1991; Cortés and Rubalcava 1991; Boltvinik 1994; Brachet-Márquez 1996; Escobar 1986). The changing political scene has been studied particularly through electoral studies and the analysis of emerging political cultures. Widespread social discontent from the magnitude of fraud in the 1988 elections, as well as the government's search for international legitimacy in the context of economic globalization, led to the strengthening of opposition parties and the reform of electoral legislation (Molinar 1989, 1992; Azíz and Peschard 1993; Crespo 1993). The process of Mexican democratization is also related to the decline of clientelistic practices, which nowadays proves to be ineffective for handling demands in both urban and rural situations (Middlebrook 1995). The political awakening of an increasingly active civil society is reflected in new social movements that in addition to their demands for services and social justice nowadays challenge the official party and focus on issues of citizenship (Krotz 1996). Middle-class actors, whose standard of living is also declining rapidly, have a considerable presence in such movements (Sergio Tamayo 1994).

The quest for democracy and citizenship is crucial for the understanding of ethnic movements in Mexico. Their importance was dramatically highlighted by the eruption of the Chiapas rebellion on January 1, 1994—the very date of the formal enactment of NAFTA—but urgent ethnic demands have been put forward by dozens of nonviolent indigenous organizations since the 1970s (Campbell 1994; Zárate 1993). Such organizations criticized official Indigenista policies because of their ineffectiveness in eradicating poverty but also because of their assimilationist practices and their blatant disregard for the cultural and political rights of the indigenous population (Arizpe 1978). This critique was reinforced by a new anthropological literature emphasizing persisting ethnicity and cultural resistance instead of acculturation and national homogeneization (Bonfil 1981; Boege 1988). A radical statement of this position argues for the existence of an Indian "deep Mexico"—the real Mexico that has been artificially covered and repressed by authoritarianism and a spurious imitation of European modernity (Bonfil 1996). Even the National Indigenist Institute adopted a discourse of cultural plurality, and the Ministry of Education reinforced its programs of bilingual education (Instituto Nacional Indigenista 1988). In 1991, the National Congress surprisingly passed a constitutional reform that recognized multiculturalism as an essential component of the Mexican nation. If this reform may be explained as related to the government's search for international legitimacy when NAFTA was being negotiated, it nevertheless opened the way to new indigenous demands and to a widespread discussion of the issue of autonomy for autochtonous peoples, where the participation of Indian representatives and authors is as important as that of non-Indian scholars (Warman and Argueta 1993; Díaz-Polanco 1997; Villoro 1998).

REFERENCES

Aguirre Beltrán, Gonzalo 1957 *El proceso de aculturación*. México, D.F.: UNAM.

Alaman, Lucas (1847) 1942 *Disertaciones*. México, D.F. Editorial Jus.

Alba, Francisco, and Joseph Potter 1982 "Population and Development in Mexico since the 1940s: An Interpretation." *Population and Development Review* 12:47–73.

Alonso, Jorge 1980 *Lucha urbana y acumulación de capital*. México, D.F.: Ediciones de la Casa Chata, CISINAH.

Arizpe, Lourdes 1978 *El reto del pluralismo cultural*. Mexico City: Instituto Nacional Indigenista.

Arroyo, Jesús 1986 *Migració a centros urbanos*. Guadalajara: Universidad de Guadalajara.

—— 1989 *El abandono rural*. Guadalajara: Universidad de Guadalajara.

Azíz, Alberto, and Jacqueline Peschard, eds. 1993 *Las elecciones federales de 1991*. Mexico City: Miguel Angel Porrúa.

Balán, Jorge, Harley Browning, and Elizabeth Jelin. 1973. *Men in a Developing Society: Geographical and Social Mobility in Monterrey, Mexico*. Austin: University of Texas Press.

Barkin, David 1990 *Distorted Development: Mexico in the World Economy*. Boulder, Colo.: Westview.

Bartra, Roger 1974 *Estructura agraria y clases sociales en México*. México, D.F.: Ediciones Era.

Benería, Lourdes, and Marta Roldán 1987 *The Cross-Roads of Class and Gender*. Chicago: University of Chicago Press.

Benítez Zenteno, Raúl, ed. 1977 *Clases sociales y crisis política en América Latina*. Mexico City: Universidad Nacional Autónoma de México/Siglo Veintiuno Editores.

Boege, Eckart 1988 *Los mazatecos ante la nación*. Mexico City: Siglo Veintiuno Editores.

Boltvinik, Julio 1994 "La satisfacción de las necesidades esenciales en México en los setenta y ochenta." In Pablo Pascual Moncayo and José Woldenberg, eds., *Desarrollo, desigualdad y medio ambiente*. Mexico City: Cal y Arena.

Bonfil, Guillermo 1996 *México profundo*. Austin: University of Texas Press.

——, ed. 1981 *Utopía y revolución*. Mexico City: Nueva Imagen.

Brachet-Márquez, Viviane 1996 *El pacto de dominación: estado, clase y reforma social en México*. Mexico City: El Colegio de México.

Bustamante, Jorge A. 1981 "La interacción social en la frontera Mexico-Estados Unidos: Un marco conceptual por la investigación." In Roque González, ed., *La frontera del norte*. México, D.F.: El Colegio de México.

Campbell, Howard 1994 *Zapotec Renaissance: Ethnic Politics and Cultural Revivalism in Southern Mexico*. Albuquerque: University of New Mexico Press.

Carrillo, Jorge V., ed. 1989 *La nueva era de la industria automotriz en México*. Tijuana, B.C.: El Colegio de la Frontera Norte.

Chant, Sylvia 1991 *Women and Survival in Mexican Cities*. Manchester, England: Manchester University Press.

Cornelius, Wayne 1975 *Politics and the Migrant Poor in Mexico City*. Stanford, Calif.: Stanford University Press.

——, and David Myhre, eds. 1998 *The Transformation of Rural Mexico. Reforming the Ejido Sector*. La Jolla: Center for U.S.-Mexican Studies. San Diego: University of California.

Cortés, Fernando, and Rosa María Rubalcava 1991 *Autoexplotación forzada y equidad por empobrecimiento*. Mexico City: El Colegio de México (Jornadas, 120).

Crespo, José Antonio 1994 "Legitimidad política y comportamiento electoral en el Distrito Federal." In Jorge Alonso, ed., *Cultura política y educación cívica*. Mexico City: Miguel Angel Porrúa/Universidad Nacional Autónoma de México.

De Janvry, Alan, Gustavo Gordillo, and Elisabeth Sadoulet 1997 *Mexico's Second Agrarian Reform. Household and Community Responses*. La Jolla: Center for U.S.-Mexican Studies, University of California, San Diego.

De la Peña, Guillermo 1981 *A Legacy of Promises. Agriculture, Politics and Ritual in the Morelos Highlands of Mexico*. Austin: University of Texas Press.

——, Juan Manuel Durán, Agustín Escobar, and Javier Garcia de Alba, eds. 1990 *Crisis, conflicto y sobrevivencia: Estudios sobre la sociedad urbana en México*. Guadalajara: Universidad de Guadalajara/CIESAS.

Díaz-Polanco, Héctor 1997 *La Rebelión Zapatista y la Autonomía*. Mexico City: Siglo Veintiuno.

Durand, Jorge, ed. 1996 *El norte es como el mar: Entrevistas a trabajadores migrantes en Estados Unidos*. Guadalajara: Universidad de Guadalajara.

Eckstein, Susan 1977 *The Poverty of Revolution: The State and the Urban Poor in Mexico*. Princeton, N.J.: Princeton University Press.

Escobar, Agustin 1986 *Con el sudor de tu frente: Mercado de trabajo y clase obrera en Guadalajara*. Guadalajara: El Colegio de Jalisco.

Esteva, Gustavo 1983 *The Struggle for Rural Mexico*. South Hadley, Mass.: Bergin and Garvey.

Fernández-Kelly, Maria Patricia 1983 *For We Are Sold: I and My People*. Albany: State University of New York Press.

Gamio, Manuel (1931) 1969 *The Mexican Immigrant*. New York: Amo.

—— (1935) 1987 *Hacia un México nuevo*. México, D.F.: Instituto Nacional Indigenista.

García, Brígida 1988 *Desarrollo económico y absorción de fuerza de trabajo en Mexíco, 1950–1980*. México, D.F.: El Colegio de México.

——, and Orlandina de Oliveira 1994 *Trabajo femenino y vida familiar en México*. Mexico City: El Colegio de México.

Garza, Gustavo 1985 *El proceso de industrialízión en la ciudad de México, 1821–1970*. México, D.F.: El Colegio de México.

González Casanova, Pablo 1972 *Democracy in Mexico*. London: Oxford University Press.

González Chávez, Humberto 1991 "Los empresarios en la agricultura de exportación en México: Un estudio de daso." *European Review of Latin American and Caribbean Studies* 50 (June):87–114.

González de la Rocha, Mercedes 1994 *The Resources of Poverty: Women and Survival in a Mexican City*. Oxford, England: Blackwell.

——, and Agustín Escobar, eds. 1991 *Social Responses to Mexico's Economic Crisis of the 1980's*. La Jolla: Center for U.S.-Mexican Studies, University of California, San Diego.

Grindle, Merilee S. 1977 *Bureaucrats, Politicians and Peasants in Mexico: A Case Study of Public Policy*. Berkeley: University of California Press.

Hewitt de Alcantara, Cynthia 1976 *Modernizing Mexican Agriculture*. Geneva: UNRISD.

Instituto de Investigaciones Sociales, ed. 1970–1973 *El perfil de México en 1980*, 3 vols. Mexico City: Universidad Nacional Autónoma de México/Siglo Veintiuno Editores.

Instituto Nacional Indigenista, ed. 1988 *INI. 40 Años*. Mexico City: INI.

Knight, Alan 1986 *The Mexican Revolution*. Cambridge, England: Cambridge University Press.

Krotz, Esteban, ed. 1996 *El Estudio de la Cultura Política en México: Perspectivas Disciplinarias y Actores Políticos*. Mexico City: Consejo Nacional para la Cultura y las Artes/CIESAS.

Lira Gonzalez, Andres 1984 *Espejo de discordias: La sociedad Mexicana vista por Lorenzo de Zavala, J. M. Luís Mora and Lucas Alaman*. México, D.F.: Secretaría de Educación Pública.

Lomnitz, Larissa Adler 1977 *Networks and Marginality. Life in a Mexican Shantytown*. New York: Academic.

——, and Marisol Pérez-Lizaur 1987 *A Mexican Elite Family, 1820–1980: Kinship, Class, and Culture*. Princeton, N.J.: Princeton University Press.

Lozano, Fernando, Frank Bean, and Bryan Roberts 1997 "The Interconnectedness of Internal and International Migration." *Soziale Welt* 12:163–179.

Massey, Douglas S., Rafael Alarcón, Jorge Durand, and Humberto González 1987 *Return to Aztlan*. Berkeley: University of California Press.

——, Luin Goldring, and Jorge Durand 1994 "Continuities in Transnational Migration: An Analysis of Nineteen Mexican Communities." *American Journal of Sociology* 99(6):1492–1533.

Middlebrook, Kevin 1995 *The Paradox of Revolution: Labor, the State, and Authoritarianism in Mexico*. Baltimore, Md.: Johns Hopkins University Press.

Molina Enriquez, Andres (1909) 1978 *Los grandes problemas nacionales*. México, D.F.: Ediciones Era.

Molinar, Juan 1989 "The Future of the Electoral System." In Wayne A. Cornelius, Judith Gentleman, and Peter H. Smith, eds., *Mexico's Alternative Political Futures*. La Jolla: Center for U.S.-Mexican Studies, University of California, San Diego.

—— 1992 *Elecciones, autoritarismo y democracia en México*. Mexico City: Cal y Arena.

Montaño, Jorge 1976 *Los pobres de la ciudad en las asentamientos espontaneos*. México, D.F.: Siglo Veintiuno Editores.

Moreno, José Luis, ed. 1992 *Ecología, recursos naturales y medio ambiente en sonora*. Hermosillo: El Colegio de Sonora.

Muñoz, Humberto, Orlandina de Oliveira, and Claudio Stern, eds. 1977 *Migración y desigualdad social en la ciudad de México*. México, D.F.: Instituto de Investigaciones Sociales/El Colegio de México.

Otero, Gerardo, ed. 1996 *Neo-Liberalism Revisited: Economic Restructuring and Mexico's Political Future*. Boulder, Colo.: Westview.

Pacheco, Edith 1997 "La población económicamente activa 1900–1995." *Demos* 10:30–31.

Padilla Dieste, Cristina 1997 *Todo queda en familia: El mercado de abastos de Guadalajara*. Guadalajara: Universidad de Guadalajara.

Pastor, Robert A., and Jorge G. Castañeda 1988 *Limits to Friendship: The United States and Mexico*. New York: Alfred A. Knopf.

Ramírez, Luis Alfonso 1994 *Secretos de familia: Libaneses y élites empresariales en Yucatán*. Mexico City: Consejo Nacional para la Cultura y las Artes.

Roberts, Bryan 1989 "Employment Structure, Life Cycle, and Life Chances: Formal and Informal Sectors in Guadalajara." In A. Portes, M. Castelis, and L. Benton, eds., *The Informal Economy–Comparative Studies in Advanced and Third World Countries*. Baltimore, Md.: Johns Hopkins University Press.

——, Reane Frank, and Fernando Lozano 1999 "Transnational Migrant Communities and Mexican Migration to the US." *Ethnic and Racial Studies* 22.

Sanderson, Steven E. 1986 *The Transformation of Mexican Agriculture: Internacional Structure and the Politics of Rural Change*. Princeton, N.J.: Princeton University Press.

Selby, Henry A., Arthur D. Murphy, and S. A. Lorenzen 1990 *Urban Life in Mexico: Coping Strategies of the Poor Majority*. Austin: University of Texas Press.

Sierra, Justo 1969 (1900–1902) *The Political Evolution of the Mexican People*. Austin: University of Texas Press.

Solís, Leopoldo 1970 *La realidad economica Mexicana: Retrovision y perspectivas*. Mexico City: Siglo Veintiuno Editores.

Solís, Patricio 1997 "Población urbana y la población rural." *Demos* 10:6–7.

Stavenhagen, Rodolfo 1969 *Las clases sociales en las sociedades agrarias*. México, D.F.: Siglo Veintiuno.

Tamayo, Jesús, and José Luis Fernandez 1983 *Zonas fronterizas*. México, D.F.: CIDE.

Tamayo, Sergio 1994 "The 20 Mexican Octobers: A Study of Citizenship and Social Movements." Ph.D. Dissertation, University of Texas at Austin.

Taylor, Paul S. 1928–1934 *Mexican Labor in the United States*, vols. 1–111. Berkeley: University of California Press.

Toledo, Alejandro 1994 *Riqueza y Pobreza en la Costa de Chiapas y Oaxaca*. México: Centro de Ecología y Desarrollo.

Tudela, Fernando, ed. 1989 *La modernización forzada del trópico: El caso de Tabasco*. Mexíco: El Colegio de México.

Unikel, Luis (with Crescencio Ruiz Chiapetto and Gustavo Garza) 1978 *El desarrollo urbano de México. Diagnóstico e implicaciones futuras*. Mexico City: El Colegio de México.

Vazquez, Luis 1995 *El leviathan arqueologico*. Leiden: University of Leiden.

Villoro, Luis 1998 *Estado plural, pluralidad de culturas*. Mexico City: Paidós/Universidad Nacional Autónoma de México.

Ward, Peter M. 1998 *Mexico City*. New York: John Wiley.

Warman, Arturo 1980 *"We Come to Object": The Peasants of Morelos and the National State*. Baltimore, Md.: Johns Hopkins University Press.

——, and Arturo Argueta 1993 *Movimientos indígenas contemporáneos en México*. Mexico City: Miguel Angel Porrúa/Universidad Nacional Autónoma de México.

Weintraub, Sidney 1990 *A Marriage of Convenience: Relations between Mexico and the United States*. New York: Oxford University Press.

Young, Gay 1994 "Household Responses to Economic Change: Migration and 'Maquiladora' Work in Ciudad Juarez, Mexico." *Social Science Quarterly* 75(3):656–671.

Zárate, Eduardo 1993 *Los señores de la utopía. Etnicidad política en una comunidad purhépecha*. Zamora: El Colegio de Michoacán.

Zea, Lepoldo 1974 *Positivism in Mexico*. Austin: University of Texas Press.

GUILLERMO DE LA PEÑA
BRYAN R. ROBERTS

MIDDLE EASTERN STUDIES

In the closing decades of the twentieth century, successive crises and cataclysmic events in the Middle East, though obviously not unique to this region, have been widely publicized by the American mass media. The 1973 Arab-Israeli War and the subsequent oil crisis, the civil war in Lebanon, the Iranian revolution of 1978–1979 and the ensuing hostage crisis, the Iraq-Iran War of 1980–1988, the Intifadah in the West Bank and Gaza, the Gulf War, the continued bombing of Iraq, the Oslo Agreement between Palestinians and Israelis, and the World Trade Center bombing have increased Americans' awareness of the Middle East but not necessarily their understanding of its culture and society. Unfortunately, the ways in which the media describe and interpret these events have created negative stereotypes about this region which are reinforced by movies such as *The Siege*. On the other hand, extensive research by anthropologists, historians, and political scientists has provided many insights into Middle Eastern societies and cultures that help counteract these stereotypes. What has been the contribution of sociologists?

More than twenty years ago, a review of a few sociological journals led me to conclude that "with the possible exception of demographers, the scholarly output of American sociologists on the Middle East is still very modest" (Sabagh 1976, p. 523). For the period 1963–1973, of the twelve articles on the Middle East published in the *American Sociological Review* and the *American Journal of Sociology*, eight were on Israel, three on Egypt, and one on Turkey. For the same period *Sociology and Social Research* had even fewer articles on the Middle East, but they were more evenly distributed (two on Israel, two on Turkey, two on Iraq, and one on Israel and Jordan).

One interpretation of this situation, which is still valid today, is that "as long as the research findings tend to be area-oriented rather than hypothesis-oriented they are not likely to be published in American sociological journals" (Sabagh 1976, p. 523). Is the state of Middle Eastern studies in sociology today any better than in the early 1970s? The objective of this review is to assess the changes that have occurred since the mid-1970s, more particularly in the 1980s and the 1990s. Four topics will be considered: (1) an overview of the salient socioeconomic and demographic characteristics of Middle Eastern countries and their implications for sociological analysis, (2) trends and distributions in the number of sociologists in the United States specializing in the Middle East, (3) a brief review of the main substantive or methodological concerns of these sociologists, and (4) some of their theoretical contributions studies to American sociology. Contributions to the sociological study of Islam will not be reviewed here since they are extensively discussed in the article "Sociology of Islam."

SOCIOECONOMIC AND DEMOGRAPHIC CHARACTERISTICS OF THE MIDDLE EAST

The Middle East includes Iran, Israel, Turkey, and the Arab countries of North Africa and southwest Asia. As shown in Table 1, countries in this vast region vary greatly, not only in population but also in levels of income, education, urbanization, and stages of demographic transition. The most telling differences are those between rich and poor countries, unmatched by the experience *of* any other Third World region. The range in gross national product (GNP) per capita in 1997 was from $169 for Somalia to $17,360 for the United Arab Emirates (UAE) and to $22,110 for Kuwait, which approaches the figure for the United States. This gap was even greater before the decline in oil prices in the mid-1980s. The least-populated countries (Kuwait, UAE, and Qatar) have the highest incomes, exceeding $10,000, and two of the most populous countries (Egypt and Iran) have lower incomes, in the range $1,000–$2,000 This income differential is in part responsible for a massive labor migration from the poor Arab countries, particularly Egypt and Yemen, to the rich Arab countries (Amin and Awny 1985; Owen 1989). One measure of the importance of this migration is provided by the figures on the share of workers' remittances in the

GNP of labor-exporting countries. In 1992, net workers' remittances constituted 19.5 and 16.5 percent of the GNP of Jordan and Egypt, respectively. Estimates of the size of the Arab labor migration streams vary widely (Amin and Awny 1985; Ibrahim 1982), but it increased rapidly in the 1970s and was substantial in 1980. For Egypt alone, one estimate places the number of workers abroad at over one million in 1980, compared with around 400,000 in 1975 (Amin and Awny 1985; Fergany 1987). There was also a considerable migration from the poor countries of southern Asia and eastern Asia to Gulf countries, with an estimated 700,000 contract workers migrating in 1987 (Stahl and Asam 1990). Prior to the Iraq-Kuwait War in 1990, there were an estimated 2.6 millions migrants in these two countries, but at least 1 million of them left within two months after the outbreak of this war (United Nations, 1996, p. 209). In addition, there was a massive exodus of Yemenis from Saudi Arabia, leading to a sharp drop of net worker remittances for Yemen within a fairly short period. There is no doubt that this massive exodus of labor migrants from Iraq, Kuwait, and Saudi Arabia created new economic problems for Arab labor-exporting countries.

The characteristics and implications of the massive labor migration of Middle Easterners and Asians to the rich Arab oil-producing countries have been analyzed by a few American demographers and sociologists (Arnold and Shah 1984; Sabagh 1993; Sell 1988). These and other studies (Amin and Awny 1985; Fergany 1987) have contributed to the analysis of (1) the process of migrant settlement in countries with stringent legislation against settlement, (2) the impact of this migration on social mobility, and (3) the consequences of labor migration on countries of origin.

While a few North Africans and Turks emigrated to the Gulf, most were attracted by expanding economic opportunities in the European community. In 1996, there was an estimated 2.6 million Turks, 1.1 million Moroccans, and about 1 million Algerians and Tunisians in Europe (OECD 1998, p. 34). Most of the Turks were in Germany, and most of the Algerians and Tunisians and half of the Moroccans resided in France.

Migration streams from the Middle East to the United States go back to the 1980s, but political

Selected Indicators: Middle Eastern Countries and the United States, 1995–1998

Country	GNP per Capita ($U.S.) mid-1997	Population (Millions), mid-1997	Total Fertility Rate, 1997	Life Expectancy, at Birth, Males, 1998	Life Expectancy, at Birth, Females, 1998	Annual Rate of Growth Total, 1995-2000	Population Urban, 1995-2000	Enrollment Ratios (%) Secondary School Female, 1995	Male, 1995	Female Economic Activity Rate as % of Male, 1995
Somalia	$169	7.1	7	45	48		5.3	6	4	NA
Yemen	$270	8.5	7.1	54	54	3.7	6.3	63	14	38
Sudan	$280	28	5.7	55	57	2.2	5	21	19	40
Mauritania	$450	2	5.4	52	55	2.5	4.9	22	11	48
Syrian AR	$1,150	11.4	4	66	71	2.5	3.4	45	40	35
Egypt	$1,180	60	3.3	64	67	1.8	2.4	80	70	40
Morocco	$1,250	27	3.3	64	68	1.8	3.1	44	34	53
Algeria	$1,490	29	3.4	68	72	2.3	3.6	65	62	32
Jordan	$1,520	4	4.8	71	75	3.3	4.1	NA	NA	27
Iran IR	$1,780	51	4.3	67	70	2.2	3.1	79	65	32
Tunisia	$2,090	9	2.8	69	71	1.8	2.9	67	64	44
Turkey	$3,130	64	2.5	66	71	1.6	3.2	74	50	56
Lebanon	$3,350	4	2.7	68	71	1.8	2.3	78	86	39
Oman	$4,950	2	5.1	69	73	4.2	6.3	68	65	16
Libyan AJ	$5,621	5	6.2	63	68	3.3	3.9	NA	NA	26
Saudi Arabia	$6,790	20	6.2	69	71	3.4	4.1	65	57	15
Bahrain	$7,820	0.5	3	72	78	2.1	2.5	91	98	24
Qatar	$11,570	0.4	3.5	71	77	1.8	2	79	77	15
Israel	$15,810	6	2.7	75	79	1.9	2	89	87	60
UAE	$17,360	3	4.7	74	76	2	2.5	77	74	15
Kuwait	$22,110	2	3.4	75	79	3	3.1	65	64	45
Iraq	NA	22	6.1	67	69	2.8	3.4	50	32	22
West Bank/ Gaza	NA	3	4.9	71	74	4.2	4.2	NA	NA	NA
United States	$28,740	268	2.1	74	80	0.8	1.1	98	99	82

Table 1

NOTE: NA=not available.

SOURCE: United Nations Development Programme 1998 *Human Development 1998*. New York: Oxford University Press; World Bank *World Development Report 1998–99*. Washington: World Bank; United Nations Home Page 1999 Statistics Division Home Page. Social Indicators Home Page. New York: United Nations.

upheavals such as the Iranian revolution, the Arab-Israeli wars of 1967 and 1973, and the Lebanese civil war as well as changes in American immigration legislation in the 1960s have led to substantial and more recent immigration to the United States. Thus, of the 1.3 million persons of Middle Eastern origin (including those of Arab, Armenian, Assyrian, Iranians, Israelis, and Turkish origins) in the United States in 1990, half were immigrants and 325,000 were very "new" immigrants who had arrived between 1990 and 1990. (U.S. Bureau of the Census 1993). As indicated by Bozorgmehr (1998, p. 5) "The Iranian revolution and its aftermath have contributed to the growth of the Iranian diaspora worldwide," so that by 1990 the United States had

285,000 Iranians "defined as persons born in Iran or Iranian ancestry." This represents a substantial growth from "small beginning of perhaps no more than 15,000 individuals in 1965" (Bozorgmehr and Sabagh 1988, p. 32).

In almost all Middle Eastern countries, rates of population growth of urban areas are higher, and in some cases much higher, than total population growth. This means that rural-urban migration constitutes an important feature of both rich and poor Middle Eastern societies. This rural exodus is most marked in some of the poorest countries but tends to be lower in poor countries with substantial international labor migration.

Differences in secondary school enrollment levels are as wide as income differences. Enrollment ratios in secondary schools in 1996 varied between a minimum of 6 for males and 4 for females in Somalia to a maximum 91 for males and 98 for females in Bahrain, almost equal to the United States (Table 1). While Bahraini's high enrollment ratios could be partly attributed to its relatively high income, wealth is no guarantee of higher education. For Kuwait, which has the highest income level, male secondary enrollment is noticeably lower (65) than it is for Egypt (80) and the Islamic Republic of Iran (79), which have much lower income. The ratios for females are about the same for these three countries, but the female-male gap is greater in Egypt and Iran. It should be noted that in 15 of the 25 Middle Eastern countries in Table 1, the female-male gap in secondary enrollment ratios is 10 percent or less. In Bahrain and Lebanon, females have a higher secondary school enrollment. These findings suggest gender equalization in education. Nevertheless, in some countries, notably Somalia, Yemen, and, surprisingly, Turkey, the gender gap is substantial. Since educational opportunities are fewer in rural areas, particularly for women, this gap could partly reflect the greater importance of these areas. Even in Middle Eastern countries where the educational gender gap is almost nil, women are still much less likely to have gainful employment outside the home than men. Nationwide data on women's employment, however, have to be interpreted carefully, since they include rural areas and also reflect different definitions of employment. Women in Israel, Turkey, and Morocco are the most likely to be employed, but even in these countries the ratio of women's to men's employment is in the range 50–60 percent (Table 1). The ratios between 40 percent and 50 percent in Kuwait, Tunisia, and Mauritania and between 30 percent and 40 percent in seven other Middle Eastern countries. By contrast, with the noticeable exception of Kuwait, in the rich Arab oil-exporting countries with little or no gender inequality in access to education, the ratio is much lower and is mainly around 15 percent. Increasing gender equality in education combined with continued gender inequality in employment in the Middle East have many consequences for women's roles and have been the subject of many analyses (Hatem 1994; Moghadam 1995; Obermeyer 1996). These analyses reveal the complex ways in which family structure, religious tradition, economic development, and state policies affect the education and employment of women.

It should be noted that even in countries with high labor-force participation by women, there is a glaring gender gap in earned income. Thus, in the United States, while there are 82 gainfully employed women for every 100 gainfully employed men, these women receive only 40 percent of men's earnings. The comparable figures are 50 women and 22 percent for Israel, 57 women and 35 percent for Turkey, and 53 women and 28 percent for Morocco. Surprisingly, this lag in working women's income is less marked in some Middle Eastern countries than in the United States (for sources, see Table 1).

During the last twenty years, fertility and mortality trend in the Middle East indicate that parts of in this region have experienced a rapid demographic transition. In 1980, all countries in this region, except Israel, Lebanon, and Turkey, had total fertility rates (TFR) of 5 or more children per women, often reaching a level above 6 children. Mortality had already declined but was still relatively high. By the end of the twentieth century, life expectancy for males had increased to about 63 years at birth and, even higher, to 74–75 years in Kuwait, Israel, and the UAE, equal to that of the United States (Table 1). There was a similar trend among females, most of whom outlive men by as much as 6 years. In nine Middle Eastern countries there was a marked decline in TFR to fewer than 3.5 children per woman, reaching as low as 2.5–2.7 in Israel, Lebanon, and Turkey in 1997 (Table 1). This is only slightly higher than the TFR for the United States. Clearly some Middle Eastern countries are rapidly undergoing a demographic transition to noticeably lower fertility and mortality, but in some other countries, even though mortality is low, fertility remains high. This is a challenge to the demographic transition theory and has been extensively analyzed by demographers and sociologists (Obermeyer 1992 and 1995).

Clearly, the Middle East is a region worthy of consideration in any analysis of the social and demographic impact of economic modernization and rising levels of income. The sudden increase in the wealth of some Arab countries is part of what Ibrahim (1982) has called the "new Arab social order," which involves the appearance of new social forces, new values, and new behavior patterns. This has resulted in a great deal of social chaos and the emergence of new social problems. Partly as a result of this social chaos, there have been significant political and social movements and revolutions that need to be analyzed from a comparative sociological perspective.

By making systematic and comparative analyses of various features of Middle Eastern societies, American sociologists could provide a foundation for a better understanding of these societies. This assumes, however, that these sociologists have incorporated the history and experience of Middle Eastern countries into their substantive concerns and theoretical models. The sections that follow will review the trends in the number of sociologists of the Middle East and in the United States, and the substantive focus of their work.

NUMBER OF SOCIOLOGISTS OF THE MIDDLE EAST IN IHE UNITED STATES

It is significant that an American sociologist, Monroe Berger of Princeton University, was active in the formation of the Middle East Studies Association of North America (MESA) in 1964 and was elected its first president. Nevertheless, in the mid-1970s there were only nine sociologists teaching courses on the sociology of the Middle East in American departments of sociology (Sabagh 1976, p. 524). While growth was slow, the 1980s and 1990s were marked by a noticeable increase in sociologists teaching or doing research on the Middle East. Sociologist members of MESA, including students, increased from 12 in 1968 to 25 in 1972, 37 in 1984, 52 in 1986, 90 in 1990, and 121 in 1998 (Sabagh 1976; Bonine 1986; MESA 1998; and special tabulation by MESA). Not all these sociologists, however, resided in the United States. In 1986 only 3 percent of MESA members were sociologists, compared to 32 percent who were historians and 21 percent who were political scientists (Bonine 1986, p. 159). In the mid-1980s Bonine could still state that "compared to Latin America, for instance, there are few sociologists and demographers specializing on the Middle East" (1986, p. 160).

While an increasing number of Middle Easterners have come to the United States to obtain Ph.D.'s in sociology, most of them have gone back home; but, as a result of the Iranian revolution and its negative effect on the teaching of Western-type sociology in Iran, many Iranians who obtained Ph.D.'s in sociology have remained in the United States as intellectual exiles. The Iranian revolution also provided a real impetus for Iranian students to major in sociology so as to gain a better understanding of the revolution.

Dr. Anne Betteridge, executive secretary of MESA, and Nancy B. Dishaw, also of MESA, kindly provided a special tabulation of the countries of birth of 1998 MESA members who indicated sociology as their discipline. There were 62 members who were residents of the United States or Canada with Ph.D.'s in sociology, of whom 44 had received their degrees since 1980, indicating a noticeable increase in the number of sociologists actively interested in Middle East studies. Most of this increase, however, may be attributed to sociologists born in the Middle East, whose numbers more than doubled, from 10 to 25. A comparison of the later and earlier Ph.D. cohorts shows that the number of sociologists born in Iran quadrupled from 3 to 12, the number of those born in Turkey increased from 0 to 7, and the number born in the United States increased more slowly from 8 to 15. By contrast, the number of sociologists born in an Arab country decreased from 7 to 6. The creation of the Association of American University Graduates in 1967 may be partly responsible for this decline.

About half of the 62 sociologists who are members of MESA and who reside in the United States or Canada are in graduate departments of sociology. By contrast, nearly all the 24 sociology student MESA members are in graduate departments of sociology. Not all sociologists with a research or teaching interest in the Middle East are members of MESA. A search of the *Guide to Graduate Departments of Sociology* of the American Sociological Association (ASA) (1999) shows that there were at least 12 who were not members of MESA.

SUBSTANTIVE FOCUS OF SOCIOLOGISTS OF THE MIDDLE EAST

It is safe to assume that sociologists who belong to MESA will focus some of their research and theoretical interest on the Middle East. The directory of ASA members (ASA 1990) provides information on fields of specialization. Unfortunately, there are no tabulations available that would allow comparisons with all sociologists or sociologists who have an interest in other world areas. There were 26 nonstudent and 9 student members of ASA in 1989 who were also members of MESA. Of the 26 nonstudent members, 15 were in graduate departments of sociology. Members were asked to check four substantive or methodological areas of sociology in order of priority, of which the first and second are below.

The three most important areas of specialization are (1) development and social change, (2) comparative sociology/macro, and (3) political sociology. Next in importance are (1) demography, (2) race/ethnic/minority, (3) sociology of sex roles, and (4) social movements. Unfortunately, no questions were asked about the extent to which sociologists focused on a given region, country, society, or community. For this, it would be necessary to analyze the publications and papers of the 35 scholars who were members of both the ASA and MESA. A survey was made of publications and papers by these scholars that were cited in *Sociological Abstracts* for the period 1985-1990. The three most frequent substantive or theoretical topics were (1) the Iranian revolution, (2) historical-sociological analyses of Turkey and Iran, with an emphasis on dependency or world system approaches, and (3) Iranian immigrants in the United States. Other topics included (1) Egyptian international migration, (2) social distance in Egypt, (3) child nutrition, (4) a review of Arab sociology, and (5) the Intifadah. It is likely, however, that there are many more contributions to Middle Eastern studies by sociologists who are not members of MESA. The task of assessing this literature is clearly beyond the scope of this article. One way to obtain this information is through a survey of these sociologists. In 1983-1984 such a survey was carried out for Arab sociologists or sociologists studying the Arab world (Sabagh and Ghazalla 1986). Ten of the sociologists residing in the United States considered social change and development and the role of Islam to have the highest priority for research on the Arab world.

One issue that needs to be considered is the extent to which sociological research on the Middle East is cited in major American sociological journals. An analysis was made of articles on the Middle East cited in *Sociological Abstracts* for the years 1985-1990 and published in the general and more specialized sociological journals. Since the number of papers on Israel was substantial, they were left out of the analysis. The results of this analysis showed that the situation was even worse now than it was in the period 1963-1973 (Sabagh 1976). On the other hand, in the 1980s a substantial number of articles on the Middle East were published in the newer or more specialized sociological journals.

An analysis of *Sociological Abstracts* for the period 1985-1990 showed that 31 specialized journals had published 104 articles pertaining to the Middle East or to Middle Easterners. The distribution of articles by country or region (exclusive of Israel) was as follows: Iran, 31; Turkey/Ottoman Empire, 14; Arab world/Middle East, 15; Egypt, 14; other Middle Eastern countries, 19; Palestinians, 5; Arab and Iranian immigrants in the United States, 6. The large number of articles on Iran may be explained by the analyses of the Iranian revolution and by the increasing number of Iranian sociologists in the United States. One issue of *State, Culture, and Society* (1985) included 8 articles devoted to "The Sociological and Ideological Dimensions of the Iranian Revolution." There were four articles on the Iranian revolution (or comparing the Iranian revolution with other revolutions) in *Theory and Society*. Five specialized journals published 10 articles on marriage and the family and the status of women, 5 of which were on Iran. The period 1985-1990 was also characterized by a substantial number of articles on the Ottoman Empire and Turkey published in the Fernand Braudel Center's *Review*. The winter 1985 issue of the *Review* included 3 articles on "From Ottoman Empire to Modem State," and the spring 1988 issue was devoted to the "Ottoman Empire: Nineteenth-Century Transformations." These articles present critical analyses of the process of incorporation of the Ottoman Empire/Turkey into the world economy. Clearly, sociologists whose research focuses on the Middle East or Middle Easterners have a better chance of getting their articles accepted in specialized sociological journals than in the major and mainstream sociological journals.

In 1996, the editor and board of *Contemporary Sociology* decided to "make a greater effort to cover sociology around the world" (Clawson 1997, p. vii). As a consequence, this journal published assessments of the development of sociology in Egypt and the Arab World (Ibrahim 1997; Naim-Ahmed

1998), Turkey (Oncu 1997), Israel (Ben-Yehuda 1997), and Palestine (Hammami 1997). Earlier, in a section of *Contemporary Sociology* entitled "Journals in Review," Mirsepassi (1995) presented an analysis of Middle Eastern journals. This is perhaps the most promising development of the 1990s, and it is hoped that it will lead to a greater impact of Middle Eastern studies on American sociology in the twenty-first century.

Although the numbers are still small, there has been a surprising increase in articles devoted to the Middle East (excluding Israel) published in the 1990s in the three major sociological journals. From 1990 to 1997, there were 7 articles, all of them devoted to Iran or the Ottoman Empire, in the *American Sociological Review*, the *American Journal of Sociology*, and *Social Forces*. This compares to only 1 article in the same journals in the 1980s.

THEORETICAL AND METHODOLOGICAL CONTRIBUTIONS OF MIDDLE EASTERN STUDIES TO SOCIOLOGY

There are two major ways in which Middle Eastern studies can contribute to sociology: (1) dramatic events in the Middle East, such as wars and revolutions, present a puzzle to sociologists studying such events, and (2) sociologists specializing in Middle Eastern studies focus on substantive issues that have consequences for sociological theory and methodology. Examples of both types of contributions will be given and discussed.

The Iranian Islamic revolution is clearly one of the most dramatic events of the last decades of the twentieth century. For Arjomand, it is a "cataclysm as significant and as unprecedented in world history as the French revolution of 1789 and the Russian revolution of 1917" (1988, p. 3). As could be expected, American sociologists of Iranian origin have contributed many important insights into the causes and consequences of this revolution, and these insights have been and will be incorporated into sociological theories about revolutions (see, e.g., Arjornand 1988; Ashraf and Banuazizi 1985; Ashraf 1988; Dabashi 1984; Moghadam 1989; Parsa 1989). For other sociologists who have studied the nature and sources of revolution, the Iranian revolution presents a real challenge. This is expressed as follows by Theda Skocpol:

The recent overthrow of the Shah, the launching of the Iranian revolution between 1977 and 1979, came as a sudden surprise to outside observers. . . . All of us have watched the unfolding of current events with fascination and, perhaps, consternation. A few of us have also been inspired to probe the Iranian sociopolitical realities behind those events . . . . Its unfolding . . . challenged expectations about revolutionary causation that I developed through comparative-historical research on the French, Russian and Chinese revolutions. (1982, p. 265)

Skocpol applied her earlier structural analysis of the causes of revolutions to the Iranian case, pointing to the involvement of urban masses in this revolution, the role of the rentier state, and the structural consequences of Shia Islam. When challenged by Nichols to the effect that she is "ready to concede the potentially revolutionary content of traditional religious teachings" (1986, p. 182). Skocpol replied that "far from offering a 'subjectivist' or 'ideational' analysis, I point out that Shi'a religion had the cultural potential to facilitate either a rebellion against or passive acquiescence to secular authority" (1986, p. 193). Arjomand criticizes Skocpol for not recognizing the normative factor of legitimacy" (1988, p. 191).

Arjomand, Ashraf, and other sociologists indicate the importance of analyzing the 1977–1979 revolution by considering its historical roots, particularly the structural, ideological, and leadership factors in previous uprisings and rebellions. Thus, for Ashraf, "The urban uprising of 1963 combined the leadership of a militant charismatic leader, the political resources of the bazaar-mosque alliance, and the sympathy of activist university students . . . a prelude to the Islamic revolution of 1977–79" (1988, p. 550). Arjomand (1988) points to the involvement of "high-ranking members" of the Shiite "clergy" or hierocracy in the constitutional revolution of 1905–1906. Arjomand (1984a, 1984b, 1988) not only traces the history of the relationship between the Shiite hierocracy, the state, and other social groups but also places his analysis of the Iranian revolution in a comparative perspective. With passage of time, on might expect a decline in the number of sociological analyses of the Iranian revolution. In fact, the opposite is true, and this revolution continues to fascinate some

American sociologists challenged by its implications for theories of revolution, social protests, and social movements. There is also increasing interest in the consequences of this revolution. Kurzman (1994) uses the material about the Iranian revolution to raise some important theoretical questions about resource mobilization theory. In a later paper (1996) he also uses this revolution to challenge the theory about structural and perceived opportunities. His argument is based on a number of interviews he carried out with Iranian expatriates in Turkey. Moaddel (1992) uses the Iranian revolution to test a the role of ideology, suggesting that ideology is a language that is used to express ideas about social problems and their solution. What is probably the first quantitative analysis of events preceding the Islamic revolution was carried out by Karen Rasler, in which she tests a number of hypotheses about the effects of governmental repression and concessions on the umber of political protests from December 1, 1977, to February 14, 1979 (1996, p. 138).

Studies of other political protest movements and revolutions in Iran have been brought together in a book edited by John Foran (1994). This book includes analyses of the Tobacco Movement of 1890–1892, the constitutional revolution of 1905–1911, the nationalist movement in Azerbaijan and Kurdistan of 1941–1946, the oil nationalization movement of 1939–1953, and social conflict in the 1960s. American historians of Iran such as Nikki Keddie and Ervand Abrahamian are, of course, very familiar with these events, but the book should inform and hopefully challenge sociologists interested in social movements and revolutions. In one chapter Foran provides an analysis of the 1977–1979 revolution, showing the importance of comparing it to those that occurred in other countries. He concludes that "its deep causes are to be sought in the same processes of dependent development, state repression, political cultures of resistance, economic downturn, and world-systemic opening that underlay other successful revolution in Mexico, Cuba, and Nicaragua" (Foran 1994, p. 181). Foran and Goodwin (1993) and Parsa (1995a) have published studies comparing the Iranian and Nicaraguan revolutions. Parsa (1995a) shows that ideological conversions and tactical considerations explain the support that entrepreneurs and workers gave to the Iranian and Nicaraguan revolution. In another paper, Parsa (1995b) presents a critical

analysis of the role of the bourgeoisie in supporting the process of democratization in Iran under the shah and in the Philippines under Marcos. Moaddel (1996) analyzes the rise of Islamic fundamentalism in Iran and Syria. Sohrabi (1995) has carried out an extensive comparative analysis of the constitutional revolutions in Iran, the Ottoman Empire, and Russia in the early 1990s. Systematic comparisons between the Iranian and other revolutions and their outcomes are the most promising development of the 1990s.

One interesting development of the last twenty years has been the application of the world system theoretical model to the Ottoman Empire and Turkey. An early issue of the Fernand Braudel Center's *Review* includes three articles on the Ottoman Empire and the world economy, one of which provides a program of research delineated by Immanuel Wallerstein (1979). The objective of this program was to analyze the process of incorporation of the Ottoman Empire into the world economy, the consequences of this incorporation, and the degree and nature of the peripheralization of the Ottoman Empire and Turkey. This program was carried out by the Research Working Group on the Ottoman Empire and was coordinated by Caglar Keyder and Immanuel Wallerstein. The work of Kasaba (1987, 1988); Keyder and Tabak (1986); Keyder (1988); Pamuk (1988); and other sociologists, economists, and historians with a world-system perspective has documented the timing and the process of incorporation of the Ottoman Empire into the world economy, the role of the Ottoman bureaucracy, and the emergence of a minority non-Muslim bourgeoisie. Kasaba (1987, p. 842) argues that "between ca. 1750 and ca. 1820 the Ottoman Empire as a whole was incorporated into the capitalist world-economy . . . [and] the history of the Ottoman Empire after the 1820's was that of its peripheralization" (Pamuk's p.). However, analysis of various indexes of foreign trade and investment (1988) shows that until 1914 the degree of integration of the Ottoman Empire into the world economy was noticeably lower than that of Latin America or that of Algeria and Egypt. Also, within the Ottoman Empire different sectors of the economy were incorporated in different periods (Cizakca 1985).

One consequence of the process of incorporation into the world economy was the emergence of a new bourgeois class of non-Muslim merchants (Kasaba 1987; Keyder 1988). While there was a social class conflict between these merchants and the Ottoman bureaucracy, this conflict "appeared on the Ottoman agenda to be acted out as Moslem-Christian ethnic-religious conflict" (Keyder 1988, p. 162). The periphery-core status of Safavid Iran and the Ottoman Empire in the seventeenth century is analyzed by Foran, who concludes that these states "were far too strong to be colonized and dominated by the core, *and* yet too weak to compete with Europe in the new peripheries of Asia, Southeast Asia, and Africa, not to mention Latin America" (1989, p. 113; italic in original). Thus, these states were neither core nor periphery.

The Fernand Braudel Center *Review* continues to publish studies of the Ottoman Empire and Turkey with a world-system perspective. Of particular interest to sociologists interested in the application of this model to urbanization is the special issue of the *Review* (fall 1993) devoted to the role of port cities in the process of incorporation of the Ottoman Empire in the nineteenth century. Included are studies of Izmir by Kasaba, Trabzon by Turgay, and Beirut by Ozveren. Keyder's study of Istanbul in the 1940s (1993) was also published in *Review*, later in the same year.

One important theoretical and methodological addition to the socio-historical studies of the Ottoman Empire is the research by Karen Barkey on conflict and contention in Turkish villages in the seventeenth century (1997). Barkley statistically analyzes court records about contentions pertaining to taxes and land. She argues that "local and small, are the most basic and common form of contention, closely linked to discontent, often preceding and underlying collective form of discontent (1997, p. 1346).

Studies of Arab immigrants in the United States provide important insights into the process of ethnicity maintenance among immigrants, showing, for example, the importance of minority status in the country of origin, religion, and entrepreneurship in the United States (Abu-Laban 1989; Abraham et al. 1983; Hagopian and Paden 1969; Sawaie 1985; Sengstock 1982; Suleiman and Abu-Laban 1989; Swan and Saba 1974). Pulcini (1993) provides a detailed review of this extensive literature.

The recent immigration from Arab countries, from Israel, and particularly from Iran, documented above, has stimulated sociological studies of the adaptation patterns of these immigrants Bozorgmehr and Feldman (1996) edited *Middle Eastern Diaspora Communities in America*, which includes chapters on all Middle Easterners, Iranians, Israelis, and Arab Muslims. It is significant that a volume edited by Waldinger, Der-Martirosian, and Bozorgmehr, which is devoted to analyses of the social and economic trajectories of major immigrant groups in the Los Angeles metropolitan region, includes a chapter entitled "Middle Easterners: A New Kind of Immigrants" (Bozorgmehr et al. 1996). It is also notable that *Iranian Studies*, which publishes only articles on Iran, devoted an entire recent issue, edited by Bozorgmehr, to the "Iranian diaspora" (1998). The articles by Bozorgmehr, Ali Modarres, Hamid Naficy, Shideh Hanassab, and Ali Akbar Mahdi cover a wide range of topics, including demographic and socioeconomic trends, patterns of settlement, music videos, sexuality and dating, and ethnic identity.

The high socioeconomic status of Iranian immigrants in the United States and their ethnoreligious diversity provide a theoretical challenge for the study of the process of immigrant adaptation. Iranian immigrants include Christian Armenians and Assyrians, Baha'is, Jews, Muslims, and Zoroastrians. A challenge for the sociological analysis of immigrant adaptation is the fact that some of these groups have their non-Iranian religious counterparts in the United States. This diversity was the focus of the first extensive study of the adaptation of Iranian immigrants in Los Angeles, which has the largest concentration of Iranians in the United States (Bozorgmehr and Sabagh 1989). Bozorgmehr (1997) has developed the concept of "internal ethnicity" for the analysis of the process of adaptation of ethnically diverse immigrant groups. This concept is applicable not only to Iranians but also to many other early and recent immigrant groups. He shows that the neglect of internal ethnicity in the literature has led to the simplification of a complex process of immigrant adaptation.

Bozorgmehr's recent comprehensive review of the studies of first- and second-generation Iranians (1998) shows the wide range of topics covered by this literature, including comparisons between immigrants and exiles, ethnicity and ethnic identity, professionals and entrepreneurs, gender, and assimilation. As the sons and daughters of Iranian immigrants are reaching adulthood, it is time for "research to direct its attention" to this second generation (Bozorgmehr 1998, p. 26). It is also time to compare the experiences of the Iranian second generation to the sons and daughters of other immigrants with equally high human and social capital, whether they are from the Middle East or from other regions of the world.

CONCLUSION

One unexpected consequence of the Iranian revolution has been an increase in the number of Iranian sociologists in the United States who have developed extensive and theoretically relevant analyses of this revolution—which, analyses in turn, have stimulated other sociologists to study this revolution. Studies of the Iranian revolution are now appearing in the mainstream sociological journals.

The world-system theoretical model has greatly benefited from extensive studies of the Ottoman Empire, especially by sociologists of Turkish origin. Ottoman archival documents are also being used to test other theoretical perspectives.

The rapid growth in the numbers of Middle Eastern immigrants in the United States in the last twenty-five years has led to the development of new concepts and insights that help us better understand the adaptation of high-status immigrants.

Still, there is much progress to be made. A continuing need exists for incorporating the experiences of this region into sociological models of wars and revolutions, of social and demographic change, of social movements, of gender roles, and the impact of religion on society. As suggested by Miresepassi (1995, p. 324), accomplishment of this work should also lead to the sociology of Middle Eastern studies becoming more relevant.

REFERENCES

Abraham, Sameer Y., Nabeel Abraham, and Barbara C. Aswad 1983 "The Southend: An Arab Muslim Working-Class Community." In Sameer Y. Abraham and Nabeel Abraham, eds., *Arabs in the New World: Studies on Arab-American Communities*. Detroit: Wayne State University Press.

Abu-Laban, Sharon M. 1989 "The Coexistence of Cohorts: Identity and Adaptation among ArabAmerican Muslims." *Arab Studies Quarterly* 11:45–83.

American Sociological Association 1990 *Biographical Directory of Members*. Washington: ASA.

—— 1999 *Guide to Graduate Departments of Sociology*. Washington: ASA.

Amin, Galal A., and Elizabeth Awny 1985 *The International Migration of Egyptian Labour. A Review of the Suite of the Arts*. Ottawa: International Development Research Centre.

Arjomand, Said A., ed. 1984a *From Nationalism to Revolutionary Islam*. Albany: State University of New York Press.

—— 1984b *The Shadow of God and the Hidden Imam*. Chicago: University of Chicago Press.

—— 1988 *The Turban and the Crown: The Islamic Revolution in Iran*. New York: Oxford University Press.

—— 1993 *The Political Dimension of Religion*. Albany: State University of New York Press.

Arnold, Fred, and Nasra M. Shah 1984 *Asian Labor Migration: Pipeline to the Middle East*. Honolulu: East-West Center.

Ashraf, Ahmad 1988 "Bazaar-Mosque Alliance: The Social Basis of Revolts and Revolutions." *Politics, Culture, and Society* 1:538–567.

——, and Ali Banuazizi 1985 "The State, Classes and Modes of Mobilization in the Iranian Revolution." *State and Society* 1:3–40.

Barakat, Halim 1993 *The Arab World: Society, Culture, and State*. Berkeley: Univrsity of California Press.

Barkey, Karen, and Ronan Van Rossem 1997 "Networks of Contention: Villages and Regional Structure in the Seventeenth-Century Ottoman Empire." *American Journal of Sociology* 102:1345–1382.

Bayat, Asef 1999 "Revolution without Movement, Movement without Revolution: Comparing Islamic Activism in Iran and Egypt." *Comparative Studies in Society and History* 40:136–169.

Ben-Yehuda, Nachman 1997 "The Dominance of the External: Israeli Sociology." *Contemporary Sociology* 26:271–274.

Bonine, Michael E. 1986 "MESA and Middle East Studies." *Middle East Studies Association Bulletin* 20:155–170.

Bozorgmehr, Mehdi 1997 "Internal Ethnicity: Iranians in Los Angeles." *Sociological Perspectives* 40:387–408.

—— 1998 "Iranians in America" *Iranian Studies* 31:1–96.

——, and Alison Feldman, eds. 1996a *Middle Eastern Diaspora Communities in America*. New York: Hagop

Kevorkian Center for Near Eastern Studies of New York University.

——, Claudia Der-Martirosian, and Georges Sabagh. 1996. "Middle Easterners: A New Kind of Immigrant." In Roger Waldinger and Mehdi. Bozorgmehr, eds., *Ethnic Los Angeles*. New York: Russell Sage.

——, and Georges Sabagh 1988 "High Status Immigrants: A Statistical Profile of Iranians in the United States." *Iranian Studies* 21:5–36.

Cizakca, Murat 1985 "Incorporation of the Middle East European World-Economy." *Review* 8:353–377.

Clawson, Dan 1997 "Editorial." *Contemporary Sociology* 26(3):vii.

Dabashi, H. 1984 "The Revolutions of Our Time: Religious Politics in Modernity." *Contemporary Sociology* 13:673–676.

Dickens, David 1989 "The Relevance of Domestic Traditions in the Development Process: Iran 1963–1979." *International Journal of Contemporary Sociology* 26:55–70.

Fergany, Nader 1987 *Differential Labour Migration: Egypt (1974–1984)*. Cairo: Cairo Demographic Centre.

Foran, John 1989 "The Making of an External Arena: Iran's Place in the World-System, 1500–1722." *Review* 12:71–120.

——, ed. 1994 *A Century of Revolution: Social Movements in Iran*. Minneapolis: University of Minnesota Press.

—— 1997 "The Future of Revolutions at the Fin-de-siecle." *Third World Quarterly* 18:791–820.

——, and Jeff Goodwin 1993 "Revolutionary Outcomes in Iran and Nicaragua: Coalition Fragmentation, War, and the Limits of Social Transformation." *Theory and Society* 22:209–247.

Hagopian, Elaine C., and Ann Paden, eds. 1969 *The Arab-Americans: Studies in Assimilation*. Wilmette, Ill.: Median University Press International.

Hammami, Rema, and Salim Tamari 1997 "Popular Paradigm: Palestinian Sociology." *Contemporary Sociology* 275–276.

Hasso, Frances S. 1998 "The 'Women's Front': Nationalism, Feminism, and Modernity in Palestine." *Gender and Society* 12:441–465.

Hatem, Mervat F. 1994 "Women in Arab Society: Work Patterns and Gender Relations in Egypt, Jordan and the Sudan." *Signs* 19:535–539.

Ibrahim, Saad E. 1982 *The New Arab Social Order: A Study of the Social Impact of Oil Wealth*. Boulder, Colo.: Westview.

—— 1997 "Cross-Eyed Sociology in Egypt and the Arab World." *Contemporary Sociology* 26:547–551.

Kasaba, Resat 1987 "Incorporation of the Ottoman Empire: 1750–1820." *Review* 10:805–847.

—— 1988 "Was There a Compradore Bourgeoisie in Mid-Nineteenth Century Western Anatolia?" *Review* 11:215–228.

Keyder, Caglar 1988 "Bureaucracy and Bourgeoisie: Reform and Revolution in the Age of Imperialism." *Fernand Braudel Center Review* 11:151–165.

—— 1994 "Globalization of a Third-World Metropolis: Istanbul in the 1980's." *Review* 17:383–421.

——, and Faruk Tabak 1986 "Eastern Mediterranean Port Cities and Their Bourgeoisie: Merchants, Political Projects, and Nation-States." *Fernand Braudel Center Review* 10:131–135.

Kurzman, Charles 1994 "A Dynamic View of Resources: Evidence from the Iranian Revolution." *Research in Social Movements, Conflicts and Change* 53–84.

—— 1996 "Structural Opportunity and Perceived Opportunity in Social-Movement Theory: The Iranian Revolution of 1979." *American Sociological Review* 61:153–170.

Middle East Studies Association 1998 *Roster of Members 1998*. Tucson, Ariz.: MESA.

Mirsepassi, Ali 1995 "Middle Eastern Studies and American Sociology." *Contemporary Sociology* 24:324–328.

Moaddel, Mansoor 1992 "Ideology as Episodic Discourse: The Case of the Iranian Revolution." *American Sociological Review* 57:353–379.

—— 1996 "The Social Bases and Discursive Context of the Rise of Islamic Fundamentalism: The Cases of Iran and Syria." *Sociological Inquiry* 330–355.

Moghadarn, Val 1989 "Populist Revolt and the Islamic State in Iran." In Terry Boswell, ed., *Revolution in the World System*. New York: Greenwood.

—— 1995 "Women's Employment Issues in Contemporary Iran: Problems and Prospects in the 1990s." *Iranian Studies* 28:175–202.

Naim-Ahmed, Samir 1998 "Sociology in the Arab World: A Self-Criticism." *Contemporary Sociology* 27:327–328.

Nichols, Elizabeth 1986 "Skocpol on Revolution: Comparative Analysis vs Historical Conjecture." *Comparative Social Research* 9:163–186.

Obermeyer, Carla Makhlouf 1992 "Islam, Women, and Politics: The Demography of Arab Countries." *Population-and-Development-Review* 18:33–60.

——, ed. 1995 *Family, Gender, and Population in the Middle East*. Cairo: American University in Cairo.

Oncu, Ayse 1997 "Crossing Borders into Turkish Sociology with Gunder Frank and Michel Foucault." *Contemporary Sociology* 26:267–270.

Organization for Economic Cooperation and Development 1998 *Continuous Reporting System on Migration. SOPEMI 1998*. Paris: OECD.

Owen, R. 1989 "The Movement of Labor In and Out of the Middle East over the Last Two Centuries: Peasants, Patterns, and Policies." In Georges Sabagh, ed., *The Modern Economic and Social History of the Middle East in World Context*. Cambridge, England: Cambridge University Press.

Pamuk, Sevket 1988 "The Ottoman Empire in Contemporary Perspective." *Fernand Braudel Center Review* 11:127–151.

Parsa, Misagh 1989 *Social Origins of the Iranian Revolution*. New Brunswick, N.J.: Rutgers University Press.

—— 1995a "Conversion or Coalition? Ideology in the Iranian and Nicaraguan Revolutions." *Political Power and Social Theory* 9:1000–1022.

—— 1995b "Entrepreneurs and Democratization: Iran and the Philippines." *Comparative Studies in Society and History* 37:803–830.

Pulcini, Theodore 1993 "Trends in Research on Arab Americans." *Journal of American Ethnic History* 12:27–60.

Rasler, Karen 1996 "Concessions, Repression, and Political Protest." *American Sociological Review* 61:132–151.

Sabagh, Georges 1976 "Sociology." In Leonard Binder, ed., *The Study of the Middle East*. New York: John Wiley.

—— 1993 "Labor Migrants in Kuwait: Will They Always Be Sojourners?" In Gema Martin Munoz, ed., *Democracia y Derechos Humanos en el Mundo Arabe*. Madrid: ICMA.

——, and Iman Ghazalla 1986 "Arab Sociology Today: A View from Within." *Annual Review of Sociology* 12:373–399.

——, and Mehdi Bozorgmehr 1987 "Are the Characteristics of Exiles Different from Immigrants? The Case of Iranians in Los Angeles." *Sociology and Social Research* 71:77–84.

Sawaie, Mohammed, ed. 1985 *Arabic-Speaking Immigrants in the United States and Canada*. Lexington, Ky.: Mazda.

Sell, Ralph R. 1988 "Egyptian International Labor Migration and Social Processes: Toward Regional Integration." *International Migration Review* 22:87–108.

Sengstock, Mary C. 1982 *Chaldean-Americans: Changing Conceptions of Ethnic Identity*. New York: Center for Migration Studies.

Skocpol, Theda 1982 "Rentier State and Shi'a Islam in the Iranian Revolution." *Theory and Society* 11:265–283.

—— 1986 "Analyzing Causal Configurations in History: A Rejoinder to Nichols." *Comparative Social Research* 9:187–194.

Sohrabi, Nader 1995 "Historicizing Revolutions: Constitutional Revolutions in the Ottoman Empire, Iran, and Russia, 1905–1908." *American Journal of Sociology* 100:1383–1447.

Stahl, Charles W., and Farooq-i-Asarn 1990 "Counting Pakistanis in the Middle East: Problems and Policy Implications." *Asian and Pacific Population Forum* 4:1–10, 24–28.

Suleiman, Michael W., and Baha Abu-Laban 1989 "The Arab Tradition in North America." *Arab Studies Quarterly* 11:1–13.

Swan, Charles L., and Leila B. Saba 1974 "The Migration of a Minority." In Barbara C. Aswad, ed., *Arabic-Speaking Communities in American Cities*. New York: Center for Migration Studies.

United Nations 1996 *World Population Monitoring 1993* New York: UN.

U.S. Bureau of the Census 1993 *1990 Census of Population Ancestry of the Population of the United States*. Washington: U.S. Government Printing Office.

Waldinger, Roger, and Mehdi Bozorgmehr, eds. 1996 *Ethnic Los Angeles*. New York: Russell Sage Foundation, 1996.

Wallerstein, Immanuel 1979 "The Ottoman Empire and the Capitalist World-Economy: Some Questions for Research." *Review* 2:389–408.

GEORGES SABAGH

MIGRATION

See Internal Migration; International Migration.

MILITARY SOCIOLOGY

Military sociology has been a relatively minor field in American sociology. Few sociologists conduct research and write on military topics, and few university departments offer courses of study in this field. To the layperson this circumstance may seem rather curious, given the sheer size and complexity of the military enterprise and the effects of war on individual societies and on the world order as a whole. The Vietnam War of the 1960s and the Persian Gulf War of 1991are reminders of the impact that military institutions and operations have on American society.

There is no single reason for this lack of emphasis. One reason may be ideological aversion to military matters. Most sociologists fall on the liberal side of the political spectrum, which has tended to emphasize the peace rather than the war aspect of international relations. Another reason may be that support for most military research requires clear policy applications, and applied research is of less interest to the majority of sociologists. Unlike other social sciences, sociology has not developed a sizable cadre of practitioners who conduct research and policy studies in those nonacademic settings where most military research takes place.

There are notable exceptions. One is the classic work of Samuel Stouffer and colleagues during World War II, *The American Soldier* (1949). Its studies of cohesion, morale, and race relations among combat units made critical contributions to both sociological theory and military personnel policies. The work of Morris Janowitz on organizational and occupational changes in the military is also a significant exception to the rule (Janowitz 1960). Charles Moskos at Northwestern University and David and Mady Segal at the University of Maryland are upholding this tradition today, and their universities are among the few that offer courses on military sociology.

In recent years most of the studies that could be classified as military sociology have been carried out in private research institutes or in military agencies, such as the Rand Corporation, the Brookings Institute, the Human Resources Research Organization (HumRRO), the Army Research Institute, and the Office of the Secretary of Defense. Study teams are generally interdisciplinary, with the fields of psychology, economics, political science, and management frequently represented. While these studies have a sociological complexion, they are not limited to sociological concepts or theory, and they usually have a military policy focus.

Much of the published work in this field consists of reports from these various organizations and agencies. No journal is devoted specifically to military sociology, although there is an American Sociological Association Section on Peace and War. *Armed Forces and Society* is an interdisciplinary journal that focuses on social science topics in the military, and *Military Psychology*, published by the Division on Military Psychology of the American Psychological Association, also covers topics of sociological interest.

This review emphasizes contemporary issues and studies in military sociology, most of which focus on the American military. For reviews that include historical perspectives the reader is referred elsewhere (D. R. Segal 1989; D. R. Segal and M. W. Segal 1991).

THE BASIS OF SERVICE

Without question the most significant issue in American military sociology following World War II is the shift from conscription to voluntary service in 1973. Indeed, many contemporary issues in military sociology—recruiting policies, social representation, and race and gender concerns—flow directly or indirectly from this change in the basis of service.

The notion of voluntary service is not new; indeed, compulsory military service has been the exception rather than the rule in the history of most Western societies, although the meaning of "involuntary" and the nature of service has changed over time. Until the Civil War, U.S. military manpower was raised through state militias, which technically encompassed all "able-bodied men" and hence might be thought of as involuntary. The raising and maintenance of militia was left to the discretion and policies of individual states, and they varied greatly in their representation and effectiveness. Although the desirability and feasibility of national conscription has been debated since the beginning of American history, until 1948 it was employed only during the Civil War and during the World Wars I and II. At all other times enlistment was voluntary (Lee and Parker 1977).

The peacetime conscription adopted in 1948 was a significant and historic departure for U.S. military policy. It was prompted by a combination of factors, including Cold War tensions with the Soviet Union, the critical role being played by the United States in defense alliances, and a perception that America had been inadequately prepared for World War II. These conditions led to proposals for a large standing, or "active-duty," military force that most believed could not be maintained by voluntary methods. The policy was supported by the American public at that time, and it was consistent with the longstanding value that all "able-bodied men" should serve their country.

The end of the peacetime draft occurred in 1973 at the end of the Vietnam War. The debate over draft policies had been intensifying during the 1960s, particularly over the issue of equity. Given the growth in the American youth population (from the post–World War II baby boom), not all men were needed for the military, and a succession of draft-exemption policies—college, occupational, marriage—fueled the debate over the fairness and equity of the draft. Not only were all able-bodied men not serving, but those exempted from service tended to be from more affluent classes. In an attempt to solve the equity problem, nearly all exemptions were eliminated during the late 1960s, and a national lottery system was adopted in 1969. These changes did not quell the debate; indeed, they probably doomed the draft, since they coincided with one of the most unpopular and unsuccessful wars in America's history. Ending exemptions for college students at a time when college students were leading the movement against the Vietnam War simply fanned the flames of opposition.

On the other side of the issue, most defense and military leaders, including many members of Congress, initially opposed ending the draft. The conditions leading to a large peacetime military force (over two million active-duty personnel) were unchanged and were not under debate. If such a large force was maintained by voluntary means, it was argued, it would be either (1) a mercenary force lacking patriotic motivation, which might be either adventuresome or ineffective in large-scale combat; or (2) socially unrepresentative, thereby placing the burden of combat on minorities, the poor, and the uneducated; or (3) too costly and therefore unaffordable (D. R. Segal 1989).

The shift to voluntary service followed definitive recommendations from a presidential commission, known as the Gates Commission, which concluded that a large peacetime force could be adequately maintained with an all-voluntary force (AVF), provided that basic pay was increased to be competitive with comparable civilian jobs. The commission argued that paying enlisted personnel below-market wages not only was unfair but entailed "opportunity" costs in the form of lost productivity of persons who are compelled to work at jobs they would not voluntarily perform. If military pay and benefits were competitive, the commission's studies concluded, a volunteer force would be socially representative and would be as effective as a drafted force. Although some attention was given to the social costs of the draft, there is little question that economic analysis and arguments formed the central basis of the commission's report (President's Commission 1970).

THE ALL-VOLUNTEER FORCE

The AVF seemed to work well for the first several years, and the dire predications of those who opposed ending the draft did not materialize. Enlistment requirements were met, and neither quality nor representation appeared much different from draft-era enlistments. The predictions of the Gates Commission seemed to be valid (Cooper 1977).

During the late 1970s, however, this positive picture faded. Military pay and benefits did not keep up with the civilian sector, and post–Vietnam War antiwar attitudes contributed to a generally negative image of the military among youth. The number and quality of new recruits began declining, and the services were forced to enlist more applicants with low aptitude scores and without high school diplomas. To make matters worse, a misnorming error was discovered in the military aptitude test (the Armed Forces Qualifying Test [AFQT]), and the quality of personnel was even lower than had been thought. By 1980 the Army was severely affected, with enlistments falling significantly below requirements and with the proportion of low-aptitude recruits—those reading at fourth- and fifth-grade levels—reaching 50 percent (Eitelberg 1988).

Some claimed that the Gates Commission had been wrong after all, and called for a return to the draft. Others, including the Secretary of the Army, proposed eliminating the aptitude and education standards that had been used since the draft era, arguing that they were not important for military job performance and were potentially discriminatory. Yet others argued that both the AVF and quality standards could be maintained but only by increasing pay and benefits to enable competition with the civilian sector. Critical to this third argument were the policy studies led by the Rand Corporation showing a relationship between aptitudes and military job performance and the feasibility of economic incentives for enlistment (Armor et al. 1982; Polich et al. 1986).

Substantial increases in pay and other benefits in the early 1980s, as well as changes in recruiting techniques including advertising, had a dramatic impact on recruiting success. By the late 1980s, all military services, including the Army, were not only meeting requirement quotas but setting new records in the quality of personnel, surpassing even the draft years in the proportion of recruits with high school diplomas and with higher aptitudes. Most military leaders, many of whom had been skeptical about ending the draft, became strong supporters of the AVF and claimed that morale and skills were at all-time highs and discipline problems were at all-time lows. Although this success did require significant increases in the military personnel budget, both the Congress and the public seemed prepared to pay this cost (Bowman et al. 1986).

The one argument against voluntary service that had never been tested empirically was the combat effectiveness of a market-motivated military. The dramatic success of the American forces in the 1991 Persian Gulf War put an end to any doubt about the ability of a volunteer military to operate successfully. Although high-technology weapons systems received much of the publicity during the war, most military leaders gave as much credit to the skill and morale of their troops, especially in comparison to the poorly trained and demoralized Iraqi soldiers.

Two major events, the collapse of the Soviet Union and the U.S. budget deficit crisis, combined to force major reductions in the size of the active military, which also meant fewer new recruits needed to sustain the smaller force. In spite of lower recruiting targets, recruit quality began edging downward again after the Persian Gulf War. The main causes were thought to be a combination of less positive attitudes toward military on the part of youth, and an increase in the proportion of youth deciding to attend college (Office of the Assistant Secretary of Defense 1998). Although some concerns have surfaced in the military community about these downward trends, by 1998 overall recruit quality was still similar to the successful levels seen during the late 1980s. A mitigating factor is the trend in the number of 18-year-olds, which declined between 1980 and 1992 but has been increasing since then and is expected to continue to grow until 2010.

SOCIAL REPRESENTATION AND ACCESS

Social representation is the degree to which an armed force represents the population from which it has been drawn. Although representation has been a longstanding issue in the United States, concerns were heightened during the AVF era, especially since that era happened to coincide with increasing emphasis on ethnic and gender diversity throughout American society. Racial representation was an issue in both the Vietnam War and the Persian Gulf War, when some civil rights leaders alleged that African Americans were overrepresented in armed forces and hence carried an unfair burden of casualties. Gender representation has developed as a major issue in concert with the women's rights movement, generating major policy changes concerning the participation of women in the military. Finally, with the election of President Bill Clinton and his campaign commitment to overturn the military ban on gays and lesbians, for the first time the issue of sexual orientation became the focus of a major military policy debate.

Debates about social representation usually divide over positions on three basic principles: equity, effectiveness, and responsiveness. The equity principle has two aspects. One is the equity of obligation, meaning that the burden of service and the risks of combat should be borne by all segments of the citizenry. Since a national military force defends the interests of an entire country and entails the risk of casualties, this obligation should be shared uniformly by all citizens, or at least all able-bodied persons. Placing this burden unequally upon certain socioeconomic or racial groups not only violates the canons of fairness in democratic societies but also potentially undermines troop morale and motivation if they perceive the disproportion as unfair (Congressional Budget Office 1989). The other aspect is the equity of access, which often means that racial minorities, women, and homosexuals should be allowed to serve in the military according to their abilities and interests, without artificial restrictions or ceilings.

The principle of effectiveness is raised because most military experts believe that the quality of military personnel in terms of education and aptitude directly influence training and combat effectiveness, and therefore a force that underrepresents quality personnel will be less effective than a representative force. Although the armed services have attained their quality goals since the late 1980s, there is no guarantee that they can always do so, particularly if military pay and benefits do not keep up with civilian compensation. The effectiveness principle is also invoked by some military experts as a counterargument to the equity position, arguing that allowing women in combat units or open homosexuals in any type of unit will undermine unit morale and cohesion, thereby reducing military effectiveness.

Finally, a representative armed force is sometimes seen as a requirement for military acceptance of civilian control as well as respect for democratic values and institutions. A military force that overrepresents particular social strata or groups (not necessarily lower strata) might place parochial interests or values over the interests and values of the society as a whole. A force drawn proportionately from all major sectors of a society—all regions, races, and social classes—is viewed as one most likely to respect and advance the shared values and goals of the total society.

Racial Representation. One of the most frequently expressed concerns about representation during the AVF era has been the overrepresentation of African Americans and lower socioeconomic groups in the armed services, especially in the Army. Given the early experience with the AVF, this concern is not without some justification, although the situation improved considerably during the 1980s.

Table 1 shows the percentage of black recruits for selected years since the end of the draft in 1973. Black overrepresentation reached its peak in 1979, before the aptitude misnorming error was discovered. Black representation declined during the early 1980s after the military corrected its screening test. It edged back up during the late 1980s, but it declined again during the early 1990s, when recruiting was scaled back in response to the smaller permanent force. Even during the draft years, black representation exceeded the black proportion of the youth population, due in part to higher voluntary enlistment and—prior to the Vietnam War—in part to college exemption policies that applied disproportionately to white youth. During most of the 1990s, black representation in the total active forces was only a few points higher than a comparable civilian population, although the trend was moving upward again toward the end of the decade, particularly in the Army.

It should not be inferred from these data that black soldiers have a risk of death or injury in combat that is disproportionately higher than that of white soldiers. In fact, black enlisted members in the active-duty forces tend to be underrepresented in combat occupations such as infantry, gun crews, and combat ships and overrepresented in administrative, clerical, and supply occupations. As a result, black casualty rates in wartime are in rough proportion to their share of the general civilian population. For example, in the Vietnam War black fatalities were approximately 12 percent of all American fatalities (Moskos and Butler 1996).

Some argue that these differences in representation present a policy problem, although there is no consensus on what, if anything, should be done about it. While some see black overrepresentation as a problem of burden, others see it as an opportunity for advancement in one of the best-integrated occupational sectors in American society. Higher black representation reflects a greater interest in military careers among African Americans, and any attempt to limit black enlistments could be viewed as a denial of equal opportunity. Indeed, the military in general, and the Army in particular, has been held up as a model for racial integration that should be emulated by other institutions (Moskos and Butler 1996).

Women in the Military. Another topic that has received considerable attention from military sociologists is the role of women in the military. Until 1967 women's participation in the military was limited to 2 percent by law, and most military jobs were closed to women. Even after the restriction was lifted by Congress, the representation of women did not change until the AVF policy and the opening of more noncombat jobs to women. After 1973 the percentage of women enlistees increased steadily, reaching a plateau during the 1980s of about 12 percent. Following major policy changes regarding combat restrictions in the early 1990s, the percentage of women recruits rose again, reaching a second plateau of about 18 percent during the late 1990s. This representation of women in the U.S. military is the highest among all NATO countries (Office of the Assistant Secretary of Defense 1998; Stanley and Segal 1988).

Percentage of Black Recruits, Active Forces

Fiscal Year	Army	Navy	Marine Corps	Air Force	Total Active Forces	U.S. Population, Ages 18–24
1973	19	11	22	14	17	12
1979	37	16	28	17	26	13
1983	22	14	17	14	18	14
1989	26	22	18	12	22	14
1991	20	17	14	11	17	14
1993	20	17	12	13	17	14
1995	22	20	13	14	18	14
1997	23	20	14	17	20	14

Table 1

The growing participation of women in the military reflects several forces, including the need for manpower in the AVF era as well as the increased demands for equity in the treatment of men and women in the workplace. Although all military services recruited more women to help alleviate shortfalls during the 1970s, the Department of Defense has also been pressured by Congress and various interest and advisory groups to enlarge the opportunities for women. The primary barriers to expanding the role of women were statutory restrictions on the assignment of women to combat units and missions. These statutes were repealed by Congress in 1993, and by 1994 the Department of Defense had substantially modified combat restriction regulations. All combat aircraft and combat ships were opened to women (except submarines, for privacy reasons), and the only units that could be closed to women were those that involved "direct ground combat" such as infantry, armor, field artillery, and special forces (Armor 1996).

In spite of the increased participation of women, gender representation continues to be a topic of debate. Arguments against allowing women in combat jobs include physical and emotional differences, privacy and sexual behavior, impacts on unit cohesion and morale, and a basic moral position that women should be protected from the high risk of death, injury, capture, or torture faced by those in ground combat units. Proponents of opening combat jobs to women counter that (1) women should be evaluated individually and not as a group for physical and emotional suitability for combat; (2) experience with women in noncombat jobs has shown no serious adverse impacts on unit cohesion or morale; and (3) women currently serve in jobs and units that are exposed to increased risks of death, injury, or capture, thereby rendering the moral argument moot and in conflict with current policies (M. W. Segal 1982). Consistent with this latter view, recent reviews on the integration of women in the military report substantial progress (Harell and Miller 1997).

A second major issue involving women in the military is sexual harassment. This problem is obviously not unique to the military; it continues to be an issue throughout American society. It may be more acute, however, in a traditional male institution like the military where women constitute small minorities in many types of jobs. Little hard evidence was available on the extent of sexual harassment in the military until a comprehensive survey was conducted at the request of a 1988 Task Force on Women in the Military. The results indicated rather serious levels of sexual harassment; altogether, 64 percent of women experienced some form of sexual harassment during a one-year period, and 5 percent reported actual or attempted rape or sexual assault (Martindale 1990). These rates of harassment were considerably higher than those found in surveys of federal civilian employees, and they presaged several serious incidents during the 1990s involving sexual harassment or other sexual improprieties in three of the four services: the 1991 Navy Tailhook incident; the 1996 Army Aberdeen Proving Grounds scandal; and the 1997 Air Force dismissal of Kelly Flinn, its first female bomber pilot, for adultery with the husband of an enlisted woman.

A follow-up survey on sexual harassment was conducted in 1995 after the military services had tightened regulations, clarified policies and practices, and increased training with regards to sexual harassment. The new survey showed some improvement, but rates of sexual harassment were still high, with 55 percent of women reporting some form of unwanted sexual behavior or advances and 4 percent reporting actual or attempted rape or some other form of sexual assault (Bastion et al. 1996).

These high rates of sexual harassment may be due to a number of factors, but are most likely associated with the increased presence of women in a traditional male workplace, and a workplace where a traditional "male" culture may be insensitive if not hostile to women. Another factor may be the attitudes and actions of military leaders and supervisors. Only about half of the women responding to the 1988 survey believed that the senior leadership of their service and their installation made "honest and reasonable" attempts to prevent sexual harassment, and only 60 percent said their immediate supervisor did so. In 1995 these rates had increased by only a few percentage points. Whether or not these figures truly reflect the behavior of military leaders, there is a perception among many military women that the military leadership is still not giving enough emphasis to the problem of sexual harassment.

Policies on Sexual Orientation. Since World War I, persons who acknowledge homosexual status or behavior have been excluded from U.S. military service, either by antisodomy provisions of the Uniform Code of Military Justice or by explicit Department of Defense regulations. This policy was challenged by President Bill Clinton in 1993, who directed the secretary of defense to prepare a "draft of an Executive Order ending discrimination on the basis of sexual orientation in determining who may serve in the Armed Forces" (Rostker and Harris 1993, p. 1). Most senior military officers opposed the change, expressing beliefs that open homosexuals would hamper maintenance of good order and discipline and would undermine unit cohesion and combat effectiveness. Various studies were commissioned, including a major study by the Rand Corporation which concluded that, based on experience in other countries and on certain U.S. police and fire departments, the homosexual ban could be lifted without serious adverse effects on unit cohesion and military performance (Rostker and Harris 1993). The Rand study also noted that nondeclared homosexuals had always served in some number in the United States and foreign militaries without undue consequences.

The center of the debate shifted to Congress, and particularly to Democratic Senator Sam Nunn, Chairman of the Armed Services Committee, who had made it clear before the 1992 election that he was skeptical about this change and would hold hearings on the matter. Based on these hearings, including testimony from both civilian experts and military leaders, a compromise proposal was crafted, which became known as the "Don't ask, don't tell" policy; this proposal became a federal statute in 1994. The statute states that sexual orientation is a private and personal matter, and is not a bar to military service. It prohibits routine questions about sexual orientation on recruiting forms, but also says that engaging in homosexual conduct is grounds for discharge, and that a voluntary statement by a person acknowledging a gay or lesbian orientation is considered homosexual conduct (Office of the Under Secretary of Defense 1998).

Needless to say, gay and lesbian activists were not satisfied with this compromise, and especially with the provision that service members continue to be discharged for merely telling someone that they are homosexual (Rimmerman 1996). The "Don't ask, don't tell" policy has been challenged in federal courts, but with the exception of several cases where a discharged gay or lesbian has been reinstated because information was obtained improperly, the statute itself has been upheld by several appellate courts.

OTHER ISSUES

There are a number of other topics that are studied by military sociologists or that raise important sociological issues. While they have not received the same degree of attention as the topics reviewed above, they deserve mention.

Sociology of Combat. A major focus of *The American Soldier* studies during World War II, the sociology of combat deals with the social processes involved in combat units, such as unit cohesion and morale, leader-troop relations, and the motivation for combat. Recent works include studies of the "fragging" incidents in the Vietnam War and the role of ideology in combat motivation (Moskos 1988).

Family Issues. The proportion of the military personnel who are married increased from around 40 percent during the draft years to 57 percent by 1995. The current active force also has a higher proportion of career personnel than the draft-era forces (50 percent compared to 25 percent), which means more families and more family concerns. Much of the increase in military benefits is related to families—housing improvements, medical insurance, overseas schools, child care. Family policy issues include the role and rights of spouses (especially officer spouses) and the issue of child care when single-parent members are deployed in a conflict (M. W. Segal 1986).

The Military as Welfare. Somewhat at odds with the social representation issue, some argue that the military should provide opportunity for educational and occupational advancement to the less advantaged in society. The most dramatic example was Project 100,000, begun in 1966 as part of President Lyndon Johnson's War on Poverty, whereby 100,000 men (mostly black) who did not meet education and aptitude requirements were offered enlistments. According to recent follow-up studies of this group as well as a group of low-aptitude recruits who entered the AVF during the misnorming era, military training and experience do not appear to offer advantages when compared to civilian experiences (D. R. Segal 1989).

Military Social Organization. Given changes in military organization at several levels—from draft to AVF, from combat-intensive jobs to technical and support jobs, and from leadership to rational management—some have argued that the military is changing from an institution or "calling" legitimized by normative values to an occupation legitimized by a market orientation (Moskos and Wood 1988). While some of these changes apply to the military as well as to many other American institutions, others suggest that the role of institutional values and traditions is still a dominant characteristic of the American military (D. R. Segal 1989).

War and Peace. The most profound impacts of national security policies and their associated military forces are on the relations between whole nations. There is very little sociological work at this level, although some of the issues would seem to be fairly critical for sociological theory (e.g., the effectiveness of deterrence policies during the Cold War; the role of effects of military alliances; the consequences of war for societal changes). One of the few sociological discussions of these broader issues is found in D. R. Segal (1989).

Comparative Perspectives. As in many other fields of sociology, comparative studies of sociomilitary issues across nations are relatively scarce. Exceptions are some comparative studies of whether the military is an institution or an occupation (Moskos and Wood 1988) and of women in military forces (Stanley and Segal 1988).

CONCLUSION

Although military sociologists are few in number, it is not a small field. The military is the largest single government agency, and it truly represents a microcosm of the larger society. The types of military issues that can be addressed by social scientists have important ramifications for military policy as well as for the development of sociology as a discipline. On the one hand, sociological concepts and perspectives have contributed to rationalizing the basis of service, studying the problems of social representation, and improving the role of women in the military. On the other hand, studies of the structure and processes of military institutions and policies can enhance sociological understanding and insights about important forms of social behavior, thereby contributing ultimately to advances in social theory.

(SEE ALSO: *Gender*; *Race*; *Peace*; *War*)

REFERENCES

Armour, D. J. 1996 "Race and Gender in the U.S. Military." *Armed Forces and Society* 23:7–27

——, R. L. Fernandez, Kathy Bers, and Donna Schwarzbach 1982 *Recruit Aptitudes and Army Job Performance*, R-2874-MRAL. Santa Monica, Calif.: Rand.

Bastian, L. D., A. R. Lancaster, and H.E. Reyst 1996 *1995 Sexual Harassment Survey*. Arlington, Va.: Defense Manpower Data Center.

Bowman, W., R. Little, and G. T. Sicilia 1986 *The All-Volunteer Force after a Decade*. Washington: Pergamon-Brassey's.

Congressional Budget Office 1989 *Social Representation in the U.S. Military*. Washington: Congress of the United States.

Cooper, Richard V. L. 1977 *Military Manpower and the All-Volunteer Force* R-1450-ARPA. Santa Monica, Calif.: Rand.

Eitelberg, Mark J. 1988 *Manpower for Military Occupations.* Alexandria, Va.: Human Resources Research Organization.

Harrell, M. C., and L. L. Miller 1997 *New Opportunities for Military Women: Effects upon Readiness, Cohesion, and Morale,* MR-896-OSD. Santa Monica, Calif.: Rand.

Janowitz, Morris 1960 *The Professional Soldier.* Glencoe, Ill.: Free Press.

Laurence, J. H., and P. F. Ramsberger 1991 *Low-Aptitude Men in the Military: Who Profits, Who Pays?* Alexandria, Va.: Human Resources Research Organization.

Lee, G. C., and G. Y. Parker 1977 *Ending the Draft: The Story of the All-Volunteer Force,* FR-PO-77-1. Alexandria, Va.: Human Resources Research Organization.

Martindale, Melanie 1990 *Sexual Harassment in the Military: 1988.* Arlington, Va.: Defense Manpower Data Center.

Moskos, C. C. 1988 *Soldiers and Sociology.* Alexandria, Va.: U.S. Army Research Institute for the Behavioral and Social Sciences.

——, and J. S. Butler 1996 *All That We Can Be.* New York: Basic.

——, and F. R. Wood 1988 *The Military: More Than Just a Job?* Washington: Pergamon-Brassey's.

Office of the Assistant Secretary of Defense (Force Management) 1998 *Population Representation in the Military Services, FY 97.* Washington: U.S. Department of Defense.

Office of the Under Secretary of Defense (Personnel and Readiness) 1998 *Review of the Effectiveness of the Application and Enforcement of the Department's Policy on Homosexual Conduct.* Washington: U.S. Department of Defense.

Polich, J. M., J. N. Dertouzos, and S. J. Press 1986 *The Enlistment Bonus Experiment,* R3353-FMP. Santa Monica, Calif.: Rand.

President's Commission 1970 *Report of the President's Commission on an All Volunteer Force.* Washington: U.S. Government Printing Office.

Rimmerman, C. A., ed. 1996 *Gay Rights, Military Wrongs.* New York: Garland.

Rostker, B. D., and S. A. Harris, study directors 1993 *Sexual Orientation and U.S. Military Personnel Policy,* MR-323-OSD. Santa Monica, Calif.: Rand.

Segal, D. R. 1989 *Recruiting for Uncle Sam.* Lawrence: University of Kansas Press.

——, and M. W. Segal 1991 "Sociology, Military." *International Military and Defense Encyclopedia.* New York: Macmillan.

Segal, M. W. 1982 "The Argument for Female Combatants." In Nancy Loring Goldman, ed., *Female Soldiers: Combatants or Noncombatants?* Westport, Conn.: Greenwood.

—— 1986 "The Military and the Family as Greedy Institutions." *Armed Forces and Society* 13:9–38.

Stanley, S. C., and M. W. Segal 1988 "Military Women in NATO: An Update." *Armed Forces and Society* 14:559–585.

Stouffer, S. A., et al. 1949 *The American Soldier.* Princeton, N.J.: Princeton University Press.

DAVID J. ARMOR

MODERNIZATION THEORY

Modernization theory is a description and explanation of the processes of transformation from traditional or underdeveloped societies to modern societies. In the words of one of the major proponents, "Historically, modernization is the process of change towards those types of social, economic, and political systems that have developed in Western Europe and North America from the seventeenth century to the nineteenth and have then spread to other European countries and in the nineteenth and twentieth centuries to the South American, Asian, and African continents" (Eisenstadt 1966, p. 1). Modernization theory has been one of the major perspectives in the sociology of national development and underdevelopment since the 1950s. Primary attention has focused on ways in which past and present premodern societies become modern (i.e., Westernized) through processes of economic growth and change in social, political, and cultural structures.

In general, modernization theorists are concerned with economic growth within societies as indicated, for example, by measures of gross national product. Mechanization or industrialization are ingredients in the process of economic growth. Modernization theorists study the social, political, and cultural consequences of economic growth and the conditions that are important for industrialization and economic growth to occur. Indeed, a degree of circularity often characterizes discussions of social and economic change involved in modernization processes because of the notion, embedded in most modernization theories, of the functional compatibility of component parts. The theoretical assumptions of modernization theories will be elaborated later.

It should be noted at the outset that the sociological concept of modernization does not refer simply to becoming current or "up to date" but rather specifies particular contents and processes of societal changes in the course of national development. Also, modernization theories of development do not necessarily bear any relationship to more recent philosophical concepts of "modernity" and "postmodernity." Modernity in philosophical and epistemological discussions refers to the perspective that there is one true descriptive and explanatory model that reflects the actual world. Postmodernity is the stance that no single true description and explanation of reality exists but rather that knowledge, ideology, and science itself are based on subjective understandings of an entirely relational nature. While their philosophical underpinnings place most modernization theories of development into the "modern" rather than the "postmodern" context, these separate uses of the term *modernity* should not be confused.

Also, modernization, industrialization, and development are often used interchangeably but in fact refer to distinguishable phenomena. Industrialization is a narrower term than modernization, while development is more general. Industrialization involves the use of inanimate sources of power to mechanize production, and it involves increases in manufacturing, wage labor, income levels, and occupational diversification. It may or may not be present where there is political, social, or cultural modernization, and, conversely, it may exist in the absence of other aspects of modernization. Development (like industrialization) implies economic growth, but not necessarily through transformation from the predominance of primary production to manufacturing, and not necessarily as characterized by modernization theory. For example, while modernization theorists may define development mainly in terms of economic output per capita, other theorists may be more concerned about development of autonomous productive capacity, equitable distribution of wealth, or meeting basic human needs. Also, while modernization theories generally envision democratic and capitalist institutions or secularization of belief systems as components of modern society,

other development perspectives may not. Indeed, dependency theorists even talk about the "development of underdevelopment" (Frank 1966).

Each of the social science disciplines pays particular attention to the determinants of modern structures within its realm (social, political, economic) and gives greater importance to structures or institutions within its realm for explaining other developments in society. Emphasis here is given to sociological modernization theory.

Although there are many versions of modernization theory, major implicit or explicit tenets are that (1) societies develop through a series of evolutionary stages; (2) these stages are based on different degrees and patterns of social differentiation and reintegration of structural and cultural components that are functionally compatible for the maintenance of society; (3) contemporary developing societies are at a premodern stage of evolution and they eventually will achieve economic growth and will take on the social, political, and economic features of western European and North American societies which have progressed to the highest stage of social evolutionary development; (4) this modernization will result as complex Western technology is imported and traditional structural and cultural features incompatible with such development are overcome.

At its core modernization theory suggests that advanced industrial technology produces not only economic growth in developing societies but also other structural and cultural changes. The common characteristics that societies tend to develop as they become modern may differ from one version of modernization theory to another, but, in general, all assume that institutional structures and individual activities become more highly specialized, differentiated, and integrated into social, political, and economic forms characteristic of advanced Western societies.

For example, in the social realm, modern societies are characterized by high levels of urbanization, literacy, research, health care, secularization, bureaucracy, mass media, and transportation facilities. Kinship ties are weaker, and nuclear conjugal family systems prevail. Birthrates and death rates are lower, and life expectancy is relatively longer. In the political realm, the society becomes more participatory in decision-making processes, and typical institutions include universal suffrage, political parties, a civil service bureaucracy, and parliaments. Traditional sources of authority are weaker as bureaucratic institutions assume responsibility and power. In the economic realm, there is more industrialization, technical upgrading of production, replacement of exchange economies with extensive money markets, increased division of labor, growth of infrastructure and commercial facilities, and the development of large-scale markets. Associated with these structural changes are cultural changes in role relations and personality variables. Social relations are more bureaucratic, social mobility increases, and status relations are based less on such ascriptive criteria as age, gender, or ethnicity and more on meritocratic criteria. There is a shift from relations based on tradition and loyalty to those based on rational exchange, competence, and other universally applied criteria. People are more receptive to change, more interested in the future, more achievement-oriented, more concerned with the rights of individuals, and less fatalistic.

Underlying the description of social features and changes that are thought to characterize modern urban industrial societies are theoretical assumptions and mechanisms to explain the shift from traditional to modern societal types. These explanatory systems draw upon the dominant theoretical perspectives in the 1950s and 1960s, growing out of classical evolutionary, diffusion, and structural-functionalist theories.

The evolutionary perspective, stemming from Spencer, Durkheim, and other nineteenth-century theorists, contributed the notion that societies evolve from lower to higher forms and progress from simple and undifferentiated to more complex types. Western industrial society is seen as superior to preindustrial society to the extent that it has progressed through specialization to more effective ways of performing societal functions. Diffusionists added the ideas that cultural patterns associated with modern society could be transferred via social interaction (trade, war, travelers, media, etc.) and that there may be several paths to development rather than linear evolution. Structural functionalists (Parsons 1951; Hoselitz 1960; Levy 1966) emphasized the idea that societies are integrated wholes composed of functionally compatible institutions and roles, and that societies

progress from one increasingly complex and efficient social system to another. This contributed to the notion that internal social and cultural factors are important determinants or obstacles of economic change.

Research by Smelser (1969) draws on all three traditions in describing modernization of society through processes of social differentiation, disturbances, and reintegration. In a manner similar to other conceptions of modernization, Smelser emphasizes four major changes: from simple to complex technology, from subsistence farming to commercial agriculture, from rural to urban populations, and, most important, from animal and human power to inanimate power and industrialization.

Parsons's later theoretical work (1964) also combines these perspectives in a neo-evolutionist modernization theory that treats societies as self-regulated structural functional wholes in which the main processes of change are social differentiation and the discovery (or acquisition through diffusion) of certain "evolutionary universals" such as bureaucratic organizations and money markets. These, in turn, increase the adaptive capacity of the society by providing more efficient social arrangements and often lead to a system of universalistic norms, "which, more than the industrial revolution itself, ushered in the *modern* era of social evolution" (Parsons 1964, p. 361). A similar neo-evolutionist social differentiation theory of modernization is provided by Eisenstadt (1970).

Another early influence on modernization theory was Weber's work on the Protestant ethic. This work stressed the influence of cultural values on the entrepreneurial behavior of individuals and the rise of capitalism. Contemporary theorists in the Weberian tradition include Lerner, McClelland, Inkeles, and Rostow. Lerner's (1958) empirical studies in several Middle Eastern societies identified empathy, the capacity to take the perspective of others, as a product of media, literacy, and urbanization and as a vital ingredient in producing rational individual behavior conducive to societal development. McClelland (1961) felt that prevalence of individuals with the psychological trait of high "need for achievement" was the key to entrepreneurial activity and modernization of society. In a similar vein, Inkeles and Smith (1974) used interview data from six societies to generate a set of personality traits by which they defined "modern man." They felt that the prevalence of individual modernity in society was determined by such factors as education and factory experience and that individual modernity contributed to the modernization of society. Finally, Rostow's (1960) well-known theory of the stages of economic growth, which he derived from studying Western economic development, emphasized the importance of new values and ideas favoring economic progress along with education, entrepreneurship, and certain other institutions as conditions for societies to "take off" into self-sustained economic growth.

All of these versions of modernization theory depict a gradual and more or less natural transition from "traditional" social structures to "modern" social structures characteristic of Western European and North American societies. More specifically, these theories tend to share to one degree or another the views that (1) modern people, values, institutions, and societies are similar to those found in the industrialized West, that is, the direction of change tends to replicate that which had already occurred in Western industrial societies; (2) tradition is opposite to and incompatible with modernity; (3) the causes of delayed economic and social development (i.e., underdevelopment) are to be found within the traditional society; (4) the mechanisms of economic development also come primarily from within societies rather than from factors outside of the society; and (5) these internal factors (in addition to industrial development) tend to involve social structures, cultural institutions, or personality types.

In keeping with this orientation, empirical studies of sociological modernization tend to deal with the internal effects of industrialization or other economic developments on traditional social institutions or with the social, political, and cultural conditions that facilitate or impede economic growth within traditional or less-developed societies. Examples might include research on the impact of factory production and employment on traditional family relations or the effects of an indigenous land tenure system on the introduction of cash crop farming in society.

Even though modernization theory since the 1960s has been dominated by and sometimes equated with Parsons's neo-evolutionary theory, it is clear that there is no single modernization theory but rather an assortment of related theories and perspectives. In addition to those mentioned, other important contributors of theoretical variants include Hagan (1962), Berger, Berger, and Kellner (1973), Bendix (1964), Moore (1967), Tiryakian (1985), and Nolan and Lenski (1999). Useful reviews include Harrison (1988), Harper (1993), and Jaffee (1998).

Since the 1960s, many critiques of modernization theory and the emergence of competing theories of development have eroded support for modernization theory. Foremost among these are dependency, world systems, and neo-Marxist theories, all of which criticize the ethnocentricity of the modernization concept and the bias in favor of dominant capitalist interests. The focus of these theories is on explaining the contemporary underdevelopment of Third World countries or regions of the world in terms of colonization, imperialist interference, and neocolonial exploitation of developing countries since their gaining of independence. In these counterperspectives, both development and underdevelopment are viewed as part of the same process by which certain "center" countries or regions become economically advanced and powerful at the expense of other "periphery" areas. Rather than explaining development and underdevelopment by the presence or absence of certain internal institutions or personalities, these alternative theories argue that both result from unequal exchange relations and coalitions of interests associated with the structural position of societies in the global economy. Rather than interpreting underdeveloped societies as traditional or archaic, both underdeveloped and developed societies are contemporary but asymmetrically linked parts of capitalist expansion. Both are relatively "modern" phenomena.

Attention to modernization theory in sociology has declined as a result of the theoretical and empirical weaknesses raised especially during the 1970s. Nevertheless, it is still the dominant perspective among government officials and international agencies concerned with third world development. Hoogvelt has noted its influence on development policies as follows:

Because modernisation theories have viewed the total transformation, that is westernisation, of developing countries to be an inescapable outcome of successful diffusion of the Western economic/technological complex, by methodological reversal it is argued that a reorganization of existing social and cultural as well as political patterns in anticipation of their compatibility with the diffused Western economic/technological complex may in fact facilitate the very process of this diffusion itself. This monumental theoretical error–which to be fair was not always committed by the theorists themselves–has in fact been made and continues to be made by modernisation policy-makers such as those employed by Western government, U.N. organizations, the World Bank, and so forth. (1978, pp. 60–61)

Thus, various *indicators* of social, political, and cultural development (such as degree of urbanization, high literacy rates, political democracy, free enterprise, secularization, birth control, etc.) have frequently been promoted as "conditions" for development.

Interestingly, as modern structures and institutions have spread around the world and created economic, political, social, and cultural linkages, an awareness of global interdependence and of the ecological consequences of industrial development and modern lifestyles has grown. It is now clear that finite natural resources and the nature of the global ecosystem could not sustain worldwide modern conditions and practices of European and North American societies even if modernization theory assumptions of evolutionary national development were correct. Thus, new visions and interpretations of national and global development have already begun to replace classical modernization theory.

Some selected publications readers may wish to consult on this topic include Billet (1993), Inglehart (1997). McMichael (1996), Roberts and Hite (1999), Roxborough (1988), and Scott (1995).

(SEE ALSO: *Global Systems Analysis; Industrialization in Less Developed Countries*)

REFERENCES

Bendix, Reinhold 1964 *Nation-Building and Citizenship: Studies of Our Changing Social Order*. New York: John Wiley.

Berger, Peter L., Brigitte Berger, and Hansfried Kellner 1973 *The Homeless Mind: Modernization and Consciousness*. New York: Vintage.

Billet, Bret L 1993 *Modernization Theory and Economic Development: Discontent in the Developing World*. Westport, Conn: Praeger.

Eisenstadt, S. N. 1966 *Modernization: Protest and Change*. Englewood Cliffs, N.J.: Prentice-Hall.

—— 1970 "Social Change and Development." In S. N. Eisenstadt, ed., *Readings in Social Evolution and Development*. Oxford: Pergamon.

Frank, Andre Gunder 1966 "The Development of Underdevelopment." *Monthly Review* 18(4):17–31.

Hagen, Everett E. 1962 *On the Theory of Social Change*. Homewood, Ill.: Dorsey.

Harper, Charles L. 1993 *Exploring Social Change*, 2nd ed. Englewood Cliffs, N.J.: Prentice Hall.

Harrison, David 1988 *The Sociology of Modernization and Development*. London: Unwin Hyman.

Hoogvelt, Ankie M. M. 1978 *The Sociology of Developing Societies*, 2nd ed. London: Macmillan.

Hoselitz, Berthold F. 1960 *Sociological Aspects of Economic Growth*. New York: Free Press.

Inglehart, Ronald 1997 *Modernization and Postmodernization: Cultural, Economic, and Political Change in 43 Societies*. Princeton, NJ: Princeton University Press.

Inkeles, Alex, and David H. Smith 1974 *Becoming Modern*. Cambridge, Mass.: Harvard University Press.

Jaffee, David 1998 *Levels of Socio-Economic Development Theory*. Westport, Conn: Praeger.

Lerner, Daniel 1958 *The Passing of Traditional Society: Modernizing the Middle East*. New York: Free Press.

Levy, Marion, Jr. 1966 *Modernization and the Structures of Societies*, vol. 1. Princeton: Princeton University Press.

McClelland, David C. 1961 *The Achieving Society*. New York: Free Press.

McMichael, Philip 1996 *Development and Social Change: A Global Perspective*. Thousand Oaks, Calif.: Pine Forge.

Moore, Barrington 1967 *Social Origins of Dictatorship and Democracy: Lord and Peasant in the Making of the Modern World*. Boston: Beacon Press.

Nolan, Patrick, and Gerhard E. Lenski 1999 *Human Societies: An Introduction to Macrosociology*, 8th ed. New York: McGraw-Hill.

Parsons, Talcott 1951 *The Social System*. New York: Free Press.

—— 1964 "Evolutionary Universals in Society." *American Sociological Review* 29:339–357.

Roberts, J. Timmons, and Amy Hite 1999 *From Modernization to Globalization: Social Perspectives on International Development*. Malden, Mass.: Blackwell.

Rostow, Walt W. 1960 *The Stages of Economic Growth: A Non-Communist Manifesto*. London: Cambridge University Press.

Roxborough, Ian 1988 "Modernization Theory Revisited." *Contemporary Studies of Society and History* 30(4):753–762.

Scott, Catherine V. 1995 *Gender and Development: Rethinking Modernization and Dependency Theory*. Boulder, Colo.: L. Rienner.

Smelser, Neil 1966 "The Modernization of Social Relations." In Myron Weiner, ed., *Modernization: The Dynamics of Growth*. New York: Basic.

So, Alvin 1990 *Social Change and Development: Modernization, Dependency and World-Systems Theories*. Newbury Park, Calif.: Sage.

Tiryakian, Edward A. 1985 "The Changing Centers of Modernity." In Erik Cohen, Moshe Lissak, and Uri Almagor, eds., *Comparative Social Dynamics: Essay in Honor of S.N. Eisenstadt*. Boulder, Colo.: Westview.

J. MICHAEL ARMER
JOHN KATSILLIS

MONEY

Sociologists treat money paradoxically: On the one hand, money is considered a central element of modern society, and yet it remains an unanalyzed sociological category. In classic interpretations of the development of the modern world, money occupies a pivotal place. As "the most abstract and 'impersonal' element that exists in human life" (Weber [1946] 1971, p. 331), it was assumed that money spearheaded the process of rationalization. For Georg Simmel and Karl Marx, money revolutionized more than economic exchange: It fundamentally transformed the basis of all social relations by turning personal bonds into calculative instrumental ties.

But by defining money as a purely objective and uniform medium of exchange, classical social theory eclipsed money's sociological significance.

If indeed money was unconstrained by subjective meanings and independent social relations, there was little left of sociological interest. As a result, economists took over the study of money: There is no systematic sociology of money. Significantly, the *International Encyclopedia of the Social Sciences* devotes over thirty pages to money but not one to its social characteristics. There are essays on the economic effect of money, on quantity theory, on velocity of circulation, and on monetary reform, but nothing on money as a "réalité sociale," using Simiand's apt term (1934).

The sociological invisibility of money is hard to pierce. For instance, the current resurgence of interest in economic sociology has led to a serious revamping of the neoclassical economic model of the market, firms, and consumption (see, e.g., Smelser and Swedberg 1994). But despite the stimulus, no full-fledged sociology of money as social process has emerged. Consider the recent literature on the culture of consumption, which boldly reverses our understanding of modern commodities. The new revisionist approach uncovers the symbolic meanings of what money buys, but, curiously, the cultural "freedom" of money itself is seldom directly challenged (see, e.g., Appadurai 1986; Bronner 1989; Brewer and Porter 1993).

A sociology of money must thus dismantle a powerful and stubborn utilitarian paradigm of a single, neutral, and rationalizing market money. It must show that money is a meaningful, socially constructed currency, continually shaped and redefined by different networks of social relations and varying systems of meanings. There is some evidence that the sociological conversion of money has begun. (See, e.g., Doyle 1992; Carruthers and Espeland 1998; Dodd 1994; Lane 1990; Mizruchi and Stearns 1994; Reddy 1987; Singh 1997; Wuthnow 1996; Mongardini 1998; Neary and Taylor 1998; Zelizer 1994, 1996.) And in anthropology, psychology, political science, geography and history there are also scattered indications that the economic model of money is starting to lose its hold. (See, e.g., Berti 1991; Bloch 1994; Cohen 1998; Guyer 1995; Heath and Soll 1996; Helleiner 1998; Kahneman and Tversky 1982; Lane 1990; Parry and Bloch 1989; Leyshon and Thrift 1997; Thaler 1990; Shafir, et al. 1997; Shell 1995.) The following two sections will first discuss the classic approach to money and then propose the basis for a sociology of money.

MARKET MONEY: A UTILITARIAN APPROACH TO MONEY

Many eighteenth-century thinkers saw the monetization of the economy as compatible with or even complementary to the maintenance of a morally coherent social life (see Hirschman 1977; Silver 1990). But the transformative powers of money captured the imagination of nineteenth- and early twentieth-century social theorists. Money turned the world, observed Simmel ([1908] 1950, p. 412), into an "arithmetic problem." On purely technical grounds, the possibility of money accounting was essential for the development of impersonal rational economic markets. But traditional social thinkers argued that the effects of money transcended the market: More significantly, money became the catalyst for the generalized instrumentalism of modern social life. As Simmel ([1900] 1978, p. 346) observed: "The complete heartlessness of money is reflected in our social culture, which is itself determined by money."

The task of social theory was thus to explain the uncontested revolutionary power of money. Presumably, it came from money's complete indifference to values. Money was perceived as the prototype of an instrumental, calculating approach; in Simmel's ([1900] 1978, p. 211) words, money was "the purest reification of means." Unlike any other known product, money was the absolute negation of quality. With money, only quantity mattered. That "uncompromising objectivity" allowed it to function as a "technically perfect" medium of modern economic exchange. Free from subjective restrictions, indifferent to "particular interests, origins, or relations," money's liquidity and divisibility were infinite, making it "absolutely interchangeable" (pp. 373, 128, 441). Noneconomic restrictions in the use of money were unequivocally dismissed as residual atavisms. As money became nothing but "mere money," its freedom was apparently unassailable and its uses unlimited. With money, all qualitative distinctions between goods were equally convertible into an arithmetically calculable "system of numbers" (p. 444).

This objectification of modern life had a dual effect. On the one hand, Simmel argued that a money economy broke the personal bondage of traditional arrangements by allowing every individual the freedom of selecting the terms and partners of economic exchange. But the quantifying alchemy of money had a more ominous chemistry. In an early essay, Marx ([1844] 1964, p. 169) had warned that the transformational powers of money subverted reality: "Confounding and compounding . . . all natural and human qualities . . . [money] serves to exchange every property for every other, even contradictory, property and object: it is the fraternization of impossibilities." As the ultimate objectifier, money not only obliterated all subjective connections between objects and individuals but also reduced personal relations to the "cash nexus." Half a century later, Simmel ([1908] 1950, p. 414) confirmed Marx's diagnosis, dubbing money a "frightful leveler" that perverted the uniqueness of personal and social values. And Max Weber ([1946] 1971, p. 331) pointed to the fundamental antagonism between a rational money economy and a "religious ethic of brotherliness."

The prevailing classic interpretation of money thus absolutized a model of market money, shaped by the following five assumptions:

1. The functions and characteristics of money are defined strictly in economic terms. As a qualityless, absolutely homogeneous, infinitely divisible, liquid object, money is a matchless tool for market exchange.

2. All monies are the same in modern society. Differences can exist in the quantity of money but not in its meaning. Thus, there is only one kind of money—market money.

3. A sharp dichotomy is established between money and nonpecuniary values. Money in modern society is defined as essentially profane and utilitarian in contrast to noninstrumental values. Money is qualitatively neutral; personal, social, and sacred values are qualitatively distinct, unexchangeable, and indivisible.

4. Monetary concerns are seen as constantly enlarging, quantifying, and often corrupting all areas of life. As an abstract medium of exchange, money has not only the freedom but also the power to draw an

increasing number of goods and services into the web of the market. Money is thus the vehicle for an inevitable commodification of society.

5. The power of money to transform nonpecuniary values is unquestioned, while the reciprocal transformation of money by values or social relations is seldom conceptualized or else is explicitly rejected.

As the classic view reasons, the monetization of the economy made a significant difference to the organization of social life. For example, it facilitated the multiplication of economic partners and promoted a rational division of labor. But a link is missing from the traditional approach to money. Impressed by the fungible, impersonal characteristics of money, classic theorists emphasized its instrumental rationality and apparently unlimited capacity to transform products, relationships, and sometimes even emotions into an abstract and objective numerical equivalent. But money is neither culturally neutral nor socially anonymous. It may well "corrupt" values and social ties into numbers, but values and social relations reciprocally corrupt money by investing it with meaning and social patterns.

TOWARD A SOCIOLOGY OF MONEY

The utilitarian model has had a remarkable grip on theorizing about money. Coleman (1990, pp. 119–131), for example, builds an extremely sophisticated analysis of social exchange yet continues to treat money as the ultimate impersonal common denominator. Even when analysts recognize the symbolic dimension of modern money, they stop short of fully transcending the utilitarian framework. Parsons (1971a, p. 241; 1971b, pp. 26–27), for instance, explicitly and forcefully called for a "sociology of money" that would treat money as one of the various generalized symbolic media of social interchange, along with political power, influence, and value commitments. In contrast to Marx's definition of money as the "material representative of wealth" ([1858–1859] 1973, p. 222), in Parsons's media theory, money was a shared symbolic language; not a commodity, but a signifier, devoid of use-value. Yet Parsons restricts the symbolism of money to the economic sphere. Money,

Parsons (1967, p. 358) contends, is the "symbolic 'embodiment' of economic value, of what economists in a technical sense call 'utility.'" Consequently, Parsons's media theory left uncharted the symbolic meaning of money outside the market: money's cultural and social significance beyond utility. Giddens (1990) complains that Parsons incorrectly equates power, language, and money, whereas for Giddens money has a distinctly different relationship to social life. As a "symbolic token," money, in Giddens's analysis, serves as a key example of the "disembedding mechanisms associated with modernity," by which he means the" 'lifting out' of social relations from local contexts of interaction and theirrestructuring across indefinite spans of time-space" (1990, pp. 22, 25, 21). Giddens's interpretation still ignores the fact that despite the transferability of money, people make every effort to embed it in particular times, places, meanings, and social relations.

Anthropologists provide some intriguing insights into the extraeconomic, symbolic meaning of money, but mostly with regards to primitive money. For instance, ethnographic studies show that in certain primitive communities, money attains special qualities and distinct values independent of quantity. How much money is less important than *which* money. Multiple currencies, or "special-purpose" money, using Polanyi's term (1957, pp. 264–266), have sometimes coexisted in one and the same village, each currency having a specified, restricted use (for purchasing only certain goods or services), special modes of allocation and forms of exchange (see, e.g., Bohannan 1959), and, sometimes, designated users.

These special moneys, which Douglas (1967) has perceptively identified as a sort of primitive coupon system, control exchange by rationing and restricting the use and allocation of currency. In the process, money sometimes performs economic functions serving as media of exchange, but it also functions as a social and sacred "marker," used to acquire or amend status, or to celebrate ritual events. The point is that primitive money is transformable, from fungible to nonfungible, from profane to sacred.

But what about modern money? Has modernization indeed stripped money of its cultural meaning? Influenced by economic models, most interpretations establish a sharp dichotomy between primitive, restricted "special-purpose" money and modern "all-purpose" money, which, as a single currency, unburdened by ritual or social controls, can function effectively as a universal medium of exchange. Curiously, when it comes to modern money, even anthropologists seem to surrender their formidable analytical tools. For instance, twenty years ago, Douglas (1967), in an important essay, suggested that modern money may not be unrestricted and "free" after all. Her evidence, however, is puzzlingly limited. Modern money, argues Douglas (p. 139), is controlled and rationed in two situations: in international exchange and at the purely individual personal level, where "many of us try to primitivize our money . . . by placing restrictions at source, by earmarking monetary instruments of certain kinds for certain purposes."

Modern money, however, is marked by more than individual whim or by the different material form of currencies. As François Simiand, one of Durkheim's students, argued, the extraeconomic, social basis of money remains as powerful in modern economic systems as it was in primitive and ancient societies (1934). Indeed, Simiand warned against an orthodox rationalist approach that mistakenly ignores the persistent symbolic, sacred, and even magical significance of modern money. In recent work, sociologists, as well as anthropologists, psychologists, historians, and political scientists, have finally heeded the warning, proposing long-overdue alternatives to the standard utilitarian model of money.

Impatient with their former theoretical blinders, some anthropologists are now claiming modern money for their disciplinary terrain, casting off the fallacy of a single, culturally neutral currency. Parry and Bloch's important collection of essays (1989) demonstrates the heterogeneity of money, showing how the multiple symbolic meanings of modern money are shaped by the cultural matrix. In psychology, new studies reject the notion that money is psychologically general, maintaining that instead money involves "multiple symbolizations" (Lea et al. 1987, p. 335). An exciting literature on "mental accounting" challenges the economists' assumption of fungibility by showing the ways individuals distinguish between kinds of money. For instance, they treat a windfall income much differently from a bonus or an inheritance, even when the sums involved are identical.

A sociological accounting of money goes even further. Anthropologists reveal the multiple symbolic representations of modern money in societies outside the centers of capitalism, and psychologists explore individual or household-based differentiations between monies. A sociological model, on the other hand, must show how, even in the most advanced capitalist societies, different networks of social relations and meaning systems mark modern money, introducing controls, restrictions, and distinctions that are as influential as the rationing of primitive money. Special money in the modern world may not be as visibly identifiable as the shells, coins, brass rods, or stones of primitive communities, but its invisible boundaries emerge from sets of historically varying formal and informal rules that regulate its uses, allocation, sources, and quantity. How else, for instance, do we distinguish a bribe from a tribute or a donation, a wage from an honorarium, or an allowance from a salary? How do we identify ransom, bonuses, tips, damages, or premiums? True, there are quantitative differences between these various payments. But surely, the special vocabulary conveys much more than diverse amounts. Detached from its qualitative differences, the world of money becomes undecipherable.

The sociological model of money thus challenges the traditional utilitarian model of market money by introducing different fundamental assumptions in the understanding of money:

1. While money does serve as a key rational tool of the modern economic market, it also exists outside the sphere of the market and is profoundly shaped by different networks of social relations and varying systems of meaning.

2. Money is not a single phenomenon. There is a plurality of different kinds of monies; each special money is shaped by a particular set of cultural and social factors and is thus qualitatively distinct. Market money does not escape extraeconomic influences but is in fact one type of special money, subject to particular social and cultural influences.

3. The classic economic inventory of money's functions and attributes, based on the assumption of a single general-purpose

type of money, is thus unsuitably narrow. By focusing exclusively on money as a market phenomenon, it fails to capture the complex range of characteristics of money as a social medium. A different, more inclusive coding is necessary, for certain monies can be indivisible (or divisible but not in mathematically predictable portions), nonfungible, nonportable, deeply subjective, and therefore qualitatively heterogeneous.

4. The assumed dichotomy between a utilitarian money and nonpecuniary values is false, for money under certain circumstances may be as singular and unexchangeable as the most personal or unique object.

5. Given the assumptions above, the alleged freedom and unchecked power of money become untenable assumptions. Culture and social structure set inevitable limits to the monetization process by introducing profound controls and restrictions on the flow and liquidity of money. Extraeconomic factors systematically constrain and shape (a) the uses of money, earmarking, for instance, certain monies for specified uses; (b) the users of money, designating different people to handle specified monies; (c) the allocation system of each particular money; (d) the control of different monies; and (e) the sources of money, linking different sources to specified uses.

Exploring the quality of multiple monies does not deny money's quantifiable and instrumental characteristics but moves beyond them; it suggests very different theoretical and empirical questions from those derived from a purely economic model of market money. In fact, a utilitarian theory of money had a straightforward task: explaining how money homogenized and commoditized modern social life. Its critics have a much more complex empirical agenda. The illusion of a fully commoditized world must be rectified by showing how different social relations and systems of meanings actively create and shape a plurality of qualitatively distinct kinds of money. Specifically, a sociological theory of money must come to grips with the remarkably different ways in which people identify, classify, interpret, organize, and use money.

Consider for instance the family economy. Domestic money—which includes wife's money, husband's money, and children's money—is a special category of money. Its meanings, uses, allocation, and even quantity are partly determined by considerations of economic efficiency, but domestic money is equally shaped by ideas about family life, by power relationships, age, gender, and social class (Zelizer 1994; Pahl 1989; Singh 1997). For instance, a wife's pin money—regardless of the amount involved—was traditionally reserved for special purchases such as clothing or vacations and kept apart from the "real" money earned by her husband. Or consider the case of gift money. When money circulates among friends or kin as a personal gift for ritual events such as weddings, christenings, bar mitzvahs, or Christmas, it is reshaped into a sentimental currency expressing care and affection. It matters who gives it, when it is given, how it is presented, and how spent. Within formal institutions, money is again redefined this time partly by bureaucratic legislation (Goffman 1961).

These cases are not anomalies or exceptions to valuefree market money but typical examples of money's heterogeneity in modern society. In fact, money used for rational instrumental exchanges is simply another socially created currency, not free from social constraints, but subject to particular networks of social relations and its own set of values and norms. A sociological theory of money must explain the sources and patterns of variation between multiple monies. How, for instance, do personal monies, such as domestic and gift monies, which emerge from the social interaction of intimates, differ from the imposed institutional money of inmates? How does the social status of transactors affect the circulation of monies? What determines the relative rigidity or permeability of boundaries between monies? And what are the patterns of conversions between them?

Developing a sociological model of multiple monies forms part of a broader challenge to neoclassical economic theory. It offers an alternative approach not only to the study of money but to all other aspects of economic life, including the market. In the long run, a proper sociological understanding of multiple monies should challenge and renew explanation of large-scale economic change and variation. It should illuminate such phenomena as aggregate expenditures on consumer durables, rates of saving, response to inflation, income redistribution, and a wide range of other phenomena in which individual consumer actions make a large macroeconomic difference. In the sociological model, economic processes of exchange and consumption are defined as one special category of social relations, much like kinship or religion. Thus, economic phenomena such as money, although partly autonomous, intertwine with historically variable systems of meanings and structures of social relations.

SEE ALSO: *Economic Sociology*

REFERENCES

Appadurai, Arjun, ed. 1986 *The Social Life of Things.* Cambridge, England: Cambridge University Press.

Berti, L., et al. 1991 "Il Denaro." *Problemi Del Socialismo* 7–8.

Bloch, Maurice 1974 "Les usages de l'argent (Money's Uses)." In Maurice Bloch, ed., "Les Usages De L' Argent." *Terrain* 23: 5–10.

Bohannan, Paul 1959 "The Impact of Money on an African Subsistence Economy." *Journal of Economic History* 19:491–503.

Brewer, John, and Roy Porter, eds. 1993 *Consumption and the World of Goods.* New York: Routledge.

Bronner, Simon J. ed. 1989 *Consuming Visions.* New York: Norton.

Carruthers, Bruce, and Wendy Nelson Espeland 1998 "Money, Meaning, and Morality." *American Behavioral Scientist* 41 (August): 1384–1408..

Cohen, Benjamin J. 1998 *The Geography of Money.* Ithaca, N.Y.: Cornell University Press.

Coleman, James 1990 *Foundations of Social Theory.* Cambridge, Mass.: Harvard University Press.

Dodd, Nigel 1994 *The Sociology of Money.* New York: Continuum.

Douglas, Mary 1967 "Primitive Rationing." In Raymond Firth, ed., *Themes in Economic Anthropology.* London: Tavistock.

Doyle, Kenneth O., ed. 1992 "The Meanings of Money." *American Behavioral Scientist* 35:637–840.

Giddens, Anthony 1990 *The Consequences of Modernity.* Stanford, Calif.: Stanford University Press.

Goffman, Erving 1961 *Asylums.* New York: Anchor.

Guyer, Jane I., ed. 1995 *Money Matters.* Portsmouth, N.H.: Heinemann.

Heath, Chip, and Jack B. Soll 1996 "Mental Budgeting and Consumer Decisions." *Journal of Consumer Research* 23:40–52.

Helleiner Eric 1998 "National Currencies and National Identities." *American Behavioral Scientist* 41 (August):1409–1436.

Hirschman, Albert O. 1977 *The Passions and the Interests.* Princeton, N.J.: Princeton University Press.

Kahneman, Daniel, and Amos Tversky 1982 "The Psychology of Preferences." *Scientific American* 246 (January):160–173.

Lane, Robert E. 1990 "Money Symbolism and Economic Rationality." Paper presented at the Second Annual Meeting of the Society for the Advancement of Socio-Economics, Washington, D.C., March.

Lea, Stephen E. G., Roger Tarpy, and Paul Webley 1987 *The Individual in the Economy.* New York: Cambridge University Press.

Leyshon, Andrew, and Nigel Thrift 1997 *Money Space: Geographies of Monetary Transformation.* London: Routledge.

Marx, Karl (1844) 1964 "The Power of Money in Bourgeois Society." In *The Economic and Philosophic Manuscripts of 1844.* New York: International Publishers.

—— (1858–1859) 1973 *Grundrisse.* New York: Vintage.

Mizruchi, M. S., and L. Brewster Stearns 1994 "Money, Banking, and Financial Markets." Pp. 313–341 in Neil Smelser and Richard Swedberg, eds., *The Handbook of Economic Sociology.* Princeton, N.J.: Princeton University Press; and New York: Russell Sage Foundation.

Mongardini, Carlo, ed. 1998 *Il denaro nella cultura moderna (Money in Modern Culture)* Roma: Bulzoni.

Neary, Michael, and Graham Taylor 1998 *Money and the Human Condition.* New York: St. Martin's.

Pahl, Jan 1989 *Money and Marriage.* New York: St. Martin's.

Parry, J., and M. Bloch, eds. 1989 *Money and the Morality of Exchange.* Cambridge, England: Cambridge University Press.

Parsons, Talcott 1967 "On the Concept of Influence." In *Sociological Theory and Modern Society.* New York: Free Press.

—— 1971a "Higher Education as a Theoretical Focus." In Herman Turk and Richard L. Simpson, eds., *Institutions and Social Exchange.* New York: Bobbs-Merrill.

—— 1971b "Levels of Organization and the Mediation of Social Interaction." In Herman Turk and Richard L. Simpson, eds., *Institutions and Social Exchange*. New York: Bobbs-Merrill.

Polanyi, Karl 1957 "The Economy as an Instituted Process." In Karl Polanyi, Conrad M. Arensberg, and Harry W. Pearson, eds., *Trade and Market in the Early Empires*. New York: Free Press.

Reddy, William 1987 *Money and Liberty in Modern Europe*. New York: Cambridge University Press.

Shafir, Eldar, Peter Diamond, and Amos Tverski 1997 "Money Illusion." *Quarterly Journal of Economics* CXII(2):341–374.

Shell, M. 1995 *Art and Money*, Chicago: University of Chicago Press.

Silver, Allan 1990 "Friendship in Commercial Society: Eighteenth-Century Social Theory and Modern Sociology." *American Journal of Sociology* 95:1,474–1,504.

Singh, Supriya 1997 *Marriage Money: The Social Shaping of Money in Marriage and Banking*. St. Leonards, Australia: Allen and Unwin.

Simiand, François 1934 "La monnaie, réalité sociales [Money: A Social Reality] *Annales sociologiques*, ser. D, pp. 1–86.

Simmel, Georg (1900) 1978 *The Philosophy of Money*, trans. Tom Bottomore and David Frisby. London: Routledge and Kegan Paul.

—— (1908) 1950 *The Sociology of Georg Simmel*, ed. Kurt H. Wolf. New York: Free Press.

Smelser, Neil J., and Richard Swedberg, eds. 1994 *The Handbook of Economic Sociology*. Princeton, N.J.: Princeton University Press; and New York: Russell Sage Foundation.

Wuthnow, Robert 1996 *Poor Richard's Principle*. Princeton, N.J.: Princeton University Press.

Zelizer, Viviana A. 1994 *The Social Meaning of Money*. New York: Basic Books.

—— 1996 "Payments and Social Ties." *Sociological Forum* 11 (September):481–495.

VIVIANA ZELIZER

MORAL DEVELOPMENT

Morality refers to the set of values that people use to determine appropriate behavior, that is, what is right versus what is wrong. Determining which behavior is morally appropriate, or "right," is essentially a cognitive decision-making process called *moral judgment*.

Moral judgment is but one component of the process leading to the actual performance of morally appropriate behavior (Rest 1986). However, research on moral development over the past forty-five years has focused primarily on the development of moral judgment. This is due in large part to the influence of psychologists Lawrence Kohlberg (1969, 1971, 1976) and Jean Piaget ([1932] 1948).

Both Piaget and Kohlberg maintained that moral behavior largely depends upon how one perceives the social world and oneself in relation to it. Furthermore, they viewed moral decision making as a rational process and thus linked the development of moral judgment to the development of rational cognition. In this way, moral development is seen largely as changes in one's *way of thinking* about questions of morality as he or she gets older.

The present discussion will provide a brief historical description of the theoretical foundation laid down by Piaget and Kohlberg; the method used by Kohlberg to assess moral development as well as alternative methods that have emerged more recently; some of the major criticisms and reconceptualizations of Kohlberg's theory of moral development; and recent research that has pursued those criticisms in the areas of cultural differences, gender differences, and continued adult development.

THEORETICAL FOUNDATION

Kohlberg built on Piaget's theory or cognitive development to hypothesize a sequence of six specific stages of moral judgment in individual development. This theory of moral development is based on a fundamental idea from Piaget that the way people think about the physical and social world is the result of an "interactional" process between the human organism's innate tendencies and influences from the environment.

This "cognitive-developmental" approach is thus distinguished from both maturational and environmental theories of development. Maturational theories (Gesell 1956) maintain that patterns of behavior express the organism's inherent tendencies. Development is seen as the natural unfolding of a process determined by hereditary factors. In contrast, environmental theories argue that behavior is determined primarily by external influences. From this point of view, behavior is not innately patterned but is essentially learned, whether as a result of conditioning processes that associate the behavior with particular stimuli, rewards, and punishment, or as a result of observing (and subsequently modeling) the behavior of others.

Social learning theory (Bandura 1977) has produced considerable research on how observational learning explains a variety of behaviors relevant to morality, including prosocial behavior (e.g., sharing, cooperation), aggression, resistance to temptation, and delayed gratification. More recent developments have pursued the question of how individuals exert control over their behavior, thus providing some balance to the theory's focus on environmental influences. Bandura's self-efficacy theory (1982), for example, emphasizes the individual's expectations as important to the successful performance of a behavior. However, social learning theory has not addressed moral action and moral character in terms of a broad developmental course (Musser and Leone 1986).

Cognitive-developmental theory, on the other hand, focuses on the developmental process by which people come to understand and organize, or "cognitively structure," their experience. It attempts to resolve the "nature-nurture" controversy by emphasizing the development of these cognitive structures as the result of the interaction between organismic tendencies and influences from the outside world. While particular ways of understanding experience may reflect innate tendencies, they develop in response to the individual's specific experiences with the environment.

Thus, development is not seen as primarily maturational, because experience is necessary for cognitive structure to take shape. However, neither is development thought to be primarily determined by the environment. Rather, cognitive developmentalists argue that, because the underlying thought organization at each stage is qualitatively different, cognitive development is more than the progressively greater acquisition of information. Furthermore, at any given stage, the current cognitive structure can influence how the world is perceived. Thus, cognitive structure is

seen to be "the result of an interaction between certain organismic structuring tendencies and the structure of the outside world, rather than reflecting either one directly" (Kohlberg 1969, p. 352).

THE DOCTRINE OF COGNITIVE STAGES

Piaget's theory of cognitive development maintains that cognitive structures are periodically transformed or restructured as they become unable to account for (or assimilate) new information from the external world adequately. These periods of restructuring result in new ways of understanding that are different from the earlier mental structures as well as from those to be developed later. This allows for the differentiation of distinct cognitive stages each identifiable by a characteristic approach to processing and organizing one's experience of external reality.

Piaget (1960) identified four main characteristics of cognitive stages. Kohlberg (1969) maintains that these characteristics accurately describe his stages of moral development. The characteristics identified by Piaget are as follows:

1. Stages refer to distinct qualitative differences in the way a person thinks about an experience or solves a problem. Although the focus of attention may be the same, the mode of thinking about it is very different.

2. The progression of stages follows an invariant sequence in the development of individuals. That is, the order in which the stages occur is universal for all human beings. It is possible that the speed or timing at which one progresses through the stages may vary with individual or cultural environments—or even that development may stop at one point or another. However, a given stage cannot be followed by any other stage than the one that is next in the sequence. Conversely, the earlier stage must first be achieved before its inadequacies become apparent and the subsequent transformation to the next stage can occur.

3. The characteristic mode of thinking represents a structured whole. Specific cognitive responses to specific tasks depend upon

the overall organizational framework within which one processes information. It is this underlying cognitive structure that produces a logical consistency to one's responses. Thus, the stage is not identified by specific responses to specific stimuli, but it is the pattern in one's responses that indicates a particular underlying cognitive structure.

4. The sequence of stages is hierarchical. At each stage, the underlying structure represents a more integrated and more complex organizational system, one that adequately accounts for information that had created discrepancies within the previous structure. For example, children in the preoperational stage of cognitive development (Piaget's second stage) cannot understand that equal-sized balls of clay formed into two different shapes still have equal amounts of clay. However, children who have achieved concrete operational thinking (Piaget's third stage) understand the principle of conservation and thus recognize that the amount of clay remains the same (is conserved) for both pieces, even though the pieces have changed in shape (Piaget and Inhelder 1969). The underlying cognitive structure of concrete operational thinking differentiates between amount and shape and integrates the information to achieve a more complex understanding of the phenomenon. It is thus logically superior to preoperational thinking. That the later stages in cognitive development are also more comprehensive and more advanced introduces a hierarchical element to the sequence. The stages of cognitive development are not just different but also hierarchical, in the sense that they provide a progressively more differentiated and more integrated—and hence more adaptive—understanding of one's interaction with the environment.

KOHLBERG'S STAGES OF MORAL DEVELOPMENT

Kohlberg's six stages of moral reasoning are divided into three levels, each consisting of two stages. The three levels are differentiated according to what serves as the basis for the person's moral judgment, specifically the significance given the prevailing, or "conventional," social expectations and authority. Briefly, the *preconventional* level, which is the level of most children under 9 years old, occurs prior to the individual's achievement of a full understanding of what is expected or required socially. The *conventional* level, which characterizes most adolescents and adults, refers to an understanding of the social conventions and a belief in conforming to and maintaining the established social order. The *postconventional* level is reached only by a minority of adults, who understand and generally accept the social rules and expectations but recognize that these have been established for the larger purpose of serving universal moral principles. Should the social conventions conflict with these principles, then moral judgment at this level will support the principles at the expense of the conventions.

Within each level, the second stage is a more advanced form than the first. More specifically, the preconventional level refers to judgment based not so much on a sense of what is right and wrong as on the physical consequences that any given act will have for the self. Accordingly, at the first stage within this level, characterized by the *punishment and obedience* orientation, the child will make judgments on the basis of avoiding trouble. This includes obeying authorities to avoid punishment.

At Stage 2, still in the preconventional level, the individual has a sense of the needs of others but still makes judgments to serve her or his own practical interests. This is called the *instrumental* orientation. Although the person is beginning to understand that social interaction involves reciprocity and exchange among participants, moral judgment is still determined by the significance that the action has for oneself. Thus a child may share candy to get some ice cream.

Next, in the conventional level, moral judgment is determined by what is considered "good" according to conventional standards. At this level, the individual has an understanding of what kind of behavior is expected. The first stage at this level (Stage 3) is characterized by the *good boy–good girl* orientation. Judgment as to what is right is based on living up to the expectations of others. It involves a trust in established authority and conformity for the sake of approval.

At Stage 4, the orientation is toward doing one's duty. This is called the *law-and-order* orientation. The individual personally subscribes to the existing social order and thus believes that obeying authority and maintaining the social order are good values in their own right. Whereas behaving according to the social conventions is desirable at Stage 3 because it produces approval from others, at Stage 4 the individual has successfully "internalized" these conventions, so that proper behavior is rewarding because it reinforces one's sense of doing one's duty and therefore produces self-approval.

At the postconventional level, one's understanding of what is right and wrong is based on one's personal values and a sense of shared rights and responsibilities. Morality is no longer determined simply by social definition, but rather by rational considerations. Stage 5 is characterized by the *social contract* orientation, which recognizes that conventions are determined by social consensus and serve a social function. There is an emphasis on utilitarian agreements about what will serve the most good for the most people. Here the person recognizes that rules or expectations are essentially arbitrary. The focus on agreement or contract produces an emphasis on what is legal and on operating "within the system" to achieve one's goals.

Stage 6, however, places the responsibility of a given moral decision firmly on the shoulders of the individual. The basis for moral judgment is found in *universal ethical principles* rather than socially established rules or expectations. One is guided by one's own conscience and recognizes the logical superiority of principles such as respect for human dignity. At Stage 6, it is thus possible to adopt a position that is in conflict with the prevailing social order, and to maintain this position as morally correct.

In Kohlberg's last theoretical paper, he and his colleagues attempt to articulate Stage 6 more completely (Kohlberg et al. 1990). They describe it as fundamentally characterized by a "respect for persons," specifically one that successfully integrates a sense of justice that is universal and impartial with an attitude of "benevolence" that is empathic and understanding of the individual (see also Lapsley 1996).

MEASURING MORAL JUDGMENT

Kohlberg's procedure for assessing moral judgment involves presenting a hypothetical "dilemma" that requires the subject to make a moral choice. The most famous example refers to "Heinz," a man whose wife is dying of cancer. The woman could possibly be saved by a new drug, but the druggist who discovered it is charging an exorbitant amount of money for it, ten times what it costs him to make it. Heinz tried but could not raise enough money, so he steals the drug. Should he have done this?

Because Kohlberg's scheme emphasizes cognitive structure, an individual's stage of moral development is indicated not by the actual behavior that is advocated but rather by the pattern of reasoning behind the decision. Thus, two people may arrive at the same decision (e.g., that Heinz should steal the drug to save the life of his dying wife) but for two entirely different reasons. An individual at the preconventional Stage 2, operating within the instrumental orientation, might recommend stealing the drug because any jail term would be short and worth saving his wife. An individual at the postconventional Stage 6 might also recommend stealing the drug but with a different understanding of the dilemma: Although stealing would violate the law, it would uphold the higher principle of valuing human life and allow Heinz to maintain his self-respect.

The difference between the actual behavioral content of a decision and the cognitive structure of the decision is also illustrated when two people arrive at different decisions but for similar reasons. Thus, the decision not to steal the drug because Heinz would go to jail and probably not be released until after his wife died is also Stage 2 thinking. Even though the ultimate decision advocates the opposite behavior of what was indicated above, it is similarly based on the consideration of what would be most instrumental to Heinz's own self-interest. On the other hand, an individual at Stage 6 might recommend not stealing the drug because, although other people would not blame Heinz if he stole it, he would nonetheless violate his own standard of honesty and lose his self-respect.

Because the stage of moral development is demonstrated not by the behavioral content but by the form of the moral judgment, the subject is allowed to respond freely to these moral dilemmas, and is asked to explain and justify his or her answer. The interviewer can probe with specific questions to elicit more information about the basis of the subject's decision. Interviewers are trained to collect relevant information without directing the subject's responses.

The subject's answers are then transcribed and coded for stage of moral development. Kohlberg identified twenty-five aspects of moral judgment, basic moral concepts that refer to such matters as rules, conscience, one's own welfare, the welfare of others, duty, punishment, reciprocity, and motives. Each of the twenty-five aspects was defined differently for each of the six stages of moral development. Originally, Kohlberg used an aspect-scoring system, whereby every statement made by the subject was coded for aspect and rated as to stage ("sentence scoring"). The subject's usage of any given stage of moral reasoning was indicated by the percentage of his or her statements that was attributed to that stage. Aspect scoring also included an overall "story rating," whereby a single stage was assigned to the subject's total response.

Coding difficulties led to the abandonment of the aspect-scoring system. Because the unit of analysis for sentence scoring was so small, coding often became dependent upon the specific content and choice of words and did not lend itself to identifying the general cognitive structure underlying the statement. Conversely, whereas story rating referred to the total response as the unit of analysis, it created some uncertainty when the subject's answer included conflicting themes.

Kohlberg and his colleagues recognized these scoring difficulties and devoted considerable attention to developing a more reliable and valid scoring system. This led to "standardized issue scoring," which relies on the use of a standardized interview format. The subject is presented with three standard dilemmas, and the interviewer probes for only two issues that are specified for each dilemma (e.g., life and punishment in the Heinz dilemma). Scoring of the subject's responses refers to a manual that describes the patterns of reasoning for Stages 1–5 on each issue (Colby et al. 1987). Stage 6 was dropped from the coding procedure, due to its empirically low incidence, but was retained as a theoretical construct (Kohlberg et al. 1990).

Because the focus of the new scoring system is directed more toward the abstract mode of reasoning, the unit of analysis is considered larger and less concrete than the single sentence. However, because this approach focuses on specifically identified issues, norms, and elements, it is considered more precise than the global story rating. Despite the qualitative nature of this approach and its potential vulnerability to rater bias, its developers report that long-term study of its inter-rater reliability, test-retest reliability, internal consistency, and validity has produced favorable results (Colby and Kohlberg 1987).

Validity has been a major concern regarding Kohlberg's moral judgment interview. Kurtines and Grief (1974) criticized the low utility of moral judgment scores for predicting moral action. Other questions have been raised about the validity of the data collected, even for the purposes of assessing moral judgment. For one, use of the "classical" dilemmas in this research has been criticized on grounds that they are not representative: Not only do they address hypothetical—as opposed to real-life—circumstances, but they refer to a limited domain of moral issues (e.g., property and punishment). Assessment may fail to indicate the extent to which the person's moral judgment is influenced by the particular context provided by the dilemma. A related matter is whether responses are affected by the characteristics (e.g., the gender) of the story's protagonist. Also the effect of differences in interviewing style, as interviewers interact with subjects and probe for further information, needs to be considered. Of particular importance is this method's dependence on the subject's verbal expression and articulation skills for the information that is collected. To the extent that the rating might be affected by either the amount of information that is provided or the manner in which it is expressed, the validity of the scoring system is called into question. (See Modgil and Modgil 1986 for discussion of these issues.)

An alternative to Kohlberg's Moral Judgment Interview is the Defining Issues Test (DIT) (Rest 1986). This is a standardized questionnaire that presents a set of six moral dilemmas and, for each dilemma, specifically identifies twelve issues that could be considered in deciding upon a course of action. The subject's task is to indicate, on a five-point scale, how important each issue is in deciding what ought to be done in the given situation. The subject also ranks the four most important issues.

Here, the term "issue" is used differently than it is in Kohlberg's new scoring procedure. The items are prototypical statements designed to represent considerations (e.g., "whether a community's laws are going to be upheld") that are characteristic of specific stages of moral reasoning as they are described in Kohlberg's theory. The importance assigned by the subject to items that represent a particular stage is taken to indicate the extent to which the subject's moral judgment is characterized by that stage's mode of thinking.

There are advantages and disadvantages to the DIT compared with the open-ended interview. Whereas the interview is helpful for originally identifying the considerations that may be relevant to resolving moral dilemmas, the DIT provides a more systematic assessment of the relative importance of such considerations. In the open-ended interview, it is never clear whether a specific concern is not identified because it is not important or because the subject failed to articulate it. Similarly, interviews are less comparable to the extent that subjects do not all address the same issues. These problems are avoided by the more structured DIT, because the task requires the subject only to recognize what is important rather than to identify and articulate it spontaneously. However, because recognition is an easier task than spontaneous production, it tends to allow higher-level responses. Another important difference is that the DIT measures the maturity of moral judgment as a continuous variable rather than in terms of the holistic step-by-step sequence of cognitive-developmental stages. Researchers must be aware of such differences when interpreting results.

A third instrument, the Moral Judgment Test (MJT) (Lind et al. 1981; Lind and Wakenhut 1985) similarly attempts to measure moral reasoning by the subject's endorsement of specific items. Hypothetical moral dilemmas are presented, and subjects respond to a series of twelve statements for each dilemma. Each of Kohlberg's six stages is represented by two statements, one in favor of and one against the particular action in question. Subjects indicate how acceptable they find each of the statements.

Citing Lind's paper (1995) extensively, Rest and colleagues (1997) focus on an important distinction between the MJT and the DIT. Instead of adding ratings to indicate how much the subject prefers a particular stage's statements (*stage preference*)—as most DIT studies do—Lind emphasizes how consistently the subject responds to different statements from the same stage (*stage consistency*). Lind argues that stage consistency is a more accurate measure of true cognitive structure, whereas stage preference is more indicative of an affective (like versus dislike) response.

Rest and colleagues (1997) use the DIT statements to construct a consistency measure that is similar to the one developed by Lind. They conclude that the stage-preference measure shows greater construct validity than the stage-consistency measures in differentiating groups with different expertise and different education. The stage-preference measure correlates more highly with moral comprehension—indicating longitudinal development—predicts both prosocial and antisocial behavior, and correlates with political attitudes.

The question of scoring for preference or consistency and what construct is measured by each approach is a legitimate methodological concern with important implications for our understanding of moral development. However, both the DIT and the MJT can be scored for preference and for consistency. Thus, they each remain a viable alternative for attempting to empirically measure moral judgment.

Another measurement tool is the Sociomoral Reflection Measure (SRM) (Gibbs and Widaman 1982; Gibbs et al. 1982), and a more recent variation is the Short Form (SRM-SF) (Gibbs et al. 1992; Basinger et al. 1995; Communian and Gielen 1995; Garmon et al. 1996). This is an open-ended, group-administrable instrument that asks subjects to rate the importance of such topics as keeping promises, affiliation, life, property, and law. It does not present specific dilemmas, but instead uses "lead-in statements" that instruct subjects to generate their own example, such as "Think about when you've made a promise to a friend," prior to providing their rating of importance. The short form consists of eleven items that can produce a score ranging from 100 (exclusively Stage 1) to 400 (exclusively Stage 4).

Proponents argue that not only is the SRM-SF suitable for assessing stages of moral judgment, but because examples are self-generated, items also can be used to assess differences in content emphasis (Basinger et al. 1995; Garmon et al. 1996). As such, it is suggested as especially useful for research on cultural differences, gender differences, everyday life (versus hypothetical) experience, and the relationship between moral judgment and moral behavior (Communian and Gielen 1995).

As discussed below, perhaps the single most influential criticism of Kohlberg's theory is Carol Gilligan's contention that it fails to describe the moral development of females (1982). Her articulation of a more female-oriented "morality of care," complete with its own sequence of stages, has led to the development of the Ethics of Care Interview (ECI) (Skoe and Marcia 1991). Similar to Kohlberg's methodology, the ECI assesses stage differences, but specifically as they are relevant to the development of care-based morality. Research with the ECI has recently been reviewed by Skoe (1998), demonstrating that the morality of care has important application to human development in general and to the development of personality in particular.

CRITICISMS AND FURTHER RESEARCH

Besides the methodological problems discussed above, Kohlberg's theory of moral development has been criticized on a number of points. The major criticisms include the following:

1. The sequence of stages is more representative of Western culture and thus not universal or invariant across all cultures. Moreover, it is culturally biased in that it maintains the ideals of Western liberalism as the highest form of moral reasoning.

2. Like many theories of personality development, Kohlberg's theory fails to describe the development of women accurately but provides a much better understanding of

male development. This is a specific variation of the first criticism, suggesting that the theory itself reflects the sexism of Western culture.

3. Kohlberg's theory fails to describe adult development adequately. In particular, its emphasis on abstract principles fails to recognize how adult moral judgment is more responsive to the specific practical matters of everyday, real-life contexts. Also, its emphasis on cognitive structure fails to recognize that changes in the content of moral reflection may be the most important aspect of adult moral development.

Cultural Bias. A cornerstone of cognitive-developmental theory is invariant sequence, the notion that the given developmental progression is universal for all human beings within all cultures. Because the conceptual organization of any given stage is considered logically necessary before the cognitive structure of the next stage can develop, each stage is said to have logical priority to subsequent stages. Shweder and LeVine (1975) take issue with both the notion of logical priority and the doctrine of invariant sequence, although they do not address the development of moral judgment per se. Specifically, they analyze dream concepts among children from the Hausa culture in Nigeria and conclude that there are multiple sequences by which such concepts develop.

Shweder (1982) follows up this initial skepticism with a fuller critique of what he sees as Kohlberg's failure to recognize cultural conceptions of morality as relative to one another. He disagrees with the assertion that there is a rational basis upon which morality can be constructed objectively. Rather, he argues that the postconventional morality that Kohlberg maintains as rationally superior is simply an example of American ideology.

Similarly, others (Broughton 1986; Simpson 1974; Sullivan 1977) argue that Kohlberg's theory is necessarily culture-bound, reflective of the Western society from which it originates. Simpson suggests that the specific moral dilemmas used in the testing situation may not have the same meaning for people of different cultures and thus the scoring system may not adequately detect legitimate cultural variations in moral structures. Thus, she maintains that the claims to universality are not valid. Sullivan goes even further, suggesting that Stage 6 reasoning is so rooted in the philosophical rationale for current Western society that it serves to defend the status quo. In doing so, it distracts attention from the injustices of such societies.

In an early response to the charge of cultural bias, Kohlberg and colleagues (1983) acknowledge the influence of Western liberal ideology on the theory. They agree there is a need to be more sensitive to cultural differences in the meaning attributed not only to the various elements of the research protocol but, consequently, also to the responses of the subjects themselves. However, they defend the claim to universality for the six-stage sequence of moral development and maintain that empirical research using the scientific method will help to determine to what extent this position is tenable.

They also maintain that, while it is appropriate to remain impartial in the study of moral judgment, this does not make it necessary to deny the relative value of certain moral positions. They assert that some positions are rationally superior to others. They thus continue to subscribe to the ideal that any given moral conflict can be brought to resolution through rational discourse.

Kohlberg's position on invariant sequence has been supported by a number of cross-cultural studies, although postconventional reasoning (Stages 5 and 6) may occur less frequently in nonurbanized cultures (Snarey 1985). However, in a sample of subjects from India, Vasudev and Hummel (1987) not only found stage of moral development to be significantly related to age, but also found postconventional thinking to occur among a substantial proportion of adults. Concluding that commonalities exist across cultures, Vasudev and Hummel also suggest there is cultural diversity in the way moral principles are expressed, interpreted, and adapted to real life.

More recent research has increasingly acknowledged the significance of cultural influences on moral development. In another study with a sample from India, Moore concludes that "the notion of justice, as defined by Western social scientists, was rarely used as a moral rationale" (1995, p.

286). Rather, results indicated moral judgment to be dependent on one's religious ideology or social status. Similarly, Okonkwo's study of Nigerians (1997) concludes that moral thinking and moral language are culture dependent. While some parallels to Kohlberg's scheme were found, some "well-articulated moral expressions could not be scored" (Okonkwo 1997, p. 117) due to the inability of Kohlberg's instrument to adequately assess certain concepts that served as the basis for subjects' moral judgments.

Ma and Cheung (1996), studying samples of Chinese, English, and American adolescents and young adults, likewise found cultural differences in the way subjects interpreted specific items on the Defining Issues Test. However, after they deleted some of the items used to indicate Kohlberg's Stage 4, their samples demonstrated a consistent heirarchical structure across the three cultures. They thus conclude that, while different cultures may encourage different perceptions of specific moral statements, there is some support for the idea of a fundamentally universal development.

Markoulis and Valanides (1997) similarly addressed the cultural bias controversy in a conciliatory fashion. Comparing students from Greece and Nigeria, they found stage differences between the two cultures, but nonetheless found that the sequence of development was similar. Again, while cultural environment is recognized as a factor, invariant sequence in development is supported.

A related concern that has been receiving more attention from researchers is the question of whether differences in political ideology within a single, larger culture may be inaccurately represented as developmental variation. Specifically, Gross (1996) compared Americans who are pro-life on the abortion issue with others who are pro-choice, and also compared Israelis who disagree on now to handle the West Bank settlement issue. As long as socioeconomic status was similar, he found no difference between the relevant ideological groups and thus concludes that there is no evidence that ideological bias is built into the stages of moral development.

Conversely, Emler and colleagues (1998) argue that differences in moral development as assessed by the DIT more accurately reflect differences in political ideology. Thoma and colleagues

(1999) acknowledge overlap between political thinking and moral judgment, but argue that Emler and colleagues and St. James (1998) provide no evidence to discount the DIT as a valid measure of moral development. Narvaez and colleagues (1999) attempt to resolve the issue with a model of moral judgment and cultural ideology as engaged in parallel development, each influencing the other to produce specific moral thinking.

Whereas recent times have been characterized by an increased sensitivity to cultural diversity and political "correctness," more attention has been drawn to the consideration of possible cultural and political bias in the theory of moral development. While some researchers have identified cultural differences in moral reasoning, this has led to an increased recognition of sociocultural factors in moral development (Eckensberger and Zimba 1997).

Shweder and colleagues (1987), for example, propose the social communication theory, which maintains that the learning of morality depends largely on the transmission of cultural ideology to children, by virtue of the evaluation and judgments that parents and others make. The point, of course, is that morality is socially constructed, not self-constructed (Emler 1998).

However, other researchers continue to maintain that, while we must make specific adjustments to our understanding of moral development, it is not necessary to abandon the general consideration of a single, universal pattern to human moral development. This area of inquiry thus promises to remain a controversial yet productive focus for several years.

Gender Bias. Carol Gilligan (1982) argues that the major theories of personality development describe males more accurately than females. She includes Kohlberg's theory in this assessment and points to the prevalence of all-male samples in his early research as a partial explanation. Gilligan contrasts two moral orientations. The first is the morality of justice, which focuses on fairness, rights, and rules for the resolution of disputes. The second is the morality of care, which focuses on relationships, a sensitivity to the needs of others, and a responsibility for others. Gilligan asserts that the orientation toward morality as justice is especially characteristic of males and, conversely, that

morality as care and responsibility is especially relevant to females. To the extent that Piaget, Freud, and Kohlberg each address morality as justice, they accurately represent male moral development but inadequately represent female moral development.

Gilligan argues that women are more likely to rely on the orientation of care to frame personal moral dilemmas. Furthermore, whereas the morality of care focuses on interpersonal relationship, it resembles the Stage 3 emphasis on satisfying the expectations of others. Gilligan believes this resemblance results in a high number of female responses being misrepresented with Stage 3 ratings.

Gilligan thus argues that Kohlberg's theory and scoring system are biased to favor men. However, Walker (1984), after systematically reviewing empirical studies that used Kohlberg's method, concludes that men do not score higher than women, when samples are controlled for education, socioeconomic status, and occupation. Similarly, Thoma (1986) reports that sex differences on the Defining Issues Test actually favor women but that the differences are trivial.

Kohlberg and colleagues (1983) address Gilligan's criticisms and agree that the care orientation is not fully assessed by their measurement but disagree that this leads to a biased downscoring of females. They suggest that care and justice may develop together and that Stage 6 nonetheless represents a mature integration of the care and justice moralities (see also Vasudev 1988).

Walker and colleagues (1987) found that both the care and the justice orientations were used by both males and females. Furthermore, the orientation used was related to the type of dilemma being discussed. If the dilemma was focused on personal relationships, both men and women tended to use the care orientation. If the dilemma was impersonal, both men and women tended to express a justice orientation. This suggests that observed gender differences in moral judgment may be more a reflection of the particular kind of dilemma they choose to discuss. Perhaps females tend to report more relationship-oriented dilemmas, the kind that pull for care-based judgments (Yussen 1977).

Wark and Krebs (1996) show just this pattern: Females did not score lower than males on

Kohlbergian dilemmas; however, females were more likely to report care-based dilemmas when asked to recall and describe moral conflicts from real life; this difference in the type of moral dilemmas accounted for differences in moral orientation from males and females.

Using the Sociomoral Reflection Measure–Short Form (SRM-SF), which does not rely on specific dilemmas provided by the researcher, Garmon and colleagues (1996) found support for gender differences in moral orientation, with females more likely to refer to a morality of care. However, they reject Gilligan's claim of a bias against females. In fact, results (Basinger et al. 1995) have indicated a possible female advantage in early adolescence. As measured by the SRM-SF, moral judgment was found to be higher among young female adolescents than among their male counterparts. No gender difference was found in late adolescence or young adulthood. Communian and Gielen (1995) found similar results in an Italian sample, with early adolescent girls scoring higher than early adolescent boys, but no gender differences in adults. In another study of seventh and eighth graders, Perry and McIntire (1995) found that subjects used a care mode, a justice mode, and a third narrowly concerned "selfish" mode to make moral decisions. The girls were more likely to use both the care and the justice modes, while the boys were more likely to choose the less developed selfish mode. Contrary to a bias against females, this research suggests that, at least in early adolescence, girls are more advanced in their moral development. Silberman and Snarey (1993) relate such a cognitive advantage to the earlier physical maturation of girls.

Consistent with the lack of evidence for a bias against females, Skoe (1995) found that Kohlberg's justice-based moral reasoning was unrelated to sex-role orientation, as measured by the Bem Sex Role Inventory (Bem 1974). However, this research indicates an interesting pattern for care-based moral reasoning. Using the Ethic of Care Interview (ECI), Skoe found that care-based reasoning was higher in women who were more androgynous and who indicated higher levels of ego identity. Skoe concludes that women who relinquish the traditional female gender role are more likely to develop a mature care-based morality than are women who retain this role.

This would seem to be inconsistent with Gilligan's argument (1982) that the morality of care depends on traditional female socialization. While this morality may be rooted in the traditional female role, Skoe's findings suggest that its advanced development may require a more integrated, androgynous identity.

Current researchers seem to be recognizing that the different moralities go beyond simple gender role differences. Woods (1996) argues that both Kohlberg and Gilligan represent polarized, sexist views, limited to a focus on gender differences. She suggests that researchers need to take a more comprehensive view of the multiple biological and cultural variables that impact moral development, without reducing it to a discussion of sexism. Gilligan's morality of care identifies a vital approach to morality that may have its origin and strength in feminine ideals, indeed that may be more salient in females than in males. However, women are not confined to it, nor is it confined to women, especially as gender roles become more relaxed.

Adult Development. A third major issue concerning Kohlberg's theory is whether or not it accurately addresses continued adult development. This issue reflects a more general concern in lifespan developmental psychology regarding the inapplicability of Piaget's model for cognitive development beyond adolescence, leading to a consideration of what has come to be called "postformal" development (Commons et al. 1984). Murphy and Gilligan (1980) found that college and postcollege subjects not only indicated a greater tendency to appreciate the importance of specific contexts in real-life dilemmas but also indicated a slight tendency to regress from Stage 5 moral reasoning on the classical dilemmas. They suggest that a more mature recognition of the significance of contextual particulars leads one to question the validity of abstract moral principles (hence the regressed score). This argument is consistent with other work suggesting that adult cognitive development in general is marked by a greater appreciation of the practical realities of day-to-day living (Denney and Palmer 1981; Labouvie-Vief 1984; W. G. Perry, Jr. 1970). Related to this emphasis on the practical is the finding of Przygotzki and Mullet (1997) that elderly adults, when attributing blame, give more importance to the consequences of an action than to the intention of the perpetrator.

Finally, Gibbs (1979) argues that adult development is characterized more by increased reflection on such existential matters as meaning, identity, and commitment than by any structural change in the way the person thinks. Similarly, Nisan and Applebaum (1995) suggest that older adults give more weight to identity-related personal considerations when considering moral choices, unless they conflict with "a moral demand" from an "unambiguous law." Gibbs (1979) suggests that Kohlberg's postconventional stages are not structural advances over the earlier stages but would be more appropriately described in terms of existential development. In response, Kohlberg et al. (1983) maintain that Stage 5 represents a legitimate cognitive structure. However, they acknowledge the possibility of further nonstructural development in the adult years with regard to both specific contextual relativity and existential reflection. They suggest that such development could be described in terms of "soft" stages that do not strictly satisfy Piaget's formal criteria for cognitive stages.

SUMMARY

In spite of the formidable criticisms that have been levied against it, Kohlberg's theory of moral development remains the centerpiece to which all other work in this area is addressed, whether as an elaboration or as a refutation. At the very least, Kohlberg has formulated a particular sequence of moral reasoning that adequately represents the prevalent sequence of development in traditional Western society. To that extent, it serves as a model, not only for building educational devices (see Modgil and Modgil 1986; Nucci 1989; Power et al. 1989), but also for comparing possible alternatives. Whether or not this sequence is in fact universal or relative to the particular culture—or a particular socialization process within the culture—is a debate that continues. Nonetheless, the scheme remains the prototype upon which further work in this area is likely to be based.

REFERENCES

Bandura, Albert 1977 *Social Learning Theory*. Englewood Cliffs, N.J.: Prentice-Hall.

—— 1982 "Self-Efficacy Mechanism in Human Agency." *American Psychologist* 37:122–147.

Basinger, Karen S., John C. Gibbs, and Dick Fuller 1995 "Context and the Measurement of Moral Judgment." *International Journal of Behavioral Development* 18:537–556.

Bem, Sandra L. 1974 "The Measurement of Psychological Androgyny." *Journal of Consulting and Clinical Psychology* 42:155–162.

Broughton, John M. 1986 "The Genesis of Moral Domination." In S. Modgil and C. Modgil, eds., *Lawrence Kohlberg: Consensus and Controversy*. Philadelphia: Falmer.

Colby, Anne, and Lawrence Kohlberg 1987 *The Measurement of Moral Judgment*, vol. 1, *Theoretical Foundations and Research Validation*. New York: Cambridge University Press.

——, Alexandra Hewer, Daniel Candee, John C. Gibbs, and Clark Power 1987 *The Measurement of Moral Judgment*, vol. 2, *Standard Issue Scoring Manual*. New York: Cambridge University Press.

Commons, Michael L., Francis A. Richards, and Cheryl Armon (eds.) 1984 *Beyond Formal Operations: Late Adolescent and Adult Cognitive Development*. New York: Praeger.

Communian, Anna Laura, and Uwe P. Gielen 1995 "Moral Reasoning and Prosocial Action in Italian Culture." *Journal of Social Psychology* 135:699–706.

Denney, Nancy W., and Ann M. Palmer 1981 "Adult Age Differences on Traditional and Practical Problem-Solving Measures." *Journal of Gerontology* 36:323–328.

Eckensberger, Lutz H., and Roderick F. Zimba 1997 "The Development of Moral Judgment." In J. W. Berry and P. R. Dasen, eds., *Handbook of Cross-Cultural Psychology*, vol. 2, *Basic Processes and Human Development*, 2nd ed. Boston: Allyn and Bacon.

Emler, Nicholas 1998 "Sociomoral Understanding." In A. Campbell and S. Muncer, eds., *The Social Child*. Hove, East Sussex: Psychology Press.

——, E. Palmer-Canton, and A. St. James 1998 "Politics, Moral Reasoning, and the Defining Issues Test: A Reply to Barnett et al. (1995)." *British Journal of Social Psychology* 37:457–476.

Garmon, Lance C., Karen S. Basinger, Virginia R. Gregg, and John C. Gibbs 1996 "Gender Differences in Stage and Expression of Moral Judgment." *Merrill-Palmer Quarterly* 42:418–437.

Gesell, Arnold 1956 *Youth: The Years from Ten to Sixteen*. New York: Harper and Row.

Gibbs, John C. 1979 "Kohlberg's Moral Stage Theory: A Piagetian Revision." *Human Development* 22:89–112.

——, Karen S. Basinger, and Dick Fuller 1992 *Moral Maturity: Measuring the Development of Sociomoral Reflection.* Hillsdale, N.J.: Erlbaum.

Gibbs, John C., and K. F. Widaman 1982 *Social Intelligence: Measuring the Development of Sociomoral Reflection.* Englewood Cliffs, N.J.: Prentice-Hall.

——, and Anne Colby 1982 "Construction and Validation of a Simplified Group-Administrable Equivalent to the Moral Judgment Interview." *Child Development* 53:875–910.

Gilligan, Carol 1982 *In a Different Voice: Psychological Theory and Women's Development.* Cambridge, Mass.: Harvard University Press.

Gross, Michael L. 1996 "Moral Reasoning and Ideological Affiliation: A Cross-National Study." *Political Psychology* 17:317–338.

Kohlberg, Lawrence 1969 "Stage and Sequence: The Cognitive-Developmental Approach to Socialization." In D. Goslin, ed., *Handbook of Socialization Theory and Research.* Chicago: Rand McNally.

—— 1971 "From *Is* to *Ought*: How to Commit the Naturalistic Fallacy and Get Away with It in the Study of Moral Development." In T. Mischel, ed., *Cognitive Development and Epistemology.* New York: Academic.

—— 1976 "Moral Stages and Moralization: The Cognitive Developmental Approach." In T. Lickona, ed., *Moral Development and Behavior: Theory, Research, and Social Issues.* New York: Holt, Rinehard, and Winston.

——, D. Boyd, and Charles Levine 1990 "The Return of Stage 6: Its Principle and Moral Point of View." In T. Wren, ed., *The Moral Domain: Essays in the Ongoing Discussion between Philosophy and the Social Sciences.* Cambridge: Massachusetts Institute of Technology Press.

Kohlberg, Lawrence, Charles Levine, and Alexandra Hewer 1983 *Moral Stages: A Current Formulation and a Response to Critics.* Basel, Switzerland: Karger.

Kurtines, William, and Esther B. Grief 1974 "The Development of Moral Thought: Review and Evaluation of Kohlberg's Approach." *Psychological Bulletin* 81:453–470.

Labouvie-Vief, Gisela 1984 "Culture, Language, and Mature Rationality." In K. McCluskey and H. W. Reese, eds., *Life-Span Developmental Psychology: Historical and Generational Effects.* New York: Academic.

Lapsley, Daniel K. 1996 *Moral Psychology.* Boulder, Colo.: Westview.

Lind, Georg 1995 "The Meaning and Measurement of Moral Competence Revisited." Paper presented at the annual meeting of the American Educational Research Association, San Francisco.

——, J. Sandberger, and T. Bargel 1981 "Moral Judgment, Ego Strength, and Democratic Orientations: Some Theoretical Contiguities and Empirical Findings." *Political Psychology* 3:70–110.

Lind, Georg, and R. Wakenhut 1985 "Testing for Moral Competence." In G. Lind, H. A. Hartmann, and R. Wakenhut, eds., *Moral Development and the Social Environment.* Chicago: Precedent.

Ma, Hing-Keung, and Chau-Kiu Cheung 1996 "A Cross-Cultural Study of Moral Stage Structure in Hong Kong Chinese, English, and Americans." *Journal of Cross-Cultural Psychology* 27:700–713.

Markoulis, Diomedes, and Nicolaos Valanides 1997 "Antecedent Variables for Sociomoral Reasoning Development: Evidence from Two Cultural Settings." *International Journal of Psychology* 32:301–313.

Modgil, Sohan, and Celia Modgil 1986 *Lawrence Kohlberg: Consensus and Controversy.* Philadelphia: Falmer.

Moore, Erin 1995 "Moral Reasoning: An Indian Case Study." *Ethos* 23:286–327.

Murphy, John M., and Carol Gilligan 1980 "Moral Development in Late Adolescence and Adulthood: A Critique and Reconstruction of Kohlberg's Theory." *Human Development* 23:77–104.

Musser, Lynn M., and Christopher Leone 1986 "Moral Character: A Social Learning Perspective." In R. T. Knowles and G. F. McLean, eds., *Psychological Foundations of Moral Education and Character Development: An Integrated Theory of Moral Development.* Lanham, Md.: University Press of America.

Narvaez, Darcia, Irene Getz, James R. Rest, and Stephen J. Thoma 1999 "Individual Moral Judgment and Cultural Ideologies." *Developmental Psychology* 35:478–488.

Nisan, Mordecai, and Barbara Applebaum 1995 "Maintaining a Balanced and Respective Identity: Moral Choice in Late Adulthood." In G. Ben-Shakhar and A. Lieblich, eds., *Studies in Psychology in Honor of Solomon Kugelmass.* Jerusalem: Magnes.

Nucci, Larry P. (ed.) 1989 *Moral Development and Character Education: A Dialogue.* Berkeley, Calif: McCutchan.

Okonkwo, Rachel U. N. 1997 "Moral Development and Culture in Kohlberg's Theory: A Nigerian (Igbo) Evidence." *IFE Psychologia: An International Journal* 5:117–128.

Perry, Constance M., and Walter G. McIntire 1995 "Modes of Moral Judgment among Early Adolescents." *Adolescence* 30:707–715.

Perry, William G., Jr. 1970 *Forms of Intellectual and Ethical Development in the College Years.* New York: Holt, Rinehart, and Winston.

Piaget, Jean (1932) 1948 *The Moral Judgment of the Child*. Glencoe, Ill.: Free Press.

—— 1960 "The General Problems of the Psychobiological Development of the Child." In J. M. Tanner and B. Inhelder, eds., *Discussions on Child Development: Proceedings of the World Health Organization Study Group on the Psychobiological Development of the Child*. New York: International Universities Press.

——, and Barbara Inhelder 1969 *The Psychology of the Child*. New York: Basic.

Power, Clark F., Ann Higgins, and Lawrence Kohlberg 1989 *Lawrence Kohlberg's Approach to Moral Education*. New York: Columbia University Press.

Przygotzki, Nathalie, and Etienne Mullet 1997 "Moral Judgment and Aging." *European Review of Applied Psychology* 47:15–21.

Rest, James R. 1986 *Moral Development: Advances in Research and Theory*. New York: Praeger.

——, Stephen Thoma, and Lynne Edwards 1997 "Designing and Validating a Measure of Moral Judgment: Stage Preference and Stage Consistency Approaches." *Journal of Educational Psychology* 89:5–28.

Shweder, Richard 1982 "Review of Lawrence Kohlberg's *Essays in Moral Development*, vol. 1, *The Philosophy of Moral Development: Liberalism as Destiny*." *Contemporary Psychology* 27:421–424.

——, and Robert A. LeVine 1975 "Dream Concepts of Hausa Children: A Critique of the 'Doctrine of Invariant Sequence' in Cognitive Development." *Ethos* 3:209–230.

——, M. Mahapatra, and Joan G. Miller 1987 "Culture and Moral Development." In J. Kagan and S. Lamb, eds., *The Emergence of Morality in Young Children*. Chicago: University of Chicago Press.

Silberman, M. A., and John Snarey 1993 "Gender Differences in Moral Development during Early Adolescence: The Contribution of Sex-Related Variations in Maturation." *Current Psychology: Developmental, Learning, Personality, and Social* 12:163–171.

Simpson, Elizabeth L. 1974 "Moral Development Research: A Case Study of Scientific Cultural Bias." *Human Development* 17:81–106.

Skoe, Eva E. 1995 "Sex Role Orientation and Its Relationship to the Development of Identity and Moral Thought." *Scandinavian Journal of Psychology* 36:235–245.

——, 1998 "The Ethic of Care: Issues in Moral Development." In E. E. A. Skoe and A. L. von der Lippe, eds., *Personality Development in Adolescence: A Cross National and Life Span Perspective*. New York: Routledge.

——, and J. E. Marcia 1991 "A Measure of Care-Based Morality and Its Relation to Ego Identity." *Merrill-Palmer Quarterly* 32:289–304.

Snarey, John R. 1985 "Cross-Cultural Universality of Social-Moral Development: A Critical Review of Kohlbergian Research." *Psychological Bulletin* 97:202–232.

Sullivan, Edmund V. 1977 "A Study of Kohlberg's Structural Theory of Moral Development: A Critique of Liberal Social Science Ideology." *Human Development* 20:352–376.

Thoma, Stephen J. 1986 "Estimating Gender Differences in the Comprehension and Preference of Moral Issues." *Developmental Review* 6:165–180.

——, Robert Barnett, James Rest, and Darcia Narvaez 1999 "What Does the DIT Measure?" *British Journal of Social Psychology* 38:103–111.

Vasudev, Jyotsna 1988 "Sex Differences in Morality and Moral Orientation: A Discussion of the Gilligan and Attanucci Study." *Merrill-Palmer Quarterly* 34:239–244.

——, and Raymond C. Hummel 1987 "Moral Stage Sequence and Principled Reasoning in an Indian Sample." *Human Development* 30:105–118.

Walker, Lawrence J. 1984 "Sex Differences in the Development of Moral Reasoning: A Critical Review of the Literature." *Child Development* 55:677–691.

——, B. deVries, and S. Trevethan 1987 "Moral Stages and Moral Orientations." *Child Development* 58:842–858.

Wark, Gillian R., and Dennis L. Krebs 1996 "Gender and Dilemma Differences in Real-Life Moral Judgment." *Developmental Psychology* 32:220–230.

Woods, Cindy J. P. 1996 "Gender Differences in Moral Development and Acquisition: A Review of Kohlberg's and Gilligan's Models of Justice and Care." *Social Behavior and Personality* 24:375–384.

Yussen, S. 1977 "Characteristics of Moral Dilemmas Written by Adolescents." *Developmental Psychology* 13:162–163.

THOMAS J. FIGURSKI

MORTALITY

See Birth and Death Rates; Infant and Child Mortality; Life Expectancy.

MULTICULTURALISM

See Ethnicity; Indigenous Peoples; Race.

MULTINATIONAL CORPORATIONS

See Corporate Organizations; Transnational Corporations.

MULTIPLE INDICATOR MODELS

A primary goal of sociology (and science in general) is to provide accurate estimates of the causal relationship between concepts of central interest to the discipline. Thus, for example, sociologists might examine the causal link between the amount of money people make and how satisfied they are with their lives in general. But in assessing the causal relationships between concepts—such as income and life satisfaction—researchers are subject to making errors stemming from a multitude of sources. In this article, we will focus on one common and especially large source of errors in making causal inferences in sociology and other social and behavioral sciences—specifically, "measurement errors." Such errors will produce biased (under- or over-) estimates of the true causal relationship between concepts.

Multiple indicator models are a method of testing and correcting for errors made in measuring a concept or "latent construct." Multiple indicators consist of two or more "alternative" measures of the same concept (e.g., two different ways of asking how satisfied you are with your life). Before examining models that use multiple indicators to assess and correct for measurement error, however, the reader should become familiar with the terms and logic underlying such models. "Latent constructs" (also described as a "latent variables") are unobservable phenomena (e.g., internal states such as the amount of "satisfaction" a person experiences) or more concrete concepts (e.g., income) that represent the hypothetical "true" or "actual" score persons would provide if we could measure a given concept without any error (e.g., a person's actual income or actual satisfaction, as opposed to their reported income or reported satisfaction).

Additionally, an "indicator" is simply another name for the empirical measure ("observed" score)

of a given construct. For instance, researchers might measure income through a single "indicator" on a questionnaire that asks people "How much money do your earn per year?"—with the response options being, say, five possible income levels ranging from "income greater than $200,000 per year" (coded as "5") to "income less than $10,000 per year" (coded as "1"). Similarly, researchers might provide a single indicator for life satisfaction by asking persons to respond to the statement "I am satisfied with my life." The response options here might be: "strongly agree" (coded as "5"), "agree" (coded as "4"), "neither agree nor disagree" (coded as "3"), "disagree" (coded as "2"), and "strongly disagree" (coded as "1").

Social scientists might expect to find a positive association between the above measures of income and life satisfaction. In fact, a review of empirical studies suggests a correlation coefficient ranging from .1 to .3 (Larson 1978; Haring et al. 1984). Correlation coefficients can have values between 1.0 and -1.0, with 0 indicating no association, and 1.0 or -1.0 indicating a perfect relationship. Thus, for example, a correlation of 1.0 for income and life satisfaction would imply that we can perfectly predict a person's life satisfaction score by knowing that person's income. In other words, individuals with the highest income (i.e., scored as a "5") consistently have the highest life satisfaction (i.e., scored as a "5"); those with the next-highest income (i.e., "4") consistently have the next-highest life satisfaction (i.e., "4"), and so on. Conversely, a -1.0 suggests the opposite relationship. That is, people with the highest income consistently have the lowest life satisfaction; those with the second-highest income consistently have the second-lowest life satisfaction, and so on.

Furthermore, a correlation coefficient of .2, as possibly found, say, between income and life satisfaction, suggests a relatively weak association. A coefficient of this size would indicate that individuals with higher incomes only *tend* to have higher life satisfaction. Hence, we should expect to find many exceptions to this "average" pattern. (More technically, one can square a correlation coefficient to obtain the amount of variance that one variable explains in another. Accordingly, squaring the $r = .2$ correlation between income and life satisfaction produces an r^2 of .04—i.e., income explains 4 percent of the variance in life satisfaction.) In sum, given a correlation of .2, we can predict life satisfaction better by knowing someone's income than if we did not have this information (we reduce our errors by 4 percent) but we will still make a lot of errors in our prediction (96 percent of the variance in life satisfaction remains unexplained).

These errors in prediction stem in part from less-than-perfect measures of income and life satisfaction analyzed (a topic covered in the next section). However, they also occur because there are many other causes of life satisfaction (e.g., physical health) in addition to income. The more of these additional causes there are, and the stronger their effects (i.e., the stronger their correlation with life satisfaction), the weaker the ability of a single construct such as income to predict life satisfaction. The same principles apply, of course, to any construct used to predict other constructs (e.g., using people's level of stress to predict the amount of aggression they will display).

Correlation coefficients and "path coefficients" are part of the "language" of causal modeling, including multiple indicator models. Like a correlation coefficient, a path coefficient describes the strength of the relationship between two variables. One can interpret a (standardized) path coefficient in a manner roughly similar to a correlation coefficient. Readers will increase their understanding of the material to follow if they familiarize themselves with these measures of strength of association. (For more information on interpreting correlation and path coefficients, see Blalock [1979]; Kline [1998].)

RELIABILITY AND VALIDITY OF MEASURES

As noted earlier, measurement errors can bias estimates of the true causal associations between constructs of interest to sociologists and other researchers. Accordingly, it is important to use measures of high quality. Specialists in the field of measurement (often labeled "psychometricans") describe high-quality measures as having strong *reliability* and *validity* (Nunnally and Bernstein 1994). Reliability concerns the consistency with

which an indicator measures a given construct; validity assesses whether one is measuring what one intends to measure or something else.

Reliability A common method of assessing reliability is to determine the strength of the correlation (consistency) between alternative (multiple) indicators of the same construct—for example, the correlation between two different measures of life satisfaction. A correlation of 1.0 would suggest that both indicators are perfectly reliable measures of life satisfaction. Conversely, a correlation of, say, .3 would suggest that the two indicators are not very reliable measures of life satisfaction.

Given the subjective nature of indicators of life satisfaction (and many other constructs found in the social and behavioral sciences), we should not be surprised to find fairly low correlations (consistency) among their many possible multiple indicators. The ambiguity inherent in agreeing or disagreeing with statements like "I am satisfied with my life," "The conditions of my life are excellent," and "In most ways my life is close to my ideal" should introduce considerable measurement error. Furthermore, we might anticipate that much of this measurement error would be *random*. That is, relative to respondents' actual ("true") scores for life satisfaction, they would provide answers (observed scores) to the subjective questions regarding life satisfaction that are likely to be nonsystematic. For example, depending on the degree of ambiguity in the multiple indicators for subjective construct like life satisfaction, a person is likely to display a random pattern of giving too high and too low scores relative to the person's true score across the set of measures.

This "noise"—unreliability due to random measurement error—will reduce the correlation of a given indicator with another indicator of the same construct. Indeed, "pure" noise (e.g., completely random responses to questions concerning respondents' life satisfaction) should not correlate with anything (i.e., $r = 0$). To the extent that researchers can reduce random noise in the indicators (e.g., by attempting to create as clearly worded self-report measures of a construct as possible) the reliability and corresponding correlations among multiple indicators should increase. Even where researchers are careful however, to select the best available indicators of constructs that represent subjective states (like life satisfaction), correlations between indicators frequently do not exceed r's of .3 to .5.

Not only does less-than-perfect reliability reduce correlations among multiple indicators of a given construct, but, more importantly, this random measurement error also reduces the degree to which indicators for one latent construct correlate with the indicators for another latent construct. That is, unreliable measures (such as each of the multiple indicators of life satisfaction) will *underestimate* the true causal linkages between constructs of interest (e.g., the effect of income on life satisfaction). These biased estimates can, of course, have adverse consequences for advancing our scientific knowledge (e.g., perceiving income as a less important source of life satisfaction than it might actually be). (Although unreliable measures will always underestimate the true relationship between two constructs, the bias of unreliable measures is more complex in "multivariate" situations where important control variables may exhibit as much unreliability as [or more unreliability than] do the predictor and outcome variables of interest.)

Psychometricians have long been aware of this problem of "attenuated correlations" from unreliable measures. In response, traditional practice is to combine each of the multiple indicators for a given construct into a single *composite* scale (e.g., sum a person's score across each life satisfaction indicator). The random errors contained in each individual indicator tend to "cancel each other out" in the composite scale (cf. Nunnally and Bernstein 1994), and the overall reliability (typically measured with Cronbach's alpha) on scale ranging from 0 to 1.0 can improve substantially relative to the reliability of individual items within the scale. Although composite scales are a definite step in the right direction, they are still less than perfectly reliable, and often much less. Consequently, researchers are still faced with the problem of biased estimates of the causal linkages among constructs of interest.

Validity. Unreliable indicators are not the only source of measurement error that can bias estimates of causal linkages among constructs. Invalid indicators can also create biased estimates. As we shall see in subsequent sections, bias from invalid measures stems from different sources and is more complex and difficult to detect and control than bias from unreliable measures.

Valid measures require at least modest reliability (i.e., correlations among indicators of a given construct cannot be $r = 0$); but reliable measures are not necessarily valid measures. One can have multiple indicators that are moderately to highly reliable (e.g., r's = .5 to .8), but they may not measure the construct they are supposed to measure (i.e., may not be valid). For example, life satisfaction indicators may display at least moderate reliability, but no one would claim that they are valid measures of, say, a person's physical health.

This example helps clarify some differences between reliability and validity, but at the risk of obscuring the difficulty that researchers typically encounter in establishing valid measures of many latent constructs. Continuing with our example, researchers may select multiple indicators of life satisfaction that critics could never plausibly argue actually measure physical health: Critics might make a very plausible argument, however, that some or all the indicators of life satisfaction also measure a more closely related concept—such as "optimism."

Note, too, that if the life satisfaction indicators do, in fact, also measure optimism, then the correlation that income has with the life satisfaction indicators could stem entirely from income's causal links with an optimistic personality, rather than from income's effect on life satisfaction itself. In other words, in this hypothetical situation, invalid ("contaminated") measures of life satisfaction could lead to *over*estimating income's effect on life satisfaction (though, as we will see in later sections, one can construct examples where invalid measures of life satisfaction could also lead to *under*estimating income's effect).

Given the many subjective, loosely defined constructs that form the core concepts of sociology and other social and behavioral sciences, the issue of what the indicators are actually measuring (i.e., their validity) is a common and often serious problem. Clearly, our scientific knowledge is not advanced where researchers claim a relationship between constructs using invalid measures of one or more of the constructs.

The sections, below, on single-indicator and multiple-indicator models will elaborate on the bias introduced by measurement error stemming from unreliability and invalidity, and how to use the multiple indicators and "path analysis" of structural equation modeling (SEM) to test and correct for the bias. This discussion continues to use the example of estimating the effect of income on life satisfaction in the face of measurement error.

SINGLE-INDICATOR MODELS

Figure 1 depicts the hypothesized causal link (solid arrow labeled "x") between the latent (unobservable) constructs of income and life satisfaction (represented with circles), and the hypothesized causal link (solid arrows labeled "a" and "b") between each latent construct (circle) and its respective empirical (observed) indicator (box). The D (disturbances) in Figure 1 represents all potential causes of life satisfaction that the researcher has not included in the causal model (stressful life events, personality characteristics, family relationships, etc.). The E's in Figure 1 represent random measurement error (and any unspecified latent constructs that have a "unique" effect on a given indicator).

Because each latent construct (circled "I" and "LS") in Figure 1 has only one indicator (boxed "I_1" or "LS_1") to measure the respective construct, researchers describe the diagram as a causal model with *single* (as opposed to multiple) indicators. Additionally, Figure 1 displays a dashed, double-headed arrow (labeled "r_1") between the box for income and the box for life satisfaction. This dashed, double-headed arrow represents the empirical or *observed* correlation between the empirical indicators of income and life satisfaction. Following the logic diagramed in Figure 1, this observed correlation is the product of actual income affecting both measured income through path a, and actual life satisfaction through path x. In turn, actual life satisfaction affects measured life satisfaction via path b. Stated in more formal "path equations," $a*x*b = r_1$.

Note, that researchers can never directly observe the *true* causal effect (i.e., path x) of actual income (I) on actual life satisfaction (LS). Researchers can only *infer* such a relationship based on the *observed* correlation (r_1) between the empirical indicators for income and life satisfaction— I_1 and LS_1. In other words, social scientists use an observed correlation—r_1—to estimate an unobservable true causal effect—path x.

Notice also that in the presence of random measurement error, the observed correlation r_1 will always be an *under*estimate of the unobservable path x representing the hypothesized true effect of income on life satisfaction. Of course, researchers hope that r_1 will equal path x. But r_1 will only equal x if our empirical measures of income and life satisfaction (I_1 and LS_1) are *perfectly reliable*—that is, have no random measurement error.

The phrase "completely reliable measures" implies that each person's observed score for income and life satisfaction indicators reflect exactly that person's actual or "true score" for income and life satisfaction. If the indicators for income and life satisfaction are indeed perfect measures, then researchers can attach a (standardized) path coefficient of 1.0 to each path (i.e, a and b) between the latent constructs and their indicator. Likewise, researchers can attach a path coefficient of 0 to each path (i.e., d and e) representing the effects of random measurement errors (E_1 and E_2) on the respective indicators for income and life satisfaction.

The path coefficient of 1.0 for a and b signifies a perfect relationship between the latent construct (i.e., true score) and the measure or indicator for the latent construct (i.e., recorded score). In other words, there is no "slippage" between the actual amount of income or life satisfaction people have and the amount of income or life satisfaction that a researcher records for each person (i.e., there is no random measurement error). Therefore, people who truly have the highest income will report the most income, those who truly have the lowest income will report the lowest income, and so on. Likewise, people who, in fact, have the most life satisfaction will always record a life satisfaction score (e.g., "5") higher than those a little less satisfied (e.g., "4"), individuals a little less satisfied will always record a life satisfaction score higher than those a little bit less satisfied yet (e.g., "3"); and so on.

Under the assumption that the measures of income and life satisfaction are perfectly reliable, social scientists can use the *observed* correlation (r_1) between the indicators I_1 and LS_1 to estimate the *true* causal effect (path x) of actual income (I) on actual life satisfaction (LS). Specifically, $r_1 = a*x*b$;

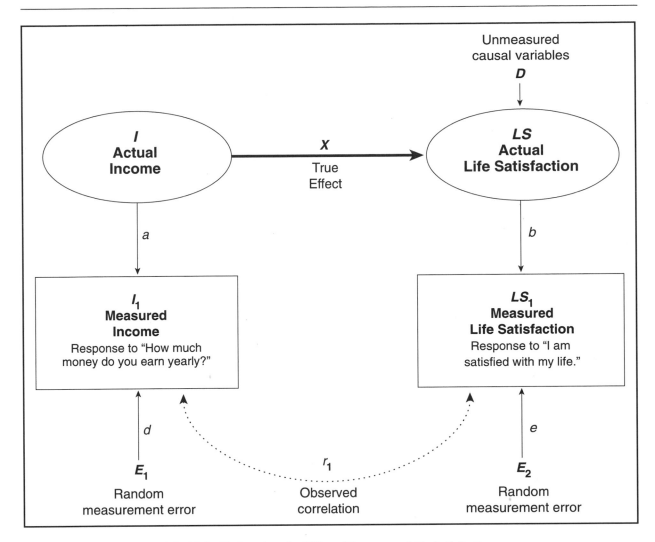

Figure 1. Single-Indicator Model for Estimating the Effect of Income on Life Satisfaction.

hence, $r_1 = 1.0 \times x \times 1.0$, or $r_1 = x$. Thus, if the observed correlation between income and life satisfaction (i.e., r_1) is, say, .2, then the true (unobservable) causal effect of income on life satisfaction (i.e., path x) would also be .2. (For more detailed explanations of how to interpret and calculate path coefficients, see Sullivan and Feldman [1979]; Loehlin [1998].)

Of course, even if researchers were to measure income and life satisfaction with perfect reliability (i.e., paths a and b each equal 1.0), there are other possible errors ("misspecifications") in the model shown in Figure 1 that could bias researchers' estimates of how strong an effect income truly has on life satisfaction. That is, Figure 1 does not

depict other possible "misspecifications" in the model such as "reverse causal order" (e.g., amount of life satisfaction determines a person's income) or "spuriousness" (e.g., education determines both income and life satisfaction and hence only makes it appear that income causes life satisfaction). (For more details on these additional sources of potential misspecification, see also Blalock [1979].)

How realistic is the assumption of perfect measurement in single indicator causal models? The answer is, "It depends." For example, to assume a path coefficient of 1.0 for path a in Figure 1 would not be too unrealistic (the actual coefficient is likely a little less than 1.0—say, .90 or .95). That is, we would not expect many errors in measuring a person's true income. Likewise, we would expect few measurement errors in recording, say, a person's age, sex, or race. As noted earlier, the measurement of subjective states (including satisfaction with life) is likely to occur with considerable error. Therefore, researchers would likely *under*estimate the true causal link between income and life satisfaction, if they assumed no random measurement error for the life satisfaction indicator—that is, if they assumed a coefficient of 1.0 for path b in Figure 1.

How badly researchers underestimate the true causal effect (i.e., path x) would depend, of course, on how much less than 1.0 was the value for path b. For the sake of illustration, assume that path b equals .5. Assume also that income is perfectly measured (i.e., path a = 1.0) and the observed correlation (r_1) between the indicators for income and life satisfaction is .2. Under these conditions, $1.0*x*.5 = .2$, and $x = .4$. In other words, researchers who report the observed correlation between income and life satisfaction ($r_1 = .2$) would substantially *under*estimate the strength of the true effect ($x = .4$) that income has on life satisfaction. Recall that an r of .2 represents an r^2 of .04, or 4 percent of the variance in life satisfaction explained by income, whereas an r of .4 represents an r^2 of .16, or 16 percent of the variance explained by income. Accounting for 16 percent of the variance in life satisfaction represents a much stronger effect for income than does 4 percent explained variance. Based on this hypothetical example, income goes from a weak to a relatively strong predictor of life satisfaction, if we have the appropriate information to allow us to correct for the bias of the unreliable measure of life satisfaction.

But how do researchers know what values to assign to the unobservable paths (such as a and b in Figure 1) linking a given latent construct to its single indicator? Unless logic, theory, or prior empirical evidence suggests that the constructs in a given model are measured with little error (i.e., the path between the circle and the box = 1.0) or indicate what might be an appropriate value less than 1.0 to assign for the path between the circle and box, researchers must turn from *single* indicator models to *multiple* indicator models. As noted earlier, multiple indicator models allow one to make corrections for measurement errors that would otherwise bias estimates of the causal relationships between constructs.

MULTIPLE INDICATOR MODELS

For researchers to claim that they are using multiple indicator models, at least one of the concepts in a causal model must have more than one indicator. "Multiple indicators" means simply that a causal model contains alternative measures of the same thing (same latent construct). Figure 2 depicts a multiple indicator model in which income still has a single indicator but life satisfaction now has three indicators (i.e., three alternative measures of the same life satisfaction latent construct). In addition to the original indicator for life satisfaction—"I am satisfied with my life"—there are two new indicators; namely, "In most ways my life is close to my ideal" and "The conditions of my life are excellent." (Recall that the possible response categories range from "strongly agree" to "strongly disagree." See also Diener et. al. [1985] for a fuller description of this measurement scale.)

As in Figure 1, the dashed, double-headed arrows represent the *observed* correlations between each pair of indicators. Recall that these observed correlations stem from the assumed operation of the latent constructs inferred in the causal model. Specifically, an increase in actual income (I) should produce an increase in measured income (I_1) through (causal) path a. Moreover, an increase in actual income should also produce an increase in actual life satisfaction (LS) through (causal) path x, which in turn should produce an increase in each of the measures of life satisfaction (LS_1, LS_2, and LS_3) through (causal) paths b, c, and d. In other words, these hypothesized causal pathways should produce observed correlations between all possible pairs of the measured variables (I_1, LS_1, LS_2, and LS_3). (We are assuming here that the underlying measurement model is one in which the unobserved constructs have a causal effect on their respective indicators. There are some types of multiple indicators, however, where a more plausible measurement model would suggest the reverse causal order—i.e., that the multiple indicators each drive the latent construct common to the set of indicators. See, Kline [1998] for a discussion of these "cause" indicator measurement models, as opposed to the more traditional "effect" indicator measurement model described here.)

The use of a single indicator for income means that researchers must use logic, theory, or prior

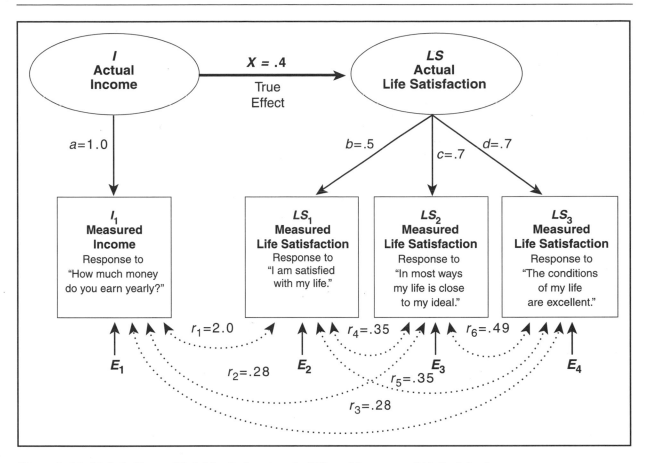

Figure 2. Multiple-Indicator Model for Estimating the Effect of Income on Life Satisfaction.

empirical evidence to assign a path coefficient to represent "slippage" between the true score (I) and the measured score (I_1). For income, path a = 1.0 (i.e., no random measurement error) seems like a reasonable estimate, and makes it easier to illustrate the path equations. (Although a coefficient of say, .95, might be more realistic, whether we use 1.0 or .95 will make little difference in the calculations that follow.) As noted earlier, however, indicators of life satisfaction are not as easily assigned path coefficients of 1.0. That is, there is likely to be considerable random error (unreliability) in measuring a subjective state such as life satisfaction. Fortunately, however, the use of *multiple indicators* for the life satisfaction construct permits researchers to provide reasonable estimates of random measurement error based on the *empirical data in the current study*—namely, the observed correlations (i.e., consistency) among the multiple indicators. Because measurement error can vary so much from one research setting to

another, it is always preferable to provide estimates of reliability based on the current rather than previous empirical studies. Likewise, reliability estimates based on the current study are much better than those estimates obtained from logic or theory, unless the latter sources can provide a compelling case for a highly reliable single indicator (such as the measure of income used in the present example).

If the multiple indicator model in Figure 2 is correctly specified, then the observed correlations among the several pairs of indicators should provide researchers with information to calculate estimates for the hypothesized (unobservable) causal paths b, c, and d (i.e., estimates of how much "slippage" there is between actual life satisfaction and each measure of life satisfaction). Researchers can use hand calculations involving simple algebra to estimate the causal paths for such simple multiple indicator models as depicted in Figure 2 (for examples, see Sullivan and Feldman 1979 and Loehlin 1998). But more complicated models are best left to "structural equation modeling" (SEM) computer software programs such as LISREL (Linear Structural Relationships; Joreskog and Sorbom 1993), EQS (Equations; Bentler 1995), or AMOS (Analysis of Moment Structures; Arbuckle 1997). Kline (1998) provides a particularly excellent and comprehensive introduction to the topic. There are two annotated bibliographies that represent almost all work related to SEM up to about 1996 (Austin and Wolfe 1991; Austin and Calderon 1996). Marcoulides and Schumacker (1996) and Schumacker and Marcoulides (1998) cover even more recent advances. Smallwaters software company has a Web site that gives a wealth of information, including other relevant Web sites: http://www.smallwaters.com/weblinks.

In essence, these SEM computer programs go through a series of trial-and-error "iterations" in which different values are substituted for the hypothesized causal paths—in Figure 2, paths b, c, d, and x. (Recall that we assigned a value of 1.0 for path a, so the SEM program does not have to estimate a value for this hypothesized path.) Ultimately, the program reaches ("converges on") a "final solution." This solution will *reproduce* as closely as possible the *observed correlations*—in Figure 2, r_1, r_2, r_3, r_4, r_5, and r_6—among each of the indicators in the proposed causal model. In the *final solution* depicted in Figure 2, the path estimates for b, c, d, and x (when combined with the "assigned" or "fixed" value for path a) exactly reproduce the observed correlations. (Note that the *final* solution will reproduce the observed correlations better than will the *initial* solutions, unless, of course, the SEM program finds the best solution on its first attempt-which is not likely in most "real-world" data analyses.)

More technically, the SEM program builds a series of (simultaneous) equations that represent the various hypothesized causal paths that determine each observed correlation. In Figure 2, the correlation (r_1 = .20) for I_1 and LS_1 involves the "path" equation: $a*x*b$ = .20; for the correlation (r_2 = .28) of I_1 and LS_2: $a*x*c$ = .28; for the correlation (r_3 = .28) of I_1 and LS_3: $a*x*d$ = .28; for the correlation (r_4 = .35) of LS_1 and LS_2: $b*c$ = .35; for the correlation (r_5 = .35) of LS_1 and LS_3: $b*d$ = .35; and for the correlation (r_6 = .49) of LS_2 and LS_3: $c*d$ =

.49. The SEM program then uses the *known* values—observed correlations and, in the causal model for Figure 2, the fixed (predetermined) value of 1.0 for path a—to simultaneously solve the set of equations to obtain a value for each of the causal paths that initially have *unknown* values.

Except in artificial examples (like Figure 2), however, the SEM program is unlikely to obtain final values for the causal paths such that the path equations exactly reproduce the observed correlations. More specifically, the program will attempt through its iterative trial-and-error procedures to find a final value for each of the causal paths b, c, d, and x that will *minimize* the "average discrepancy" across each of the six model-*implied* correlations (i.e., predicted by the path equations) versus the six empirically *observed* correlations.

For example, to reproduce the observed correlation (r_4 = .35) between LS_1 and LS_2 (recall that empirical correlations among indicators of subjective states like life satisfaction often range between .3 and .5), the SEM program would have to start with values for causal paths b and c (i.e., estimates of "slippage" between actual life satisfaction and measured life satisfaction) considerably lower than 1.0. In other words, the software program would need to allow for some random measurement error. If, instead, the initial solution of the SEM program assumed perfect reliability, there would be a substantial discrepancy between at least some of the implied versus observed correlations among the indicators. That is, multiplying the path b = 1.0 by the path c = 1.0 (i.e., assuming perfect reliability of each indicator) would imply an observed correlation of 1.0 (i.e., perfect consistency) between LS_1 and LS_2—an implied (i.e., predicted) correlation that far exceeds the r_4 = .35 correlation we actually observe. (Keep in mind that, as depicted in Figure 2, the *best values* for b and c are .5 and .7, respectively, which the SEM program will eventually converge on as it "iterates" to a final solution).

If, at the next iteration, the SEM program were to substitute equal values for b and c of about .59 each (to allow for less than perfect reliability), this solution would exactly reproduce the observed correlation of .35 (i.e., .59*.59 = .35) between LS_1 and LS_2. But using a value of .59 for both b and c would *not* allow the program to reproduce the observed correlations for LS_1 and LS_2 with I_1 (the indicator for income). To obtain the observed correlation of .20 between I_1 and LS_1, the program needs to multiply the paths $a*x*b$. Accordingly, r_1 (.20) should equal $a*x*b$—that is, $1.0*x*.59 = .20$. Solving for x, the program would obtain a path value of about .35. Likewise, to obtain the observed correlation of .28 between I_1 and LS_2, the program needs to multiply the paths $a*x*b$. Accordingly, r_2 (.28) must equal $a*x*c$—that is, $1.0*x*.59 = .28$. Solving for x, the program would obtain a path value of about .47. In other words, the program cannot find a solution for the preceding two equations that uses the *same value* for x. That is, for the first equation $x \simeq .35$. But for the second equation $x \simeq .47$.

Given the SEM program's need to come up with a *unique* (i.e., single) value for x (and for all the other causal paths the program must estimate), a possible compromise might be to use a value of .41. Substituting this value into the preceding two equations—$a*x*b$ and $a*x*c$—would provide an *implied* correlations of about .24—$1.0*.41*.59$ . .24—for both equations. Comparing this implied correlation with the *observed* correlations of .20 and .28 for I_1/LS_1 and I_1/LS_2, respectively, the discrepancy in these two situations is $+/- .04$.

Although this is not a large discrepancy between the implied and the observed correlations, the SEM program can do better (at least in this hypothetical example). If the SEM program subsequently estimates values of .50 and .70 for causal paths b and c, respectively, then it is possible to use the same value of x (specifically, .40) for each path equation involving I_1/LS_1 and I_1/LS_2, and reproduce exactly the observed correlations for r_1 (i.e., $1.0*.40*.50 = .20$) and r_2 (i.e., $1.0*.40*.70 = .28$). By using these estimated values of .5 and .7 for paths b and c in place of the .6 and .6 values initially estimated, the program can also reproduce exactly the observed correlation ($r_4 = .35$) between LS_1 and LS_2—that is, $.5*.7 = .35$. Furthermore, by using an estimated value of .7 for causal path d, the program can exactly reproduce *all* the remaining observed correlations in Figure 2—$r_3 = .28$, $r_5 = .35$, and $r_6 = .49$—that involve path d, that is, $a*x*d$, $b*d$, and $c*d$, respectively. (We leave to the reader the task of solving the equations.)

In sum, by using the fixed (a priori) value of $a = 1.0$ and the estimated values of $x = .4$, $b = .5$, $c = .7$, and $d = .7$, the six implied correlations exactly match the six observed correlations depicted in Figure 2. In other words, the hypothesized causal paths in our model provide a "perfect fit" to the "data" (empirical correlations).

Reproducing the observed correlations among indicators does not, however, establish that the proposed model is correct. In the logic of hypothesis testing, one can only disconfirm models, not prove them. Indeed, there is generally a large number of alternative models, often with entirely different causal structures, that would reproduce the observable correlations just as well as the original model specified (see Kim and Mueller 1978 for examples). It should be apparent, therefore, that social scientists must provide rigorous logic and theory in building multiple indicator models, that is, in providing support for one model among a wide variety of possible models. In other words, multiple indicator procedures require that researchers think very carefully about how measures are linked to latent constructs, and how latent constructs are linked to other latent constructs.

Additionally, it is highly desirable that a model contain more observable correlations among indicators than unobservable causal paths to be estimated—that is, the model should be "overidentified." For example, Figure 2 has *six* observed correlations (r_1, r_2, r_3, r_4, r_5, and r_6) but only *four* hypothesized causal paths (x, b, c, and d) to estimate. Thus, Figure 2 is overidentified—with *two* "degrees of freedom" (df) By having an excess of observed correlations versus hypothesized causal paths (i.e., by having at least one and preferably many degrees of freedom), a researcher can provide tests of "model fit" to assess the probability that there exist alternative causal paths not specified in the original model. (Where the fit between the implied vs. observed correlations is poor, researchers typically seek to revise their causal model to better fit the data.)

Conversely, "just-identified" models will contain exactly as many observable correlations as hypothesized causal paths to be estimated (i.e., will have 0 degrees of freedom). Such models will *always* produce estimates (solutions) for the causal paths that *exactly* reproduce the observable correlations—no matter how badly misspecified the proposed causal pathways may be. In other words, "perfect" fit is inevitable and provides no useful information regarding whether the model is correctly specified or not. This result occurs because, unlike an overidentified model, a just-identified model does not have any degrees of freedom with which to detect alternative causal pathways to those specified in the original model. Accordingly, just-identified models are not very interesting to SEM practitioners.

Finally, the worst possible model is one that is "underidentified," that is, has fewer observable correlations than unobservable causal paths to be estimated. Such models can provide no single (unique) solutions for the unobservable paths. In other words, an infinite variety of alternative estimates for the causal paths is possible. For example, if we restricted Figure 2 to include only LS_1 and LS_2 (i.e., dropping LS_3 and I_1), the resulting two-indicator model of life satisfaction would be underidentified. That is, we would have *two* causal paths to estimate—from the latent construct to each of the two indicators (i.e., paths b and c)—but only *one* observed correlation ($r_4 = .35$). Under this situation, there is no *unique* solution. We can literally substitute an infinite set of values for paths b and c to exactly reproduce the observed correlation (e.g., given $b*c = .35$, we can use $.7*.5$ or $.5*.7$, or two values slightly less than .6 each, and so on).

The number of indicators per latent construct helps determine whether a model will be overidentified or not. In general, one should have at least three and preferably four or more indicators per latent construct—unless one can assume a single indicator, such as income in Figure 2, has little measurement error. Adding more indicators for a latent construct rapidly increases the "overidentifying" pieces of empirical information (i.e., degrees of freedom). That is to say, observable correlations (between indicators) grow faster than the unobservable causal paths (between a given latent construct and indicator) to be estimated.

For example, adding a fourth indicator for life satisfaction in Figure 2 would require estimating *one* additional causal path (linking the life satisfaction latent construct to the fourth indicator), but would also produce *four* more observed correlations (LS_4 with LS_3, LS_2, LS_1, and I_1). The modified model would thus have *three* more degrees of freedom, and correspondingly greater *power* to

determine how well the model fits the empirical data (observed correlations). Including a fifth indicator for life satisfaction would produce *four* more degrees of freedom, and even more power to detect a misspecified model. (The issue of model identification is more complicated than outlined here. The requirement that an identified model have at least as many observed correlations as causal paths to be estimated is a necessary but not sufficient condition; cf. Kline [1998].)

Some additional points regarding multiple indicator models require clarification. For instance, in "real life" a researcher would never encounter such a perfect reproduction of the (noncausal) observable correlations from the unobservable (causal) paths as Figure 2 depicts. (We are assuming here that the causal model tested in "real life," like that model tested in Figure 2, is "overidentified." Recall that a "just-identified" model always exactly reproduces the observed correlations.) Indeed, even if the researcher's model is correctly specified, the researcher should expect at least *some* minor discrepancies in comparing the observed correlations among indicators with the correlations among indicators predicted (implied) by the hypothesized causal paths.

Researchers can dismiss as "sampling error" (i.e., "chance") any discrepancies that are not too large (given a specific sample size). At some point, however, the discrepancies do become too large to dismiss as "chance." At that point, researchers may determine that they have not specified a proper model. Poor model fit is strong grounds for reevaluating and respecifying the original causal model—typically by adding and (less often) subtracting causal paths to obtain a better fitting model. Just because an overidentified model can detect that a model is misspecified does not mean, however, that it is easy to then tell where the misspecification is occurring. Finding and correcting misspecification is a complex "art form" that we cannot describe here (but see Kline 1998 for an overview).

The next section will describe how nonrandom measurement error can create a misfitting multiple indicator model and corresponding bias in estimates of causal pathways. Additionally, we will demonstrate how a just-identified model, in contrast to an overidentified model, will fail to detect and thus correct for this misspecification, resulting in considerable bias in estimating the true effect of income on life satisfaction.

MULTIPLE-INDICATOR MODELS WITH NONRANDOM MEASUREMENT ERROR

We have discussed how poor quality measures—low reliability and low validity—can bias the estimates of the true effects of one latent construct on another. Our specific modeling examples (Figures 1 and 2), however, have focused on the bias introduced by unreliable measures only. That is, our causal diagrams have assumed that all measurement error is *random*. For example, Figure 2 depicts the error terms (*E*'s) for each of three multiple indicators of life satisfaction to be *unconnected*. Such random measurement error can occur for any number of reasons: ambiguous questions, coding errors, respondent fatigue, and so forth. But none of these sources of measurement error should *increase* correlations among the multiple indicators. Indeed, as noted in previous sections, random measurement error should *reduce* the correlations (consistency) among multiple indicators of a given latent construct—less-than-perfect correlations that researchers can then use to estimate reliability and thereby correct for the bias that would otherwise occur in underestimating the true effect of one latent construct on another (e.g., income on life satisfaction).

Conversely, where measurement error *increases* correlations among indicators, social scientists describe it as systematic or *nonrandom*. Under these conditions, the measurement errors of two or more indicators have a common source (a latent construct) other than or in addition to the concept that the indicators were suppose to measure. The focus now becomes the *validity* of measures. Are you measuring what you claim to measure or something else? (See the section above entitled "Reliability and Validity of Measures" for a more general discussion.)

Failure to include nonrandom—linked or "correlated"—errors in a multiple-indicator model will bias the estimates of other causal paths in the model. Figure 3 depicts such a linkage of error terms through the personality variable "optimism" (O). Based on the hypothetical model in Figure 3,

the observed correlation (r_6) between the indicators LS_2 and LS_3 would not be entirely the consequence of the effects of life satisfaction (*LS*) operating through the causal paths *c* and *d*. In fact, part of this observed correlation would occur as a consequence of the causal paths *e* and *f* (which in this hypothetical example, we have constrained to be equal). In other words, the indicators LS_2 and LS_3 measure some of life satisfaction but also optimism. That is, they measure something in addition to what they were intended to measure. Stated in still other words, the two indicators are not "pure" (completely valid) measures of life satisfaction because they are "contaminated" by also tapping optimism.

Note that r_6 is the only observed correlation that differs in strength in comparing Figures 2 and 3. For Figure 2, this correlation equals .49; for Figure 3, this correlation equals .85. The higher observed correlation for r_6 in Figure 3 stems from the "inflated" correlation produced by the effects of optimism through paths *e* (.6) and *f* (.6). Note, also, that .6*.6 equals .36. If we add .36 to the original observed correlation for r_6 (i.e., .49) in Figure 2, we obtain the observed correlation of .85 in Figure 3. All other paths estimates and observed correlation remain the same across the two figures. Furthermore, like Figure 2, Figure 3 depicts path estimates for a final solution that exactly reproduce all observed correlations.

Note, too, if we had not added the causal paths (*e* and *f*) to represent the hypothesized effect of optimism on two measures of life satisfaction, we could not obtain a "good fit" for the observed correlations in Figure 3. Indeed, *without* these additional paths, the SEM computer program would have to increase the path coefficients for *c* and *d*—say, to about .92 each—in order to reproduce the observed correlation of .85 for r_6. But then the program would fail to reproduce the observed correlations involving LS_2 and LS_3 with the other indicators in the model (LS_1 and I_1). For example, the observed correlation between I_1 and LS_2 (r_2 = .28) would now be *overestimated*, based on the product of the causal paths—*a**x*c—that the model in Figure 3 suggests determines r_2. That is, 1.0*.4*.92 results in an implied (predicted) correlation of about .37, which leaves a discrepancy of .09 relative to the correlation (.28) actually observed.

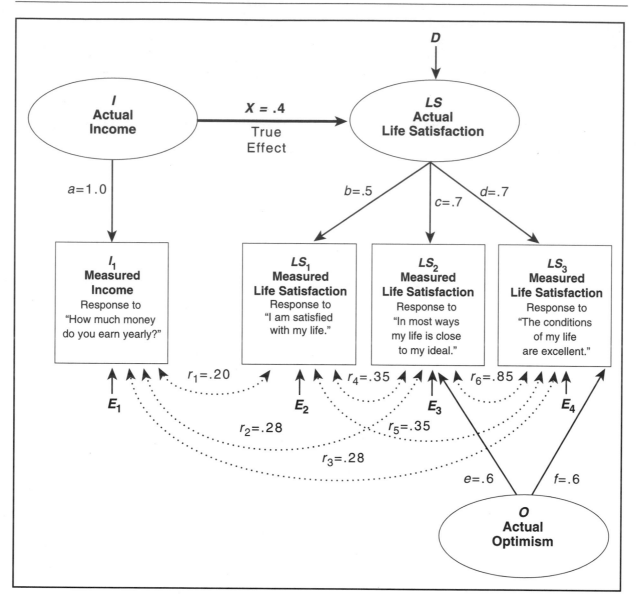

Figure 3. Multiple-Indicator Model for Estimating the Effect of Income on Life Satisfaction with Nonrandom Measurement Error for Optimism.

NOTE: *To obtain an overidentified model, paths k and l are "constrained" to have equal path coefficients.

In the absence of good fit—as a consequence of not allowing paths e and f to be included in the model to be tested (i.e., not specifying the "correct" model)—the SEM program might continue to "iterate" by substituting new estimates for c and the other causal paths in Figure 3—b, d, and x—which initially have unknown values. No matter what values are estimated for each of these causal paths, however, the program will not be able to eliminate a discrepancy between the implied and

the observed correlations for at least some of the pairs of indicators—a discrepancy that, as noted previously, the program will attempt to minimize based on the criterion of finding path estimates that result in the lowest average discrepancy summed across all possible comparisons of implied versus observed correlations in the model.

Indeed, a misspecification in one part of a model (in this instance, failure to model nonrandom measurement error in LS_1 and LS_2 indicators) generally "reverberates" throughout the causal model, as the SEM program attempts to make adjustments in all path coefficients to minimize the average discrepancy. In other words, estimates for each path coefficient are most often at least slightly biased by misspecified models (the greater the misspecification, the greater the bias). Most importantly, the failure to model (and thus correct for) nonrandom measurement error will typically result in the SEM program's estimating a value for the true effect of one construct on another—in the present example, the true effect (path x) of income on life satisfaction—that will be biased (either over- or underestimated). For example, when we use a SEM program (EQS) to calculate estimates for the hypothesized causal paths in Figure 3 (excluding the paths for the contamination of optimism), we obtain a final solution with the following estimates: $b= .38$, $c= .92$, $d= .92$, and $x = .31$. Thus, in the present example, the failure to model nonrandom measurement error has led to an underestimate ($x= .31$) of income's true effect ($x = .40$) on life satisfaction. Interestingly, by far the largest discrepancy in fit occurs between I_1 and LS_1 (the implied correlation is .08 less than the observed correlation), not between LS_2 and LS_3 (where there is 0 discrepancy)—demonstrating that misfit in one part of the model can produce misfit (reverberate) elsewhere in the model.

The hypothetical model depicted in Figure 3 is necessarily artificial (to provide simple illustrations of SEM principles). In real-life situations, it is unlikely (though still possible) that sources of contamination, when present, would impact only some of the multiple indicators for a given construct (e.g., only two of the three measures of life satisfaction). Furthermore, researchers would be on shaky ground if they were to actually claim that the correlated measurement error modeled in the present example stemmed from an identifiable source—such as optimism. (Indeed, to avoid specifically labeling the source of the inflated correlation between LS_1 and LS_2, researchers would most likely model a curved, double-headed arrow between E_3 and E_4 in Figure 3, and have the SEM program simply estimate the appropriate value—.36—for this new path representing correlated measurement error.) To make a legitimate claim that a construct like optimism contaminates a construct such as life satisfaction, researchers would also need to provide traditional measures of the suspected source of contamination (e.g., include established multiple indicators for optimism).

As a final example of the need to use *overidentified* multiple indicator models in order to detect misspecified models, consider a modification of Figure 3 in which we have access to the single indicator for income (I_1) but have only two indicators for life satisfaction available to us—LS_2 and LS_3. Assume, further, that we are unaware that optimism contaminates the two life satisfaction indicators. Note that this new model is *just identified*. That is, there are three observed correlations (r_2, r_3, and r_6) and three hypothesized causal paths to estimate (x, c, and d). Accordingly, this model will perfectly fit the data, despite the fact that we have not modeled (i.e., misspecified) the correlated measurement error (.36) that we've built into the .85 observed correlation (r_6) between LS_2 and LS_3.

More specifically, in order to reproduce the .85 correlation, the SEM program will increase the estimate of reliability for the LS_2 and LS_3 life satisfaction indicators by increasing the c and d paths from their original (true) value of .7 each to new (biased) values of about .92 each. To reproduce the observed correlation of .28 for both I_1/LS_2 and I_1/LS_3 (r_2 and r_3), the program can simply decrease the x path (i.e., the estimate of the true effect of income on life satisfaction) from its original (true) value of .40 to a new (biased) value of about .30—that is, for both path equations $a*x*c$ and $a*x*d$: $1.0*.3*.92 . .28$.

In sum, our just-identified model perfectly fits the data despite the fact our model has failed to include (i.e., has misspecified) the correlated measurement error created by optimism contaminating the two life satisfaction indicators. More importantly, the failure to model the nonrandom measurement error in these two indicators has led us to a biased underestimate of the true effect of income and life satisfaction: Income explains $.3^2 = 9\%$ of the variance in life satisfaction for the current (biased) model, but explains $.4^2 = 16\%$ variance in life satisfaction for the earlier (correctly specified) model.

As noted earlier, the debilitating effects of nonrandom measurement error are extremely diverse in their potential forms and correspondingly complex in their potential bias in under- or overestimating causal links among latent constructs. The present discussion only touches on the issues and possible multiple indicator models for detecting and correcting this type of measurement error. The reader is encouraged to consult other sources that provide additional details (starting with Kline 1998).

STRENGTHS AND WEAKNESSES OF MULTIPLE-INDICATOR MODELS USING SEM

As we have seen, by incorporating multiple indicators of constructs, structural equation modeling procedures allow more rigorous tests of causal models than possible when using single indicators. With sufficient multiple indicators to provide an overidentified model, SEM procedures are particularly powerful in detecting and correcting for the bias created by less than perfectly reliable and valid measures of latent constructs of interest. In other words, by building a more accurate *measurement model*—that is, providing a more correct specification of the causal linkages between latent constructs and their indicators—SEM researchers can obtain more accurate estimates of the causal linkages in the *structural model*—that is, the effect of one latent variable on another.

A correct specification of the measurement model is, then, a means to the ultimate goal of obtaining accurate path estimates (also described as "parameter estimates") for the structural model (e.g., obtaining the true effect of income on life satisfaction by correcting for measurement error). Some research, however, makes the measurement model the central focus (e.g., whether the three indicators of life satisfaction correlate with each other in a manner consistent with their measuring a single latent construct). In this situation, the SEM procedure is known as "confirmatory factor analysis" (CFA). The CFA uses the typical SEM principle of positing a measurement model in which latent constructs (now described as "factors") impact multiple indicators (the path coefficient now described as a "factor loading"). Unlike a "full-blown" SEM analysis, however, the CFA does not specify causal links among the latent constructs (factors), that is, does not specify a structural model (e.g., there is no interest in whether income affects life satisfaction). Instead, the CFA treats potential relationships among any two factors as simply a "correlation" (typically represented in diagrams with a curved, double-headed arrow between the factors); that is, the causal ordering among latent constructs is *not specified*.

Researchers have developed especially powerful CFA procedures for establishing the validity of measures through significant enhancements to traditional construct validity techniques based on multitrait/multimethods (MTMM), second-order factor structures, and testing the invariance of measurement models across diverse subsamples (again, see Kline 1998 for an introduction). CFA has also been at the vanguard in developing "nonlinear" factor analysis to help reduce the presence of "spurious" or "superfluous" latent constructs (referred to as "methods" or "difficulty" factors) that can occur as a consequence of using multiple indicators that are highly skewed (i.e., non-normally distributed) (Muthen 1993, 1998). These nonlinear factor analysis procedures also provide a bridge to recent advances in psychometric techniques based on item-response theory (cf. Reise et al. 1993; Waller et al. 1996).

CFA provides access to such powerful psychometric procedures as a consequence of its enormous flexibility in specifying the structure of a measurement model. But this strength is also its weakness. CFA requires that the researcher specify all aspects of the measurement model a priori. Accordingly, one must have considerable knowledge (based on logic, theory, or prior empirical evidence) of what the underlying structure of the measurement model is likely to be. In the absence of such knowledge, measurement models are likely to be badly misspecified. Although SEM has available particularly sophisticated techniques for detecting misspecification, simulation studies indicate that these techniques do not do well when the hypothesized model is at some distance from the true model (cf. Kline 1998).

Under these circumstances of less certainty about the underlying measurement model, researchers often use "exploratory factor analysis" (EFA). Unlike CFA, EFA requires no a priori specification of the measurement model (though it still works best if researchers have some idea of at least the likely number of factors that underlie the set of indicators submitted to the program). Individual indicators are free to "load on" any factor. Which indicators load on which factor is, essentially, a consequence of the EFA using the empirical correlations among the multiple indicators to seek out "clusters" of items that have the highest correlations with each other, and designating a factor to represent the underlying latent construct that is creating (is the "common cause" of) the correlations among items. Of course, designating these factors is easier said then done, given that the EFA can continue to extract additional factors, contingent on how stringent the standards are for what constitutes indicators that are "more" versus "less" correlated with each other. (For example, does a set of items with correlations of, say, .5 with each other constitute the same or a different "cluster" relative to other indicators that correlate .4 with the first cluster and .5 with each other? Extracting more factors will tend to separate these clusters into different factors; extracting fewer factors is more likely to combine the clusters into one factor.) The issue of the number of factors to extract is, then, a major dilemma in using EFA, with a number of criteria available, including the preferred method, where possible, of specifying a priori the number of factors to extract (cf. Floydand Widaman 1995).

A potential weakness with EFA is that it works best with relatively "simple" measurement models. EFA falters in situations where the reasons for the "clustering" of indicators (i.e., interitem correlations) stem from complex sources (see Bollen 1989 for an example). As an aspect of this inability to handle complex measurement models, EFA cannot match CFA in the sophistication of its tests for validity of measures. On the other hand, because CFA is more sensitive to even slight misspecifications, it is often more difficult to obtain satisfactory model "fit" with CFA.

Exploratory and confirmatory factor analysis can complement each other (but see Floyd and Widaman 1995 for caveats). Researchers may initially develop their measurement models based on EFA, then follow that analysis with CFA (preferably on a second random subsample, in order to avoid modeling "sampling error"). In this context, the EFA serves as a crude "first cut," which it is hoped, results in a measurement model that is close enough to the "true model" that a subsequent CFA can further refine the initial model,

using the more sophisticated procedures available with the confirmatory procedure.

Even though researchers use EFA and CFA to focus exclusively on *measurement models*, these psychometric studies are really a preamble to subsequent work in which the measures previously developed are now used to test causal linkages among constructs in *structural models*. Most of these subsequent tests of causal linkages among constructs (e.g., the effect of income on life satisfaction) use data analytic procedures, such as ordinary least squares (OLS) regression or analysis of variance (ANOVA) that assume no underlying latent structure. Accordingly, these traditional analyses of structural models work with measured (observable) variables only, can accommodate only a *single indicator* per construct of interest and, therefore, must assume (in essence) that each single indicator is perfectly reliable and valid. In other words, in the absence of a multiple indicators measurement model for each construct, there is no way to make adjustments for less-than-perfect reliability or validity.

In an attempt to enhance the reliability of the single-indicator measures that traditional data analyses procedures require, researchers often combine into a single *composite* scale the set of multiple indicators (e.g., the three indicators of life satisfaction) that prior EFA and CFA research has established as measuring a given latent construct (factor). Although, as noted earlier, a single-indicator composite scale (e.g., summing a respondent's score on each of the three life satisfaction indicators) is generally preferable to a noncomposite single indicator (at least when measuring more subjective and abstract phenomena), a composite scale is still less than perfectly reliable (often, much less). Accordingly, using such an enhanced (more reliable) measure will still result in biased parameter estimates in the structural model.

Validity also remains a concern. Even if prior psychometric work on measures has rigorously addressed validity (though this is often not the case), there is always a question of how valid the measure of a given construct is in the context of other constructs in the current structural model (e.g., what sort of "cross-contamination" of measures may be occurring among the constructs that might bias estimates of their causal linkages).

SEM remains a viable alternative to the more traditional and widely used data analysis procedures for assessing causal effects in structural models. Indeed, SEM is so flexible in specifying the structural, as well as measurement part of a causal model, that it can literally "mimic" most of the traditional, single indicator, data analysis procedures based on the general linear model (e.g., Analysis of Variance [ANOVA], Multivariate Analysis of Variance [MANOVA], Ordinary Least Squares [OLS] regression), as well as the newer developments in these statistical techniques (e.g., Hierarchical Linear Modeling [HLM]). SEM can even incorporate the single-indicator measurement models (i.e., based on observable variables only) that these other data analysis procedures use. The power to adjust for random and nonrandom measurement error (unreliability and invalidity) is realized, however, only if the SEM includes a multiple-indicator (latent variable) measurement model.

A multiple-indicator measurement model also provides SEM procedures with a particularly powerful tool for modeling (and thus adjusting for) correlated measurement errors that inevitably occur in analyses of *longitudinal* data (cf. Bollen 1989). Likewise, multiple-indicator models allow SEM programs to combine latent growth curves and multiple subgroups of cohorts in a "cohort-sequential" design through which researchers can examine potential cohort effects and developmental sequences over longer time frames than the period of data collection in the study. By also forming subgroups based on their pattern of attrition, (i.e., at what wave of data collection do respondents drop out of the study), SEM researchers can analyze the "extended" growth curves while adjusting for the potential bias from nonrandom missing data (Duncan and Duncan 1995)—a combination of important features that non-SEM methods cannot match. Furthermore, although SEM is rarely used with *experimental* research designs, multiple-indicator models provide exceptionally powerful methods of incorporating "manipulation checks" (i.e., whether the experimental treatment manipulates the independent variable that was intended) and various "experimental artifacts" (e.g., "demand characteristics") as alternative causal pathways to the outcome variable of interest (cf. Blalock 1985).

Although this article has focused on strengths of the SEM multiple indicator measurement model, the advantages of SEM extend beyond its ability to model random and nonrandom measurement error. Particularly noteworthy in this regard is SEM's power to assess both contemporaneous and lagged *reciprocal* effects using nonexperimental longitudinal data. Likewise, SEM has an especially elegant way of incorporating maximum likelihood full-information imputation procedures for handling missing data (e.g., Arbuckle 1996; Schafer and Olsen 1998), as an alternative to conventional listwise, pairwise, and mean substitution options. Simulation studies show that the full-information procedures for missing data, relative to standard methods, reduce both the bias and inefficiency that can otherwise occur in estimating factor loadings in measurement models and causal paths in structural models.

So given all the apparent advantages of SEM, why might researchers hesitate to use this technique? As noted earlier in discussing limitations of confirmatory factor analysis, SEM requires that a field of study be mature enough in its development so that researchers can build the a priori causal models that SEM demands as input. SEM also requires relatively large sample sizes to work properly. Although recommendations vary, a minimum sample size of 100 to 200 would appear necessary in order to have a reasonable chance of getting solutions that "converge" or that provide parameter (path) estimates that are not "out of range" (e.g., a negative variance estimate) or otherwise implausible. Experts often also suggest that the "power" to obtain stable parameter estimates (i.e. the ability to detect path coefficients that differ from zero) requires the ratio of subjects-to-parameters-estimated be between 5:1 and 20:1 (the minimum ratio increasing as variables become less normally distributed). In other words, more complex models demand even larger sample sizes.

Apart from the issue of needed a larger N to accommodate more complex causal models, there also is some agreement among SEM experts that models should be kept simpler in order to have a reasonable chance to get the models to fit well (cf., Floyd and Widaman 1995). In other words, SEM works better where the total number of empirical indicators in a model is not extremely large (say 30 or less). Accordingly, if researchers wish to test causal models with many predictors (latent constructs) or wish to model fewer constructs with many indicators per construct, SEM may not be the most viable option. Alternatively, one might consider "trimming" the proposed model of constructs and indicators through more "exploratory" SEM procedures of testing and respecifying models, possibly buttressed by preliminary model trimming runs with statistical techniques that can accommodate a larger number of predictors (e.g., OLS regression), and with the final model hopefully tested (confirmed) on a second random subsample. Combining pairs or larger "parcels" from a common set of multiple indicators is another option for reducing the number of total indicators, and has the added benefit of providing measures that have more normal distributions and fewer correlated errors from idiosyncratic "content overlap." (One needs to be careful, however, of eliminating too many indicators, given that MacCallum et al. [1996] have shown that the power to detect good-fitting models is substantially reduced as degrees of freedom decline.)

An additional limitation on using SEM has been the complex set of procedures (based on matrix algebra) one has had to go through to input the model to be tested—accompanied by output that was also less than user-friendly. Fortunately, newer versions of several SEM programs can now use causal diagrams for both input and output of the structural and measurement models. Indeed, these simple diagramming options threaten to surpass the user-friendliness of the more popular mainstream software packages (e.g., Statistical Package for the Social Sciences [SPSS]) that implement the more traditional statistical procedures. This statement is not meant to be sanguine, however, about the knowledge and experience required, and the care one must exercise, in using SEM packages. In this regard, Kline (1998) has a particularly excellent summary of "how to fool yourself with SEM." The reader is also encouraged to read Joreskog (1993) on how to use SEM to build more complex models from simpler models.

As the preceding discussion implies, using multiple-indicator models requires more thought and more complicated procedures than does using more common data analytic procedures. However, given the serious distortions that measurement errors can produce in estimating the true causal links among concepts, the extra effort in using multiple-indicator models can pay large dividends.

REFERENCES

Arbuckle, J. L. 1996 "Full Information Estimation in the Presence of Incomplete Data. In G. Marcoulides and R. Schumacker eds., *Advanced Structural Equation Modeling: Issues and Techniques.* Mahwah, N. J.: Lawrence Erlbaum.

—— 1997 *Amos User's Guide Version 3.6.* Chicago: SPSS.

Austin, J., and R. Calderon 1996 "Theoretical and Technical Contributions to Structural Equation Modeling: An Updated Annotated Bibliography." *Structural Equation Modeling* 3:105–175.

——, and L. Wolfe 1991 "Annotated Bibliography of Structural Equation Modeling: Technical Work." *British Journal of Mathematical and Statistical Psychology* 44:93–152.

Bentler, P.M. 1995. *EQS: Structural Equations Program Manual.* Encino, Calif.: Multivariate Software.

Blalock, H. M. 1979 *Social Statistics,* 2nd ed. New York: McGraw-Hill.

——, ed. 1985 *Causal Model in Panel and Experimental Designs.* New York: Aldine.

Bollen, K. A. 1989 *Structural Equations with Latent Variables.* New York: John Wiley.

Diener, E., R. A. Emmons, R. J. Larsen, and S. Griffin 1985 "The Satisfaction with Life Scale." *Journal of Personality Assessment* 49:71–75.

Duncan, T. E., and S. C. Duncan 1995 "Modeling the Processes of Development via Latent Variable Growth Curve Methodology." *Structural Equation Modeling* 2:187–213.

Floyd, F. J., and K. F. Widaman 1995 "Factor Analysis in the Development and Refinement of Clinical Assessment Instruments." *Psychological Assessment* 7:286–299.

Haring, M. J., W. A. Stock, and M. A. Okun 1984 "A Research Synthesis of Gender and Social Class as Correlates of Subjective Well-Being." *Human Relations* 37: 645–657.

Joreskog, K. G. 1993 "Testing Structural Equation Models." In K. A. Bollen and J. S. Long, eds., *Testing Structural Equation Models.* Thousand Oaks, Calif.: Sage.

——, and D. Sorbom 1993 *Lisrel 8: User's Reference Guide.* Chicago: Scientific Software.

Kim, J., and C. W. Mueller 1978 *Introduction to Factor Analysis: What It Is and How to Do It.* Beverly Hills, Calif.: Sage.

Kline, R. B. 1998 *Principles and Practice of Structural Equation Modeling.* New York: Guilford.

Larson, R. 1978 "Thirty Years of Research on the Subjective Well-Being of Older Americans. *Journal of Gerontology* 33:109–125.

Loehlin, J. C. 1998 *Latent Variable Models: An Introduction to Factor, Path, and Structural Analysis*, 3rd ed. Hillsdale, N.J.: Lawrence Erlbaum.

Marcoulides, G. A., and R. E. Schumacker, eds. 1996 *Advanced Structural Equation Modeling: Issues and Techniques*. Mahwah, N.J.: Lawrence Erlbaum.

Muthen, B. O. 1993 "Goodness of Fit with Categorical and Other Nonnormal Variables." In K. A. Bollen and J. S. Long, eds., *Testing Structural Equation Models*. Thousand Oaks, Calif.: Sage.

—— 1998 *Mplus User's Guide: The Comprehensive Modeling Program for Applied Researchers*. Los Angeles, Calif.: Muthen and Muthen.

Nunnally, J. C., and I. H. Bernstein 1994 *Psychometric Theory*, 3rd ed. New York: McGraw-Hill.

Randall, R. E., and G. A. Marcoulides (eds.) 1998 *Interaction and Nonlinear Effects in Structural Equation Modeling*. Mahwah, N. J.: Lawrence Erlbaum.

Reise, S. P., K. F. Widaman, and R. H. Pugh 1993 "Confirmatory Factor Analysis and Item Response Theory: Two Approaches for Exploring Measurement Invariance." *Psychological Bulletin* 114:552–566.

Schafer, J. L., and M. K. Olsen 1998 "Multiple Imputation for Multivariate Missing-Data Problems: A Data Analyst's Perspective." Unpublished manuscript, Pennsylvania State University. http://www.stat.psu.edu/~jls/index.html/#res.

Sullivan, J. L., and S. Feldman 1979 *Multiple Indicators: An Introduction*. Beverly Hills, Calif.: Sage.

Waller, N. G., A. Tellegen, R. P. McDonald, and D. T. Lykken 1996 "Exploring Nonlinear Models in Personality Assessment: Development and Preliminary Validation of a Negative Emotionality Scale." *Journal of Personality* 64:545–576.

KYLE KERCHER

MUSIC

From the earliest days of the discipline, music has been a focus of sociological inquiry. Max Weber, for example, used the development of the system of musical notation as a prime illustration of what he saw as the increasing rationalization of European society since the Middle Ages (Max Weber 1958). Like Weber, many since have used music

and music making as a strategic research site for answering sociologically important questions. Nevertheless, music has not become the focus of a distinctive fundamental approach in sociology comparable to topics like "socialization," "organization," "deviance," and "culture." That is why the subject of this entry is the "sociology of music" and not "musical sociology" and why it takes such a long bibliography to suggest the range of work in the field.

While no musical sociology has developed, over the decades numerous aspects of music making or appreciation have been the substantive research site for addressing central questions in sociology. Broadly, these can be grouped together as six ongoing research concerns, and together they can be said to constitute the scattered but rich sociology of music. These six focuses will be considered in turn.

MACROSOCIOLOGY

Many sociologists have been concerned with the relationship between society and culture. Talcott Parsons, among others, believed that there was a close fit between the two, so that it would be possible to compare societies and changes taking place in society by studying elements of their cultures including music. This is what led Max Weber (1958) to focus on music as an example of the rationalization of Western society and led another early sociologist, Georg Simmel ([1882] 1968), to see music as a mirror of socio-psychological processes. The most ambitious cross-national attempt to directly link the structure of society with musical expression has been that of Lomax (1968).

Contemporary scholars see the links between social structure and music not as natural but as deliberately constructed, and they focus on the circumstances of that process. For example, Cerulo (1999) has found an association between the circumstances of a nation's founding and its national anthem. Whisnant (1983) examined the politics of culture involved in constructing the idea of Appalachian folk culture, and Cloonan (1997) examines how "Englishness" is constructed in contemporary British pop music.

Another line of contemporary studies exploring the society-music link focuses on the globalization of music culture. The specific focuses and methods of these researchers vary widely, but together they show the resilience of local forms of musical expression in the context of the globalization of the media. See, for example, Wallis and Malm (1984), Nettl (1985, 1998), Hebdige (1987), Guilbault (1993), and Manuel (1993).

THE SOCIAL CONSTRUCTION OF AESTHETICS

In line with the constructivist orientation just mentioned, a number of scholars have examined the processes by which aesthetic standards are set and changed. The seminal works in this line are by Meyer (1956) and Becker (1982). Hennion (1993) studies the evolution of standards in the Paris music world. Monson (1996) carefully examines the conventions of jazz improvisation. Ellison (1995) shows the close interplay between country music artists and their fans in defining the country music experience, and Frith (1996) examines many of the same issues in the world of rock music.

Alternative kinds of aesthetic standards have been contrasted. The most widely compared are "fine art," "folk," and "popular" aesthetics (Gans 1974). Using the example of jazz, Peterson (1972) shows that music can evolve from folk to pop and then to fine art. Frith (1996) perceptively shows that all three standards are used simultaneously in the rock world and elsewhere.

THE STUDY OF MUSIC WORLDS

In his early studies of interaction among dance-hall musicians, Becker pioneered the study of the conventions that musicians use in making their kind of music together (summarized in Becker 1982). This line of activity has been continued in musical scenes varying from a group of coldly calculating recording session musicians (Peterson and White 1979; Faulkner 1983) to an impassioned gay community (DeChaine 1997). See also Zolberg (1980), Etzkorn (1982), Gilmore (1987), MacLeod (1993), Rose (1994), Monson (1996), Devereaux (1997), and Nettl (1998).

A related and often overlapping line of studies focuses on the socialization of performers. See, for example, Bennett (1980), Kingsbury (1988), Freeman (1996), DeChaine (1997), and Levine and Levine (1996). The socialization of audiences has also been the focus of considerable attention. The focus of inquiry has included popular music fans (Hebdige 1979, Frith 1981, 1996), the Viennese supporters of Ludwig van Beethoven (DeNora 1995), country music fans (Ellison 1995), and hip-hop fans (Rose 1995).

THE INSTITUTIONALIZATION OF MUSIC FIELDS

While the art-world perspective focuses on the interaction of individuals and groups in making and appreciating music, research on institutionalization has to do with the creation of the organizations and the infrastructure that support distinctive music fields. DiMaggio (1982), for example, shows the entrepreneurial processes by which the classical music field was established in the United States. Menger (1983) and Hennion (1993) show the structure of the contemporary art music fields of France. Peterson (1990) and Ennis (1992) trace the reconfiguration of the pop music field into rock in the 1940s and 1950s, and Peterson (1997) traces the institutionalization of the country music field and its articulation with the larger field of commercial music in the mid-1950s.

Based on the production of culture perspective, some researchers have shown how elements of the production process, including law, technology, industry structure, industrial organization, careers, and market structures, profoundly shape the sort of music that is produced. The interplay between these processes is traced by Peterson (1990) to show why rock music emerged in the mid-1950s. For other examples of work in the production of culture perspective, see Keil (1966), Ryan (1985), Lopes (1992), Jones (1992), Frith (1993), Manuel (1993), Freeman (1996), and Levine and Levine (1996).

A number of studies have traced the development of specific music organizations and organization fields. Ahlquist (1997) shows the structure of the early-nineteenth-century entrepreneurial opera world, and Martorella (1982) shows the remarkably different field of opera that emerged following the American Civil War. Arian (1971) and Hart (1975) focus on the classical music orchestra. Peterson and White (1979) and Faulkner (1983) discuss the organization of the apparently purely competitive world of recording studio session musicians. Gilmore (1987) focuses on three distinct contemporary classical music fields in New York City. MacLeod traces the field of club-date musicians in the same city. Guilbault (1993) shows the shaping of World Music in the West Indies. Negus (1999) compares the very different methods the major music industry corporations use in exploiting country music, rap, and reggae.

One specific line of studies focuses on the "concentration-diversity" hypothesis. Peterson and Berger (1975) show that periods of competition in the popular music field lead to a great diversity in the music that becomes popular, while concentration of the industry in a few firms leads to homogeneity in popular music. Using later data, Burnett (1990) challenges this finding, and Lopes (1992) shows how large multinational firms are able to control the industry while at the same time producing a wide array of musical styles.

MUSIC FOR MAKING DISTINCTIONS

All known societies employ music as a means of expressing identity and marking boundaries between groups (Lomax 1968), and a number of authors have shown the place of music in social class and status displays. DeNora (1995) shows the role that Beethoven's music played in the Vienna of 1800 by marking off the rising business aristocracy from the older court-based aristocracy that championed the music of Haydn and Mozart. DiMaggio (1982) shows how the rising commercial elite of nineteenth-century Boston used support for classical music as a status marker, and recent survey research studies show how music preferences have been used in making social class distinctions. See, for example, Bryson (1996) and Peterson and Kern (1996).

Numerous studies have explored issues of racism in the meanings ascribed to music and its creators. Reidiger (1991), for example, shows how immigrant Irish, Germans, Jews, Swedes, and the like developed the "black-faced" minstrel show to satirize African-Americans and show their own affinity with the dominant English-speaking class as part of what they came to call the "white race." Leonard (1962) and Peterson (1972) show the evolving attitudes of whites toward jazz and African-American culture. The most extensive line of work on race focuses on how jazz was created and interpreted by African-American intellectuals as a form of resistance to the dominant white culture. See especially Jones (1963), Kofsky (1970), Vincent (1995), Devereax (1997), and Panish (1997). The racial shaping of blues, gospel, and rap have been explored, respectively, by Keil (1966), Heilbut (1997), and Rose (1994).

Music is gendered in many ways. Men are more likely to be producers, women consumers; women are often demeaned in the lyrics of rock, rap, and heavy metal, but they are characterized as strong in country music lyrics. Yet, compared to other topics, there has not been much research on gender in music and music making. Four different books suggest the range of topics that could be explored: McClary (1991) on the gendering of opera in which strong female leads do not succeed; Buffwack and Oermann (1993) on the decades of struggle of female country music entertainers for equality with men; Lewis (1990) on the gendered nature of rock videos; and Nehring (1997) on gender issues in pop music.

At least since the "jazz age" of the 1920s, music has been one of the primary ways in which generations are defined and define themselves. In the 1990s, for example, one slogan of the young was "If it's 'too loud,' you're too old." Hebdige (1979), Frith (1981), Laing (1985), Liew (1993), Lahusen 1993, Epstein (1994), Weinstein (1994), Shevory (1995), and DeChaine (1997), among many others, show how specific contemporary youth groups use music to state distinctions not only between themselves and their parents but between themselves and other youth groups as well.

THE EFFECTS OF MUSIC

As just noted, new musical forms are identified with each new generation, and adults have tended to equate the music of young people with youthful deviance. Jazz, swing, rock, punk, disco, heavy metal, and rap, in turn, have been seen as the causes of juvenile delinquency, drug taking, and overt sexuality. See, for example, Leonard (1962), Hebdige (1977), and Laing (1985). Jazz was under attack for most of the first half of the twentieth century, and more recently heavy metal music has come in for the most sustained attention (Raschke 1990; Walser 1993; Weinstein 1994; Binder 1993; and Arnett 1996).

One of the most persistent research topics involving music has been the content analysis of song lyrics, on the often unwarranted assumption that one can tell the meaning a song has for its fans by simply interrogating lyrics (Frith 1996). Content analyses can be divided roughly into two types, holistic and systematic.

Systematic content analyses identify a universe of songs, draw a systematic sample from the universe, and analyze the lyrics in terms of a standard set of categories, typically using statistics to represent their results. Examples of systematic content analysis include Horton (1957), Carey (1969), Rogers (1989), and Ryan et al.(1996). Most such content analyses have focused on popular music, but one of the most remarkable is John H. Muller's study of the changing repertoire of classical music over the first half of the twentieth century (1951)—a study that clearly deserves updating. Kate Muller (1973) makes a start. Holistic content analyses typically involve selecting songs that fit the research interest of their author and making judgments of the meaning of a song, or groups of songs, as a whole (Lewis 1990; McLurin 1992; Lahusen 1993; Ritzel 1998).

Finally the "effects" focus in social movements research returns the sociological study of music full circle to more macro-sociological concerns. Music has been an integral part of most social movements, as has been shown by a number of studies. For example, Denisoff and Peterson (1972) provide a collection of essays that describe the place of music in movements ranging from the International Workers of the World, Nazi youth groups, and folk protest music to avant-garde jazz, country music, rock, and religious fundamentalism. Denisoff (1971) has made an analysis of the use of music in the political protest movement of the 1960s and 1970s, and Neil Rosenberg (1993) has assembled a set of essays on the politicization of folk music in that same era. Treece (1997) describes the role of bossa nova in Brazil's popular protest movement, and Eyerman and Jamison (1998) examine the place of music in more recent social movements.

Something approaching one-half the works cited here are by scholars who research music topics relevant to sociology, but who are not themselves sociologists. This openness and diversity is important to the continuing vitality of the sociology of music. It is to be hoped that, in forthcoming decades, self-conscious efforts to bring more order to the scatter will facilitate the systematic articulation of research questions, stimulate research on more diverse music worlds, and encourage more cumulation of research findings. These efforts may also show the ways in which music can become a fundamental perspective in sociology similar to socialization, organization, deviance, culture, and the like.

REFERENCES

Ahlquist, Karen 1997 *Democracy in the Opera: Music, Theater, and Culture in New York City, 1915–69*. Urbana: University of Illinois Press.

Arian, Edward 1971 *Bach, Beethoven and Bureaucracy*. University: University of Alabama Press.

Arnett, Jeffrey 1996 *Metal Heads: Heavy Metal Music and Adolescent Alienation*. Boulder, Colo: Westview.

Atali, Jacques 1985 *Noise: The Political Economy of Sound*. Minneapolis: University of Minnesota Press.

Becker, Howard S. 1982 *Art Worlds*. Berkeley: University of California Press.

Bennett, Stit 1980 *Becoming a Rock Musician*. Amherst: University of Massachusetts Press.

Binder, Amy 1993 "Media Depictions of Harm in Heavy Metal and Rap Music." *American Sociological Review* 58:753–767.

Bryson, Bethany 1996 "'Anything but Heavy Metal': Symbolic Exclusion and Musical Dislikes." *American Sociological Review* 61:884–899.

Bufwack, Mary A., and Robert K. Oermann 1993 *Finding Her Voice: The Saga of Women in Country Music*. New York: Crown.

Burnett, Robert 1990 *Concentration and Diversity in the International Phonogram Industry*. Gothenburg, Sweden: University of Gothenburg Press.

Carey, James T. 1969 "Changing Courtship Patterns in Popular Song." *American Journal of Sociology* 74:720–731.

Cerulo, Karen 1999 *Identity Designs: The Sights and Sounds of a Nation*. New Brunswick, N.H.: University Press of New England.

Cloonan, Martin 1997 "State of the Nation: 'Englishness,' Pop and Politics in the Mid-1990s." *Popular Music and Society* 21(2):47–70.

DeChaine, D. Robert 1997 "Mapping Subversion: Queercore Music's Playful Discourse of Resistance." *Popular Music and Society* 21(1):7–38.

Denisoff, R. Serge 1971 *Great Day Coming: Folk Music and the American Left*. Urbana: University of Illinois Press.

———, and Richard A. Peterson 1972 *The Sounds of Social Change*. Chicago: Rand McNally.

DeNora, Tia 1995 *beethoven and the construction of Genius: Musical Politics in Vienna, 1792–1803*. Berkeley: University of California Press.

Devereaux, Scott 1997 *The Birth of Bebop: A Social and Musical History*. Berkeley: University of California Press.

DiMaggio, Paul J. 1982 "Cultural Entrepreneurship in Nineteenth Century Boston, Part 1: The Creation of an Organizational Base for High Culture in America." *Media, Culture and Society* 4:33–50.

Ellison, Curtis W. 1995 *Country Music Culture*. Jackson: University Press of Mississippi.

Ennis, Philip 1992 *The Seventh Stream*. Hanover, N.H.: University Press of New England.

Epstein, Jonathon S. (ed.) 1994 *Adolescents and Their Music: If It's Too Loud, You're Too Old*. New York: Garland.

Etzkorn, K. Peter 1982 "On the Sociology of Musical Practice and Social Groups." *International Social Science Journal* 34:555–569.

Eyerman, Ron, and Andrew Jamison 1998 *Music and Social Movements*. Cambridge, England: University of Cambridge Press.

Faulkner, Robert 1983 *Music on Demand*. New Brunswick, N.J.: Transaction Books.

Freeman, Robert 1996 "On the Future of America's Orchestras." *Harmony* 3:11–22.

Frith, Simon 1981 *Sound Effects: Youth Leisure and the Politics of Rock 'N' Roll*. New York: Pantheon.

——— 1996 *Performing Rites*. Cambridge, Mass.: Harvard University Press.

Frith, Simon (ed.) 1993 *Music and Copyright*. Edinburgh: University of Edinburgh Press.

Gans, Herbert J. 1974 *Popular Culture and High Culture*. New York: Basic Books.

Gilmore, Samuel 1987 "Coordination and Convention: The Organization of the Concert World." *Symbolic Interaction*. 10:209–227.

——— 1988 "Schools of Activity and Innovation." *Sociological Quarterly* 29:203–219.

——— 1990 "Tradition and Novelty in Concert Programming: Bringing the Artist Back In." *Sociological Forum* 8:221–242.

Guilbault, Jocelyne 1993 *Zouk: World Music in the West Indies*. Chicago: University of Chicago Press.

Hart, Philip 1975 *Orpheus in the New World: The Symphony Orchestra as an American Cultural Institution*. New York: W.W. Norton.

Hebdige, Dick 1979 *Subcultures: The Meaning of Sytle*. London: Methuen.

——— 1987 *Cut and Mix: Cultural Identity and Caribbean Music*. London: Methuen.

Heilbut, Anthony 1997 *The Gospel Sound: Good News and Bad Times*. New York: Limehouse Editions.

hennion, Antoine 1993 *La Passion Musicale: Une Sociologie de la Mediation*. Paris: Edition Metailie.

Horton, Donald 1957 "The Dialogue of courtship in American Popular Songs." *American Journal of Sociology* 62:569–578.

Jones, Leroy 1963 *Blues People: The Negro Experience in America and the Music That Developed from It*. New York: William Murrow.

Jones, Steve 1992 *rock Formation: Music, Technology, and Mass Communication*. Newbury Park, Calif.: Sage.

Keil, Charles 1966 *Urban Blues*. Chicago: University of Chicago Press.

Kingsbury, Henry A. 1988 *Talent and Performance: A Conservatory Culture System*. Philadelphia: Temple University Press.

Kofsky, Frank 1970 *Black Nationalism and the Revolution in Music*. New York: Pathfinder.

Lahusen, Christian 1993 "The Aesthetics of Radicalism: The Relationship between Punk and the Patriotic Nationalist Movement of the Basque Country." *Popular Music* 12:263–280.

Laing, Dave 1985 *One Chord Wonders: Power and Meaning in Punk Rock*. Milton Keynes, England: Open University Press.

Leonard, Neil 1962 *Jazz and the White Americans*. Chicago: University of Chicago Press.

Levine, Syemour, and Robert Levine 1996 "Stress and Discontent in the the Orchestra Workplace." *Harmony* 2:15–26.

Lewis, Lisa A. 1990 *Gender Politics and MTV*. Philadelphia: Temple University Press.

Liew, Maria van 1993 "The Scent of Catalan Rock: Els Pets' Ideology and the Rock and Roll Industry." *Popular Music* 12:245–261.

Lomax, John 1968 *Folk Song Style and Culture*. Washington, D.C.: American Association for the Advancement of Science.

Lopes, Paul 1992 "Innovation and Diversity in the Popular Music Industry." *American Sociological Review* 57:56–71.

McClary, Susan 1991 *Feminine Endings: Music, Gender, and Sexuality*. Minneapolis: University of Minnesota Press.

McLaurin, Melton A. 1992 "The changing Image of the South in Country Music." In Melton A. McLaurin and Richard A. Peterson, eds., *You Wrote My Life: Lyrical Themes in Country Music*. Philadelphia: Gordon and Beach.

MacLeod, Bruce A. 1993 *Club Date Musicians: Playing the New York Party Circuit*. Urbana: University of Illinois Press.

McPhee, William 1963 "When Music becomes a Business." In Joseph Berger, Maurice Zeitlin, and B. Anderson, eds., *When Music becomes a business*. Boston: Houghton-Mifflin.

Menger, Pierre-Michel 1983 *Le Paradoxe du Musicien: Le Compositeur, le Mélomaine et l'État dans la Société Contemporaraine*. Paris: Harmoniques Flammarion.

Meyer, Leonard B. 1956 *Emotion and Meaning in Music*. Chicago: University of Chicago Press.

Middleton, Richard 1990 *Studying Popular Music*. Milton Keynes, England: Open University Press.

Monson, Ingrid 1996 *Saying Something: Jazz Improvisation and Interaction*. Chicago: University of Chicago Press.

Muller, John H. 1951 *The American Symphony Orchestra: A Social history of Taste*. Bloomington: Indiana University Press.

Muller, Kate 1973 *Twenty Seven Major American Symphony Orchestras*. Bloomington: University of Indiana.

Negus, Keith 1993 *Producing Pop: Culture and Conflict in the Popular Music Industry*. London and New York: E. Arnold.

—— 1997 *Popular Music in Theory: An Introduction*. Hanover, N.H.: University Press of New England.

—— 1999 *Music Genres and Corporate Cultures*. London: Routledge.

Nehring, Neil 1997 *Popular Music, Gender, and Postmodernism: Anger Is an Energy*. Thousand Oaks, Calif.: Sage.

Nettl, Bruno 1985 *The Western Impact on World Music*. New York: Schirmer.

—— (ed.) 1998 *In the Course of Performance: Studies in the World of Musical Improvisation*. Chicago: University of Chicago Press.

Panish, Jon 1997 *The Color of Jazz: Race and Representation in Postwar American Culture*. Jackson: University Press of Mississippi.

Peterson, Richard A. 1972 "A Process Model of the Folk, Pop, and Fine Art Stages of Jazz." In Charles Nanry, ed., *American Music: From Storyville to Woodstock*. New Brunswick, N.J.: Rutgers University Press.

—— 1990 "Why 1955? Explaining the Advent of Popular Music." *Popular Music* 9:97–116.

—— 1997 *Creating Country Music: Fabricating Authenticity*. Chicago: University of Chicago Press.

——, and David G. Berger 1975 "Cycles in Symbol Production: The Case of Popular Music." *American Sociological Review* 40(2):158–173.

——, and Roger Kern 1996 "Changing Highbrow Taste: From Snob to Omnivore." *American Sociological Review* 61:900–907.

——, and Howard White 1979 "The Simplex Located in Art Worlds." *Urban Life* 7:411–439.

Raschke, Carl A. 1990 *Painted Black: From Drug Killings to heavy Metal: The Alarming True Story of how Satanism Is Terrorizing Our Communities*. San Francisco: Harper and Row.

Reidiger, David R. 1991 *The Wages of Whiteness: Race and the Making of the American Working Class*. London: Verso.

Ritzel, Fred 1998 "*Was ist ous uns geworden?—Ein Haufchen Sand am Meer*: Emotions of Post War Germany as Extracted from Examples of popular Music." *Popular Music* 17:293–309.

Rogers, Jimmie N. 1989 *The Country Music Message*. Fayetteville: University of Arkansas Press.

Rose, Tricia 1994 *Black Noise: Rap Music and Black Culture in Contemporary America*. Hanover, N.H.: University Press of New England.

Rosenberg, Neil V. 1985 *Bluegrass: A History*. Urbana: University of Illinois Press.

——, ed. 1993 *Transforming Tradition: Folk Music Revival Examined*. Urbana: University of Illinois Press.

Ryan, John 1985 *The Production of Culture in the Music Industry*. Lanham, Md.: University Press of America.

——, Legarde H. Calhoun, and William M. Wentworth 1996 "Gender or Genre: Emotion Models in Rap and Country Music." *Popular Music and Society* 20(2):121–154.

Shevory, Thomas C. 1995 "bleached Resistance: the Politics of Grunge." *Popular Music and Society* 19(2):23–48.

Simmel, Georg (1882) 1968 *the Conflict in Modern Culture*. New York: Teachers College Press.

Treece, Davide 1997 "Bosa Nova and Brazil's Music of Popular Protest." *Popular Music* 16:1–30.

Vincent, Ted 1995 *Keeping Cool: The Black Activists Who Built the Jazz Age*. London: Pluto.

Wallis, Roger, and Krister Malm 1984 *Big Sounds from Small Peoples: The Music Industry in Small Countries.* Londn: Constable.

Walser, Robert 1993 *Running with the Devil: Power, Gender, and Madness in Heavy Metal Music.* Hanover, N.H.: University Press of New England.

Weber, Max 1958 *The Rational and Social Foundations of Music.* Carbondale: Southern Illinois University Press.

Weber, William 1986 "The Rise of Classical Repertoire in Nineteenth-Century Orchestral concerts." In Joan Peyser, ed., *The Orchestra.* New York: Scribners.

Weinstein, Deena 1994 *Heavy Metal: A Cultural Sociology.* New York: Lexington.

Whisnant, David E. 1983 *All That Is Native and Fine: The Politics of Culture and an American Region.* Chapel Hill: University of North Carolina Press.

Zolberg, Vera 1980 "Displaced Art and Performed Music: selective Innovation and the Strucure of Artistic Media." *Sociological Quarterly* 21:219–231.

—— 1990 *Constructing a Sociology of the Arts.* Cambridge, England: Cambridge University Press.

RICHARD A. PETERSON

N

NATIONAL BORDER RELATIONS

Are the processes commonly described as globalization presenting us with a borderless future? Are borders, the limits of state authority, traditionally the instrument by which states and nations define themselves, changing beyond recognition at the threshold of the twenty-first century? Are borders, in the classical sense of the age of the nationstate, being abolished, as part of the erosion of the nation-state itself? Are they withering, or are they undergoing functional change? Are there regional differences between the developments in Europe (EU), America (NAFTA), Asia, and Africa?

A full answer to such very practical questions would perhaps benefit from a grounding in a "general theory of boundaries" conceived as an integral part of the "general theory of systems" (Strassoldo 1976–77, 1979, 1982). States and nations are just a genus of social (societal) systems, and it can be argued that social systems are just a specific kind of (general) systems. For instance, the study of boundary (or interface, as they are sometimes also called) processes, osmotic processes taking place through cell membranes, is one of the frontiers of biological research. In fact, the boundary became a basic concept in system theories in the 1960s and 1970s (Miller 1977). The boundary has an important place in several other disciplines, beginning perhaps with Gestalt psychology (boundary as the line that activates *Gestalten*) and philosophical anthropology, according to which the drawing of neat boundary lines—around concepts, in the definition of categories, in the classification of phenomena, in staking out domains and setting rules—is one of the hallmarks of formal, rational discourse (Bateson 1972). That most elusive concept, form, can best be defined as a "marked space" (Brown 1969). We can only conceive objects, that is, chunks of reality that have a form, a line around them: "Epistemology is about where you draw the line" (Wilden 1972).

Restricting our view to sociological system theories, we find the concept of boundary ("boundary maintenance," "boundary articulation," etc.) recurring throughout Parsons's voluminous works. He seems to have borrowed the idea from earlier anthropologists; and it was another anthropologist, Barth, who has given it renewed popularity in more recent times (Barth 1969).

The logical and ontological primacy of boundaries over any other system element has been emphasized by Luhmann, arguably the sociologists who has most systematically grappled with this problem. For him, any system first emerges as a difference—that is, a boundary—between the inside and the outside, the system and the environment. Later, a difference between a center and a periphery emerges within the system (Luhmann 1982).

It must be admitted, however, that run-of-the-mill sociology has not paid much attention to the concept and problem of boundaries, although every time one meets such dichotomies and expressions as "in–out," "internal–external," "backstage–frontstage," "cross-cutting," "center and periphery," "marginality," "stranger," "distinction," "identity," "closure," and so on, a boundary is implied. Several hypotheses have been suggested for this widespread blindness of sociologists to such a pervasive reality. One is the necessity, typical of all sciences, to isolate phenomena in order to make them manageable for study; this leads researchers to focus on the "core" of social objects, dismissing their margins as though they just "die out" in a surrounding vacuum. Alternatively, it may well be that it is just the inevitable interconnectedness of social phenomena, the generally overlapping, uncertain, and fuzzy character of empirical social boundaries that has kept sociologists clear of them.

On the other hand, it is always possible to find forerunners and prophets for every sociological concept and theory. So one can be referred to Simmel's fascinating musings on the "criss-crossing of social circles," on the "door," the "bridge," and the "handle" as different means of overcoming the boundary-line between different domains. In fact, his whole "formal" approach to sociology is built on the notion that social life is a system of "frames"—that is, boundaries—that are an essential part of its dynamics. This notion, of course, has fed many other, later theorists, from Schutz to Goffman. In the case of territorial borders, one can refer to what Sorokin (1928) called the "geographic school" of nineteenth-century sociology (Le Play, Des Moulins) and to Durkheim's claim that "frontiers" are a central feature of "social morphology." The fullest early sociological treatise on borders is by a follower of Durkheim, the Belgian sociologist and social reformer De Greef, who developed a complex and suggestive theory of an evolutionary interaction between national, political, and territorial ("horizontal") borders on one side, and social ("vertical") boundaries (between groups, classes, organisations etc.) on the other (De Greef, 1908).

Borders—or frontiers, or boundaries—can be studied in a variety of ways: as limits of state sovereignty or as limits of administrative units within states, but also as cultural markers—markers of ethnicity, group or individual identity, and as form. Here, we are predominantly interested in the political borders between nations and states rather than substate boundaries or cultural and anthropological concepts of boundaries (Cohen 1986). Borders, thus, are products of human attempts at organizing territories. They may change location as well as function. "Frontiers are inseparable from the entities which they enclose" (M. Anderson 1996, p. 178); they are "a geographical instrument . . . for the organization of space" (Guichonnet and Raffestin 1974, p. 9). Political borders are human constructs, not natural givens. "Frontiers between states are institutions and processes." (M. Anderson 1996, p. 1).

Borders are institutionalized in legal texts and international agreements, and as such are the expression of political will and social organization. They mark the limits of political decision making, the limits of a legal space, the limits within which state identities and rights and duties of citizenship operate. Looking at borders as processes, Malcolm Anderson defines four dimensions (M. Anderson 1996, p. 2): (1) They are instruments of state policy, protecting and promoting interests; (2) the de facto control states exercise over their borders is indicative of the nature of the state; (3) frontiers are markers of identities of "imagined communities" (B. Anderson 1983); and (4) the "frontier" is a term of discourse, affecting "not only the physical flow of goods and persons, which can be measured; much more important, they affect the culture and consciousness of people, which is much more difficult to assess" (Strassoldo 1998, p. 87).

Historically, the development of the idea of the border has been closely linked to the idea of the development of the state (Breuilly 1993). As the idea of the state changed, so did the functions of borders. Ancient empires, like the Greek or the Roman, had clearly defined boundaries within them—to define citizenship rights and duties—but the outer limits were 'fuzzy'. The claim was that the limits of the empire were the limits of the (civilized) world; the empire could not be bounded. In practice, the Romans developed the idea of the *limes*, a frontier line well within the boundaries within which Roman authority ruled, with a zone of influence beyond, which would act as a buffer against the "barbarians." Even in the Middle Ages, empires preferred to be separated by spaces—"marches" (lat. *margo*)—rather than by fixed lines. In premodern times, feudal, vertical bonds of fealty were of greater importance than territorial frontiers, and local borders—city limits, customs and toll collection points—exceeded state borders in their practical impact on everyday life. Only the decline of the feudal and the rise of the absolutist order, and then of the nation-state, necessitated greater reliance on clearly defined and defendable boundaries.

Borders became the defining feature of the emerging territorial states, as fixed in the Westphalian system (1648), following the Thirty-Years' War, with its "permanent and unalterable" international frontiers. They were neither permanent nor unalterable. The next attempt to achieve and fix a balanced international state system was undertaken in the Treaty of Utrecht (1713); and then again at the Congress of Vienna (1815) after the Napoleonic Wars.

Social contract theories highlighted the right to exit a territory (if an individual or a group found that the territorial government had broken the contract)—a stipulation closely linked with the discovery of "uninhabited" lands, particularly in the New World. Right of entry, on the other hand, rested solely with the sovereign (with the emerging exception of diplomatic immunity).

Of particular importance was the concept of borders for the emerging European nation-states in the wake of the French Revolution: Homogenization within (i.e., erosion of cultural and linguistic boundaries) and "rational" or "natural" external frontiers exactly delineated frontiers to mark the limits of exclusive authority and sovereignty, guaranteeing and safeguarding the modern state's claim to be the "sole, exclusive fount of all powers and prerogatives of rule" (Poggi 1978, p. 92).

Nation-states established the "classical" functions of frontiers—limits of state jurisdiction, fiscal limits, lines of military protection and defense, customs borders, and sociocultural boundaries. Borders serve to safeguard stability within and protect against external threats. All these functions aim at differentiating between inside and outside, between "us" and "them"; they are means of inclusion and exclusion. In this sense, they are, first and foremost, barriers, enclosing a "security community" (Deutsch et al. 1957). Wilson and Donnan define borders as "political membranes through which people, goods, wealth and information must pass in order to be deemed acceptable by the state. Thus," they argue, "borders are agents of a state's security and sovereignty, and a physical record of a state's past and present relations with its neighbours." In their view, borders consist of three elements: (1) "the legal borderline which simultaneously separates and joins states;" (2) "the physical structures of the state which exist to demarcate and protect the borderline, composed of people and institutions which often penetrate deeply into the territory of the state;" and (3) "territorial zones of varying width which stretch across and away from borders, within which people negotiate a variety of behaviours and meanings associated with their membership in nations and states." (Wilson and Donnan 1998, p. 9).

In the late nineteenth and early twentieth centuries, concepts of the border assumed, under the auspices of "geopolitics," a Darwinian—biological or organic—interpretation. Friedrich Ratzel (1897) argued that states were living organisms, with frontiers as their skins. And as the organism grew (or shrunk), the skin would adapt, or have to be adapted. States, in his view, were striving to secure the necessary "living space" (*Lebensraum*) for their people and the most effective borders to safeguard them. While Lucien Febvre (1922) rejected such ideas of a "natural" border, seeing it closely linked to the militarization of the modern state, Ratzel's disciple Karl Haushofer paved the way for the Nazi interpretation of the state ruthlessly pursuing the frontiers deemed necessary for expansionist policies based on racial superiority (Haushofer 1986; Murphy 1997).

In the United States, Frederick Jackson Turner, from the perspective of the settlement of the NorthAmerican continent, saw the "frontier" as a moving section where wilderness and civilization meet, having profound implications for an American "frontier mentality" (Turner 1894). This dynamic concept of frontier as a moving space led to purchase of territory (Louisiana, 1803, from France; Florida, 1819, from Spain) and territorial conquest through war (New Mexico, Arizona, Nevada, Utah, California, part of Colorado, 1848, from Mexico), creating the Rio Grande border. The northwestern frontier with Canada was settled, after decades of controversy with Britain, in 1846, following the 49th parallel.

Frontiers in South America have been products of European colonialism. Yet, in contrast to

Africa, they developed over a longer period of time. South American independence, on the other hand, preceded African decolonization by about 150 years. According to the principle of *uti possidetis*, the administrative boundaries of the Spanish colonial government were generally accepted, but disputes about the exact location of frontiers have led to military conflicts up to the present day (Peru and Ecuador signed a peace treaty in 1998).

African boundaries were mostly drawn by the colonizing European powers in the late nineteenth century (Berlin Conference 1884–1885) in the "scramble for Africa," largely ignoring ethnic, tribal, and linguistic structures on the continent (Asiwaju 1985). These artificial boundaries, sometimes modified in the implementation process *in loco*, were accepted by the Organization of African Unity (OAU) at their first postcolonial conference in Cairo, in 1964, in order to guarantee stability. Recent events, such as those in Rwanda and Somalia, have given rise to fundamental questioning of these colonial frontiers and the state system exported from Europe along with them.

The literature relating to frontiers and boundaries in recent times is extensive (M. Anderson 1983; Anzaldua 1987; Barth 1969; Brownlie 1979; Day 1987; Foucher 1988; Herzog 1990; Heyman 1991; Koptyoff 1987; Kratochwil 1986; Lamb 1968; Luard 1970; Martinez 1994a; Prescott 1987; Sahlins 1989; Strassoldo 1973; Strassoldo and Delli Zotti 1982; Tägil 1977). Particularly since the fall of the Berlin Wall, frontiers have increasingly returned to the political and academic discourse in Europe (M. Anderson 1996; M. Anderson and Bort, eds. 1998; Blake 1994; Brunn and Schmitt-Egner 1998; Donnan and Wilson 1994; Eger and Langer 1996; Eskelinen et al. 1998; Foucher 1990; Ganster et al. 1997; Kramer 1997; Martinez 1994b; Murray and Holmes 1998; Neuss et al. 1998; O'Dowd and Wilson 1996; Raich 1995; Rupich 1994; Wilson and Donnan 1994–1998a).

New international frontiers have been created (e.g., the Baltic states, the former Yugoslavia, the Czecho-Slovakian "velvet divorce," Moldova); other boundaries have changed their function fundamentally, particularly in the case of the former Iron Curtain. Resurgent nationalisms in the former Soviet Union and in the Balkans, emulating the classic European claim to independent nationstates in multinational contexts, have highlighted the inherent contradiction between the international community's accepted principles of "sanctity of borders" and the "right to national self-determination (Hayden 1992; Sluga 1998).

At the same time, the rhetoric about a borderless Europe (i.e. the retreat of the classic nation state within the European Union) has been, at least partially, translated into reality. Free movement of goods and people was already envisaged in the Treaty of Rome (1957), the founding document of the European (Economic) Community. With the introduction of the Single Market in 1993, based on the 1986 Single European Act, the economic functions (customs, tariffs, etc) of borders inside the EU have been eroded. Since 1995, the 1985 Schengen Agreement and the 1990 Schengen Convention have been progressively implemented, in the process blurring the distinction between international and substate boundaries within the EU (den Boer 1998).

Political frontiers as limits of sovereign states were a European invention and were subsequently exported through colonialism and imperialism. Europe is now facing the biggest challenges to the traditional role of borders. The Schengen Convention, as of 1999 signed by all but two EU member states (the United Kingdom and Ireland) and implemented in ten member states, abolished border controls (passport controls, border police checkpoints) at the internal frontiers and transferred those border controls, standardized and supervised by the Schengen Control Committee, to the external frontiers of "Schengenland." "The general purpose of frontiers in the sovereign state was to establish absolute physical control over a finite area and to exercise exclusive legal, administrivve and social controls over its inhabitants. But the traditional attributes of 'sovereignty' are clearly being eroded in Europe and frontiers are losing their hard-edged clarity" (M. Anderson 1996, p. 89). Pooling of sovereignty, the legal prerogative of EU law over national law, and economic and monetary union (with the introduction of the euro in 1999) are often cited as indicators of the demise of the nation-state. This may be exaggerated. Milward (1992) has argued that the EU actually came to the rescue of the nation-state by providing the material benefits that secure its legitimacy. Yet

Milward did not take into account the developments in the 1990s, as expressed in the 1992 Maastricht and 1997 Amsterdam Treaties on European Union, the latter incorporating, for example, the Schengen *acquis* into the institutional framework of the EU.

Will the processes that can be observed in Europe have repercussions elswhere? Commentators from areas where the European border experience was exported have taken a keen interest (Asiwaju 1996). If borders lose their symbolic and real functions in security and control, will other functions—such as markers of identity and culture—become more salient? Fernand Braudel (1985) observed how the Roman "frontier between the Rhine and the Danube was . . . a cultural frontier *par excellence*," exercising tangible influence long after its historical demise (p. 66).

The Schengen Convention already entails a transformation of the border-line into a spatial concept of borders, which, in the light of advancing surveillance technology and the need to combat cross-border crime at the locus of its origin (or destination), rather than at the border has been seen as a return of the marches, or *limes* (Foucher 1998).

In addition, and orchestrating this process of erosion, institutionalized cross-border cooperation has become a common feature at nearly all European frontiers, having started along the German–Dutch and German–French frontiers and subsequently expanded with every phase of EU enlargement.

This, against the backdrop of the demise of the Iron Curtain, has also helped to focus attention on the fact that although borders may be barriers, they can also be (or become) points of contact, channels of communication and interaction. Martinez (1994b) describes four types of interaction at borders, arranged on a continuum from closed to open:

1. "Alienated borderlands," characterized by political and military tensions that allow for very little, if any, exchange across the border. The border is closed; borderlanders on each side perceive of each other as aliens.

2. "Coexistent borderlands," where contacts are possible and limited exchange takes place but long-term cooperation seems undesirable for political or military reasons.

3. "Interdependent borderlands," where contacts are frequent, mutual trade and exchange across the frontier has assumed complementary character, and a common borderland mentality is being developed both sides of the border. The border, however, is still closely monitored and only open in so far as the states' interests are not damaged.

4. "Integrated borderlands," where all barriers and obstacles to cross-border communication, exchange, and movement of people, goods, services, and capital have been removed and a common cultural cross-border identity is developing.

Although these are "ideal-typical" definitions, it is not difficult to find practical examples to these four stages, which can, as envisaged by Martinez, be seen as stages in an evolution. Number 1 would be the historical example of the bipolar Cold War frontier, the Iron Curtain, as symbolized by the Berlin Wall, or, perhaps, by the "Green Line" separating Turkish and Greek Cypriots. Number 2 could be the borders between former Soviet republics, such as Belarus and Poland. Number 3 is clearly Martinez's model for the U.S.–Mexican border, where, under the umbrella of NAFTA, goods and capital may flow relatively unhindered across the internal border of the free-trade area, but movement of people is restricted and border control is a high priority. Number 4 would be the internal frontiers of the post-Schengen European Union, classically expressed in the close cross-border relations along the German–Dutch (Euregio) or German–French borders, including the German provision of transferring sovereignty rights to institutions straddling the frontier (Beyerlin 1998).

Yet opening frontiers is not seen solely as a positive process. What is apparent is that people in Europe and the United States seem to harbor an unfocused, general anxiety about frontiers no longer providing the protection they once did. Organized cross-border crime, trafficking of drugs and other smuggled goods, and organized human trafficking seem to indicate that frontier controls are no longer as effective as they once were. This may be changing as populations become more accustomed to the absence of frontier controls at the internal frontiers. This absence is widely welcomed in frontier regions. In general, the French—normally very sensitive to these matters—seem to have adopted a reasonably relaxed attitude about open frontiers, and those living in the frontier regions seem very pleased with the new situation. Law enforcement agencies seem to have adapted to the new situation without undue difficulty. The nature of frontiers is perceived as changing. New information technology for surveillance and identity control is widely seen as a key factor in securing efficient frontier controls.

The dangers of cross-border crime—drug trafficking, illegal weapons trade, car and cigarette smugggling, money laundering, fraud and corruption, human smuggling, and so on—must not be underestimated. At "their most extreme, substantial rises in the proportion of illegality in international economic activity can destabilize national economies" (Holmes 1999). The rise in internal and cross-border crime in Eastern Europe, particularly in the countries of the former Soviet Union, can be attributed to the difficult transitional situation in these countries: post-communist states attempting, in Claus Offe's (1996) term, a "triple transition": the rapid and simultaneous transformation of their political systems, their economic systems, and their boundaries and identities.

The discourse of migration control has become intricately linked with the discourses on crime and security in a process of "securization" (Bigo 1999; Huysmans 1995). Security has become a much broader concept, compared with the focus on military concerns that dominated the discourse until the changes of 1989–1990, encompassing new risks and threats to society, the economy, and the polity itself (Zielonka 1991). This constitution of a security continuum, including the control of frontiers and immigration among police activities in the fight against crime, is, Bigo argues, "not a natural response to the changes in criminality," but rather a proactive mixing of crime and immigration issues (Bigo 1999, p. 67–68). Buzan has coined the term "societal security" to describe the shift of security concerns from protection of the state to protection against threats, or perceived

threats, against society and identity or against the identity and security of groups within a society (Buzan 1991).

The southern and eastern frontiers of the European Union, as well as the U.S.–Mexican border, demonstrate that the "promotion of borderless economies based on free market principles in many ways contradicts and undermines . . . efforts to keep borders closed to the clandestine movements of drugs and migrant labor." (Andreas 1996, p. 51). Yet despite these efforts at tightening border controls, even erecting what has euphemistically been dubbed the "tortilla curtain"–a metal wall along the border south of San Diego—and combining military and law enforcement agencies, "many clandestine border crossers are adapting rather than being deterred." (Andreas 1996, p. 64). Economic factors, "underlying push-pull factors" (Andreas 1996, p. 68), have frustrated repeated attempts at closing the U.S.–Mexican border to illegal migrants. Operation "Wetback" (under Richard Nixon) and, more recently, operation "Gatekeeper," caused "immediate economic damage, tensions between social groups and [had] almost zero effect on illegal immigration." (Bigo 1998, p. 159).

Clearly, these functional changes of states will be reflected in the functional changes of their borders, and vice versa. Borders, Foucher (1998) reminds us, "are time inscribed into space or, more appropriately, time written in territories" (p. 249). Thus, "different conceptions of the frontier as an institution existed before the modern sovereign state and other kinds will emerge after its demise" (M. Anderson 1996, p. 5). If we are not witnessing the demise of the nation-state, under the dual pressures of globalization and regional responses, the least we can state is that it is "diversifying, developing," if "not dying" (Mann 1996).

Or will the new security architecture being created in Europe establish or cement dividing lines that will echo the maintenance of global inequalities? Is the hardening of the external frontier of—perhaps an enlarged—EU part of the Huntingtonian scenario of a "clash of civilizations" (Huntington 1996)? In view of the complexities within what Huntington losely defines as "civilizations" as well as between them, this is unlikely (Holmes 1998), but frontiers will remain instruments of politics and instruments for the protection of interests.

REFERENCES

Anderson, B. 1983 *Imagined Communities: Reflexions on the Origin and Spread of Nationalism*. London: Verso.

Anderson, M. 1996 *Frontiers: Territory and State Formation in the Modern World*. Cambridge: Polity Press.

——, ed. 1983 *Frontier Regions in Western Europe*. London: Frank Cass.

——, and E. Bort, cds. 1998 *The Frontiers of Europe*. London: Pinter.

Anzaldua, G. 1987 *Borderlands/La Frontera: The New Mestiza*. San Francisco: Spinsters/Aunt Lute.

Asiwaju, A. I., ed. 1985 *Partitioned Africans: Ethnic Relations Across Africa's International Boundaries, 1884–1984*. London: Hurst and University of Lagos Press.

—— 1996 "Public Policy for Overcoming Marginalization: Borderlands in Africa, North America and Western Europe." In S. Nolutshungu, ed., *Margins of Insecurity: Minorities and International Security*. Rochester, N.Y.: Rochester University Press.

Barth, F., ed. 1969 *Ethnic Groups and Boundaries: The Social Organisation of Cultural Difference*. London: Allen and Unwin.

Bateson, G. 1972 *Steps to an Ecology of Mind*. San Francisco: Chandler.

Beyerlin, U. 1998 "Neue rechtliche Entwicklungen der regionalen und grenzüberschreitenden Zusammenarbeit." In G Brunn and P Schmitt-Egner, eds., *Grenzüberschreitende Zusammenarbeit in Europa: Theorie–Empirie–Praxis*. Baden-Baden: Nomos.

Bigo, D. 1998 "Frontiers and Security in the European Union: The Illusion of Migration Control." In M Anderson and E Bort, eds., *The Frontiers of Europe*. London: Pinter.

—— 1999 "'The Landscape of Police Co-operation." In E. Bort and R. Keat, eds., *The Boundaries of Understanding*. Edinburgh: ISSI.

Blake, G., ed. 1994 *World Boundaries Series*, 5 vols. London: Routledge.

Braudel, F. 1985 *Civilisation and Capitalism: Vol 3. The Perspective of the World*. London: Collins.

Breuilly, J. 1993 *Nationalism and the State*. Manchester, U.K.: Manchester University Press.

Brown, G. S. 1969 *Laws of Form*. London: Allen and Unwin.

Brownlie, I. 1979 *African Boundaries: A Legal and Diplomatic Encyclopedia*. London: Hurst.

Brunn, G., and P Schmitt-Egner, eds. 1998 *Grenzüberschreitende Zusammenarbeit in Europa–Theorie–Empirie–Praxis*. Baden-Baden: Nomos.

Buzan, B. 1991 *People, States and Fear: An Agenda for International Security Studies in the Post Cold War Era*. London: Harvester Wheatsheaf.

Cohen, A. P., ed. 1986 *Symbolising Boundaries*. Manchester, U.K.: Manchester University Press.

Day, A. J., ed. 1987 *Border and Territorial Disputes*. London: Keeesings Reference Publications.

De Greef, G. 1908 *La structure generale de la societe, III: La theorie des frontieres et des classes*. Brussels; Larcier; Paris: Alcan.

den Boer, M., ed. 1998 *Schengen's Final Days*. Maastricht, Netherlands: European Institute of Public Administration.

Deutsch, K. W., et al. 1957 *Political Community and the North Atlantic Area: International Organization in the Light of Historical Experience*. Princeton, N.J.: Princeton University Press.

Éger, G. and J. Langer, eds. 1996 *Border, Region and Ethnicity in Central Europe*. Klagenfurt, Austria: Norea.

Eskelinen, H., I. Liikanen, and J. Oksa, eds. 1998 *Curtains of Iron and Gold: Reconstructing Borders and Scales of Interaction*. Aldershot, U.K.: Ashgate.

Febvre, L. 1922 *La Terre et l'évolution humaine*. Paris: La Renaissance du Livre.

Foucher, M. 1988 *Frons et frontières*. Paris: Fayard.

Ganster, P., A. Sweedler, J. Scott, and W. D. Eberwein, eds. 1997 *Borders and Border Regions in Europe and North America*. San Diego: San Diego State University Press.

Guichonnet, P., and C Raffestin 1974 *Géographie des frontières*. Paris: Presses Universitaires de France.

Haushofer, K. 1986 *De la Géopolitique*. Paris: Fayard.

Hayden, R. M. 1992 "Constitutional Nationalism in the Formerly Yugoslav Republics." *Slavic Review* Winter.

Herzog, L. A. 1990 *Where North Meets South: Cities, Space and Politics on the US–Mexico Border*. Austin: University of Texas Press.

Heyman, J. 1991 *Land, Labor and Capital at the Mexican Border*. Flagstaff: University of Arizona Press.

Holmes, L. 1998 "Europe's Changing Boundaries and the Clash of Civilzations Thesis." In P. Murray and L. Holmes, eds., *Europe: Rethinking the Boundaries*. Aldershots, U.K.: Ashgate.

—— 1999 "Crime, Corruption and Politics: International and Transnational Factors." In J. Zielonka and A. Pravda, eds., *Democratic Consolidation in Eastern Europe: International and Transnational Factors.* Forthcoming.

Huntington, S. 1996 *The Clash of Civilizations and the Remaking of the New World Order.* New York: Simon and Schuster.

Huysmans, J. 1995 "Migrants as a Security Problem: Dangers of 'Securitizing Societal Issues." In R. Miles and D. Thränhardt, eds., *Migration and European Integration: The Dynamics of Inclusion and Exclusion.* London: Pinter.

Koptyoff, I., ed. 1987 *The African Frontier.* Bloomington: Indiana University Press.

Krämer, R. 1997 *Grenzen der Europäischen Union.* Potsdam, Germany: Brandenburgische Landeszentrale für Politische Bildung.

Kratochwil, F. 1986 "Of Systems, Boundaries and Territoriality: An Inquiry into the Formation of the State System." *World Politics* 1: .

Lamb, A. 1968 *Asian Frontiers: Studies in a Continuing Problem.* London: Pall Mall Press.

Luard, E., ed. 1970 *The International Regulation of Frontier Disputes.* London: Thames and Hudson.

Luhmann, N. 1982 "Territorial Boundaries as System Boundaries." In R. Strassoldo and G. Delli Zotti, eds., *Cooperation and Conflict in Border Areas.* Milan: Angeli.

Mann, M. 1996 "Nation States in Europe and Other Continents: Diversifying, Developing, Not Dying." In G. Balakrishnan, ed., *Mapping the Nation.* London: Verso.

Martinez, O. J. 1994a *Border People: Life and Society in the US–Mexico Borderlands.* Tucson: University of Arizona Press.

—— 1994b "The Dynamics of Border Interaction: New Approaches to Border Analysis." In C. H. Schofield, ed., *Global Boundaries.* London: Routledge.

Miller, J. G. 1977 *Living Systems.* New York: McGraw-Hill.

Milward, A. 1992 *The European Rescue of the Nation State.* London: Routledge.

Murphy, D. T. 1997 *The Heroic Earth: Geopolitical Thought in Weimar Germany, 1918–1933.* Kent, Ohio: Kent State University Press.

Murray, P., and L. Holmes, eds. 1998 *Europe: Rethinking the Boundaries.* Aldershot, U.K.: Ashgate.

Neuss, B., P. Jurczek, and W. Hilz, eds. 1998 *Grenzübergreifende Kooperation im östlichen Mitteleuropa.* Tübingen: Europäisches Zentrum für Föderalismus Forschung.

O'Dowd, L., and T. M. Wilson, eds. 1996 *Borders, Nations and States.* Aldershot, U.K.: Avebury.

Offe, C. 1996 "Capitalism by Design? Democratic Theory Facing the Triple Transition in Eastern Europe." *Social Research* 58(2):3–13.

Poggi, G. 1978 *The Development of the Modern State.* London: Hutchinson.

Prescott, J. R. V. 1987 *Political Frontiers and Boundaries.* London: Allen and Unwin.

Raich, S. 1995 *Grenzüberschreitende und interregionale Zusammenarbeit in einem "Europa der Regionen."* Baden-Baden: Nomos.

Ratzel, F. 1897 *Politische Geographie.* Münich: Oldenberg.

Rupnik, J. 1994 "Europe's New Frontiers." *Daedalus* Summer.

Sahlins, P. 1989 *Boundaries: The Making of France and Spain in the Pyrenees.* Berkeley: University of California Press.

Sluga, G. 1998 "Balkan Boundaries: Writing History and Identity into Territory." In P Murray and L Holmes, eds., *Europe: Rethinking the Boundaries.* Aldershot, U.K.; Ashgate.

Strassoldo, R., ed. 1973 *Confini e Regioni.* Trieste, Italy: Lint.

—— 1976–1977 "The Study of Boundaries: A Systems-Oriented, Multidisciplinary, Bibliographical Essay." *The Jerusalem Journal of International Relations* 2(2):81–107.

—— 1979 "La teoria del confine." In *Temi di sociologia delle relazioni internazionali.* Gorizia, Italy: ISIG.

—— 1982 "Boundaries in Sociological Theory, a Reassessment." In R. Strassoldo and G. Delli Zotti, eds., *Cooperation and Conflict in Border Areas.* Milan: Angeli.

—— 1998 "Perspectives on Frontiers: The Case of Alpe Adria." In M. Anderson and E. Bort, eds., *The Frontiers of Europe.* London: Pinter.

Strassoldo, R., and G. Delli Zotti, eds. 1982 *Cooperation and Conflict in Border Areas.* Milan: Angeli.

Tägil, S. 1977 *Studying Boundary Conflicts.* Stockholm: Scandinavian University Books.

Turner, F. J. 1894 *The Frontier in American History.* Madison: State Historical Society of Wisconsin.

Wilden, A. 1972 *System and Structure.* London: Tavistock.

Wilson, T. M., and H. Donnan, eds. 1994 *Border Approaches: Anthropological Perspectives on Frontiers.* Lanham, Md.: University Press of America.

——, eds. 1998 *Border Identities: Nation and State at International Frontiers.* Cambridge, U.K.: Cambridge University Press.

—— 1998 "Nation, State, and Identity at International Borders." In T. M. Wilson and H. Donnan, eds., *Border Identities: Nation and State at International Frontiers.* Cambridge, U.K.: Cambridge University Press.

Zielonka, J. 1991 "Europe's Security: A Great Confusion." *International Affairs* 67(1):127–137.

RAIMONDO STRASSOLDO
EBERHARD BORT

NATIONALISM

Nationalism has been defined in a variety of ways at different levels of analysis (e.g., Kohn 1955, 1968; Symmons-Symonolewicz 1970; Kamenka 1973; Plamenatz 1973; Smith 1976, 1981; Snyder 1984). The concept combines a sense of identification with a people, an ideology of common history and destiny, and a social movement addressed to shared objectives. This definition raises questions about what differentiates a people or a nation from others, the nature of identification, the conditions under which nationalist ideologies develop, and the course and aims of nationalist movements.

Historically the term *nationalism* was applied to attempts to follow early European models "to make the boundaries of the state and those of the nation coincide" (Minogue 1967, p. 12), that is, to create loyalty to a nation-state (Kohn 1968). It was also applied to struggles, proliferating after World War II, to gain independence from colonial domination and join the community of sovereign states. More recently, however, analysts have found the confusion between the concepts of state and nation to be a hindrance to understanding contemporary nationalism. Only rarely, if at all, do the boundaries of a state coincide with those of a nation. By *nation* we mean an ethnic group that (1) shares one or more identifying characteristics, such as language, religion, racial background, culture, and/or territory; and (2) is politically mobilized or is amenable to such mobilization. Thus, *nationalism* should be distinguished from *patriotism*, in that the identification and loyalty in the former is to an ethnic group or nation, and in the latter to the state.

IDENTIFICATION

Debates centering on the intrinsic nature of collective ethnic identification feature variations on two general themes—primordialism and structuralism. Implied in the primordial perspective is a deemphasis on an instrumental view of ethnic ties. These ties are seen as ends in themselves shaped by forces other than material self-interest; they are persistent and they resist the homogenization predicted by convergence and modernization theorists. The essence of these ties "is a psychological bond that joins a people and differentiates it in the subconscious conviction of its members from all other people in the most vital way" (Connor 1978, quoted in Stack 1986, pp. 3, 4). These bonds stem from "immediate contiguity and kin connection mainly, but beyond them . . . from being born into a particular religious community, speaking a particular language, or even a dialect of a language, and following particular social practice" (Geertz 1963, pp. 14, 15). Thus, there can be multiple identities—for instance, a Moroccan may identify with an ethnic group within Morocco, the Maghrebs of North Africa, the Arabic speaking people, and the Muslim people at large. These identities assume varying significance depending on the context, lending credence to the old saying "My brother and I against my cousin, and my cousin and I against the stranger." To structuralists, "ethnic identity results instead from objective intergroup differences in the distribution of economic resources and authority" (Hechter 1986, p. 109). Implied here is rational choice and self-interest, that ethnic ties are means to certain ends, and that the boundaries of ethnic groups are changeable.

Neither primordialists nor structuralists would deny the obvious variations in the intensity of identification and in the potential for nationalist movements cross-culturally and over time. Several factors are expected to contribute to these variations. Among the more important of these factors is coterminality of characteristics. In most instances multiple characteristics are involved in distinguishing among ethnic groups—in an overlapping manner at times and coterminously at others. The United States offers an example of overlapping identities where people from different racial backgrounds share the same religious orientation, people with different religious orientation share a common language, and there is no territorial exclusiveness. This overlap in ethnic identification is credited in part with lowering intergroup tensions (Williams 1947). At the other extreme are peoples in southern Sudan, Eritrea, Tibet, the Tamils and Sinhalese in Sri Lanka, the republics of the former Soviet Union, the republics of former Yugoslavia, and other places where all or a combination of racial, religious, linguistic, cultural, and territorial maps largely coincide. The greater the number of factors that coincide, the greater the gulf or "social fault" among ethnic groups along which nationalist sentiments and tensions are likely to intensify (Nagi 1992).

In addition to differentiating attributes and geographic distributions, a number of features of the social structure contribute heavily to variance in intensity and patterns of nationalism. Hechter (1986) suggests two types of such factors. One is the institutionalization of ethnic differences in legal and normative rules, especially those governing property and civil rights, as was the case in South Africa. The other is differentiation in positions in the division of labor that shape "specialization experiences as well as material interests." Deutsch offers another factor in nationalism, attributing membership in a people essentially to a "wide complementarity of social communication" that "consists in the ability to communicate more effectively, and over a wide range of subjects, with members of one large group than with outsiders" (1953, p. 71). Communication is subject not only to commonality of language and cultural background, but also to available means. These include networks of social relations as well as the ever-advancing technological means of mass communication.

NATIONALISM

In addition to identification and "consciousness of kind," nationalism involves ideology and mobilization for social movement and political action. The ideology stems from identification, the sense of uniqueness of group origin, history, culture, collective authority, and destiny (Smith 1981). Political mobilization and the course of nationalist movements are greatly influenced by a host of internal and external factors. Important among the internal factors are uneven economic conditions and disparities along cultural lines in control of resources, access to goods, and distribution of

positions in the occupational structure. The collective perception of an ethnic group of its deprivation or exploitation may challenge the legitimacy not only of the regime but also of the state itself. The theme of "relative deprivation" has been central to explanations of political violence (e.g., Gurr 1970).

The political system allocates power and authority. An uneven distribution among ethnic groups can be the direct result of exclusionary rules and practices, as in the case of Apartheid in South Africa, or the indirect result of socioeconomic disparities and associated discriminatory practices, as characterized in the relationships between Catholics and Protestants in Northern Ireland. Whatever the reason, a cultural distribution of power is as evocative of a nationalist sense of deprivation as a cultural distribution of resources. The close relationship between power and resources led Lasswell to observe that politics is "Who Gets What, When, How" (1936, p. ii).

Applying a developmental perspective, Huntington (1968) connects political stability or instability to the balance between "institutionalization" and "participation." This line of reasoning suggests to some analysts (e.g., Sanders 1981) a linear relationship between political development and political instability—in this case arising from nationalism, which is credited with having been the most prevalent reason for state-level violence (Said and Simmons 1976). Support for such a pattern of relationships derives also from the expectation that the national integration and political assimilation characteristic of developed societies contribute to a shift from culturally based to functionally based cleavages. The net result is a reduction in the prevalence and intensity of ethnic mobilization in the more politically developed countries. However, clearly implied in Huntington's discussion of relations between demand for participation and institutional capacity is a balance at low levels in the least developed countries and at high levels in the developed ones. Imbalances can be expected at early and middle states of development, which suggests a curvilinear pattern.

There is no unanimity on the relationships between development and nationalism. This is understandable in view of the complexity of both phenomena and the current state of research. An important voice on these relationships is that of

Walker Connor (e.g., 1972), who contends that modernization, the spread of education, and improved means of mass communication are responsible for a resurgence in ethnic nationalism. Juan Linz observes that "in the modern world the aim seems to be to build nations rather than states, a task that is probably beyond the capacity of any state that has not achieved the characteristics of a nation-state before the era of nationalism" (1978, p. 62). The distinction between "level" and "process" of modernization and development is useful in understanding the rise in nationalist sentiments. As Smith has noted, "Perhaps, then, it is not the fact of economic progress or decline that is relevant to ethnic revival, but simply economic change per se. Most change . . . is painful and uprooting" (1981, p. 34). Tensions, strains, and dislocations associated with change in the structure and distribution of power—political change—are no less painful or uprooting. Attempts by central governments to secularize and to shift loyalties from ethnic groups to the state underlie much of contemporary nationalism.

NATIONALIST MOVEMENTS

The literature offers two perspectives in explaining the formation of social movements—collective behavior and resource mobilization. In the former, social movements are viewed as responses to a rise in grievances and the actors are seen as "arational" if not "irrational"; in the latter they are considered as goal-oriented, rational responses dependent on organization and mobilization of resources (Jenkins 1983). Debates concerning the strengths and limitations of these two perspectives are yet to be settled. Important to a discussion of nationalism, however, is that literature on social movements, especially on resource mobilization, is primarily Western in conceptualization and empirical foundations. Significant in this respect are differences in aims that guide social movements. More common to Western societies is "changing some elements of the social structure and/or reward distribution of a society" (McCarthy and Zald 1977, pp. 1217, 1218), as compared to nationalist movements that press for autonomy, if not for secession. The first type of movement seeks change through influencing political institutions, the legitimacy of which is not in question (e.g., civil rights in the United States and labor movements in many countries). Nationalist movements, on the

other hand, often challenge, if not outright reject, the legitimacy of the state (e.g., Croatia, Slovenia, Bangladesh, Eritrea, and others that eventually seceded from larger states, as well as Biafra, Southern Sudan, Quebec, and others where no separation has occurred). This is not to cast doubt on the applicability of theories of social movements to ethnic nationalism but, rather, to point out that the influence of differences among societies in levels of development, political institutions, types of regimes, and movements' aims has not been adequately explored (see McCarthy and Zald 1977; Tilly 1978; Jenkins 1983).

In the following paragraphs we shall outline some of the important features of nationalist movements and the processes of mobilization. More specifically, we shall consider the role of grievance, resources, repertoires of expression, and aims.

The role of grievances remains unresolved. While traditional analysis places grievances stemming from structural strains associated with social change at the root of movements (e.g., Smelser 1962; Gurr 1970; Gusfield 1970), resource mobilization proponents favor structural "causal" explanations (e.g., Tilly 1978). Some feel discontent is ubiquitous and therefore, by itself, cannot explain the emergence of social movements. McCarthy and Zald go even further: "For some purposes, grievances and discontent may be defined, created and manipulated by issue entrepreneurs and organizations" (1977, p. 1215). In line with this perspective is Smith's account of "ethnic revival" (1981). Smith maintains that the unique and distinguishing rationale of an ethnic group is the emphasis on group belonging and group uniqueness that links successive generations of the group with specific origins and history. Driving the engines of "historicism" and "nationalism" are discontented intellectuals, educators, and professional intelligentsia. Blocked mobility, opposition and repression by traditional authorities, and frustrated expectations concerning recognition, especially on the part of Third World intellectuals, are factors in the radicalization of these groups, which then turn to historicism and inward to their ethnic communities (Smith 1981).

In explaining the spread of "value-oriented movements," Smelser (1962) refers to "structural conduciveness." Two elements of conduciveness are highly applicable to ethnonationalist movements. One relates to the importance of communication in "disseminating a generalized belief"—a position consistent with that of Deutsch (1953) and Connor (1972), cited earlier. The other is "the availability of means to express grievances" during troubled or uncertain times in order to redress problems.

Attempts to explain nationalist movements must account for the mobilization of resources. McCarthy and Zald outline five central considerations: (1) "aggregation of resources (money and labor)"; (2) the form of organization these resources entail; (3) involvement of individuals and organizations outside the movement; (4) the flow of resources to and from the movement; and (5) "the importance of costs and rewards in explaining individual and organizational involvement" (1977, p. 1216).

The prevailing patterns of social relations are expected to influence the potential for, and forms of, organization and mobilization. Tilly (1978) maintains that combined strength in identification and interpersonal bonds lead to high levels of organization and to greater possibilities for mobilization. In a similar vein Oberschall (1973) offers a classification for patterns of organization. Along one dimension—relations within collectivities—he identifies three types: "communal," "associational," and "weakly [organized] or unorganized." Mobilization, which is facilitated by communal and associational forms, is rendered difficult by the weakly organized and unorganized structures. Along another dimension, Oberschall distinguishes between "vertical" and "horizontal" relations to other collectives and segments of society. Social and political bonds across classes and collectivities can influence mobilization; however, the direction of influence can be expected to vary depending on the type of movement. For example, Oberschall observes: "If in a stratified society there exist [sic] strong vertical social and political bonds between upper and lower classes, mobilization into protest movements among lower classes is not likely to take place" (1973, p. 120). While this may be the case in regard to class conflicts, vertical bonds within an ethnic group can significantly facilitate mobilization.

Strength in family and kinship relations underlies Tilly's networks of interpersonal bonds

and Oberschall's communal organization. Houseknecht sees strength here as referring "to the extent to which family/kinship obligations and rights take precedence over their nonkinship counterparts" (1990, p. 1). She outlines important ways in which kinship relates to ethnic identification, nationalism, and the organization of movements. Early socialization builds identification with an ethnic culture and commitment to its values and norms, which continue to be strengthened and enforced through kinship ties. Commonality in cultural background facilitates social communication, and the networks of kinship ties are readily available channels for the mobilization of human and material resources. Furthermore, the traditional authority structure afforded by strong family and kinship systems provides protection in resisting pressures applied by the state's central authorities.

While informal networks of kinship and interpersonal relations are important to nationalist movements, the role of formal organizations cannot be overstated. As pointed out by McCarthy and Zald (1977), a social movement may include more than one organization; and all organizations in a movement compose a "social movement industry." Competition over resources can arise between a movement industry and other commitments, as well as among organizations within the same movement industry. The latter form of competition is common to nationalist movements, as in the case of the Kurds. This frequently encourages the involvement of neighboring states or major powers, and often leads to internal conflicts within movements.

These lines of reasoning concerning the role of kinship and interpersonal relations bring up the unresolved debate over the relative effectiveness of bureaucratic centralized movement organizations compared with those of an informal decentralized nature. While some argue that "a formalized structure with a clear division of labor maximizes mobilization by transforming diffuse commitments into clearly defined roles and . . . centralized decision making," others maintain that "decentralized movements with a minimum division of labor and integrated by informal networks and an overarching ideology are more effective" (Jenkins 1983, p. 539).

Why would individuals and organizations contribute their labor and resources to ethnonationalist movements? To primordialists, the answer is that they do so in order to preserve cultural integrity and a way of life, to maintain group solidarity and social bonds, and to advance the cause of a community from which a sense of security and pride is derived. These are valued ends in themselves. To collective behavior theorists, the answer is in the collective mood, the social contagion, and the state of mind that are engendered in response to the perception of grievances. To structuralists and resource mobilization proponents, the answer lies in rational collective action and the pursuit of interests.

Opportunities for mobilization are also enhanced by the quality of leadership and its effectiveness in articulating the interests of the group. Smelser explains the significance of charismatic leadership to value-oriented movements. Such forms as "the dreamer prophet of the cult, the nationalist crusader, and the totalitarian demagogue" (1962, p. 355) are compatible with the character of these movements in certain phases of their development. He goes on to point out, however, that "Insofar as a value-oriented movement receives material from outside sources, and insofar as it inherits an organizational structure, the need for charismatic leadership lessens" (p. 356). Useful here are categories identified by Hermann (1986) to analyze political leaders. Particularly important are such contextual factors as to whom the leaders are accountable, forms of interaction with followers, the constraints defined by constituents' beliefs and norms, the strength and nature of opposition, and available resources.

Repertoires of expression of ethnic nationalist movements vary along a wide spectrum that includes interest articulation, passive resistance, demonstrations and riots, sabotage and terrorist acts, and internal wars. Patterns of expression are shaped by the style of leadership, the level of organization, and resources. They are also influenced by the reactions of the state as well as by external forces. These expressions represent events in the life history of movements. The points at which these movements begin and end are generally difficult, if not impossible, to ascertain. Thus, what might be referred to as beginnings or outcomes may well represent only arbitrarily defined points in a process.

Ethnic movements differ in aims and strategies. Smith identifies six types:

1. Isolation . . . . was the most common strategy for smaller ethnic communities in the past. The ethnic community chooses to stay aloof from society as a whole. 2. Accommodation. Here the ethnic community aims to adjust to its host society by encouraging its members to participate in the social and political life of the society and its state. Often, individual members try to assimilate to the host society, or at least become acculturated, for individual advancement. 3. Communalism . . . . is simply a more dynamic and active form of accommodation . . . . The aim is communal control over communal affairs in those geographical areas where the ethnic community forms a demographic majority. 4. Autonomism. There are . . . various forms and degrees of autonomy . . . . Cultural autonomy implies full control by representatives of the ethnic community over every aspect of its cultural life, notably education, the press and mass media, and the courts. Political autonomy or "home rule" extends this to cover every aspect of social, political, and economic life, except for foreign affairs and defense. Ideally, autonomists demand a federal state structure, and this strategy is really only open to communities with a secure regional base. 5. Separatism. This is the classic political goal of ethnonational self-determination . . . . In each case, the aim is to secede and form one's own sovereign state, with little or no connection with former rulers. 6. Irredentism. Here an ethnic community, whose members are divided and fragmented in separate states, seeks reunification and recovery of the "lost" or "unredeemed" territories occupied by its members. In general, this is only possible where the ethnic community has its membership living in adjoining states or areas. (1981, pp. 15–17)

Seeking independent rule, as in secessionist or separatist movements, poses the most serious threat to the state. Such movements challenge not only the legitimacy of the government or regime, but also the integrity of the state itself.

It is reasonable to expect that factors shaping the intensity of nationalist movements will, in turn, influence the formation of secessionist goals.

Territorial coterminality with lines of ethnic identification is a strong contributor, with distance from the ruling center adding to the potential for secessionist claims (Young 1975; Islam 1985; Pankhurst 1988). Timing seems to be important to the rise of such claims as well as to their success. Based on the experiences of several African countries, Young (1975) points out that time is conducive when polity in the parent state falls into disrepute, calling its legitimacy into question because of mismanagement, corruption, and discrimination. He also concludes that times of cataclysmic events in the lives of states offer opportunities for secessionist claims because of the fluidity these events engender, the options they open, and the push for choices to be made. Young cites other antecedents that provide a basis for solidarity and mobilization, such as regional differentials in concentration of wealth and representation in power positions, and at least the minimum political resources to make independent status possible even when economic sacrifice is required. To this list of contributing factors, Islam (1985) adds the magnitude of suffering, the impact of the secession of a region on the rest of the country, whether the seceding region represents a majority or a minority of the population, and the involvement of outside powers.

REGIONAL AND GLOBAL INFLUENCES

The rise of nationalism and the forms and directions it takes are significantly influenced by forces external to the respective states—regional and global socioeconomic and political conditions, and by the spread of ideologies. The power vacuum created by the liquidation of colonialism after World War II tended to be filled by newly created states where borders had been frequently drawn arbitrarily vis-à-vis ethnic distributions. Regional power struggles, territorial disputes, economic competition, and ideological differences have left many regions of the world fraught with turmoil. Since cultural pluralism is characteristic of most, if not all, of the new states, ethnic nationalism often figures prominently in regional conflicts—as a cause at times, and as a consequence at others. The regional dynamics of ethnonationalism can take many forms. It has been a force behind the formation of alliances among independent states, for instance, the Arab League (1945), the Arab Magreb

Union (1989), and the Gulf Co-operation Council (1981). It was also influential in rare cases of voluntary fusion of independent states. Egypt and Syria formed the United Arab Republic (1958) which "was open to other Arab states to join, but only Yemen entered a loose association" (*Encyclopedia of World History* 1998, p. 689). A military coup in Syria ended its union with Egypt in 1961, and Yemen pulled out in 1966. Ethnonationalism was also used as justification for annexation by force as in Germany's invasion of Austria and the Sudetenland (late 1930s); China's occupation of Tibet (1950s); and Iraq's invasion of Kuwait (early 1990s), which was repelled by an international coalition led by the United States and including several Arab countries.

The phenomenal advancements in means of communication and transportation have enormously increased the intensity and scope of global relations. Four features of these relations are particularly relevant to nationalism. First is the spread of ideologies related to human rights and the right to self-determination. Reports of abuses of these rights are communicated in a graphic and rapid, if not an instant, manner. They galvanize global public opinion and prod governments to intercede. The intervention of the Northa Atlantic Treaty Organization (NATO) countries and others in opposition to "ethnic cleansing" in Bosnia and Kosovo is a case in point. Rapid communication also brings to ethnic communities the successes of others who are engaged in struggles or have succeeded in attaining varying measures of autonomy. Second is the presence of world forums to address these issues and bring to bear the weight of the global community, such as the United Nations General Assembly, the Security Council, the International Court of Justice, and other governmental and nongovernmental organizations. Third is the increasing globalization of the economy, which makes it possible for small sociopolitical units to find multilateral niches, thereby reducing dependency on bilateral economic relations with either former colonial powers or states from which they have seceded. Fourth is the geopolitical relations among major powers. When the world was polarized between the two superpowers—the United States and the former Soviet Union—they frequently supported different sides of conflicts within pluralistic societies, either directly or through proxies. In the past, both countries have taken positions in support of the doctrine of "self-determination." President Wilson was a staunch spokesman for the principle during and after World War I. Around the same time, "at the Seventh All Russian Democratic Labor Party Conference of May 12, 1917 . . . in a resolution drafted by Lenin, the conference unequivocally endorsed the right of all of the nations forming part of Russia freely to secede and form independent states" (Connor 1984, p. 45). In contemporary global relations both countries have shown less commitment to the principle. This became clearly evident in the resistance of the former Soviet Union to the independence of the Baltic States, and in the use of military force to keep Chechnya within the fold of the Russian Federation. The approaches of these powers to nationalism have become subject to strategic and economic interests, tempered by the balance of force that can be brought to the situation. The ebb and flow of relations among these powers exerted considerable influence on ethnonationalism for decades.

The vested interests of other states are usually rooted in resources, trade, security, geopolitical advantage, ethnic affinity, or other ideology. More recently, humanitarian considerations have been assuming greater significance in the foreign policy of the West, most notably the United States, progressing "from the call for moral pressure in the 1970s, to economic sanctions in the 1980s, to military intervention in the 1990s" (Kissinger 1999, p. 43), as in the case of Kosovo. While the large states "are likely to intervene for instrumental reasons," the small ones "are more likely to intervene for affective reasons" (Heraclides 1990, p. 377). Regional and global influences may strengthen or weaken the state's means of control and repression, contribute to the movement's resources and sanctuary, and/or raise awareness and help mobilize regional and global public opinion. These interests and their expression, directly or through international organizations, expand or inhibit opportunities for nationalist movements including those with secessionist aims.

The spread of the ideology of minority rights and self-determination plays a special role in secessionist movements. In a comparative analysis, Sigler concludes: "There is historical weight to the charge that minority rights is a guise for separatist sentiment" (1983, p. 188). He maintains that the "concept of minority rights briefly blossomed under the minorities treaties system" (p.190) that followed from the Treaty of Versailles. The system was to protect the rights of minorities in many countries, mostly in Europe, after World War I. It gave jurisdiction to the Permanent Court of International Justice, but litigations became protracted and difficult to adjudicate, thus severely limiting the court's role. It gave power to the Council of the League of Nations to intervene but did not guarantee that disciplinary actions would be carried out against states for infractions. Mutual reinforcement of a system of states as a basis for international relations restrained the various states from interfering in each other's internal affairs. "The collapse of the minorities treaties system . . . has encouraged minority separatist movements . . . . In the absence of a strong international system for the protection of minority rights, resort to separatist politics may have become more prevalent" (Sigler 1983, p. 190). This reinforces Smelser's ideas about structural conduciveness mentioned earlier.

If the odds facing secessionists are great, those facing irredentists are much greater. By definition, irredentism involves multiple secessions, which means contending with forces of more than one state. Consider the difficulties facing the Kurds for whom fulfilling the aim of a unified independent homeland (Kurdistan) is resisted by all the states among which they are divided (Azerbaijan, Iran, Iraq, Syria, and Turkey). An exception was when an ethnic group in one state seeks to attach itself to a neighboring state that includes part of the same group. This tactic is used by some separatists to obtain external support (Young 1975), as in the case of Kashmir that has attracted the backing of Pakistan in its struggle to secede from India. Potential annexation is not necessary for a state to intervene in support of related groups in another state. In the course of extending protection to the Greek and Turkish subpopulations of the island state of Cyprus, war almost erupted between Greece and Turkey.

REACTIONS OF THE STATE

Actions by the authorities and the means of control they employ are largely shaped by the objectives of nationalist movements and greatly affect their course. When perceived as threats to the stability of state and government, they are usually met with repression. However, nationalist movements that remain clandestine and limited under conditions of severe repression tend to gather momentum and erupt into open expression when a new regime, or change in policy, reduces coercion. Recent events in the former Soviet Union and other countries illustrate the point.

Repression is not the only means used by states in responding to threats of ethnonationalism. Some states, such as the former Soviet Union and the People's Republic of China, adopted population redistribution policies aimed at diluting the coterminalitiy of ethnicity with territory. Language policies in education are also used to increase homogenization. Data and other information about Russia and the former Soviet Union are more readily available than about China. The "russification" of Central Asia involved "several migration waves . . . the most recent of which occurred from the mid-nineteenth century to the 1960's . . . conquest and incorporation of the region was accompanied by Russian in-migration, first of peasants in search of new farmland and later of semiskilled industrial workers who entered with regional economic development under socialism" (Kaiser 1994, p. 238). For example, between 1926 and 1959, the proportion of Russians in the population of Kazakhstan increased from 19.7 to 42.7 percent, and from 11.7 to 30.2 percent in Kurgyzstan (Koslov 1975, quoted in Kaiser 1994). These policies seem to have been counterproductive because of heightening nationalist sentiments among the native populations who did, and continue to, view the Russians as colonialists who enjoy greater power and resources (Kaiser 1994). Migration is not the only means used in population redistribution; native populations may be driven out in a process of "ethnic cleansing" as occurred in Bosnia and Kosovo. Central governments in some pluralist states may adopt redistributive policies in regard to resources to assist economic development in lagging regions. Tito's regime in Yugoslavia introduced such policies which ignited a feeling of being exploited on the part of ethnic groups in the more advanced republics (e.g., Slovenia and Croatia).

Other means in the state's arsenal are arrangements for power sharing in governance and mechanisms for conflict regulation. Nordlinger (1972) outlines six such mechanisms: (1) a stable governing coalition of political parties involving all major conflict groups, (2) proportional distribution of elective and appointive positions, (3) mutual veto by which government decisions must be acceptable to major conflict organizations, (4) purposive depoliticization in which leaders of conflict groups agree to keep government out of policy areas that impinge upon the various segments' values and interests, (5) regulation by compromise over conflictual issues, and (6) one group granting concessions to another as a way of managing conflicts. He also sees four motives for leaders to engage in conflict regulation: (1) external threats or pressure, (2) negative effects on the economic well-being of the groups involved, (3) aversion to risking violence and human suffering that might result from unregulated conflicts, and (4) the protection of leaders' own power position.

Lijphart places equal emphasis on leaders "whose cooperative attitudes and behavior are needed to counteract the centrifugal tendencies inherent in plural societies" (1977, p. 1). The forms he outlines for "consociational" democracies overlap in many ways with Nordlinger's mechanisms for conflict regulation. One important difference, however, is Lijphart's inclusion of "segmental autonomy," that is, federalism. Nordlinger specifically excluded federalism as a mechanism for regulating conflicts because he saw in it a recipe for a breakup of the state.

Emphasis in the foregoing discussion has been on strategies to prevent the breakup of the state. An alternative, however, is to carry out an orderly and peaceful separation. The division of Czeckoslovakia (1993) into two countries (the Czeck and the Slovak Republics), although a rare example, renders this alternative real rather than just theoretical.

OUTLOOK ON THE FUTURE

While forecasting is a hazardous endeavor, especially in regard to such complex and volatile phenomena as nationalism, disciplined consideration of important trends and their implications for the future is warranted. Interest here is in long-term change that may span generations and many decades of evolution. As implied earlier, the forces of modernization and development are intricately interrelated to the prevalence, severity, and modes of resolving nationalist tensions. By modernization, we mean the forces of change in institutions, organization, and behavior in adaptation to the vast and rapid advancement in knowledge and its technological application. In a classic analysis, Black describes the awesome significance of this process:

The change in human affairs now taking place is of the scope and intensity that mankind has experienced on only two previous occasions, and its significance cannot be appreciated except in the context of the entire course of world history. The first revolutionary transformation was the emergence of human beings, about a million years ago, after many thousands of years of evolution from primate life . . .

The second great revolutionary transformation in human affairs was that from primitive to civilized societies, culminating seven thousand years ago. . . . Three [early civilizations]—the Mesopotamian, the Egyptian, and the Cretan—have transmitted their knowledge and institutions to later societies.

The process of change in the modern era is of the same order of magnitude as that from prehuman life and from primitive to civilized societies; it is the most dynamic of the great revolutionary transformations in the conduct of human affairs. What is distinctive about the modern era is the phenomenal growth of knowledge since the scientific revolution and the unprecedented effort at adaptation to this knowledge that has come to be demanded of the whole mankind. (1966, pp. 2–4).

Emerging through this process is change in institutions toward greater capacity for political participation, expanding and more productive economies, and increasing cultural neutrality in the formulation of laws and universality in their application. As has been noted by many analysts of social change, this transformation has been accompanied by change in value orientation toward increasing emphasis on achievement, secularization, individualism, rational choice, the rule of law, and tolerance for differences. Powering this process are mutually reinforcing systems of education, research, and development. Several points are important in explaining the connections between modernization and nationalism.

First, the course of modernization is highly influenced by the ability of leaders "to keep the delicate balance required for survival between the maintenance of the traditional pattern of values that serves as the basis for cohesion and adaptation to new knowledge that requires a revision of the traditional value system" (Black 1966, p. 4). This "clash of civilizations" is common to developing and transitional societies; it is often seized upon in mobilizing nationalist sentiments. The resulting mixes tend to negate the notion that modernization means turning other societies into clones of those of the West. In fact, there are pronounced differences among the advanced countries in the configurations of institutions, organizations, and values they have evolved.

Second, "the challenge . . . in the societies that modernized earlier was internal, the processes of transformation took place generally over centuries. In the later modernizing societies this challenge has been increasingly external, hence more rapid and even abrupt" (Black 1966, p. 8). As pointed out earlier, rapid and abrupt change in itself can create considerable dislocation in institutions and unpredictability in behavior—conditions of anomie—that are fertile grounds for mobilizing fervor for such emotional causes as nationalism.

Third, with halts at times and set backs at others, modernization is a continual process with different countries, and different peoples within countries, being at varying stages of the process. Certain levels of transformation bring about institutional arrangements, modes of organization, and value orientations favorable to prospects for peaceful and orderly resolution of nationalist tensions. It is no accident that the ethnic sub-populations in Switzerland (French, German, Italian, and others), in former Czechoslovakia (Czechs and Slovaks), in the United Kingdom (English, Scottish, and Welsh), in Belgium (Flemings and Walloons), and in Canada (citizens of Quebec and others), found ways to resolve, or to go about resolving, these issues within peaceful legal frameworks. To be sure, there remain instances of violent conflicts as in the case of Northern Ireland.

The point to be made here is that, in the long run—over an extended span of history—the process of modernization can be expected to lessen ethnic tensions and promote peaceful resolution. At present and in the short run, however, the ubiquity of ethnic conflicts and the escalation in associated violence are to be expected in many regions and countries of the world. In part, this is because of the abruptness of change in general, the pressure built over decades of ethnic differentiation in the distribution of power and resources, and fluidity in the structure of central authorities that suppressed their expression as happened in Yugoslavia and the former Soviet Union. The influence of fluidity in power structures is illustrated by Naimark in his foreword to a volume aptly entitled *The Revenge of the Past*:

> *The collapse of the Soviet Union was caused by nationalism, that is, by the demands of the subject nationalities of the USSR for genuine independence and autonomy. Unified in their hostility to the Kremlin's authority, the fifteen constituent Union Republics, including the Russian republic, declared sovereignty and began to build state institutions of their own . . . . With the failure of the August 1992 putsch attempt, sovereign republics obtained their independence. Nationalism reigned supreme"* (1993, p. ix).

Another major trend expected to have significant dampening effects on violent nationalism is the development of global and regional governmental and nongovernmental organizations addressed, in part or in whole, to investigating, reporting, and intervening with cases of discrimination and abuses of human rights. Precedents, of historic importance, were introduced in 1999 with the military intervention of the NATO countries in attempting to reverse "ethnic cleansing" in Kosovo, and the indictment of a head of state and high officials in a serving government by a United Nations Tribunal for "crimes of war and against humanity." To focus on the United Nations for a moment, among its achievements over the first fifty years, Alger cites the following:

> *It has invented new tools such as peacekeeping. It has extended its mission to include violent conflicts within states. It has broadened peace-keeping to include an array of supportive humanitarian operations. It has drafted a broad array of human rights conventions covering economic, social, cultural, civil, and political dimensions. (1998, p. 422).*

Finally, other trends with potential impacts on nationalism include the *voluntary* formation of economic and political federations among states such as the European Union, and the globalization of the economy. The growing interdependence among countries brings to bear the weight of regional and global communities in containing the risks of disruptive violence. Furthermore, these trends facilitate greater autonomy for small sociopolitical units by offering multilateral niches that reduce dependence on bilateral economic relations with the countries in which they are part or from which they have seceded. In other words, globalization and regionalization tend to transfer power and authority from the states upward to the larger structures and downward to local levels, thus, increasing local autonomy. As has already been explained, a host of other factors particular to each situation are also at work.

CONCLUSIONS

In conclusion, it can be said that the current pervasiveness of nationalism should be self-evident. The socioeconomic, political, and other human costs are frequently staggering. In the short and intermediate term, the ubiquity of the phenomenon can be expected to continue. In addition to Africa and the Balkans, there remain significant ethnic tensions, if not risks of violence, in many countries of Asia—Russia, China, and India, among others. However, in the long run, major trends of modernization, economic globalization and interdependence, and the development of international organizations and forums to address the problem, all point to conditions less conducive to the mobilization of nationalist sentiments and more tending to peaceful resolutions of such tensions.

As a major feature of social structure, ethnicity is of central theoretical importance. However, many (and often large) gaps in the state of knowledge exist, both in theory and in accumulated data. Basically, three shortcomings in the literature account for this. First, there are conceptual and theoretical limitations, especially at the intermediate levels of abstraction that connect abstract explanatory schemes—of which a notable few exist—with concrete events. Second, the preponderance of empirical work in this area is in the form of case studies that are mostly historical. These case studies offer uniformity neither in concepts nor in evidence. The third problem with literature on ethnic nationalism is its fragmentation. A coherent picture must draw upon concepts and propositions from a number of traditions, and there are many overriding concepts with which to assemble frameworks to advance theory and to guide the collection of evidence. While they are difficult to plan and execute, there is compelling need for comparative studies to advance understanding of the underlying principles. Clear understanding of nationalism, and of the processes involved, is essential to the evolving of appropriate educational, policy, constitutional, and other legal means for accommodating cultural diversity.

(SEE ALSO: *Ethnicity*; *Social Movements*)

REFERENCES

Alger, Chadwick F. 1998 "Conclusion: The Potential of the United Nations System." In Chadwick F. Alger, ed., *The Future of the United Nations System*. Tokyo: United Nations University Press.

Black, Cyril E. 1966 *The Dynamics of Modernization: A Comparative Study of History*. New York: Harper and Row.

Connor, Walker 1972 "Nation-Building or Nation-Destroying?" *World Politics* 24:319–355.

—— 1978 "A Nation Is a Nation, Is a State, Is an Ethnic Group, Is a. . . ." *Ethnic and Racial Studies* I(4):377–400.

—— 1984 *The National Question in Marxist-Leninist Theory and Strategy*. Princeton, N.J.: Princeton University Press.

Deutsch, Karl W. 1953 *Nationalism and Social Communication*. Cambridge, Mass.: Massachusetts Institute of Technology Press.

Encyclopedia of World History 1998 New York: Oxford University Press.

Geertz, Clifford 1963 "The Integrative Revolution: Primordial Sentiments and Civil Politics in the New States." In Clifford Geertz, ed., *Old Societies and New States: The Quest for Modernity in Asia and Africa*. New York: Free Press.

Gurr, Ted Robert 1970 *Why Men Rebel*. Princeton, N.J.: Princeton University Press.

Gusfield, Joseph R. 1970 "Introduction: A Definition of the Subject." In Joseph R. Gusfield, ed., *Protest, Reform, and Revolt: A Reader in Social Movements*. New York: John Wiley.

Hechter, Michael 1986 "Theories of Ethnic Relations." In John F. Stack, Jr., ed., *The Primordial Challenge: Ethnicity in the Contemporary World*. New York: Greenwood.

Heraclides, Alexis 1990 "Secessionist Minorities and External Involvement." *Internal Organization* 44(3):341–378.

Hermann, Margaret G. 1986 "Ingredients of Leadership." In Margaret G. Hermann, ed., *Political Psychology: Contemporary Problems and Issues*. San Francisco: Jossey-Bass.

Houseknecht, Sharon K. 1990 "The Role of Family and Kinship in Ethnic Nationalist Movements." Columbus: Mershon Center, Ohio State University. Mimeograph.

Huntington, Samuel P. 1968 *Political Order in Changing Societies*. New Haven: Yale University Press.

Islam, Rafiqul 1985 "Secessionist Self-Determination: Some Lessons from Katanga, Biafra and Bangladesh." *Journal of Peace Research* 22(3):211–221.

Jenkins, J. Craig 1983 "Resource Mobilization Theory and the Study of Social Movements." *Annual Review of Sociology* 9:527–553.

Kaiser, Robert A. 1994 "Ethnic Demography and Interstate Relations in Central Asia." In Roman Szporluk, ed., *National Identity and Ethnicity in Russia and the New States of Eurasia*. Armonk, N.Y.: M. E. Sharpe.

Kamenka, Eugene, ed. 1973 *Nationalism, the Nature and Evolution of an Idea*. London: Edward Arnold.

Kissinger, Henry 1999 "New World Disorder." *Newsweek* (May 31):41–43.

Kohn, Hans 1955 *Nationalism*. Princeton, N.J.: D. Van Nostrand.

—— 1968 "Nationalism." In David L. Sills, ed., *International Encyclopedia of the Social Sciences*, vol. 11. New York: Macmillan/Free Press.

Koslov, Victor 1975 *Natsional'nosti SSSR*. Moscow: Statistika: 86–88.

Lasswell, Harold D. 1936 *Politics: Who Gets What, When, How*. New York: McGraw-Hill.

Lijphart, Arend 1977 *Democracy in Plural Societies: A Comparative Exploration*. New Haven, Conn.: Yale University Press.

Linz, Juan J. 1978 "The Breakdown of Democratic Regimes: Crisis Breakdown and Reequilibrium." In Juan J. Linz and Alfred Stepan, eds., *The Breakdown of Democratic Regimes*. Baltimore, Md.: Johns Hopkins University Press.

McCarthy, John D., and Mayer N. Zald 1977 "Resource Mobilization and Social Movements: A Partial Theory." *American Journal of Sociology* 82:1212–1241.

Minogue, K. R. 1967 *Nationalism*. New York: Basic.

Nagi, Saad Z. 1992 "Ethnic Identification and Nationalist Movements." *Human Organization* 51(4):304–317.

Naimark, Norman M. 1993 "Forward." In Ronald G. Suny, *The Revenge of the Past: Nationalism Revolution, and the Collapse of the Soviet Union*. Stanford, Calif.: Stanford University Press.

Nordlinger, Eric 1972 *Conflict Regulation in Divided Societies*. Cambridge, Mass.: Center for International Affairs, Harvard University.

Oberschall, A. 1973 *Social Conflict and Social Movements*. Englewood Cliffs, N.J.: Prentice-Hall.

Pankhurst, Jerry G. 1988 "Muslims in Communist Nations: The Cases of Albania, Bulgaria, Yugoslavia, and the Soviet Union." In Anson Shupe and Jeffery Hadden, eds., *The Politics of Religion and Social Change: Religion and Political Order*, vol. 2. New York: Paragon.

Plamenatz, John P. 1973 "Two Types of Nationalism." In Eugene Kamenka, ed., *Nationalism, the Nature and Evolution of an Idea*. London: Edward Arnold.

Said, Abdul, and Luis Simmons 1976 *Ethnicity in the International Context*. New Brunswick, N.J.: Transaction.

Sanders, David 1981 *Patterns of Political Instability*. London: Macmillan.

Sigler, Jay A. 1983 *Minority Rights: A Comparative Analysis*. Westport, Conn.: Greenwood.

Smelser, Neal 1962 *Theory of Collective Behavior*. New York: Free Press.

Smith, Anthony D. 1976 "Introduction: The Formation of Nationalist Movements." In Anthony D. Smith, ed., *Nationalist Movements*. London: Macmillan.

—— 1981 *The Ethnic Revival*. Cambridge [England]; New York: Cambridge University Press.

Snyder, Louis L. 1984 *Macro-Nationalism: A History of the Pan-Movements*. Westport, Conn.: Greenwood.

Stack, John F., Jr. 1986 "Ethnic Mobilization in World Politics: The Primordial Perspective." In John F. Stack, Jr., ed., *The Primordial Challenge*. New York: Greenwood.

Symmons-Symonolewicz, Konstantin 1970 *Nationalist Movements: A Comparative View*. Meadville, Pa.: Maplewood.

Tilly, Charles 1978 *From Mobilization to Revolution*. Reading, Mass.: Addison-Wesley.

Williams, Robin M., Jr. 1947 *The Reduction of Intergroup Tensions*. New York: Social Science Research Council.

Young, M. Crawford 1975 "Nationalism and Separatism in Africa." In Martin Kilson, ed., *New States in the Modern World*. Cambridge, Mass.: Harvard University Press.

SAAD Z. NAGI

NATURE VS. NURTURE

See Gender; Intelligence; Sex Differences; Socialization.

NEGOTIATION OF POWER

In ordinary usage, *negotiation* signifies contracting, bargaining, and attempting to reach an agreement. Many studies of negotiation have been carried out particularly with respect to commercial, diplomatic, political, and trade union relations. Recently, acquisitions from the study of negotiation (modalities, styles, strategies, and so on) have been applied to the analysis of interpersonal and social dynamics, ranging from one-to-one relationships to more complex social situations and the management of organizations. Negotiation has also found a specific field of application in the solution of conflicts (Pruitt and Carnevale 1993).

Negotiation is, briefly, a process in which two or more parties try to reach a satisfactory solution to a shared problem. To be more specific, it is a process in which the actors define their own obligations, costs, and benefits to achieve a common result. It is important to emphasize that negotiation is a process, that is to say, it is a dynamic—and not an instantaneous situation—that may be adopted as a way of regulating relationships. Negotiation is a process of exchange (of information, threats, favors, and so on) that goes on until compromises beneficial for all parties involved begin to become apparent. It is a process that advances cautiously and methodically, so that the interests and the expectations of the parties involved are able to emerge gradually. Only when the parties have succeeded in deciphering the real interests and intentions that lie behind their respective declared positions can possible solutions be identified.

Negotiation processes can be analyzed from various points of view, using various techniques. It is possible, for example, to use macrostructural variables. In this case, the outcome is explained on the basis of variables in the context where the negotiation is carried out. Alternatively, it is possible to use psychological variables, interpreting the result of negotiation in the light of the personal characteristics of the actors and of the psychodynamics that develop between them. A third possibility is the "strategic" approach. A strategic analysis does not ignore context-defined effects and limits on the negotiation process nor the importance of the psychodynamic relationship established by the participants but it assumes that the outcome of negotiation will be primarily the result of strategic actions by the negotiators. According to this approach, a negotiation process can only be reconstructed by starting from the actual choices made from the alternative strategies available by actors in specific situations.

It is in this perspective that the special case of "interpower" negotiation (where the term "power" is used as an abbreviation for "institutional power" or "branch of government") has emerged. The topic has become important because in modern political systems the traditional concept of such powers has been modified; because the opportunities for conflict between them have multiplied; and finally because an increasing number of social and economic issues involving values of fundamental importance for individuals and communities have become the target of decisions, interventions, or actions taken or promoted by the various institutional powers.

During the twentieth century, the state has everywhere become increasingly interventionist, while respecting, in democratic societies, traditional civil and political freedoms. State intervention involves, on one hand, the economy and, on the other, various aspects of everyday life. In the economy, the state regulates private initiative relatively strictly, striving to guarantee the "social rights" of less favored groups without yielding to socialist collectivism. As well as impacting, sometimes significantly, on the lives of individuals, groups, communities, and enterprises, the intervention of the contemporary state upsets the parameters of the classic division of powers (legislative, executive, judicial), threatening its survival.

Indeed, it has led to the gradual rise of a new pattern of division of powers.

State intervention involves a massive increase in the production of regulations and therefore in the opportunities for violating such regulations and promoting legal action. It also exacerbates competition and conflicts among powers, among the various branches of state administration, and between decision-making centers and citizens (Field 1996). Normative activity has expanded so much that it can no longer remain the prerogative of parliament. For practical reasons, it is widely delegated to the executive and to administrative authorities. Moreover, a first decision on many conflicts must be referred to the administrative authorities, so that the classic principle of the exclusive attribution of fundamental functions to separate, corresponding powers is violated. The principle of the clear-cut division of powers has ceased to exist.

On the other hand, the very nature of public administration has changed. It not only carries out normative functions but also possesses wide-ranging discretionary power in defining and safeguarding the public interest. To do this, either official decrees or contractual instruments may be used.

Public administration has become a huge—indeed excessively large, according to many commentators—bureaucratic body. Formally, it continues to be subject to the law (which often leaves the administration a high degree of freedom for discretionary action) and to the directives of the executive. But there are many fields in which the law itself concedes considerable autonomy from the executive to administrative organs.

In addition, the nature of the work of the judiciary has changed. The system of sources for precedent is getting more complex and the number of regulations is mushrooming. Interpretation by judges therefore must involve strongly creative elements. There has also arisen a new area of intervention connected with the increasing number of functions assigned to public administration and the growing role of government. Judges are prompted to set aside their old self-image of being the "voice of the law "and to undertake an independent "political" role, inspired partly by new developments in legal theory, such as the law of interests and values, the sociology of law, and judicial pragmatism.

At the same time, Western states are experiencing two new and extremely important functions that are not comparable to the traditional ones. The first is that of *political orientation*. The intervention of the state must necessarily be organized around a program if it is to have significance and coherence. The program must be one on which the electorate expresses itself at elections and which an organ of the state has the task of translating into concrete provisions for the period of office of the legislature (at the next election, the electorate will decide whether to continue or to change program and governing team).

The body of the state delegated to administer the *political orientation* could only be the former executive. The executive, however, having been charged with its new task, has completely transformed its structures and authority. It has changed from a mainly executive body into a *governing power* that lasts for at least one legislature. Generally, it is the main initiator of the laws necessary to implement the *political orientation* and is followed in such action by both the legislative power and the public administration.

The second new function is that of guaranteeing the principles of the constitution. The United States provided a valid example in this respect, although for many years it was not followed by other countries. The much faster rate of change of the normative system makes it more likely that the laws themselves may violate fundamental values, as well as personal and social rights that the community wants to maintain intact. Parliaments have ceased to be reliable champions of the freedoms and the rights of the citizen. Frequently, they have been transformed into assemblies that merely represent sectarian or corporate interests. For that reason, there has emerged a demand to entrust the defense of those values and freedoms to a body that does not have to face a periodic electoral test. Constitutional courts were therefore created in nearly all political systems of the twentieth century. The interventionist state does not disclaim the division of power as such. The division must remain effective to avoid an excessive or even total concentration of power that would threaten citizens' civil and political freedoms and social rights, or would jeopardize the proper, efficient government of society and the economy. But as we have noted, the modern state can no longer be considered a harmonic whole made up of separate powers organized around the three functions of legislative, executive, and judicial power.

The division of the powers remains, but it has assumed a different form (O'Toole 1993). It has become a Weberian ideal-type with new features that can be summarily described as follows. There are at least five powers instead of the traditional three:

1. *The governing power* carries out the function of political orientation, defining the main policies. Whether it is embodied in a president, a prime minister, a chancellor, or some other figure, the governing power is an organ that enjoys guaranteed stability, which is indispensable for translating political orientation into action. In general, the governing power will attempt to perform a broader normative function than the one attributed to it, thus entering into conflict or competition with the parliament.

2. *The legislative branch* has taken on the function of confirming the political orientation decided by the governing power when its majority belongs to the same party. Where the majority belongs to a different party, the function is more political and relationships are competitive, because the overriding aim is to win the next election. Nevertheless, obstruction of the policies of the governing power, or its formal removal, must remain absolutely exceptional eventualities. The legislative branch also has other checks and controls over the governing power (formal questioning, inquiries, and so on).

3. *Public administration* has become one of the powers because, although it is subject to law and the directives of the governing power, its sheer size and the growing range of functions assigned to it enable the public administration to pursue objectives in the public interest which it identifies independently with discretionary freedom. The aims of the public administration are achieved by regulation and sanctions.

4. *The judicial power* is the power that guarantees in complete autonomy the proper application of the law to specific cases. The judiciary contributes creatively to the evolution of the normative system. For this reason, it may perform, intentionally or not, an important "political" role.

5. *The supreme court (constitutional court)* has the function of guaranteeing supreme political and social values for all the other powers, especially the governing and legislative powers. These values have to be removed from the cut and thrust of day-to-day politics and constantly defended. In fact, the supreme court identifies these values with wide discretion.

The new model of the division of powers places the governing—and not the legislative—power at the center of the state's organization. It is the governing power that provides the driving force. The other powers act as potential brakes, the legislative branch on the political front and the supreme (constitutional) court on the legal side.

The governing power cannot therefore be compared to a medieval absolute (albeit elective) monarch. Still less can it be compared to the dictators of contemporary authoritarian and totalitarian regimes. It acts in a context of free democracy and in a system of the division of powers that places limits on it and prevents it from taking the place of other powers in the exercise of functions that do not properly belong to it. Realistically, its position within the organization of the state is probably less strong than might appear from the above model.

If we examine what has happened to the former legislative, executive, and judicial functions that today are no longer attributed to or exercised by a specific power, it will become apparent that they are distributed among the new powers without the rigid distinctions that once prevailed. Although every political system has mechanisms for blocking democracy-threatening initiatives (for example, penal norms can be only introduced by acts of parliament), the vagueness and fluidity of the new political situation demands the introduction of new procedures to regulate the relationships of the new powers. New procedures are necessary to avoid the risk of permanent conflict, the blocking of all political plans, and the struggle to occupy ever-wider areas of influence.

Almost all the major Western nations have, to some extent, adapted to the new model. Of course, each system has chosen its own way of allowing a governing power to emerge and of defining a corresponding series of complementary authorities and checks. Indeed, a surprising variety of solutions has been devised to ensure the optimal functioning of the interventionist state. Since it is impossible to illustrate here the performance and the details of the models established by the major Western nations, we shall merely list some of the most important changes.

Great Britain in the twentieth century has transformed its classic parliamentarian government into government by the prime minister, who represents the governing power. This has been possible thanks to the rigid bipartite nature of the British political system, which guarantees the alternation of parties in power; to the adoption of a first-past-the-post voting system that reinforces the two-party system; and to the strict internal discipline in the parties.

France under the Fifth Republic has overcome the disadvantages of its extreme parliamentarianism, which were due to the excessive fragmentation and lack of internal discipline of the parties. This has been achieved through the direct election of the president of the republic, the reinforcement of the position of the government with respect to parliament, and the return to a majority electoral law with two ballots. The governing power in France is the president, except when the parliamentary majority is hostile (policies are decided with the prime minister). The Constitutional Council safeguards the ideals of French constitutionalism. In Germany, the governing power is represented by the chancellor. Elected by majority vote in the Bundestag, the chancellor enjoys remarkable stability, partly because of the principle of the constructive vote of no confidence. It is up to the chancellor to dictate the political orientation, which parliament normally backs. The strength of the German political parties, the federal organization of the state, and an effective constitutional court provide an effective counterweight to the power of the chancellor.

In the nineteenth century, Congress was the real center of American political life. During the twentieth century, however, the presidential system of the United States has become actual rather than nominal, and the true driving force of the nation today is the president. Congress has nevertheless kept a significant portion of its former power and is currently the most powerful of all the Western parliaments. The Supreme Court is also rather more than a mere check on the governing power.

Italy is something of an anomaly because its constitution enshrines the model of the social interventionist state, but the country has not succeeded in developing the structures for a new division of powers. The Italian parliament has jealously preserved all its normative functions, but the public administration interprets and applies the regulations with such a high degree of autonomy that it distorts the intentions of the legislator. The strict two-chamber structure slows down parliamentary activity; the government has only weak prerogatives over parliament; and the judiciary, originally conceived as a mere instrument to apply the laws, has actually been performing a largely political role in recent years. These modifications to the institutional order have been fostered by major changes in the political process, especially concerning the demands and behavior of citizens. Two aspects, in particular, deserve attention. First, increasingly frequently, public policy disputes among social or special-interest groups are taken to the legislator, the administrative branch, or the judicial arena for resolution. Second, more and more people request government intervention to solve private problems or to further group interests. The new powers therefore have to tackle new tasks and satisfy additional social demand.

The breakdown of the traditional division of powers, whose roles, functions and relationships are very clearly defined, at least formally, leads to a fluid situation in which the new powers are forced to negotiate with each other.

There are two aspects that coexist in interpower negotiation. The first is negotiation on matters of substance and—albeit generally in less explicit terms—for the attribution of roles. On fundamental issues, it is necessary to make a distinction between topics that involve nonnegotiable values

and interests on which it is possible to reach a compromise or to find some way of compensating the losing party.

Even though the present era is characterized by the spread of secularism and cultural relativism, there are topics on which people—and therefore institutions—are deeply divided. Abortion is one example, for it involves worldviews and values that are not negotiable. In such cases, the majority will impose its position without attempting to mediate an agreement with the minority. The decision adopted, whatever it is, will obviously produce resentment, the undermining of authority, and conflict. The process of developing a common-ground culture and fostering empathy on sensitive topics, such as abortion, is complex, although it may be effective with small groups of participants (LeBaron and Carstarphen 1997). Another such example is the question of worship in schools. Moreover, people are becoming very sensitive about issues such as environment, health, and safety: Divisions and conflicts go through not only interests but values, ideologies, deep-rooted ideas. If the area of decisions imposed by a majority on the minority or the minorities were to extend, the already serious fractures in society would deepen, with consequences that could threaten the very continuance of coexistence.

In addition, negotiation over the attribution of roles can develop at two different levels, the institutional and the political. The subject of negotiation is always the same, concerning the organizational model to be applied to the powers, the levels of government (federal, state, and local), and the sphere in which each power will exercise its influence. All participants claim to be pursuing the public interest but the context in which negotiation is carried out changes. In the first case, constitutional principles, values, and rights are the benchmarks. In political negotiation, however, concrete policy priority decisions are negotiated as well as the allocation of financial and other resources and standards for crucial areas such as health, public safety, and education.

It is also important to bear in mind that other factors apart from those already mentioned play a part in interpower negotiation, including each actor's unique characteristics and awareness of its source of legitimization. The president, or governing power, will be more sensitive to general public opinion. The legislative power cannot ignore strong pressures exercised both by constituencies and by lobbies. The judiciary is the guardian of the laws, and the public administration bases its position on technical competence and a professed impartiality. The ensuing system looks rather unstable, so the problem then becomes how to combine diverse, conflicting interests, styles, and sensitivities, which all claim to be pursuing a common goal: the public interest and the satisfaction of individual and social needs.

In order to achieve this agreement, it is necessary, first of all, to establish common definitions of what is meant by the "public interest" and by "social and individual needs". Second, negotiating procedures must be agreed upon since the checks-and-balances principle, a feature of political systems with a traditional division of powers and well-defined functions, is no longer adequate. The checks-and-balances principle loses much of its value in a continuously changing situation with different actors. Third, it is necessary to seek the consent of the governed to clear the way for negotiations, enabling citizens to be informed and to exercise some kind of control (Susskind and Cruikshank 1989).

Interpower negotiation should not aim for minimum levels of agreements but should seek to create bargains that improve the working of the political system and produce a genuine gain for citizens. In contrast with normal conditions of negotiation, when powers are involved it is not appropriate to seek the victory of one or other of the parties. Instead, the actors must perceive that they should exploit their differences to achieve benefits jointly.

Taking advantage of differences of interest does not mean helping the other party in order to receive help in turn (do ut des) or making a simple exchange. It signifies, above all, learning how to recognize the priorities, responsibilities, and interests of each actor. The first problem to be resolved in interpower negotiation is to identify a limit beyond which it is in no one's interest to go. In the literature on the subject, some analysts propose "best alternatives to nonagreement" (BATNA) as a criterion for verifying the motivation and interests underlying negotiation (Fisher and Ury 1981). Negotiation is thus the key to improvement. If

powers wage battle, each trying to impose its own interests and strengthen its own position, the result may be to block the political system, thus losing the confidence of citizens. Conflict between the courts, the political authorities, and the public administration is not the most effective way to deal with the breakdown of the traditional division of powers.

REFERENCES

Aharoni, Y., ed. 1997 *Changing Roles of State Intervention in Services in an Era of Open International Markets*. Albany: State University of New York Press.

Baruch Bush, R. A., and J. P. Folger 1994 *The Promise of Mediation*. San Francisco: Jossey-Bass.

Bercovitch, J., and J. Rubin, eds. 1992 *Mediation in International Relations: Multiple Approaches to Conflict Management*. New York: St. Martin's Press.

Breslin, J., and S. Rubin, eds. 1995 *Negotiation Theory and Practice*. Cambridge, Mass.: Program on Negotiation at Harvard Law School.

Dukes, F. E. 1996 *Resolving Public Conflict: Transforming Community and Governance*. Manchester, England: Manchester University Press.

Fisher, R., and W. Ury 1981 *Getting to Yes: Negotiation Agreement without Giving In*. Boston: Hougton Mifflin.

Goodwin, C. S. 1996 *The Arc of the Pendulum: A Philosophy for Government in the 21st Century*. Lanham, Md.: University Press of America.

Hanson, R. L. 1998 *Governing Partners: State-Local Relations in the United States*. Boulder, Colo.: Westview.

Lavinia, H. *Negotiation, Strategies for Mutual Gain*. Beverly Hills, Calif.: Sage.

Lax, D. A., and J. K. Sebinius 1986 *The Manager as Negotiator: Bargaining for Cooperation and Competitive Gain*. New York: Free Press.

LeBaron, M., and N. Carstarphen 1997 "Negotiating Intricable Conflict: The Common Ground Dialogue Process and Abortion." *Negotiating Journal* (October):341–363.

Leowenstein, K. 1965 *Political Power and the Governmental Process*. Chicago: University of Chicago Press.

Lewicki, R. J., D. M. Saunders, and J. W. Minton 1997 *Essentials of Negotiation*. Homewood, Ill.: Richard D. Irwin.

O'Toole, L. J., ed. 1993 *American Intergovernmental Relations: Foundations, Perspectives, and Issues*. Washington, D.C.: Congressional Quarterly Press.

Pruitt, D. G., and P. J. Carnevale 1993 *Negotiation in Social Conflict*. Pacific Grove, Calif.: Brooks/Cole.

Raiffa, H. 1985 *The Art and Science of Negotiation*. Cambridge, Mass.: Harvard University Press.

Simeon, R. 1985 *Division of Powers and Public Policy*. Toronto: University of Toronto Press.

Susskind, L., et al. 1999 *Negotiating Environmental Health and Safety Agreements*. Washington D.C.: Island Press.

——, and P. T. Field 1996 *Dealing with an Angry Public: The Mutual Gain*. New York: Free Press.

——, and J. Cruikshank 1987 *Breaking the Impasse: Consensual Approaches to Resolve Public Disputes*. New York: Basic Book.

Ursel, J. 1992 *Private Lives, Public Policy: 100 Years of State Intervention in the Family*. London: Women's Press.

Weiss, D. S. 1996 *Beyond the Walls of Conflict: Mutual Gains Negotiating for Unions and Management*. Homewood, Ill.: Irwin Professional.

BRUNO TELLIA

NETWORK ANALYSIS

See Social Networks.

NONPARAMETRIC STATISTICS

Parameters are characteristics of the population being studied such as a mean (μ), standard deviation (σ) or median (Md). Statistics describe characteristics of a sample. Sample mean ($\bar{x}$) and sample median (m) are two examples. In traditional or classical parametric statistics, making inferences from a sample or samples to a population or populations necessitates assumptions about the nature of the population distribution such as a normal population distribution.

Nonparametric statistics may be defined as statistical methods that contribute valid testing and estimation procedures under less stringent assumptions than the classical parametric statistics. However, there is no general agreement in the literature regarding the exact specification of the term "nonparametric statistics." In the past, nonparametric statistics and the term "distribution-free methods" were commonly used interchangeably in the literature, although they have different implications. Nonparametric statistics were often referred to as distribution-free statistics because they are not based on a particular type of a distribution in the population such as a normal distribution. It is, however, generally agreed that nonparametric statistics require fewer, or less stringent, assumptions about the nature of the population distribution being studied, compared to classical parametric statistics. It is important to note that nonparametric statistics are not totally assumption-free either, since they must be based on some assumptions applicable to specific tests, such as lack of ties or the independence of two random samples included in the study. They are flexible in their use and are generally quite robust. Nonparametric statistics allow researchers to arrive at conclusions based on exact probability values and the confidence interval.

The major advantages of nonparametric statistics compared to parametric statistics are that: (1) they can be applied to a large number of situations; (2) they can be more easily understood intuitively; (3) they can be used with smaller sample sizes; (4) they can be used with more types of data; (5) they need fewer or less stringent assumptions about the nature of the population distribution; (6) they are generally more robust and not often seriously affected by extreme values in data such as outliers; (7) they have, in many cases, a high level of asymptotic relative efficiency compared to the classical parametric tests; (8) the introduction of jackknife, bootstrap, and other resampling techniques has increased their range of applicability; and (9) they provide a number of supplemental or alternative tests and techniques to currently existing parametric tests.

Many critics of nonparametric tests have pointed out some major drawbacks of the tests: (1) they are usually neither as powerful nor as efficient as the parametric tests; (2) they are not as precise or as accurate as parametric tests in many cases (e.g., ranking tests with a large number of ties); (3) they might lead to erroneous decisions about rejecting or not rejecting the null hypothesis because of lack of precision in the test; (4) many of these tests utilize data inadequately in the analysis because they transform observed values into ranks and groups; and (5) the sampling distribution and distribution tables for nonparametric statistics are too numerous, are often cumbersome, and are limited to small sample sizes. The critics also claim that new parametric techniques and the availability of computers have reduced the need to use nonparametric statistics. Given these advantages and disadvantages, how does one choose between parametric and nonparametric tests?

Many criteria are available for this purpose. Statistical results are expected to be unbiased, consistent, or robust, or to have a combination of these characteristics. If both tests under consideration are applicable and appropriate, what other criteria may be used in the choice of a preferred test? The power and efficiency of a test are very widely used in comparing parametric and nonparametric tests.

The power of a test is the probability of rejecting the null hypothesis H_0 when it is false. It is defined as $1 - \text{ß}$, where ß is the probability of a Type II error, or acceptance of a false null hypothesis. If test A and test B would have the same alpha level of significance and the same sample sizes, and test B has a higher power, then test B is considered a preferred choice. However, calculations of the power of a test are often cumbersome. Another way of addressing the issue of the power of a test is through an asymptotic relative efficiency measure. The relative efficiency of a test in comparison to another test is the ratio of the sample size needed to achieve the same power with similar assumptions about significance levels and population distribution. Asymptotic relative efficiency of a test (sometimes called Pitman efficiency) is measured without a limit on the increase in sample size of that test. Thus, for example, when an asymptotic efficiency of Kendall's τ relative to Personian r is given as .912, it means that the τ with a sample size of 1000 is as efficient as an r with a sample size of 912. The test for asymptotic relative efficiency is now routinely used in the literature to compare two tests.

Based on these criteria, it can be generalized that nonparametric tests and techniques tend to be preferred when: (1) nominal or ordinal data are involved; (2) robust tests are needed because of outliers in the data; (3) probability distribution or density function of the data is unknown or cannot be assumed, as in the case of small sample sizes; (4) the effects of violations of specific test assumptions are unknown, or only weak assumptions can be made; (5) analogous parametric tests are not available, as in the case of runs tests and goodness-of-fit tests; and (6) preliminary trials, supplemental or alternative techniques for parametric techniques are needed.

NONPARAMETRIC STATISTICAL LITERATURE

The term *nonparametric statistics* was introduced in the statistical literature in the 1940s (Noether 1984). The historical roots of nonparametric statistics are supposed to go as far back as 1710 when John Arbuthnot did a study that included the proportion of male births in London (Daniel 1990; Hettmansperger 1984) using a sign test which is a nonparametric procedure. Spearman's rank correlation coefficient, which is widely used even today, was the forerunner of the chi-square test, which was introduced in 1900.

Initial major developments in the field that introduced and popularized the study of nonparametric methods appeared in the late 1940s and early 1950s, though a few nonparametric tests were published in the late 1920s such as the Fisher-Pitman test, Kendall's coefficient of concordance, and Hotelling and Pabst's paper on rank correlation in the 1930s. Contributions by Wilcoxon and Mann-Whitney were introduced during the 1940s. The term *nonparametric* reportedly appeared for the first time in 1942 in a paper by Wolfowitz (Noether 1984). The 1956 publication of Siegel's text on nonparametric statistics popularized the subject to such an extent that the text was one of the most widely cited textbooks in the field of statistics for a few years. It was during this time that computer software for nonparametric tests was introduced.

The major emphasis in the 1960s and 1970s was on the extension of the field into regression analysis, and analysis of variance to develop tests analogous to the classical parametric tests. It was also discovered during this period that nonparametric tests were more robust and more efficient than previously expected. The basis for the asymptotic distribution theory was developed during this time period.

A number of texts have been published recently (see, e.g., Conover 1999; Daniel 1990; Hollander and Wolfe 1999; Krauth 1988; Neave and Worthington 1988; Siegel and Castellan 1988; Sprent 1989). Some of these texts can be used without an extensive statistical background; they have excellent bibliographies and provide adequate examples of assumptions, applications, scope, and limitations of the field of nonparametric statistics. In addition, the *Encyclopedia of Statistical Sciences* (Kotz and Johnson 1982–1989) and the *International Encyclopedia of Statistics* (Kruskal and Tanur 1978) should serve as excellent sources of reference material pertaining to nonparametric statistics.

The literature on nonparametric statistics is extensive. The bibliography published in 1962 by Savage had approximately 3,000 entries. More recent bibliographies have made substantial additions to that list.

TESTS AND TECHNIQUES

Nonparametric statistics may be divided into three major categories: (1) noninferential statistical measures; (2) inferential estimation techniques for point and interval estimation of parametric values of the population; and (3) hypothesis testing, which is considered the primary purpose of nonparametric statistics. (Estimation techniques included in the category above are often used as a first step in hypothesis testing.) These three categories include different types of problems dealing with location, dispersion, goodness-of fit, association, runs and randomness, regression, trends, and proportions. They are presented in Table 1 and illustrated briefly in the text.

Table 1, which includes a short list of some commonly used nonparametric statistical methods and techniques, is illustrative in nature. It is not intended to be an exhaustive list. The literature literally consists of scores of nonparametric tests. More exhaustive tables are available in the literature (e.g., Hollander and Wolfe 1999). The six columns in the table describe the nature of the sample, and the eight categories of rows identify the major types of problems addressed in

nonparametric statistics. Types of data used in nonparametric tests are not included in the table, though references to levels of data are made in the text. Tables that relate tests to different types of data levels are presented in some texts (e.g., Conover 1999). A different type of table provided by Bradley (1968) identifies the family to which the nonparametric derivations belong.

The first column in Table 1 consists of tests involving a single sample. The statistics in this category include both inferential and descriptive measurements. They would be used to decide whether a particular sample could have been drawn from a presumed population, or to calculate estimates, or to test the null hypothesis. The next column is for two independent samples. The independent samples may be randomly drawn from two populations, or randomly assigned to two treatments. In the case of two related samples, the statistical tests are intended to examine whether both samples are drawn from the same (or identical) populations. The case of k (three or more) independent samples and k related samples are extensions of the two sample cases.

The eight categories in the table identify the main focus of problems in nonparametric statistics and are briefly described later. Only selected tests and techniques are listed in table 1. Log linear analyses are not included in this table, although they deal with proportions and meet some criteria for nonparametric tests. The argument against their inclusion is that they are rather highly developed specialized techniques with some very specific properties.

It may be noted that: (1) many tests cross over into different types of problems (e.g. the chi-square test is included in three types of problems); (2) the same probability distribution may be used for a variety of tests (e.g., in addition to association, proportion, and goodness-of-fit, the chi-square approximation may also be used in Friedman's two-way analysis of variance and Kruskal-Wallis test); (3) many of the tests listed in the table are extensions or modifications of other tests (e.g., the original median test was later extended to three or more independent samples; e.g., the Jonckheere test); (4) the general assumptions and procedures that underlie some of these tests have been extended beyond their original scope (e.g. Hájek's extension of the Kolmogorov-Smirnov test to regression

Selected Nonparametric Tests and Techniques

TYPE OF DATA

Type of Problem	One Sample	Two Independent Samples	Two Related, Paired, or Matched Samples	k Independent Samples	k Related Samples
Location	Sign test Wilcoxon signed ranks test	Mann-Whitney-Wilcoxon rank-sum test Permutation test Fisher tests Fisher-Pitman test Terry Hoeffding and van der Waerden/normal scores tests Tukey's confidence interval	Sign test Wilcoxon matched-pairs signed rank test Confidence interval based on sign test Confidence interval based on the Wilcoxon matched-pairs signed-ranks test	Extension of Brown-Mood median test Kruskal-Wallis one-way analysis of variance test Jonckheer test for ordered alternatives Multiple comparisons	Extension of Brown-Mood median test Kruskal-Wallis one-way analysis of variance test Jonckheer test for ordered alternatives Multiple comparisons Friedman two-way analysis of variance
Dispersion (Scale Problems)		Siegel-Tukey test Moses's ranklike tests Normal scores tests Test of the Freund, Ansari-Bradley, David, or Barton type			
Goodness-of-fit	Chi-square goodness-of-fit Kolmogorov-Smirnov test Lilliefors test	Chi-square test Kolmogorov-Smirnov test		Chi-square test Kolmogorov-Smirnov test	
Association	Spearman's rank correlation Kendall's tau_a tau_b tau_c Olmstead-Tukey test Phi coefficient Yule coefficient Goodman-Kruskal coefficients Cramer's statistic Point biserial coefficient	Chi-square test of independence	Spearman rank correlation coefficient Kendall's tau_a tau_b tau_c Olmstead-Tukey corner test	Chi-square test of independence Kendall's Partial rank correlations Kendall's coefficient of agreement Kendall's coefficient of concordance	Kendall's coefficient of concordance

(continued)

Selected Nonparametric Tests and Techniques (continued)

TYPE OF DATA

Type of Problem	One Sample	Two Independent Samples	Two Related, Paired, or Matched Samples	k Independent Samples	k Related Samples
Runs and Randomness	Runs test Runs above and below the median Runs up-and-down test	Wald-Wolfowitz runs test			
Regression		Hollander and Wolfe test for parallelism Confidence interval for difference between two slopes		Brown-Mood test	
Trends and Changes	Cox-Stuart test Kendall's tau Spearman's rank correlation coefficient McNemar change test Runs up-and-down test		McNemar Change test		
Proportion and Ratios	Binomial test	Fisher's exact test Chi-square test of homogeneity		Chi-square test of homogeneity	Cochran's Q test

Table 1

analysis and extension of the two-sample Wilcoxon test for testing the parallelism between two linear regression slopes); (5) many of these tests have corresponding techniques of confidence interval estimates, only a few of which are listed in Table 1; (6) many tests have other equivalent or alternative tests (e.g., when only two samples are used, the Kruskal-Wallis test is equivalent to the Mann-Whitney test); (7) sometimes similar tests are lumped together in spite of differences as in the case of the Mann-Whitney-Wilcoxon test or the Ansari-Bradley type tests or multiple comparison tests; (8) some tests can be used with one or more samples in which case the tests are listed in one or more categories, depending on common usage; (9) most of these tests have analogous parametric tests; and (10) a very large majority of nonparametric tests and techniques are not included in the table.

Only a few of the commonly used tests and techniques are selected from Table 1 for illustrative purposes in the sections below. The assumptions listed for the tests are not meant to be exhaustive, and hypothetical data are used in order to simplify the computational examples. Discussions about the strengths and weaknesses of these tests is also omitted. Most of the illustrations are either two-tailed or two-sided hypotheses at the

0.05 level. Tables of critical values for the tests illustrated here are included in most statistical texts. Modified formulas for ties are not emphasized, nor are measures of estimates illustrated. Generally, only simplified formulas are presented. A very brief description of the eight major categories of problems follows.

Location. Making inferences about location of parameters has been a major concern in the field of statistics. In addition to the mean, which is a parameter of great importance in the field of inferential statistics, the median is a parameter of great importance in nonparametric statistics because of its robustness. The robust quality of the median can be easily ascertained. If the values in a sample of five observations are 5, 7, 9, 11, 13, both the mean and the median are 9. If two observations are added to the sample, 1 and 94 (an outlier), the median is still 9, but the mean is changed to 20. Typical location problems include estimating the median, determining confidence intervals for the median, and testing whether two samples have equal medians.

Sign Test This is the earliest known nonparametric test used. It is also one of the easiest to understand intuitively because the test statistic is based on the number of positive or negative differences or signs from the hypothesized median. A binomial probability test can be applied to a sign test because of the dichotomous nature of outcomes that are specified by a plus (+) which indicates a difference in one direction or a minus (−) sign which indicates a difference in another direction. Observations with no change or no difference are eliminated from the analysis. The sign test may be a one-tailed or a two-tailed test. A sign test may be used whenever a *t*-test is inappropriate because the actual values may be missing or not known, but the direction of change can be determined, as in the case of a therapist who believes that her client is improving. The sign test only uses the direction of change and not the magnitude of differences in the data.

Wilcoxon Matched-Pairs Signed-Rank Test The sign test analysis includes only the positive or negative direction of difference between two measures; the Wilcoxon matched-pairs signed-rank test will also take into account the magnitude of differences in ordering the data.

Example: A matched sample of students in a school were enrolled in diving classes with different training techniques. Is there a difference? The scores are listed in Table 2.

Illustrative Assumptions: (1) The random sample data consist of pairs; (2) the differences in pair values have an ordered metric or interval scale, are continuous, and independent of one another; and (3) the distribution of differences is symmetric.

Hypotheses: A two-sided test is used in this example.

H_0: Sum of positive ranks = sum of negative ranks in population

H_1: Sum of positive ranks ≠ sum of negative ranks in population

(1)

Test statistic or procedures: The differences between the pairs of observations are obtained and ranked by magnitude. T is the smaller of the sum of ranks with positive or negative signs. Ties may be either eliminated or the average value of the ranks assigned to them. The decision is based on the value of T for a specified N. Z can be used as an approximation even with a small N except in cases with a relatively large number of ties. The formula for Z may be substituted when $N > 25$.

$$Z = \frac{T - N(N+1)/4}{\sqrt{N(N+1)(2N+1)/24}} \quad (2)$$

This formula is not applicable to the data in Table 2 because the N is < 25 and the calculations in Table 2 will be used in deciding whether to reject or fail to reject ("accept") the null hypothesis. In this example in Table 2, the N is 7 and the value of the smaller T is 9.5.

Decision: The researchers fail to reject the null hypothesis (or "accept" the null hypothesis) of no difference between the two groups, with an N of 7 at the 0.05 level, for a two-sided test, concluding that there is no statistically significant difference in the two types of training at the 0.05 level.

Efficiency: The asymptomatic related efficiency of the test varies around 95 percent, based on the sample sizes.

Total Scores for Five Diving Trials

Pairs	X Team A	Y Team B	Y - X Differences	Signed Rank of Differences T_+	Negative Ranks T_-
1	37	35	-2	-1	1
2	39	46	7	+4	
3	32	24	-8	-5.5	5.5
4	21	34	13	+7	
5	20	28	8	+5.5	
6	9	12	3	+2	
7	14	9	-5	-3	3
				$T_+ = 18.5$, $T_- = 9.5$	9.5

Table 2

Related parametric test: The *t*-test for matched pairs.

Analogous nonparametric tests: Sign test; randomization test for matched pairs; Walsh test for pairs.

Kruskal-Wallis One-Way Analysis of Variance Test This is a location measure with three or more independent samples. It is a one-way analysis of variance that utilizes ranking procedures.

Example: The weight loss in kilograms for 13 randomly assigned patients to one of the three diet programs is listed in Table 3 along with the rankings. Is there a significant difference in the sample medians?

Illustrative Assumptions: (1) Ordinal data; (2) three or more random samples; and (3) independent observations.

Hypotheses: A two-sided test without ties is used in this example.

$H_0:$ $Md_1 = Md_2 = Md_3$. The populations have the same median values.

$H_1:$ $Md_1 \neq Md_2 \neq Md_3$ All the populations do not have the same median value. (3)

Test statistics or procedures: The procedure is to rank the values and compute the sums of those ranks for each group and calculate the *H* statistic. The formula for *H* is as follows:

$$H = \left(\frac{12}{N(N+1)} \sum_{i=1}^{k} \frac{R_i^2}{N_i} \right) - 3(N+1) \quad (4)$$

where N_1 = the case in the *i*th category of rank sums R_i = the sum of ranks in the *i*th sample.

$$H = \frac{12}{13(13+1)} \left[\frac{(46)^2}{5} + \frac{(16)^2}{4} + \frac{(29)^2}{4} \right]$$
$$-3(13+1) = 45,9857 - 42 \quad (5)$$
$$H = 3.99$$

Decision: Do not reject the null hypothesis, as the chi-square value for 2 df at the 0.05 level is 5.99 and the *H* value of 3.99 is less than the critical value.

Efficiency: Asymptotic relative efficiency of Kruskal-Wallis test to *F* test is 0.955 if the population is normally distributed.

Related parametric test: *F* test. Analogous nonparametric test(s): Jonckheere test for ordered alternatives.

Friedman Two-Way Analysis of Variance This is a nonparametric two-way analysis of variance based on ranks and is a good substitute for the parametric *F* test when the assumptions for the *F* test cannot be met.

Example: Three groups of telephone employees from each of the work shifts were tested for their ability to recall fifteen-digit random numbers, under four conditions or treatments of sleep

Diet Programs and Weight-Loss Rankings

Group 1	Rank	Group 2	Rank	Group 3	Rank
2.8	3	2.2	1	2.9	4
3.5	7	2.7	2	3.1	6
4.0	11	3.0	5	3.7	9
4.1	12	3.6	8	3.8	10
4.9	13				
	$R_1 = 46$		$R_2 = 16$		$R_3 = 29$

Table 3

deprivation. The observations and rankings are listed in Tables 4 and 5. Is there a difference in the population medians?

$$F_\tau = \left[\frac{12}{Nk(k+1)} \sum_{j=1}^{k} R_j^2 \right] - 3N(k+1)$$

N = number of rows (subjects)

k = number of columns (variables or conditions or treatments)

R_j = sum of ranks in the jth column

(6)

$$F_\tau = \left[\frac{12}{3(4)(4+1)} \right] [(11)^2 + (6)^2 + (3)^2 + (10)^2]$$
$$- 3(3)(4+1)$$

(7)

$$F_\tau = (0.20)(266) - 45 = 8.2 \qquad (8)$$

Illustrative Assumptions: (1) There is no interaction between blocks and treatment; and (2) ordinal data with observable magnitude or interval data are needed.

Hypotheses:

H_0: $Md_1 = Md_2 = Md_3 = Md_4$. The different levels of sleep deprivation do not have differential effects.

H_1: One or more equality is violated. The different levels of sleep deprivation have differential effects.

(9)

Test statistic or procedures: The formula and computations are listed above.

Decision: The critical value at the 0.05 level of significance in this case for $N=3$ and $k=4$ is 7.4. Reject the null hypothesis because the F value is higher than the critical value. Conclude that the ability to recall is affected.

Efficiency: The asymptotic relative efficiency of this test depends on the nature of the underlying population distribution. With $k=2$ (number of samples), the asymptotic relative efficiency is reported to be 0.637 relative to the t test and is higher in cases of larger number of samples. In the case of three samples, for example, the asymptotic relative efficiency increases to 0.648 relative to the F test, and in the case of nine samples it is at least 0.777.

Related parametric test: F test.

Analogous nonparametric tests: Page test for ordered alternatives.

Mann-Whitney-Wilcoxon Test A combination of different procedures is used to calculate the probability of two independent samples being drawn from the same population or two populations with equal means. This group of tests is analogous to the t-test, it uses rank sums, and it can be used with fewer assumptions.

Example: Table 6 lists the verbal ability scores for a group of boys and a group of girls who are less than 1 year old. (The scores are arranged in ascending order for each of the groups.) Do the data provide evidence for significant differences in verbal ability of boys and girls?

Scores of Three Groups by Four Levels of Sleep Deprivation

Conditions	I	II	III	IV
Group 1	7	4	2	6
Group 2	6	4	2	9
Group 3	10	3	2	7

Table 4

Rank of Three Groups by Four Levels of Sleep Deprivation

Ranks	I	II	III	IV
Group 1	4	2	1	3
Group 2	3	2	1	4
Group 3	4	2	1	3
R_j	11	6	3	10

Table 5

Illustrative Assumptions: (1) Samples are independent and (2) ordinal data.

Hypotheses: A two-sided test is used in this example.

H_0: $Md_1 = Md_2$. There are no significant differences in the verbal ability of boys and girls.

H_1: $Md_1 \neq Md_2$. There is a significant difference in the verbal ability of boys and girls. (10)

Test statistic or procedures: Rearrange all the scores in an ascending or descending order (see Table 7). The test statistics are U_1 and U_2 and the calculations are illustrated below.

Mann-Whitney Wilcoxon U Test The following formulas may be used to calculate U.

$$U_1 = N_1N_2 + \frac{N_1(N_1+1)}{2} - R_2 \quad (11)$$

$$U_2 = N_1N_2 + \frac{N_2(N_2+1)}{2} - R_2 \quad (12)$$

$R_1 = 1+4+5+9 = 19$

$R_2 = 2+3+6+7+8+10.5+10.5 +12+13 = 72$

R_1 and R_2 refer to the sum of ranks for group 1 and group 2, respectively. (13)

$U_2 = (4)(9) = [9(9+1)/2] - 72 = 9$ and $U_1 = 27$, for $U_1 + U_2 = (N_1N_2) = 36$

Decision: Retain null hypothesis. At the 0.05 level, we fail to reject the null hypotheses of no differences in verbal ability. The rejection region for U in this case is 4 or smaller, for sample sizes of 4 and 9 respectively.

Efficiency: For large samples, the asymptomatic relative efficiency approaches 95 percent.

Related Parametric Test: F test.

Analogous Nonparametric Tests: Behrens-Fisher problem test, robust rank-order test.

Z can be used as a normal approximation if $N > 12$, or N_1, or $N_2 > 10$, and the formula is given below.

$$Z = \frac{R_1 - R_2(N_1-N_2)(N+1)/2}{\sqrt{N_1N_2(N+1)/3}} \quad (14)$$

Dispersion. Dispersion refers to spread or variability. Dispersion measures are intended to test for equality of dispersion in two populations.

The two-tailed null hypothesis in the Ansari-Bradley-type tests and Moses-type tests assumes that there are no differences in the dispersion of the populations. The Ansari-Bradley test assumes equal medians in the population. The Moses test has wider applicability because it does not make that assumption.

Dispersion tests are not widely used because of the limitations on the tests imposed by the assumptions and the low asymptotic related efficiency of the tests, or both.

Goodness-of-Fit. A goodness-of-fit test is used to test different types of problems—for example, the likelihood of observed sample data's being drawn from a prespecified population distribution, or comparisons of two independent samples

Verbal Scores for Boys and Girls Less than 1 Year Old

Boys N_1 (sample A):	10	15	18	28					
Girls N_2 (sample B):	12	14	20	22	25	30	30	31	32

Table 6

being drawn from populations with a similar distribution. The first problem mentioned above is illustrated here using the chi-square goodness-of-fit procedures.

X_2, or the chi-square test, is among the most widely used nonparametric tests in the social sciences. The four major types of analyses conducted through the use of chi-square are: (1) goodness-of-fit tests, (2) tests of homogeneity, (3) tests for differences in probability, and (4) test of independence. Of the four types of tests, the last one is the most widely used. The goodness-of-fit test and the test of independence will be illustrated in this article because the assumptions, formulas, and testing procedures are very similar to one another. The X_2 test for independence is presented in the section on measures of association.

Goodness-of-fit tests would be used in making decisions based on the prior knowledge of the population; for example, sentence length in a new manuscript could be compared with other works of an author to decide whether the manuscript is by the same author; or a manager's observation of a greater number of accidents in the factory on some days of the week as compared to the average figures could be tested for significant differences. The expected frequency of accidents given in table 8 below is based on the assumption of no differences in the number of accidents by days of the week.

Illustrative Assumptions: (1) The data are nominal or of a higher order such as ordinal, categorical, interval or ratio data. (2) The data are collected from a random sample.

Hypothesis:

Test Statistic or Procedures: The formula for calculating this is the same as for the chi-square test of independence. A short-cut formula is also provided and is used in this illustration:

H_0 : The distribution of accidents during the week is uniform.

H_1 : The distribution of accidents during the week is not uniform.

(15)

$$\chi^2 = \Sigma \frac{(f_o - f_e)^2}{f_e}$$

$$\chi^2 = \Sigma \frac{(f_o)^2}{f_e} - N$$

(16)

The notation f_0 refers to the frequency of actual observations and f_e is the frequency of expected observations.

$$\chi^2 = \frac{225}{30} + \frac{900}{30} + ... + \frac{1600}{30}$$
$$+ \frac{2025}{30} - N = 230 - 210 = 20$$

(17)

Decision: With seven observations, there are six degrees of freedom. The value for χv_2 is 12.59 at the .05 level of significance. Therefore, the null hypothesis of equal distribution of accidents over the 7 days is rejected at the .05 level of significance.

Asymptotic Relative Efficiency: There is no discussion in the literature about this because nominal data can be used in this analysis and the test is often used when there are no alternatives available. Asymptotic relative efficiency is meaningless with nominal data.

Related Parametric Test. t test.

Analogous Nonparametric Tests. The Kolmogrov-Smirnov one-sample test, and the binomial test for dichotomous variables.

The Kolmogrov-Smirnov test is another major goodness-of-fit test. It has two versions, the one-sample and the two-sample tests. It is different from the chi-square goodness-of-fit in that the

Ranked Verbal Scores for Boys and Girls Less than 1 Year Old												
Scores: 10	12	14	15	18	20	22	25	28	30	30	31	32
Rank: 1	2	3	4	5	6	7	8	9	10.5	10.5	12	13
Comp: A	B	B	A	A	B	B	B	A	B	B	B	B

Table 7

Kolmogrov-Smirnov test, which is based on observed and expected differences in cumulative distribution functions and can be used with individual values instead of having to group them.

Association. There are two major types of measures of association. They consist of: (1) measures to test the existence (relationship) or nonexistence (independence) of association among the variables, and (2) measures of the degree or strength of association among the variables. Different tests of association are utilized in the analysis of nominal and nominal data, nominal and ordinal data, nominal and interval data, ordinal and ordinal data, and ordinal and interval data.

Chi-Square Test of Independence In addition to goodness-of-fit, χ_2 can also be used as a test of independence between two variables. The test can be used with nominal data and may consist of one or more samples.

Example: A large firm employs both married and single women. The manager suspects that there is a difference in the absenteeism rates between the two groups. How would you test for it? Data are included in Table 9.

Illustrative Assumptions: (1) The data are nominal or of a higher order such as ordinal, categorical, interval, or ratio data. (2) The data are collected from a random sample.

Hypothesis:

Test statistic or procedures: The formula for χ_2 is given below. Differences between observed and expected frequencies are calculated, and the resultant value is indicated below.

The expected frequencies are obtained by multiplying the corresponding column marginal totals by row marginal totals for each cell divided by the total number of observations. For example, the expected frequency for the cell with an observed frequency of 40 is $(100 \times 100)/400 = 25$.

H_0: The two variables are independent or there is no difference between married and single women with respect to absenteeism.

H_1: The two variables are not independent (i.e., they are related), or there is no difference between married women and single women with respect to absenteeism. (18)

$$\chi^2 = \Sigma \frac{(f_o - f_e)^2}{f_e}$$

f_o – observed frequency,

f_e – expected frequency (19)

Similarly, the expected frequency for the cell with an observed frequency of 170 is $(200 \times 300)/400 = 150$.

$$(30-25)^2/25 + (70-75)^2/75 + (40-25)^2/$$
$$25 + (60-75)^2/75 + (30-50)^2/$$
$$50 + (170-150)^2/150$$
$$\chi^2 = 1 + .33 + 9 + 3 + 8 + 2.67 = 24$$
(20)

$$df = (\text{number of rows} - 1) \times (\text{number of columns} - 1) = (3-1)(2-1) = 2$$ (21)

Decision: As the critical χ^2 value with two *df* is 5.99, we reject the null hypothesis, at the 0.05 level. We accept the alternate hypothesis of the existence of a statistically significant difference in the ratio of absenteeism per year between the two groups of married and single women.

Efficiency: The asymptotic relative efficiency of a χ^2 test is hard to assess because it is affected by the number of cells in the contingency table and the sample size as well. The asymptotic related efficiency of a 2×2 contingency table is very low,

Frequency of Traffic Accidents for One Week during May

Day	S	M	T	W	T	F	S	Total
Traffic Accidents	15	30	30	25	25	40	45	210
Expected Frequencies	30	30	30	30	30	30	30	210

Table 8

but the power distribution of χ^2 starts approximating closer to 1 as the sample size starts getting larger. However, a large number of cells in a χ^2 table, especially with a combination of large sample sizes, tend to yield large χ^2 values which are statistically significant because of the size of the sample. In the past, Yate's correction for continuity was often used in a 2 × 2 contingency table if the cell frequencies were small. Because of the criticism of this procedure, this correction procedure is no longer widely used. Other tests such as Fisher's Exact Test can be used in cases of small cell frequencies.

Related Parametric Test: There are no clear-cut related parametric tests because the χ^2 test can be used with nominal data.

Analogous Nonparametric Tests: The Fisher Exact Test (limited to 2 × 2 tables and small tables) and the median test (limited to central tendencies) can be used as alternatives. In addition, a large number of tests such as phi, gamma, and Cramer's V statistic, can be used as alternatives, provided the data characteristics meet the assumptions of these tests. The χ^2 distribution is used in many other nonparametric tests.

The chi-square tests of contingency tables allow partitioning of tables, combining tables, and using more than two-way tables with control variables.

The second type of association tests measure the actual strength of association. Some of these tests also indicate the direction of the relationship and the test values in most cases extend from −1.00 to +1.00 indicating a negative or a positive relationship. The values of some other nondirectional tests fall between 0.00 and 1.00. Contingency table formats are commonly used to measure this type of association. Among the more widely used tests are the following, arranged by the types of data used: *Nominal by Nominal Data:*

Phi coefficient—limited to a 2 × 2 contingency table. A square of these test values is used to interpret a proportional reduction error.

Contingency coefficient based on the chi-square values. The lowest limit for this test is 0.00, but the upper limit does not attain unity (value of 1.00).

Cramer's V statistic—not affected by an increase in the size of cells as long as it is related to similar changes in the other cells.

Lambda—the range of lambda is from 0.00 to 1.00, and thus it has only positive values.

Ordinal by Ordinal Data:

Gamma—uses ordinal data for two or more variables. Test values are between −1.00 and +1.00.

Somer's D—used for predicting a dependent variable from the independent variable.

Kendall's tau—described in more detail below.

Spearman's rho—described in more detail below.

Categorical by Interval Data

Kappa—The table for this test needs to have the same categories in the columns and the rows. Kappa is a measure of agreement, for example, between two judges.

The tests described above are intended for two-dimensional contingency tables. Tests for three-dimensional tables have been developed recently in both parametric and nonparametric statistics.

Two other major measures of association referenced above are presented below. They are Kendall's τ (the forerunner of this test is also one

Annual Absences for Single and Married Women

Days Absent	Married Women		Single Women		Row Totals
	f_o	(f_e)	f_o	(f_e)	
Low (0–5)	30	(25)	70	(75)	100
Medium (6–10)	40	(25)	60	(75)	100
High (11+)	30	(50)	170	(150)	200
Column Totals	100		300		400

Table 9

of the oldest test statistics) and Spearman's ρ (one of the oldest nonparametric techniques). They are measures of association based on ordinal data.

τ is a measure of rank-order correlation. It also tests for independence of the two variables observed. It assumes at least ordinal data. The test scores of τ range between −1.00 and +1.0 by convention. A score of +1.00 indicates a perfect agreement between rankings of the two sets of observations. A score of −1.00 indicates a perfect negative correlation which means the ranking in one observation is in the reverse order of the other set of observations. All other scores fall between these two values. The test statistics for data with no ties is given below.

The test statistic:

$$\tau = \frac{S}{n(n-1)/2} \qquad (22)$$

S measures the difference between the pairs of observations in natural order. A number of students are ranked according to their mathematical and verbal test scores. The six students are identified by letters A to F. There is no need to know the actual scores, and if actual scores are known, they will be converted to ranks as in Table 10.

What is being measured here with τ is the degree of correspondence between the two rankings based on mathematical and verbal scores. The calculations can be simplified if one of the values is arranged in the natural ascending order from the lowest value to the highest value. The lack of correspondence between the two rankings can be measured by just using the second set of rankings which, in this case, is verbal ability.

Illustrative Assumptions: (1) The data are at least ordinal. (2) Variables in the study are continuous.

Hypothesis:

H_0: Mathematical and verbal test scores are independent.

H_1: Mathematical and verbal test scores are related positively or negatively.

(23)

The number of concordant pairs is measured by the agreement between the two pairs based on their corresponding standing in their own ranking, and discordant pairs are calculated on the basis of the disagreement between them. The example given below in Table 11 consists of no tied ranks.

$$S = 8 - 7 = 1$$

$$\tau = \frac{S}{n(n-1)/2} = \frac{8-7}{6(5)/2} = \frac{1}{15} = 0.067 \qquad (24)$$

Decision: With $n = 6$, the researcher fails to reject the null hypothesis H_0 at 0.05 level since tau = 0.067 is smaller than tau = 0.600, which is the critical value for a two-tailed test.

Efficiency: The asymptotic relative efficiency: Both Kendall's τ and Spearman's ρ have an asymptotic relative efficiency of .912 compared to the Personian r (correlation coefficient) which is a parametric test and can go up to 1.12 in exponential type of distribution data.

Related Parametric Test: Personian correlation coefficient (in case of interval or ratio data).

Analogous Nonparametric Tests: Spearman's ρ (rho).

Mathematical (X) and Verbal (Y) Test Scores for Six Students

	A	B	C	D	E	F
X Math	9	15	8	10	12	7
Y Verbal	10	13	9	11	4	12

Table 10

In many studies, however, the same values may occur more than once within X observations, within Y observations, or within both observations—in which case there will be a tie. In the case of tied ranks, different formulas for tau$_a$, tau$_b$, tau$_c$ are used. There is, however, no general agreement in the literature about the usage of subscripts. More detailed treatment of this topic is provided in Kendall and Gibbons (1990). Kendall's τ measures the association between two variables, and when there are more than two variables, Kendall's coefficient of concordance can be used to measure the association among multiple variables.

Spearman's ρ (rho) is another popular measure of a rank-correlation technique. The technique is based on using the ranks of the observations, and a Personian correlation is computed for the ranks. Spearman's rank correlation coefficient is used to test independence between two rank-ordered variables. It resembles Kendall's tau in that regard, and the two tests tend to be similar in their results of hypothesis testing.

Runs and Randomness. A run is a gambling term that in statistics refers to a sequence or an order of occurrence of event. For example, if a coin were tossed ten times, it could result in the following sequence of heads and tails: H T H H H T T H H T. The purpose of runs test is to determine whether the run or sequence of events occurs in a random order.

Another type of runs test would be to test whether the run scores are higher or lower than the median scores. A runs up-and-down test compares each observation with the one immediately preceding it in the sequence. Runs tests are not very robust, as they are very sensitive to variations in the data.

As there are no direct parallel parametric tests for testing the random order or sequence of a series of events, the concept of power or efficiency is not really relevant in the case of runs tests.

Regression. The purpose of regression tests and techniques is to predict one variable based on its relationship with one or more other variables. The procedure most often used is to try to fit a regression line based on observed data. Though only a few simple regression techniques are included in Table 1, this is one of the more active areas in the field of nonparametric statistics.

The problems relating to regression analysis are similar to those in parametric statistics such as finding a slope, finding confidence intervals for slope coefficients, finding confidence intervals for median differences, curve fitting, interpolation, and smoothing. For example, the Brown-Mood method for finding a slope consists of graphing the observations on a scatter diagram; then a vertical line is drawn representing the median value, and points on both sides of the vertical line are joined. This gives the initial slope, which is later modified through iterative procedures if necessary. Some other tests are based on an extension of the rank order of correlation techniques discussed earlier.

Trends and Changes. Comparisons between, before, and after experiment scores are among the most commonly used procedures of research designs. The obvious question in such cases is whether there is a pattern of change and, if so, whether the trends can be detected. Demographers, economists, executives in business and industry, and federal and state departments of commerce are always interested in trends—whether downward, upward, or existing at all. The Cox-Stuart change test, or test for trend, is a procedure intended to answer these kinds of questions. It is a modification of the sign test. The procedures are very similar to the sign test.

Mathematical (X) and Verbal (Y) Test Scores in Rank Order

Values (X, Y)	Rankings (X, Y)	(Y is similar in natural order to X)	Y is reverse of natural order of X
(7, 12)	(1, 5)	1	4
(8, 9)	(2, 2)	3	1
(9, 10)	(3, 3)	2	1
(10, 11)	(4, 4)	1	1
(12, 4)	(5,1)	1	0
(15, 13)	(6, 6)	0	0
		8	7

Table 11

Example: We want to test a statement in the newspaper that there is no changing trend in snowfall in Seattle between the last twenty years and the twenty years before that. The assumptions, procedures, and test procedures are similar to the sign test. These data constitute twenty sets of paired observations. If the data are not chronological, then values below the median and above the median would be matched in order. The value in the second observation in the set is compared to the first and would be coded as either positive or plus, negative or minus, and no change. A large number of positive or negative signs would indicate a trend, and the same number of positive and negative signs would indicate no trend. The distribution here is dichotomous, and, hence, a binomial test would be used. If there are seven positive signs and thirteen negative signs, it can be concluded that there is no statistically significant upward or downward trend in snowfall at the 0.05 level as $p(k = 7/20/0.50)$ is greater, k being the number of positive signs. The asymptotic relative efficiency of the test compared to rank correlation is 0.79. Spearman's coefficient of rank correlation and Kendall's Tau may also be used to test for trends.

Proportion. The term "portion" or the term "share" may be used to convey the same idea as "proportion" in day-to-day usage. A sociologist might be interested in the proportion of working and nonworking mothers in the labor force, or in comparing the differences in the proportion of people who voted in a local election and the voter turnout in a national election. In case of a dichotomous situation, a binomial test can be used as a test of proportion; but there are many other situations where more than two categories and two or more independent samples are involved. In such cases, the chi-square distribution may also be viewed as a test of differences in proportion between two or more samples.

Cochran's Q test is another test of proportions that is applicable to situations with dichotomous choices or outcomes for three or more related samples. For example, in the context of an experimental situation, the null hypothesis would be that there is no difference in the effectiveness of treatments. Restated, it is a statement of equal proportions of success or failures in the treatments.

NEW DEVELOPMENTS

The field of nonparametric statistics has matured, and the growth of the field has slowed down compared to the fast pace in the 1940s and 1950s. Among the reasons for some of these changes are the development of new techniques in parametric statistics and log linear probability models, such as logit analysis for categorical data analysis, and the widespread availability of computers that perform lengthy calculations. Log linear analysis has occasionally been treated in nonparametric statistics literature because it allows the analysis of dichotomous or ordered categorical data and allows the application of nonparametric tests. As indicated earlier, it was not included in the tests discussed in this article because it is a categorical response analog to regression or variance models.

There is further research being conducted in the field of nonparametric robust statistics. The field of robust statistics is also in the process of developing into a new subspecialty of its own. At the same time, development of new tools—jackknife, bootstrapping, and other resampling techniques that are used both in parametric and nonparametric statistics—has positively impacted the use of nonparametric techniques. Based on the contents of popular computer software, the field of nonparametric statistics cannot yet be considered part of the mainstream of statistics, although some individual nonparametric tests are widely used.

There are many new developments taking place in the field of nonparametric statistics. Only three major trends are referenced here. The scope of application of nonparametric tests is gradually expanding. Often, more than one nonparametric test may be available to test the same or similar hypotheses. Again, many new, appropriate, and powerful nonparametric tests are being developed to replace or supplement the original parametric tests. Last, new techniques such as bootstrapping are making nonparametric tests more versatile.

As in the case of bootstrapping, many other topics and subtopics in nonparametric statistics, have developed into full-fledged specialties or subspecialties—for example, extreme value statistics, which is used in studying floods and air pollution. Similarly, a large number of new techniques and concepts—such as (1) the influence curve for comparing different robust estimators, (2) M-estimators for generalizations that extend the scope of traditional location tests, and (3) adaptive estimation procedures for dealing with unknown distribution—are being developed in the field of inferential statistics. Attention is also being directed to the developments of measures and tests with nonlinear data. In addition, attempts are being made by nonparametric statisticians to incorporate techniques from other branches of statistics, such as Bayesian statistics.

Parallel Trends in Development. There are two parallel developments in nonparametric and parametric statistics. First, the field of nonparametric statistics is being extended to develop more tests analogous to parametric tests. Recent developments in computer software include many of the new nonparametric tests and alternatives to parametric tests. Second, the field of parametric statistics is being extended to develop and incorporate more robust tests to increase the stability of parametric tests. The study of outliers, for example, is now gaining significant attention in the field of parametric statistics as well.

Recent advancements have accelerated developments in nonparametric and parametric statistics, narrowing many distinctions and bridging some of the differences between the two types, bringing the two fields conceptually closer.

REFERENCES

Bradley, James B. 1968 *Distribution-Free Statistical Tests.* Englewood Cliffs, N.J.: Prentice-Hall.

Conover, W. J. 1999 *Practical Nonparametric Statistics*, 3rd ed. New York: John Wiley.

Daniel, Wayne W. 1990 *Applied Nonparametric Statistics*, 2nd ed. Boston: PWS-KENT.

Kotz, Samuel, and Normal L. Johnson, editors-in-chief 1982–1989 *Encyclopedia of Statistical Sciences*, vols. I-IX. New York: John Wiley.

Gibbons, Jean Dixon 1986 "Distribution-Free Methods." In S. Kotz and N. L. Johnson, eds., *Encyclopedia of Statistical Sciences*, vol. 2. New York: John Wiley.

Hettmansperger, Thomas P. 1984 *Statistical Inference Based on Ranks.* New York: John Wiley.

Hollander, Myles, and Douglas A. Wolfe 1999 *Nonparametric Statistical Methods*, 2nd ed. New York: John Wiley.

Kendall, Maurice G., and Jean Dickinson Gibbons 1990 *Rank Correlation Methods*, 5th ed. London: Oxford University Press.

Kotz, Samuel, Norman L. Johnson, Campbell, and B. Read 1982–1989 *Encyclopedia of Statistical Sciences*, vols. 1–9 and supplement. New York: John Wiley.

Krauth, Joachim 1988 *Distribution-Free Statistics: An Application-Oriented Approach.* Amsterdam: Elsevier.

Kruskal, William H., and Judith M. Tanur, eds. 1978 *International Encyclopedia of Statistics*, vols. I-II. New York: Free Press.

Neave, H. R., and P. L. Worthington 1988 *Distribution-Free Tests.* London: Unwin Hyman.

Noether, Gottfried E. 1984 "Nonparametriccs: The Early Years-Impressions and Recollections." *American Statistician* 38(3):173–178.

Savage I. R. 1962 *Bibliography of Nonparametric Statistics.* Cambridge, Mass.: Harvard University Press.

Siegel, Sidney 1956 *Nonparametric Statistics for the Behavioral Sciences.* New York: McGraw-Hill.

Siegel, Sidney, and N. John Castellan, Jr. 1988 *Nonparametric Statistics for the Behavioral Sciences*, 2nd ed. New York: McGraw-Hill.

Sprent, P. 1989 *Applied Nonparametric Statistical Methods.* London: Chapman and Hall.

SUBHASH R. SONNAD

NURSING HOMES

See Long Term Care Facilities.

O

OBJECTIVITY

See Epistemology; Measurement; Scientific Explanation.

OBSERVATION SYSTEMS

The most sensitive, sophisticated, and flexible instrument of observation available today is the human being. All the recent advances in technology have not changed this central fact; we can monitor communications, transcribe conversations using language processing software, and conduct computer-assisted content analysis of the results. Still, at some point a person who understands the social context must infer the meaning of the communications. Systematic methods of observation may vary the unit of analysis, shift the boundaries of categories, and adjust the level of judgment allowed, but sociologists are ultimately left with the basic reality of human beings watching other human beings. The role of the methodologist is to make this process more systematic.

Most sociological data are filtered through the perceptions of informants in an idiosyncratic manner. Retrospective accounts of events, opinion polls, and surveys measure the output of the social perception process. Only systematic observation, with valid and reliable instruments, provides a record of the events themselves rather than the retrospective reconstruction of the events. The more rigorously defined the categories, the more confident the researcher can be that the data reflect the events and not just the biases and preconceptions of the informants.

While some of the systems that are described below were developed for specific purposes such as the observation of business case-study groups or the diagnosis of psychiatric patients, most attempt to capture the full range of social behavior and may thus be applied to a wide range of settings. Not included here are specialized systems that have been developed for single contexts, such as the classroom behavior of small children, the responses of subjects in tightly controlled laboratory experiments, and the evaluation of employees. One fast-food restaurant, for example, has developed a thirty-one-category observation system that managers can use to observe and evaluate counter staff. Items include "There is a smile," "The bag is double folded," and "Change is counted efficiently."

Observation systems have been used for a wide variety of purposes over the years. Early uses included psychiatric diagnosis, job placement, and basic research into group process and development. As corporate assessment centers came into widespread use for the selection of executives, early observation systems reappeared for the analysis of leaderless-group exercises. More recent applications have included research and consulting on team building and training, the evaluation of social workers, the prediction of success and failure of military cadets, the study of leadership networks in large corporations, the evaluation and treatment of problem children in the classroom, the evaluation of psychiatric interventions, the analysis of delinquent behavior, and resocialization, and consultation on mergers and consolidations (Polley et al. 1988). In the past ten years, direct observation has been in decline. As a result of the high costs in terms of time and money, systematic observation has often given way to retrospective rating systems (Bales 1998). Such methods are, however, a poor substitute for direct observation.

SINGLE-CATEGORY SYSTEMS

Elliot D. Chapple introduced the *interaction chronograph* in 1940. It was a simple device that consisted of two telegraph keys. Observers were instructed to press key A when person A spoke and key B when person B spoke. A record of the conversation was kept on a moving paper tape. Not surprisingly, inter-rater reliabilities were nearly perfect. Twenty-five years later, the human observers wee replaced by voice-activated microphones attached to analog-digital converters (Wiens et al. 1965). That such a simple device could replace the human observer suggests that the systems were not taking full advantage of the observers' capabilities. In reality, the decision to record such objective and basic information simply shifted the burden of interpretation from the observer to the researcher. Elliot Chapple (1940) and his successors developed elaborate schemes for interpreting the patterns of lines and blanks that appeared on their paper tapes. At the peak of its popularity, the interaction chronograph was used for everything from psychiatric diagnosis to employee placement.

MULTIPLE CATEGORY SYSTEMS

Chapple's work serves as an important benchmark. The near-perfect reliability is achieved at the cost of validity. The observation systems that followed it generally traded off a measure of reliability for greater validity. More meaningful sets of categories will almost certainly be harder to employ with any degree of inter-rater reliability.

Interaction Process Analysis (IPA) was one of the earliest attempts to devise more meaningful categories. Bales (1950) began with an encyclopedic list of behaviors and gradually consolidated them into an elegant set of twelve basic categories. Fifty years later, his original system is still one of the most widely applied observation methods.

The IPA category list was evolving at the same time that Parsons and Bales (1955) were developing a model of family socialization. They saw family leadership in the 1940s and 1950s as divided between the father and the mother. IPA perpetuates this somewhat dated division through its primary dimension; six categories are provided for coding task-oriented behaviors and six are for coding socioemotional behaviors (Table 1). When Slater (1955) suggested that this role differentiation could be extended to a general model of effective leadership in groups, he sparked a continuing controversy. But it must be remembered that this conceptualization preceded any serious consideration of either androgyny or flexibility in sex roles.

Additional symmetries are built into IPA. Three of the six socioemotional categories carry positive affect, and each has a direct counterpart on the negative side. Task-oriented behavior is seen as the process of asking questions and offering answers, though the answers—in the form of suggestions, opinions, and orientation (or information)—may be in response to questions asked or implied. Finally, the functionalist orientation of Parsons and Bales (1955) appears in the identification of six problems faced by groups: communication, evaluation, control, decision, tension reduction, and reintegration.

Following Chapple's lead, Bales developed and marketed a moving paper-tape recording device. The interaction recorder allowed for observation of groups rather than just dyads; the tape was divided into twelve rows and moved past a window at a constant speed so that the observer could write a code, indicating who was speaking to whom, within a category-by-time sector on the tape. This added complexity and enlarged the unit of analysis. The interaction recorder provided a continuous on-off record while IPA recorded discrete acts. The coding unity was, however, kept small. IPA coders often record two or three acts for a single sentence and are expected to record *all* acts. The first serious challenge to Bales's IPA system was Borgatta's Interaction Process Scores (IPS) system (1963). Borgatta argued that the twelve categories failed to make some crucial distinctions. His redefinition of the boundaries resulted in an eighteen-category system that had the advantage of greater precision and the disadvantages of greater

Interaction Process Analysis

	Category	Emotion	Task	Problem
1.	Shows solidarity	Positive		Reintegration
2.	Shows tension release	Positive		Tension reduction
3.	Agrees	Positive		Decision
4.	Gives suggestion		Answer	Control
5.	Gives opinion		Answer	Evaluation
6.	Gives orientation		Answer	Communication
7.	Asks for orientation		Question	Communication
8.	Asks for opinion		Question	Evaluation
9.	Asks for suggestion		Question	Control
10.	Disagrees	Negative		Decision
11.	Shows tension	Negative		Tension reduction
12.	Shows antagonism	Negative		Reintegration

Table 1

SOURCE: Adapted from Bales (1950) p. 14.

complexity and a lack of symmetry. The former problem was largely solved by the availability of a self-training workbook (Borgatta and Crowther 1965). Such a manual has never been widely available for IPA.

The next logical step after categorization is the organization of categories. IPA had an implicit organization that was lacking in IPS. This, and the fact that IPA had twelve rather than eighteen categories, made IPA the easier system to learn and use. As Weick (1985) points out, however, there is a problem of "requisite variety." A system for understanding a phenomenon must be at least as complex as the phenomenon itself. Weick uses the metaphor of a camera with variable focal length. In order to photograph objects at twenty different distances, the camera must have at least twenty focal settings or the pictures will not all be of equal clarity. This creates real problems for the interaction chronograph. Clearly, social behavior is more complex than Chapple's on-off category system. Unfortunately for researchers, it is also more complex than IPA's twelve-category system. This creates a dilemma. The mind can hold only so many categories at once; even with twelve categories, most observers tend to forget the rarer ones in an attempt to simplify their task.

MULTIDIMENSIONAL SYSTEMS

Timothy Leary (1957) proposed one of the first observation systems based primarily on dimensions rather than categories. His interpersonal diagnosis system placed sixteen categories at the compass points of a two-dimensional circumplex. The dimensions, dominance-submission and love-hate, would prove to be the two most common dimensions among the systems that followed. While intended primarily for the diagnosis of psychiatric disorders, the system also identified the "normal," or less intense, variant of each behavior as well as the likely response that each behavior would generate in other people. For example, the general behavior in the direction of dominance is "manage, direct, lead"; this behavior is likely to "obedience" in others. The extreme version of the category is "dominate, boss, order." This falls into the larger category of behavior that is described as "managerial" when in the normal range and "autocratic" when in the abnormal range. More than a method of observation, the interpersonal diagnosis system was a remarkably well-articulated theory of interpersonal relations. Were it not for Leary's well-publicized advocacy of lysergic acid diethylamide (LSD), the system might very well be in common use today. While the research was briefly resurrected by McLemore and Benjamin (1979), it never had a major impact on either social psychology or psychiatry. Leary claimed that the system worked so well for psychiatric diagnosis that a receptionist trained in its use could provide diagnoses based on observations in the waiting room that rivaled those obtained by psychiatrists after conducting a diagnostic interview.

Leary's two dimensions were theoretically derived. In a 1960 doctoral dissertation, Arthur Couch pioneered the application of factor analysis to interpersonal behavior, thus offering an empirical alternative for the derivation of dimensions. Couch's six dimensions of interpersonal behavior were derived from the factor analysis of a vast amount of data on twelve groups of five undergraduates each. The individuals were given a large battery of personality tests and the twelve groups were observed participating in a wide variety of tasks across five meetings each. While the factor analysis is not independent of the original categories of measurement and observation, Couch's data set was so exhaustive as to deserve credence.

MULTILEVEL SYSTEMS

The three dimensions of Bales and colleagues' SYMLOG (System for the Multiple Level Observation of Groups) (1979) owe much both to IPA and to Couch's empirical work. They also reflect the legacy of Leary's circumplex. Dominant-submissive (up-down, or U-D) was the first factor from Couch's analysis; in IPA it corresponds to total amount of talking rather than to interaction in any specific set of categories; Leary's interpersonal diagnosis system had already identified the primary dimension as dominant-submissive. In essence, this was also the dimension that Chapple's interaction chronograph measured. Friendly-unfriendly (Positive-negative, or P-N), Couch's second factor, was represented in IPA by the three positive and three negative socioemotional categories, and it corresponds to love-hate in Leary's system. Task-oriented–emotional expressive (forward-backward, or F-B), the controversial distinction from IPA, was a compromise that created one bipolar dimension out of two of Couch's remaining factors. These three dimensions, generally referred to by the code letters shown above, define a three-dimensional conceptual space. Following Leary, Bales

and his colleagues then defined the compass points of the space. In this case, definitions were produced for all twenty-six vectors in the three-dimensional space. Thus, a dominant, unfriendly, task-oriented act (UNF) is defined as "authoritarian and controlling," and a submissive, unfriendly, emotional act (DNB) is described as "withdrawn and alienated." This was a creative solution to the dilemma of providing requisite variety while keeping the number of categories reasonable. While there are twenty-six categories, they are organized into three dimensions, so coders can hold the three-dimensional space rather than the twenty-six categories in mind. The twenty-six category descriptions then become a reference to be used when first learning the system and trying to understand where specific behaviors fit.

In addition to the basic level of behavior described above, SYMLOG also provides definitions for the twenty-six vectors on the level of nonverbal behavior. This level is coded when unintentional messages are sent through nonverbal behaviors or when the nonverbal—or paralinguistic—cues are at variance with the overt verbal cues. In developing his descriptions of facial expression and nonverbal cues, Bales drew on the work of the eighteenth-century French Encyclopedists. He found that Diderot and his colleagues had developed a more sophisticated understanding of facial expression and nonverbal nuance than have modern social scientists.

SYMLOG also allows for the coding of verbal content. Theoretically, the two levels of behavior—overt and nonverbal—could be coded without reference to the content of the message. Conversely, the content of messages could be coded from written transcripts without reference to the behaviors of the speakers. The content coding level attends only to evaluative statements. Each statement is first coded PRO (for statements in favor of something) or CON (statements against something). The content of the value statement is then coded in the same three-dimensional space that was used for behavior. Finally, the level of the value statement is recorded. Levels begin with the self and move outward: self, other, group, situation, society, and fantasy.

When the full SYMLOG system is used for coding a conversation, the result is a set of simple sentences written in code. For example, Figure 1 records a brief exchange that took place from 1:23 to 1:24. Joe ordered Bill to stop contradicting him. The behavior was authoritarian (UNF) and the value statement was against negativity in Bill (CON N BIL). Bill responded in a rebellious manner (UNB) and made a value statement against Joe's authoritarianism (CON UNF JOE). Ron intervened in a "purposeful and considerate" manner (UPF) and made a value statement in favor of reducing the level of conflict (PRO DP GRP). If we see contradictions between the overt and nonverbal behavior, we could add lines such as 123 JOE GRP N DN. This would indicate that underneath Joe's authoritarianism is a note of insecurity and nervousness. (The first "N" in the message stands for "nonverbal," the "A" in each of the messages in Figure 1 stands for "act.") Clearly, the system requires fairly extensive training of coders. Most SYMLOG coders went through a fifteen-week course that was run as a self-analytic group. During this time, they alternated between serving as group participants and retreating behind a mirror to serve as coders. While there remain some universities in which such courses are still taught, the use of this method peaked in the late 1970s and early 1980s. Most work being done with SYMLOG at this time uses a parallel system of retrospective rating which requires no special training. This has resulted in time and cost savings, but at the expense of sacrificing the dynamic moment-to-moment process measurement that the original SYMLOG observation system made possible.

SYMLOG adds depth and sophistication to the coding of social interaction but again enlarges the unit of measurement. While IPA is an act-by-act coding system, SYMLOG is a "salient-act" coding scheme. Since it takes longer to record a SYMLOG observation, the coder must select the most important acts for recording. Clearly, this results in a loss of reliability as disagreements may result not only from two observers interpreting the same act differently but also from two observers selecting different acts for recording. Because of this, two observers are generally sufficient for IPA, but five or more are recommended for SYMLOG. Alternatively, interaction can be coded from video recordings. By going over the record repeatedly and picking up different acts with each pass, a higher percentage of acts can be picked up

by each coder, thus increasing the inter-rater reliability and decreasing the number of coders required. The only problem with this alternative is that SYMLOG does not record intensity. When multiple coders are used, more intense acts are likely to be selected as salient by more coders and will thus be weighted more heavily than the less intense acts that may be picked up by only one or two coders. Using only two coders and allowing them multiple passes in order to pick up a higher percentage of acts eliminates this implicit weighting effect.

The issue of reduced reliability is directly related to the problem of subjectivity. Moreno (1953) was an early critic of IPA; he argued that the observations of nonparticipants were meaningless because they could not possibly comprehend the life of a group to which they did not belong. While his position was extreme, it raised a difficult problem for any system that relies on the observations of outsiders. By standing outside the group, the outsider gains distance and "objectivity." Unfortunately, it is not clear that objectivity has any real meaning when speaking of interpersonal interaction. IPA sidestepped the problem by providing very clear specifications of categories. SYMLOG confronts the problem directly since observers are required to make fairly strong inferences as to the meaning of behavior. The coder is instructed to take the role of the "generalized other," or the "average" group member. When a group is polarized, this may be impossible. Half the group is likely to interpret an act in one way and the other half in a different way. This is another reason for having multiple observers. It is hoped that the various biases of the observers will cancel one another out if five or more people observe. Polley (1979) goes a step further by providing "descriptive reliabilities." Instead of simply reporting a reliability figure, descriptive reliabilities allow for a systematic analysis of observer bias. It is argued that observations tell us as much about the observer as about the observed. This is particularly true when group members are trained to serve as observers, as is the case in the self-analytic groups that are often the subject of SYMLOG observations.

Both IPA and SYMLOG have been repeatedly criticized for their use of a bipolar model of the relationship between "task-oriented" and "emotional" behavior. Two of these critiques have proposed adding a fourth dimension. Hare (1976)

Time	Who	To Whom	Act/Non	Direction	Description	Pro/Con	Direction	Level
123	JOE	BIL	A	UNF	Stop contradicting me!	C	N	BIL
123	BIL	JOE	A	UNB	Don't give me orders.	C	UNF	JOE
124	RON	GRP	A	UPF	I think we should all calm down.	P	DP	GRP

Figure 1. Sample SYMLOG Coding

went back to Parsons' original Adaptation, Goal Attainment, Integration, Latent Pattern Maintenance (AGIL) system and concluded that the task dimension should be divided into two dimensions: serious versus expressive and conforming versus nonconforming. Wish and colleagues (1976) proposed leaving the task-emotion dimension intact, even though it did not seem to be quite bipolar, and adding a fourth dimension: intensity. Polley (1987) has argued that emotionality is already captured in the friendly-unfriendly dimension and that the third dimension should be reserved for recording conventional versus unconventional behavior. This solution contends that the polarization of task and emotion is an artifact from the 1950s and has largely lost its meaning since then. If work is defined as devoid of emotional satisfaction, then task and emotion are bipolar. As soon as we recognize the possibility of having an emotional reaction—positive or negative—to work, the two dimensions become orthogonal. As Stone points out, the task-emotion polarity "implies that most work involves sublimation of the libido, and demands impulse control. Moreover, it becomes difficult to imagine management's orientation . . . fostering individual creativity as some so-called excellent companies have been able to do" (1988, p. 18). It is becoming increasingly apparent that no "universal" scheme for coding interpersonal interaction exists totally independent of cultural and temporal context.

SPECIALIZED SYSTEMS

While Leary's system was intended primarily for psychiatric diagnosis, and IPA was originally designed for the coding of case discussion groups at Harvard Business School, the methods described above represent attempts to develop comprehensive and general coding schemes. In addition to these all-purpose methods, observation systems have been devised for somewhat more specific relationships or channels of communication.

Richard Mann's (1967) sixteen-category system codes only one-way relationships from members to leaders. By narrowly defining the relationships to be observed, Mann was able to provide a much more detailed picture. Coding categories are provided for four types of impulse, four different expressions of affect, three variations of dependency, and five ego states. The additional sophistication is achieved by drastically reducing the number of observed relationships. If we observe a ten-person group using Mann's leader-member relationship scheme, we are looking at nine one-way relationships. If we use one of the all-purpose methods, we are coding forty-five two-way relationships.

The most thoroughly studies channel of communication is probably the nonverbal. While this is a small part of the SYMLOG system, proxemic behavior has been exhaustively categorized by Hall (1963) in terms of posture, orientation of bodies, kinesthetic factors, touch code, visual code, thermal code, olfaction code, and voice loudness. The potential complexity of this mode of communication is further illustrated by the fact that Birdwhistell (1970) developed an equally elaborate system for the coding of movement. While Hall's system codes states, Birdwhistell's codes state-to-state transitions. Each of these coding schemes concentrates on the physical nature of nonverbal behavior. In contrast, Mehrabian's system (1970) attempts to directly record the meaning of the behavior via a three-dimensional model that closely parallels SYMLOG. Again, the difference is in whether meaning is inferred by the observer or deferred to the researcher.

The other channel of communication that has been studied in depth is content. Again, this is a small part of SYMLOG; all content that does not carry a positive or negative evaluation is ignored.

In 1977, Philip Stone and his colleagues published *The General Inquirer*, a computerized content analysis system. While many of the applications involve the coding of written text, it has also been used for the coding of transcribed conversations. In one of the first applications of the method, Dexter Dunphy used *The General Inquirer* to code descriptions that group members had written of recent sessions. The great advantage of the methods is that it allows the user to define a dictionary. Three of the earliest dictionaries were the *Harvard III Psychosocial Dictionary*, the *Stanford Political Dictionary*, and the *Need-Achievement Dictionary*. It would also be possible to develop a SYMLOG value-level dictionary. In the case of a computerized content analysis system, the dictionary designer infers meaning *before* the behavior is coded.

RECENT DEVELOPMENTS

Observation systems only flourish when supported by a substantial research group. Because of the expense and the need for multiple coders, it is difficult to use observation systems as an isolated researcher. For three decades (the 1950s through the 1970s) such a group existed at Harvard. Bales and his colleagues had a well-equipped observation room and plenty of graduate student labor available. When Bales retired in 1985, the observation laboratory ceased to function as a research center. For most of the 1980s there were really no major research centers conducting observation work.

In the 1990s Joseph McGrath and his colleagues at the University of Illinois established a major research agenda around McGrath's theory of time, interaction, and performance (TIP) (1991). While much less method-driven than Bales's IPA and SYMLOG research groups, McGrath's group uses an observation method known as "time-by-event-by-member pattern observation" (TEMPO) (Futoran et al. 1989).

TEMPO was designed as a general observation method for the analysis of a wide range of group performance settings. It is divided into two sets of categories. The first codes on four performance functions:

1. Propose content—solutions, ideas.
2. Propose process—goals, strategies, acts.

3. Evaluate content—agreement, disagreement, clarification.
4. Evaluate process—agree, modify, disagree.

The two "proposal categories" are further classified as: (1) new—a new proposal; (2) prior—previously proposed; or (3) dictate—repeat content for clarification or emphasis. The two evaluation categories are further classified as: (1) agree, (2) clarify or modify, (3) disagree, or (4) reject/veto.

The second set of categories codes seven nonproduction function categories:

T. Task digression

P. Personal comments

I. Interpersonal comments

R. React to experiment

D. Digressions

U. Uninterpretable

S. Silence

McGrath's group devised their own methodology rather than relying on IPA or SYMLOG because they were concerned with both process and activity. They felt that the existing systems did not allow for the level of temporal pattern recognition that they were looking for. Their primary criteria for the system were that it: (1) be time-based, (2) identify individual member behavior, (3) recognize multiple acts within a single speech, (4) allow for multiple simultaneous acts and periods of inactivity, and (5) relate act to task products. Virtually all their observation studies are based on the analysis of videotaped records of interacting groups. The TIP theory and the TEMPO method are central to the line of research that McGrath and his colleagues conducted in the 1990s. *Small Group Research* devoted an special issue to six articles that resulted from a single large research project known as "The JEMCO Workshop Study" (McGrath 1993), but additional work from this research team has resulted in numerous journal articles and books.

Another major research effort that has produced its own observation system is led by Susan Wheelan. The work of Wheelan and her colleagues focused on group development. The Group Development Observation System (GDOS) is based in Wilfred Bion's concept of basic assumption and work groups (1959). It consists of seven categories (Wheelan et al. 1993):

1. Dependency statement
2. Counterdependency statement
3. Fight statement
4. Flight statement
5. Pairing statement
6. Counter-pairing statement
7. Work statement

Like McGrath's group, Wheelan's group is primarily concerned with temporal patterns in group development. The conceptual underpinnings of the two lines of research are, however, very different. Again, GDOS has resulted in numerous journal articles and books. A special issue of *Small Group Research* was also devoted to this line of research (Wheelan 1999).

While there have been a number of other observation systems to emerge in the past decade, these two represent extended lines of research. Most of the publications that have used observation systems since 1980 have used either modifications of existing systems or idiosyncratic systems that were used once or twice and so did not generate a comparative body of work.

A DECADE OF SMALL GROUP RESEARCH

In 1990, *International Journal of Small Group Research* and *Small Group Behavior* merged to form a new international and interdisciplinary journal known as *Small Group Research*. This journal publishes research on small groups that ranges across sociology, psychology, organizational behavior, social work, group psychotherapy, communications, and management information systems. As the only interdisciplinary journal in the field of small groups, it is a good indicator of the popularity of the observation systems in general and also of specific systems. Table 2 presents the results of an inventory of the past decade of research published in *Small Group Research*. In addition to tabulating the total number of articles using observation systems each year, it also indicates whether the articles used direct observation, videotapes, or transcriptions and whether they used one of the

four most popular general-purpose methods (IPA, SYMLOG, TEMPO, and GDOS) or some other method.

Of the 270 articles published in *Small Group Research* over the past decade, 41 used observation methods. IPA and SYMLOG are still in use; the other most common methods were TEMPO and GDOS, described above. However, the majority of articles (28) used idiosyncratic observation methods. While many represent real contributions to the literature, the lack of a common method makes comparisons across studies difficult. The other trend that is evident from Table 1 is that relatively few studies (9) used live observation. The remaining studies were almost equally split between the coding of videotapes and the coding of transcriptions. Perhaps the real loss in this shift of methodology is that so many rely on transcripts. One of the strengths of observation methods is that they capture paralinguistic cues; these data are lost to systems that rely on transcriptions.

THE FUTURE OF OBSERVATION SYSTEMS

Observation systems have been used less and less in recent years for a mundane reason: cost. Training observers is time consuming, as is the actual process of observing and coding behavior. At this point, serious research using direct SYMLOG observation is being done at only two or three institutions. In contrast, the much less time-consuming method of SYMLOG retrospective rating (using either the Bales items or the Polley revisions) is currently in use in at least fifty institutions around the world. While there is some indication of a resurgence of interest in direct observation, as evidenced by the studies cited in the preceding sections, it is clear that the method requires a substantial commitment of time and money on the part of the researcher.

While the costs of direct observation are high, it is clear that there are a great many aspects of social behavior that simply cannot be understood without it. Basic research still needs to be done on group development, particularly as it relates to team building in organizations. The effects of various leadership styles and decision-making processes on group functioning are still not thoroughly understood. A wide range of styles is currently

Small Group Research

Year	No. of Articles	No. Using Observation	No. Using Direct	No. Using Videotape	No. Using Transcripts	IPA	SYMLOG	TEMPO	GDOS	Other
1999*	22	4		1	3			1	1	2
1998	31	5	2	1	2					5
1997	27	2		1	1				1	1
1996	26	2	1		1					2
1995	25	3	1	1	1					3
1994	27	2		1	1					2
1993	28	10	3	5	2		1	4	1	4
1992	26	3	1		2		1			2
1991	28	5		4	1	1				4
1990	30	5	1	3	1	1		1		3
Total	270	41	9	17	15	2	2	6	3	28

Table 2

NOTE: *February through August.

used by group therapists, but these styles are more often backed by rival schools of thought than empirical evidence.

As with content analysis, the future of observation systems may well lie with computerization. Johansen (1989) coined the term *groupware* to refer to computer systems for the support of groups or teams. To date, most of the systems have provided little more than an "electronic flipchart" for nominal group technique sessions. With advances in artificial intelligence, more sophisticated examples of groupware have been gradually emerging. Speech-recognition programs for the automatic transcription of meetings could greatly reduce the cost of using content analysis. Programs have been developed for recognizing emotional content in speech. If these were to be combined with voice-activated, some automatic scoring of behavior—at least at the paralinguistic level—should be possible. Until technology substantially reduces the costs, a return to the widespread use of observation systems seems unlikely.

REFERENCES

Bales, Robert F. 1950 *Interaction Process Analysis*. Chicago: University of Chicago Press.

——— 1998 *Social Interaction Systems: Theory and Measurement*. New Brunswick, N.J.: Transaction Publishers.

———, Stephen P. Cohen, and Stephen A. Williamson 1979 *SYMLOG: A System for the Multiple Level Observation of Groups*. New York: Free Press.

Bion, Wilfred 1959 *Experiences in Groups*. New York: Basic.

Birdwhistell, Ray 1970 *Kinesics and Context*. Philadelphia: University of Pennsylvania Press.

Borgatta, Edgar 1963 "A New Systematic Interaction Observation System." *Journal of Psychological Studies* 14:24–44.

———, and Betty Crowther 1965 *A Workbook for the Study of Social Interaction Processes*. Chicago: Rand McNally.

Chapple, Elliot D. 1940 "Measuring Human Relations: An Introduction to the Study of the Interaction of Individuals." *Genetic Psychology Monographs* 27:3–147.

Couch, Arthur S. 1960 Personality determinants of interpersonal behavior. Ph.D. diss, Harvard University.

Futoran, Gail K., Janice R. Kelly, and Joseph E. McGrath 1989 "TEMPO: A Time-Based System for Analysis of Group Process." *Basic and Applied Social Psychology* 10(3):211–232.

Hall, Edward T. 1963 "A System for the Notation of Proxemic Behavior." *American Anthropologist* 65:1003–1026.

Hare, A. Paul 1976 *Handbook of Small Group Research*, 2nd ed. New York: Free Press.

Johansen, Robert 1989 *Groupware*. New York: Free Press.

Leary, Timothy 1957 *Interpersonal Diagnosis of Personality*. New York: Ronald.

McGrath, Joseph E. 1991 "Time, Interaction, and Performance (TIP): A Theory of Groups." *Small Group Research* 22:147–174.

—— (ed.) 1993 "Time, Task, and Technology in Work Groups: The JEMCO Workshop Study." *Small Group Research* (Special issue). 24:285–420.

McLemore, Clinton, and Lorna Benjamin 1979 "Whatever Happened to Interpersonal Diagnosis?" *American Psychologist* 34:17–34.

Mann, Richard D. 1967 *Interpersonal Styles and Group Development*. New York: John Wiley.

Mehrabian, Albert 1970 "A Semantic Space for Nonverbal Behavior." *Journal of Consulting and Clinical Psychology* 35:248–257.

Moreno, Jacob 1953 *Who Shall Survive?* Beacon, N.Y.: Beacon House.

Parsons, Talcott, and Robert F. Bales 1955 *Family, Socialization, and Interaction Process*. New York: Free Press.

Polley, Richard B. 1979 "Investigating Individual Perceptual Biases of Group Members in Rating and of Observers in SYMLOG Interaction Scoring." In R. F. Bales, S. P. Cohen, and S. A. Williamson, eds., *SYMLOG: A System for the Multiple Level Observation of Groups*. New York: Free Press.

—— 1987 "The Dimensions of Interpersonal Behavior: A Method for Improving Rating Scales." *Social Psychology Quarterly* 50:72–82.

——, A. Paul Hare, and Philip J. Stone (eds.) 1988 *The SYMLOG Practitioner: Applications of Small Group Research*. New York: Praeger.

Slater, Philip J. 1955 "Role Differentiation in Small Groups." *American Sociological Review* 20:300–310.

Stone, Philip J. 1988 "SYMLOG for Skeptics." In R. B. Polley, A. P. Hare, and P. J. Stone, eds., *The SYMLOG Practitioner: Applications of Small Group Research*. New York: Praeger.

——, Dexter C. Dunphy, Marshall S. Smith, and Daniel M. Ogilvie 1966 *The General Inquirer: A Computer Approach to Content Analysis*. Cambridge, Mass.: Massachusetts Institute of Technology Press.

Weick, Karl E. 1985 "Systematic Observation Methods." In G. Lindzey and E. Aronson, eds., *The Handbook of Social Psychology*, 3rd ed. New York: Random House.

Wheelan, Susan A. (ed.) 1999 "Group Development." *Small Group Research* (Special Issue). 30:3–129.

——, A. F. Verdi, and R. McKeage 1993 *The Group Observation Development System: Origins and Applications*. Philadelphia: PEP.

Wiens, A. N., J. D. Matarazzo, and G. Saslow 1965 "The Interaction Recorder: An Electronic Punched Paper Tape Unity for Recording Speech Behavior during Interviews." *Journal of Clinical Psychology* 21:142–145.

Wish, Myron, Morton Deutsch, and S. Kaplan 1976 "Perceived Dimensions of Interpersonal Relations." *Journal of Personality and Social Psychology* 33:409–420.

RICHARD B. KETTNER-POLLEY

OCCUPATIONAL AND CAREER MOBILITY

Occupational and career mobility in adulthood is often referred to as intragenerational social mobility. It involves change in an individual's position in the labor market over the adult life course. Change is studied with respect to both type of work and the rewards derived from work. The term *career* refers to an individual's job history. Empirical *regularity* in the careers of individuals in the labor force defines what we call a "career line" or "job trajectory," since a work history common to a portion of the labor force reflects the existence of structurally determined linkages among jobs in the economy. Jobs are located in particular firms, whereas occupations and industries encompass jobs in many firms. An individual may remain in the same occupation or industry but change firms (and jobs within the same firm) any number of times. Since the process of job change does not necessarily involve a change of occupation or industry, but a change of occupation or industry always involves a job change, the process of job change provides a more detailed account of career movement. Changes in the rewards derived from work usually accompany job changes but can also occur during the course of tenure in a job.

Research on intragenerational mobility has focused on the labor force as a whole and on employees in particular occupations and firms. Research on the labor force as a whole has usually considered change in occupation and industry, as measured for detailed categories or more aggregated groupings that define broad occupational and industrial groups. It has also considered change in the rewards derived from work, focusing primarily on occupational prestige and earnings. Research on particular occupations and firms has usually focused on job status and authority changes within organizational hierarchies and on changes in work rewards.

Early work on intragenerational mobility involved the mathematical modeling of transition probabilities, usually among a few, highly aggregated categories (see Mayer 1972 for a review). This work used Markov models and semi-Markov models to analyze transition probabilities in a sequence under the assumption that the job category an individual will occupy in the future depends only on the job category occupied in the present and not on job categories occupied previously. Although there was empirical support for this assumption in some studies, it was not found to be broadly applicable. In semi-Markov models, transition probabilities are permitted to vary with time and for subgroups of the population. These models capture declines in mobility with age or duration of stay and allow for the fact that some individuals are more likely to move than others. There is evidence that mobility is an exponentially declining function of time (Mayer 1972) and that some individuals become "movers" while others become "stayers" (Blumen et al. 1955).

Later analyses have considered more refined models of job change, focusing on job shifts as elementary acts in the mobility process. Job shifts may be either voluntary or involuntary, and may occur at a decreasing rate with time in the labor market. They are also more likely to occur within a firm than between firms as labor market experience increases (Rosenfeld 1992; DiPrete and Nonnemaker 1997). As time spent in a firm increases, both rates of promotion and rates of leaving the firm also decline (Petersen and Spilerman 1990; DiPrete and Nonnemaker 1997). When the effect of labor market experience is considered simultaneously, firm tenure may have a positive effect on within-firm job mobility, but this effect indicates that the rate of within-firm job mobility declines with labor market experience more slowly for each year of tenure with an employer than for each year of pre-employer labor market experience. Job shifts (both voluntary and involuntary) are strongly and negatively related to job tenure. As the duration of a job increases, the probability

of leaving it declines. Most of this decline occurs in the first year of a job, after which there is a leveling off (Topel and Ward 1992). Within firms, however, job tenure has a positive effect on the probability of promotion, in some instances increasing up to a point and then decreasing (Felmlee 1982; Althauser and Kalleberg 1990; Petersen and Spilerman 1990). The rate of mobility varies with characteristics of the individual, the job, the occupation, the employing organization, and the economic environment.

Change in the rewards derived from work usually accompanies a job shift (Sørensen 1974; Rosenbaum 1984; Topel and Ward 1992). Voluntary job shifts are associated with increases in prestige and wages; involuntary job shifts, with losses. Job shifts *within* firms and occupations are more often associated with gains in prestige and wages than those *between* firms and occupations (DiPrete and Krecker 1991; DiPrete and McManus 1996; Cheng and Kalleberg 1996). In general, the rewards of changing jobs decline with labor market experience and job tenure. Wages, as well as the opportunity for wage growth and promotion, bear a negative relationship to the probability of a job shift (Petersen and Spilerman 1990; Topel and Ward 1992). Change in wages also occurs during the course of a job (Topel 1991), declining with labor market experience and, at a decreasing rate, with job tenure (Topel and Ward 1992). For the labor force as a whole, occupational prestige and earnings increase over the adult working life. The shape of these trajectories tends to be concave downward—with a rise early in the career, a plateau during the middle years, and a slight decline as the end of the work career approaches. Status and earnings trajectories have the same form, but the former is flatter (Mincer 1974; Rosenfeld 1980). There is also variation in the shape of these trajectories for those in different career lines (Spilerman 1986).

Given the heterogeneity of career lines and the important role that age, or duration since career entry, plays in shaping career lines, there have been attempts to study the path of careers in recent years. Not only does mobility decline sharply with age, and therefore with the proximity of a job to the end of a career line, but job changes that occur later in an individual's work life tend to involve jobs requiring skills that are more similar than those that occur earlier in the work life

(Spenner et al. 1982; Althauser and Kalleberg 1990). There is also evidence that early career experiences have an important effect on later career outcomes. This evidence indicates not only that those entering *different* career lines, who receive different rewards at career entry, can expect different career outcomes (Marini 1980; Spenner et al. 1982), but also that early experiences *within* a career line can condition subsequent progression and the level of reward attained relative to others who enter the same career line (Stewman and Konda 1983; Rosenbaum 1984). The career lines most often studied have been trajectories within institutional structures, but there have also been attempts to describe career lines that cross institutional boundaries (Spilerman 1977; Spenner et al. 1982; Althauser and Kalleberg 1990).

LABOR MARKET STRUCTURE

The concept of "career line" or "job trajectory" derives from the view that the labor market is structured in a way that makes some types of job changes more likely than others. Early work on career mobility ignored this structural differentiation, estimating the overall (linear) relationship between the status and earnings of an individual's first job and the status and earnings of a job held later in the career (Blau and Duncan 1967; Coleman et al. 1972; Marini 1980). Jobs resembling each other in status, pay, and working conditions, however, are sometimes part of a career line and sometimes not, even if part of a career line can be attached to different career lines. Jobs providing similar current rewards may therefore not offer the same prospects for future mobility.

Since career lines are rooted in labor-market structure, their existence demonstrates that intragenerational mobility is influenced by the structure of the labor market and changes in that structure, as well as by the demography of the labor force and individual characteristics that affect movement within segments of the labor market. If jobs have entry requirements and confer rewards, the structure of jobs plays a critical role in establishing the link between the attributes of individuals and work rewards. Recognition that the labor market is structured in a way that produces segmentation among career lines has led to attempts not only to describe career lines but to identify the forces shaping them.

Pioneering work by White (1970) directed attention to the importance of social structure in shaping careers by modeling the way in which vacancies in a structured labor market trigger career movement. More recent models of vacancy-based movement have further delineated the ways in which vacancy chains, job distributions, and managerial staffing and hiring practice structure the relative career chances of individuals (Sørensen 1977; Skvoretz 1984; Stewman and Konda 1983; Stewman 1986). In these models the availability of job openings determines career advancement possibilities, and the shape of organizational hierarchies affects the probability of advancement. Since most organizational hierarchies are pyramidal, with many more low-level than high-level positions, the average employee's advancement must slow down over time. Aggregate age-promotion curves appear to be described empirically by an exponential-decline function where the highest promotion chances occur at the outset, declines are a fixed proportion of an individual's current chances, and promotion chances become increasingly rare but not impossible. In short, promotion favors youth, declines gradually, but does not disappear for older workers. There may also be chances for an increase in promotion during the initial career years when most on-the-job training occurs.

Although career advancement often occurs as a result of job change to fill a vacant position, not all career movement depends on or is affected by a job opening. New jobs in organizations are sometimes created for particular individuals, and jobs that are vacated may be eliminated rather than filled. New jobs can also be created by individual moves to become self-employed, and the termination of self-employment does not necessarily create a vacancy. Within organizations, career advancement occurs through upgrading as well as vacancy filling. An employee receives an upgrade promotion when a certain level of seniority or a certain performance marker is reached. Such promotions involve reclassification to a higher rank and do not depend on a vacancy's being present (Stewman and Yeh 1991; Barnett and Miner 1992). Both upgrade promotions and vacancy promotions may occur during the course of an individual's career. These alternative advancement mechanisms, however, are not necessarily found equally throughout an organizational hierarchy. In several occupational categories studied in one organization, most lower-level promotions were vacancy based, and a higher proportion of upper-level promotions occurred through upgrading (Barnett and Miner 1992). The mechanisms available for promotion affect an individual's promotion chances. It has been found that if promotion occurs through upgrading based on performance rather than vacancy filling, salary grade level is not necessarily associated with a lower probability of promotion (Petersen and Spilerman 1990). Similarly, the effect of hiring temporary workers on the promotion chances of permanent workers depends on the extent to which promotion occurs through vacancy filling rather than upgrading (Barnett and Miner 1992).

Because the structure of the labor market affects career movement, there have been attempts to understand the structural bases of segmentation among career lines. During the 1940s and 1950s, institutional economists called for an understanding of well-defined systems of jobs and firms, drawing a distinction between internal and external labor markets. For example, Dunlop (1957) argued that within a firm there are groups of jobs, or "job clusters," each of which is linked together by technology, the administrative organization of the production process, and the social customs of the work community. A job cluster usually contains one or more key jobs and a group of associated jobs, and the wage rates for the key jobs mediate the effects of labor market influences, including union and government wage policies, and forces in the market for products on the wage structure of the firm. The distinction between internal and external labor markets was later reintroduced by Doeringer and Piore (1971), who discussed what they called a "mobility cluster." The central idea was that administrative rules and procedures tend to set up separate markets for those already hired (an internal labor market) and those seeking employment (an external labor market). A firm hires workers from the outside labor market into "entry jobs," and other jobs are filled internally as workers progress on well-defined career ladders by acquiring job related skills, many of which are firm-specific. Thus, firms make investments in individuals, and these investments segment the workforce with respect to advancement opportunity.

The concept of the internal labor market was developed further in what was first called *dual* and then *segmented* labor market theory (Gordon 1972; Kalleberg and Sørensen 1979). This theory draws a distinction between primary and secondary jobs, arguing that the internal labor market is only one kind of work setting. *Primary* jobs emphasize long-term attachment between workers and firms and offer built-in career ladders and promotion opportunities, whereas *secondary* jobs do not offer these advantages. The distinction between primary and secondary jobs may occur within the same firm or between firms, since primary jobs are considered more likely to be found in oligopolistic, unionized industries, and secondary jobs in competitive industries.

Dual and other segmented labor-market theories have come under attack as being too crude to meaningfully characterize the multiple dimensions on which labor markets vary. Attempts to measure labor-market segmentation by crude topologies, including industrial and occupational categories, have also been criticized. Because there is extensive heterogeneity within industrial and occupational categories, and because there is no way to link them to the kinds of job clusters hypothesized to exist, it has been argued that more disaggregated analyses of jobs and firms are needed. Many subsequent analyses have focused on particular bureaucracies or firms, and those examining larger segments of the labor market have sought to measure the characteristics on which employing organizations and occupations vary.

Attempting to develop a systematic conceptual scheme for studying labor market segmentation, Althauser and Kalleberg argued that "the concept of an internal labor market should include any cluster of jobs, regardless of occupational titles or employing organizations, that have three basic structural features: (a) a job ladder, with (b) entry only at the bottom, and (c) movement up this ladder, which is associated with a progressive development of knowledge and skill" (1981, p. 130). Based on four possible pairings of type of control and prospects for advancement, they differentiated four types of labor market structures: (1) firm internal labor markets, which are internal labor markets controlled by firms; (2) occupational internal labor markets, which are internal labor markets controlled by occupational incumbents; (3) firm labor markets, which provide firm-specific security without advancement prospects; and (4) occupational labor markets, which provide occupational security without advancement prospects.

Within a firm or an occupation, there may be multiple job ladders that vary in length and shape, and there are structured relationships among job ladders. Job mobility occurs not only along formal organizational and occupational ladders but across them (Baron et al. 1986; Stewman 1986; DiPrete 1989). For example, job ladders often cross detailed and even aggregated occupational boundaries. DiPrete (1987) described the permeability of these boundaries as depending on several types of contingencies: (1) skill-based contingencies, (2) information-based contingencies, (3) contingencies due to the configuration of positions in an organization, and (4) contingencies that emerge from the institutionalization of formal structure. Internal labor markets limit competition from outsiders by offering a combination of closed and restricted mobility contests that involve movement on and across job ladders (DiPrete and Krecker 1991; Stewman and Yeh 1991).

Because employing organizations vary in the kinds of jobs they offer, the occupational groupings in which those jobs fall, and the wages they pay, there has been some attempt to examine the effect of organizational characteristics on job mobility. Large organizations offer better pay, have more job ladders offering opportunities for promotion and wage growth, and offer better employee benefits. Organization size is therefore positively related to mobility within an organization and negatively related to voluntary movement out of an organization (Hachen 1992; DiPrete 1993; Cheng and Kalleberg 1996). Organizations in concentrated industries and industries dominated by conglomerates experience both lower rates of within-firm mobility and lower rates of voluntary exit because they have higher average wage levels, and there is a negative relationship between the average wage level of an industry and the probability of both within-firm mobility and voluntary firm exit. High-wage industries have lower rates of within-firm mobility than low-wage industries because, net of organizational size, internal labor markets are less prevalent in firms in high-wage industries. Capital-intensive industries have higher rates of

both within-firm mobility and voluntary firm exit but lower rates of involuntary exit. These differences are linked to the greater prevalence of internal labor markets in firms in capital-intensive industries (Hachen 1992).

Although there is general agreement that the technical character of work influences organizational development, existing variation in institutional and personnel structures, especially cross-nationally, indicates that the technical character of work alone does not determine job ladders and career lines. These are affected by the historical circumstances surrounding an organization's founding, including the gender, racial, and ethnic composition of the workforce; by market and other social conditions that affect organizational change and employment growth; and by the negotiating strength of various bargaining units.

A number of explanations have been advanced for the emergence of internal labor markets. One focuses on the development of specialized knowledge and skill relevant to employment in particular occupations, jobs, and firms. Becker (1964) noted that when a worker receives training specific to the needs of an employer, the worker's value to the employer increases since a new employee would have to receive similar training before being able to perform at the same level. It is therefore in the interest of the employer to retain workers with such specific training by providing them with opportunities for promotion, salary growth, and employment security. When firm-specific skills are rewarded, workers also have an interest in remaining with the employer because the wages and other benefits they could obtain from another employer are lower. Based on this reasoning, Williamson (1975) argued that internal labor markets emerged because they were preferable to long-term contracts for maintaining the employment relationship. Thus, internal labor markets are seen as resulting from employers' needs for renewable supplies of otherwise scarce, highly skilled workers. Substantial empirical evidence is consistent with this view. Another explanation, offered by Bulow and Summers (1986), is that job hierarchies offering promotion prospects and wage increases are an important means of motivating workers when individual performance is not easily monitored.

The emergence and spread of internal labor markets is also seen as related to the development of personnel departments, formalized rules, and the rise of bureaucratic control. Although there is some empirical support for this view, at least some internal labor markets preceded the emergence of bureaucratic control systems and rules (Althauser 1989; Stovel et al. 1996). Spilerman (1986) has noted that workers have an interest in barring lateral entry and in having high-level positions filled through promotion. Workers may also wish to limit employer discretion by having decisions about promotion and layoff tied to seniority. These worker interests cause labor unions to work to create more widespread job hierarchies and promotion. Although internal labor markets have been argued to be a result of unionization, evidence suggests that they are to some degree an alternative to unionization (Pfeffer and Cohen 1984). In manufacturing establishments, the technology of production helps to manage the workforce, binding workers to a specific organization with specific machines and production technology, and providing necessary skills and training. Unionization reduces turnover by providing workers with a voice, skewing compensation toward deferred benefits over current wages and bonuses, and paying a larger proportion of total compensation as fringe benefits valued particularly by senior workers. In the presence of a governance system under unionization, the internal labor market and other forms of bureaucratic control are redundant if not in competition with union mechanisms.

Because the prevalence of internal labor markets varies across organizations, there has been some attempt to explain why they are found more often in some organizations than others. It was initially argued that firms characterized by high profit levels, oligopolistic pricing, and large organization size were more likely to create internal labor markets because they could better afford to. However, there is evidence that internal labor markets are not merely a derivative feature of core-economy organization (Althauser 1989). Hachen (1992) has suggested that they are affected by three characteristics of employer personnel policy: the need to retain workers, the availability of alternative mechanisms for retention, and the ability to use specific mechanisms. In labor-intensive industries where labor costs are substantial and worker replacement is used as a strategy to maintain or even lower wage levels, retaining workers is less important. As a result, within-firm mobility rates are low, and involuntary exit rates are high. When an organization desires to retain workers, offering higher wages and increasing internal opportunities are two means of retention, but organizations vary in their ability to use these mechanisms. A large organization will be better able to offer internal opportunities. An organization that can offer high wages may have less need to offer advancement opportunities.

Career lines not only involve substantial movement between job ladders within firms but often cross firm and industry boundaries rather than remaining within them. In the U.S. economy, most job change involves a change of employer (DiPrete and Krecker 1991). It has been estimated that only somewhat over a quarter of U.S. workers are continuously employed by the same employer for twenty years or more (Hall 1982). In some careers, such as the salaried professions, crafts, and "secondary" labor-market positions, firm and industry are not a locus of career line structure. Nevertheless, moves between firms and industries often occur between related positions, so that labor-market segmentation emerges even without institutional barriers.

Aspects of the structure of labor markets, other than internal labor markets, that have implications for occupational and career mobility have been documented in cross-national research. One type of cross-national variation is in the relationship between the educational system and the labor market, which varies according to the structure of the educational system. In countries with more stratified and standardized educational systems, such as Germany, Austria, France, and Norway, there is a tighter linkage between educational preparation and labor-market position than in the United States. In these countries, reliance on educational degrees and other credentials as screening devices is greater, and rates of occupational and job mobility are lower (Haller et al. 1985; Allmendinger 1989; DiPrete and McManus 1996). In the United States, where schooling is more open and comprehensive, the number of years of education attained matters more, and career mobility is higher because a larger proportion of employees are allocated to low-level entry positions in organizations. In Great Britain, which has a stratified educational system, similar to those of the other European countries, occupational mobility is higher than in the United States because the linkage between education and training prior to labor-market entry and job placement is weaker. Workers are also more likely to attain part-time education after labor-market entry that leads to occupational change (Winfield et al. 1989).

Another aspect of labor market structure that varies cross-nationally is the degree of institutional separation between manual and white-collar work, which affects mobility across this boundary. Existing throughout Europe, but strongest in the German-speaking middle-European countries, is the institution of apprenticeship for manual work, which restricts access to jobs for skilled workers to those who complete an apprenticeship after elementary schooling. In countries where the institution of apprenticeship is less strong, as in France and the United States, access to a job as a skilled worker is more dependent on affiliation with a specific enterprise and is open to those moving up from unskilled jobs. The greater stratification of the educational system in countries where the institution of apprenticeship is strong also restricts upward mobility from manual to nonmanual jobs.

Another variation observed cross-nationally is in the degree of separation between hierarchically ranked white-collar positions. In Austria and France, there is greater separation among hierarchical layers of white-collar work than in the United States, where the higher levels of white-collar work are more open to entry from below (Haller et al. 1985). In the United States, both the highest and lowest categories in the occupational structure are less separated from the middle layers than they are in Austria and France. As a result, mobility over relatively long distances is more common in the United States. This difference may be due in part to the less stratified educational system in the United States.

Another type of variation in labor market structure found across countries is in the links of the labor market to other national institutions such as the state and centralized employer and labor associations. In some countries, such as China, the state remains the major employer (Zhou et al. 1997); in others, such as Austria and France, large enterprises and whole industrial sectors are nationalized (Haller at al. 1985). Labor markets in Europe have also been described as less flexible than those in the United States because "corporatist"

institutional arrangements of various types coordinate and regulate the labor markets. Countries described as corporatist have relatively centralized wage-setting institutions that result in less volatility in wages and smaller wage differences (DiPrete and McManus 1996; Gottschalk and Smeeding 1997). They may also have greater employment security that reduces involuntary job mobility, but restrictions on wages may result in relatively high unemployment as well.

Because the availability of vacancies in organizational hierarchies affects career advancement, and the supply of labor affects both the probability of advancement and wages, career progress in all countries is affected by demographic factors such as the size and distribution of education and skills in various age cohorts and the rate of exit from positions (Stewman and Konda 1983). It is also affected by organizational growth and contraction that result in the creation and termination of jobs. Change in the actual structure of jobs occurs in response to social and economic influences, including technological development. At the level of the firm, expansion increases the rate of promotion, and contraction decreases it (Stewman and Konda 1983; Barnett and Miner 1992). Expansion of an industry, as measured by growth in the average size of firms or the establishment of new firms, increases the rate of job shifts within and between firms in the industry and decreases the rate of involuntary exit (Hachen 1992; DiPrete 1993; Haveman and Cohen 1994; DiPrete and Nonnemaker 1997). Contraction of an industry, as measured by decline in the average size of firms or the closing of firms, decreases the rate of job shifts between firms in the industry and increases the rate of movement out of the industry, including movement to unemployment. Contraction of an industry may either decrease or increase the rate of within-firm mobility, since contraction may lead to the internal redeployment of labor as a substitute for new hiring. Internal mobility that reflects reorganization occurs primarily among lower white-collar, service, and blue-collar workers. Movement out of the industry and to unemployment occurs primarily among service and blue-collar workers (DiPrete 1993). Change that involves merger and acquisition within an industry has fewer effects, but they tend to be similar to the effects of industry contraction (DiPrete 1993; Haveman and Cohen 1994). The effects of *occupational* expansion and contraction differ somewhat from those of *industrial* expansion and contraction. Expansion of an occupation increases the rate of mobility between firms in an industry but not within firms. Contraction of an occupation increases the rate of mobility within firms (due to the redeployment of labor) and increases the rate of movement to unemployment but does not increase the rate of movement out of the industry (DiPrete and Nonnemaker 1997). The adverse effects of economic turbulence in either an industry or occupation are dampened by employer tenure.

Since the structure of the labor market affects both job mobility and wage growth, aspects of labor market structure account for the aggregate declines in job mobility and wage gain observed over the course of workers' careers. One aspect of labor-market structure that plays a role in explaining the declining change in career rewards is the pyramidal shape of organizational and occupational hierarchies, which contain many more lower-level than higher-level positions. Given this structure and the role of vacancy filling in promotion, the chances of promotion and wage growth linked to promotion decline with labor-market experience. To the extent that upward mobility is possible, workers entering a career line are in competition with others at the same level for advancement to the next highest level. Because jobs at the next level are filled from those occupying positions in the level below, entry to a job ladder and performance at each step on the ladder affect ultimate career attainments. Rosenbaum (1984) has described the process by which employees in a cohort are progressively differentiated throughout their careers in a series of implicit competitions as being like a tournament. Selections among the members of a cohort occur continually as careers unfold, and each selection affects the opportunity to advance further. As a result, individuals are distributed more and more to "winner "and "loser" paths, and interpersonal variance in wages rises with labor-market experience and firm tenure. Those who are not promoted are more likely to leave the firm, but their gain from doing so is less than the gain of those who are promoted internally.

According to human capital theory, the shape of wage trajectories over the career course is a function of the changing productivity of workers. Wage growth through labor-market experience results from learning on the job that increases a worker's productivity and value to the employer. On-the-job training occurs in formal training programs provided by employers or as a result of informal instruction by supervisors and coworkers and simply by doing the job. Time away from the job, in contrast, can lead to skill depreciation. Because investments in training are costly, these are concentrated in the early part of careers, leading to greater wage growth at early rather than later career stages. Formal and informal training in a particular firm and on particular jobs can provide knowledge and skills that are general or specific. General knowledge and skills are applicable in other firms and other jobs, whereas specific knowledge and skills are applicable only in the firm or job where they are acquired. As workers develop firm- and job-specific human capital, they are less likely to leave that firm or job because their productivity and resulting wages are higher than they would be in another firm or job. Although productivity may be greater in the firm or job where specific human capital is acquired, increments in productivity decline over time. As a result of this decline and biological aging, productivity may be lower at the end of a career than it was earlier.

One problem with human capital theory is that the relationship between labor market experience and worker productivity has not been adequately tested. Labor-market experience may affect wages because it is a proxy for seniority if wages rise with seniority and job tenure regardless of productivity. For women, labor-market experience may be an outcome rather than a determinant of career mobility if entry into career lines offering little opportunity for advancement affects labor-force participation (Marini 1980; Marini and Fan 1995). Evidence on the relationship between labor market experience and productivity within occupations suggests that, although labor market experience has some bearing on productivity, its effect on career advancement is largely independent of productivity (Horowitz and Sherman 1980; Medoff and Abraham 1980, 1981; Maranto and Rodgers 1984). Much variability is also seen across occupations and work contexts in the extent to which work experience affects either productivity or earnings (Horowitz and Sherman 1980; Spilerman 1986). Evidence also contradicts the "tradeoff hypothesis"—that individuals sacrifice earnings at the beginning of their careers for better long-term career prospects. Individuals with lower earnings early in their careers actually have lower rather than higher job status and earnings later.

More recent economic explanations of the relationship between labor-market experience and wage growth have focused on new arguments about the role of productivity in shaping the desire of employers, especially those who make large investments in screening and training employees, to retain workers and motivate high performance over time (Lazear 1981; Lazear and Rosen 1981; Malcomson 1984; Bulow and Summers 1986). Promotions and wage increases are seen as a means of eliciting effort from workers when the monitoring of their efforts and outputs is prohibitively expensive. These explanations deviate from the view that labor is paid its marginal product in each short period, assuming that workers are paid their marginal product over the life cycle or in some cases in excess of their marginal product. So far, none of these explanations has an empirical basis, and, as single-factor explanations, they are unlikely to account for the diverse compensation schemes observed across occupations and work settings (Talbert and Bose 1977; Spilerman 1986). A further problem is that they ignore the role of nonmonetary incentives in retaining workers and motivating high performance.

Other economic explanations of career mobility have combined human capital theory and information theory to consider the role of imperfect information and the acquiring of additional information as influences on career decision making (e.g., Jovanovic 1979). As in human capital theory, voluntary job mobility is assumed to result from a comparison of the benefits derived from one's current job with those that could be obtained from another job. The decision to search for or accept another job is argued to be affected by new information about either the current job or a possible alternative. Because certain aspects of a job cannot be assessed prior to employment, new information is argued to be acquired through actually working on the job, and this information affects assessment of the quality of the person-job match. Jobs that survive are those evaluated as a good match, or at least as a better match than could be obtained elsewhere. With increases in labor-market experience, workers acquire more information about the labor market and are better

able to demonstrate their performance, which in turn provides more information to employers. As a result, matches improve over the course of a career, and, because it becomes increasingly less likely that a better match can be found, job mobility declines. Although the role of information is implicit, a related argument is linked to the vacancy-based model of career advancement (Sørensen 1977). According to this argument, as time in the labor market increases, people who enter the labor market in a position below their optimum level because a better vacancy is unavailable have more time to take advantage of vacancies and to close the gap between their current and potential rewards. What these models do not consider is the path dependency of careers, whereby there are long-term effects of early job placements on later career outcomes. Job placement early in a career not only shapes worker experience and training but is used as a basis for screening by employers that affects later career opportunities.

Information about the labor market and specific alternative jobs may also change with labor-market experience in ways that affect assessments of the likelihood that a better alternative is available. At labor-market entry and during the early career, both occupational aspirations and the importance attached to a variety of job attributes decline. These changes suggest a diminished view of the labor market, which makes it less likely that a better alternative to one's current job will be perceived to be available. As firm and job tenure increase, it is also likely that knowledge of specific alternative job opportunities declines, since the time since the worker's last involvement in job search is longer and contacts with others who would be sources of information are fewer.

If opportunities for career advancement and wage growth are used by employers to retain workers who have firm- and job-specific knowledge and skill, career advancement and wage growth may also decline over the course of individual careers because they become less necessary means of retaining workers. They become less necessary because increases in firm- and job-specific knowledge and skills increase the extent to which a worker will be more valuable to the current employer than to an alternative employer and because the value of accrued employee benefits, including retirement benefits, makes it increasingly costly for a worker to change employers. As firm and job tenure increase, personal relationships and familiarity with the work environment also increase, reducing the likelihood that a worker will change employers or jobs. There is also less time left as a career advances to recover the costs of a change of employer or job and achieve the same level of functioning as was attained with the current employer or a higher level (Groot and Verberne 1997).

WORKER CHARACTERISTICS

Given the structure of the labor market, particularly the local labor market where most job search occurs, entry into a career line is affected by worker characteristics, such as job-related credentials (e.g., education, intelligence, physical attributes), job preferences, and access to resources (e.g., information, material support, sponsorship by influential others). In some career lines, worker characteristics at entry may also influence career progression, whereas in others such characteristics may have little effect after access to a career line is obtained. If worker characteristics at entry continue to have an effect, they may do so in part because they influence subsequent on-the-job training and performance.

Most theoretical attempts to explain individual differences in career mobility have focused on individual differences in worker performance. In human capital theory, workers are seen as rational actors who make investments in their productive capacities to maximize lifetime income (Becker 1964; Mincer 1974). The investments usually studied are education and on-the-job training, although the theory applies to other investments, such as effort, job search, geographic mobility, and health. It is assumed that labor markets offer open opportunity and that earnings growth is a function of change in productivity due to how hard individuals work and to the ability, education, and training they possess. Individuals can increase their productivity not only through formal education but by learning on the job. Because investments in education and training are costly, workers concentrate their investments in the early part of their careers, sacrificing immediate earnings for better long-term career prospects. Although worker qualifications that may affect productivity have been found to be associated with advancement, these

associations are consistent with explanations other than that afforded by human capital theory. In the theory of vacancy-based competition, workers' performance-related resources are also assumed to affect career advancement, but the mechanism by which they affect advancement is left unspecified (e.g., Sørensen 1977).

Sociologists generally view the relationships between education and experience, on the one hand, and career advancement on the other, as influenced primarily by the organizational, and even the broader societal, context in which the administrative arrangements that govern promotions and salary advancement arise. Spilerman (1986) has suggested that education and experience bear weaker relationships to promotion and earnings when organizational rules rigidly prescribe the temporal paths of occupational and earnings advancement. These rigid schedules are usually found in workplaces where the majority of workers are engaged in a very few career lines, or where multiple career lines exist, but there is little opportunity for transferring among them. Such schedules often result from unionization, since labor unions seek to standardize work arrangements. Even the effects of education and experience that exist under this type of personnel system vary across cities in ways suggesting an influence of general societal beliefs that educated and experienced workers should be paid more. Because such beliefs do not specify how much more, compensation schedules vary widely. Education and experience appear to bear stronger relationships to earnings in large nonunionized organizations that encompass many occupational specialties. However, even in these organizations, societal notions of equity and custom may affect wage structures. In Japan, for example, both seniority and family size are major determinants of salary in large companies (Dore 1973).

Sociological accounts differ from economic explanations in recognizing that the rewards of work derive from job occupancy and that a relatively enduring structure of jobs determines the relationships of individual effort, ability, and performance to work rewards. In the sociological view, jobs are assigned wage rates via processes operating at the societal and organizational levels; and the mechanisms that match individuals to jobs produce associations between individual effort, ability, and training, on the one hand, and work rewards, on the other. Jobs differ in the routes by which they are entered and in the extent to which performance can affect work rewards.

What influences advancement is not the attributes of individuals per se, but their attributes in relation to organizational positions. Organizations define the criteria by which ability is identified. To the extent that ability is not tied to those criteria, it will not be recognized and rewarded. If individuals of limited ability are able by chance or other more calculated means to meet the criteria by which ability is identified, they will be assumed to have ability by an inference process in which the direction of causality is reversed. An important consequence of this system is that factors affecting access to positions, of which ability is only one, and factors affecting performance in accordance with organizationally recognized criteria, including the willingness to conform to organizational goals and practices, have an important influence on long-term career outcomes.

Given the importance of the structure of jobs in mediating the relationship between individual attributes such as education and experience and job rewards, it is not surprising that unchanging attributes have little direct effect on rewards within job status categories. However, they have an important effect on careers via their influence on access to positions in the structure of jobs. Education is a major determinant of access to job ladders and career lines, and movement within these produces relationships between education and experience and work rewards. The organizational hierarchies to which college graduates, especially those from preferred colleges, have access increase the effects of college on career attainments over time. These hierarchies are moved through via experience. Within at least some career lines, education increases rates of promotion and wage gain (Rosenbaum 1984; Petersen and Spilerman 1990; Sicherman and Galor 1990). Education bears a positive relationship to within-firm and within-occupation mobility and a negative relationship to mobility between occupations, firms, and industries, as well as a negative relationship to moves to unemployment (Sicherman and Galor 1990; Cheng and Kalleberg 1996; DiPrete and Nonnemaker 1997). When mobility does occur between occupations and firms, education increases the likelihood that these moves are voluntary and in an upward direction. Education also helps to buffer workers

from economic turbulence. Young, educated workers are both helped less by organizational expansion and hurt less by organizational contraction (Rosenbaum 1984; DiPrete 1993; DiPrete and Nonnemaker 1997).

Over time, career histories become differentiated in the timing and occurrence of advancement. Early recognition and achievement relative to members of the same entry cohort have long-term effects on career mobility. Those receiving early promotions have more rapidly advancing subsequent careers and ultimately attain higher-level positions and higher earnings than those not receiving early recognition (Stewman and Konda 1983; Rosenbaum 1984). The age when a person enters a position bears a negative relationship at career advancement (Petersen and Spilerman 1990; Rosenfeld 1992). The early recognition of "stars" and its cumulative effect on subsequent career movement has been argued to occur as a result of labeling processes that identify such individuals as especially able—as high achievers who are likely to achieve more.

One problem in research on career mobility has been the limited availability of actual measures of worker ability and performance. Most research has studied the effects of education; formal on-the-job training; and informal training acquired through experience in the labor market, in a firm, or on a job. This set of influences is not only limited, but measures of these influences have tended to be crude and indirect. Informal training through experience has usually been inferred from the durations of time spent in the labor market, in a firm, or on a job. Since direct measures of ability and performance have rarely been obtained, knowledge of the effects of ability and performance on career mobility remains limited.

In both theory and research, there has been relatively little attention paid to the influence of worker characteristics other than ability and performance. There is evidence that individual differences in work and job values affect entry into career lines and that these change over the career course, in part as a result of experiences in the labor market (Lindsay and Knox 1984; Judge and Bretz 1992). However, the effect of workers' values, normative beliefs, preferences, and personality characteristics on career mobility has not been studied, and individual variation in these characteristics has often been assumed to be either unimportant or nonexistent. Similarly, little attention has been paid to the influence of noncareer events and activities on career advancement. There has been some limited study of the effects of family roles, which indicates that marriage and children have different effects on the career advancement of women and men, but relatively little is known about the effects of family and other noncareer events and activities on career mobility.

Apart from ability and performance, the worker characteristics receiving the most attention in research on career mobility have been ascriptive characteristics such as gender, race, and ethnicity. The structure of the labor market mediates the relationship of these characteristics to job rewards, since these characteristics become a basis for the differentiation of job ladders and career lines, as well as a basis for access to the jobs within them (Spilerman 1977; DiPrete 1989; Marini and Fan 1995; Yamagata et al. 1997). Because other measures of worker characteristics and the process of employer evaluation and selection have received little research attention, however, understanding of the multiple factors that produce differences in career mobility among groups defined by ascriptive characteristics remains limited.

Another type of worker characteristic that has received some research attention is the social ties of workers, particularly as used in the process of job change. It has been argued that social networks provide a kind of capital—social capital—that is useful to workers in career advancement. Social ties of high status are seen as furthering career advancement more than those of low status, and it has also been argued that weak social ties are more helpful than strong social ties because weak ties provide a less redundant source of information and influence (Granovetter 1974; Lin 1990). There is evidence that workers do rely on others whom they know in the process of job change, but the extent to which social ties are a source of information and influence varies with the structure of the labor market and a worker's place in it. In China's largely state-controlled economy, a worker's social ties are not used as a source of information but are a source of influence on state authorities with decision-making power over jobs. In market economies, social ties are used as a source of both

information and influence, although the extent to which they are used varies across countries and for different types of career lines (Wegener 1991; Bian and Ang 1997). In at least some countries, workers in lower-status positions are more likely to use social ties when changing jobs than workers in higher-status positions. Evidence has been inconsistent on whether the use of social ties in obtaining jobs produces better outcomes, but when social ties are used and have an effect, obtaining help from those of high status rather than low status increases job rewards. Empirical evidence on the influence of the strength of social ties has been inconsistent, in part because the strength of social ties has been defined and operationalized in a variety of ways. In some countries strong social ties have been shown to be more helpful than weak ones. In other countries weak social ties are more helpful for workers in jobs of high status, whereas strong social ties are more helpful for workers in jobs of lower status (Wegener 1991; Bian and Ang 1997).

SELECTION BY EMPLOYERS

Movement within a career line is affected not only by the characteristics of workers but by the characteristics and actions of those empowered by employers to make hiring and promotion decisions. Evaluation of performance and ability is usually based on incomplete information. In many jobs, performance is difficult to assess. Ability is even harder to assess, because it is inferred from performance. In addition, human perceptive capabilities are limited and variable. As a result, employers tend to rely on readily available information, or "signals," such as the amount of education attained, where it was attained, the amount and types of prior job experience, observable personal attributes, and evidence of past performance such as the rate of career advancement and prior job status and earnings (Spence 1974). The use of such signals is particularly likely when job shifts are made between organizations and between job ladders within an organization rather than within an organization or a job ladder (Rosenfeld 1992). The criteria on which individuals are evaluated are therefore often superficial, and having the resources (i.e., money, knowledge, and skill) to identify the way the evaluation process works and acquire an appropriate set of signals plays an important role in career advancement. Because of the difficulty of obtaining information, employers are susceptible to employees' attempts to supply and manipulate information about themselves as well as others.

Another influence on the evaluation of ability and performance is attitudes and beliefs previously acquired by those with decision-making authority. Information is unconsciously filtered and interpreted through that cognitive lens. The effect of prior attitudes and beliefs is evident in the prejudice and stereotyping triggered by ascriptive characteristics such as gender, race, and ethnicity (Hamilton 1981; Marini 1989), which have been a focus of theories of discrimination in the labor market (see, e.g., Blau 1984).

In addition to the difficulties that arise in assessing performance and ability, personal relationships and political coalitions influence mobility. As noted, there is growing evidence that personal contacts and relationships can constitute important sources of information and influence in gaining access to jobs. For workers seeking advancement, they can provide information about available positions and how to apply or present oneself favorably as a candidate. They can also result in preferential treatment based on personal liking and trust, shared interests, or expected gain on the part of those making hiring and promotion decisions. For employees responsible for hiring and promotion, personal contacts and relationships can provide information about candidates that reduces the risk of error in the selection process and increases the likelihood that individuals with similar interests and a sense of loyalty or indebtedness to them will be advanced. Personal contacts and relationships can also affect decisions if they lead to a desire to gain favor with others supportive of a candidate. Because those making hiring and promotion decisions can act to advance their own interests and the interests of others, a candidate's position in workplace political coalitions can affect advancement prospects.

REFERENCES

Allmendinger, Jutta 1989 *Career Mobility Dynamics: A Comparative Analysis of the United States, Norway, and West Germany*. Berlin: Max-Planck-Institut für Bilungsforschung.

Althauser, Robert P. 1989 "Internal Labor Markets." *Annual Review of Sociology* 15:143–161.

——, and Arne L. Kalleberg 1981 "Firms, Occupations and the Structure of Labor Markets: A Conceptual Analysis." In I. Berg, ed., *Sociological Perspectives on Labor Markets*. New York: Academic.

—— 1990 "Identifying Career Lines and Internal Labor Markets within Firms: A Study in the Interrelationships of Theory and Methods." In R. L. Breiger, ed., *Social Mobility and Social Structure*. New York: Cambridge University Press.

Barnett, William P., and Ann S. Miner 1992 "Standing on the Shoulders of Others: Career Interdependence in Job Mobility." *Administrative Science Quarterly* 37:262–281.

Baron, James N., Alison Davis-Blake, and William T. Biebly 1986 "The Structure of Opportunity: How Promotion Ladders Vary within and among Organizations." *Administrative Science Quarterly* 31:248–273.

Becker, Gary S. 1964 *Human Capital*. New York: National Bureau of Economic Research.

Bian, Yanjie, and Soon Ang 1997 "Guanxi Networks and Job Mobility in China and Singapore." *Social Forces* 75:981–1005.

Blau, Francine D. 1984 "Discrimination against Women: Theory and Evidence." In W. Darity, Jr., ed., *Labor Economics: Modern Views*. Boston: Kluwer-Nijhoff.

Blau, Peter M., and Otis Dudly Duncan 1967 *The American Occupational Structure*. New York: John Wiley.

Blumen, Isadore, M. Kogan, and P. J. McCarthy 1955 *The Industrial Mobility of Labor as a Probability Process. Cornell Studies in Industrial and Labor Relations*, vol. 6. Ithaca: New York State School of Industrial and Labor Relations, Cornell University.

Bulow, J .I., and Larry H. Summers 1986 "A Theory of Dual Labor Markets with Application to Industrial Policy, Discrimination, and Keynesian Unemployment." *Journal of Labor Economics* 4:376–414.

Cheng, Mariah Mantsun, and Arne L. Kalleberg 1996 "Labor Market Structures in Japan: An Analysis of Organizational and Occupational Mobility." *Social Forces* 74:1235–1260.

Coleman, James S., Zahava D. Blum, Aage B. Sørensen, and Peter H. Rossi 1972 "White and Black Careers during the First Decade of Labor Force Experience. I. Occupational Status." *Social Science Research* 1:243–270.

DiPrete, Thomas A. 1987 "Horizontal and Vertical Mobility in Organizations." *Administrative Science Quarterly* 32:422–444.

—— 1989 *The Bureaucratic Labor Market*. New York: Plenum.

—— 1993 "Industrial Restructuring and the Mobility Response of American Workers in the 1980s." *American Sociological Review* 58:74–96.

——, and Margaret L. Krecker 1991 "Occupational Linkages and Job Mobility within and across Organizations." *Research in Social Stratification and Mobility* 10:91–131.

DiPrete, Thomas A., and Patricia A. McManus 1996 "Institutions, Technical Change, and Diverging Life Chances: Earnings Mobility in the United States and Germany." *American Journal of Sociology* 102:34–79.

DiPrete, Thomas A., and K. Lynn Nonnemaker 1997 "Structural Change, Labor Market Turbulence, and Labor Market Outcomes." *American Sociological Review* 62:386–404.

Doeringer, Peter B., and M. J. Piore 1971 *Internal Labor Markets and Manpower Analysis*. Lexington, Mass.: Heath.

Dore, Ronald P. 1973 *British Factory–Japanese Factory*. Berkeley: University of California Press.

Dunlop, John 1957 "The Task of Contemporary Wage Theory." In G. W. Taylor and F. C. Pierson, eds., *New Concepts in Wage Determination*. New York: McGraw-Hill.

Felmlee, Diane H. 1982 "Women's Job Mobility Processes within and between Employers." *American Journal of Sociology* 80:44–57.

Gordon, David M. 1972 *Theories of Poverty and Underemployment*. Lexington, Mass.: Heath.

Gottschalk, Peter, and Timothy M. Smeeding 1997 "Cross-National Comparisons of Earnings and Earnings Inequality." *Journal of Economic Literature* 35:633–687.

Granovetter, Mark 1974 *Getting a Job: A Study of Contacts and Careers*. Cambridge, Mass.: Harvard University Press.

Groot, Wim, and Maartje Verberne 1997 "Aging, Job Mobility, and Compensation." *Oxford Economic Papers* 49:380–403.

Hachen, David S., Jr. 1992 "Industrial Characteristics and Job Mobility." *American Sociological Review* 57:39–55.

Hall, Robert L. 1982 "The Importance of Lifetime Jobs in the U.S. Economy." *American Economic Review* 72:716–724.

Haller, Max, Wolfgang König, Peter Krause, and Karin Kurz 1985 "Patterns of Career Mobility and Structural Positions in Advanced Capitalist Societies: A Comparison of Men in Austria, France, and the United States." *American Sociological Review* 50:579–603.

Hamilton, David L. 1981 *Cognitive Processes in Stereotyping and Intergroup Behavior*. Hillsdale, N.J.: Erlbaum.

Haveman, Heather A., and Lisa E. Cohen 1994 "The Ecological Dynamics of Careers: The Impact of Organizational Founding, Dissolution, and Merger on Job Mobility." *American Journal of Sociology* 100:104–152.

Horowitz, Stanley A., and Allen Sherman 1980 "A Direct Measure of the Relationship between Human Capital and Productivity." *Journal of Human Resources* 15:67–76.

Jovanovic, Boyan 1979 "Job Matching and the Theory of Turnover." *Journal of Political Economy* 87:972–990.

Judge, Timothy A., and Robert D. Bretz, Jr. 1992 "Effects of Work Values on Job Choice Decisions." *Journal of Applied Psychology* 77:261–271.

Kalleberg, Arne, and Aage B. Sørensen 1979 "The Sociology of Labor Markets." *Annual Review of Sociology* 5:351–379.

Lazear, Edward P. 1981 "Agency, Earnings Profiles, Productivity, and Hours Restrictions." *American Economic Review* 71:606–620.

——, and Sherwin Rosen 1981 "Rank-Order Tournaments as Optimum Labor Contracts." *Journal of Political Economy* 89:841–864.

Lin, Nan 1990 "Social Resources and Social Mobility: A Structural Theory of Status Attainment." In R. L. Breiger, ed., *Social Mobility and Social Structure*. Cambridge: Cambridge University Press.

Lindsay, Paul, and William E. Knox 1984 "Continuity and Change in Work Values Among Young Adults." *American Journal of Sociology* 89:918–931.

Malcomson, James M. 1984 "Work Incentives, Hierarchy, and Internal Labor Markets." *Journal of Political Economy* 92:486–507.

Maranto, Cheryl L., and Robert C. Rodgers 1984 "Does Work Experience Increase Productivity? A Test of the On-the-Job Training Hypothesis." *Journal of Human Resources* 19:341–357.

Marini, Margaret Mooney 1980 "Sex Differences in the Process of Occupational Attainment: A Closer Look." *Social Science Research* 9:307–361.

—— 1989 "Sex Differences in Earnings in the United States." *Annual Review of Sociology* 15:343–380.

——, and Pi-Ling Fan 1995 "The Gender Gap in Earnings at Career Entry." *American Sociological Review* 62:588–604.

Mayer, Thomas 1972 "Models in Intragenerational Mobility." In J. Berger, M. Zelditch, Jr., and B. Anderson, eds., *Sociological Theories in Progress*, vol. 2. Boston: Houghton Mifflin.

Medoff, James L., and Katherine G. Abraham 1980 "Experience, Performance, and Earnings." *Quarterly Journal of Economy* 95:703–736.

——— 1981 "Are Those Paid More Really More Productive? The Case of Experience." *Journal of Human Resources* 16:186–216.

Mincer, Jacob 1974 *Schooling, Experience, and Earnings.* New York: National Bureau of Economic Research.

Petersen, Trond, and Seymour Spilerman 1990 "Job Quits from an Internal Labor Market." In K. U. Mayer and N. B. Tuma, eds., *Event History Analysis in Life Course Research.* Madison: University of Wisconsin.

Pfeffer, Jeffrey, and Yinon Cohen 1984 "Determinants of Internal Labor Markets in Organizations." *Administrative Science Quarterly* 29:550–572.

Rosenbaum, James L. 1984 *Career Mobility in a Corporate Hierarchy.* New York: Academic.

Rosenfeld, Rachel A. 1980 "Race and Sex Differences in Career Dynamics." *American Sociological Review* 45:583–609.

——— 1992 "Job Mobility and Career Processes." *Annual Review of Sociology* 18:39–61.

Sicherman, Nachum, and Oded Galor 1990 "A Theory of Career Mobility." *Journal of Political Economy* 98:169–192.

Skvoretz, John 1984 "The Logic of Opportunity and Mobility." *Social Forces* 63:72–97.

Sørensen, Aage B. 1974 "A Model for Occupational Careers." *American Journal of Sociology* 80:44–57.

——— 1977 "The Structure of Inequality and the Process of Attainment." *American Sociological Review* 42:965–978.

Spence, Michael A. 1974 *Market Signaling.* Cambridge, Mass.: Harvard University Press.

Spenner, Kenneth I., Luther B. Otto, and Vaughn R. A. Call 1982 *Career Lines and Careers.* Lexington, Mass.: Lexington Books.

Spilerman, Seymour 1977 "Careers, Labor Market Structure, and Socioeconomic Achievement." *American Journal of Sociology* 83:551–593.

——— 1986 "Organizational Rules and the Features of Work Careers." *Research in Social Stratification and Mobility* 5:41–102.

Stewman, Shelby 1986 "Demographic Models of Internal Labor Markets." *Administrative Science Quarterly* 31:212–247.

———, and S. L. Konda 1983 "Careers and Organizational Labor Markets: Demographic Models of Organizational Behavior." *American Journal of Sociology* 88:637–685.

Stewman, Shelby, and Kuang S. Yeh 1991 "Structural Pathways and Switching Mechanisms for Individual Careers." *Research in Social Stratification and Mobility* 10:133–168.

Stiglitz, Joseph E. 1973 "Approaches to the Economics of Discrimination." *American Economic Review* 63:287–295.

Stovel, Katherine, Michael Savage, and Peter Bearmen 1996 "Ascription and Achievement: Models of Career Systems at Lloyds Bank, 1890–1970." *American Journal of Sociology* 102:358–399.

Talbert, Joan, and Christine E. Bose 1977 "Wage Attainment Processes: The Retail Clerk Case." *American Journal of Sociology* 83:403–424.

Topel, Robert H. 1991 "Specific Capital, Mobility, and Wages: Wages Rise with Job Seniority." *Journal of Political Economy* 99:145–176.

———, and Michael P. Ward 1992 "Job Mobility and the Careers of Young Men." *Quarterly Journal of Economics* 107:439–479.

Wegener, Bernd 1991 "Job Mobility and Social Ties: Social Resources, Prior Job, and Status Attainment." *American Sociological Review* 56:60–71.

White, Harrison C. 1970 *Chains of Opportunity.* Cambridge, Mass.: Harvard University Press.

Williamson, Oliver E. 1975 *Markets and Hierarchies: Analysis and Antitrust Implications.* New York: Free Press.

Winfield, Idee, Richard T. Campbell, Alan C. Kerckhoff, Diane D. Everett, and Jerry M. Trott 1989 "Career Processes in Great Britain and the United States." *Social Forces* 68:284–308.

Yamagata, Hisashi, Kuang S. Yeh, Shelby Stewman, and Hiroko Dodge 1997 "Sex Segregation and Glass Ceilings: A Comparative Statics Model of Women's Career Opportunities in the Federal Government over a Quarter Century." *American Journal of Sociology* 103:566–632.

Zhou, Xueguang, Nancy Brandon Tuma, and Phyllis Moen 1997 "Institutional Change and Job Shift Patterns in Urban China, 1949 to 1994." *American Sociological Review* 62:339–365.

MARGARET MOONEY MARINI

OCCUPATIONAL PRESTIGE

Individuals have repeatedly demonstrated an ability to rank occupations according to their prestige, a relative social standing in a society. Occupational prestige is one of the most empirically studied aspects of stratification structure in modern societies. Social stratification theories, however, differ in their views of the concept of prestige. Wegener points out that theories vary primarily in their suppositions of the foundation on which prestige is based, that is, achievement, esteem, honor, or charisma. Wegener also distinguishes two types of stratification theories, one that views prestige as a hierarchy of positions and the other as an attribute of socially closed groups.

> *By and large, stratification theories that emphasize order in society (e.g., functionalist theories) conceive prestige as an attribute of individuals or of individual social positions that form a hierarchy. Stratification theories that emphasize conflict (e.g., Weber) think of prestige as designating social aggregates, or individuals within social aggregates, influenced by social closure processes.* (Wegener 1992, p. 255)

Despite such variation in theoretical views, most empirical studies share the notion that occupational positions are hierarchically ordered along a single dimension as judged by the individuals in the society. Efforts to measure such a concept involve a reputational approach in which respondents are asked to evaluate occupations.

The modern study of occupational prestige dates to a landmark survey fielded in 1947 by the National Opinion Research Center under the direction of Cecil C. North and Paul K. Hatt (Reiss 1961). Although others had conducted earlier investigations in the United States. NORC's national sample and broad coverage of the occupational hierarchy became the model for later inquiries. Perhaps the best known product of the North-Hatt study was Duncan's Socioeconomic Index (SEI) (1961), which assigned to each detailed occupational category a predicted prestige score based on the age-standardized education and income characteristics of occupational incumbents reported by the 1950 Census of Population. Although this index proved to have somewhat different properties than prestige, it exploited the limited occupational titles evaluated by the North-Hatt study to construct the first metric scale of socioeconomic status for all occupations.

In the 1960s, a second generation of studies was carried out by NORC (Hodge et al. 1964). Piecing together surveys from 1963, 1964, and 1965, Siegel (1971) generated the first prestige scale for all Census occupations. This scale served for twenty years as the foundation of socioeconomic status scores, and it became the backbone of Treiman's International Prestige Scale (1977). In 1980, however, a major change in the occupational classification system employed by the U.S. Bureau of the Census called into question scores based on earlier classifications of occupational titles, since there was no sensible way to match old and new categories. In 1989, the NORC General Social Survey undertook another periodic sounding of Americans' evaluations of the general social standing of occupations (Nakao and Treas 1994). In the 1989 survey, a total of 740 occupational titles were selected to ensure reasonable coverage of the 503 detailed occupational categories of the 1980 census classification system. These titles were rated by a sample of 1,166 respondents, each of whom rated 110 occupations. The evaluation involved sorting cards, each bearing one occupational title, onto a sheet displaying a nine-rung ladder of social standing (from "1" for the lowest possible social standing to "9" for the highest possible). Based on their ratings, a score was calculated for each occupation and was converted to a scale so as to have a logical range from 0 (lowest) to 100 (highest) of prestige scores. For use in data analyses of most social surveys, in which occupations are coded according to occupational categories, scores assigned to categories, not titles, become necessary. Thus, using the scores for occupational titles in respective categories, a score was computed for each of the 503 detailed occupational categories of the 1980 census. The 1989 survey, which was the first to collect evaluations for all occupational categories at one time, yielded new prestige scores. These scores became the basis for updating the Socioeconomic Index (Hauser and Warren 1997).

Five generalizations may be drawn from the empirical research on occupational prestige.

First, very different methods for soliciting occupational evaluations yield very similar prestige hierarchies. Presenting respondents with an occupational title (e.g., electrician), the North-Hatt study asked them to "pick out the statement that best gives your personal opinion of the general standing that such a job has." Five response categories, ranging from "excellent standing" to "poor standing," were presented, along with a "don't know" option. One might readily fault the ambiguous instructions calling for both a "personal" opinion and a reading of "general" standing. Nonetheless, the results proved virtually identical to those of the 1964 and 1989 surveys, which asked respondents to sort cards bearing occupational titles onto a "ladder of social standing," the method that became the primary standard against which all other inquiries are evaluated (Nakao et al. 1990). The 1964 study went on to ask respondents to sort occupations onto a horizontal ruler according to another specific dimension (e.g., freedom and independence, perceived income, how interesting the work). However different the tasks, the correlation with social standing evaluations was over .90 for eight of nine dimensions.

Even when respondents are instructed to cluster occupations according to their similarity (rather than to rank them by social standing), multidimensional scaling methods reveal that one of the organizing principles behind judged similarity is a prestige hierarchy. Burton (1972) first demonstrated this with a nonrandom subsample of volunteers solicited from an advertisement in the Harvard student newspaper. Kraus et al. (1978) achieved similar results with a representative sample of 463 urban Israelis. To confirm that people view occupations in terms of an up/down classification scheme, Schwartz (1981) showed that ranking occupations according to "vertical" paired adjectives (e.g., top/bottom) yields results highly correlated with prestige scores, while rankings based on evaluative (e.g., kind/cruel), potency (e.g., big/little), and activity (e.g., slow/fast) dimensions fail to replicate prestige orderings. Studies that directly asked the respondents on what basis they rated occupations, or that asked them to rate occupations on selected dimensions such as "value to the society" or "power," did not culminate in conclusive results. Individuals' evaluations seem to be based on their judgments of the "overall desirability" of occupations (Goldthorpe and Hope 1974; Hauser and Featherman 1977). In short, the prestige hierarchy is so central to how we evaluate occupations that it emerges from virtually any reasonable effort to elicit it.

Second, overall prestige rankings are very stable over time. Hodge et al. (1964) reported a correlation of .99 between the 1947 North-Hatt study and their own in the mid-1960s. Nakao and Treas (1994) found a correlation of .96 between

the mid-1960s and 1989. This stability is not surprising. First, the relative income and education levels associated with various occupations are quite stable over time (Treiman and Terrell 1975). Second, to the extent that prestige is fixed by the division of labor and workplace authority, we do not expect the prestige of flight attendants to soar above that of pilots.

This is not to say that prestige never changes. Hodge et al. (1964) noted modest gains for blue-collar occupations, an upswing in scientific occupations and the "free" professions (e.g., "physician"), and a downturn in artistic, cultural, and communication occupations. Nakao and Treas (1994) compared the scores for 160 occupational titles evaluated in both 1964 and 1989 and found that the mean score moved up from 45.2 to 47.5 while the standard deviation declined from 17.3 to 15.8. They noted especially that the bottom of the American occupational prestige distribution shifted upward between 1964 and 1989. Low-status service and farming occupations especially came to be more favorably evaluated (see Table 1). This may be, in part, due to changes in the occupation itself. Farmers, for example, have undergone changes and have come to be seen as "agribusiness" owners. Thus, change in prestige may occur not only because of the succession of new generations who hold different views, but also because all age groups change their thinking about the relative standing of occupations. Changes in the general public's familiarity with an occupation can also affect its rating, as demonstrated for "nuclear physicist" between 1947 and 1963 (Hodge et al. 1964). Thus, individual occupations change even though the overall ranking of occupations remains quite stable over time. The growing prestige of low-status occupational titles warrants further study, especially because it is inconsistent with socioeconomic trends observed in the workforce and in the workplace-the growing inequality in earnings, the decline of unionized blue-collar employment, the influx of traditionally devalued workers like women and immigrants, and the absence of systematic skill upgrading for blue-collar workers (Nakao and Treas 1994).

Third, prestige evaluations are surprisingly comparable from one society to another. Arguing that industrialization everywhere demands a similar organization and reward of work, Treiman

**Prestige Scores for Selected Occupations in the United States, 1964 and 1989
(1980 Census Major Occupational Categories)**

Occupational Title	1964	1989
Managerial and Professional Specialty Occupations		
Department head in a state government	80	76
Banker	72	63
General manager of a manufacturing plant	64	62
Lunchroom operator	31	27
Accountant	57	65
Chemist	69	73
Public grade school teacher	60	64
Clergyman	69	67
Lawyer	76	75
Musician in a symphony orchestra	59	59
Technical, Sales, and Administrative Support Occupations		
Medical technician	61	68
Manager of a supermarket	47	48
Insurance agent	47	46
Travel agent	43	41
Cashier in a supermarket	31	33
Telephone solicitor	26	22
Secretary	46	46
Post office clerk	43	42
Shipping clerk	29	33
Bill collector	26	24
Bank teller	50	43
Service Occupations		
Housekeeper in a private home	25	34
Policeman	48	59
Bartender	20	25
Cook in a restaurant	26	34
Janitor	16	22
Barber	38	36
Farming, Forestry, and Fishing Occupations		
Farm owner and operator	44	53
Gardener	23	29
Logger	26	31
Precision Production, Craft, and Repair Occupations		
Airplane mechanic	48	53
Superintendent of a construction job	51	57
House painter	30	34
Baker	34	35
Operators, Fabricators, and Laborers		
Saw sharpener	19	23
Welder	40	42
Assembly line worker	27	35
Bus driver	32	32
Locomotive engineer	48	48
Filling station attendant	22	21

Table 1

SOURCE: Nakoa and Treas (1994); Siegel (1971).

(1977) assembled eighty-five prestige studies of sixty nations, tribal societies, and territories. Comparing the United States with fifty-nine other societies yielded an average intercorrelation of .837; in other words, about 70 percent of the variation in U.S. prestige evaluations is shared in common with the "average" society available to Treiman. To be sure, the correlations ranged from .98 for Canada to .54 for Zaire. Prestige hierarchies are similar, but not identical. Notable differences relate to level of economic development (Treiman 1977) and the greater appreciation of manual labor in socialist societies (Penn 1975; for a Chinese exception, see Lin and Xie 1988).

Fourth, subgroups within a society also tend to agree about the relative ranking of occupations. Efforts to discern differences between blacks and whites, between those employed in more versus less prestigious jobs, have typically found little effect of the respondent's social location on his or her view of the occupational hierarchy (e.g., Goldthorpe and Hope, 1972; Kraus et al. 1978). To be sure, higher-status groups assign somewhat higher absolute rankings to high-status jobs than do lower-status groups, who tend to boost lower-status jobs somewhat (Hodge and Rossi 1978). Apparently, this phenomenon does not arise because groups hold self-serving views of the social order. Instead, high-status individuals agree more among themselves and, thus, avoid random ranking errors that move both high- and low-status occupations toward the middle of the distribution. In comparison to the differences among individuals in their ratings (i.e., reported interrater correlations range from .42 to .745), the variation between groups is smaller than the variation within groups (Hodge et al. 1982). Since location in the social structure has been shown to influence so many other attitudes, it is surprising that groups agree so closely on the order of occupations. The mechanisms leading to this consensus are not well understood. By early adolescence, however, children can agree on how jobs rank (Gunn 1964).

Fifth, the main factors associated with an occupation's prestige are its education and income levels, the basic logic behind the original construction of the Socioeconomic Index (Duncan 1961). Socioeconomic scores based on these two factors account for about 80 percent of the variation in prestige attributed to different occupations (Hodge 1981). Based on the 1989 prestige scores and the occupational data from the 1990 U.S. Census, Hauser and Warren (1997) also reported that in several models they used, between 70 and 80 percent of the variance in occupational prestige was accounted for by occupational education and earnings.

In the studies of status attainment models, socioeconomic status scores were demonstrated to be superior to prestige scores in accounting for a son's occupational achievement using his father's status (Featherman et al. 1975; Featherman

and Hauser 1976; Treas and Tyree 1979). It would be a mistake, however, to dismiss occupational prestige. Subgroups of raters agree not only on the prestige of an occupation, but also on how prestige differs from the occupation's socioeconomic location (Hodge 1981). Furthermore, a more recent study by Kerckhoff et al. (1989) showed in a comparative study of status attainment in the United States and Great Britain, that differences between the two countries were illuminated in the models using prestige scores, but not in the models using the Socioeconomic Index. The British data yielded stronger intergenerational effect on the respondents' occupations than did the United States data when prestige scores were used. This implies that the prestige scale captures different aspects of the status attainment process than the Socioeconomic Index does.

However important the educational requirements and economic rewards of occupations, they are not alone in determining the prestige accorded occupations. The racial or age composition of jobs may also figure in their public evaluation. Even controlling for education and occupation, a higher proportion of nonwhites in an occupation is associated with a lower prestige rating (Siegel 1971). Occupations dominated by the very young or the very old are similarly disadvantaged (Siegel 1971). However, the proportion of women in an occupation was shown to have no or little effect on prestige (England 1979; Bose and Rossi 1983; Fox and Suschnigg 1989).

There is no conclusive evidence that American respondents consistently downgrade the status of female-gendered occupational titles (e.g., policewoman) as compared with male titles (e.g., policeman). However, male (but not female) respondents do downgrade the standing of occupations in which women find employment—a relation that holds after the income and education levels of workers are taken into account (Meyer 1978). Further studies are warranted investigating systematic associations between gender and occupational evaluation.

Empirical studies of occupational prestige are based on the notion that prestige represents a hierarchy of social standing of individuals or aggregates based on their occupations. This notion is widely used in analyses of social survey data as a

variable indicating an individual's social status. While it is a useful index, the assumption behind its application as a measure of social status is that individuals' social positions are manifested by the occupations they hold. This assumption is rooted in the fact that occupation is a means through which social and economic resources are distributed. Furthermore, occupation is salient in one's life, providing not only economic needs, but also social relations that establish one's role in a society. This assumption may hold true in most industrialized countries, yet it perhaps deserves a further consideration in future research. As to what measure is appropriate as an index of social status in what context (for example, socioeconomic scale versus prestige scale), further research is called for that would lead us to a more thorough understanding of the stratification system and the process of individuals' attainment of social positions within it.

REFERENCES

Bose, C. E., and P. H Rossi 1983 "Gender and Jobs: Prestige Standings of Occupations as Affected by Gender." *American Sociological Review* 48:316–330.

Burton, M. 1972 "Semantic Dimensions of Occupational Names." In A. Kimball Romney, Roger N. Shepard, and Sara Nerlove, eds., *Multidimensional Scaling: Theory and Applications in the Behavioral Sciences, Vol. 2, Applications*. New York: Seminar.

Duncan, O. D. 1961 "A Socioeconomic Index for All Occupations." In Albert J. Reiss, Jr., et al., eds., *Occupations and Social Status*. New York: Free Press.

England, P. 1979 "Women and Occupational Prestige: A Vacuous Sex Inequality." *Signs* 5:252–265.

Featherman, D. L., F. L. Jones, and R. M. Hauser 1975 "Assumptions of Social Mobility Research in the U.S.: The Case of Occupational Status." *Social Science Research* 4:329–360.

Featherman, D. L., and R. M. Hauser 1976 "Prestige or Socioeconomic Scales in the Study of Occupational Achievement?" *Sociological Methods and Research* 4:402–422.

Fox, J., and C. Suschinigg 1989 "A Note on Gender and the Prestige of Occupations." *Canadian Journal of Sociology* 14(3):353–360.

Goldthorpe, J. H., and K. Hope 1972 "Occupational Grading and Occupational Prestige." In Keith Hope, ed., *The Analysis of Social Mobility: Methods and Approaches*. Oxford, U.K.: Clarendon Press.

Goldthorpe, J. H., and K. Hope 1974 *The Social Grading of Occupations. A New Scale and Approach*. Oxford, U.K.: Clarendon Press.

Gunn, B. 1964 "Children's Conceptions of Occupational Prestige." *Personnel and Guidance Journal* 558–563.

Hauser, R. M., and J. R. Warren 1997 "Socioeconomic Indexes for Occupations: A Review, Update, and Critique." *Sociological Methodology* 27:177–298.

Hodge, R. W. 1981 "The Measurement of Occupational Prestige." *Social Science Research* 10:396–415.

——, and P. M. Rossi 1978 "Intergroup Consensus in Occupational Prestige Ratings: A Case of Serendipity Lost and Regained." *Sozialwissenschaftliche Annelen* 2:B59–B73.

Hodge, R. W, P. M. Siegel, and P. Rossi 1964 "Occupational Prestige in the United States, 1925–1963." *American Journal of Sociology* 70:286–302.

Kerckhoff, A. C., R. T. Campbell, J. M. Trott, and V. Kraus 1989 "The Transmission of Socioeconomic Status and Prestige in Great Britain and the United States." *Sociological Forum* 4:155–177.

Kraus, V., E. O. Schild, and R. W. Hodge 1978 "Occupational Prestige in the Collective Conscience." *Social Forces* 56:900–918.

Lin, N., and W. Xie 1988 "Occupational Prestige in Urban China." *American Journal of Sociology* 93:793–832.

Meyer, G. S. 1978 "Sex and Marriage of Raters in the Evaluation of Occupations "*Social Science Research* 7:366–388.

Nakao, K., R. W. Hodge, and J. Treas 1990 *On Revising Prestige Scores for All Occupations. General Social Survey Methodological Report No. 69*.

Nakao, K., and J. Treas 1994 "Updating Occupational Prestige and Socioeconomic Scores: How the New Measures Measure Up." *Sociological Methodology* 24:1–72.

Penn, R. 1975 "Occupational Prestige Hierarchies: A Great Empirical Invariant?" *Social Forces* 54:352–364.

Reiss, A. J., Jr., O. D. Duncan, P. K. Hatt, and C. C. North 1961 *Occupations and Social Status*. New York: Free Press of Glencoe.

Schwartz, B. 1981 *Vertical Classification: A Study in Structuralism and the Sociology of Knowledge*. Chicago: University of Chicago Press.

Siegel, P. M. 1971 Prestige in the American Occupational Structure. Ph.D. diss, University of Chicago.

Treas, J., and A. Tyree 1979 "Prestige Versus Socioeconomic Status in the Attainment Processes of American Men and Women." *Social Science Research* 8:201–221.

Treiman, D. J. 1977 *Occupational Prestige in Comparative Perspective*. New York: Academic Press.

Treiman, D. J., and K. Terrell 1975 "Women, Work and Wages-Trends in the Female Occupation Structure." In Kenneth C. Land and Seymour Spilerman, eds., *Social Indicator Models*. New York: Russell Sage Foundation.

Wegener, B. 1992 "Concepts and Measurement of Prestige." *Annual Review of Sociology* 18:253–280.

KEIKO NAKAO

OCCUPATIONS

See Professions; Work and Occupations.

ORGANIZATIONAL EFFECTIVENESS

See Bureaucracy; Complex Organizations; Industrial Sociology; Organizational Structure; Social Organization.

ORGANIZATIONAL STRUCTURE

Organizations are composed of a variety of elements. Perhaps the fundamental component is *organizational structure*, the set of interrelationships (social bonds) between positions. Even organizations of globe-encircling proportions, such as multinational corporations, demonstrate "the consciously coordinated activities of two or more people" (Barnard 1938, p. 73). Similarly, it may be argued that relationships between and among sets of such organizations form the social structure of whole societies.

Within an organizational structure, groups or sets of social relationships can be differentiated by task specialization, known as the *division of labor*. People are assigned to specific positions within an organizational structure to increase the specificity of tasks and the reliability with which they are performed. Organizational structure is both (1) an outcome resulting from interactive processes between elements within the organization, as well as between the environment and the organization, and (2) a determinant of those interactive processes. Organizational structure calls forth or inhibits particular behaviors by organizational participants.

Interaction among parties to a relationship results in shared understandings that become part of an organization's culture. Focusing as it does on relationships constituting organizational structure, the social systems perspective for organizational analysis has been criticized as having a static cast. By contrast, organizational theorists contend that studying social processes among constituent parties *is* dynamic because it examines how social change occurs as participants grant or withhold their consent for collective actions. When the volitional and cognitive exigencies among constituents change, their behavior toward each is altered. Negotiation among organizational participants leads to the creation of new relationships, fluidity in existing relationships, and the potential for breaking off longstanding relationships. Processes influencing expectation and negotiation are complicated by the structural advantages enjoyed by dominant constituent parties. Whether change in agreed-upon relations is viewed as desirable often depends on whether a given constituent party perceives change to be disproportionately beneficial to itself when compared with the benefits to other specific constituent groups or to the overall organization. Moreover, more powerful constituents can, to their own benefit, cloud less powerful constituents' perceptions of what is actually in the latter's self-interest.

Much traditional theory and research on organizations, almost always implicitly (sometimes explicitly), assumes that decisions by upper participants benefit the entire collectivity. Most analyses do not differentiate benefit to the collectivity from benefit to upper-, middle-, or lower-level participants. Most researchers simply proceed on the implicit assumption that owners and managers are prime, if not sole, legitimate participants in and *entitled* beneficiaries of organizational structure. It is assumed, moreover, that lower-level employees in particular, and lower level participants generally, are incidental to the social construction of the organization, and are thus passive contributors to and beneficiaries of organizational structure. By contrast, modern sociological theory (as expressed throughout the present discussion of organizational structure and its correlates) increasingly differentiates among upper-, middle-, and lower-level participants as well as, separately, the organization as a whole. Thus, in this view, a much broader array of constituents contributes directly

or indirectly to organizational survival and therefore merit an appropriate share of rewards. Researchers need explicitly to identify and differentiate all participants and constituents that contribute directly or indirectly to an organization. Allocation of resources to an organization's tasks, defined through the division of labor, critically affects the power balance between participants, thus raising important and politically disturbing questions. Organizational structure, composed of collectively endorsed and enacted resource allocation agreements, can be usefully understood from an "organizational justice" perspective.

Organizational justice research seeks to understand how resources are allocated in ways believed to be "fair" by various interactants. The perceived fairness of resource allocations by organizational participants is distributive justice; the perceived fairness of the process through which resource allocation decisions are made is procedural justice. Both distributive justice and procedural justice interact to influence organizational participants' perceptions of fairness. Distributive justice may follow underlying norms of allocation, including an assessment of both the quantity and the quality of participants' contribution to a given effort (thus, their earned equity in the organization), as well as the extent to which resources are evenly allocated among participants (thus, their right to equal treatment) and, moreover, how much participants *need* the resources they receive (thus, their right to basic means for survival) (Linkey and Alexander 1998). These norms underlying the allocation of resources may affect the satisfaction of organizational participants through the outcomes of allocation decisions. Procedural justice has two components: the structure and form of procedures through which resources are allocated, and the social and emotional relations between parties in an exchange relationship (interactive justice). As Brockner and Siegel (1995) point out, the difference between these two components may signal the difference between how much control participants have over the process of allocative decisions, and their intent toward others in making such decisions.

Researchers have proposed two different viewpoints to explain variations in organizational participants' satisfaction with procedural and distributive justice. The self-interest explanation is that individuals wish to maximize their resources and are more satisfied when their rewards are greater. The group-values explanation is that individuals evaluate themselves in the context of group membership; the perception of an individual as fair is colored by perceptions of the fairness of his or her group, and how resources are allocated to an individual indicates his or her worth relative to other members of the group. Both the self-interest and the group-values explanations have helped to explain organizational participants' satisfaction with the allocation of resources. These two approaches are reflected in the focus of allocation rules based on the *attributes* and *contributions* of recipients (Cook and Yamagishi 1983). *Attributes* are personal characteristics such as gender, age, and ethnicity that are used to determine social status. *Contributions* refer to valued inputs made by participants in an exchange relationship; among these valued inputs are performance and effort. Classification is not always clear-cut; for example, *ability* might be classified as an attribute in some circumstances but as a contribution otherwise.

While most of the organizational justice literature focuses on the contributions of organizational participants, a growing number of studies focus on their attributes. Evidence suggests that the degree to which organizational participants endorse norms for resource allocation to individuals is associated with their own placement within an organizational structure. Moreover, endorsement of these norms may also vary according to demographic characteristics such as age, gender, and income, as well as cultural factors such as political affiliation and religious affiliation (Jason S. Lee and Stolte 1994; Linkey and Alexander 1998). An important question for further research is whether individuals with given attributes alter their endorsement of allocative norms as their own placement within the organization's structure varies over the course of their own tenure in the organization. Further, *satisfaction* with resource allocation outcomes is associated with structural, demographic, and cultural factors (Huo et al. 1996; Irwin 1996); although the evidence for a consistent association between gender and satisfaction is mixed (e.g., Sweeney and McFarlin 1997; Lee and Fahr 1999). Given the level of ethnic and gender segregation within the workforce, particular tasks appear to be associated with certain attributes as workers are distributed into organizational positions. Additionally, institutional factors, such as state legislation, and cultural values may affect allocators' distribution norms. In some cases, distribution norms for external constituents related to a given organization through its impact on their culture, economy, or community may differ from distribution rules for those participating directly in an organization. These factors contribute to differential allocation of resources to participants within organizational structures, and their different perceptions of, and satisfaction with, allocation outcomes.

Blau and Scott's *cui bono* criterion (1962) explicitly raises the question of who benefits from particular policies and characteristics of organizational structure. Blau and Scott suggest a fourfold topology of organizations: (1) mutual benefit organizations, such as clubs, where presumably egalitarian *members* are prime beneficiaries; (2) business or industrial organizations, where *owners* are prime beneficiaries; (3) service organizations, such as hospitals, where *clients* are prime beneficiaries; (4) commonweal organizations, such as the State Department, in which the *public-at-large* is prime beneficiary. For each type of organization, researchers should systematically examine patterns of benefit by virtue of a constituency's location either (1) externally in an input-output exchange relationship to the organization or (2) internally as upper-, middle-, or lower-level participants in its organizational structure (Etzioni 1961). A fully developed distributive justice perspective would evaluate the benefit a constituency derives from the organization relative to its contribution to the organization's *sustained* existence (Alvarez 1979).

Not only does the allocation of resources impact organizational structure, it also affects assessments of organizational structure in terms of effectiveness and efficiency. *Organizational effectiveness* may be defined as the capacity of an organization to produce intended and unintended outcomes. An organization may unknowingly, unintendedly, or inadvertently serve the interest of a given constituency. Such "latent" functional consequences are seldom explored and documented in advance by social scientists. More usually, latent functions are discovered when they become manifest because organizational activities are dramatically altered or the organization ceases to exist, with the consequence that former latent beneficiaries are severely affected. Indeed, previously unrecognized support from such latent beneficiaries may have

been critical to organizational well-being (perhaps survival), and the disaffection of such beneficiaries might threaten future organizational survival. But the concept of "latent" functions has not yet produced a research literature.

Notwithstanding vexing conceptual problems raised by the issue of "latency," research on organizational effectiveness has traditionally overemphasized manifest purposive action, by reference to the organization's *intended* outcomes (or formal goals). It is obvious, but critical to note, that if the organization goes out of existence, it can no longer accomplish anything. Hence, perhaps the most important task (latent or manifest) for any organization is its continued survival. While some organizations are designed, and are prepared from the outset, to go out of existence upon completion of the task for which they were initially created, many, perhaps most, organizations are quick to acquire new purposes so as to maintain themselves in existence. Indeed, some organizations such as political parties and governments have been known to kill their own people in attempts to remain in existence. Thus, the "cost" per se of getting things done is, at least theoretically, of no consequence in assessing organizational effectiveness. Traditionally, assessing effectiveness requires the comparison of organizational activities to an optimal standard outlined in organizational goals. Since different organizational constituencies (or stakeholders) may have different and sometimes conflicting expectations, this traditional approach has serious limitations.

By contrast, the "cost" of getting things done is paramount in any assessment of *organizational efficiency*. "Costs" of accomplishing any given task can be of various kinds; and each type of cost may be assessed by various techniques, with varying degrees of efficacy. Unfortunately, social science has not reached any consensus on what types of costs and benefits are worth measuring. Thus, in its broadest sense, *efficiency* may be viewed as the assessment of an organization's inputs (either in kind or in the distribution of those inputs) relative to its output, in a more narrow view it is simply cost per unit of production. Traditionally, efficiency is reflected in economic analyses and cost-accounting techniques (e.g., Rossi and Freeman 1993). However, it may reflect other kinds of resources, such as opportunity costs; risk; and political, social, and social benefits. Like effectiveness, the attributes and positions of organizational stakeholders influence how efficiency is perceived and assessed.

This review is categorized into four functional requirements for social system survival, as posited by Parsons (1960): (1) adaptation to the environment, (2) goal attainment, (3) integration of its members into a "whole," and (4) creation of cultural understandings (often latent) among members by which the meaning of collective action can be judged. We do not suggest Parsons's AGIL scheme is the only or the definitive way to classify organizational structures or attendant activities. Rather, AGIL focuses on the totality of a particular organization (as a social system) and raises questions of how its organizational structures come into being, change, and persist; within each category we question "who benefits" from consensual, consciously coordinated activities.

ADAPTATION TO THE ENVIRONMENT

"Environment" refers to a broad array of elements that are "outside" organizational boundaries but are relevant to organizational functioning. Organizational boundaries are the set of agreed-upon relationships that constitute organizational structure. Dill defines the task, or technical, environment as all features of the environment "potentially relevant to goal setting and goal attainment" (1958, p. 410). Established beliefs and practices embedded within the organization may systematically affect the shape and operation of the focal organization's structure. Scott (1998) terms these influences the *institutional environment* of organizations; others refer to it as *organizational culture*. An organization may seek to control or reshape all or some elements in its environment as a means to lessen uncertainty about its capacity to endure. An organization might reshape its own organizational structures if it is unable to reshape the environment (e.g., Aldrich 1979). Dess and Beard (1984) suggest that Aldrich's topology of environmental characteristics (1979) may be classified into three categories: (1) munificence, or the environmental availability of resources needed by organizations; (2) complexity, or the similarity or dissimilarity of environmental entities and their distribution across the environment; and (3) dynamism, or the degree of change in the environment.

Organizations are embedded within larger societies. The societal culture (relatively integrated sets of values and value-based orientations) of a given society directly affects the kinds of organizational structures that can be sustained by organizations. Nevertheless, organizational structures and their internal organizational cultures might be a stronger determinative force than the outer societal culture. Hence, some organizations are often viewed as determinative importers of social change into some societies (e.g., technology transfers by multinational corporations). Organizational culture and the external societal culture inevitably affect one another; exploring specific nuances at the interface between these two cultural arenas is still a matter for future research. Blau (1994) notes that differential mobility among social groups may alter organizational structures, either increasing or constraining opportunities. Gains in social equity made by groups characterized by gender, ethnicity, age, or socioeconomic status may result in the alteration of organizational structures. The ability of workers to form coalitions both within and outside organizations may alter organizational hiring, promotion, and retention practices. Such restructuring may increase the mobility of groups in gaining more equitable organizational positions, or it may retain inequalities through the eventual resegregation of occupations (Cohen et al. 1998).

Neither effectiveness nor efficiency is an unalloyed universal good. As given constituencies gain stature and power, they are able to reform, reconstitute, or create relationships accordingly; but what makes one constituency more effective and/or more efficient may impact negatively on either the effectiveness or the efficiency of another. Hence, while not its sole determinant, the *net balance of power* between constituencies is an important variable in the formation and maintenance of organizational structure. When environmental conditions remain relatively constant, the stratification of organizational structure may also remain relatively constant as it is being reified, recreated, and reenacted, given that those already well placed are advantaged within each new round of structured interactions. However, when environmental conditions are visited by strong or rapid changes for example, in political culture, technology, or rapid changes (for example, in political culture, technology, or demographic characteristics), these may precipitate renegotiation and recalibration of social structures within the organization. Because modern organizations seldom resemble a zero-sum model, not all gains by one constituency constitute a loss for another. However, unless the organization continues to grow, prosper, and reward formerly well-rewarded constituencies, a sense of relative deprivation due to perceived loss of effectiveness and efficiency in obtaining organizational rewards may lead to intergroup conflict.

Thus, organizations are affected by the exchange of resources between organizations and various constituencies, including those providing resource inputs to an organization, the exchange of labor for wages, and those between organizations and consumers of outputs. Environmental pressures, including competition for resources, may influence organizations to change structure, including strategic alliances, mergers, joint ventures, downsizing, and divestitures. Organizations may choose to maintain or change relationships on the basis of competition, power to create stable market relations, and institutional attachments through interpersonal and interorganizational relationships (Baker et al. 1998). Such changes presumably allow organizations more flexibility in responding to turbulent and uncertain environments, and each changes the stance of an organization in relation to others that compete for related resources in a market. This is accomplished by increased organizational efficiency, in which decreased labor force size, or hierarchy, and increased organizational interdependence results in fewer costs in producing outputs. The impacts of such strategies have been consequential for workers' expectations of long-term connections to workplaces, and expectations about their careers. Workers increasingly expect duties to be assigned on the basis of experience and training rather than organizational structure (Powell 1996). Pugh and Hickson (1996) argue that as organizational environments become more turbulent and uncertain, organizations require a "redundancy of function" in which individuals are called on to have a wide variety of skills and fill multiple functions in a highly interdependent environment. Thus, workers develop flexible organizational "roles" rather than fulfilling a function based on a hierarchical position (Powell 1996). Older and younger workers may experience a sense of relative deprivation as a result of changes in organizational structure

and as their own expectations of future employment opportunities decrease (Lerner 1996). Lerner concludes that procedural justice in organizational restructuring has not led to distributive justice in terms of employment opportunities and expectations.

The *state* (the system of governance in a society) is another global element with pervasive repercussions for organizational functioning. The state may regulate the organizations directly by instituting programs within them or indirectly by state regulation of what an organization may produce or how it may transact with other organizations such as suppliers or consumers. Organizations may attempt to influence governmental actions so that public policy does not constrain them or so that it will actively benefit them. Organizations frequently influence legislation directly, as by activities of lobbyists on retainer. Organizations often mount campaigns either to achieve or to prevent the enactment of specific legislation by directly influencing general public opinion and particular voters. Even if legislation is passed over their opposition, organizations can achieve their purposes by subsequently influencing the allocation of resources for its enforcement. Fligstein and Mara-Drita (1996) note that market relations between buyers, sellers, and the state are characterized by a power struggle in which each participant mobilizes resources to enact its own interests in maintaining (or altering) current relationships.

Communities are attentive to organizations located in their midst since changes in organizational structure can have considerable repercussions for the community at large. As Scott (1998) points out, not all organizations are strongly tied to the communities in which they are located. Locally based firms have a greater vested interest in community prosperity than do geographically dispersed firms, and they may act to assure continued community prosperity. Organizations may strongly affect the allocation of public goods and services as well as specifications in local policies, such as zoning and tax laws. Organizations may affect communities in which they are located through either implicit or explicit threats of "exit" as well as by directly impacting regulatory and economic conditions. The number, size, and type of organizations located in a community also have widespread consequences for individual local residents. South and Xu (1990) compared industries that dominate their local metropolitan economy with those that do not, finding that employees in dominant industries earn higher wages. Thus, organizations have important political, economic, and normative effects on individuals with or without organizational membership and on their community's organized power structures.

We now explore how organizations respond to and create their own environments. "Gatekeepers" are organizational participants at various levels who "selectively" permit information and people to traverse boundaries into and out of an organization. They "legitimate" particular environmental constituencies, with whom the organization then establishes institutional relations. Relations with constituencies not so "selected" become invisible, neutralized, or illegitimate. The breadth of the environmental domain that an organization claims in this manner has consequences for its stability. Narrow domains are associated with greater stability, while broad, inconsistently defined domains are associated with loss of function (Meyer 1975). At the same time, normative and regulatory forces outside organizations may exert pressures on gate-keepers to allow or disallow certain pieces of information or particular people.

"Loose coupling," or a seemingly weak relationship between parts of an organization (Pfeffer and Salancik 1978), is one of many ways in which organizations learn to deal with a broad environmental domain. This weak relationship allows change in one part of an organization to precipitate minimal or no change in other parts. Relationships between subunits or individuals in organizations, and relationships between the organization and other environmental entities, may be loosely coupled. Organizations may respond to potentially disruptive threats by very limited conformity in a specific sector, and yet this limited conformity projects an aura of complete organizational compliance. In reality, components of organizational structure affected by a given threat may be effectively uncoupled from many other components and processes, resulting merely in the appearance of compliance (DiMaggio and Powell 1983). Loose coupling can also lead to structural "inertia" in an organization's response to environmental changes, causing "lags" between environmental changes and adaptations to them on the part of various organizational structures. However, the degree to which loose coupling is useful as a strategy depends on the particular situation and linkages involved. Loose coupling in terms of outsourcing labor, autonomous work teams, organizational networking, and increasingly separated divisional organizational forms have all been adopted in the last decade as a response to increased market competition and technical complexity. Such modifications of organizational structure are most often justified by upper-level participants as attempts to increase either or both the organization's efficiency and *responsiveness* (effectiveness) to environmental challenges perceived to threaten organizational survival. What is left unsaid, however, is that a narrow economic conception of what constitutes efficiency or effectiveness by upper-level participants, such as executives and stockholders, may have devastating consequences for middle- and lower-level participants as well as for the surrounding community. Indeed, the very fact that they are essentially disenfranchised from organizational decision making may engender a confrontational relationship with upper-level participants that may render all parties inefficient and ineffective for the process of inventing alternative problem-solving solutions that contribute to the organization's holistic and long-term well-being.

Assessing the effectiveness of an organization's capacity to adapt may be less focused on outcomes than on the processes of organizational change. Organizational theorists have suggested that organizational effectiveness is reflected in how well an organization acquires and processes information and with what flexibility and adaptability (Weick 1977). Galbraith (1977) contends that organizations reduce environmental complexity by changing communication structures within organizations. Other researchers suggest that organizations are effective when their subunits are congruent with the specific environment with which they interact, and when organizations overall are congruent with their environments (Lawrence and Lorsch 1967). Such perspectives of organizational effectiveness may not be linked to the achievement of goals but, from a managerial perspective, may rest in the survival, or profitability of organizations. As Lerner (and maybe others) demonstrate, such goals may not be satisfactory to middle- and lower-level participants whose employment opportunities and expectations may be adversely affected by a particular organizational adaptation.

Further, since organizational participation is affected by the demographic characteristics of participants, the specific demographic consequences (whether intended or unintended) of environmental adaptation must be examined.

Who benefits in the adaptation of organizations to the environment? Elites (fiduciaries, executives, and high-level managers) are only one kind of constituency vying for potential benefits derived from organizational structure. Middle- and lower-level organizational participants are often neglected in the research literature on organizational structure. Often, when research findings indicate that either an "organization" or a "community" benefits from a particular activity, what is really meant is that *upper*-level participants benefit. Certain populations (women and ethnic minorities, for example) participate differentially at upper, middle, and lower levels of organizational structure; thus, a focus on upper-level participants is insufficient to fully describe patterns of benefit.

GOAL ATTAINMENT

"Goal" refers to a desirable future state of affairs. *Official* goals are the formal statements put forth by organizations to state their general purposes (Perrow 1961). *Operative* goals, on the other hand, refer to "what the organization is actually trying to do" (Perrow 1961, p. 855). The degree of congruency between official and operative goals is variable. It is important to distinguish organizational goals from the motives of individual organizational participants (Simon 1964). However, researchers need to clarify how particular goal activity differentially benefits specific internal or external constituencies. Goals limit and direct organizational decision making and suggest criteria by which organizational performance can be measured.

Over time, organizations establish multiple, often disparate, and sometimes conflicting goals. Kochan and colleagues (1976) argue that goal multiplicity and conflict are associated with both horizontal (number of tasks at the same level of structure) and vertical (number of levels between the "highest" and "lowest" units) differentiation of organizational structure. In the pursuit of multiple goals, coordination of effort is necessary, leading to vertical differentiation of organizational

structure. Organizations change their goals over time, for both external and internal reasons. Thompson and McEwen (1958) contend that goals vary because interaction with elements *external* to the organization can be of two kinds: competitive or cooperative. The only competitive option in their discussion we call *bounded competition*, referring to the fact that the interaction takes place within the bounds of the normative structure (institutional environment) of the larger social system. By contrast, we conceive of *raw* or *unbounded competition* as taking place outside any normative order common to the contending parties and is not accounted for by Thompson and McEwen's discussion. In the extreme absence of common normative understandings, hostility between contending parties can rise to a level wherein one party believes itself justified in attempts to annihilate another. Accordingly, Thompson and McEwen define competition as rivalry between two or more organizations mediated by a third party. Organizations compete for resources viewed as desirable for organizational functioning. Thompson and McEwen discuss three cooperative styles of interaction between organizations and external elements, each underscored by a decreasing level of hostility: co-optation, bargaining, and coalition. Co-optation is the absorption of an external element into the organization, neutralizing its potential hostility by incorporating it within the organization's structure. Bargaining is direct interaction with environmental entities in which some kind of exchange takes place so that the organization can get what it desires. Coalition is an agreement, usually of specific duration for specific collective purposes, combining the efforts of two or more organizations, and restricting the right of each to set goals unilaterally. Notice that coalition requires very low levels of hostility between an organization and its partners; indeed, a potential outcome may be loss of separate identity and structural unification. These strategies can increase or decrease the size and complexity of organizational structure and the allocation of resources within it.

Organizational goals also change for *internal* reasons. Constituencies within the organization frequently form *coalitions*, initially for self-protection against real or imagined threats to the pursuit of their own interests. Each unable to impose its will on others, but fearing imposition, makes alliances with other constituencies perceived to be friendly. Some such alliances capture key positions of the organizational structure, thus giving greater access to the allocation of organizational resources. This dominance can be maintained over time by securing the cooperation of other elements and coalitions within the organization through the selective distribution of resources. How central a given goal is to an organization may depend on the composition of the dominant coalition and the relative balance of power within it.

This discussion has emphasized the complexity of goals and goal setting, given a variety of internal and external factors. The processes by which groups or members of organizations gain power, and the loose coupling between goals and motivations, have a large impact on goal setting. It is useful to discuss the processes of power in organizations in more depth. Many theorists have proposed definitions of power, but it was Emerson who proposed one of the most useful: *Power* resides in the dependency of one on the resources of another (1962). Resource control theorists believe that individuals or organizational subunits exercise power because they allocate resources needed by others to reduce uncertainty or because their resources are specialized or are central to the workflow of the organization (Lachman 1989). Researchers have paid much attention to structural conditions associated with power in organizations. Spaeth (1985) found that resource allocation is central to task performance since lower-level employees are assigned to produce given outputs and are provided with the necessary resources to do so. The higher the level of the worker, the more discretionary resources she or he will have to allocate. Recently, researchers have explored the relationship between technological innovation and shifts of power among organizational members. Burkhardt and Brass (1990) found that early adopters of a computerized information system in a federal agency increased their centrality and power in organizational networks. These shifts did not completely alter the power structure since those in power were not completely displaced by early technology adopters. Barley (1986) makes clear that technology provides organizational members an occasion for structuring." The same technological system may have different implications and may cause different social changes in different organizational structures. Thus, Barley disputes the claims by some researchers that technology has objective material consequences regardless of the social contexts within which it exists.

Scott (1998) writes that organizations attempt to build structures not only to accomplish a division of labor, but also to create a structure of authority. As organizations become more formalized—that is, as procedures and rules are explicitly formulated—power differentials are built into the system and institutionalized. The distributive advantage of upper participants is not obvious since hierarchy is presumably built on specific task competence and power is vested for specific task achievement. Those with institutionalized power need not mobilize to have their interests served, since they control the flow of resources and information. The institutionalization of power contradicts resource control theory, which asserts that those who control the contingencies for change in organizations gain power. Lachman (1989) emphasizes that when the relative power of subunits changes, the previous power structure significantly affects the new one. He found that the greatest predictor of subunit power after organizational change was its degree of power before the change, regardless of its control over organizational contingencies or changes.

The complexity of goals within organizations creates a number of difficulties in assessing effectiveness. The use of *goals* as virtually the sole criterion for effectiveness places excessive focus on the outcomes, rather than the processes, of organizational activities. While some goals may be universally held within an organization, these are usually held with varying degrees of intensity by various constituencies. Moreover, multiple, and sometimes conflicting, goals are held by various organizational constituencies; notably those at different hierarchical levels, but also those defined by a variety of other factors. Goals may be difficult to operationalize for organizations such as human service agencies, and "fuzzy goals" may be adaptive in avoiding conflict or in concealing operative goals (Weiss 1972). Often, the evaluation of organizational effectiveness is skewed toward one or another constituency's view of what constitute legitimate organizational goals or the priority assigned to given goals. Also, goal displacement may occur when compliance with indicators of good job performance (such as the number of calls taken per hour at a computer help desk) supplants the intended outcome of job performance (solving computer users' technical problems).

Accordingly, evaluation researchers have suggested a number of strategies for resolving some of the conflicts in determining and measuring goals. Stake (1975) suggests "responsive" evaluation that takes into account multiple and conflicting constituencies' goals, treating each as a separate and valid view of organizational functioning. One of the goals of responsive evaluation is to inform each group of the others' perspectives. Patton (1997) suggests a shift from goals to outcomes, focusing on expected changes, maintenance, or prevention that are the intended focus of organizational activity. Scriven (1975) suggests "goal-free" evaluation that focuses on only the actual, measurable outcomes of organizational activities compared to a profile of the demonstrated needs of participants. "Goal-free" evaluation does not include a formal elicitation of goals nor a review of formal organizational documents, but focuses instead on the needs of organizational participants, whether these are formally stated or not. The success that these alternative perspectives have in circumventing goals as the focus of effectiveness evaluation is variable, but they do constitute an acknowledgement of the difficulties in assessing organizational effectiveness solely through goal attainment.

Organizational *efficiency*, like *effectiveness*, is also tied to the attainment of organizational goals, but measures attainment against its costs. Cost-effectiveness analysis measures the monetary benefits of a program against the financial costs of implementing it. Cost-benefit analysis can estimate the broadly conceived benefits of a program versus its various costs, but usually also monetizes the benefits and compares them. Not only do these types of analyses face the same challenges described above in determining how the effectiveness of organizational activity is to be determined, they must choose a cost-accounting perspective that also reflects a particular "interest group" perspective. Freeman and Rossi (1993) describe three cost-accounting perspectives: (1) The individual level weighs costs, benefits, and effectiveness from the perspective of the unit targeted by an organization (people, groups, or organizations). (2) The program sponsor level takes the perspective of the sponsor in valuing benefits and accounting for costs, and examines the profitability of a given organizational activity. 3) The communal (or societal) perspective assesses both the direct and the indirect effects of organizational activity in a broad context and for a wide variety of participants. Both upper-level organizational participants and researchers have overemphasized the program-sponsor perspective, emphasizing short-term impacts and economic outcomes and short-changing factors that are integral to self-perceived well-being of often less powerful constituencies, such as the impact on their psychic, social, cultural, or political condition. Recent developments in "socioeconomics" seek to develop theoretical approaches that may bring these considerations under systematic analysis (Etzioni 1990, 1996, 1998; Granovetter 1985, 1992; Granovetter and Swedberg 1992). Monetizing such factors is difficult and controversial, but the costs and benefits of broader social and cultural factors both in monetary and other forms is included in efficiency studies using the communal perspective.

Economic analyses, however, frame their results in a monetary context for use by managers or policy makers, framing outcomes in ways that are less relevant to mid- and low-level workers, who do not control the allocation of resources. Additionally, it is difficult (and controversial) to monetize benefits, especially those involving complex social contexts, such as cultural and political changes. It may be difficult to combine multiple and/or conflicting goals in economic analyses, including the unintended consequences of organizational action. Finally, by definition, economic analysis takes an incremental approach to change, assuming that benefit is achieved if the benefits outweigh the costs. For some kinds of organizational activities, an incremental approach toward cost-effectiveness or cost-benefit analysis may not be appropriate if a partial change in outcomes is not desirable. For example, many programs designed to prevent drug use do not measure outcomes in terms of decreased drug use among participants, but in the extent to which total nonuse of drugs may be effectuated.

Setting and attainment of goals are complex processes affected by factors internal and external to organizations and by processes for power distribution. The *cui bono* criterion alerts the researcher not to take formal goals at face value but to identify how key actors and groups in coalitions differentially benefit from goal activity. In spite of its tendency to persist, organizational structure can be and is altered to reflect the power of new alliances among internal and external constituencies who benefit from new institutional arrangements. Organizations survive because powerful constituent alliances continue to derive benefit from them.

THE INTERNAL INTEGRATION OF ORGANIZATIONAL STRUCTURE

Organizations cohere in part because some elements of organizational structure are designated to coordinate other organizational elements into a collective "whole" in the pursuit of goals. This discussion of integration will examine (1) how some organizational variables affect composition of organizational structural; (2) structure's differential outcomes for stratified groups; and (3) who benefits from integration.

One factor important to integrating organizational members is technology, knowledge about how to get things done. Organizations often must increase coordination to achieve technically complicated tasks. Galbraith (1977) notes four mechanisms for increasing task coordination: (1) Rules standardize both acceptable actions and agreed-upon ends. (2) Schedules coordinate interdependent activities or multiple activities occurring at the same time. (3) Departmentalization routinizes the division of labor by grouping homogeneous tasks together. (4) Organizational hierarchy helps to coordinate tasks that are interrelated among departments. Organizational size can be an important factor affecting internal structure. Several measures have been used for size, including the physical plant, number of clients, or number of employees (Kimberly 1976). Most researchers have treated size as a determinant of organizational structure. It can be an indicator of demand for organizational services or products, providing constraints or opportunities for structural change.

These two variables are related to a number of structural outcomes, the most important of which are complexity or differentiation, formalization, and centralization. Complexity is the diversity of factors that must be simultaneously coordinated to get a task done. Horizontal differentiation is the specification of component elements of tasks performed at the same level of organizational structure. Vertical differentiation is the number of levels of importance, power, and control among units. Multiple and complex technologics are associated with increased structural differentiation (Dewar and Hage 1978). Increased size (number of participants) is necessary to achieve high degrees of structural differentiation, although a large organization may be minimally differentiated and simply coordinated. Nevertheless, larger organizations are generally more structurally differentiated and more complexly coordinated (cf. Blau and Schoenherr 1971).

Formalization is the extent to which rules for behaviors and relations in organizations are explicitly specified for participants directly or indirectly associated with particular tasks. This means that formalized positions have standardized powers and duties, regardless of the particular individual incumbent. Organizations with routine technology have a greater degree of formalization (Dornbusch and Scott 1975) at a more minute level of detail. Glisson (1978) contends that routinized technology may produce greater formalization. Formalization, however, is only moderately associated with organizational size (e.g., Blau and Schoenherr 1971).

Centralization refers to the extent to which decision making in an organization is concentrated or dispersed. Dornbusch and Scott (1975) point out that organizations may engage multiple technologies that vary in terms of clarity, predictability, and efficacy. Tasks high on these dimensions are more likely to be centralized, but tasks low on the dimensions are likely to be allocated to specialists, decentralizing organizational authority. Centralization through rules is associated with use of routine technology (Hage and Aiken 1967). There is an inverse relationship between size and centralization: Larger organizations tend to decentralize decision making.

Recent organizational restructuring in the United States has resulted in some organizations becoming "smaller" in size than they were three decades ago. The adoption of new technologies including computer-assisted production and just-in-time inventory systems have resulted in a decrease in vertical hierarchy, and a flattened lateral hierarchy. At the same time, the complexity of the technology and the need for increased coordination has increased interdependence of organizational subunits or "teams," while centralization has decreased (Galbraith and Lawler 1993). Reengineering technologies has often resulted in changing the processes of work, rather than directly changing organizational structures, but has contributed to the increasingly interdependent relations among organizational subunits (Keidel 1994). Such reengineering has led to flexibility in team function, resulting in "semistructures" in which some aspects of performance are prescribed, but the processes through which teams operate are not (Brown and Eisenhardt 1995). Scott (1998) notes, however, that the resources needed to successfully alter structure to function in a more lateral, independent fashion are considerable, and many organizations do not have the resources to make this kind of structural transformation.

Consistently with generalized values in the host society, organizational structure has differential outcomes for people of diverse identities. Labor theorists offer various explanations for *occupational segregation*, the organizational practice of reserving specific kinds of jobs for people of given ethnicity or gender. Occupational segregation results in lower earnings in jobs traditionally held by relatively powerless groups-minority men and white and minority women. Kaufman (1986) found that black men were more likely than white men to be employed in highly routinized, less skilled jobs and were less likely to be in job ladders involving increasing levels of status dominance over other workers. Tienda and colleagues (1987) found that, although women's earnings increase as they move into jobs traditionally held by males, male incumbents experience a greater increase in earnings than their female counterparts. Some researchers contend that market forces have created an occupationally segregated labor force, while others believe that organizational practices are responsible. Bridges and Nelson (1989) argue that although market forces produce gender-related inequalities (as expected), these are exacerbated by intraorganizational decisions resulting in preservation of occupational segregation.

Although hierarchy appears to be determined rationally by high-level managers and by owners, labor theorists reveal that organizational structure has differential outcomes for people based on ethnicity and gender. Further, the structural inequalities between wages and perquisites for workers at various levels of the organization may be quite large and not necessary to maintain a task-oriented division of labor on which an organization's survival might depend. Marxists, work redesign theorists, and researchers exploring organizational "structuring" explicitly address how organizations benefit, or fail to benefit, worker categories. These perspectives challenge the presumption of rationality for organizational structures imbalanced in favor of a given constituency. Problems in assessing benefit are due to the assumption that managers or the environment determine what middle and lower participants do without exploring resistance to more generally beneficial institutional policies by upper participants. Researchers examining the impact of variables such as size on formalization frequently exclude human agents, and thereby reify organizational structure. Such research fails to give due consideration to how organizational structuring might account for these phenomena. To the extent that workers successfully and persistently subvert, modify, or resist organizational structuring of their activities, researchers cannot justify the assumption that structure is the sole result of owner, managerial, or environmental influences.

LATENT FACTORS IN STRATEGIC PLANNING

Values guide and give meaning to activities. A set of activities, however, may be variously interpreted from alternative value perspectives. Activities that are rational and meaningfully appropriate for an organizational task (in a bank, for example) may also be in substantial congruity with prescriptions and proscriptions of, say, an ostensibly unrelated religious organization serving the same client population. This hidden or latent positive affinity might make a bank clerk appear particularly productive as new customers are attracted to the bank and give favorable reactions for service received from the bank in spite of, rather than because of, role performance as bank clerk. The latent import could be negative, in which case the bank clerk might look particularly unproductive.

Although there is no assurance an organizational structure staffed with a demographically diverse population has a higher probability of survival, rational theorists believe its chances are increased. As an organization takes in participants with demographic characteristics different from those of previous participants, modalities of personal values at different participant levels will change. This creates a latent potential for future pressure to change goals and procedures. For effective long-term strategic planning, decision makers are well advised to consider implications of alternative demographic concentrations among actual or potential external constituencies and among each internal participant level. Cultivation of new markets to absorb organizational output may require recruitment from populations with new attributes as much as recruitment from new populations to reduce labor costs may require acceptance of new types of participant contributions. Such changes inherently precipitate structural change. An organization that sets narrow limits to organizational culture may as a latent consequence inadvertently limit its capacity to adapt to altered environmental conditions and thus decrease its capacity to survive.

Research examining the link between organizational culture and effectiveness has reflected managerial interest in improving organizational performance through the control and directed change of organizational culture. Research examining the link has been mixed, finding a direct relationship between the two (e.g., Petty et al. 1995), examining culture as a set of mediating variables in organizational performance (e.g., Saffold 1988), and finding no relationship between the two (e.g., Reynolds 1986). While most studies have examined factors internal to organizations in the construction of culture, some have examined the links between culture and organizational markets, networks, and environmental factors (e.g., Burt et al. 1994). One reason for the mixed findings in the association between organizational culture and effectiveness is a difficulty in defining and measuring culture. Culture has been variously defined as underlying shared values and beliefs among participants (Schein 1991); meanings of actions among individual participants (Golden 1992), and means of governing transactions among individual participants (Ouchi 1980). Culture has therefore been measured in terms of strength, meaning the congruence of managerial beliefs to managerial practices (Denison 1990);

individual practices, affect, and cognitions (Silvester et al. 1999); and organizational types governing transactions among participants, which exhibit traits such as the degree of hierarchy or flexibility (Ouchi 1980). These differences in the definitions of culture and in its measurement account for some of the variability of findings in the organizational culture literature. Additionally, differences in organization types and criteria of effectiveness may also account for differential findings of the link between culture and organizational performance. A struggle between proponents of qualitative and quantitative methods has led to a bifurcated literature and a lack of multimethod studies examining the complexities of organizational culture (Martin and Frost 1996). Most studies on organizational culture and effectiveness focus on overall performance, profit, and productivity from the perspectives of the organizational elite, upper management, and administrators while purporting to describe a "whole" organization's culture and outcomes.

While organizational culture is both an important *result* and a *determinant* of organizational structure, it appears to have been given both narrow and exaggerated importance by writers whose focus is on profit-making organizations. In the mid-1980s researchers contended that centralized control of corporate culture by managers was correlated with organizational success (e.g., Deal and Kennedy 1982). Meyerson and Martin (1987) call this the integrationist perspective, but argue that organizational theory has encompassed at least two other perspectives, the differentiation perspective and the fragmentation perspective. The differentiation perspective acknowledges that there may be "nested" cultures and subcultures within organizations that may embrace different forms, ideologies, and rituals. The fragmentation perspective observes that clearly conflicting cultural understandings and practices in organizations may exist, and may shift as coalitions form around specific tasks and as organization members deal with the ambiguity of their tasks.

Martin (1992) notes that one or all of these cultural characteristics may be present within organizations, but that participants' positions throughout the organizational structure may affect how they perceive an organization's culture. Management may take an integrationist view of culture, seeing it as a way of controlling and coordinating organizational activity. Rank-and-file workers may be more likely to adopt a differentiation perspective instead, and those whose jobs are characterized by a high degree of ambiguity and environmental uncertainty may be more likely to adopt a fragmentation perspective. The issue here is how much of values essential to its own well-being each constituency will surrender in return for real or imagined benefits derived from continued organizational participation. Upper participants are only one constituency potentially benefiting from organizational culture. Other constituencies may use it as a vehicle to express resistance to, or interest in, a wide array of organizational and environmental conditions. If upper participants seek effectiveness in goal achievement and efficient productivity for increased profits, lower participants might seek security of employment and quality of working conditions. Participants may see the organization as a forum within which each subgroup expresses its own array of self-interests for potential incorporation into organizational culture in the context of collective, perhaps universal, concern for organizational survival. Depending on their relative power (location) within the organization's structure, constituents may be limited in the degree to which they can enact and establish understandings about the distribution of rewards (of various kinds including but not limited to economic rewards) relative to their own structural positions and to their self-perceived contributions to organizational survival.

If participants decide the distribution of rewards is unsatisfactory or inequitable relative to some other comparison group or individual, relative deprivation theorists argue that participants will then attempt systemic or individual remedies. Indeed, lower participants may choose to treat "official" cultural accounts with disbelief or to subvert them (Smircich 1983). The form that perceived unfairness takes influences the actions that people are likely to take; Skarlicki and Folger (1997) found that if participants perceive organizations as having low procedural justice and low distributive justice, they are more likely to take retributive action against an organization for perceived injustices than those who believe that only procedural or distributive justice is low. However, researchers have failed to demonstrate how unfavorable comparisons cause behavioral outcomes.

Historically, groups of workers have understood existence of ethnicity and gender inequality in the work place, but not all groups have taken steps to remedy the problems. The organizational justice perspective may allow exploration of organizational structuring as a process in which agency exists on the parts of participants and constituents of organizations at both aggregate and individual levels in accord with their cultural orientation.

CONCLUDING REMARKS

Current theory and research on organizational structure have been characterized by both managerial determinism and by a vague environmental determinism used to exonerate owners and managers from detrimental consequences of their structural designs upon middle and lower participants within the organization. Owners and higher-level managers often overemphasize short-term gains achieved by production and managerial techniques undermining relative empowerment of lower participants. On their behalf, organizational theorists and researchers contribute unwittingly to intensification of unnecessary control over workers, consumers, community residents, and other types of participants (Clegg 1981). Research guided by a organizational justice perspective may reduce an overemphasis on the competitive advantage of upper participants (disguised as advantage by the *organization* against external adversaries) and open new vistas on cooperative actions beneficial to all participants and related to the perceived value of their contributions to organizational survival. In the final analysis, perhaps the only justification for rewards received by a category of organizational participants is the contribution it makes to the essential task of organizational survival (Alvarez 1979).

(SEE ALSO: *Complex Organizations*; *Work and Occupations*; *Professions*)

REFERENCES

Aldrich, Howard E. 1979 *Organizations and Environments*. Englewood Cliffs, N.J.: Prentice-Hall.

Alvarez, Rodolfo 1979 "Institutional Discrimination in Organizations and Their Environments." In R. Alvarez and K. Lutterman, eds., *Discrimination in Organizations: Using Social Indicators to Manage Social Change*. San Francisco: Jossey-Bass.

Baker, Wayne E., Robert R Faulkner, and Gene A. Fisher "Hazards of the Market: The Continuity and Dissolution of Interorganizational Market Relationships." *American Sociological Review* 63(2):147–177.

Barnard, Chester I. 1938 *The Functions of the Executive.* Cambridge, Mass.: Harvard University Press.

Barley, Stephen R. 1986 "Technology as an Occasion for Structuring: Evidence from Observations of CT Scanners and the Social Order of Radiology Departments." *Administrative Science Quarterly* 31:78–108.

Blau, Peter M. 1994 *The Structural Contexts of Opportunities.* Chicago, Ill.: University of Chicago Press.

——, and Richard Schoenherr 1971 *The Structure of Organizations.* New York: Basic Books.

Blau, Peter, and W. Richard Scott 1962 *Formal Organizations.* New York: John Wiley.

Bridges, William P., and Robert L. Nelson 1989 "Markets in Hierarchies: Organizational and Market Influences on Gender Inequality in a State Pay System." *American Journal of Sociology* 95:616–658.

Brockner, Joel, and Phyllis Siegel. 1995 "Understanding the Interaction Between Procedural and Distributive Justice: The Role of Trust." In Roderick M. Kramer and Tom R. Tyler, eds., *Trust in Organizations: Frontiers of Theory and Research.* Thousand Oaks, Calif.: Sage.

Brown, Shona L., and Kathleen M. Eisenhardt 1995 "Product Innovation as Core Capacity: The Art of Continuous Change." *Academy of Management Review* 20(2):343–375.

Burkhardt, Malene E., and Daniel J. Brass 1990 "Changing Patterns or Patterns of Change: The Effects of a Change in Technology of Social Network Structure and Power." *Administrative Science Quarterly* 35:104–127.

Burt, Ronald S., Shaul M. Gabbay, Gerhard Holt, and Peter Moran 1994 "Contingent Organization as a Network Theory: The Culture-Performance Contingency Function." *Acta Sociologica* 37:345–370.

Clegg, Stewart 1981 "Organization and Control." *Administrative Science Quarterly* 33:24–60.

Cohen, Lisa E., Joseph E. Brosehak, and Heather A. Haveman 1998 "And Then There Were More? The Effect of Organizational Sex Composition on the Hiring and Promotion of Managers." *American Sociological Review* 63:711–727.

Cook, Karen S., and Toshio Yamagishi 1983 "Social Determinants of Equity judgments." In David M. Messick and Karen Cook, eds., *Equity Theory.* New York: Praeger.

Deal, Terrence, and Allan Kennedy 1982 *Corporate Cultures.* Reading, Mass.: Addison-Wesley.

Dess, Gregory G., and Donald W. Beard 1984 "Dimensions of Organizational Task Environment." *Administrative Science Quarterly* 29:52–73.

Denison, D. 1990 *Corporate Culture and Organizational Effectiveness.* New York: John Wiley.

Dewar, Robert D., and Jerald Hage 1978 "Size, Technology, Complexity and Structural Differentiation: Toward a Theoretical Synthesis." *Administrative Science Quarterly* 23:111–136.

Dill, William R. 1958 "Environment as an Influence on Managerial Autonomy." *Administrative Science Quarterly* 2:409–443.

DiMaggio, Paul J., and Walter W. Powell 1983 "The Iron Cage Revisited: Institutional Isomorphism and Collective Rationality in Organizational Fields." *American Sociological Review* 147–160.

Dornbusch, Sanford M., and W. Richard Scott 1975 *Evaluation and the Exercise of Authority.* San Francisco: Jossey-Bass.

Emerson, Richard M. 1962 "Power-Dependence Relations." *American Sociological Review* 31–40.

Etzioni, Amitai 1961 *A Comparative Analysis of Complex Organization.* New York: Free Press.

—— 1990 "A New Kind of Socio-Economics (The Ascent of Socio-Economics)." *Challenge* 33(1):31.

—— 1996 "How to Make a Humane Market: Quality of Life or Economic Success?" *New Statesman* 127(4412):25–28.

—— 1998 "A Communitarian Note on Stakeholder Theory." *Business Ethics Quarterly* 8(4):679.

Fligstein, Neil, and Iona Mara-Drita 1996 "How to Make a Market: Reflections on the Attempt to Create a Single Market in the European Union." *American Journal of Sociology* 102:1–33.

Freeman, David M., and Peter Rossi 1993 "Using Theory to Improve Program and Policy Education." *Social Forces* 71(4):1102–1103.

Galbraith, Jay 1977 *Organization Design.* Reading, Mass.: Addison-Wesley.

——, and Edward E. Lawler, III (eds.) 1993 *Organizing for the Future: The New Logic for Managing Complex Organizations.* San Francisco, Calif.: Jossey-Bass.

Glisson, Charles 1978 "Dependence of Technological Routinizations of Structural Variables in Human Service Organizations." *Administrative Science Quarterly* 23:383–395.

Golden, K. A. 1992 "The Individual and Organizational Culture: Strategies for Action in Highly-Ordered Contexts." *Journal of Management Studies* 29:1–21.

Granovetter, Mark 1985 "Economic Action and Social Structure: The Problem of Embeddedness." *American Journal of Sociology* 91:481–510.

—— 1992 "Economic Institutions as Social Constructions: A Framework for Analysis." *Acta Sociologica* 35(1):3–12.

——, and Richard Swedberg 1992 *The Sociology of Economic Life*. San Francisco: Westview.

Hage, Jerald, and Michael Aiken 1967 "Relationship of Centralization to Other Structural Properties." *Administrative Science Quarterly* 12:72–91.

Huo, Juen J., Heather J. Smith, Tom R. Tyler, and E. Allan Lind 1996 "Superordinate Identification, Subgroup Identification, and Justice Concerns: Is Separatism the Problem; Is Assimilation the Answer?" *Psychological Science* 7(1):40–45.

Irwin, Sarah 1996 "Age Related Distributive Justice and Claims on Resources." *British Journal of Sociology* 47(1):68–92.

Kaufman, Robert L. 1986 "The Impact of Industrial and Occupational Structure on Black-White Employment Allocation." *American Sociological Review* 310–323.

Keidel, Robert W. 1994 "Rethinking Organizational Design." *Academy of Management Executives* 8(4):12–30.

Kimberly, John 1976 "Organizational Size and the Structuralist Perspective." *Administrative Science Quarterly* 29:571–597.

Kochan, Thomas, George Cummings, and Larry Huber 1976 "Operationalizing the Concepts of Goals and Goal Incompatibility in Organizational Behavior Research." *Human Relations* 29:544–577.

Lachman, Alan 1989 "Power from What?" *Administrative Science Quarterly* 34:231–251.

Lawrence, Paul R., and Jay W. Lorsch 1967 *Organization and Environment: Managing Differentiation and Integration*. Boston: Graduate School of Business Administration, Harvard University.

Lee, Cynthia, and Jiing-Lih Farh 1999 "The Effects of Gender in Organizational Justice Perception." *Journal of Organizational Behavior* 20:133–143.

Lee, Jason S., and John F. Stolte 1994 "Cultural and Structural Determinants of Justice Reactions in the Economic Domain." *Social Behavior and Personality* 22(4):319–328.

Lerner, Melvin J. 1996 "Victims without Harmdoers: Human Casualties in the Pursuit of Corporate Efficiency." In Leo Montada and Melvin J. Lerner, eds., *Current Societal Concerns about Justice*. New York: Plenum.

Linkey, Helen, and Sheldon Alexander 1998 "Need Norm, Demographic Influence, Social Role, and Justice Judgement." *Current Psychology* 17(2–3):152–162.

Martin, Joanne 1992 *Cultures in Organizations: Three Perspectives*. New York: Oxford University Press.

——, and Peter Frost 1996 "The Organizational Culture War Games: a Struggle for Intellectual Dominance." In Stewart R. Clegg, Cynthia Hardy, and Walter R. Nord, eds., *Handbook of Organizational Studies*. Thousand Oaks, Calif.: Sage.

Meyer, Marshall W. 1975 "Leadership and Organizational Structure." *American Journal of Sociology* 81:514–542.

Meyerson, D., and J. Martin 1987 "Cultural Change: An Integration of Three Different Views." *Journal of Management Studies* 24:623–647.

Oliver, Amalya 1997 "On the Nexus of Organizations and Professions: Networking through Trust." *Sociological Inquiry* 67(2):227–245.

Ouchi, William G. 1980 "Markets, Bureaucracies and Clans." *Administrative Science Quarterly* 25:129–141.

Parsons, Talbot 1960 *Structure and Process in Modern Society*. New York: Free Press.

Patton, Michael Quinn 1997 *Utilization-Focused Evaluation*. Thousand Oaks, Calif.: Sage.

Perrow, Charles 1961 "The Analysis of Goals in Complex Organizations." *American Sociological Review* 26:854–866.

Petty, M. M., A. Beadles, II, Christopher M. Lowery, Deborah F. Chapman, and David W. Connell 1995 "Relationships between Organizational Culture and Organizational Performance." *Psychological Reports* 76:483–492.

Pfeffer, Jeffrey, and Gerald R. Salancik 1978 *The External Control of Organizations*. New York: Harper and Row.

Powell, Walter W. 1996 "The Capitalist Firm in the 21st Century: Emerging Patterns." Paper presented at the Annual Meetings of the American Sociological Association, New York, August.

Pugh D. S., and D. J. Hickson 1996 *Writers on Organizations*, 5th ed. Thousand Oaks, Calif.: Sage.

Reynolds, P. D., 1986 "Organizational Culture as Related to Industry, Position, and Performance: A Preliminary Report." *Journal of Management Studies* 23:333–345.

Rossi, Peter H., and Howard E. Freeman 1993 *Evaluation: A Systematic Approach*. Thousand Oaks, Calif.: Sage.

Saffold, G. S., III 1988 "Culture Traits, Strength, and Organizational Performance." *Academy of Management Review* 12(4):546–558.

Schein, Edgar H. 1991 "What is Culture?" In Peter J Frost, Larry F. Moore, Meryl Reis Louis, Craig C.

Lundber, and Joanne Martin, eds., *Reframing Organizational Culture*. Thousand Oaks, Calif.: Sage.

Scott, W. Richard 1998 *Organizations*. Englewood Cliffs, N.J.: Prentice-Hall.

Scriven, Michael 1972 "Pros and Cons about Goal-Free Evaluation." *Evalaution: The Journal of Educational Evaluation* (Center for the Study of Evaluation, UCLA) 3(4):1–7.

Silvester, Joanne, Neil R. Anderson, and Fiona Patterson 1999 "Organizational Culture Change: An Inter-Group Attributional Analysis." *Journal of Occupational and Organizational Psychology* 72:1–23.

Simon, Herbert A. 1964 "On the Concept of Organizational Goals." *Administrative Science Quarterly* 9:122.

Skarlicki, Daniel P., and Robert Folger 1997 "Retaliation in the Workplace: The Roles of Distributive, Procedural, and Interactional Justice." *Journal of Applied Psychology* 82(3):434–443.

Smircich, Linda 1983 "Organizations as Shared Meanings." In Louis Pondy, ed., *Organizational Symbolism*. Greenwich, Conn.: JAI.

South, Scott J., and Woman Xu 1990 "Local Industrial Dominance and Earnings Attainment." *American Sociological Review* 55:591–599.

Spaeth, Joe L. 1985 "Job Power and Earnings." *American Sociological Review* 50:603–617.

Stake, Robert E. 1975 *Evaluating the Arts in Education: A Responsive Approach*. Columbus, Ohio: Charles E. Merrill.

Sweeney, Paul D., and Dean B. McFarlin 1997 "Process and Outcome: Gender Differences in the Assessment of Judgement." *Journal of Organizational Behavior* 18:83–98.

Thompson, James D., and William McEwen 1958 "Organizational Goals and Environments: Goal Setting as an Interaction Process." *American Sociological Review* 23:23–31.

Tienda, Marta, Shelley A. Smith, and Villma Ortiz 1987 "Industrial Restructuring, Gender Segregation, and Sex Differences in Earnings." *American Sociological Review* 52:195–210.

Weick, Karl E. 1977 "Re-Punctuating the Problem." In Paul S. Goodman and Johnnes M. Pennings, eds., *New Perspectives on Organizational Effectiveness*. San Francisco: Jossey-Bass.

Weiss, Carol H. 1972 *Evaluation Research: Methods of Assessing Program Effectiveness*. Englewood Cliffs, N.J.: Prentice- Hall.

RODOLFO ALVAREZ
LEAH ROBIN

ORGANIZED CRIME

NOTE: *Although the following article has not been revised for this edition of the Encyclopedia, the substantive coverage is currently appropriate. The editors have provided a list of recent works at the end of the article to facilitate research and exploration of the topic.*

Organized crime is considered one of the most serious forms of crime for two reasons: (1) It is so often lucrative and successful; and (2) it is so difficult to counteract. In the broadest terms, organized crime can be viewed as any form of group conduct designed to take advantage of criminal opportunities, whether on a one-time or a recurring basis. More commonly, the label *organized crime* has more restricted usage.

It should not be a surprise to find criminals associating for the purpose of committing crime. The achievement of goals through cooperative efforts is a common element of contemporary life. Association with other criminals creates an interesting dilemma for the individual criminal. Having coconspirators increases the visibility of criminal conduct, the risks of apprehension, and, upon apprehension, the risk of betrayal. On the other hand, some types of criminal opportunities can be exploited only through group behavior. Offenders who fail to join with others may thereby limit their rewards from criminal conduct. For organized crime to persist, it must function both to overcome the risks of associating with others and result in positive benefits and increased rewards for those who participate.

No one knows how much organized crime is committed every year. Rather than being measured in numbers of events, the significance of organized crime is generally recorded in the dollar volume of activities. Some have argued that revenue estimates for organized crime are advanced more in the interest of drama than of accuracy, but the estimates are nonetheless staggering. For example, annual revenue from the sale of drugs is placed in the $40 to $60 billion range, and annual revenue from illicit gambling operations, at $20 to $40 billion.

Organized crime is unlikely to be reflected in official crime statistics for three reasons: first, crime statistics record information about individual criminal events rather than about the individuals or groups committing them; second, many of the activities of organized crime groups involve so-called victimless crimes where no report of a crime is made; and third, persons who are victimized by organized crime groups may be unlikely or unwilling to come forward and report their victimization.

Organized crime is best understood by examining the nature of ongoing criminal organizations, their activities, and societal response to the behavior of these organizations. A secondary use of the term, referring to criminal support systems that aid all offenders, is also briefly noted.

ONGOING CRIMINAL ORGANIZATIONS

Organized crime usually refers to the activities of stable groups or gangs that commit crimes on an ongoing basis. While not all group crime is properly labeled "organized crime," there exists no standard definition of the term. Instead, the phenomenon has been variously described as "a cancerous growth on American society" (Andreoli 1976, p. 21); "one of the queer ladders of social mobility" (Bell 1970, p. 166); "a society that seeks to operate outside the control of the American people and its governments" (President's Commission 1967, p. 1); and "the product of a self-perpetuating criminal conspiracy to wring exorbitant profits from our society by any means" (Salerno and Tompkins 1969, p. 303).

Scholars have identified the following as elements that characterize all groups labeled as organized crime: a hierarchical organizational structure, dominated by a strong leader; a territorial imperative, exhibited in attempts to monopolize all lucrative criminal opportunities within a geographic area; a predilection to violence both to enforce internal norms and to advance economic objectives; and a desire to influence the social response to criminal conduct, as demonstrated in significant investments in public corruption. Cressey (1969) identified these latter two characteristics—the "element of enforcement" and the "element of corruption"—as the essential features of organized crime.

In the United States, organized crime has been personified in ethnically based criminal organizations and, in particular, the twenty-four fictive "families" believed to make up the American Mafia. Joseph Valachi, in testimony before the United States Senate in 1963, revealed a sordid and secret world in which he claimed these criminal organizations operated and prospered.

While some scholars pointed to inconsistencies in Valachi's statements, and other criminals would later question the depth of his experience and knowledge, his testimony spawned a series of books and movies that placed Italian criminal organizations in the forefront of the public's consciousness with respect to organized crime.

The term *mafia* (with either upper- or lower-case letters) is used variously to apply to a secret criminal organization or to a life-style and philosophy that developed in sixteenth- and seventeenth-century southern Italy and Sicily in opposition to a series of foreign rulers who dominated the area. The life-style combines the idea of manliness in the face of adversity with an antagonism to authority and a closeness and reliance on family and clan.

Smith (1975) argues that applying the "mafia" label to Italian criminal organizations in the United States was both fateful and calculated. It was fateful because it imbued these organizations with international connections that there was little evidence they had. This may in turn have helped these organizations consolidate and solidify their power, in competition with other ethnic (primarily Irish) criminal organizations that were actually more prevalent in the early decades of the twentieth century. Use of the label was calculated in that it gave Italian criminal organizations a subversive and sinister character designed to ensure public support for extraordinary law enforcement efforts to eradicate these groups.

Overlooked in much of the attention paid to Mafia "families" was the fact that bands of brigands and smugglers, displaying many of the same organizational attributes as "mafia," were well established in Elizabethan England; that criminal organizations linked to a life-style based on the primacy of male-dominated families and the concept of dignity and manliness are common in Central and latin America; and that criminal societies and associations have been successful vehicles for social mobility in many cultures, for example, the Chinese Triads or the Japanese Yakuza.

Also overlooked were some significant changes occurring during the late 1960s and early 1970s in the major cities in which the Mafia "families" were believed to operate. These changes signaled what Ianni (1974) called "ethnic succession" in organized crime: That is, as the populations of inner cities came to be dominated by racial minorities, so too were the ranks of those running criminal organizations. This gave rise to law enforcement characterizations of such groups as the "Mexican Mafia" or the "Black Mafia," not because of their associations with Mafia "families" but as a shorthand way of communicating their organizational style and methods of operating.

By the 1980s, the term *organized crime* had lost its ethnic distinction. Instead, the label started being applied to many more criminal associations, from motorcycle and prison gangs to terrorist groups to some juvenile gangs. Observed in all these groups were the organizational characteristics that had first been identified as distinctive of Mafia "families."

ACTIVITIES OF ORGANIZED CRIME GROUPS

The activities in which organized crime groups are involved constitute another distinctive hallmark. Broadly defined, the term *organized crime* can be used to describe the activities of a band of pickpockets, a gang of train robbers, or a cartel of drug smugglers. Practically speaking, however, use of the term is somewhat more restrictive.

Commentators, scholars, and lawmakers generally use the term when referring to criminal conspiracies of an entrepreneurial nature—in particular, enterprises focused in black-market goods and services. Black markets are those in which contraband or illegal goods and services are exchanged. In this more restrictive use of the term, the activities of drug smugglers would be included while the conduct of pickpockets or train robbers would not.

These latter groups, and others involved in various forms of theft and extortion, commit what are best termed *predatory crimes*. As such, they are generally regarded as social pariahs. Society and the forces of social control will actively seek to root out such groups and bring them to justice. This is despite the fact that such groups may display a highly evolved organizational structure, a strong sense of territory, and a tendency toward violence.

Contrast this with groups engaged in entrepreneurial conduct. These groups supply the society with goods and services that are illegal but in demand. While some in society may still view these criminals as social pariahs, many in society will not. Instead, the criminal group establishes patron—business relationships with criminal and noncriminal clients alike. The forces of social control are not so bent on eradicating these groups because of the widespread social support they garner. This support, when added to the profits reaped as criminal entrepreneurs, creates both the means and the conditions for corruption.

If any one activity can be considered the incubator for organized crime in the United States, it would be the distribution and sale of illegal alcohol during Prohibition. The period of Prohibition (1920–1933) took a widely used and highly desired commodity and made it illegal; it also created the opportunity for a number of predatory criminal gangs to evolve as entrepreneurs. These entrepreneurs then developed important client and business relationships and emerged from Prohibition as wealthy and somewhat more respectable members of their communities.

Gambling and other vices have similar social support profiles. Purveyors of these services are widely perceived as engaged in victimless crimes, that is, black-market transactions involving willing buyers and sellers. Their activities, while morally unacceptable to many, arouse little social concern.

Societal ambivalence becomes even more pronounced where gray-market goods and services are involved. These are situations where legal goods or services are being provided in an illicit manner or to persons ineligible to receive them. Abuses of wartime rations is a good example of a gray-market situation, as is the negotiation of so-called sweetheart labor contracts or the illegal disposal of hazardous waste.

Criminal groups involved in gray-market activities are very tightly meshed in the economic and social fabric of the legitimate community. The persona of such groups is more likely to be legal than illegal, and the capacity of their members to become closely affiliated with persons of power and authority is likely to be great. Public corruption becomes not only likely but inevitable.

Combined with the characteristics that groups of criminals exhibit, the activities in which they engage are also likely to define such groups as organized crime. Some commentators feel it is impossible to separate a group's character from the nature of the crimes it commits. To this way of thinking, selling drugs requires a certain level of organization, but it is impossible to tell whether a group has evolved an organizational style in order to sell drugs or began to sell drugs as a consequence of its organizational capacity.

What is clear is that the capacity to exploit one type of criminal opportunity can be parlayed into other legal and illegal endeavors. Similarly, profits from organized crime activities can permit individual criminals to climb that "queer ladder of social mobility" that wealth creates.

SOCIETY AND ORGANIZED CRIME GROUPS

The final aspect of organized crime that distinguishes it from other forms of crime is its relationship with the society in which it operates. Organized crime is the one form of crime that assesses criminal opportunities in light of the probable social response as well as the possible economic and social rewards.

Cressey (1969) identified this capacity of organized crime as a "strategic planning" capability. Using this capability, organized crime groups choose "safe crime": where there is high social tolerance or at least ambivalence toward the conduct; where the chances of apprehension are therefore not great; where, even if apprehended, the chances of conviction are small; and where, even if convicted, the likelihood of serious consequences is also small.

In this assessment, society's attitudes toward various criminal activities become a key determinant in the nature of organized crime activities that will be displayed. Society's attitudes, as embodied in the criminal law, become even more significant.

Packer (1969) argued that in black- and gray-market situations, the criminal law may actually serve as a protective tariff. As such, the law limits the entry of entrepreneurs into the proscribed marketplace while guaranteeing, for those who do enter the market, exorbitant profits. The theory of deterrence does not work in such markets because as the sanction increases so do the likely rewards.

A similar analysis by Smith (1978) suggests that the law operates in many marketplaces to segment genetic demand, labeling some legal and some illegal. By so doing, the law does not reduce demand; what it does is change the dynamics of the market, creating the "domain" or market share of organized crime. In this sense, it is society—through its legislative enactments—that generates and structures the dynamics of organized crime opportunities.

Social institutions also play a role in structuring the nature and success of organized crime. The nature of government and the underpinnings of justice systems loom large in determining how organized crime groups will operate and succeed. Anglo-American legal systems, founded on the principle of individual responsibility for criminal acts, deal at best ineptly with group crime. When faced with more sophisticated criminal conspiracies, they appear to falter.

Where criminal organizations are armed with investments in public corruption, justice systems will not operate properly. Where government operates ineffectively or unfairly, the black market will flourish. Where there is the tendency to proscribe what cannot be controlled, criminal organizations will reap social support and financial rewards.

CRIMINAL SUPPORT SYSTEMS

A secondary use of the term *organized crime* refers to support systems that aid the criminal activities of all offenders. The typical list of support systems includes the tipster, the fix, the fence, and the corrupt public official. Each of these mechanisms serves to reduce the risks of criminal conduct or to lessen its consequences.

For example, tipsters function to provide criminals with information critical to committing a crime, such as the internal security schedule for a building or the timing of valuable cargo shipments. By doing so, they reduce the uncertainties the offenders face and enhance the chances for success. As a reward, tipsters receive a percentage of the "take," or proceeds of the crime.

The fix arranges for special disposition of a criminal's case, once it is in the justice system. This might mean seeing that paperwork is lost, or that a light sentence is imposed. Usually, the fix operates with the aid of corrupt public officials who are in a position to accomplish the required improper acts.

The fence serves as the market for stolen property, transforming it into cash or drugs for thieves. In the role of middleman, the fence determines what thieves steal, how much they are paid to do so, and, consequently, how often they steal. Fences provide structure and stability to a wide range of offenders. Like other criminal support systems, they impose organization on the activities of criminal groups and individual criminals.

Not all criminals can access the services of criminal support systems. These mechanisms will not act to serve the notorious or the psychotic. In this way, criminal elites are established and preserved. For those who use these support systems, crime is organized, the justice system is predictable, and success is likely.

There was a time when the "criminal underworld" was a physical place, a true sanctuary to hide and protect criminals. Now the underworld exists as a communication system, an important dimension of which involves support systems that can aid and protect offenders. The manner in which these systems function provides stability and organization to the underworld.

SUMMARY

Organized crime refers primarily to the broad range of activities undertaken by permanent criminal organizations having the following characteristics: a hierarchical organizational structure; a territorial imperative; a predilection for violence; and the capacity and funds to corrupt public officials.

These groups tend to locate in gray or black markets where they establish patron-client relationships with much of society. The funds they earn as entrepreneurs, combined with social support for their activities, permit them to influence the social response to their acts. They may become upwardly mobile as a result of investing their profits in both legal and illegal endeavors.

Organized crime also refers to criminal support systems such as the tipster, the fix, the fence,

and the corrupt official, who impose organization and stability in the underworld.

(SEE ALSO: *Criminology*)

REFERENCES

Abadinsky, Howard 1981 *Organized Crime*. Boston: Allyn and Bacon.

Anderson, Annelise Graebner 1979 *The Business of Organized Crime*. Stanford, Calif.: Hoover Institution Press.

Andreoli, P. D. 1976 "Organized Crime Enterprises—Legal." In S. A. Yefsky, ed., *Law Enforcement Science and Technology: Proceedings of the First National Conference on Law Enforcement Science and Technology*. Chicago: IITRI.

Arlacchi, Pino 1996 "Mafia: The Sicilian Cosa Nostra." *South European Society and Politics* 1:74–94.

Bell, Daniel 1970 "Crime as an American Way of Life." In M. E. Wolfgang, L. Savitz, and N. Johnson, eds., *The Sociology of Crime and Delinquency*. New York: Wiley.

Chambliss, William J. 1978 *On the Take: From Petty Crooks to Presidents*. Bloomington: Indiana University Press.

Chubb, Judith 1996 "The Mafia, the Market and the State in Italy and Russia." *Journal of Modern Italian Studies* 1:273–291.

Cressey, Donald R 1969 *Theft of the Nation: The Structure and Operations of Organized Crime in America*. New York: Harper and Row.

Frisby, Tanya 1998 "The Rise of Organised Crime in Russia: Its Roots and Social Significance." *Europe Asia Studies* 50:27–49.

Godson, Roy, and William J. Olson 1995 "International Organized Crime." *Society* 2:18–29.

Homer, Frederic D. 1974 *Guns and Garlic: Myths and Realities of Organized Crime*. West Lafayette, Ind.: Purdue University Press.

Huang, Frank F. Y., and Michael S. Vaughn 1992 "A Descriptive Analysis of Japanese Organized Crime: The Boryokudan from 1945 to 1988." *International Criminal Justice Review* 2:19–57.

Huey-Long-Song, John, and John Dombrink 1994 "Asian Emerging Crime Groups: Examining the Definition of Organized Crime." *Criminal Justice Review* 19:228–243.

Ianni, Francis A. J. 1974 *Black Mafia: Ethnic Succession in Organized Crime*. New York: Simon and Schuster.

Joe, Karen A. 1994 "The New Criminal Conspiracy? Asian Gangs and Organized Crime in San Francisco." *Journal of Research in Crime and Delinquency* 31:390–415.

Kelly, Robert J., Ko-Lin Chin, and Jeffrey A. Fagan 1993 "The Dragon Breathes Fire: Chinese Organized Crime in New York City." *Crime, Law and Social Change* 19:245–269.

Kwitny, Jonathan 1979 *Vicious Circles: The Mafia in the Marketplace.* New York: Morton.

Maas, Peter 1968 *The Valachi Papers.* New York: Putnam.

Packer, Herbert L. 1969 *The Limits of the Criminal Sanction.* Stanford, Calif.: Stanford University Press.

Pons, Philippe 1996 "Social Order in Modern Japan [17th-20th Centuries]. Mobster Control of Vagrancy; Ordre marginal dans le japon moderne (17e-20e siecle). Les Voyous canalisateurs de l'errance." *Annales* 51:1155–1178.

President's Commission on Law Enforcement and the Administration of Justice 1967 *Task Force Report: Organized Crime.* Washington, D.C.: U.S. Government Printing Office.

Robertson, Frank 1977 *Triangle of Death: The Inside Story of the Triads–The Chinese Mafia.* London: Routledge and Kegan Paul.

Salerno, Ralph, and John S. Tompkins 1969 *The Crime Confederation: Cosa Nostra and Allied Operations in Organized Crime.* Garden City, N.Y.: Doubleday.

Smith, Dwight C., Jr. 1975 *The Mafia Mystique.* New York: Basic Books.

——1978 "Organized Crime and Entrepreneurship." *International Journal of Criminology and Penology* 6:161–177.

Walsh, Marilyn E. 1977 *The Fence: A New Look at the World of Property Theft.* Westport, Conn.: Greenwood Press.

MARILYN E. WALSH

OVERPOPULATION

See Human Ecology and Environmental Analysis; Environmental Sociology; Population.

P

PARADIGMS AND MODELS

The terms "paradigm" and "model" have enjoyed considerable popularity in sociology, in part because the terms have a range of meanings. In everyday language, *model* has two senses: (1) a replica of an object being modeled, for example, a "model of a building," and (2) an exemplar to be emulated, as in "role model." "Paradigm" is somewhat more esoteric in everyday usage, but has become quite important in academic disciplines including sociology, largely due to Thomas S. Kuhn's 1962 book, *The Structure of Scientific Revolutions*.

The original meaning of *paradigm* overlaps that of "model" in the sense of exemplar. The term comes from the study of grammar where a paradigm provides a model of, for example, the way to conjugate all the regular verbs of a particular type (I love, you love, he or she loves, etc.). Its appearance in sociology predates Kuhn, but since Kuhn, it has become a much grander idea. Merton used the device of analytical paradigms for presenting codified materials, by which he means a technique for exposing the "complete array of assumptions, concepts and basic propositions employed in a sociological analysis" (1949, p. 13). Parsons treated "paradigm" in a similar way when he presented paradigms for social interaction and social change and emphasized that these are distinct from theories (1951, p. 485).

It is quite clear, however, that Kuhn's work has brought "paradigm" from relative obscurity to a central place in the discourses of the humanities, the social sciences, and the history and philosophy of science. Kuhn's paradigm and his model of change in science are highly controversial; yet, they have had considerable influence in these academic fields. Some of the effects Kuhn intended; many effects, however, were unintended, causing Kuhn to disavow explicitly some of the interpretations of his work (Kuhn 1970, 1974). Crews (1986) comments that a loose reading of Kuhn's book—which he calls the most frequently cited academic book of modern times—even justifies the rejection of science as empirical.

WORKING DEFINITIONS

A useful definition of *model* draws on Kaplan:

> *Any system A is a model of a system B if the elements and relationships of A aid in the understanding of B without regard to any direct or indirect causal connection between A and B.* (1964, p. 263)

For example, one could use ideas about political change (system A)—stable government, crisis, revolution, new government attains stability—to model change in science (system B). Models range from informal analogies or metaphors (e.g., society as an organism) to highly formal equation systems.

A model contains elements that have (or are given) properties—that is, are characterized by descriptive terms, and connections among some or all of these elements. One could construct a physical model of a social network using balls with holes in them and rods that fit into the holes. The rods would connect some but not all of the balls;

the balls (elements of the model) would represent individuals in the network and the rods (connections) would link those individuals who communicate with one another.

The critical property of a model is an isomorphism with its object, the thing being modeled. Strictly speaking, *isomorphism* is a one-to-one correspondence between the elements and relationships in the model and the elements and relationships in its object. Needless to say, strict isomorphism is not satisfied by many metaphors and analogies even though these can aid understanding; the lack of strict isomorphism, however, should serve as a caution in taking analogies too literally. Similar caution applies to models in general since it is all too easy to reify the model, that is, confuse the model with its object. Models do not capture all the properties of their objects, so that even with strict isomorphism, a model inevitably omits significant aspects of the object. As long as those concerned with a model recognize this limitation, they can employ the model fruitfully and unproblematically.

A loose usage of "model" treats it as synonymous with "theory" or as theory expressed in mathematical symbols. While it is possible to have a model of a theory, the working definition given above rules out synonymous usage because a model of *x* must resemble *x* in terms of pattern or structure, whereas a theory about *x*, that predicts or explains *x*, need not, and generally does not, resemble *x*. In short, theories of *x* do not have to be isomorphic with *x*; models do.

In formulating a working definition of *paradigm*, it would seem reasonable to follow Kuhn since he is largely responsible for the contemporary significance of the idea. This presents serious difficulties, however, for as Laudan observes, "Kuhn's notion of paradigm has been shown to be systematically ambiguous . . . and thus difficult to characterize accurately" (1977, p. 73). While constructing a definition of "paradigm" is a formidable task, it is an essential one because the paradigm is critical to an understanding of Kuhn, and Kuhn's work plays an important role in many of the current controversies in sociology. Some of the ambiguity disappears if one distinguishes between what a paradigm *is* and what a paradigm *does*; still, it would be presumptuous to believe that one could fully capture Kuhn's concept with all its nuances. The following working definition has the more modest goal of representing many of his key ideas:

> A paradigm *is a significant scientific achievement recognized by a particular community of scientists that provides a model from which springs a coherent tradition of scientific research and also a general way of looking at the world.*

The principal functions of a paradigm include: (1) determining what kinds of problems are appropriate objects of study, (2) specifying appropriate ways to study these problems, and (3) delimiting the types of theories and explanations that are acceptable. For example, one could consider Durkheim's *Suicide* ([1897] 1951) as a paradigm for many sociologists that provides a model for research and a way to look at phenomena. For Durkheimians, *Suicide* is an exemplar that specifies ways to look for and at social facts, and that limits explanations of given social facts to other social facts, rather than, for example, explaining social facts with psychological ideas like motives.

It is important to distinguish "paradigm" from "theory." While a well-developed paradigm may contain a number of specific theories, a paradigm is "metatheoretical." A theory makes statements about the world, whereas a paradigm involves statements about the nature of acceptable theory, the appropriate entities to investigate, and the correct approaches to these investigations. As an exemplar, a paradigm serves as a normative standard; hence, it is a special type of model, a model of what the given scientific community considers to be exemplary work.

KUHN'S MODEL OF SCIENTIFIC CHANGE

Kuhn developed a model of change in science built around his concept of paradigm. The model employs several concepts related to "paradigm" that extend its meaning: normal science, anomaly, crisis, revolution, paradigm shift, and incommensurability. Brief explications of these ideas follow. (Page references below are to Kuhn 1970.)

Normal Science. When a paradigm gains acceptance in a scientific community, it is largely in terms of a promise of success if researchers in the community follow the exemplar. "Normal science consists in the actualization of that promise, an actualization achieved by extending the knowledge of those facts that the paradigm displays as particularly revealing, by increasing the extent of the match between those facts and the paradigm's predictions, and by further articulation of the paradigm itself" (p. 24). To Kuhn, normal science involves "mopping-up operations [that] engage most scientists throughout their careers" (p. 24), and is primarily devoted to puzzle solving: "Perhaps, the most striking feature of the normal research problems . . . is how little they aim to produce major novelties, conceptual or phenomenal" (p. 35).

Anomaly. The term *anomaly* refers to "the recognition that nature has somehow violated the paradigm-induced expectations that govern normal science" (p. 52).

Crisis. A *crisis*, a period of "pronounced professional insecurity" (p. 68–69), occurs when enough anomalies accumulate so that scientists question the appropriateness of the paradigm.

Revolution. Kuhn takes scientific *revolutions* to be "those non-cumulative developmental episodes in which an older paradigm is replaced in whole or in part by an incompatible new one" (p. 92).

Paradigm shift. Kuhn argues that scientists with a new paradigm do not merely have new interpretations for what they observe, but rather "see" things differently. This difference in perception, or paradigm shift, is in a sense similar to the Gestalt switch studied by psychologists, in which the same figure can yield a right-hand face or a left-hand face depending on how it is viewed.

Incommensurability. During crisis periods, rival paradigms coexist and advocates of rival paradigms cannot understand one another because they have different ways of seeing the world, different standards for appraisal, and different objectives for their scientific community; that is, there is *incommensurability*. Consequently, paradigm conflicts are not resolvable by appeal to a set of shared criteria.

These concepts allow a sketch of Kuhn's model:

Paradigm I → Normal Science → Anomalies → Crisis → Revolution → Paradigm II

When the members of a scientific community accept a paradigm, that acceptance generates a set of shared commitments to objectives, methods for achieving those objectives and criteria for appraising theories and research. These commitments are the foundation for a period of normal science, since what to study, how to study it, and what constitutes adequate explanations are not problematic. During normal science, the community regards the paradigm itself as unalterable and immune to challenge. Scientists work to solve the puzzles that the paradigm presents and for which the paradigm guarantees solutions; in this process of puzzle solving, refutations for theories contained in the paradigm arise and empirical studies come up with unexpected findings. The more serious refutations and the more surprising findings come to be regarded as anomalies, and as these anomalies accumulate, scientists are at a loss as to how to deal with them. In the crisis period, rival paradigms arise, but because paradigms are incommensurable, scientists adhering to rivals have no common basis for choosing among the competitors. Paradigm II wins out because some scientists undergo the conversion experience of a paradigm shift where they see the world in a new way, because the adherents of Paradigm II are especially persuasive, or because the adherents of Paradigm I die off.

Kuhn's model questions ideas of cumulation and progress in science. While normal science is cumulative, revolutions do not preserve all, or even the most important, achievements of previous paradigms. "There are losses as well as gains in scientific revolutions" (p. 167). Furthermore, the incommensurablity thesis argues that Paradigm II does not win out because it is better or more progressive; the lack of shared standards precludes definitive judgments.

CRITIQUE

Kuhn's work has raised important questions for scholars in the history, philosophy, and sociology of science and has generated a large literature in these areas. Interestingly enough, it has also had broad appeal to intellectuals outside of these specialized fields. Although Kuhn presented his basic model in 1962, his ideas continue to command attention and engender controversy, both within relevant technical fields and in broader academic circles. His work seems to have had less impact in the natural sciences, although it attacks the conventional views of many natural scientists.

Kuhn's emphasis on scientific communities and on noncognitive factors in the development of science clearly appeals to sociologists, especially sociologists of science—for instance, those who study social networks among scientists or the effects of reward systems. His model provides an antidote to the mythology of cumulative, linear growth of knowledge, the view that characterizes science as building one discovery on another and, with each increment, coming closer to total truth about nature. Nearly forty years after his initial publication, it is difficult to appreciate how dominant such mythology was when Kuhn challenged it.

If prior views overemphasized cognitive and rational factors and held to a naive and simplistic view of progress in science, many post-Kuhnians underemphasize the cognitive and the rational or overemphasize the social and the political; moreover, some totally deny the possibility of scientific progress. For many, Kuhn provides the license to remove science from its pedestal, to deny that science has any distinctive character or special claim on society's attention or support, and to demand that social sciences cease their attempts to be scientific. Close examination of a few of Kuhn's key ideas indicates how Kuhn came to be used in ways he, himself, disavowed.

The first problem is the ambiguity of the term "paradigm." Masterman (1970), a sympathetic critic, has pointed to twenty-one different senses of "paradigm" in the 1962 book, and Kuhn has added to the problem with later modifications of his ideas (1970, 1974). Laudan notes, "Since 1962 most of Kuhn's philosophical writings have been devoted to clearing up some of the ambiguities and confusions generated [by the 1962 book] . . . to such an extent that . . . [m]ore than one commentator has accused the later Kuhn of taking back much of what made his message interesting and provocative in the first place" (1984, pp. 67–68).

The metaphorical language in Kuhn's model poses a second serious problem. As Laudan puts it:

Notoriously, he speaks of the acceptance of a new paradigm as a "conversion experience," conjuring up a picture of the scientific revolutionary as a born-again Christian, long on zeal and short on argument. At other times

he likens paradigm change to an "irreversible Gestalt-shift." . . . Such language does not encourage one to imagine that paradigm change is exactly the result of a careful and deliberate weighing-up of the respective strengths of rival contenders. (1984, p. 70)

Although Laudan believes that problems of misinterpretation can be "rectified by cleaning up some of the vocabulary," and although Kuhn has assumed some responsibility for the misunderstandings due to his own rhetoric (1970, pp. 259–260), it should be noted that Kuhn's ambiguity and his vivid metaphors are important reasons for much of the enthusiastic embracing of his model. The possibility of reading into the meaning of "paradigm" and "paradigm shift" enables the model to serve a variety of agendas.

Kuhn's incommensurability thesis is both the most frequently criticized and the most frequently misused element of his model. It has provided ammunition for a radical subjectivism that denies all standards (Scheffler 1967). In attacking those who use Kuhn to justify any sweeping paradigm of their own, Crews writes, "By incommensurability Kuhn never meant that competing theories are incomparable but only that the choice between them cannot be *entirely* consigned to the verdict of theory-neutral rules and data" (1986, p. 39; emphasis added). Since Kuhn never clearly specified how rules and evidence entered into paradigm change and since he understated the degree to which different scientific communities can share rules and objectives, it is not surprising that this thesis became a rallying point for attacks on scientific rationality.

Another major criticism—and one that goes to the heart of Kuhn's model—involves the indivisible character of paradigms. Paradigm shift is an all-or-nothing process; a paradigm is accepted or rejected as a whole. Treating the parts of a paradigm as inseparable almost requires the transition from one paradigm to another to be a conversion experience; moreover, such a holistic view does not provide an accurate picture of how large-scale changes of scientific allegiance occur (Laudan 1984, pp. 71–72).

Many of these criticisms are widely held. Nevertheless, Kuhn's model remains important to many disciplines including sociology. Some scholars remain adherents to the basic features of the model; others believe they must respond to the model's challenges to contemporary philosophy and methodology of science.

USE OF "PARADIGM" IN SOCIOLOGY

While several leading British sociologists of science who focus on the sociology of knowledge reflect the intellectual mood of Kuhnian analysis (Collins 1983), the main applications of "paradigm" have occurred in either descriptive or normative efforts in the sociology of sociology.

Analysts have employed versions of Kuhn's concept to classify sociological activities as belonging to one or another paradigm; for example, Ritzer (1975) distinguishes three paradigms for the field at large: social facts, social definition, and social behavior. Bottomore (1975) identifies four paradigms of macrosociology: structural-functionalist, evolutionist, phenomenologist, and structuralist. Other sociologists discriminate varying numbers of paradigms from as few as two to as many as eight for a single subfield. Some writers classify theories into different paradigms; others categorize research strategies; still others codify more general philosophical orientations. In addition to disputing the number of paradigms, sociologists also disagree about whether paradigm applies to the field in general or only to subfields and whether there are any paradigms at all in sociology, that is, whether the field is preparadigmatic.

A few studies have applied Kuhn to examine historical development of a paradigm. Colclough and Horan (1983), for example, use content analysis of status attainment studies to illustrate Kuhn's model. Their analysis finds evidence for a stage of normal science and a stage in which anomalies arise, and they suggest the onset of a crisis for status attainment research.

Sociologists who use Kuhn focus on different properties of paradigms and debate the utility of their approaches or their faithfulness to Kuhn (cf. Ritzer 1975, 1981a, 1981b; Eckberg and Hill 1979; Hill and Eckberg 1981; Harvey 1982). Compounding the confusion are the many interpreters who read their own meanings into Kuhn. One critic argues:

[F]or the most part the use of the term paradigm in sociology fails to reflect the analytic elements of Kuhn's concept . . . Arbitrary pigeon-holing schemes of varying degrees of sophistication, are constructed and theories of, ideas about, and approaches to, sociology are dropped in. The result is a personalized schematic device that . . . plays little part in providing . . . any explanation or understanding of the growth of knowledge. The labeling of such pigeon-holes as paradigms legitimizes the scheme and implies an authority it does not possess. (Harvey 1982, p. 86)

The disarray led Bell to ask "Does the term "paradigm" carry too many possible meanings for rigorous thinking? Has it become quasi-mystical? Is it time to review its many usages and to consider discarding it in favor of more precise terms that convey to others more accurately what we mean to say?" (1990, p. 17) Bell went on to answer yes to all three questions.

MODELS IN SOCIOLOGY

The first basic distinction necessary to characterize the use of models in sociology is among substantive, measurement, and statistical models. The substantive modeler's objective is to model a specific theory, phenomenon, or process in order to learn (or teach) something about the specific object of the model. For example, Pfeffer and Salancik (1978) use a theory of interpersonal power and dependence (Emerson 1962) to model interorganizational relations, or Gamson (1969) creates an elaborate game that simulates the operation of key features of a society. In both examples, the model focuses on a particular problem—to learn about organizational relations in the first, or to teach students about major aspects of society in the second.

The objective of a measurement model is to create and justify a measuring instrument that has a wide range of applicability. One measurement area to which sociologists were early contributors is attitude measurement; sociologists were among the first to develop models for scaling attitudes. These scaling models provide the rationale for assigning numbers to represent different expressions of the attitude. For example, Bogardus (1925), in a classic work, created a measure of social distance on the analogy of physical distance, in which allowing a member of some ethnic group into your family represented less social distance than only allowing that person to live in your neighborhood. Guttman (1950) developed one of the most frequently used attitude scaling models, which defines and justifies procedures for ordering a set of attitude questions.

Statistical models are the basis for the systematic quantitative analysis of sociological data, and most empirical research in the field employs one or more statistical models. These models are general tools, broadly applicable to diverse problems; the nature of the subject matter that the data reflect is largely irrelevant to the model as long as the data have certain properties (e.g., as long as they are drawn randomly from some population). A large number of different statistical models appear in the sociological literature. Some are simple, for example, using the analogy of coin tossing to evaluate the likelihood that a given event occurred by chance; others are highly complex, using systems of equations to represent the structure of relationships in a set of variables. Models for multivariate analysis have become extremely important to sociology, including, for example, structural equation models, also known as path or causal models (Bielby and Hauser 1977), and log-linear models (Goodman 1984).

In recent years, models have become a central feature of the sociological literature. Researchers have constructed verbal, mathematical, and computer models to deal with a range of substantive phenomena and measurement issues. The application of statistical models to sociological data has increased dramatically in both the diversity of models employed and their mathematical sophistication. The most significant developments, however, have occurred in the creation, elaboration, and testing of formalized models of substantive phenomena, that is, models involving mathematics or logic.

In the early years of model building, substantive sociologists did not regard formal models as central to their concerns. Many mainline researchers were dubious about the utility of formal models in advancing knowledge about a substantive problem and often considered model construction as primarily an intellectual exercise, stimulating to the creator but of little relevance to anyone else. Articles presenting models appeared mainly in esoteric journals read by small audiences of the initiated.

A striking feature of recent sociological work is the emergence of formal models as a central feature of several research traditions. Papers presenting formal models, extensions of these models, critiques of them, and empirical studies testing the models have appeared regularly in journals such as the *American Sociological Review*. While specialized journals such as the *Journal of Mathematical Sociology* still publish many articles dealing with substantive models, the fact that general sociological journals also publish reports dealing with formal models indicates that formal modeling has become much more integrated with substantive research in several problem areas of the discipline.

Recent research involving formal models has dealt with a diversity of substantive problems, employed a variety of mathematical tools, and used many different types of data to evaluate the empirical predictions of the models. Sociologists have constructed models for collective behavior (Heckathorn 1996; Kim and Bearman 1997), demographic processes (Yamaguchi and Ferguson 1995), exchange processes (Lawler and Yoon 1996; Yamaguchi 1996; Molm 1997; Burke 1997), geographic mobility (Herting et al. 1997), organization ecology (Gábor et al. 1994; Hannan et al. 1995) performance expectations and power-prestige orders (Troyer and Younts 1997; Berger et al. 1998), and social differentiation-inequality (Rickson and Palange 1994; Nielsen 1995; Orbell et al. 1996; Mark 1998). What has changed from the past is that highly developed models in each of these lines of research have become part of the core of theory building rather than merely interesting adjuncts.

FUNCTIONS OF MODELS

A model, first of all, is an abstract representation of what the modeler regards as important aspects of the object being modeled. It involves assumptions, explicit or tacit, about that object, its elements, and the relationships among these elements. The definition given above requires that modeling lead to increased understanding; examining the relationships assumed in the model and ascertaining those that fit the object well, those that fit the object somewhat, and those that do not fit at all serves this most important function. In other words, scrutinizing ways the model resembles the object and ways it does not can uncover previously unrecognized features of the object. Formal models, as noted earlier, employ logical or mathematical tools to derive conclusions from the model's assumptions, and researchers then test whether these conclusions represent hitherto unknown properties of the object. A model, in general, provides the means to ask new questions about the phenomenon it represents and thus functions to generate new ideas.

A model provides a vehicle for communication. Since a model is more abstract than its object and since it omits many properties of the object, it is easier for writer and audience to share understanding of the model than of the object. Caution, however, is necessary, particularly when the model is a vague analogy (e.g., society as a living organism). The possibility of reading into analogies and metaphors can defeat shared understanding when the audience focuses on aspects that are unintended. A model may display the complexities of the object. Attempting to represent the ties among members of a social group, for example, may require the elaboration of a simple model that represents only the presence or absence of a relationship to one that distinguishes types of relationships—attraction, task interdependence, relative status, and so on. Even if a model inadequately represents its object, it can enhance the understanding of that object by exposing issues that need to be addressed. One important class of models—those known as "baseline models"—are developed in order to study how the object deviates from the model's minimal representation. Investigating discrepancies between a baseline representation and the object can direct the construction of a more complex model (Cohen 1963).

The last general function to be noted is that a model can serve to relate what appear to be different phenomena. An abstract model can apply to a variety of different objects, thus calling attention to their common aspects; sometimes, particularly with metaphors and analogies, the features of one phenomenon serve as the model for another. Using drama as a model for everyday interaction calls attention to some common elements (e.g., what it means to play a role).

Berger and colleagues (1980) present a typology of models based upon more specific functions. Although their concern is mathematical models, their typology has more general application; they distinguish: (1) explicational models, (2) representational models, and (3) theoretical construct models. Explicational models are those for which the primary goal is to explicate or render precise one or more concepts. Many social network models are explicational models in that they provide an explication of the concept of social structure (Marsden and Lin 1982). While all models are representational, in this typology the term refers to those models that attempt to represent a particular observed social phenomenon. The majority of models developed in sociology are representational in this sense as long as one has some latitude in interpreting "observed," in many cases, the object of the model is a generalization from observed phenomena. Coleman (1964, 1973) has formulated a number of representational models dealing with social change and with collective action.

Theoretical construct models are those which formalize an explanatory theory. In sociology, these models have focused on a variety of substantive topics as the following examples illustrate: Fararo and Skvoretz (1989) have devised a model drawing on social structural theories of Blau (1977) and Granovetter (1973); Hannan and Freeman (1989) have constructed models of organizational birth and death processes based on bioecological theories; Berger and colleagues (1977) have formulated a model of status characteristic theory (Berger et al. 1966, 1972).

Sociological models are models in a sense that is close to the everyday meaning of model as a replica or representation. It is even reasonable to think of many of them in the other everyday sense, as exemplars, since we can point to sociological research traditions devoted to their development and test. Only with the benefit of more hindsight than is presently available, however, will it be possible to judge whether any of these models are paradigmatic.

REFERENCES

Bell, Wendell 1990 "What Do We Mean by 'Paradigm.'" *Footnote* 18:17.

Berger, Joseph, Bernard P. Cohen, and Morris Zelditch, Jr., 1966 "Status Characteristics and Expectation States." In Joseph Berger, Morris Zelditch Jr., and Bo Anderson, eds., *Sociological Theories in Progress*, vol. 1. Newbury Park, Calif.: Sage.

—— 1966 "Status Characteristics and Social Interaction." *American Sociological Review* 37:241–255.

—— and J. Laurie Snell 1980 *Types of Formalization in Small-Group Research*. Westport, Conn.: Greenwood.

Berger, Joseph, M. Hamit Fisek, Robert Z. Norman, and Morris Zelditch, Jr. 1977 *Status Characteristics and Social Interaction: An Expectation-States Approach*. New York: Elsevier.

Berger, Joseph, Cecilia Ridgeway, M. Hamit Fisek, and Robert Z. Norman 1998 "The Legitimation of Power and Prestige Orders." *American Sociological Review* 63:379–405.

Bielby, William T., and Robert M. Hauser 1977 "Structural Equation Models." *Annual Review of Sociology* 3:137–161.

Blau, Peter 1977 *Inequality and Heterogeneity*. New York: Free Press.

Bogardus, Emery S. 1925 "Measuring Social Distance." *Journal of Applied Sociology* 9:299–308.

Bottomore, Tom 1975 "Competing Paradigms in Macrosociology." *Annual Review of Sociology* 1:191–202.

Burke, Peter 1997 "An Identity Model for Network Exchange." *American Sociological Review* 62:134–150.

Cohen, Bernard P. 1963 *Conflict and Conformity: A Probability Model and Its Application*. Cambridge, Mass.: MIT Press.

Colclough, Glenna, and Patrick M. Horan 1983 "The Status Attainment Paradigm: An Application of the Kuhnian Perspective." *Sociological Quarterly* 24:25–42.

Coleman, James 1964 *Models of Change and Response Uncertainty*. Englewood Cliffs, N.J.: Prentice-Hall.

—— 1973 *The Mathematics of Collective Actions*. Chicago: Aldine.

Collins, H. M. 1983 "The Sociology of Scientific Knowledge: Studies of Contemporary Science." *Annual Review of Sociology* 9:265–285.

Crews, Frederick 1986 "In the Big House of Theory." *New York Review of Books*. (May 29).

Durkheim, Emile (1897) 1951 *Suicide*. New York: Free Press.

Eckberg, Douglas L., and Lester Hill, Jr. 1979 "The Paradigm Concept and Sociology: A Critical Review." *American Sociological Review* 44:925–937.

Emerson, Richard 1962 "Power-Dependence Relations." *American Sociological Review* 27:31–41.

Fararo, Thomas J., and John Skvoretz 1989 "The Biased Net Theory of Social Structures and the Problem of Integration." In Joseph Berger, Morris Zelditch, Jr., and Bo Anderson, eds., *Sociological Theories in Progress: New Formulations*. Newbury Park, Calif.: Sage.

Péli, Gábor, Jeroen Bruggeman, Michael Masuch, and Breanndán Ó. Nualláin 1994 "A Logical Approach to Formalizing Organization Ecology." *American Sociological Review* 59:571–593.

Gamson, William A. 1969 *SIMSOC: Simulated Society*. New York: Free Press.

Goodman, Leo A. 1984 *The Analysis of Cross-Classified Data Having Ordered Categories*. Cambridge, Mass.: Harvard University Press.

Granovetter, Mark S. 1973 "The Strength of Weak Ties." *American Journal of Sociology* 78:1360–1380.

Guttman, Louis 1950 "The Basis for Scalogram Analysis." In Samuel A. Stouffer, et al., eds., *Measurement and Prediction*. Princeton, N.J.: Princeton University Press.

Hannan, Michael T., Glenn R. Carroll, Elizabeth A. Dundon, and John Charles Torres 1995 "Organizational Evolution in a Multinational Context: Entries of Automobile Manufacturers in Belgium, Britain, France and Italy." *American Sociological Review* 60:509–528.

Hannan, Michael T., and John Freeman 1989 *Organizational Ecology*. Cambridge, Mass.: Harvard University Press.

Harvey, Lee 1982 "The Use and Abuse of Kuhnian Paradigms in the Sociology of Knowledge." *Sociology* 16:85–101.

Heckathorn, Douglas D. 1996 "The Dynamics and Dilemmas of Collective Action." *American Sociological Review* 61:250–277.

Herting, Jerald R., David Grusky, and Stephen E. Van Rompaey 1997 "The Social Geography of Interstate Mobility and Persistence." *American Sociological Review* 62:267–287.

Hill, Lester, Jr., and Douglas L. Eckberg 1981 "Clarifying Confusions about Paradigms: A Reply to Ritzer." *American Sociological Review* 46:248–252.

Kaplan, Abraham 1964 *The Conduct of Inquiry*. San Francisco: Chandler.

Kim, Hyojoung, and Peter S. Bearman 1997 "The Structure and Dynamics of Movement Participation." *American Sociological Review* 62:70–93.

Kuhn, Thomas S. 1962 *The Structure of Scientific Revolutions*. Chicago: University of Chicago Press.

—— 1970 "Postscript." *The Structure of Scientific Revolutions*, 2nd ed. Chicago: University of Chicago Press.

—— 1974 "Second Thoughts on Paradigms." In Frederick Suppe, ed., *The Structure of Scientific Theories*. Urbana, Ill.: University of Illinois Press.

Laudan, Larry 1977 *Progress and Its Problems: Towards a Theory of Scientific Growth*. Berkeley: University of California Press.

—— 1984 *Science and Values: The Aims of Science and Their Role in Scientific Debate*. Berkeley: University of California Press.

Lawler, Edward J., and Jeongkoo Yoon 1996 "Commitment in Exchange Relations: Test of a Theory of Relational Cohesion." *American Sociological Review* 61:89–108.

Mark, Noah 1998 "Beyond Individual Differences: Social Differentiation from First Principles." *American Sociological Review* 63:309–330.

Marsden, Peter V., and Nan Lin (eds.) 1982 *Social Structure and Network Analysis*. Beverly Hills, Calif.: Sage.

Masterman, Margaret 1970 "The Nature of a Paradigm." In Imre Lakatos and Alan Musgrave, eds., *Criticism and the Growth of Knowledge*. Cambridge: Cambridge University Press.

Merton, Robert K. 1949 *Social Theory and Social Structure*. Glencoe, Ill.: Free Press.

Molm, Linda 1997 "Risk and Power Use: Constraints on the Use of Coercion in Exchange." *American Sociological Review* 62:113–133.

Nielsen, Francois 1995 "Meritocratic and Monopoly Inequality: A Computer Simulation of Income Distribution." *Journal of Mathematical Sociology* 20:319–350.

Orbell, John, Zeng Langche, and Matthew Mulford 1996 "Individual Experience and the Fragmentation of Societies." *American Sociological Review* 61:1018–1032.

Parsons, Talcott 1951 *The Social System*. Glencoe, Ill.: Free Press.

Pfeffer, Jeffrey, and Gerald R. Salancik 1978 *The External Control of Organizations*. New York: Harper and Row.

Rickson, Roy E., and Jean-Yves Parlange 1994 "Structural Differentiation and Size in Organizations: A Thermodynamic Formulation and Generalization." *Journal of Mathematical Sociology* 19:69–90.

Ritzer, George 1975 *Sociology: A Multiple Paradigm Science*. Boston: Allyn and Bacon.

—— 1981a "Paradigm Analysis in Sociology: Clarifying the Issues." *American Sociological Review* 46:245–248.

—— 1981b *Toward an Integrated Sociological Paradigm: The Search for an Exemplar and an Image of the Subject Matter*. Boston: Allyn and Bacon.

Scheffler, Israel 1967 *Science and Subjectivity*. Indianapolis, Ind.: Bobbs Merrill.

Troyer, Lisa, and C. Wesley Younts 1997 "Whose Expectations Matter? The Relative Power of First- and Second-Order Expectations in Determining Social Influence." *American Journal of Sociology* 103:692–732.

Yamaguchi, Kazuo 1996 "Power in Networks of Substitutable and Complementary Exchange Relations: A Rational Choice Model and an Analysis of Power Centralization." *American Sociological Review* 61:308–332.

——, and Linda R. Ferguson 1995 "The Stopping and Spacing of Childbirths and Their Birth-History Predictors: Rational Choice Theory and Event-History Analysis." *American Sociological Review* 60:272–298.

BERNARD P. COHEN

PARENTAL ROLES

In the opening years of the twenty-first century, most adults are or will become parents. The ages at which they start having children, as well as the number of children they have, differ significantly from earlier generations and from culture to culture, as do the social and economic conditions of parenthood. In this article, several major aspects of parenthood in the contemporary United States— and other industrialized nations—are discussed. First, several *demographic patterns* associated with parenting are reviewed. Second, the *rewards and costs* associated with parenting are examined. Third, *changes in the responsibilities of parents*, as defined by social perceptions of the nature of childhood, are discussed. In this section, special attention is given to gender differences in parenting styles. The fourth section examines *the impact of the first child's birth* on the parents. The paper closes with a discussion of *parent-child relations in middle and later life*.

DEMOGRAPHIC TRENDS IN PARENTING

Average Number of Births per Woman. One of the most dramatic changes in the nature of parenthood in industrialized nations has been the *decline* *in the average number of births to each woman.* In the United States, this number has decreased from seven births per woman to two, over the past 200 years. This downward trend has not been steady or consistent, however. During some periods, such as the Great Depression of the 1930s, the rate of decline was much more pronounced, while at other times, most notably during the post-World War II baby boom (1946–1962), the number of births per woman actually increased. In 1936, the middle of the Depression, American women were giving birth to two children, on the average. At the peak of the baby boom, in 1957, the number reached 3.6 births per woman. For nearly twenty years following this peak, the birth rate dropped dramatically. Since the mid-1970s, the birth rate has been fairly stable. There are, however, racial and socioeconomic differences in fertility. In the United States, white women have the fewest births, followed by black and Hispanic women. White women aged 40 to 44 have given birth to an average of 1.9 children, while African-American and Hispanic women have had 2.1 and 2.6 children, respectively (U.S. Bureau of the Census 1999).

Reasons for the Declining Birth Rate. Why has the average number of births per woman decreased over the past 200 years? One major reason is that in the past women had little control over their childbearing. Through the eighteenth and nineteenth centuries, married women gave birth to as many children as they were biologically capable of having. This pattern persisted into the twentieth century for many women, although by the end of the nineteenth century many middle-class women were beginning to use birth control. Childbearing in the United States is now largely controlled through the use of various contraceptive methods and, to a lesser extent, through medically induced abortion. Most people have the number of children they want to have, and generally, they want no more than two children. Only a small percentage of couples want, and actually have, more than two children (Shehan and Kammeyer 1997, pp. 183–184).

A second reason for the historical decline in childbearing is that children are no longer economic assets for their families. Through much of the nineteenth century, the labor of children helped families survive. Most Americans lived on farms, where children could help out in many ways. Even

the children who lived in small towns and cities often worked at young ages to help support their families. When laws pertaining to child labor and mandatory education were passed in the late nineteenth and early twentieth centuries, children became less valuable to their parents in economic terms. Today, children require large economic expenditures from their parents, as discussed later in this article. Most people have the number of children they think can afford, and thus, the number they have is much lower than in the past (Shehan and Kammeyer 1997, p. 184).

A third reason for today's low fertility rate is the high number of women who are in the paid labor force. Economic need has led to a dramatic increase in the employment of mothers, married as well as divorced. In 1960, fewer than one in every five mothers of preschool children was employed. Today, over 60 percent are employed. The increased demand for substitute child care has become one of the most pressing social problems in industrial nations. Child-rearing duties decrease the amount of time and energy women can devote to their jobs; therefore, those who are career oriented may choose to forego childbearing altogether or to limit the number of children they have (Shehan and Kammeyer 1997).

Changes in the Characteristics of Parents. Social change in the twentieth century has not only reduced the average number of children born per woman in industrialized nations but has also seen a change in the marital status and age at which women begin to have children. The childbearing period seems to be expanding, as some women continue to become mothers in their teen years while others wait until they are in their late twenties, thirties, or early forties. Developments in reproductive biology have even made it possible for women who have gone through menopause (which typically occurs in the early fifties) to have babies. Teenage childbearing was fairly common in the post–World War II baby boom, but most of the teenagers who had babies during that era were married. Teen birth rates fell from the mid-1950s to the mid-1980s then increased in the early 1990s. Today, the rate of teen childbearing is lower than it was at the beginning of the 1990s, but most teen births (71 percent) occur outside of marriage (Shehan and Kammeyer 1997, p. 186).

Another significant change in fertility is the increase in births to unmarried women. Today, American women spend fewer years in marriage because they are marrying at older ages and are more likely to get divorced. As a result, there is less time available to them to have children within the context of marriage. One-third of all births in the United States today are to unwed mothers. The rate is higher among blacks than it is among whites. Childbearing outside marriage actually varies widely among industrialized nations, from Japan, where only 1 percent of all babies are born to unmarried women, to Sweden, where the comparable figure is 53 percent.

As a consequence of the high out-of-wedlock birth rate and the high divorce rate, an increasing number of adults are engaging in solo parenting. In 1995, about twelve million American families—or about one-fourth of all families with children—had only one parent (U.S. Bureau of the Census 1995). While the majority of single parents are women, men are also raising children alone. Today, about one-sixth of all single-parent homes are headed by men.

THE CHANGING SOCIAL CIRCUMSTANCES OF PARENTING

The demographic shifts that have occurred in industrial nations since World War II—particularly the increases in divorce and out-of-wedlock births—have increased the likelihood that children will have little or no contact with one of their biological parents during some period of their childhood. Only one in every four children of divorced parents who live with their mothers sees his or her father once a week; and close to half have little or no personal contact of any type with their fathers after divorce. Men's contact with their biological children from previous marriages is reduced when they remarry and become involved in the lives of stepchildren or have children with their new partner. Other adults, however, may step in to fill the gap in children's access to their biological parents. For instance, three-fourths of the children who live with their fathers share their homes with other adults. About one-third live in multigenerational households (with grandparents and other relatives), and another third

live with their father and his intimate partner. Children in these homes may or may not benefit from the added financial and emotional resources that nonrelated adults can offer (Shehan and Seccombe 1996).

Single-parent families headed by women often have financial problems. Many live below the poverty level. A major contributing factor to this "feminization of poverty" is the fact that not all noncustodial fathers are ordered by the courts to pay child support after divorce, and, of those who are, fewer than half actually pay the full amount.

GOVERNMENT SUPPORT FOR PARENTS

The major changes in family patterns that have occurred over the past twenty-five years have made government leaders from around the world very aware of family problems. Concerns about declining birthrates and the aging of the population have been widespread throughout industrial nations. Many governments have adopted "pro-family" attitudes and attempted to create more supportive environments for families. But industrial nations have differed significantly in the extent to which they have provided support for families. The U.S. government has been reluctant to assume public responsibility for care of children, instead passing laws that reinforce the private nature of child support obligations. According to one indicator of "family friendliness," the United States, along with Portugal, Italy, Ireland, Spain, and Greece, is among the least generous of the industrialized nations in terms of its benefits packages for families with children (Gauthier 1999, p. 7).

As women's labor-force participation increased in industrialized nations in the 1970s, renewed attention was given to the provision of maternity leave plans. In most countries, these plans were upgraded, at least in terms of their duration, increasing by six weeks, on average across eighteen industrialized nations. Major increases in maternity pay also occurred in most countries. But in the United States, where only thirty states had provisions for maternity leave, no pay was mandated. In 1992, the Family and Medical Leave Act was passed by the U.S. Congress and signed into law by President Bill Clinton. The legislation provides public and private employees in companies with fifty or more workers the right to take up to twelve weeks leave each year to care for a newborn or newly adopted child; or for a seriously ill child, spouse, or parent; or for their own serious health conditions (Gauthier 1999).

THE CHILDBEARING DECISION: THE REWARDS AND COSTS OF PARENTING

Since individuals are now better able to control their reproductive functions due to advances in contraceptive technology and access to legal abortion, it is important to examine why the majority of adults still choose to become parents. For most people, becoming a parent involves a decision-making process in which the anticipated rewards and costs of parenting are weighed. One major influence on this choice is societal pressure. While most societies encourage fertility among their members, the United States is considered to be particularly *pronatalist*, which means its dominant values and attitudes promote and encourage childbearing (Schoen 1997).

Rewards of Parenting. In earlier historical periods, children were valued in large part because their labor could greatly enhance a family's economic survival. Today, children may continue to have economic value for parents who view them as a type of old age insurance. A small minority of parents, typically those from rural areas, also see children's ability to participate in household labor as a valuable asset. Having children may also enable a family to maintain control over property or a family-owned or family-operated farm or business. For most families, though, children may be more of an economic liability than a benefit. Their primary value to their parents is emotional and symbolic. Understanding the noneconomic benefits of child rearing helps in understanding why most people choose to become parents when they are no longer forced to do so by biological necessity.

Studies of the value of children to their parents have identified many major rewards that child rearing provides. One reward is *family continuity or personal immortality*. The birth of children ensures that the father's family name will continue into the future, at least for one more generation, and may give the parents a sense of immortality, a feeling that part of them will survive after death.

Becoming a parent can also lead to a *change in social identity*. It bestows adult status, which carries with it implications of maturity and stability. In fact, for many people, parenthood is *the* event that gives them a sense of feeling like an adult. Having children may also produce a sense of achievement, not only for the physical fact of conception but also for the challenges of raising a child. Moreover, many parents also feel a sense of accomplishment through their children's achievements. Finally, during the child-rearing years, the legitimate authority that is attached to the parent role, as well as the resulting power and influence parents have over their children's lives, may increase parents' self-esteem, especially for those who have little control over other aspects of their lives.

The most frequently mentioned reward of child rearing involves primary group ties and affection. Children help their parents establish new relationships with their own parents, grandparents, aunts and uncles, siblings, and friends; such relationships can provide emotional support and practical assistance. Children are also expected to help prevent loneliness and to provide love and companionship for their parents. Many people regard childbearing as a sacred duty and may feel that by becoming parents they are fulfilling a divine commandment. Moreover, the physical and symbolic sacrifices involved in child rearing are perceived by some as a sign that parents are more virtuous and altruistic than childless adults (Shehan and Kammeyer 1997, pp. 187–189).

The Costs of Parenting. There are also numerous costs associated with parenting. These costs are economic as well as social and emotional. Over the years, economists have estimated the *direct economic costs* (e.g., food, clothing, shelter, medical and dental care, toys, recreation, leisure, and education) and the *indirect economic costs* (e.g., foregone savings and investments, lower standards of living, and loss of potential income for parents who leave the labor market to care for the child) of child rearing. The direct costs of raising a child to age 18 have risen by more than 20 percent in recent decades, after adjustments for inflation and for changes in family size have been made. In 1998, raising a child to adulthood, which includes sending her or him to a state university for four years, costs middle-income parents an average of

$459,014; that's $301,183 in direct costs and $157,831 in costs associated with college education (Longman 1998).

Another important economic cost of parenthood that must be considered is the current or future family income that is given up when parents leave the labor force—or reduce their hours in employment—to care for children. Virtually all parents face some opportunity costs in having children. Using estimates and procedures developed by the U.S. Department of Agriculture—which provides reports on the costs of child rearing annually—the following example of the opportunity costs encountered by parents is offered. A married woman with an annual salary of $23,600 who stays home to care for a child from birth until kindergarten age (at which point she reenters the labor force on a half-time basis) can expect to sacrifice nearly $1 million in lost income by the time that child reaches age 21 (Longman 1998). When opportunity costs are added to the direct costs of child rearing that were listed above, a middle-income couple can expect to spend slightly more than $1.45 million on one child by the time she or he completes college.

In the United States and other industrialized nations, however, parents receive some governmental subsidies for raising children. In the United States in 1998, each dependent child was worth a $2,650 deduction on his or her parents' federal income taxes. Parents are also able to take a tax credit for child care expenses—a maximum of $720 for one child in a low-income family to a maximum of $1,440 for two or more children (Longman 1998).

The presence of children may also be costly to adults through the restriction of their activities and the resulting loss of freedom. Parents are responsible for the mental, emotional, physical, spiritual, and social development of their offspring. Obviously, such responsibility may consume much of the parents' time and attention and may require a readjustment of lifestyle to take the children's needs and activities into account. Consequently, parenting may have negative effects on marriage. Studies have shown that the birth of children may hurt a couple's affectional and sexual relationship, due largely to frequent interruptions, a loss of privacy, and increased demands on time and energy. The birth of children often results in role segregation, which means that spouses engage in fewer joint activities as they attempt to fulfill their parental responsibilities (Walzer 1998).

When the Costs Outweigh the Rewards. For a small minority of adults in industrialized nations, the anticipated costs of having children outweigh the anticipated rewards, and they decide to have no children. Throughout most of the twentieth century, the proportion of childless marriages in the United States was only 5 to 10 percent. The rates of childlessness increased in the last decades of the century, however. In the late 1990s, nearly one in every five American women aged 40 to 44 (considered the final years of the childbearing period in women) was childless (U.S. Bureau of the Census 1995, 1999).

The individuals with the highest education in our society are the ones least likely to have children, because they experience the highest opportunity costs associated with childbearing and child rearing. In the United States, middle-aged women with graduate degrees are three times more likely than those who drop out of high school to be childless. Two-income couples who earn more than $75,000 are much more likely than those who make less than $20,000 to be childless (Longman 1998).

Adults who choose to remain childless may believe that having children would interfere with their ability to achieve in their careers or in other types of public service. They may feel that caring for children would drain away the time and energy that could be devoted to other highly valued pursuits. Another important consideration for such adults is the expectation that the commitment to parenthood would reduce the time available to devote to their marriage. To voluntarily childless couples, marriage rather than children may be the primary source of affection and sense of belonging.

THE CHANGING RESPONSIBILITIES OF PARENTS

Views of children and childhood, and of parental responsibilities, have changed over the centuries. For most of human history, simple physical survival of children was the dominant issue in child rearing. Prior to the seventeenth century, parental love was rarely identified by child-rearing experts as a critical factor in the development of a child. In medieval societies, there was no recognition of any characteristics that distinguished children from adults; children merged naturally into adult society from about the age of 7. There were no boundaries separating the adult world from the world of children (Cunningham 1995). It wasn't until the sixteenth century that childhood was viewed as a period of innocence. Children were idolized and valued as a source of amusement or escape for adults. Later in the sixteenth century, and carrying over into the seventeenth and eighteenth centuries, childhood began to be seen as a time of immaturity and children were believed to need discipline and guidance as they prepared for adulthood. Parents were expected to provide physical care, consistent discipline, and a model for proper behavior.

At the close of the nineteenth century, during the Victorian age, awareness of the vulnerability of children and a belief in the sacredness of childhood emerged. Compulsory schooling, which removed children from the labor force, was introduced and drew a sharp line between childhood and adulthood. Once children were regarded as different from—and inferior to—adults, they became dependent on older persons for survival (Shehan 1999). In some segments of American society today, there is a belief that parents alone can—and should—meet all their children's needs. Parents are responsible not only for their children's physical well-being but also for their psychological adjustment. Often, flaws in a person's adjustment are traced to a lack of parental love or some other parental shortcoming.

The Mother Role. To many people, parenting is synonymous with mothering, and mothering is believed by many to be an instinct found in all women. While scientists have yet to find an instinctual motive for motherhood among humans, they have demonstrated a strong learned need among women to have children. Most women, given the choice to become mothers, would choose to do so, and most women who are already mothers would choose the role again (Genevie and Margolies 1987).

The belief that motherhood is necessary for women's fulfillment and for the normal healthy development of children has waxed and waned throughout our history, largely in response to economic conditions. When women's labor is not needed outside the home, the mother role is glorified and exalted; when women's labor is essential to the economy, the importance of the mother-child bond is downplayed (Margolis 1984). Earlier in our history, when our economy was agrarian, parenting was more of a joint venture. Child rearing was shared among a larger number of adults and the mother-child bond was not regarded as primary. Only after industrialization and urbanization changed the nature of work and family life did the role of mother in child development become preeminent. As will be discussed below, similar changes are under way in regard to the father role.

The Father Role. While the verb *to mother* is used to refer to the nurturance and care given to children, usually by women, the verb *to father* has a much more restricted meaning. To many, this simply refers to the male role in procreation. The responsibilities attached to the father role have traditionally been economic. To be a good father, a man had to be a good provider. Participation in the daily custodial care of the child was not expected, nor was companionship or nurturance. In recent decades, with the entrance of large numbers of mothers into the labor force, the expectations attached to the father role have begun to change. Men can no longer be good fathers simply by being good providers. They must also participate more fully in the daily care of their children and in the socialization process (Griswold 1993).

It appears that these expectations are being reflected in changed behavior. More fathers are attending childbirth education classes with their wives and are present at the births of their children, and the average amount of time men spend with their children has increased since the early 1970s. These changes support the argument that men are psychologically capable of participating in all parenting behaviors. Perhaps the most telling evidence of the extent to which Americans' ideas about the father role have changed since the 1940s can be found in the expert advice on parenting. In the first edition of his classic book about child care, which was published in 1945, Dr. Benjamin Spock reminded fathers that they need not be as involved in child care as mothers, at most preparing a bottle for the baby on Sundays. By the

1980s, Dr. Spock was admonishing fathers to take on half of all child care and housework tasks.

TRANSITION TO PARENTHOOD

Some sociological studies have found that many couples experience the birth of their first child as a crisis. The changes brought about by the addition of a baby to a household are indeed extensive. Occupational commitments, particularly of the mother, may be reduced, and family economics must be reorganized as spending increases and earnings are reduced. Household space must be reallocated to accommodate the infant's lifestyle. The parents' time and attention must be redirected toward the infant. Relationships with kin, neighbors, and friends must be redefined to include the baby's schedule. The marital relationship itself may be disrupted due to the enormous demands for time, energy, and attention made by the baby. As a result, new mothers frequently report unexpected fatigue, confinement to the home and a sharp reduction in social contacts, and the loss of the satisfaction that accompanied outside employment. New fathers may feel added economic pressure (Walzer 1998).

The severity of the crisis experienced by new parents does not seem to be related to the quality of the marital relationship before the birth of the child or to the degree to which the child was planned and wanted. Instead, it may be the degree to which the parents had romanticized parenthood in conjunction with their lack of preparation for the role that leads to a feeling of crisis. As a result of the tremendous changes brought about by the presence of children and the burdens associated with child rearing, marital satisfaction appears to decline sharply around the time of the first child's birth and to remain low until children leave the home (Shehan and Kammeyer 1997, pp. 213–214).

PARENTING IN THE MIDDLE YEARS

During the twentieth century, there was a steady increase in the number of young adults who returned to their parents' homes to live. When children return home to live with their parents, there are both advantages and disadvantages. Many of the problems are caused by the ambiguity of the situation. Parents may wonder whether they should establish and enforce rules governing their children's behavior (e.g., curfews, financial obligations, use of drugs and alcohol, and guests). Both parents and their young adult children are likely to revert to the roles they played when the children were adolescents. Young adults may revert to being emotionally, physically, and financially dependent on their parents but may find it stressful being "adult teenagers." Parents, too, are likely to feel stress when their young adult children return home to live. They are often forced to make major changes in their daily routines, and to take on unwanted burdens such as extra cooking, cleaning, and laundry when children return home. There can also be financial strains for the parents, associated with larger food bills and greater utilities costs. Conflicts between parents and their adult children may arise simply because of crowded household conditions. When adult children bring their furniture, sports equipment, pets, and clothing back home, the "empty nest" can become a "cluttered nest." But in spite of the problems that can arise when young adults live with their parents, both groups typically feel that the situation has many benefits (Shehan and Kammeyer 1997, pp. 260–265).

PARENTING IN THE LATER YEARS OF LIFE

The rewards of parenting can persist throughout life. Continued attachment to their children helps to minimize elderly parents' sense of isolation and loneliness. Children's readiness to take care of parents' needs helps to build a sense of security in old age and is important in day-to-day survival. However, elderly parents also want to continue to help their children. Their contributions to their adult children occur in many forms, from providing financial assistance to help with housework and care of grandchildren. Elderly persons derive a great sense of pride and satisfaction from their parental role, even when their sons and daughters are middle-aged adults with children of their own. Being recognized by their children for their value and competence as parents helps them to maintain high levels of self-esteem. When adult children provide aid and assistance to their elderly parents—especially if they take a condescending attitude toward their parents and make all decisions for them—the latter may find it demoralizing. The ideal situation is one where elderly parents and their adult children help each other and make decisions together. All things considered, the relationships between elderly parents and their adult children are very positive (Shehan and Kammeyer 1997, pp. 273–275).

(SEE ALSO: *American Families; Family Roles; Fertility; Socialization*)

REFERENCES

Cunningham, Hugh 1995 *Children and Childhood in Western Society since 1500*. London: Longman.

Gauthier, Anne Helene 1999 *The State and the Family: A Comparative Analysis of Family Policies in Industrialized Countries*. Oxford: Clarendon Press.

Genevie, Lou, and Eva Margolies 1987 *The Motherhood Report: How Women Feel about Being Mothers*. New York: Macmillan.

Griswold, Robert L. 1993 *Fatherhood in America: A History*. New York: Basic Books.

Longman, Phillip J. 1998 "The Cost of Children." *U.S. News and World Report* 124 (March 30):50–57.

Margolis, Maxine L. 1984 *Mothers and Such: Views of American Women and How They've Changed*. Berkeley: University of California Press.

Schoen, Robert 1997 "Why Do Americans Want Children?" *Population and Development Review* 23(2):333–359.

Shehan, Constance L. 1999 "No Longer Place for Innocence: The Re-Submergence of Childhood in Postindustrial Societies." In Constance Shehan, ed., *Through the Eyes of the Child: Re-Visioning Children as Active Agents of Family Life*, vol. 1 in *Contemporary Perspectives on Family Research*. Stanford, Conn.: JAI.

——, and Kenneth C. W. Kammeyer 1997 *Marriages and Families: Reflections of a Gendered Society*. Needham Heights, Mass.: Allyn and Bacon.

Shehan, Constance L., and Karen Seccombe 1996 "The Changing Social Circumstances of Children's Lives." *Journal of Family Issues* 17(4):435–440.

U.S. Bureau of the Census 1995 *Fertility of American Women: June 1995*, P-20-499.

—— 1999 *Census Bureau Facts for Features* (CB99-FF.07), Mother's Day 1999, released on April 29.

Walzer, Susan 1998 *Thinking about the Baby: Gender and Transitions into Parenthood*. Philadelphia: Temple University Press.

CONSTANCE L. SHEHAN

PARTICIPANT OBSERVATION

See Ethnography; Qualitative Methods; Sociocultural Anthropology.

PARTICIPATORY RESEARCH

Participatory research integrates scientific investigation with education and political action. Researchers work with members of a community to understand and resolve community problems, to empower community members, and to democratize research. The methods of participatory research include group discussions of personal experience, interviews, surveys, and analysis of public documents. Topics that have been investigated with this approach include community issues such as polluted water supplies and the school curriculum, employment issues such as working conditions and unionization, and theoretical issues about consent and resistance to domination. For social scientists who question the traditions of being detached and value-free, and who seek an approach that is less hierarchical and that serves the interests of those with little power, participatory research is a valuable alternative.

Participatory research can be identified by five characteristics: (1) participation by the people being studied; (2) inclusion of popular knowledge; (3) a focus on power and empowerment; (4) consciousness raising and education of the participants; and (5) political action. A precise definition should be avoided so that each group that does participatory research can be free to develop some of its own methods.

Participation in the research process by the people being studied is best viewed as a continuum that includes low levels of participation, such as asking people who are interviewed to read and comment on the transcripts of their interviews, as well as high levels of participation. Ideally, community members have a significant degree of participation *and control*, and help to determine the major questions and overall design of the study.

Second, participatory research validates popular knowledge, personal experience and feelings, and artistic and spiritual expressions as useful ways of knowing. If researchers are to work with community members as co-investigators, they must respect people's knowledge. Moreover, one of the rationales for community participation in research is the assumption that people understand many aspects of their situation better than outsiders do. Practitioners have used group discussions, photography, theater, and traditional tales to draw on popular knowledge (Barndt 1980; Luttrell 1988).

A focus on power and empowerment also distinguishes most participatory research. "The core issue in participatory research is power. . . the transformation of power structures and relationships as well as the empowerment of oppressed people," states Patricia Maguire in her excellent analysis of the field (1987, p. 37). Participatory researchers differ widely in their positions on empowerment, and include radicals who try to transform the power structure by mobilizing peasants to wrest land from the ruling class, as well as conservatives who ignore power relations and focus on limited improvements such as building a clinic or a collective irrigation system.

The fourth characteristic of participatory research—consciousness raising and education—is closely related to power. Group discussions and projects typically attempt to reduce participants' feelings of self-blame and incompetence, and try to relate personal problems to unequal distributions of power in the community and the society. Participants often become visibly more confident and effective as they speak out in discussions, learn that others share some of their experiences, and learn research skills and relevant technical information.

Finally, participatory research includes political action, especially action that cultivates "critical consciousness" and is oriented toward structural change, not toward adjusting people to oppressive environments (Brown and Tandon 1983). Some scholars argue that "real" participatory research must include actions that radically reduce inequality and produce "social transformation." Research and action, from this perspective, should be guided by a general theory like Marxism to help identify the underlying causes of inequality and the best strategies for changing society. Others

caution against expecting to achieve radical changes because "social transformation requires . . . organizing, mobilizing, struggle" as well as knowledge (Tandon 1988, p. 12). These researchers point to the value of small collective actions in educating people about the local power structure, creating greater solidarity and feelings of power, and providing new knowledge about how power is maintained and challenged. Many projects include little or no collective action and are limited to changing the behavior of individual participants, strengthening or "creating a community network" and "fostering critical knowledge" (Park 1978, p. 20).

In some cases, participatory research produces major changes, as exemplified by a project with residents of a small town in the state of Washington. The town was going to be destroyed by the expansion of a dam, and the U.S. Army Corps of Engineers was planning to disperse the community. But with the assistance of Professor Russell Fox and numerous undergraduates from Evergreen State College, residents clarified their own goals for a new community, learned about the planning process, and produced a town-sponsored plan for a new town. Their plan was accepted by the Corps of Engineers after prolonged struggle involving the courts and the U.S. Congress. The new town thrived and continued to involve the entire community in planning decisions (Comstock and Fox 1982).

A study of the working conditions of bus drivers in Leeds, England, illustrates the mixed results that are more typical of participatory research. As a result of greater pressure at work accompanying Prime Minister Margaret Thatcher's program of deregulation, bus drivers were experiencing increasing stress, accidents, and conflicts at home (Forrester and Ward 1989). With the help of professors from the University of Leeds who were running an adult education program for workers, a group of eight bus drivers, selected by their local union, decided to do research that would investigate stress at work and motivate the drivers' union to take action. They designed and carried out a survey of a sample of drivers and their families, studied accident records, and measured physical signs of stress. Although the report presenting their findings failed to produce the desired action by the union, the project was successful in many other ways—workers' stress became part of the agenda for the union and the national government, and the report was used by workers in other countries to document the need for improved working conditions. The participants in the research gained research skills and knowledge about work stress, and the professors produced academic papers on work stress and participatory research. The professors had a dual accountability (as they put it) both to the bus workers and to the university; their projects produced results that were valuable to both groups.

THE HISTORY OF THE FIELD AND RELATIONS TO OTHER FIELDS

Participatory research was developed primarily by Third World researchers, and most projects have been in Third World communities. In the 1970s it became clear that mainstream economic development projects were failing to reduce poverty and inequality. In response, researchers began to develop alternative approaches that increased the participation of the poor in development programs and aimed at empowering poor rural and urban communities as well as improving their standard of living (Huizer 1979; Tandon 1981, 1988). For example, in the Jipemoyo Project in Tanzania, researchers and villagers investigated traditional music and dance practices and developed cooperative, small-scale industries based on these traditions, such as the production of "selo drums" for sale in urban areas (Kassam and Mustafa 1982). In other projects, peasants and farmers participated with agricultural and social scientists to determine the most appropriate and productive farming methods. Several projects in Latin America, led by Orlando Fals Borda and labeled "participatory action research," integrated the knowledge of peasant activists and academics to build rural organizations and social movements.

Participatory researchers in the Third World are closely associated with Paulo Freire, an exiled Brazilian educator with roots in Marxism and critical theory. His book *Pedagogy of the Oppressed* is the most influential work in participatory research. Freire argues that teaching and research should not be dominated by experts but should be based on dialogue with a community of oppressed people. Through dialogue and collective action, people can develop critical consciousness, learn the skills they need to improve their situation, and liberate themselves. A similar approach has been developed by the influential Highlander Research and Education Center in the southern United States. Organized by Myles Horton and others in the 1930s, Highlander has inspired many participatory researchers with its success in educating and empowering poor rural people (Gaventa and Horton 1981; Gaventa et al. 1990). Another important center of participatory research has been the Participatory Research Network in Toronto, focusing on adult education (Hall 1975, 1981).

The development of participatory research in the 1970s was also fostered by challenges to positivist social science by feminists, Marxists, critical theorists, and others (Bernstein 1983; Harding 1986). The critics emphasized the links between knowledge and power. They argued that the positivists' emphasis on objectivity, detachment, and valuefree inquiry often masked a hidden conservative political agenda, and encouraged research that justified domination by experts and elites and devalued oppressed people. The critics proposed alternative paradigms that integrated research and theory with political action, and gave the people being studied more power over the research (Carr and Kemmis 1986; Lather 1986; Rose 1983).

The development of alternative paradigms, together with the emergence of participatory research in the Third World and the politicial activism accompanying social movements of the 1960s and 1970s, sparked a variety of participatory research projects by North American social scientists. John Gaventa investigated political and economic oppression in Appalachian communities, and grass-roots efforts to challenge the status quo, and Peter Park criticized mainstream sociology from the perspective of participatory research and critical theory. Health-related issues such as wifebattering, health collectives, and toxic wastes were studied by Patricia Maguire and others, while researchers in education examined community efforts to improve public schools and participatory methods of teaching (Luttrell 1988). Issues at the workplace such as struggles for unionization have been investigated by many participatory researchers; they have documented the impact of factors such as ethnic divisions and women's work culture on the success of unionization (Bookman and Morgen 1988).

Participatory research is closely related to several other fields. Feminist approaches to research and teaching often closely resemble participatory research and emphasize nonhierarchical relations between researcher and researched, raising consciousness, taking action against sexism and other forms of domination, and valuing expressive forms of knowledge (see Smith 1987; Stanley and Wise 1983). Feminists have done the majority of the participatory research projects in North America, but they do not use the label, and feminists and participatory researchers rarely consult each other's work.

A similar approach has been developed by William F. Whyte, who works with representatives of managment and workers to study organizational problems such as reducing production costs, or redesigning training programs. His approach differs from participatory research in that it gives little attention to power and empowerment, or to consciousness raising and education, and the action component of the projects is coordinated with management and does not directly challenge the existing power structure. Whyte labels his approach "participatory action research," which will cause confusion since the same term is used to describe Orlando Fals Borda's very different, more radical approach.

Participatory research also overlaps with several traditional social science methods, especially participant observation, ethnography, and intensive interviews, all of which rely on empathic interpretation of popular knowledge and everyday experience and that lead researchers to be engaged with the people being studied, not detached from them. Applied research also focuses on social action, but usually for the privileged—those with the money and sophistication to employ researchers or consultants.

ISSUES IN PARTICIPATORY RESEARCH

Two issues underlie many of the problems confronted by academic participatory researchers: the relations between researchers and the researched; and the tensions between being politically active and producing objective, academic studies.

Relations between researchers and researched are problematic at each stage of a participatory research project (on stages, see Maguire 1987; Vio Grossi 1981; Hall 1981). At the beginning of the project the researchers must consider what segments of the community will participate. Although some participatory researchers talk about "the oppressed" people in a community or "the poor" as if they were a homogeneous group, most communities are complex and internally stratified, and the more powerless people usually are more difficult to include.

The power of the researcher versus the researched also is problematic in the next stage of a project, when participants identify and discuss community problems. Researchers have specific skills in facilitating the group and obtaining information, and typically have more time, money, and other resources. Therefore, they can take more responsibility (and power) in the project, and community members often want a researcher to take charge in some areas. There are also conflicts during group discussions between validating participants' knowledge and power versus educating for critical consciousness and validating the researchers' power (Vio Grossi 1981).

When the project moves to the stage of designing research on community problems, researchers are especially likely to have a power advantage, since community members typically lack the skills and the interest to carry out this task. If community members are to be equal participants in designing a complex research project, they first need an extended educational program like the adult education classes for the Leeds bus drivers. Otherwise, the research probably will have to be fairly limited, or the researchers will control the research design, while community members participate as consultants and trained research assistants. In this case it becomes especially important that community members have substantial power in setting the research agenda (e.g., Merrifield 1989).

Conflicts between activism and involvement versus academic objectivity and detachment are another source of problems. However, many of the problems can be resolved by questioning the assumed incompatibility between being involved with the people one is studying and producing objective or valid evidence. On the one hand, involved researchers often produce valid knowledge. Sociology and anthropology include many examples of systematic, highly regarded ethnographies and interview studies by researchers who were very involved with the community. Moreover, participating as an activist probably yields just as valid an account as being a traditional participant observer. On the other hand, research methods associated with being detached, such as surveys and quantitative analysis, often contribute to effective political action. For example, a research group in Bombay organized a participatory census of pavement dwellers in a large slum. Their results documented that slum dwellers had been underenumerated by the official census and had been unjustly denied census-dependent services. Participants also created strong community organizations and learned how to use existing services (Patel 1988). In this project, community involvement and academic standards were compatible. In other projects, participatory researchers have experienced many conflicts between serving the interests of the community being researched, and producing knowledge that is valuable to the academic community.

RECENT DEVELOPMENTS

Participatory research methods have gradually spread through the social sciences and related fields in recent years. Researchers in health (Cornwall and Jewkes 1995; Mishra et. al. 1998), family sociology (Small 1995), community psychology (Stoecker and Beckwith 1992; Yeich and Levine 1992), and other fields are using participatory research methods. Several journals have devoted special issues to participatory research, including *American Sociologist* (Stoecker and Bonacich 1992, 1993), *The Journal of Social Issues* (Bryden-Miller 1997) and *Human Relations* (Chisholm and Elden 1993). New books on participatory research also have appeared (De Koning and Martin 1996; Fals-Borda and Roshman 1991; Park et al. 1993).

The growing numbers of studies using participatory research methods vary widely in the degree to which they depart from traditional social science methods. In most studies, control over the research design remains with the researcher, although the researched may have power over a limited component of the project. In addition, many studies do not include social action as part of the project. As participatory research continues to

develop, researchers will continue to struggle with balancing the power of the researcher and the researched, and with the conflicting demands of activism and academic standards.

(SEE ALSO: *Field Research Methods; Qualitative Methods; Social Movements*)

REFERENCES

Acker, Joan, Kate Berry, and Joke Esseveld 1983 "Objectivity and Truth: Problems in Doing Feminist Research." *Women's Studies International Forum* 6:423–435.

Barndt, Deborah 1980 *Education and Social Change: A Photographic Study of Peru.* Dubuque, Iowa: Kendal/ Hunt.

Bernstein, Richard 1983 *Beyond Objectivism and Relativism.* Philadelphia: University of Pennsylvania Press.

Bookman, Ann, and Sandra Morgen (eds.) 1988 *Women and the Politics of Empowerment.* Philadelphia: Temple University Press.

Bredo, Eric, and Walter Feinberg (eds.) 1982 *Knowledge and Values in Social and Educational Research.* Philadelphia: Temple University Press.

Brown, L. David, and Rajesh Tandon 1983 "The Ideology and Political Economy of Inquiry: Action Research and Participatory Research." *Journal of Applied Behavioral Science and Technology: An International Perspective* 19:277–294.

Brydon-Miller, Mary, and Deborah Tolman (eds.) 1997 *Journal of Social Issues* 53(4):597–827. Special Issue on Transforming Psychology: Interpretive and Participatory Research Methods.

Carr, Wilfred, and Stephen Kemmis 1986 *Becoming Critical: Education, Knowledge and Action Research.* London: Falmer.

Chisholm, R. G., and M. Elden (eds.) 1993 *Human Relations* 46(2):121–298. Special Issue: Action Research.

Comstock, Donald, and Russell Fox 1982 "Participatory Research as Critical Theory: North Bonneville U.S.A. Experience." Paper presented at 10th World Congress of Sociology, Mexico City. (Available from Russell Fox, Evergreen State College, Olympia, Wash. 98505.)

Cornwall, Andrea, and Rachel Jewkes 1995 "What Is Participatory Research?" *Social Science and Medicine* 41:1667–1677.

De Koning, Korrie, and Marion Martin (eds.) 1996 *Participatory Research in Health.* London: Zed.

Fals Borda, Orlando 1988 *Knowledge and People's Power: Lessons with Peasants: Nicaragua, Mexico and Colombia.* New York: New Horizons.

——, and Mohammed Roshman (eds.) 1991 *Action and Knowledge: Breaking the Monopoly with Participatory Action Research.* New York: Apex.

Forrester, Keith, and Kevin Ward 1989 "The Potential and Limitations: Participatory Research in a University Context." Participatory Research Conference Case Study, Division of International Development, International Centre, Calgary, Alberta.

Freire, Paulo 1970 *Pedagogy of the Oppressed.* New York: Continuum.

Gaventa, John 1980 *Power and Powerlessness: Quiescence and Rebellion in an Appalachian Valley.* Urbana: University of Illinois Press.

—— 1988 "Participatory Research in North America." *Convergence* 21:19–29.

——, and Billy Horton 1981 "A Citizen's Research Project in Appalachia, U.S.A." *Convergence* 14:30–40.

——, Barbara Smith, and Alex Willingham (eds.) 1990 *Communities in Economic Crisis.* Philadelphia: Temple University Press.

Hall, Bud 1975 "Participatory Research: An Approach for Change." *Prospects* 8:24–31.

—— 1981 "The Democratization of Research in Adult and Non-Formal Education." In P. Reason and J. Rowan, eds., *Human Inquiry.* New York: John Wiley.

Harding, Sandra 1986 *The Science Question in Feminism.* Ithaca, N.Y.: Cornell University Press.

Huizer, Gerrit, and Bruce Mannheim (eds.) 1979 *The Politics of Anthropology: From Colonialism and Sexism Toward a View from Below.* Paris: Mouton.

Kassam, Yusuf, and Mustafa Kemal (eds.) 1982 *Participatory Research: An Emerging Alternative Methodology in Social Science Research.* New Delhi: Society for Participatory Research in Asia.

Lather, Patti 1986 "Research as Praxis." *Harvard Educational Review* 56:257–277.

Luttrell, Wendy 1988 *Claiming What Is Ours: An Economics Experience Workbook.* New Market, Tenn.: Highlander Research and Education Center.

Maguire, Patricia 1987 *Doing Participatory Research: A Feminist Approach.* Amherst: Center for International Education, School of Education, University of Massachusetts.

Merrifield, Juliet 1989 "Putting the Scientists in Their Place: Participatory Research in Environmental and Occupational Health." *Highlander Center Working Paper* New Market, Tenn.: Highlander Research and Education Center.

Mies, Maria 1983 "Towards a Methodology for Feminist Research." In G. Bowles and R. Klein, eds., *Theories of Women's Studies.* London: Routledge and Kegan Paul.

Mishra, Shirz, Leo Chavez, J. Raul Magana, Patricia Nava, R. Burciaga Valdez, and F. Allan Hubbell 1998 "Improving Breast Cancer Control among Latinas: Evaluation of a Theory-Based Educational Program." *Health Education and Behavior* 25:653–670.

Park, Peter 1978 "Social Research and Radical Change." Presentation at 9th World Congress of Sociology, Uppsala, Sweden.

——, Mary Brydon-Miller, Budd Hall, and Edward T. Jackson (eds.) 1993 *Voices for Change: Participatory Research in the U.S. and Canada.* Westport, Conn.: Greenwood.

——, Budd Hall, and Ted Jackson (eds.) Forthcoming *Knowledge, Action and Power: An Introduction to Participatory Research.* South Hadley, Mass.: Bergin and Garvey.

Participatory Research Network 1982 *Participatory Research: An Introduction.* New Delhi: Society for Participatory Research in Asia.

Patel, Sheela 1988 "Enumeration as a Tool for Mass Mobilization: Dharavi Census." *Convergence* 21:120–135.

Rose, Hilary 1983 "Hand, Brain and Heart: A Feminist Epistemology for the Natural Sciences." *Signs: Journal of Women in Culture and Society* 9:73–94.

Shor, Ira (ed.) 1987 *Freire for the Classroom: A Sourcebook.* Portsmouth, N.H.: Heinemann.

Small, Stephen A. 1995 "Action-Oriented Research: Models and Methods." *Journal of Marriage and the Family* 57:941–956.

Smith, Dorothy 1987 *The Everyday World as Problematic: A Feminist Sociology.* Boston: Northeastern University Press.

Stanley, Liz, and Sue Wise 1983 *Breaking Out: Feminist Consciousness and Feminist Research.* London: Routledge and Kegan Paul.

Stoecker, Randy, and David Beckwith 1992 "Advancing Toledo's Neighborhood Movement through Participatory Action Research: Integrating Activist and Academic Approaches." *Clinical Sociology Review* 10:198–213.

Stoecker, Randy, and Edna Bonacich (eds.) 1992, 1993 *American Sociologist.* Special Issues on Participatory Research, Part I, 23 no. 4 (Winter 1992); Part II, 24, no. 1 (Spring 1993).

Tandon, Rajesh 1981 "Participatory Research in the Empowerment of People." *Convergence* 14:20–29.

—— 1988 "Social Transformation and Participatory Research." *Convergence* 21:5–18.

Vio Grossi, Francisco 1981 "Socio-Political Implications of Participatory Research." *Convergence* 14:43–51.

Whyte, William F. 1989 "Advancing Scientific Knowledge through Participatory Action Research." *Sociological Forum* 4:367–386.

Yeich, S., and R. Levine 1992 "Participatory Research's Contribution to a Conceptualization of Empowerment." *Journal of Applied Social Psychology* 22:1894–1908.

FRANCESCA M. CANCIAN
CATHLEEN ARMSTEAD

PEACE

Humans have always prized and sought peace. The conditions believed to foster peace and the very conception of peace, however, have varied in different periods and cultures. In this article, we examine contemporary scholarly understandings of peace and how to achieve and maintain peace (Barash 1991; Galtung 1996; Stephenson 1994). In particular, we discuss the views of American sociologists and other social scientists who regard themselves as engaged in peace studies, peace research, conflict resolution, and related fields.

The concept of peace is contested. Some analysts use the term "peace" in opposition to war; this is *negative peace*, defined as the absence of direct physical violence. Other analysts stress *positive peace*, defined as social relations marked by considerable equality in life chances, by justice, or even by harmony. Some writers use the term "peace" to refer only to relations among global actors in a world system, while others include relations among persons and groups as well as among countries. Finally, some observers regard peace as a stable condition and others think of it as many never-ending processes.

In this article, we discuss certain aspects of positive peace, while focusing on negative peace. Furthermore, we emphasize international peace, but also consider large-scale relations within societies. With these focuses, we examine three categories of peace processes: (1) *building peace*, developing processes that prevent the emergence of destructive conflicts; (2) *making peace*, developing processes that contribute to deescalation and settlement of conflicts; and (3) *keeping and restoring peace*, fostering processes that help maintain peace and construct equitable relations.

BUILDING PEACE

The analysts providing the research and theorizing examined here and in the next sections vary in the relative importance they give to variables and conditions from different sources: from within one or more of the contending parties, from the relationship among them, and from their social context. Each is discussed in turn.

Internal Factors. Considerable work has been done about the processes and the conditions within countries that contribute to international peace or war and within large-scale groups that contribute to societal peace or destructive conflict. One such body of work stresses the role of self-serving elites in arousing, sustaining, and exacerbating antagonisms against other countries or groups. For example, during the years of the Cold War, many observers analyzed the existence and effects of a political–military–industrial complex in promoting the arms buildup in the United States and in the Soviet Union (Mills 1956; Sanders 1983).

More recently, peace workers have been directing their attention to political and intellectual elites who develop and promote ethno-nationalist ideologies. The way such ideologies are based on a socially constructed history and shared community is the subject of considerable analyses (Anderson 1991). In addition, many analysts stress the contribution that such ideologies make to the emergence and exacerbation of bitter fights and of genocide (Anthony Smith 1991). Finally, observers often examine how military, political, and intellectual leaders promote such ideologies for their personal benefit.

Peace workers believe that analyzing such processes demystifies them and their products. Furthermore, they believe that such unmasking undermines the effectiveness of those seeking to mobilize followers to wage struggles that deny legitimacy to their opponents. This kind of critical analysis is a major form of peace research.

Another large body of writing about building peace examines the education and socialization of members of a society or group in ways that promote peace. This includes research and theorizing about the ways this has been done and about the ways that it might be done. The feminist scholarly perspective is an influential source for important contributions to this body of work. For example, using this perspective, the invisibility of women in studies of conflicts and peace processes becomes apparent, and feminist scholars provide new insights into international and domestic conflicts by paying attention to the roles women play in such conflicts (Enloe 1989). Furthermore, considerable research demonstrates consistent differences between women and men regarding support for the use of military means in international conflicts. The popular expectations, however, tend to exaggerate the degree to which men and women differ in their conduct in conflicts and negotiations (Stephenson 1996; Taylor and Miller 1994).

Feminist work tends to emphasize that the gender differences that do exist result significantly from past socialization of males and females into gender roles and from patriarchal social structures. Men learn to be relatively competitive and hierarchical, while women emphasize integrative relations. The feminist perspective fosters a vision that social relationships could be less patriarchal and therefore less unjust and less prone to destructive conflict than they generally have been.

How language and imagery are used to give meaning to conflicts helps frame conflicts and thus affects how they are waged. For example, analysts examine how the mass media and films contribute to an overreliance on violence and the threat of violence to wage conflicts (Gibson 1995). Such work also illuminates the processes of dehumanization of opponents in social conflicts, as well as revealing how such dehumanization contributes to the destructive escalation of struggles.

Since conflicts are inherent in social life, the role of social structure and culture in shaping how conflicts are waged is highly significant for building peace. Analysts are giving increasing attention to variations in the repertoire of methods used to conduct conflicts, including constructive ones, that are available for different people in different historical periods (Tilly 1978). Efforts to study and to train people in the methods of nonviolent action and problem-solving conflict resolution methods therefore contribute to building peace internationally and domestically (Kriesberg 1998).

Relational Factors. Several aspects of the relations among global and among societal actors

affect the likelihood that those actors will interact peacefully. One long-standing area of peace studies has been the effect of integration between societies and of sectors within societies. Integration is indicated by the high rate of exchange of goods, peoples, and ideas across societal and group lines, relative to exchanges within. Research findings support the generalization that such integration enhances mutual security and reduces the probability of countries' waging wars or threatening each other's security. Increased integration not only creates greater bonds of mutual interest and identity, but also improves communication and exchanges that parties regard as equitable. Furthermore, research on ethnic and other cleavages within societies also indicates the importance of integration, cross-cutting ties, and shared identities in preventing such cleavages from manifesting themselves in destructive conflicts (Dahrendorf 1959; Kriesberg 1998).

Considerable evidence has been reported indicating that democratic countries do not make war against each other (Gleditsch and Heegre 1997). Although the finding and particularly its interpretation are contested, the finding seems robust, given particular definitions of democracy and war. The finding may be explained by the tendency of governments in democratic societies to accord legitimacy to each other and credibility to each other's claims. Furthermore, negotiating differences may tend to be regarded as more acceptable and more skillfully practiced in democratic than in nondemocratic societies.

Contextual Factors. The social context within which possible adversaries interact certainly affects their relations. The context includes the social system within which adversaries interact, including the overall level of integration, the nature of institutional structures, the likelihood of external intervention in conflicts, and the kind of norms that are shared. The concepts of positive peace and structural violence help in understanding the relationship between social context and peace. Unlike personal violence, structural violence is indirect. It refers to the "avoidable denial of what is needed to satisfy fundamental needs" (Galtung 1980, p. 67). Thus, structural conditions may damage and cut short people's lives by restrictions of human rights or by malnutrition and illness, while other people using available knowledge and resources do not suffer the same deprivations. Such inequities are built into the global order and constitute negative peace. This influential idea has stimulated various studies, particularly regarding conditions in peripheral or underdeveloped regions. The literature about the development of the world system and of colonialism obviously bears on this matter (Chase-Dunn and Hall 1997).

The expansion in the number, scope, and size of international nongovernmental organizations (INGOs) is a subject of growing sociological attention, reflecting INGOs' increasing global importance. Many kinds of transnational organizations perform activities and are arenas for interactions that supplement or even compete with states and with international governmental organizations. INGOs include multinational corporations, religious and ideological organizations, professional and trade associations, trade union federations, and ethnic associations. These groupings provide important bases of transnational identity and action (Smith et al. 1997).

Critical analysts view these developments as part of a new global order in which a transnational elite exercises hegemonic domination. Their work stresses the increasing global inequality and the development of a transnational elite that fosters globalization and profits from it. From this perspective, the U.S. government's promotion of democracy throughout the world is a method of maintaining order while promoting free markets and capitalism. Democracy, in this context, means *polyarchy*, a system in which a small group rules and mass participation is limited to choosing leaders in managed elections (Robinson 1996, p. 49).

International and supranational governmental organizations are also taking on increasing importance; witness the peacekeeping activities of the United Nations after the Cold War. Social scientists, including sociologists, have examined the conditions in which such institutions emerge and survive, how they serve to improve the quality of life, and how they may help to prevent conflicts from erupting and escalating destructively (Etzioni 1965).

The people of the world are already highly interdependent and are becoming increasingly so. This is true at the societal and at the global level. The flow of goods, capital, labor, ideas, and information is ever faster, ever less expensive, and ever more extensive. Consequently, the people of the world share problems relating to environmental threats, governmental abuse and brutal conflicts spurring large-scale refugee flows, dislocations resulting from rapid social change, and challenging social relations among groups that are culturally different.

These phenomena contribute to the growing homogenization of the world. More and more people share images, ideas, and norms relating to consumer preferences, forms of entertainment, the protection of human rights, and economic development. But these phenomena also generate particularistic reactions and threaten destructive conflicts within and between societies. Experiences with these phenomena around the world and within each society are not the same for everyone. Some people reject the spreading secularism and the dominance of Western, particularly American, ideas and power. The empirical contradictions and the moral dilemmas arising from these developments are increasingly matters of inquiry among peace workers (Boulding 1990).

MAKING PEACE

Recent peace work has focused on limiting the destructive escalation of conflicts, fostering transitions toward deescalation, and conducting negotiations that help end conflicts constructively. Internal, relational, and contextual factors contribute to these ways of making peace.

Internal Factors. Among internal factors, sociological work attends particularly to popular forces that pressure governments to move toward accommodations with external adversaries. This interest combines with the growth in theory and research about social movements to generate many studies of peace movements (Lofland 1993; Marullo and Lofland 1990). Analyses of campaigns against nuclear weapons and other evidence indicate that, at least within the United States and western Europe, public opinion and organized public pressure have influenced governments, often in the direction of peacemaking (Joseph 1993; Klandermans 1991).

In addition, certain internal structural factors can help leaders to recognize the needs of the other side and to communicate responsiveness. Such factors may include leaders who are accorded legitimacy, openness to considering alternative courses of action, sources of good information about outside groups, and norms limiting intolerance. Such factors and specific policy-making procedures can help limit escalation, manage crises, and negotiate settlements (Wilensky 1967).

Relational Factors. Most work on peacemaking focuses on the relations between adversaries, including analyses of tacit bargaining, formal and informal negotiations, and providing mutual reassurance about security. The relationship between the United States and the Soviet Union, and their alliances during the Cold War, has been the subject of considerable study. Contributions have been made about the extent to which that conflict and the proxy wars associated with it were based on misunderstandings and on processes of dehumanization that fostered conflict escalation (Gamson and Modigliani 1971).

Other writing has drawn from and contributes to studies of problem-solving conflict resolution and conflict transformation. This work includes the analysis of ways of waging struggles constructively so that escalation is limited, and so that possibilities of reaching mutually acceptable accommodations are not foreclosed. This is an argument examined in studies of the use of nonviolent action, as in the American civil rights struggle and in many other conflicts (Powers and Vogele 1997; Wehr et al. 1994; Sharp 1973).

Work on relational aspects of peacemaking also includes analyses of conciliatory gestures and other initiatives to deescalate conflicts, of the management of crises, of the transformation of intractable conflicts into tractable ones, and of strategies and techniques for negotiating mutually acceptable agreements (Patchen 1988). It also includes the efforts by persons in one camp to exchange information and possible options for peacemaking with their counterparts in the opposing camp, through conferences, dialogue groups, and ongoing workshops.

The ending of the Cold War illustrates the success of some of these methods (Kriesberg 1992). Specifically, such methods include negotiating mutual assurances that vital interests would not be threatened, as was done in the Conference for Security and Cooperation in Europe, resulting in the Helsinki Accords, signed in 1975. Included in the Accords was a shared commitment to norms, for example, about protecting human rights, which fostered increased mutual exchanges. In addition, the American and Soviet military alliances established confidence-building measures and later restructured their military forces to be less provocative. Nonofficial channels such as the Pugwash meetings and the Dartmouth conference assisted in reaching agreements that helped to transform the Cold War. These developments have served as inspirations for efforts to limit or transform other regional conflicts.

The transformation of the conflict in South Africa about apartheid is another important illustration of the effectiveness of some of these methods (Kriesberg 1998). For example, the African National Congress (ANC), with the leadership of Nelson Mandela, consistently pursued nonracist goals, thus offering assurance that whites were and would remain recognized as South Africans. The means used in the struggle to end apartheid were considered in that light; they were initially nonviolent, and even when the decision to wage armed struggle was undertaken, terrorism was excluded. Informal and unofficial communications prepared the adversaries for working out an agreement that was acceptable to all the major adversaries in the seemingly intractable conflict in South Africa (van der Merwe 1989).

Of course, in some cases when challengers initiated nonviolent struggles, they were repressed or the conflicts escalated destructively. Such cases, as in China and in Northern Ireland, deserve and have received attention. However, there are many case studies and quantitative analyses indicating that reliance on violence and threat of violence is frequently counterproductive and often mutually destructive (Vasquez 1993).

Contextual Relations. One important aspect of a conflict's context, affecting its transformation and its peaceful settlement, is the involvement of intermediaries. Analysts using a sociological approach give attention to the role of nonofficial persons and groups as well as official intermediaries. Such intermediaries often provide a variety of mediating services, including helping bring adversaries to the negotiating table, facilitating meetings, aiding in developing new options, building support for an agreement, and helping to implement and to sustain an agreement that is reached (Burton 1990; Laue 1973). Persons and groups providing such services vary greatly in the way adversaries understand their role and in the resources they bring with them. For example, unofficial mediators with relatively few material resources may be able to provide exploratory services relatively well, since their engagement generally involves low risks for the antagonists. Mediators with a major stake in the fight and with great resources can provide compensations and assurances that are relatively important in closing negotiations and implementing them.

The U.S. government and U.S. private citizens have played important mediating roles in many international and even internal conflicts in other countries (Kriesberg 1992). American mediation in Israeli-Arab conflicts has been particularly extensive and often crucially effective. U.S. secretaries of state and U.S. presidents have conducted major mediating efforts, often using considerable resources to induce the negotiating parties to conclude an agreement and to implement it. Among the notable agreements reached are those mediated by Secretary of State Henry Kissinger in 1974 between Israel and Egypt and between Israel and Syria, and the 1978 Camp David agreements between Israel and Egypt, mediated by President Jimmy Carter and leading to the two countries' signing a peace treaty.

Nonofficial persons and groups from the United States have also provided mediation services, for example in the conflict between Israeli Jews and Palestinians. Nonofficial channels have been particularly important due to the long-standing refusal of the Israeli government to recognize the Palestine Liberation Organization (PLO) as the representative of the Palestinians. Jewish and Palestinian Americans have often had the knowledge, interest, and contacts to provide useful channels for exploring possible options and ways of taking steps toward official mediation and negotiation.

Mediation efforts, obviously, do not always succeed. Many efforts never result in agreements. In some cases, agreements are reached but not ratified or not implemented. On occasion, agreements are followed by disastrous breakdowns, as happened in Rwanda in 1994. Of course, failing to mediate probably would not have yielded better results. Nevertheless, this indicates that we need to know much more about the type of mediation that tends to be effective at each stage of various kinds of conflicts.

Among the many other relevant contextual factors, we note only a few. First, changes in prevailing norms and understandings sometimes embolden one party in a conflict and undermine the faith of its opponent. The result is that a conflict that has long persisted can move toward resolution. For example, changing views about human rights and democracy contributed to ending the civil wars in Central America and apartheid in South Africa.

The context also includes a wide range of international governmental and nongovernmental organizations, with varying capabilities of contributing to peacemaking. The mass media are also increasing the global attention to especially terrible events at particular times. Finally, the increasing availability of weapons of all kinds enables more and more people to challenge existing conditions, as well as enabling those in authority to resort to violent means of control.

KEEPING AND RESTORING PEACE

The recent transformation and settlement of protracted international and societal conflicts and the radical transformation of previously authoritarian and repressive societies have heightened attention to the challenges of building postconflict relations that are enduring and just (Lederach 1997). Changes within one or more antagonist camps and between former antagonists are crucial in meeting these challenges. In recent years, analysts have given particular attention to the role of intermediaries, standards of human rights, and other elements of the antagonists' social context.

Internal Factors. A fundamental change in ways of thinking among members of one or more antagonistic sides can be a powerful factor in producing an enduring peace between them. This does sometimes happen. For example, most Germans after the defeat of Nazism repudiated what they themselves had believed and done; instead, they welcomed beliefs, values, and institutions shared with the victors. To some extent, a similar transformation occurred among Russians as the Cold War ended. As a result of the American civil rights struggle of the 1950s and 1960s, most southern American whites became convinced that they were wrong to resist ending the Jim Crow system of discrimination. Similarly, most South African whites would now concur that the ending of apartheid was right and just.

Changes in internal social structure also are frequently crucial. Countries that have had internal conditions engendering overreliance on military means and goals that threatened vital interests of other countries may reduce their external threat only after undergoing a fundamental internal restructuring. The restructuring may entail civilian control of the military and the development of a civil society and democratic institutions. Peaceful accommodations in postconflict relations within a country may also depend upon fundamental changes in one or more sides of the past conflict. This occurs as governments change or as the leadership of an ethnic, a religious, or a class movement undergoes change.

Relational Factors. Traditionally, efforts to restore peace after a conflict ends include policies to redress the grievances that were viewed as the conflict's source. For communal differences within a country, this may entail more autonomy for citizens with different languages or religions and provisions for popular participation in determining the form and degree of autonomy. For example, during the early 1950s, the status of Puerto Rico in relationship to the rest of the United States was being reconstituted. A Puerto Rican nationalist group resorted to violence in seeking independence. The suppression of violent attacks while avoiding general repression, the availability of a legitimate electoral political process, social and economic improvements, and programs of integration and autonomy, including cultural nationalism, combined to produce a generally peaceful relationship in which alternative arrangements are contested within the established political system.

In the United States, a wide variety of methods and strategies are employed to redress grievances and increase equity; they include programs of affirmative action for women and minorities. Such programs, however, have become subject to challenge and have been reduced. This demonstrates the ongoing nature of conflicts related to socially constructed differences between citizens.

In recent years, peace workers have been giving considerable attention to fostering mutual understanding and tolerance among peoples with different cultural backgrounds living in the same society (Weiner 1998). This attention extends to reconciliation between peoples who perpetrated gross human rights violations and peoples who suffered profound losses during periods of repression or of violent struggle. Reconciliation is complex, variously combining several processes: (1) acknowledging the truth of what happened; (2) administering justice for past misdeeds, and ensuring future justice and security; (3) extending forgiveness to members of the group that committed wrongs (sometimes in response to expressions of remorse); and (4) accepting responsibility by those who committed wrongs or failed to oppose them. In postapartheid South Africa, for example, the work of the Truth and Reconciliation Commission represents one way to deal with these postconflict issues.

A variety of recent developments contribute to reconciliation among the different peoples making up the United States. The truth about discrimination, violent repression, and other injustices regarding Native Americans, African Americans, and other groups has been more frequently acknowledged; this is evident in the mass media, in scholarly work, and in governmental statements. In addition, religious and other community organizations, corporations, and local governments have promoted or provided education programs, workshops, training, and dialogue groups to help persons of different communities learn about each other's experiences and perspectives.

Furthermore, long-standing policies have been instituted to strengthen a shared identity as Americans. The conception of Americans as belonging to a single ethnic group or an assortment of people melting into a single ethnicity, however, is changing. Instead, the multicultural character of America is increasingly accepted and even celebrated.

Contextual Factors. International organizations are increasingly expected to play critical roles in keeping and restoring the peace. United Nations and other peacekeeping forces have undertaken many more such tasks since the Cold War ended. Regional organizations and individual countries, particularly the United States, have intervened to restore and sustain peace (Moskos 1976; Segal and Segal 1993). Even after an agreement ending civil strife has been reached, the continuing engagement of external governments is crucial for the survival of the agreement and its implementation (Hampson 1996).

International nongovernmental humanitarian and advocacy organizations have grown greatly and are often helpful in restoring and maintaining peace (Lederach 1997). They may support the development of civil organizations that sustain peace. Even in the postconflict reconstruction of what was Yugoslavia, some success may be found. For example, many governmental and nongovernmental activities have helped the people in Macedonia manage external threats and the dangers of internal strife.

CONCLUSIONS

Peace work and the ways of thinking about peace have greatly expanded in recent decades. Peace is increasingly understood to be multidimensional and dynamic. Consequently, the ways of promoting peace are also manifold, and they vary in different settings for different actors. Theory and research about aspects of peace and their promotion draws from and contributes to social theory and social practice.

Recent applied and scholarly peace work is based on past experience, but the realities of the current world necessitate fresh thinking and innovative practices. New approaches and ideas are developing, combining knowledge and experience from many new interdisciplinary fields, including conflict resolution, feminist studies, security studies, and international relations.

Much more work needs to be done to understand the nature of peace and how its various aspects can be promoted. Peace is not easily advanced, is never total, and is never wholly secure. Whatever peaceful gains may be made must be energetically defended against the inevitable threats arising from new challenges.

REFERENCES

Anderson, Benedict 1991 *Imagined Communities: Reflections on the Origin and Spread of Nationalism*. London: Verson.

Barash, David P. 1991 *Introduction to Peace Studies*. Belmont, Calif.: Wadsworth.

Boulding, Elise 1990 *Building a Global Civic Culture: Education for an Independent World*. Syracuse, N.Y.: Syracuse University Press.

Burton, John 1990 *Conflict: Resolution and Provention*. New York: St. Martin's.

Chase-Dunn, Christopher, and Thomas D. Hall 1997 *Rise and Demise: Comparing World-Systems*. Boulder, Colo.: Westview.

Dahrendorf, Ralf 1959 *Class and Class Conflict in Industrial Society*. Stanford, Calif.: Stanford University Press.

Enloe, Cynthia 1989 *Bananas, Beaches and Bases*. Berkeley and Los Angeles: University of California Press.

Etzioni, Amitai 1965 *Political Unification*. New York: Holt, Rinehart and Winston.

Galtung, Johan 1980 *The True Worlds: A Transnational Perspective*. New York: Free Press.

—— 1996 *Peace by Peaceful Means: Peace and Conflict, Development and Civilization*. Thousand Oaks, Calif.: Sage.

Gamson, William A., and Andre Modigliani 1971 *Untangling the Cold War*. Boston: Little, Brown.

Gibson, James William 1995 *Warrior Dreams: Violence and Manhood in Post-Vietnam America*. New York: Hill and Wang.

Gleditsch, Nils Petter, and Havard Heegre 1997 "Peace and Democracy." *Journal of Conflict Resolution* 41:283–310.

Hampson, Fen Osler 1996 *Nurturing Peace: Why Peace Settlements Succeed of Fail*. Washington, D.C.: U.S. Institute of Peace Press.

Joseph, Paul 1993 *Peace Politics: The United States between the Old and New World Orders*. Philadelphia: Temple University Press.

Klandermans, Bert (ed.) 1991 *Peace Movements in Western Europe and the United States*. Greenwich, Conn.: JAI Press.

Kriesberg, Louis 1992 *International Conflict Resolution: The US–USSR and Middle East Cases*. New Haven, Conn.: Yale University Press.

—— 1998 *Constructive Conflicts: From Escalation to Resolution*. Lanham, Md.: Rowman and Littlefield.

Laue, James 1973 "Intervenor Roles: A Review." *Crisis and Change* III:4–5.

Lederach, John Paul 1997 *Building Peace: Sustainable Reconciliation in Divided Societies*. Washington, D.C.: U.S. Institute of Peace Press.

Lofland, John 1993 *Polite Protestors: The American Peace Movement of the 1980's*. Syracuse, N.Y.: Syracuse University Press.

Marullo, Sam, and John Lofland (eds.) 1990 *Peace Action in the Eighties*. New Brunswick, N.J.: Rutgers University Press.

Mills, C. Wright 1956 *The Power Elite*. New York: Oxford University Press.

Moskos, Charles C. 1976 *Peace Soldiers*. Chicago: University of Chicago Press.

Patchen, Martin 1988 *Resolving Disputes between Nations: Coercion or Conciliation*. Durham, N.C.: Duke University Press.

Powers, Roger S., and William B. Vogele (eds.) with Christopher Kruegler and Ronald M. McCarthy, associate eds. 1997 *Protest, Power, and Change: An Encyclopedia of Nonviolent Action from ACT-Up to Women's Suffrage*. New York: Garland.

Robinson, William I. 1996 *Promoting Polyarchy: Globalization, U.S. Intervention, and Hegemony*. New York: Cambridge University Press.

Sanders, Jerry W. 1983 *Peddlers of Crisis*. Boston: South End Press.

Segal, David R., and Mady Wechsler Segal 1993 *Peacekeepers and their Wives: American Participation in the Multinational Force and Observers*. Westport, Conn.: Greenwood.

Sharp, Gene 1973 *The Politics of Nonviolent Action*. Boston: Porter Sargent.

Smith, Anthony 1991 *National Identity*. Reno: University of Nevada Press.

Smith, Jackie, Charles Chatfield, and Ron Pagnucco (eds.) 1997 *Transnational Social Movements and Global Politics: Solidarity beyond the State*. Syracuse, N.Y.: Syracuse University Press.

Stephenson, Carolyn M. 1994 "*New Approaches to International Peacemaking in the Post–Cold War World*." In Michael T. Klare, ed., *Peace and World Security Studies: A Curriculum Guide*. Boulder, Colo.: Lynne Reinner.

—— 1996 "Gender Differences in Conflict Resolution." In *Report of the Expert Group Meeting on Political Decision-Making and Conflict Resolution: The Impact of Gender Difference*. Santo Domingo, Dominican Republic: United Nations Division for the Advancement of Women (EGM/PDCR/1996/rep.1).

Taylor, Anita, and Judi Beinstein Miller (eds.) 1994 *Conflict and Gender*. Cresskill, N.J.: Hampton Press.

Tilly, Charles 1978 *From Mobilization to Revolution*. Reading, Mass.: Addison-Wesley.

van der Merwe, Hendrik 1989 *Pursuing Justice and Peace in South Africa*. New York: Routledge.

Vasquez, John A. 1993 *The War Puzzle*. Cambridge: Cambridge University Press.

Wehr, Paul, Heidi Burgess, and Guy Burgess (eds.) 1994 *Justice without Violence*. Boulder, Colo.: Lynne Rienner.

Weiner, Eugene (ed.) 1998 *The Handbook of Interethnic Coexistence*. New York: Continuum.

Wilensky, Harold L. 1967 *Organizational Intelligence: Knowledge and Policy in Government and Industry*. New York: Basic Books.

LOUIS KRIESBERG

PENOLOGY

Penology, an applied field of sociology, is the theoretical study of prison policy, prison management, and the resulting prison culture. The sociological contributions to prison issues are applicable worldwide and offer practical solutions to problems relating to overcrowding, prison violence, and prison culture. While there is a rich European and American history of prison (e.g., Howard 1777; Beccaria 1819; Bentham 1843; Foucault 1977; Hirsh 1992), the focus here is on American prisons from the 1940s to the commencement of the twenty-first century. The following discussion begins with major sociological analyses of prison and concludes with changes in American prison policy over the past fifty years.

With a few exceptions (e.g., Goffman 1966), prison sociology has traditionally followed some variety of structural analysis. This theoretical perspective is concerned with a societal member's values, attitudes, roles, activities, and relationships that are assumed to be significantly influenced by the organization and structure of the member's environment. There are two broad types of this perspective that have been utilized in prison analysis; both focus on the structural components of prison and the members of that system. The first type, structural functionalism, focuses on how these components affect order in prison. The second type, conflict theory, focuses on how the structural components of prison and the larger society create conflict in prison.

THEORETICAL ANALYSIS

Structural Functionalism. Clemmer's *The Prison Community* (1940) is an early form of structural functional analysis. Based on interviews with staff and inmates, Clemmer's exploratory study is an ethnography of prison. This pioneering work set forth the argument that administrative policy (i.e., authoritative control over inmates, or the lack of control over inmates) influenced inmate subculture. This subculture included behavior, rules, and attitudes. Inmates could be unruly, and could prey on each other and staff if control was lacking.

This behavior would disrupt prison order and inmate adjustment to prison life. The prison administration would attempt to reestablish order by increasing control efforts, and inmates would counter these efforts through a process of "prisonization." "Prisonization" was a socialization process through which seasoned inmates inducted new inmates into the inmate subculture. The content of this socialization for new inmates included the learning of negative attitudes toward work, government, family, and inmate groups other than their own. Inmate behavior would become resistant, obstructive, and subterfugal. Clemmer saw this "prisonization" and the resultant inmate subculture as unfortunate and unintended consequences of the administrative controls. He believed the negativism and hostility perpetuated by the inmate subculture was disruptive to the inmates' reform and was "a stronger force for evil than the programs are for good" (Clemmer 1940, p. xiii).

Sykes's *The Society of Captives* (1958) was a qualitative, exploratory, and ex post facto study that also applied a structural functional analysis. Attempting to determine the cause of a series of prison riots, Sykes studied institutional records and interviewed correctional officers, civilian work supervisors, and inmates. Sykes found the cause of the prison disequilibrium to be rooted in the prison structure and values that followed from a policy of control. He argued that management's major task was to control the inmates, but the prison's system of power was flawed with structural weaknesses that left administrators serious difficulties in imposing their control regime on the inmates. These structural weaknesses involved the inmates' lack of a sense of duty to obey correctional officers, and the correctional officers' lack of legitimate rewards and punishments, with which they could encourage inmate submission.

Power based on authority, Sykes claimed, has two essential elements: the legitimacy of control efforts and a sense of duty to obey by those who are controlled (1958, pp. 46–47). He found the latter to be present down to the correctional officer level at the New Jersey State Prison, which operated under a traditional organizational hierarchy. The sense of duty to obey disappeared,

however, when the control efforts were applied to inmates. The correctional officers had to make deals (i.e., giving correctional officer duties to trusted inmates in exchange for their help in preventing trouble) and compromises (i.e., overlooking rule violations) with inmates to achieve compliance and order. Sykes argues that correctional officer corruption (i.e., reciprocity) could not be eliminated by replacing the correctional officers. New correctional officers were aggressively pressured by the inmates (i.e., threats of riots, blackmailing staff) until they, too, compromised the rules and regulations.

The problem was a weakness of the prison system. "The effort of the custodians to 'tighten up' the prison undermines the cohesive forces at work in the inmate population and it is these forces which play a critical part in keeping the society of the prison on an even keel" (Sykes 1958, p. 124). The cohesive forces are the less violent and more stable inmates who are given illicit privileges in exchange for their help in encouraging inmate cohesiveness and prison equilibrium. If the prison officials strip these inmates of their power (tighten up), the more violent and less stable inmates rise to power.

In addition to providing the structural functional analysis described above, Sykes argued that the result of imprisonment on inmate values, attitudes, and behaviors is a product of the patterns of interaction the inmate experiences on a daily basis (1958, p. 134). For example, inmates feel helpless and frustrated when staff refuse to explain bureaucratic decisions. Sykes described the hardships of imprisonment (i.e., rejection, degradation, deprivation, alienation, and lack of safety) felt by the inmates, and he acknowledged that "Somehow the imprisoned criminal must find a device for rejecting his rejectors, if he is to endure psychologically" (1958, p. 67). Sykes also depicted the correctional officers' work environment as dangerous and tense. He reported that the correctional officers were heavily outnumbered in a potentially violent setting, and were often frustrated by the administrative pressure to maintain order while they lacked unconditional compliance from the inmates.

The Prison: Studies in Institutional Organization and Change by Cressey (1961) and *Theoretical Studies in Social Organization of the Prison*, by Cloward and colleagues (1960) were also structural functional analyses. Both studies depicted prisons as authoritarian systems governed by bureaucratic hierarchy and empowered to control inmates. They described how the control policy in prison affects the power structure which, in turn, influences communication and values (i.e., staff pursuit of power over inmates, inmate restraint from talking to staff). Cressey (1961) found that two different prison policies, one emphasizing custody and the other treatment, had different hierarchies with contradictory purposes. The two hierarchies, with different models of decision making, one authoritative and the other participatory, had to increase their efforts to communicate with each other to facilitate the security desired by the custody branch and the programming desired by the treatment branch. It was also reported in the Cressey study (1961) that inmates and staff can work together effectively when the role expectations of their respective groups are not involved. Effective communication deteriorates when inmates and staff allow their respective group pressures to interfere with their relationships (1961, pp. 229–259).

Webb and Morris's *Prison Guards* (1978) focused on the organization of prison structure, which Clemmer (1940) had felt contributed to the maintenance of prison order (or disorder) and determined the inmates' prison experience. They focused on the correctional officers' subculture, and concluded that the officers saw maintaining security as their main function. While discipline was expressed as the means for carrying out the policy, poor prison facilities and inexperienced administrators were seen as barriers to prison order and safety.

Webb and Morris (1978) reported that the officers' major complaints about administrators were lack of communication and failure to consult the officers when decisions had to be made. This suggests that those making the decisions were distrustful of the officers' ability to participate in decision making, and preferred to monopolize power at the top. It also means that information that the officers would know best (i.e., security issues relating to certain inmates) was not being considered by those making the decisions. The correctional officers saw their safety compromised. The frustration caused by this poor communication process led to correctional officers being openly critical of the administration, and to their finding ways of undermining the administration's authority (i.e., doing no more than they were told).

Webb and Morris (1978) described how the officers developed their own protective society. The veteran correctional officers pressured the new to become "hardened" and "con-wise," and if, after six months to a year, the officers were not seen as "con-wise," then they were given the derogatory label "pro inmate." This pressure to be estranged and nonsympathetic in their attitudes toward inmates was the correctional officers' way of protecting themselves from "getting conned" or "being burned" by the inmates.

Kauffman's *Prison Officers and Their World* (1988) was another structural functional analysis of the correctional officer subculture. Correctional officers had been blamed by the central administration for the riots and inmate violence that had plagued the Massachusetts prison system in the 1970s. Based on interviews with sixty correctional officers, Kauffman describes the rite of passage that many new correctional officers went through: how the recruits were assigned the high-inmate-contact positions in cellblocks, abandoned by the administration and veteran officers, and aggressively tested by the inmates. The general result of this treatment was an emotional hardening toward the inmates, and the acceptance of violence by staff as a means of controlling inmates. Kauffman concludes that the power veteran officers had over staff recruits was an unintended consequence of the lack of a clear administrative policy for bringing order to the prison system. She found that the administration was determined to find someone to blame for the rite of passage many recruits went through, rather than adopting a policy "to counter the continuing legacy of chaos and violence" (1988, p. 199).

The influence of prison policy on the structure, process, behavior, and attitudes in the prison (a focus typical of both structural perspectives) is also represented in DiIulio's *Governing Prisons* (1987). He shows how prison management problems have been addressed in Texas, California, and Michigan through the development and use of different management policies. He refers to the Texas policy as one of "control," where authority is centralized and where the use of administratively controlled inmates to control other inmates ("building tendering") prevailed until the decision in *Ruiz v. Estelle* (1980) ruled the system illegal. DiIulio claims that California has a "consensus" policy, in which each warden works to get inmate "consensus" on classification systems, there are elaborate in-service training programs for correctional officers, and there are community-related educational/vocational programs for inmates. DiIulio (1987) found that Michigan has a third alternative, which emphasizes a bureaucratic system of measuring and dispensing different levels of inmate "responsibility" and accountability. DiIulio found the quality of life for inmates inside the Michigan prisons better than what he had found in other state prisons. Staff had a difficult time accepting the responsibility model, however.

Conflict Theory. The second theoretical strand of prison sociology, conflict theory, saw tight controls on inmates as unjust and called for the sharing of power with them. Wright's *The Politics of Punishment* (1973) is the first of three works representing this second branch of structural analysis that will be reviewed here. Wright is more critical of prison operations than the structural functionalists. He thought rehabilitation was manipulative in the way that it attempted "to coerce the prisoner to conform to established authority" (1973, p. 325), and then use this conformity as the basic criterion for parole. Wright believed inmates were almost totally helpless to protect themselves against the dehumanization of "liberal" totalitarian rule he found in most prisons.

The prison administration's focus on rehabilitation was an individualistic solution that avoided and disguised the real causes of criminality. Wright claimed that it was the structural flaws in the capitalist system (i.e., unemployment and the lack of opportunities outside the prison), not individual failings, that were the problem. Wright believed that crime could be reduced, and prisons reformed, by moving the American capitalist society toward socialism. Within this context, prisons could be decentralized and not controlled by a "self-perpetuating, unrestrained bureaucracy" (1973, p. 342). The administration of punishment could be placed under public surveillance. The prison under this system would "serve the interests of the people rather than of the elite" (1973, p. 337). Wright suggests that prison management has typically held to the position that prison order can be obtained only with traditional control strategies (i.e., correctional officer power over inmates), and that the effect of these strategies has been oppressive and inhumane prison conditions.

Hawkins's *The Prison: Policy and Practice* (1976) is another critical analysis of prisons and prison management. Although Hawkins's prison experience was gained in the United Kingdom, his message was relevant to American prison practitioners and researchers. Among his claims was that correctional officers had only been superficially studied by the functional branch of sociologists, who presented them as stereotypes acting out assigned roles (1976, p. 81). Hawkins saw the correctional officers in a situation of role conflict (security versus treatment) that was due to the absence of clear job descriptions and training. The results of this conflict for the correctional officers were negative attitudes toward the administration and obstructive behavior. These results, along with the conflicting goals of imprisonment (punishment versus rehabilitation), were seen by Hawkins as impediments to prison reform. Hawkins also urged that prison evaluations should be more than just "eulogistic and imprecise descriptions of success stories" (1976, p. 178).

In his assessment of the Attica prison in New York, Hawkins also found that the relationship between correctional officers and inmates was a crucial factor in the 1971 riot. The problem was mostly structural. The officers were assigned to large blocks of inmates, rather than to small units where they could have established rapport with the inmates. In the large units the officers worked with different inmates each day, thus reducing the opportunities and motivations for staff and inmates to development mutual respect and understanding. The structural problem went further, however. Hawkins, citing a New York State Special Commission's report on Attica, reported that there were unnecessary priorities in the correctional officer recruitment policies (i.e., age, physical size, and strength were more important than skills in persuasion, leadership, and interpersonal relations).

Irwin's *Prisons in Turmoil* (1980) also represents this "conflict" branch of sociological theorizing. Irwin, an ex-felon and past leader in the prison reform movement of the 1970s, shows how American penal policy has followed changes in the economic and political conditions in the United States.

His thinking ran against the usual functionalist sociology, which explained prison policy and activity largely in terms of internal events. Irwin believed that sociologists (e.g., Clemmer 1940; Sykes 1958) who studied prison cultures were blinded by their focus on prison structure, and therefore failed to recognize the fact that when inmates enter prison, they bring their outside values with them. He also believed that if prisons are to be safe and free from malicious authoritarianism, staff and inmates should have more formal input into policy and grievance decisions.

These sociological analyses of prison were written in different phases of the development of penal policy. It is very difficult to determine whether the literature influenced the policy, or vice versa. Most likely, they shaped each other. The point of the following brief history of the development of American penal policy over the past fifty years is not to make the causal argument, but to help the reader get a sense of the changing ideologies leading to the current management model.

CHANGES IN AMERICAN PENAL POLICY

Retribution to Rehabilitation. Prisons in the United States have traditionally been centralized hierarchical organizations with authoritarian and coercive management. Policies and procedures have been formulated at the central administrative offices and passed down in military fashion to prison administrations for implementation. This is assuredly true of the management style that administered the penal philosophies of the 1950s. The decade began with a "Big House" warehousing of inmates that implemented a classical penal philosophy embracing retribution, "care," and the notion that punishment should fit the crime. The decade ended with a changed perspective on crime and punishment, emphasizing that punishment should fit the individual and the inmate should be rehabilitated. By 1958, a noncustodial treatment branch of prison management shared an uneasy coexistence with the custody branch. Three types of treatment programs (psychological, educational, and economic) were centrally administered under the rubric of the rehabilitative ideal (Irwin 1980). The idea was to treat the individual problem that "caused" the individual to commit the crime. By the end of this decade, most prison

administrators had implemented this rehabilitative model without any interference from federal and state governments.

Rehabilitation to Reintegration. The early 1960s saw variations of the rehabilitative or treatment model of the late 1950s sharing an uneasy coexistence with an authoritative management style that had traditionally maintained order and control in large prison bureaucracies. Public and prison administrative acceptance of the "rehabilitative ideal" as a penal policy was partly rooted in its advocates' view that the new scientifically based treatment model could provide a remedy for crime.

By the middle 1960s, the call for community involvement in rehabilitation was signaled in a report by the President's Commission on Law Enforcement and Administration of Justice. Advocating a shift to a policy of reintegration, the report advised that rehabilitation might be best done outside prison, and that community programs should be designed that could change both the inmate and society (U.S. President's Commission 1967, pp. 27–37). It took a few years to catch on, but in the late 1960s a number of community alternatives to prison were developed and heavily underwritten by federal revenues.

Reintegration to Retribution. This reintegration policy continued into the 1970s. Prison administrators were pressed to design reentry programs such as work and educational release, and home furloughs. But public support waned in the mid-1970s, when the "get-tough-with-criminals" and antirehabilitative mood became dominant. The second theoretical strand of prison sociology, conflict structuralism, began around this time. This orientation was influenced by the 1960s societal reaction and critical theories that denounced the 1950s conservative structural functionalism. Riots and litigation forced federal courts to scrutinize the repressive management of correctional facilities and community-based treatment programs to ensure compliance with the Eighth Amendment right to protection from cruel and unusual punishment.

If prisons were being unfair in their partiality toward manipulative rehabilitation (e.g., Wright 1973; Hawkins 1976: the liberal critique), then retribution ought to replace it as a penal goal. The mid- to late 1970s saw a readoption of the early classical policy—"let the punishment fit the crime"—rather than the rehabilitative or positivist policy of "letting the punishment fit the criminal." A different argument was that rehabilitation rarely worked (e.g., Martinson 1974: the conservative critique). Prison technologies had not successfully rehabilitated inmates despite prison administrators' repeated claims of success. The Martinson survey (1974) of 231 treatment reports in New York concluded that treatment had not worked. The publication of this survey ended any lingering hope for serious rehabilitative programming.

The "new" word in penal policy was "retribution." Though it had been criticized by many social scientists and judges since the early 1900s, in 1972 the U.S. Supreme Court offered retribution as an appropriate reason for capital punishment (*Furman v. Georgia*, 408 U.S. 238, 1972). The neoclassical doctrine generally implies deterrence as a function of punishment. Wilson and Herrstein (1985) are among those who take this position. There are others, however, who argue that retribution is the main function, and that there does not have to be any further utilitarian purpose such as deterrence. The argument these penologists make for retribution is that inmates are incarcerated because they deserve to be, not because they should be treated and not because their punishment should serve as a deterrent. Many penologists credit the retributive model with encouraging prison management to create an environment where inmates can serve their time safely and productively, rather than a harsh environment designed to deter crime. The deprivation of freedom was a harsh enough punishment: Prisons did not have to be punishing beyond that.

As the 1980s commenced, national policy emphasized broad reductions in domestic welfare programs. The criminal justice system warmed to the reacceptance of the classical notion that punishment should fit the crime rather than the criminal. The widespread adoption of determinate sentencing continued throughout the 1980s and 1990s, as it became increasingly difficult for social theorists to agree on definitive causes of crime. By 1999, most states had determinate sentencing, action supportive of the classical model. This, along with the conservative "get even tougher" response to violent crimes and drug offenses, was why the U.S. prison population more than tripled from 1980 to 1998. With 1,277,866 inmates in state and federal prisons (U.S. Department of Justice 1999), the United States ranks with Russia as having the highest-known incarceration rates of any industrialized nation in the world.

The Penal Debate. One contemporary justification for prison is its crime deterrence function, for which there is considerable public support. Many sociologists take the neoclassical position that an appropriate and updated crime control policy should include an increase in the swiftness and certainty of punishment for street offenders, and that control efforts should focus on both the before-sentencing work of police and prosecution, and the after-sentencing work of corrections. The deterrence advocates' penal policy is based on the theory of criminality that proposes that the frequency of an individual's criminal behavior is a matter of the individual's choice, and a consequence of that behavior's reinforcement or punishment in the past. The individual's choice is based on the expectation of subsequent reward or punishment.

Despite the general public's belief that prison is a deterrent to crime, there is considerable research evidence to the contrary, leaning some sociologists against deterrence. They argue that crimes of passion are less apt to be deterred by prison sentences than crimes committed for monetary gain. The threat of prison is less likely to deter someone of lower socioeconomic status, who has less "good life" and status to lose, than someone of wealth and higher status. Additionally, the courts are so overcrowded that the possibility of swift and certain punishment is diminished.

Entering the twenty-first century, the prevailing model of sentencing is still grounded in the neoclassical deterrence ideology. When it comes to the serving of the sentence, however, the neoclassical retributive, nondeterrence doctrine prevails. This retribution policy requires a correctional system that does not abuse individual treatment, but instead makes rehabilitation programs voluntary, restricts autonomy of movement, specifies the length of sentence in advance (determinate), and implements it in a fair and safe environment. Since about 1973, prison administrators have addressed these fairness and safety issues, specified in the retribution policy, by attempting to minimize the potential violence associated with overcrowding, gang membership, and racism. They have tried to do this by separating the inmate populations into small functional housing units (Levinson and Gerard 1973) that are supervised by a decentralized "unit management" team. Current research (i.e., Farmer 1994) has shown that, if implemented properly, this method of managing inmates can facilitate increased communication, safer conditions, a more satisfying work environment for staff, and more personal programming for inmates.

Sociologists and penologists generally expect the twenty-first-century prison situation to continue its current trends. Incarceration rates will continue to climb as sentences become longer, and as good-time awards and parole options decrease. Acquired immune deficiency syndrome (AIDS) and racism in prison will be more closely watched and more rigorously dealt with. Inmates will become more violent as confinement, with less programming, becomes more Spartan and harsher. Gang membership in prison will increase, along with management efforts to combat the membership. Prison "privatization" in areas of prison construction and management, inmate work, and services (i.e., food, health, counseling, education) will become a more widely accepted solution to increasing prison costs and decreasing prison budgets.

REFERENCES

Beccaria, Cesare 1819 "*Crimes and Punishments*," transl. from Italian by M. D. Voltaire. In F. P. Williams, III and Marilyn D. McShane, ed., 1998 *Criminology Theory: Selected Classis Readings*, 2nd ed. Cincinnati: Anderson Publishing

Bentham, Jeremy 1843 "Introduction to the Principles of Morals and Legislation." In F. P. Williams, III and Marilyn D. McShane, ed., 1998. *Crime Theory: Selected Classic Readings*, 2nd ed. Cincinnati: Anderson Publishing.

Clemmer, Donald 1940 *The Prison Community*. Boston: Christopher.

Cloward, Richard A., Donald R. Cressey, George H. Grosser, Richard McCleery, Lloyd E. Ohlin, Gresham M. Sykes, and Sheldon L. Messiger 1975 *Theoretical Studies in Social Organization of the Prison*. Millwood, N.Y.: Kraus.

Cressey, Donald (ed.) 1961 *The Prison: Studies in Institutional Organization and Change*. New York: Holt, Rinehart, and Winston.

DiIulio, John J. 1987 *Governing Prisons: A Comparative Study of Correctional Management*. New York: Free Press.

Farmer, J Forbes 1994 "Decentralized Management in Prison: A Comparative Case Study." *Journal of Offender Rehabilitation* 20 (Fall–Winter):117–130.

Foucault, Michel 1977 *Discipline and Punish*. New York: Pantheon.

Goffman, Irving 1966 "On the Characteristics of Total Institutions: Staff-Inmate Relations." In D. R. Cressey, ed., *The Prison*. New York: Holt, Rinehart and Winston.

Hawkins, Gordon 1976 *The Prison: Policy and Practice*. Chicago: University of Chicago Press.

Hirsh, Adam J. 1992 *The Rise of the Penitentiary*. New Haven, Conn.: Yale University Press.

Howard, John 1777 *The State of Prisons in England and Wales*. London: E. Eyres

Irwin, John 1980 *Prisons in Turmoil*. Boston: Little Brown.

Kauffman, Kelsey 1988 *Prison Officers and Their World*. Cambridge, Mass.: Harvard University Press.

Levinson, Robert B., and Roy E. Gerard 1973 "Functional Units: A Different Correctional Approach." *Federal Probation* 37(4):8–16.

Martinson, Robert 1974 "What Works? Questions and Answers about Prison Reform" *Public Interest* 35:22–54.

Sykes, Gresham M. 1958 *The Society of Captives*. Princeton: Princeton University Press.

U.S. Department of Justice, Bureau of Justice Statistics 1999 http://www.ojp.usdoj.gov/bjs.

U.S. President's Commission on Law Enforcement and Administration of Justice 1967 *The Challenge of Crime in a Free Society*. Washington, D.C.: Government Printing Office.

Webb, G. L., and David G. Morris 1978 *Prison Guards: The Culture and Perspective of an Occupational Group*. Houston, Tex.: Coker.

Wilson, James Q., and Richard J. Herrnstein 1985 *Crime and Human Nature*. New York: Simon and Schuster.

Wright, Erik O. 1973 *The Politics of Punishment*. New York: Harper Row.

J FORBES FARMER

PENSION SYSTEMS

See Retirement; Social Security Systems.

PERSONAL AUTONOMY

Personal autonomy refers to a person's sense of self-determination, of being able to make choices regarding the direction of her or his own actions, including the freedom to pursue those choices. With personal autonomy, an individual is able to engage in effective self-regulation—successfully monitoring needs and values; responding adaptively to the environment, and initiating, organizing, and directing actions toward the achievement of needs. For some theorists, the psychological experience of autonomy has its origin in the organism's natural tendency to organize both itself and its environment in the pursuit of goals. In this view, a sense of autonomy requires the absence of restraining forces that can limit this natural tendency. Importantly, feelings of autonomy are not only crucial for adequate intrapersonal functioning—competent action and adequate psychological health—but are also essential for the adequate functioning of a healthy society.

CONCEPTIONS OF PERSONAL AUTONOMY

Early personality theorists viewed autonomy as one element of a dialectical process in the developing self. Angyal (1941), for example, proposed that personality develops in the context of two conflicting pressures, autonomy and surrender (or homonomy). A pull toward autonomy leads toward differentiation from other people and the physical environment, connoting individuation, separation, independence, freedom, and the like. The tendency toward autonomy, however, is met by a countervailing pull toward surrender, felt by the individual as a desire to become part of something greater than oneself, uniting with others and with the physical environment. Surrender is reflected in concepts such as community, union, interdependence, and obligation. A similar dialectic can be seen in the theorizing of Otto Rank (1929) and David Bakan (1966). For instance, in Bakan's approach, a concept comparable to autonomy is agency, a tendency toward manipulation that results in aloofness and differentiation of the personality. Agency is viewed as occurring in conflict with communion, a tendency that pushes a person toward connectedness and personality coherence.

The dialectical view of autonomy is interesting, suggesting as it does that autonomy has little meaning outside some notion of wholeness or integration against which the individuating, segregating pressure of autonomy can push. More recent theorists also seem to understand that the concept of autonomy implies the question "Autonomy from what?" But rather than viewing autonomy as one element in an intrapsychic union of opposites, current conceptualizations focus on conflicts between an individual's need for self-determination and potential external constraints encountered in the social environment (Deci and Ryan 1985; Ryan et al. 1997). In this view, autonomy is conceptualized as reflecting the organism's natural developmental trajectory toward increasing complexity and the concomitant press toward greater organization of its environment in the process of self-development (Ryan et al. 1997). But, of course this natural development is not guaranteed. Insufficient resources—such as insecure attachment in infancy, emotional detachment in adolescence, inadequate social support in adulthood, or even neurobiological deficits in the individual—represent potential oppositional forces to the expression of autonomy. Desires for interpersonal relatedness do not stand in conflict with autonomy needs from such a perspective, but rather play a supportive role (Ryan 1991). Thus, the development of autonomy requires responsive parental nurturing, including recognition of and support for the child's expression of autonomy. In adulthood, the sense of autonomy is facilitated by an interpersonal environment that allows the individual to view his or her intentions to act as being caused by internal, personal motivations rather than being caused by external sources.

THEORIES OF AUTONOMY

Theories relevant to an understanding of autonomy all share the assumption that individuals are motivated in some way to have the freedom to determine their own fate. For instance, deCharms (1968) proposed a general motivational tendency to strive to be an agent of causality. Individuals who initiate an intentional behavior experience themselves as the causal origin of the action and as intrinsically motivated. Individuals who do not experience personal causation, but rather view themselves as pawns being impelled by external causes will experience action as being extrinsically motivated.

Causality Orientations Theory. Intrinsic motivation is viewed as a basic ongoing motivational propensity of all individuals that directs activity unless it is blocked in some way (Deci and Ryan 1985). Major constraints on experiencing intrinsic motivation can include stable or transient individual differences in the ways that individuals make sense of events. The most important causal orientations for understanding autonomy are the autonomy orientation and the control orientation. Individuals experiencing an autonomy orientation do not feel their behavior to be controlled by external contingencies. Instead, the individuals' experiences are ones of choice, flexibility, awareness of needs, effective accommodation to the environment, and responsiveness to available information. Such individuals are able to effectively seek out situations that allow them to experience autonomy, to use information in initiating action, and to be resilient in the face of difficulties. Only in an individual experiencing a "control orientation" does the tension between desired autonomy and controlling forces become salient and intrinsic motivation become reduced. In situations requiring action, such individuals experience feelings of pressure and anxiety, and action comes to be viewed as controlled by either internal factors not of their making (e.g., perceived obligations) or external forces (Deci and Ryan 1985). An individual's causal orientation is important because failure to experience autonomy is associated with reduced functioning, poorer health, and increased psychopathology (Deci and Ryan 1987; Ryan et al. 1995).

Undermining Effects of Reward on Intrinsic Motivation. Intrinsic and extrinsic motivation are affected not only by individuals' orientations toward explaining the causes of their actions, but also by the presence of external rewards or punishments for engaging in certain actions. Engaging in an intrinsically motivated activity means that it is the feelings of enjoyment and excitement that result from the activity that are rewarding. Presence of other rewards is unnecessary to such experiences (Deci and Ryan 1985). In fact, an important finding is that receiving rewards can be detrimental for behavior that is normally intrinsically motivated. Children or adults who begin receiving rewards for engaging in such behavior may find motivation for that activity to become extrinsic in nature (Lepper and Greene 1978). Paradigmatic demonstrations of this phenomenon involve paying college students for performing enjoyable tasks such as solving puzzles and giving children a ribbon and gold star as a good-player award for playing with magic markers (Deci 1971; Lepper et al. 1973). Subsequent to receiving rewards, interest in the activity can be decreased once rewards are again absent. This decrease in task interest is thought to indicate a shift toward extrinsic motivation for performance of the task. Moreover, rewards can have similarly deleterious effects on tasks that require an individual to be creative.

Both the pervasiveness and the interpretation of these negative effects on task interest and creativity remain matters of heated debate (Eisenberger and Cameron 1996, 1998; Hennessey and Amabile 1998; Lepper 1998; Sansone and Harackiewicz 1998). There do, however, appear to be some reliable conditions under which tangible rewards such as money, candy, or gold stars decrease intrinsic motivation. Receiving expected rewards regardless of the quality of one's performance leads participants to subsequently spend less time engaging in a task once the reward is removed.

Cognitive Evaluation Theory. The primary autonomy-based interpretation for reduced task interest comes from cognitive evaluation theory (Deci and Ryan 1985). Cognitive evaluation theory suggests that, to the extent that rewards are controlling, intrinsic motivation will be decreased. Controlling events are ones that make individuals feel pressured to behave in a certain way. The presence of controlling events decreases feelings of self-determination by leading perceivers to believe that they are acting in order to receive a desired outcome. For example, tangible rewards like money or physical awards that are given regardless of the quality of the work can lead an individual to view actions as being instrumental for getting a desired outcome, and thus as controlled by those rewards. But receiving rewards can also be informative, conveying that one is competent. Such feedback about performance increases intrinsic motivation. Thus, in some contexts the informational function of a reward may override the decrease in intrinsic motivation that results from its controlling function. This is particularly the case, according to cognitive evaluation theory, for unexpected or intangible rewards such as praise. In addition, when receipt of a reward is contingent on performance, a tangible cue highly symbolic of one's achievement can also be intrinsically motivating (Harackiewicz et al. 1984; Sansone and Harackiewicz 1998). Related research on creativity has been explained in terms of how rewards can orient the individual toward goal-relevant stimuli. For creativity tasks where one's thinking needs to be divergent and less stimulus-bound, such a goal-related focus can be counterproductive, reducing the cognitive flexibility and intense involvement in a task needed for producing novel solutions (Amabile 1983).

The findings regarding intrinsic and extrinsic motivation have important implications for the ideal socialization of members of a society (Ryan et al. 1997). One task of a society is appropriate socialization of its members, directing their behavior in productive avenues. In a sense, a major task of culture is to provide individuals with appropriate means of determining how their lives can contribute to a fuller development of humankind, offering as it were, an appropriate avenue for "heroism" (Becker 1971). Ryan and colleagues (1991, 1997) argue that creating individuals who are cooperative and not alienated from society requires that socializing agents provide opportunities for autonomy within a supportive context of belongingness. Behavior that is experienced as occurring either under social pressures or from internal forces of incompletely integrated, or introjected, societal values will not be experienced as autonomous. Successful internalization of societal values such that they result in intrinsically motivated behavior is thus ideal for effective functioning of a society.

Reactance Theory. A second theory that has implications for understanding decreased interest in a task after receiving controlling rewards is reactance theory. From this perspective, loss of autonomy, of ability to choose to engage in some action, means loss of freedom. Thus, when individuals begin to anticipate a reward for behavior that was previously driven solely by intrinsic motives, they may in some contexts come to see that reward as an attempt to impose on them some type of action-outcome contingency. They may feel a sense that the attempt is intended to restrict their ability to freely engage or not engage in the activity at will. This loss of expected freedom induces a state of psychological tension known as reactance (Brehm 1993; Brehm and Brehm 1981). Reactance involves the experience of active, negative emotional states such as frustration and anger, and results in an individual's engaging in active attempts to regain the lost freedoms. From this perspective, reduced interest in a task is not a result of declining intrinsic motivation per se, but is merely an expression of a general motivation to regain lost freedom of choice. It is important to note that defiant rebellion against controlling influences does not necessarily mean regaining freedom. Automatically withdrawing effort from activities that were previously pleasing means that one's choices are being controlled in an oppositional way by those external influences (Deci and Ryan 1985).

AUTONOMY IN THE CONTEXT OF CONTROL NEEDS

The recent conception of autonomy proposed by Deci and Ryan (1985) is similar in many ways to an earlier notion of the motivation to have effective interaction with one's environment, effectance motivation (White 1959). White proposed that a variety of behaviors of the active organism, such as play, exploration, and active curiosity, can best be explained by proposing a need to engage in activities that lead to feelings of efficacy, and that allow the developing organism to become competent. Thus the notion of an effectance or mastery motive is closely related to a motive for autonomy in that both reflect a force that directs the organism toward increasing competence in managing the self and personal goals, or in managing one's environment. Indeed, the need for autonomy, mastery, and a third motive, power (Winter 1973) can all be viewed as reflections of an organism's need for personal control over various domains of their life (Marsh et al. 1998). Personal control involves a contingency between actions and outcomes, a sense of having in one's repertoire actions that can increase the likelihood of getting desired outcomes. Thus needs for power reflect a need for control over the social environment, and needs for mastery reflect a need for control over the physical and nonsocial environment; autonomy reflects intrapersonal control needs.

From such a control motivation perspective, autonomy is reflected in controlling the self, regulating emotional responses, and making decisions regarding one's actions. A key assumption of such an approach is that autonomy involves beliefs about contingency—notions about oneself as a causal force, consistent with deCharm's (1968) notion of origins versus pawns. A particularly distinguishing feature of need for autonomy as a control motive is that it becomes defined in large part as reflecting a need to resist others' controlling influence. From Deci and Ryan's (1985) perspective, however, autonomy is about the choice over what action-outcome contingencies to explore, *not* about control per se. From their perspective, need for self-determination is quite independent of control needs; it is in a sense prior to control. Thus, if control needs are about whether the individual can have a shot at winning a game through his or her actions, autonomy is about having the choice of whether to enter the game—to decide whether to try to explore the contingencies, regardless of whether or not there are contingencies once the choice is made. Such need for autonomy is a proactive, ever-present force, not a reactive force that emerges in response to *loss* of intrapersonal control. In this way autonomy has an element much like early notions of mastery needs; effectance motivation was explicitly hypothesized to not be a deficit-based need and thus was viewed as dissimilar to tissue-deficit drives like hunger (White 1959).

However, the research on the effects of reward on intrinsic motivation makes it clear how sensitive the experience of autonomy is to deficits of autonomy. Autonomy is uniquely about freedom from control, in that having the freedom to explore contingencies in the world, to attend to intrinsic experiences of action rather than having to attend to the controlling features of a situation, is, in a real sense, about the ability to have control over oneself. In fact, individuals who have greater needs for autonomy show somewhat greater ability to detect another's nonverbal displays in which affect and expression of dominance versus passivity are expressed; needs for power, in contrast, are uncorrelated with such skill (Marsh et al. 1999). Perhaps the nonverbal behavior of others is more informative to an individual with greater need for autonomy because the intentions of others might offer some threat to one's own freedom. Thus,

considering autonomy within a context of control needs, and as potentially involving homeostatic processes (Pittman and Heller 1987), seems to have utility.

In general, though, understanding autonomy and its relationship to different domains of control needs, and understanding the effects of loss of autonomy, seem to be important factors not yet fully explored by social scientists. In particular, many of the cognitive processes that have been explored with loss of control in mastery domains have been less frequently explored in the domain of autonomy. Control motivation research demonstrates that individuals have strong tendencies toward biased perceptions that events are under their personal control, and that cognitive processes function to help maintain such biases. The extent to which autonomy-based action is similarly mediated by biased cognitive processes suggests important questions for future study.

Perhaps the most fundamental question not addressed in current research on autonomy harkens back to personality theorists' beliefs that autonomy motives should be understood as standing in perpetual intrapsychic conflict with the need of the individual for surrender and communion with others. If such forces operate independently of one another, separate theories for autonomy and control and for belongingness processes are reasonable. On the other hand, early theorists may be correct in the belief that the desire for autonomy, control, and independence act in a continual creative conflict with the individual's desire for social acceptance, integration, and union. From such a perspective, the tension may result in emergent phenomena not otherwise predicted by considering the needs independently of one another. Reexamining this dynamic tension may provide a useful next direction for developing a more complete picture of the impact of autonomy needs on the individual and on his or her connection with other individuals, important social groups, and society.

REFERENCES

Amabile, T. M. 1983 *The Social Psychology of Creativity.* New York: Springer-Verlag.

Angyal, A. 1941 *Foundations for a Science of Personality.* New York: Commonwealth Fund.

Bakan, D. 1966 *The Duality of Human Existence*. Chicago: Rand McNally.

Becker, E. 1971 *The Birth and Death of Meaning: An Interdisciplinary Perspective on the Problem of Man*, 2nd ed. New York: Free Press.

Brehm, J. W. 1993 "Control, Its Loss, and Psychological Reactance." In G. Weary, F. Gleicher, and K. L. Marsh, eds., *Control Motivation and Social Cognition*. New York: Springer-Verlag.

Brehm, S., and J. W. Brehm 1981 *Psychological Reactance: A Theory of Freedom and Control*. New York: Academic Press.

deCharms, R. 1968 *Personal Causation*. New York: Academic Press.

Deci, E. L. 1971 "Effects of Externally Mediated Rewards on Intrinsic Motivation." *Journal of Personality and Social Psychology* 18:105–115.

——, and R. M. Ryan 1985 *Intrinsic Motivation and Self-Determination in Human Behavior*. New York: Plenum.

—— 1987 "The Support of Autonomy and the Control of Behavior." *Journal of Personality and Social Psychology* 53:1024–1037.

Eisenberger, R., and J. Cameron 1996 "Detrimental Effects of Reward: Reality or Myth?" *American Psychologist* 51:1153–1166.

—— 1998 "Reward, Intrinsic Interest, and Creativity: New Findings." *American Psychologist* 53:676–679.

Harackiewicz, J. M., G. Manderlink, and C. Sansone 1984 "Rewarding Pinball Wizardry: Effects of Evaluation and Cue Value on Intrinsic Interest." *Journal of Personality and Social Psychology* 47:287–300.

Hennessey, B. A., and T. M. Amabile 1988 "Reward, Intrinsic Motivation, and Creativity." *American Psychologist* 53:674.

Lepper, M. R. 1998 "A Whole Much Less than the Sum of its Parts." *American Psychologist* 53:675–676.

——, and D. Greene 1978 *The Hidden Costs of Rewards*. Hillsdale, N.J.: Erlbaum.

——, and R. E. Nisbett 1973 "Undermining Children's Intrinsic Interest with Extrinsic Reward: A Test of the 'Overjustification' Hypothesis." *Journal of Personality and Social Psychology* 28:129–137.

Marsh, K. L., S. A. Nasco, D. Hilton, G. S. Bains, and W. M. Webb 1999 "Domain-Specific Control: Individual Differences in Motivations for Mastery, Power, and Autonomy." Manuscript under review.

Pittman, T. S., and J. F. Heller 1987 "Social Motivation." *Annual Review of Psychology* 38:461–489.

Rank, O. 1929 *The Trauma of Birth*. New York: Harcourt, Brace.

Ryan, R. M. 1991 "The Nature of the Self in Autonomy and Relatedness." In J. Strauss and G. R. Goethals, eds., *The Self: Interdisciplinary Approaches*. New York: Springer-Verlag.

——, J. Kuhl, and E. L. Deci 1997 "Nature and Autonomy: An Organizational View of Social and Neurobiological Aspects of Self-Regulation in Behavior and Development." *Development and Psychopathology* 9:701–728.

Ryan, R. M., R. W. Plant, and S. O'Malley 1995 "Initial Motivations for Alcohol Treatment: Relations with Patient Characteristics, Treatment Involvement and Dropout." *Addictive Behaviors* 20:279–297.

Sansone, C., and J. M. Harackiewicz 1998 "'Reality' is Complicated." *American Psychologist* 53:673.

White, R. W. 1959 "Motivation Reconsidered: The Concept of Competence." *Psychological Review* 66:297–333.

Winter, D. G. 1973 *The Power Motive*. New York: Free Press.

KERRY L. MARSH

PERSONAL DEPENDENCY

Personal dependency is the tendency to seek support, security, reassurance, and guidance from outside the self. The object of dependency may be another person, a social unit (e.g., family, a religious group), or a symbolic belief system from which people receive positive outcomes, such as assistance, love, and/or the attainment of personal goals. The support requested can be physical (dependency on a caregiver by infants and persons who are very old, sick, or disabled), cognitive (a student's reliance on his or her teacher), and/or emotional (reliance on another person for reassurance and love). A dependent relationship implies the existence of interpersonal bonding, commitment, involvement, obligation, and trust.

An analysis of social science literature clearly reveals that personal dependency has been conceptualized in either negative or positive terms. On the one hand, personal dependency has been equated with weakness, immaturity, and passivity, and it has been viewed as an obstacle to the development of an autonomous and mature person. On the another hand, personal dependency has been viewed as a basic human motivation, which accomplishes important adaptive functions. It seems to contribute to the process of coping with life adversities and to set the basis for the formation of close relationships and social ties as well as for social cooperation and hierarchical social structures. In this article, I first present negative and positive conceptualizations of personal dependency. I then attempt to provide a more integrative conceptualization of dependency, in which its positive and negative aspects can coexist.

NEGATIVE VIEWS OF PERSONAL DEPENDENCY

During the last century, several social science professionals have viewed personal dependency in adulthood as a sign of weakness and immaturity. For example, Bornstein (1993) defines personal dependency in terms of negatively valued beliefs and emotions. Dependency-related beliefs refer to mental representations of the self and the social world that justify the tendency to seek support from other persons in times of need. Specifically, they include the perception of the self as weak, helpless, and ineffectual, as well as the beliefs that other persons are powerful and have the ability and skills to solve life problems and to control the course and outcomes of environmental events. Dependency-related emotions include the arousal of anxiety and worry upon external demands to deal with life tasks in an independent manner as well as fears of criticism, rejection, and separation. According to Bornstein (1993), these beliefs and emotions detract from independence, reinforce dependency over the life span, and facilitate its generalization across different interpersonal situations and social settings.

The emphasis on the negative aspects of personal dependency seems to reflect Western societies' values of independence, autonomy, and mastery. It also seems to reflect the view that mature, well-adjusted persons should attempt to cope with life tasks in an autonomous and self-directed way. As a result, the tendency to turn to others for support, assistance, and reassurance in times of need can be equated with immaturity, helplessness, and powerlessness, as well as with the failure to meet cultural expectations and standards. Moreover, it can be viewed as a risk factor for psychological problems, such as depression, anxiety, alcoholism, and eating disorders, as well as for negative social phenomena, such as loss of personal identity and blind obedience to totalitarian leaders. In extreme cases, when people suffer from persistent and severe interpersonal or occupational problems, personal dependency is considered to be a specific type of diagnosable psychological disorder.

The negative view of dependency can be traced to early writings of Freud, who argued that dependency in adulthood consists of immature and infantile forms of behaviors. In his view, a dependent orientation toward life is related to gratifying and frustrating breast-feeding experiences during the first year of life, when infants' survival completely depends on their mother's goodwill. Abrupt weaning, frustrations related to rigid and insensitive feeding schedules, and/or the failure to end the nursing period are hypothesized to result in a failure to adequately deal with conflicts regarding dependency and autonomy. This failure is reflected in the arousal of anxiety every time one is required to act in an independent manner; the experience of serious doubts about one's own ability to be an autonomous person; and the longing for the infantile, dependent relationship with the feeding mother. Problematic breast-feeding experiences are also hypothesized to lead people to believe that the solution for their problems is outside and that others can take care of them in the same way that their mothers fed them.

The problem with Freud's ideas is that they are not supported by empirical findings (see Bornstein 1993, for a review). First, studies have failed to find a coherent and meaningful pattern of association between feeding experiences in infancy and self-reports of personal dependency in adulthood. Second, there is no strong evidence that personal dependency in adulthood is associated with mouth- and food-related activities as well as with oral behaviors (e.g., thumbsucking). Third, mixed results have been found in studies assessing the association between personal dependency and psychological disorders that have an oral component, such as eating disorders, alcoholism, and tobacco addiction. However, although findings do not support Freud's premise that dependency equals immaturity and infantilism, it still continues to exert a major influence in psychological writings.

A related approach to personal dependency can be found in object relation theories, which emphasize the crucial role that the early child-parent relationship plays in social and emotional development (Greenberg and Mitchell 1983). Like Freudian theory, these theories view events occurring during the first one or two years of life as critical for the development of personal dependency. However, unlike Freud, the proponents of object relations theories do not emphasize feeding experiences. Rather, they focus on the child's relationship with his or her parents and the failure to resolve conflicts around nurture and closeness, on the one hand, and separation and autonomy, on the other. In these terms, personal dependency reflects an infantile desire to merge with other persons and to be cared for by them. Furthermore, it is related to the search for absolute love and enmeshed relationships, the use of psychotropic drugs, and the identification with strong leaders and highly cohesive groups.

One basic hypothesis derived from object relation theories is that parenting style during infancy and childhood may be critical for an understanding of the development of offspring's personal dependency. Bornstein (1993) follows this idea and contends that overprotective and/or authoritarian parenting may create a vicious circle that increases the likelihood of offspring's dependency. Specifically, overprotective and/or authoritarian parents may prevent their children from engaging in exploratory and trial-and-error activities that promote a sense of mastery and autonomy. As a result, these children may perceive themselves as weak and may tend to seek others' help when confronted with life tasks. This support-seeking tendency may elicit others' helping behaviors, which, in turn, may further reinforce personal dependency. Along this reasoning, personal dependency would be overtly expressed mainly when the other (e.g., a parent, a teacher) is perceived as a powerful authority, and may underlie the blind pursuit of strong and authoritarian leaders who can offer protection and help.

The contribution of parenting style to personal dependency has also been acknowledged in social learning theories, which focus on the type of behaviors that parents reinforce throughout childhood and adolescence (Rotter 1982). Specifically, children whose parents positively reinforce passive and dependent behaviors are hypothesized to become dependent adult persons. These children may learn that dependent behaviors are adequate instrumental means for obtaining positive outcomes (e.g., love, esteem) from parents and that active and autonomous behaviors should be inhibited if they want to maintain a good relationship with parents. Social learning theories also hypothesize that this learning would be generalized across situations, leading people to behave in a dependent manner in a wide variety of social contexts. Like object relation theories, social learning theories suggest that overprotective and/or authoritarian parenting would lead to offspring's dependency, because such parents may reinforce passive and dependent behaviors. However, social learning theories differ from object relation theories in that they view personal dependency as an active instrumental means for obtaining positive outcomes from authority figures.

In emphasizing parental reinforcement and learning processes, social learning theories also highlight the role that the learning of gender roles—the learning of cultural norms and expectations regarding feminine and masculine traits and behaviors—may play in the development of personal dependency (Mischell 1970). This is particularly noted in Western cultures, where the equation between dependency and femininity may lead parents to reinforce dependent behaviors among girls and to punish these behaviors in boys. In this way, parents may provide differential reinforcement for boys and girls, leading children to meet cultural expectations concerning the expression of dependency. However, one should recall that the "dependency = femininity" equation reflects Western societies' norms and that other cultural contexts can produce different gender-role expectations and different patterns of parental reinforcement.

The negative aspects of dependency have been also emphasized by interpersonal theories of personality (e.g., Leary 1957). In these theories, dependency has been equated with personal characteristics of weaknesses, passivity, and helplessness. Moreover, it has been associated with suggestibility, compliance, and the adherence to others' beliefs and interests as a means for obtaining love, approval, and support. Interpersonal theories also emphasize that dependency is associated with fear of negative evaluation and test anxiety, which, in turn, may further exacerbate dependency. These worries may divert cognitive resources away from active, self-directed behaviors and may lead people to escape or avoid any situation that demands autonomy and independence.

Like psychoanalytic theories, interpersonal theories also suggest that personal dependency in adulthood increases the risk for psychological problems. In this context, studies have examined the association between self-reports of dependency, on the one hand, and depression, anxiety, substance abuse, and eating disorders, on the other. However, results are mixed. Whereas some studies have indeed found a positive association between self-reports of dependency and psychological disorders, other studies have failed to find such an association. Moreover, there is evidence that dependency may be an outcome rather than a cause of psychological disorders (Bornstein 1993). For examples, there are studies showing that the onset of depression and the resulting increase in helplessness and powerlessness feelings promote passive and dependent behavior. Accordingly, longitudinal studies have shown that the onset of alcoholism is followed by an increase in dependent behavior.

The above findings put into question the view that dependency is a negative personal characteristic. Rather, they may imply that dependent behavior reflects a cry for help, reassurance, and support in dealing with emotional and social problems. As such, dependent behavior may be an adaptive means for overcoming life difficulties with the help of others. In these cases, avoiding support seeking and maintaining a facade of autonomy and self-reliance may have detrimental consequences for people who really need help and support to overcome their predicaments.

POSITIVE VIEWS OF PERSONAL DEPENDENCY

The positive sides of personal dependency have been emphasized by psychological and sociological theories that focus on the development and stability of social relations, contracts, and organizations. In terms of Kelley's interdependence theory (1979)—the most influential theory on interpersonal relationships—the reliance of person on a partner for the satisfaction of his or her own needs is a basic requirement for the development and stability of close and positive relationships. In fact, Kelley suggests that there can be no stable relationship when a person is unable or unwilling to rely on his or her partner. Dependency is the psychological glue that maintains a close relationship over time. Moreover, it seems to prevent people from moving toward alternative relationships.

Along the above reasoning, personal dependency is considered to be one core component of the experience of love and to be associated with other components of this phenomenon, such as commitment, intimacy, and trust. For example, theory and research have emphasized that a person's dependency on a romantic partner precedes commitment to the relationship—precedes the intention to maintain the relationship in the future. Accordingly, dependency seems to play a critical role in the development of closeness and intimacy within love relationships. People who can rely on their partners for need satisfaction have been found to develop a sense of trust and confidence in their partner's goodwill, which, in turn, may facilitate the taking of risks in the relationship and the sharing of intimate feelings and thoughts with the partner. As a result, people may strengthen their willingness to initiate and maintain intimate patterns of communication while developing a sense of togetherness with the partner.

Personal dependency has been also viewed to play a positive role in group dynamics as well as in the stability of hierarchical relationships within social organizations. In this context, personal dependency seems to precede a person's willingness to participate in group activities and to collaborate with others in teamwork, mainly when others are at a higher rank in the organizational hierarchy. People who are unable or unwilling to rely on others for goal achievement and task completion may be reluctant to participate in teamwork, may prefer to work alone, and may react negatively to authority figures who threaten their independence. Only when people feel that they need support and guidance from others may they be positively oriented toward teamwork and authority figures. In fact, there is evidence that the level of dependency members of a group feel toward each other is a sign of group cohesion and a positive predictor of group effectiveness. In a broader perspective, personal dependency seems to be a prerequisite for the phylogenetic development of social ties and structures.

Theory and research have also highlighted the association between dependency and positive personal characteristics. First, research has shown that the equation between dependency and passivity is not always true. In fact, there are many situations in which dependency leads to active forms of behavior, such as attempts to outperform others in order to attract the attention of an authority figure. Second, positive associations have been found between dependency and sensitivity to interpersonal cues—the ability to decode and understand others' messages. Third, there is evidence that personal dependency is related to health-promotion behaviors, such as seeking of medical treatments and compliance with them, as well as to relationship-enhancing traits, such as sociability, self-disclosure, and cooperative orientation in social interactions.

Studies in the field of stress and coping have shown that people who seek support and guidance from others in times of need possess positive mental representations of the self and the social world. In these studies, the tendency to rely on support seeking as a coping strategy has been found to be related to the perception of the self as capable of coping with stressful events and environmental demands. This tendency has been also found to be associated with optimistic beliefs about distress management as well as about others' ability and willingness to provide support and guidance.

Personal dependency has also been found to result in adaptive behavior. The tendency to seek support from others has been conceptualized as a basic behavioral strategy that people use in coping with life adversities. In Lazarus and Folkman's model (1984), the most influential theory in the field of stress and coping, support seeking is considered to be one of the most frequently used coping strategies. More important, research has consistently found that reliance on this coping strategy leads to positive psychological and social outcomes. Specifically, people who cope with life problems by seeking support from others tend to feel better, to experience less distress, and to show fewer problems in social functioning than people who rely only on themselves. Moreover, the belief that one can depend on others in times of need has been found to facilitate social adjustment.

Studies in the field of stress and coping have also shown that a reluctance to seek support in times of need has negative health and adjustment outcomes. People who rely exclusively on themselves in dealing with intense and persistent stressful events have been found to experience, in the long run, high levels of distress and serious problems in physical health and social functioning. These findings may reflect the fragile nature of the "pseudo-safe" world of a person who believes that he or she can deal alone with all life problems and does not need the help of others. It seems that the lack of others to depend upon leaves this person vulnerable and helpless in face of stressful events.

The adaptive advantage of personal dependency has been particularly emphasized in Bowlby's attachment theory (1969). In his terms, human infants are born with a prewired repertoire of behaviors aimed at maintaining proximity to other persons and seeking their support in times of need. These behaviors seem to reflect a basic human motivation and to accomplish a crucial adaptive function—to guarantee the survival of the helpless infant by eliciting helping behaviors in parents. According to Bowlby, this motivation persists over the entire life span, even among mature and autonomous adults. In fact, Bowlby does not view dependency as a sign of immaturity and infantilism, but as a healthy motivation that facilitates the process of coping with life problems and the development of positive social ties.

According to Bowlby, the tendency to rely on others in times of need is an inborn affect regulation device, which is automatically activated upon the experience of distress. In these cases, other persons function as a "haven of safety" to which people can retreat for comfort and reassurance and as a "secure base" from which they can develop their unique personalities in a loving and approving atmosphere. As a result, the overt expression of dependency needs and behaviors may have beneficial effects on the process of distress management as well as on the individual's psychological wellbeing.

Bowlby also proposes that actual experiences related to the expression of dependency needs exert tremendous influence on social and emotional development. On the one hand, interactions with significant others who are responsive to one's dependency needs may lead to the experience of more and longer episodes of positive affect and the development of positive feelings toward the world and the self. On the other hand, interactions with rejecting others may elicit chronic distress, serious doubts about others' intentions, and problems around dependency-autonomy themes.

Along the above reasoning, actual experiences related to the expression of dependency needs may shape the way people cope with life adversities. Specifically, interactions with significant others who are responsive to one's dependency needs set the basis for the construction of effective distress management strategies. People may find out that acknowledgment and display of distress elicits positive responses from significant others. They may also learn that they are capable of eliciting helping responses from others and that support seeking is an effective way of coping. In this way, the satisfaction of dependency needs would lead people to regulate affect by overtly expressing distress and engaging in active seeking of support.

Interestingly, Bowlby does not conceptualize dependency and autonomy as antagonistic motivations. Rather, he suggests that the satisfaction of dependency needs might facilitate the development of an autonomous person. In his terms, autonomous activities in infancy are activated when a caregiver satisfies infants' dependency needs and when he or she is perceived as a "secure base" to which infants can retreat in case of danger. Thus, infants who can use the caregiver as a "secure base" can show a balance between dependency and autonomy. They can move away from the caregiver without being anxious about his or her availability, can return to him or her when danger arises, and can recommence autonomous activities (e.g., play, exploration) as the proximity to the caregiver is reestablished. Overall, the expression of dependency needs does not necessarily mean that the person cannot engage in autonomous behavior. Rather, the expression and satisfaction of these needs seems to set the basis for a confident and pleasurable development of autonomy.

AN INTEGRATIVE VIEW OF PERSONAL DEPENDENCY

The above-reviewed literature clearly indicates that personal dependency may have both negative and positive implications for the individual and the society. The main question here is whether and how the negative and positive aspects of personal dependency can coexist. In other words, one should

attempt to present a more integrative view of personal dependency, which can explain how this phenomenon may be an adaptive device and at the same time may lead to maladjustment and social problems.

As noted earlier, Bowlby argues that personal dependency is a healthy human behavior and that the tendency to seek support from others has positive psychological and social effects. However, this healthy pattern of behavior can become dysfunctional upon the recurrent frustration of one's cry for help. According to Bowlby, when people perceive significant others as nonresponsive to their dependency needs, they may learn that support seeking fails to bring the expected relief and that other defensive strategies should be developed. One of these strategies is a "fight" response, by which people attempt to compulsively elicit others' love and support through controlling and clinging responses. That is, these persons seem to develop an overly dependent pattern of behavior. The problem with this strategy is that it may create an anxious focus around social relationships; doubts about one's autonomy; anxious demands for proximity; fears of separation, rejection, and criticism; and inability to leave frustrating social interactions. As can be seen, this defensive strategy seems to result in all the negative consequences that psychoanalytic and social learning theories have linked to personal dependency.

Along the above reasoning, personal dependency per se is not a pathological sign of weakness and immaturity. Only when healthy dependency needs are frustrated and a person adopts an overly dependent defensive strategy is he or she caught in a vicious circle of anxiety, helplessness, maladjustment, and increasing dependency. In this view, psychoanalytic and social learning theories have in fact dealt with overdependency rather than with the normal expression of dependency needs. Moreover, most of the findings relating dependency to emotional and social problems have been obtained from self-report questionnaires that tap overdependency rather than the tendency to seek support from others in times of need. These questionnaires include items about fears of rejection, separation, and criticism; need for approval; and doubts about autonomy.

The above reasoning receives strong support in studies that focus on the interpersonal and intrapersonal correlates of adult attachment styles. Shaver and Hazan (1993) define attachment styles as stable patterns of beliefs, emotions, and behaviors in social relationships, and divide them into three types: secure, avoidant, and preoccupied. The "secure" style is defined by feelings of comfort with dependent relationships as well as by the tendency to seek support from others. The "avoidant" style is defined by reluctance to depend on others, avoidance of close relationships, and an overemphasis on autonomy and self-reliance. The "preoccupied" style is defined by compulsive attempts to minimize distance from others via clinging behaviors and fears of rejection, separation, and criticism. Overall, these three styles can be organized along a dependency continuum, with the "avoidant" style reflecting underdependency, the "secure" style the normal expression of these needs, and the "preoccupied" style overdependency.

Studies in adult attachment styles have consistently documented the adaptive advantage of the normal expression of dependency needs, as manifested in the secure style. First, securely attached persons have been found to report on more positive interactions with parents than avoidant and preoccupied persons. Second, persons addressing the secure style have been found to show less distress in times of stress than persons who address either an avoidant or a preoccupied style. Third, secure persons have been found to have more positive and stable close relationships and to be more positively involved in social activities than avoidant and preoccupied persons. That is, the overt expression of dependency needs is related to positive personal and social outcomes. In contrast, either the inhibition of these needs or the adoption of an overly dependent pattern of behavior seems to have detrimental effects on psychological and social functioning.

In conclusion, the above line of thinking and findings emphasize the balance between dependency and autonomy needs. The overt expression of dependency needs in adulthood does not necessarily compete with or inhibit autonomy needs. Rather, as Bowlby suggests, the satisfaction of dependency needs may facilitate the expression of autonomy needs. In these cases, people can freely move back and forth between dependency and autonomy, can flexibly accommodate to social demands, and then can maintain an adequate level of social adjustment and functioning. Only when this balance is disrupted, either among persons who overemphasize autonomy or among those who behave in an overly dependent manner, is adjustment at risk. In these cases, people may be unable and/or unwilling to flexibly adjust to the social world, in which they should act autonomously at same times and rely on others at other times.

Of course, a person's balance between dependency and autonomy needs depends not only on psychological factors. Rather, it also results from cultural and societal norms, values, and expectations. In fact, this balance would be different in societies that emphasize collectivist values (e.g., acceptance of social roles, family maintenance, and security) and in societies that emphasize individualistic values (e.g., personal achievement, mastery, freedom, and autonomy). Theory and research should attempt to provide a better understanding of the interface between cultural norms and values, a person's history of social interactions, and his or her expression of personal dependency. Moreover, they should throw away anachronistic and simplistic views of personal dependency and adopt a more integrative view of this basic human motivation.

REFERENCES

Bornstein, R. F. 1993 *The Dependent Personality*. New York: Guilford.

Bowlby, J. 1969 *Attachment and Loss: Attachment*. New York: Basic Books.

Greenberg, J. R., and Mitchell, S. A. 1983 *Object Relations in Psychoanalytic Theory*. Cambridge, Mass.: Harvard University Press.

Kelley, H. H. 1979 *Personal Relationships: Their Structure and Processes*. Hillsdale, N.J.: Erlbaum.

Lazarus, R. S., and S. Folkman 1984 *Stress, Appraisal, and Coping*. New York: Springer.

Leary, T. 1957 *Interpersonal Diagnosis of Personality*. New York: Ronald Press.

Mischell, W. 1970 "Sex Typing and Socialization." In P. H. Mussen, ed., *Carmichael's Manual of Child Psychology*, 3rd ed. New York: Wiley.

Rotter, J. 1982 *The Development and Application of Social Learning Theory*. New York: Praeger.

Shaver, P. R., and C. Hazan 1993 "Adult Romantic Attachment: Theory and Evidence." In D. Perlman and W. Jones, eds., *Advances in Personal Relationships*, vol. 4. London: Jessica Kingsley.

MARIO MIKULINCER

PERSONAL RELATIONSHIPS

See Interpersonal Power; Symbolic Interaction Theory.

PERSONALITY AND SOCIAL STRUCTURE

Three questions underlie the study of social structure and personality: What is social structure? What is personality? And, what is the relationship between the two? The history of this area and the current state of knowledge contain tremendous variability in the answers to these questions.

For example, social structure includes whole cultural configurations, social institutions such as family and the state, social stratification and class, the nature of roles, organizational structures, group dynamics, and micro-features of day-to-day interactions. Social structure also includes process and change at the group level, such as economic depression-recession, modernization, revolution, war, organizational growth and decline, human development and aging, and life-course transitions (school-to-work, retirement).

Concepts and approaches to personality also have a rich history in this area, with many variations. These include attitudes, abilities, affective and attributional styles, values, beliefs, cognitive schema, identities, aspirations, views of the self and others, and individual behaviors. The concept of personality, too, connotes both structure and process or change. Most contemporary observers would agree with a definition of personality as "regularities and consistencies in the behavior of individuals in their lives" (Snyder and Ickes 1985, p. 883). In some approaches, attitude and the self precede and determine behavior; in other approaches, people observe behavior and infer their own mental states and features of self.

Neither a simple answer nor close consensus exists among scholars on the nature of the relationship between social structure and personality, although most would agree that the relationship is reciprocal rather than asymmetric, and modest rather than extremely strong or extremely weak (House and Mortimer 1990; Miller-Loessi 1995; Mortimer and Lorence 1995). That is, multiple areas of research provide clear evidence that variations in social structures shape components of personality, *and* that variations in personality in turn affect social structure. Humans are not completely pawns in the face of social forces, nor are they entirely independent, autonomous agents, unfettered by social influences. The study of human lives shows clear evidence of both forms.

The study of social structure and personality has its roots in the disciplines of sociology, psychology, and anthropology. Scholars whose ideas and research offer inspiration include Marx (1963), Freud (1928), Mead (1934), Lewin (1951), Gerth and Mills (1953), Inkeles and Levinson (1954), Smelser and Smelser (1963), and Turner (1956).

The focus of scholarship in the 1930s, 1940s, and early 1950s was to define the basic concepts and processes for personality, for social structure, and for the relationship between the two. This era produced and elaborated developments such as field theory, role theory, and interactionist perspectives on the self, along with concepts such as self, significant other, role taking, socialization, the authoritarian personality, modal personality, and national character.

In the 1950s, the sociological research on social structure and personality focused on macroscopic empirical studies of national character: What was national character? How did it vary? Could it be defined in terms of modal personality types? A long tradition of comparative anthropological studies of culture and personality informed these studies. For example, some of these studies considered the relationship between social class and personality, with *social class* defined as white-collar–blue-collar. *Personality* referred to some underlying continuum of "adjustment," and the link between social class and personality occurred in socialization, in particular in child-rearing practices.

The 1960s produced major changes in the study of personality and social structure. First, the quantity of research increased significantly, concurrently with the massive growth of sociology and psychology as disciplines and with the growth of higher education. Second, research in the area became more diffuse and more differentiated. What had been a fairly identifiable area of research scattered to subareas of scientific disciplines, such as the sociology of medicine, social stratification, small group dynamics, or attitude-behavior research. The research problems multiplied; research methods and strategies multiplied; theories and explanations multiplied; and journal outlets and books multiplied. At the same time, communication, integration, and cross-fertilization across the research fragments declined, although in recent years this may be changing. In short, during this era "social structure and personality" became an umbrella description for many different lines of investigation that were only loosely connected.

The third major change in the 1960s was a refocusing of research on social structure and personality, one that continues into the 1990s. The empirical macroscopic studies of national character, and the emphasis on holistic conceptions of culture and national character, declined. On the sociological side, the emphasis shifted to studying "*aspects* of societies in relation to *aspects* of individuals" (House 1981, p. 526). On the psychological side, a looser, multidimensional approach to personality replaced the earlier Freudian approach, which was based on a coherent dynamic system and on personality types and structures (DiRenzo 1977).

House (1981) describes this major refocusing of research in terms of three principles, which also define ideals for the investigation of personality and social structure. First, the *components* principle suggests that social structures such as roles, positions, and systems are multidimensional, and theory should specify which dimensions are important for which personality phenomena (such as stress, self-esteem, and locus of control). Second, the *proximity* principle suggests focusing first on understanding the more proximate stimuli that affect people and then mapping the causal patterns across broader levels of social structure in time and space. Third, the *psychological* principle identifies the importance of specifying the psychological processes involved when social structures and processes affect the self, personality, and attitudes. House's three principles nicely summarize many of the recent advances in the study of social structure and personality. They also define the nature

of limitations in current knowledge, and identify research frontiers.

The contemporary landscape of research on social structure and personality in sociology is a patchwork of problems and areas. These include social stratification, work, and personality (Kohn et al. 1983); social structure and health, both physical and psychological (Mirowsky and Ross 1986); disjunctive social changes (war, economic depression) and individual adjustment (Elder 1974); role transitions and psychological changes (O'Brien 1986); variations in self-concept by structural position (Gecas and Burke 1995); human development, aging, and social change (Featherman and Lerner 1985; Alwin et al. 1991); and political and discriminatory attitudes, social institutions, and change (Kiecolt 1988), to mention just a few.

One of the most substantial and important areas of research involves the study of social stratification, work and personality, and the program of research of Kohn, Schooler, and colleagues (1983; Kohn and Slomczynski 1990; Kohn et al. 1997). The Kohn-Schooler model reflects the dominant approach in this particular area, and illustrates the major sociological approach to the study of social structure and personality. Spenner (1988a, 1988b, 1998) provides detailed review of this research. In comparison, approaches in psychology are more microscopic—in focusing on shorter intervals of time and smaller arenas of social space—and more likely to rely on experiments and lab studies, or field research versus large-scale survey research of people's work lives and personality histories.

The Kohn-Schooler model begins with dimensions of jobs that are defined and measured as objectively as possible (versus subjective dimensions and measures of individual's jobs). These structural imperatives of jobs include: occupational self-direction (substantive complexity of work, closeness of supervision, and routinization); job pressures (time pressure, heaviness, dirtiness, and hours worked per week); extrinsic risks and rewards (the probability of being held responsible for things outside one's control, the risk of losing one's job or business, job protections, and job income); and organizational location (ownership, bureaucratization, and hierarchical position). The three basic dimensions of personality in this research include intellectual flexibility, self-directedness of orientation, and sense of well-being or distress.

Among the subdimensions of these organizing dimensions are authoritarian conservatism, personally responsible standards of morality, trustfulness, self-confidence, self-deprecation, fatalism, anxiety, and idea conformity.

The type of analysis used in the Kohn-Schooler research estimates the lagged and contemporaneous reciprocal relationships between conditions of work and dimensions of personality in nonexperimental, panel, survey data. The major data come from a national sample of over 3,000 persons, representative of the male, full-time labor force, age 16 and over in 1974. About one-third of these men were reinterviewed about ten years later, with measures being taken of work conditions and personality at both points in time. Most of the studies of women in this tradition refer to wives of men in the sample. In a series of structural equation model analyses that adjust for measurement error in dimensions of jobs and personality, the authors document an intricate pattern of lagged (over time) and contemporaneous selection and socialization effects. *Selection effects* refers to the effects of personality on work and social structure; *socialization effects* refers to the effects of work (social structure) on self and personality. Most of the effects of personality on work are lagged, as workers appear to select jobs of a given type depending on measured aspects of their personality, or to slowly mold jobs to match their personalities. Conversely, the effects of jobs on personalities appear to be somewhat larger and to involve both contemporaneous and lagged effects. The largest relationships center on components of occupational self-direction, in particular, on substantive complexity of work. For example, substantive complexity of work environments increases intellectual flexibility for men by an amount that is one-fourth as great as the effect of intellectual flexibility a decade earlier, net of controls for other variables and confounding influences.

Kohn, Schooler, and colleagues interpret their findings with a "learning-generalization" explanation. In it, people learn from their jobs and generalize the lessons to spheres of their lives away from the job. Rather than using alternate psychological mechanisms such as displacement or compensation, the structural imperatives of jobs affect a worker's values; orientations to self, children, and society; and cognitive functioning. They do this primarily through a direct process of learning from the job and generalization of what has been learned to off-job realities. The collected research shows that these generalizations appear to hold under a broad range of controls for spuriousness, alternate explanations, and extensions. The extensions include men's and women's work lives, self-direction in leisure activities, housework, and educational domains, as well as a number of replications of the basic model including careful comparisons with samples from Poland and Japan, and more recently from the Ukraine (Kohn et al. 1997).

Similar summaries exist for many other areas of research in social structure and personality, but this line of research has been one of the most important. The limitations of the Kohn-Schooler program of research illustrate some of the frontiers facing research on work and personality. First, are these conditions of work the most important dimensions of social structure? Do they combine and exert their effects in a more complicated recipe? Are there other features of context that should be considered? Second, are these the appropriate dimensions and combinations or personality? Are there left-out dimensions or other larger meta- or organizing dimensions of personality, such as flexibility-rigidity or general affectivity (Spenner 1988a) or processual dimensions of personality, that might be more important?

Third, there are many alternate explanations that replace or extend the learning-generalization explanation for how jobs and personality reciprocally relate (for review, see O'Brien 1986). They include: (1) fit hypotheses, in which the quality of the match between dimensions of personality and dimensions of social structure determines the effects of the person on the job and vice versa; (2) needs and expectancy explanations, in which additional layers of cognitive weighting, interpretation, and processing mediate the relationships among job attributes, personality dimensions, and work attitude outcomes; (3) buffering and mediational hypotheses, in which the effects of social structure on personality (or vice versa) are accentuated or damped for certain extreme combinations of work conditions, or outside influences such as social support buffer the effects of social structure on personality; and (4) social information processing and attributional explanations, which posit additional perceptual or judgmental, evaluative or choice, or attributional processes that affect job-attitude and attitude-behavior linkages.

At more microscopic levels (shorter time intervals such as seconds or minutes, and smaller domains of social space, such as intrapsychic, or face-to-face interactions) the challenge for research on social structure and personality is to discover the meanings and processes that underlie longer-term, larger-scale correlations between the two. This challenge applies not only to how job or social structure affects personality, but also to how a domain of personality selects a worker into an occupational or another role, or serves as a catalyst for human agency and leads to attempts by people to modify their roles and circumstances. For example, if learning generalization operates as hypothesized, what does that mean? Is the learning part of the process as straightforward as textbook images of reinforcement psychology and social learning theory imply it is? Survey research designs, the dominant methodology, typically assume and rarely observe, specify, or test the social-psychological and psychological concomitants of learning generalization. What are the associated perceptual, affective, cognitive, and behavioral concomitants of learning generalization? What are the supporting and disconfirming attribution patterns and mediations? Or is the learning process below the level of cognitive operations and attributuional web of inferences that people use to make sense of their world? Experimental and observational design may be more informative than the typical survey research approach. The field understands many of the ingredients but not the specific recipe.

At a mezzoscopic level—careers, the human life span, organizations, and other institutional settings and mechanisms—the challenge to research on social structure and personality is to put the snapshots of relationships in motion and understand the dynamics over longer periods of time. For example, in the Kohn-Schooler model, how are its findings nested in adult development, and how is adult development affected by the dynamics implied in this model? Age and developmental variations have received only limited attention in the Kohn-Schooler approach. Further, much of our knowledge about relationships between various social structures and personality assumes a system in equilibrium (for example, a single coefficient capturing an effect over five or ten years). We know much less about the dynamics of social

structure–personality relationships, including estimation of trajectories, threshold effects, and rates of change. Here too, different types of research and data designs will be required to advance the state of knowledge.

Finally, at a larger, macroscopic level—encompassing decades and centuries, and whole institutional spheres and societies—the challenges confronting research in social structure and personality are multiple. They include discovering the larger sociohistorical, psychological, and biological contexts and processes in which social structure–personality relationships are embedded, and then mapping and tracing the lines of influence across levels. For example, many research streams are exclusively national or subnational, in terms of generalizations . The Kohn-Schooler approach, with systematic studies in the United States, Poland, Japan, and the Ukraine, is a notable exception, but even here we are still early on in understanding how the models vary in comparative studies of national and subnational contexts. Further, the state of knowledge is young in our understanding of how historical variations in the content and composition of work, the labor process, and the family, or in organizational form and practice altered relationships between social structure and personality. This larger challenge also includes discovering how long-term variations in human personality feed back on long-term variations in social structures, shaping history and defining what is possible for the evolution of social forms and processes.

REFERENCES

Alwin, D. F., R. L. Cohen, and T. M. Newcomb 1991 *Aging, Personality and Social Change: Attitude Persistence and Change over the Life-Span.* Madison: University of Wisconsin Press.

DiRenzo, Gordon J. 1977 "Socialization, Personality and Social Systems." In A. Inkeles, J. Coleman, and N. Smelser, eds., *Annual Review of Sociology*, vol. 3. Palo Alto, Calif.: Annual Reviews.

Elder, Glen H., Jr. 1974 *Children of the Great Depression.* Chicago: University of Chicago Press.

Featherman, David L., and Richard M. Lerner 1985 "Ontogeneses and Sociogenesis: Problematics for Theory and Research about Development and Socialization across the Life-Span." *American Sociological Review* 50:659–676.

Freud, Sigmund 1928 *The Basic Writings of Sigmund Freud*. Edited and translated by A. A. Brill. New York: Random House.

Gecas, Victor, and Peter Burke 1995 "Self and Identity." In K. S. Cook, G. A. Fine, and J. S. House, eds., *Sociological Perspectives on Social Psychology*. Needham Heights, Mass.: Allyn and Bacon.

Gerth, Hans, and C. Wright Mills 1953 *Character and Social Structure*. New York: Harcourt.

House, James S. 1981 "Social Structure and Personality." In M. Rosenberg and R. H. Turner, eds., *Social Psychology: Sociological Perspectives*. New York: Basic Books.

——, and Jeylan T. Mortimer 1990 "Social Structure and the Individual: Emerging Themes and New Directions." *Social Psychology Quarterly* 53:71–80.

Inkeles, Alex, and Daniel Levinson 1954 "National Character: The Study of Modal Personality and Social Systems." In G. Lindzey, ed., *Handbook of Social Psychology*. Cambridge, Mass.: Addison-Wesley.

Kiecolt, K. Jill 1988. "Recent Developments in Attitudes and Social Structure." In W. R. Scott, and J. Blake, eds., *Annual Review of Sociology*, vol. 14. Palo Alto, Calif.: Annual Reviews.

Kohn, Melvin L., and Carmie Schooler, with the collaboration of J. Miller, K. Miller, C. Schoenbach, and R. Schoenberg 1983 *Work and Personality: An Inquiry into the Impact of Social Stratification*. Norwood, N.J.: Ablex.

Kohn, Melvin L., and Kazimierz M. Slomczynski 1990 *Social Structure and Self-Direction: A Comparative Analysis of the United States and Poland*. Cambridge, Mass.: Basil Blackwell.

——, Kazimierz M. Slomczynski, Krystyna Janicka, Valeri Khmelko, Bogdan W. Mach, Vladimir Paniotto, Wojciech Zaborowski, Roberto Gutierrez, and Cory Heyman 1997 "Social Structure and Personality under Conditions of Radical Social Change: A Comparative Analysis of Poland and Ukraine." *American Sociological Review* 62:614–638.

Lewin, Kurt 1951 *Field Theory in Social Science*. New York: Harper.

Marx, Karl 1963 *Karl Marx: Early Writings*. Edited and translated by T. B. Bottomore. New York: McGraw-Hill.

Mead, George H. 1934 *Mind, Self and Society*. Chicago: University of Chicago Press.

Miller-Loessi, Karen 1995 "Comparative Social Psychology: Cross-Cultural and Cross- National." In K. S.

Cook, G. A. Fine, and J. S. House, eds., *Sociological Perspectives on Social Psychology*. Needham Heights, Mass.: Allyn and Bacon.

Mirowsky, John, and Catherine E. Ross 1986 "Social Patterns of Distress." In R. Turner and J. Short, eds., *Annual Review of Sociology*, vol. 12. Palo Alto, Calif.: Annual Reviews.

Mortimer, Jeylan, and John Lorence 1995 "Social Psychology of Work." In K. S. Cook, G. A. Fine, and J. S. House, eds., *Sociological Perspectives on Social Psychology*. Needham Heights, Mass.: Allyn and Bacon.

O'Brien, Gordon E. 1986 *Psychology of Work and Unemployment*. New York: Wiley.

Smelser, Neil J., and William T. Smelser 1963 *Personality and Social Systems*. New York: Wiley.

Snyder, Mark, and William Ickes 1985 "Personality and Social Behavior." In G. Lindzey and E. Aronson, eds., *Handbook of Social Psychology, Special Fields and Applications*, vol. II. New York: Random House.

Spenner, Kenneth I. 1988a "Social Stratification, Work and Personality." In W. R. Scott and J. Blake, eds., *Annual Review of Sociology*, vol 14. Palo Alto, Calif.: Annual Reviews.

—— 1988b "Occupations, Work Settings and the Course of Adult Development: Tracing the Implications of Select Historical Changes." In P. B. Baltes, D. L. Featherman, and R. M. Lerner, eds., *Life-Span Development and Behavior*, vol. 9. Hillsdale, N.J.: Lawrence Erlbaum.

—— 1998 "Reflections on a 30-Year Career of Research on Work and Personality by Melvin Kohn and Colleagues." *Sociological Forum* 13:169–181.

Turner, Ralph. H. 1956 "Role-taking, Role Standpoint, and Reference Group Behavior." *American Journal of Sociology* 61:316–328.

KENNETH I. SPENNER

PERSONALITY MEASUREMENT

WHAT IS PERSONALITY?

"Personality" is an ambiguous term derived from the natural language, and not necessarily a scientific concept. Consensus among interested scientists as to its precise meaning has been fairly modest. One major cleavage is between views of personality as core dynamic processes inherent in all people and views that emphasize characteristics on which individuals differ. Because the second sort of view defines personality in a way as to make it far more conducive to measurement, this article focuses on personality as certain potentially measurable characteristics of individuals.

Which measurable characteristics? There are many kinds of characteristics, and useful ways of categorizing characteristics have been developed (Norman 1967; Angleitner et al. 1990). Characteristics that fall into many of the categories do not fit common definitions of personality. Descriptors of physical characteristics (e.g., short, muscular) lack sufficient reference to psychological (behavioral, affective, cognitive) features. Descriptors invoking social roles (e.g., motherly, professional) and social effects (e.g., famous, neglected) involve social-contextualization and relativization too heavily to give inferences about an individual's personality attributes. Descriptors of emotions (e.g., elated, afraid) and many motivational and intentional states (e.g., hungry, reluctant, inspired) are too prone to reference relatively transient characteristics. And some descriptors (e.g., awful, impressive) are so purely evaluative that they provide insufficient specificity with respect to psychological features.

Among descriptors that refer to presumably more internal and enduring psychological attributes, three categories stand out. Abilities or talents (e.g., skillful, creative, athletic) refer to maximum rather than typical levels of performance on tasks. Beliefs and attitudes (e.g., religious, racist, environmentalist) concern affectively tinged habits of mind pertaining to specific objects and concepts. Although personality models have frequently contained some ability- and attitude-related content, at their core are traits (e.g., daring, patient) that are more directly related to typical behavioral patterns. Because they are expressed behaviorally, enduring motivational patterns (e.g., need for achievement) might also be easily fit within definitions of personality that emphasize typical behavior patterns. "Temperament" usually denotes the more clearly inborn and genetically derived aspects of personality, whereas "character" is often used to denote acquired moral qualities. But these terms are otherwise synonymous with personality, which can be defined as consistencies in patterns of behavior—where behavior is defined broadly to include affect, cognition, and motivation—on which individuals differ. Overall, personality is a lay concept of sufficient importance and usefulness to have been taken up and refined by scientists.

In natural languages, personality descriptors are alternately represented as adjectives (e.g., adventurous), attribute nouns (e.g., adventurousness), or type nouns (e.g., adventurer). Because adjectives differentiate properties, personality adjectives are inherently central to personality description, although some languages lack an adjective class and carry on this adjective function in other ways (Dixon 1977). Psychologists move easily between adjectives and attribute-noun characterizations of the same trait (as with extraverted and extraversion): Either form suggests properties that exist in varying degrees. Type-noun characterizations, in contrast, imply a categorization—one either is an extravert or one is not—which in turn suggests the assumption of a bimodal frequency distribution of individuals on the trait. Such bimodal distributions appear to be rare. Although type-noun characterizations of personality traits have great popular appeal, their use by academic psychologists has become quite limited. There has been a search for categorical taxons underlying the traits related to certain mental disorders (e.g., Meehl 1995), but this task is not easy. Recent correlational studies indicate that symptoms of mental disorders, and of personality disorders in particular, are continuously distributed in the population, and have substantial overlap with measures of various personality traits (Costa and Widiger 1994).

In the last three decades, many psychologists have addressed the fundamental issue of whether personality traits are real, or whether they exist only in the eye of the beholder. Mischel's early review (1968) suggested that personality measures were at best modest predictors of relevant actual behaviors. However, a consensus has emerged that when criterion behaviors are aggregated, across time or across situations, personality measures can become quite highly predictive (Kenrick and Funder 1988). This follows, of course, from definitions of personality offered above: Personality does not denote single behaviors but rather consistent patterns in multiple behaviors. Moreover, studies involving twins and adoptees have repeatedly indicated that personality-trait scores are partially (as much as 50 percent) heritable, implying biological underpinnings. Such behavior-genetic findings have stimulated the development of models that set forth biological explanations for personality variation, attempting to delineate phenotypic constructs so that they correspond directly to known biological mechanisms (e.g., Gray 1987; Rothbart et al. 1994; Zuckerman 1995). Nonetheless, studies with twins and adoptees also indicate that differences in experience, mainly of the type *not* shared by family members, have a profound effect on personality characteristics (Plomin 1990). There are also some indications of important effects of culture.

Although personality traits reflect behavioral consistencies across situations, a variety of research findings indicate that some situations facilitate expression of personality traits more than do other situations (Caspi and Moffitt 1993). Highly structured or ritualized social settings (e.g., a funeral home, a lecture hall) tend to attenuate the expression of personality differences, whereas relatively unstructured settings (e.g., a nightclub, a playground) bring out personality differences. This pattern has three important consequences for personality measurement. First, to the extent that a society's social milieux are age-stratified, one might expect across-time continuity in apparent traits to be somewhat "heterotypic"—leading to different surface characteristics at different ages. Second, personality characteristics are best assessed by placing the individual in a relatively unstructured situation in which responses are relatively unconstrained by social norms; therefore, the stimuli on personality measures should not have correct responses. Third, to the extent that a cultural milieu is highly structured and ritualized, one might expect to see less emphasis on personality differences than would be found in relatively individualistic cultural mileux (Miller 1984).

PERSONALITY MEASUREMENT CAPTURES CONSISTENCIES

Measurement can be defined as a set of rules for assigning numbers to entities (such as individuals) in such a way that attributes of the entities are faithfully represented. Measurement procedures typically set up, or specify, regularized administration conditions. Thus, measurement generally involves consistency of procedure; but personality measurement has an even deeper relation to consistency.

As noted above, a consensual definition of personality would emphasize characteristics that are internally rather than externally caused, psychological rather than overtly physical, and stable and enduring rather than transient. Because of the emphasis on stable and enduring qualities, reliability—relative absence of measurement error—is of first importance in personality measurement. A reliable measure by definition registers characteristics that are consistent across time, as indicated by test-retest reliability coefficients or across situations. Internal consistency, or inter-item reliability, is an analogue of cross-situational stability. Each item represents a unique situation in either of two ways: (1) its referent content may refer to a distinct situation (e.g., "I talk a lot at parties"), or (2) simply being presented with this item as distinguished from another item (e.g., "I talk very little at parties") is a unique immediate situation for the respondent. Reliability is most often measured either by a stability coefficient, indicating the correlation between scores at one time and those at another, or by an internal consistency coefficient (e.g., coefficient alpha) that represents the average correlation between pairs of all possible split halves of the test items, although a variety of alternative reliability models are available. Until cross-time stability is established, a trait's stability is only presumed and it might be better termed an attribute, since the latter term has fewer implications as to stability.

Another criterion for the reliability of personality judgments is the extent to which different observers agree in rating a target. This is a more demanding criterion; ideally, to the degree an individual has a characteristic it will be obvious to both self and observers. However, a number of influences tend to attenuate agreement between observers. Some characteristics (e.g., sociability) are highly observable, whereas others (e.g., anxiety level) are less so. Interobserver agreement is typically reduced by having observed the target at different times or in different situations. Generally, we might expect the self to be the most privileged observer, but in certain ways the self-viewpoint can be misleading. Personality characterizations have social functions and, understandably, self-observer agreement is prone to be affected by conscious impression management and unconscious self-enhancement tendencies (Paulhus and

Reid 1991). Finally, quite independently of content, observers differ in their use of measurement scales (e.g., differential tendencies to agree or disagree, respond extremely, or use the middle option if available). Given this minefield of potential difficulties, the moderate level of interobserver agreement documented in the research literature may be quite remarkable. It makes sense to capitalize on the conjoint perspective of multiple judges: the best arbiter of the degree to which an individual can be characterized with a certain trait may be the pooled judgments of several observers well acquainted with the subject (Hofstee 1994; Kolar et al. 1996), perhaps conjoined with self-ratings. Though greater acquaintance clearly increases judges' accuracy, there is, particularly for the more observable traits, surprisingly good consensus among near strangers for the traits of a target (Borkenau and Liebler 1993).

Another important, but demanding, index of consistency is across-time stability: within a sample of individuals, the extent to which one's relative standing at time 1 correlates with that at time 2. Across-time stabilities tend to be very high for short intervals (e.g., a day or a week) but diminish with greater intervals to a more moderate level. Even across long intervals, cross-time stabilities in adulthood—particularly after age 30—for most personality traits are impressively high (Costa and McCrae 1997). It appears, however, that the further the measurement intervals reach into childhood and especially infancy, the lower the stabilities become; judgments of infant temperament may not do much better than chance in predicting judgments of later adult personality. Stabilities may be held down by the incommensurability of the contexts within which infant and adult temperaments function: It is difficult to apply many adult traits (e.g., industrious, artistic, unselfish) to infants, so that any forms of continuity would have to be heterotypic. It seems likely, however, that levels of traits often do change from childhood to adulthood. Part of this change could be genetically programmed, as a different set of genes comes on-line with greater maturity, and an initial set goes off-line; on the other hand, much may change under the influence of experience. To Wordsworth's assertion that "the child is father of the man," psychometricians offer an assent beset with caveats: "usually," "in many ways," "with definite exceptions."

PERSONALITY DATA HAS MULTIPLE SOURCES

Data on behavior patterns are most commonly elicited from self and observers or acquaintances using standardized measures of personality traits. Scores on these structured measures are compared within a sample in a "nomothetic" manner, that is, seeking generalizations that can be applied to all individuals. Historically, the dominant position of this structured, nomothetic approach stems from the success of well-known inventories like (1) the Minnesota Multiphasic Personality Inventory (MMPI), which is actually more of a psychiatric symptom inventory than a personality inventory; (2) the California Psychological Inventory (CPI), which resembles the MMPI in numerous respects but taps rather different content, with scales labeled so as to stress the presence (or absence) of adaptive traits; and (3) the Myers-Briggs Type Indicator (MBTI), a measure based on parts of C. G. Jung's typology. The MBTI has been criticized by psychometricians, ignored by academic researchers, yet bought up by the millions in other circles. Today, these older inventories have competition from numerous new inventories that in some cases are shorter and more efficient.

Nonetheless, there are potentially useful alternatives to the questionnaire. Some embody an idiographic approach—seeking individually unique constructs that are not generalized to all people—rather than a nomothetic one. For example, in George Kelly's Role-Construct Repertory Test, each testee nominates a set of personally significant acquaintances, then derives idiographic constructs by comparing subsets of them. Such idiographic measures undoubtedly have a unique contribution: They may generate results that are more meaningful to the individual measured. But knowledge of general laws illuminates understanding of the individual case; it is possible to adapt many nomothetic measures to serve idiographic ends. Thus, improved nomothetic understanding lays the groundwork for improved idiographic understandings.

Questionnaires, whether used nomothetically or idiographically, are essentially overt and direct in their measurement approach. A trait is assessed with reference to a person's behaviors, emotions, and cognitions. Descriptions, which may be at a rather broad level, are collected. This overt method can be highly efficient, but has a significant disadvantage: Because the descriptive content provides clues to what is being measured, respondents completing the measure could, if motivated, intentionally present an inaccurate picture. Moreover, responses can be provided thoughtlessly. Some of those who are dissimulating or not paying attention can be identified using so-called validity indexes. These indexes are computed by scouring the response pattern for various signs of less than honest and accurate responding: unusual levels of agreement with unfavorable items, disagreement with favorable items, denying common vices, claiming rare virtues, responding dissimilarly to items with similar content, or responding similarly to items with contradictory content.

Projective measures, in contrast, are covert measures of personality that are more resistant to dissimulating or inattentive responding. These measures assume a "projective hypothesis" first defined by Rorschach, Jung, and others early in this century: If an individual is presented with a vague or ambiguous stimulus, that individual's response will be determined by habitual internal tendencies, preoccupations, and cognitive styles, rather than being affected by features of the stimulus. In a word, respondents "project" their proclivities onto the stimulus. Projective measures are potentially very sensitive receptors for personality variation. As noted above, personality differences are clearest when individuals are confronted with unstructured situations; vague and ambiguous stimuli are unstructured situations. One might simply place the individual in an unstructured situation and observe which behaviors, emotions, and thoughts ensue.

The most popular unstructured stimuli for these purposes have been inkblots (e.g., the Rorschach and Holtzman stimulus sets), sets of pictures—selected for their ambiguity—about which stories are elicited (e.g., the Thematic Apperception Test [TAT] and its derivatives), and figure drawings; in the last case the individual is presented with blank paper and asked to draw a certain object (e.g., person, house, tree). Other commonly used unstructured stimuli include incomplete sentences (e.g., "Most people __.") and single words for which an association is elicited. The raw material provided by the respondent must then be coded and interpreted with reference to response patterns of aggregate respondents. These measures capture aspects of personality covertly and indirectly; due to the ambiguity of the test materials, respondents are unlikely to guess what is being measured.

Though attractive in theory, projective measures have been problematic in practice. The rock upon which they are prone to founder is the crucial one of reliability. A first problem is that individuals' responses to projective stimuli are affected by social context and environment, and to a considerable degree they change from one day to another. This problem may be partially solved by gathering responses to many stimuli, preferably on multiple occasions, and looking for consistent patterns across time and across stimuli. A second problem is that observers often have low levels of agreement with regard to coding and interpreting the stimuli; that is, there is often a great deal of interobserver noise obscuring any underlying signal. There have been recent attempts to create interpretive coding schemes with better reliability. The best example is Exner's comprehensive system for the Rorschach (1986), which integrates features of several previous Rorschach scoring systems.

The Rorschach and the TAT remain fairly popular measures in clinical settings, and continue to generate a stream of research. Presently, however, many psychologists are skeptical about the usefulness of these measures, given the laborious, complex procedures for collecting and scoring data. One problem may be the sheer volume and range of the data that such free-response methods bring in; perhaps only a fraction of these data are of any importance, and we are not yet sure which fraction deserves the most attention. Projective measures might in the future become increasingly important, to the extent that they can be made more reliable, parsimonious, and efficient.

Other forms of data can be coded using the interpretive schemes developed for projective measures. For example, politician's speeches, reports of early memories, and virtually any autobiographical material can be analyzed in much the same way as stories elicited from the TAT. Most often, such material has been analyzed in terms of implicit motivational features (e.g., achievement, power, intimacy), and evidence suggests that such covertly measured motivation is not substantially correlated with indexes of similar content derived from structured measures of self-attributed motivation (McClelland et al. 1989). In general, autobiographical data seems to provide information outside that provided by personality questionnaires, given that individuals seem to store schematic beliefs about traits separately from autobiographical memories (Klein and Loftus 1993). Therefore, autobiographical data could become an important part of the comprehensive assessment of individuals.

WHICH TRAITS ARE WORTH MEASURING?

Whether the measurement method is overt or covert, another crucial issue concerns the particular traits that one ought to measure. Most commonly, this issue has been handled within a scale-construction strategy that might be called "rational": A researcher decides which trait (i.e., construct) he or she wants to measure, creates a pool of potential items, tries them out on a sample of respondents, and perhaps iterates between data and preconceived theory to create a relatively efficient measure of the construct. A second, "empirical" strategy is in some ways a variant of the first. The researcher includes in the sample of respondents one or more criterion groups (e.g., introverts, psychopaths, artists) and determines the set of items that best differentiates each criterion group from a control sample, thus leading to a "criterion-keyed" scale for the construct (e.g., introversion, psychopathy, creative temperament). In either strategy, the researcher begins with an a priori conception of what ought to be measured, but in the empirical strategy this conception is identified with a criterion group. It is not difficult to combine rational and empirical strategies, as was done in the only major revision of the original MMPI.

Unfortunately, a field that accumulates a great host of a priori conceptions can become quite chaotic, and this was the predominant state of affairs in personality measurement until at least the 1970s, when expert compendiums on personality traits could still be organized alphabetically by trait (e.g., London and Exner 1978), as if there were no other way to order them. There were many constructs, and it was clear that some of them were related to others, but the structure underlying the whole set of constructs was unclear. From the early decades of the twentieth century, investigators seeking an ordering framework turned to a statistical technique called "factor analysis." *Factor analysis* is a method for reducing a large number of observed variables to a smaller number of hypothetical variables (factors), by analyzing the covariances among the observed variables and identifying redundancies in the set of variables. Factor analysis can be used to identify parsimonious sets of variables within sets of items built by any scale-construction strategy. Historically, reviews of factor analyses of various collections of personality scales (e.g., French, 1953) have not led to a consensus on a common framework (Goldberg 1972).

Significant progress on the structural problem came largely by temporarily averting attention from the a priori constructs of experts in order to study those personality conceptions of laypersons that are embedded in the natural language. As noted at the outset, personality traits are socially meaningful phenomena about which laypersons comment and generalize, and the lexicon of any language is a repository of descriptors referencing a wide variety of human characteristics. The lexical hypothesis formalizes this state of affairs into a strategy for identifying necessary features for an organizing framework, or taxonomy, of personality attributes (Goldberg 1981). This hypothesis essentially states that the more important the attribute, the more likely people are to develop a word for it. The most important attributes will then be those represented by numerous terms (often representing specific aspects of broader concepts) within one language, and by recurrence across many languages. Once descriptors are gathered, for example from a dictionary, they can be used by individuals to describe themselves or others. Factor analysis of this data, in any language, can be used to search for a few dimensions underlying numerous descriptors.

Expert personality constructs are typically based on certain aspects of the lay descriptive vocabulary, but scientists may refine and extend lay distinctions in useful ways. Therefore, one cannot obtain a *sufficient* model of personality traits by studying lexical descriptors, but one can find *necessary* features for such a model, aspects that—based on their salience to lay observers—are too important to leave out. In this respect, lexical models of personality dimensions offer minimum-content criteria for other personality models, pointing clearly to some (but not all) of the trait concepts important enough to measure. In practice, lexical models have helped focus attention on important variables previously omitted from expert-derived models.

Lexical studies involve (1) culling descriptors from a dictionary; (2) omitting descriptors that are infrequently used or, by the consensus of multiple judges, refer to categories less relevant to personality (e.g., physical traits, temporary states); (3) aggregating the remaining descriptors (typically 300 to 400) into a questionnaire format with a multipoint (e.g., 1 to 5) rating scale; (4) administering the forms so constructed to a large (usually >400) sample of respondents for description of self, a well-acquainted peer, or sometimes both; and (5) factor-analyzing the descriptors to derive an indigenous or "emic" personality structure for that language. Such studies have been conducted in over a dozen languages, including English, German, Dutch, Italian, Spanish, Hungarian, Czech, Polish, Filipino, Korean, Turkish, and Hebrew.

Findings of these lexical studies (reviewed by Saucier 1997) show some variations, probably due to differences in sampling of subjects and variables as much as to actual differences between languages. But the most common result has been a robust structure of five independent (uncorrelated) factors, with apparent cross-language universality for the three largest of these factors: extraversion (which includes sociability, activity, and assertiveness), agreeableness (which includes warmth, generosity, humility, patience, and nonaggressiveness), and conscientiousness (which includes dependability, orderliness, and consistency). The remaining two factors (one referencing aspects of emotional stability, the other aspects of intellect, imagination, and unconventionality) are generally smaller and more variant from one study to another. Despite these partial inconsistencies between one emic structure and another, the five-factor structure, often labeled the "Big Five," has been shown to be easily translatable into a large number of languages (McCrae et al. 1998). Moreover, the

Big Five appears to capture the structure of trait judgments about children as well as adults (Digman and Shmelyov 1996).

The Big Five has had considerable influence on personality questionnaires. For example, one prominent three-factor inventory (the NEO Personality Inventory) was revised to add the two missing factors from the Big Five, in this case agreeableness and conscientiousness (McCrae and Costa 1985). Moreover, the five factors have strong relations to the constructs measured by other prominent inventories, including the Myers-Briggs Type Indicator, the 16PF inventory, and the Personality Research Form. Four of the five factors (excluding intellect/imagination) are substantially correlated with measures of personality disorder symptoms and some mood, anxiety, and impulse control disorders cataloged in current psychiatric nosologies; a safe generalization seems to be that disorders tend to co-occur with extreme scores on personality dimensions (like the Big Five) on which there is wide variation in the general population (Costa and Widiger 1994). However, psychotic syndromes map rather poorly onto the Big Five, as do a few other clearly important individual-differences constructs, like religiousness and attractiveness (Saucier and Goldberg 1998)

Although the Big Five have obtained some degree of consensus as an organizing framework for personality characteristics, there are at least five remaining issues whose resolution might lead to a different consensual structure: (1) The generalizability of the Big Five factors to languages spoken in non-Western, nonindustrialized nations, and indeed in less complex societies, is as yet uncertain. (2) The Big Five represent very broad, global trait constructs, and groups of more specific constructs are typically more useful in prediction contexts; however, there is as yet little consensus about the particular specific subcomponents that make up each of the broad factors. (3) There may be factors in related domains, such as abilities or attitudes, that could arguably be added to the model. (4) The organization of personality variables into factors based on lexical representation might be reasonably superseded by a set of factors based on a superior rationale, for example, correspondence to main lines of biological or environmental influence. And (5) there may be constructs well represented among natural-language descriptors that will prove to be of great importance. Personality-relevant constructs with apparently meager representation in natural language descriptors, but attracting much current research interest, include those having to do with (1) defense mechanisms (Paulhus et al. 1997), (2) coping styles (Suls et al. 1996), and (3) personal goals and strivings (Pervin 1989).

One important criterion by which personality constructs might be added to, or eliminated from, a basic descriptive model is validity. Validity should be clearly distinguished from reliability: *Reliability* concerns whether a scale is measuring anything at all, and is a prerequisite to any form of validity. *Validity* concerns the meaning of a scale score, that is, the accuracy of the inferences one can make from the scale. For a construct that demonstrates validity, there is a good argument for meaningfulness and usefulness with respect to other phenomena. Validity evidence is gathered in an ongoing process, rather than in any single study.

A prior question, of course, is whether personality measures have a substantial enough degree of validity to make them worthwhile. Mischel's early critique (1968) suggested they did not. An increasingly large volume of studies documents the many ways in which they do. For example, conscientiousness is a valuable predictor of effective job-related performance (even after the predictive value of intelligence is accounted for and removed), and has also been associated with increased longevity. Low scores on emotional stability (i.e., high scores on neuroticism) are predictive of higher rates of divorce, of male midlife crises, and of health-related complaints (though not actually greater illness). Agreeableness has associations with aspects of conflict (or absence of conflict) in close relationships, and extraversion predicts variation in a wide range of social-interaction variables.

PROSPECTS AND FURTHER APPLICATIONS

As the foregoing review indicates, the science of personality measurement is no longer at the primitive stage represented by early taxonomies of virtues (such as those of Plato or Confucius), of physiological humors (such as that of Galen), or by

the pseudoscience of astrological signs which beckons from magazine racks. Unlike these approaches, current personality measurement is far more explicit about (1) defining personality, (2) measuring attributes in a standardized, reliable manner, (3) attending to multiple sources of data, (4) checking the validity of hypothesized models, and (5) placing the plethora of possible constructs within a parsimonious and empirically justifiable organizing framework. Nonetheless, current scientific practices are inevitably based on assumptions that are subject to being overturned. Rorer (1990) provides a conceptual review of personality assessment with attention to differences between the assumptions of mainstream and alternative paradigms.

Personality as a discipline has come to be located mainly within the larger umbrella of psychology. This is reasonable, given that personality deals with the behavior, affect, and cognitions of individuals, and with individual differences. But certain aspects of personality seem to be equally relevant to other sciences. Many of the more inborn, dispositional aspects of personality are clearly rooted in biology and genetics, and personality change may well be associated with physiological changes—as cause or effect. Moreover, humans are social as well as biological beings, and personality functions within a social context. The sociological aspects of personality need more attention: Although Goffman (1972) proposed aspects of one useful sociological theory of personality, and Bellah et al. (1985) described certain social-structural contexts that may foster narcissism, generally the relation of personality variation to its broader social context is but dimly understood.

In anthropology, one finds a rich tradition of studies of "culture and personality." Past work in this area has been hindered by use of less than adequate personality measurement models. For example, many studies used projective personality measures with insufficiently developed reliability. If improvements are made in analysis of projective data, it may be possible to take a new look at old data. Moreover, linguists and anthropologists may be uniquely well equipped to gather and judge evidence pertinent to the cross-cultural universality of basic personality dimensions, and help answer several important questions: Which dimensions of interindividual variation are not only measurable in any culture, but derivable from the indigenous language of any culture? What is the meaning of between-culture variation in the classification of personality characteristics? To what extent is "modal personality" a viable way of differentiating societies, or of mapping cultural change, and how do temperament and social structure interact? Do cultures differ in how they organize the heterogeneity that personality variation introduces?

The fascinating generalizations offered by Mead, Benedict, and others must be considered provisional, given the probably limited range and value of data upon which they are based. If waves of advancement in personality measurement were joined to waves of advancement in other social sciences, a powerful current might ensue, which would yield a far better understanding of societies in terms of the diverse range of humans within each of these societies.

REFERENCES

Angleitner, Alois, Fritz Ostendorf, and Oliver P. John 1990 "Towards a Taxonomy of Personality Descriptors in German: A Psycho-Lexical Study." *European Journal of Personality* (4):89–118.

Bellah, Robert, Richard Madsen, William M. Sullivan, Ann Swidler, and Steven M. Tipton 1985 *Habits of the Heart: Individualism and Commitment in American Life*. Berkeley: University of California Press.

Borkenau, Peter, and Anette Liebler 1993 "Consensus and Self-Other Agreement for Trait Inferences from Minimal Information." *Journal of Personality* (61):477–496.

Caspi, Avshalom, and Terrie E. Moffitt 1993 "When Do Individual Differences Matter: A Paradoxical Theory of Personality Coherence." *Psychological Inquiry* (4):247–271.

Costa, Paul T., Jr., and Robert R. McCrae 1997 "Longitudinal Stability of Adult Personality." In Robert Hogan, John A. Johnson, and Stephen R. Briggs, eds., *Handbook of Personality Psychology*. San Diego, Calif.: Academic Press.

Costa, Paul T., Jr. and Thomas A. Widiger (eds.) 1994 *Personality Disorders and the Five-Factor Model of Personality*. Washington, D.C.: American Psychological Association.

Digman, John M., and Alexander G. Shmelyov 1996 "The Structure of Temperament and Personality in Russian Children." *Journal of Personality and Social Psychology* (71):341–351.

Dixon, R. M. W. 1977 "Where Have All the Adjectives Gone?" *Studies in Language* (1):19–80.

Exner, John E., Jr. 1986 *The Rorschach: A Comprehensive System, Vol. 1, Basic Foundations*, 2nd ed. New York: Wiley.

French, John W. 1953 *The Description of Personality Measurements in Terms of Rotated Factors*. Princeton, N.J.: Educational Testing Service.

Goffman, Erving 1972 *The Presentation of Self in Everyday Life*. Woodstock, N.Y.: Overlook Press.

Goldberg, Lewis R. 1972 "A Historical Survey of Personality Scales and Inventories." In Paul McReynolds, ed., *Advances in Psychological Assessment*, vol. 2. Palo Alto, Calif.: Science and Behavior Books.

—— 1981 "Language and Individual Differences: The Search for Universals in Personality Lexicons." In Ladd Wheeler, ed., *Review of Personality and Social Psychology*, vol. 2. Beverly Hills, Calif.: Sage.

Gray, Jeffrey A. 1987 "The Neuropsychology of Emotions and Personality." In Stephen M. Stahl, Susan D. Iverson, and Elisabeth C. Goodman, eds., *Cognitive Neurochemistry*. Oxford: Oxford University Press.

Hofstee, Willem K. B. 1994 "Who Should Own the Definition of Personality?" *European Journal of Personality* 8:149–162.

Kenrick, Douglas T., and David C. Funder 1988 "Profiting from Controversy: Lessons from the Person-Situation Debate." *American Psychologist* 43:23–34.

Klein, Stanley B., and Judith Loftus 1993 "The Mental Representation of Trait and Autobiographical Knowledge about the Self." In Thomas K. Srull and Robert S. Wyer, Jr., eds., *Advances in Social Cognition, vol. 5, The Representation of Trait and Autobiographical Knowledge about the Self*. Hillsdale, N.J.: Lawrence Erlbaum.

Kolar, David W., David C. Funder, and Randall C. Colvin 1996 "Comparing the Accuracy of Personality Judgements by the Self and Knowledgeable Others." *Journal of Personality* 64:311–337.

London, Harvey, and John E. Exner, Jr. 1978 *Dimensions of Personality*. New York: John Wiley.

McClelland, David C., Richard Koestner, and Joel Weinberger 1989 "How Do Self-Attributed and Implicit Motives Differ?" *Psychological Review* 96:690–702.

McCrae, Robert R., and Paul T. Costa, Jr. 1985 "Updating Norman's Adequate Taxonomy: Intelligence and Personality Dimensions in Natural Language and in Questionnaires." *Journal of Personality and Social Psychology* 49:710–721.

——, Gregorio H. Del Pilar, Jean-Pierre Rolland, and Wayne D. Parker 1998 "Cross-Cultural Assessment of the Five-Factor Model: The Revised NEO Personality Inventory." *Journal of Cross-Cultural Psychology* 29:171–188.

Meehl, Paul E. 1995 "Bootstraps Taxometrics: Solving the Classification Problem in Psychopathology." *American Psychologist* 50:266–275.

Miller, Joan G. 1984 "Culture and the Development of Everyday Social Explanation." *Journal of Personality and Social Psychology* 46:961–978.

Mischel, Walter 1968 *Personality and Assessment.* New York: John Wiley.

Norman, Warren T. 1967 *2800 Personality Trait Descriptors: Normative Operating Characteristics for a University Population.* Ann Arbor: University of Michigan Press.

Paulhus, Delroy L., and Douglas B. Reid 1991 "Enhancement and Denial in Socially Desirable Responding." *Journal of Personality and Social Psychology* 60:307–317.

Paulhus, Delroy L., Bram Fridhandler, and Sean Hayes 1997 "Psychological Defense: Contemporary Theory and Research." In Robert Hogan, John A. Johnson, and Stephen R. Briggs, eds., *Handbook of Personality Psychology.* San Diego, Calif.: Academic Press.

Pervin, Lawrence A. (ed.) 1989 *Goal Concepts in Personality and Social Psychology.* Hillsdale, N.J.: Lawrence Erlbaum.

Plomin, Robert 1990 "The Role of Inheritance in Behavior." *Science* 248:183–188.

Rorer, Leonard G. 1990 "Personality Assessment: A Conceptual Survey." In Lawrence A. Pervin et al., eds., *Handbook of Personality: Theory and Research.* New York: Guilford.

Rothbart, Mary K., Douglas Derryberry, and Michael I. Posner 1994 "A Psychobiological Approach to the Development of Temperament." In John E. Bates, and Theodore D. Wachs, eds., *Temperament: Individual Differences at the Interface of Biology and Behavior.* Washington, D.C.: American Psychological Association.

Saucier, Gerard 1997 "Effects of Variable Selection on the Factor Structure of Person Descriptors." *Journal of Personality and Social Psychology* 73:1296–1312.

——, and Lewis R. Goldberg 1998 "What Is Beyond the Big Five?" *Journal of Personality* 66:495–524.

Suls, Jerry, James P. David, and John H. Harvey 1996 "Personality and Coping: Three Generations of Research." *Journal of Personality* 64:711–735.

Zuckerman, Marvin 1995 "Good and Bad Humors: Biochemical Bases of Personality and Its Disorders." *Psychological Science* 6:325–332.

GERARD SAUCIER

PERSONALITY THEORY

WHAT IS PERSONALITY?

A definition of *personality*, and there are many such definitions, must precede a treatment of personality theory. One must note at the start that personality is not an entity or a thing. It is a mentalistic construct that serves as an abstract cognitive device for understanding (1) the characteristic ways human beings behave or are inclined to behave; (2) their perceptions of their defining characteristics; and in the view of many, (3) the common (in some cases measured) perception that others have of them. This view of "personality" overlaps to a great extent with William James's view of self ([1890]1952), both psychological and social. Though personologists may at times refer to personality as if it had been reified, this stems less from their intention than from a limitation of the language used. Given this condition, one can only strive to assure as close a correspondence as is possible of the definition of this word with the complex reality it is intended to reflect and capture.

Definitions of personality vary depending on the standpoint—scientific, philosophical, humanistic, or strictly psychological—that one adopts. Personality for our purposes is one or another heuristic enabling social scientists to understand and predict human behavior, both overt and tacit, and individuals' complex responses to the events that sweep over them daily. To speak of individuals' personalities is to allude to all their longstanding, characterological properties that dispose them, given any set of circumstances, to respond in a predictable way. In popular parlance "to really know someone" is to understand that person's self-concept and the idiosyncratic manner in which he or she deals with problems of daily life, whether social, political, or purely intrapsychic. In short, to know someone is to have a knowledge of their personality; but the personality of an individual is not a simple matter to assess. To realize this, one has only to consider that there is a shifting presentation of self as a function of the multifarious situations in which one can find oneself. The same person with a single personality has a number of personae at his or her disposal for (generally) adaptive use.

It is useful to quote in this context a classic statement by William James:

Properly speaking, a man has as many social selves as there are individuals who recognize him *and carry an image of him in their mind. To wound any one of these images is to wound him. But as the individuals who carry the images fall naturally into classes, we may practically say that he has as many different social selves as there are distinct* groups *of persons about whose opinion he cares. He generally shows a different side of himself to each of these different groups. Many a youth who is demure enough before his teachers and parents, swears and swaggers like a pirate among his "tough" young friends. We do not show ourselves to our children as to our club-companions, to our customers as to the laborers we employ, to our own masters and employers as to our intimate friends.* ([1890] 1952, chap. X, "The Consciousness of Self," pp. 189–190)

This statement, written in the 1880s, has a modern ring, and clearly presages the later work of, say, Hartshorne and May (1928) and Walter Mischel (1968). Clearly it represents a theory of personality that is relativistic and relational. Relative to the former aspect, it invokes a double perspective. The first is the perspective of individuals as they present themselves very differently and even inconsistently in various contexts to different classes of people. The second is the perception of observers who make judgments about individuals' personalities (or characters) based on the limited sampling of behavior they have witnessed either directly or indirectly. As such, it also presents the notion of self and of personality, though these two terms do not have identical meanings, as much more complex when viewed from within by the individual than when viewed from without by society. Relative to the relational aspect, personality appears to be shaped by the demand characteristics of the social group within which the individual performs. In this Jamesian perspective, personality is the flip side of self, that

is, observers' characterizations of others as distinguished from the views that those latter individuals have of themselves. Indeed the everyday language that individuals use to describe themselves (as well as others) has provided the vocabulary (e.g., altruistic, aggressive, nurturant, inquisitive, venturesome) for defining the components of the construct, personality (e.g., Cattell 1964, 1965). Further, the equivalents of these terms, used to personologically distinguish individuals, can be found in most of the world's languages. (This notion has been labeled the "fundamental lexical hypothesis," and is addressed below.)

An individual's identity—understanding of his or her character and typical patterns of behavioral responses to social and other environmental stimuli—is the result not simply of their personal history, but of his or her construal of that history and of the either vivid or tacit memories that form the warp and weft of their self-understanding. It is generally accepted that memories are never absolutely veridical. The fact that false memories are more or less richly interlarded with relatively true memories suggests that personality as viewed from its owner's standpoint is partially self-constructed. William James stated that "False memories are by no means rare occurrences in most of us, and, whenever they occur, they distort the consciousness of the me . . . The most frequent source of false memory is the accounts we give to others of our experiences" ([1890]1952, p. 241). He asserts that this is a source of the errors in testimony that the individual has every intention of making honest. This is confirmed in more recent analyses (e.g., Laurence et al. 1998) that demonstrate that people's characterization's of themselves or others can be compellingly shaped by the situational as well as by intrapsychic demands that subjects experience when they must make judgments about personality. That these dynamics may be at work when individuals are completing even the best-validated and most reliable of personality inventories is reason to draw conclusions from such inventories with caution.

THEORIES IN GENERAL

Theories that have been developed to explain the dimensions of personality and the way personality develops are too numerous to describe (see Table

Selected Personality and Related Theories, and Their Originators

Adler, Alfred	Developed a holistic theory, individual psychology, characterized by teleological, sociobiological, and self-actualizing dynamics. Utilized notion of unconscious, but used a rational, commonsense approach to remediating problems.
Allport, Gordon	Theorized that structural elements of personality comprised traits disposing individuals to respond to stimulus fields in predictable patterns. Traits are viewed as both individualizing and nomothetic.
Angyll, Andreas	Developed a partial theory that stressed the human's need to serve superordinate group goals, while striving for self-individualization.
Bandura, Albert	Developed a social cognitive theory of human development in which the modeling of behavior by important others shapes each person's behavior and character. This theory has a strong teleological emphasis meshed with sense of self-efficacy.
Berne, Eric	Posited a phenomenological theory of human personality, *transactional analysis,* comprising three distinct ego states: parent, adult, and child.
Binswanger, Ludwig	An existential psychologist, a disciple of Heidegger, who elaborated a phenomenological approach to the understanding of human behavior, especially in the face of the most difficult aspects of life.
Burrow, Trigant	Pioneered view of humans as profoundly social, interactive, personologically shaped by group activity. An early group therapist.
Boss, Medard	A Heideggerian whose antitheoretical approach nevertheless limns a view of human nature that is constructivist, but with traces of the psychoanalytic and the phenomenological.
Cattell, Raymond	Developed a complex trait theory and psychometric measure (16 PF) through factor-analysis of vernacular trait expressions.
Corsini, Raymond	Formulated a developmental theory of personality of Adlerian and Rogerian inspiration, involving a strong genetic component; emphasized formative influence of parental values, educational experiences, and critical stochastological events.
Digman, John	(*See* McDougall, W.)
Dollard, John	Developed (with Neal Miller) a theory of personality of behavioral inspiration, constituted largely of evolving habits; drives and stimulus-response connections account for dynamics of changing personality structures.
Erikson, Erik	Elaborated a stage-based, life-span model of human development that was psychosocial and psychoanalytic in inspiration. A major focus is on personal identity development.
Eysenck, Hans	Fashioned a psychometrically supported model of human personality that is biologically trait-based and hierarchically organized.
Frankl, Viktor	Developed a life-span, noninstinctual, teleological model of human development in which the dominant motivational force is the will to meaning, underpinned by values and ideals.
Freud, Sigmund	Developed a state-based, conflict theory of personality that is pansexual and deterministic. The central construct is the Oedipal conflict, the resolution of which enables, especially for the male, the full expansion of the psyche.
Horney, Karen	Developed a revisionist psychoanalysis that shed its androcentric features; her sociopsychological theory later evolved along Adlerian lines and generated a cogent feminine psychology.
Jackson, Don	With J. Haley, P. Watzlawick, J. Beavin, and others at the Mental Research Institute in Palo Alto, California, formulated a humanistic, systems-oriented approach to understanding human character and behavior.
Janet, Pierre	Founder of *psychological analysis.* Formulated a holistic psychology of the person, including a theory of rapport, the unconscious, and the complexes that drive human behavior. A nineteenth-century empiricist, he developed, inter alia, notions of transference and suggestibility.
Jung, Carl	Founder of *analytic psychotherapy.* Posited a holistic psychology of the person, including a theory of the unconscious and the complexes that drive human behavior.
Kelly, George	Developed *personal construct theory,* a constructivist system of human personality development, predicated on the assumption that individuals construe reality in light of their life history. These construals govern anticipation and realization of events.

(continued)

Selected Personality and Related Theories, and Their Originators *(continued)*

Lewin, Kurt	Developed a topological psychology predicated on Gestalt psychological principles; this is a psychophysical model for human behavior utilizing geometric constructs to conceptualize personality determinants.
Lowen, Alexander	Reichian in inspiration, Lowen developed *bioenergetic analysis,* predicated on a multifactorial model of human personality, heavily organicist in character. Therapy involves body work.
Maslow, Abraham	Fashioned the *psychology of being,* a model of human nature as self-actualizing, holistic, creative, and joyful. This nomothetic model postulates a hierarchy of psychophysical needs that will sequentially assert themselves, if not impeded.
May, Rollo	Developed an existential personology that accents the dynamic. This *continental existentialism* provided the elements and "givens" for conflicts at the core of personality development.
McDougall, W.	The *five-factor model* of personality has a distinguished lineage: Formulated by W. McDougall and developed by L. Klages, F. Baumgartner, G. Allport, E. Borgatta, D. Fiske, E. Tupes and R. Christal, and J. Digman, among other more recent investigators, it involves a strong heritability component; this model is cross-cultural and statistically and psychometrically generated.
Mead, George	Developed *social interaction theory,* a system of social behaviorism in which individuals symbolically interiorize their roles and status as a function of the interactive perceptions of others.
Miller, Neal	(*See* Dollard, John)
Meyer, Adolf	Developed a psychobiological theory of personality, stressing the unity of mind and body, the former a function of the latter. The theory has a strong orientation to the organismic in the genesis of psychopathology.
Murray, Henry	Elaborated a comprehensive, holistic theory that stressed motivation, environment, the psychodynamic, the idiographic-nomothetic spectrum, the personal, the life-span history, and specifically the cerebral determinants of one's ever-in-flux personality.
Piaget, Jean	Developed a partial theory of personality comprising a seminal model of cognitive development that deliberately made abstraction of emotions and social matrices. The model is characterized by an ineluctably sequenced, linear series of cognitive stages.
Rank, Otto	A polymath, he developed a humanistic personology based on minimizing primordial fears (of life and death) and developing one's will, which integrates a person's sense of who he or she is. Influenced Carl Rogers.
Rogers, Carl	Developed a theory of human nature characterized by self-actualization and holism; an innate organismic valuing process, if left unimpeded, leads individuals to live fully effloresced, authentic, and healthful lives.
Skinner, Burrhus	Developed an operant conditioning theory, which serves as a scientific heuristic for understanding the development of behavioral habits and capabilities of any organism; mistakenly thought by some to deny existence of intrapsychic realities.
Sullivan, Harry	Developed an interpersonal theory of personality that focuses on the social situation rather than the person; this theory postulates that individuals' personalities are a reflection of the assessment others make, or are imagined to make, of them.
Wolpe, Joseph	Rejecting psychodynamic methodologies, he evolved a theory of personality development that was of Pavlovian inspiration. His theory is of interest principally to psychotherapists.

Table 1

1 for a partial list). They each have been zealously defended and propagated by their adherents. In spite of the paucity of empirical validation for most of them, this has not assured their demise. Though most of the large-scale, molar theories that are still studied have been developed in the twentieth century, the study of human personality has veered in the second half of the century toward the manageably molecular. The trend to fine, multivariate analyses of human behavior in the established experimentalism of academia has created its own tension with the countervailing movement to holistic conceptualizations of personality. The synthesizing of psychosociological findings with those that are cognitive, affective, and psycho-neuro-endocrinological is a work in progress. At the end of the day, this scientific project has eventuated in scholarly specialization in numerous subdisciplines, which can only, with great difficulty and some contortions, be articulated

into a unified and coherent theoretical system. The task still needs to be addressed.

HISTORICAL PRECURSORS

It needs to be noted that theorizing about the determinants of human behavior in individuals as well as their social groups has its origins in antiquity and has progressed throughout history. There is a rich vein of philosophical speculation on this subject in the Greco-Roman civilization that was the seedbed of Western culture. Hellenistic thinkers and playwrights bequeathed a rich assortment of treatises and ideas to what would become Euro-American concepts of the nature of personality and its development. The ideas that are most salient for us and that have had the greatest impact on modern Western thought have come from the great Hellenistic thinkers that preceded the era of Roman cultural and military hegemony. Among the pre-Socratics, physiological theories of the development of personality can be traced at least to Empedocles. Later Hippocrates (fourth century B.C.E.) and still later Galen (second century C.E.) (Kagan 1994) postulated that the physical humors of the body are related to temperament. Blood, black bile, yellow bile, and phlegm were linked, as these nouns suggest, to sanguine, melancholic, choleric, and phlegmatic temperaments, respectively. The specifics of this theory are given no credence today, but the principle that personality has physiological determinants (or at least correlates) is very much alive.

Plato and Aristotle proposed powerful models of human psychological development. In *Laws*, for example, Plato proposed an environmental perspective relative to the problems that are occasioned by parents' overreactions to children's spontaneous and immature behaviors.

The privacy of home life screens from general observation many little incidents, too readily occasioned by a child's pains, pleasures, and passions which are not in keeping with a legislator's recommendations, and tend to bring a medley of incongruities into the characters of our citizens. (Book 7, sec. 788)

He does not exclude a genetic perspective as the following passage from the same work attests.

Now of all wild young things a boy is the most difficult to handle. Just because he more than

any other has a fount of intelligence in him that has not yet "run clear," he is the craftiest, most mischievous, and most unruly of brutes. So the creature must be held in check, as we may say, by more than one bridle—in the first place, when once he is out of the mother's and the nurse's hand, by attendants to care for his childish helplessness, and then further, by all the masters who teach him anything. (Book 7, sec. 808)

Plato's student, Aristotle, was a more entrenched environmentalist than Plato. He affirmed the principle of tabula rasa in his treatise "On the Human Mind."

Mind is in a sense potentially whatever is thinkable, although actually it is nothing until it has thought. What it thinks must be in it just as characters may be said to be on a writing-tablet on which as yet nothing stands written. This is exactly what happens with the mind. (Book 3, chap. 4, sec. 430)

That the human personality evolves as a function of the myriad contingencies that befall a person during the course of life has been entrenched since classical times. Plato asserted that

While spoiling of children makes their tempers fretful, peevish and easily upset by mere trifles, severe and unconditional tyranny makes its victims spiritless, servile, and sullen, rendering them unfit for the intercourse of domestic and civic life. (Book 7, sec. 791)

RELIGION AND THE PATHOGNOMONIC

That the human character has dysfunctional and even evil propensities is a nomothetic principle that was propagated in Western thought as a salient dogma of the Christian church. Although widely rejected, it pervaded much of political and social theorizing up to and even beyond the seventeenth century. Its most radical expression was in the homilies of such divines as Jonathan Edwards. The biblical dictum "I was shapen in iniquity and in sin did my mother conceive me" (Psalm 51) founded in part the traditional Christian view that human nature is fundamentally flawed by "original sin." It found expression in various vehicles of social thought and intellectual discussion of that time. The philosophers of the Enlightenment in

Europe repudiated this doctrine, although it continued to be propagated in religious circles and adumbrated in secular writings. The notion that human nature was essentially corrupt persisted in many of the systems of philosophy that flourished in the nineteenth century.

The dominant personality theorists of that period were clinicians with medical training. This professional background reinforced the pathological slant they gave to their descriptions of the human personality. Their theories of human psychological development gave prominence to the causes of deviant behavior rather than to the conditions for normal growth. Models of human personality were larded with dispositions to aggressive and narcissistic behavior. Freud in his more mature writings designated the aggressive instinct as one of the two pillars of his drive theory; the other, of course, was the erotic, a notion conceived in variously narrow and broad terms. His expansive pleasure principle was anticipated in the eighteenth century in the philosophy of Utilitarianism. Jeremy Bentham, a member of that school, stated that humans routinely engage in a "felicific calculus" ordained to maximize pleasure and minimize pain.

Twentieth-century theoreticians, principally university-based experimentalists, have striven to develop personological models focusing on wellness rather than on the pathognomonic. Gordon Allport is one of the outstanding representatives of this movement. Nevertheless the vocabulary, grammar, and notions of dysfunction and pathology continue to be woven into modern trait psychology. For example, Eysenck's three-factor model of personality contains a psychoticism factor and a neuroticism factor, and neuroticism is one of the factors in the influential five-factor model of human personality postulated by William McDougall and most recently associated with the work of Paul T. Costa and Robert R. McCrae.

SELF-ACTUALIZATION

A contrary movement, often termed "humanistic," is based on the self-actualizing and growth-oriented models of Kurt Goldstein, Otto Rank, Carl Rogers, Abraham Maslow, the cognitive psychologist Jean Piaget, and many others in which

pathology is conceptualized as a departure from normality rather than a component of it. Rogers, for example, asserted that just as plants are shaped by the directions they must take in seeking sources of light, human beings evolve throughout their life spans by reaching for the emotional and social sustenance that will allow the "organismic valuing process" to shape them into fully effloresced and functioning persons. Intrinsic wickedness and pathology have no place in these models of human nature. And although human nature can be thought of in terms of fundamental human needs, as in Maslow's *Psychology of Being*, the needs are not directed to destruction of self and others but to the fullest expression of a creative, generous, and joyful life expression. This is clearly in conflict with the psychodynamic models of nineteenth-century psychiatry, among them the Freudian system, which explained the engine of human development in terms of libidinal drives and tension reduction.

Self-disclosure and social transparency is one of the more healthful aspects of this model of the normal personality. O. Hobart Mowrer stated that psychological health depends on conditions that ensure transparency, and he traced its historical roots as far back as the ancient practice of *exomologesis*, in which a community of believers periodically engaged in collective confession of their violations of community mores, as in the monastic communities of the (Semitic) Essenes. This principle finds its most celebrated expressions in the psychotherapeutic literature. Moritz Benedikt, in the last third of the nineteenth century, and Carl Gustav Jung, in the twentieth, made it central to their therapeutic systems. They emphasized the critical importance for patients of divulging the "pathogenic secrets" that are woven into the fabric of their lives. A modern expression of this burgeoned in the 1960s in the therapeutic community (TC) movement, in locations such as Daytop Village and Phoenix House, where each day began with a morning meeting in which each member of the "family" publicly recounted his or her failures of the preceding day.

That we know more than we can tell and that we know more than we are aware that we know has been postulated since the pre-Socratics of Hellenistic Greece. Johann Christian Reil's seminal work, "Rhapsodien," published in 1803, describes the phenomenon of multiple personalities, and a complex topographical model of the human psyche. It is rarely questioned as we approach the twenty-first century that our behavior is influenced and our personality shaped by information that is sedimented in the organism, to paraphrase Merleau-Ponty, but which exists at a subsymbolic level and cannot in every instance be consciously accessed. The somatic-marker hypothesis of Antonio Damasio (1994; see chap. 8, pp. 165–201) is a recent expression of this position, which has profound implications for our conceptualization of what "personality" is and how it is shaped.

DEVELOPMENTAL PSYCHOLOGY AND PERSONALITY THEORY

It is self-evident to the psychologist that one cannot treat the construct of personality without grounding it in a scientific developmental psychology. This is true even of those theories that are simply descriptive rather than causal-explanatory. Persons are not born with personalities, although Thomas and Chess (1980), for example, have demonstrated in their widely cited New York Longitudinal Study that temperamental traits, constituents of some models of personality, are strongly influenced by hereditary factors. Personalities develop from infancy to adulthood and, indeed, across the life span. If the developmental psychology on which a personality theory is based is seriously flawed, then it is highly probable that that personality theory, itself, is also flawed. Ausubel et al. (1980) have reviewed a large number of developmental theories and their derivative personality theories. These theories range from the preformationist and quaintly theological to the most social and educationist systems that have flourished in the humanist climate of late-twentieth-century Western thought. They are, it must be emphasized, of unequal value. It flows from this that as the prevailing models of developmental psychology have evolved in the light of empirical research, personality theories have also had to evolve. For example, in the measure that the psychosexual stage theory of human development proposed by Freud a hundred years ago has been superseded and, arguably, discredited, to that extent has Freudian personality theory become superannuated. This can be stated of a number of personality theories whose value to scholars is now largely of a historical character. It is useful to add at this point that a theory of developmental psychology *is* a theory of personality as long as it

provides an integrative and broad-scale view of the way human beings develop socially, psychically, and characterologically.

THE MOVEMENT TO HOLISM

Holism, a much-used term of Greek etymology, characterizes an approach to understanding human personality that integrates all aspects of the person and, more recently, the social matrix in which it has been shaped and finds expression. Human psychology that attempts to explain behavior by appeal to only one "faculty" or one dimension of the human organism, that restricts itself to, say, simply rationalist or neuroendocrinological processes without understanding the systemic character of personality, has largely fallen into disfavor. Jan Christian Smuts, Alfred Adler, and Kurt Goldstein were early proponents of an integrative and holistic approach to the study of human beings, integrating organicist as well as social dimensions in a comprehensive view of personality and its determinants. Abandonment of fragmentary models has increased the appeal of Maturana and Varela's work (1980). Situated in a constructivist tradition, this work is not only biological but also profoundly social-psychological in its conceptualization of the human person. For example, these researchers' concept of "autopoiesis" is that the integrity and unity of the organism is generated from within, even as it interacts with and accommodates its surroundings. Every person is a self-organizing entity. The feed-forward mechanisms of which modern constructivists speak indicate that knowledge is to a great extent the construction of schemas involving the total organism. In this respect even the human's immunological system is part of a larger knowing system. The congruence between this vision and the self-actualizing models of Goldstein, Maslow, and Rogers is obvious. Unidimensional systems have evolved toward multidimensionality. Personologists have increasingly pursued the goal of formulating integrative models of human experience.

"Holism," as an approach to understanding human personality, can now be characterized more broadly as biopsychosocial. The knowledge that individuals have of themselves, whether tacit or conscious, is not simply intrapsychically determined. That knowledge is a function of what they have been told they are by those who are most meaningful to them. The principle of Harry Stack Sullivan that our self-concept is the image that we see reflected in the eyes of those who are making appraisals of us had its antecedents in the concept of the "looking-glass" self, developed by Charles Horton Cooley, George Herbert Mead, and James Mark Baldwin at the beginning of the twentieth century. A broadly systemic view of the development of the human person has come into focus, and it is profoundly sociologized.

THE FEMINIST DYNAMIC

It is a commonplace notion of modern psychology that nomothetic models of the person have in the past been formulated by Caucasian males who unreflectively based them on male psychological norms. If, as Nietzsche said, all theory is autobiographical, it would follow that theories of personality developed by males reflect in part their personal and culturally circumscribed experiences. Sigmund Freud's, Lawrence Kohlberg's, and Erik Erikson's theories of moral development and evolution of human identity have been identified, among others, as based on male norms. Deviations from this male template have been considered abnormal. Karen Horney was among the first to repudiate psychoanalytic assertions that women were endowed with a moral sense inferior to that of males because they could not as children resolve the "Oedipal conflict" in the univocal sense that boys could. Feminists, including Inge K. Broverman, Pat Chesler, Carol Gilligan, and Carolyn Z. Enns have detailed the distortions implicit in characterizations of the typical female personality as submissive, conformist, masochistic, depression-prone, and so forth. The internalization of social roles by both men and women inevitably results in personality profiles that reflect those roles. The argument is made that establishing a template for normality that derives from a culture-circumscribed social role for men necessarily casts the typical feminine personality in the realm of the deficient, at least to the extent that it is laden with the deficits of the roles in which women have been socialized.

Whether there are universal, that is, nomothetic psychological differences between men and women arising from genetic determinants of gender-related behavior is an empirical question that is still being studied by behavioral geneticists. If indeed there is no significant difference in the psychological development of the two sexes independent of fluid, relativistic cultural variables, it would not seem to matter which sex one used as the nomothetic template for healthy human development. The focus of analysis would necessarily shift to the socially constructed roles that are imposed on females. Assessing women as inferior by virtue of their possession of personality traits they have internalized in a society that has prescribed them would seem patently unjust.

NEUROPSYCHOLOGICAL INFLUENCES IN PERSONOLOGY

Just as there are no two Coke bottles and no two newly minted pennies that are perfectly identical, a fortiori there are no two humans beings who are truly identical. Reminded that the preponderance of the human genome endows each of us with characteristics that are universal, we must also acknowledge that there are at least 20,000 genes, called "polymorphic genes," that come in many varieties, that get randomly assorted at conception, and that endow us in part with our individuality. The genes that define us as human are called "monomorphic genes." They account for the fact that we all look recognizably human and normally act so. Whatever nomothetic principles have been truly (or purportedly) established relative to the psychobiological and behavioral properties of the human, they derive, by definition, from these genes.

Behavioral geneticists such as Robert Plomin and Thomas Bouchard (among other researchers in this field) have established the contribution of heredity to personality. For example, Bouchard has done well-regarded studies on twins reared apart that have shed light on the heritability of personality traits. Although his findings and those of other behavioral geneticists have excited controversy and negative comment, there is a convergence of evidence to show that indeed some of the variance one finds in certain personality traits is of genetic origin. But one needs to recognize that the controversy is fraught as much with ideological and political concerns as with strictly scientific ones, and the values embedded in these conflicting opinions can tilt arguments in one direction as well as another. The flashpoint, par excellence, for this controversy is the position taken on the personality trait "intelligence," a construct referring to certain adaptive and creative human capabilities. That these capabilities are still imperfectly understood ensures that the various constructs purported to define them are even more imperfectly formulated. Psychometricians are placed at an even further remove from these nebulous realities when they attempt to measure them, often by paper-and-pencil instruments.

The power of environment to shape or mis-shape personality is incontestable. Attachment Theory, associated with the work of John Bowlby, among others, offers a cogent explanation of the conditions for healthful psychological development. This theory has an affinity with the principles evolved by such ethologists as Tinbergen, Lorenz, Hinde, and other students of the social life of animals. Failure to develop a strong infant–primary caregiver bond during the period of primary socialization (that is, between the appearance of the first social smile at several weeks of age and the appearance of stranger anxiety at, say, six to eight months of age) is thought to lay the groundwork for developmental psychopathy—and the rupture of this bond in the first years of life, is thought to lay the groundwork for later affective disorders. A related perspective is that of Object-Relations theorists, whose views on "mothering" and its influence on development are more (human) relational and less instinct- or drive-based than the classical psychoanalytic model.

Although the influence of childhood experiences, both positive and negative, on adult personality is not in dispute, the partial reversibility of these effects is asserted by Michael Rutter, Jerome Kagan, and others. The variables at issue, for example, bonding in infancy to a primary caregiver and stimulus deprivation in toddlerhood are, after all, continuous and complex. The strength and duration of the variables, and their interaction with genetic variables of an idiographic and often unknown character, produce personality effects that are not predictable with any accuracy. The principle of *neoteny*, that is, the slowing of developmental rates and the retention of plasticity and developmental capabilities well into adulthood, is at issue here. Humans enjoy a relatively long period of growth from infancy to adulthood, a period in which earlier psychological deformity can be mitigated, if not entirely undone. In the wake of a traumatic infancy and childhood, prolonged immaturity provides humans with the affordances of redemption.

HOMUNCULARISM

Theories of personality development range on a continuum from the most rigidly preformationist at one end to the most malleable and environmentally sensitive at the other. Historically, Western psychology has been shifting toward the latter. In his remarkable work, *Centuries of Childhood* (1962), Philippe Ariès has demonstrated the long tradition of viewing children as miniature adults, *homunculi*, so to speak. The homuncular theory in its most primitive form postulated that the human organism, a little man (i.e., homunculus), contained in the semen of the male, is deposited in the uterus of the mother. It is presumedly organically and morphologically complete. It merely needs to be nurtured to a mature status. The term has been extended as we know to embrace the postulate that not only the organic features of the mature human reside in the neonate but also the psychological features.

Children are, in this view, born with preformed characters and the cognitive structures of adults. To quote Ausubel et al.,

> *The basic human properties and behavioral capacities–personality, values, and motives; perceptual, cognitive, emotional, and social reaction tendencies–are not conceived as undergoing qualitative differentiation and transformation over the life-span but are presumed to exist preformed at birth.* (1980 p. 15).

Vestiges of homuncularism remain in the work of twentieth-century personality theorists who attribute to infants and older children cognitions and emotions that, in a univocal sense, can only be the product of adult mentation. Confusing infantile sexuality with adult sexuality, as in classical psychoanalysis, is an example of this (cf., e.g., Thomas and Chess 1980, chap. IV, for a broader look at this issue). Among the more important of these innate schemas are the "racial unconscious" of Carl Gustav Jung and the "phylogenetic unconscious" of Sigmund Freud. They both have important implications for personological features and specific behaviors that are predicated on them.

It is widely recognized that the younger the organism, the more plastic it is in terms of acquiring and altering the learnings and adaptations it needs in order to thrive. Early-twentieth-century theories of human development postulated rigid and clearly delineated stages. These stages are no longer considered to have the rigid boundaries they were once supposed to have. In the earlier stage models it was presumed, but never demonstrated, that personality structure was established and firmly set by the age of, say, six or seven. In this view, the principal features of the personality did not change; they were only elaborated. This prescientific homuncularism has yielded to life-span developmental models.

There exists a countervailing point of view. Research has revealed the profound and subtle possibilities for change in the human personality that exist throughout the maturational process. Critical to this process of differentiation are education and other environmental factors, not excluding the benign and nurturant conditions that need to prevail during infancy in the home. Relevant to this orientation to human development is, again, the principle of neoten. The slowing of humans' development from infancy to adulthood, has afforded humans the opportunity for evolving the complex and diverse personalities that, in the view of these theorists, is the hallmark of this species.

THE NOMOTHETIC AND THE IDIOGRAPHIC

That the psychologist as scientist has, in the past, inclined to a nomothetic and deterministic understanding of human beings is understandable. After all, it is difficult to build a science on the idiographic. Nevertheless, the concern of rank-and-file persons not to see themselves simply as one of billions of "knock-off's" from a universal template is also understandable. This may underlie some of the concern about cloning. "If there are clones about, how will you know who people really are?" ask some. Though there is a misconception about the phenomenon of cloning that underlies that question (after all, identical twins meet the definition of clones, and we come to know *who they are*), it indicates the concern about personal identity found in Western society. More specifically, the need to be an individual and to be different (but not too different) from everyone else is evident in many Western and Westernized cultures. This plays out in the theorizing of personologists who have developed personality theories that give emphasis to the environmental factors that impinge on individuals in all phases of their lives, and that individuate them. It is this diversity in personal histories that accounts to a large extent for the uniqueness of each person. That members of the same family who have similar histories still mature to adulthood with very different personality profiles attests to the interaction of genetic factors with education, not excluding stochastic events that may have powerful formative impact on development.

THEORIES: DICHOTOMIES AND STAGES

The study of personality has addressed the question of what dynamics operate in all human beings to shape their behavior throughout the life span. This question assumes that there are some species-wide principles governing the development of human traits from conception to demise. It also addresses the question of what factors effect the individuation of human beings such that no one person is like any other person though they all share the same monomorphic genic substrate. Social scientists will recognize the ancient dichotomy for conceptualizing the relative contributions of nature as distinguished from life experiences. The code for this derives from Shakespeare's characterization of Caliban in *The Tempest*. Prospero refers to him as "a born devil, on whose nature Nurture can never stick." The expressions "nomothetic" and "idiographic" also refer to this dual factor—to wit, the universal principles governing the set "human beings" vis-à-vis relative principles governing the development of individuals within the set. In reality these are not true dichotomies except insofar as we wish to logically make them so. As in other conceptual polarities, explaining the emergence of a human being into adulthood admits of varying theoretical frameworks. A comparable perspective is reflected in the anthropological and linguistic distinctions between the *etic* (that is, the most general, often universal, frame for analyzing cultural behavior) and the *emic* frame (which examines social subsets of the species). An example of the former is Francis Galton's hypothesis, recently labeled "fundamental lexical hypothesis (cf. Goldberg 1990, p.

1216), which affirms that the world's languages all contain terms describing similar personality traits, albeit traits that, although they have the same meaning, are valued differently, and present themselves with varying intensity and frequencies. An example of the latter is the principle (inherent in most multicultural perspectives on personality development) that the geohistorical background of any distinct society profoundly shapes the ideals of human behavior, morals, and social conduct, which get incarnated as "personality" in the majority of its members. The Sapir-Whorf hypothesis goes even further and states that the very structure of the language that a cultural subset of the human race speaks affects the character of their ideation and the consequent conduct of the group's affairs. But earlier, Nietzsche affirmed that "philosophers within the domain of the Ural-Altaic languages" look into the world differently and take different paths than "Indo-Germans and Moslems: the spell of grammatical functions is in the last resort the spell of physiological value judgments and racial conditions" ([1885]1952, p. 472)

There have been zealous partisans of theories explaining human behavior that have, for reasons ideological as much as scientific, conceptualized personality into sets of dichotomies, in which they have emphasized one polarity rather than another. This antipodal schema has been with us since antiquity. The motifs of heroism and cowardice, of altruism and selfishness, of loyalty and betrayal, of candor and duplicity, of anguish and ecstatic joy, among other descriptors of the human experience that can play out in all human lives, received their finest expression in the works of such tragedians as Sophocles and Shakespeare. On the other hand, the uniqueness of each person and the passion for establishing one's personal identity is no less prominent in the great literature of the West. One has only to review, for example, the plays of Tennessee Williams, the great oeuvre of Cervantes, the vast range of characters in the novels of Balzac or Dickens, or in, say, Thomas Mann's *Magic Mountain*, to grasp the diversity that artists have displayed in limning the contours of these distinct personalities, to which readers have been able to resonate.

That human personality evolves and becomes different as an individual proceeds through a series of life stages would seem to be self-evident.

This view presumes, of course, that the construct "stage" is grounded in something real in human development. There are a number of complications to this view. First, the scope for change gets narrowed in the measure that variance in personality factors is explained by genetic factors. Obversely, the scope for change gets broadened in the measure that it is explained by education and other experience. Obviously, stage theory is less plausible, or less coercive in its implications, in the measure that personality development is fluidly malleable and educationally structured. The opposite seems true if biologically prestructured. But there is a second-order level for explaining personality change in a genetic perspective. One can accept a measure of predetermination in the psychoneurological substrate for personality, but it is not illogical to allow room in this model for a series of hardwired developmental periods. The model of Arnold Gesell, for example, though predeterministic, allows for qualitative stage-based shifts in the cognitive, psycho-motoric, interpersonal, and affective preferences and capabilities of the person.

As Piaget noted, whether or not one "sees" human development progressing from infancy to adulthood in stages is a function of how fine-grained and molecular one makes one's analysis. It is a question of scale. Standing inches from a *pointillist* painting, say, by Seurat, one sees only a multitude of tiny dots of pigment. It is only in distancing oneself so that the entire painting or large sections of it come into focus that the transitions from beach to sea to boats to trees to bathers become apparent. The phases of the panorama stand out as one macroscopically scans the canvas. It is difficult (but not impossible) to discern the shape of a galaxy when one is part of it.

As the analysis of personality development has assumed a more scientific, microscopic focus, there has been a tendency for the stage-based theories to fall into disrepute. This may account for the decline in popularity of the schemas developed by Freud, Erikson, Piaget, Sullivan, and Kohlberg, for example. Though these conceptualizations of human personality development continue to enjoy widespread support in part, if not in whole, they are partially in eclipse by virtue of advances in the newer human sciences. Cognitive science, psychoneurology, endocrinology, and social and developmental psychology, among other disciplines, have inevitably superannuated all these grand systems to a greater or lesser degree.

SUMMARY

On entering the twenty-first century, the Zeitgeist will favor, it appears, theories of personality that are life-span developmental, less instinct-driven but more persons-relational, constructivist, process-oriented and dynamic, that is, Heraclitean, holistic, teleonomic, evolutionary, genetics-based, gender-equal, emic, sociological, and idiographic. Clearly, personality theories that predate World War II are not, by and large, consistent with these descriptors. It appears that the era of the grand systems is past. Personology will reconcile itself to more modest paradigms for describing, explaining, and predicting human behavior.

Students who wish to follow the development of this discipline are urged to regularly consult the *Annual Review of Psychology*, the *Journal of Personality and Social Psychology*, the *European Journal of Personality*, *Developmental Psychology*, and other respected periodicals that publish articles in this domain. An excellent and more detailed analysis of many of the issues raised above can be found in *Theories of Personality* by Hall, et al. (1998, chap. 1, 15).

REFERENCES

Ariès, P. 1962 *Centuries of Childhood: A Social History of Family Life*. New York: Random House.

Ausubel, D. P., E. V. Sullivan, and S. W. Ives 1980 *The Theory and Problems of Child Development*, 3rd ed. Grune and Stratton.

Cattell, R. B. 1964 *Personality and Social Psychology*. San Diego: Knapp.

Cattell, R. B. 1965 *The Scientific Analysis of Personality*. Baltimore: Penguin Books.

Damasio, A. R. 1994 *Descartes' Error: Emotion, Reason, and the Human Brain*. New York: Avon Books.

Goldberg, L. R. 1990 "An Alternative 'Description of Personality': The Big-Five Factor Structure." *Journal of Personality and Social Psychology* 59:1216–1229.

Hall, C. S., G. Lindzey, and J. B. Campbell 1997 *Theories of Personality*, 4th ed. New York: John Wiley.

Hartshorne, H., and M. A. May 1928 *Studies in the Nature of Character*, vol. I, *Studies in Deceit*. New York: Macmillan.

James, W. (1890) 1952 *The Principles of Psychology*. vol. 53 in *Great Books of the Western World*. Chicago: Encyclopedia Britannica.

Kagan, J. 1994 *Galen's Prophecy: Temperament in Human Nature*. New York: Basic Books.

Laurence, J. R., D. Day, and L. Gaston 1998 "From Memories of Abuse to the Abuse of Memories." In S. J. Lynn, ed., *Truth in Memory*. New York: American Psychological Association Press.

Mahoney, M. 1991 *Human Changes Processes: The Scientific Foundations of Psychotherapy*. New York: Basic Books.

Maturana, H. R., and F. J. Varela 1980 *Autopoiesis and Cognition: The Realization of the Living*. Boston: Reidel.

Mischel, W. 1968 *Personality and Assessment*. New York: John Wiley.

Nietzsche, F. (1885) 1952 *Beyond Good and Evil*. vol. 43 in *Great Books of the Western World*. Chicago: Encyclopedia Britannica.

Pervin, L. A. 1996 *The Science of Personality*. New York: John Wiley.

Thomas, A., and S. Chess 1980 *The Dynamics of Psychological Development*. New York: Brunner/Mazel.

FRANK DUMONT

PERSUASION

The average number of hours the television set is on in American households is 6.8 hours a day (Peterson 1981). When not watching their 6.8 hours of television, most people spend the bulk of their time in talk with others. Much of this talk is geared not just to making oneself understood but to convincing someone else of the value and correctness of one's viewpoint. The average adult spends the majority of his or her waking hours at work, where, depending on the job, much activity involves efforts to get others to do one's bidding or being the object of such efforts. All this television watching, conversation, and work takes place in a social and political climate that, in theory if not in practice, encourages the exchange and dissemination of ideas among large numbers of people.

These facts have led some to conclude that this is an era of persuasion in which understanding who says what to whom in what way and with what effect is of critical importance (Lasswell 1948). In fact, some argue that the current era of persuasion is one of the few periods in the four millennia of

Western history characterized by such a degree of openness to argument (McGuire 1985).

Whether or not the present era is unique in this manner, more and more people are becoming conscious of the persuasive contexts in which they spend most of their time. Indeed, if the increasingly ingenious efforts of advertisers to pique interest and shape tastes and habits are any indication, people are becoming increasingly savvy about others' efforts at persuasion. This means that we have a very practical interest in understanding just how persuasion works. It also means that social scientists, and social psychologists in particular, have an interest in understanding and explaining a pervasive social phenomenon.

As one aspect of understanding persuasion, social psychologists have long studied attitude formation and change. During the 1920s and 1930s psychologists focused on describing the attitudes people hold. This led to the development of techniques for measuring attitudes, primarily scales such as the Likert scale, which continue to be used today by persuasion researchers. The second period of interest in attitude research occurred during the 1950s and 1960s, with the main focus moving from description to the study of attitude change and the effects of attitudes on behavior. (For a review of the research on attitude-behavior consistency, see Ajzen and Fishbein 1977.) This interest waned considerably during the next two decades as social psychologists became increasingly interested in social perception, or how people selectively interpret and respond to their social environments. The resurgence of interest in attitudes, and particularly in persuasion, that followed is thus largely informed by social psychology's more general emphasis on how people process the information they take in from their environment.

One might speculate that the interest in explaining persuasion and attitude change over mere attitude description reflects the increasing influence of mass media. However, this coincidence of research interest and social change is belied by the lack of communication between those studying the effects of mass media on attitudes and those studying persuasion in more immediately interpersonal contests (Roberts and Maccoby 1985). The discussion here reflects this split in research focuses, concentrating solely on persuasion research in face-to-face, interpersonal contexts and

dealing only peripherally with research on the effects of mass media on attitudes. (See Roberts and Maccoby 1985 for a review of this literature.) The issue of brainwashing, an extreme form and method of persuasion, is considered only when it has direct relevance to less extreme persuasion contests and processes.

Of relevance to research on persuasion is the study of normative compliance occurring in settings where no active attempt is made to influence, but people change their opinions or judgments nonetheless. Asch's (1951) research on conformity demonstrated that subjects involved in a simple task of judging the length of a line were highly influenced by the judgments of others present, even when no overt influence attempts were made. In these studies people working with the experimenter gave incorrect assessments of the relative lengths of lines viewed. Even in cases of obviously incorrect judgments, most subjects conformed to the majority's assessment. Normative compliance is found to be greater the closer to unanimity the majority view, the larger the number holding it, and the more the conforming subject is attracted to and invested in group membership.

The persistence of findings of normative compliance, even in the absence of overt influence attempts, raises an obvious question: What happens when such overt attempts at persuasion are made? This and related questions are the focus of persuasion research. The focus in persuasion research is on attitude change "occurring in people exposed to relatively complex messages consisting of a position advocated by a communicator and usually one or more arguments designed to support that position" (Eagly and Chaiken 1984, p. 256). More simply defined, *persuasion* is an effort to change people's attitudes, these being the emotional and cognitive responses they have to objects, people, experiences, and so on.

FACTORS AFFECTING THE LIKELIHOOD OF PERSUASION

The guiding question of who says what to whom in what way with what effect has largely determined what factors researchers look to in explaining and predicting persuasion. These factors fall into four general classes: source or communicator variables, message variables, channel variables, and receiver variables. Reflecting two decades of research on social cognition, studies of the effects of these variables on persuasion investigate how these factors affect persuasion by shaping the way in which people process information in the persuasion context. Indeed, the term *process* reflects the computer analogy often used to capture the manner in which people perceive, interpret, and respond to their environment.

For example, in studying the effects of source characteristics (the characteristics of the person communicating the persuasive message) researchers might examine how the likability of the source leads the receiver (the object of persuasion) either to attend to or to ignore the quality of the arguments accompanying the message. Similarly, researchers examine other aspects of cognition (e.g., attention, comprehension, receptivity, retention) for the manner in which they mediate the effects on persuasion of source, message, channel, and receiver variables.

Source Variables. The source variable of greatest interest is the credibility of the person communicating the persuasive message, including the communicator's apparent knowledge, social class, attractiveness, and likability. Consistently with common sense, the more credible the source, the more persuasive the source and the more likely that the receiver will change his or her attitude in the direction of the persuasive message. More interesting, however, is the combination of source credibility with other factors, and their combined effect on persuasion. For example, if the target person is not personally involved with the issue at hand, source credibility is more likely to enhance persuasion than if the person is highly involved in the issue. This is because personal involvement is likely to be associated with greater argument scrutiny by the target person, reducing the likelihood of immediate acceptance of even a credible source's position (Chaiken 1980).

The effects of source credibility on persuasion are thus mediated by the extent to which the target is motivated to thoughtfully scrutinize the supporting arguments presented by the source. Personal involvement in the issue is one such motivation, but specific knowledge of the topic (without any particularly emotionally charged investment in it) and being educated in general are also factors that mediate the effect of source credibility because of their impact on the manner in which the

target processes information at his or her disposal. Level of involvement, knowledge, and education are all characteristics of the receiver. The above example thus reveals the complex relationships between the factors that affect persuasion and their joint effects on information processing.

Message Variables. Many aspects of the persuasive message itself have been examined by research on persuasion. These include message style, ordering of arguments presented, speed of delivery, and message repetition. The effects of message repetition on persuasion are particularly interesting because they reveal the often unexpected combined effects of variables. For example, a study by Cacioppo and Petty (1979) revealed that only if supporting arguments are strong does repetition enhance persuasion, since repetition leads to greater argument scrutiny by the receiver, which enhances persuasion only to the extent that arguments are convincing.

Common sense might tell us that the use of humor in a message will enhance its persuasiveness by increasing the attractiveness of the source or, in the case of weak supporting arguments, distracting the target's attention from the content. Researchers have hypothesized that humor should enhance persuasion with a highly credible source, but not with a less credible source, since humor is likely to further reduce credibility in the latter case. However, there is little evidence to support the expected effects of humor on persuasion. The observed effects are rarely significant, and are as often negative as positive. Furthermore, the combined effects of humor with source credibility, or humor's impact on interest, retention, or source evaluation, are not found (McGuire 1985).

Channel Variables. Channel variables refer to the medium in which the message is communicated. For example, message persuasiveness varies depending on whether the message is given in person or in verbal, written, audio, or video form. In addition, channel variables include factors such as distraction—either direct distraction created by the behavior of the source or indirect distraction such as repeated external noise during the communication.

Petty and Cacioppo (1981) studied the effects of distraction on persuasion and found that its effects are mediated by cognitive factors such as the target's ability or motivation to scrutinize the arguments. If the message is accompanied by a distracting noise, for example, this will enhance persuasion if accompanying arguments are weak, since it decreases the receiver's ability or motivation to pay close attention to the supporting arguments. Conversely, if the supporting arguments are strong, distraction decreases the likelihood of persuasion, especially with knowledgeable targets, since it makes it unlikely they will pay attention to the strong arguments designed to persuade them.

Similarly, other channel variables, such as the use of catchy music in television ads, affect persuasion to the extent that they motivate the receiver to generate positive rather than negative thoughts in response to the message. Generating thoughts is distinguished from argument scrutiny because it refers to the additional arguments or ideas the receiver brings to bear in evaluating a message, not to the supporting arguments provided by the communicator. Channel or other variables enhance persuasion to the extent that they generate positive thoughts or supporting arguments in the target (Greenwald 1968). Like other factors affecting persuasion then, the impact of channel variables on persuasion is mediated by the resulting cognitive processes engaged in by the target of the persuasive message.

Receiver Variables. Since persuasion is oriented toward convincing someone to adopt a particular viewpoint or opinion, it makes sense that the person himself or herself has some impact on the persuasion process. Interest in the personality correlates of persuasion was high during the 1950s but waned in the following decades as individual-level explanations of social phenomena became less popular among social psychologists. However, more recent work has revived interest in the effect of receiver variables on persuasion.

A variety of receiver variables relating to personality characteristics have been studied to determine receiver susceptibility and resistance to persuasion. With respect to self-esteem, researchers predict that greater self-esteem will decrease the likelihood of persuasion to the extent that it increases the likelihood that the receiver will carefully scrutinize the arguments, and decreases the likelihood of the receiver's being swayed by a credible source in the absence of strong supporting arguments. Therefore, like the other factors

affecting persuasion, self-esteem exerts its effects on persuasion through the variables related to the manner in which the receiver processes the information available in the persuasion context.

Results of studies of self-esteem and persuasion offer mixed results, some indicating negligible effects (Barber 1964) and others suggesting that the lower the self-esteem, the greater the tendency to conform, especially when the aspect of self-esteem involved is closely related to the issue at hand (Endler et al. 1972). The effects of self-esteem are complex, especially when combined with other variables. For example, greater influenceability is associated with higher, not lower, self-esteem as the complexity of the persuasive message increases.

More consistent findings have been produced on the effects of receiver's mood on responses to persuasive attempts. Interestingly, research has shown that neutral or bad moods decrease susceptibility to persuasive attempts, largely because targets are more likely to scrutinize messages when in a neutral or bad mood than when in a good mood (Wegener et al. 1995; Rosseli et al. 1995).

The effects of authoritarianism or dogmatism have also received considerable research attention. *Dogmatism* is defined as a general inclination to be closed-minded, intolerant, and deferential to authority. Research has shown that receivers low in dogmatism are persuaded by strong, but not by weak, arguments. Dogmatic receivers, in contrast, are persuaded by strong arguments only when the source is nonexpert. With expert sources, dogmatic individuals are equally persuaded by strong and weak arguments (DeBono and Klein 1993).

Aside from personality characteristics, persuasion researchers, like other social researchers, have shown a longstanding interest in the issue of gender differences. A summary of 148 studies of the effects of gender on persuasion (Eagly and Carli 1981) indicates that women are more easily influenced than men. However, as consistent as these findings are, the magnitude of gender differences in influenceability is small enough to raise doubts about its practical significance for people's everyday lives (McGuire 1985).

However trivial these differences may be, they have inspired persuasion researchers to search for an explanation. One plausible account is that "greater female susceptibility and greater male predictability might derive from socialization differences such that conforming pressures are exerted more strongly and uniformly on women, compressing them into a narrow band of high influenceability" (McGuire 1985, p. 288). Thus, the effects of gender on influenceability result from the different social experiences of men and women (for example, the greater likelihood that women will hold jobs in which they will receive more persuasion attempts than they themselves perform).

METHODOLOGICAL AND THEORETICAL ISSUES IN THE STUDY OF PERSUASION

While all studies of persuasion tend to focus on some combination of the variables discussed above, more general research orientations have not been uniform. One way of dividing research approaches to persuasion is to distinguish between the descriptive and the mathematical models. The former may focus on any combination of variables affecting persuasion, but their predictions tend to be stated in the form of verbal argument or a set of hypotheses. Mathematical or probabilistic models, on the other hand, cast their predictions about persuasion in the form of equations, with variables and their relationships represented in algebraic terms. While the choice of research approach does not dictate which variables the researcher focuses on, some argue that the greater precision of probabilistic models makes for a more exact understanding of the conditions likely to produce persuasion (McGuire 1985). Others (e.g., Eagly and Chaiken 1984) refer to these models as "normative," meaning that they describe how persuasion ought to work, not necessarily how it works in reality.

Whatever the relative merits of descriptive and probabilistic approaches, there is some consensus among persuasion researchers that a more general theory of persuasion is necessary if the vast research findings in the area are to be integrated in a meaningful manner (Eagly and Chaiken 1984). As this discussion shows, the research on persuasion is blessed with a large number of well-conceptualized variables, most of which are easy to operationalize, that is, to create in a laboratory setting. The discussion also shows, however, that even when a small portion of all the possible combinations of these variables are matched with one or two of the mediating cognitive processes, the resulting insights into persuasion are far from some of the commonsense notions alluded to throughout this discussion. This fact lends support for the call for a more unifying theory of persuasion to integrate the somewhat fragmented picture that emerges from a combining-of-variables approach.

SUSCEPTIBILITY AND RESISTANCE TO PERSUASION

This discussion raises important questions about issues of susceptibility and resistance to persuasion. When is being easily persuaded good? When is resistance good, and how can it be taught? If Americans are spending between six and seven hours a day in front of their television sets, and the rest of their waking hours in persuasive communications with others on the job or at leisure, teaching resistance to all this persuasion might become a top priority. For example, when research reveals that motivating people to generate reasons for their attitudes toward a product ultimately causes them to change their initial attitude, and even to purchase a product on the basis of their changed attitude (only to regret it later) attention is called to the conditions under which enhancing resistance might be warranted (Wilson et al. 1989). On the other hand, when research shows that two years of viewing *Sesame Street* caused both black and white children to manifest more positive attitudes towards black and Hispanics, something is learned about the conditions under which enhancing attitude change and persuasion is desirable (Bogatz and Ball 1971).

Whether one values resistance or openness to persuasion, our understanding of resistance to persuasion is enhanced by our understanding of what increases the likelihood of persuasion. As this discussion has shown, source variables (e.g., credibility), channel variables (e.g., distractions), message variables (e.g., argument strength), and receiver variables (e.g. personality characteristics) can all affect the receiver's susceptibility or resistance to persuasion. In addition, research has shown that when people perceive persuasive messages as threats to their freedom, they resist persuasion and maintain their original position or, in some cases, adopt a position opposite to the one advocated in the message (Brehm 1966).

More recent research on values reveals another factor involved in susceptibility and resistance to persuasion. In general, people are more susceptible to messages which are consistent with their own values, and more resistant to those that are not. For example, Han and Shavitt (1994) have shown that receivers with individualistic values (e.g., Americans) are more persuaded by advertising messages emphasizing individualistic themes (e.g., "Take care of number one!"). In contrast, receivers with collectivistic values (e.g., Koreans) are more persuaded by advertising messages emphasizing collectivistic themes (e.g., "For you and your family!"). Thus, whether we are interested in enhancing persuasion or increasing resistance to it, understanding the role of values in the persuasion process is crucial.

Ultimately, resistance to the potential loss of autonomy involved in persuasion is not surprising in a culture that places a premium on such individuality and freedom. In addition, such concerns are not unwarranted, given the fact that many of the attempts at persuasion people face in natural settings are specifically designed to minimize the threatening aspects of such attempts and thus to reduce resistance (hence the use of the word "seductive" to refer to arguments, advertisements, etc.). Are people continually at risk, then, of potentially harmful persuasion?

One could argue that in people's ability to be persuaded lies the possibility of autonomy. If people are easily persuaded, then they are in similar measure unlikely to be overwhelmingly persuaded by a particular viewpoint over all others. They may be likely to resist total indoctrination, if only because they are susceptible to some other credible source sending a convincing message in a captivating medium.

REFERENCES

Ajzen, I., and M. Fishbein 1977 "Attitude-Behavior Relations: A Theoretical Analysis and Review of Empirical Research." *Psychological Bulletin* 84:888–918.

Asch, S. E. 1951 "The Effects of Group Pressure upon the Modification and Distortion of Judgments." In H. Guetzkow, ed., *Groups, Leadership and Men*. Pittsburgh, Pa.: Carnegie Press.

Barber, T. X. 1964 "Hypnotizability, Suggestibility and Personality: V. A Critical Review of Research Findings." *Psychological Reports* 14:299–320.

Bogatz, G. A., and S. J. Ball 1971 *The Second Year of Sesame Street: A Continuing Evaluation*, 2 vols. Princeton, N.J.: Educational Testing Service.

Brehm, J. W. 1966 *A Theory of Psychological Reactance*. New York: Academic Press.

Cacioppo, J., and R. Petty 1979 "Effects of Message Repetition and Position on Cognitive Response, Recall, and Persuasion." *Journal of Personality and Social Psychology* 37:97–109.

Chaiken, S. 1980 "Heuristic versus Systematic Information Processing and the Use of Source Versus Message Cues in Persuasion." *Journal of Personality and Social Psychology* 39:752–766.

DeBono, K. G., and C. Klein 1993 "Source Expertise and Persuasion: The Moderating Role of Recipient Dogmatism." *Personality and Social Psychology Bulletin* 19:167–173.

Eagly, A. H. and L. L. Carli 1981 "Sex of Researchers and Sex-typed Communications as Determinants of Sex Differences in Influenceability: A Meta-analysis of Influence Studies." *Psychological Bulletin* 90:1–20.

Eagly, A. H., and S. Chaiken 1984 "Cognitive Theories of Persuasion." In L. Berkowitz, ed., *Advances in Experimental Social Psychology*, vol. 17. New York: Academic Press.

Endler, N. S., D. L. Weisenthal, and S. H. Geller 1972 "The Generalization Effects of Agreement and Correctness on Relative Competence Mediating Conformity." *Canadian Journal of the Behavioral Sciences* 4:322–329.

Han, S., and S. Shavitt 1994 "Persuasion and Culture: Advertising Appeals in Individualistic and Collectivistic Societies." *Journal of Experimental Social Psychology* 30:326–350.

Greenwald, A. G. 1968 "Cognitive Learning, Cognitive Response to Persuasion, and Attitude Change." In A. G. Greenwald, T. S. Brock, and T. M. Ostrom, eds., *Psychological Foundations of Attitudes*. New York: Academic Press.

Lasswell, H. D. 1948 "The Structure and Function of Communication in Society." In L. Bryson, ed., *Communication Ideas*. New York: Harper.

McGuire, W. J. 1985 "Attitudes and Attitude Change." In G. Lindzey and E. Aronson, eds., *The Handbook of Social Psychology*, vol. 2. New York: Random House.

Peterson, R. A. 1981 "Measuring Culture, Leisure, and Time Use." *Annals of the American Academy of Political and Social Science* 453:1969–1979.

Petty, R. E., and J. T. Cacioppo 1981 *Attitudes and Persuasion: Classic and Contemporary Approaches*. Debuque Ia.: W. C. Brown.

Roberts, D. F., and N. Maccoby 1985 "Effects of Mass Communication." In G. Lindzey and E. Aronson, eds., *The Handbook of Social Psychology*, vol. 2. New York: Random House.

Rosselli F., J. Skelly, and D. M. Mackie 1995 "Processing Rational and Emotional Messages: The Cognitive and Affective Mediation of Persuasion." *Journal of Experimental Social Psychology* 31:163–190.

Wegener, D. T., R. E. Petty, and S. M. Smith 1995 "Positive Mood Can Increase or Decrease Message Scrutiny: The Hedonic Contingency View of Mood and Message Processing." *Journal of Personality and Social Psychology* 69:5–15.

Wilson, T. D., D. S. Dunn, D. Kraft, and D. J. Lisle 1989 "Introspection, Attitude Change, and Attitude Behavior Consistency: The Disruptive Effects of Explaining Why We Feel the Way We Do." In L. Berkowitz, ed., *Advances in Experimental Social Psychology*, vol. 22. New York: Academic Press.

SUSAN McWILLIAMS

PHENOMENOLOGY

Phenomenology is a movement in philosophy that has been adapted by certain sociologists to promote an understanding of the relationship between states of individual consciousness and social life. As an approach within sociology, *phenomenology* seeks to reveal how human awareness is implicated in the production of social action, social situations and social worlds (Natanson 1970).

Phenomenology was initially developed by Edmund Husserl (1859–1938), a German mathematician who felt that the objectivism of science precluded an adequate apprehension of the world (Husserl 1931, 1954). He presented various philosophical conceptualizations and techniques designed to locate the sources or essences of reality in the human consciousness. It was not until Alfred Schutz (1899–1959) came upon some problems in Max Weber's theory of action that phenomenology entered the domain of sociology (Schutz 1967). Schutz distilled from Husserl's rather dense writings a sociologically relevant approach. Schutz set about describing how subjective meanings give rise to an apparently objective social world (Schutz 1954, 1962, 1964, 1966, 1996; Schutz and Luckmann 1973; Wagner 1983).

Schutz's migration to the United States prior to World War II, along with that of other phenomenologically inclined scholars, resulted in the transmission of this approach to American academic circles and to its ultimate transformation into interpretive sociology. Two expressions of this approach have been called *reality constructionism* and *ethnomethodology*. Reality constructionism synthesizes Schutz's distillation of phenomenology and the corpus of classical sociological thought to account for the possibility of social reality (Berger 1963, 1967; Berger and Berger 1972; Berger and Kellner 1981; Berger and Luckmann 1966; Potter 1996). Ethnomethodology integrates the Parsonian concern for social order into phenomenology and examines the means by which actors make ordinary life possible (Garfinkel 1967; Garfinkel and Sacks 1970). Reality constructionism and ethnomethodology are recognized to be among the most fertile orientations in the field of sociology (Ritzer 1996).

Phenomenology is used in two basic ways in sociology: (1) to theorize about substantive sociological problems and (2) to enhance the adequacy of sociological research methods. Since phenomenology insists that society is a human construction, sociology itself and its theories and methods are also constructions (Cicourel 1964, 1973). Thus, phenomenology seeks to offer a corrective to the field's emphasis on positivist conceptualizations and research methods that may take for granted the very issues that phenomenologists find of interest. Phenomenology presents theoretical techniques and qualitative methods that illuminate the human meanings of social life.

Phenomenology has until recently been viewed as at most a challenger of the more conventional styles of sociological work and at the least an irritant. Increasingly, phenomenology is coming to be viewed as an adjunctive or even integral part of the discipline, contributing useful analytic tools to balance objectivist approaches (Aho 1998; Levesque-Lopman 1988; Luckmann 1978; Psathas 1973; Rogers 1983).

TECHNIQUES

Phenomenology operates rather differently from conventional social science (Darroch and Silvers 1982). Phenomenology is a theoretical orientation, but it does not generate deductions from propositions that can be empirically tested. It operates more on a metasociological level, demonstrating its premises through descriptive analyses of the procedures of self-, situational, and social constitution. Through its demonstrations, audiences apprehend the means by which phenomena, originating in human consciousness, come to be experienced as features of the world.

Current phenomenological techniques in sociology include the method of "bracketing" (Bentz 1995; Ihde 1977). This approach lifts an item under investigation from its meaning context in the commonsense world, with all judgments suspended. For example, the item "alcoholism as a disease" (Peele 1985; Truan 1993) is not evaluated within phenomenological brackets as being either true or false. Rather, a *reduction* is performed in which the item is assessed in terms of how it operates in consciousness: What does the disease notion do for those who define themselves within its domain? A phenomenological reduction both plummets to the essentials of the notion and ascertains its meanings independent of all particular occasions of its use. The reduction of a bracketed phenomenon is thus a technique to gain theoretical insight into the meaning of elements of consciousness.

Phenomenological tools include the use of introspective and *Verstehen* methods to offer a detailed description of how consciousness itself operates (Hitzler and Keller 1989). Introspection requires the phenomenologist to use his or her own subjective process as a resource for study, while *Verstehen* requires an empathic effort to move into the mind of the other (Helle 1991; Truzzi 1974). Not only are introspection and *Verstehen* tools of phenomenological analysis, but they are procedures used by ordinary individuals to carry out their projects. Thus, the phenomenologist as analyst might study himself or herself as an ordinary subject dissecting his or her own self-consciousness and action schemes (Bleicher 1982). In this technique, an analytic attitude toward the role of consciousness in designing everyday life is developed.

Since cognition is a crucial element of phenomenology, some theorists focus on social knowledge as the cornerstone of their technique (Berger and Luckmann 1966). They are concerned with how commonsense knowledge is produced,

disseminated, and internalized. The technique relies on theoretical discourse and historical excavation of the usually taken for granted foundations of knowledge. Frequently, religious thought is given primacy in the study of the sources and legitimations of mundane knowledge (Berger 1967).

Phenomenological concerns are frequently researched using qualitative methods (Bogdan and Taylor 1975; Denzin and Lincoln 1994, 1998). Phenomenological researchers frequently undertake analyses of small groups, social situations, and organizations using face-to-face techniques of participant observation (Bruyn 1966; Psathas and Ten Have 1994; Turner 1974). Ethnographic research frequently utilizes phenomenological tools (Fielding 1988). Intensive interviewing to uncover the subject's orientations or his or her "life world" is also widely practiced (Costelloe 1996; Grekova, 1996; Porter 1995). Qualitative tools are used in phenomenological research either to yield insight into the microdynamics of particular spheres of human life for its own sake or to exhibit the constitutive activity of human consciousness (Langsdorf 1995).

Techniques particular to the ethnomethodological branch of phenomenology have been developed to unveil the practices used by people to produce a sense of social order and thereby accomplish everyday life (Cuff 1993; Leiter 1980; Mehan and Wood 1975). At one time, "breaching demonstrations" were conducted to reveal the essentiality of taken-for-granted routines and the means by which threats to these routines were handled. Since breaching these routines sometimes resulted in serious disruptions of relationships, this technique has been virtually abandoned. Social situations are video- and audiotaped to permit the painstaking demonstration of the means by which participants construct their identities, their interpretations of the meanings of acts, and their sense of the structure of the situation (Blum-Kulka 1994; Jordan and Henderson 1995). Conversational analysis is a technique that is frequently used to describe how people make sense of each other through talk and how they make sense of their talk through their common background knowledge (Psathas 1994; Schegloff and Sacks 1974; Silverman, 1998). The interrelations between mundane reasoning and abstract reasoning are also examined in great depth as researchers expose, for example, the socially constituted bases of scientific and mathematical practice in commonsense thinking (Knorr-Cetina and Mulkay 1983; Livingston, 1995; Lynch, 1993).

THEORY

The central task in social phenomenology is to demonstrate the reciprocal interactions among the processes of human action, situational structuring, and reality construction. Rather than contending that any aspect is a causal factor, phenomenology views all dimensions as constitutive of all others. Phenomenologists use the term *reflexivity* to characterize the way in which constituent dimensions serve as both foundation and consequence of all human projects. The task of phenomenology, then, is to make manifest the incessant tangle or reflexivity of action, situation, and reality in the various modes of *being in the world*.

Phenomenology commences with an analysis of the *natural attitude*. This is understood as the way ordinary individuals participate in the world, taking its existence for granted, assuming its objectivity, and undertaking action projects as if they were predetermined. Language, culture, and common sense are experienced in the natural attitude as objective features of an external world that are learned by actors in the course of their lives.

Human beings are open to patterned social experience and strive toward meaningful involvement in a knowable world. They are characterized by a typifying mode of consciousness tending to classify sense data. In phenomenological terms humans experience the world in terms of *typifications*: Children are exposed to the common sounds and sights of their environments, including their own bodies, people, animals, and vehicles. They come to apprehend the categorical identity and *typified* meanings of each in terms of conventional linguistic forms. In a similar manner, children learn the formulas for doing common activities. These practical means of doing are called *recipes for action*. Typifications and recipes, once internalized, tend to settle beneath the level of full awareness, that is, to become *sedimented*, as do layers of rock. Thus, in the natural attitude, the foundations of actors' knowledge of meaning and action are obscured to the actors themselves.

Actors assume that knowledge is objective and that all people reason in a like manner. Each actor assumes that every other actor knows what he or she knows of this world: All believe that they share common sense. However, each person's biography is unique, and each person develops a relatively distinct stock of typifications and recipes. Therefore, interpretations may diverge. Everyday social interaction is replete with ways in which actors create feelings that common sense is shared, that mutual understanding is occurring, and that everything is all right. Phenomenology emphasizes that humans live within an intersubjective world, yet they at best approximate shared realities. While a *paramount reality* is commonly experienced in this manner, particular realities or *finite provinces of meaning* are also constructed and experienced by diverse cultural, social, or occupational groupings.

For phenomenology, all human consciousness is practical—it is always consciousness of something. Actors intend to introduce projects into the world; they act in order to implement goals based on their typifications and recipes, their *stock of knowledge* at hand. Consciousness as an *intentional process* is composed of thinking, perceiving, feeling, remembering, imagining, and anticipating directed toward the world. The objects of consciousness, these intentional acts, are the sources of all social realities, which are, in turn, the materials of commonsense.

Thus, typifications derived from common sense are internalized, becoming the tools that individual consciousness uses to constitute a *lifeworld*, the unified arena of human awareness and action. Common sense serves as an ever-present resource to assure actors that the reality that is projected from human subjectivity is an objective reality. Since all actors are involved in this intentional work, they sustain the collaborative effort to reify their projections and thereby reinforce the very frameworks that provide the construction tools.

Social interaction is viewed phenomenologically as a process of reciprocal interpretive constructions of actors applying their stock of knowledge at hand to the occasion. Interactors orient themselves to others by taking into account typified meanings of actors in typified situations known to them through common sense. Action schemes are geared by each to the presumed projects of others. The conduct resulting from the intersection of intentional acts indicates to members of the collectivity that communication or coordination or something of the like is occurring among them. For these members, conduct and utterances serve as *indexical* expressions of the properties of the situation, enabling each to proceed with the interaction while interpreting others, context, and self. Through the use of certain interpretive practices, members order the situation for themselves in sensical and coherent terms: In their talk they gloss over apparent irrelevancies, fill in innumerable gaps, ignore inconsistencies, and assume a continuity of meaning, thereby formulating the occasion itself.

Ongoing social situations manifest patterned routine conduct that appears to positivist investigators to be normative or rule guided. Phenomenologically, rules are indexical expressions of the interpretive processes applied by members in the course of their interactions. Rules are enacted in and through their applications. In order to play by the book, an interpreter endeavors to use a rule as an apparent guide. However, he or she must use all sorts of background expectancies to manage the fit somehow between the particular and the general under the contexted conditions of the interaction, and in so doing is acting creatively. Rules, policies, hierarchy, and organization are accomplished through the interpretive acts or negotiations of members in their concerted efforts to formulate a sense of operating in accord with a rational, accountable system. This work of doing structure to the situation further sustains its commonsensical foundations as well as its facticity.

Phenomenologists analyze the ordering of social reality and how the usage of certain forms of knowledge contributes to that ordering. It is posited that typified action and interaction become *habitualized*. Through sedimentation in layered consciousness, human authorship of habitualized conduct is obscured and the product is externalized. As meaning-striving beings, humans create theoretical explanations and moral justifications in order to legitimate the habitualized conduct. Located in higher contexts of meaning, the conduct becomes objectivated. When internalized by succeeding generations, the conduct is fully institutionalized and exerts compelling constraints over individual volition. Periodically, the institutions might be repaired in response to threats, or individuals might be realigned if they cognitively or affectively migrate.

The reality that ordinary people inhabit is constituted by these legitimations of habitualized conduct. Ranging from commonsense typifications of ordinary language to theological constructions to sophisticated philosophical, cosmological, and scientific conceptualizations, these legitimations compose the paramount reality of everyday life. Moreover, segmented modern life, with its proliferation of meaning-generating sectors, produces multiple realities, some in competition with each other for adherents. In the current marketplace of realities, consumers, to varying degrees, may select their legitimations, as they select their occupations and, increasingly, their religions (Berger 1967).

PRACTICE

Doing phenomenological sociology involves using procedures that are distinct from positivist research. Phenomenological practice is increasingly evident in the discipline as more subjectivist work is published. The phenomenological analysis of mass media culture content, for example, applies the elements of the approach to yield an understanding of the reflexive interplay of audience lifeworlds and program material (Wilson 1996). Thus, TV talk show discourses may be described as social texts that are refracted by programmers from commonsense identity constructs. The visual realization yields narrative images that audiences are seduced into processing using their own experiences. The viewers' lifeworlds and the TV representations are blended into reality proxies that provide viewers with schemata to use in configuring their personal orientations. Subsequently, programmers draw upon these orientations as additional identity material for new content development.

Phenomenological work with young children examines how both family interactions and the practices of everyday life are related to the construction of childhood (Davila and Pearson 1994). It reveals how the children's elemental typifications of family life and common sense are actualized through ordinary interaction. Penetrating the inner world of children requires that the phenomenological practitioner view the subjects in children's own terms, from their levels and viewpoints

(Waksler 1991; Shehan 1999). Such investigation shuns adult authoritative and particularly scientific perspectives, and seeks to give voice to the children's experience of their own worlds. Infants' and children's communicative and interactive competencies are respected and are not diminished by the drive toward higher-level functioning (Sheets-Johnstone 1996).

At the other end of the lifecycle, phenomenologists investigate how aging and its associated traumas are constituted in the consciousness of members and helpers. The struggle for meaning during aging accompanied by chronic pain may be facilitated or impaired by the availability of constructs that permit the smoother processing of the experiences. Members of cultures that stock typifications and recipes for managing aging and pain skillfully may well be more likely than others to construct beneficial interpretations in the face of these challenges (Encandela 1997). Phenomenological work encourages the helpers of the elderly to gain empathic appreciation of their clients' lifeworlds and enhanced affiliation with them through the use of biographical narratives that highlight their individuality and humanity (Heliker 1997).

The healing professions, particularly nursing, seem to be deeply imbued with a phenomenological focus on the provision of care based on a rigorous emphasis on the patient's subjective experience (Benner 1995). Substantial attention has been devoted to the ethical implications of various disease definitions, to how language shapes the response to illness, and to how disease definitions and paradigmatic models impact communication between health professionals and patients (Rosenberg and Golden 1992). Significant work on the phenomenology of disability has demonstrated how the *lived body* is experienced in altered form and how taken-for-granted routines are disrupted by invoking new action recipes (Toombs 1995). Nonconventional healing practices have also been examined, revealing how embodiment and the actor's subjective orientation reflexively interrelate with cultural imagery and discourse to transfigure the self (Csordas 1997). Further, phenomenological work has suggested that emotions are best analyzed as interpreted processes embedded within experiential contexts (Blum 1996; Solomon 1997).

IMPLICATIONS

For phenomenology, society, social reality, social order, institutions, organizations, situations, interactions, and individual actions are constructions that appear as suprahuman entities. What does this suggest regarding humanity and sociology? Phenomenology advances the notion that humans are creative agents in the construction of social worlds (Ainlay 1986). It is from their consciousness that all being emerges. The alternative to their creative work is meaninglessness, solipsism, and chaos: a world of dumb puppets, in which each is disconnected from the other and life is formless (Abercrombie 1980). This is the nightmare of phenomenology. Its practitioners fear that positivist sociologists actually theorize about such a world (Phillipson 1972).

Phenomenologists ask sociologists to note the misleading substantiality of social products and to avoid the pitfalls of reification. For the sociologist to view social phenomena within the natural attitude as objects is to legitimate rather than to analyze. Phenomenological sociologists investigate social products as humanly meaningful acts, whether these products are termed attitudes, behaviors, families, aging, ethnic groups, classes, societies, or otherwise (Armstrong 1979; Gubrium and Holstein 1987; Herek 1986; Petersen 1987; Starr 1982). The sociological production of these fictive entities is understood within the context of their accomplishment, that is, the interview setting, the observational location, the data collection situation, the field, the research instrument, and so forth (Schwartz and Jacobs 1979). The meaning contexts applied by the analyst correlates with those of the subjects under investigation and explicates the points of view of the actors as well as expressing their lifeworlds. Phenomenological sociology strives to reveal how actors construe themselves, all the while recognizing that they themselves are actors construing their subjects and themselves.

Phenomenologically understood, society is a fragile human construction, thinly veneered by abstract ideas. Phenomenology itself is evaluatively and politically neutral. Inherently, it promotes neither transformative projects nor stabilization. In the work of a conservatively inclined practitioner, the legitimation process might be supported, while the liberative practitioner might seek to puncture or debunk the legitimations (Morris 1975). Phenomenology can be used to reveal and endorse the great constructions of humankind or to uncover the theoretical grounds of oppression and repression (Smart 1976). Phenomenologists insist upon the human requirements for meaning, subjective connectedess, and a sense of order. These requirements may be fulfilled within existent or emancipative realities (Murphy 1986).

The phenomenological influence upon contemporary sociology can be seen in the increased humanization of theoretical works, research methods, educational assessment procedures, and instructional modes (Aho 1998; Darroch and Silvers 1982; O'Neill 1985; Potter 1996). Phenomenological thought has influenced the work of postmodernist, poststructuralist, critical, and neofunctional theory (Ritzer 1996). Notions such as constructionism, situationalism, and reflexivity that are at the core of phenomenology also provide the grounds for these recent formulations. For example, the premise of poststructuralism that language is socially constituted denying the possibility of objective meaning is clearly rooted in phenomenology. The procedure known as *deconstruction* essentially reverses the reification process highlighted in phenomenology (Dickens and Fontana 1994). The postmodernist argument that knowledge and reality do not exist apart from discourse is also clearly rooted in phenomenology. Postmodernism's emphasis on the representational world as reality constructor further exemplifies the phenomenological bent toward reflexivity (Bourdieu 1992). On the other hand, phenomenology has been used to reverse nihilistic excesses of postmodernism and poststructuralism (O'Neil 1994). The emphases of the critical school on the constitution of the liberative lifeworld by the autonomous, creative agent via the transcendence of linguistic constraint echoes a theme of phenomenological thought (Bowring 1996). Neofunctionalism, a looser and more inclusive version of its predecessor, finds room for a microsocial foundation focusing on the actor as a constructive agent (Layder 1997).

Phenomenology, while remaining an identifiable movement within the discipline of sociology, has influenced mainstream research. Inclusion of qualitative research approaches in conventional research generally expresses this accommodation (Bentz and Shapiro 1998). The greater acceptance of intensive interviewing, participant observation, and focus groups reflect the willingness of nonphenomenological sociologists to integrate subjectivist approaches into their work. The study of constructive consciousness as a method of research has broadened and strengthened the standing of sociology in the community of scholars (Aho 1998).

Phenomenology has made a particular mark in the area of educational policy on a number of levels. The flaws of objective testing have been addressed using phenomenological tools. The issue of construct validity, the link between observation and measurement, has been studied ethnographically as a discursive activity to clarify the practices employed by education researchers to establish validity (Cherryholmes 1988). Testing of children has increasingly respected the subjectivity of the test taker (Gilliatt and Hayward 1996; Hwang 1996). Educators are more alert to the need for understanding the learner's social and cognitive processes, for taking into account the constraining parameters of consciousness, and for encouraging self-conscious reflection. Instructional practices that emphasize constructivist approaches have gained great support among professionals and have been broadly implemented to the benefit of learners (Marlowe and Page 1997).

The future impact of phenomenology will depend on its resonance with the needs and aspirations of the rising generations of sociologists. The drive of some among this emerging generation is to examine the obvious with the infinite patience and endurance that is required to come up with penetrating insight. The arena of discourse analysis perhaps holds the greatest promise of this achievement and will likely elicit substantial effort. The phenomenology of emotions also appears to entice young scholars. The reflexive analyses of popular and mediated culture in relation to identity formation will likely draw further interest, as will the study of virtuality, cyberspace, and computer simulcra. The study of children, the family, and education will increasingly be informed by an emphasis on constructive consciousness. Due to its lack of presumption and openness, the phenomenological movement in sociology has proved hardy during the closing decades of the twentieth century and is well situated to encounter the new millennium.

(SEE ALSO: *Ethnomethodology*; *Qualitative Methods*; *Postmodernism*; *Poststructuralism*)

REFERENCES

Abercrombie, Nicholas 1980 *Class, Structure and Knowledge*. New York: New York University Press.

Aho, James A. 1998 *The Things of the World: A Social Phenomenology*. Westport, Conn.: Praeger.

Ainlay, Stephen C. 1986 "The Encounter with Phenomenology." In James Davison Hunter and Stephen C. Ainlay, eds., *Making Sense of Modern Times: Peter L. Berger and the Vision of Interpretive Sociology*. London: Routledge and Kegan Paul.

Armstrong, Edward G. 1979 "Black Sociology and Phenomenological Sociology." *Sociological Quarterly* 20:387–397.

Benner, Patricia 1995 *Interpretive Phenomenology: Embodiment, Caring and Ethics in Health and Illness*. Thousand Oaks, Calif.: Sage.

Bentz, Valerie Malhotra 1995 "Experiments in Husserlian Phenomenological Sociology." *Studies in Symbolic Interaction* 17:133–161.

——, and Jeremy J. Shapiro 1998 *Mindful Inquiry in Social Research*. Thousand Oaks, Calif.: Sage.

Berger, Peter L. 1963 *Invitation to Sociology: A Humanistic Perspective*. New York: Anchor.

—— 1967 *The Sacred Canopy: Elements of a Sociological Theory of Religion*. New York: Doubleday.

——, and Brigitte Berger 1972 *Sociology: A Biographical Approach*. New York: Basic Books.

Berger, Peter L., and Hansfred Kellner 1981 *Sociology Reinterpreted*. New York: Doubleday.

Berger, Peter L., and Thomas Luckmann 1966 *The Social Construction of Reality: A Treatise in the Sociology of Knowledge*. New York: Doubleday.

Bleicher, Josef 1982 *The Hermeneutic Imagination: Outline of a Positive Critique of Scientism and Sociology*. London: Routledge and Kegan Paul.

Blum, Alan 1996 "Panic and Fear: On the Phenomenology of Desperation." *Sociological Quarterly* 37:673–698.

Blum-Kulka, Shoshana 1994 "The Dynamics of Family Dinner Talk: Cultural Contexts for Children's Passages to Adult Discourse." *Research on Language and Social Interaction* 27:1–50.

Bogdan, Robert, and Steven J. Taylor 1975 *Introduction to Qualitative Research Methods: A Phenomenological Approach to the Social Sciences*. New York: John Wiley.

Bowring, Finn 1996 "A Lifeworld without a Subject: Habermas and the Pathologies of Modernity." *Telos* 106:77–104.

Bourdieu, Pierre 1992 *An Invitation to Reflexive Sociology*. Chicago: University of Chicago Press.

Bruyn, Severn T. 1966 *The Human Perspective in Sociology: The Methodology of Participant Observation*. Englewood Cliffs, N.J.: Prentice-Hall.

Cherryholmes, Cleo H. 1988 "Construct Validity and the Discourses of Research." *American Journal of Education* 96:421–457

Cicourel, Aaron V. 1964 *Method and Measurement in Sociology*. New York: Free Press.

—— 1973 *Theory and Method in a Study of Argentine Fertility*. New York: John Wiley.

Costelloe, Timothy M. 1996 "Between the Subject and Sociology: Alfred Schutz's Phenomenology of the Life-World." *Human Studies* 19:247–266.

Csordas, Thomas J. 1997 *The Sacred Self: A Cultural Phenomenology of Charismatic Healing*. Berkley: University of California Press.

Cuff, E. C. 1993 *Problems of Versions in Everyday Situations*. Lanham, Md.: University Press of America.

Darroch, Vivian, and Ronald J. Silvers (eds.) 1982 *Interpretive Human Studies: An Introduction to Phenomenological Research*. Washington, D.C.: University Press of America.

Davilla, Roberta A., and Judy C. Pearson 1994 "Children's Perspectives of the Family: A Phenomenogical Inquiry." *Human Studies* 17:325–341.

Denzin, Norman K., and Yvonna S. Lincoln 1994 *Handbook of Qualitative Research*. Thousand Oaks, Calif.: Sage.

—— (eds.) 1998 *Collecting and Interpreting Qualitative Materials*. Thousand Oaks, Calif.: Sage.

Dickens, David R., and Andrea Fontana (eds.) 1994 *Postmodernism and Social Inquiry*. New York: Guilford Press.

Encandela, John A. 1997 "Social Construction of Pain and Aging: Individual Artfulness within Interpretive Structures." *Symbolic Interaction* 20:251–273.

Fielding, Nigel G. (ed.) 1988 *Actions and Structure: Research Methods and Social Theory*. London: Sage.

Garfinkel, Harold 1967 *Studies in Ethnomethodology*. Englewood Cliffs, N.J.: Prentice-Hall.

——, and Harvey Sacks 1970 "The Formal Properties of Practical Actions." In John C. McKinney and Edward A. Tiryakian, eds., *Theoretical Sociology*. New York: Appleton-Century-Crofts.

Gilliatt, Stephen E., and Nicholas F. Hayward 1996 "A Testing Time: The Role of Subjective Practices in Making Sense of Student Performance." *Assessment and Evaluation in Higher Education* 21:161–171.

Grekova, Maya 1996 "Restructuring of 'The Life-World of Socialism.'" *International Sociology* 11:63–78.

Gubrium, Jaber F., and James A. Holstein 1987 "The Private Image: Experiential Location and Method in Family Studies." *Journal of Marriage and the Family* 49:773–786.

Heliker, Diane M. 1997 "A Narrative Approach to Quality Care in Long-Term Care Facilities." *Journal of Holistic Nursing* 15:68–81.

Helle, Horst J. (ed.) 1991 *Verstehen and Pragmatism: Essays in Interpretative Sociology*. Frankfurt, Federal Republic of Germany: Peter Lang.

Herek, Gregory M. 1986 "The Instrumentality of Attitudes: Toward a Neofunctional Theory." *Journal of Social Issues* 42:99–114.

Hitzler, Ronald, and Reiner Keller 1989 "On Sociological and Common-Sense *Verstehen*." *Current Sociology* 37:91–101.

Husserl, Edmund 1931 *Ideas: General Introduction to Pure Phenomenology*. W. R. Boyce Gibson, trans. New York: Humanities Press.

—— 1970 *The Crisis of European Sciences and Transcendental Phenomenology*. David Carr, trans. Evanston, Ill.: Northwestern University Press.

Hwang, Ahn-Sook 1996 "Positivist and Constructivist Persuasions in Instructional Development." *Instructional Science* 24:343–356.

Ihde, Don 1977 *Experimental Phenomenology: An Introduction*. New York: Putnam.

Jordan, Brigitte, and Austin Henderson 1995 "Interaction Analysis: Foundations and Practice." *Journal of the Learning Sciences* 4:39–103.

Knorr-Cetina, Karin, and Michael J. Mulkay (eds.) 1983 *Science Observed*. London: Sage.

Langsdorf, Lenore 1995 "Treating Method and Form as Phenomena: An Appreciation of Garfinkel's Phenomenology of Social Action." *Human Studies* 18:177–188.

Layder, Derek 1997 *Modern Social Theory: Key Debates and New Directions*. London: UCL Press.

Leiter, Kenneth 1980 *A Primer on Ethnomethodology*. New York: Oxford University Press.

Levesque-Lopman, Louise 1988 *Claiming Reality: Phenomenology and Women's Experience*. Totowa, N.J.: Rowman and Littlefield.

Livingston, Eric 1995 "The Idiosyncratic Specificity of the Methods of Physical Experimentation." *Australian and New Zealand Journal of Sociology* 31:1–21.

Luckmann, Thomas (ed.) 1978 *Phenomenology and Sociology: Selected Readings*. New York: Penguin.

Lynch, Michael 1993 *Scientific Practice and Ordinary Action: Ethnomethodology and Social Studies of Science*. Cambridge: Cambridge University Press.

Marlowe, Bruce A., and Marilyn L. Page 1997 *Creating and Sustaining the Constructivist Classroom*. Thousand Oaks, Calif.: Corwin.

Mehan, Hugh, and Houston Wood 1975 *The Reality of Ethnomethodology*. New York: John Wiley.

Morris, Monica B. 1975 "Creative Sociology: Conservative or Revolutionary?" *American Sociologist* 10:168–178.

Murphy, John W. 1986 "Phenomenological Social Science: Research in the Public Interest." *Social Science Journal* 23:327–343.

Natanson, Maurice 1970 "Alfred Schutz on Social Reality and Social Science." In Maurice Natanson, ed., *Phenomenology and Social Reality*. The Hague: Nijhoff.

O'Neill, John 1985 "Phenomenological Sociology." *Canadian Review of Sociology and Anthropology* 22:748–770.

—— 1994 *The Poverty of Postmodernism* London: Routledge.

Peele, Stanton 1985 *The Meaning of Addiction: Compulsive Experience and Its Interpretation*. Lexington, Mass.: Lexington Books.

Petersen, Eric E. 1987 "The Stories of Pregnancy: On Interpretation of Small-Group Cultures." *Communication Quarterly* 35:39–47.

Phillipson, Michael 1972 "Phenomenological Philosophy and Sociology." In Paul Filmer, Michael Phillipson, David Silverman, and David Walsh, eds., *New Directions in Sociological Theory*. Cambridge: Massachusetts Institute of Technology Press.

Porter, Eileen Jones 1995 "The Life-World of Older Widows: The Context of Lived Experience." *Journal of Women and Aging* 7:31–46.

Potter, Jonathan 1996 *Representing Reality: Discourse, Rhetoric and Social Construction*. Thousand Oaks, Calif.: Sage.

Psathas, George 1994 *Conversation Analysis : The Study of Talk-in-Interaction*. Thousand Oaks, Calif.: Sage.

—— (ed.) 1973 *Phenomenological Sociology: Issues and Applications*. New York: John Wiley.

Ritzer, George 1996 *Modern Sociological Theory*. New York: McGraw-Hill.

Rogers, Mary F. 1983 *Sociology, Ethnomethodology, and Experience: A Pheomenological Critique*. New York: Cambridge University Press.

Rosenberg, Charles E., and Janet Golden (eds.) 1992 *Framing Disease: Studies in Cultural History*. New Brunswick, N.J.: Rutgers University Press.

Schegloff, Emmanuel, and Harvey Sacks 1974 "Opening Up Closings." In Roy Turner, ed., *Ethnomethodology*. Baltimore: Penguin.

Schutz, Alfred 1996 *Collected Papers IV*. In Helmut Wagner and George Psathas, eds., in collaboration with Fred Kersten, *Phaenomenologica Series*, vol. 136. Boston: Kluwer Academic.

—— 1962 *Collected Papers I: The Problem of Social Reality*. Maurice Natanson, ed. The Hague: Nijhoff.

—— 1964 *Collected Papers II: Studies in Social Theory*. Arvid Brodersen, ed. The Hague: Nijhoff.

—— 1966 *Collected Papers III: Studies in Phenomenological Philosophy*. I. Schutz, ed. The Hague: Nijhoff.

—— 1967 *The Phenomenology of the Social World*. George Walsh and Frederick Lehnert, trans. Evanston, Ill.: Northwestern University Press.

—— 1970 *Reflections on the Problem of Relevance*. Richard Zaner, ed. New Haven: Yale University Press.

——, and Thomas Luckmann 1973 *The Structure of the Life World*. Evanston, Ill.: Northwestern University Press.

Schwartz, Howard, and Jerry Jacobs 1979 *Qualitative Sociology: A Method to the Madness*. New York: Free Press.

Sheets-Johnstone, Maxine 1996 "An Empirical-Phenomenological Critique of the Social Construction of Infancy." *Human Studies* 19:1–16.

Shehan, Constance L. (ed.) 1999 *Through the Eyes of the Child: Revisioning Children as Active Agents of Family Life*. Greenwich, Conn.: JAI Press.

Silverman, David 1998 *Harvey Sacks: Social Science and Conversation Analysis*. New York: Oxford University Press.

Smart, Barry 1976 *Sociology, Phenomenology, and Marxian Analysis: A Critical Discussion of the Theory and Practice of a Science of Society*. London: Routledge and Kegan Paul.

Solomon, Robert C. 1997 "Beyond Ontology: Ideation, Phenomenology and the Cross Cultural Study of Emotion." *Journal for the Theory of Social Behaviour* 27:289–303.

Starr, Jerold M. 1982 "Toward a Social Phenomenology of Aging: Studying the Self Process in Biographical Work." *International Journal of Aging and Human Development* 16:255–270.

Ten Have, Paul, and George Psathas 1994 *Situated Order: Studies in the Social Organization of Talk and Embodied?* Lanham, Md.: University Press of America.

Toombs, S. Kay 1995 "The Lived Experience of Disability." *Human Studies* 18:9–23.

Truan, Franklin 1993 "Addiction as a Social Construction: A Postempirical View." *Journal of Psychology* 127:489–499.

Truzzi, Marcello 1974 *Verstehen: Subjective Understanding in the Social Sciences*. Reading, Mass.: Addison-Wesley.

Turner, Roy (ed.) 1974 *Ethnomethodology: Selected Readings*. Baltimore: Penguin.

Waksler, Frances Chaput (ed.) 1991 *Studying the Social Worlds of Children: Sociological Readings*. London: Falmer Press.

Wagner, Helmut R. 1983 *Alfred Schutz: An Intellectual Biography*. Chicago: University of Chicago Press.

Wilson, Tony 1996 "Television's Everyday Life: Towards a Phenomenology of the 'Televisual Subject.'" *Journal of Communication Inquiry* 20:49–66.

Web Sites of Interest

Center for Advanced Research in Phenomenology: http://www.flinet.com/~carp/

Internet Resources

http://mills.edu/ACAD_INFO/SOC/SOC153/internet.html

MYRON ORLEANS

POLICE

For modern sociology the core problem of police has been, and continues to be, the extrication of the concept *police* from the forms and institutions in which it has been realized and the symbols and concealments in which it has been wrapped. Doing so is essential to the interpretive understanding of the idea of police and is prerequisite to mature answers to the question of what policing means, has meant, and can mean. In one form or another it is the project that has occupied sociologists of police since the early 1960s, and although there is occasional overlap and interchange, attention to it is primarily what distinguishes contributions to the sociology of police from scholarly efforts in the study of police administration, jurisprudence, criminalistics, and police science.

THE POLICE: A SOCIOLOGICAL DEFINITION

By the end of the 1960s a small number of now-classic empirical studies of police had made it apparent that conventional understandings of the idea of police were fundamentally and irreparably flawed. In the face of large-scale studies by Reiss (1971) and Black (1971) which showed that the model tour of duty of a patrol officer in the high-crime areas of the nation's largest cities did not involve the arrest of a single person, it became impossible for sociologists to continue to speak of police as "law enforcers" or of their work as "law enforcement." Likewise, both Skolnick's *Justice without Trial* (1966) and Wilson's *Varieties of Police Behavior* (1968) illustrated dramatic differences in the way police were organized and the relationships they elected to enjoy with courts and law. Similarly, early studies of both the exercise of patrol officer discretion (Bittner 1967a, 1967b) and requests for police service (Cumming et al. 1965; Bercal 1970) cast substantial doubt on the notion that a substantial, much less a defining, activity of police was "fighting crime."

Police Role and Functions. The task of extricating the concept of police from these common misconceptions was assumed by Egon Bittner in *The Functions of Police in Modern Society* (1970). A fundamental theme of Bittner's work was that to define police as "law enforcers," "peacekeepers," "agents of social control," "officers of the court," or, indeed, in any terms that suppose what police should do, confuses police role and function. Throughout history, in this country and in others, police have performed all sorts of functions. In fact, the functions, both manifest and latent, that police have performed are so numerous and so contradictory that any attempt to define police in terms of the functions they are supposed to perform or the ends they are supposed to achieve is doomed to failure.

Force as the Core of the Police Role. Sociologically, policing cannot be defined in terms of its ends; it must be defined in terms of its means. In *Functions* Bittner advanced an approach to understanding the role of the police that was based on the single means that was common to all police, irrespective of the ends to which they aspired or were employed. The means Bittner found to define police was a right to use coercive force. Police, said Bittner, are "a mechanism for the distribution of non-negotiably coercive force" (1971). No police had ever existed, nor is it possible to conceive of an entity that could be called police ever existing, that did not claim the right to use coercive force.

Sociologically, Bittner's formulation had three major virtues. First, it was universal. It was applicable to police everywhere and at all times, police as diverse as the sheriff's posse of the old West, the London bobby, the FBI, or the police of Hitler's Third Reich or Castro's Cuba. Second, it was politically and morally neutral. It could be used to refer to police whose behavior was exemplary as readily as it could be applied to police whose behavior was appalling. Third, it made it possible to make explicit and to probe in systematic ways a host of questions about the role of police that could not previously be explored because they had been concealed in the confusion between role and function: Why do all modern societies, from the most totalitarian and most tyrannical to the most open and democratic, have police? What does having police make available to society that no other institution can supply? What functions are appropriate to assign to police and what are best left to other institutions?

These questions are of such enormous consequence and so fundamental to an understanding of the role of the police that it is difficult to conceive of a sociology of police existing prior to their recognition.

Why Police? If police are a "mechanism for the distribution of non-negotiably coercive force," why should all modern societies find it necessary to create and sustain such a mechanism? What does having such a mechanism make available to modern societies that no other institution can provide?

Bittner's answer is that no other institution has the special competence required to attend to "situations which ought not to be happening and about which something ought to be done NOW!" (1974, p. 30). The critical word in Bittner's careful formulation of the role of the police is "now." What the right to distribute coercive force gives to police is the ability to resolve situations that cannot await a later resolution. The crucial element is time. Turning off a fire hydrant against the wishes of inner-city street bathers, preventing the escape of a serial murderer, halting the escalation of a domestic dispute, or moving back the curious at the scene of a fire so that emergency equipment can pass—these and hundreds of other tasks fall to police because their capacity to use force may be required to achieve them "now."

This view of police radically inverts some conventional conceptions. While popular opinion holds that police acquire their right to use coercive force from their duty to enforce the law, the sociology of police holds that police acquire the duty to enforce the law because doing so may require them to invoke their right to use coercive force. Similarly, focus by police on the crimes and misdemeanors of the poor and humble, and their relative lack of attention to white-collar and corporate offenders, is often promoted as reflecting a class or race bias in institutions of social control. While not denying that such biases can exist and do sometimes influence the direction of police attention, if such biases were eliminated entirely, the distribution of police effort and attention would undoubtedly remain unchanged. It would remain unchanged because the special competence of police, their right to use coercive force, is essential in enforcement efforts in which offenders are likely to physically resist or to flee. In white-collar and corporate crime investigations, the special competence of lawyers and accountants is essential, while the special competence of police is largely unnecessary.

INSTITUTIONAL FORMS

Although all modern societies have found it necessary to create and maintain some form of police, it is obvious that any institution that bears the right to use coercive force is extraordinarily dangerous and highly subject to abuse and corruption. The danger of the institution of police would appear to be magnified when it gains a monopoly, or a near-monopoly, on the right to use coercive force, and when those who exercise that monopoly are almost exclusively direct and full-time employees of the state. Appearances and dangers notwithstanding, these are nevertheless the major terms of the institutional arrangement of police in every modern democracy. Some comment on the sociology of this institutional uniformity may be helpful.

Avocational Policing. For most of human history most policing has been done by individuals, groups, associations, and organizations in the private sector. This type of private-sector policing, done by citizens not as a job but as an avocation, may be classified into at least three types, each of which offered a somewhat different kind of motivation to private citizens for doing it (Klockars 1985). Historically, the most common type is *obligatory avocational policing*. Under its terms private citizens are compelled to police by the threat of some kind of punishment if they fail to do so. In American police history the sheriff's posse is perhaps the most familiar variety of this type of policing. The English systems of frankpledge (Morris 1910) and parish constable (Webb and Webb 1906) were also of this type.

A second type of private-sector policing, *voluntary avocational policing*, is done by private citizens not because they are obliged by a threat of punishment but because they, for their own reasons, want to do it. The most familiar American example of this type of policing is vigilante groups, over three hundred of which are known to have operated throughout the United States up to the end of the nineteenth century (Brown 1975).

A third type, *entrepreneurial avocational policing*, includes private citizens who as English thief takers, American bounty hunters, French agents provocateurs, and miscellaneous paid informants police on a per-head, per-crime basis for money.

The institutional history of these avocational forms of policing is thoroughly disappointing, and modern societies have largely abandoned these ways of getting police work done. The central flaw in all systems of obligatory avocational policing is that as the work of policing becomes more difficult or demanding, obligatory avocational policing takes on the character of forced labor. Motivated only by the threat of punishment, those who do it become unwilling and resistant, a situation offering no one any reason to learn or cultivate the skill to do it well. All forms of voluntary avocational policing suffer from the exact opposite problem. Voluntary avocational police, vigilantes and the like, typically approach their work with passion. The problem is that because the passionate motives of voluntary avocational police are their own, it is almost impossible to control who and where and what form of police work they do and on whom they do it. Finally, the experience with entrepreneurial forms of avocational policing—thief takers, bounty hunters, and paid informants—has been the most disappointing of all. The abuse and corruption of entrepreneurial avocational police has demonstrated unequivocally that greed is too narrow a basis on which to build a police system.

Sociologically, the shortcoming of all forms of avocational policing is that none of them offers adequate means of controlling the police. This observation leads directly to the question of why one might have reason to suspect that a full-time, paid police should be easier to control than its avocational precedents. What new means of control is created by establishing a full-time, paid, police vocation?

The answer to this problem is that only when policing becomes a full-time, paid occupation is it possible to dismiss, to *fire*, any particular person who makes his or her living doing it. The state can only hire entrepreneurial avocational police, bounty hunters, paid informants, and thief takers; it cannot fire them. Vigilantes are driven by their own motives and cannot be discharged from them. Obligatory avocational police are threatened with punishment if they don't work; most would love to be sacked. Because the option to fire, to take police officers' jobs away from them, is the only essential means of controlling police work that separates the police vocation from all avocational arrangements for policing, how that option is used will, more than anything else, determine the shape and substance of the police vocation.

The Police Vocation. The English, who in 1829 created the first modern police, were intimately familiar with the shortcomings of all forms of avocational policing. They had, in fact, resisted the creation of a paid, full-time police for more than a century, out of fear that such an institution would be used as a weapon of political oppression by the administrative branch of government. To allay the fears that the "New Police" would become such a weapon, the architects of the first modern police, Home Secretary Robert Peel and the first commissioners of the New Police, Richard Mayne and Charles Rowan, imposed three major political controls on them. Peel, Mayne, and Rowan insisted that the New Police of London would be unarmed, uniformed, and confined to preventive patrol. Each of these features shaped in profound ways the institution of the New Police and, in turn, the police of the United States and other Western democracies that explicitly copied the English model.

Unarmed. Politically, the virtue of an unarmed police is that its strength can be gauged as a rough equivalent of its numbers. Weapons serve as multipliers of the strength of individuals and can increase the coercive capacity of individuals to levels that are incalculable. One person with a rifle can dominate a dozen citizens; with a machine gun, hundreds; with a nuclear missile, thousands. One person with a police truncheon is only slightly stronger than another, and that advantage can be quickly eliminated by the other's picking up a stick or a stone. In 1829 the individual strength of the 3,000 constable, unarmed New Police offered little to fear to London's 1.3 million citizens.

While this political virtue of an unarmed police helped overcome resistance to the establishment of the institution, the long-run sociological virtue of an unarmed police proved far more important. Policing is, by definition, a coercive enterprise. Police must, on occasion, compel compliance from persons who would do otherwise. Force is, however, not the only means to compel compliance. Sociologically, at least three other bases for control are possible: authority, power, and persuasion.

Unarmed and outnumbered, the New Police "bobby" could not hope to police effectively on the basis of force. Peel, Mayne, and Rowan knew that if the New Police were to coerce successfully, they would have to do so on the basis of popular respect for the authority and power of the institution of which they were a part. The respect owed each constable was not owed to an individual but to a single, uniform temperament, code of conduct, style of work, and standard of behavior that every constable was expected to embody.

In order to achieve this uniformity of temperament, style, conduct, and behavior, the architects of the New Police employed the option to dismiss with a passion. "Between 1830 and 1838, to hold the ranks of the New Police of London at a level of 3300 men required nearly 5,000 dismissals and 6,000 resignations, most of the latter not being altogether voluntary" (Lee 1971; p. 240). During the first eight years of its organization, every position on the entire force was fired or forced to resign more than three times over!

Unlike their earlier London counterparts, the new American police were undisciplined by the firing option. What prevented the effective use of the firing option by early American police administrators was that police positions were, by and large, patronage appointments of municipal politicians. In New York, for example, the first chief of police did not have the right to fire any officer under his command. So while London bobbies were being dismissed for showing up late to work or behaving discourteously toward citizens, American police were assaulting superior officers, taking bribes, refusing to go on patrol, extorting money from prisoners, and releasing prisoners from the custody of other officers.

In New York, Boston, Chicago, and other American cities the modern police began, in imitation of London's bobbies, as unarmed forces; but, being corrupt, undisciplined, and disobedient, they could not inspire respect for either their power or their authority. In controlling citizens they had no option but to rely on their capacity to use force. The difficulty with doing so unarmed is that someone armed with a multiplier of strength can always prove to be stronger. Gradually, against orders, American police armed themselves, at first with the quiet complicity of superior officers and later, as the practice became widespread, in open defiance of departmental regulations. Eventually, in an effort to control the types of weapons their officers carried, the first municipal police agencies began issuing standard service revolvers.

The long-run sociological consequence of arming the American police can be understood only by appreciating how it shaped American police officers' sense of the source of their capacity to control the citizens with whom they dealt. While the London bobbies drew their capacity for control from the profoundly social power and authority of the institution of which they were a part, American police officers understood their capacities for control to spring largely from their own personal, individual strength, multiplied if necessary by the weapon they carried on their hips. This understanding of the source of their capacity for control led American police officers to see the work they did and the choices they made in everyday policing to be largely matters of their individual discretion. Thus, the truly long-run sociological

effect of the arming of the American police has been to drive discretionary decision making to the lowest and least public levels of American police agencies. Today how an American police officer handles a drunk, a domestic disturbance, an unruly juvenile, a marijuana smoker, or a belligerent motorist is largely a reflection not of law or agency policy but of that particular officer's personal style. This is not to say that law or agency policy cannot have influence over how officers handle these types of incidents. However, one of the major lessons of recent attempts by sociologists to measure the impact of changes in law or police policy in both domestic violence and drunken driving enforcement is that officers can resist those changes vigorously when the new law or policy goes against their views of proper police response (see Dunford et al. 1990;Mastrofski et al. 1988).

Uniformed. Politically, the requirement that police be uniformed is a guarantee that they will not be used as spies; that they will be given information only when their identity as police is known; that those who give them information, at least when they do so in public, are likely to be noticed doing so; and that they can be held accountable, as agents of the state, for their behavior. The English, who had long experience with uniformed employees of many types, understood these political virtues of the uniform completely. In fact, an incident in 1833 in which a police sergeant assumed an ununiformed undercover role resulted in such a scandal that it nearly forced the abolition of the New Police.

By contrast, the early American understanding of the uniform was totally different. Initially it was seen to be a sign of undemocratic superiority. Later it was criticized by officers themselves as a demeaning costume and resisted on those grounds. For twelve years, despite regulations that required them to do so, early New York policemen successfully refused to wear uniforms. In 1856 a compromise was reached by allowing officers in each political ward to decide on the color and style they liked best.

Despite the early resistance to the uniform and the lack of appreciation for its political virtues, American police eventually became a uniformed force. While the London bobby's uniform was explicitly designed to have a certain "homey" quality and to reflect restraint, the modern American police officer's uniform is festooned with the forceful tools of the police trade. The gun, ammunition, nightstick, blackjack, handcuffs, and Mace, all tightly holstered in shiny black leather and set off with chromium buckles, snaps, badges, stars, flags, ribbons, patches, and insignia, suggest a decidely military bearing. The impression intended is clearly one not of restraint but of the capacity to overcome the most fearsome of enemies by force.

The Military Analogy and the War on Crime. To understand the sociology of the American police uniform, it is necessary to see in it a reflection of a major reform movement in the history of the American police. Around 1890 American police administrators began to speak about the agencies they administered as if they were domestic armies engaged in a war on crime (Fogelson 1977).

The analogy was powerful and simple. It drew upon three compelling sources. First, it sought to connect police with the victories and heroes of the military and to dissociate them from the corruption and incompetence of municipal politics. Second, it evoked a sense of urgency and emergency in calls for additional resources. From the turn of the century to the present day, the war on crime has proved a useful device for getting municipal governments and taxpayers to part with money for police salaries and equipment. Third and most important, the war on crime and the military analogy sought to create a relationship between police administrators and politicians at the municipal level that was similar to the relationship enjoyed by military generals and politicians at the national level. At the national level Americans have always conceded that the decision on whether to fight a war was a politicians' decision, but how that war was to be fought and the day-to-day discipline of the troops was best left to the generals. By getting the public and the politicians to accept these terms of the police-politics relationship, the early police administrators found a way to wrest from the hands of politicians the tool they needed to discipline their troops: the option to fire disobedient officers.

The uniform of the war-ready American police officer is testimony to the fact that since the 1940s, American police administrators have won the battle to conceive of police as engaged in a war on crime. In doing so they have gained control of the option to fire for administrative purposes. However, the cost of that victory has been enormous.

A major problem is the idea of a war on crime and the expectation police have promoted that they can, in some sense, fight or win it. In point of fact, a war on crime is something police can neither fight nor win for some fundamental sociological reasons. It is simply not within the capacity of police to change those things—unemployment, the age distribution of the population, moral education, civil liberties, ambition and the social and economic opportunities to realize it—that influence the amount and type of crime in any society. These are the major social correlates of crime, and despite presentments to the contrary, police are but a small tail on a gigantic social kite. Moreover, any kind of real "war on crime" is something that no democratic society would be prepared to let its police fight. No democratic society would be able to tolerate the kinds of abuses to the civil liberties of innocent citizens that fighting any real "war" on crime would necessarily involve. It is a major contribution of the sociology of police since the 1960s to demonstrate that almost nothing police do can be shown to have any substantial effect on reducing crime.

The problems of policing in the name of crime when one cannot do much of anything about it are enormous. It is not uncommon for patrol officers to see their employers as hypocritical promoters of a crime-fighting image that is far removed from what they know to be the reality of everyday police work. They may seek to explain what they know to be their failure to do much about crime in terms of the lack of courage of their chief, the incompetence of police administration, or sinister political forces seeking to "handcuff" the police. They often close off what they regard as the disappointing reality of what they do in cynicism, secrecy, and silence—the "blue curtain," the occupational culture of policing.

Equally problematic as a spoil of the early chiefs' victory in their war on crime is the quasi-military police administrative structure. Once heralded as a model of efficiency, it is now regarded as an organizationally primitive mode of management. It works, to the extent that it works, by creating hundreds and sometimes even thousands of rules and by punishing departures from those rules severely. The central failing of such an administrative model is that it rests on the unwarranted assumption that employees will not discover that the best way to avoid punishment for doing something wrong is to do as little as possible. The administration can, in turn, respond by setting quotas for the minimum amount of work it will tolerate from employees before it moves to punish them, but if it does so, that minimal amount of work is, by and large, all it will get.

Preventive Patrol. The third major mechanism with which architects of the New Police sought to neutralize their political uses was to confine police to preventive patrol. This restriction was understood to have the effect of limiting the uniformed, patrolling constable to two relatively apolitical types of interventions: situations in which constables would be called upon for help by persons who approached them on the street and situations that, from the street, constables could see required their attention. These political virtues of patrol impressed the architects of the New Police, particularly Sir Richard Mayne. Mayne postponed the formation of any detective unit in the New Police until 1842, and during his forty years as commissioner held its ranks to fewer than 15 detectives in a force of more than 3,500.

In the early American experience, uniformed patrol served the principal purpose of imposing some semblance of order on unruly officers. Patrol offered some semblance of assurance that officers could be found at least somewhere near the area to which they were assigned. And while American police created detective forces almost immediately after they were organized, patrol has become in the United States, as in Britain and other modern democracies, the major means of getting police work done.

Sociologically, patrol has had tremendous consequences for the form and substance of policing. It has, for example, been extraordinarily amenable to the three most profound technological developments of the past century: the automobile, the telephone, and the wireless radio. And while there is no evidence that increasing or decreasing the amount of patrol has any influence whatsoever on the crime rate, each of these technological developments has made police patrol more convenient

and more attractive to citizens who wish to call for police service. It is not an exaggeration to say that the vast majority of the activity of most modern police agencies is driven by a need to manage citizen demand for patrol service.

In recent years, attempts to manage this demand have taken many forms. Among the most common are the creation of computer-aided dispatch systems that prioritize the order in which patrol officers are assigned to complaints and increasingly stringent policies governing the types of problems for which police will provide assistance. Also increasingly common are attempts to handle complaints that merely require a written report, by taking that report over the telephone or having the complainant complete a mail-in form. In no small part, such efforts at eliminating unnecessary police response and making necessary police response efficient have produced some of the increasing cost for police labor.

REORIENTING POLICING

Despite efforts at prioritization, limitation of direct police response, and development of alternative ways of registering citizen complaints, demand for police service continues to grow. Despite the fact that individual citizens appear to want this form of police service more than any other, some contemporary approaches suggest that the entire idea of "dial-a-cop," "incident-driven" policing requires reconsideration. Two such approaches, "community-oriented policing" (Skolnick and Bayley 1986) and "problem-oriented policing" (Goldstein 1979, 1990), have been advanced as the next generation of "reform" movements in American policing (Greene and Mastrofski 1988).

As theories of police reform, both "problem-oriented" and "community-oriented" policing are grounded in the suspicion that the traditional police response of dispatching patrol officers in quick response to citizen complaints does little to correct the underlying problem that produced the complaint. To some degree at least, this suspicion is confirmed by studies that tend to show that a fairly small number of addresses tend to generate disproportionate numbers of calls for police service, and that patrol officers commonly return to such "hot spots" again and again to attend to similar problems (Sherman et al. 1989).

Both problem-oriented and community-oriented policing offer strategies to deal with such problems that go beyond merely dispatching an officer to the scene. Problem-oriented policing offers a generic, four-step, problem-solving strategy—scanning, analysis, response, and assessment—that police can use to identify problems and experiment with solutions. Community-oriented policing, by contrast, does not offer a mechanism for problem analysis and solution. It is, however, committed to a general strategy that calls for cooperative, police-community efforts in problem solving. In such efforts it encourages the employment of a variety of police tactics—foot patrol, storefront police stations, neighborhood watch programs—that tend to involve citizens directly in the police mission.

While both approaches to reorienting policing have been heralded as revolutionary in their implications for the future of policing, both confront some major obstacles to their realization. The first is that neither problem-oriented nor community-oriented police efforts have been able to reduce the demand for traditional patrol response. Unless that demand is reduced or police resources are increased to allow it to be satisfied along with nontraditional approaches, the community- and problem-oriented policing approaches will most likely be relegated, at best, to a secondary, peripheral role.

The second problem confronting both community- and problem-oriented policing stems from the definition of police and the role appropriate to it in a modern democratic society. The special competence of police is their capacity to use force, and for that reason all modern societies find it necessary and appropriate to have them attend to situations that cannot await a later resolution. Reactive, incident-driven, dial-a-cop patrol is a highly popular, extremely efficient, and (as nearly as possible) politically neutral means of delivering that special competence. To expand the police role to include responsibility for solving the root problems of neighborhoods and communities is an admirable aspiration; but it is a responsibility that seems to go beyond the special competence of police and to require, more appropriately, the special competence of other institutions.

In the past quarter of a century, the scholarly literature on police has grown so dramatically that a guide is quite helpful if not essential for the reader who seeks to explore the sociology of police. There are seven classic works in the sociology of police that continue to frame most modern dialogues: Michael Bantons's *The Policeman in the Community* (1968), Egon Bittner's *Functions of Police in Modern Society* (1970), Herbert Packer's *The Limits of the Criminal Sanction* (1968), Jerome Skolnick's *Justice without Trial* (1966), William Westley's *Violence and the Police* (1970), and James Q. Wilson's *Varieties of Police Behavior* (1968). These classic works are informed, dramatized, broadened, and otherwise enhanced by a second generation consisting of five extraordinary empirical and theoretical works: Donald Black's *Manners and Customs of the Police* (1980), David Bayley's *Forces of Order: Police Behavior in Japan and the United States* (1976), William Ker Muir, Jr.'s *Police: Streetcorner Politicians* (1977), Peter Manning's *Police Work: The Social Organization of Policing* (1977), and Jonathan Rubinstein's *City Police* (1973).

Beginning in the 1980s, the literature on the sociology of police may be thought of as dividing into three tracks. One track continues the general reflections on the nature of the police institution and its enterprise and includes Richard Ericson's *Making Crime* (1982), Carl Klockars's *The Idea of Police* (1983), Robert Reiner's *The Politics of the Police* (1985), and most recently Richard Ericson and Kevin Haggarty's *Policing the Risk Society* (1997). A second track includes a collection of studies that focus on particular types of or particular problems in policing. Among them are Geoffrey Alpert and Laurie Fridell's *Police Vehicles and Firearms: Instruments of Deadly Force* (1992), Gary Marx's *Undercover* (1988), Maurice Punch's *Conduct Unbecoming: The Social Construction of Police Deviance and Control* (1985), and Lawrence W. Sherman's *Policing Domestic Violence* (1992), as well as two collections, *Modern Policing*, edited by Michael Tonrey and Norval Morris (1992), *Police Violence: Understanding and Controlling Police Abuse of Force*, edited by William A. Geller and Hans Toch (1996). The third track is, of course, the enormous literature on community policing. The collection edited by Jack Greene and Stephen Mastrofski and entitled *Community Policing: Rhetoric or Reality* (1988) is a good guide to the early literature. Herman Goldstein's *Problem-Oriented Policing* (1990) is, of course, essential. Malcolm Sparrow, Mark Moore, and David

Kennedy's *Beyond 911* (1995), and George Kelling and C. Coles's *Fixing Broken Windows* (1996) are two works of some influence in contemporary discussions of the promise of community policing.

(SEE ALSO: *Criminal Sanctions; Criminology; Social Control*)

REFERENCES

Alpert, Geoffrey, and Laurie Fridell 1992 *Police Vehicles and Firearms: Instruments of Deadly Force.* Prospect Heights, Ill.: Waveland.

Bayley, David 1976 *Forces of Order: Police Behavior in Japan and the United States.* Berkeley: University of California Press.

Bercal, T. E. 1970 "Calls for Police Assistance: Consumer Demand for Governmental Service." *American Behavioral Scientist* 13, no. 2 (May–August):221–238.

Bittner, E. 1967a "Police Discretion in Apprehension of Mentally Ill Persons." *Social Problems* 14 (Winter):278–292.

—— 1967b "The Police on Skid Row: A Study of Peace Keeping." *American Sociological Review* 32 (October):699–715.

—— 1970 *The Functions of Police in Modern Society.* Washington: U.S. Government Printing Office.

—— 1974 "Florence Nightingale in Pursuit of Willie Sutton: A Theory of Police." In H. Jacob, ed., *The Potential for Reform of Criminal Justice.* Beverly Hills, Calif.: Sage.

Black, D. 1971 "The Social Organization of Arrest." *Stanford Law Review* 23 (June):1087–1111.

—— 1980 *Manners and Customs of the Police.* New York: Academic.

Brown, R. M. 1975 *Strain of Violence: Historical Studies of American Violence and Vigilantism.* Oxford: Oxford University Press.

Cumming, E., I. Cumming, and L. Edell 1965 "Policeman as Philosopher, Guide, and Friend." *Social Forces* 12(3):276–286.

Dunford, F. W., D. Huizinga, and D. S. Elliott 1990 "The Role of Arrest in Domestic Assault: The Omaha Police Experiment." *Criminology* 28(2):183–206.

Ericson, Richard 1982 *Making Crime.* Toronto: University of Toronto Press.

——, and Kevin Haggarty 1997 *Policing the Risk Society.* Toronto: University of Toronto Press.

Fogelson, R. 1977 *Big City Police.* Cambridge, Mass.: Harvard University Press.

Geller, William, and Hans Toch 1996 *Police Violence: Understanding and Controlling Police Abuse of Force.* New Haven, Conn.: Yale University Press.

Goldstein, H. 1979 "Improving Policing: A Problem-Oriented Approach." *Crime and Delinquency* 25 (April):236–258.

—— 1990 *Problem-Oriented Policing.* New York: McGraw-Hill.

Greene, J., and S. Mastrofski 1988 *Community Policing: Rhetoric or Reality.* New York: Praeger.

Kelling, George, and C. Coles 1996 *Fixing Broken Windows.* New York: Free Press.

Klockars, C. B. 1985 *The Idea of Police.* Beverly Hills, Calif.: Sage.

Lee, M. 1971 *A History of Police in England.* Montclair, N.J.: Patterson Smith.

Manning, Peter 1977 *Police Work: The Social Organization of Policing.* Prospect Heights, Ill.: Waveland.

Mastrofski, S., R. R. Ritti, and D. Hoffmaster 1988 "Organizational Determinants of Police Discretion: The Case of Drunk Driving." *Journal of Criminal Justice* 15:387–402.

Morris, W. A. 1910 *The Frankpledge System.* New York: Longmans, Green.

Muir, William, Jr. 1977 *Police: Streetcorner Politicians.* Chicago: University of Chicago Press.

Packer, Herbert 1968 *The Limits of the Criminal Sanction.* Stanford, Calif.: Stanford University Press.

Punch, Maurice 1985 *Conduct Unbecoming: The Social Construction of Police Deviance and Control.* London: Tavistock.

Reiner, Robert 1985 *The Politics of the Police.* Brighton: Weatsheaf.

Reiss, A. J., Jr. 1971 *Police and the Public.* New Haven, Conn.: Yale University Press.

Rubinstein Jonathan 1973 *City Police.* New York: Farrar, Strauss and Giroux.

Sherman, L. W., P. Gartin, and M. E. Buerger 1989 "Hot Spots of Predatory Crime: Routine Activities and the Criminology of Place." *Criminology* 27:27–55.

Sherman, Lawrence 1992 *Policing Modern Violence.* New York: Free Press.

Skolnick, J. K. 1966 *Justice Without Trial.* New York: John Wiley.

——, and D. Bayley 1986 *The New Blue Line.* New York: Free Press.

Sparrow, Malcolm, Mark Moore, and David Kennedy 1995 *Beyond 911*. New York: Basic.

Tonrey, Michael, and Norval Morris (eds.) 1992 *Modern Policing*. Chicago: University of Chicago Press.

Webb, S., and B. Webb 1906 *English Local Government from the Revolution to the Municipal Corporations Act: The Parish and the County*. New York: Longmans, Green.

Westley, William 1970 *Violence and the Police*. Cambridge: Massachusetts Institute of Technology Press.

Wilson, J. Q. 1968 *Varieties of Police Behavior: The Management of Law and Order in Eight Communities*. Cambridge, Mass.: Harvard University Press.

CARL B. KLOCKARS

POLISH AND EASTERN EUROPEAN SOCIOLOGY

CENTRAL AND EASTERN EUROPEAN SOCIOLOGY

There is no doubt that central and eastern European sociologies have similar intellectual, historical, and political roots and can be treated as one block, in contrast to western European sociologies, which are not characterized by uniformity (Nedelmann and Sztompka 1993). This holds true especially for the postwar period in the development of eastern European sociologies. The only exception to this pattern is Polish sociology, which is why we analyze the history and current state of Polish sociology separately. In this brief analysis of central and eastern European sociology we focus on Russian, Hungarian, Czech, Bulgarian, and Rumanian sociologies (see Kolaja and Das 1988; Genov 1989; Keen and Mucha 1994).

Overall, we do not evaluate these sociologies as very impressive, especially in comparison to western European sociologies, on the one hand, and American sociology, on the other. Central and eastern European sociologies have not produced important contributions either to classical tradition or to contemporary sociology. The only contribution to classical world sociology that should be mentioned here comes from Russian tradition and belongs to Pitrim Sorokin (1959, 1962).

The postwar period in the development of eastern and central European sociology is marked by the imposition of the communist system on the societies in that region. This historical development had overwhelming impact on the development of sociology in these societies. In Russia we witness further expansion of orthodox Marxism—the development that began right after the Bolshevik revolution in 1917, when sociology was removed from universities along with "bourgeois" professors. Historical materialism was proclaimed the only true scientific sociology, whereas the critique of "bourgeois sociology" was the only way of dealing with Western social thought and adopting Western sociological ideas. In the 1950s and 1960s in Russia, a kind of "empirical" Marxist sociology was established. Because of this development, survey research on the conditions of the working class on a large scale was launched and has continued up to this day. This continuing research is atheoretical and purely descriptive.

The so-called Stalinist period, which began right after World War II and lasted until the late fifties, or in some countries even the early sixties, was marked by the almost complete defeat of academic sociology. Sociology was labeled a "bourgeois pseudo-science" (Kolosi and Szelenyi 1993, p. 146), and was abolished as an academic and autonomous discipline. It is hard to overestimate the negative outcomes of this period and the entire period of the communist system in the eastern and central European countries. The development of sociology has been substantially slowed down if not, in some cases, completely stopped. This is why it was only in the 1960s that debates about the scientific character of sociology reemerged in Hungarian and other sociologies in this region. During most of the time after the Stalinist period and until the 1990s, sociologies of this region were trying to free themselves from Marxist ideology, which was not easy since communist regimes always treated sociology as dangerous discipline. These factors are basically responsible for the retardation of these sociologies, as compared to the rest of European sociology. Another important factor that should be mentioned here is the intellectual tradition. As opposed to such countries as Germany, France, Great Britain, and even Poland, the central and eastern European countries have had no tradition of sociological thought.

In this context it is easy to see why, during the communist period and even after the collapse of the communist system, there was little significant achievement in sociological theory and research in eastern and central European countries.

For example, in Bulgaria it was only in 1985 that sociology began as an academic discipline at few universities. The factor that ignited this development was the fact that Bulgarian Sociological Association organized the VII World Congress of International Sociological Association (ISA) in Varna in 1970. However, the organization of the World Congress of ISA was possible due to purely political decision made by Bulgarian communist government and ISA authorities, but not as the result of advancement of Bulgarian sociology itself.

In Rumania and Czechoslovakia the condition of sociology was very bad, and practically until 1989 the discipline of sociology in these countries was subjected to special controls by the communist regimes. For example, in Czechoslovakia, to have any sort of academic career, communist party membership was required. In East Germany it was only after 1980 that earning a Ph.D. in sociology was allowed for East German academics. Even in the former Yugoslavia, sociology was strictly controlled by the government; this control, in conjunction with the lack of a sociological research tradition, created a situation in which substantial development of the discipline of sociology was very difficult (Keen and Mucha 1994).

Only in Hungary were there important contributions to sociology. These were made by Gyorgy Konrad and Ivan Szelenyi in urban sociology and especially in the sociology of inequalities, classes, and intelligentsia. Their book, *The Intellectuals on the Road to Class Power*, is probably the most famous contribution of Hungarian sociology to world sociological literature (Konrad and Szelenyi 1979). Research on economical sociology by Istvan Gabor, Janos Kornai, and Elmer Hankiss, and on social structure and stratification by Tamas Kolosi, was also significant, not only for our understanding of Hungarian society but also for a general understanding of the phenomena studied.

As mentioned previously, Polish sociology is a special and different case, which is why we treat it separately. There is a rich tradition of sociological thought in Poland. Important contributions to sociology that have significance for this discipline were made by Polish sociologists. Even during the communist period, sociology in Poland remained

relatively free in terms of research, the process of institutionalization of academic life, and contact with Western sociology.

THE ORIGINS OF SOCIOLOGY IN POLAND

To understand the past and present status of Polish sociology, one should take into account its peculiarity, namely, its particularly tight, intrinsic link with the course of Polish national history, overabundant with uprisings, wars, revivals and transformations. The nineteenth century and the period up to World War II were characterized by the reception of the dominant European trends of social thought. The organicism of Herbert Spencer is reflected in the works of Jozef Supinski (1804–1893), called the founder of Polish sociology. He formulated, for the first time, the problem of the interplay between the nation and the state, which became persistent later on in Polish sociology. Ludwik Gumplowicz (1838–1909) was one of the classic exponents of the conflict tradition and probably the only Polish sociologist of that period who entered the standard textbooks of the history of sociology. He published several works, mainly in German: *Der Rassenkampf* (1883), *Grundriss der Soziologie* (1885), *Die soziologische Staatsidee* (1892), and *Soziologie und Politik* (1892). Gumplowicz's peculiarity consisted in his being an advocate of sociologism before Émile Durkheim. His approach to social life was that the emergence and functioning of social organizations are marked by enduring conflict between social groups, for example, ethnic groups. This is why in some textbooks he is also called a social Darwinist.

The psychologism of Gabriel Tarde and Gustave Le Bon influenced the ideas of Leon Petrazycki (1867–1931), whose three fundamental works were originally published in Russian: *The Introduction to the Study of Politics and Law* (1892), *An Introduction to the Study of Law and Morality* (1905), and *The Theory of Law and State* (1907). His *Die Lehre vom Einkommen* (two volumes, 1893–1895) was published in Berlin. For Petrazycki, observation is a basic method of investigating and studying objects and phenomena. As regards psychic phenomena, the observation consists in self-observation, or introspection. The task of sociology is to detect objective tendencies of social phenomena. Unconscious adaptation processes might be replaced by deliberate steering of man's destiny with the help of law. The ideal pursued by Petrazycki consisted in the human psyche's being so fitted to the requirements of social life that normative systems (e.g., morality) would prove unnecessary.

Another advocate of psychologism was Edward Abramowski (1868–1918). His main writings include *Individual Elements in Sociology* (1899), and *Theory of Psychical Units* (1899), in which he sketched his theory of sociological phenomenalism. Its main thesis was that the development of societies is based on the constant interaction between objective phenomena and human consciousness, which are causes and effects alternately. In three works—*Problems of Socialism, Ethics and Revolution*, and *Socialism and the State*, all written before 1899 and published in *Social Philosophy: Selected Writings* (1965)—he applied sociological phenomenalism to the analysis of the strategy of class struggle and to the realization of the socialist system. Social revolution should be preceded by "moral revolution"—a deep transformation of conscience. A cooperative is a germ of a socialist society, while the state is its enemy. A cooperative can be transformed into a real republic—a cooperative *res publica*.

Ludwik Krzywicki (1859–1941) was the foremost representative of the first Polish Marxists' generation. Among his works are: *Modern Social Issue* (1888), *Political Economy* (1899), *Sociological Studies* (1923), and *Idea and Life* (1957). Krzywicki was under substantial influence from Darwin and Comte, which led him to the idea of society as a section of natural phenomena and social evolution as a part of universal evolution. The merging of historical materialism with positivistic scientific criteria produced a natural-evolutionistic branch of Marxism comprising the canon of "iron historical laws," of which Krzywicki himself was the representative. His conception of "historical background" allowed him to invent the original typology of social systems. Also, he was the author of original conception of "industrial feudalism," being the precursor of the "welfare state" theory.

Another follower of Marx's ideas, Kazimierz Kelles-Krauz (1872–1906), published, among other works, *The Law of Revolutionary Retrospection* (1895), *Sociological Law of Retrospection* (1898), *Economic Basis of Primitive Forms of the Family* (1900), *A Glimpse of XIX Century Sociology* (1901), and *Economic Materialism* (1908). Kelles-Krauz defined the sociological theory of Marxism as monoeconomism, according to which the whole of social life is determined by the mode of production. However, the central point of his sociological conception was the law of revolutionary retrospection. It referred exclusively to the sphere of social consciousness and was supposed to explain the origins of the revolutionary ideal in a way parallel to monoeconomics: The ideals by which the whole reformatory movement wishes to substitute the existing social norms are always similar to norms from the more or less distant past.

Stefan Czarnowski (1879–1937), in his *Leading Ideas of Humanity* (1928), *Culture* (1938), and *Works*, (2 vols., 1956), continued Durkheim's ideas. *Culture* is Czarnowski's top achievement, in which he claims that culture is the whole of objective elements of social heritage, common for several groups and because of its generality able to expand in space. Czarnowski overcame the dualism of Durkheim's conception, granting both society and culture the character of reality *sui generis*. Characteristic of all these conceptions was the overt impact of the actual sociopolitical conditions on the content of social theory.

The soliology of Florian Znaniecki (1882–1958) and the social (or cultural) anthropology of Bronislaw Malinowski (1884–1942) were different from the above-mentioned bodies of work in at least two respects. First, the works of both Znaniecki and Malinowski gained worldwide recognition; second, both consisted of general conceptions not restricted in scope by particular conditions of time, place, and culture. Znaniecki was coauthor (with W. I. Thomas) of *The Polish Peasant in Europe and America* (1918–1920) and author of numerous books, such as *Cultural Reality* (1919), *Introduction to Sociology* (1922), *The Laws of Social Psychology* (1925), *Sociology of Education* (2 vols., 1928–1930), *The Method of Sociology* (1934), *Social Actions* (1936), *The Social Role of the Man of Knowledge* (1940), *Cultural Sciences* (1952), and the posthumous volume *Social Relations and Social Roles*. He is well known as the author of the concept of "humanistic coefficient," and of a theoretical system unfolding the postulate of universal cultural order and axionormatively ordered social actions. Bronislaw Malinowski, author of *Argonauts of Western Pacific* (1922), *The Sexual Life of Savages in North-Western Melanesia* (1929), *Coral Gardens and Their Magic* (1935), *A Scientific Theory of Culture and Other Essays* (1944), and *Freedom and Civilization* (1947), among other works, found world esteem as one of the most influential scholars in establishing the functional approach in cultural anthropology.

BETWEEN POST-WAR YEARS AND THE COLLAPSE OF COMMUNISM, 1949–1989

The history of Polish sociology in this period has yet to be written. Among the best attempts to characterize Polish sociology under communism are Wladyslaw Kwasniewicz's articles: "Dialectics of Systemic Constraint and Academic Freedom: Polish Sociology under Socialist Regime," and "Between Universal and Native: The Case of Polish Sociology" (Kwasniewicz 1993, 1994). It was a time when sociology underwent severe criticism (including condemnation in the period 1949–1956), a time of a great shift toward Marxist orientation, but also a time of continuation of traditional lines of theorizing and of implementing in Polish sociology several novelties emerging in Western sociology (especially after 1956, when Polish sociology was brought back to life). The revival and development of Polish sociology was possible at that time thanks to the following outstanding intellectuals of the older generation: Jozef Chalasinski (1904–1979), who wrote *Young Generation of Peasants* (1938), *Society and Education* (1948), *Young Generation of the Villagers in People's Poland* (a series of volumes, 1964–69), and *Culture and Nation* (1968). He was a prominent student of Polish intelligentsia, peasantry, and youth. Stanislaw Ossowski (1897–1963), who wrote *On the Peculiarities of Social Sciences* (1962) and *Class Structure in the Social Consciousness* (1963, English ed.). The latter contained fresh, stimulating, and critical overviews of theories of both class and social stratification. Maria Ossowska (1896–1974), who wrote *Foundations of the Study of Morality* (1947) and *Social Determinants of Moral Ideas* (1970). Andrzej Malewski (1929–1963), whose work will be mentioned in the next section. Stefan Nowak (1925–1990), whose work will also be mentioned in the next section.

While Ossowski studied class structure and stratification theoretically, Jan Szczepanski initiated empirical research around the problems of the emergence of a socialist-grown working class and an intelligentsia. His book *Polish Society* (1970) summarizes about thirty monographs that emerged from this research project between 1956 and 1965.

The period from 1956 up to the 1970s was certainly the time of a strong group of Marxist sociologists, including among others Zygmunt Bauman, Julian Hochfeld, Wladyslaw Markiewicz, and Jerzy Wiatr.

MAJOR CONTEMPORARY CONTRIBUTIONS

The major group of Polish sociologists consequently avoided pure theorizing. However, a large number of works present novel interpretations of contemporary sociological theories. Functionalistic orientation was extensively studied by several sociologists, among them Piotr Sztompka (*System and Function: Toward a Theory of Society*, 1974), and by social anthropologists like Andrzej Paluch (*Conflict, Modernization and Social Change: An Analysis and Critique of the Functional Theory*, 1976). Another extensively studied orientation is interactionist theory by such theoreticians as Marek Czyzewski (*The Sociologist and Everyday Life: A Study in Ethnomethodology and Modern Sociology of Interacton*, 1984), Elzbieta Halas (*The Social Context of Meanings in the Theory of Symbolic Interactionism*, 1987), Zdzislaw Krasnodebski (*Understanding Human Behavior: On Philosophical Foundations of Humanistic and Social Sciences*, 1986), Ireneusz Krzeminski (*Symbolic Interactionism and Sociology*, 1986), and Marek Ziolkowski (*Meaning, Interaction, Understanding: A Study of Symbolic Interactionism and Phenomenological Sociology as a Current of Humanistic Sociology*, 1981).

There are also good examples of innovative works within the domain of conflict theory by Janusz Mucha (*Conflict and Society*, 1978), Marxist theory by Andrzej Flis (*Antinomies of the Great Vision*, 1990), social exchange theory by Marian Kempny (*Exchange and Society: An Image of Social Reality in Sociological and Anthropological Theories of Exchange*, 1988), and "sociological theory of an individual's identity" by Zbigniew Bokszanski (*Identity–Interaction–Group: Individual's Identity in Perspective of Sociological Theory*, 1989). Since social anthropology used to be treated in Poland as closely related to sociology, I should mention Piotr Chmielewski's work, *Culture and Evolution* (1988), in which he gives penetrating theoretic insight into evolutionistic theory from Darwin through his own contemporaries, and Zdzislaw Mach's book, *The Culture and Personality Approach in American*

Anthropology (1989), which presents a critical evaluation of this influential theoretical paradigm.

Original, creative efforts at the level of history of social thought, metatheory, and sociological theory have been quite substantial in the postwar period. In the domain of history of sociology an important achievement is the monumental, two-volume *History of Sociological Thought* by Jerzy Szacki (1979). The work is not just a simple presentation of theories of significant social thinkers from social philosophy of antiquity to contemporary sociological controversies of the 1970s. Critical analysis of each conception is accompanied by a penetrating account of its place in intellectual history, its relation to other orientations, and its role in the development of the social sciences. It can be said that this work presents the "true history of social thought." The work does not have its equivalent in world literature.

We should also mention another original, creative work in the domain of history of sociology. Edited by Piotr Sztompka, *Masters of Polish Sociology* (1984) presents a comprehensive account of Polish sociology from its beginnings up to martial law in 1981 and after—a period that has been described as initiating a search for a new perspective for Polish sociology.

The greatest achievements in the fields of metatheory and/or philosophy of social sciences include two books by Stefan Nowak and Edmund Mokrzycki. Nowak's book, *Understanding and Prediction: Essays in Methodology of Social and Behavioral Sciences* (1976), can be considered the vehicle by which Polish sociology entered metatheoretical debates of contemporary social sciences as a fully mature partner. Nowak discusses several issues crucial for sociological metatheory, such as the usefulness of the "humanistic coefficient," laws of science versus historical generalizations, inductionism versus deductionism, the time dimension, causal explanations, reduction of one theory to another, and axiomatized theories. The solutions he proposes are novel and enlightening. The same can be said about Edmund Mokrzycki's book, *Philosophy and Sociology: From the Methodological Doctrine to Research Practice* (1983). Mokrzycki argues that since early positivism began circulating in the 1950s as the methodological foundation of sociology, the result has been that empirical sociology has lost the character of a humanistic discipline without acquiring the status of a true scientific discipline. As a way out, Mokrzycki proposes to put sociology within the framework of a broadly understood theory of culture.

In the field of sociological theory, the following achievements should be pointed out. First, we should mention the theoretical group dealing with class, social structure, and stratification. This group is headed by Wlodzimierz Wesolowski, whose *Classes, Strata, and Power* (Wesolowski 1979) serves as their leading theoretical achievement. The crux of the argument is that while, theoretically, relationship to the means of production determines attributes of social position (such as income, work, and prestige), the uniformity of that relationship created under socialism makes the means of production lose their determining properties. In this circumstance, status becomes disengaged from class and tends to "decompose" so that we encounter the phenomenon of "leapfrogging" by groups along certain dimensions. This statement was the point of departure for further studies on meritocratic justice, educational meritocracy, and stratification and structure in comparative perspective (Slomczynski et al. 1981; Slomczynski 1989; Kohn and Slomczynski 1990), social mobility (Wesolowski and Mach 1986), as well as for other studies.

A second group of works deals with problems in the field of sociology but bordering on microsociology and social philosophy. Pawel Rybicki's *The Structure of the Social World* (1979) introduces to sociological debates in Poland, for the first time in a very comprehensive way, problems of micro-macro link, the problematics of a small group, and ontological dilemmas especially related to individualism versus holism controversy. On the other hand, Andrzej Malewski's work (1975), aimed primarily at modification and experimental testing of the social-psychological theories of L. Festinger, M. Rokeach, and N. E. Miller, also undertakes fundamental methodological and theoretical problems of the integration of social sciences, which Malewski tries to solve through the procedure of theoretical reduction. Jacek Szmatka's work *Small Social Structures: An Introduction to Structural Microsociology* (1989), tries to reach virtually all the same goals that his predecessors, mentioned above, tried to reach. The final result of these endeavors is his structural microsociology, based on assumptions of emergent sociological structuralism, the structural conception of the small group, and specific conception of short- and long-range social structures.

Still another type of theorizing is present in the next two important theoretical works, Sztompka's *Theory of Social Becoming* (1990) and Jadwiga Staniszkis's *The Ontology of Socialism* (1989). The two works are very different in terms of style of theorizing and level of abstraction, but they have one goal in common: to produce theoretical conceptions that would account for tensions, problems, and processes of Polish society. Sztompka, who develops his conception around such categories as human agency and social movements, is highly abstract and stays within the Marxian tradition. Staniszkis engages in her analysis categories such as power, politics, legitimization, and ideology. She is less abstract and refers frequently to concrete societies. However, she too stays within the Marxian tradition.

Sociology of Culture, by Antonina Kloskowska (1983), continues vital traditions of this field in Polish sociology and also provides several theoretical innovations. The term *sociology of culture* is understood here to refer to a branch of sociological theory that is culture oriented and that operates with various types of cultural data. Basic subject matter for this theory is symbolic culture, while basic factors are conditions and functions of symbolic culture in the domain of societal culture. Kloskowska develops, among other theories, communication theory of symbolic culture and theory of symbolic culture development; one of her statements is that symbolic culture can perform its functions only when it preserves its original character, and its values remain intrinsic and autotelic, and are sought for their own sake.

The most vital and extensively cultivated, however, is empirical sociology of Polish society. Its standards of research procedures do not differ from western European ones. Polish sociology owes many important methodological and technical improvements to two prominent and in some sense classical methodologists: Stefan Nowak and Jan Lutyñski. The empirical branch of Polish sociology is very diversified and multifaceted. Especially extensive are studies on several aspects of

social consciousness of Polish society (continuing Ossowski's 1963 work); its changes in time perspective (Koralewicz 1987), value system, attitudes, aspirations (Nowak 1980, 1982, 1989), class consciousness, and political participation (Ziolkowski 1988); and collective subconsciousness and the concept of collective sense (Marody 1987, 1988). Another important and vital field of research are studies on political and legal system of Polish society (Staniszkis 1987), legitimation of the social order (Rychard 1987), repressive tolerance of the political system (Gorlach 1989), local power elite (Wasilewski 1989), and deviance and social control (Kwasniewski 1987). The third domain of research consists of different aspects of social and economic organization of the Polish society, namely self-management and current economical crisis (Morawski 1987), determinants of economical interests (Kolarska-Bobinska 1988), and conditions of social dimorphism (Wnuk-Lipinski 1987). There are also interesting studies on the life values of youth in Poland (Sulek 1985), the role of the army in the Polish political and social scene (Wiatr 1988), and the birth and the role of the Solidarity movement (Staniszkis 1984). We should also mention the Polish attempt to develop the framework of sociotechnics by Adam Podgorecki (1966), which convinced many academics to switch to the study of practical applications of sociology.

CURRENT TRENDS AND PERSPECTIVES IN POLISH SOCIOLOGY

The events of 1989, which marked the beginning of an economical, political, and social transformation in Poland, gave Polish sociologists rich empirical material to study. The great interest in research on Polish transition provoked even the suppositions of overpolitization of Polish sociology. Nevertheless, new perspectives appeared in the field of social structure, stratification, and mobility (Wnuk-Lipinski 1989, 1996; Domanski 1994). Attempts to construct a model of the middle class in postcommunist societies have been made by H. Domanski and J. Kurczewski. There is a special focus on the consolidation of young central and eastern European democracies and political and party systems in studies by Ewa Nalewajko (1997). Another well-developed field is the study of power and business elites, their roots and integration by Jacek Wasilewski (Wasilewski 1997, 1998) and

Wlodzimierz Wesolowski (1995, 1996). The mainstream of current Polish sociology is focused on society in transition, but this does not mean that there are no pure theoretical studies being in process. The basic science type endeavor is being pursued in the tradition of structural social psychology (i.e., group processes). The theoretical research program in network exchange theory developed by Szmatka, Mazur, and Sozanski is one of the most methodologically advanced in sociology, and their new studies on network conflict theory gained some recognition in world sociology (Szmatka et al. 1997, 1998; Szmatka and Mazur 1998).

REFERENCES

Domanski, Henryk 1994 "The Recomposition of Social Stratification in Poland." *Polish Sociological Review* 4:335–358.

Genov, Nikolai (ed.) 1989 *National Traditions in Sociology*. London: Sage.

Gorlach, Krzysztof 1989 "On Repressive Tolerance: State and Peasant Farm in Poland." *Sociologia Ruralis* 28:23–33.

Keen, Mike Forrest, and Janusz Mucha (eds.) 1994 *Eastern Europe in Transformation. The Impact on Sociology*. Westport, Conn.: Greenwood.

Kloskowska, Antonina 1983 *Sociology of Culture*. Warszawa: Polish Scientific Publishers. (In Polish).

Kohn, Melvin L., and Kazimierz M. Slomczynski 1990 *Social Structure and Self-Direction: A Comparative Analysis of the United States and Poland*. Cambridge, Mass.: Basil Blackwell.

Kolaja, Juri, and Man Singh Das (eds.) 1988 *Sociology in Eastern Europe*. India: Books and Periodicals.

Kolarska-Bobinska, Lena 1988 "Social Interests, Egalitarian Attitudes, and the Change of Economic Order." *Social Research* 55:111–138.

Kolosi, Tamas, and Ivan Szelenyi 1993 "Social Change and Research on Social Structure in Hungary." In Birgitta Nedelmann and Piotr Sztompka, eds., *Sociology in Europe: In Search of Identity*. New York: Walter de Gruyter.

Konrad, Gyorgy, and Ivan Szelenyi 1979 *The Intellectuals on the Road to Class Power*. New York: Harcourt Brace Jovanovich.

Koralewicz, Jadwiga 1987 "Changes in Polish Social Consciousness during the 1970s and 1980s: Opportunism and Identity." In J. Koralewicz, I. Bialecki,
and M. Watson, eds., *Crisis and Transition: Polish Society in the 1980s*. Oxford: Berg.

Kwasniewicz, Wladyslaw 1993 "Between Universal and Native: The Case of Polish Sociology." In Brigitta Nedelmann and Piotr Sztompka, eds., *Sociology in Europe: In Search of Identity*. New York: Walter de Gruyter.

—— 1994 "Dialectics of Systemic Constraint and Academic Freedom: Polish Sociology under Socialist Regime." In Mike Forrest Keen and Jonusz Mucha, eds., *Eastern Europe In Transformation: The Impact on Sociology*. Westport, Conn.: Greenwood.

Kwasniewski, Jerzy 1987 *Society and Deviance in Communist Poland: Attitudes to Social Control*. Oxford, England: Berg.

Malewski, Andrzej 1975 *For a New Shape of the Social Sciences: Collected Papers*. Warszawa: Polish Scientific Publishers. (In Polish).

Marody, Miroslawa 1987 "Social Stability and the Concept of Collective Sense." In J. Koralewicz, I. Bialecki, and M. Watson, eds., *Crisis and Transition: Polish Society in the 1980s*. Oxford, England: Berg.

—— 1988 "Antinomies of Collective Subconsciousness." *Social Research* 55:97–110.

Mokrzycki, Edmund 1983 *Philosophy and Sociology: From the Methodological Doctrine to Research Practice*. London: Routledge and Kegan Paul.

Morawski, Witold 1987 "Self-Management and Economic Reform." In J. Koralewicz, I. Bialecki, and M. Watson, eds., *Crisis and Transition: Polish Society in the 1980s*. Oxford, England: Berg.

Nalewajko, Ewa 1997 *Proto-Parties and Proto-System? An Outline of Emerging Polish Multipartism*. Warszawa: Instytut Studiow Politycznych PAN (In Polish).

Nedelmann, Birgitta, and Piotr Sztompka (eds.) 1993 *Sociology in Europe: In Search of Identity*. New York: Walter de Gruyter.

Nowak, Stefan 1976 *Understanding and Prediction: Essays in Methodology of Social and Behavioral Sciences*. Dordrecht: Reidel.

—— 1980 "Value System of the Polish Society." *Polish Sociological Bulletin* 2:5–20.

—— 1982 "Value System and Social Change in Contemporary Poland." *Polish Sociological Bulletin* 1–4:119–132.

—— 1989 "The Attitudes, Values and Aspirations of Polish Society." *Sisyphus: Sociological Studies* 5:133–163.

Podgorecki, Adam 1966 *Principles of Sociotechnics*. Warszawa: Wieolza Powszechna. (In Polish).

Rybicki, Pawel 1979 *The Structure of the Social World.* Warszawa: Polish Scientific Publishers.

Rychard, Andrzej 1987 "The Legitimation and Stability of the Social Order in Poland." In J. Koralewicz, I. Bialecki, and M. Watson, eds., *Crisis and Transition: Polish Society in the 1980s.* Oxford, England: Berg.

Slomczynski, Kazimierz M. 1989 *Social Structure and Mobility: Poland, Japan, and the United States.* Warszawa: Polish Academy of Sciences, Institute of Philosophy and Sociology.

——, Joanne Miller, and Melvin L. Kohn 1981 "Stratification, Work, and Values: A Polish-United States Comparison." *American Sociological Review* 46:720–744.

Sorokin, Pitirim A. 1959 *Social and Cultural Mobility.* Glencoe, Ill.: Free Press.

—— 1962 *Social and Cultural Dynamics*, 4 vols. Englewood Cliffs, N.J.: Bedminister Press.

Staniszkis, Jadwiga 1984 *Poland: Self-Limiting Revolution.* Princeton, N.J.: Princeton University Press.

—— 1987 "The Political Articulation of Property Rights: Some Reflections on the University "Inert Structure." In J. Koralewicz, I. Bialecki, and M. Watson, eds., *Crisis and Transition: Polish Society in the 1980s.* Oxford, England: Berg.

—— 1989 *The Ontology of Socialism.* Warszawa: In Plus. (In Polish).

Sulek, Antoni 1985 "Life Values of Two Generations: From a Study of the Generational Gap in Poland." *Polish Sociological Bulletin* 1–4:31–42.

Szacki, Jerzy 1979 *History of Sociological Thought.* Westport, Conn.: Greenwood.

Szczepanski, Jan 1970 *Polish Society.* New York: Random House.

Szmatka, Jacek 1989 *Small Social Structures: An Introduction to Structural Microsociology.* Warszawa: Polish Scientific Publishers. (In Polish).

——, and Joanna Mazur 1998 "Power Distribution in Conflict Networks: An Extension of Elementary Theory to Conflict Networks." In John Skvoretz and Jacek Szmatka, eds., *Advances in Group Processes*, vol. 15. Greenwich, Conn.: JAI.

Szmatka, Jacek, John Skvoretz, and Joseph Berger (eds.) 1997 *Status, Network, and Structure: Theory Development in Group Processes.* Stanford, Calif.: Stanford University Press.

Szmatka, Jacek, John Skvoretz, Tadeusz Sozanski, and Joanna Mazur 1998 "Conflict in Networks." *Sociological Perspectives* 41:49–66.

Sztompka, Piots 1990 *Theory of Social Becoming.* Cambridge, England: Polity.

—— (ed.) 1984 *Masters of Polish Sociology.* Krakow: Ossolimeum. (In Polish).

Wasilewski, Jacek 1989 "Social Processes of Power Elite Recruitment." *Sisyphus: Sociological Studies.* 5:205–224.

—— 1997 "Elite Research in Poland: 1989–1995." In Heinrich Best and Ulrike Becker, eds., *Elites in Transition: Elite Research in Central and Eastern Europe.* Opladen, Germany: Leske and Budrich.

—— 1998 "Elite Circulation and Consolidation of Democracy in Poland." In John Higley, Jan Pakulski, and Wlodzimierz Wesolowski, eds., *Postcommunist Elites and Democracy in Eastern Europe.* London: Macmillan.

Wesolowski, Wlodzimierz 1979 *Classes, Strata, and Power.* London: Routledge and Kegan Paul.

—— 1995 "Formation of Political Parties in Post-Communist Poland." *Sisyphus. Social Studies* 11(1):9–32.

—— 1996 "New Beginnings of the Entrepreneurial Classes. The Case of Poland." *The Polish Sociological Review* 1(113):79–96.

——, and Bogdan W. Mach 1986 "Unfulfilled Systemic Functions of Social Mobility I: A Theoretical Scheme." *International Sociology* 1:19–35.

Wiatr, Jerzy 1988 *The Soldier and the Nation.* Washington: Westview.

Wnuk-Lipinski, Edmund 1987 "Social Dimorphism and Its Implications." In J. Koralewicz, I. Bialecki, and M. Watson, eds., *Crisis and Transition: Polish Society in the 1980s.* Oxford, England: Berg.

—— 1989 "Inequality and Social Crisis." In Wladyslaw Adamski and Edmund Wnuk-Lipinski, eds., *Poland in the 1980s: Reassessment of Crises and Conflicts.* Warszawa: PWN.

—— 1996 *Democratic Reconstruction: From Sociology of Radical Social Change.* Warszawa: PWN. (In Polish).

Ziolkowski, Marek 1988 "Individuals and the Social System: Values, Perceptions, and Behavioral Strategies." *Social Research* 55:139–177.

KINGA WYSIENSKA
JACEK SZMATKA

POLITICAL AND GOVERNMENTAL CORRUPTION

Everyone knows what political corruption is, but it is notoriously hard to define. Different cultures have different conceptions of corruption: what would be considered corrupt in Denmark might be seen as simply polite in Indonesia. This understanding also varies across time: buying office was standard procedure in eighteenth-century Britain but would be inexcusable today. Arnold Heidenheimer has divided corruption into three categories (Heidenheimer et al. 1978). *"White" corruption* includes acts that a majority of people would not consider worthy of punishment. *"Gray" corruption* includes acts that "some elements" would want to see punished, but others would not. *"Black" corruption* includes acts that a "majority consensus . . . would condemn and would want to see punished on the grounds of principle." Heidenheimer suggests that as societies modernize, behavior that was once seen as "white" becomes "gray," and may eventually turn "black." Others have suggested that the concept of "corruption" develops as societies move from seeing governmental offices as private property to believing them to be public trusts.

The American political scientist V. O. Key Jr. (1936) defines *graft* as "an abuse of power for personal or party profit." Joseph Nye, another American political scientist, calls corruption:

> *[B]ehavior which deviates from the formal duties of a public role because of private-regarding (family, close family, private clique) pecuniary or status gains; or violates rules against the exercise of certain types of private-regarding influence. This includes such behavior as bribery (use of a reward to pervert the judgment of a person in a position of trust); nepotism (bestowal of patronage by reason of ascriptive relationship rather than merit); and misappropriation (illegal appropriation of public resources for private-regarding uses)* (Nye 1967).

One long-running controversy in political science is whether corruption can serve a useful purpose for society. The most traditional school of thought, the "moralist" school, insists that corruption is always a breach of the public trust and must never be tolerated. Foremost in the ranks of this school were the "muckrakers," American journalists who wrote books, during the early twentieth century, denouncing big business and public corruption. But in a review of a muckraking classic,

Lincoln Steffens's *The Shame of the Cities*, the American political scientist Henry Jones Ford (1904, p. 678) argued that corruption was better than "slackness and decay." If businessmen had to corrupt politicians in order to get things done, that was an acceptable cost of progress. Ford's heirs, the so-called revisionists, became important in social science during the 1960s. Such revisionists as Nye and Samuel Huntington argued that corruption could serve useful social purposes. Corruption could bridge gaps between otherwise antagonistic groups. It could ease the path to modernization by overcoming bureaucratic inertia. It could foster social integration by binding people closer to the state.

More recently, scholars have returned to emphasizing the ill effects of corruption. It can increase the costs of administration, bloating national budgets. Rather than cutting bureaucracy, corruption tends to expand it, as officials seek more opportunities to shake down citizens. If businessmen must bribe in order to function in a particular country, they may take their investments elsewhere. Corruption can weaken the private sector into dependence and degrade the public sector into banditry. The economic collapse of Indonesia, a country previously seen as an example of the coexistence of corruption and prosperity, has fueled this school of thought. Recent research by Paolo Mauro (1997), an economist at the International Monetary Fund, has shown that highly corrupt countries tend to invest less of their gross domestic product, spend less on education, and have lower economic growth rates than their cleaner counterparts.

CORRUPTION IN THE UNITED STATES

The United States is less corrupt than almost all Third World countries. Its capitalist economy and democratic government offer fewer opportunities for massive political graft than the socialist kleptocracies of Africa. American government's dispersal of power prevents the sort of presidential corruption that has characterized Latin America. The American press, its freedom constitutionally guaranteed, is quick to jump on accusations of malfeasance, often blowing them out of proportion. The American legal system has inherited the English tradition of protecting private property and respecting individual rights.

But for most of its history, the United States has had a reputation of being more corrupt than most western European countries. British observers such as Lord Bryce expressed this sentiment most often, contrasting the probity of the Victorian era to the iniquity of the Gilded Age. The exuberant democracy of the nineteenth century spawned extensive patronage, widespread vote fraud, and a venal political class. Indeed, Bryce and Alexis de Tocqueville noted that the most able Americans went into business rather than government; when they needed political favors, they bought them from those lesser talents who had won office. Civil servants continue to have a lower status in the United States than in Europe. In addition, the American system is much more permeable than its European counterparts. Its numerous state and local governments encourage popular participation. They also give citizens more chances to corrupt bureaucrats.

As a general rule, corruption in the United States has been greater at the state and local levels than in the federal government. While no president has ever been imprisoned, many mayors and governors have. Fixated on Washington, the media often ignores what happens in city halls or, especially, state capitols. This gives boodlers more confidence that their misdeeds will go unpunished. Since city governments conduct most law enforcement, more scandals take place in local police departments than in the Federal Bureau of Investigation (FBI). Since state and local governments conduct most construction, contractors develop more shady relationships with governors or mayors than with presidents. Many defense firms, however, have cozy ties with Congress members and Pentagon officials.

While there was corruption in colonial America (even George Washington used liquor to buy votes during his candidacy for the Virginia legislature), municipal graft did not truly take off until the nineteenth century. Powered by the Industrial Revolution, and fed by waves of immigration, American cities boomed during this period. While governmental institutions were weak, a new form of organization filled this gap: the political machine. Michael Johnston defines a political machine as a "party organization within which power is highly centralized, and whose members are motivated and rewarded by divisible material incentives rather than by considerations of ideology or long-term goals of public policy" (1982, p. 38). While they would sometimes advocate social reform if they believed it would win votes, machine politicians were primarily interested in the spoils of office: jobs and favors for their supporters and graft for themselves. Machines developed close ties to business interests seeking contracts or other concessions: construction contractors, real estate developers, insurance agencies, law firms, organized crime. Ward leaders mobilized machine supporters, often the immigrant poor, through small favors such as Christmas baskets; the fixing of minor crimes; or, for the most loyal, undemanding government jobs.

While the stereotypical machine was Democratic, there were many Republican machines until the New Deal made urban workers loyal Democrats. City machines were the most common, but there were rural machines (most notably in southern Texas), suburban machines, and even statewide machines. While one normally associates machine politics with the inner-city poor, one of the strongest remaining machines in the country is the Republican organization of Nassau County, New York—a New York City suburb that is one of the wealthiest counties in the United States. (It is probably best known as the political base of former U.S. Senator Alfonse D'Amato.)

Probably the most famous machine was Tammany Hall, which dominated Manhattan's Democratic organization from the early nineteenth century until the early 1960s. Descended from the Sons of Liberty of the Revolutionary era, it rose to supremacy after the Civil War under the leadership of William "Boss" Tweed and Richard Croker, and reached its zenith of power around World War I under the guidance of the unusually shrewd Charles F. Murphy. In the 1930s, Murphy's successors made a series of miscalculations that crippled Tammany. They alienated both President Franklin D. Roosevelt and Governor Herbert Lehman, and they supported John O'Brien, an inept hack, as the successor to the discredited Mayor James J. Walker. O'Brien lost the 1933 mayoral race to Fiorello LaGuardia, a nominal Republican, staunch New Dealer, and sworn Tammany foe. LaGuardia's three terms in office helped pound the nails into Tammany's coffin. Other Democratic organizations in New York City, particularly those in the Bronx and Brooklyn, became more important.

While Tammany enjoyed a brief comeback in the 1950s under Carmine DeSapio, its fate was sealed when DeSapio lost his race for Democratic district leader in 1961. Manhattan had become gentrified, and its new, wealthier residents had no interest in Tammany-style politics.

Many cities had machines. Until the New Deal, Chicago had rival Democratic and Republican organizations whose battles for power occasionally turned violent. After the New Deal, the Democratic organization dominated Chicago and some of its leaders, especially Mayor Richard J. Daley (1955–1976), became national figures. Philadelphia had a Republican machine of legendary rapaciousness that managed to hold onto City Hall until 1951. Once it became clear that the GOP would not return to power, many longtime Republican ward bosses switched parties and built a powerful Democratic machine. Kansas City had its Pendergast organization, which produced President Harry Truman. Jersey City's two machine mayors, Frank "I Am the Law" Hague and John V. Kenny, dominated its politics from 1917 to 1971. Machines were not confined to the North: Edward "Boss" Crump ruled Memphis for many years, while San Antonio became notorious for its vote buying and graft.

Political machines have declined throughout the twentieth century. Prompted by Lincoln Steffens's *The Shame of the Cities* (1904), Progressive reformers strengthened the civil service and reduced machine influence in city government, sometimes by making elections nonpartisan or by replacing elected mayors with the council-manager system. While Franklin D. Roosevelt rewarded those machine Democrats who backed him (most notably Chicago Mayor Edward Kelly and Edward Flynn, "the Boss of the Bronx"), some observers have argued that his New Deal eventually undermined machines by replacing their handouts with bureaucratic programs (although Richard J. Daley could show them how those could be turned to a machine's advantage).

The postwar years brought many changes to American cities that hurt machines. Television gave candidates a means to reach voters without the help of local bosses. Court decisions greatly restricted the amount of patronage leaders could bestow upon their followers. The rise of public sector unions further restricted bosses' ability to hand out jobs, and in some cities, unions replaced party bosses as the main support for politicians. Inquiries such as the 1951 Kefauver hearings exposed the links between many urban politicians and organized crime.

Political scientists and journalists have offered varying assessments of political machines. Some praise them for integrating immigrants into American politics. Many of the newcomers had little experience with democracy and little understanding of the Anglo-American tradition. Machine politicians gave them something concrete for their vote, whether that was a small gift, help with the law, or a job. Machines have also been praised for making government function; Richard J. Daley boasted that Chicago was "the city that works." Others have criticized machines for corrupting government, enriching political hacks, and providing poor public services.

While few machines still operate, American cities still see plenty of graft. Periodic scandals rock urban police departments, most recently in New Orleans and Washington. Frequently, there are revelations about the scandalous relations between construction firms and politicians. In the mid-1980s, a scandal concerning the Parking Violations Bureau ended the careers of many New York City politicians. Marion Barry, the four-term mayor of Washington, made himself a synonym for graft and misgovernment.

There have also been many scandals concerning state government. During the late nineteenth century, businessmen, especially railroad magnates, bribed state legislators en masse. From Arizona to South Carolina, recent sting operations have found state legislators pathetically eager to accept payoffs. The cozy relationships between state officials and the construction industry have had national implications. In 1973, Vice President Spiro Agnew resigned as part of a plea bargain stemming from bribes he accepted as governor of Maryland.

There are large regional differences in attitudes toward corruption. What is considered scandalous in Minnesota may be seen as merely inappropriate in New York and harmless in Louisiana. Daniel Elazar argues for a theory of political culture that explains these differences. Puritan New England developed a "moralistic" conception of governance that emphasized the common good. When New Englanders settled the states of the northern tier, from Michigan to the Pacific Northwest, they brought this culture with them. These states continue to be intolerant of corruption. The Middle Colonies attracted a diverse ethnic mix that made it difficult to agree on a common good. Instead, they developed an "individualistic" political culture that saw politics as a business and tolerated politicians' pursuit of self-interest. States in a belt running west from New York and New Jersey to Illinois and Missouri continue to accept petty graft as part of the normal way of conducting politics. The South developed politics dominated by elite factions and low public participation. Elazar calls this culture "traditionalistic." Particular states have developed their own cultures tolerant of or antagonistic to corruption. The Scandinavians who settled the upper Midwest brought their squeaky-clean politics with them. Louisiana's French heritage bestowed upon it the Napoleonic Code, with its emphasis on state power and a certain lassitude about graft.

CORRUPTION AT THE FEDERAL LEVEL

While there were scandals during the Republic's early years, corruption did not become a major problem until the Jacksonian era of the 1820s and 1830s. Mass political parties brought with them the "spoils system" through which the president bestowed government jobs upon his supporters. The "spoils system" came to dominate government to the extent that some presidents spent most of their time fulfilling the demands of state party leaders for rewards for their followers. After a disappointed office seeker assassinated President James Garfield in 1881, demands for reform led Congress to pass the Pendleton Act two years later, which created the modern civil service; but it was not until the early twentieth century that merit came to predominate in government employment.

The Industrial Revolution increased business influence in government. The Civil War saw a series of military procurement scandals, beginning a long tradition in American life. During the years after the war, there were several scandals concerning the relationships between politicians and railroads (many of which received government subsidies). In addition, during this period,

many prominent officials were found to have taken bribes, most notably William Belknap, Ulysses Grant's secretary of war.

While the Progressive era saw a general reform of American politics, the United States experienced several scandals during the 1920s. The sale and production of alcoholic beverages was forbidden during the Prohibition era (1920–1933), but the public's continuing thirst spawned a vast underground liquor trade that fueled the rise of organized crime and corrupted many public officials. The administration of President Warren Harding (1921–1923) is usually considered the most corrupt in American history. Charles Forbes, head of the Veterans' Bureau, was convicted of fraud, conspiracy, and bribery. In the "Teapot Dome" scandal, Interior Secretary Albert Fall secretly leased federal oil reserves to two businessmen in return for cash gifts and no-interest loans; Fall was eventually imprisoned for bribery.

The succeeding decades saw few high-level scandals. There were many congressional peccadilloes, but the worst that could be discovered about any high officials was influence peddling by some of Harry Truman's cronies and acceptance of small gifts by Dwight Eisenhower's chief of staff. The Watergate scandal (1972–1974) made up for lost time, bringing down President Richard Nixon and sending many of his closest allies to jail. While it is beyond the scope of this article to explain the details of this affair—there are entire books that do that—we should note that little about Watergate concerned financial corruption, primarily Nixon's tax evasion and massive illegal contributions to his 1972 reelection campaign. Watergate was mostly a matter of abuse of power, especially Nixon's use of the government to harass his political enemies and his cover-up thereof.

Watergate led to a flood of legislation. The 1971 Federal Election Campaign Act was extensively amended in 1974. The Ethics in Government Act of 1978 created the institution of the independent counsel to investigate official malfeasance. The Foreign Corrupt Practices Act of 1977 forbade American companies to bribe overseas officials. Prosecutors and journalists became more aggressive in their investigations of corruption. Two major scandals rocked Congress: the revelation of corrupt links between a South Korean lobbyist and several congressmen ("Koreagate") and the willingness of some senators and representatives to take bribes in a sting investigation ("Abscam").

The 1980s saw their share of scandals. The Iran-Contra affair, which involved the covert sale of arms to Iran and the illegal diversion of the profits to Nicaraguan anti-communist rebels (the "contras"), tarnished the last years of the Reagan Administration. A long investigation found favoritism and influence peddling to be rife within the Department of Housing and Urban Development (HUD). The collapse of many savings and loans (S&Ls), which cost the government $500 billion to pay back depositors, revealed suspicious relationships between some thrift operators and prominent politicians, most notably House Speaker Jim Wright. The so-called Keating Five senators lobbied for easier treatment for S&L owner Charles Keating; revelations about their activities ended the careers of three of the five.

While Bill Clinton promised to run the "most ethical administration in history," he has instead presided over an era as sleazy as those of his predecessors. Scandals forced out HUD Secretary Henry Cisneros and Agriculture Secretary Mike Espy. There were charges that foreigners made large illegal donations to the Democratic National Committee during the 1996 election. The most explosive charges surrounded Clinton himself. Allegations of corrupt real estate deals by Clinton when he was governor of Arkansas led to an independent counsel investigation that began in 1993 and continues as of this writing. This investigation eventually produced the charge that Clinton had perjured himself and had obstructed an inquiry into his affair with a White House intern. Clinton was questioned about this affair as part of a sexual harassment lawsuit. Clinton was eventually impeached, but the Senate failed to convict him.

CORRUPTION IN WESTERN EUROPE

Italy is probably considered the most corrupt country in western Europe. Southern Italy has a long history of patron-client relationships that take precedence over written law. In this highly stratified society, landowners and professionals serve as natural patrons to their clientele of laborers and peasants. The Mafia, of course, is part of this system of patronage. Italy's complex administrative law undermines efficiency, and so requires mediation in order to function. Politicians and local notables help citizens, especially businessmen, navigate the maze of red tape—for a price.

After World War II, Italy developed a strong party system that permeated all of society. While Italy had many small parties, three dominated politics until 1993: the Christian Democrats, the Socialists, and the Communists. In order to keep the Communists out of power, the Christian Democrats dominated every government from 1947 to 1993; after 1962, they usually governed with the support of the Socialists. Both the Christian Democrats and the Socialists were deeply factionalized, with politicians commanding their own followings. As such, the parties could only be held together through bargaining—which often included graft. The Christian Democrats, in particular, were dependent upon the support of local leaders in the South and in Sicily (which were both far behind the rest of country economically), many of them with ties to the Mafia. Southern politicians used the national government's resources to support their local economies. Often this meant public works boondoggles, which enriched politically connected (and Mafia-owned) construction firms and which only increased the contempt held by northern Italians for their southern countrymen.

Because many Italians feared that a communist government would bring their country into the Soviet bloc, the Christian Democrats were essentially a perpetual governing party. Proportional representation meant that no party would ever gain a majority, so coalition governed Italy. While squabbling among factions meant that particular governments usually lasted a year or less, the same parties always came out on top. The Christian Democrats and the Socialists used their power to create a vast web of patronage, which enmeshed Italy's many state-owned firms, the national broadcasting system, executive agencies, and public banks. The lack of turnover loosened what few inhibitions Italian politicians had about exploiting their positions for financial gain. While the Communists remained out of power, they cut backroom deals with the ruling parties to enrich themselves, especially after the 1970s, when they distanced themselves from the Soviet Union and when regional autonomy gave Communists more chances to govern.

These arrangements collapsed in 1992–1993. There were a number of reasons for this change. Under the pressure of global competition, Italian business owners grew weary of the high taxes and inefficient government produced by widespread corruption. The drive for European monetary union required Italy to reduce its huge budget deficit. The end of the Cold War made communist control less unthinkable (especially when the party renounced communism and renamed itself the Democratic Party of the Left).

It was a team of prosecutors investigating corruption in Milan's construction industry who really rocked Italy's political world. Led by Antonio Di Pietro (who now sits in Italy's Senate and may be the next president), the so-called clean hands brigade demolished the Italian establishment during 1992–1994. Prosecutors exposed massive patronage, political awarding of contracts, and bribery. It became clear that organized crime had friends at the highest levels. Former Prime Minister Bettino Craxi, a Socialist, was convicted of corruption after he fled to Tunisia. Giulio Andreotti, a Christian Democrat who had served as prime minister seven times, is, as of this writing, on trial for being a member of the Mafia.

The corruption investigations touched even those who benefited from them. After the Italian party system collapsed in 1993, the media tycoon Silvio Berlusconi led a conservative coalition to victory in the March 1994 elections. Berlusconi's government collapsed when prosecutors announced that they were investigating him. In 1998, Berlusconi was convicted of bribing tax inspectors (although he was later acquitted of other charges), but he remains leader of his Forza Italia party.

Spain also has a long history of corruption and patronage. Governments have long relied on local notables to administer the law. While Francisco Franco strengthened the state during his long rule (1939–1975), he made appointments more on the basis of loyalty than competence. The return of democracy brought greater professionalism, but local patrons remain important. It was corruption on a national scale that grabbed the headlines in the 1990s. A series of scandals embarrassed the socialist government of Prime Minister Felipe Gonzalez, who led Spain from 1982 to 1996. Many observers attributed the corruption to the socialists' arrogance after so many years in power. In 1991, Deputy Prime Minister Alfonso Guerra resigned after his brother Juan was accused of using party facilities for private gain. A series of scandals surrounded Socialist party finances. The heads of the Bank of Spain and the Civil Guard were besmirched by corruption. This wave of "sleaze" helped lead to the socialists' defeat in 1996.

France has had many scandals throughout its history. Some have even threatened the stability of the regime. Conservatives opposed to the Republic used the Panama Canal scandal (1892–1993) and the Stavisky affair (1934) to attack the legitimacy of democratic government. Others have simply been embarrassing, as when it was revealed that President Valéry Giscard d'Estaing had accepted diamonds from the infamous tyrant Jean-Bedel Bokassa, president of the Central African Republic and a longtime French client. Overall, the French tend to have a cynical view of government, accepting corruption and the abuse of power as the way the world works.

The "long presidency" of François Mitterand (1981–1995) included a series of scandals, many of them concerning the finances of Mitterand's Socialist Party. Rising campaign costs forced socialists, who lacked conservatives' constituency among business, to raise money in irregular ways. Contractors who sought business with socialist-governed municipalities were told to contribute to party-controlled consultancies, which funneled the money to the national party. The exposure of this practice embarrassed the socialists, but they could plausibly claim that other parties engaged in similar schemes. The businessman Roger-Patrice Pelat, who was indicted for insider trading before his death in 1989, had questionable relationships with many politicians, including his close friend Mitterand and Prime Minister Pierre Bérégovoy, who committed suicide in 1993 after it was revealed that Pelat had given him an interest-free loan.

Two other leading French politicians have come under fire in recent years. Alan Juppé, a conservative former prime minister, has been charged with obtaining fraudulent jobs for Gaullist party activists when he worked for then–Paris Mayor Jacques Chirac, who is now president. Roland Dumas, a former foreign minister and chief of the Constitutional Court, is under investigation for his ties to a defense contractor, which hired his mistress and paid her a $9 million commission.

Greece is another southern European country notorious for corruption and clientelistic politics. The governments of Andreas Papandreou (1981–1989, 1993–1996), longtime leader of the Pan-Hellenic Socialist Movement (PASOK), were widely perceived as crooked and patronage ridden, but Papandreou himself was acquitted of embezzlement charges in 1992. Tax evasion is common, and the economy remains dependent upon state patronage and contracts.

Many of the countries of northern Europe have become bywords for clean government. The governments of Scandinavia, the Netherlands, and Switzerland, in particular, are known for their honesty. A typical "scandal" in these countries would be a politician using party funds to pay for diapers for her baby. One major exception is Belgium, which is known as the "Italy of the North" for its corruption and cronyism. The government was shaken by a case of the pedophile murderer Marc Dutroux, who had conducted his activities in such a way that it appeared he had official protection. The 1991 murder of a Socialist Party boss remains unsolved, and many suspect the involvement of leading politicians and the Mafia. Willy Claes, former North Atlantic Treaty Organization (NATO) secretary general, was convicted in December 1998 of accepting a bribe from a defense contractor when he was economic affairs minister. Two other prominent Belgian politicians were also convicted.

Corruption was widespread in British politics during the eighteenth and early nineteenth centuries, but the Northcote-Trevelyan reforms of 1854 established the modern British civil service, which is world renowned for its honesty. Indeed, many former British colonies, such as Singapore, have benefited from their reputation for sound administration. The conservative governments of Margaret Thatcher (1979–1990) and John Major (1990–1997) saw their share of scandals, notably some involving large donations to the Conservative Party by questionable characters. (The United Kingdom does not limit donations to parties, nor does it require them to be disclosed.) Years of one-party rule led to a certain degree of arrogance and self-satisfaction, but little real corruption. While many observers attributed Major's defeat in 1997 to "sleaze," it appears that is just another way of saying, "The Tories had been in power for too long and it was time to give someone else a chance."

Germany is also known as a relatively corruption-free country, although, contrary to popular belief, the Nazi regime was filled with petty graft and party patronage. In the 1980s, it was revealed that the Flick industrial group had made illegal donations to the major political parties, while this embarrassed the government of Chancellor Helmut Kohl (1982–1998), it never threatened its stability. More recently, there have been scandals about bribery in the construction industry and about the involvement of big-city police with the drug trade and prostitution. Probably the most serious threat is the large network of ex-communists in the former East Germany, which has become known for favoritism and intimidation.

The most conspicuous European scandal of the late 1990s has concerned the European Commission, the governing body of the European Union. An internal audit, leaked to members of the European Parliament, revealed waste, corruption, and cronyism in many Euro-programs. It revealed that Edith Cresson, commissioner for research policy and a former French prime minister, had appointed her dentist to coordinate acquired immune deficiency syndrome (AIDS) research and had presided over a fraud-ridden job training program. In order to stem a parliamentary drive to censure or remove the commissioners, commission president Jacques Santer appointed the Committee of Independent Experts to investigate the audit's charges. The panel produced a report that essentially found the allegations to be true. Faced with a parliamentary revolt, and with Cresson unwilling to quit alone, all twenty European Commissioners resigned in March 1999.

CORRUPTION IN EAST ASIA

During the last quarter of the twentieth century, East Asia has had the fastest-growing economy in the world, but the economic crisis of 1997–1998 exposed the vast corruption of some countries. Indonesia was the most conspicuous case. During his 1966–1998 reign, Suharto amassed a fortune that may reach into the tens of billions of dollars. His children enriched themselves by acting as middlemen between state-owned firms and contractors; serving as the Indonesian partners of many foreign investors; and acquiring interests in aviation, broadcasting, automobiles and many other industries. Businessmen close to Suharto, such as industrialist Liem Sioe Liong and timber magnate Mohammed "Bob" Hasan, came to dominate the economy. As long as Indonesia kept growing, most citizens and businessmen accepted Suharto's banditry. Indonesia's economic and political collapse in 1998 led to demonstrations against his rule and to bloody riots in Jakarta, the capital. Suharto quit in May 1998; B. J. Habibie, his successor, found his associates implicated in a multimillion-dollar banking scandal. Abdurrahman Wahid, elected president in October 1999, announced that he would pardon Suharto should be ever be convicted of corruption.

The Philippines has a long history of corruption. A small group of families has long dominated Philippine politics, buying off their supporters through graft and patronage. Filipino culture emphasizes personal relationships, rather than formal institutions. As such, written law has little connection with the workings of the Philippine government. The Philippine civil service, police, and congress have particularly corrupt reputations. After independence in 1946, several Philippine presidents were known to be corrupt, especially Elpidio Quirino (1948–1953) and Carlos García (1957–1961). Ferdinand Marcos (1965–1986) put them all to shame, especially after he declared martial law in 1972. Philippine Airlines became a private commuter line for the Marcos family. Marcos bullied wealthy families into giving up their holdings to his family and friends. The Central Intelligence Agency (CIA) estimated that Marcos himself was worth $10 billion, but after Marcos fell from power, investigators were able to track down only a fraction of that sum. Despite her promises of a new era, the administration of Corazon Aquino (1986–1992) was also wracked with corruption. Fidel Ramos (1992–1996), however, built a reputation for honesty and presided over a period of prosperity.

Thailand is world renowned for its tolerance for drug trafficking and prostitution, and it is widely alleged that these businesses have allies in the government. The country also has a political culture dominated by patronage, bribery, vote buying, and crony capitalism. Prime Minister Banharn Silpa-Archa (1995–1996) was particularly identified with these practices, but the crisis of 1997–1998 disrupted many of Thailand's arrangements. The country has now adopted a more democratic constitution and has banned vote buying and insider deals.

South Korea has a political system that concentrates power in the presidency. It is not surprising that corruption has been concentrated there, too. Park Chung-hee seized power in 1961, vowing to end the sleaze of South Korea's early years. Park amassed enormous power over South Korea's economy and government. While most observers agree that he mostly used that power to his country's betterment, his dominance convinced many businessmen that they needed to donate to Park's party if they wanted to win his favor. After Park was assassinated in 1979, Chun Doo Hwan assumed the presidency. There were rumors of corruption surrounding Chun, which were confirmed in 1996 when he and his successor, Roh Tae Woo, were convicted of corruption and sedition. Chun was sentenced to life in prison; Roh received seventeen years. Kim Young Sam, who succeeded Roh in 1993, had a clean image that was soiled when his son Kim Hyun Chul was convicted in 1997 of receiving bribes. The collapse of one of the nation's leading conglomerates sparked charges that it had corrupt ties with Kim's government.

The Liberal Democratic Party (LDP) dominated Japanese politics from 1955 to 1993; it still leads most governing coalitions. On the international stage, it projected an image of serene competence. Behind the scenes, Japanese back rooms saw wheeling and dealing that would put any Chicago pol to shame. Kakuei Tanaka, prime minister from 1972 to 1974, ran a pork-barrel-fueled machine that dominated the LDP. Tanaka forced the government to extend the bullet train line into his mountainous home base, nearly bankrupting the national railroad in the process. In 1983, Tanaka was finally convicted of accepting bribes from the American aircraft manufacturer Lockheed, which had spread around $22 million among Japanese politicians in the 1970s. While the LDP's rule was broken in 1993, it regained control in 1994, and by 1996 an old Tanaka ally, Ryutaro Hashimoto, was serving as prime minister. In recent years, scandals have rocked the Ministry of Finance, which wields great power over the Japanese economy. Finance officials have been accused of covering up banks' financial troubles and of leaking sensitive information to bank executives.

CORRUPTION IN SOUTH ASIA

The nations of South Asia (India, Pakistan, Bangladesh, and Sri Lanka) are all former British colonies that benefited from the United Kingdom's common law tradition and bureaucratic honesty; but all have sunk into a morass of corruption. Pakistan is now considered one of the most corrupt countries in the world. Tax evasion is ubiquitous: only about half of assessed taxes are actually collected. Businessmen believe that they must pay government officials if they seek a public contract. Civil servants are poorly paid, and believe they must take bribes in order to survive. The two most recent prime ministers, Benazir Bhutto (1988–1990, 1993–1996) and Nawaz Sharif (1990–1995, 1997–present), have presided over administrations rife with corruption. In April 1999, Bhutto and her husband were convicted of taking kickbacks on government contracts. They were each sentenced to five years in prison.

A recent book on India and Pakistan calls corruption in India "pervasive, systematic, structured, and graded . . . running from the bottom to the top of the political order." The British gave India an honest civil service, but Indira Gandhi's state of emergency (1975–1977) destroyed its integrity and morale by forcing bureaucrats to break the law. Now India's estimated fifteen million civil servants shake down citizens for every service imaginable, from installing phone lines to permitting people to enter the country. Corrupt politicians hold power on a national scale. Jayalitha Jayaram, the notorious boss of Tamil Nadu state, brought down the government of Prime Minister Atal Bihari Vajpayee through her defection in April 1999. A 1996 corruption investigation discovered that Jayaram owned 10,000 saris and 350 pairs of shoes.

CORRUPTION IN THE MIDDLE EAST

The Middle East is a nation bereft of functioning democracies, save Israel and Turkey. The predominance of authoritarian regimes has created a situation ripe for corruption. The Saudi royal family has a reputation for corruption on a massive scale. It treats the national income as royal revenue and distributes it at whim. There are 7,000 royal princes, whom the *Economist* described as "lawless and hedonistic." Not content with their generous allowances, they collect huge commissions on foreign contracts and muscle in on private business. Public anger at royal corruption, particularly that of King Saud, fueled an Islamic fundamentalist movement for a time. Crown Prince Abdullah assumed management of the government in January 1996, and his honesty and ruthlessness have defused the threat from the opposition.

Egypt is world renowned for its bureaucratic corruption. Its one million civil servants are notoriously indolent and graft hungry. Bribes are necessary to engage in any government transaction. The government is unable to provide most public services, opening the door for Islamist groups to fill the void. Morocco, Tunisia, and Algeria are also known for their corruption. In Algeria, years of corrupt rule by the military and the National Liberation Front fueled an Islamist revolt that has led to a savage civil war.

Turkey's fragile democracy has been besieged by corruption. Its parties are far more concerned with seeking patronage and state contracts than with promoting ideological agendas. Former Prime Minister Tansu Ciller (1993–1996) has become vastly wealthy while in politics, and allegations of graft and cronyism have swirled about her. A staunch secularist, she nevertheless formed a coalition government with Islamic leader Necmetin Erbakan in 1996, because he promised to prevent an investigation of Ciller's finances. She made a similar deal with Erbakan's successor, Mesult Yilmaz, who had his own skeletons to hide. Yilmaz's government finally fell in November 1998 because of continuing allegations about corruption. There have also been charges that the police are in league with gangsters, right-wing hit squads, and drug traffickers.

CORRUPTION IN SUB-SAHARAN AFRICA

With the possible exception of the former Soviet Union, sub-Saharan Africa is the most corrupt region in the world. Colonial rule left weak governments and few educated administrators. Socialist-minded leaders created state-dominated economies that failed disastrously and offered numerous opportunities for graft. With arbitrary boundaries left over from colonial times, few states have developed a sense of "nationhood," and political actors' first loyalty is usually to their ethnic group.

"Personal rulership" is perhaps the most common political system in Africa. The ruler has almost unlimited legal competence. He is not concerned with building a following among the general public; instead he attends to the needs of his more powerful supporters, usually in the military or in state-owned firms. But state power is too limited to implement any policy except pillage. Personal rulership tends to be corrupt and arbitrary, but also weak and unstable.

The most extreme form of personal rulership is what Max Weber called a "sultanistic" regime. Such a state has no claim to legitimacy, whether based on tradition, ideology, charisma, or social order. The ruler runs the state to benefit him and his allies. He treats the public treasury as an extension of his personal fortune. He sells import and export licenses to the highest bidders, and appoints his cronies to run state-owned firms where they can exploit their nation's resources. Because the ruler's whims (and those of his supporters) supersede the written law, there is no predictability to the state's actions. This discourages private enterprise, since businessmen cannot know whether their property will be confiscated. The only path to success is through winning the ruler's fickle favors. While sultanistic states rarely function well enough to collect taxes, that did not bother many African leaders, who had their own streams of revenue: exporting natural resources through state-owned firms (especially during the high-commodity-price 1970s) and collecting foreign aid from the Cold War rivals. The French have remained active in their former colonies and have propped up many an unsavory dictator.

Mobutu Sese Seko, who ruled Zaire (now the Democratic Republic of Congo) from 1965 to 1997, was a perfect example of a sultanistic ruler who treated the state as his personal property. The *Economist* (1997, p.21) described his rule as the "systematic theft of the state from top to bottom." Mobutu accumulated a fortune that amounted between $4 and $9 billion. Bribes, kickbacks, the public treasury, the returns from Zaire's mineral wealth, French and American aid—all went into Mobutu's Swiss bank accounts. By the end of his reign, he owned nine villas in Belgium; a Brazilian coffee plantation; a mansion in Spain; property in several African cities; and estates in Portugal, Switzerland, and the French Riviera. He also owned tens of thousands of bottles of wine bottled in the year of his birth.

Mobutu found Zaire a poor country—and left it destitute. In the name of Zairean nationalism, he seized expatriate-owned businesses in 1973 and gave them to his cronies, who promptly ran them into the ground. (Uganda's Idi Amin did much the same thing at the same time with Asian-owned businesses, with the same results.) Zaire is world-renowned for its mineral resources, including cobalt, diamonds and copper. Mobutu nationalized the mining industry—and wrecked it. Rather than paying them, Mobutu let his soldiers work for their money by robbing ordinary citizens. Pity the poor businessman trying to import goods into Zaire, for he had to pass a gauntlet of nine state agencies, all of them demanding bribes. The end of the Cold War meant that Mobutu's Western allies would no longer subsidize his regime. By the mid-1990s, Mobutu's government had stopped functioning, and a guerrilla uprising took root. With his army more interested in looting than in fighting, Mobutu fled the country in May 1997 and died soon after. By that point, Zaireans' purchasing power was only one-fourth what it had been in the 1950s, when they still lived under Belgian rule. The Belgians left behind an excellent system of roads. By the 1990s, it had deteriorated to the point where it was no longer possible to drive across Zaire.

While Mobutu set an impressive standard for banditry, other African rulers did their best to keep up. Mali's Moussa Traoré, Niger's Gnassingbe Eyadema, Cameroon's Paul Biya, and Gabon's Omar Bongo are some of the more noteworthy kleptocrats who have misgoverned Africa over the past generation. Few have had the panache of Jean-Bedel Bokassa of the Central African Republic (1965–1979). Like Mobutu, Bokassa treated his land as his private domain. Unlike Mobutu, Bokassa went so far as to crown himself emperor in a ceremony modeled after Napoleon's coronation. Through his control of the diamond trade, Bokassa accumulated a truly imperial fortune. His antics became an embarrassment to his French masters, who overthrew him after he personally led a massacre of children who were protesting the cost of school uniforms. The French spread a rumor that Bokassa ate his political opponents; distraught by this charge, Bokassa revealed that he had given diamonds to leading French politicians, including then–President Valéry Giscard d'Estaing.

Of all African countries, Nigeria is probably the most notorious for corruption. Bribery is universal and scamming seems to be the national pastime. With its vast reserves of petroleum, Nigeria experienced an economic boom during the 1970s oil crisis. The returns from that wealth mostly went to the military and to corrupt politicians. The nation's schools, hospitals and roads are in dreadful condition. President Shehu Shagari's administration (1979–1983) was so corrupt that the army overthrew him so they could get in on the action. More recently, Sani Abacha stole billions of dollars from the national treasury during his 1993–1998 dictatorship. Abacha realized that distributing import licenses for fuel was a good way to reward his cronies. He allowed the nation's oil refineries to deteriorate, forcing this oil-producing nation to import gasoline, and thereby enriched his pals. Alas, poor Abacha did not get to enjoy his wealth for long: He died suddenly in June 1998, allegedly in the company of prostitutes. (Some have suggested that Abacha's rivals poisoned his Viagra.)

CORRUPTION IN LATIN AMERICA

While Latin America has not been pillaged as thoroughly as Africa, corruption is a serious problem in most countries in the region. Only Chile, Costa Rica, and Uruguay have reputations for being relatively clean. Latin America's corruption is rooted in its Spanish and Portuguese colonial past. Far from home, colonial bureaucrats were able to exploit their positions for profit, often treating their offices as their private possessions. Mercantilistic regulation meant that merchants and landowners often had to bribe officials in order to do business. Independence changed little. Hispanic traditions of paternalism meant extensive involvement by the state in the economy, which created great opportunities for bribery and smuggling. A foreign investment boom in the late nineteenth century strengthened local economies, but often primarily enriched a few leaders at the top. Nationalists attacked foreign investment, especially in the oil industry, and replaced it with state-owned firms, which frequently became deeply corrupt. The domestic private sector remained underdeveloped and dependent on the state.

Much of Latin America's corruption has swirled about the various strongmen who have held power over the years. Alfredo Stroessner, who dominated Paraguay from 1954 to 1989, turned his country into a gangster's paradise. Nazi war criminals and international drug traffickers flocked to live under Stroessner's protection. Stroessner treated Paraguay's government as his personal fiefdom, distributing patronage to his supporters and providing few services to ordinary citizens. Stroessner ensured his longevity by spreading the graft around. High tariffs in neighboring Argentina and Brazil spawned a thriving smuggling trade. Many military officers became millionaires through this trade, buying Rolls-Royces and building mansions. Eventually, the armed forces were wholly funded by the smuggling of cigarettes, whiskey, cocaine, and heroin. The costs of the vast Itaipú hydroelectric project mushroomed from a 1973 estimate of $2 billion to a final figure of $21 billion in 1991. Much of the overrun appears to have gone into officials' pockets through kickbacks and bribery.

Venezuela saw a series of *caudillos* who made huge fortunes off the nation's oil wealth. General Juan Vicente Gomez (1910–1935) accumulated $200 million and became the nation's largest landowner. Major Marcos Pérez Jiménez did even better during his short reign (1951–1957), building a fortune of more than $250 million. The Somoza clan ruled Nicaragua from 1936 to 1979, dominating the economy and stashing away tens of millions of dollars. Haiti has had scarcely one uncorrupt leader in its entire history, but the Duvaliers (François 1957–1971; Jean-Claude 1971–1986) stand out even in that wretched lot. When Jean-Claude fled Haiti in 1986, he was said to be worth $800 million. Fulgencio Batista, president of Cuba from 1940 to 1944 and from 1952 to 1958, accumulated a fortune of between $100 and $300 million. Rafael Trujillo treated the Dominican Republic as his personal fiefdom during his 1930–1961 reign. At one point, Trujillo acquired the country's only shoe factory and then forbade Dominicans to go barefoot. Visitors to Santo Domingo noted that the country's poverty must be exaggerated: After all, everyone wore shoes! Trujillo's practice of requiring a 10 percent bribe on every governmental transaction helped him fill his bank accounts with up to $500 million.

While presidential corruption is a long tradition in Latin America, a newer plague is infecting states from the Rio Grande to the Andes: drug trafficking. *Norteamericanos'* insatiable appetite for cocaine, marijuana, and heroin (and their government's insistence on maintaining the ban on such substances) is undermining political stability in several Latin American countries. Cocaine cartels have been a fixture in Colombia since the 1970s. In the 1980s, the Medellín cartel threatened the stability of the Colombian government. More recently, it was revealed that the Calí cartel had partially funded the presidential campaign of Ernesto Samper (1994–1998). The Revolutionary Armed Forces of Colombia (FARC), guerrillas funded by the drug trade, now control much of the country. Many observers fear that Colombia will become the hemisphere's first "narco-state."

However, Mexico may get there first. Because of the extensive border it shares with the United States, Mexico has long been an ideal location for smugglers. When the Drug Enforcement Administration (DEA) increased surveillance in South Florida and the Caribbean during the late 1980s, the cocaine trade moved into Mexico. Since then the drug trade has boomed in Mexico, corrupting nearly every area of the Mexican government. Even General Jesús Gutierrez Rebollo, who was leading Mexico's war on drugs, was arrested for accepting bribes from a major drug trafficker. The Mexican police are universally believed to be corrupt. State governors, army officers, party leaders—the drug traffickers have ties to them all.

Several leaders have made their countries havens for the drug trade. The most famous, of course, is Manuel Antonio Noriega, who dominated Panama from 1983 to 1989. An American invasion brought him to the United States, where he now serves a sentence for drug trafficking and racketeering. Vinicio Cerezo, president of Guatemala from 1985 to 1990, was widely suspected of being friendly to the drug trade. For a time during the 1980s, Bolivia was run by a group of military officers known as the "cocaine colonels."

Some of the larger nations in Latin America have developed large, clientelistic political party machines. Probably the most famous is Mexico's Institutional Revolutionary Party (PRI), which has (under different names) dominated Mexican politics since 1929. Since then, the PRI has won every presidential elections and most state ones, often

fraudulently. Since the 1980s, however, the National Action Party (PAN) and the Democratic Revolutionary Party (PRD) have become serious competitors for power. The PRI's influence permeates Mexican society through corporatist labor and business organizations. PRI patronage dominates many institutions. Mexico's state-owned oil company, Petroleos Mexicanos, is notoriously corrupt. Mexico has a long history of presidents who retired wealthy. José Lopez Portillo, president from 1976 to 1982, parlayed the oil boom of those years into a fortune of at least $5 billion. Carlos Salinas de Gortari (president, 1988–1994) moved to Ireland under widespread suspicion of massive corruption. His brother, Raul, was later convicted of arranging the murder of a prominent PRI politician. While Salinas privatized many of Mexico's state-owned firms, thereby opening up its economy, some of these companies went to PRI allies under suspicious circumstances.

From 1958 to 1998, two political parties dominated Venezuela in close cooperation. Vast oil wealth provided the necessary resources for patronage (a country of 22 million has 1.3 million government employees) and subsidies. The state nationalized many industries, providing more opportunities for patronage and graft, but also leaving the private sector weak and dependent. During the boom of the 1970s, politicians could indulge their penchant for cronyism and corruption. The decline in oil prices in the 1980s diminished the parties' ability to mollify dissent. Jaime Lusinchi, president from 1983 to 1988, had to remain in exile for several years to avoid prosecution for misuse of state property. Carlos Andres Pérez, a fixture in Venezuelan politics since the 1950s and twice president (1974–1979, 1988–1993), was impeached in 1993 for abuse of public funds. Hugo Chavez, who had led an attempted coup d'état against Pérez, was elected president in 1998 without the support of the major parties.

Brazil lacks strong political parties, but it does not lack for patronage. Especially in rural areas, there is a tradition of machine politics dominated by local elites who use public resources to win mass support. President Fernando Collor de Mello (1990–1992) emerged from this background. While other Brazilian presidents had corrupt reputations, such as Juscelino Kubitschek de Oliveira (1956–1962) and José Sarney (1985–1990), Collor became the first president to be impeached by Congress. He resigned before he could be removed from office. Corruption under the Collor regime included overpricing on government contracts, rigging public bidding, insider deals, and illegal fundraising. Collor's campaign treasurer, Paulo César Farias, collected $2 billion in kickbacks from leading contractors. Collor himself spent $2.5 million on a garden at his home. One corrupt Collor ally in the Brazilian Congress claimed his wealth came from winning the lottery 333 times; he used the lottery as a means of laundering his corrupt wealth. Some observers argued the Collor era's corruption stemmed from changes in Brazil's electoral law that made it more difficult for the president to form stable coalitions in Congress. Brazil's economic crisis reduced the public resources available for bargaining, forcing Collor to turn to private sources.

CORRUPTION IN COMMUNIST AND POST-COMMUNIST STATES

Nowhere in the world does corruption pervade society more thoroughly than in communist and post-communist states. The absolute command of resources that characterizes communist states, and many post-communist states, makes them perfect loci for massive corruption. Under Joseph Stalin and Mao Zedong, terror kept corruption from getting out of line. As communist states aged, corruption became more flagrant. In the USSR, the regime of Leonid Brezhnev (1964–1982) became a synonym for graft and inefficiency. Almost all Communist Party officials took bribes; most exploited their offices for all the privileges they were worth. Organized crime, which has a centuries-old history in Russia, established close ties with party leaders. Indeed, the black market often was all that kept the USSR from collapsing. Managers of state factories and farms had to be corrupt to survive. They lacked the material necessary to meet their goals, so they bribed officials to approve their production. Ordinary citizens had to bribe, too, in order to get consumer goods, medical care, and housing.

Other communist countries featured extensive corruption that came to light after the revolution of 1989–1991. Exposure of the lavish lifestyles of the East German elite—who had always preached Marxist simplicity—led to massive demonstrations and helped trigger the end of the communist regime. The leaders of Bulgaria and Romania have also been revealed to be corrupt.

The communist era bequeathed a legacy that made massive corruption inevitable in most post-communist countries: a contempt for written law, a complete lack of protections for private property, a cynical public, an arrogant officialdom, a state-dominated economy, an absence of any institutions independent of the state. Some post-communist states made the transition relatively easily and with relatively little corruption: Poland, Hungary, the Czech Republic, Slovenia, and the Baltic states. But the states of the former USSR (with the exception of the Baltics) have traveled a rockier path that has mostly led in to a swamp of corruption.

When Russia privatized many of its state firms in 1992, the bulk of them went to former communist apparatchiks, ex-KGB agents, *mafiya* leaders, and a few well-connected businessmen. These "oligarchs" generally paid bargain-basement prices. They have dominated Russian politics in the post-communist era and have supplied crucial support for President Boris Yeltsin. The crash of the ruble in the summer of 1998 damaged both their political credibility and their economic clout. Former Prime Minister Viktor Chernomyrdin is widely believed to have made a multi-billion-dollar fortune from the privatization of the state natural gas monopoly, Gazprom—one of the few Soviet-era companies that makes something that anybody wants. Allegations of massive corruption have swirled about former Finance Minister Anatoly Chubais, once the great hope of reform.

Paid poorly or not at all, military officers have turned to selling their own equipment. During the conflict in Chechnya, some Russian soldiers actually sold weapons to the Chechen separatists. Officers often would rather smuggle than perform their military duties. Some even sell nuclear material or chemical weaponry to rogue states. Customs officials are so corrupt and obstreperous that the U.S. government actually trains Russian businessmen in techniques for avoiding them.

Despite all the talk of Russian capitalism, the state still dominates the economy. Most Russians still work for state firms. Businessmen must obtain licenses for most activities, which creates great opportunity for extortion. More important, Russia has not created the kind of legal system necessary for private enterprise to flourish. With few laws to govern the emerging capitalist economy, bureaucrats can take away a company's assets at a whim. With their property at the mercy of corrupt officials, even honest businessmen must bribe to stay afloat. There is little tradition of respecting private property in Russia. Even under the czars, all land belonged to the sovereign; even the wealthiest landowner was legally a tenant.

Taking advantage of this time of troubles, organized crime has taken over much of the Russian economy, with the help of their old communist and Komitet Gosudarstvennos Bezopasnoti (Committee for State Security) (KGB) allies. The police and other law enforcement agencies are underpaid, undermanned, and demoralized. With domination of their home territory assured, Russian gangsters are now spreading their activities worldwide.

Other post-communist states have their own patterns of massive corruption. Foreign investors have shied away from Ukraine, despite its rich farmland and modern factories, because its all-encompassing graft and labyrinthine bureaucracy makes doing business almost impossible. As in Russia, former communist officials and *mafiya* gangsters dominate the economy. Ex-communists made Bulgaria and Romania bywords for corruption until the voters booted them out.

China has moved toward a market economy while retaining the Communist Party's monopoly on political power. This has created many opportunities for corruption. Party leaders have plundered state firms, received state loans, and embezzled state funds. The People's Liberation Army has entered a variety of businesses, some legal, some not. The children of communist leaders—the so-called "princelings"—have used their positions to build fortunes. Some observers have argued that corruption has smoothed the transition to capitalism by circumventing bureaucratic rules. It is true that corruption has been most visible in the fastest-growing parts of China, especially in the southern province of Guangdong, where it may well have opened doors that strict legality would have kept shut. Corruption may now be harming commerce.

Like Russia, China lacks a system of property law, so businessmen remain at the mercy of officialdom and cannot settle their disputes in court. They must instead rely on bribery and *guangxi* (connections), which often translates into giving local bosses a cut of their profits. Foreign investors are losing patience. There are also signs that corruption is impairing governance. During the Yangtze River floods of the summer of 1998, water washed away many "bean-curd" dams and bridges. Officials had embezzled the money that would have strengthened these structures. Premier Zhu Rongji has used these disasters to justify his current anticorruption campaign.

North Korea has not moved away from communism one bit, so there is no private sector to shake down. Instead, the state itself has become a criminal enterprise. With its economy in ruins, North Korea has become a "gangster state" that sells narcotics and counterfeit money around the world. It can no longer pay its diplomats, so they support themselves by smuggling. North Korea's fake $100 bills are so convincing that they led the United States to redesign its currency. To fuel its drug trade, the state runs its own methamphetamine factories and opium poppy farms.

THE OUTLOOK FOR THE FUTURE

The global trend toward democracy and capitalism may decrease corruption in the long term, but in the short term it may increase the perception of corruption. The openness brought by democracy allows for greater disclosures of official malfeasance. Graft that would have remained secret under an authoritarian regime instead comes out, perhaps damaging the public's opinion of politicians. While capitalism reduces the state's role in the economy, thereby decreasing the opportunity for officials to enrich themselves, the privatization schemes necessary for the transition to free markets often become a bonanza for those in power.

There are several attempts to fight corruption on an international level. Transparency International, founded in 1993, organizes anticorruption efforts across the world. Its annual survey of perceptions of corruption has embarrassed many graft-ridden countries. Transparency International now has chapters in seventy countries. In 1997, twenty-nine members of the Organization for Economic Cooperation and Development (OECD) signed the Convention on Combating Bribery of Foreign Public Officials. This accord, which went into effect in February 1999, forbids the bribery of foreign executive, legislative, and judicial officials. Countries that signed the accord had to agree to punish offenders severely, to help each other prosecute offenders, and to encourage the wider use of sound accounting and auditing practices. The International Monetary Fund (IMF) and the World Bank now often condition their loans on steps to reduce corruption and "crony capitalism." In 1997, the World Bank established a comprehensive anticorruption program.

REFERENCES

Elazar, Daniel J. 1984 *American Federalism: A View from the Stars*, 3rd ed. New York: Harper and Row.

Elliott, Kimberly Ann (ed.) 1997 *Corruption and the Global Economy*. Washington, D.C.: Institute for International Economics.

Ford, Henry Jones 1904 "Municipal Corruption." *Political Science Quarterly* 19:673–686.

Heidenheimer, Arnold J., Michael Johnston, and Victor T. LeVine (eds.) 1989 *Political Corruption: A Handbook*. New Brunswick, N.J.: Transaction.

Huntington, Samuel P. 1968 *Political Order in Changing Societies*. New Haven, Conn.: Yale University Press.

Johnston, Michael 1982 *Political Corruption and Public Policy in America*. Monterey, Calif.: Brooks/Cole.

Little, Walter, and Eduardo Posada-Carbó (eds.) 1996 *Political Corruption in Europe and Latin America*. New York: St. Martin's.

Key, V. O., Jr. 1936 *The Techniques of Political Graft in the United States*. Chicago: University of Chicago Press.

Mauro, Paolo 1997 *Why Worry about Corruption?* Washington, D.C.: International Monetary Fund.

Noonan, John T., Jr. 1984 *Bribes*. New York: Macmillan.

Nye, Joseph S. 1967 "Corruption and Political Development: A Cost-Benefit Analysis." *American Political Science Review* 66 (June):417.

Sabato, Larry J., and Glenn R. Simpson 1996 *Dirty Little Secrets: The Persistence of Corruption in American Politics*. New York: Times Books.

Steffens, Lincoln. (1904) 1968 *The Shame of the Cities*. New York: Hill & Wany.

"The Last Days of Mobutu." 1997 *The Economist* March 22: 21.

RICHARD MCGRATH SKINNER

POLITICAL CORRECTNESS

THE HISTORY OF POLITICAL CORRECTNESS

While the term *political correctness* (hereafter, PC) entered common parlance only in the mid-1990s and may soon lose its popularity, the phenomenon to which it refers, namely ideological conformity with the views of those in power or in fashion, is millenia old. To have PC, there must be ideology, and ideology developed with the formation of states. To the extent that all states use violence or the threat thereof to serve the interests of the few who control the state by extracting resources from the many who do not, states always face a problem of legitimacy. If they are to minimize their use of coercive violence to extract surplus production, states must try to convince their subjects that the state serves the interests not only of the ruling class but of the society as a whole. Such is the role of ideology, whether religious or secular.

Until the French Revolution, most states tried to legitimate themselves by identifying themselves with a religion, for instance, Confucianism in China, various branches of Christianity in Europe, and Islam from Morocco to Indonesia. In these "premodern" states, PC was virtually synonymous with religious orthodoxy, as defined by the political and religious elites in control. It was enforced by sanctions ranging from execution, torture, and expulsion to expropriation, ostracism, disfranchisement, discrimination, and segregation. In the late eighteenth century, the American and French revolutions abruptly shifted the onus of state legitimation from religious orthodoxy to a secular ideology of "liberty, equality, fraternity." This ideology was, however, widely at variance with the structure of highly stratified societies (such as the United States, a slave society) and the practice of coercive states that were often democratic in name only. The bourgeois liberal ideology of the French Revolution gradually spread to much of the world in the nineteenth and twentieth centuries, briefly challenged by two large countermovements, one reactionary (fascism), one radical (Marxism). Both challenges collapsed, fascism after a quarter-century, in mid-twentieth century, and Marxism in three-quarters of a century, some forty years later.

All these political movements thrived on the elaboration of ideology that served not only to legitimate state power, but to obscure the enormous discrepancy between the democratic, egalitarian ideals and the oppressive, exploitative reality. What the priesthood had been to religiously based PC, the intelligentsia and the bureaucracy became to secular PC. The actual term "political correctness" began to be used principally in the Marxist tradition, which claimed the ability to perform scientific analysis of social and political events, and thus allowed for the possibility of being correct or incorrect in one's analysis. The "party line," as defined by the ruling elite in communist regimes, invariably claimed correctness, of course, and invented elaborate ex post facto rationalizations for even the most radical policy changes (e.g., the 1939–1941 Soviet-Nazi alliance to gobble up Poland). Soon, however, the concept of PC was adopted by opponents of Marxism to ridicule the dogmatism and obvious opportunism of communist regimes, as, for instance, in George Orwell's brilliant satire *Animal Farm*.

More recently, in the 1990s, the term PC was revived in the English-speaking world, and rapidly gained currency as a description of the self-imposed ideological conformity and censorship practiced by intellectual, business, and governmental elites in the United States, Canada, Britain, and elsewhere. While the term is principally a weapon used by conservatives to ridicule liberals, it is used across the ideological spectrum, sometimes in healthy, self-deprecatory criticism of fellow liberals or radicals.

CONTEMPORARY POLITICAL CORRECTNESS

In the current context, PC has several interesting features, as follows:

1. While PC is often supported by state regulations, legislation, and a wide range of legal and extralegal measures (covering such things as "hate speech," sexual harassment, homosexuality, and affirmative action), its principal focus of conformity enforcement is situated in the intellectual, bureaucratic, and business elites that "voluntarily" adhere to the PC ideology, exercise extensive self-censorship, and practice more or less subtle forms of ostracism against mavericks.

2. PC ideology is widely at variance with what the majority of the population regards as commonsensical, and it conflicts with the interests and beliefs of many large groups (e.g. males, whites, religious fundamentalists, the poorly educated). It thus pits the liberal ruling elites against the populist masses. The colleges and universities, especially the elite institutions among them, are the most vocal and articulate proponents of PC, as are, of course, the graduates of such institutions when they accede to the command posts of government and business.

3. PC is not a coherent political movement aimed at changing the fundamental structure of society, as were Marxism and fascism, for example. Rather, it is an inchoate cultural movement aimed at imposing on a supposedly benighted populous the values, lifestyles, and speech patterns of the elites. It attacks almost exclusively the symbolic aspects of popular culture, rather than the fundamental features of social inequality and injustice. One of its principal cultural products is a rich crop of rapidly changing euphemistic neologisms, the use or nonuse of which serves as evidence of whether one is PC or not.

The central tenets of this elite PC ideology in the United States include the elements discussed below.

1. *PC is a theoretical celebration of "diversity" on many fronts: religious, ethnic, racial, linguistic, and sexual.* The corollary of this celebration of diversity is the rejection of the older ideology of the melting pot, of cultural assimilation, of English-language dominance, and an alternative vision of American society as a mosaic of racial, ethnic, linguistic, religious, and "lifestyle" groups clamoring for recognition of special status, and competing for scarce resources.

This diversity tenet has led in practice not so much to *tolerance* of "otherness," a widely accepted value, but to institutionalized, officialized recognition of group affiliation, rights and quota in employment, education, contracts, and so on. These "affirmative action" programs have often been "voluntary" and flexible, but they have faced massive resentment because they violated many values held dear by masses of Americans. They flew in the face of the principle that *individuals* have legal rights, not groups, and that these rights are *equal*. They also squarely violated universalistic norms, such as that merit, competence, or seniority should govern allocation of resources, rather than ethnic or racial membership. A massive backlash against affirmative action, bilingual education, and other "special group rights" programs resulted, because PC is seen, not only as creating division and dissension in American society, but as imposing a double standard of tolerance. For instance, black students are allowed to autosegregate on campuses in a way that white students are not. Hate speech codes are also asymmetrically enforced for blacks and whites, men and women, heterosexuals and homosexuals. Indeed, the very same "hate" words, such as "queer" and "nigger," are differently evaluated depending on who uses them!

2. *PC embraces a libertarian ideology holding that individual freedom is, in principle, only limited by respect for the rights of others.* Again, if PC libertarianism were evenhandedly applied, it would meet little opposition. This, however, is not the case. Take two examples: drug use and hate speech. The PC position on drug use is one of unequivocal condemnation of tobacco use (increasingly a lower-class habit), even those forms of it that do not pollute the air (such as chewing tobacco). Alcohol use, on the other hand, is widely tolerated, even though its lethality is second only to that of tobacco. As for the illegal drugs, there is no clear PC line, although many self-styled libertarians are amazingly tolerant of heavy state repression and suspension of civil rights involved in the "war against drugs."

Attempts to control hate speech on campuses and elsewhere is another glaring example of PC double standards. First, many PC proponents have little trouble reconciling their self-styled libertarianism and defense of free speech with attempts to restrict the latter for those with whom they disagree. Second, there is blatant lack of evenhandedness in ostracizing certain kinds of hate speech but not others. Thus, college professors may with impunity refer to their opponents as "male chauvinist pigs," "racist honkies," or "fascist cops," but not as "dumb broads," "ignorant niggers," or "flaming faggots." "Afrocentrist" teachers are allowed to spread anti-Semitic venom by alleging that African slavery was dominated by Jews, but psychometricians and psychologists like Arthur Jensen, Philippe Rushton, and Richard Herrnstein are virulently attacked for suggesting that part of the persistent difference in performance of whites and blacks on intelligence quotient (IQ) and other standardized tests may be genetic in origin. Examples of this double standard of PC enforcement in academia are legion, as documented in Dinesh D'Souza's *Illiberal Education.*

The offence, it seems, lies as much in the gender, skin pigmentation, or sexual preference of the offender as in the hate speech itself. Only certain combinations are taboo. Others are tolerated, or even found amusing. (Stand-up comedy is an excellent barometer of PC, for instance, and most stand-up comics are acutely attuned to PC. Women may, with impunity, insult men; gays may insult straights; and blacks may insult whites—but not vice versa.)

3. *PC embraces conservationist, environmentalist causes; these, again, would receive wider acceptance if PC were not so elitist, selective, and sentimentalist.* PC ecologism is usually cast as a morality play between good guys (Native Americans, Aborigines, Greenpeace, the Sierra Club) and bad guys (loggers, oil companies, maquiladoras). The reality, of course, is much more nuanced. Native peoples, for

example, began to show as great a proclivity to overfish, overhunt, overgraze, overlog, and otherwise degrade their environment as that of more "advanced" peoples, as soon as they gained access to the destructive technology (steel axes, nylon nets, firearms, chain saws) that make these activities possible. There is also now a powerful backlash against ecologism among Third World intellectuals who argue, rather persuasively, that the ecological movement in the West is highly elitist. The "Green" movement is spearheaded, they say, by leisured romantics, intellectuals, biologists, and other educated members of affluent societies who, after despoiling their own countries, want to convince the poor countries to stop development in order to preserve unspoiled playgrounds for the scientists and eco-tourists of the rich countries.

4. *PC shows a concern for equality, which, once more, would be widely shared in the general population, if it had not been extended by PC proponents in two radically new directions.* The first extension concerns the transformation of the notion of *individual* equality of *opportunity* into *group* equality of *results*. The latter is as controversial as the former is almost universally accepted. The PC model of the ideal society is no longer one in which social rewards are fairly distributed to individuals according to their abilities, efforts, and ethics, but one in which socially defined racial and ethnic groups achieve proportional representation in every sphere of activity. Such a model of a quota society is not only absurd and unrealizable; it is also a prescription for perpetual conflict. The definition of groups is arbitrary and manipulable for gain. Millions of people are of mixed descent, a disallowed category in contemporary America. The population base for establishing proportionality is elastic. (For instance, should blacks be 2 percent of the students at the University of Washington, their percentage in the population of the State of Washington, which it serves, or 12 percent, the percentage of blacks in the United States?) Why should some

groups (e.g., Hispanics) be represented, but not others (e.g., Arabs)? Why is an overrepresentation of whites among physics professors objectionable, but not an overrepresentation of blacks on basketball teams, or of Hassidic Jews in the diamond trade? Why do PC liberals, who proclaim that race does not matter, defend, in the same breath, race-based affirmative action? (Even a formerly sensible Nathan Glazer reversed himself recently on this score and now believes in the necessity for a proportional black presence at elite universities. If blacks, why not poor rural whites, surely another oppressed minority?) In short, the quota society is a bad idea that deserves a quick burial. South Africa just abolished racial apartheid. Why should the United States perpetuate it?

The second controversial extension of the concept of equality by the PC proponents is on the gender front. Few Americans would contest the ideas that women's worth is equal to that of men, that women should have equal rights with men, that they should be able to compete with men on equal terms, and that they should receive equal pay and benefits for equal work. But the PC agenda goes well beyond that consensual definition of gender equality. PC feminists are generally quite ambivalent about accepting the obvious differences between men and women; if they do accept these differences, they generally ascribe them more to nurture than to nature, and they seek either to ignore or to minimize them; and, quite inconsistently, they want to preserve gender segregation where it favors women (e.g., in sports). PC feminists, in short, want a unisex society, except where it suits them. Finally, PC feminists want the right to be protected against "sexual harassment" whenever they *feel* they have been harassed. Many, in addition, would want to subject sexual relations to a code of conduct involving repeated, explicit verbal assent (unilaterally imposed on men) for every sexual act. Some colleges have gone as far as institutionalizing this nonsense.

Needless to say, the common sense of most Americans, women as well as men, refuses to accept an ideology that flies in the face of experience, and there is a substantial backlash against radical feminism. Yet PC feminist dogma still rules supreme in many policy domains—for instance, in the military, which tries not only to achieve full gender integration but to rule sex out of existence in its ranks. Any officer bold enough to suggest that this is impossible immediately jeopardizes his or her career.

5. *PC takes a secular outlook that has its roots in eighteenth-century Enlightenment and has dominated Western intellectual life ever since, but that arouses deep antagonism in the half or more of the American population that considers itself religious, and, even more so, in the quarter or so who are fundamentalist Christians.* PC secularism is more than Jeffersonian separation of church and state in that it also frontally attacks the "religious right" on moral issues such as contraception, divorce, and marriage, as well as most controversially—abortion and homosexuality. PC secularism is also at variance with its classical Enlightenment expression in that it does not automatically align itself with the scientific mainstream. For example, many PC secularists reject the mounting evidence supporting the partially genetic underpinning of human behavior, of gender differences, and of basic abilities and character traits. While they may ridicule biblical creationism, they espouse an extreme "social constructionist" view of human behavior and human relations, which is, in fact, a form of secular creationism.

THE EFFECTS OF POLITICAL CORRECTNESS

Because the current form of American PC is such an elite phenomenon, its effect has been limited to the relatively small class of literate bureaucrats and academics who take it seriously. It did stifle intellectual discourse on American campuses and did promote the teaching of a good deal of nonsense masquerading as scholarship. But there is little evidence that it makes many converts, and considerable evidence that it brings out a conservative

backlash. Indeed, PC ideology already seems on the defensive, vulnerable as it is to ridicule. American cultural products always have some resonance in other countries, especially English-speaking and Western European ones: the United Kingdom, Canada, Australia, Scandinavia, the Netherlands, and Germany in particular. But in those countries as well, its influence has been limited to the intellectual elite. In much of the rest of the world, American-style PC has had even less resonance, either because the issues it addresses have little relevance there (e.g., race relations), or because other political and economic problems (such as human rights violations or poverty) give such issues as feminism or conservation much lower priority. Indeed, many PC tenets may even clash more openly with the values of non-Western cultures than they do with the common sense of Westerners.

The probability is, thus, high that the current wave of American-style PC has already crested and that it will be ephemeral. But then, a new brand will crop up, probably no more sane than the current one. Intellectuals, alas, often prove themselves to be much more the sycophants of power than the guardians of reason.

REFERENCES

Devine, Philip E. 1996 *Human Diversity and the Culture Wars*. Westport, Conn.: Praeger.

D'Souza, Dinesh 1992 *Illiberal Education*. New York: Vintage.

Fish, Stanley Eugene 1995 *Professional Correctness*. New York: Claredon.

Friedman, Marilyn, and Jan Narveson 1995 *Political Correctness: For and Against*. Lanham, Md.: Rowman and Littlefield.

Glazer, Nathan 1975 *Affirmative Discrimination*. New York: Basic.

Orwell, George 1946 *Animal Farm*. New York: Harcourt.

Wilson, John K. 1995 *Myth of Political Correctness*. Durham, N.C.: Duke University Press.

PIERRE L. VAN DEN BERGHE

POLITICAL CRIME

Political crime has been more often an object of partisan assertion than of independent research.

Passions are easily aroused, facts are difficult to establish. Nevertheless, a growing number of studies have contributed to (1) articulating the issues in defining political criminality, (2) describing instances and patterns of resistance to political-legal authority, (3) cataloging and analyzing governmental efforts to prevent and counter such challenges, and (4) proposing research agendas.

THE PROBLEM OF DEFINITION

Political criminality may be narrowly or broadly defined, with greater or lesser regard for definitions offered by laws and interpretations by authorities. Moreover, the values and politics of observers frequently influence their conceptions of what and who is politically criminal. The resulting mélange of definitions has led Kittrie and Wedlock to conclude pessimistically, "It may be that an objective and neutral definition of political crime is impossible, because the term seems to involve relativistic relationships between the motives and acts of individuals and the perspectives of government toward their conduct and allegiances" (1998, p. xxxvi). However, an alternative view is implicit in their understanding of political criminality as perceptual and relational, defined in interaction between opposing parties.

Whose perceptions decide what is to be called political crime? Apart from partisan and subjective answers, the empirical reality of political criminality is that it is defined by those with enough power to impose their perceptions. Insofar as a political authority structure has been established, one may argue that the dominant parties within it by definition have the power to define criminality (Turk 1982a, pp. 11–68, 1984; pp. 119–121; for more restrictive legalistic definitions, see Ingraham 1979, pp. 13, 19; Frank Hagan 1997, p. 2). However, this view leaves unsettled the question of how authorities themselves may be defined as political criminals.

The most common resolution is to expand the definition to include anyone who commits extralegal acts defending or attacking an authority structure. For example, Roebuck and Weeber consider political crime to be any illegal or disapproved act committed by "government or capitalistic agents" or by "the people against the government" (1978, pp. 16–17). This very subjective definition (disapproved by whom?) leaves one unable to distinguish either between acts against and on behalf of

authority or between legal and nonlegal behavior. A more promising approach is to recognize that criminality may be defined at different levels of political organization—international as well as national.

International conventions, treaties, and judicial decisions have gone far toward formally defining war crimes, genocide, terrorism, violations of human rights, and environmental depredations. Such international standards may be invoked as criteria for labeling not only individuals but also agencies and regimes as political criminals guilty of "state crimes" (Barak 1991; Ross 1995). Even when formal legal criteria have not been articulated, evidence of harmful consequences of governmental policies and corporate practices may be used to define as political crimes "acts of commission and omission that result in grave social harm" (Tunnell 1993, p. xiv).

Formal pronouncements and unofficial assertions, however, may not have much significance. Accusations against governmental and corporate regimes are unlikely to impact on them unless there is a significant likelihood that they will be penalized for their actions. Within nations, acts by subnational authorities have sometimes been effectively treated as political crimes by national authorities who saw them as endangering societal or elite interests. An example is the American federal government's historic crackdown on state and local violations of constitutionally guaranteed civil rights in the South.

At the international level, it is still rare for even gross violations of human rights to result in sanctioning. Though often accompanied by rhetorical accusations of criminality, expeditions such as the Kosovo intervention by the North Atlantic Treaty Organization (NATO) have typically been launched more out of geopolitical concerns than legal or moral ones, and tend to end in new political and economic accommodations rather than criminal trials. For the present, the lack or weakness of international policing and judicial institutions leaves powerful nations such as the United States free to reject or ignore such charges as practicing genocidal policies toward Native Americans, holding political prisoners, torturing detainees and convicts, and illegally authorizing operations in other countries by the Federal Bureau of Investigation (FBI), the Drug Enforcement

Agency (DEA), and the Central Intelligence Agency (CIA). With little or no chance of their enforcement, invoking international or national laws to define political crimes will continue to amount to little more than largely subjective and partisan ideological tactics.

Another question is whether political criminality is to be defined only as behavior. While one may agree that only specified harmful acts *should* be punishable, the historical fact is that, in addition to offending behavior, nonbehavioral attributes such as ethncity and class background have frequently been used by antagonists as criteria of intolerable political deviance. Moreover, imputed as well as observed deviations or threats have been used. Anticipation as well as reaction are involved in the identification of political criminality. At the beginning of World War II, Japanese immigrants and their descendants in the United States were officially defined as security risks and forcibly relocated to prison camps, and during both world wars many German nationals and immigrants were subjected to surveillance and orders restricting their freedom to travel outside the areas where they lived.

In sum, political criminality is most realistically defined as whatever is treated as such by specified actors (usually governments, dominant groups, or their agents) who have the power to impose their conceptions in particular historical situations.

RESISTING AUTHORITY

Resistance to political authority may be more or less deliberate, organized, or planned. As noted above, even the appearance or potential of resistance may be sufficient for authorities to act against perceived challengers. Actual resisters may be engaged in activities ranging from merely disrespectful comments to the most violent assaults, from spontaneous eruptions to carefully orchestrated attacks, from individually motivated acts to organized strategies of rebellion. Acts of resistance may be categorized as evasion, dissent, disobedience, or violence.

Resisters may simply evade the orders and demands of the powerful. Avoiding masters, bosses, tax collectors, and military conscription has generally been safer than explicit defiance—because open defiance tends to force authorities to respond, while tacit evasion is more easily ignored or minimized. Russian serfs learned in such instances as the St. Petersburg massacre how ruthless the Cossacks could be in suppressing dissenters and petitioners—the kind of lesson that has been taught to peasants and workers over the centuries in many lands. As Karl Marx complained, peasants and industrial workers tend to settle for mere survival and small gains instead of becoming revolutionaries. Fear of brutal repression is not groundless, and those with little social power are realistically skeptical even in democratic societies (as regularly shown in legal and political attitude polls) of notions that they can expect protection because they have legal rights.

The right to speak out against authority is enshrined in many legal traditions but in practice is limited by the varying tolerance of authorities and people—decidedly lower in wartime and economic hard times. After centuries of attempting to deter such offenses as seditious libel and treasonous utterances, more democratic governments have de facto concluded that the effort is incompatible with the concept of free speech (Law Commission 1977; Stone 1983; Hurst 1983; cf. Franks 1989). However, other labels may be invoked to authorize punishing those whose dissent is especially galling, especially when authorities feel particularly threatened. U.S. Senator Joseph McCarthy, for instance, achieved the lasting notoriety of "McCarthyism" by making freewheeling accusations of "subversion" against a wide spectrum of targets—from known communists to President Dwight Eisenhower. Though McCarthy's failure to refrain from smearing the president and the army, both icons in 1950s America, resulted in his downfall, the political climate remained one in which public objections to capitalism, American foreign policies, and even racial segregation carried the risk of being labeled a "communist" or at least a "fellow traveler."

Dissenting is one thing, but actually disobeying rules and commands is another. Lower-class people have historically suffered many demonstrations of their vulnerability, and so have characteristically been less likely than higher-class people either to dissent or to disobey overtly (Turk 1982a, pp. 69–114). On the other hand, dissenting or disobedient higher-class, especially youthful, resisters have typically been subjected to less punitive treatment. For instance, sentences of Vietnam draft resisters decreased in response to the political repercussions of imprisoning growing numbers of higher-class young men (Hagan and Bernstein 1979). Not surprisingly, civil disobedience has been more likely to be a higher-class than a lower-class mode of resistance—that is, a tactic of those whose backgrounds encourage them to believe, perhaps erroneously, in their own significance and efficacy and in legal rights and protections. Certainly in the 1960s, in the early stages of the civil rights movement, marchers against southern segregation were far more likely to be students, intellectuals, and "bourgeois" than laborers, farmers, and "proletarians."

Violent resistance by individuals and small organizations seldom threatens authority structures directly, but does indirectly weaken them in that authorities facing or fearing violence typically adopt extralegal and repressive control measures—which contradict beliefs in legal restraints on governmental power. The more actually and ideologically democratic the political order, the greater the contradiction—which is associated with the greater vulnerability of democratic than despotic regimes to terrorism (Turk 1982b, p. 127).

Political violence tends to escalate from coercive to injurious to destructive forms, in an interaction spiral generated by decreasing hope on the side of one or both parties of an acceptable accommodation and/or by perceived advantages in escalation (Turk 1996). Coercive violence, which may complement or succeed verbal or legal appeals and arguments, is intended to pressure opponents to change their policies or practices—typical acts being telephoned threats, disruption of communications, and rioting. Injurious violence is aimed at causing limited damage to property or persons, with little or no risk of lethal damage, when opponents do not respond satisfactorily to coercion—as when Quebec separatists blew up mailboxes and American student radicals firebombed Reserve Officers Training Corps (ROTC) buildings on university campuses. Torture and execution mark the transition from injurious to destructive violence. Destructive violence seeks to terrify active and potential opponents and to eliminate the enemy's resources of personnel, supplies, and facilities; examples include the assassinations of governmental (or revolutionary) leaders, as well as acts of terrorism (e.g., the Oklahoma City bombing).

Political offenders have commonly been viewed as morally or mentally defective. However, even the most violent assassins and terrorists appear unlikely to exhibit psychopathology (Turk 1983, 1984, p. 123; cf. Schafer 1974; also Robins and Post 1997). The effort to understand political resisters begins in recognizing that they may vary enormously in political consciousness and motivation, organizational involvement, and readiness to commit violent acts, in addition to other characteristics, such as class origins. Distinctions must be made among deliberate political actors, emotional reactors to climates of political instability and violence, and apolitical opportunists such as ordinary criminals who merely seek to profit from their contacts with resistance figures and movements.

ASSERTING AUTHORITY

Political dominance is defended legally and often extralegally at all institutional levels. The highest and broadest level is typified by national (and increasingly international) policies of insulation (regulating access and mobility, e.g., through immigration and licensing laws), sanctioning (defining and enforcing behavioral rules, e.g., through criminal laws), and persuasion (disseminating favored communications, e.g., through education and censorship)—that is, through *statecraft*, governing strategies designed to ensure that potential resisters lack the opportunities, resources, and will to challenge authority (Gamson 1968). More specifically focused on controlling resistance is political policing—the organized effort to gather relevant intelligence, manipulate channels of communication, neutralize opposition, and deter challenges.

Because the value of information can never be fully anticipated, intelligence gathering is inherently limitless. Advancing technologies of surveillance and analysis enable ever more extensive and intensive monitoring of human behavior and relationships. The distinction between public and private is increasingly dubious in both law and practice. Recurring legislative and judicial efforts to impose legal restraints have occasionally slowed but never stopped the trend (Marx 1988). One of the most celebrated efforts—to end surveillance of civilians by U.S. Army intelligence officers—failed when the highest court ruled in 1972 "that it was not the business of the Supreme Court but of

Congress to monitor executive practices like surveillance" (Jensen 1991, p. 255).

Authorities have never been entirely comfortable with the ideal of free and open communications. Even where that ideal has been most firmly asserted in law, in practice the right to disseminate critical information and ideas has been limited (Kittrie and Wedlock 1998, *passim*). Openly or subtly, communications favoring the status quo have been facilitated, while dissent has been inhibited to a greater or lesser degree. For example, Eugene Debs (leader of the Socialist Party) was convicted and imprisoned not explicitly for his outspoken opposition to American involvement in World War I, but instead for "conspiracy" to obstruct military conscription and war production—a charge under the Espionage Act of 1917, which required no direct evidence of either conspiracy or obstructive actions.

When resistance is encountered, some blend of enclosure and terror tactics is used—that is, a combination of methods designed not only to suppress resistance but also to convince offenders that apprehension is inevitable and punishment unbearably severe. Psychological as well as physical coercion is accomplished by subjecting targets to sanctions varying from character assassination to torture and extermination. An example of the first is the FBI's effort to discredit Martin Luther King, Jr., as a subversive agitator, a communist sympathizer or dupe, and an immoral womanizer. As for the second, South African apartheid forces provided many instances, including the beating death under interrogation of Steve Biko, leading voice of the "black consciousness" movement.

International covenants notwithstanding, torture and other violations of human rights continue throughout the world (regularly documented by Amnesty International and other organizations). Extreme human rights abuses are reported not only in dictatorships such as Iraq and authoritarian regimes such as Sri Lanka but also in democracies such as Britain, India, Israel, and the United States. Clearly, authorities facing serious challenges are unlikely to be restrained by legal or other norms.

The ultimate goal of political policing is general deterrence. Insofar as the subject population does not knowingly and willingly accept the political order, fear and ignorance may still ensure acquiescence. Surveillance, censorship, and neutralization are designed not only to repress political deviance but also to discourage any inclination to question the social order. But intimidation must be supplemented by persuasion if superior power is to be legitimated—transformed into authority. A classic technique is the political trial, in which legal formalities are used to portray the accused as a threat to society, to convey the impression that political policing is legally restrained, and to reinforce the sense that political dominance is both right and irresistible. Such trials have not been limited to totalitarian states such as Nazi Germany and the Soviet Union (Kirchheimer 1961), but have also occurred with some regularity in democratic nations such as the United States. Historically, examples have occurred from the Puritans' legalistic suppression of Anne Hutchinson to the Chicago trial for "conspiracy" of eight assorted radicals with varied causes, whose only link was that they "represented the spectrum of leftist dissidents" (Belknap 1994, p. 240; see also Christenson 1986).

RESEARCH AGENDAS

Studies of political criminality have raised far more questions than they have answered. In the future, it will be not isolated, small-scale investigations but ongoing research programs, that will be essential if the quest for systematic explanations of political criminality is to be successful. Such programs will necessarily be multilevel, integrating research on the political socialization of individuals, the radicalization of defenders as well as challengers of authority, the interaction of resistance and policing strategies, and the conditions under which the political organization of social life is relatively visible (low rates of both resistance and repression).

The viability of a political authority structure can in principle be objectively defined: The probability of its survival increases or decreases. Accordingly, research can identify progressive actions (which increase viability) and destructive actions (which decrease viability) by anyone involved in political conflict. Turk (1982a, pp. 181–191) hypothesizes that random violence, economic exploitation, and weakening social bonds are destructive, while nonviolent actions increasing the life chances of everyone instead of only some people are likely to be progressive.

REFERENCES

Barak, Gregg 1991 *Crimes by the Capitalist State*. Albany: State University of New York Press.

Belknap, Michal R. (ed.) 1994 *American Political Trials*. Westport, Conn.: Praeger.

Christenson, Ron 1986 *Political Trials: Gordian Knots in the Law*. New Brunswick, N.J.: Transaction.

Franks, C. E. S. (ed.) 1989 *Dissent and the State*. Toronto: Oxford University Press.

Gamson, William A. 1968 *Power and Discontent*. Homewood, Ill.: Dorsey.

Hagan, Frank E. 1997 *Political Crime: Ideology and Criminality*. Needham Heights, Mass.: Allyn and Bacon.

Hagan, John, and Ilene Bernstein 1979 "Conflict in Context: The Sanctioning of Draft Resisters, 1963–76." *Social Problems* 27:109–122.

Hurst, James Willard 1983 "Treason" In Sanford H. Kadish, ed., *Encyclopedia of Crime and Justice*, vol. 4. New York: Free Press.

Ingraham, Barton L. 1979 *Political Crime in Europe: A Comparative Study of France, Germany and England*. Berkeley: University of California Press.

Jensen, Joan M. 1991 *Army Surveillance in America, 1775–1980*. New Haven, Conn.: Yale University Press.

Kirchheimer, Otto 1961 *Political Justice: The Use of Legal Procedure for Political Ends*. Princeton, N.J.: Princeton University Press.

Kittrie, Nicholas N., and Eldon D. Wedlock, Jr. (eds.) 1998 *The Tree of Liberty: A Documentary History of Rebellion and Political Crime in America*. Baltimore, Md.: Johns Hopkins University Press.

Law Commission 1977 *Codification of the Criminal Law: Treason, Sedition, and Allied Offences*. Working Paper 72. London: Her Majesty's Stationery Office.

Marx, Gary T. 1988 *Undercover: Police Surveillance in America*. Berkeley: University of California Press.

Robins, Robert S., and Jerrold M. Post 1997 *Political Paranoia: The Psychopolitics of Hatred*. New Haven, Conn.: Yale University Press.

Roebuck, Julian, and Stanley C. Weeber 1978 *Political Crime in the United States: Analyzing Crimes by and against Government*. New York: Praeger.

Ross, Jeffery Ian (ed.) 1995 *Controlling State Crime: An Introduction*. New York: Garland.

Schafer, Stephen 1974 *The Political Criminal: The Problem of Morality and Crime*. New York: Macmillan.

Stone, Geoffrey R. 1983 "Sedition" In Sanford H. Kadish, ed., *Encyclopedia of Crime and Justice*, vol. 4. New York: Free Press.

Tunnell, Kenneth D. (ed.) 1993 *Political Crime in Contemporary America: A Critical Approach*. New York: Garland.

Turk, Austin T. 1982a *Political Criminality: The Defiance and Defense of Authority*. Newbury Park, Calif.: Sage.

—— 1982b "Social Dynamics of Terrorism." *Annals of the American Academy of Political and Social Science* 463:119–128.

—— 1983 "Assassination" In Sanford H. Kadish, ed., *Encyclopedia of Crime and Justice*, vol. 1. New York: Free Press.

—— 1984 "Political Crime." In Robert F. Meier, ed., *Major Forms of Crime*. Newbury Park, Calif.: Sage.

—— 1996 "La violencia politica desde una perspectiva criminologica." (Political Violence in Criminological Perspective) *Sistema* 132–133 (Junio):41–55.

AUSTIN T. TURK

POLITICAL ORGANIZATIONS

Investigations of the behaviors of political organizations occur at an intersection of sociology, political science, and organizations studies. This interdisciplinary perspective offers great potential for richly informed understanding and comprehensive theoretical explanation of numerous facets of these crucial social actors and their relationships with the larger society and polity in which they are embedded. Four fundamental questions have dominated research and theorizing in this field over the past several decades: (1) What sociopolitical conditions encourage the creation of political organizations? (2) How are participants recruited and induced to provide crucial resources for political action? (3) What mobilization processes enable political organizations to work together most effectively toward collective ends? (4) What strategies and tactics exert the greatest impact on public policy makers' decisions? This article attempts to provide brief answers to these questions. Although most of the empirical research on political organizations concentrates on the United States, some recent evidence from European nations is examined.

The least restrictive definition of a political organization is any formally organized, named group that tries to influence the policy decisions of public officials. Most political organizations take the form of a voluntary association of persons or organizations that pools its members' and constituents' financial and other resources, and engages in conventional political actions to affect policy-making outcomes. Common synonyms for this type of organization are "interest groups," "pressure groups," and "collective action organizations." Ironically, political parties are not political organizations, because their primary purpose is to elect candidates to public office and only incidentally to press for specific policy agendas. Most public bureaucracies should be excluded, unless they act regularly to promote their own policy preferences within a government. Another questionable type is the social movement organization whose primary political tactics involve rallies, demonstrations, and violent forms of protest (including revolutionary actions intended to overthrow the government) rather than working within routine channels of the political system. Some social movement organizations eventually transform into conventional political interest groups, if they survive their turbulent youths as outside challengers. However, certain profit-making corporations might be considered quasi-political organizations, in instances where their government affairs officers lobby for preferential treatment from legislators and regulators (Salisbury 1994).

Political organizations—including such types as labor unions, professional societies, business and trade associations, churches, neighborhood and community organizations, fraternities and sororities, nationality and racial-ethnic federations, civic service, philanthropic, and cooperative groups, medical and legal societies, conservation leagues, and even recreational and hobby clubs—encompass a broad range of formal goals. Political purposes need not be their primary goal nor compose the majority of their activities, but the critical requirement is that they go beyond merely providing direct services to their members by seeking to change or preserve the social, economic, cultural, or legal conditions faced by their members or those on whose behalf they operate. One interesting type is the so-called citizens' group or public interest group (PIG), which purports not to benefit narrow sectarian or economic self-interests but to promote the broader collective values of the society (Berry 1977). For example, civil rights, civil liberties, environmental protection, feminist, and consumer advocacy associations frequently proclaim a disinterested agenda. A close examination of their supporters and activities suggests that they do not differ fundamentally from other political organizations in methods of operation (Schlozman and Tierney 1986, pp. 30–35). Based on listings compiled by various American directories, perhaps as many as 23,000 voluntary associations operate at the U.S. national level (many with dozens or hundreds of chapters and branches in state and local communities). Of these, perhaps half qualify as political organizations based on their efforts to communicate their positions on national policy issues to the federal government (Knoke 1990, p. 208). They range in size from the American Association of Retired Persons (AARP), with more than twenty-five million members, to small staff organizations with fewer than a dozen operatives bankrolled by foundations or public donations.

The creation, growth, and expansion of U.S. political organizations seem to occur in cycles corresponding to national political and economic events, including shifts in the legislative, regulatory, and judicial climate (Berry 1977, p. 13; Schlozman and Tierney 1986, pp. 74–82; Gray and Lowery 1996). American labor unions established a national policy presence during the New Deal, and public interest groups blossomed during the civil rights, antiwar, and feminist social movements of the 1960s. Business advocacy associations flocked to Washington in the 1970s and 1980s in reaction to restrictions imposed by newly established federal regulatory agencies for environment, occupational safety and health, consumer protection, and equal employment opportunity (Vogel 1996). Increasingly, mass membership associations have yielded ground to institutionally based organizations, including corporations; universities; foreign firms and governments; and confederations of U.S. state and local governments, such as the National League of Cities.

Interest groups rarely form spontaneously but require leadership and resources. Interest group foundings and expansions may be best understood as involving exchanges between entrepreneurial organizers, who invest capital in a set of benefits offered to potential members as the price of membership, and members who pay dues in order to receive these benefits. Intergroup subsidies may occur; for example, the American Federation of Labor–Congress of Industrial Organization (AFL-CIO) founded the National Council of

Senior Citizens, helped to recruit its early members from unions, and continued to underwrite its activities. Although committed citizen activists, such as Ralph Nader or John Gardner, occasionally provide an energizing impetus for launching new organizations, many public interest groups rely on patronage from wealthy individuals or foundation sponsors to get launched (Walker 1983), as well as on favorable mass media treatment to bolster their legitimacy. Once an organization is formed, its survival, growth, and effectiveness depend on its ability to attract and hold new members and other organizational sponsors. Labor unions and business associations can acquire substantial war chests through dues and assessments on their members, but PIGs have more limited capacities to tap potential diffuse constituents' money. The virtual collapse of Greenpeace in the 1990s underscores the vulnerability of many activist organizations to quickly dwindling support.

For more than three decades, a central paradigm to explain member contributions has been the economic or rational choice model developed in Mancur Olson Jr.'s *Logic of Collective Action* (1965). Olson considered the conditions under which people would voluntarily contribute their resources to an organized group seeking a public good (such as a governmental farm crop subsidy) from which no eligible recipients could be excluded. Olson argued that utility-maximizing actors would refuse to pay for public goods that will be produced regardless of their contributions, and thus would take a "free ride" on the efforts of other members. As a result, the model predicts that most political organizations should fail to mobilize their potential supporters if they were to rely solely on public goods to obtain sustenance. Olson concluded that such entities are viable only if they offer "selective incentives" to prospective members in exchange for their contributions toward the organization's public-good lobbying efforts. These inducements might include magazine subscriptions, group insurance, social gatherings, certification and training programs, and similar benefits from which the organization could effectively exclude noncontributors unless they pay dues and assessments. In Olson's formulation, a political organization's policy objectives are reduced to a secondary "by-product" of its members' and supporters' interests in obtaining personal material benefits. Despite his appealing analytical arguments, Olson's propositions were repeatedly challenged by empirical investigations of the incentive systems of real voluntary organizations. Members often respond to diverse inducements apart from personal material gains, including normative and purposive appeals and organizational lobbying for public goods (Moe 1980, pp. 201–231; Knoke 1988, 1990, pp. 123–140). For example, right-to-life organizations appeal to their supporters' religious, ideological, and emotional convictions about the illegitimacy of abortion and the necessity to take direct action to shut down clinics as well as to campaign on behalf of prolife politicians. The availability of picnics or T-shirts could hardly provide a compelling motivation for most participants in these groups. The internal economies of political organizations turn out to be more complex than originally believed. Organizational leaders have an important role in defining the conditions and prospects for their members and in persuading them to contribute to collective efforts that may run counter to the members' short-term personal interests.

The governance of political organizations is often posed as a choice between oligarchic or democratic alternatives. Persistent leadership and staff cliques in labor unions, trade associations, fraternal organizations, professional societies, and other types of associations are frequently interpreted as evidence of an inevitable "iron law of oligarchy." However, apart from labor unions (with their legal monopolies on occupational representation within certain industries), most voluntary groups are too dependent on their members for critical resources to enable officials to flout the memberships' interests in the long run. Consequently, most political organizations' constitutions provide for an array of democratic institutions, including competitive elections, membership meetings, referenda, and committee systems (Berry 1984, pp. 92–113; Knoke 1990, pp. 143–161). But actual practices of consulting members to formulate collective actions vary widely, and researchers have only begun to examine how the democratic control of political organizations shapes their capacities to mobilize their members for collective actions. The analytic task is further complicated by the complex interactions of formal governance processes with executive and leadership actions, bureaucratic administration, environmental conditions, and the internal economy of member incentives.

Political organizations serve a dual function for a political system. First, they aggregate the interests of citizens holding similar preferences, enabling them to press their demands on government officials more effectively. By articulating member demands and pooling the scarce resources of weak individuals, interest groups fashion a louder voice that is not readily dismissed by those in positions charged with public policy making. However, not all interests are created equal. Because higher-socioeconomic-status groups are more likely to join and participate in political organizations, the pressure-group system is biased against representing the views of less organized class, race, gender, and ethnic interests (Verba et al. 1995; Van Deth 1997). Second, political organizations provide public authorities with channels to communicate policy information and provide benefits to their electoral constituencies. Adroit politicians can manipulate public opinion to some degree by selectively targeting which interest groups will receive coveted access to present a case for modifications to pending policy decisions. Public officials and political organizations have a mutual interest in delivering policy successes that permit them both to survive to play the influence game again and again (Browne 1998, pp. 226–228). The fragmentation of political power among numerous policy arenas in the American federal system offers many aggrieved groups several institutional pressure points—legislatures; executive agencies; regulatory bodies; and courts at the local, state, and national levels—through which to raise their demands and promote their preferred solutions onto the public policy agenda for debate and resolution. This duality of political organizations at the interface between the state and its citizenry assures that the interest-group system exerts a crucial, if constitutionally ambiguous, impact on shaping many outcomes of collective political action.

Researchers have made substantial progress in uncovering the evolving techniques deployed by political organizations in lobbying public policy makers on specific issues (Schlozman and Tierney 1986, pp. 261–385; Knoke 1990, pp. 187–213; Baumgartner and Leech 1998, pp. 147–167). Campaign contributions and litigation are relatively rare methods, while contacting governmental officials (legislative, executive, regulatory), testifying at hearings, presenting research findings, and mobilizing their mass memberships are the most prevalent tactics. But mustering the appearance of grassroots support by hiring consultant firms and lobbying specialists to generate calls and letters may be quickly discredited as phony "astroturf" (Kollman 1998, pp. 157–160). The Internet and the World Wide Web are only the most recent technological innovations to be pressed into the interest-group battle. The impact of political money, primarily unlimited political action committee (PAC) "soft money" election campaign contributions, is a highly emotional topic. Some researchers conclude that a corrupt campaign financing system allows large corporations to enjoy disproportionate political access and influence (Clawson et al. 1998), while others see the corporate capacity to act in unison on political affairs as more problematic and conditional (Mizruchi 1992; Grier et al. 1994). All lobbying methods aim at gaining organizational access to policy makers by winning their attention, communicating with contacts about mutual information needs, and reinforcing for those targets the importance of continuing to pay attention to the organization's issues (Browne 1998, pp. 68–82). However, the precise conditions under which diverse lobbying tactics exert demonstrable impacts on policy decisions remain elusive.

One increasingly important strategy is collective action by a coalition of political organizations, often competing against an opposing coalition that advocates the contrary policy position. The organizational-state conceptualization of national policy domains emphasizes the shifting nature of short-term networks among organized interest groups mobilizing and coordinating their collective resources in campaigns to pass or defeat particular legislative proposals. The processes by which interorganizational communication networks generate collective action were examined in empirical studies of the U.S. national energy, health, agriculture, and labor policy domains (Laumann and Knoke 1987; Heinz et al. 1993), and in a comparison of U.S., German, and Japanese labor policy making (Knoke et al. 1996). European political scientists have been especially energetic in applying a policy network perspective to understanding how informal bargaining between interest groups and officials shapes policy outcomes in complex institutional settings (Peterson 1992; Verdier 1995).

Debates among European scholars about the organized representation of societal interests initially concentrated on corporatism as a distinctive form of interest intermediation. Although many definitions of corporatism and neocorporatism abound (Cox and O'Sullivan 1988), the dominant theme concerns how interest groups become incorporated into public policy-making processes through institutionalized access to the levers of state power rather than as seekers of intermittent influence and access that characterize fragmented, pluralist systems such as the United States (Baumgartner and Walker 1989). A corporatist arrangement involves explicit policy negotiations between state agencies and interest groups, followed by implementation of policy agreements through these political organizations, which enforce compliance by their members. The corporatist state takes a highly interventionist role by forming private sector "peak" (encompassing, nonvoluntary, monopolistic) interests groups; delegating to them quasi-public authority to determine binding public policy decisions; and brokering solutions to conflicts (Hirst 1995). In return for a stable share of power, privileged corporatist organizations are expected to discipline their members to accept the imposed policy decisions. Within national labor and other policy domains a closed tripartite network of state agencies, business, and labor organizations collaborates on solutions to such problems as workplace regulation and income distribution, and imposes these compromises on the society. Although much corporatist bargaining occurs primarily within the executive and regulatory sectors, the social partnership aspect of negotiated class conflicts should carry over into the parliamentary arena. The corporatist organizations representing capital, labor, and state interests jointly sponsor legislative proposals originated by agreement with the executive branch. Other interest groups are effectively excluded from participating in these corporatist agreements, resulting in a pattern of cumulative cleavages between them and the corporatist core. These disgruntled, excluded status groups are sources of new social movements against the corporatist monopolies; ecological, antinuclear, feminist, homeless, and immigrant groups are examples of these deprived segments.

This well-ordered corporatist framework seems to be breaking down as a result of the 1986 Single European Act that leads inexorably to an integrated internal market (Mazey and Richardson 1993; Fligstein and Mara-Drita 1996). Simultaneously, a "Europe of regions" is developing, with such areas as Scotland, Brittany, and the Basque country of Spain attaining formal representation and integration into European Union (EU) affairs. The Union is not yet a state, because it still lacks full sovereign power to make and enforce many types of decisions, particularly taxation. Rather, EU policy making is nonhierarchical, open, complex, conflictful, and unpredictable. With Brussels emerging as a supranational forum for resolving social, environmental, producer, and consumer conflicts, new forms of interest representation and lobbying are arising to tackle the expanding EU policy agenda. To varying degrees across different policy domains, the member states are steadily losing control over intergovernmental bargains, while "networks of actors . . . have become guardians of the policy agenda at the subsystemic level of EU governance, over which political controls are often weak or attenuated" (Peterson 1997, p. 7). In sum, the European Union is embarked on a huge, unforeseeable natural experiment that seems likely to transform traditional corporatist state-society relations into a system more closely resembling the "disjointed pluralism" of United States (Mazey and Richardson 1993, p. 24). The situation offers unbounded theoretical and research opportunities.

Despite occasional pessimistic appraisals that "interest-group studies have defined themselves into a position of elegant irrelevance" (Baumgartner and Leech 1998, p. xvii), research on political organizations is thriving at several levels of analysis, from the individual members to organizational political economies to the integration of societal interests into national and supranational polities. Analysts must exert greater effort to link these diverse focuses into a comprehensive explanation of interest organization behaviors situated within their sociopolitical environments. Especially promising avenues include developing formal models of rational social choice at the micro and macro levels; developing models of intra- and interorganizational exchange network; accounting for historical and institutional differences in interest representation processes across diverse national settings; and the functions of nongovernmental agencies (such as the World Health Organization) and pressure groups (such as Amnesty International) in the world system. Given the vastly expanded sociopolitical functions of modern states in all their permutations, a better understanding of the roles that political organizations play as developers, mediators, expresser, and manipulators of societal interests is indispensable.

(SEE ALSO: *Political Party Systems; Voluntary Associations*)

REFERENCES

Baumgartner, Frank R., and Beth L. Leech 1998 *Basic Interests: The Importance of Groups in Politics and in Political Science*. Princeton, N.J.: Princeton University Press.

Baumgartner, Frank R., and Jack L. Walker 1989 "Educational Policymaking and the Interest Group Structure in France and the United States." *Comparative Politics* 21:273–288.

Berry, Jeffrey M. 1984 *The Interest Group Society*. Boston: Little, Brown.

—— 1977 *Lobbying for the People: The Political Behavior of Public Interest Groups*. Princeton, N.J.: Princeton University Press.

Browne, William P. 1998 *Groups, Interests, and U.S. Public Policy*. Washington, D.C.: Georgetown University Press.

Clawson, Dan, Alan Neustadtl, and Mark Weller 1998 *Dollars and Votes: How Business Campaign Contributions Subvert Democracy*. Philadelphia: Temple University Press.

Cox, Andrew, and Noel O'Sullivan (eds.) 1988 *The Corporate State: Corporatism and the State Tradition in Western Europe*. Hants, England: Edward Elgar.

Fligstein, Neil, and Iona Mara-Drita 1996 "How to Make a Market: Reflections on the European Union's Single Market Program." *American Journal of Sociology* 102:1–34.

Gray, Virginia, and David Lowery 1996 *The Population Ecology of Interest Representation: Lobbying Communities in the American States*. Ann Arbor: University of Michigan Press.

Grier, Kevin B., Michael C. Munger, and Brian E. Roberts 1994 "The Determinants of Industry Political Activity, 1978–1986." *American Political Science Review* 88:911–926.

Heinz, John P., Edward O. Laumann, Robert L. Nelson, and Robert H. Salisbury 1993 *The Hollow Core: Private Interests in National Policymaking*. Cambridge, Mass.: Harvard University Press.

Hirst, Paul 1995 "Quangos and Democratic Government." *Parliamentary Affairs* 48:341–359.

Knoke, David 1990 *Organizing for Collective Action: The Political Economies of Associations*. New York: Aldine de Gruyter.

—— 1988 "Incentives in Collective Action Organizations." *American Sociological Review* 53 (June): 311–329.

——, Franz Urban Pappi, Jeffrey Broadbent, and Yutaka Tsujinaka 1996 *Comparing Policy Networks: Labor Politics in the U.S., Germany, and Japan*. New York: Cambridge University Press.

Kollman, Ken 1998 *Outside Lobbying: Public Opinion and Interest Group Strategies*. Princeton, N.J.: Princeton University Press.

Laumann, Edward O., and David Knoke 1987 *The Organizational State: A Perspective on the Social Organization of National Energy and Health Policy Domains*. Madison: University of Wisconsin Press.

Mazey, Sonia, and Jeremy Richardson 1993 "Introduction: Transference of Power, Decision Rules, and Rules of the Game." In Sonia Mazey and Jeremy Richardson, eds., *Lobbying in the European Community*. New York: Oxford University Press.

Mizruchi, Mark S. 1992 *The Structure of Corporate Political Action: Interfirm Relations and Their Consequences*. Cambridge: Harvard University Press.

Moe, Terry 1980 *The Organization of Interests: Incentives and the Internal Dynamics of Political Interest Groups*. Chicago: University of Chicago Press.

Olson, Mancur, Jr. 1965 *The Logic of Collective Action*. Cambridge: Harvard University Press.

Peterson, John 1997 "States, Societies and the European Union." *West European Politics* 20(4):1–23.

—— 1992 "The European Technology Community: Policy Networks in a Supranational Setting." In David Marsh and R. A. W. Rhodes, eds., *Policy Networks in British Government*. Oxford: Oxford University Press.

Salisbury, Robert H. 1994 "Interest Structures and Policy Domains: A Focus for Research." In William Crotty, Mildred A. Schwartz, and John C. Green, eds., *Representing Interests and Interest Group Representation*. Washington: University Press of America.

Schlozman, Kay L., and John T. Tierney 1986 *Organized Interests and American Democracy*. New York: Harper and Row.

Van Deth, Jan W. (ed.) 1997 *Private Groups and Public Life: Social Participation, Voluntary Associations and Political Involvement in Representative Democracies*. London: Routledge.

Verba, Sidney, Kay Lehman Schlozman, and Henry E. Brady 1995 *Voice and Equality: Civic Voluntarism in American Politics*. Cambridge, Mass.: Harvard University Press.

Verdier, Daniel 1995 "The Politics of Public Aid to Private Industry: The Role of Policy Networks." *Comparative Political Studies* 28:3–42.

Vogel, David 1996 *Kindred Strangers: The Uneasy Relationship between Politics and Business in America*. Princeton, N.J.: Princeton University Press.

Walker, Jack L. 1983 "The Origins and Maintenance of Interest Groups in America." *American Political Science Review* 77:390–406.

DAVID KNOKE

POLITICAL PARTY SYSTEMS

DEFINITIONS

Political parties have been defined both normatively, with respect to the preferences of the analyst, and descriptively, with respect to the activities in which parties actually engage. Normative definitions tend to focus on the representative or educational functions of parties. Parties translate citizens' preferences into policy and also shape citizens' preferences. Parties are characterized as "policy seeking." Thus, Lawson (1980) defines parties in terms of their role in linking levels of government to levels of society. She states, "Parties are seen, both by their members and by others, as agencies for forging links between citizens and policy-makers." Von Beyme (1985, p. 13) lists four "functions" that political parties generally fulfill: (1) the identification of goals (ideology and program); (2) the articulation and aggregation of social interests; (3) the mobilization and socialization of the general public within the system, particularly at elections; and (4) elite recruitment and government formation.

Descriptive definitions usually stay closer to Max Weber's observation that parties are organizations that attempt to gain power for their members, regardless of constituent wishes or policy considerations. Parties are characterized as "office seeking." "Parties reside in the sphere of power. Their action is oriented toward the acquisition of social power . . . no matter what its content may be" (Weber 1968, p. 938). Schumpeter ([1950] 1975) applies this type of definition to a democratic setting. He argues that parties are organizations

of elites who compete in elections for the right to rule for a period. Or as Sartori (1976, p. 63) puts it, "a party is any political group identified by an official label that presents at elections, and is capable of placing through elections (free or nonfree), candidates for public office."

The present article employs a descriptive definition but also investigates how well parties perform functions described in the normative definitions. Thus, a party system may be characterized as the array or configuration of parties competing for power in a given polity. The focus here will be almost exclusively on Western-style democracies.

ORIGINS

Von Beyme (1985) suggests three main theoretical approaches to explain the emergence of political parties: institutional theories, historical crisis situation theories, and modernization theories. (Also see LaPalombara and Weiner 1966.)

Institutional Theories. Institutional theories explain the emergence of parties as largely due to the way representative institutions function. Parties first emerge from opposing factions in parliaments. Continuity, according to such theories, gives rise to stable party constellations based on structured cleavages. These theories seem most relevant to countries with continuously functioning representative bodies, such as the United States, Britain, Scandinavia, Belgium, and the Netherlands. However, institutional theories do not explain developments well in some countries, such as France, because continuity of parliament has been absent, and the parliament's strength and independence has come repeatedly into question. The timing of the franchise is also relevant, but its effect is indeterminate because a party system has often been partly established before the franchise was fully extended. Moreover, liberal bourgeois parties that have helped establish parliamentary government have often been opposed to extending the franchise to the lower classes, while leaders such as Bismarck or Napoleon III have sometimes extended the franchise in nonparliamentary systems for tactical political reasons (von Beyme 1985, p. 16). Likewise, Lipset (1985, chap. 6) argues that a late and sudden extension of the franchise has sometimes contributed to working-class radicalism because the lower classes were not slowly integrated into an existing party system. Voting laws can also affect the structure of the party system. Single-member districts, with a first-past-the-post plurality winner, as in the United States and in Britain, are said to encourage a small number of parties and ideological moderation (competition for the center). National lists, with proportional representation (PR), are said to encourage multipartism (fractionalization) and ideological polarization. However, PR may have this effect only if it is implemented concurrently with the extension of the franchise, because already-established parties may otherwise be well entrenched and leave little room for the generation of new parties. Lijphart (1985) notes that voting laws may also affect other features of political life, such as voter turnout and efficacy or system legitimation, but that these effects have not been extensively investigated.

Crisis Theories. Critical junctures in a polity's history may generate new political tendencies or parties. Crisis theories are especially associated with the Social Science Research Council's (SSRC's) project on Political Development (e.g., LaPalombara and Weiner 1966; Grew 1978). According to SSRC scholars, five such crises can be identified in political development: the crises of national identity, state legitimacy, political participation, distribution of resources, and state penetration of society. The sequence in which these crises are resolved (if only temporarily) and the extent to which they may coincide can affect the emerging party system. Thus, Britain's well-spaced sequence contributed to the moderation of its party system. The recurrent piling up of crises in Germany from the mid-nineteenth century to the mid-twentieth century, and the attempt to solve problems with penetration (strong-state measures) contributed to the fragmentation, polarization, and instability of its party system. The piling up of all five crises in mid-nineteenth century America contributed to the emergence of the Republican Party—and the second party system. From a slightly different perspective, von Beyme (1985) notes three historical crisis points that have generated parties. First, the forces of nationalism and of integration during the nation-building process have often taken on roles as political parties. Second, party systems have been effected by breaks in legitimacy as a result of dynastic rivalries, as between Legitimists, Orleanists, and Bonapartists in mid-nineteenth

century France. Third, the collapse of parliamentary democracy to fascism has produced characteristic features in the party systems of post-authoritarian democracies: "a deep distrust of the traditional right; an attempt to unify the centre right; [and] a split on the left between the socialists and the Communists" (p. 19).

Modernization Theories. Some theories, following the tenets of structural functionalism, argue that "parties will not in fact materialize unless a measure of modernization has occurred" (LaPalombara and Weiner 1966). Modernization includes such factors as a market economy and an entrepreneurial class, acceleration of communications and transportation, increases in social and geographic mobility, increased education and urbanization, an increase in societal trust, and secularization. LaPalombara and Weiner argue that the emergence of parties requires one, or both, of two circumstances: citizens' attitudes may change, so that they come to perceive a "right to influence the exercise of power," or some group of elites or potential elites may aspire to gain or maintain power through public support. Clearly, not all elements of modernization are necessary, since the first party systems (in the United States and Britain) emerged in premodern, agrarian, and religious societies. Also, not all modernization theories are functionalist. Thus, Moore (1966) and others have suggested the emergence of a bourgeoisie increases the probability of the emergence of democracy.

Probably the most influential theory of the origins of party systems is by Lipset and Rokkan (1966) and Lipset (1983). While ostensibly anchored in Parsonsian functionalism, theirs is a comparative-historical approach that borrows from each of the categories listed here. According to Lipset and Rokkan, the contours of the party systems for western European states can be understood in the context of the specific outcomes of three historical episodes. The three crucial junctures are (1) the Reformation, "the struggle for the control of the ecclesiastical organizations within the national territory"; (2) the "Democratic Revolution," related to a conflict over clerical/secular control of education beginning with the French Revolution; and (3) the opposition between landed and the rising commercial interests in the towns early in the "Industrial Revolution." A significant fourth struggle between owners and workers emerges in the later stages of the Industrial Revolution. Lipset and Rokkan suggest that the shape of current party systems was largely determined during the stages of mass mobilization in the pre–World War I West.

Following Lipset and Rokkan, von Beyme (1985, pp. 23–24) lists ten types of parties that have emerged from this historical development: (1) liberals in conflict with the old regime, that is, in conflict with: (2) conservatives; (3) workers' parties against the bourgeois system (after c. 1848) and against left-wing socialist parties (after 1916); (4) agrarian parties against the industrial system; (5) regional parties against the centralist system; (6) Christian parties against the secular system; (7) communist parties against the social democrats (after 1916–1917) and anti-revisionist parties against "real Socialism"; (8) fascist parties against democratic systems; (9) protest parties in the petty bourgeoisie against the bureaucratic welfare state system (e.g., Poujadisme in France); (10) ecological parties against a growth-oriented society. No one country contains all ten sorts of parties, unless one includes splinter groups and small movements.

PARTY SYSTEMS AND SOCIETY

Even under a purely office-seeking definition, parties in a democracy must have some connection to society since they have to appeal to voters' material or ideal interests. Yet the connection between the party system and social structure or social values is rather weak in most countries—and much weaker than would be expected under a theory that sees parties as mediating between society and the state. In many cases, organizational or institutional factors may be much more important than social factors in determining party strength.

Social Cleavages. The party types listed above clearly have some connection to divisions or cleavages in society. Parties may seek to represent social classes, religious denominations, linguistic communities, or other particular interests. Three types of politically relevant social cleavages may be identified:

1. Positional cleavages correspond to a party supporter's place in the social structure. This may be an ascriptive position into which one is born, such as race, ethnicity, or gender, or it may be a social structural

position, such as social class or religious denomination, which one might be able to change in the course of a lifetime. Of course, the distinction between ascriptive and social structural position is not absolute, but may itself be partly determined by social norms. Also, against Marxist expectations, class determinants of party support are generally overshadowed by racial, ethnic, religious, regional, or linguistic determinants, when these are also present. One explanation for this finding is that, while one can split differences on class (especially monetary) policies, similar compromises are much more difficult where social "identity" is concerned.

2. "Behavioral" cleavages, especially membership, generally have a greater impact on party support than positional cleavages. Studies have shown that while working-class status is mildly correlated to support for leftist parties, union membership is quite strongly correlated. And while religious denomination is correlated to support for religious parties (e.g., Catholics and Christian Democrats in Germany), strength of belief or church attendance is much more strongly correlated.

3. Ideological cleavages are preferences, values, worldviews, and the like, which may not correspond entirely to one's position in society. Indeed, ideological orientations may overshadow positional cleavages as a determinant of partisan preferences. For instance, several of the ostensibly working-class communist parties of western Europe have traditionally drawn large percentages of their support from middle-class leftists.

Not all cleavages or issues that exist in a society are politically relevant at any given time, or if they are, they may not correspond to party support. One can distinguish between latent and actual cleavages around which politics are mobilized. Some cleavages may remain latent for a very long time before becoming politicized. For instance, women's issues had been relevant for decades before the "gender gap" emerged in the elections of the 1980s. One can also consider the process of politicization as a continuum that begins when a new social division or issue emerges, develops into a (protest) movement, then a politicized movement, and ends—at an extreme—with the creation of a new political party or the capture of an existing party. Of course, this process may be halted or redirected at any stage.

Party Loyalty and Party System Change: Alignment, Realignment, Dealignment. Parties may persist over time, and the party system alignment may be stable. There are several possible reasons for this:

1. The social cleavages around which a party was built may persist.

2. Voters may grow up in a stable party system and be socialized to support one or another party. Studies show that when a new cleavage line emerges in party alignment, it begins with the youngest generations. These generations then carry their new party loyalties with them throughout their lives, though perhaps to a decreasing extent if the events that originally motivated them fade over time. Likewise, older generations tend to resist alignments along newly emerging cleavage lines because they remain loyal to the parties they began to support in their own youth.

3. Parties may become organizationally entrenched and difficult to dislodge. Even if cleavages or issues emerge that cause voter dissatisfaction with existing parties, these parties may have the organizational resources to outmaneuver new movements or parties. They may be able to "steal" the new parties' issues and absorb or coopt their constituencies, or they may be able to stress other issues that distract voters from the new issues.

However, newly emerging cleavage structures may overwhelm these inertial tendencies. The party system may respond in three ways to new social cleavages. The first two are processes of party "realignment":

1. New parties may be formed to appeal to the new constituencies. A classical example is the emergence of the British Labour Party in the late nineteenth and early twentieth centuries when the Liberals and Conservatives did not pay sufficient attention to the concerns of the growing working classes. The more recent emergence of Green parties in some European countries is another example. The creation of the American Republican Party in the 1850s shows the explosive impact a new party can have: Lincoln's election precipitated the South's secession.

2. Existing parties may change their policies to appeal to new constituencies. For instance, existing parties seem now to be in the process of killing the European Greens by adopting their issues. Perhaps the best example of this process is found in American history. Bryan's Democrats moved to absorb the Populist Party, and Al Smith's and Franklin Roosevelt's Democrats moved to absorb the growing urban ethnic constituencies (Burnham 1970; Chambers and Burnham 1975).

3. If neither of these changes occurs, there may be a period of "dealignment" in which much of the population—especially new constituencies—is alienated from all parties, and turnout or political participation declines. New constituencies may organize themselves into pressure groups or social movements that fail either to form new parties or to capture existing parties. Existing parties may become internally more heterogeneous and polarized, single-issue actions may proliferate, referenda may increase, and citizen action groups may simply bypass parties. Scholars since the mid-1960s have debated whether Western polities are going through a period of realignment or dealignment (Dalton et al. 1984). Of course, both processes may be occurring: dealignment may be a way-station on the road to party realignment.

STRUCTURAL FEATURES

Certain structural features of the party system may be important independently of parties' connections to society.

Representativeness. The electoral system determines how votes are translated into seats in the legislature. The results can vary widely. At one extreme, a system of proportional representation

(PR) with a single national list enables even tiny parties to get representatives into the legislature. Thus, if 100 parties each received 1 percent of the vote, each would receive 1 seat in a 100-seat legislature. Such systems put no obstacles in the way of party system fragmentation. At the other extreme, first-past-the-post plurality voting with single-member constituencies tends to overrepresent larger parties and underrepresent smaller parties. Thus, if party A won 40 percent of the vote in every district, and parties B and C each won 30 percent of the vote in every district, party A would get all the seats in the legislature, and parties B and C would get none at all. Such systems discourage party system fragmentation. Still, regionally concentrated minority parties tend to be less underrepresented than minority parties whose support is spread across all districts. If 100 parties were completely concentrated in each of 100 districts, the electoral system could not prevent fragmentation. Some election systems combine features. German voters have two votes, one for a district candidate and one for a party list. If any candidate receives a majority in his or her district, that candidate gets a seat. The remaining seats are allocated proportionately according to the list votes. Furthermore, a party must receive at least 5 percent of the national vote to get any seats from the list portion. This system attempts to reduce party system fragmentation and at the same time to reduce overrepresentation and underrepresentation. It was once thought that PR reduces government stability and endangers democracy. However, recent research gives little support for this proposition: "electoral systems are not of overriding importance in times of crisis and even less in ordinary times" (Taagepera and Shugart 1989, p. 236).

Volatility. Party system volatility, or fluctuations in electoral strength, encompasses several different processes (Dalton et al. 1984; Crewe and Denver 1985). It includes the gross and net flow of voters between parties, as well as into and out of the electorate because of maturity, migration, death, and abstention. It also includes realignment and dealignment: changes in the electoral alignment of various constituencies, and the overall weakening of party attachments. Scholars have long debated whether electoral volatility contributed to the collapse of democracies in the 1930s, especially the mobilization of first-time or previously alienated voters. Recently, Zimmermann and Saalfeld (1988) concluded that volatility encouraged democratic collapse in some, but not all, countries. Studies also show that most postwar antidemocratic "surge" parties draw support disproportionately from voters who are weakly attached to parties or weakly integrated in politically mobilized subcultures such as labor, religious, or ethnic organizations. Yet volatility and protest do not always flow in an antidemocratic direction. On the contrary, they are also normal components of democratic politics. Few would argue that the New Deal realignment harmed American democracy or that most new-left or ecology movements are antidemocratic. In order for volatility to cause trouble for democracy, it must be accompanied by antidemocratic sentiments. Indeed, massive vote switching among *democratic* parties may be the best hope for *saving* democracy during a crisis. Everything depends on the propensity of voters to support antidemocratic parties.

Fragmentation. In the wake of World War II, some scholars argued that the fragmentation of party systems, partly caused by proportional representation, contributed to the collapse of European democracies. In a fragmented party system, they argued, there are too many small parties for democratic representation and effective government. Citizens are confused and alienated by the large array of choices. Because parties have to form coalitions to govern, voters' influence over policy is limited, and they become further disenchanted with democracy. With so many small parties, governing coalitions can be held hostage to the wishes of very minor parties. Empirical studies show some support for these theses. Fragmentation is associated with reduced confidence in government and satisfaction with democracy. Governments in fragmented party systems tend to be unstable, weak, and ineffective in addressing major problems. However, other scholars argue that party-system fragmentation is not the main culprit. Fragmentation contributes to problems, but other factors are more important. Since fragmented party systems are often composed of blocs of parties (as in, e.g., the Netherlands and Italy), voters have less difficulty reading the terrain than alleged. Besides, party system polarization may contribute to governmental instability and ineffectiveness more than to fragmentation. Scholars have looked at this possibility in both the interwar period and the postwar period. While the evidence is not overwhelming, it tends to support the thesis.

Polarization. Sartori's model of "polarized pluralism" (1966, 1976) is the most influential account of party system polarization. In a polarized party system, according to Sartori, a large (but not majority) party governs more or less permanently in unstable coalitions with various other parties. At least one extremist (antisystem) party is in quasi-permanent opposition. Extremist parties are sufficiently unacceptable to others that they cannot form alternative coalitions, but they are strong enough to block alternative coalitions that do not include themselves. Sartori argues that this leads to stagnation and corruption at the center, frustration and radicalization at the periphery, and instability among governing coalitions. He cites Weimar Germany, Fourth Republic France, and contemporary Italy as examples. Much empirical evidence supports Sartori's model. Polarization is associated with illiberal values in postauthoritarian democracies such as West Germany, Austria, Italy, and Spain.

The dynamic may also work in reverse. When intolerant and distrustful relations among political actors were institutionalized by constitutional guarantees in some postauthoritarian countries, they became crystallized in a polarized party system. Cross-national research shows that polarization harms other aspects of democracy, as well. Polarization is negatively related to democratic legitimation and trust in government, and is positively associated with cabinet instability. However, other elements of Sartori's model have been disputed. In particular, studies in the early 1980s of Italy—the model's current exemplar—called into question Sartori's claim that polarized pluralism generates extremism and thus harms democracy. These studies claimed that the Italian Communists had moderated and that the centrist Christian Democrats had become less intolerant of them. However, the studies' own evidence were not entirely persuasive, and subsequent developments—while not reversing course—do not present a decisive break with earlier patterns.

COALITIONS

Single-party government in Western democracies is relatively rare (Laver and Schofield 1990). The multiparty systems of most countries necessitates coalition government. Even in two-party America, a president and Congress of different parties produce a kind of coalition government. (Indeed, internal party discipline is so weak in America, as well as in some parties in Italy, Japan, and other countries, that one can characterize parties themselves as coalitions of political actors.) Most work on coalition government attempts to predict which parties get into office. One of the most influential theories predicts that "minimum connected winning" (MCW) will form most often. This theory combines office-seeking and policy-seeking approaches, predicting that parties will form bare-majority coalitions (so that the spoils can be divided among the smallest number of winners) among contiguous parties on the ideological dimension (so that there is not too much disagreement about policy). MCW theory succeeds fairly well in predicting coalitions in unidimensional party systems, but less well in multidimensional systems, which are often fragmented, polarized, and/or based on rather heterogeneous societies. Likewise, research suggests that in unidimensional systems, offices are most often allocated among the winning parties proportionately to their electoral strength. In multidimensional systems, however, offices are allocated less according to parties' electoral strength than according to their "bargaining" strength, that is, how much they are needed to complete the majority. Thus, if three parties won 45 percent, 10 percent, and 45 percent of the vote, the small party would have just as much bargaining strength as either of the larger parties.

Research also shows that party-system fragmentation and polarization and the presence of antisystem parties all contribute to cabinet instability. Theorists have sometimes posited that cabinet instability leads to instability of democracy—that it may reduce governments' capacity to solve problems effectively, and that this may reduce the regime's legitimacy. Yet research gives only mixed support for this conjecture. Investigators have found that cabinet instability tends to depress the electorate's evaluation of "the way democracy works," but its effects on other measures of democratic legitimation and confidence in government are inconsistent. Research on contemporary democracies shows that cabinet instability is related to civil disorder and governmental ineffectiveness. But research on the period between the world wars indicates that cabinet instability cannot be definitely tied to the collapse of democracy. Cabinets in France and Belgium were as unstable as those in Germany and Austria, but only the latter democracies collapsed (British and Dutch cabinets were more stable). Why is cabinet instability not more clearly tied to problems for democracy? One possibility is that cabinet instability simply reflects the severity of problems. Just as electoral volatility may reflect citizens' desire for change, cabinet instability may reflect elites' flexible response to the problems. Neither of these need reflect a desire for a regime change, simply for a policy change. Indeed, cabinet *immobility* might be more damaging to effectiveness and democratic legitimation if problems are severe enough. In this respect, cabinet instability, like electoral volatility, probably has an indeterminate effect on democratic survival.

Oversized grand-coalition governments also have ambiguous effects on liberal democracy. The most important theory is Lijphart's (1977, 1984) model of "consociational democracies," plural societies with high levels of intercommunal conflict. In such polities, parties are unwilling to go into opposition because they risk losing too much and because party strength—closely tied to the size of the ascriptive communities—changes too slowly to make their return to office likely. Thus, formal opposition could lead to more extreme conflict. The alternative is a grand coalition government of all major parties, combined with a degree of federalism and proportional allocation of state services according to party or community size. Since potential conflict is too dangerous, open opposition is delegitimated and suppressed. In this respect, consociational procedures are intended to be a method for *reducing* extreme underlying intercommunal conflict through contact among opponents (at the elite level), which promotes trust. If these measures succeed, the "game among players" can move to one in which moderate conflict and tolerance of opponents becomes legitimated. This appears to have succeeded in the Netherlands and Austria, and failed most miserably in Lebanon. On the other hand, if grand coalitions are formed in societies *without* extreme underlying conflict, they may *initiate* a vicious circle of intolerance and delegitimation. To form a grand coalition, prosystem parties generally move closer to the center of the policy spectrum than

they would otherwise do. This move may leave their more militant (but still prosystem) constituents politically homeless, and they may seek harder positions in a more extremist party or movement. These constituents do not so much abandon their party as the party abandons them. Thus, if a grand coalition submerges a moderate competitive structure, it can generate polarization. The grand coalition government of 1966–1969 in West Germany, a country with little intercommunal conflict, was probably largely responsible for the rise of antisystem voting at the time. If the grand coalition government had not ended fairly quickly, it might have caused serious problems for West German democracy.

RESEARCH DEVELOPMENTS IN THE 1990s

Research on political parties and party systems has continued to stream unabated in the 1990s, yet many of the basic principles outlined above continue to hold true. Three important research areas may be mentioned. First, scholars have sought to understand the role of party systems in democratization, especially in central and eastern Europe, but in other regions as well. Second, the study of political extremism has been knit more closely with the study of party systems. Third, recent stock taking in the field of political legitimation has highlighted the importance of party systems.

The "third wave" of democratization, beginning with transitions in southern Europe in the mid-1970s, and continuing with transitions in Latin America, East Asia, and central and eastern Europe, is one of the most important social and political developments of the last quarter of the twentieth century. Scholars seeking explanations for the relative success or failure of democratic transition and, especially, consolidation have generally highlighted the importance of well-functioning party systems. Thus, Huntington (1991, chap. 6) argues that party-system polarization is one of the greatest hazards to democratization (also see Di Palma 1990; Lipset 1994). Theorists of democratic transitions have pointed to the importance of "pacting" between authoritarian-regime softliners and democratic-opposition moderates, and to the exclusion of regime hard-liners and antiregime extremists (O'Donnell and Schmitter 1986; Karl and Schmitter 1991). The importance of moderation during the transition period, prior to the legalization of a party system, parallels the importance of moderation of a party system within an existing democracy (Weil 1989). Empirical studies of democratization in Latin America (Remmer 1991), Central and Eastern Europe (Fuchs and Roller 1994; Toka 1996; Wessels and Klingemann 1994), and East Asia (Shin 1995) tend to support this thesis—as do general, comparative treatments of democratization (Linz and Stepan 1996).

The study of political extremism has taken party systems into account more fully in the 1990s than had perhaps previously been the case. Earlier studies often characterized extremism in terms of psychological predispositions, socialization, or economic dislocations. These accounts tended to focus on personal distress—sometimes in absolute terms, but sometimes in terms of reference groups and relative deprivation—and were often couched in functionalist theories of social dislocation in the course of social modernization. A later wave of extremism research focused more on resource mobilization within social movements. It was not deprivation (absolute or relative) that created extremism, according to this view, but the ability to organize. A third wave of extremism research has emphasized political "opportunity space," gaps or niches in the opposition structure, which political entrepreneurs can fill if they are skillful. Extremism often arises not so much because conditions have worsened, nor because groups have newly organized, as because existing parties within the party system have vacated certain ideological positions and opened competitive opportunities or niches for extremists. Mainstream parties may vacate these niches because they enter or leave office, or because they feel they need to compete more effectively with another party. The reader will notice that it is not so much that these three accounts contradict each other as that they are nested, with the first most specific and the last most general. Perhaps the most important recent study of right-wing extremism in Western polities is Kitschelt and McGann (1995). Other useful recent collections of essays include Weil (1996) and McAdam and colleagues (1996).

Studies of legitimation, confidence, and trust continue to attend to the effects of parties and party systems. Recent surveys of the literature show that party systems do not always or uniformly have an influence, but when they do, a moderate opposition structure is most conducive to these forms of political support. Polarization, grand coalitions, and "cohabitation" ("divided government" in America) do not tend to promote legitimation, confidence, and trust (see Fuchs et al. 1995; Listhaug 1995; Listhaug and Wiberg 1995).

Finally, a few recent general contributions to the literature may be listed. Important recent books that bring the field up to date include Ware (1996) and Mair (1997). Also, a new journal devoted to political parties and party systems, *Party Politics*, from Sage Publications, began publication in 1995 and has become a major outlet for scholarship in this field.

REFERENCES

Burnham, Walter Dean 1970 *Critical Elections and the Mainsprings of American Politics*. New York: Norton.

Chambers, William Nisbet, and Walter Dean Burnham (eds.) 1975 *The American Party Systems*, 2nd ed. New York: Norton.

Crewe, Ivor, and David Denver (eds.) 1985 *Electoral Change in Western Democracies: Patterns and Sources of Electoral Volatility*. New York: St. Martin's.

Dalton, Russell J., Stephen C. Flanagan, and Paul A. Beck 1984 *Electoral Change in Advanced Industrial Democracies*. Princeton, N.J.: Princeton University Press.

Di Palma, Giuseppe 1990 *To Craft Democracies: An Essay on Democratic Transitions*. Berkeley: University of California Press.

Fuchs, Dieter, Giovanna Guidorossi, and Palle Svensson 1995 "Support for the Democratic System." In H. D. Klingemann and D. Fuchs, eds., *Citizens and the State*. New York: Oxford University Press.

Fuchs, Dieter, and Edeltraud Roller 1994 "Cultural Conditions of the Transformation to Liberal Democracies in Central and Eastern Europe," WZB Discussion Paper FS III 94-202. Wissenschaftszentrum Berlin, Berlin.

Grew, Raymond (ed.) 1978 *Crises of Political Development in Europe and the United States*. Princeton, N.J.: Princeton University Press.

Huntington, Samuel P. 1991 *The Third Wave: Democratization in the Late Twentieth Century*. Norman: University of Oklahoma Press.

Karl, Terry Lynn, and Philippe C. Schmitter 1991 "Modes of Transition in Latin America, Southern and Eastern Europe." *International Social Science Journal* 128:269–284.

Kitschelt, Herbert, and Anthony J. McGann 1995 *The Radical Right in Western Europe: A Comparative Analysis*. Ann Arbor: University of Michigan Press.

La Palombara, Joseph, and Myron Weiner (eds). 1966 *Political Parties and Political Development*. Princeton, N.J.: Princeton University Press.

Laver, Michael, and Norman Schofield 1990 *Multiparty Government. The Politics of Coalition in Europe*. New York: Oxford University Press.

Lawson, Kay (ed.) 1980 *Political Parties and Linkage*. New Haven, Conn.: Yale University Press.

Lijphart, Arend 1977 *Democracy in Plural Societies*. New Haven, Conn.: Yale University Press.

—— 1984 *Democracies: Patterns of Majoritarian and Consensus Government in Twenty-One Countries*. New Haven, Conn.: Yale University Press.

—— 1985 "The Field of Electoral Systems Research: A Critical Survey." *Electoral Studies* 4:3–14.

Linz, Juan J., and Alfred Stepan 1996 *Problems of Democratic Transition and Consolidation: Southern Europe, South America, and Post-Communist Europe*. Baltimore: Johns Hopkins University Press.

Lipset, Seymour Martin 1983 "Radicalism or Reformism: The Sources of Working-Class Politics." *American Political Science Review* 77:1–18.

—— 1994 "The Social Requisites of Democracy Revisited." *American Sociological Review* 59:1–22.

——, and Stein Rokkan (eds.) 1967 "Cleavage Structures, Party Systems and Voter Alignments." In Seymour Lipset and Stein Rokkan *Party Systems and Voter Alignments*. New York: Free Press.

Listhaug, Ola 1995 "The Dynamics of Trust in Politicians." In H. D. Klingemann and D. Fuchs, eds., *Citizens and the State*. New York: Oxford University Press.

——, and Matti Wiberg 1995 "Confidence in Political and Private Institutions." In H. D. Klingemann and D. Fuchs, eds., *Citizens and the State*. New York: Oxford University Press.

McAdam, Doug, John D. McCarthy, and Mayer N. Zald 1996 *Comparative Perspectives on Social Movements: Political Opportunities, Mobilizing Structures, and Cultural Framings*. New York: Cambridge University Press.

Mair, Peter 1997 *Party System Change: Approaches and Interpretations*. New York: Oxford University Press.

Moore, Barrington, Jr. 1966 *Social Origins of Dictatorship and Democracy*. Boston: Beacon.

O'Donnell, Guillermo, and Philippe C. Schmitter 1986 *Transitions from Authoritarian Rule: Tentative Conclusions about Uncertain Democracies*. Baltimore: Johns Hopkins University Press.

Remmer, Karen L. 1991 "The Political Impact of Economic Crisis in Latin America in the 1980s." *American Political Science Review* 85:777–800.

Sartori, Giovanni 1966 "European Political Parties: The Case of Polarized Pluralism." In Joseph LaPalombara and Myron Weiner, eds., *Political Parties and Political Development*. Princeton: Princeton University Press.

—— 1976 *Parties and Party Systems: A Framework for Analysis*. Cambridge: Cambridge University Press.

Schumpeter, Joseph (1950) 1975 *Capitalism, Socialism and Democracy*. New York: Harper Colophon.

Shin, Doh Chull 1995 "The Democratization of Korean Politics and Culture in Progress and Repose: Public Opinion Survey Findings, 1988–1994." Paper presented at the International Conference, 50 Years of Korean Independence, 50 Years of Korean Politics. Sponsored by the Korena Political Science Association, Seoul.

Taagepera, Rein, and Matthew Soberg Shugart 1989 *Seats and Votes. The Effects and Determinants of Electoral Systems*. New Haven, Conn.: Yale University Press.

Toka, Gabor 1996 "Parties and Electoral Choices in East-Central Europe." In G. Pridham and P. G. Lewis, eds., *Stabilising Fragile Democracies: Comparing New Party Systems in Southern and East Europe*. London: Routledge.

von Beyme, Klaus 1985 *Political Parties in Western Democracies*. Gower, Wales: Aldershot.

Ware, Alan 1996 *Political Parties and Party Systems*. New York: Oxford University Press.

Weber, Max 1968 *Economy and Society*. Berkeley: University of California Press.

Weil, Frederick D. 1989 "The Sources and Structure of Legitimation in Western Democracies: A Consolidated Model Tested with Time-Series Data in Six Countries since World War II." *American Sociological Review* 54:682–706.

—— 1996 *Research on Democracy and Society: Volume 3, Extremism, Protest, Social Movements, and Democracy*. Greenwich, Conn.: JAI.

Wessels, Bernhard, and Hans Dieter Klingemann 1994 "Democratic Transformation and the Prerequisites of Democratic Opposition in East and Central Europe," Working Paper FS III 94-201. Wissenschaftszentrum Berlin für Sozialforschung, Berlin.

Zimmermann, Ekkart, and Thomas Saalfeld 1988 "Economic and Political Reactions to the World Economic Crisis of the 1930s in Six European Countries." *International Studies Quarterly* 32:305–334.

FREDERICK D. WEIL

POLITICAL SOCIOLOGY

Two distinct but converging intelllectual traditions have defined the field of political sociology: the social stratification tradition pioneered by Karl Marx and Frederick Engels; and the organizational tradition originated by Max Weber and Robert Michels (Lipset 1981). In the first, political sociology is defined broadly as the study of social power in all institutional sectors of society with a primary emphasis on the state and its structural roots in the class system. This tradition takes a holistic view of social structure and change, arguing that the class system determines the organization of the state and political action. The state is conceived as the institutional structure whose central function is maintaining the social order and is thus examined in terms of its functions. The second tradition defines political sociology more narrowly in terms of the organization of political groups and political leadership with primary emphasis on the structure of the state and the groups that compete for control over the state. The state is conceived as the legitimate monopoly on the means of violence. This approach emphasizes the informal and formal organization of political parties, interest groups and social movements, their links to the governmental bureaucracy and formal centers of policy making, the legitimating myths that are used to justify the system of rule, the organization of the legal system, and the sources and impact of public opinion, including the organization of the mass media and electoral politics.

As societies modernize and become more complex, it becomes increasingly difficult to distinguish these two traditions. Institutions become more complex and differentiated, thus developing their own distinctive autonomy while at the same time being shaped by the larger system of power. In response, analysts have blended these approaches together, synthesizing arguments drawn from the competing perspectives. We begin with a brief summary of the classic ideas and their bearing on contemporary work and then examine attempts to integrate these approaches.

KARL MARX AND THE THEORY OF THE STATE

Karl Marx and Frederick Engels developed two distinct theories of the state: an instrumental theory; and a structuralist argument (Carnoy 1979). In the first, the state is a tool or instrument of the dominant class, used to protect the property system and impose order through force and ideological manipulation. The dominant class is a ruling class, meaning that it simultaneously dominates the economy and the political system. This class is socially cohesive and politically unified, which gives it direct control over the state. The state is the institutionalization of power or, to draw on Max Weber's conception (1947), the legitimate monopoly on the means for force in society and, as a tool of the upper class, consolidates upper-class power by force and fraud.

In the contemporary period, this argument inspired Mills's theory of the "power elite" (1956), defined in terms of the cohesive leadership group that unifies the corporate rich, the political directorate, and the military elite, as well as Domhoff's theory of business dominance (1979, 1990, 1998) and Useems's inner-circle thesis (1984). In these arguments, the capitalist class is seen as socially cohesive—integrated through exclusive private clubs, prep schools and universities, debutante balls, and interlocking corporate directorships. These networks create an inner-circle leadership group that controls the largest multinational corporations and is central to these various networks. Domhoff (1998) argues that this upper class rules through four processes: (1) policy planning in which leading inner-circle-controlled policy organizations, such as the Business Roundtable, the U.S. Chamber of Commerce, and the Brookings Institution, develop the major policy proposals that are eventually adopted; (2) campaign contributions that select the candidates for electoral office (Clawson et al. 1992); (3) special-interest lobbying for specific firms and industries; and (4) ideological control through publicity campaigns that control the political agenda and mold public opinion so as to minimize opposition. Thus the ruling class constitutes an organized leadership group with considerable cohesion and political unity.

Marx and Engels also advanced a structural theory of state, treating it as the autonomous product of class struggles. Thus, in his essay *The Eighteeth Brumaire of Louis Bonaparte* ([1852] 1964), Marx argued that the political development of the working-class movement combined with disorganization and internal conflicts within the ruling class led to a military dictatorship. The capitalist class was too divided to rule directly and thus had to be protected by a military dictator. Extending this argument, Neumann (1942) explained the rise of fascist dictatorship in Germany during the 1930s in terms of a combination of working-class mobilization, a disorganized bourgeoisie and strong autocratic political traditions. Drawing on Gramsci's ideas about the "modern prince" of modern bourgeois civil society (1957), Poulantzas (1973) advanced a structuralist theory of the state, arguing that market competition disorganizes the capitalist class, requiring that the state operate as a "relatively autonomous" institution that organizes the capitalist class into a hegemonic bloc while disorganizing the working class. Critics have pointed out that this functionalist argument lacks a specific mechanism for class rule (Skocpol 1981). In response, Offe (1984) and Block (1987) argued that in capitalism the state is barred from entering profit-making enterprise, which makes state managers structurally dependent on capitalists to make investments and thereby create employment, taxes, and economic growth. State managers are thus structurally pressured to create capital accumulation and act autonomously to promote reforms that rationalize and stabilize the capitalist system.

Thus the stratification tradition has gradually incorporated arguments from the organizational tradition, focusing on leadership groups and the autonomy of political institutions. By conceiving political institutions as independent but structurally dependent on the capitalist economy, these analysts have synthesized Marxian arguments with organizational arguments. Still this position has been subjected to several criticisms. First is that social stratification is not primarily a question of class but one of prestige and exclusionary social practices (Weber 1947; Parkin 1979). As Weber (1947) argued, classes are defined by their market position, which rarely provides sufficient cohesion for successful political mobilization. Status groups,

in contrast, are based on shared values and a code of honor, thus readily mobilizing for political action. Thus the political struggle over the state is typically not about class but about the lifestyles and prestige of status communities. Second, political institutions have their own autonomous logic and interests, operating independent of the interests and action of classes and other organized groups. Thus Michels ([1911] 1962) argued that formal organization creates oligarchic leadership which is able to divert political organizations from their official goals to promoting the interests of the permanent staff. Similarly, Weber (1947) argued that rational-legal authority and bureaucratic organization tend to replace traditional and charismatic rule, thus creating the "iron cage" of the modern bureaucratic state. Both arguments underscore the independent importance of political organizations, to which we now turn.

MAX WEBER, ROBERT MICHELS, AND THE ORGANIZATIONAL APPROACH

The second major approach is rooted in the work of Weber and Michels as well as the classic elite theorists Gaetano Mosca ([1896] 1939) and Vilfredo Pareto ([1935] 1963). Their core argument is that rule by the few (or the elite) is inevitable. This is due to the scarcity of leadership talent, the psychological need of masses for leadership, and the imperatives of complex organization. The central political question, then, is not the elimination of a ruling class or the creation of a classless society but the institutional mechanisms that regulate elite recruitment and the effectiveness of various formulas for legitimating elite rule. Thus Michels's thesis about the "iron law of oligarchy" ([1911] 1961) took as its primary target the German Social Democratic Party (SPD), contending that, despite its formal goal of promoting working-class democracy and internationalism, the SPD was in fact controlled by the permanent staff who used it to promote their own careers and positions. This proved prescient when, a few years later, the SPD rallied to the autocratic German Kaiser to support World War I against the French working class. Similarly, Weber's arguments about the "iron cage" of bureaucracy (1947) were borne out by the creation of the Soviet Union which created a highly rationalized political economy more oppressive than any in western Europe. It thus came to dominate human conduct independent of its formal goals. In a similar vein, Mosca ([1896] 1939) and Pareto ([1935] 1963) argued that participatory or "direct" democracy is not feasible and that, at its core, modern democracy is a system for institutionalizing elite turnover by requiring that elites peacefully compete for popular support in competitive elections. Thus democracy is really a system for selecting among competing elites and thus reducing the risks of incompetent hereditary leaders and violent struggles for power. It also legitimizes the system by encouraging mass to assume that they have a say in their rulers and thus contributes to political stability.

Schumpter (1942) developed this further into the pluralist theory of democracy, arguing that by forcing candidates to compete for popular votes in elections with multiple political parties, providing adult suffrage, and protecting rights to speech and assembly, modern representative democracy also disperses power and creates a degree of popular accountability. Electoral competition means that elites have to mobilize popular support and thus respond to public concerns. Dahl (1957, 1982) and Rose (1968) argued that this creates a countervailing power system that ensures that all significant groups have a voice and a vehicle for countering more powerful groups. In this vein, Duverger (1962) shows that electoral rules determine the number and type of political parties. Majoritarian systems with single-member districts and "winner-take-all" elections (e.g., the United States and Britain) create two-party systems with nonideological parties because voters are unwilling to throw away their ballots to support third parties. Proportional systems that allocate legislative seats based on their proportion to the popular vote create multiple ideological parties. This, in turn, creates different opportunities for political expression with majoritarian systems experiencing more protest and conflict because they are less responsive while proportional systems have greater governmental instability due to the number and contentiousness of political parties (Powell 1982).

This pluralist thesis has come under several criticisms. First, competitive elections and rules protecting freedom of association and speech do not counteract the institutional bias of politics. Thus Schattschneider (1960) argued that the interest groups and parties in the United States overwhelmingly represent the upper class. Business and the professions are well represented, while workers, consumers, and disadvantaged groups are weakly represented (Schlozman and Tierney 1986; Berry 1997; Form 1995). Second, pluralist institutions provide no guarantee that disadvantaged groups will be able to mobilize and secure access to the system (Gamson 1975; Piven and Cloward 1979). Thus McAdam (1982) and Jenkins (1985) show that movements on behalf of African-Americans and farm workers were politically blocked by their upper-class opponents until the 1960s, when electoral realignments and increased resources for these groups allowed them to successfully mobilize. Thus political opportunities for the excluded and disorganized are historically variable and by no means institutionally guaranteed. Third is the organizational argument that oligarchy undermines the responsiveness of political parties and interest groups to their supporters (Schattschneider 1960; McConnell 1966). Thus, despite a plurality of organizations, these are internally autocratic and largely unresponsive to member interests.

Arguing that pluralists and stratification theorists share a similar "society-centered" approach, "state-centered" analysts have analyzed the role of state managers as autonomous agents of political change (Nordlinger 1981; Evans et al. 1985; Skocpol and Amenta 1986). Thus, instead of being the tools of special-interest groups (pluralism) or of the upper class and class struggles (neo-Marxism), these state managers independently develop policies that promote their ideological visions and politico-administrative interests. This ability is rooted in the growing autonomy and resources of the state, which is becoming more rationalized and more central to contemporary political economies. Bureaucracy and professionalization insulate government agencies from outside control, thus making them more independent. Because many policies are responses to problems that have previously been addressed, policy precedents have a strong positive feedback effect on the development of new policies. Thus the greater the policy development and administrative capacities of governmental bodies, the greater the ability of state managers to initiate rationalizing reforms (Finegold and Skocpol 1995; Amenta 1998).

This perspective (also called "historical institutionalism" [Skocpol and Campbell 1995]) is a useful corrective to society-centered theories. It shares with classic elite theory the idea that policy making can be independent of societal constraint, and it develops the idea of state capacities. It has been criticized, however, for overemphasizing the autonomy of state managers and failing to specify the conditions under which political institutions are autonomous (Domhoff 1996). In response, Amenta (1998) has synthesized state-centered arguments with resource mobilization theory (Tilly 1978; McAdam 1982; Jenkins 1983) to explain how political institutions mediate the impact of social movements on policy change. Likewise, Finegold and Skocpol (1995) show how political leaders during the New Deal mobilized business support for their policies but also became dependent on business leaders. Some contend that this perspective applies better to the more rationalized stronger states in western Europe and Japan, where state managers and coordinated corporatist bargaining have been central to post–World War II economic policy (Schmitter 1981; Katzenstein 1985). The United States is a strong case for capitalist dominance, thus supporting the stratification approach, while other states display stronger state institutions and thus support the organizational approach.

POSSIBILITIES FOR SYNTHESIS

Since both traditions have proved useful, several have attempted to synthesize them. One approach has been treating these theories contextually, arguing that each theory bears in particular settings or with specific aspects of political change. Thus Laumann and Knoke (1987) argue that some policy arenas are organized pluralistically with multiple competing groups and considerable fluidity, while others are more centralized with a smaller number of actors and a more hierarchical relationship among them. Thus they compare the more pluralistic health care arena with the more centralized field of energy policy. Similarly, Dye (1995) argues that pluralism better explains patterns of elite recruitment while a hierarchical "power elite" model better explains decision making. The challenge for such a contextual synthesis is to develop a rationale for the conditions under which neo-Marxist, pluralist, and state-centered arguments are relevant.

A second approach is to integrate these arguments into a more comprehensive theoretical framework. Lukes (1974) and Alford and Friedland (1985) have advanced a multidimensional theory of political power that conceptually integrates these perspectives. The starting point is Weber's classic conception of power as the ability to secure one's will against that of others even if against their resistance (1947). Thus power is always relational, involving interactions among at least two or more parties. It is also hierarchical, in the sense that one party or group is stronger or controls the other. It is also a potential or capacity. History shows that power is often based on force—whether physical or psychological coercion—but that such force is inherently unstable. No society can be organized solely on the basis of force because, at the first opportunity, people will break the rules. Terror is not only unstable but also inefficient. Thus power holders attempt to institutionalize their power; that is, they try to make it more stable by being seen by subordinates as legitimate. Authority is power that is widely perceived by subordinates as fair and just, and thus is more likely to be stable. Manipulated authority is power that power holders have attempted to legitimize by controlling information and creating false images among subordinates. Authentic authority is freely accepted by subordinates as fair and just (Habermas 1976).

Lukes (1974) distinguishes three dimensions of power: decision-making power, agenda control, and systemic power. *Decision-making power* exists when subordinants are aware of an underlying conflict of interest with power holders but are induced to act in the power holder's interest. Resources, such as wealth, charismatic claims, or the threat of violence, allow power holders to control subjects against their will. Even if compliance is not total, claimants with superior resources will typically control the behavior of subordinates. This is the aspect of power on which pluralists and state-centered analysts focus.

In *agenda control*, power holders prevail because they control what issues will be decided and what potential issues are removed from the political agenda. Such processes constitute "nondecisions" (Bachrach and Baratz 1970) in that power holders decide not to decide. Agenda control is more subtle than decision-making power, and is difficult to study but is nonetheless central to the political system. Thus, in a community power study of Gary, Indiana, Crenson (1971) found that powerful industrialists pressured local government to ignore local pollution problems created by the steel plants. Similarly, Perrucci (1994) found that state and local officials mounted joint publicity campaigns with Japanese auto corporations that convinced local voters that the large tax breaks granted to these foreign auto companies would create jobs and tax revenues despite unequal tax burdens. Because the mass media are central to creating public issues, they are typically key. Domhoff (1998) argues that upper-class control over the mass media, the leading universities, and the major policy organizations prevents issues such as unemployment and redistributive tax reform from becoming topics of decision making. News stories are largely created by press releases and interviews with government officials, which gives government officials considerable say over what issues will be aired in the mass media. Subordinates may be aware that power is being wielded, but they cannot force their own perspectives onto the political agenda. Thus this second dimension strongly controls the decision-making process by determining what issues and views get included or ignored. Elite theorists are the key architects of this type of work.

In *systemic power*, power holders benefit by structural arrangements, such as the distribution of wealth or superior political organization. Subordinates may not be aware of their conflicting interests with power holders and may, in fact, be ideologically indoctrinated to accept the authority of power holders. This may stem from several processes. One is the inability of subordinates to mobilize and press their interests. Disorganized and resource-poor groups are often unable to mobilize (Gaventa 1985; Jenkins 1985). Second are ideologies that legitimize power. Under slavery, slave owners successfully promoted the idea that they were paternalistic "father figures" who cared for and protected their childlike slaves. Insofar as slaves accepted this ideology, they were reluctant to rebel and resisted in ways that were controllable (Genovese 1974). Neo-Marxists advance this type of analysis.

Alford and Friedland (1985) contend that different theories of power have different objects of explanation and different time scales, with systemic arguments focusing on long-term structural change, agenda setting about moderate-term institutional changes, and decision making about short-term behavior. These are hierarchically organized

with systemic power-setting limits on the agenda-setting processs, which in turn sets limits on decision making. Thus studies that focus solely on first- or second-dimensional power without including the systemic context are limited and potentially flawed. Seemingly conflicting theories of political power can be synthesized once we specify their objects of explanation and integrate them into a larger theoretical framework.

Hicks and Misra (1993) advance an alternative synthetic "political resource" theory, arguing that institutional contexts define the infraresources or facilitative conditions that enable specific groups to mobilize and secure their interests (called "instrumental resources"). Thus neo-Marxian and pluralist arguments about the political actions of specific groups need to be combined with state-centered and elite arguments about institutional capacities and policy precedents. They show that factors identified by all these theories affect the amount of social welfare spending in Western democracies. Similarly, in a study of the adoption of public venture capital firms by state governments in the United States, Leicht and Jenkins (1998) show that corporatist bargaining between big capital and labor combine with strong administrative capacities of state governments to create new entrepreneurial economic development policies. Thus, instead of specifying a causal hierarchy among theories, this approach identifies interactive combinations of factors identified by these various power theories.

At this point, it is unclear which approach will eventually prevail. The contextual approach has considerable flexibility but needs to explain the conditions under which different power theories hold. The multidimensional power argument has conceptual breadth but lacks clear empirical relevance. Unless competing theories can be tested simultaneously in empirical analyses, it is difficult to evaluate how useful a purely conceptual synthesis is. In effect, Alford and Friedland (1985) have simply demonstrated that structural, institutional, and behavioral explanations refer to different objects. The political resource theory has strong empirical promise but needs greater specification as to the interactive combinations that integrate these power theories. Single-factor theories clearly need to be surpassed so that a broader theory of power and the state can be developed that will account for a variety of contexts as well as different power processes within an inclusive theoretical framework.

REFERENCES

Alford, Robert, and Roger Friedland 1985 *The Powers of Theory*. New York: Cambridge University Press.

Amenta, Edwin 1998 *Bold Relief*. Princeton, N.J.: Princeton University Press.

Bachrach, Peter, and Morton Baratz 1970 *Power and Poverty*. New York: Oxford University Press.

Berry, Jeffrey 1997 *The Interest Group Society*, 3rd ed. New York: Longmann.

Block, Fred 1987 *Revising State Theory*. Philadelphia, Pa.: Temple University Press.

Carnoy, Martin 1984 *The State and Political Theory*. Princeton, N.J.: Princeton University Press.

Clawson, Dan, Alan Neustadtl, and Denise Scott 1992 *Money Talks*. New York: Basic.

Crenson, Matthew 1971 *The Un-Politics of Air Pollution*. Baltimore, Md.: Johns Hopkins University Press.

Dahl, Robert 1957 *A Preface to Democratic Theory*. New Haven, Conn.: Yale University Press.

—— 1982 *Dilemmas of Pluralist Democracy*. New Haven, Conn.: Yale University Press.

Domhoff, G. William 1979 *The Powers That Be*. New York: Random House.

—— 1990 *The Power Elite and the State*. New York: Aldine DeGruyter.

—— 1996 *State Autonomy or Class Dominance?* New York: Aldine DeGruyter.

—— 1998 *Who Rules America?* 3rd ed. Mountain View, Calif.: Mayfield.

Dye, Thomas 1995 *Who's Running America?* 6th ed. Englewood Cliffs, N.J.: Prentice-Hall.

Duverger, Maurice 1962 *Political Parties*, 2nd ed. New York: John Wiley.

Evans, Peter, Dietrich Rueschemeyer, and Theda Skocpol (eds.) 1985 *Bringing the State Back In*. New York: Cambridge University Press.

Finegold, Kenneth, and Theda Skocpol 1995 *State and Party in America's New Deal*. Madison: University of Wisconsin Press.

Form, William 1996 *Segmented Labor, Fractured Politics*. New York: Plenum.

Gamson, William 1975 *The Strategy of Social Protest*. Homewood, Ill.: Dorsey.

Gaventa, John 1985 *Power and Powerlessness*. Urbana: University of Illinois Press.

Genovese, Eugene G. 1974 *Roll, Jordan, Roll! The World the Slaves Made*. New York: Vintage.

Gramsci, Antonio 1957 *The Modern Prince and Other Writings*. New York: International.

Habermas, Jurgen 1976 *Legitimation Crisis*. Boston: Beacon.

Hicks, Alexander, and Joya Mishra 1993 "Political Resources and the Growth of Welfare in Affluent Democracies, 1960–1982." *American Journal of Sociology* 99:668–710.

Jenkins, J. Craig 1983 "Resource Mobilization Theory and the Study of Social Movements." *Annual Review of Sociology* 9:527–553.

—— 1985 *The Politics of Insurgency*. New York: Columbia University Press.

Katzenstein, Peter 1985 *Small States in World Markets*. Ithaca, N.Y.: Cornell University Press.

Laumann, Edward, and David Knoke 1987 *The Organizational State*. Madison: University of Wisconsin Press.

Leicht, Kevin, and J. Craig Jenkins 1998 "Political Resources and Direct State Intervention." *Social Forces* 76:1323–1345.

Lipset, Seymour Martin 1981 *Political Man*, 2nd ed. Baltimore, Md.: Johns Hopkins University Press.

Lukes, Steven 1974 *Power*. London: Macmillan.

McAdam, Doug 1982 *Political Process and the Development of Black Insurgency*. Chicago: University of Chicago Press.

McConnell, Grant 1966 *Political Power and American Democracy*. New York: Vintage.

Marx, Karl (1852) 1964 *The Eighteenth Brumaire of Louis Bonaparte*. New York: International.

Michels, Robert (1911) 1962 *Political Parties*. Chicago: Dover.

Mills, C. Wright 1956 *The Power Elite*. New York: Oxford University Press.

Mosca, Gaetano (1896) 1939 *The Ruling Class*. New York: McGraw-Hill.

Neumann, Franz 1942 *Behemoth*. New York: Octagon.

Nordlinger, Eric A. 1981 *On the Autonomy of the Democratic State*. Cambridge, Mass.: Harvard University Press.

Offe, Claus 1984 *Contradictions of the Welfare State*. London: Hutchinson.

Pareto, Vilfredo (1935) 1963 *Mind and Society*. New York: Dover.

Parkin, Frank 1979 *Marxism and Class Theory*. London: Tavistock.

Perrucci, Robert 1994 *Japanese Auto Transplants in the Heartland*. New York: Aldine DeGruyter.

Piven, Frances, and Richard Cloward 1979 *Poor Peoples Movements*. New York: Pantheon.

Powell, G. Bingham 1982 *Contemporary Democracies*. Cambridge, Mass.: Harvard University Press.

Poulantzas, Nicos 1973 *Political Power and Social Classes* London: New Left.

Rose, Arnold 1968 *The Power Structure*. New York: Oxford University Press.

Schattschneider, E. E. 1960 *The Semi-Sovereign People*. New York: Holt, Reinhart and Winston.

Schlozman, Kay Lehman, and John T. Tierney 1986 *Organized Interests in American Democracy*. New York: Harper and Row.

Schmitter, Phillipe 1981 "Interest Intermediation and Regime Governability in Contemporary Western Europe and North America." In Suzanne Berger, ed., *Organizing Interests in Western Europe*. New York: Cambridge University Press.

Schumpeter, Joseph 1942 *Capitalism, Socialism and Democracy*. New York: Harper and Row.

Skocpol, Theda 1981 "Political Response to Capitalist Crisis." *Politics and Society* 10:155–201.

——, and Edwin Amenta 1986 "States and Social Policies." *Annual Review of Sociology*. vol. 131–157.

Skocpol, Theda, and John L. Campbell (eds.) 1995 *American Society and Politics*. New York: McGraw-Hill.

Tilly, Charles 1978 *From Mobilization to Revolution*. Reading, Pa.: Addison-Wesley.

Useem, Michael 1984 *The Inner Circle*. New York: Oxford University Press.

Weber, Max 1947 *From Max Weber*. Hans Gerth and C. Wright Mills, eds. New York: Oxford University Press.

J. CRAIG JENKINS

POPULAR CULTURE

Since the 1960s, studies of popular culture in the United States have proliferated and a range of novel arguments have been proposed, linking patterns of popular culture production and consumption to systems of stratification and power. Before the 1960s in Europe, Roland Barthes ([1957] 1972) and Fernand Braudel ([1949] 1966) championed (for quite different reasons) increased attention to everyday culture and its social significance, and members of the Frankfurt school emigrating to the United States brought new theories of mass culture to American academics (Rosenberg and White 1957; Lowenthal 1961), but American scholars still did not generally see any value in studying popular culture.

Beginning in the mid-1960s, as the American middle class began to be targeted by the mass media as the desired audience, more American educators started to show more interest in media-based popular culture, even though in much of academia, studying popular culture was either declassé or taboo (Ross 1989). A few hardy souls from sociology and literary criticism looked at popular culture as a realm of interesting fads and fashions, ephemeral cultural forms that plummeted though modern urban life with regularity, gave rise to much cultural entrepreneurship, and left ordinary citizens running to keep up with what was "happening." Sociologists found it a bit easier to justify ongoing attention to these social ephemera because of the established tradition in sociology of examining urban and suburban communities and their cultures (Park 1955; Lynd and Lynd 1929). By the mid-1960s a quite active community of scholars around Bowling Green University proliferated empirical and descriptive accounts of everything from fast-food restaurants to rock and roll (Keil 1966; Nye 1972; Cawelti 1972; Browne 1982). At roughly the same time, a small group of literary scholars drew on longstanding literary interest in the voices of the people in literature (Shiach 1989, chap. 2, 4), and argued that to understand contemporary uses of language, one had to study commercial language in popular culture (McQuade and Atwan 1974). This work did not have much success in changing either sociology or literature. In sociology, it was eclipsed conceptually by sociological work that linked patterns of popular culture to systems of institutional control (Cantor 1971; Denisoff 1974; Hirsh 1972).This work had greater legitimacy because it addressed the organizations' literature, but it also reinforced the sense that the study of popular culture was not really important enough to stand on its own.

By the end of the 1960s, as the political climate shifted, radical scholars began to champion studies of popular culture either to understand the world of "the people" (disregarded by elites) or to account for the political passivity of the working class and poor. They tried to resuscitate questions about elite distaste for popular culture itself and its relation to systems of social control. These questions gave popular culture new importance, not as an aesthetic or commercial system but as a political actor in systems of stratification and power (Schiller 1969; Guback 1969; Aronowitz 1973; Gans 1974).

This legacy has been carried into present-day popular culture research as it has spread through sociology, literature, anthropology, history, and cultural studies. Ongoing fascination with "politics from below" has made this subfield a conceptually complex and politically "left" branch of cultural studies, not concerned so much with the moral fabric of society or the ideational sources of its integration (subjects derived from the Weberian tradition of cultural studies), but rather with the use of culture to exert or avoid systematic domination from above.

Many contemporary attempts to explain patterns of cultural domination through popular culture are indebted to (and in different ways critical of) the work on mass culture and consciousness begun by the Frankfurt school. Members of the Frankfurt Institute of Social Research originally organized themselves to examine the philosophical underpinnings of Marxism, but when Hitler came to power, since most of the leading members of the group were Jewish, this project was disrupted and many figures came to the United States. The work on mass culture that developed from this group was (not surprisingly) devoted to understanding the success of Nazism by dissecting and analyzing the psychological and political effects of mass society (Jay 1973). Members of the Frankfurt school perceived mass culture as aesthetically and politically debilitating, reducing the capacities of audiences to think critically and functioning as an ideological tool to manipulate the political sentiments of the mass public. They argued that in modern industrial societies, the pursuit of economic and scientific rationality provided an impoverished environment for human life. The realm of culture, which might have provided respite from the drudgery of everyday life, was itself being industrialized, yielding a commercial mass culture that atomized audiences and lulled them with emotionally unsatisfactory conventionality. This world of commodities only added to the dissatisfactions that deflected people from their desires. The dulling of their senses made them politically passive, and their emotional discontent made them easy targets for propaganda that addressed their

powerful inner feelings. This combination, according to theory, was what made the propaganda in Nazi Germany so effective (Horkheimer and Adorno 1972).

During the 1960s, critical theory, as the work of the Frankfurt school came to be known, continued in U.S. intellectual circles to be used to explain the political conservatism of the working class, but it was also taken up in the student movement as a critique of commercial mass culture that justified the efforts by "flower children" to create radical social change through cultural experimentation. The problem was that, for the latter purpose, critical theory was too deterministic to have much room for human agency, including cultural strategies for change. Constructivist models from the sociology of culture could be and were used to explain how ordinary people could break the hold of political institutions over their imaginations (Blumer 1969; Goffman 1959; Berger and Luckmann 1966; Schutz 1967; Becker 1963), but they did not explain how ideological control of populations by elites could work. The insights of the Italian communist political writer Antonio Gramsci (1971) about hegemony seemed a better scheme for explaining both the role of ideology in systems of power and the constructed nature of social reality. According to Gramsci, elites maintained their power and legitimacy by creating hegemonic definitions of reality that were accepted as common sense by the population. By subscribing to these views, nonelites collaborated in their own oppression. Gramsci's work, available in English translations and popularized in the academic community in the 1970s, gave the study of culture and power in the English-speaking world new direction.

By the 1970s, much innovative work on popular culture was coming out of Great Britain. The British school of cultural studies drew attention to the role of nonelites in systems of power, but it focused more on working-class culture—particularly its role as a crucible for cultural resistance, innovation, and change. This school had its roots in the work of E. P. Thompson (1963) and Raymond Williams (1961; 1977; 1980). These authors began from the premise that the working class is not defined just by relations of production, but also by a self-consciousness bred in a class-based way of life. The working class has its own history and traditions that give its members distinct values and a complex relation to societal level systems of power. In their own cultural enclaves, class members are active producers of their own political institutions and popular entertainments (and through them defined social realities). So while the public culture of Western industrialized societies may be dominated by elites who control the mass media and who try to use cultural systems for exerting power, their hegemonic control is circumscribed by the cultures of subordinated groups. The realm of popular culture, in this tradition, is an arena of conflict in which cultural identity, authority, and autonomy are contested. Social rifts are made manifest in the multiplicity of points of view that enter into the public sphere along with the hegemonic messages of much mass culture (Curran, Gurevitch, and Woolacott 1979; Hall and Whannel 1965).

While early British cultural studies paid greatest attention to working-class culture, the ideas about cultural resistance were easily transferred to the analysis of other subordinated groups such as women, youth, and minorities. This broader approach to cultures of resistance gave birth to the kind of subcultural analysis conducted, for example, by Dich Hebdige (1979). He argues that innovations in youth culture come from marginalized working-class youths rebelling against both their parents and hegemonic culture. New developments in music and dress are culled from the cultural possibilities made available in mass society, both in commercial commodities and local cultures. These cultural resources are mixed and reassembled to create new subcultural styles. Much innovation of this sort comes from minority communities and is picked up by middle-class kids in part because it is so offensive to their parents. The irony, of course, is that if they make these styles popular, they end up making them part of the world of mass culture, economic mainstays of the entertainment industry.

One of the most interesting literatures spawned in America by this British school comes from historians looking to the realm of popular culture to try to understand class, gender, and ethnic relations in the United States. Roy Rosenzweig (1983), Kathy Peiss (1985), and George Lipsitz (1990) look at how class, gender, and ethnic culture are sustained and dissolved over time in patterns of resistance, co-optation, mutual influence, and change. They identify ways that residues of older cultural traditions both resist and are incorporated into the cultural mainstream, and

ways that different groups have absorbed and used elements of both traditional and mass culture to fashion distinct identities and ways of life.

Rosenzweig (1983), studying the white working class in nineteenth-century America, treats popular culture as a site of resistance to work discipline in the factory. The division of life into periods of work and leisure for workers in this period was not, to Rosenzweig, the articulation of two spheres of activity, but a political division that was part of a struggle over control of time by workers.

Peiss (1985) looks at women workers in nineteenth-century cities. She demonstrates that young working women used their new economic independence to resist the constraints of the family as well as of the factory. They were able to develop new styles of dress, dancing, and play, but could not free themselves from their highly structured gender relations.

Lipsitz (1990) looks at how ethnic and class cultures have been sustained and dissolved in the late twentieth century in the United States. He sees popular culture forming a kind of popular memory, obscuring and yet reviving the U.S. working class's immigrant past and ethnic complexity. Centralized mass media such as television have helped to create and record the decline of immigrant identity under the force of consumerism. In contrast, more participatory cultural forms like street dancing and parading during Mardi Gras and some popular music forms have allowed ethnic groups to play their identities and create an urban mixed culture that simultaneously embraces and rejects traditional ethnic identity.

Another direction in the analysis of class and culture has been developed by Pierre Bourdieu (1984) and his colleagues in France. They have been looking for the mechanisms by which domination has been sustained across generations. If social constructivists are right and social life must necessarily be "created" by each new generation, then social *stability* over time needs theoretical explanation. To Bourdieu, culture is a main source of class stability. He argues that each rank has its own kind of cultural tastes, some systems of taste constituting cultural capital that can be exchanged for economic capital. People at the top of the hierarchy have a class culture with a high amount of cultural capital. They teach this culture to their children and thereby give them an economic edge. This kind of elite culture is also taught in school, but kids from less affluent backgrounds often resist learning it. This cultural resistance by the working class is not a victory, according to Bourdieu; rather, it is a trap for reproducing the class system.

Bourdieu's theory of cultural and social stratification is interestingly unlike most models found in the United States and Britain because it has no special place for a homogenizing mass culture. Bourdieu argues that members of different social ranks may see the same films (or other forms of mass culture), but they see them in different ways and they like or dislike them for different reasons. Elite culture is more abstract and formal than working-class culture, so elite filmgoers pay more attention to film language while nonelites care more about plots and stars. These differences in cultural consumption are more significant to Bourdieu than differences of cultural production (mass versus handmade culture) because elites identify with formal approaches to culture and prefer to associate with (and hire) those who share their views.

Scholars in both Britain and the United States have been profoundly influenced by Bourdieu. Paul DiMaggio (1982), in a study of the Boston Symphony and its development in the nineteenth century, paid attention to the differentiation of tastes and social ranks at issue when concerts for elite audiences were purged of popular songs and were used to define a special repertoire of classical music. This happened when the symphony was established as an elite musical institution and drove out competing musical organizations that had more "democratic" tastes. DiMaggio argues that this cultural differentiation took place when immigrant groups grew dramatically in Boston and took over local politics there. The superiority of traditional elites was no longer visible in the public sphere, but it remained central to the economy. The creation of cultural institutions identifying this elite with elevated tastes helped to make class power visible and to sustain it over time by giving upper-class Bostonians a distinctive culture.

In Britain, Paul Willis (1977) has confirmed Bourdieu's perceptions about class reproduction through his study of the education of working-class youths. He argues that distaste for the "elevated" values of the school among working-class youths is expressed in school by resistance to lessons. This resistance does not have the optimistic possibilities found in the theories of Williams (1977) or Hebdige (1979), but results in class reproduction. Working-class youths, in eschewing elite cultural values, end up reproducing their own domination within the class system. MacLeod (1987) in the United States finds much the same thing, although he focuses on differences between blacks and whites. Members of gangs from both ethnic communities who lived in the same housing project found difficulty escaping their social rank because of difficulties at school. The blacks believed that by going to school they could achieve mobility, while the white kids did not. Still, both groups were kept in their "places" by a lack of cultural capital.

Since the end of the 1970s, there has been a growing literature, stimulated by the women's movement, on gender stratification and popular culture. The bulk of it addresses two media—novels and film—because of the centrality of women to the economic development of these two areas of popular entertainment. As Ann Douglas (1977) pointed out in her seminal and controversial book, *Feminization of American Culture*, women readers and women writers helped to establish this form of popular novel writing in the United States during the nineteenth century. Sentimental novels were tailored to the domesticated women in the period, who had to stay home and devote their attention to familial relations and child rearing. The novels focused on interpersonal relations and problems of individuals' morals (as opposed to large issues of morality)—just the kind of thing that both fit and justified middle-class women's highly circumscribed lives. Douglas decries the role of women writers in shaping this disempowering literature for women and praises in contrast more "masculine" and male writings from the period (hence generating much controversy about her easy acceptance of the literary canon). Most important for students of popular culture, she argues that the sentimental novels were models of mass culture that have been used ever since in romance novels and soap operas.

Janice Radway (1984) questioned this easy dismissal of romance novels, and went out to study in a quasi-ethnographic fashion the readers of contemporary romance novels to see how they were affected by their reading. She found that the novels had more mixed effects than Douglas supposed. While they taught traditional gender relations (including male violence toward women), they also celebrated the gentler side of men and (more important) were used by women readers as a reason to deflect demands on their time by husbands and children. Women claimed their reading time as their own, and used it to withdraw temporarily from the uninterrupted flow of demands on their attention.

Gaye Tuchman's book (1989) provides some interesting history that serves as a vantage point from which to view the controversy between Douglas and Radway. She shows that, around the turn of the century, publishing houses began to reject the women novelists and their sentimental novels and to favor male novelists. Publishers were central to the switch to the canons of modernism, and the "expulsion" of women from the profession of novel writing. Women readers still constituted the major market for novels, but their market had become so lucrative that high-status male poets, who had eschewed the novel before, began to be interested in it. Once this occurred, their tastes were taken as authoritative and the novel was quickly placed in their hands. Tuchman makes clear that changes in taste like this were neither arbitrary nor grounded purely in aesthetics; they were the result of economic changes in the literary market, institutional decisions about how to address them, and institutional trivialization of women and their culture.

The attention to gender and film has been inspired not by the importance of the female audience or the centrality of women to the film industry (the opposite is the case), but rather by the importance of actresses, of the faces and bodies of film stars, to the commercial and cultural success of the industry. When feminist studies of film began in the 1970s, most of the work was on the exploitation of the female body in films by male filmmakers and for a male audience. This kind of analysis stressed how commercial films used male-centered notions of sexuality and power, presenting women in films as objects of desire and/or violence (Weibel 1977; Tuchman et al. 1978). In the 1980s, researchers turned away from the study of film production and toward analyses of film language and film consumption to construct a psychology of film watching (Modleski

1982; Mulvey 1989). Much of this literature focuses on the voyeuristic pleasure film watching provides men by allowing them to gaze at women's bodies while sitting in a dark theater where the female objects of the gaze cannot look back. Scholars in this tradition examine in shot-by-shot detail how men and women are differentially presented on film: men are generally in medium shots, carrying the action of films, while women stand in the background (or are dissected in close-ups to appear as faces or other body parts, available to the male gaze).

Because this type of analysis seemed to prove so decisively that films are constructed for a male audience, feminists wondered why women seem to find so much pleasure in going to the movies. One answer is that some films contain strong and interesting female characters who address issues of concern to female audiences. Another is that interpretations of films are not so controlled by authorial intentions, and are much more a matter of audiences' active readings of messages. Drawing on Nancy Chodorow's ideas about female psychology (1978), Carol Gilligan's ideas about female reasoning (1982), Lacanian psychology, and poststructuralist views of the politics of interpretation (Eagleton 1983), a psychology of film emerged around how audiences (particularly women) construct meaning from film texts (Mulvey 1985, 1989; Erens 1979). The most recent works of media analysis have rejected altogether such a dualistic approach to gender. Learning from studies of sexuality itself, they have considered how gender categories are at stake in popular culture. They examine how gender dualism is enforced and contested in the mass media (Gamson 1998).

In the 1980s, two opposite developments in culture theory have emerged from renewed attention (in poststructuralism in general and in the film theory described above) to the multivocality of texts and the proliferation of meanings through multiple readings. The upbeat one emphasizes the liberatory nature of culture, and is related to: (1) the poststructuralist argument that asserting alternative interpretations undermines the authority of canonical readings; (2) feminist versions of reader response theory that contend that how you use culture is central to what it is; and (3) the idea from the British school of cultural studies that competing social voices enter into the public sphere and are available for readers or audiences to find.

Advocates of this position claim that efforts at social control through culture do not work very well because, in their own life worlds, people use the cultural resources around them in their own ways. These new constructivists—for example, Robert Bellah (Bellah et al. 1985) Ann Swidler (1986), Joseph Gusfield (1989), and Michael Schudson (1989)—are much like Goffman (1959) and earlier symbolic interactionists who presented everyday life as a cultural achievement, but they see the construction of meaning in everyday life (in an optimistic reversal of Foucault and other poststructuralists) as a healthy exercise of power as well as symbolic manipulation (Foucault 1970, 1975, 1979; Jameson 1984; Zukin 1988).

This optimistic view of the proliferation of meanings in everyday life is countered by students of postmodernism who derive from structuralism and poststructuralism an interest in the languages of culture and see in modern urban society a loss of meaning resulting from the multiplication of signs and their decontextualization or reappropriation. They argue that commercial culture has such a need to assign meaning to objects (in order to make sense of their consumption and use) that signs are proliferated, reappropriated, mixed, and reused until they lose their meaning. For example, as famous paintings are used to sell cosmetics, images of the Old West are used to signify the solidity of banks, and bits and pieces of past architecture are mixed to construct a new built environment, history is made meaningless. The play with signs goes on without serious thought to what this does to human life. The result is (to postmodernists) a politically debilitating alienation. Cultural production and counterproduction, the argument goes, may reduce hegemony by undermining attempts to define "common sense," and may give people pleasure through the free play of signs, but they provide only an illusion of freedom, and breed a loss of meaning in life. This view of modern urban life contains some of the unremitting pessimism of the Frankfurt school, but it is tied to a view of cultural decentralization that is at odds with traditional critical theory.

The diverse approaches to popular culture that have developed since the 1960s seem to have produced a proliferation of meanings for popular culture itself, but the result has not been alienation. Popular culture research has gained an analytic richness that it lacked when few scholars dared or cared to approach it. Conflicting theoretical views about what makes popular culture significant may make it more difficult to define and characterize (much less understand) the field. But all the debates consider how groups come to understand the world they live in, and how those understandings subordinate or alienate them (on the one hand) or liberate them to make meaningful lives, in spite of efforts by others to control them (Long 1997). This heritage is clear, and gives both meaning and direction to popular culture studies.

(SEE ALSO: *Mass Media Research; Postmodernism; Social Movements*)

REFERENCES

Aronowitz, Stanley 1973 *False Promises*. New York: McGraw-Hill.

Barthes, Roland (1957) 1972 *Mythologies*. New York: Hill and Wang.

Becker, Howard 1963 *Outsiders: Studies in the Sociology of Deviance*. New York: Free Press.

Bellah, Robert N., et al. 1985 *Habits of the Heart*. Berkeley: University of California Press.

Berger, Peter, and T. Luckmann 1966 *Social Construction of Reality*. Garden City, N.Y.: Doubleday.

Blumer, Herbert 1969 *Symbolic Interactionism: Perspective and Method*. Berkeley: University of California Press.

Bourdieu, Pierre 1984 *Distinction: A Social Critique of the Judgment of Taste*. Cambridge, Mass.: Harvard University Press.

Braudel, Fernand (1949) 1966 *The Mediterranean and the Mediterranean World in the Age of Phillip II*. New York: Harper.

Browne, Ray 1982 *Objects of Special Devotion*. Bowling Green, Ohio: Popular Press.

Cantor, Muriel 1971 *The Hollywood Producer*. New York: Basic.

Cawelti, J. G. 1972 *The Six-Gun Mystique*. Bowling Green, Ohio: Popular Press.

Chodorow, Nancy 1978 *Reproduction of Mothering*. Berkeley: University of California Press.

Curran, James, Michael Gurevitch, and Janet Woolacott 1979 *Mass Communication and Society*. New York: Russell Sage Foundation.

Denisoff, Serge 1974 *Solid Gold: The Popular Record Industry*. New Brunswick, N.J.: Transaction Books.

DiMaggio, Paul 1982 "Cultural Entrepreneurship in Nineteenth-Century Boston: The Creation of an Organizational Base for High Culture in America." *Media, Culture and Society* 4:33–50.

Douglas, Ann 1977 *Feminization of American Culture*. New York: Knopf.

Eagleton, Terry 1983 *Literary Theory*. Minneapolis: University of Minnesota Press.

Erens, P. 1979 *Sexual Stratagems*. New York: Horizon.

Foucault, Michel 1970 *The Order of Things*. New York: Random House.

—— 1975 "What Is an Author?" *Partisan Review* 4:603–614.

—— 1979 *Discipline and Punish*. New York: Vintage.

Gamson, Joshua 1998 *Freaks Talk Back*. Chicago: University of Chicago Press.

Gans, Herbert 1974 *Popular Culture and High Culture*. New York: Basic.

Gilligan, Carol 1982 *In a Different Voice*. Cambridge, Mass.: Harvard University Press.

Goffman, Erving 1959 *Presentation of Self in Everyday Life*. Garden City, N.Y.: Anchor.

Gramsci, Antonio 1971 *Selections from the Prison Notebooks*. New York: International.

Guback, Thomas 1969 *The International Film Industry: Western Europe and America since 1945*. Bloomington: Indiana University Press.

Gusfield, Joseph 1989 *On Symbols and Society*. Chicago: University of Chicago Press.

Hall, Stuart, and Paddy Whannel 1965 *The Popular Arts*. New York: Pantheon.

Hartounic, Valerie 1997 *Cultural Conceptions*. Minneapolis: University of Minnesota Press.

Hebdige, Dick 1979 *Subculture: The Meaning of Style*. New York: Methuen.

Hirsh, Paul 1972 "Processing Fads and Fashions: An Organization-Set Analysis of Cultural Industry Systems." *American Journal of Sociology* 77:639–659.

Horkheimer, Max, and Theodor Adorno (1944) 1972 *Dialectic of Enlightenment*. New York: Seabury.

Jameson, Frederic 1984 "Postmodernism, of the Cultural Logic of Late Capitalism." *New Left Review* 146:53–93.

Jay, Martin 1973 *The Dialectical Imagination: A History of the Frankfurt School and the Institute of Social Research 1923–50*. Boston: Little, Brown.

Keil, C. 1966 *Urban Blues*. Chicago: University of Chicago Press.

Lipsitz, George 1990 *Time Passages*. Minneapolis: University of Minnesota Press.

Long, Elizabeth 1997 *From Sociology to Cultural Studies*. Malden, Mass: Blackwell.

Lowenthal, Leo 1961 *Literature, Popular Culture and Society*. Englewood Cliffs, N.J.: Prentice-Hall.

Lynd, Robert, and H. Lynd 1929 *Middletown*. New York: Harcourt, Brace, and World.

MacLeod, Jay 1987 *Ain't No Making It*. Boulder, Colo.: Westview.

McQuade, Donald, and Robert Atwan 1974 *Popular Writing in America*. New York: Oxford University Press.

Modleski, Tania 1982 *Loving with a Vengeance*. Hamden, Conn.: Archon.

Mulvey, Laura 1985 "Film and Visual Pleasure." In G. Mast and M. Cohen, eds., *Film Theory and Criticism*. New York: Oxford University Press.

—— 1989 *Visual and Other Pleasures*. Bloomington: Indiana University Press.

Nye, R. B. 1972 *New Dimensions in Popular Culture*. Bowling Green, Ohio: Popular Press.

Park, Robert 1955 *Society*. New York: Free Press.

Peiss, Kathy 1985 *Cheap Amusements: Working Women and Leisure in New York City, 1880 to 1920*. Philadelphia: Temple University Press.

Radway, Janice 1984 *Reading the Romance*. Chapel Hill: University of North Carolina Press.

Rosenberg, Bernard, and David Manning White 1957 *Mass Culture*. New York: Free Press.

Rosenzweig, Roy 1983 *Eight Hours for What We Will: Workers and Leisure in an Industrial City, 1870–1920*. New York: Cambridge University Press.

Ross, Andrew 1989 *No Respect: Intellectuals and Popular Culture*. New York: Routledge and Kegan Paul.

Schiller, Herbert 1969 *Mass Communication and American Empire*. New York: Kelly.

Schudson, Michael 1989 "How Culture Works." *Theory and Society* 18:153–180.

Schutz, Alfred 1967 *Collected Papers*, vol. 3, *The Problem of Social Reality*. The Hague: Martinus Nijhoff.

Shiach, Morag 1989 *Discourse on Popular Culture*. Stanford, Calif.: Stanford University Press.

Swidler, Ann 1986 "Culture in Action: Symbols and Strategies." *American Sociological Review* 51:273–286.

Thompson, E. P. 1963 *The Making of the English Working Class*. New York: Vintage.

Tuchman, Gaye 1989 *Edging Women Out*. New Haven, Conn.: Yale University Press.

——, Arlene Daniels, and James Benet 1978 *Hearth and Home*. New York: Oxford University Press.

Weibel, Kathryn 1977 *Mirror, Mirror*. Garden City, N.Y.: Anchor.

Williams, Raymond 1961 *The Long Revolution*. New York: Columbia University Press.

—— 1977 *Marxism and Literature*. Oxford: Oxford University Press.

—— 1980 *Problems in Materialism and Culture*. London: Verso.

Willis, Paul 1977 *Learning to Labor*. New York: Columbia University Press.

Zukin, Sharon 1988 "The Post-Modern Debate over Urban Form." *Theory, Culture and Society* 5:431–446.

CHANDRA MUKERJI

POPULATION

As a topic, *population* refers to the size and composition of social groupings and the dynamics of change in these characteristics. It extends to the determinants and consequences of levels, differentials, and changes in fertility, mortality, and spatial distribution. Within the social sciences, population study has a broad concern with the cultural, social, economic, and psychological causes and consequences of these characteristics (see Hauser and Duncan 1959; Coleman and Schofield 1986; Stycos 1987; Namboodiri 1988). Within sociology, the main concern is with linkages between social institutions and the dynamics of population change and equilibrium (see Taeuber, Bumpass, and Sweet 1978; Nam 1994; Greenhalgh 1996). *Demography* is an important component of population study that focuses on data collection, measurement, and description. (Though it would be impossible to cite all articles relevant to the general topic of population, a number of useful articles are cross-referenced at the end of this article.)

OVERVIEW OF POPULATION HISTORY

A brief overview of major changes in the characteristics of human populations will suggest some of the linkages between social life and these characteristics. (For a more detailed discussion see, for example, Wrigley 1969; Petersen 1975.)

During Neolithic times, hunting and gathering groups probably consisted of only a few dozen individuals. Based on the technology and the area believed to have been populated, it is estimated that in about 8000–6000 B.C. the population of the world was only five million to ten million (Yaukey 1985, p. 38). Probably about half of all children died before age 5. Mainly because of the high mortality of infants and children, life expectancy was probably only about 20 years, although some adults would have survived to advanced ages. Maternal mortality was also high, probably resulting in considerably shorter life expectancy for females than for males (United Nations 1973, p. 115). In such a setting, the social consequences of these fundamental demographic facts would have been enormous. Many of our current social values and institutions have their roots in this harsh environment.

Death was sudden, random, and frequent—at least five times as common, in a population of a given size, as in a developed country today. A major function of religion was to enable people to interpret death as a part of the life course and to surround it with rituals. New births to offset these deaths were essential for the survival of a group. There can be no doubt that many groups, of various sizes, failed in this effort, but the survivors were our ancestors. Children were important to the economy of the household and community from an early age, and young adults were crucial to the welfare of older adults. Practices and institutions to encourage fertility—of humans, as well as of the environment of plants and animals—were essential. Marital unions of some type would have been virtually universal and would have begun at an early age. It is likely that unions would have been arranged by the parents, partly because they occurred at such early ages, as well as because of the social advantages of arranged marriages for strengthening an intergenerational network of social obligations. Thus the social institutions of religion, marriage, and the extended family, among others, had some of their original impetus in the extremely high mortality of human prehistory and the consequent imperative for high fertility and child survivorship.

One of the most remarkable functions of social institutions is that they provide valves or mechanisms by which population size can be regulated to be compatible with the prevailing environmental circumstances and the level of technology (Davis 1963). As just mentioned, high mortality must be accompanied by comparably high fertility if a population is to sustain itself. For the most part, it is the level of mortality that drives the level of fertility, through various intervening mechanisms, although mortality (infanticide) has sometimes served as a means of population control. The social regulation of population size usually takes the form of increasing or decreasing the average number of births per woman, to compensate for uncontrollable influences on mortality.

Humans have a much greater capacity to reproduce than is often recognized, and even in situations of very high mortality and fertility there is usually an untapped potential for even higher fertility. There are well-documented "natural fertility" populations in which the *average* woman who survives the childbearing ages has 10 to 11 children after age 20, and it is estimated that the average after age 15 could be as high as 16 children under some circumstances. (Of course, if maternal mortality is high, many women will not survive the childbearing years.) The potential supply of births is adequate to balance even the most severe conditions; if it were not, the species would not have survived.

Over the long run, there has been a pattern of increased life expectancy with two major transitions. The transition from hunting and gathering to settled agriculture and larger human settlements produced a net increase in life expectancy, although with some shifts in causes of death. Larger settlements have a higher incidence of infectious diseases because of inadequate sanitation and sources of clean drinking water. The second major transition began in the seventeenth century with industrialization and the progressive reduction of deaths from infectious diseases. Fluctuations in mortality due to transitory influences have been superimposed on these two main transitions (Tilly 1978; Wrigley and Schofield 1981). Some of the short-term increases in mortality, due to wars, famines, and epidemics, have been devastating. For example, the Black Death in fourteenth-century Europe eliminated more than one-third of the population in several areas.

During the transition to agriculture and larger settlements, mortality fell and population size increased. It is believed that, starting in roughly 5000 B.C., world population approximately doubled every 1,000 years, reaching 100 million around 500 B.C. It doubled again in the next 1,000 years, reaching 200 million around 500 A.D., and again in the next 1,000 years, reaching 425 million in 1500 A.D. (McEvedy and Jones 1978). Most of the growth was in Europe and the Middle East. This is obviously an extremely low rate of growth by modern standards, around 0.07 percent per year, but it was a marked increase from the hunting and gathering era.

The increase in carrying capacity with a new technology and social organization probably had its principal effect on reproduction at the household level (Laslett and Wall 1972; Goody 1976, 1983). If territory for new settlements is absent or inaccessible, having too many children will lead to excessive division of land and property. Some kind of limitation on reproduction will result.

The most important social mechanism or lever for regulating fertility has probably been limitation of exposure to the risk of conception—in short, regulation of sexual activity. Thus, in preindustrial Europe, the age at marriage was high—on average, in the mid-twenties. The motivation for delaying marriage and the formation of new households probably arose because the parental generation had limited land to pass to their children. Marriage and childbearing were deferred until a viable household could be established. These household-level motives led to a general consensus that marriage at later ages was preferable. Associated with late age at marriage were voluntary rather than arranged marriages, and apprenticeships or domestic service for many young people. Alternatives to married life developed—for example, celibate religious communities. These behaviors can be viewed as mechanisms for fertility limitation, even though they certainly had more direct functions as well. Within marriage there was probably very little use, or even knowledge, of contraception.

When short-term increases in mortality occurred, as with a famine, war, or epidemic, the social response was an increase in the prevalence of marriage and/or a reduction in the mean age at marriage. Again, these motivations operated primarily at the household level, in the sense that when mortality rose, there were increased opportunities for land division and settlement, and new households could be formed more quickly.

The attempt here is to characterize population growth and homeostasis in the broadest terms, up to the beginning of the industrial era in the West. Because of limited space, this description glosses over enormous differences worldwide in the patterns of reproduction and social structure and their linkages. There have several ethnographic and historical analyses of these variations (see, e.g., Hanley and Wolf 1985).

The growth of population that accompanied industrialization is indicated by the following estimates. World population was about 545 million in 1600; 610 million in 1700; 900 million in 1800; 1,625 million in 1900. It is expected to be about 6,100 million in 2000 (McEvedy and Jones 1978; United Nations 1998). The period saw an acceleration in the rate of growth, as well as enormous increases in sheer numbers of people. Prior to 1900, Europe increased most rapidly. In other parts of the world, most of the increase was concentrated in the twentieth century. This period of rapid growth is described as the *demographic transition*. It is discussed briefly below. (See the end of this article for relevant cross-references.)

MORTALITY DECLINE

The transformation of mortality from a common event, occurring most often to children, to a relatively rare event, occurring most often to the elderly, arose from a confluence of technological and social developments. Most important among these was the control of infectious diseases spread by microorganisms in the air and water. An improved understanding of the etiology of these diseases, together with technical capacity and political support for public health measures, led to childhood vaccinations, clean drinking water, and improved sanitation (McKeown 1976). Standards of personal hygiene and cleanliness of clothing improved. There is little evidence that improvements in diet were important, and curative (as contrasted to preventive) medicine played a relatively small role in the main part of the transformation.

In developed countries, the infant mortality rate has steadily fallen from about 250 deaths (in the first year of life) per 1,000 births to a present level of fewer than 10 per 1,000 births (Mosley and Chen 1984). One consequence of a decline in the risk of infant and child deaths is to increase the sense of parental control over reproduction. It is more rational to develop notions of desired numbers of children when the survivorship of children is less random. Similarly, as survivorship improves, it is more rational to invest in children's future by providing them with formal education. The cost of children, to their parents and to the larger society, increases as child mortality falls and life expectancy improves (see, e.g., Easterlin 1976).

The increase in life expectancy, currently about 73 years in the developed countries, has also resulted in a rise in the mean age of the population, in a substantial increase in the proportion who are elderly or retired, and in a shift to causes of death associated with old age. These trends have broad social implications—for the employment of and advancement in opportunities for young people, the resilience of political structures, and the cost of retirement programs and medical care for the elderly, for example.

Fewer births per woman, together with the now negligible rates of maternal mortality in developed countries, have resulted in a substantially greater life expectancy for women than for men. Although at birth there are about 104 males for every 100 females, there are progressively more females, per male, for every age after about age 30 in the United States. The elderly population consists disproportionately of women. Also, because women tend to be younger than their husbands, they typically experience much longer periods of widowhood than men do.

In today's developing countries, mortality decline has been much more rapid than it was in the developed countries, because an accumulation of Western public health measures could be introduced nearly simultaneously. Most of the decline has occurred since World War II and the ensuing independence of most of these countries from colonial powers, although some of it can be traced back to earlier decades of the twentieth century. The rapidity of the mortality decline and its largely exogenous nature have been factors in the delay of a subsequent fertility decline in many cases (see

Preston 1978). (See the end of this article for relevant cross-references.)

FERTILITY DECLINE

Within Europe, the onset of substantial reductions in fertility occurred first in France early in the nineteenth century, and last in Ireland early in the twentieth century. In the earliest cases, the onset of fertility control coincided with mortality decline rather than following it. In general, a lag between the decline in mortality and the decline in fertility resulted in substantial population growth. In the United States and Britain, 1880 is regarded as a watershed year for the widespread initiation of contraception.

With no exceptions, from the cases of France through Ireland, the initiation and the bulk of the modern fertility declines occurred mainly as a result of contraception rather than delayed marriage, and in contexts in which contraception was publicly regarded as immoral, supplies and information were illegal, and methods were primitive by today's standards. As a generalization, births were not intentionally spaced or postponed; rather, attempts were made to terminate childbearing at some earlier parity than would have been the case without intervention. Some married couples appear even to have chosen to have no children or only one child. The main contraceptive method was withdrawal (*coitus interruptus*). Abstinence was probably not infrequently used as a last resort. Rhythm may have been used, but probably incorrectly; douching was common but was probably ineffective. Sterilization was not available, although it is likely that a high proportion of hysterectomies served the same function. Condoms were not widely available until the twentieth century.

It is clear that the motivation to control fertility was both powerful and personal. It is unfortunate that it is so difficult at this distance to reconstruct the specific strategies that were employed, patterns of communication between couples, and sources of information. However, at least two generalizations can be made. One is that the practice of contraception required an ideational justification, to the effect that individual couples have a personal right to control their family size. From a modern perspective it is easy to overlook the fundamental importance of this concept. It is not just a coincidence that France was the first country to experience contraception on a wide scale, that it was the home of the Enlightenment, and that it was also the first European country to experience a fundamental political revolution. Intervention to prevent a birth rests on the premise that it is legitimate for an individual—or a couple—to make critical choices affecting personal welfare. Contraception can be viewed as a manifestation of a value for personal freedom, even in the face of strong pronatalist pressures from both church and state.

A secondary condition for contraceptive use in the West appears to have been some degree of local development, as evidenced by higher literacy and a higher standard of living. Historical research continues into the importance of specific factors such as the relative status of women, the transition to a wage-earning class, local industrialization, improvements in social security and public welfare, and so on. (For more details on specific countries, see, e.g., Ryder [1969]; Livi Bacci [1977]; Teitelbaum [1984]. For a general discussion of these factors in Europe, see van de Walle and Knodel [1980]. For theoretical discussions, see Caldwell [1976, 1978]. See also Nam [1994].)

Turning to the transition in economically less developed countries, one to two generations of reduced mortality, combined with a traditional high level of fertility, resulted in annual growth rates of 3 percent or more. However, beginning in the late 1960s, some Asian countries, particularly Taiwan and South Korea, began to experience rapid declines in fertility. At present these countries have reached approximate equilibrium between fertility and mortality rates, although they continue to grow because of their youthful age distributions. About a decade later, Thailand, Indonesia, and several Latin American countries such as Colombia and Mexico showed rapid reductions in their fertility rates. By the late 1990s, dramatic fertility declines were under way in nearly all countries outside of sub-Saharan Africa and Pakistan, and even these countries have shown clear declines among better-educated urban couples. The declines are due in small part to delayed marriage, but for the most part to use of contraception—primarily sterilization, and secondarily reversible methods such as intrauterine devices and the pill (see Bulatao and Lee [1983]; Cleland and Hobcraft [1985]; see also the country reports published on the Demographic and Health Surveys Project by Macro International [1985–2000]).

The conditions for these fertility declines show both similarities to and differences from the Western declines. It appears critical for couples to accept the idea that it is appropriate to intervene in the procreative process. In Pakistan, for example, it is commonly held that the number of births, as well as their gender and survivorship, is in the hands of Allah, and it would be wrong to interfere with his will. (It must be noted that a stated religious rationale for high fertility often masks other factors, such as a subordinate role for women. In other Islamic countries, such as Indonesia, Bangladesh, and even Iran, family planning is considered to be consistent with Islam.) Contraception tends to be found where the concepts of political and economic self-determination are better established, particularly among women. Female education is the single strongest correlate of fertility change.

In contrast with the Western experience, however, it also appears critical to have institutional support for contraception. The countries that have shown the clearest declines in fertility had national family planning programs with visible support from the highest levels of the government. The most effective programs have integrated family planning services into a general program of maternal and child health, and provide couples with easy access to a range of alternative methods (see Lapham and Mauldin 1987). Many countries are actually passing beyond this phase of the contraceptive transition, beginning in the 1990s, so that government-subsidized programs are being replaced by privatized services, at least for the middle class.

The consequences of population growth for economic development have been much debated (Simon 1977; Birdsall 1980). There have been some cases, such as Japan and South Korea, in which rapid economic expansion occurred simultaneously with rapid increases in population. Virtually all such cases were transitional, and the fertility of those countries is currently at replacement level, so the debate is now of mainly historical interest. There is a general consensus that low growth facilitates development. A growing population has a young age distribution, with many new entrants to the labor force and relatively few old people in need of pensions and health care. These factors may stimulate economic growth, but they must be balanced against the costs of supporting and educating large numbers of children. In several countries, such as the Philippines, the economy is unable to employ large cohorts of young people satisfactorily, especially those who are better educated, and they emigrate in large numbers. In addition, household welfare can be adversely affected by large numbers of children, even in situations of economic expansion at the macro level. The negative consequences of rapid growth extend beyond the economy and into the areas of health, social welfare, political stability, and the environment. (See the end of this article for relevant cross-references.)

CHANGES IN POPULATION DISTRIBUTION

Enormous changes in geographical distribution have been superimposed on the major trends in population size described above. Many of the social problems attributed to rapid population growth are more accurately diagnosed as consequences of increasing concentration. Urban areas, in particular the megalopolises of developing countries such as Mexico City, Buenos Aires, and New Delhi, have been growing during the twentieth century at more than twice the rate of the countries in which they are located. Cities are centers of concentration of economic, intellectual, and political life (see Hawley 1981), but rapid growth has exacerbated the problems of inadequate housing, sanitation, transportation, schooling, unemployment, and the crime associated with urban life. It is estimated that, in the year 2000, 76 percent of the population of developed countries is urban (compared to 26 percent in 1900 and 55 percent in 1950). In the developing countries, 41 percent is urban in 2000 (compared to 7 percent in 1900 and 18 percent in 1950).

The growth of cities has resulted in part from the excess of births over deaths in rural areas. With out-migration serving as one of the household-level valves for population regulation, individuals have been displaced from areas that cannot absorb them and have moved to cities, which are perceived to have better economic opportunities. Often that perception is incorrect. With a few exceptions, fertility is lower in cities than in rural areas.

A second major type of population redistribution in recent centuries has, of course, been across national borders. Movement to the Americas was greatest during the half-century between 1880 and 1930, and continues to the present. There are many streams of both short-term and long-term international migration, for example out of South and Southeast Asia and into the Middle East, Europe, and North America, and from Africa into Europe and North America, and the economies of several sending countries are strengthened by monthly remittances from their emigrants (United Nations 1979, 1997). (See the end of this article for relevant cross-references.)

POPULATION OF THE UNITED STATES

The United States has a population of approximately 278 million in the year 2000 and a growth rate of somewhat less than 1 percent annually, roughly one-third of which is due to immigration and two-thirds to natural increase. Fertility is slightly below replacement level, but there are more births than deaths because of the large size of the baby boom cohort, born from the late 1940s through the early 1960s. Age-specific fertility rates are increasing gradually for women in their thirties and forties, mainly because of postponed first and second births rather than later births. Otherwise, rates have been remarkably stable since the early 1970s. Rates below age 20 were dropping in the late 1990s but are still higher than in most other developed countries. For several excellent articles on fertility levels, differentials, and trends in the United States, see Casterline and colleagues (1996). See also National Center for Health Statistics (1999) and more recent annual reports in the same series.

Perhaps the most serious issues related to fertility are the large numbers of unplanned births to young women and the high numbers of abortions—about 2 for every 5 births—that could have been averted by contraception. Few developed countries have a range of contraceptive methods as limited as that of the United States. For example, intrauterine devices (IUDs) and progesterone-based pills are the two main nonsurgical methods in the rest of the world, but IUDs are not available in the United States. As mentioned earlier, most of the fertility decline in the West occurred while contraception was considered immoral and was explicitly illegal. Although contraception and even abortion are now legal, deep cultural ambiguities remain in the linkage between sexuality and procreation. A litigious environment has inhibited both the development of new contraceptives by American pharmaceutical companies and the marketing of new contraceptives developed elsewhere, and the U.S. government plays a minimal role in such development.

Life expectancy in the late 1990s was 73 years for males and 79 years for females (PRB 1998). Although life expectancy is increasing for both males and females, the female advantage is also gradually increasing. The female advantage was nearly 3 years at the beginning of the twentieth century, nearly 4 years at the middle, and nearly 7 years at the end of the century (Gelbard et al. 1999). The greatest improvements in mortality are in the highest age groups, especially after age 85. Because of increases in the number of elderly and projected changes in the age distribution of the labor force, the age at receipt of full Social Security benefits is scheduled to increase gradually, from 65 to 66 by the year 2009 and to 67 by the year 2027 (Binstock and George 1990).

Among males, whites have approximately a 5-year advantage over nonwhites, and among females, whites have approximately a 4-year advantage (National Center for Health Statistics 1989; and more recent annual reports in the same series). Life expectancy for black males is falling, due mainly to deaths by homicides to black males in their twenties and a greater prevalence of cardiovascular disease among blacks (Keith and Smith 1988). Infant mortality rates for nonwhite babies are increasing, due to low birth weights and inadequate prenatal care. These reversals of earlier long-term improvements are indicators of worsening conditions among poorer Americans. (For more description of the population of the United States, see Bogue [1985]; Lieberson and Waters [1988]; Sweet and Bumpass [1988]; Nam [1994].) (See the end of this article for cross-references to articles containing more discussions of the population of the United States.)

FUTURE POPULATION

The overriding concern of world population policy in recent years has been the achievement of a new equilibrium between fertility and mortality, so that growth will be slowed or stopped. Sometimes this policy is stated in terms of enabling couples to have the number of children they want to have, and no more, because surveys in most developing countries indicate that couples desire smaller families than they actually have (see the country reports published by Macro International [1985–2000].).

The concept of *replacement fertility* is important for understanding population projections. Normally stated in terms of the female population, the reproductive value of a woman of a given age is equal to the number of daughters she will have who will survive to (at least) this same age. If the average reproductive value is exactly 1, then fertility is at replacement level. This occurs when the average woman has about 2.1 births in her lifetime (a little above 2.0, to compensate for children who do not survive). If there has been a history of higher fertility, then the population has been growing and is relatively young, with many women in the peak ages of childbearing. As a result, there can continue to be more births than deaths (i.e., population growth) for a very long time after the net reproduction rate has reached or even fallen below the replacement value of 1.0. However, in the long term, replacement fertility will lead to a no-growth population, and below-replacement fertility will lead to population decline.

Strictly speaking, reproduction is intergenerational, but it is estimated with the net reproduction rate, a synthetic measure calculated from age-specific fertility and survival rates within an interval of time such as one year. If an artificial cohort of women is subjected to these rates and does not replace itself, then current fertility is interpreted to be below replacement.

Projected improvements in mortality would have a relatively low impact on population growth. For reproduction, it is survivorship up to and through the childbearing ages that matters. Improvements in survivorship after age 45 or so have little impact. Projections do require some assumptions about the future of the human immunovirus (HIV) and acquired immune deficiency syndrome (AIDS) epidemic, primarily in sub-Saharan Africa and also in South and Southeast Asia.

In the year 2000, world population is estimated to be 6.1 billion, with a growth rate of about 1.8 percent annually. If the current rate were to continue, world population would reach 9.2 billion by the year 2025. Even if reproduction immediately came into balance with mortality, as just described, world population would continue to increase. Population momentum, due to the youthful age distribution, would produce an excess of births over deaths (i.e., growth) for more than a century. World population would reach 7.5 billion by 2025, eventually stabilizing at nearly 10 billion. Substantial future growth is inevitable, but there is a wide range of possible scenarios.

Projections developed by the United Nations (United Nations 1998) for the year 2025 range from a low variant of 7.3 billion to a medium variant of 7.8 billion and a high variant of 8.4 billion, depending on assumptions about about future mortality and (more important) future fertility. By comparison, ten years earlier (United Nations 1988) the *low* projection for 2025 was 8.5 billion, slightly above the current *high* projection. This substantial downward revision reflects a general optimism that the threat of a world population explosion has largely receded. (It also implies that little credibility should be attached to longer-term projections, and for that reason this article will not cite projections beyond 2025.)

All the current projection scenarios assume that fertility will decline. The lowest estimate is based on an assumption that it will decline to below-replacement levels very soon, after 2005, and will decline steadily thereafter. This assumption is highly improbable, but even the medium variant assumes that worldwide fertility will be below replacement by 2030. This is a remarkable change from earlier projections, because prior to the late 1990s almost all scenarios assumed that fertility would ultimately converge to replacement level, with uncertainty only about when that would occur. Now that better data are available on actual changes during the 1980s and 1990s, it is considered likely that fertility will fall *below* replacement level early in the twenty-first century.

The net reproduction rate is currently less than 1.0 (that is, fertility is below the long-term level needed to balance mortality) in virtually all the more developed countries. The one-fifth of the world's population that resides in those countries will increase scarcely at all, and much of that growth will be the result of immigration from developing countries. Around the year 2000, compared to a standard of replacement fertility, Europe is at 68 percent of replacement level and North America is at 93 percent, while Asia is 10 percent above replacement, Latin America is 20 percent above, and Africa is 84 percent above. (These percentages come from estimates and medium-variant projections for 2000 by the United Nations [1998].) It is projected that low growth in Europe will cause the median age to rise to the mid-forties by 2025, with a fifth of the population above 65 years of age, a situation that the United States will approach a few years later. An excellent discussion of the causes and effects of future population change, and of many of the other topics in this article, can be found in Gelbard and colleagues, Haub, and Kent (1999).

Although world growth has been the preoccupation of recent decades, the possibility of population decline has long been acknowledged in Europe. In the United States, fertility has been below replacement since approximately 1970, and if it were not for high levels of immigration, this country would also face the prospect of population decline. Policies directed at increasing fertility in European countries have met with little success (see Calot and Blayo 1982; van de Kaa 1987). In urban settings with a high standard of living, children lose much of their earlier value as a source of economic activity, household wealth, and security in old age. They become increasingly expensive in terms of direct costs such as clothing, housing, and education, and in terms of opportunity costs such as forgone labor force activity by the mother.

In brief, there are probably two main reasons why fertility has not declined even further in the developed countries. One is the adherence to a powerful norm for two children that was consolidated around the middle of the twentieth century. Surveys show an overwhelming preference for exactly two children—preferably one boy and one girl, especially in the United States—with little flexibility either above or below that number. Actual childbearing often departs from the norm, more commonly by being below two children, so that fertility is below replacement. A high proportion of childbearing beyond two children is due to a desire for at least one child of each sex. Reliable methods to achieve the desired sex composition would result in a noticeable reduction of third and later births.

Second, children provide parents with a primary social group. There is no longer an expectation that they will provide support in old age, nor an important concern with carrying on the family name, but children do provide psychic and social rewards. To bear children is to emulate the behavior of one's parents and to replicate the family of orientation. However, this goal can be largely attained with only one child, as is being demonstrated in the lowest-fertility countries of Europe and in urban China. As increasing numbers of women opt for no children or only one child, it is possible that the widespread preference for two will weaken, even in the United States. For further discussion of fertility preferences in the United States, see Schoen and colleagues (1997).

Although the world as a whole is far from experiencing a decline in population, the low reproductivity of some countries and subpopulations raises questions about future mechanisms for restraining an indefinite decline in fertility, and eventually in population (see Teitelbaum and Winter 1985; Davis et al. 1986). It is reasonable to speculate on whether the cultural and social props for replacement fertility will continue to hold, or whether, as in the low and medium UN projections, worldwide fertility will decline to below-replacement levels early in the twenty-first century.

Major reductions in fertility in the past have been the result of delayed marriage and contraception and have been motivated at the level of the household. Maintenance of equilibrium in the future will require an increase in desired family size and less use of contraception. Many household-level factors associated with economic development would seem to support a projection of continued decline in fertility—for example, increased labor-force participation and autonomy for women, declines in marriage rates, increased costs for the education of children, and increased emphasis on consumption and leisure. It is easier to project a continued decline in fertility, rather than a significant upturn, in the absence of major changes or interventions in the microeconomy of the household. However, it also seems plausible that children will take on an increased (noneconomic) value as they become scarcer, or that subpopulations that favor high fertility will come to dominate, in which case the world will return to the previous pattern of long-term homeostasis at some level, or will establish a new pattern of very gradual growth, rather than allowing an inexorable decline.

(SEE ALSO: *Birth and Death Rates; Demographic Transition; Demography; Ethnicity; Family Planning; Infant and Child Mortality; Internal Migration; International Migration; Life Expectancy; Race; Retirement; Urbanization*)

REFERENCES

Binstock, Robert H., and Linda K. George (eds.) 1990 *Handbook of Aging and the Social Sciences*. London: Academic.

Birdsall, Nancy 1980 "Population Growth and Poverty in the Developing World." *Population Bulletin* 35 (5).

Bogue, Donald J. 1985 *The Population of the United States: Historical Trends and Future Projections*. New York: Free Press.

Bulatao, Rodolfo, and Ronald D. Lee 1983 *Determinants of Fertility in Developing Countries*. New York: Academic.

Caldwell, John G. 1976 "Toward a Restatement of Demographic Transition Theory." *Population and Development Review* 2:321–366.

—— 1978 "A Theory of Fertility: From High Plateau to Destabilization." *Population and Development Review* 4:553–577.

Calot, G., and Chantal Blayo 1982 "The Recent Course of Fertility in Western Europe." *Population Studies* 36:349–372.

Casterline, John B., Ronald D. Lee, and Karen A. Foote (eds.) 1996 *Fertility in the United States: New Patterns, New Theories. Population and Development Review*, a supplement to vol. 22.

Cleland, John, and John Hobcraft (eds.) 1985 *Reproductive Change in Developing Countries*. Oxford: Oxford University Press.

Coleman, David, and Roger Schofield (eds.) 1986 *The State of Population Theory*. Oxford: Basil Blackwell.

Davis, Kingsley 1963 "The Theory of Change and Response in Modern Demographic History." *Population Index* 29:345–366.

——, Mikhail S. Bernstam, and Rita Ricardo-Campbell (eds.) 1986 *Below-Replacement Fertility in Industrial Societies: Causes, Consequences, Policies. Population and Development Review*, a supplement to vol. 12.

Easterlin, Richard A. 1976 "The Conflict between Resources and Aspirations." *Population and Development Review* 2:417–425.

Gelbard, Alene, Carl Haub, and Mary M. Kent 1999 "World Population beyond Six Billion." *Population Bulletin* 54(1): Population Reference Bureau.

Goody, Jack 1976 *Production and Reproduction*. Cambridge: Cambridge University Press.

—— 1983 *The Development of the Family and Marriage in Europe*. Cambridge: Cambridge University Press.

Greenhalgh, Susan 1996 "The Social Construction of Population Science: An Intellectual, Institutional, and Political History of Twentieth Century Demography." *Comparative Studies in Society and History* 38:26–66.

Hanley, Susan B., and Arthur P. Wolf (eds.) 1985 *Family and Population in East Asian History*. Stanford, Calif.: Stanford University Press.

Hauser, Philip M., and Otis Dudley Duncan (eds.) 1959 *The Study of Population*. Chicago: University of Chicago Press.

Hawley, Amos H. 1981 *Urban Society*. New York: John Wiley.

Keith, Verna M., and David P. Smith 1988 "The Current Differential in Black and White Life Expectancy." *Demography* 25:625–632.

Lapham, Robert J., and W. Parker Mauldin 1987 "The Effects of Family Planning on Fertility: Research Findings." In R. J. Lapham and G. B. Simmons, eds., *Organizing for Effective Family Planning Programs*. Washington: National Academy Press.

Laslett, Peter, and Richard Wall (eds.) 1972 *Household and Family in Past Time*. Cambridge, England: Cambridge University Press.

Lieberson, Stanley, and Mary C. Waters 1988 *Ethnic and Racial Groups in Contemporary America*. New York: Russell Sage Foundation.

Livi Bacci, M. 1977 *A History of Italian Fertility*. Princeton, N.J.: Princeton University Press.

McEvedy, Colin, and Richard Jones 1978 *Atlas of World Population History*. New York: Facts on File.

McKeown, Thomas 1976 *The Modern Rise of Population*. New York: Academic.

Macro International, Inc. 1985–2000 Country reports from the Demographic and Health Surveys Project, Calverton, Md.

Mosley, W. Henry, and Lincoln C. Chen (eds.) 1984 *Child Survival: Strategies for Research. Population and Development Review*, a supplement to vol. 10.

Nam, Charles 1994 *Understanding Population Change*. Itasca, Ill.: F.E. Peacock.

Namboodiri, Krishnan 1988 "Ecological Demography: Its Place in Sociology." *American Sociological Review* 53:619–633.

National Center for Health Statistics 1999 "Births: Final Data for 1997." *National Vital Statistics Reports* 47(18). See also more recent annual reports in the same series.

Petersen, William 1975 *Population*. New York: Macmillan.

Population Reference Bureau (PRB) 1998 *World Population Data Sheet*. Washington: PRB. See also more recent publications in the same series.

Preston, Samuel H. 1978 *Mortality Patterns in National Populations*. New York: Academic.

Ryder, Norman B. 1969 "The Emergence of a Modern Fertility Pattern: United States 1917–1966." In S. J. Behrman, ed., *Family Planning. A World View*. Ann Arbor: University of Michigan Press.

Schoen, Robert, Young J. Kim, Constance A. Nathanson, Jason Fields, and Nan Marie Astone 1997 "Why Do Americans Want Children?" *Population and Development Review* 23:333–358.

Simon, Julian 1977 *The Economics of Population Growth*. Princeton, N.J.: Princeton University Press.

Stycos, J. Mayonne (ed.) 1987 *Demography as an Interdiscipline. Sociological Forum* 2 (4). Special issue.

Sweet, James A., and Larry L. Bumpass 1988 *American Families and Households*. New York: Russell Sage Foundation.

Taeuber, Karl E., Larry L. Bumpass, and James A. Sweet (eds.) 1978 *Social Demography*. New York: Academic.

Teitelbaum, Michael S. 1984 *The British Fertility Decline: Demographic Transition in the Crucible of the Industrial Revolution*. Princeton, N.J.: Princeton University Press.

——, and Jay M. Winter 1985 *The Fear of Population Decline*. San Diego, Calif.: Academic.

Tilly, Charles (ed.) 1978 *Historical Studies of Changing Fertility*. Princeton, N.J.: Princeton University Press.

United Nations 1973 *The Determinants and Consequences of Population Trends: New Summary of Findings on Interaction of Demographic, Economic and Social Factors*, vol. 1. *Population Studies* 50. New York: UN.

—— 1979 *Trends and Characteristics of International Migration Since 1950*. New York: UN.

—— 1988 *World Demographic Estimates and Projections, 1950–2025*. New York: UN.

—— 1997 *World Urbanization Prospects: The 1996 Revision*. New York: UN.

—— 1998 *World Population Prospects: The 1998 Revision*. New York: UN.

van de Kaa, Dirk J. 1987 "Europe's Second Demographic Transition." *Population Bulletin* 42(1).

van de Walle, Etienne, and John Knodel 1980 "Europe's Fertility Transition: New Evidence and Lessons for Today's Developing World." *Population Bulletin* 34 (6).

World Bank 1990 *World Development Report 1990*. Washington: Oxford University Press.

Wrigley, E. A. 1969 *Population and History*. New York: McGraw-Hill.

——, and R. S. Schofield 1981 *The Population History of England, 1541–1871: A Reconstruction*. London: Edward Arnold.

Yaukey, David 1985 *Demography: The Study of Human Population*. New York: St. Martin's.

THOMAS W. PULLUM

PORNOGRAPHY

Most societies have some kinds of sexually explicit words, images, and other materials that are disapproved, prohibited, illegal, or restricted in circulation; that are portrayed in a manner that is generally unacceptable; and that are classified as pornography. The term *pornography* often denotes subjective disapproval of materials rather than their content or effect.

Historically, attitudes toward pornography tend to be cyclical. The most recent expansion in the United States of the availability of such materials began in the 1960s, as a result of larger social trends, including the civil rights movement, the counterculture and antiwar movement, approval of the contraceptive pill, and liberal U.S. Supreme Court decisions providing access to previously banned novels and films. These trends contributed to continuing discussion on whether new forms of social control would be necessary to cope with pornography, and federal government investigations into pornography's impact were launched in 1968 and 1985.

Both the President's Commission on Obscenity and Pornography (1971) and the Attorney General's Commission on Obscenity and Pornography (1986) felt that it was not possible to define pornography clearly. The term has no legal definition, although certain sexual content is not protected by the free speech guarantees of the First Amendment to the U.S. Constitution and can be prosecuted under federal and state laws regulating obscenity.

Over the last several decades, the connotations of pornography have changed from a generic descriptor of explicit sexual content to more pejorative representations of sexual material. Pornography is often distinguished from erotica, which is a more tender, humanistic, and artistic type of sexual representation.

The divergence in opinion on how to deal with the pornography problem could be seen in the different recommendations of the two federal commissions established to examine it. The President's Commission recommended that the laws on obscenity should be repealed, because the material represented an insignificant social problem and had no lasting negative effect on its users. The report of the Attorney General's Commission urged that the obscenity laws should be strictly enforced, because the material had significant negative impact and constituted an important national problem. One possible reason for this disagreement was the change in the market for explicit materials between 1970 and 1986, but another factor could have been differences in the time available, composition, and resources of the two commissions.

Because sexually explicit content is often initially excluded from mainstream channels of communication, its creators have usually been alert to newly emerging outlets for distribution. One of the first books to appear in print after Gutenberg developed printing around 1448 was Boccaccio's erotic masterpiece, *The Decameron*. Soon after Edison developed moving pictures in 1891, underground "blue" movies began to appear. Super 8mm movies presenting sexually explicit content could be found in 1970, the very first year that the new technology appeared.

In the 1980s, soon after deregulation of the telephone business, many sex telephone services offered both recorded messages and the opportunity to have individualized "audiotext" conversations. Around the same time, sexually explicit movies became available via pay-per-view cable systems servicing homes and hotel chains.

In 1979, when fewer than 1 percent of American homes had videocassette recorders (VCRs), 80 percent of VCR owners bought or rented sexually explicit tapes. Some stores boosted sales of VCRs by giving a sexually explicit videotape as a gift with every purchase. During the 1990s, perhaps one-third of adult males and one-fifth of adult females have seen a sexually explicit videotape in a given year. The VCR is especially popular for viewing sexual content because it permits the user to speed up, slow down, replay, or freeze images. America is the world's largest producer of sexually explicit videotapes, churning out approximately 7,500 per year. The huge growth in the explicit video market during the 1980s and 1990s paralleled an increase in the number of large strip clubs around the country. The videos have become a way of promoting the careers of the actresses who appear at the clubs, who also can be seen in men's magazines.

CD-ROM and Internet income from sex-related content cannot be accurately measured but is believed to be enormous. A series of U.S. Supreme Court decisions has established the Internet as a public forum that is entitled to the highest level of protection by the First Amendment, including the representation of sexually explicit materials. Several laws that restricted access of children to the Internet have been declared unconstitutional by federal courts.

Rating systems represent one approach to social control of sexual content. The 1968 original movie rating system, by assigning sexually explicit materials to a special Adult X category and the development of similar kinds of ratings for television programs and popular music, further helped legitimate sexual content.

Within several years after the movie rating system began, X-rated films began to be shown at major theaters. The X-rated *Last Tango in Paris*, starring Marlon Brando, the country's most celebrated actor, was one of the most popular films of 1973, the same year in which *Deep Throat* became a national sensation because of its enormous commercial success and humor. The X-rated *Midnight Cowboy* had already received an Academy Award as Best Picture in 1969.

In addition to ratings, technological approaches have been used as a way of regulating children's access to sexual content. A special chip was developed so that parents could block children's access to objectionable materials on television. Such approaches attempt to strike a balance between the American abhorrence of censorship and parents' concern about their children's exposure to inappropriate material.

The ultimate weapon in blocking the availability of offensive sexual material has always been the application of the laws against obscenity. Three criteria for obscenity were promulgated by the U.S. Supreme Court in the case of *Miller v. California* (413 U.S. 15, 1973): the material had to be patently offensive; it must appeal to the prurient interest of the average adult applying contemporary standards; and it must have no literary, artistic, political, or scientific value.

Because the Court no longer wanted to deal with the stream of cases that it had been handling, "community" was newly defined to be a local county, state, or federal court district, so that each area could have whatever level of sexual material it found acceptable. The number of indictments and convictions declined after 1973 because of juries' reluctance to convict, prosecutorial predictability, changes in the political climate that led to antipornography becoming a less salient and less attractive political theme, and communities' views that criminal justice resources should give less attention to obscenity and focus more on crimes against persons.

The decline in implementation of criminal justice sanctions encouraged new entrepreneurs to produce and distribute sex-oriented materials. Another spur to entrepreneurs, in the 1980s, was the Federal Communications Commission's decision not to regulate cable television, and this was followed in 1984 by the television networks' decision to eliminate their national code of broadcast standards. The continuing competition for audiences between media further increased the likelihood that sexual content would receive more prominence, in a situation in which administrative barriers to representation of sex content were clearly diminishing.

Instead of criminal prosecution of materials for violation of the obscenity laws, a number of cities adopted a totally different approach in the 1990s. These communities use zoning laws against theaters, strip clubs, bookstores, and other sex-related industries in order to break up their concentration and minimize visual pollution. The new approach accepted these establishments' right to sell sexually explicit products or services but challenged their right to maintain their location.

The zoning laws rely on a U.S. Supreme Court decision which held that if "adult" businesses could be shown to have adverse secondary effects (decline in real estate values and quality of life and increase in crime), the community could make zoning changes, provided that reasonable alternative avenues of communication were available to the businesses (*Playtime Theatres v. City of Renton*, 106 U.S. 925, 1986).

An example of the zoning approach could be seen in New York City where a 1997 law required that "adult" bookstores, strip clubs, peepshows, and theaters be at least 500 feet from each other and at least 500 feet from residences and public buildings, thus eliminating the concentration of such establishments in Times Square. Any challenges to such zoning changes have been handled in the civil rather than the criminal courts.

One way in which producers of these materials attempt to minimize legal problems is to make publications, movies, and videotapes in both hard-core and soft-core versions, for targeted distribution to specific markets. The hard-core materials usually show some form of actual sexual interaction and the soft-core content generally presents simulated interaction. Any representation of sexual material involving children has been the target of intensive law enforcement and is very scarce.

There seems to be no relationship between sexually explicit materials and prostitution; consumers of these materials are not likely to be customers of prostitutes, because of differences in the gratifications provided by the two activities. There also seems to be no significant relationship between the production and distribution of such materials and organized crime. There are now so many producers and distributors and the prices are so competitively low that organized crime groups cannot make a large enough profit to justify participation in the business.

Although there is no unified and consistent feminist attitude toward pornography, feminist opposition to pornography has generated much attention. One sustained feminist attack on pornography, jointly led by writer Andrea Dworkin and attorney Catherine A. MacKinnon, argued that pornography is misogynistic and dehumanizing, graphically presenting the sexually explicit subordination of women. They developed a model ordinance for Indianapolis that represented a civil rights approach, which identified pornography as a violation of the equality guarantee of the Fourteenth Amendment. However, the ordinance was found to be unconstitutional by a federal appeals court (*American Booksellers Association v. Hudnut*, 771 F. 2d, 7th Circuit, 1985). A comparable approach was upheld by the highest court in Canada (*Butler v. The Queen*, 1 SCR 452, 199, 1992), where it has been primarily used to prosecute gay publications.

A collateral approach involved dissemination of feminist writer Robin Morgan's slogan, "Pornography is the theory, rape is the practice." Around the same time that feminist theorists were arguing that the growing availability of misogynistic pornography was the direct cause of increasing rates of rape, a number of mass communication researchers conducted laboratory experiments that attempted to prove the connection between exposure to such materials and the development of callous attitudes toward women and rape. One of the problems with these studies is that they were usually conducted with college students, who were exposed to materials that they would not ordinarily see. There is also the possibility of an experimenter effect and the difficulty of proving the carrying over of an attitude from viewing a film to a real rape situation. Several researchers have expressed the view that to interpret their largely laboratory-based studies as confirming a causal nexus between exposure to sexually explicit films and subsequent sexually violent behavior would represent overgeneralization.

Another problem in arguing for such a nexus is that no large-scale content studies prove that there has been any increase in the amount of sexual violence in the media. An examination of the available data suggests that there has been a decline since 1977 in the amount of sexual violence in the media, but there has probably been an increase in violence in nonpornographic fare, such as action, slasher, and horror films. To single out pornography for stringent legal action and to ignore ideas about rape and violence that are otherwise so pervasive in our culture is not justified by the available evidence.

A number of natural experiments have provided information on the possible relationship between media sex content and rape and other sex crimes. In the United States, four states that eliminated all obscenity statutes and had a concomitant increase in the availability of sexually explicit materials for varying periods between 1973 and 1986 were studied. During the period of obscenity nonprosecution, the mean annual arrest rates for sex offenses in these four states declined significantly in comparison to the other forty-six states. A study of the first three countries to legalize sexually explicit materials (Denmark, Sweden, Germany) concluded that legalization did not lead to increased sexual violence in any of them.

Researchers using other indirect measures have similarly attempted to correlate sex offenses with previous exposure to sexually explicit materials. A large-scale study by the Kinsey Institute for Sex Research of convicted sex offenders found no relation between sex crimes and offenders' exposure to such materials. Another study of nonincarcerated sex offenders reported no significant differences between the exposure to such materials of the offenders and the general adult male population. Whether on an individual, a regional, or a national basis, empirical studies have failed to find any consistent correlation between availability of and exposure to explicit materials and sex crimes against women.

A number of producers are actively distributing sexually explicit materials targeted for women consumers, and other producers have developed such materials for feminist audiences. Some feminists have produced their own explicit films and others have made videotapes for women and couples that are sold in mainstream superstores and direct mail catalogs. A number of performers who became known from appearing in explicit movies and tapes are obtaining roles in mainstream studio or independent films.

Research has identified a number of functions served by sexually explicit materials. They provide information that is not otherwise available, as well as fantasy outlets and sexual stimulation. They also provide reassurance about one's body and about shame or guilt relating to specific practices. The materials can desensitize people so that they are better able to consider and discuss sexual matters, and can facilitate communication between sexual partners. The materials may provide a socially acceptable functional equivalent for masturbation and for acting out otherwise socially harmful sexual behavior. For members of a group audience, as in a strip club or a movie theater, the social context can reinforce the experience. The materials and performers also may provide a vehicle for connoisseurship.

Plausible next steps in sociological investigations of pornography could include cross-media content analyses, naturalistic studies of effects, systematic case studies of the role of the various interest groups involved in promoting or blocking pornography, investigation of the structure of the pornography industry, and studies of the role of the home environment in contributing to how explicit materials are used.

In Denmark, the first country to legalize pornography (1969), the market for such materials declined sharply, as a result of satiation of the audience. Tracking the cycle of acceptance of pornography in America, to see whether the Danish experience is relevant, could represent an important study. A collateral study could determine whether there are specific subgroups in the population for whom these materials are becoming more or less important. The extent to which pornography continues to be a feature of the political culture wars and a vehicle for obtaining support for larger economic and policy initiatives represents an important social indicator, as is the alliance between feminists and moral conservatives in opposing pornography. Another activity that will surely bear watching in the future is how the effort to regulate pornography on the Internet, for children or adults, can be accomplished by a state or a country that does not have legal jurisdiction over the global information network that is the Internet.

REFERENCES

Attorney General's Committee on Obscenity and Pornography 1986 *Final Report*. Washington, D.C.: U.S. Government Printing Office.

Gebhard, P. H., J. H. Gagnon, W. B. Pomeroy, and C. Christenson 1965 *Sex Offenders*. New York: Harper and Row.

Kimmel, M. (ed.) 1989 *Men Confront Pornography*. New York: Crown.

Lederer, L. (ed.) 1980 *Take Back the Night: Women on Pornography*. New York: William Morrow.

MacKinnon, C. A. 1993 *Only Words*. Cambridge, Mass.: Harvard University Press.

President's Commission on Obscenity and Pornography 1971 *Final Report*. Washington, D.C.: U.S. Government Printing Office.

Strossen, N. 1995 *Defending Pornography: Free Speech, Sex, and the Fight for Women's Rights*. New York: Scribner.

Winick, C. 1977 "From Deviant to Normative: Changes in the Social Acceptability of Sexually Explicit Material." In E. Sagarin, ed., *Deviance and Social Change*. Beverly Hills, Calif.: Sage.

Zillman, D., and J. Bryant (eds.) 1989 *Pornography: Research Advances and Policy Considerations*. Hillsdale, N.J.: Lawrence Erlbaum.

CHARLES WINICK

POSITIVE MENTAL HEALTH

The concept of positive mental health was developed by Marie Jahoda, who argues that positive mental health can be viewed as an enduring personality characteristic or as a less permanent function of personality and the social situation (Jahoda 1958). This article summarizes Jahoda's approach to positive mental health, reviews other discussions of the concept, describes a challenge to the assumption that positive mental health requires the accurate perception of reality, examines the value assumptions inherent in the concept, and compares the notions of normality and positive mental health.

In her classic book, *Current Concepts of Positive Mental Health* (1958), Jahoda identified the following six approaches to the definition of positive mental health, which are described in detail below: (1) attitude toward own self; (2) growth, development, and self-actualization; (3) integration; (4) autonomy; (5) perception of reality; and (6) environmental mastery.

1. Acceptance of self, self-confidence, and self-reliance characterize the mentally healthy person. An important attribute of positive mental health includes the understanding of one's strengths and weaknesses, coupled with the conviction that one's positive characteristics outweigh the negative traits. Independence, initiative, and self-esteem are other indictors of positive mental health.

2. The realization of one's potential is the underlying assumption of this dimension of positive mental health. Maslow (1954) explains that

self-actualization is a motive that encourages the person to maximize capabilities and talents. It is hypothesized that growth motivation is related to positive mental health. Rather than meeting basic human needs, self-actualization implies movement toward higher goals. This dimension of positive mental health also implies an investment in living—a concern with other people and one's environment, rather than a primary focus on satisfying one's own needs.

3. The person with positive mental health has a balance of psychic forces, a unified outlook on life, and resistance to stress. Psychoanalysts view integration as the balance of the id, the ego, and the superego. This balance is viewed as changeable, with flexibility as the desired end result. Positive mental health refers to integration at the cognitive level, which implies a unifying philosophy of life that shapes feelings and behaviors. Finally, resistance to stress characterizes the integrated person. The mentally healthy person can adapt to stress without deteriorating. Everyone experiences anxiety when encountering a stressful situation. A mentally healthy response to anxiety and stress suggests some tolerance of tension, ambiguity, and frustration.

4. Autonomy refers to self-determination and independence in decision making. The concept suggests that the person with positive mental health is self-directed and self-controlled. The individual acts independently of the outside world; behavior is not dictated by environmental circumstances.

Jahoda points out that some authors have a different interpretation of autonomy. Autonomy may be defined as having freedom of choice about conforming to societal norms. This perspective implies that the person is not independent of the environment, but does have free choice to decide how to respond to societal demands.

5. "As a rule, the perception of reality is called mentally healthy when what the individual sees corresponds to what is actually there" (Jahoda 1958, p. 49). Mentally healthy reality perception includes perception free from need distortion. A mentally healthy person views the world without distortions, fitting the perception to objective cues that are present, and does not reject evidence because it does not fit his or her wishes or needs.

Jahoda argues that this dimension of positive mental health implies the ability to perceive others in an empathetic manner. This social sensitivity enables a healthy person to put himself or herself in another person's place and anticipate that person's behavior in a given social situation.

6. Mastery of the environment refers to achieving success in some social roles and appropriate function in those roles. Positive mental health also includes the ability to have positive affective interpersonal relations. The social roles involved in environmental mastery may include sexual partner, parent, and worker. Environmental mastery suggests the ability to adapt, adjust, and solve problems in an efficient manner.

OTHER DEFINITIONS OF POSITIVE MENTAL HEALTH

Jourard and Landsman propose similar criteria for positive mental health: positive self-regard, ability to care about others, ability to care about the natural world, openness to new ideas and to people, creativity, ability to work productively, ability to love, and realistic perception of self (1980, p. 131).

Jensen and Bergin (1988) conducted a nationwide survey of 425 professional therapists (clinical psychologists, marriage and family therapists, social workers, and psychiatrists) to determine values associated with mental health. Eight themes were identified as important for a positive, mentally healthy lifestyle: (1) competent perception and expression of feelings (sensitivity, honesty, openness with others); (2) freedom/autonomy/responsibility (self-control, appropriate feelings of guilt, responsibility for one's actions, increasing one's alternatives at a choice point); (3) integration, coping, and work (effective coping strategies, work satisfaction, striving to achieve); (4) self-awareness/growth (awareness of potential, self-discipline); (5) human relatedness/interpersonal and family commitment (ability to give and receive affection, faithfulness in marriage, commitment to family needs, self-sacrifice); (6) self-maintenance/physical fitness (healthful habits, self-discipline in use of alcohol, drugs, tobacco); (7) mature values (purpose for living, having principles and ideals); and (8) forgiveness (making restitution, forgiving others) (Jensen and Bergin 1988, p. 292). They found a high level of consensus among the practitioners. Many of these values are consistent with the six approaches identified by Jahoda in 1958.

ILLUSIONS AND POSITIVE MENTAL HEALTH

The validity of one of the components of positive mental health has been questioned (Snyder 1989). Is accurate reality perception the hallmark of positive mental health? Taylor and Brown argue that "certain illusions may be adaptive for mental health and well being" (1988, p. 193). They explain that mentally healthy persons have an unrealistic positive self-evaluation. Normal individuals are more aware of their strengths and less aware of their weaknesses, perceiving themselves as better than the average person and viewing themselves more positively than others see them.

Another illusion held by mentally healthy persons is an exaggerated sense of self-control. Taylor and Brown (1988) cite evidence that depressed individuals are more likely to have realistic perceptions of personal control than are nondepressed persons. Positive illusions of personal control over the environment, self-worth, and hopefulness about the future imply mental health, and these illusions enable people to function in an adaptive manner.

According to Taylor and Brown (1988), illusions can promote several criteria of mental health, including happiness or contentment, the ability to care for others, and the capacity for intellectually creative and productive work. While mentally healthy people learn from negative experiences, their illusions help them to cope with stresses and strains (Taylor et al. 1989).

Taylor and Brown conclude, "the mentally healthy person appears to have the enviable capacity to distort reality in a direction that enhances self-esteem, maintains beliefs in personal efficacy, and promotes an optimistic view of the future" (1988, p. 204).

THE ROLE OF UNDERLYING VALUE ASSUMPTIONS

Jahoda (1980) argues that the definition of positive mental health depends upon underlying value assumptions. Schwartz and Link explain, "What is viewed as good and functional is often dependent on who is doing the viewing and what value hierarchy is being applied" (1991, p. 240). The definition of positive mental health varies across societies. In addition, there may be variance across social groups within one society (e.g., social class, gender, race, and ethnicity). It is also the case that the definition of positive mental health may be a function of the situation.

Different societies have their own definition of positive mental health. In some societies, a mentally healthy individual is supposed to be autonomous, while in other societies, the mentally healthy person is expected to be compliant, conforming to particular rules imposed by others.

Variance across social groups within one society is illustrated by evidence that there are different standards of positive mental health for men and women. Broverman et al. (1981) report sex role stereotypes in the clinical judgments of mental health among seventy-nine psychotherapists. The therapists were asked to identify the characteristics that portrayed healthy, mature, and socially competent adults. Broverman et al. found "that healthy women differ from healthy men by being more submissive; less independent; less adventurous; more easily influenced; less aggressive; less competitive" (1981, p. 92).

The definition of positive mental health is situational. While a particular behavior is mentally healthy in one situation, it may represent mentally ill behavior in another situation. For example, behavior in a life-threatening situation may be defined as adaptive, given the stresses of the environment. In normal everyday life the same behavior may be defined as bizarre. This observation leads Foote and Cottrell to ask, "What are the psychologically relevant attributes of an environment which permit the manifestations of psychologically healthy behavior?" (1959, p. 44).

Finally, according to Jahoda (1988), the definition of positive mental health is also influenced by the following four assumptions: (1) the criteria for judging health and illness are debatable; (2) neither mental illness nor mental health can be defined by the absence of the other; (3) there are degrees of mental health; and (4) a low level of mental health is not synonymous with mental illness.

NORMALITY OR POSITIVE MENTAL HEALTH?

There is continued debate on the definition of and relationship between normality and positive mental health. There is general agreement among researchers who study normatology that the definition of psychopathology is more precise than the definition of normal behavior (Offer and Sabshin 1991; Strack and Lorr 1997). While psychiatrists have developed sets of very specific criteria for defining mental illness (American Psychiatric Association 1994), there are no set criteria for defining either normal behavior or positive mental health. As is the case for the definition of positive mental health, the determination of normality varies across societies, subgroups within one society, and situations. What is normal (or positive mental health) in one time and place is abnormal (or mentally ill) in another. Both concepts are fluid in nature. Additional research is needed to understand how the definitions of positive mental health and normality are created. What are the underlying assumptions of these definitions, and how do they vary across societies and situations?

While normality implies the absence of psychopathology, positive mental health goes *beyond* normality. Researchers agree that positive mental health is more than the absence of mental illness; it represents the enhancement of human potential. Although a person may not have symptoms of mental illness, he or she may not have positive mental health, especially in the absence of self-confidence, self-actualization, integration, autonomy, reality perception, and environmental mastery. To have positive mental health implies fulfilling one's potential to the fullest. One might argue that positive mental health is a moving target, representing goals that are established, evaluated, and then revised as a person's circumstance change. The concept of positive mental health is utopian. While many strive to achieve positive mental health, only a few fulfill the goal of maximizing their potential.

REFERENCES

American Psychiatric Association 1994 *Diagnostic and Statistical Manual of Mental Disorders*, 4th ed. Washington: American Psychiatric Association.

Broverman, Inge K., S. R. Vogel, D. M. Broverman, F. E. Clarkson, P. S. Rosenkranz 1981 "Sex-Role Stereotypes and Clinical Judgments of Mental Health." In Elizabeth Howell and Marjorie Bayes, eds., *Women and Mental Health*. New York: Basic Books.

Foote, Nelson N., and Leonard S. Cottrell, Jr. 1959 *Identity and Interpersonal Competence: A New Direction in Family Research*. Chicago: University of Chicago Press.

Jahoda, Marie 1958 *Current Concepts of Positive Mental Health*. New York: Basic Books.

—— 1980 *Current Concepts of Positive Mental Health*, rev. ed. New York: Arno.

—— 1988 "Economic Recession and Mental Health: Some Conceptual Issues." *Journal of Social Issues* 44:13–23.

Jensen, Jay P., and Allen E. Bergin 1988 "Mental Health Values of Professional Therapists: A National Interdisciplinary Survey." *Professional Psychology: Research and Practice* 19:290–297.

Jourard, S. M., and T. Landsman 1980 *Healthy Personality: An Approach from the Viewpoint of Humanistic Psychology*, 4th ed. New York: Macmillan.

Maslow, Abraham H. 1954 *Motivation and Personality*. New York: Harper and Row.

Offer, Daniel, and Melvin Sabshin (eds.) 1991 *The Diversity of Normal Behavior: Further Contributions to Normatology*. New York: Basic Books.

Schwartz, Sharon, and Bruce G. Link 1991 "Sociological Perspectives on Mental Health: An Integrative Approach." In Daniel Offer and Melvin Sabshin, eds., *The Diversity of Normal Behavior: Further Contributions to Normatology*. New York: Basic Books.

Snyder, C. R. 1989 "Reality Negotiation: From Excuses to Hope and Beyond." *Journal of Social and Clinical Psychology* 8:130–157.

Strack, Stephen, and Maurice Lorr 1997 "Invited Essay: The Challenge of Differentiating Normal and Disordered Personality." *Journal of Personality Disorders* 11:105–122.

Taylor, Shelley, and Jonathan Brown 1988 "Illusion and Well Being: A Social Psychological Perspective on Mental Health." *Psychological Bulletin* 103:193–210.

Taylor, Shelley, Rebecca L. Collins, Laurie A. Skokan, and Lisa G. Aspinwall 1989 "Maintaining Positive Illusions in the Face of Negative Information: Getting the Facts without Letting Them Get to You." *Journal of Social and Clinical Psychology* 8:114–129.

JANET HANKIN

POSITIVISM

The concept of "positivism" was originally used to denote the scientific study of social phenomena, but today the term *positivism* has become vague. Most often, it is used as a pejorative smear for certain kinds of intellectual activity in the social sciences, sociology in particular. Most frequently, at least within sociology, positivism is associated with such undesirable states as "raw empiricism," "mindless quantification," "antihumanism," "legitimation of the status quo," and "scientific pretentiousness." With few exceptions (e.g., Turner 1985), sociologists are unwilling to label themselves "positivists." Yet, the titular founder of sociology—Auguste Comte—used this label as a rallying cry for developing formal and abstract theory that could still be used to remake society; so, the current use of the term does not correspond to its original meaning. If anything, the term connotes almost the exact opposite of Comte's vision (1830–1842). It is proper, therefore, to review Comte's original conception of positivism and its use in early sociology, and then we can discover how and why the meaning of positivism changed.

In *Cours de philosophie positive*, Comte began by asserting that "the first characteristic of Positive Philosophy is that it regards all phenomena as subject to natural *Laws*" (1830–1842, p. 5). Moreover, he emphasized that "research into what are called *causes*, whether first or final," is "in vain" (1830–1842, p. 6); and by the time he was well into *Cours de philosophie positive*, he stressed that a "great hindrance to the use of observation is the empiricism which is introduced into it by those who ... would interdict the use of any theory whatever" because "no real observation of any kind of phenomena is possible, except in as far as it is first directed, and finally interpreted, by some theory" (1830–1842, p. 242). Rather, the goal of positivistic sociology is to "pursue an accurate discovery of ... Laws, with a view to reducing them to the smallest possible number," and "our real business is to analyze accurately the circumstance of phenomena, to connote them by natural relations of succession and resemblance" (1830–1842, p. 6). Comte's exemplar for this advocacy was Newton's law of gravitation, an affirmation of his early preference to label sociology as "social physics." Moreover, such laws were to be used to reconstruct society; and while Comte went off the deep end on this point, proclaiming himself, late in his career, to be the "high priest of humanity" (Comte 1851–1854), it is difficult to see Comte's positivism as antihumanistic, as conservative, or as legitimating the status quo.

How, then, did Comte get turned on his head? The answer to this question cannot be found in nineteenth-century sociology, for the most positivistic sociologists of this period—Herbert Spencer (1874–1896) and Émile Durkheim ([1893] 1947; [1895] 1934)—could hardly be accused of "raw" and "mindless" empiricism, nor could they in the context of their times be considered antihumanistic, conservative, and apologists for the status quo (the label "conservative" for these thinkers is imposed retrospectively, through the refraction of contemporary eyeglasses). Moreover, early American sociologists—Albion Small, Frank Lester Ward, Robert Park, William Graham Sumner, and even the father of statistical methods and empiricism in American sociology, Franklin Giddings—all advocated Comtean and Spencerian positivism before World War I. Thus, the answer to this question is to be found in the natural sciences, particularly in a group of scientist-philosophers who are sometimes grouped under the rubric "the Vienna Circle," despite the fact that several intellectual generations of very different thinkers were part of this circle.

Before the "circle" was evident, the nature of the issues was anticipated by Ernst Mach (1893), who argued that the best theory employs a minimum of variables and does not speculate on unobservable processes and forces. Mach emphasized reliance on immediate sense data, rejecting all speculation about causes and mechanisms to explain observed relations among variables. Indeed, he rejected all conceptions of the universe as being regulated by "natural laws" and insisted that theory represent mathematical descriptions of relations among observable variables. Although Mach was not a member of the Vienna Circle, his ideas framed the issues for those who are more closely identified with this group. Yet, his ideas did not dictate their resolution. Many in the Vienna Circle were concerned primarily with logic and systems of formal thought, almost to the exclusion of observation (or, at least, to the point of subordinating it to their primary concerns). A split thus developed in the Vienna Circle over the relative emphasis on empirical observation and systems of logic; a radical faction emphasized that truth can be "measured solely by logical coherence of statements" (which had been reduced to mathematics), whereas a more moderate group insisted that there is a "material truth of observation" supplementing "formal truths" (Johnston 1983, p. 189). Karl Popper, who was a somewhat marginal figure in the Vienna Circle of the 1930s, is perhaps the best-known mediator of this split, for he clearly tried to keep the two points of emphasis together. But even here the reconciliation is somewhat negative (Popper 1959, 1969): A formal theory can never be proved, only disproved; and so, data are to be used to mount assaults on abstract theories from which empirical hypotheses and predictions are formally "deduced."

Why did the philosopher-scientists in the Vienna Circle have any impact on sociology, especially American sociology? In Europe, of course, sociology had always been firmly anchored in philosophy, but in American sociology during the 1920s and 1930s, the rise of quantitative sociology was accelerating as the students of Franklin Giddings assumed key positions in academia and as Comtean and Spencerian sociology became a distant memory. (It should be noted, however, that Marx, Weber, and Durkheim had yet to have much impact on American sociology in the late 1920s or early 1930s.) But American sociology was concerned with its status as science and, hence, was receptive to philosophical arguments that could legitimate its scientific aspirations (Turner and Turner 1990). Mach was appealing because his advocacy legitimated statistical analysis of empirical regularities as variables; and Popper was to win converts with his uneasy reconciliation of observation and abstract theory. Both legitimated variable analyses; and for American sociologists in the 1930s and later from the 1940s through the early 1960s, this meant sampling, scaling, statistically aggregating, and analyzing empirical "observations." Members of the Vienna circle had even developed an appealing terminology, *logical positivism*, to describe this relation between theory (abstract statements organized by a formal calculus) and research (quantitative data for testing hypotheses logically deduced from abstract statements). The wartime migration of key figures in the late Vienna Circle to the United States no doubt increased their impact on the social sciences in the United States (despite the fact that the "logical" part of this new label for "positivism" was redundant in Comte's original formulation). But logical positivism legitimated American empiricism in this sense: The quantitative data could be used to "test" theories, and so it was important to improve upon methods of gathering data and analyzing methodologies in order to realize this lofty goal. Along the way, the connection of theory and research was mysteriously lost, and positivism became increasingly associated with empiricism and quantification, per se.

There was a brief and highly visible effort, reaching a peak in the late 1960s and early 1970s, to revive the "logical" side of positivism by explaining to sociologists the process of "theory construction." Indeed, numerous texts on theory construction were produced (e.g., Zetterberg 1965; Dubin 1969; Blalock 1969; Reynolds 1971; Gibbs 1972; Hage 1972), but the somewhat mechanical, cookbook quality of these texts won few converts, and so the empiricist connotations of positivism were never successfully reconnected to abstract theory. Even the rather odd academic alliance of functional theory with quantitative sociology—for example, Merton and Lazarsfeld at Columbia and Parsons and Stouffer at Harvard—was unsuccessful in merging theory and research, once again leaving positivism to denote quantitative research divorced from theory.

Other intellectual events, anticipated by various figures of the Vienna Circle, created a new skepticism and cynicism about the capacity to develop "objective" science, especially social science. This skepticism stressed the arbitrary nature of symbols and signs and hence their capacity to represent and denote the universe independently of the context in which such signs are produced and used. Such thinking was supplemented by Kuhn's landmark work (1970) and by the sociology of science's emphasis (e.g., Whitley 1984) on the politico-organizational dynamics distorting the idealized theory-data connection as advocated by Popper (1969). Out of all this ferment, a new label increasingly began to appear: *postpositivism*. This label appears to mean somewhat different things to varying audiences, but it connotes that Comte's original vision and Popper's effort to sustain the connection between empirical observations and theory are things of the past—just as "rationalism" and "modernity" are giving away to "postmodernism." Thus, one hears about a "postpositivist" philosophy of science, which, despite the vagueness and diversity of usages for this label, is intended to signal the death of positivism. Curiously, this postpositivism is meant as an obituary for the older Comtean positivism or its resurrection as logical positivism by the Vienna Circle, where abstract logic and observation were more happily joined together.

The result is that the term "positivism" no longer has a clear referent, but it is evident that, for many, being a positivist is not a good thing. It is unlikely, then, that "positivism" will ever be an unambiguous and neutral term for sociological activity revolving around the formulation and testing of theory and the use of plausible theories for social engineering (or in more muted form, for "sociological practice"). Other labels are likely to be employed in light of the negative connotations of positivism in an intellectual climate dominated by "post-isms."

Despite this apparent eclipse of positivism by various post-isms, positivistic sociology remains a vibrant activity, albeit by other names. Because of the pejorative use of the label "positivism," few are willing to embrace it, but many practice positivistic sociology. What, then, are the main tenets of positivism? This question can be answered under ten general points.

First, positivism assumes that there is a "real world" that can be studied scientifically. The social world is not an illusion, or a total fabrication of sociologists' imaginations. It is there; it has properties amenable to investigation.

Second, positivism assumes that there are fundamental properties of the social universe that are always operative when people act, interact, and organize. While the properties can manifest themselves in a wide variety of forms in varying contexts, they nonetheless exist; and they are what drive the dynamics of the social universe. The goal of positivism is to uncover these fundamental properties, to see how they work, to develop theories on their operation, and to test these theories with systematically collected data.

Third, the theories developed by positivists should strive for some degree of formality. The making of formal statements need not invoke mathematics or some other system of formal argument; rather, all that is necessary is that concepts denoting processes be explicitly defined and that relations among concepts be stated clearly. These goals can be met with ordinary language, although if they can be converted into mathematics, this is seen by most positivists as useful though not absolutely necessary.

Fourth, in defining concepts formally, these definitions should denote aspects of the social universe such that what is encompassed by the concept is clear and, equally important, what is not is also explicit. In stating relations among concepts denoting fundamental properties of the social world, these relations can be stated in three basic ways. One is functional (in the mathematical sense), whereby variation in one concept is seen to be related to another (e.g., the level of differentiation in a population is a positive function of its size). A second way to state relations is through analytical models that specify the direct, indirect, and reverse causal effects among those forces of the universe that are seen as connected. A third procedure is historical in which events at earlier points in time are seen to cause directly, or in combination with other events, an outcome. A fourth, though less desirable (and at best, preliminary), procedure is to find the place of particular forces in an abstract category system that juxtaposes phenomena (e.g., the periodic table in chemistry or Parsonian four-functions analysis).

Fifth, the goal of all positivistic theories statements is parsimony. Reducing theories to their simplest form is always desired, whether this be a simple equation, an analytical model, a historical sequence of cause, or even a simple set of categories.

Sixth, at the same time that statements move toward parsimony, they should become ever more abstract and should seek to explain as large a portion of reality as is possible. The goal is always to explain as much of the social universe with as few principles and models as can do justice to the dynamics of the social world.

Seventh, all theoretical statements must be testable, at least in principle. Some statements can be tested directly with existing methodologies; others must be transformed (e.g., from deductions to hypotheses); and still others may have to wait for new methodologies or for specific classes of events to occur. The critical criterion is that theories be testable, now or in the future.

They must suggest by their formulation ways of operationalization.

Eighth, theories can be tested by all relevant methods: historical, comparative, experimental, survey, observational, and even simulational. No one method identifies positivism; all are useful in assessing the plausibility of theories.

Ninth, tests must always be used to assess the plausibility of theories. When tests do not support the theory, the theory must be rejected and/or revised.

Tenth, theories that remain plausible constitute, for the time being, the best explanations of the social universe. And the more theories remain plausible, the more they are made parsimonious, and the more new theories are developed to explain what has not yet been explained, the more knowledge of the nature and operative dynamics of the social universe accumulates.

REFERENCES

Blalock, Hubert M., Jr. 1969 *Theory Construction: From Verbal to Mathematical Formulations*. Englewood Cliffs, N.J.: Prentice-Hall.

Comte, Auguste 1830–1842 *Cours de philosophie positive: Les Préliminaires généraux et la philosophie mathématique*. Paris: Bachelier.

—— 1851–1854 *Système de politique: ou, traite de sociologie, instituant la religion de l'humanite*. Paris: L. Mathias.

Dubin, Robert 1969 *Theory Building*. New York: Free Press.

Durkheim, Emile (1895) 1934 *The Rules of the Sociological Method*. New York: Free Press.

—— (1893) 1947 *The Division of Labor in Society*. New York: Free Press.

Gibbs, Jack 1972 *Sociological Theory Construction*. Hinsdale, Ill.: Dryden Press.

Hage, Jerald 1972 *Techniques and Problems of Theory Construction in Sociology*. New York: John Wiley.

Johnston, William M. 1983 *The Austrian Mind: An Intellectual and Social History 1848–1938*. Berkeley: University of California Press.

Kuhn, Thomas 1970 *The Structure of Scientific Revolutions*, 2nd ed. Chicago: University of Chicago Press.

Mach, Ernst 1893 *The Science of Mechanics*, trans. T. J. McCormack. La Salle, Ill: Open Court.

Popper, Karl 1969 *Conjectures and Refutations*. London: Routledge and Kegan Paul.

—— 1959 *The Logic of Scientific Discovery*. London: Hutchinson.

Reynolds, Paul Davidson 1971 *A Primer in Theory Construction*. Indianapolis: Bobbs-Merrill.

Spencer, Herbert 1874–1896 *The Principles of Sociology*, 3 vols. New York: Appleton.

Turner, Jonathan H. 1985 "In Defense of Positivism." *Sociological Theory* 3:24–30.

Turner, Stephen Park, and Jonathan H. Turner 1990 *The Impossible Science: An Institutional Analysis of American Sociology*. Newbury Park, Calif.: Sage.

Whitley, Richard 1984 *The Intellectual and Social Organization of the Sciences*. Oxford: Clarendon Press.

Zetterberg, Hans L. 1965 *On Theory and Verification in Sociology*, 3rd ed. New York: Bedminster Press.

JONATHAN H. TURNER

POSTINDUSTRIAL SOCIETY

Postindustrial society is a concept used to characterize the structure, dynamics, and possible future of advanced industrial societies. Like the more recent concepts of postmodern and radically modern society, the concept of postindustrial society attempts to make sense of the substantial changes experienced by advanced industrial societies since the end of World War II. In providing a depiction of the character and future of these societies, analyses usually attempt to shape the futures they describe. Such efforts illustrate an awareness among sociologists of the "reflexive" character of much social science—that is, an awareness that analyses of society become elements of the social world that have the potential to shape the future.

Social analysts have long been aware of the potential effects of their ideas, at times engaging in work precisely because it may have an effect on the future through such mechanisms as social engineering, social movements, and the application of technology. The nineteenth-century theorists of "industrial" society, like postindustrial theorists a century later, tried to make sense of the diverse changes surrounding them, oftentimes in an effort to help shape the future. In the early nineteenth century, Claude-Henri de Saint-Simon attempted to provide an image of what was then a barely emerging industrial society, an image he hoped would enable scientists and industrialists to see the crucial roles they were to play in a society consciously directed by scientific knowledge. Similarly, in the mid-nineteenth century, Karl Marx and Fredrich Engels were outlining the characteristics of industrial capitalism, including the revolutionary role of the proletariat, when the factory system in England was still in its infancy, and the workforce "was still heavily concentrated in agriculture and domestic service, with the remainder mostly employed in the old craft industries." (Kumar 1978, p. 133) Although theorists of industrial society may not have been fully correct in all areas, their recognition of some major correlates of industrialization provided a surprisingly accurate portrait of a form of society qualitatively different from prior modes of human organization. The emerging industrial society was one that increasingly utilized technology and machinery for work; a society with substantial increases in communications, transportation, markets, and income; a society within which urbanism became a way of life, and the division of labor became increasingly complex; a society marked by an increasing role for the state, and bureaucratization in government and the economy; and a society marked by increasing secularization and rationalization.

The concept of postindustrial society indicates significant changes in some of these central characteristics of industrial society. In probably the earliest use of the concept, the Guild Socialist Arthur Penty (1917) called for development of a postindustrial state that reversed key characteristics of industrial society. Penty called for development of a mode of organization reflecting the artisan workshop, in which work, leisure, and family would be once again brought together. Although Penty may have been the first to use the concept of postindustrial society, it was not until the 1960s that the concept took on its present character, focusing on quantitative changes separating postindustrial from industrial society. Interest in the future, and in postindustrial society, developed at this time as a response to the dramatic changes occurring in advanced industrial societies. These changes included the technological and organizational expansion accompanying economic growth in the post–World War II era, the expansion of the welfare state and an increased concern over the dark side of industrialism. An array of terms emerged to characterize the social

milieu of advanced industrial societies, including the technocratic era (Brzezinski 1970), service class society (Dahrendorf 1967), personal service society (Halmos 1970), postscarcity society (Bookchin 1971), posteconomic society (Kahn and Wiener 1967), knowledge society (Drucker 1969), postmodern society (Etzioni 1968), and postindustrial society (Touraine 1971; Richta et al. 1969). Although differing in focus, the analyses overlapped considerably with Daniel Bell's work on postindustrial society (1973, 1989), which has been considered the best known and most complete analysis (Kumar 1978). Thus, the following effort to characterize postindustrial society uses Bell's analysis as the organizing framework. This is followed by an examination of the related concepts of postmodern and radically modern society.

CHARACTERISTICS OF POSTINDUSTRIAL SOCIETY

For analytical purposes Bell divides society into three parts: social structure, culture, and the polity. The concept of postindustrial society focuses primarily on changes in social structure, that is, changes in the economy, in technology, and in occupational structure. Although the social structure, polity, and culture may influence one another, it is not assumed there is a harmonious relation between the three. In fact, changes in any one may pose problems for the others (Bell 1976).

Bell's depiction of postindustrial society (1973, 1989) focuses on two dimensions: the centrality of codified theoretical knowledge, and the expansion of the service sector, especially professional and human services. The centrality of theoretical knowledge is viewed as the most important dimension, or axial principle, of postindustrial society. The institutions that most embody this dimension are the university and the research institute. In postindustrial society major innovations are more a product of the application of theoretical knowledge (e.g., Albert Einstein's discussion of the photoelectric effect for the development of lasers, holography, photonics), than the product of persons skilled in the use of equipment (e.g., Alexander Graham Bell and Thomas Edison). The use of theoretical knowledge increases the importance of advanced education, reflected in substantial enrollments in colleges and universities, as well as substantial numbers of scientists, engineers, and persons with advanced degrees. For example, between 1939 and 1964, as the United States moved from an industrial to a postindustrial society, the number of scientists and engineers increased over fivefold, from 263,000 to 1,475,000 (Bell 1973). Relatedly, the percentage of 20- to 24-year-olds studying for college degrees went from 4 percent in 1900 to 15 percent in 1940, 26 percent in 1950, and 34 percent in 1960 (estimated from Bell 1973, table 3–4). Related estimates show tertiary enrollment rates going from 32 percent in 1960 to 56 percent in 1980 and 81 percent in 1993 (World Bank 1980, 1997). Accompanying the importance of science and theoretical knowledge is an occupational structure in which more persons are involved in services, with professional and helping services especially important. This includes increased employment in education, science, and engineering, which is a natural consequence of a society committed to science and education. It also includes expansion of the number of white-collar workers and professionals in government and the helping services, resulting from an expanded welfare state and increased attention to health care. Such trends are illustrated in the following data (Table 1) on employment trends in the percentage of the workforce in white-collar and professional occupations in the United States, and in seventeen developed countries (twelve western European countries, plus Canada, Australia, New Zealand, Japan, and Israel) (U.S. Bureau of the Census 1975, 1998; ILO 1965–1988, 1997). Also included are related data for agriculture, mining, and manufacturing for the United States.

Increased employment in white-collar and professional occupations occurs largely at the expense of agricultural employment and, to a lesser extent, of manufacturing employment. The economic dynamic behind such changes consists of shifts in relative demand toward services as disposable income increases (Clark 1960), and to the greater responsiveness of agriculture and manufacturing to technical innovation (Fuchs 1968). As incomes rise, the *percentage* of total income used for food and agricultural products declines, and the need for basic manufactured products is more easily met. Thus, relative demand for health, education, and an array of other services may increase. At the same time, technical innovations increase productivity in agriculture and manufacturing, lowering the demand for labor in these sectors. However,

technical change is less able to displace workers in services, even though technical advances aid productivity. This is most clearly seen in health care, where technical change may increase the services available and the need for personnel to provide new services. Thus, economic and technical developments shift relative consumer demand and labor toward services. Such economic dynamics point out that development of an increasingly service-oriented postindustrial economy does not mean agriculture and manufacturing are ignored (Cohen and Zysman 1987). It means that technology takes over much of what people formerly did, and shifts productive efforts and labor toward services.

Accompanying the rising importance of theoretical knowledge and the service sector are several other changes. These include changes in women's roles, especially increased participation in the formal labor force. Additionally, the class structure of postindustrial society comes to increasingly center around education and technical expertise, creating possible tensions between expertise and populist sentiments. New political issues and attitudes concerned with the environment and quality of life move onto the political agenda (Ingelhart 1977; Lipset 1976). Technocratic rule may begin to take hold in organizations, and confront the problem of rationalized means becoming ends. Corporations may come under pressure to take into account objectives other than profit maximization. Efforts at social planning increase, and confront the problem of establishing a rational calculus for maximizing benefits throughout the society. The society becomes more politicized and conflictive as citizenship expands and groups seek a place in the polity.

Such conditions provide the basis for changes in consciousness and cosmology, as individuals confront a world of information and expanding specialized knowledge. The world becomes less one in which the individual interacts with nature and machines, and more one of persons interacting with persons. The reciprocal consciousness of self and other becomes increasingly important in defining the world. The culture may come to show contradictions between values of self-restraint, discipline, and work as a calling, on the one hand, and emerging postindustrial values of consumption and the negation of traditional bourgeoisie life, on the other (Bell 1976).

	1900	1940	1960	1970	1980	1990	1995
Percentage of White-Collar Occupations							
United States	17.6	31.1	40.1	44.8	48.0	59.9	61.8
Percentage of Professional Occupations							
United States	4.3	7.5	10.8	13.8	14.1	16.5	17.6
Seventeen Developed Countries			6.1	9.1	14.3	18.5	
Percentage of Agriculture, Mining, Manufacturing							
United States			31.4	26.5	21.3	19.2	

Table 1

The image of postindustrial society provided by Bell and other social analysts is one in which technological advances have made possible development of a society characterized by the expansion and use of theoretical knowledge, and the concomitant expansion of white-collar and especially professional employment. A commitment to human welfare and social planning facilitates expansion of the welfare state and human services, further increasing white-collar and professional employment. Yet, such a society is not without tensions and conflict, both within the social structure and between the social structure, polity, and culture. It is by pointing out such tensions and problems that postindustrial theorists attempt not only to describe the present and the future but also to shape the future. In one of the more recent contributions to the postindustrial literature, Fred Block is clear about the role social analysis plays in shaping the future. He points out that "[social theory] has real consequences, because individuals cannot do without some kind of conception of the type of society in which [they] live" (Block 1990, p. 2). Block's book represents a return to the analysis of postindustrial society after a brief hiatus during the 1980s that Block attributes to the breakdown of mainstream and leftist social theory, and the reemergence of a tradition of economic liberalism quiescent since the Great Depression. Block's analysis carries forward the focus of prior postindustrial theory on social structure, yet gives scant attention to the role of codified theoretical knowledge, the university and professional groups. Instead, Block looks at key aspects of the changing postindustrial economy of the United States in an effort to develop alternative possibilities for the future. He notes that a postindustrial economy utilizing advanced technology, and having a substantial service sector, would be most productive if it kept some distance from the dictates of classical economic theory. Specifically, productivity is likely enhanced by: (1) relatively low levels of marketness, allowing for greater predictability and more accurate information; (2) labor relations emphasizing cooperation between labor and management, since skilled labor in technologically sophisticated industries and the professions has substantial knowledge and is expensive to replace; (3) treating capital not merely as a physical asset, but as part of a productive process that includes the organization of persons working with capital; (4) developing measures of economic well-being that incorporate positive and negative utilities currently excluded from measures like gross national product (e.g., child care and pollution as positive and negative utilities); and (5) using various hybrid forms of market, state, and other regulatory mechanisms to enhance quality growth.

Block's work provides a useful extension of postindustrial theory into the more traditional economic domains of labor, capital, and measured economic output. The book may represent a revival of analyses of postindustrial society, perhaps under the alternative concept of postmodern society. However, before considering the notion of postmodern society, some criticisms of the concept of postindustrial society need to be mentioned. Much of the critical literature focuses on Bell's work, since it is viewed as one of the best expressions of postindustrial theory. One criticism of postindustrial theory is that it overemphasizes the role of theoretical knowledge in decision making. Although critics acknowledge that formal knowledge is more important than ever before, they contend that technical experts and scientific knowledge have not come to play the central role in decision making in government or corporations that postindustrial theorists said they would. Within government, political dynamics of the industrial era persist, and within the corporation "the expert and his knowledge are, for the most part, embedded in the corporate bureaucracy" (Cohen and Zysman 1987, p. 260). Also, critics point out that while there may be more scientists, more persons with advanced education, and more money spent on research and development, these may be only tenuously related to increases in the amount and effective use of theoretical knowledge (Kumar 1978).

Critics also question the attention given by postindustrial theorists to the service sector, and to white-collar and professional work. As with theoretical knowledge, critics agree the service sector has grown, yet question the focus of postindustrial theorists. Critics remind us that the service sector has always been a major segment of preindustrial and industrial society (Hartwell 1973), that most service employment is in low-skilled, low-paid work, and that increases in white-collar and professional employment are a consequence of dynamics embedded in industrial society. Relatedly, most of the increases in white-collar and professional employment are in clerical positions and jobs like teaching and nursing, jobs that carry less autonomy and income than traditional professional occupations. Perhaps most important, critics argue that a focus on the service sector fails to adequately acknowledge the key role that manufacturing would play in a postindustrial economy, including the dependence of the service sector on a dynamic manufacturing sector (Cohen and Zysman 1987).

One response to these and other criticisms (e.g., see Ritzer 1989; Frankel 1987) would be to point out that postindustrial theory often acknowledged points made by critics, such as the fact that the political order could check trends in the economy; that the bulk of services are in low-skilled, low-paid labor; and that a sophisticated and dynamic manufacturing sector is important for an economy as large as that of the United States. Postindustrial theory merely chose to focus on other developments that may hold insights into the future of advanced industrial society. A related response to criticisms is to point out that critics have frequently acknowledged the validity of postindustrial claims of an increasing role for formal and theoretical knowledge, the increasing importance of technical developments in information processing, and the rise of a service sector with a good number of white-collar and professional workers. The points of contention between postindustrial theory and

its critics appear to center on the general portrait of society provided by postindustrial theorists: Is this society best seen as a new type of society, or as a logical extension of advancing industrialization (Kumar 1978; 1988; 1995; Ritzer 1989; Giddens 1990)? Also, what are the implications of this image of society, not only for describing the present and future, but for shaping both?

POSTMODERN SOCIETY

Recent discussions of the character and future of advanced industrial societies have been framed within the concept of postmodern society. Although the variety of work dealing with postmodern society makes a clear definition difficult (Smart 1990; Kumar 1995), it seems reasonable to say postmodern society differs from postindustrial society in having the more nebulous reference point of a type of society coming after "modern" society. Whereas studies of postindustrial society understandably give substantial attention to technical and economic factors, studies of postmodern society broaden the focus to bring political and especially cultural phenomenon more to the center of analysis (Kumar 1995). This shift in focus helps explain why analyses of the cultural dynamics of postindustrial society are frequently considered in terms of the dynamics of postmodern society (e.g., Baudrillard 1983), and why studies of the economic characteristics of postmodern society look very much like studies of postindustrialism (e.g., Clegg 1990). For many authors, postmodernism is the culture of a postindustrial society (e.g., Lyotard 1984; Lash 1990; Jameson 1992; Mandel 1978).

Analyses of postmodern society may differ from postindustrial analyses not only in substantive focus, but also in basic presuppositions regarding the nature of social reality. While studies of postmodern society can reflect a standard social science framework, what has come to be called postmodern theory often includes a critique of science that undermines traditional social scientific inquiry (Turner 1998; Bogard 1990). Although the central tenants of postmodern theory are still unclear (Smart 1990; Ritzer 1997; Rosenau 1992), it is possible to note some major themes. Reflecting the influence of literary criticism, postmodern theory often views "social and cultural reality, and the social sciences themselves [as] linguistic constructions" (Brown 1990, p. 188). Authoritative images of what is real are seen to emerge through rhetorical processes in which "people establish repertoires of categories by which certain aspects of what is to be the case are fixed, focused, or forbidden" (Brown 1990, p. 191). Postmodern theory critiques the notion that signs and symbols adequately capture reality, and posits that signs and symbols are the only reality we truly know (Brown 1987). The reality of the social world described by social scientists is viewed as inseparable from the discourse through which social scientists come to signify some descriptions of the world as more legitimate than others (Lemert 1990). The traditional hierarchy in which reality occupies a privileged status separate from the symbols used to describe it is broken down, or deconstructed. The deconstruction project of postmodern theory not only critiques the separation of reality from symbols describing it, but also critiques other hierarchies, such as those separating expert knowledge from common knowledge, and high culture from low. The project even moves to deconstruct the very possibility of a generalizing social science, and the idea of a social world (Foucault 1980; Baudrillard 1983). In such bold forms a postmodern sociology becomes a contradiction in terms, undermining its own basis for existence (J. H. Turner 1998; B. Turner 1990; Smart 1990; Bauman 1988). However, although a postmodern sociology may be difficult to establish, a sociology of postmodernism that examines postmodern society, and draws from postmodern theory, is possible.

Attempts to characterize postmodern society reflect the contributions of postmodern theory, as well as more conventional sociological approaches. From postmodern theory comes a view of postmodern society as a technologically sophisticated high-speed society, with access to vast amounts of information, and fascinated by consumer goods and media images. Mass consumption of goods and information is seen as facilitating a breakdown of hierarchies of taste, and development of an explicit populism. Technology and speed blur lines separating reality from simulation, as television, videos, movies, advertising, and computer models provide simulations of reality more real than real. People may realize this hyperreality is simulation, yet be fascinated by it, and come to

make it part of their lives, thus transforming much of reality into simulation (Baudrillard 1983). Under such conditions history comes to have little meaning, and the fast-paced present becomes increasingly important. People may attempt to come to grips with such a world, but the world comes to undermine major assumptions, or grand narratives, of rationality and progress, thus generating a sense of exhaustion (Lyotard 1984). An acute sense of self-consciousness and unease may develop, as "the current age stumbles upon the very transvaluation of Western values and vocabularies that Nietche urged more than a century ago" (Baker 1990, p. 232).

Views of postmodern society from more conventional social science frameworks echo some of these themes. For example, both Daniel Bell (1976) and Christopher Lasch (1979) point to the development of cultural themes in postindustrial society emphasizing consumption and personal gratification at the expense of themes emphasizing self-restraint, work, commitment, and a sense of historical connection and continuity. In a Marxist analysis, Fredric Jameson (1984) points to the loss of a sense of historical connection in the consumer-oriented world of late capitalism.

One productive approach to postmodern society starts from the assumption that a central process defining modern society is differentiation. Thus, the type of society coming after modern society is viewed as reversing this process. The process of de-differentiation is illustrated in the cultural arena in the conflation of high and popular culture noted above, as well as the general deconstruction project of postmodernist theory (see also Lash 1988). Within the economic arena de-differentiation appears in the reversal of the processes of bureaucratization and the division of labor characteristic of the assembly line (Clegg 1990). Such trends have been viewed as part of the changing character of production in the world economy since 1960, and have been examined under such terms as the second industrial divide (Piore and Sable 1984), or the emergence of disorganized capitalism (Lash and Urry 1987). The changes frequently include a shift to smaller organizations or subunits of organizations, a less formalized and more flexible division of labor, increased variation in the character of products, more decentralized managerial structures, and the use of computers. Such organizations are engaged in services, information processing, or production using computer controlled flexible production techniques (Burris 1989; Heyderbrand 1989; Clegg 1990). The postbureaucratic character of these organizations is made possible by computers that do routine tasks, as well as by the need to respond flexibly to diverse clientele and markets, and the sophisticated capabilities of employees that operate complex manufacturing equipment and provide professional services.

Although postmodern production techniques and organizations are becoming more prominent and important in advanced industrial societies, they may express themselves in different ways and do not eclipse other forms of production and organization. Low-skilled tasks in manufacturing and services will likely compose a substantial segment of the workforce far into the future, creating the possibility of increased variation in skill and income in postmodern society. Also, postmodern organizations can vary substantially among themselves. For example, Clegg (1990) argues that Japan and Sweden stand as alternative expressions of postmodernist futures. Sweden provides the more optimistic democratic scenario with fairly broad representational rights of workers in organizations. Japan represents a less optimistic view with an enclave of privileged workers formed on exclusive principles of social identity, such as gender, ethnicity, and age.

RADICALLY MODERN SOCIETY

Much as critics of the concept of postindustrial society pointed out that postindustrial trends were best seen as the logical extension of major characteristics of industrial society, so Anthony Giddens (1990) has questioned the notion that postmodern trends actually represent a break with modern society. Giddens acknowledges current trends of complexity and widespread change accompanied by lack of a clear sense of progress, and would also likely admit to trends of de-differentiation in some organizations. However, Giddens does not see this as constituting postmodernity. Instead he refers to such trends as characterizing radically modern societies, for these societies represent the logical extension of three essential characteristics of modernity. The first characteristic is an increase in complexity, as the major processes of industrialization, class formation, and rationalization proceed

apace and shape one another. The second key element of modernity is the separation of much of what humans experience as social reality from concrete instances of time and space. Thus, money represents an element of social reality that designates a mechanism of exchange not bound to any specific instance of exchange. Even more abstractly, experts and expert systems represent specialized knowledge that may be called upon for a variety of purposes at a number of times and places. Science is one of the clearer expressions of such knowledge, with its esoteric and changing images of the character of the natural and physical universe. As societies become more modern, humans are viewed as increasingly experiencing the world through such abstract, or "disembedded," categories as money, expertise, and science. Realization of the disembedded nature of social life helps facilitate development of the third characteristic of modernity, its reflexivity. As noted earlier, *reflexivity* refers to the fact that efforts and information used to understand social reality become part of reality, and thus help shape the present and the future. According to Giddens, awareness of reflexivity is not confined to social scientists, but is embedded in the nature of modernity. Modern societies generate theories of what they are, which become important constitutive elements that shape society, including the future character of theories. All three of the characteristics of modernity find expression in each of four interrelated institutional complexes: capitalism, the nation-state, the military, and industrialization. Thus, radically modern societies are those in which major institutions are highly complex, abstract or disembedded, and reflexive. Such societies will be more difficult for individuals to concretely understand; will require substantial amounts of "trust" in abstract and expert systems; and will generate high levels of self-consciousness, as persons seek to use personal resources to more reflexively construct personal identity and meaning. Thus, radically modern societies may produce the unease and sense of powerlessness that some postmodern theorists see in postmodern societies. By avoiding the concept of postmodern society, Giddens is able to illustrate how current trends are part of the logic of modernity, and is able to provide a view of the future more optimistic than the view of some postmodern theorists by underscoring the reflexive and transformative power of ideas and action.

POSTMODERN SOCIETY AND THE WORLD SYSTEM

Most analyses of postindustrial, postmodern, and radically modern societies carry with them a view of societal change occurring within an increasingly interconnected world system. Giddens is quite explicit in this regard, pointing out how the complexity, abstractness, and reflexive character of modernity moves beyond the nation-state to become a world-level phenomenon (1990). This is most clearly expressed in the development of a world capitalist system, a nation-state system, a world military order, and an international division of labor. Although Giddens does not systematically consider the dynamics of these aspects of the world system in discussing radical modernity, his conceptualization is a useful reminder of the possible utility of considering multiple dimensions of the world system in efforts to understand postmodern societies. As the review of postindustrial and postmodern literature suggested, most analyses consider the role of the world system in terms of economic exchanges (Bell 1989), new technologies, and new modes of economic organization (Piore and Sable 1984; Lash and Urry 1987; Clegg 1990).

Recently, analysts have drawn increasing attention to cultural dimensions of the world system (e.g., Featherstone 1990; Boli and Thomas 1997), pointing out how themes associated with modern, postmodern, and postindustrial society have become elements of an emerging world culture (Meyer et al. 1997; Meyer 1991; Smith 1990; Robertson 1989, 1990). Giddens touched on these themes when he noted how the abstract and reflexive character of modernity has become a global phenomenon, making theories of modernity part of contemporary culture. Meyer (1980, 1991) and others (Meyer et al. 1997) also note the role that ideologies of modernity and postindustrialism may play in the contemporary world, pointing out how rationalized conceptions of modern society, including social scientific discourse, have become part of a contemporary world cultural framework. For example, modern images of society that view economic development, national integration, and personal and societal progress as the product of individuals with specialized knowledge are said to have become a world-level assumption, and generated expansion of educational enrollments between 1950 and 1970 (Meyer et al. 1977; Boli and Ramirez 1986; Fiala and Lanford 1987). Relatedly, postindustrial images of the role of specialized knowledge in society are viewed as an important factor affecting the worldwide expansion of higher education and professional employment in the post–World War II era (Meyer and Hannan 1979). Such images may account for part of the increase from 3.7 percent to 9.2 percent between 1960 and 1990 in the percentage of the labor force employed in professional occupations among twenty-two developing countries, a significant increase considering the substantial population and labor-force growth during this period. This contrasts with the increase from 6.1 percent to 18.5 percent for the seventeen developed countries reported earlier, and with the increase from 10.8 percent to 16.5 percent for the United States. While economic growth may account for some of these increases in professional employment, the substantial expansion for developing countries, especially compared to the United States, indicates other variables likely play a role. It seems plausible that postindustrial images regarding the importance of specialized knowledge and personnel may have an effect.

CONCLUSION

Efforts to understand the character and future of advanced industrial societies in the latter half of the twentieth century have been done under the rubric of at least three major concepts. The concept of postindustrial society focused attention on social structural or economic dimensions of society, especially the changing character of technology, knowledge, occupations, and the market. The concept of postmodern society continued to bring attention to structural and economic aspects of society, yet gave increased attention to political, cultural, and psychological dimensions, at times with an explicit critique of standard social science methodology. The concept of radically modern society underscored the links between contemporary changes and the basic dynamics of modernity, while introducing the useful idea that radically modern societies are characterized by high levels of abstractness and reflexivity. Each of the three concepts acknowledges that changes are occurring within an increasingly interconnected world system.

The current review clearly illustrates the reflexive character of much social science. In postindustrial theory this was largely a recognition that formal scientific knowledge may shape the future. In postmodern theory, and especially in radically modern theory, this reflexivity also became part of the culture itself, affecting the consciousness of much of the population. This creates a vastly more complex image of society, with a diverse array of possible futures, and may account for the unease postmodern theory sees as characterizing postmodern society.

While work on postmodern and radically modern society offers insightful ideas, most empirical research has been done on postindustrial society, and economic aspects of postmodern society. Future studies should attempt to examine some of the major elements of postmodern and radically modern approaches, as well as continue to clarify areas of ambiguity within postindustrial theory. For example, within the postindustrial framework, attention should be given to understanding the influence of various segments of a knowledge class on specific institutions in society, and to trying to explain national variation in the expansion of various types of service employment.

Within the postmodernist framework, it would be informative to assess claims of pessimism, self-consciousness, and declines of grand narratives, noting their variation across social groups and societies. Examination of variation across time and space in the way individuals, communities, and societies experience exposure to media might help clarify the provocative hypothesis of the increasing salience of simulation in social life. Efforts to rethink extant research in terms of the simulation hypothesis could also prove informative.

Drawing from the view of radically modern societies, it would be useful to examine the idea that modern cultures increasingly incorporate reflexive elements. Analysis of the changing role of evaluation studies, news presentations and commentaries, and economic projections and predictions could help clarify the developing reflexive character of human societies.

Last, to assess hypotheses regarding the effects of world cultural themes, research could examine the effects of an ideology of specialized knowledge and expertise on expansion of professional employment. The data presented above suggest the plausibility of such an effect, yet do not offer firm support.

Issues such as those above are but a few of the avenues of research that may help provide a clearer image of the character and future of advanced industrial societies. In posing the issues, and in providing answers, social science will likely help shape the future it describes.

REFERENCES

Baker, Scott 1990 "Reflection, Doubt, and the Place of Rhetoric in Postmodern Social Theory." *Sociological Theory* 8:232–245.

Baudrillard, Jean 1983 *Simulations*. New York: Semiotext(e).

Bauman, Zygmunt 1988 "Is There a Postmodern Sociology?" *Theory, Culture and Society* 5:217–237.

Bell, Daniel 1989 "The Third Technological Revolution." *Dissent* 36:164–176.

—— 1976 *The Cultural Contradictions of Capitalism*. New York: Basic Books.

—— 1973 *The Coming of Post-Industrial Society: A Venture in Social Forecasting*. New York: Basic Books.

Block, Fred 1990 *Postindustrial Possibilities: A Critique of Economic Discourse*. Berkeley: University of California Press.

Bogard, William 1990 "Closing Down the Social: Baudrillard's Challenge to Contemporary Sociology." *Sociological Theory* 8:1–15.

Boli, John, and Francisco Ramirez 1986 "World Culture and the Institutional Development of Mass Education." In John Richardson, ed., *Handbook of Theory and Research for the Sociology of Education*. Westport, Conn.: Greenwood.

Boli, John, and George M. Thomas 1997 "World Culture in the World Polity: A Century of International Non-Governmental Organization." *American Sociological Review* 62:171–190.

Bookchin, Murray 1971 *Post-Scarcity Anarchism*. Berkeley, Calif.: Ramparts Press.

Brzezinski, Zbigniew 1970 *Between Two Ages: America's Role in the Technocratic Era*. New York: Viking Press.

Brown, Richard Harvey 1990 "Rhetoric, Textuality, and the Postmodern Turn in Sociological Theory." *Sociological Theory* 8:188–197.

—— 1987 *Society as Text: Essays on Rhetoric, Reason, and Reality*. Chicago: University of Chicago Press.

Burris, Beverly 1989 "Technocratic Organization and Control." *Organization Studies* 10:1–22.

Clark, Colin 1960 *The Conditions of Economic Progress*, 3rd ed. New York: Macmillan.

Clegg, Stewart R. 1990 *Modern Organizations: Organization Studies in the Postmodern World.* Newbury Park, Calif.: Sage.

Cohen, Stephen, and John Zysman 1987 *Manufacturing Matters: The Myth of the Post-Industrial Economy.* New York: Basic Books.

Dahrendorf, Ralf 1967 *Society and Democracy in Germany.* Garden City, N.Y.: Doubleday.

Drucker, Peter 1969 *The Age of Discontinuity: Guidelines to Our Changing Society.* New York: Harper and Row.

Etzioni, Amitai 1968 *The Active Society.* New York: Free Press.

Featherstone, Mike 1990 *Global Culture: Nationalism, Globalization and Modernity.* Newbury Park, Calif.: Sage.

Fiala, Robert, and Audri Gordon Lanford 1987 "Educational Ideology and the World Educational Revolution 1950–1970." *Comparative Education Review* 31:315–332.

Foucault, Michel 1980 *Power/Knowledge: Selected Interviews and Other Writings, 1972–1977.* Colin Gordon, ed. New York: Pantheon.

Frankel, Boris 1987 *The Post-Industrial Utopians.* Great Britain: Polity Press.

Fuchs, Victor 1968 *The Service Economy.* New York: Columbia University Press.

Giddens, Anthony 1990 *The Consequences of Modernity.* Stanford Calif.: Stanford University Press.

Halmos, P. 1970 *The Personal Service Society.* Great Britain: Constable.

Hartwell R. M. 1973 "The Service Revolution: The Growth of Services in the Modern Economy." In *The Industrial Revolution, 1700–1914.* Brighton, England: Harvester Press.

Heyderbrand, Wolf 1989 "New Organizational Forms." *Work and Occupations* 16:323–357.

Ingelhart, Ronald 1977 *The Silent Revolution: Changing Values and Political Styles Among Western Publics.* Princeton, N.J.: Princeton University Press.

International Labor Organization (1965–1988) 1997 *Yearbook of Labor Statistics.* Geneva: ILO.

Jameson, Fredric 1992 *Postmodernism, or the Cultural Logic of Late Capitalism.* London: Verso.

—— 1984 "Postmodernism, or the Cultural Logic of Late Capitalism." *New Left Review* 146:59–92.

Kahn, Herman, and Anthony Wiener 1967 *The Year 2000.* New York: Macmillan.

Kumar, Krishan 1995 *From Postindustrial to Postmodern Society.* Cambridge: Basil Blackwell.

—— 1988 *The Rise of Modern Society.* New York: Basil Blackwell.

—— 1978 *Prophecy and Progress: The Sociology of Industrial and Post-Industrial Society.* London: Allen Lane.

Lasch, Christopher 1979 *The Culture of Narcissism.* New York: Warner.

Lash, Scott 1990 *Sociology of Postmodernism.* New York: Routledge.

—— 1988 "Postmodernism as a Regime of Signification." *Theory, Culture and Society* 5:311–336.

——, and John Urry 1987 *The End of Organized Capitalism.* Madison: University of Wisconsin Press.

Lemert, Charles 1990 "General Social Theory, Irony, Postmodernism." In Steven Seidman and David G. Wagner, eds., *Postmodernism and Social Theory.* Cambridge, Mass.: Blackwell.

Lipset, Seymour 1976 *Rebellion in the University.* Chicago: University of Chicago Press.

Lyotard, Jean-Francois 1984 *The Postmodern Condition.* Minneapolis: University of Minnesota Press.

Mandel, Ernst 1978 *Late Capitalism.* London: Verso.

Meyer, John 1991 "Concluding Commentary: The Evolution of Modern Stratification Systems." In David Grusky, ed., *Social Stratification: Class, Race and Gender in Sociological Perspective.* Boulder, Colo.: Westview.

—— 1980 "The World Polity and the Authority of the Nation State." In Albert Bergesen, ed., *Studies of the Modern World System.* New York: Academic Press.

——, John Boli, George M. Thomas, and Francisco O. Ramirez 1997 "World Society and the Nation State." *American Journal of Sociology* 103:144–181.

Meyer, John, and Michael Hannan 1979 "National Development in a Changing World System: An Overview." In *National Development and the World System: Educational, Economic, and Political Change, 1950–1970.* Chicago: University of Chicago Press.

Meyer, John, Francisco Ramirez, Richard Rubinson, and John Boli-Bennett 1977 "The World Educational Revolution, 1950–1970." *Sociology of Education* 50:242–258.

Penty, Arthur 1917 *Old Worlds for New: A Study of the Post-Industrial State.* London: Allen and Unwin.

Piore, Michael, and Charles Sabel 1984 *The Second Industrial Divide: Possibilities for Prosperity.* New York: Basic Books.

Richta, Radovan, et al. 1969 *Civilization at the Crossroads: Social and Human Implications of the Scientific and Technological Revolution*, 3rd ed. New York: International Arts and Sciences Press.

Ritzer, George 1997 *Postmodern Social Theory.* New York: McGraw-Hill.

—— 1989 "The Permanently New Economy: The Case for Reviving Economic Sociology." *Work and Occupations* 16:243–272.

Robertson, Roland 1990 "Mapping the Global Condition: Globalization as the Central Concept." In Mike Featherston, ed., *Global Culture: Nationalism, Globalization and Modernity.* Newbury Park, Calif.: Sage.

—— 1989 "Globalization, Politics and Religion." In J. A. Beckford and T. Luckmann, eds., *The Changing Face of Religion.* Newbury Park, Calif.: Sage.

Rosenau, Pauline Marie 1992 *Post-Modernism and the Social Sciences: Insights, Inroads, and Intrusions.* Princeton, N.J.: Princeton University Press.

Smart, Barry 1990 "Modernity, Postmodernity and the Present." In Bryan S. Turner, ed., *Theories of Modernity and Postmodernity.* Newbury Park, Calif.: Sage.

Smith, Anthony 1990 "Towards a Global Culture?" In Mike Featherstone, ed., *Global Culture: Nationalism, Globalization and Modernity.* Newbury Park, Calif.: Sage.

Touraine, Alain 1971 *The Post-Industrial Society.* New York: Random House.

Turner, Bryan 1990 "Periodization and Politics in the Postmodern." In Bryan S. Turner, ed., *Theories of Modernity and Postmodernity.* Newbury Park, Calif.: Sage.

Turner, Jonathan H. 1998 *The Structure of Sociological Theory,* 6th ed. Belmont, Calif.: Wadsworth.

U.S. Bureau of the Census 1998 *Statistical Abstract of the United States 1998: The National Data Book.* Washington: U.S. Government Printing Office.

—— 1975 *Historical Statistics of the United States, Part I. Colonial Times to 1970.* Washington: U.S. Government Printing Office.

World Bank 1997 *World Development Report, 1997.* New York: Oxford University Press.

—— 1980 *World Development Report, 1980.* New York: Oxford University Press.

ROBERT FIALA

POSTMODERNISM

In 1959, C. Wright Mills speculated that "the Modern Age is being succeeded by a post-modern period" in which assumptions about the coherence of the Enlightenment values of scientific rationality and political freedom were being challenged (1959, p. 166). Critical theorists had earlier speculated about how the revolutionary potential of the urban laboring classes of the nineteenth century was co-opted by the shift to a postindustrial twentieth-century society, a society characterized by mass consumerism and war economies. The characteristics of postindustrial societies were explored more recently in Daniel Bell's analysis of contemporary capitalism (1976). In the modern information societies, Bell argues that the class forces that drove nineteenth-century social change have been replaced by new processes. Under welfare capitalist states, scientists, technicians, managers, and bureaucrats formulate social tensions as administrative and technical issues based on political consensus. For Bell, postindustrial societies with their information bases hold the key to social harmony and the end of misery.

Alain Touraine's view (1984) is different. He also stresses how class antagonism has changed under welfare capitalism, but for Touraine the information managers, guided by technological thinking, tend to "steer the entire social order toward the perfectly programmed society, the ultimate technocratic prison" (Baum 1990, p. 5). Touraine also writes that the categories of basic sociological analysis have become out of touch with changes in contemporary societies. In particular, he rejects the modernist supposition of evolutionary progress over time, culminating in what he calls "the impoverishing homogeneity of modern civilization" (Touraine 1984, p. 38), the sociologist's conception of the national states as units of analysis, and the gradual expunging of the cultural diversity of traditional societies. The collapse of modernism arises from a failure of sociology to keep abreast of the developing autonomy of cultural products, the globalization of capital, and the rise of new forms of social control and of public resistance to them. In this analysis, "the crisis of modernity . . . is not all-encompassing . . . the crisis in modernity is not considered to be total or terminal but limited in scope, if deep" (Smart 1990, p. 408). Though Bell and Touraine have been associated with critiques of postindustrial societies, the meaning of "postmodernism" has become far more radical, and draws on earlier sources.

De Saussure's "structural" theory of linguistics (1959) distinguished the "sign" from the "signified" and developed a science based on the discovery that symbolic systems might have formal properties that were unrelated to the meanings of the objects they signified but that might hold across different systems of symbols. The system for describing, for example, the animal kingdom and the protocols for siting teepees might reflect the same logic—without any inherent equivalence to the things they described or organized (Giddens 1987). "Poststructuralism" deepened this disinterest in the signified objects by dismissing any link binding words/symbols to things. Things were only the hypostatizations of language. All analysis was "deconstruction," or unmasking of phenomena in terms of their underlying rhetorical conventions. For poststructuralists, texts only pointed to other texts. The world was viewed as an intertwining of systems of representation without any derivation from or basis within "terra firma." Everything became text—including violent speech and violent symbolic acts such as incest, war, or spousal abuse.

The postmodern twist is the application of the linguistic implications of poststructuralism to the three core principles connecting contemporary civilizations with the project of the Enlightenment: scientific knowledge (Truth), aesthetics (Beauty), and morality (the Good). The Enlightenment project—"modernism"—refers to the rise of the Age of Reason. It was characterized by the gradual shift away from religious sensibilities and to scientific objectivity, the rational exploitation of nature for human needs, the perspectival representation of nature in art and humanistic truth in fiction, and the struggle for a humane society. Modernism was realist in its epistemology and progressive in its politics. Truth could be attained—particularly with scientific advances. Beauty could be distinguished from trash. Humanism could nurture moral conduct and decent conditions of life. And history was purposive and progressive.

Postmodernism is the sensibility that arises when the credibility of these "master narratives" is questioned. The postmodern period, as described by Lyotard (1984) and Baudrillard (1983), is the one we now confront. Though it is often dated as a creature of the post–World War II period, it is thought only to have become generalized with mass consumerism in the age of electronics and to have been initiated by dramatic changes in contemporary capitalism. Capitalism has ushered in global communication and exchange, and has created a self-sustaining cybernetic system that almost completely transcends the ability of individual governments to control their directions and objectives. As a result, postmodernity is sometimes referred to as posthistorical society in the sense that the mission or sense of purpose that guided nation-states in the past through events such as the French Revolution has been overtaken by global consumerism. The view of history as a struggle for the gradual liberation of humanity and progressive evolution of more humane societies is dismissed by Lyotard as mythic. In addition, the transcendence of communities by electronic representations makes the idea of "the social" purely illusory (Bogard 1990). The objectivity of societies, nation-states, communities, and history is viewed only as "narratives" or "simulacra" (Baudrillard 1983). Referents disappear in favor of a world of simulations, models, performatives, and codes—in short, "information" (broadly conceived), which becomes the predominant phenomenon of exchange among the masses through the mass media.

One of the important theoretical aspects of the postmodernist position is its explicit rejection of Marxism in general and Habermas' theorizing about creating a rational society through communicative competence. Where Habermas (1973, p. 105) speculates that a rational community might be able to "arrive at the conviction that in the given circumstances the proposed norms are 'right,'" Lyotard rejects the myth of reason behind the Habermasian project. The project implies that there is a correct moral and scientific standard to which communities ought to aspire. Enforcement of such standards valorize conformity and, as witnessed in the fascist European states in the 1920s and 1930s, promote terrorism to extract it. This introduces a tension within postmodernism that has not been worked through (Frank 1990). On the positive side, the supposition of "multivocality" in scientific and moral discourse promotes the "excavation" of minority voices and minority experiences which have been occluded in "master" modernist ways of thinking. Every point of view can be heard, none can be privileged. On the other side, postmodernism seems ill equipped to distinguish between any particular moral or objective position and any other, including the fascist discourse that is associated with modernism. Choosing between Holocaust history and Holocaust denial would seem in principle to be a matter of rhetorical preference—which is clearly nihilistic.

When we move away from epistemology to postmodernity's impact on art and architecture, the situation is different. Postmodernism celebrates a rejection of hegemonic traditions and styles by mixing elements from competing schools and by bringing the rim of representation into focus as an organic element of the depiction. Novels exploit the discontinuities in perspective and the fragmentations in contemporary society. In architecture, postmodernism represents a repudiation of high-density ("efficient") functionality based on centralized city planning with an emphasis on no-frill construction. Decentralized planning emphasizes collage and eclecticism and the development of spaces to heighten aesthetic possibilities (Harvey 1989). The globalization of experience encourages such exchanges and experimentation. However, the replacement of "efficient" spaces like public housing, with their brutalizing side effects, with more particularistic designs is part of the emancipatory interest of modernity—so that at least here, postmodernity is still part and parcel of the Enlightenment. This raises three questions.

First, to what extent has the case been made that the changes in capitalism during the past two decades have been so profound as to represent a destruction of modernist society and a disappearance of history and "the social" (i.e., real face-to-face community)? Some critics dispute the claim (Baum 1990); others point out that Baudrillard's evidence is unconvincing since his own postmodern manner of exposition is self-consciously rhetorical, inflationary, and, consistent with the idiom, only one possible reading of recent history (Smart 1990). Second, if we have no careful (i.e., modernist) analysis of the factors that have contributed to the demise of our confidence in the "master narratives" of modernism, would it not seem to be impossible to discern which ones have been shaken, and how seriously our confidence in them has been eroded? Skepticism is insufficient. Finally, under these circumstances, is it not predictable that there is no consensus about the meaning of postmodernism? Arguably this dissensus is inherent in the perspective. For Baudrillard (1983), postmodernism spells the end of sociology (and other modernist subjects); for Bauman (1988), it is simply a new topic—a sociology of postmodernism, but not a postmodern sociology. For Brown (1990), it is an opportunity to rethink the continuing relevance of the role of rhetoric in politics and science in order to employ knowledge in guiding human conduct. Under these circumstances, the proclamation of the death of modernism would seem premature.

Over the past decade two debates have emerged which raise questions about the postmodern project and which deal respectively with the issues of (1) epistemology, or the postmodern struggle with truth and the special standing of the natural sciences, and (2) of morality and the struggle to define and achieve the "good society" within democratic politics.

The first issue is raised by the famous hoax perpetrated by Alan Sokal, professor of physics at New York University, a left-leaning radical who taught math in Nicaragua under the rule of the Sandanistas. His "transformative hermeneutics of quantum gravity" was a spoof of the pretentious claims about science running through the leading figures of the French intellectual establishment—Derrida, Lacan, and Lyotard—spiked, according to Sokal, with the usual nonsensical and impenetrable jargon and buzzwords (Sokal 1996b). The parody was published in a special issue of *Social Text* designed by the editors to rebuke the criticisms of their antiscientific agenda by leading scientists. Sokal published an exposé at the same time in *Lingua Franca* (1996a). The hoax ignited a storm of criticism on both sides which some have referred to as "the science wars" (Natoli 1997, pp. 115 ff.; Kingwell 1999). The hoax continues to provoke debate today (see *http://www.physics.nyu.edu/faculty/sokal/index.html*). Although Sokal abused the good faith of the editors of a journal in a humanities discipline, he justified his behavior by reference to the naïveté of those editors, whose credentials could scarely permit them to draw the conclusions about the purely rhetorical foundations of science or to discredit centuries of scientific progress. Yet in neither side was the "demonstration" definitive. The validity of the scientific method is neither established by the hoax, nor rubbished by what Richard Dawkins writing in *Nature* dubbed "the vacuous rhetoric of montebanks and charlatans" on the Left Bank (1988, p. 141). Nor is it undermined on this side of the Atlantic by Steven Seidman's claims in *Contested Knowledge* that the scientific community in eighteenth-century Europe prevailed over aristocracy and the

Church because it provided the forces of liberalism with a convenient but essentially vacuous cudgel with which to rout the older order: "Is the claim that only science ensures true knowledge . . . not merely another ruse on the part of a rising social elite wishing to legitimate their own aspirations for privilege? . . . [S]cience, just like religion, rests upon a series of assumptions that cannot be scientifically proven . . . Enlightenment science is as weak a guarantor of truth as religion." (1994, p. 24). Science for Seidman and the other postmodernists is just faith in a secular vein without any special epistemological leverage. The proponents of the Enlightenment were simply replacing priests with scientists, and religion with another form of superstition. Sokal and Bricmont's *Fashionable Nonsense* (1998) calls the postmodernists' bluff on such charges. At this point, it is premature to draw conclusions about the future of this controversy. Suffice it to say for the time being that poetry and physics should be cataloged separately.

On the issue of morality and everyday politics, John O'Neill's *The Poverty of Posmodernism* takes a similarly critical view of "the academic trendiness" of advocates of cynicism and fragmentation who have forsaken humanism and the critique of social injustice as part of the postmodern turn. "Today we are told to jettison the old-fashioned belief in unique values . . . we are wholly ruled by prejudice and politics . . . we are asked to believe that human beings are now so speciated by gender and race—though we are silent about class—that there can be no universal knowledge, politics, or morality." As O'Neill stresses, "these ideas have not grown up among the masses who have sickened of the injustices and exploitation that grinds their life . . . it is not these people who have abandoned idealism, universalism, truth and justice. It is those who already enjoy these things who have denounced them on behalf of the others" (1995, p. 1)—the new "illiterati" of the simulacrum, the Disney World theorists and the esthetes of the radically chic. "Too much of the world still starves, dies young and is wasted by systematic greed and evil for anyone to write the obituaries of philosophy, ideology and humanism" (p. 196). O'Neill argues that there are good philosophical foundations in the phenomenology of everyday life, the transcendental instinct of reason to fasten on the contradictions of existence, and commonsense scepticism

to keep alive the distinction between truth and falsity, freedom and slavery, and justice and injustice. The idea that political discourse has been reduced to mere perspective, that there is nothing outside language or that there is no "extratextuality" deny the vision of history and community, and exhaust culture with cultural industry, communication with fashion. "The claim that there are no longer any grand stories capable of under-writing common sense . . . gives comfort only to those who lack community at any level of society other than intellectual fashion" (p. 198). O'Neill's own inspiration for criticizing the antirationalism of postmodernism is founded on what he describes as the tension between language and vision, between elites and masses, between reality and possibility. The static linguisticality of postmodernism is a trap, an illusion. The current celebration of relativism by what used to be the progressive left is not only ill founded but politically nihilistic. It valorizes only minoritarianism while leaving unexamined the consequences of globalization and the dismantling of the welfare state by the political right. That state, with all its blemishes, has been an achievement in which civic democracy took root, in which politics was driven in part for reasons other than naked self-interest. In his vision, O'Neill says that postmodernism undermines our sense of cultural debt to the past and removes the duty which each generation has to pass on what it has learned to the future. "Those of us who own knowledge, who enjoy literacy, health, self-respect and social status have chosen to rage against our own gifts rather than to fight for their enlargement in the general public. We have chosen to invalidate our science, to psychiatrize our arts, to vulgarize our culture, to make it unusable and undesirable by those who have yet to know it. We honour no legacy. We receive no gifts. We hand on nothing" (1995, p. 2). Yet if O'Neill's critique of antirationalism is sound, all this changes and his self-flagellation is premature.

The moral and epistemological concerns of O'Neill and Sokal are quite different from the critiques of commodity esthetics in George Ritzer's *The McDonaldization of Society*, which provides a useful point of comparison. Following Weber's insight about the intrusiveness of rationalization, Ritzer shows how the McDonald fast-food franchise led to a widespread adoption of commodity production and consumption based on standardization, efficiency, leveling of tastes, and the stifling of worker experiences that has come to set the model for our individual relationships with the market, if not the world generally. But McDonaldization calls forth that critical posture which Veblen labeled "the instinct of craftmanship" ([1899] 1962, p. 75), without which waste and conspicuous consumption would be unbridled. Like Veblen, Ritzer applauds the resistance to such trends; but his perspective is Weberian and transcendental. By contrast, for students of postmodernism, scientific truths and emancipatory projects are merely further commodities, fashions, or fictions caught up in the McDonalization of empirical truth and the social good. Sokal and O'Neill represent the opening of serious dialogues on these engaging issues.

(SEE ALSO: *Popular Culture; Postindustrial Society; Social Philosophy*)

REFERENCES

Baudrillard, Jean 1983 *In the Shadow of the Silent Majorities*. New York: Semiotext(e).

Baum, Gregory 1990 "The Postmodern Age." *Canadian Forum* (May):5–7.

Bauman, Z. 1988 "Is There a Postmodern Sociology?" *Postmodernism*, special issue of *Theory, Culture and Society* 5(2–3):217–238.

Bell, Daniel 1976 *The Cultural Contradictions of Capitalism*. New York: Basic.

Bogard, William 1990 "Closing Down the Social: Baudrillard's Challenge to Contemporary Sociology." *Sociological Theory* 8(1):1–15.

Brown, Richard H. 1990 "Rhetoric, Textuality, and the Postmodern Turn in Sociological Theory." *Sociological Theory* 8(2):188–197.

Dawkins, Richard 1998 "Postmodernism Disrobed." *Nature* 394(9 July):141–143.

de Saussure, Ferdinand 1959 *Course in General Linguistics*. C. Bally and A. Sechehaye, eds., Wade Baskin, trans. New York: McGraw-Hill.

Frank, Arthur 1990, "Postmodern Sociology/Postmodern Review." *Symbolic Interactionism* 14(1):93–100.

Giddens, Anthony 1987 "Structuralism, Post-structuralism and the Production of Culture." In A. Giddens and J. Turner, eds., *Social Theory Today*. Stanford, Calif.: Stanford University Press.

Habermas, J. 1973 *Legitimation Crisis*. Boston: Beacon.

Harvey, David 1989 *The Condition of Postmodernity*. Oxford: Blackwell.

Kingwell, Mark 1999 "Peace in the Science Wars?" *Globe and Mail* (May 29). (Review Essay, Toronto.)

Lyotard, Jean-Francois 1984 *The Postmodern Condition: A Report on Knowledge*. Minneapolis: University of Minnesota Press.

Mills, C. Wright 1959 *The Sociological Imagination*. New York: Oxford University Press.

Natoli, Joseph 1997 "Postmodernity's War with Science." In *A Primer on Postmodernity*. Malden, Mass.: Blackwell.

O'Neill, John 1995 *The Poverty of Postmodernism*. New York: Blackwell.

Ritzer, George 1996 *The McDonaldization of Society*. Thousand Oaks, Calif.: Pine Forge.

Seidman, Steven 1994 *Contested Knowledge: Social Theory in the Postmodern Era*. Malden, Mass.: Blackwell.

Smart, Barry 1990 "On the Disorder of Things: Sociology, Postmodernity and 'The End of the Social.'" *Sociology* 24:397–416.

Sokal, Alan D. 1996a "A Physicist Experiments with Cultural Studies." *Lingua Franca* 6(4):62–64.

—— 1996b "Transgressing the Boundaries: Towards a Transformative Hermeneutics of Quantum Gravity." *Social Text* 14(1, 2):217–252.

——, and Jean Bricmont 1998 *Fashionable Nonsense: Post Modern Intellectuals' Abuse of Science*. New York: St. Martin's.

Touraine, Alain 1984 "The Waning Sociological Image of Social Life." *International Journal of Comparative Sociology* 25:33–44.

Veblen, Thorsten (1899) 1962 *The Theory of the Leisure Class*. New York: Mentor.

AUGUSTINE BRANNIGAN

POVERTY

Scholarly as well as ideological debate has long centered around the most elementary questions concerning poverty. What is poverty? How can it be measured? What causes it? Is it a natural phenomenon or a symptom of a poorly ordered society? Though answers to all these questions abound, there is no definitive answer to any one of them, nor can there ever be, for the questions are not purely demographic, but moral, ethical, and political as well. Poverty is a concept, not a fact, and must be understood as such. Even though no definitive answers are possible, this does not mean that all answers are thereby equal; many are based on ignorant assumptions and ill-formed judgments. Sociologists involved in poverty research seek to make sure that all understand the meaning and consequences of various points of view, and that both theoretical and policy research is based soundly upon clear definitions and reliable data.

Even the definition of "poverty" is problematic. The word is derived from the French *pauvre*, meaning "poor." Poverty is simply the state of lacking material possessions, of having little or no means to support oneself. All would agree that anyone lacking the means necessary to remain alive is in poverty, but beyond that there is little agreement. Some scholars and policy makers would draw the poverty line at the bare subsistence level, like Rowntree's "the minimum necessaries for the maintenance of merely physical efficiency" (1901, p. viii). Others argue for poverty definitions that include persons whose level of living is above subsistence but who have inadequate means; among those holding to the latter, further arguments concern the definition of adequacy. Social science cannot resolve the most basic arguments. For example, the level of living implied by the poverty threshold in the United States would be seen as desirable and unattainable in many other countries, yet few would suggest that poverty in the United States be defined by such outside standards. Sociologists can evaluate the demographic and economic assumptions underlying standards of poverty, but not the standards themselves.

CONCEPTIONS OF POVERTY

Poverty can be defined in absolute or relative terms. The subsistence line is a good example of an absolute definition (i.e., below this line one does not have sufficient resources to survive). A criterion based on some arbitrary formula, such that poverty equals some fraction of the median income or below, is a good example of a relative definition (e.g., "All persons earning less than 25 percent of the median income are poor"). In all industrial societies an absolute definition will have far fewer persons officially in poverty than will a relative definition, creating natural political pressure for absolute definitions. For example, a study in 1976 revealed that if poverty was defined as

having 50 percent of the median income, data on income distributions would show that an unchanging 19 percent of the population had been poor for almost the past two decades (U.S. DHEW 1976). Absolute definitions show declines in poverty over time in industrial nations. There are valid arguments for both types of definitions. Some argue that relative definitions of poverty render the term meaningless in affluent societies, and make cross-national comparisons difficult—for example, in an advanced industrial society, 50 percent of national median income could leave one adequately provided for, while the same percentage in many less industrialized societies would not provide basic necessities to sustain life. On the other hand, within societies there is evidence that most people see poverty in relative terms rather than as an absolute standard (Rainwater 1974; Kilpatrick 1973). That is, popular conceptions of what level of living constitutes poverty have been found to change as general affluence goes up and down. Advocates of relative measures point out that any absolute measure is arbitrary and thus meaningless. A reasonable definition of the poor, they argue, should be one that demarcates the lower tail of the income distribution as the poor, whatever the absolute metric represented by that tail, for those persons will be poor by the standards of that time and place. As the average level of income rises and falls, they argue, what is seen as poverty will, and should, change. Advocates of absolute measures of poverty do not deny that perception of poverty is intimately tied to distributional inequality, but argue that relative definitions are too vague for policy purposes. An absolute standard, defined on some concrete level of living, is a goal that can possibly be attained. Once it is attained, they say, a new goal could be set. Eliminating poverty as defined by relative standards is a far more difficult goal, both practically and politically. T. H. Marshall noted, "the question of what range of inequality is acceptable above the 'poverty line' can only marginally, if at all, be affected by or affect the decision of where that line should be drawn" (1981, p. 52).

Relative versus absolute poverty is a distributional distinction, but there are other important distinctions as well. A social distinction, and one with considerable political import, is usually made between the "deserving poor" and the "undeserving poor." In their brief summary of the historical origins of this distinction, Morris and Williamson (1986, pp. 6–12) maintain that it became significant in the fourteenth century, when, for a variety of reasons (the decline of feudalism, the rise of a market economy with concomitant periodic labor dislocations, bubonic plague–induced regional labor shortages), the poor became geographically mobile for the first time. Before that, the local Catholic parish, with its "Blessed are the poor" theology, was the primary caretaker of the indigent. Mobility caused an increase in the number of able-bodied individuals needing temporary assistance, and troubles arising from their presence contributed to a growing antipathy toward the able-bodied poor.

Katz (1989) also traces the origins of the "undeserving poor" in part to demographic factors. He points out that, prior to the twentieth century, poverty was a seemingly unalterable fact of life, and most people would spend their lives in it. Thus no moral taint was attached to poverty. The only policy question usually involved the locus of responsibility for aid, and the answer was a simple one: Responsibility was local, and those needy persons not belonging to the community could be "resettled." Increased population mobility made the settlement provisions unworkable, and the original distinction between the genuinely needy and "rogues, vagabonds, and sturdy beggars" hardened into a moral distinction between the poor, who needed no public relief, and "paupers," those needing assistance because of personal failings (Katz 1989, pp. 12–14).

Feagin (1975, chap. 2) locates the origins of negative attitudes toward the poor in the Protestant Reformation. Under Protestantism, he notes, the "work ethic"—the ideology of individualism—became a central tenet of the Western belief system. Poverty, in the extreme Calvinist version of this viewpoint, is largely a consequence of laziness and vice, and can even be regarded as just punishment from a righteous God. The rise of Puritan thought contributed to the increasing disfavor with which the unemployed and destitute were regarded. It became a matter of faith that poverty was individually caused and must thereby be individually cured. These ideas became secularized, and programs to aid the poor thereafter focused on curing the individual faults that led to poverty: Potential problems in the structure of society that caused unemployment and underemployment were not to be scrutinized in search of a solution. The notion of poverty continues to be in flux. As Marshall (1981) noted, the concept has been with us since antiquity, but its meaning has not been constant through the ages.

Most sociologists today distinguish among three major types of explanations of poverty: individual, situational, and structural theories. Individual theories attribute the primary cause of poverty to individual failings or, more neutrally, to individual differences—the central argument being that the poor are different from the nonpoor in some significant way. Situational theories agree that the poor are different from the nonpoor, but argue that the differences are a result of poverty, not a cause of it. Structural theories see differences in individual attributes as irrelevant, and argue that poverty has only societal-level origins: The characteristics of economic systems create poverty, not the characteristics of individuals.

THEORY AND POLICY

The epitome of the individual viewpoint in the social sciences was the once-dominant "culture of poverty" explanation for destitution. Oscar Lewis (1961, 1966) is usually credited with this idea, which sees poverty not only as economic deprivation, or the absence of something, but also as a way of life, the presence of specific subcultural values and attitudes passed down from generation to generation. Lewis saw the structure of life among the poor as functional, a set of coping mechanisms without which the poor could not survive their harsh circumstances. But there were negative consequences of the value system as well, he noted. Family life was disorganized, there was an absence of childhood as a prolonged lifecycle stage, a proliferation of consensual marriages, and a very high incidence of spouse and child abandonment—all of which left individuals unprepared and unable to take advantage of opportunities. Exacerbating the problem, the poor were divorced from participation in and integration into the major institutions of society, leading to constant hostility, suspicion, and apathy. Many have maintained that the culture-of-poverty viewpoint dovetailed perfectly with a politically liberal view of the world. It blamed the poor as a group for their poverty, but held no single person individually responsible, nor did it blame the structure of the economy or the society. This view of the poor led to antipoverty policies directed at changing the attitudes and values of those in poverty, so that they could "break out" of the dysfunctional cultural traits they had inherited. It led political liberals and radicals to attempts to "organize the poor." Political conservatives transformed the explanation into one that held the poor more culpable individually and the problem into one that was intractable—"benign neglect" being then the only sensible solution (Banfield 1958, 1970; Katz 1989). There were many problems with the culture-of-poverty explanation. Most serious was the fact that the cultural scenario simply doesn't fit. Only a minority of the poor are poor throughout their lives; most move in and out of poverty. Also, a substantial proportion of those in poverty are either women with children who fell into poverty when abandoned by a spouse, or the elderly who became poor when their worklives ended: Neither event could be explainable by the culture of the class of destination. Many studies falsified specific aspects of the culture-of-poverty thesis (for a review, see Katz 1989, pp. 41 ff.), and Hyman Rodman's influential notion of the "lower-class value stretch" (1971) offered an alternative explanation (the poor actually share mainstream values, but must "stretch" them to fit their circumstances—remove the poverty, and they fit neatly into dominant culture—attempts to alter their "culture" are unnecessary, and meaningless, since "culture" is not the problem). Nonetheless, the culture-of-poverty thesis was (and to some extent still is) a very popular explanation for poverty. This is probably so in part because it fits so well the individualistic biases of most Americans. Surveys of attitudes toward poverty have shown that most persons prefer "individualistic" explanations of poverty, which place the responsibility for poverty primarily on the poor themselves. A minority of Americans subscribe to "structural" explanations that blame external social and economic factors, and this minority consists largely of the young, the less educated, lower income groups, nonwhites, and Jews (Feagin 1975, p. 98).

A more sophisticated recent treatment incorporating some of the explanatory power of the culture of poverty argument without that theory's untenable assumptions is William Wilson's depiction of the "underclass" (1987). This recent work by Wilson on the underclass has been criticized by some as a return to classical culture of poverty theory in a new guise. It is not, of course, and represents a very different type of explanation. Wilson defines the underclass as an economically disadvantaged group whose marginal economic position and weak attachment to the labor force is "uniquely reinforced by the neighborhood or social milieu" (Wilson 1993, p. 23). Changes in the geography of employment, industrial specialization, and other factors have resulted in a rise in joblessness among urban minorities, which has in turn led to an increase in other social dislocations. Primary among those other factors has been the steady out-migration of working-class and middle-class families from the inner cities, which groups would normally provide a social buffer. Wilson notes: "in a neighborhood with a paucity of regularly employed families and with the overwhelming majority of families having spells of long-term joblessness, people experience a social isolation that excludes them from the job network system that permeates other neighborhoods and that is so important . . . other alternatives such as welfare . . . are not only increasingly relied on, they come to be seen as a way of life" (1987, p. 57). The 1990 U.S. Census showed that about 15 percent of the poor lived in neighborhoods where the poverty rate was at least 40 percent (O'Hare 1996). In these neighborhoods, where few are likely to have resources or job networks, reside Wilson's "underclass." Unlike the culture-of-poverty theory, Wilson's theory analyzes the structural and cultural resources of poor places, rather than the socialized attitudes and values of poor people. Wilson contends that "ghetto-specific cultural traits" are relevant in understanding the behavior of inner-city poor people, but these traits, contra culture-of-poverty theory, do not have a life of their own. That is, they are an effect of deprivation and social isolation, not a cause of it, and they command very little commitment—they are not self-perpetuating. "Social isolation," Wilson's key concept, implies not differential socialization of the inner-city poor, but rather their lack of cultural resources supporting the desirability and possibility of achieving culturally normative aspirations. The individual characteristics normally associated with a culture of poverty argument represent expected and even rational responses to adverse environments, not socialized belief systems.

While Wilson's work has been very influential in the social sciences, one of the most politically influential recent works on poverty policy has been that of Murray (1984). Murray argued that the viewpoint that individuals ultimately cause their own poverty changed in the 1960s to the viewpoint that the structure of society was ultimately responsible. This alteration in the intellectual consensus, which freed the poor from responsibility for their poverty, was fatally misguided, he argues, and caused great damage to the poor. Despite enormously increased expenditures on social welfare from 1965 on, he maintains, progress against poverty ceased at that point. In the face of steadily improving economic conditions, the period 1965–1980 was marked by increases in poverty, family breakdown, crime, and voluntary unemployment. Murray argues that this occurred precisely because of the increased expenditures on social welfare, not despite them. Work incentive declined during these years because of government policies that rewarded lack of employment and nonintact family structure. It is a standard economic principle that any activity that is subsidized will tend to increase. Murray's arguments have had policy impact, but have been subject to extensive criticism by students of the field.

As evidence of the disincentive to work brought about by social welfare payments, Murray cites the Negative Income Tax (NIT) experiments. These were large social experiments designed to assess the effects of a guaranteed income. The first NIT experiment was a four-year study in New Jersey from the late 1960s to the early 1970s. In this study, 1,375 intact "permanently poor" families were selected, and 725 of them were assigned to one of eight NIT plans. It was found that the reduction in labor-market activity for males caused by a guaranteed income was not significant, but that there were some reductions for females (5–10 percent of activity), most of which could be explained by the substitution of labor-market activity for increased child care (home employment). In a larger NIT study conducted throughout the 1970s, the Seattle-Denver Income Maintenance Experiment (usually referred to in the literature as the SIME-DIME study), much larger work disincentives were found, about 10 percent for men, 20 percent for their spouses, and up to 30 percent for women heading single-family households (see Haveman 1987, chap. 9, for an excellent summary of the many NIT experiments). Murray offered these findings as evidence that existing welfare programs contributed to poverty by creating work disincentives. Cain (1985) pointed out that the experiments provided much higher benefits than existing welfare programs, and also noted that, given the low pay for women at that level, the 20 percent reduction for wives would have a trivial effect on family income. If it resulted in a proportionate substitution of work at home, the reduction could actually lead to an improvement in the lives of the poor. Commentators have presented arguments against almost every point made by Murray, insisting that either his measures or his interpretations are wrong. For example, Murray's measure of economic growth, the gross national product (GNP), did increase throughout the 1970s, but real wages declined, and inflation and unemployment increased—poverty was not increasing during good times, as he argues. His other assertions have been similarly challenged (for summaries, see McLanahan et al. 1985; Katz 1989, chap. 4), but though his arguments and empirical findings simply do not stand up to close scrutiny, the broad viewpoint his work represents remains important in policy deliberations, probably because they offer pseudoscientific support for the biases of many.

MEASURES OF POVERTY

In the United States, official poverty estimates are based on the Orshansky Index. The index is named for Mollie Orshansky of the Social Security Administration, who first proposed it (Orshansky 1965). It is an absolute poverty measure, based on the calculated cost of food sufficient for an adequate nutritional level and on the assumption that persons must spend one-third of their after-tax income on food. Thus, the poverty level is theoretically three times the annual cost of a nutritionally adequate "market basket." This cost was refined by stratifying poor families by size, composition, and farm/nonfarm, and by creating different income cutoffs for poverty for families of differing types. Originally there were 124 income cutoff points, but by 1980 the separate thresholds for farm families and female-headed households had been eliminated, and the number of thresholds reduced to 48. Since 1969 the poverty line has been regularly updated using the Consumer Price Index (CPI) to adjust for increased costs. The original index was based on the least costly of four nutritionally adequate food plans developed by the Department of Agriculture. Since a 1955 Department of Agriculture survey of food consumption patterns had determined that families of three or more spent approximately one-third of their income on food, the original poverty index was simply triple the average cost of the economy food plan. This index was altered for smaller families to compensate for their higher fixed costs, and for farm families to compensate for their lower costs (the farm threshold began as 70 percent of the nonfarm for an equivalent household, and was raised to 85 percent in 1969). Originally, the poverty index was adjusted yearly by taking into account the cost of the food items in the Department of Agriculture economy budget, but this changed in 1969 to a simple CPI adjustment (U.S. Bureau of the Census 1982).

Over the years there have been many criticisms of the official poverty measure and its assumptions (for summaries and extended discussion, see U.S. DHEW 1976; Haveman 1987). The first set of problems, some argue, come from the fact that the very basis of the measure is flawed. The economy food budget at the measure's core is derived from an outdated survey that may not reflect changes in tastes and options. Further, the multiplication of food costs by three is only appropriate for some types of families, other types must spend greater or lesser proportions on food. Some estimates indicate that the poor spend half or more of their income on food; the more well-to-do spend one-third or less. Even if the multiplier was correct, the original Department of Agriculture survey discovered it for posttax income; in the poverty measure it is applied to pretax income, though the poor pay little in taxes. Other problems often cited include the fact that the "economy budget" assumes sufficient knowledge for wise shopping—a dubious assumption for the poor— and the fact that the poor are often locked into paying much higher prices than average because of a lack of transportation. An additional problem is that the poverty thresholds are not updated by using changes in the actual price of food, but instead by changes in the CPI, which includes changes in the price of many other items such as clothing, shelter, transportation, fuel, medical fees, recreation, furniture, appliances, personal services, and many other items probably irrelevant to the expenses of the poor. Findings are mixed, but it is generally agreed that the losses in purchasing power suffered by the poor in inflationary periods is understated by the CPI (see Oster et al. 1978, p. 25). A second set of problems derives from the fact that the definition is based on income only. Both in-kind transfers and assets are excluded. Excluding in-kind transfers means that government-provided food, shelter, or medical care is not counted. Excluding assets means that a wealthy family with little current income could be counted as poor.

DEMOGRAPHY OF POVERTY

In 1987 the average poverty threshold for a family of four was $11,611 per year (all figures in this paragraph are from U.S. Bureau of the Census 1989a, p. 163; 1989b, p. 166; 1990). This means the assumed annual cost of an adequate diet for four persons was $3,870.33, or about 88 cents per meal per person. For a single person the poverty threshold was $5,778, and the food allowance $1.76 per meal. In 1986 the poverty threshold was $11,203, allowing 85 cents per meal, and in 1988 it had risen to $12,091, or 92 cents per meal. In the United States in 1987 there were 32,341,000 persons below the poverty threshold, or 13.4 percent of the population. In 1988 there were 31,878,000, or 13.1 percent, almost a half-million fewer persons below official poverty than the year before. These figures underestimate official poverty somewhat, since they are based on the Current Population Survey, which is primarily a household survey and thus does not count the homeless not in shelters. The decline from 1987 to 1988 in the number in poverty is part of a long-term trend. In 1960 there were 8 million more—39,851,000 persons—who by today's guidelines would have been counted as officially in poverty, representing 22.2 percent of the population. By the official, absolute standard, poverty has greatly decreased over the past three decades, both in terms of the actual number of persons below the threshold and, even more dramatically, by the percentage of the population in poverty (U.S. Bureau of the Census 1989). This decrease actually took place over two decades, since the number of people in poverty in 1970 had declined to only 25,420,000, or 12.6 percent of the population, and the number and percentage have risen since then, but never back as high as the 1960 levels. Poverty is not evenly spread over the population. Of those below the official poverty level in 1988, 57.1 percent were female, 29.6 percent were black, and 16.9 percent were Hispanic. Female-headed families with children were disproportionately poor. In poverty in 1988 were 38.2 percent of all such white families and 56.3 percent of all such black families (this is a gender phenomenon, not a single-parent one, since in 1988 only 18 percent of male-headed single parent families were below the poverty threshold). The age composition of the poor population has changed. In 1968, 38.6 percent of those in poverty were of working age (18–64), while twenty years later 49.6 percent of those in poverty were of working age. From 1968 to 1988 the percentage of the poor population over 65 declined from 18.2 percent to 10.9 percent, and the percentage who were children under 18 declined from 43.1 percent to 39.5 percent. A higher percentage of working-age poor is seen by some as a sign of worse times. It almost certainly reflects not only economic downturns but also in part ideological biases toward helping the presumably able-bodied poor; most antipoverty programs have been specifically aimed at the old or the young. O'Hare (1996) points out that the poverty rate and the number of poor in the 1990s exceed those figures in the 1970s. He notes that all the dramatic postwar decline in poverty rates occurred before 1973. After that, poverty rates in the United States rose through the early 1980s, then declined, but never back to the 1973 level.

Despite extensive debate about the policy implications of various definitions of poverty, and the inherent difficulty of locating this population, one can have confidence that the poor are being counted with reasonable precision. More than one generation of social scientists have contributed to the refinement of the measures of poverty, and existing statistical series are based on data collected by the U.S. Bureau of the Census—an organization with very high technical competence. Nonetheless, there is one group, the extremely poor, whose numbers are in doubt. All current measurement relies on the household unit, and assumes some standard type of domicile. As Rossi puts it, "our national unemployment and poverty statistics pertain only to that portion of the domiciled population that lives in conventional housing" (1989, p. 73). An extremely poor person living, perhaps temporarily, in a household where other adults had sufficient income would not be counted

as being in poverty. Even more important, the literally homeless who live on the street, and those whose homes consist of hotels, motels, rooming houses, or shelters are not counted at all in the yearly Current Population Survey (the decennial census does attempt to count those in temporary quarters, but the 1990 census was the first to even attempt to count those housed in unconventional ways or not at all). The studies of Rossi and his colleagues indicate that the number of extremely poor people in the United States (those whose income is less than two-thirds of the poverty level) is somewhere between four and seven million. The number of literally homeless poor people, those who do not figure into the official poverty counts, must be estimated. The best available estimate is that they number between 250,000 and 350,000, about 5–8 percent of the extremely poor population (Rossi 1989). The number of extremely poor people has more than doubled since 1970, while the population was increasing only by 20 percent (Rossi 1989, p. 78). The extremely poor are at considerable risk of becoming literally homeless. When they do so, they will disappear from official statistics (just as the unemployed cease being officially unemployed soon after they give up the search for work). To see that official statistics remain reliable in the face of increasing extreme poverty is the most recent methodological challenge in the field.

POVERTY IN LOW-INCOME COUNTRIES

Most of the discussion thus far has concerned poverty in the United States. Comparing poverty across countries is a difficult enterprise, but is important to do if one is to put poverty in any individual country in perspective. Poverty in the United States and in other highly industrialized countries simply does not fall into the same category as poverty in less industrialized nations. Many of those classified as in poverty in the United States would be seen as reasonably well off by international standards. This means that, although many countries report a "percentage-in-poverty" figure for their populations, these figures cannot be sensibly compared, since the concept of what constitutes poverty varies so widely. Statistics from the United Nations Development Program 1998 Human Development Report can illustrate this stark contrast. In 1998, in the forty-four countries the U.N. classifies as "least developed," about 29 percent of the population was not expected to survive to age 40. Compare this to the 5 percent not expected to survive to that age in the industrial countries. In the least developed countries, 43 percent of the population has no access to safe water, 64 percent no access to sanitation, and 51 percent no access to health services (considering all developing countries rather than just the poorest, those figures would be 29 percent, 20 percent, and 58 percent, respectively). This level of living is characteristic of very few people in industrial nations, making poverty comparisons almost meaningless. The World Bank has attempted to provide international comparisons of poverty by creating a measure of the percentage of a country's population living on less than $1 a day, calculated in 1985 international prices and "adjusted to local currency using purchasing power parities" (World Bank 1999, p. 69). The $1-a-day figure was chosen because this is the typical poverty line in low-income countries. World Bank figures indicate that about 1.3 billion people live on less than $1 a day. Twenty-seven countries in which over 25 percent of the population lives with resources at less than this level were counted, as were fourteen countries (Guatemala, Guinea-Bissau, Honduras, India, Kenya, Lesotho, Madagascar, Nepal, Niger, Peru, Rwanda, Senegal, Uganda, Zambia) where approximately half or more of the population lives on less than $1 a day.

It is clear that while relative poverty is a serious moral and political issue in industrial countries, absolute poverty—at levels unheard of in industrial countries—is a far more serious problem in much of the rest of the world.

The study of poverty is a difficult field, and is not properly a purely sociological endeavor. As even this brief overview shows, a thorough understanding requires the combined talents of sociologists, economists, demographers, political scientists, historians, and philosophers. All these fields have contributed to our understanding of the phenomenon.

REFERENCES

Banfield, Edward C. 1958 *The Moral Basis of a Backward Society*. New York: Free Press.

—— 1970 *The Unheavenly City*. Boston: Little, Brown.

Cain, Glen 1985 "Comments on Murray's Analysis of the Impact of the War on Poverty on the Labor Market Behavior of the Poor." In Sara McLanahan, et al., eds., *Losing Ground: A Critique*, Special Report No. 38. Institute for Research on Poverty, University of Wisconsin.

Feagin, Joe R. 1975 *Subordinating the Poor: Welfare and American Beliefs*. Englewood Cliffs, N.J.: Prentice-Hall.

Haveman, Robert H. 1987 *Poverty Policy and Poverty Research: The Great Society and the Social Sciences*. Madison: University of Wisconsin Press.

Katz, Michael B. 1989 *The Undeserving Poor: From the War on Poverty to the War on Welfare*. New York: Pantheon.

Kilpatrick, R. W. 1973 "The Income Elasticity of the Poverty Line." *Review of Economics and Statistics* 55:327–332.

Lewis, Oscar 1961 *The Children of Sanchez*. New York: Random House.

—— 1966 *La Vida: A Puerto Rican Family in the Culture of Poverty–San Juan and New York* New York: Random House.

McLanahan Sara, Glen Cain, Michael Olneck, Irving Piliavin, Sheldon Danziger, and Peter Gottschalk 1985 *Losing Ground: A Critique*, Special Report No. 38. Institute for Research on Poverty, University of Wisconsin.

Marshall, T. H. 1981 *The Right to Welfare and Other Essays*. New York: Free Press.

Morris, Michael, and John B. Williamson 1986 *Poverty and Public Policy: An Analysis of Federal Intervention Efforts*. Westport, Conn.: Greenwood.

Murray, Charles 1984 *Losing Ground: American Social Policy, 1950-1980*. New York: Basic.

O'Hare, William P. 1996 "A New Look at Poverty in America." *Population Bulletin* 51(2):1–48.

Orshansky, Mollie 1965 "Counting the Poor: Another Look at the Poverty Profile." *Social Security Bulletin* 28(1):3–29.

Oster, Sharon M., Elizabeth E. Lake, and Conchita Gene Oksman 1978 *The Definition and Measurement of Poverty*. Boulder, Colo.: Westview.

Rainwater, Lee 1974 *What Money Buys: Inequality and the Social Meaning of Income*. New York: Basic.

Rodman, Hyman 1971 *Lower-Class Families: The Culture of Poverty in Negro Trinidad*. London: Oxford University Press.

Rossi, Peter H. 1989 *Down and Out in America: The Origins of Homelessness*. Chicago: University of Chicago Press.

Rowntree, B. S. 1901 *Poverty: A Study of Town Life*. London: Macmillan.

U.S. Bureau of the Census 1982 "Changes in the Definition of Poverty." *Current Population Reports*, Series P-60, No. 133. Washington, D.C.: U.S. Government Printing Office.

—— 1989a "Poverty in the United States: 1987." *Current Population Reports*, Series P-60, No. 163. Washington, D.C.: U.S. Government Printing Office.

—— 1989 "Money Income and Poverty Status in the United States: 1988." *Current Population Reports*, Series P-60, No. 166. Washington, D.C.: U.S. Government Printing Office.

—— 1990 "Measuring the Effect of Benefits and Taxes on Income and Poverty: 1989." *Current Population Reports*, Series P-60, No. 169-RD. Washington, D.C.: U.S. Government Printing Office.

U.S. Department of Health, Education, and Welfare (DHEW) 1976 *The Measure of Poverty: A Report to Congress as Mandated by the Education Amendments of 1974.* Washington, D.C.: U.S. Government Printing Office.

United Nations 1998 *Human Development Report.* Oxford: Oxford University Press.

Wilson, William Julius 1987 *The Truly Disadvantaged: The Inner City, the Underclass, and Public Policy.* Chicago: University of Chicago Press.

—— 1993 *The Ghetto Underclass: Social Science Perspectives.* Newbury Park, Calif.: Sage.

World Bank 1999 *World Development Indicators, 1999.* Washington: International Bank for Reconstruction and Development/World Bank.

WAYNE J. VILLEMEZ

POWER

See Bureaucracy; Interpersonal Power; Social Organization.

PRAGMATISM

Pragmatism, the Greek root word of which means "action," grew out of a turn-of-the-century reaction in American philosophy to Enlightenment conceptions of science, human nature, and social order. Generally, it has sought to reconcile incompatibilities between philosophical idealism and realism. In the former, reality is conceived of as existing only in human experience and subjectivity, and is given in the form of perceptions and ideas. In the latter, reality is proposed as existing in the form of essences or absolutes that are independent of human experience. These two traditions have grounded different approaches to empiricism and in their extremes can be found, respectively, in the solipsism of the British philosopher George Berkeley and the positivistic embracement of natural law by the French sociologist Auguste Comte.

As a response and an alternative to these traditions, pragmatism has not been developed as a unified philosophical system. Rather, it has existed as a related set of core ideas and precepts that are expressed as versions or applications of pragmatic thought. Variation within that thought ranges across the realism–idealism continuum and is largely a function of different analytical agendas. Despite that variation, however, pragmatism has become quite broad in its application to theoretical and research problems. Acknowledged as the most distinctive and profound contribution of American intellectual thought, its influence can be found in all contemporary disciplines in the humanities and social sciences. Its intellectual roots are described in Rucker (1969), Martindale (1960), and Konvitz and Kennedy (1960), and its core ideas are described in Shalin (1986), Rochberg-Halton (1986), and Rosenthal (1986).

MAIN IDEAS AND VARIATIONS

In summary form, the main ideas embodying the thrust of pragmatism are as follows. First, humans are active, creative organisms, empowered with agency rather than passive responders to stimuli. Second, human life is a dialectical process of continuity and discontinuity and therefore is inherently emergent. Third, humans shape their worlds and thus actively produce the conditions of freedom and constraint. Fourth, subjectivity is not prior to social conduct but instead flows from it. Minds (intelligence) and selves (consciousness) are emergent from action and exist dialectically as social and psychical processes rather than only as psychic states. Fifth, intelligence and consciousness are potential solutions to practical problems of human survival and quality of life. Sixth, science is a form of adjustive intelligibility and action that is useful in guiding society. Seventh, truth and value reside simultaneously in group perspectives and the human consequences of action. Eighth, human nature and society exist in and are sustained by symbolic communication and language. In these core ideas can be seen the neo-Hegelian focus on dialectical processes and the concurrent rejection of Cartesian dualisms, the Darwinian focus on the emergence of forms and variation through adjustive processes, and the behavioristic focus on actual conduct as the locus of reality and understanding. These ideas were embraced and developed by a variety of scholars and thinkers, including Ralph Waldo Emerson, Percy Bridgman, C. I. Lewis, Morris Cohen, Sidney Hook, Charles Morris, Charles Peirce, William James, Charles Horton Cooley, John Dewey, and George Herbert Mead. Of these, Peirce, James, Cooley, Dewey, and Mead will be reviewed here for purposes of assessing the relevance of pragmatism to social science and sociology.

Charles S. Peirce (1839–1914) is generally credited as the originator of the term *pragmatism* and the formulation of some of its basic tenets. One of his earliest statements (1877–1878) pertained to methods for resolving doubt about conclusions, in which he argued in favor of science because of its flexibility and self-correcting processes. This view contrasts sharply with the Cartesian basis of science in subjectivism and individualism proposed by Descartes. Rather than focusing on belief and consciousness as definitive, Peirce focused on probability. Both truth and scientific rationality rest in a community of opinion in the form of perpetual doubt and through a process of revisions are measured in terms of movement toward the clarification of ideas. The emphasis in this process is both evolutionary, since Peirce saw modes of representing knowledge moving from chance (firstness) to brute existence (secondness) to generality or order (thirdness), and pragmatic, since truth is meaningful only in terms of future consequences for human conduct (the "pragmatic rule").

William James (1842–1910) was driven by the problem of determinism and free will. This problem was expressed in his monumental *Principles of Psychology* (1890), in which he established a functional view assimilating biology and psychology and treated intelligence as an instrument of human survival, and in his brilliant analysis of consciousness (1904), in which he characterized human experience as an ongoing flow instead of a series of psychic states. Pragmatist principles were sharply articulated in these works. James accepted

Peirce's pragmatic rule that the meaning of anything resides in experimental consequences. Accordingly, the distinction between subject and object as fundamental was denied and was replaced with the idea that relations between the knower and the known are produced by and in ongoing experience. This more dialectical conceptualization informed his theory of emotions, which stressed bodily responses as producers of emotional responses (e.g., we feel afraid because we tremble) and his theory of the self, emphasizing the "I" (self as knower) and the "Me" (self as known) as tied to multiple networks of group affiliation. His focus throughout was on the operations of ongoing experience, and his formulations not only specified and elaborated pragmatist principles but anticipated or contributed to behaviorism, gestalt psychology, and operationalism.

Charles Horton Cooley (1864–1929), building on the work of James, rejected the legitimacy of all dualisms. In his famous statement that "self and society are twin-born," he asserted the inseparability of individuals and society. Individuals, he proposed, are merely the distributive phase and societies the collective phase of the same social processes. The indissoluble connection of self and society, which was the dominant theme of Cooley's writings, is manifested in their necessary interdependence. His theory of the social self held that self-concepts are behaviorally derived through reflected appraisals of the actions of others—the looking-glass self. Especially important in the process of self-acquisition are primary groups (family, friends), which link the person to society. Correspondingly, society significantly exists in the form of personal imaginations or mental constructs; society, Cooley stated, is an interweaving and interworking of mental selves. Cooley's approach was thoroughly holistic and organic, with human consciousness and communication being the most critical processes, and his work added further to the pragmatist's dismantling of the Cartesian split between mind and society.

John Dewey (1859–1952) was perhaps the most influential and prolific of the early pragmatists. Coming philosophically to pragmatism from Hegelianism, he emphasized intelligence, process, and the notion that organisms are constantly reconstructing their environments as they are being determined by them. He contributed forcefully to the critique of dualistic thought in his analysis of stimulus-response theory (1896). Instead of constituting an arc, in which the stimulus leads to a response (a dualistic conception), Dewey argued that they are merely moments in an overall division of labor in a reciprocal, mutually constitutive process (a dialectical conception). Central to those dialectics was communication, which according to Dewey was the foundation and core mechanism of social order. He developed an instrumentalist theory of language (1925)—language as a tool—which was generalized into a broader instrumentalism. One of his central interests was moral and social repair through the application of intelligence and scientific methods. He merged theory and practice in the view that ideas are instruments for reconstructing and reconstituting problematic situations. Those ideas may be moral judgements or scientific findings, but both take the general form of hypotheses, which are proposals for action in response to difficulties. Dewey thus built upon Peirce's and James's pragmatic rule by arguing that validity and truth statements, whether theological or scientific, are established by examining the consequences of action derived from hypotheses.

George Herbert Mead (1863–1931) sought understanding of emergent human properties, such as the ability to think in abstractions, self-consciousness, and moral and purposive conduct. His central argument was that these properties are grounded in the development of language and social interaction as humans adjust to the conditions of their environments and group life (Mead 1934). His position is said to be one of social behaviorism, in which the social act is the unit of analysis and out of which minds and selves develop. The act has covert and overt phases. It begins in the form of an attitude (an incipient act), is constructed through role-taking processes (imaginatively placing oneself in the position of others), and is manifested in overt conduct. All social behavior involves a conflation of subjective and objective processes through which persons adjustively contend with the facts of their environments and simultaneously create social situations. Mead's explicit theory of time and sociality places these adjustments squarely in the dialectics of continuity and discontinuity (Maines et al. 1983).

In these five brief summaries can be seen how the early pragmatists wove together strands of scientific method, evolutionary theory, language, and behaviorism into a radically new perspective. Pragmatism provided a clear alternative to perspectives based on Cartesian dualisms and reconstituted science, morality, aesthetics, political theory, and social development in terms of dialectical transactions. Philosophical idealism and realism were brought into a common framework in the proposition that human experience and facts of nature and society (the "world that is there," as Mead called them) are only phases of ongoing social processes that mediate persons and their environments in terms of transacted meanings. The variation within pragmatism hinges largely on individual affinities for idealism and realism: James and Cooley tended toward idealism, Peirce toward realism, and Dewey and Mead toward a transactional midpoint between the two. Moreover, there is variation in pragmatism's influence in the social sciences and humanities. Dewey has been enormously influential in education and communication, Mead and Cooley in sociology and social psychology, Peirce in semiotics, and James in psychology. That variation, however, only represents modal tendencies, since pragmatism as a whole has had a significant impact across disciplines.

INFLUENCE IN SOCIAL SCIENCE

Since 1980 there has been a major resurgence of interest in pragmatism (Bernstein 1986). Its compatibilities with quantum mechanics and relativity theory have been articulated, as has its relevance for the development of a more social semiotics and discourse analysis (Perinbanayagam 1986). The relation of pragmatism to hermeneutics, from the tradition of German Idealism, has been reexamined (Dallmayr 1987), as has its relation to critical theory in the work of Jürgen Habermas (McCarthy 1984), literary criticism (Rorty 1982), phenomenology (Ricoeur 1985), cultural studies (Carey 1989), and modernization theory (Rochberg-Halton 1986). According to some, such as Richard Bernstein and more recently John Diggins (1994), this resurgence indicates that the early pragmatists were ahead of their time. Some scholars in the 1990s have continued to revise pragmatist thought on its own terms. Wiley (1995) has proposed a sophisticated modification of Mead's theory of the self through Peirce's triadic, semiotic perspective. Joas (1993), while not writing on pragmatism, per se, has shown how pragmatist precepts have been intrinsic both to classical and contemporary theory. He also (Joas 1996) has retheorized creativity, long at the heart of pragmatism's emphasis on novelty and indeterminism, for dominant sociological models based on structural differentiation, rational adaptation, and self-enhancement.

Other scholars have sought to reinvigorate pragmatism's relevance for contemporary political and cultural agendas. Noting that the seeds of a feminist pragmatism existed in the work and practices of the classical thinkers (Mead, Dewey, James), Seigfried (1996) politicizes pragmatism in the common struggles of women, ethnic minorities, and the sexually marginalized. While retaining the traditional center of the perspective, she seeks to move it toward a reconsideration of contextual ethics and reciprocal moral responsibility and to promote the search for pragmatic truths that would emancipate people from distorted beliefs and values that become sedimented into accepted fact. These scholars also include Cornell West (1989), who articulated his version of "prophetic pragmatism" in *The American Evasion of Philosophy* and followed it with his influential *Race Matters* (1994), which was more politically engaged and contributed to a more vibrant democracy that better empowers local participation in institutional concerns. Still others have sought more radical revisions of pragmatism. Denzin (1992, 1996), drawing in part from West, provides a revision of pragmatism in postmodernist, cultural studies terms that seeks to transform it into a mechanism of cultural critique. Such works find audiences in humanistic circles, but have met with mixed reactions among social scientists. Farberman (1991) and Lyman (1997) reject the postmodernist project partly on the grounds of its nihilistic implications, Van Den Berg (1996) because of its limited vision of Enlightenment philosophy, and Maines (1996) because its core concepts are already contained in pragmatist thought. Others, such as Seidman (1996) have attempted more even-handed critiques and seek the common ground of postmodernism and pragmatism. Regardless of recent interpretations of pragmatism, the collapse of hegemonic theories and the corresponding import of post-positivistic debate in social scientific theorizing has brought

the basic tenets of pragmatism back into the search for new paradigms in social theory.

These recent influences and developments notwithstanding, there has been a long tradition of direct influence of pragmatism on social science research and theory. Sociology's first research classic was Thomas and Znaniecki's (1918–1920) study of Polish immigrant adaptation to American urban life. They were interested in questions of personal adjustment, family relations, neighborhood formation, delinquency, and cultural assimilation, and they used the principles of pragmatism, especially as expressed by G. H. Mead, to answer those questions. Their monumental five-volume work presented their attitude-value scheme as a general theory of the adjustive relations between individuals and society. "Attitudes" referred to the individual's tendencies to act and represented human subjectivity; "values" referred to the constraining facts of a society's social organization and represented the objective social environment. Both are present in any instance of human social conduct, they argued, but the relationships between the two are established in processes of interpretation that they called "definitions of the situation." Thomas and Znaniecki thus placed human agency at the center of their explanations, and they conceptualized society as the organization of dialectical transactions.

That research contained pragmatist ideas pertaining to the social psychological and social organizational aspects of human behavior. These aspects were developed during the 1920s and 1930s at the University of Chicago by Ellsworth Faris and Robert Park. Faris (1928) examined attitudes, especially in terms of the nature of their influence on behavior. He argued that human subjectivity is a natural datum for sociological research and proposed that wishes and desires, not attitudes, have a direct bearing on overt conduct. Park (1926) was more interested in large-scale historical issues such as urban organization and racial stratification. He directly applied Dewey's focus on society as communication to his research on urban communities. These communities, he argued, have objective spatial patterns, but those patterns are not separable from human consciousness. Urban ecology thus has a moral dimension composed of meanings that collectivities attribute to urban areas. The pragmatist roots of Park's sociology recently has been reemphasized in his theory of human ecology (Maines et al. 1996), his influence on applied sociology (Reitzes and Reitzes 1992; see also Maines 1997), and as a framework for describing and theorizing urban public space (Lofland 1998).

The pragmatist themes of individual/society inseparability and human behavior as transactions were pursued by other sociologists. In 1937, Herbert Blumer coined the phrase *symbolic interaction* to refer simultaneously to how humans communicate and to a sociological perspective. He applied that perspective to a wide range of research areas such as social psychology, collective behavior, race relations, and social problems (Maines 1989). Blumer's posthumous volume on industrialization and social change (1990) elaborates the Thomas and Znaniecki formulations by presenting a conceptualization of causal influences that hinge on human agency and interpretation. Stone's research on clothing and fashion (1962) similarly focuses on human behavior as transactions. In particular, his analysis of identity establishment identifies dialectical processes of communication through which individuals are located and placed in the social organization of society. His treatment of interpersonal identities is sympathetic to Cooley's emphasis on the importance of primary groups, while his treatment of structural relations corresponds with Thomas and Znaniecki's concept of values and predates contemporary social psychological research on individuals and social structure.

Studies of social organization have been directly influenced by pragmatist principles, as previously mentioned, but that influence has been especially apparent since the early 1970s (see Hall 1987 and Fine 1993 for summaries). Anselm Strauss's research on occupations and formal organizations has been prominent in this recent work and has led to the development of the "negotiated order" perspective (Strauss 1978). Negotiations, he argues, are processes through which collective actions occur and tasks are accomplished. These processes are influenced by actor characteristics, the immediate situation, and larger structural contexts. However, those larger contexts are also influenced reciprocally by actual negotiations and their situations. Strauss's model of social organization thus is a recursive and dialectical one. Stryker (1980) presents a slightly different version but one that is no less pragmatist. He incorporates

traditional role theory to argue that social structural arrangements limit options and opportunities by channeling people into status and role positions. So located, people construct their identities in terms of social meanings that are hierarchically organized. Both Strauss's and Stryker's applications of pragmatism have stimulated considerable research and theoretical development.

Such development has continued with some vigor throughout the 1990s. Pestello and Saxton (2000) draw on explicit principles of pragmatism to reframe the study of deviance in terms of the dialectics of inclusion and exclusion. While closer to the classical statements, they share with the neopragmatists such as West, Seigfried, and Rorty the interest in reclaiming the vision of emancipatory democracy that has always been present in the perspective. Other scholars have used pragmatist principles to further develop areas of sociological theory. Fine (1992) addresses the relationship between agency and structure, and theorizes both the obdurate and interpretive dimensions of the relations among contexts of action. Musolf (1998) shows how agency and structure relations are expressed in an array of standard sociological areas (socialization, gender, deviance, power, society), while Hall (1997) offers an updated version of his earlier conceptual framework (Hall 1987) that allows analysts to better specify dimensions of agency-structure relations. Five dimensions are identified: strategic agency, rules and conventions, structuring situations, culture construction, and empowering delegates. He then shows how power is expressed along these dimensions and links together situations and contexts.

In a related approach to matters of agency and structure, Strauss (1993) builds on his earlier theory of negotiations to focus analysis on ordering processes. He begins by articulating over a dozen assumptions drawn from pragmatism that guide his analysis. He then presents a "processual order" theory that focuses on how larger scale processes and structures condition organizations and situations within which people interpret and construct their conduct and how local decisions have consequences for larger scale processes and structures. This theory has been used in research by Fischer and Dirsmith (1995) to examine organizational strategies and technology use in large accounting firms. Ulmer (1997) also has used the theory to explain how state sentencing guidelines are filtered through state and local political processes, and how local court communities set "going rates" for actual criminal sentencing. Ulmer's research is especially relevant because it simultaneously presents data on statewide sentencing outcomes and the contextual practices that produce those outcomes.

Yet another related line of development has focused on what W. I. Thomas ([1927] 1966) called "situational analysis," which examines the interplay of actors' interpretations and the obdurate qualities of situations. Katovich and Couch (1992) draw on Mead's theory of time to show how pasts are used by people to become socially situated. Situations, they argue, are not merely settings in which human conduct occurs, but rather are forms of conduct themselves and exist as transactions of pasts and futures. Gusfield (1996) presents his long line of research on alcohol problems, and addresses how those problems are constructed. He discusses various claims-makers within the alcoholism movement, and then dissects actual alcohol problems in terms of their situations—situations of drinking, of driving, of accountability—and the ideologies and logics-in-use that connect them. Hall and McGinty (1997) analyze educational policy processes from the "transformation of intentions" perspective. In a statewide study of the Missouri career ladder program, they show how various contexts (state legislature, advisory committees, bureaucratic offices, school districts, local schools) influence the original intended policy. Actual policy effects, accordingly, are strongly influenced by situational contingencies that render policy processes themselves less-than-rational. Similarly, Deutscher and colleagues (1993) analyze the contradictory findings from decades of attitude-behavior research, and provide a situational approach for explaining the inconsistencies between attitudes (what people say about themselves) and behavior (what people do). To understand consistency and inconsistencies between attitudes and behavior, they argue, we must understand the situations that produce those kinds of relationships.

One of the distinctive characteristics of social science research and theory that has been grounded in pragmatism is the reluctance to give credence to dualisms such as micro–macro or individual–society. While issues of scale have always been acknowledged and used, as the work of Park, Blumer,

Stone, Stryker, Strauss, Hall, and Fine has demonstrated, the focus has been on the examination of social processes that produce, maintain, and change social orders. These social processes have generally been conceptualized as communicative in nature, and the central thrust has been on how large- and small-scale phenomena are simultaneously or similarly transacted by individuals and groups. The focus on those processes has maintained the action orientation of pragmatism, and the central precepts of the perspective are finding increasing currency and relevance in contemporary work in the social sciences and humanities.

(SEE ALSO: *Social Philosophy*; *Social Psychology*)

REFERENCES

Bernstein, Richard 1986 *Philosophical Profiles*. Philadelphia: University of Pennsylvania Press.

Blumer, Herbert 1990 *Industrialization as an Agent of Social Change: A Critical Analysis*. Hawthorne, N.Y.: Aldine de Gruyter.

Carey, James 1989 *Communication as Culture*. Boston: Unwin Hyman.

Dallmayr, Fred 1987 *Critical Encounters between Philosophy and Politics*. Notre Dame, Ind.: University of Notre Dame Press.

Denzin, Norman 1992 *Symbolic Interactionism and Cultural Studies*. Cambridge, Mass.: Blackwell

—— 1996 "Sociology at the End of the Century." *Sociological Quarterly* 37:743–752.

Deutscher, Irwin, Fred Pestello, and H. Frances G. Pestello 1993 *Sentiments and Acts*. Hawthorne, N.Y.: Aldine de Gruyter.

Dewey, John 1896 "The Reflex Arc Concept in Psychology." *Psychological Review* 3:363–370.

—— 1925 *Experience and Nature*. Chicago: Open Court.

Diggins, John Patrick 1994 *The Promise of Pragmatism: Modernism and the Crisis of Knowledge and Authority*. Chicago: University of Chicago Press.

Farberman, Harvey 1991 "Symbolic Interactionism and Postmodernism: Close Encounter of a Dubious Kind." *Symbolic Interaction* 14:471–488.

Faris, Ellsworth 1928 "Attitudes and Behavior." *American Journal of Sociology* 33:271–281.

Fine, Gary Alan 1992 "Agency, Structure and Comparative Contexts: Toward a Synthetic Interactionism" *Symbolic Interaction* 15:87–107.

—— 1993 "The Sad Semise, Mysterious Disappearance, and Glorious Triumph of Symbolic Interactionism." *Annual Review of Sociology* 19:61–87.

Fischer, Michael, and Mark Dirsmith 1995 "Strategy, Technology, and Social Processes Within Professional Cultures: A Negotiated Order, Ethnographic Perspective." *Symbolic Interaction* 18:381–412.

Gusfield, Joseph 1996 *Contested Meanings: The Construction of Alcohol Problems*. Madison: University of Wisconsin Press.

Hall, Peter 1987 "Interactionism and the Study of Social Organization." *Sociological Quarterly* 28:1–22.

—— 1997 "Meta-Power, Social Organization, and the Shaping of Social Action." *Symbolic Interaction* 20:397–418.

——, and Patrick McGinty 1997 "Policy as Transformation of Intentions: Producing Program from Statute." *Sociological Quarterly* 38:439–467.

James, William 1890 *Principles of Psychology*. New York: Henry Holt.

—— 1904 "Does Consciousness Exist?" *Journal of Philosophy, Psychology, and Scientific Method* 1:477–491.

Joas, Hans 1993 *Pragmatism and Social Action*. Chicago: University of Chicago Press.

—— 1996 *The Creativity of Action*. Chicago: University of Chicago Press.

Katovich, Michael, and Carl Couch 1992 "The Nature of Social Pasts and Their Use as Foundations for Situated Action." *Symbolic Interaction* 15:25–47.

Konvitz, Milton, and Gail Kennedy (eds.) 1960 *The American Pragmatists*. Cleveland, Ohio: World.

Lofland, Lyn 1998 *The Public Realm*. Hawthorne, N.Y.: Aldine de Gruyter.

Lyman, Stanford 1997 *Postmodernism and the Sociology of the Absurd*. Fayetteville: University of Arkansas Press.

McCarthy, Thomas 1984 *The Critical Theory of Jürgen Habermas*. Cambridge, England: Polity.

Maines, David 1989 "Repackaging Blumer: The Myth of Herbert Blumer's Astructural bias." In Norman Denzin, ed., *Studies in Symbolic Interaction*. Greenwich, Conn.: JAI.

—— 1996 "On Postmodernism, Pragmatism, and Plasterers: Some Interactionist Thoughts and Queries" *Symbolic Interaction* 19:323–340.

—— (ed.) 1997 "Interactionism and Practice." *Applied Behavioral Science Review* 5:1–139. (Special Issue.)

——, Jeffrey Bridger, and Jeffery Ulmer 1996 "Mythic Facts and Park's Pragmatism: On Predecessor-Selection and Theorizing in Human Ecology" *Sociological Quarterly* 37:521–549.

——, Noreen Sugrue, and Michael Katovich 1983 "The Sociological Import of G. H. Mead's Theory of the Past." *American Sociological Review* 48:151–173.

Martindale, Don 1960 *The Nature and Types of Sociological Theory*. Boston: Houghton Mifflin.

Mead, George Herbert 1934 *Mind, Self, and Society*. Chicago: University of Chicago Press.

Musolf, Gil Richard 1998 *Structure and Agency in Everyday Life*. Dix Hills, N.J.: General-Hall.

Park, Robert 1926 "The Urban Community as a Spatial and Moral Order." In Ernest Burgess, ed., *The Urban Community*. Chicago: University of Chicago Press.

Peirce, Charles 1877–1878 "Illustrations of the Logic of Science." *Popular Science Monthly* 12:1–15, 286–302, 604–615, 705–718; 13:203–217, 470–482.

Perinbanayagam, Robert 1986 "The Meaning of Uncertainty and the Uncertainty of Meaning." *Symbolic Interaction* 9:105–126.

Pestello, Frances, and Stanley Saxton 2000 "Renewing the Promise of Pragmatism: Towards a Sociology of Difference." *Studies in Symbolic Interaction* 23:(In press.)

Reitzes, Donald, and Dietrich Reitzes 1992 "Saul Alinsky: An Applied Urban Symbolic Interactionist." *Symbolic Interaction* 15:1–24.

Ricoeur, Paul 1985 *Time and Narrative*. Chicago: University of Chicago Press.

Rochberg-Halton, Eugene 1986 *Meaning and Modernity: Social Theory in the Pragmatic Attitude*. Chicago: University of Chicago Press.

Rorty, Richard 1982 *Consequences of Pragmatism*. Minneapolis: University of Minnesota Press.

Rosenthal, Sandra 1986 *Speculative Pragmatism*. Amherst: University of Massachusetts Press.

Rucker, Darnell 1969 *The Chicago Pragmatists*. Minneapolis: University of Minnesota Press.

Seidman, Steven 1996 "Pragmatism and Sociology: A Response to Clough, Denzin, and Richardson." *Sociological Quarterly* 37:753–759.

Seigfried, Charlene Haddock 1996 *Pragmatism and Feminism: Reweaving the Social Fabric*. Chicago: University of Chicago Press.

Shalin, Dmitri 1986 "Pragmatism and Social Interactionism." *American Sociological Review* 51:9–29.

Stone, Gregory 1962 "Appearance and the Self." In Arnold Rose, ed., *Human Behavior and Social Processes*. Boston: Houghton Mifflin.

Strauss, Anselm 1978 *Negotiations*. San Francisco: Jossey-Bass.

—— 1993 *Continual Permutations of Action*. Hawthorne, N.Y.: Aldine de Gruyter.

Stryker, Sheldon 1980 *Symbolic Interactionism: A Social Structural Version*. Menlo Park, Calif.: Benjamin/ Cummings.

Thomas, W. I. 1966 "Situational Analysis: The Behavior Pattern and the Situation." In M. Janowitz, ed., *W. I. Thomas on Social Organization and Social Personality*. Chicago: University of Chicago Press. (Originally published in 1927 in *Publications of the American Sociological Society* 22:1–12.)

——, and Florian Znaniecki 1918–1920 *The Polish Peasant in Europe and America*, 5 vols. Chicago: University of Chicago Press.

Ulmer, Jeffery 1997 *The Social Worlds of Sentencing: Court Communities under Sentencing Guidelines*. Albany, N.Y.: State University of New York Press.

Van Den Berg, Axel 1996 "Liberalism without Reason?" *Contemporary Sociology* 24:153–158.

West, Cornell 1989 *The American Evasion of Philosophy*. Madison: University of Wisconsin Press.

—— 1994 *Race Matters*. N.Y.: Vintage.

Wiley, Norbert 1995 *The Semiotic Self*. Chicago: University of Chicago Press.

DAVID R. MAINES

PREDICTION AND FUTURES STUDIES

PREDICTION AND SOCIETY

Meaning. Prediction (*previsione*) is "seeing before-hand" how the future will be; that is, the situation that will come about in the short, medium, and long term. This, however, is a "seeing before-hand" that is not content with simply knowing what the final situation will be but it is also concerned with knowing with how it will be reached. It is concerned not only with the end-point but also with the process that the present situation will undergo to transform itself into (or remain as) the end-point. This two-part nature of prediction (end-point and development/process) enables us to take prediction into a scientific dimension, because the process by which the end-point is reached is comprehensible by means of the elaboration of a standardized method of identifying variables and their positions in a model of relationships that connect the before to the after, and carry the before to the after, and lead from the starting point to the end-point. Without this scientific attention to the passage from the former point to the latter, prediction could simply be a matter of taking the present and reading its evolution by means of an external "operator," such as a magic formula, casting stones, or the interpretation of animal innards.

This scientific attention to the process leading to the end-point—the prediction—is so crucial because by identifing elements of the process we can modify their developments to bring about the prediction we postulated. In other words, the variable now to be discovered and defined is not so much the prediction (with the extrapolative method) as the scientific process to be predicted so as to achieve a situation we desire (with the normative method).

In the light of the above, the term "prediction" as a name for this discipline is clearly less appropriate than others, such as "futurology," "future thinking," or "futures studies." A distinction may be drawn between two of these in that "futurology" is more of a disciplinary name and "futures studies" is more of an agenda of scientific activity aimed at achieving and discriminating between possible, probable, and desired futures.

In fact, if prediction is all of these things, it is of fundamental importance for taking action; that is, for deciding a priori how to achieve a given objective or to discover what a particular action will lead to.

Prediction is basically a scientific process in both of the senses just described, but it is also strongly related to other cognitive dimensions, such as ideology, ideas of utopia, action, and change. The theories underpinning prediction therefore combine or conflict with the theories and cognitive dimensions of reality. The links between these concepts should therefore be made clear.

Prediction, Utopia, and the Future of Traditional Society. A link of some kind between prediction, ideas of utopia, planning, and change certainly exists. We shall try to highlight it, starting from the problematic identified for prediction. Utopia is a "nonplace" in which is located a perfect society (perfect for he who first conceives it) dominated by a "cold synchrony," that is, by mechanical relations that serve only to maintain the utopian system without creating the emotional "warmth" or interests, including conflicting interests, whose relational outcome is unpredictable and therefore transforms the time-one system into something different from the time-zero system. Utopia is therefore the end-point of prediction, static and without relations, whose outcome cannot be predicted—an absolute end-point beyond which is nothingness. And between the present and the utopian state is "non-sense," that is, a black box whose contents do not interest us—the contents being the process that enables us to pass from the past to utopia.

What relation is there between prediction and utopia? We can interpret utopia as a residue of traditional society in which everything is tied to the past, but experienced in the pre-modern European society of the fifteenth and sixteenth centuries. In traditional society, real prediction, and therefore the future situation, is *deduced by* the past: Action is prescriptive, change is an aberration, organizations are similar because they all have the same structural contents and perform the same functions. Everything comes from the past: Rules are written in the past and actions are already perfected in the past. In these conditions, the process generating the future is a dejà-vu—not a perfect one, but a human condition and a destiny. The end-point that is different from such a prediction is not of this earthly condition but of the other life, in heaven or in hell. Utopia represents a sort of rebellion against the placing of heaven beyond earthly life—it is the secular dream of human omnipotence because it dares to place social perfection "not here" but nonetheless on earth. This utopia, an expression of the rebellion—no matter how fantastic—of traditional man, comes to represent a piece of "heaven" brought to earth, in which relations between people and social structures are so "sweet and delicate" as to strengthen the sweetness we have inside us rather than producing new situations and without automatically creating new equilibriums and new states. Because of all this, we can understand why constuctors of utopia do not need to know the process enabling us to pass from the present to the future (because it is a copy of the past) and why it is dominated by a static equilibrium that does not change once it has been achieved.

Thus prediction, utopia, and change in a society in which change is an aberration mean at the most bringing the perfection of the nonearthly world into the earthly world, but leaving it detached from reality, which also remains immutable. In other words, prediction is a game left to forces that are untameable and therefore ineluctable and at bottom mechanical, perpetuating positive and negative flows ad infinitum.

Prediction and the Objective as a Reference for the Plan: Ideology and the Future of Modern Society. Prediction becomes practically useful—able not only to reveal what will be but how this future may be controlled—when we lose sight of the perfections of the state we have called utopia and it takes on the role of an objective to be striven for, when an active value is ascribed to social ideals and single individuals' capacity for action. Here, society activates ideology as a resource and at the same time recognizes the ability of individual action, and above all the synthesis of individual actions, to create new situations.

Modern society thus shifts the focus from *the perfection of utopia*, which needs no modification since it is by definition perfect, and which is (an unreachable) vaguely defined objective, to the *laboratory of process*, which is concerned with relations and objectives to be achieved. If such an objective happens to be clearly defined, it is so accepted as provisional and therefore "adjustable," because certainty is only to be found in highly generic values such as justice, equality, and self-fulfillment in a fair, egalitarian, individual-enhancing society. This process of achieving the desired or probable prediction is guided by two resources activated by society. The first is ideology, the cognitive representation of the world used to guide practical action toward the objective that is the subject of prediction. The second resource is trust in the individual whose initiative may contribute to achieving the prediction, with the proviso that the action of this individual must be combined with that of other individuals to thus produce positive results for the predicted state of interpersonal and social relations.

In this view of modern society, it seems that the focus—aside from the objective defined in the probable or desired prediction that in its most complete form takes on the configuration of a plan—shifts for the most part to the process from which the prediction (and the predicted plan) emerges and thus to how this process is rationally manifested, how it may be scientifically explained, and what may be done to bend it to the achievement of the prediction.

All this comes about in modern society because change is conceived as normal, a factor built into the trajectory toward the future, tendentially and plausibly different from the present and above all from the past. All that remains of the past is the genetic origin of the present and a certain limited influence on it. If we have thus conceptually severed the deterministic link (at least in ideological terms) between past and future, modern society clearly has to focus very sharply on the processes and interdependent relations of the present in order to predict and dominate the future.

Determinism and Creativity in Prediction. To understand how prediction is to be orientated and manifested, rationality and the scientific method are essential because rationality and the scientific method provide the most effective and efficient ways of bringing about the realization of what we want to happen or what "must" happen. Hence the importance of method in obtaining a prediction and controlling it.

Methods have both deterministic components and creative components that are selected and embedded into techniques proper; these will be considered below. For the time being, it is sufficient simply to mention some features of these components. Deterministic components ground the formation of the end-point (prediction) in relations among the social, economic, environmental, and value structures defined in a model. Creative components include those that highlight the identification and pursuit of new and "invented" ways of controlling or accelerating the achievement of a prediction. Around such components, objective or subjective methodological techniques are developed that highlight the workings of a model and its simulation or formation of decisions.

METHODS OF PREDICTION

The Scientific Problem of Prediction. Not only is the scientific nature of social sciences considered suspect by people outside the social sciences, but certain social scientists themselves consider the social disciplines nonscientific because the most they can do is provide a way of "reading" a social reality composed of individuals, groups, mutual

relations, and formal organizations. For such people, the social sciences are not sciences but opinions. The reason is that—apart from some concepts providing interpretative keys for human, social and organizational action, mutual relations, and the products of those relations—interpretative theories stand the test of falsifiability only for a short time, often only until an event outside the phenomenon under investigation undermines the equilibrium and internal stability achieved by the phenomenon and explained by the theory. In the short term, the interpretative weakness of the theory even throws doubt on the ability of social science to explain the phenomenon. And this weakness of explanation obviously affects the strength of the prediction and consequently what has to be done to change it, that is, what is to be done to carry the present into the future.

Yet particular attention has been focused on four of the activities or purposes of which science is composed: (1) description as a pre-scientific stage and (2) explanation, (3) prediction, and (4) control as scientific activities proper. In point of fact, causal explanation is the central activity of the scientific process, since prediction is deduced from explanation and control is a "political" manipulation (and as such outside the phenomenon explained) of the variables of the explanatory model, undertaken deductively to achieve a modification of the prediction.

It may therefore be said that induction is at the root of description and explanation and deduction is at the root of prediction and control. But it is for precisely this reason that the first two activities are "more scientific," in that they are caught up in the bond between theory and theory-testing empirical research, whereas prediction and control are more rooted in utilization and change, in the final analysis in technical application. It is probably in this logic that we should see the contradiction between prediction as a science, whereby methods and techniques are elaborated as a deductive extension of methods for description and explanation or the perfection of methods, and prediction as techniques to help elites who have to make decisions to modify predictions and the explanatory picture deriving from them.

In other words, making predictions becomes scientific activity on the basis of data that are absent but that are plausible or possible or probable or desired, and whose relations may give rise to situations and scenarios that are equally possible, probable, and desired, but not certain.

The scientific nature of prediction is therefore based on rationality and the logic implicit in the links between events that have already come about and implicit in the possible reactions of, or to, a behavior that may come about. It is thus a matter of *reasoning by analogy*: Such-and-such has happened before in certain situations, so it may happen now in similar situations.

The scientific nature of prediction is also based on the fact that from the level of spatial analogy (if we have verified that an effect comes about *here*, we may infer that it will come about *there* in culturally analogous conditions) we may pass to the level of temporal analogy (if we have verified in the causal explanation that something comes about *today*, we may infer that it will come about *tomorrow*).

In more general terms, in prediction there is a "low-profile science," which becomes the rational study of what could happen in the future and above all how this might be more adequately dealt with so as best to guide or govern it.

Given these epistemological premises for prediction, the techniques that manifest its methodological paths are the result of the combination of certain features of the methods: qualitative and quantitative, those based on objective data or the opinions of elites (of power or knowledge), and extrapolative or normative. The predictive specificity of these three features increases from the first to the third. *Quantitative and qualitative* refer to the level of research and knowledge concerning a given phenomenon; the higher the level, the greater the chance of having indicators that are tried and tested and therefore more practically defined. *Objective data and elite opinions* are more closely tied to the usefulness ascribed to prediction. The objective datum reconstructs the model in a system, identifies the causal process and objective to which it leads, and starts from the assumption that it is "technically" possible to act on the structure of the process to modify its consequences. Leaders' opinions are privileged in that the basic assumption is that it will be their ideas and expectations, "true" or "false" as they may be, that condition, or even produce, the change in the

objective/end-point. In the first of these approaches, there is extreme confidence in the scientific character of the epistemological canons of science; in the second, there is substantial lack of confidence that science can produce reality control—it becomes merely a formal exercise, though rationally useful. The *extrapolative and normative* features introduce action aimed at controlling the objective/end-point: Extrapolation is the projection of present processes and mechanisms into the future to postulate how it may possibly and probably be configured; the normative feature is fixing the desired future to identify the processes and mechanisms to achieve it. This is a dual approach to the future that is complementary rather than contradictory, in that its second (normative) part begins where the first (extrapolative) has served its purpose.

Table 1 shows the various techniques of prediction in relation to the three dimensions defined by the three features: qualitative–quantitative, objective–leaders' opinions, and normative–exploratory.

This plotting enables us to make some statements and develop some assessments of methods, especially of their function in establishing the various dimensions of prediction in terms of future studies.

Objective and Quantitative Techniques. Objective and quantitative techniques are common to all research. They are standardized and consolidated in practice. Scenarios, time series, causal models, simulations, and so on provide potent instruments for translating quantitative results into explained variance and high probability, although their considerable rigidity leaves them unable to cope with interference from new and sudden exogenous variables. These highly statistical methods are more effective in short-term prediction and for circumscribed rather than global events. They are also used in combined form to achieve both exploratory and normative prediction. Here the methodology may be used to explain the causal process by means of which a given trend is manifested, after which a "mission" is decided upon—a defined objective, such as a plan—and modifications are introduced into the contextual variables and their relational flows in order to achieve the objective. An example of these combined methodologies may be found in the research carried out

Methods of Prediction in the Combination of the Three Criteria

		normative method	extrapolative method
objective data	quantitative	scenarios	scenarios
		gaming and simulation	time series
			regression analysis and canonical analysis
			econometrics and causal models
			nonlinear models
			trend impact analysis
			cross impact analysis
			gaming and simulation
	qualitative	scenarios	scenarios
		relevance trees	gaming and simulation
		science fiction	
opinions of leaders	quantitative	scenarios	scenarios
		Delphi	Delphi
		cross impact analysis	cross impact analysis
			trend impact analysis
	qualitative	"expert group meetings," in-depth interviews, "genius forecasting"	"expert group meetings," in-depth interviews, "genius forecasting," intuitive logic
		intuitive logic	
		Delphi	Delphi
		cross impact analysis	cross impact analysis
		scenarios	scenarios

Table 1

on the Italian situation by Alberto Gasparini under the auspices of the Istituto di Sociologia Internazionale di Gorizia (ISIG) (Gasparini et al. 1983, 1988).

The first research project set out to identify how to meet the housing needs of a metropolitan area in accordance with a preestablished norm, which in this case was the habitation standard expressed in terms of the acceptable ratio between living space and family sizes. Housing needs were identified by applying several habitation standards, after which exploratory techniques were used, simulating natural demographic and social trends, simulating new housing markets and vacant housing markets, introducing factors such as filtering and vacancy chains. The result was the determination of how much of future housing needs (for example, ten years later) would remain with no intervention, that is, by leaving the area's housing situation to develop under its own impetus. Subsequently interventions were carried out on single variables: incentives for building new housing or for putting vacant housing on the market or for restoring existing housing or for providing financial help for needy families, and so on. The observation of the effects of interventions on the variables of the housing needs model indicated whether the objective had been achieved and, if it had not, provided indications as to the most appropriate modifications to be applied to single variables in order to achieve the objective.

The second project was on the quality of the environment in daily life in Italian towns. The questions were the following: What type of environment is it? How can quality be defined? What is the current state of environmental quality? How can high environmental quality be achieved in the daily life of the town? To answer these questions, prediction was developed over the following stages: (1) Quality of the environment was defined according to people's expectations in terms of services (number) and their spread or concentration in the town area, all placed in relation to individual and community values expressed by the local inhabitants. Surveys were carried out in each town by giving a questionnaire to 137 samples in as many communities, for a total of 33,000 interviewees. The result was the *model of desired environmental quality for daily life* as derived from subjective data converted into objective data. (2) This desired model was applied to each town (how many and what services existed and their location), which gave *the model of environmental quality for daily life lived.* (3) Observations were carried out on the context in which the above model was placed and the variables producing it, in order to identify the variables that influence the quality of the environment in it. These independent variables (clusters of multiple variables reduced in number by factor analysis and causally related to environmental quality through canonical analysis) represented the various features of community life: population, town territory, values, economic structure, social structure, local government, endogenous resources, exogenous resources, communications with the outside world, and so on. (4) The achievement of the desired environmental quality for daily life was explored by intervening on the variables that were causally most important for environmental quality (as they emerged from stage 3) and by simulating the effects that these interventions would have on environmental quality. This may entail further interventions on single variables until the

achievement of the desired environmental quality, which is the subject of the prediction.

A third project was the definition of task environments and their dynamics in agricultural production organizations. This research was basically exploratory in nature, concluding with normative assessments. The exploration was not carried out by inquiring into how company task environments are modified over time (an inquiry into process), because the starting theory (to be subjected to verification) was that proposed by Emery and Trist (1965), whereby task environments are modified as companies expand and become increasingly causally important and disruptive, introducing irrationality into the decisions companies have to make. In this research, then, predictive exploration was not based on the projection of variables into the future, but on the investigation of two situations (small-company and large-company task environments) and their comparison in accordance with the Emery–Trist theory, reconstructing the dynamics by comparing the two potential stages of a single company that grows from a small one into a large one (Gasparini 1983). By means of defining the role of the agricultural entrepreneur and his relations with the task environment organizations, synthesising these into a few factors (by factor analysis) and linking them through canonical analysis, task environments were identified and articulated according to their influential and direct relations with the company, according to contacts not generating real influences in that relations were based on sporadic contacts, and so on. One substantial difference emerged between small and large companies. In small companies, there are few influential relations and a great many casual and sporadic contacts. In large companies, the relational task environment is very rich in relations, influences, and dependency on company decisions; the structure of the sporadic contact task environment is by contrast marked by relational links that are weak and few and far between. This exploratory projection produced by the hypothetical transformation of a small company into a large one therefore showed a radical change in the functional and power relationships of the task environment. The identification of concrete relations and contacts and their respective influence clearly leads to the intention to intervene according to the normative objective, which in this case is a rethinking of entrepreneurship, or an operational intervention in the agricultural economy to make sure that small and large entrepreneurs retain the power and responsibility assigned to them by the theory.

These three research examples show the great versatility of quantitative and objective techniques, that they need to be integrated with one another, and that they can be used in the exploratory dimension and some normative functions. These techniques are inextricably intertwined, as is exemplified by the fact that the exploratory dimension itself must be defined by reference to the *criterion* implicit in the normative dimension.

Leader's Opinions and Qualitative Techniques. The methods and techniques based on leaders' opinions, be they decision makers or experts in a particular field, are fundamentally qualitative in nature, that is, they are based on assessments that can be conventionally ordered in numerical values from which relations can then be highlighted. This can be done, as in the case of cross-impact analysis, but it should not be forgotten that the quantitative values manipulated are derived from percentages attributed intuitively to the occurrence of one event rather than another. Nevertheless, there are slightly differing degrees of formalization between these methods, and they are expressed in terms of their internal logic, reasoning experience that discriminates the more possible from the less possible, the ability to progressively refine judgments (the Delphi method), the compatibility between the reasoning and the context in which it is used, and the compatibility that has to give rise to the prediction for the phenomenon placed in the context.

This type of technique also contains scenarios, but they derive more from leaders' judgments than from the (highly implicit) model at the basis of the issues at stake and therefore of the variables defining the features of the model itself.

These are thus methods that can be used for the study and prediction of phenomena whose details are not known and/or which are relatively new, which means that recourse is made to qualified individuals equipped, for one reason or another, to see their own knowledge and predictions through the prism of research experience or familiarity with decision-making processes. If such is the case, the next step might be to transform the results of these subjective predictions into indicators and formal explanatory models, to be tested with exploratory methods and normative methods to obtain a (concrete) measurement of the projection or process required to achieve the predetermined objective–norm–criterion.

But it may also be the case that the simple results derived from these opinions are considered sufficient (expressed to various degrees of sophistication by means of in-depth interviews, the Delphi method, cross-impact analysis and the qualitative scenario), and this happens because, or probably because, the scientific component in the prediction is not held to be very important; it is considered as a set of rational instruments for reasoning about the plausibility of the prediction itself. Taking into account that these rationalized judgments come from policymakers (at the summit of the decision-making process) or opinion makers, this ascientific factor is even more worrisome.

In this case, the implicit conviction is that these are the players who will have a major role in the achievement of their own prediction—in which case, we are faced squarely with the principle of self-fulfilling prophecies.

Techniques in a Band of Abivalence. From Table 1 we still have to analyze the two intermediate bands in which predictive techniques are to be placed. Though these are conceptually different in some respects, they are also instrumentally contiguous, which in practice means that they often overlap, or are at least complementary, when being used. Objective qualitative methods indicate that phenomena are analyzed structurally with no measured data; methods that are quantitative but based on leaders' opinions provide judgments strongly based on facts, or at least measurable data, which involves a strong tendency to apply leaders' opinions to a concrete context.

Prediction techniques placed in these two bands of ambivalence are very similar to those devised for the predictive analysis of leaders' opinions, but they rely heavily on a detailed knowledge of context. Thus they also make use not only of the Delphi method, cross-impact analysis, and scenarios, but also simulation in objective quantitative methods. However, the most typical of these two bands are relevance trees, science fiction, and tendency impact.

An example of predictive research in this context of ambivalence is condensed in what Igor Bestuzhev-Lada (1997) calls "technological prediction." It comprises seven procedures that use methods which are both quantitative and qualitative, objective and subjective. The procedures are: program elaboration, construction and analysis of the starting model, construction and analysis of the predictive background model, exploratory prediction, normative prediction, prediction verification, and formulation of recommendations for a proper management of technological prediction. Indicators are often measured quantitatively, but their treatment and assessment are mostly qualitative.

In summary, the combination of the three criteria detailed in Table 1 indicates the following:

1. There are more specific techniques in the objective–quantitative methods and the leaders' opinions–qualitative methods.

2. In the ambivalence band, methods that are typically objective and bound to opinion leaders tend to extend toward the quantitative and qualitative.

3. The exploratory and normative methods are not alternatives but are fairly well integrated with one another. An exploratory projection is implicit in the normative method, and the exploratory method requires a criterion that is able to be transformed into the desired prediction–norm.

4. Many methods are multivalent in prediction in that they are used to construct many types of prediction, but also in that they are technically versatile because they can be used with measured data and opinions alike. The most important example of this is the scenario.

5. The effectiveness of the methods varies according to the type of prediction in question. For short-term predictions and those on a circumscribed subject, the quantitative–objective method is most effective. The longer the period involved and the broader the subject, the more effective are qualitative methods and methods based on leaders' opinion. This means that a broad to medium to long-term framework analyzed with qualitative methods contains specific short-term subjects studied with mathematical formalization.

6. The scientific nature of prediction methods therefore varies with the variation of frames and times of reference, or at least there is a variation of the forms of expression of the scientific activities of description, explanation, and control.

From the above it thus emerges that the complexity of *prediction of the future* entails a multiplicity of studies because the future expresses itself in very different ways. This is why it is more than legitimate to speak in methodological terms of *futures studies*.

THE DISTRIBUTION OF FUTURES STUDIES IN TIME AND SPACE

It is well known that studying the future becomes a strongly felt need in times of transition. The rules of the past no longer hold, and the rules for the future do not yet exist or are still untried. In addition, globalization accentuates the need to build niches within which some form of autonomy may be regained. But what does niche autonomy mean when globalization bombards it with the upheaval external to it, upheaval which is therefore experienced as irrational?

This question gives rise to the need to predict and to achieve prediction through studies on the future or futures. It is hardly surprising that many public and private institutions have set up study centers for prediction. An indicator of this growth is provided by the large number of Web sites for such centers, which are being put together to form a *Futures Studies Internet Society*.

An ISIG study (Apuzzo et al. 1999) has found that worldwide two hundred and eight institutions working in futures studies have Web sites. Of these, one hundred and forty publish papers, one hundred and twenty-three provide links, sixty-nine publish their own journals on-line and conduct training, sixty-four advertise books, fifty-seven provide on-line shopping, forty-seven pass on chat news, thirty-eight make available projects, thirty-four are concerned with software, and twenty-eight deal with methods and techniques.

Most of the sites are American (one hundred and seventeen futures studies institutes) and only twenty-three are international; fourteen are in Britian; eleven in France; eight in Australia; six in Sweden; five in Canada; three each in Germany, Finland, Belgium, Norway, and Italy; two in Switzerland; and one each in Argentina, Denmark, Zaire, Austria, Israel, and Russia.

There can be no doubt that the future, especially in the United States, is strongly perceived as a subject requiring analysis. We have interpreted this as a way of finding autonomous futures for individual niches in the context of sweeping globalization. But it may also happen that despite this intention, the incipient Futures Studies Internet Society will accentuate the very standardization of feeling, thinking about, and planning the future that such great efforts are being made to curtail.

Bibliography

Aa.Vv 1987 *Futuro e complessità*. Milan: Angeli.

Apuzzo, Gian Matteo, Bruno Maltoni, and Moreno Zago 1999 "Futures Studies Bookmarks." *Quaderni di Futuribili* 3:98.

Bell, Wendell 1994 "Futuro." In *Enciclopedia delle Scienze Sociali*, vol. IV. Rome: Istituto Enciclopedia Italiana.

—— 1997 *Foundations of Futures Studies*. London: Transaction publishers. Vol. I and vol. II.

——, and J. A. Mau (eds.) 1971 *The Sciology of the Future*. New York: Russell Sage Foundation.

Bestuzhev-Lada, Igor 1997 "I fondamenti metodologici della previsione tecnologica." *Quaderni di Futuribili* 1:110.

de Jouvenel, Bertrand 1967 *The Art of Conjecture*. New York: Basic Books.

Emery, F. E., and E. L. Trist 1965 "The Causal Texture of Organizational Environment." *Human Relations* 18:21–32.

Flechtheim, Ossip K. 1966 *History and Futurology*. Meisenheim am Glau, Germany: Verlag Anton Hain.

Gasparini, Alberto 1983 *Ambiente operativo e azienda agricola*. Milan: Angeli.

——, Aldo de Marco, and Roberto Costa (eds.) 1988 *Il futuro della città*. Milan: Angeli.

Glenn, Jerome C. 1994 *Introduction to the Futures Research Methodology Series*. Washington, D.C.: Unu Millennium Project Feasibility Study.

Godet, Michel 1979 *The Crisis in Forecasting and the Emergence of the Prospective Approach*. New York: Unitar, Pergamon Policy Studies.

—— 1994 *De la anticipation a la accion*. Barcelona: Editorial Marcombo.

—— 1995 "Global Scenarios: Morphological and Probability Analysis." In *1995 profutures meeting*, Ipts, Jrc, Ec: 17–30.

Gordon, Theodore J. 1992 "The Methods of Futures Research." *Annals* 522(July):25–35.

Irvine, J., and B. Martin 1984 *Foresight in Science; Picking the Winners*. London: Pinter Publishers.

Jantsch, Eric 1967 *Technological Forecasting in Perspective*. Paris: OECD.

Kahn, Herman, and Antony Wiener *The Year 2000–A Framework for Speculation in the Next 33 Years*. London: Macmillan.

Land, Kenneth C., and Stepeh H. Schneider (eds.) 1987 *Forecasting in the Social and Natural Sciences*. Dordrecht, The Netherlands: D. Reidel.

Malaska, Pentti 1995 "Survey of the Use of the Multiple Scenario Approach in Big European Companies Since 1973." In *1995 profutures meeting*, Ipts, Jrc, Ec.: 42–46.

Mannermaa, Mika, Sohail Inayatullah, and Richard Slaughter (eds.) 1994 *Coherence and Chaos in Our Uncommon Futures. Visions, Means, Actions*. Turku, Finland: World Futures Studies Federation.

Masini, Eleonora 1993 *Why Futures Studies?* London: Grey Seal.

—— (ed.) 1994 "La previsione. Idee, protagonisti, nodi problematici." *Futuribili* 1:223.

——, and Giorgio Nebbia (eds.) 1997 "I limiti dello sviluppo. 1972–2022. Che cosa resta dopo 25 anni, che cosa resterà fra 25 anni." *Futuribili* 3:193.

McHale, John 1969 *The Future of the Future*. New York: George Braziller.

Meadows, Donella H., Dennis L. Meadows, Jurgen Randers, and William W. Behrens, III 1972 *The Limits to Growth*. New York: Universe Books.

Norse, David 1979 "Scenario Analysis in Interfutures." *Futures* October.

Ortegon, Edgar, and Javier E. Medina Vasquez (eds.) 1997 *Prospectiva: construccion social del futuro*. Santiago de Calí, Colombia: Ilpes.

Pocecco, A. (ed.) 1994 *Il futuro come progetto degli scienziati sociali*. Gorizia, Italy: ISIG (Institute of International Sociology).

Polak, Fred 1971 *Prognostic: A Science in the Making*. Amsterdam: Elsevier.

—— 1973 *The Image of the Future*. Amsterdam: Elsevier.

Schwartz, Peter 1996 *The Art of the Long View. Planning for the Future in Uncertain World.* New York: Currency Doubleday.

Slaughter, Richard A. (ed.) 1993 "The Knowledge Base of Futures Studies." *Futures* 25:3.

Wilson, Ian 1978 "Scenario." In *Handbook of Futures Research.* Westport, Conn.: Greenwood Press.

ALBERTO GASPARINI

PREGNANCY AND PREGNANCY TERMINATION

Pregnancy is one of the most important events in a woman's life. For many women, pregnancy defines, enhances, or determines their economic, social, or personal value. Pregnancy and childbearing can be highly desired for personal reasons, or to meet social expectations. In some circumstances, childlessness may be grounds for suspicion, divorce, or worse. Pregnancy in the wrong situation may be undesirable to an equivalent degree. Traditionally, the woman with an unacceptable pregnancy may be abandoned, lose her prospects for marriage, be forced into prostitution, or suffer an even worse fate. Other pregnancies, even though they occur within a socially sanctioned circumstance, may result in loss of opportunities for social or economic advancement. Control over the occurrence and outcome of pregnancy is integral to women's control over their lives. This concept was strongly stated at the International Conference on Population and Development in Cairo in 1994.

Menarche, the first menstrual period, marks the beginning of a woman's reproductive period, and menopause, the last menstrual period, marks the end. Menarche occurs between ages 8 and 14 for most well-nourished women, but may come later if there is malnutrition or chronic disease. If the first menstrual period follows ovulation (release of an egg or ovum from the ovary), the woman may be fertile before menarche has occurred. For most women, fertility increases rapidly in the first year after menarche, as ovulation becomes more regular, so that as many as 95 percent of women in their late teenage years may be fertile. Infertility in the first years after menarche may be due to malnutrition, malformations of the uterus and reproductive organs, hormone abnormalities leading to anovulation, or genetic diseases. After the early twenties, fertility declines, as sexually transmitted diseases; endometriosis (occurrence in abnormal sites of tissue normally found in the lining of the uterus); and other inflammatory, infectious, and vascular diseases affect reproductive organs. Menopause occurs between ages 40 and 55 in most women, but most women over 40 are infertile, and very few live births occur to women over 45.

PREGNANCY

Pregnancy is typically divided into trimesters, which are uneven in length. Obstetricians invariably refer to "weeks" of pregnancy, meaning the number of weeks from last menstrual period, or when the last menstrual period should have occurred. The first trimester lasts from 3 to 12–14 weeks, the second from 12–14 to 24–26, and the third from 24–26 to delivery. The terminology is confusing, as menstrual age (the time since the last period) is not the same as gestational age (the time since fertilization, the union of the sperm and ovum). Therefore gestational age will be 2 weeks less than menstrual age. The system evolved in an era when many or most women could recall a last menstrual cycle, but few knew when conception or fertilization occurred. Now, more women may be aware of the date when conception occurred, and some pregnancies occur after assisted reproductive technologies (ART), when the time of fertilization may be known exactly. Either way, pregnancy itself begins immediately after implantation. This occurs about 3 weeks after the menstrual period and about 1 week after fertilization (therefore the first trimester starts at 3 weeks). A blood pregnancy test becomes positive within a day or two of implantation, and a urine test becomes positive a few days later. By the time the menses are missed, 4 weeks after the last menses, a urine pregnancy test will be positive if fertilization occurred at the expected time.

Between 10 percent and 40 percent of pregnancies result in *spontaneous abortion* in the first trimester. The wide variation in incidence reflects difficulty in recognizing very early abortion as well as differences in abortion rates among different age groups. Most spontaneous abortions are the result of chromosomal or developmental abnormalities of the pregnancy and are unavoidable; 1–2 percent of pregnancies abort spontaneously in the second trimester, often due to infection, and about 1 percent of pregnancies have serious anomalies. About 1 percent of pregnancies are *ectopic*, occurring outside of the uterus. Most *ectopic pregnancies* require medical or surgical treatment to avoid hemorrhage. Ectopic pregnancy is one of the major causes of maternal mortality; in the United States, it is still associated with about 10 percent of maternal deaths (Cunningham et al. 1997).

RESPONSE TO PREGNANCY

Women typically pass through several stages of reaction to pregnancy. The first reaction may be denial, particularly when the pregnancy is unwanted, or delight, when the pregnancy is wanted. Later, desired or planned pregnancy may still be accompanied by periods of ambivalence or anxiety (Affonso 1997). The concern may be about personal or work changes, financial stresses, health concerns, or concern about fetal health. At some point in the pregnancy, typically first or second trimester, the pregnancy is usually accepted. The fetus is visualized as a baby, and planning for birth and beyond ensues (Taylor 1980).

The pregnancy may not be accepted; the woman may choose to abort the pregnancy, or she may deny existence of the pregnancy, or she may never accept it even though she eventually gives birth. The lack of acceptance may follow a situation where abortion was unavailable; this may be an individual situation or a matter of political policy. During wartime, impregnation of "enemy" women (which may be accompanied by denial of abortion) is a form of terrorism (Swiss 1993).

Pregnancy itself does not impart any ability to deal with stress, nor does it decrease ability to manage stress. Women who have difficulty caring for themselves adequately when not pregnant, such as adolescents and women with severe psychiatric or developmental handicaps, may have difficulty caring for themselves while pregnant, to the detriment of the fetus. Pregnancy may be an incentive to stop self-abusive behavior such as drug use, but while pregnancy may be the motivating factor, it does not supply the emotional organization to change behavior. Domestic abuse of women does not usually stop with pregnancy; it often escalates (American College of Obstetricians and Gynecologists 1995b).

PREGNANCY AND BIRTHRATES

The *pregnancy rate* is the number of pregnancies occurring per 1,000 women of reproductive age (considered to be ages 15–45 inclusive), per year. The *fertility rate* is the number of all births (liveborn and stillborn) per 1,000 women age 15–45 per year; this is the *birth rate for reproductive-age women*. The term *birthrate*, unmodified, usually means the number of live births per 1,000 population (male and female of all ages).

Pregnancy rates increase during the teenage years and generally peak during the late twenties in most societies, before declining in the thirties and forties. Birthrates follow a similar trend, although the peak birthrate may occur later than the peak pregnancy rate, and the difference between pregnancy rates and birthrates is more pronounced at the extremes of reproductive life. At the beginning and the end of reproductive life more pregnancies are likely to be terminated by abortion.

More pregnancies than are wanted occur. Some are mistimed, occurring earlier than wanted, and some are unwanted at any time. In the United States, between 40 percent and 50 percent of pregnancies are unintended (Horton 1995; Henshaw 1998a). Overall, mistimed pregnancies are more frequent than unwanted pregnancies, but the relationship may be reversed in some groups, such as women over 40. Rates of unplanned pregnancy are generally lowest in countries with wide availability of effective contraception combined with public education, such as western Europe (Paul 1999). Unplanned pregnancy may occur because of contraceptive failure or non-use of contraception. In the United States noncontracepting women, about 8 percent of women at risk for unintended pregnancy, account for about 50 percent of unplanned pregnancies (Gold 1990).

Unplanned pregnancy may result in birth, spontaneous abortion, or induced abortion. The *abortion ratio* (ratio of pregnancies aborted to pregnancies occurring) in the United States for unplanned pregnancy is about 0.5 (Gold 1990). In other countries the rates may be lower, where unplanned pregnancies are accepted or abortion is not readily available, or higher, where unplanned pregnancy is not tolerated personally, socially, or economically (Henshaw et al. 1999).

Teenage pregnancy rates have been of concern because of adverse medical and economic outcomes, which are intertwined (Fraser et al. 1995). For most of the century, pregnancy rates for U.S. teenagers have been declining. Rates began to rise in the 1980s, reaching a recent high of 117 per 1,000 (women ages 15–19) in 1990 (Alan Guttmacher Institute 1999). By 1997 rates had declined about 10 percent to 97 per 1,000. Birthrates have shown a parallel decline from 60 per 1,000 to 54 per 1,000, and abortion rate declined as well.

In contrast to teenage women, women in their twenties have higher pregnancy and birthrates. Birthrates are currently about 110 per 1,000 women in this age group (National Center for Health Statistics 1999). Crude abortion rates are similar to those of adolescents, 20–30 per 1,000 women. Since adolescents have fewer pregnancies and births, the abortion ratio is higher than for women in their twenties or thirties. Overall, more than 40 percent of teenage pregnancies resulted in induced abortion. There are large variations in pregnancy, birth, and abortion rates by state, ethnic group, and age (Horton 1998). Nineteen-year-olds have a much higher pregnancy rate than 15-year-olds. Nonwhite and black teenage pregnancy rates are approximately twice those of white teenage rates. Nonwhite and younger teenagers are more likely to have induced abortions (National Center for Health Statistics 1999).

Comparison of birth and abortion rates can be cumbersome. Distribution of women's age, ethnic group, geographic location, time of collection of statistics, event definition, and accuracy of reporting will affect rates.

CONDUCT OF PREGNANCY

A comprehensive discussion of pregnancy is outside the scope of this encyclopedia; for more complete information, an obstetrics textbook (e.g., Cunningham et al. 1997; Gabbe et al. 1996) should be consulted.

The first trimester of pregnancy is often accompanied by nausea and vomiting, which is typically short-lived but may be severe enough to interfere with daily activities. Some women have hyperemesis, vomiting which is severe enough to result in dehydration or even death; it is treated with intravenous fluids, antinausea drugs, and sometimes intravenous feeding. Although a link between hyperemesis and ambivalence or anxiety about pregnancy has been postulated, the strength and the relevance of any such link is uncertain.

Women often note changes in food likes and dislikes, but there is no medical reason to restrict types of food. There are often cultural restrictions and prescriptions, and there is seldom any reason to interfere with custom. In the second half of pregnancy many women have heartburn, because of the pressure of the pregnancy on the bowel and stomach, and because of relaxation of the esophagus. Changes in diet or eating habits, or using antacids, may help.

Women need additional calories during the second 2 trimesters; the amount is about 300 kcal per day for most women, the equivalent of a modest sandwich. The additional calories should consist mostly of complex carbohydrates; most Americans have adequate protein intake. Women who receive protein supplements may have higher rates of preterm birth than women receiving carbohydrate supplements or no supplements at all. The U.S. Department of Agriculture administers a food supplement program called WIC (Women, Infants, and Children), which provides food to low-income pregnant and lactating women, infants, and children up to 5 years of age. Supplementation is associated with small decreases in the rate of low-birthweight delivery and a decrease in cost of caring for newborns (Merkatz 1990).

Folic acid, a vitamin, has been shown to decrease the incidence of neural tube defects, a complex of birth defects of the brain or spine. Since the neural tube fuses in the fifth menstrual week, often before pregnancy is noticed, women should take adequate folic acid before pregnancy (Czeizel and Dudas 1992; Rosenberg 1992). The recommended daily allowance of folic acid prior to pregnancy, 400 mg, is easily achieved with a well-balanced diet. Since bread and cereals are now fortified with folic acid, it is becoming harder to avoid adequate folic acid. However, residents of closed communities, producing their own food may not have access to fortified food. Overconsumption of most vitamins is harmless, and the excess is excreted in urine. However, fat-soluble vitamins may accumulate and reach levels that are toxic to the fetus. Iron is useful for women who are anemic because of iron deficiency.

Prenatal medical care is available to most women in the United States through a patchwork of public and private funding (Alan Guttmacher Institute 1994). Public funding has increased over the last decades as it became evident that the cost of caring for low-birthweight infants could be decreased by providing prenatal care (Merkatz 1990). The relative importance of individual facets of prenatal care is not certain (e.g., Crane et al. 1994; Higby et al. 1993), and some usual practices are probably useless but are persistent (AAP and ACOG 1997; Merkatz 1990). Efforts to assess prenatal care are complicated by the observation that women who actively seek prenatal care have better outcomes than those who do not, even when the latter group receives the same care.

OUTCOMES OF PREGNANCY

A normal pregnancy lasts 38–42 menstrual weeks (*term*). Infants over 37 weeks are considered *full-term*. Infants under 37 weeks are considered *preterm*. *Low birthweight* (or under 2,500 grams at birth), includes both preterm infants and full-term infants who weigh less than expected. The *low-birthweight rate* is the percentage of births under 2,500 grams.

The low-birthweight rate is an indicator of maternal health and of the effectiveness of prenatal and intrapartum care. However, the low birthweight numbers may be affected by the definition of live births. In some locations, live births are considered to be births over 28 weeks and/or 750 or 1,000 grams. In the United States the usual definition is any birth over 500 grams or showing movement or cardiac activity after birth; birth of a fetus under 500 grams without movement is classified as a spontaneous abortion. However, the definition varies by state and some states have adopted 350 grams as the threshold (Horton 1998). A 350-gram threshold will appear to raise the rate of low birthweight and the mortality rate of low-birthweight infants, as virtually no fetus born between 350 and 500 grams will survive (see ACOG 1995a).

Low birthweight is the leading cause of *perinatal death*. Perinatal deaths consist of *antepartum deaths* (in which the fetus dies before delivery), *intrapartum death* (in which the fetus dies during labor or

delivery), and *neonatal deaths* (in which a liveborn infant dies in the first 28 days). In contrast to the low-birthweight rate, which is usually expressed as a percentage, the death rate is usually expressed as the rate per thousand births (both live and stillbirths). Death rates vary according to policies on inclusion of the smallest fetuses and infants.

A *viable fetus* is a fetus that can survive outside the uterus. Viability may affect a decision to use an intrauterine treatment versus delivery and treatment of the infant. Viability has also played a role in some debates about abortion, as the gestational age of viability has decreased with advances in perinatal care.

For most healthy women, the physical stress of pregnancy is easily managed. Pregnancy is much more dangerous to women with underlying anemia, heart, or kidney disease, who cannot manage the necessary increase in blood supply and circulation, and to women who do not have adequate nutrition. Family planning, by allowing adequate nutrition before pregnancy and recovery between pregnancies, is critical to women's health status during pregnancy (Alan Guttmacher Institute 1997). Women who are poorly nourished or ill have a much higher chance of delivering a low-birthweight baby, who in turn is more likely to have chronic illnesses and disabilities.

Delivery has additional risks to all women. In the nineteenth century, with the best available care, maternal mortality was about 1 percent per pregnancy, and it remains at that level, or higher, in some parts of the world. It is estimated that each year 600,000 women die from pregnancy and childbirth (Berg et al. 1996; WHO 1998a). The three most common causes of morbidity and mortality are hemorrhage, infection, and pre-eclampsia (high blood pressure and blood vessel disease unique to pregnancy). Morbidity and mortality from all 3 of these situations are less likely where there are trained birth attendants (midwives or physicians) with access to a short list of medications (Rooks 1997). Relatively simple interventions may make a major difference in outcome (e.g., Wallace et al. 1994). In contrast, the incremental increase of complex technology is relatively small, although it may be dramatic in some situations. The widespread application of some technologies has been harmful by creating additional problems, such as interference with normal

Some Commonly Used Prenatal Tests

Test	Rationale	Limitations
Anemia screening	Allows supplementation.	
Gonorrhea	Treatment prevents infection of the fetus.	Screening cost-effective in high-prevalence populations.
Syphilis	Treatment prevents infection of the fetus.	
Human immunodeficiency virus (HIV)	Allows treatment with anti-retroviral medications during delivery, planning for . infant feeding	Effective if antiretroviral drugs are available and safe alternatives to breastfeeding are available.
Bacterial vaginosis	Treatment prevents preterm labor.	Data on effectiveness are conflicting.
Glucose	Identify diabetic women early enough for treatment.	Effective in high-prevalence groups; may not be cost-effective in low-prevalence groups.
Rubella	Identification of nonimmune women identifies pregnancies at risk.	Vaccination of most young women has reduced incidence.
Hepatitis B	Identification of carrier women allows vaccination of infants.	In high-prevalence areas universal vaccination without screening is cost-efficient and simpler.
Rh typing	Identify fetuses at risk for Rh disease, and prevent sensitization.	
Alpha-fetoprotein	Identify fetuses with spine and brain malformations.	Can identify 90% of affected fetuses. 2-5% of women will need additional testing
"Triple screen"	Screen for Down syndrome.	Can identify 60% of affected fetuses; 5% of women will need additional testing.
Ultrasound	Identify twins, fetal defects, nonviable pregnancy.	Will identify most twins. Screening for birth defects not supported by randomized controlled trial.
Amniocentesis	Identify chromosomal abnormalities in fetus.	Carries some risk, expensive. CVS more versatile and faster.
Chorionic villus sampling (CVS)	Identify chromosomal and metabolic abnormalities in fetus.	May be riskier than amniocentesis, less available.

Table 1

labor by restriction of movement (Butler et al. 1993) or by diversion of resources from other beneficial programs.

Births are classified as *spontaneous* (vaginal), *operative vaginal*, or *operative abdominal*. Spontaneous birth includes births that are assisted by a birth attendant's hands. Operative vaginal births include forceps and vacuum extractor (suction cup applied to the baby's head); rates range from as low as 1 percent to 30 percent or higher in some settings. Operative abdominal births are "cesarean sections," and rates vary widely. In western Europe rates are generally 8–15 percent of total births. In the United States, rates had risen steadily for several decades before decreasing very slightly in the last several years to about 22 percent of all births (National Center for Health Statistics 1999). In some cities throughout the world there is a local demand for elective abdominal delivery as an alternative to labor, generally restricted to women who can afford to pay for the request. With such widely varying rates of operative intervention there is no consensus on optimal rates, although there are many opinions. For instance, there has been no decline in the rate of mental retardation in the

United States, although both fetal monitoring and operative delivery were purported to prevent at least some retardation (ACOG 1992; Rosen and Dickinson 1992).

After birth, women and babies do best when they are kept together and allowed to establish lactation (WHO 1998b). Separation of mother and baby as practiced in many hospitals is not only unpleasant, but inappropriate in terms of infection control and infant nutrition. The effect of labor and delivery routines on "bonding" or attachment has been debated; whether any simple intervention can influence parenting is questionable at this point. The social and educational support of trained lay women has measurable success in some studies on labor outcome and breastfeeding success (Rooks 1997). More intensive programs of pregnancy, delivery, and postpartum peer care have not been fully evaluated (O'Connor 1998).

TERMINATION OF PREGNANCY

Abortion is an event, other than a birth, that terminates a pregnancy. Abortion may be *spontaneous*, if it begins without intervention from the woman and without medical intervention, or *induced*, if some agent or procedure is used to cause the abortion. Induced abortion may also be classified as *legal* or *illegal*. Other terminology is neither uniform nor clear. *Therapeutic* abortion may refer to all legal induced abortions performed under medical supervision, or to those performed for medical indication such as severe illness in the woman. Spontaneous abortion may be classified as *inevitable* if it has not yet occurred but will occur, as *incomplete* if the pregnancy has been partially passed, or as *complete* if all tissue has been expelled or removed.

A *viable pregnancy* may refer to a pregnancy in which the baby is apparently healthy and growing; the pregnancy would be expected to continue if there were no intervention. A *nonviable pregnancy* will result in spontaneous abortion. Nonviable pregnancies are also called *blighted ovum* (which is technically incorrect since the ovum or egg has already divided), *empty sac*, or *fetal demise*. Abnormal pregnancies are sometimes detected by ultrasound or by blood testing, before there are any symptoms of spontaneous abortion.

Most abortions are requested because the pregnancy was unwanted, but there are other reasons, some of which are listed in Table 2.

In the United States, 90 percent of abortions occur in the first trimester; half of all women request abortion before 8 menstrual weeks. Ten percent of women request abortion after 12 weeks. Between 1 and 2 percent of all abortions performed are for fetal malformations; these are almost all second-trimester procedures. Fewer than 1 percent of abortions are performed in the third trimester. Generally, as the length of gestation increases, the cost of abortion increases, and the number of providers decreases (Gold 1990).

There are several types of procedures in use (for a more complete discussion, see Paul 1999). In the first trimester, there are both medical and surgical techniques. Surgical techniques consist of variations of suction curettage. In this procedure the cervix is stretched open if necessary; in very early pregnancy (fewer than 6 menstrual weeks) no opening may be necessary. The inside of the uterus is suctioned using a plastic tube and a vacuum created by an electric or manual pump. "Sharp" curettage, the traditional dilatation and curettage (D&C) is more traumatic and has been largely replaced by suction curettage.

Several medications are used for early medical abortion, depending on availability. Methotrexate is a medication that blocks folic acid, a vitamin. Several days later the woman takes a second drug, misoprostol (a prostaglandin drug), which makes the uterus contract and expel the pregnancy. The process is similar in both timing and feeling to a spontaneous abortion. The exact time sequence is difficult to predict; about 75 percent of women abort within 1 week. Vaginal bleeding occurs for a mean of about 10 days, but may last longer. The medication may fail to produce an abortion about 1 percent of the time, and about 1 percent of women need a suction curettage because of heavy bleeding. Methotrexate can be used up to 7 or 8 menstrual weeks, and is the most common agent in use in the United States, because it is FDA approved for other uses, and therefore easily available.

Mifepristone (formerly called RU 486) has been used in millions of women in China, France, Sweden, and the United Kingdom for medical

Reasons Offered for Abortion

Health concerns (e.g., severe hyperemesis)

Change in circumstances since conception:

Abandonment by partner or family
Change in finances or social situation
Illness of other family member

Abnormal pregnancy

Exposure to teratogen

Table 2

abortion since 1986, but has had to overcome numerous political roadblocks in the United States. Mifepristone, a different class of medication from methotrexate, blocks progesterone hormone binding sites. It requires use of a second drug, a prostaglandin drug such as misoprostol, several days later to expel the pregnancy. In contrast to methotrexate, 75 percent of women abort within 2 days, and 90–95 percent abort within 1 week. Mifepristone can be used up to 7 to 9 menstrual weeks depending on the selection of the second drug.

After 7 to 9 menstrual weeks, suction curettage is the main technique. At the end of the first trimester and in second trimester, opening the cervix sufficiently becomes more challenging. Osmotic dilators are used over several hours or several days; osmotic dilators are placed in the cervix, where they absorb water and swell. Preparation for abortion in the mid- and late second trimester may take several days. Surgical procedures, often called dilatation and evacuation (D&E), are variations of early pregnancy techniques using suction and extraction instruments. After 16 weeks, medical (induction) techniques can be used to induce labor. All the agents—prostaglandin, oxytocin, and saline—are unpredictable, may take several hours to several days, and may involve a curettage to remove placenta if it is not completely expelled. Hospitalization is the rule, and therefore induction techniques are more costly than surgical techniques in an out-patient setting.

Legal abortion has very few serious complications. Term pregnancy has a death rate at least ten times higher than first-trimester abortion (10–12 deaths per 100,000 versus 0. 5–1.0 deaths per 100,000 women in the United States) (Berg et al.

1996; Paul et al. 1999), and a morbidity rate (serious medical outcomes such as major operations) hundreds of times higher. There is virtually no situation in which it is safer for a woman to continue a pregnancy than to abort a pregnancy, although there are sometimes situations in which abortion should be delayed briefly. However, abortion is safest if it is performed early (Gold 1990; Paul et al. 1999). Early abortion by suction curettage does not have an effect on future fertility. Abortion itself is not associated with adverse psychological sequelae; unwanted pregnancy may have adverse associations regardless of whether the pregnancy is aborted or continued. In second trimester the medical risks are higher than in first trimester (Paul et al. 1999).

It is difficult to ascertain the numbers and types of abortions performed in the United States. In most states abortion is a reportable procedure; however, many procedures are not reported, probably for reasons of confidentiality of both provider and patient (Fu et al. 1998). Some abortions may be misclassified as treatment of a spontaneous abortion, since the suction procedure is identical; or the reverse may be true. In hospitals, some induced abortions may be classified as spontaneous abortion. The Alan Guttmacher Institute estimates abortion procedures using both governmental and nongovernmental sources. The CDC also publishes "Abortion Surveillance" as a supplement to *Mortality and Morbidity Weekly Review*. Small variations in abortion rates may be related to reporting and surveillance issues as well as varying rates of pregnancy and abortion.

Currently, early medical abortion accounts for fewer than 1 percent of all abortions in the United States, as methotrexate is the only agent available. In other countries, medical abortion may account for up to a third of all abortion procedures. In France, half of all women seeking abortion request abortion early enough to be eligible for medical abortion, and two-thirds of them choose medical abortion. This shift to medical abortion in France has been accompanied by a shift to earlier abortion in general, while overall abortion rates have remained the same (Paul et al. 1999). Medical abortion is highly acceptable to women in many countries. Acceptability studies consistently estimate that 60–80 percent of women would choose medical abortion over surgical abortion were it available (Winikoff 1994).

However, despite the preference for medical abortion over surgical abortion, surgical abortion remains the only method available to most women, if they have access to any method at all. In the United States the number of abortion providers has dropped over the last two decades. Abortion is available in a minority of counties in the United States, most of them in urban areas (Lichter et al. 1998). The majority of abortion procedures take place in free-standing medical facilities, many of them primarily devoted to abortion provision (Henshaw 1998b). Planned Parenthood clinics provide about 12 percent of all abortions. About 10 percent of abortions occur in hospitals or hospital-affiliated clinics. At least 5 percent of abortions occur in doctors' offices that are not identified as providing primarily abortion-related care.

Most physicians providing abortions in the United States are obstetrician-gynecologists, but other physicians provide abortions. Only about a third of gynecologists provide abortions, so most women needing abortion are referred to an unfamiliar caregiver. First-trimester abortions are also provided in several states by physicians' assistants (PAs) and midwives. Most states have "physician-only" statutes that limit the provision of abortion to physicians. However, these statutes were written before the increase in utilization of advanced practice nurses, such as midwives, and "physician extenders," such as PAs, who currently perform other procedures of comparable complexity and skill (Freedman et al. 1986). In a few countries (e.g., Bangladesh) midwives provide most abortion services.

Costs for abortions range form several hundred dollars for a first-trimester procedure in an office or clinic setting, to thousands of dollars for procedures performed in hospitals. Many insurance policies cover abortion, although reimbursement rates vary. Some forms of insurance do not cover abortion at all, for example, insurance provided to U.S. federal employees. Publicly funded insurance for indigent women covers "medically indicated" abortions in some states but not others. Finally, many women requesting abortion do not have any insurance at all, most commonly because their employment does not provide insurance. Women who need specialized procedures because of underlying medical illnesses may have additional barriers; there are several states in which no hospital will allow an abortion to be performed.

In the United States the majority of people polled supported the availability of abortion, but many were in favor of some restrictions. Parental consent laws for minors have been passed in nearly half the states. Any such law must contain a "judicial bypass" to be considered constitutional, so that minors can petition a judge if they cannot tell a parent (Paul et al. 1999). In practice, most minors do involve a parent with or without parental consent laws. The main effect of such laws is to delay abortion for those minors without good family support.

In the United States there is a vocal and well-funded minority with the goal of criminalizing abortion. Mandatory waiting periods and mandatory consent processes have also been passed. These increase the amount of time and expense necessary for a woman to obtain an abortion, particularly where there are few providers. Other quasi-legal attempts to decrease abortion include passage of laws that are either unenforceable or unconstitutional. These include restrictions on the type of facility that can perform abortion and "partial-birth abortion" laws. The resulting legal challenges are expensive, and this tactic can be considered a sustained economic assault (Reproductive Freedom News 1999). Antiabortion groups in the United States have been increasingly involved in terrorist activities, including harassment, arson, violence, and even murder. Several thousand incidents or harassment and arson are reported annually to the National Abortion Federation (National Abortion Federation 1999).

Abortion is generally legal in most European countries and in much of Asia, but is illegal in most of South America and Africa (WHO 1998b). The effect of government-sanctioned denial of abortion rights is not to decrease the number of abortions significantly. Abortion rates are correlated with multiple factors such as patterns of sexual activity, type of contraceptive use, desired family size, and tolerance of unwanted pregnancy. In the United States it has been estimated that the number of abortions performed annually before widespread legalization was 600,000 to 1.2 million per year (Gold 1990). The number reported the first year after legalization was 615,831 (Koonin et al. 1996). The effect of criminalizing abortion is to delay abortion for some women and to make it riskier for almost all women, resulting in increased

death rates (Population Reports 1997). As an example, after abortion was criminalized in Romania, the death rate from abortions quintupled; while maternal mortality doubled (WHO 1998b). In South American and East Africa, the rates of illegal abortion are similar, about 35 per 1,000 women of childbearing age, but death rates are dissimilar (0.3 percent and 1.5 percent, respectively, of women undergoing abortion), related to underlying health status and access to postabortion care (WHO 1998b).

Increases in the provision of contraceptive services are associated with decreases in abortion rates (Henshaw et al. 1999; Estrin 1999). However, the United States has consistently refused to fund contraceptive services adequately, particularly services in developing countries, because of right-wing political pressure (Alan Guttmacher Institute 1996).

Pregnancy carries an intrinsic risk to women's health, which can be minimized by appropriate medical care to women who are in good health to start. Family planning is essential to women's health during pregnancy, and essential to the health of their infants. Women who do not want to be pregnant will risk health and life to end the pregnancy. Denying or criminalizing abortion care results in additional health risks for women while diverting health resources that could be used for maternity services for other women.

REFERENCES

Affonso, Dyanne D., Chong-Yeu Lui-Chang, and Linda J. Mayberry 1997 "Worry: Conceptual Dimensions and Relevance to Childbearing Women." *Health Care for Women International* 20:227–236.

Alan Guttmacher Institute 1994 *Uneven and Unequal: Insurance Coverage and Reproductive Health Services*. New York: Alan Guttmacher Institute.

—— 1996 *Endangered: U.S. Aid for Family Planning Overseas*. New York: Alan Guttmacher Institute.

—— 1997 *Family Planning Improves Child Survival and Health*. New York: Alan Guttmacher Institute.

—— 1999 *Teenage Pregnancy: Overall Trends and State-by-State Information*. New York: Alan Guttmacher Institute (April).

American Academy of Pediatrics and American College of Obstetricians and Gynecologists 1997 *Guidelines for Perinatal Care*, 4th ed. Elk Grove Village, Ill.: AAP.

American College of Obstetricians and Gynecologists 1992 *Fetal and Neonatal Neurologic Injury*. Technical Bulletin. Washington, D.C.: ACOG.

—— 1995a *Committee Opinion: Perinatal and Infant Mortality Statistics*. Washington, D.C.: ACOG.

—— 1995b *Domestic Violence*. Washington, D.C.: ACOG

—— 1998 *Committee Opinion: Vitamin A Supplementation during Pregnancy*. Washington, D.C.: ACOG.

Berg, Cynthia J., Hani K. Atrash, Lisa M. Koonin, and Myra Tucker 1996 "Pregnancy-Related Mortality in the United States, 1987–1990." *Obstetrics and Gyneclogy* 88:161–167.

Crane, James P., Michael L. LeFevre, Renee C. Winborn, Joni K. Evans, Bernard G. Ewigman, Raymond P. Bain, Frederic P. Frigoletto, Donald McNellis, and the RADIUS Study Group 1994 "A Randomized Trial of Prenatal Ultrasonographic Screening: Impact on the Detection, Management, and Outcome of Anomalous Fetuses." *American Journal of Obstetrics and Gynecology* 171:382–399.

Butler, Jane, Barbara Abrams, Jennifer Parker, James M. Roberts, and Russell K. Laros 1993 "Supportive Nurse-Midwife Care is Associated with a Reduced Incidence of Cesarean Section." *American Journal of Obstetrics and Gynecology* 168:1407–1413.

Cunningham, E. Gary, Paul C. MacDonald, Norman F. Gant, Kenneth J. Leveno, Larry C. Gilstrap, Gary D. V. Hankins, and Steven L. Clark 1997 *Williams Obstetrics*, 20th ed. Stamford, Conn.: Appleton and Lange.

Czeizel, Andrew E., and Istvan Dudas 1992 "Prevention of the First Occurrence of Neural-Tube Defects by Periconceptional Vitamin Supplementation." *New England Journal of Medicine* 327:1832–1835.

Estrin, D. J. 1999 "In Three Former Soviet States, Rates of Abortion Are Declining as Contraceptive Prevalence Increases." *International Family Planning Perspectives* 25:49–50.

Fraser, Alison M., John E. Brockert, and R. H. Ward 1995 "Association of Young Maternal Age with Adverse Reproductive Outcomes." *New England Journal of Medicine* 332:1113–1117.

Freedman, Mary Anne, David A. Jillson, Roberta R. Coffin, and Lloyd F. Novick 1986 "Comparison of Complication Rates in First Trimester Abortions Performed by Physician Assistants and Physicians." *American Journal of Public Health* 76:550–554.

Fu, Haishan, Jacqueline E. Darroch, Stanley K. Henshaw, and Elizabeth Kolb 1998 "Measuring the Extent of Abortion Underreporting in the 1995 National Survey of Family Growth." *Family Planning Perspectives* 30:128–133, 138.

Gabbe, S., J. R. Niebyl, and J. L. Simpson 1996 *Obstetrics: Normal and Problem Pregnancies*, 3rd ed. New York: Churchill-Livingston.

Gold, Rachel Benson 1990 *Abortion and Women's Health*. New York: Alan Guttmacher Institute.

Henshaw, Stanley K. 1998a "Unintended Pregnancy in the United States." *Family Planning Perspectives* 30:24–29, 46.

—— 1998b "Abortion Incidence and Services in the United States, 1995–1996." *Family Planning Perspectives* 30:263–270, 287.

——, Susheela Singh, and Taylor Haas 1999 "Recent Trends in Abortion Rates Worldwide." *International Family Planning Perspectives* 25:44–48.

Higby, Kenneth, Elly M. J. Xenakis, and Carl J. Pauerstein 1993 "Do Tocolytic Agents Stop Preterm Labor? A Critical and Comprehensive Review of Efficacy and Safety." *American Journal of Obstetrics and Gynecology* 168:1247–1259.

Horton, Jacqueline A. (ed.) 1995 *The Women's Health Data Book, A Profile of Women's Health in the United States*. Washington, D.C.: Jacobs Institute of Women's Health.

—— 1998 *State Profiles of Women's Health*. Washington, D.C.: Jacobs Institute of Women's Health.

Koonin, Lisa M., Jack C. Smith, Merrell Ramick, and Clarice A. Green 1996 "Abortion Surveillance—United States, 1992." *Morbidity and Mortality Weekly Review*, vol. 45, supp. 3. Atlanta, Ga.: Center for Disease Control.

Lichter, Daniel T., Diane K. McLaughlin, and David C. Ribar 1998 "State Abortion Policy, Geographic Access to Abortion Providers and Changing Family Formation." *Family Planning Perspectives* 30:281–287.

National Abortion Federation 1999 "Clinic Support Update." Washington, D.C.: NAF (April).

National Center for Health Statistics 1999 *Births: Final Data for 1997*. Atlanta, Ga.: Center for Disease Control and Prevention.

O'Connor, M. L. 1998 "Home Nurse Visits from Pregnancy until Child's Second Birthday Have Sustained Benefits for Mother and Child." *Family Planning Perspectives* 30:47–48.

Paul, Maureen, E. Steve Lichtenberg, Lynn Borgatta, David A. Grimes, and Phillip G. Stubblefield 1999 *A Clinician's Guide to Medical and Surgical Abortion*. New York: Churchill-Livingston.

Population Reports 1997 *Caring for Postabortion Complications: Saving Women's Lives*. Baltimore, Md.: Population Information Center (September).

Reproductive Freedom News 1999 *Anti-Abortion Legislature Swamps Choice Activists*. New York: Center for Law and Reproductive Policy (May).

Rooks, Judith S. 1997 *Midwifery and Childbirth in America*. Philadelphia, Pa.: Temple University Press.

Rosen, Mortimer G., and Janet C. Dickinson 1992 "The Incidence of Cerebral Palsy." *American Journal of Obstetrics and Gynecology* 167:417–423.

Rosenberg, Irwin H. 1992 "Folic Acid and Neutral-Tube Defects—Time for Action?" *New England Journal of Medicine* 327:1875–1877.

Swiss, S. 1993 "Rape as a Crime of War: A Medical Perspective." *Journal of the American Medical Association* 270:612–615.

Taylor, Paul (ed.) 1980 "Parent-Infant Relationships." New York: Grune and Stratton.

Wallace, H. M., R. P. Nelson, and P. J. Sweeney 1994 *Maternal and Child Health Practices*, 4th ed. Oakland, Calif.: Third Party.

Winikoff, Beverly 1994 *Acceptability of First Trimester Medical Abortion*. New York: Population Council.

World Health Organization, Division of Reproductive Health 1998a *Postpartum Care of the Mother and Newborn: A Practical Guide*. Geneva, Switzerland: WHO.

—— 1998b *Unsafe Abortion*, 3rd ed. Geneva, Switzerland: WHO.

LYNN BORGOTTA

PREJUDICE

Gordon Allport, in his classic *The Nature of Prejudice*, defined prejudice as "an antipathy based upon a faulty and inflexible generalization" (1954, p. 9). This phrasing neatly captures the notion that both inaccurate beliefs and negative feelings are implicated in prejudice. To these "cognitive" and "affective" dimensions of prejudice, some analysts add "conative," referring to action orientation (Klineberg 1972) and prescription (Harding et al. 1969). Allport's circumspection on the conative implications of prejudice—he said "(prejudice) may be felt or expressed" (1954, p. 9)—foreshadowed our growing understanding that the correspondence of behavior with cognitions and feelings is uncertain, a research issue in its own right (Schuman and Johnson 1976).

Racial and ethnic prejudice was Allport's primary interest. Emerging social issues have brought

expanded attention to other forms of prejudice—against women, the elderly, handicapped persons, AIDS patients, and others. This discussion will focus on racial prejudice among white Americans, in the expectation that parallels and points of contrast will continue to make race relations research relevant to other forms of prejudice.

TRENDS AND PATTERNS

For many years, derogatory stereotypes, blatant aversion to interracial contact, and opposition in principle to racial equality were seen as the central manifestations of race prejudice, virtually defining the social science view of the problem. Indicators of these beliefs and feelings show a clear positive trend (Jaynes and Williams 1989; Schuman et al. 1997). White Americans' belief in the innate intellectual inferiority of blacks declined from 53 percent in 1942 to about 20 percent in the 1960s, when the question was discontinued in major national surveys. The percentage of whites who said it would make no difference to them if a Negro of equal social status moved into their block rose from 36 percent to 85 percent between 1942 and 1972. White opinion that blacks should have "as good a chance as white people to get any kind of job" climbed from 45 percent in 1944 to 97 percent in 1972. Thomas Smith and Paul Sheatsley sum up this picture without equivocation: "Looking over this forty-year span, we are struck by the steady, massive growth in racial tolerance" (1984, p. 14).

Recurrent outbursts of overt racial hostility and public acts of discrimination (Feagin 1991) serve as unfortunate reminders that some white Americans still cling to blatant prejudice. More importantly, even the majority of whites, those on whom Smith and Sheatsley focus, appear unambiguously tolerant only if attention is confined to such traditional survey indicators as those described above. A confluence of developments has broadened the study of race prejudice and transformed our understanding of white racial attitudes. First, evidence of widespread, subtle prejudice has been revealed in research using disguised, "nonreactive" methods. Second, "social cognition" scholarship, paramount for two decades in the psychological wing of social psychology, has been powerfully applied to intergroup relations. Recent scholarship is broadened and balanced by its acknowledgment of the crucial role of affect along with cognition. Third, evolution of the struggle for racial equality in the United States has shifted attention to a new domain of racial policy-related beliefs and feelings. These perspectives provide ample evidence that white racial prejudice is not a thing of the past, but exists today in complex forms that have yet to be thoroughly charted.

Evidence from "Nonreactive" Studies. Given the clear dominance of "liberal" racial norms evinced in public opinion data, it might be expected that needs for social acceptability and self-esteem would lead many whites to withhold evidence of negative racial feelings and cognitions whenever possible. Disguised, "nonreactive" research (Webb 1981) provides substantial evidence that, indeed, traditional survey approaches underestimate negative racial feeling. Field experiments reveal that whites often provide less help to victims who are black (Crosby et al. 1980), sometimes redefining the situation so as to justify their lack of response (Gaertner 1976). Such elements of nonverbal behavior as voice tone (Weitz 1972) and seating proximity (Word et al. 1974) have been found to reveal negative racial feelings and avoidance. Recent reaction time and word completion studies similarly document the existence of "implicit" racial prejudice among many whites who score low on self-reported "explicit" prejudice (Dovidio et al. 1997). Thus, accumulating American evidence reveals that "microaggressions" (Pettigrew 1989) often accompany self-portrayals of liberalism. Parallel research in western Europe has uncovered similar forms of microaggression against that continent's new immigrant minorities (Den Uyl et al. 1986; Klink and Wagner 1999; Sissons 1981).

Social Cognition Perspectives, Now Acknowledging the Role of Affect. In recognizing aspects of prejudice as predictable outgrowths of "natural" cognitive processes, Allport (1954) was ahead of his time. A wave of social cognition research on intergroup relations was set in motion by Henri Tajfel (1969), who demonstrated that mere categorization—of physical objects or of people—encourages exaggerated perception of intragroup homogeneity and intergroup difference. Even in "minimal groups" arbitrarily created in psychology laboratories, these effects of social categorization are often accompanied by ingroup favoritism and outgroup discrimination (Brewer 1979, 1991; Hamilton 1979). Accumulating evidence of the negative consequences of ingroup/outgroup categorization has spurred research aimed at identifying conditions of intergroup contact that are likely to decrease category salience and promote "individuation" or "decategorization" (Brewer and Miller 1988; Wilder 1978), or at least to reduce the negativity of outgroup stereotypes (Rothbart and John 1985; Wilder 1984). Recent attention to the role of motivation in guiding cognition (Fiske 1998) contributes to this effort.

The study of attributional processes (Heider 1958) also has been usefully applied to intergroup relations, calling attention to such issues as whether white perceivers believe that black economic hardship results from discrimination or lack of effort. Research evidence has linked stereotypic thinking to attributions of outgroup behavior (David L. Hamilton 1979). Specific predictions are developed in Pettigrew's discussion of the "ultimate attributional error" (1979a), the tendency to hold outgroups personally responsible for their failures, but to "discount" their responsibility for successes, attributing successes to such factors as luck or unfair advantage.

The intense research scrutiny given cognitive factors meant that the critical affective component of prejudice was often ignored. That imbalance is being corrected. The 1993 publication of *Affect, Cognition, and Stereotyping*, edited by Mackie and Hamilton (1993), marked the dramatic shift in emphasis in social psychology. Varied research, from American laboratory experimentation (Stangor et al. 1991; Dovidio et al. 1989) to European surveys (Pettigrew 1997; Pettigrew and Meertens 1995), demonstrates that emotional factors not only are central to intergroup prejudice but have special characteristics of their own and are highly predictive of policy attitudes. One attempt at synthesis outlines a tripartite conception of prejudice as stereotypes, affect, and "symbolic beliefs" (Esses et al. 1993; Zanna 1994).

Expanding the Racial Attitude Domain to Policy Views. Over the past twenty-five years, evolution in the struggle for racial equality has brought new complexity to the public debate about racial issues. Notions that barriers to black equality consist solely of white hostility and aversion, and formal denial of rights, now appear naive. Advocates insist that structural barriers far more complex and far more pervasive than formal denial of access prevent actual desegregation and equality of opportunity, making questions about acceptance by white individuals a moot point for millions of black Americans.

In the current era of U.S. race relations, traditional manifestations of race prejudice recede in relevance, and different forms of race-related belief and feeling take center stage—reactions to agitation for change, recognition and interpretation of continuing inequality, and support for proposed remedies. By all indications, such white "perceptions, explanations, and prescriptions" (Apostle et al. 1983, p. 18) show far less consensus and support for racial change than appeared in traditional race survey data. Asked about specific policies and programs designed to increase racial equality—fair housing guarantees, school desegregation plans, affirmative action in hiring and college admission—white Americans show substantially less support than they voice for racial equality in principle (Pettigrew 1979b; Schuman et al. 1997). Many white Americans exaggerate recent black gains and benefits of affirmative action (Steeh and Krysan 1996) and underestimate the remaining inequality (Kluegel and Smith 1982). There is substantial white resentment of black activism and perceived progress (Bobo 1988a; Schuman et al. 1997).

Attribution research in social psychology and earlier societal analyses (Ryan 1971; Feagin 1975) converge with recent studies of racial policy opinion to tell a clear story: Whites explain the economic plight of black Americans more often as the result of such "individualistic" factors as lack of motivation than in terms of such "structural" factors as discrimination (Apostle et al. 1983; Kluegel and Smith 1986). In addition, individualistic attributions along with denial of discrimination are linked to a variety of policy-relevant beliefs and opinions, including opposition to affirmative action (Bobo and Kluegel 1993; Kluegel and Smith 1983, 1986).

CHARACTERIZATIONS OF WHITE RACIAL ATTITUDES

Efforts to characterize the complex pattern of racial attitudes held by white Americans emphasize an array of themes, as discussed below.

"Natural" Cognitive Processing. As noted earlier, social cognition analyses claim that a substantial part of the racial prejudice once thought to have sociocultural or psychodynamic roots actually stems from ordinary cognitive processing, particularly categorization (David L. Hamilton 1979). Social cognition portrayals increasingly acknowledge motivational and social influences (David A. Hamilton and Tina K. Trolier 1986; Fiske 1987, 1998). And there are recent powerful calls to acknowledge the joint influence on prejudice of cognition and affect (Esses et al. 1993; Pettigrew 1997; Smith 1993).

Strain Between Individualism and Egalitarianism. Current racial policy issues are said to pull whites between two cherished American values, individualism and egalitarianism (Lipset and Schneider 1978). *Qualified* support for social programs exists, in this view, because egalitarian sentiments prevail only until a proposal challenges individualistic values.

Ambivalence. Adding psychodynamic flavor to the individualism/egalitarianism value strain idea, some analysts describe current white feelings as an ambivalence that produces an unpredictable mix of amplified positive and negative responses (Katz et al. 1986).

"Aversive" Racism. A desire to avoid interracial contact, muted negative feeling, and egalitarian self-concept are the mix Kovel (1970) characterized as aversive racism. The outcome is avoidance of positive interracial behavior when the situation can be defined to permit it, and expression of negative feelings when there are ostensible nonracial justifications (Gaertner 1976; Gaertner and Dovidio 1986).

"Symbolic" or "Modern" Racism and "Racial Resentment." Antiblack affect instilled by childhood socialization and the sense that racial change threatens fondly held individualistic values, *not* self-interest, are claimed as the twin foundations of Sears's "symbolic" racism (1988). "Modern"

racism contains the added ingredient of denying continuing racial inequality (McConahay 1986). "Racial resentment" (Kinder and Sanders 1996) is a recent addition to this family of "new racism" constructs. The label serves as a reminder that whatever the roots of new racism, a primary manifestation is anger that blacks' gains have exceeded their entitlement.

"Subtle" Prejudice. Using probability survey data from western Europe, Pettigrew and Meertens (1995) developed scales for both blatant and subtle prejudice that proved highly predictive of attitudes toward immigrants across four nations, six target outgroups, and seven samples. Their conception of subtle prejudice contains three components: perceived threat to traditional values (similar to symbolic racism), exaggeration of intergroup differences, and the absence of positive affect (admiration and sympathy) for the outgroup. Rejecting the claims of Sniderman and his colleagues (1991), Meertens and Pettigrew (1997) demonstrate that their subtle prejudice is distinctly different from political conservatism.

"Dominant Stratification Ideology." A belief that opportunity is plentiful and equally distributed, and thus effort is economically rewarded and economic failure is deserved—these compose the "dominant stratification ideology" (Huber and Form 1973; Kluegel and Smith 1986), a sociological elaboration on the individualism theme. Although personal status and strands of American "social liberalism" also play a role, unyielding adherence to this American "dominant ideology" is portrayed as a major impediment to public support for redistributional claims in general, and to calls for racial change in particular (Kluegel and Smith 1986). On a backdrop of ignorance bred of social segregation, whites' own experiences of economic success work to prevent recognition of the continuing barriers to full opportunity for black Americans (Kluegel 1985).

Self-Interest. Collective self-interest is sometimes identified as the primary basis of whites' interracial beliefs and feelings (Jackman 1994; Wellman 1993). If zero-sum assumptions prevail, redistribution in favor of blacks will be seen as a losing proposition to whites. Self-interest is at the heart of what Bobo (1988b) called an "ideology of bounded racial change" and what Bobo and colleagues (1997) have dubbed "laissez-faire racism": White acceptance of racial change and efforts to promote it end when continued change is perceived to threaten the well-being of whites.

PRESCRIPTIONS FOR MODERN PREJUDICE

When the lessons from cognitive social psychology are counterposed with those from other perspectives on modern race prejudice, an apparent dilemma is revealed. Though social cognition findings indicate that category salience can promote stereotype change under some circumstances (Cook 1984; Pettigrew 1998), much of the cognitive literature insists that categorization is a central contributor to race prejudice and negative race relations: Color consciousness is often portrayed as an evil, color blindness the ideal. From other scholars of modern prejudice, the analysis and prescription are nearly a mirror image of this view. Color blindness is said to impede forthright problem solving in desegregated institutions (Schofield 1986); to represent ignorance of the structural barriers faced by black Americans (Kluegel 1985); and to be used as a weapon by those opposing black claims of collective rights (Jackman and Muha 1984; Omi and Winant 1986). The solution implied or stated by these analysts is for whites to adopt a color consciousness that fully acknowledges the historical impact of racial subordination and the continuing liabilities of direct and indirect discrimination. The two streams of advice present this challenge: How to promote a racial understanding in the white public that minimizes the psychological liabilities of ingroup/outgroup categorization while acknowledging the full sociological implications of the past and continuing color line.

(SEE ALSO: *Discrimination*)

REFERENCES

Allport, Gordon 1954 *The Nature of Prejudice*. Cambridge, Mass.: Addison-Wesley.

Apostle, Richard A., Charles Y. Glock, Thomas Piazza, and Marijean Suelzle 1983 *The Anatomy of Racial Attitudes*. Berkeley: University of California Press.

Bobo, Lawrence 1988a "Attitudes toward the Black Political Movement: Trends, Meaning, and Effects on Racial Policy Preferences." *Social Psychology Quarterly* 51:287–302.

—— 1988b "Group Conflict, Prejudice, and the Paradox of Contemporary Racial Attitudes." In Phyllis A. Katz and Dalmas A. Taylor, eds., *Eliminating Racism*. New York: Plenum.

——, and James R. Kluegel 1993 "Opposition to Race-Targeting: Self-Interest, Stratification Ideology, or Racial Attitude?" *American Sociological Review* 58:443–464.

——, and Ryan A. Smith 1997 "Laissez Faire Racism: The Crystallization of a 'Kinder Gentler' Anti-Black Ideology." In Steven A. Tuch and Jack K. Martin, eds., *Racial Attitudes in the 1990s: Continuity and Change*. Greenwood, Conn.: Praeger.

Brewer, Marilynn B. 1979 "Ingroup Bias in the Minimal Intergroup Situation: A Cognitive-Motivational Analysis." *Psychological Bulletin* 86:307–324.

—— 1991 "The Social Self: On Being the Same and Different at the Same Time. *Personality and Social Psychology Bulletin* 17:475–482.

——, and Norman Miller 1988 "Contact and Cooperation: When Do They Work?" In Phyllis A. Katz and Dalmas A. Taylor, eds., *Eliminating Racism*. New York: Plenum.

Cook, Stuart W. 1984 "Cooperative Interaction in Multiethnic Contexts." In Norman Miller and Marilynn B. Brewer, eds., *Groups in Contact: The Psychology of Desegregation*. New York: Academic.

Crosby, Faye J., Stephanie Bromley, and Leonard Saxe 1980 "Recent Unobtrusive Studies of Black and White Discrimination and Prejudice: A Literature Review." *Psychological Bulletin* 87:546–563.

Den Uyl, Roger, C. E. Choenni, and Frank Bovenkerk 1986 "Mag Het Ook Een Buitenlander Wezen? Discriminatie Bij Uitzendburo's." Utrecht, The Netherlands: National Bureau against Racism.

Dovidio, John F., Kerry Kawakami, Craig Johnson, Brenda Johnson, and Adaiah Howard 1997 "On the Nature of Prejudice: Automatic and Controlled Processes." *Journal of Experimental Social Psychology* 33:510–540.

Dovidio, John F., Jeffrey Mann, and Samuel L. Gaertner 1989 "Resistance to Affirmative Action: The Implications of Aversive Racism." In Faye J. Crosby and Fletcher A. Blanchard, eds., *Affirmative Action in Perspective*. New York: Springer-Verlag.

Esses, Victoria M., Geoffrey Haddock, and Mark P. Zanna 1993 In Diane M. Mackie and David L. Hamilton, eds., *Affect, Cognition, and Stereotyping: Interactive Processes in Group Perception*. San Diego, Calif.: Academic.

Feagin, Joe R. 1975 *Subordinating the Poor*. Englewood Cliffs, N.J.: Prentice-Hall.

—— 1991 "The Continuing Significance of Race: Antiblack Discrimination in Public Places." *American Sociological Review* 56:101–116.

Fiske, Susan T. 1987 "On the Road: Comment on the Cognitive Stereotyping Literature in Pettigrew and Martin." *Journal of Social Issues* 43:113–118.

—— 1998 "Stereotyping, Prejudice, and Discrimination. In Daniel T. Gilbert, Susan T. Fiske, and Gardner Lindzey, eds., *The Handbook of Social Psychology*, 4th ed. New York: McGraw-Hill.

Gaertner, Samuel L. 1976 "Nonreactive Measures in Racial Attitude Research: A Focus on 'Liberals.'" In Phyllis A. Katz, ed., *Toward the Elimination of Racism*. New York: Pergamon.

——, and John F. Dovidio 1986 "The Aversive Form of Racism." In John F. Dovidio and Samuel L. Gaertner, eds., *Prejudice, Discrimination, and Racism*. Orlando, Fla.: Academic.

Hamilton, David A., and Tina K. Trolier 1986 "Stereotypes and Stereotyping: An Overview of the Cognitive Approach." In Phyllis A. Katz and Dalmas A. Taylor, eds., *Eliminating Racism*. New York: Plenum.

Hamilton, David L. 1997 "A Cognitive-Attributional Analysis of Stereotyping." In Leonard Berkowitz, ed., *Advances in Experimental Social Psychology*, vol. 12. New York: Academic.

Harding, John, Harold Proshansky, Bernard Kutner, and Isador Chein 1969 "Prejudice and Intergroup Relations." In Gardner Lindzey and Elliot Aronson, eds., *Handbook of Social Psychology, Volume V*, 2nd ed. Reading, Mass.: Addison-Wesley.

Heider, Fritz 1958 *The Psychology of Interpersonal Relations*. New York: John Wiley.

Huber, Joan, and William H. Form 1973 *Income and Ideology*. New York: Free Press.

Jackman, Mary R. 1994 *The Velvet Glove: Paternalism and Conflict in Gender, Class, and Race Relations*. Los Angeles, Calif.: University of California Press.

——, and Michael J. Muha 1984 "Education and Intergroup Attitudes: Moral Enlightenment, Superficial Democratic Commitment, or Ideological Refinement?" *American Sociological Review* 49:751–769.

Jaynes, David Gerald, and Robin M. Williams, Jr. 1989 *A Common Destiny: Blacks and American Society*. Washington, D.C.: National Academy Press.

Katz, Irwin, Joyce Wackenhut, and R. Glen Hass 1986 "Racial Ambivalence, Value Duality, and Behavior." In John F. Dovidio and Samuel L. Gaertner, eds., *Prejudice, Discrimination, and Racism*. Orlando, Fla.: Academic.

Kinder, Donald R., and Lynn M. Sanders 1996 *Divided by Color: Racial Politics and Democratic Ideals*. Chicago: University of Chicago Press.

Klineberg, Otto 1972 "Prejudice. The Concept." In David L. Sills, ed., *International Encyclopedia of the Social Sciences*, reprint ed. New York: Macmillan Free Press.

Klink, Andreas, and Ulrich Wagner 1999 "Discrimination against Ethnic Minorities in Germany: Going Back to the Field." *Journal of Applied Social Psychology* 29:402–423.

Kluegel, James R. 1985 "If There Isn't a Problem, You Don't Need a Solution." *American Behavioral Scientist* 28:761–784.

——, and Eliot R. Smith 1982 "Whites' Beliefs about Blacks' Opportunity." *American Sociological Review* 47:518–532.

—— 1983 "Affirmative Action Attitudes: Effects of Self-Interest, Racial Affect, and Stratification Beliefs on Whites' Views." *Social Forces* 61:797–824.

—— 1986 *Beliefs about Inequality: Americans' Views of What Is and What Ought to Be*. New York: Aldine de Gruyter.

Kovel, Joel 1970 *White Racism: A Psychohistory*. New York: Pantheon.

Lipset, Seymour Martin, and William Schneider 1978 "The Bakke Case: How Would It Be Decided at the Bar of Public Opinion?" *Public Opinion* 1:38–44.

McConahay, John B. 1986 "Modern Racism, Ambivalence, and the Modern Racism Scale." In John F. Dovidio and Samuel L. Gaertner, eds., *Prejudice, Discrimination, and Racism*. Orlando, Fla.: Academic Press.

Mackie, Diane M., and David L. Hamilton (eds.) 1993 *Affect, Cognition, and Stereotyping: Interactive Processes in Group Perception*. San Diego, Calif.: Academic Press.

Meertens, Roel W., and Thomas F. Pettigrew 1997 "Is Subtle Prejudice Really Prejudice?" *Public Opinion Quarterly* 6:54–71.

Omi, Michael, and Howard Winant 1986 *Racial Formation in the United States from the 1960s to the 1980s*. New York: Routledge and Kegan Paul.

Pettigrew, Thomas F. 1979a "The Ultimate Attribution Error: Extending Allport's Cognitive Analysis of Prejudice." *Personality and Social Psychology Bulletin* 5:461–476.

—— 1979b "Racial Change and Social Policy." *Annals of the American Academy of Political and Social Science* 441:114–131.

—— 1989 "The Nature of Modern Racism." *Revue Internationale de Psychologie Sociale* 2:291–305.

—— 1997 "The Affective Component of Prejudice: Results from Western Europe." In Steven A. Tuch and Jack K. Martin, eds., *Racial Attitudes in the 1990s: Continuity and Change*. Westport, Conn.: Praeger.

—— 1998 "Intergroup Contact Theory." *Annual Review of Psychology* 49:65–85.

——, and Roel W. Meertens 1995 "Subtle and Blatant Prejudice in Western Europe." *European Journal of Social Psychology* 25:57–75.

Rothbart, Myron, and Oliver P. John 1985 "Social Categorization and Behavioral Episodes: A Cognitive Analysis of the Effects of Intergroup Contact." *Journal of Social Issues* 41:81–104.

Ryan, William 1971 *Blaming the Victim*. New York: Vintage.

Schofield, Janet Ward 1986 "Causes and Consequences of the Colorblind Perspective." In John F. Dovidio and Samuel L. Gaertner, eds., *Prejudice, Discrimination, and Racism*. Orlando, Fla.: Academic.

Schuman, Howard, and Michael P. Johnson 1976 "Attitudes and Behavior." *Annual Review of Sociology* 2:161–207.

Schuman, Howard, Charlotte Steeh, Lawrence Bobo, and Maria Krysan 1997 *Racial Attitudes in America: Trends and Interpretations*, 2nd ed. Cambridge, Mass.: Harvard University Press.

Sears, David O. 1988 "Symbolic Racism." In Phyllis A. Katz and Dalmas A. Taylor, eds., *Eliminating Racism*. New York: Plenum Press.

Sissons, Mary 1981 "Race, Sex and Helping Behavior." *British Journal of Social Psychology* 20:285–292.

Smith, Eliot R. 1993 "Social Identity and Social Emotions: Toward New Conceptualizations of Prejudice." In Diane M. Mackie and David L. Hamilton, eds., *Affect, Cognition, and Stereotyping: Interactive Processes in Group Perception*. San Diego, Calif: Academic.

Smith, Thomas W., and Paul B. Sheatsley 1984 "American Attitudes toward Race Relations." *Public Opinion* 6:14–15, 50–53.

Sniderman, Paul M., Thomas Piazza, Philip E. Tetlock, and Ann Kendrick 1991 "The New Racism." *American Journal of Political Science* 35:423–447.

Stangor, Charles, Sullivan, Linda A., and Thomas E. Ford 1991 "Affective and Cognitive Determinants of Prejudice." *Social Cognition* 9:359–380.

Steeh, Charlotte, and Maria Krysan 1996 "The Polls—Trends: Affirmative Action and the Public, 1970–1995." *Public Opinion Quarterly* 60:128–158.

Tajfel, Henri 1969 "Cognitive Aspects of Prejudice." *Journal of Social Issues* 4:79–97.

Webb, Eugene J. 1981 *Nonreactive Measures in the Social Sciences*, 2nd ed. Boston: Houghton Mifflin.

Wellman, David T. 1993 *Portraits of White Racism*, 2nd ed. New York: Cambridge University Press.

Weitz, Shirley 1972 "Attitude, Voice, and Behavior: A Repressed Affect Model of Interracial Interaction." *Journal of Personality and Social Psychology* 32:857–864.

Wilder, David A. 1978 "Reduction of Intergroup Discrimination Through Individuation of the Out-Group." *Journal of Personality and Social Psychology* 36:1361–1374.

—— 1984 "Intergroup Contact: The Typical Member and the Exception to the Rule." *Journal of Experimental Social Psychology* 20:177–194.

Word, Carl O., Mark P. Zanna, and Joel Cooper 1974 "The Nonverbal Mediation of Self-Fulfilling Prophecies in Interracial Interaction." *Journal of Experimental Social Psychology* 10:109–120.

Zanna, Mark P. 1994 "On the Nature of Prejudice." *Canadian Psychology* 31:11–23.

MARYLEE C. TAYLOR
THOMAS F. PETTIGREW

PROBABILITY THEORY

Sociologists, as much as researchers in any field perhaps, use a variety of approaches in the investigation of their subject matter. Quite successful and important are the historical and exegetical approaches and those in the traditions of anthropology and philosophy. Also of great importance are the systematic approaches that use mathematical models. Here the social investigator proposes a model, a mathematical depiction of social phenomena. A successful mathematical model can be very powerful, providing not only confidence in the theory from which the model was derived, giving us an explanation of the phenomena, but producing as well a method for predicting, giving us a practical means for controlling or affecting the social phenomena.

The social mathematical model is first of all a description of the relationship of the properties of social objects—groups, states, institutions, organizations, even people. If the model is derived from a theory, or if it contains features implied by a theory, and if the model fits data (i.e., has been found to satisfy some criterion of performance), the model can in addition be regarded as evidence to support that theory. In this case we can think of a true, underlying model that generated the observations we are studying and a proposed model that will be tested against data. Quantitative analysis begins, then, with some theoretical understanding of the properties of groups of social objects; this understanding leads to the specification of a model of the interaction of these properties, after which observations of these properties on a sample of the objects are collected. The performance of the model is then evaluated to determine to what degree the model truly describes the underlying process.

The measurement of a property of a social object is called a *variable*. Variables can be either fixed or random. Fixed variables are those determined by the investigator; they usually occur in experiments and will not be of concern in this chapter. All other variables are random. The random nature of these variables is the unavoidable consequence of two things; first, the fact that our observations are *samples*, that is, groups of instances of social objects drawn from a population (that is, a very large number of possible instances to be observed); second, the fact that our theories and data collection are often unable to account for all the relevant variables affecting the variables included in the analysis. Probability theory in social models, or, equivalently, random variables in social models, will derive from these two subtopics: sampling and the specification of residual or excluded variables in the models.

A certain philosophical difference of opinion arises among probability theorists about the nature of the true source of the randomness in nature. One group argues that these features are inherent in reality, and another argues they are simply the consequence of ignorance. The primary modeling tool of the former group is the *stochastic process* (Chung 1974), while that of the latter is the *Bayesian statistical model* (de Finetti 1974).

MAIN CONCEPTS

Probability is a name assigned to the relative frequency of an event in an event space, that is, a set of possible events. For example, we might define the event space as the two sides of a single coin labeled heads (*H*) and tails (*T*): {*T*, *H*}. The actual outcome of a coin flip is a random variable, *X*, say, and the probability of the outcome *H* is $P(X = H)$. The probability distribution function (or PDF)

assigns a quantity to this probability. By definition, for a fair coin $P(X = H) = .5$. Since the event space is composed of only two events, then $P(X = T) + P(X = H) = 1$, that is, one or the other event occurs for certain, and $P(X - T) - 1 - P(X = H) = .5$. Thus the probability of *T* is equal to the probability of *H* and the coin is fair.

In general we assign numbers to the events in our event space, allowing us to use mathematical language to describe the probabilities. For example, the event space of the number of people arriving at a bank's automatic teller machine (ATM) is {0, 1, 2, . . .} over a given time interval Δt. Given certain assumptions, such as that the arrival time of each person is independent of anyone else's, we can derive a theoretical PDF. For a given time interval Δt, the probability of the number of people *X* can be shown to be

$$P(X = k \mid \Delta t) = \frac{(\lambda \Delta t)^k e^{-(\lambda \Delta t)}}{k!}$$

where λ is the mean rate of people arriving at the ATM over the time interval Δt, and $k = 0, 1, 2, . . .$

Suppose from bank records we are able to determine that 100 people per hour complete a transaction at a particular ATM during normal working hours. For Δt equal to one minute or 1/60 an hour, the PDF is

$$P(X = k) = \frac{1.6667^k e^{-1.6667}}{k!}$$

For some selected values of *k* we have

k	P(X = k)
0	.1889
1	.3148
2	.2623
3	.1457
4	.0607
...	...

If we assume that each person spends about a minute at the ATM, we should expect one or more people standing in line behind someone at the

ATM about 50 percent of the time since the probability of two or more people arriving during a one minute interval is

$$P(X \geq 2) = 1 - P(X = 0) - P(X = 1) = .4963$$

The event spaces for the examples above are discrete, but continuous event spaces are also widely used. A common PDF for continuous event spaces is the normal distribution:

$$p(X = x) = \frac{1}{\sqrt{2\pi\sigma^2}} e^{-\frac{(x-\mu)^2}{2\sigma^2}}$$

where μ and σ^2, commonly called the mean and variance respectively, are parameters of the distribution, and χ is a real number greater than minus infinity and less than plus infinity. The normal PDF is the most widely used distribution in social models, first because it had advantageous mathematical properties and second because its specification in many cases can be justified on the basis of the central limit theorem (Hogg and Tanis 1977, p. 155).

Other important concepts in probability theory are the *cumulative distribution function* (or CDF), *joint distributions* (distributions involving more than one variable), and *conditional distributions*. The CDF is the probability of X being less than or equal to x, that is, $Pr(X \leq x)$. An accessible introduction to probability may be found in Hogg and Tanis (1977).

SAMPLING

In physics all protons behave similarly. To determine their properties, any given instance of a proton will do. Social objects, on the other hand, tend to be complex, and their properties can vary considerably from instance to instance. It is not possible to draw conclusions about all instances of a social object from a given one in the same manner we might from single instance of a proton. Given equivalent circumstances, we cannot expect everyone to respond the same way to a question about their attitudes toward political issues or to behave the same way when presented with a set of options.

For example, suppose we wish to determine the extent to which a person's education affects his or her attitudes towards abortion. Let A_i represent a measurement of the attitude of some person, labeled the ith person, scored 0 if they are opposed to abortion or 1 if not. Let B_i be the measurement of the person's education, scored 0 for less than high school, 1 for high school but no college, or 2 for at least some college.

Given measurements on a sample of people, we would find that they would be distributed in some fashion across all the six possible categories of the two variables. Dividing the number that fall into each category by the total number in the sample would give us estimates of the empirical distribution for the probabilities: $PR(A = 0, B = 1)$, $PR(A = 0, B = 2)$, and so on. We might also model this distribution. For example, an important type of model is the loglinear model (Goodman 1972; Haberman 1979; Agresti 1990), which models the log of the probability:

$$\log PR(A = i, \ B = j) = \lambda_i^A + \lambda_j^B + \lambda_{ij}^{AB}$$

where λ_i^A, λ_j^B and λ_{ij}^{AB} are parameters (actually sets of parameters). In this model the λ_{ij}^{AB} parameters represent the associations between A and B, and an estimate of these quantities might have important implications for a theory.

Given a sample distribution, computing an estimate of λ_{ij}^{AB} is straightforward (Bishop, Fienberg, and Holland 1975). It is important, however, to realize that such an estimate is itself a random variable, that is, we can expect the estimate to vary with every sample of observations we produce. If the sample is properly selected, in particular if it is a simple random sample in which each person has an equal chance of being included in the sample, it can be shown that the estimates of λ_{ij}^{AB} have, in large samples at least, a normal distribution (Haberman 1973). Our estimates, then, are themselves parameters of a distribution, usually the means of a normal distribution. It follows that the fundamental parameters upon which a theory will depend can never be directly observed and that we must infer its true value from sample data.

All research on social objects is unavoidably research on samples of observations. Therefore all such research will necessarily entail at the very least a probabilistic sampling model, and the conclusions drawn will require properly conceived statistical inference.

MODELS WITH EXCLUDED VARIABLES

The Regression Model. The most well-known and widely used statistical model is the regression model. It is a simple linear hypersurface model with an added feature: a disturbance term, which represents the effects on the dependent variable of variables that have not been measured. To the extent that the claims or implications of a theory may be put into linear form, or at least transformed into linear form, the parameters (or regression coefficients) may be estimated and statistical inference drawn by making some reasonably benign assumptions about the behavior of the variables that have been excluded from measurement. The key assumption is that the excluded variables are uncorrelated with included variables. The failure of this assumption gives rise to *spurious* effects; that is, parameters may be under- or overestimated, and this results in faulty conclusions. The statistical inference also requires a homogeneity of variance of the disturbance variables, called *homoscedasticity*. The variation of the excluded variables must be the same across the range of the independent variables. This is not a critical assumption, however, because the consequence of the violation of this assumption is inefficiency rather than bias, as in the case of the spurious effects. Moreover, the underlying process generating the heteroscedasticity may be specified, which would yield efficient estimates, or a modified inference may be computed, based on revised estimates of the variances of the distribution of the parameter estimates (White 1980).

For example, a simple regression of income, say, on years of education may be described, $y_i = b_0 + b_1 x_i + \varepsilon_i$, where y_i and x_i are observations on income and years of education, respectively, of the *i*th person b_0 and b_1 are regression coefficients, and ε_i is the disturbance term. Estimates of b_0 and b_1 may be found (without making any assumptions about the functional form of the distribution of ε_i by using perhaps the most celebrated theorem in statistics, the Gauss-Markov theorem, and they are usually called *ordinary least squares estimates*.

If we gather the observations into matrices, we can rewrite the regression equation as functions of matrices: $Y = XB + E$, where Y is an N x 1 vector of observations on the dependent variable. X an N x K matrix of observations on K independent variables, B a K x 1 vector of regression coefficients,

and E an N x 1 vector of disturbances. With this notation the estimates in B may be described $B\hat{} = (X'X)^{-1} X'Y$, where; the "^" over the B emphasizes that they are estimates of the parameters.

Our observations are samples, and since our estimates of B will vary from sample to sample, it follows that these estimates will themselves be random variables. Appealing again to the Gauss-Markov theorem, it is possible to show that the ordinary least squares estimates have a normal distribution with variance-covariance matrix equal to $\text{VarCov}(\hat{B}) = \sigma^2_\varepsilon (X'X)^{-1} X'Y$, where σ^2_ε is estimated by $\sigma^2_\varepsilon = (Y - XB)'(Y - XB)/(N - K - 1)$.

Other models. The regression model in the previous section is a "single equation" model, that is, it contains one dependent variable. A generalization of the regression model incorporates multiple dependent variables. This model may be represented in matrix notation as $BY = \Gamma X + Z$, where Y is an N x L matrix of L *endogenous* variables (i.e., variables that are dependent in at least one equation), B is an L x L matrix of coefficients relating endogenous variables among themselves, X is an N x K matrix of K *exogenous* variables (i.e., variables that are never dependent), Γ is an L x K matrix of coefficients relating the exogenous variables to the endogenous variables, and Z is an N x L matrix of disturbances. Techniques have been developed to produce estimates and statistical inference for these kinds of models (Judge et al. 1982; Fox 1984).

Measurement error is another kind of excluded variable, and models have been developed to incorporate them into the regression and simultaneous equation models. One method for handling measurement error is to use multiple measures of an underlying *latent* variable (Bollen 1989; Jöreskog and Sörbom 1988). A model that incorporates both measurement error and excluded variable disturbances may be described in the following way:

$$Y = \Lambda_y \eta + \varepsilon_y$$
$$X = \Lambda_x \xi + \varepsilon_x$$
$$B\eta = \Gamma \xi + \zeta$$

where Y and X are our observations on the endogenous and exogenous variables respectively, Λ_y, and Λ_x are coefficient matrices relating the underlying variables to the observed variables, η and ξ are the latent endogenous and exogenous variables respectively, B and Γ are coefficient matrices relating the latent variables among themselves ε_y and ε_z are the measurement error disturbances, and ζ is the excluded variable disturbance.

This model incorporates three sources of randomness, measurement error disturbance, excluded variable disturbance, and sampling error. Models of the future may contain a fourth source of randomness: a structural disturbance in the coefficients. These latter models are called random coefficient models and are a special case of the most general kind of probabilistic model called the *mixture model* (Judge et al. 1982; Everitt 1984).

The models described to this point have been linear. Linearity can be a useful approximation that renders the problem tractable. Nonlinearity may be an important aspect of a theoretical specification, however, and methods to incorporate nonlinearity in large-scale models have been developed (Amemiya 1985). It also appears to be the fact that most social measures are not continuous, real variables, which is what is assumed by the regression and simultaneous models described above. Thus, much work is now being devoted to the development of models that may be used with measures that are limited in a variety of ways— they are categorical, ordinal, truncated, or censored, for example (Muthén 1984; Maddala 1983). Limited variable methods also include methods for handling variations on the simple random method of sampling.

Probability theory has had a profound effect on the modeling of social processes. It has helped solve the sampling problem, permitted the specification of models with excluded variables, and provided a method for handling measurement.

REFERENCES

Agresti, A. 1990 *Categorical Data Analysis*. New York: John Wiley.

Amemiya, T. 1985 *Advanced Econometrics*. Cambridge, Mass.: Harvard University Press.

Bishop, Y. M. M., S. E. Fienberg, and P. W. Holland 1975 *Discrete Multivariate Analysis: Theory and Practice*. Cambridge, Mass.: MIT Press.

Bollen, K. A. 1989 *Structural Equations with Latent Variables*. New York: John Wiley.

Chung, K. L. 1974 *Elementary Probability Theory with Stochastic Processes*. Berlin: Springer-Verlag.

de Finetti, B. 1974 *Theory of Probability*, 2 vols. New York: John Wiley.

Everitt, B. S. 1984 *An Introduction to Latent Variable Models*. London: Chapman and Hall.

Fox, J. 1984 *Linear Statistical Models and Related Methods*. New York: John Wiley.

Goodman, L. A. 1972 "A General Model for the Analysis of Surveys." *American Journal of Sociology* 37:28–46.

Haberman, S. J. 1973 "Loglinear Models for Frequency Data: Sufficient Statistics and Likelihood Equations." *Annals of Mathematical Statistics* 1:617–632.

—— 1979 *Analysis of Qualitative Data*, vol. 2, *New Developments*. Orlando, Fla.: Academic.

Hogg, Robert V., and Elliot A. Tanis 1977 *Probability and Statistical Inference*. New York: Macmillan.

Jöreskog, K. G., and Dag Sörbom 1988 *LISREL VII*. Chicago: SPSS.

Judge, George G., R. Carter Hill, William Griffiths, Helmut Lutkepohl, and Tsoung-Chao Lee 1982 *Introduction to the Theory and Practice of Econometrics*. New York: John Wiley.

Maddala, G. 1983 *Limited-Dependent and Qualitative Variables in Econometrics*. Cambridge, England: Cambridge University Press.

Muthén, B. 1984 "A General Structural Equation Model with Dichotomous, Ordered Categorical, and Continuous Latent Variable Indicators." *Psychometrika* 49:115–132.

Tuma, Nancy Brandon, and Michael T. Hannan 1984 *Social Dynamics: Models and Methods*. Orlando, Fla.: Academic.

White, H. 1980 "A Heteroskedasticity-Consistent Covariance Matrix Estimator and a Direct Test for Heteroskedasticity." *Econometrica* 48:817–838.

RONALD SCHOENBERG

PROBATION AND PAROLE

The criminal justice system is the primary institution responsible for the formal social control of criminal deviance. Those who violate the criminal law are subject to a variety of sanctions, ranging from the reprimand of a police officer to execution by hanging. Most offenders are not apprehended, and among those who are arrested many are not prosecuted nor convicted of a crime. For offenders who are found guilty, either by trial or more often by negotiated guilty plea, the sentence handed down by the court typically mandates correctional supervision, usually either some form of probation or incarceration with early release to some form of parole.

Even though probation and parole have been integral components of corrections since the nineteenth century, the differences between them are not always clear. Both are postconviction alternatives to incarceration that include supervision in the community by a probation or parole officer, who, depending on the jurisdiction, may be the same person. They are conditional releases to the community that are contingent on compliance with stipulated conditions, which if violated, may lead to revocation. Many probation and parole programs are similar (e.g., intensive supervision) or they share clientele. Last, as alternatives to incarceration, both are less expensive, less punitive, and probably more effective strategies of crime control.

The major difference between probation and parole is that probationers are sentenced directly to community supervision without being incarcerated, while parolees serve part of their sentence incarcerated before they are released to parole. Parole is a conditional release from confinement, whereas probation is a conditional suspension of a sentence to confinement. In both cases, a new crime or technical violation of conditions may lead to enhanced restrictions or incarceration. A general definition of *probation* is the conditional supervised release of a convicted offender into the community in lieu of incarceration (Allen et al. 1985). *Parole* is the conditional supervised release of an incarcerated offender into the community after serving part of the sentence in confinement (Clear and Cole 1986).

PROBATION

Before informal probation was created in Boston in 1841 by philanthropist John Augustus, and the first statewide probation law was enacted in Massachusetts in 1978, convicted offenders were typically fined or imprisoned, often serving their full sentence. Probation was instituted as an alternative to incarceration at a time when jail and prison overcrowding became a critical management and humanitarian issue. Probation was considered a front-end sentencing solution to overcrowding,

intended specifically for less serious, first-time, and juvenile offenders amenable to "rehabilitation."

Over the years, rehabilitation has remained the primary goal of probation, and to this end, probation facilitates behavioral reform in a variety of ways. First, the often negative practical and symbolic consequences of the stigma of being an "ex-con" are neutralized. As less notorious and visible "probationers," the label will have less deleterious effects on the rehabilitative process. Second, the contaminating effects of imprisonment are avoided. This is particularly important for the less experienced offender, who may learn more about crime from more sophisticated, and sometimes predatory, inmates. The "pains of imprisonment" also produce anger, resentment, hostility, cynicism, and many other dysfunctional attitudes and feelings that make it more difficult to reform. Third, probation supports the existing social integration of the offender in the free community of noncriminals, including family, neighbors, employers and coworkers, friends, teachers and classmates, and others who are critical to the informal social control of crime. The offender released from incarceration will have the more difficult task of "reintegration." Fourth, the rehabilitative programs and services available to probationers are generally less coercive and more varied, flexible, and effective than those provided for prisoners. Fifth, the implied trust in leaving an offender in the community to demonstrate the ability to conform reinforces a positive attribution of self and expectations of appropriate behavior. Probation is more likely than incarceration to contribute to a self-fulfilling prophecy of rehabilitation.

Secondary goals of probation are more punitive. Probation is a penal sanction by virtue of the restrictions placed on the freedom of the offender. The conditions range from very lenient (e.g., weekly phone contact with a probation officer) to very punitive (e.g., twenty-four-hour home confinement), depending on the nature of the offense and offender characteristics. The goal of crime control can also be addressed by enhanced monitoring of probationers' compliance with the terms of probation, particularly their whereabouts. This can be accomplished by increasing the number and duration of meaningful (namely, face-to-face) contacts between probationer and probation officer, in the department's office, at home, at work, in a residential or nonresidential program facility, or anywhere else in the community. More comprehensive control is possible with electronic monitoring devices; for example, transmitter anklets can verify the location of a probationer within, or outside of, a stipulated free movement area. The goal of deterrence is served to the extent that rehabilitation and punishment succeed in preventing probationers from committing more crimes and returning to the criminal justice system. Finally, justice is achieved when probation is the appropriate sentence for the offense and offender, and its application is equitable and uniform across race, sex, and socioeconomic status categories (McAnany et al. 1984).

The decision to grant probation is the product of a complex organization of legal actors, sentencing procedures, decision criteria, and system capacity. The decision may be initiated by the prosecutor, who negotiates a guilty plea in exchange for a recommendation to the judge that the defendant be sentenced to probation. Or it may await conviction at trial. In either case, a presentence investigation report prepared by a probation officer may support the recommendation by providing background information on the offender and an assessment of the public risks and prospects for probation success.

There are intense organizational pressures to minimize the number of trials and to divert convicted offenders from incarceration: There are huge case backlogs in the courts (Meeker and Pontell 1985) and tremendous overcrowding in jails and prisons, as evidenced by the almost forty states in 1988 that were under court order to reduce inmate populations in order to meet a variety of correctional standards (Petersilia 1987). Incredibly, it has been estimated that more than 90 percent of convictions for felonies are the result of negotiated guilty pleas (McDonald 1985), and a high percentage of those receive probation since, by state, from 25 to 70 percent of convicted felons are sentenced to probation (Petersilia 1985). It is clearly in the personal and organizational interests of the defendant, prosecutor, judge, and even the jailer and prison superintendent to support "copping" a plea for probation.

Whether the conviction is negotiated or decided at trial, the judge sentences the offender, within the constraints imposed by the sentencing model and guidelines used in the jurisdiction. Most states use indeterminate sentencing, where judges have substantial discretion in rendering sentences and parole authorities are responsible for release decisions of incarcerated offenders. The trend is toward determinate sentencing, where judges and parole boards have much less influence on sentence and release decisions. In both models, probation is a widely used sentencing option, especially for less serious offenders but even for many serious offenders: Nationally, as high as 20 percent of violent offenders receive probation, including 13 percent of defendants convicted of rape and 9 percent of those convicted of homicide (Lisefski and Manson 1988).

Despite the confluence of the trend toward determinate sentencing, more pervasive justice model practices in corrections, and increased public pressure to be more punitive with criminals, there are relatively more offenders on probation than incarcerated or on parole than there were two decades ago (Petersilia et al. 1985). More serious offenders are being incarcerated for more fixed sentences, but the concomitant institutional overcrowding has produced a greater utilization of probation, as well as a variety of types of probation designed to meet the needs of both less serious and middle-range offenders, who in the past would have been more likely to be incarcerated. In addition to "standard probation," characterized by assignment to a probation officer with a caseload of as many as two hundred probationers and nominal contact, supervision, and rehabilitative services, a whole range of "intermediate sanctions" has been created that includes programs that are typically more punitive, restrictive, intensive, and effective than standard probation (Petersilia 1987; Morris and Tonry 1990). Judges now have a diversity of probation alternatives at sentencing: intensive supervised probation, home confinement, electronic monitoring, residential centers (halfway houses), and split sentences (jail/probation). These alternatives are often combined and coupled with other probation conditions that require restitution to victims, employment or education, payment of program costs, random urinalysis, specialized treatment or classes (e.g., Alcoholics Anonymous), or community service. Many of the intermediate sanctions are also used in the supervision of parolees.

PAROLE

Like probation, parole in the United States was created to relieve the serious overcrowding problem in prisons at the beginning of the nineteenth century. Years before informal probation began, some prison wardens and correctional administrators were releasing prisoners before their full sentence was served. They were either released outright, much as if they had received a pardon, or monitored informally by the police. Based on the European correctional innovations of "good time" and "ticket of leave," formal parole emerged toward the end of the nineteenth century, with the first indeterminate sentencing law passed in 1876 in New York (Champion 1990).

Until Maine abolished parole in 1976, all states had indeterminate sentencing and parole authorities. In general, within these systems a prisoner earns good time by productive participation in institutional programs and good conduct. The accumulated good time is subtracted from the sentence to determine the time incarcerated. This decision is typically made by a parole board, which is often a group of political appointees from a variety of occupations and constituencies. The offender is then released (or awarded a leave) to the supervision of a parole officer. If an offender does not commit a new crime or violate the conditions upon which release to parole is contingent, he or she can complete the remainder of the sentence as a parolee, to the time of discharge and freedom.

The goals of parole are anchored in indeterminate sentencing and the tenets of the rehabilitative ideal. It is assumed that offenders are amenable to reformation, through both the rehabilitation provided by the prison's treatment, educational, and vocational programs and the reintegration back into the free world facilitated by the transitional programs and services of parole. These twin primary goals of "rehabilitation" and "reintegration" drive the decisions and actions of the parole system. Parole is granted when the prisoner is considered ready for release, based on behavior during confinement, the extent to which rehabilitation is evident, and the apparent risk to public safety. In practice, many offenders spend a relatively small proportion of their sentence incarcerated; for instance, a convicted murderer with a life sentence may "do hard time" for as few as, say, ten years and serve the rest of the sentence on parole. Parole is revoked, or modified, when there are indications that reintegration is in jeopardy or unlikely, owing to violation of parole conditions. A new crime, in particular, but even a technical violation may be sufficient for the parole board to reincarcerate a parolee. The parole board also has the discretionary authority to set dates for parole hearings, fix minimum terms and release dates, determine good time credits, and specify parole conditions and requirements.

Like probation, the secondary goals of parole include punishment, crime control, and deterrence. After all, parole is a part of the penal sanction defined by the sentence to imprisonment, and, depending on the type of parole and stipulated conditions, the parole experience can be very restrictive and quasi-custodial. Effective rehabilitation, supervision, and monitoring of parolees should also produce deterrent effects—the combination of reformation and punishment should prevent future criminal conduct among parolees.

Unfortunately, by the mid-1970s, evidence had accumulated that suggested that parole was not an especially effective crime control strategy (Martinson 1974), and the shift away from the rehabilitative ideal to a more punitive justice philosophy (von Hirsch 1976) began in earnest. About one-third of states have returned to some form of determinate sentencing, and more are likely to follow. The discretionary power of judges in rendering sentences and of parole boards in implementing them has been abridged, in order to make decisions more rational and fair by linking them to the severity of the offense rather than the characteristics of the offender. Offenders are now more likely to be serving sentences in confinement; since 1980, the rate of incarceration has increased by 76 percent (Bureau of Justice Statistics 1989). They are also less likely to be placed on parole by a paroling authority; between 1977 and 1987, releases from imprisonment decided by parole boards dropped from about 70 percent to 40 percent of all releases, while mandatory releases increased from roughly 5 percent to 30 percent of the total (Hester 1988). With determinate sentencing, many states simply do not have paroling authorities or parole supervision in the community.

These changes have also affected the types of parole that are still available in a majority of states. Although many parole and probation programs are similar, the usually more serious offenses and criminal histories of parolees and the shift toward more punitive correctional systems have led to a hardening of the conditions of (cf. U.S. Sentencing Commission 1987), less utilization of "standard parole," and a greater emphasis on protecting public safety by extending custody from the institution to the community. The goals of rehabilitation and reintegration have become less important, while crime control and deterrence have become more important. Consequently, there is greater reliance on transitional programs that maximize monitoring and supervision, while providing opportunities and services (e.g., employment, school, counseling, drug treatment) intended to facilitate reentry into the community and desistance from crime during parole and, ultimately, after discharge from correctional supervision. These programs are more intensive and custodial, often involving residential placement in a halfway house, intensive parole supervision, or home confinement with electronic monitoring. From these community bases, parolees may participate in work or school releases, home furloughs, counseling, religious services, and a variety of other reintegrative activities.

Although parole is not used to the extent that it was before the advent of determinate sentencing, and there are those who believe that it should be abolished in all states, some research suggests that determinate sentencing is no more a panacea than prior correctional reforms. There may be a leveling of sentencing disparities, and more offenders are being incarcerated. But they, on the average, are doing less time and, after release, may be as likely to be reconvicted and reincarcerated (Covey and Mande 1985).

RESEARCH

While the research evidence on the efficacy of determinate sentencing may be sketchy, there are many studies of other issues in probation and parole that have produced more substantive results. Social scientific research on probation and parole has tended to revolve around a set of related issues that are common to both: program effectiveness, recidivism, and classification and

prediction. The overriding empirical and policy question is "What works?" Attempts to address the question vary in rigor and quality, and the answers are neither direct nor simple.

There are innumerable studies of program effectiveness, most of them not producing useful, much less compelling, evidence of program success or failure. For example, many studies conclude that a probation program is successful because 30 percent of participants recidivate or that a parole program is successful because 40 percent of participants recidivate. There are serious problems with those kinds of studies. First, they do not compare the program being evaluated with others, either with other probation or parole programs, or across correctional alternatives (e.g., release, probation, incarceration, and parole).

Second, without comparison groups, one can only evaluate program effectiveness in relation to some standard of success. But preordained acceptable levels of recidivism are determined normatively, not empirically. Normative criteria of success cannot be applied uniformly across the incredible variation in probation and parole programs. For instance, some probation programs, because of the very low risk participants, should probably generate recidivism rates that are closer to 5 percent than 30 percent.

Third, recidivism is often not defined or measured adequately. Generically, recidivism has come to mean "reoffending," particularly by offenders who have had contact with the criminal justice system, as measured typically by rearrest, reconviction, reincarceration, or some variation or combination thereof. But what does a probationer or parolee relapse to, and what is the most appropriate and accurate measure? The answers are complicated by the fact that probation and parole can be revoked if an offender commits a crime that becomes known to criminal justice authorities or by a noncriminal violation of release conditions (a "technical violation"). Paradoxically, practically all studies ignore the substantial amount of successful criminal behavior that remains hidden from officials, but many use both revocation criteria as measures of recidivism. Which measure is used can dramatically affect judgments about program effectiveness. Evaluations of three intensive probation supervision programs show that technical violations, as compared to new crimes, account for the majority of revocations. The revocation rates due to technical violations for these programs were 56 percent, 70 percent, and 85 percent, respectively. However, if the technical violations are not counted in the recidivism rates, the rates drop to 7 percent, 8 percent, and 5 percent, respectively (Petersilia 1987). Depending on program objectives, recidivism, no matter how measured, may not be the only or most appropriate criterion of program effectiveness. What may also be useful is assessment of relative costs and savings, impacts on jail and prison overcrowding, effects on public perceptions of safety, performance at school or in the workplace, changes in offenders' attitudes and self-concept, and so on.

More rigorous studies utilize comparison groups in order to assess the relative effectiveness of different correctional strategies. A typical study compares the recidivism rates of various combinations of offenders on probation, incarcerated, and on parole, and concludes that probationers are least likely and ex-prisoners are most likely to recidivate. Of course, one would predict those results based on the differences between the groups in their risk to recidivate. The selection biases of the court place the least serious, low-risk offenders on probation and the most serious, high-risk offenders in institutions. The observed differences in recidivism do not reflect the relative effectiveness of the programs, but the original differences in the recidivism risks of the comparison groups.

Some studies attempt to produce more comparable groups by using more objective probation and parole prediction instruments to classify and then compare offenders by level of recidivism risk across programs. That is, they try improve comparability by "matching" offenders within the different program groups. For example, a study of the relative effectiveness of standard probation, intensive supervision probation, and incarceration with parole classified offenders within each group into low-, medium-, high-, and maximum-risk levels. Comparisons of recidivism, measured by rearrest, reconviction, and reincarceration, across the three program alternatives for each of the four categories of offenders (namely, least likely to most likely to recidivate) show that parole is least effective in preventing recidivism at all levels of recidivism risk. The differences between standard and intensive probation are not as consistent: no matter how recidivism is measured,

the rate is higher among intensive supervision probationers who are low- and high-risk offenders; among medium-risk offenders, it varies by the measure of recidivism; and for maximum-risk probationers, there seems to be little difference in the effectiveness of standard or intensive supervision, except for the somewhat higher reincarceration rate among intensive supervision probationers (Erwin 1986).

The equivocal findings of this and many similar studies reflect the difficulty in predicting recidivism risk with any degree of accuracy. The most comprehensive and statistically sophisticated techniques (e.g., cluster analyses, linear models, complex contingency tables) are not much more accurate than bivariate tabular procedures developed seventy years ago by Ernest Burgess. And no technique is able to predict recidivism with higher than 70 percent accuracy, with most slightly better than chance (Blumstein et al. 1986). Therefore, it is virtually impossible to make groups comparable on the basis of recidivism risk, or any other prediction criteria, which compromises the validity of the findings regarding differential program effectiveness.

The mixed results probably also reflect the paradox of intensive supervision programs in general: Increasing supervision and monitoring may increase, rather than decrease, the probability of recidivism. The offender is at greater risk to recidivate, simply because there is a better chance that unacceptable conduct will be observed. However, depending on the declared program goals, this may indicate success rather than failure: If intensive supervision of probation and parole are intended to enhance crime control and public safety, rather than to rehabilitate, higher rates of recidivism may demonstrate program effectiveness (Gottfredson and Gottfredson 1988).

Research on probation and parole effectiveness cannot produce compelling findings from studies that depend on comparisons of typically noncomparable groups. What is necessary are "equivalent" groups that are created through random assignment within experiments. Unfortunately, experimental designs are usually more expensive and more difficult to implement and complete in natural settings. Consequently, they are extremely rare in research on probation and parole. For instance, there are more than one hundred studies of the effectiveness of intensive probation supervision, but none have an experimental design with random assignment to program conditions (Petersilia 1987). There are some current efforts to implement studies of probation and parole that have experimental designs, but if the objective is to produce valid and useful knowledge on "what works," there must be a greater commitment on the part of the criminal justice system, funding agencies, and the social science research community.

The field of probation and parole research and study will continue to be important for social scientists. While there is no indication that the description and analysis presented here is changing at this time, the concern with the issues is active. Some more recent writings add to the character of the presentation here, and are well worth reviewing for persons who wish to pursue the development of the field. (See Albonetti and Hepburn 1997; Heilbrun 1999; Geerken and Hayes 1993; Gendreau et al. 1994; McCorkle and Crank 1992; and Turner et al. 1992.)

(SEE ALSO: *Court Systems of the United States; Criminal Sanctions; Criminology; Social Control*)

REFERENCES

Albonetti, Celesta, and John Hepburn 1997 "Probation Revocation: A Proportional Hazards Model of the Conditioning Effects of Social Disadvantage." *Social Problems* 44(1):124–138.

Allen, Harry E., Chris Eskridge, Edward Latessa, and Gennaro Vito 1985 *Probation and Parole in America*. New York: Free Press.

Blumstein, Alfred, Jacqueline Cohen, Jeffrey Roth, and Christy Visher (eds.) 1986 *Criminal Careers and "Career Criminals."* Washington, D.C.: National Academy Press.

Bureau of Justice Statistics 1989 *Prisoners in 1988* (bulletin). Washington, D.C.: U.S. Department of Justice.

Champion, Dean J. 1990 *Probation and Parole in the United States*. Columbus, Ohio: Merrill.

Clear, Todd, and George F. Cole 1986 *American Corrections*. Belmont, Calif.: Brooks/Cole.

Covey, Herbert C., and Mary Mande 1985 "Determinate Sentencing in Colorado." *Justice Quarterly* 2:259–270.

Erwin, Billie S. 1986 "Turning Up the Heat on Probationers in Georgia." *Federal Probation* 50:17–24.

Geerken, Michael, and Hennessey Hayes 1993 "Probation and Parole: Public Risk and the Future of Incarceration Alternatives." *Criminology* 31(4):549–564.

Gendreau, Paul, Francis Cullen, and James Bonta 1994 "Intensive Rehabilitation Supervision: The Next Generation in Community Corrections?" *Federal Probation* 58(1):72–78.

Gottfredson, Michael, and Don M. Gottfredson 1988 *Decision Making in Criminal Justice*. New York: Plenum.

Heilbrun, Alfred 1999 "Recommending Probation and Parole." In Allen Hess and Irving Weiner, eds., *The Handbook of Forensic Psychology*. New York: John Wiley.

Hester, Thomas 1988 *Probation and Parole, 1987*. Washington, D.C.: U.S. Department of Justice.

Lisefski, Edward, and Donald Manson 1988 *Tracking Offenders*. Washington, D.C.: U.S. Department of Justice.

McAnany, Patrick D., Doug Thomson, and David Fogel (eds.) 1984 *Probation and Justice: Reconsideration of a Mission*. Cambridge, Mass.: Oelgeschlager, Gunn and Hain.

McCorkle, Richard, and John Crank 1997 "Meet the New Boss: Institutional Change and Loose Coupling in Parole and Probation." *American Journal of Criminal Justice* 21(1):1–26.

McDonald, William F. 1985 *Plea Bargaining: Critical Issues and Common Practices*. Washington, D.C.: U.S. Department of Justice.

Martinson, Robert 1974 "What Works? Questions and Answers about Prison Reform." *Public Interest* 35:22–54.

Meeker, James, and Henry M. Pontell 1985 "Court Caseloads, Plea Bargains, and Criminal Sanctions: The Effects of Section 17 P.C. in California." *Criminology* 23:119–143.

Morris, Norval, and Michael Tonry 1990 *Between Prison and Probation: Intermediate Punishments in a Rational Sentencing System*. New York: Oxford.

Petersilia, Joan 1985 *Probation and Felony Offenders*. Washington, D.C.: U.S. Department of Justice.

—— 1987 *Expanding Options for Criminal Sentencing*. Santa Monica, Calif.: Rand.

——, Susan Turner, James Kahan, and Joyce Peterson 1985 *Granting Felons Probation: Public Risks and Alternatives*. Santa Monica, Calif.: Rand.

Quinn, James, and John Holman. "Electronic Monitoring and Family Control in Probation and Parole." *Journal of Offender Rehabilitation* 17(3–4):77–87.

Turner, Susan, Joan Petersilia, and Elizabeth Deschenes 1992 "Evaluating Intensive Supervision Probation/Parole (ISP) for Drug Offenders." *Crime and Delinquency* 38(4):539–556.

U.S. Sentencing Commission 1987 *United States Sentencing Commission Guidelines Manual*. Washington, D.C.: U.S. Sentencing Commission.

von Hirsch, Andrew 1976 *Doing Justice*. New York: Hill and Wang.

JOSEPH G. WEIS

PROFESSIONS

The idea of a "profession" did not exist in ancient times. Although there were people who did what is currently denoted as professional work, these "professionals" often labored in dependent positions. For example, physicians in the Roman Empire were slaves in wealthy households, and architects worked as salaried public employees. Lawyers in ancient Greece were merely friends of the litigants who spoke before a gathering of their peers. Neither lawyers nor physicians received formal training (Carr-Saunders and Wilson 1937). By medieval times, the three classic professions—medicine, law, and the clergy (which included university teaching)—began to approximate more closely the modern conception of professions. With the development of universities, then under religious auspices, would-be professionals completed lengthy training in their chosen fields. They also began to constitute a new class of intellectuals. As society increasingly secularized, the professions emerged from under religious control and began to organize professional associations. By the eighteenth century, they had achieved independent status.

In the nineteenth century, middle-class occupations such as dentistry, architecture, and engineering began to professionalize, aspiring to the gentlemanly status of the classic, learned professions (Dingwall and Lewis 1983). "Gentlemanly" was the appropriate description, since the majority of professionals were men. It was not until the 1970s that women began to make significant inroads into these occupations, and even today men predominate in the status professions.

In the nineteenth and early twentieth centuries, professionalism developed in concert with the increasing division of labor and rationalization characteristic of industrializing Europe and the United States. As competitors in market economies, occupational incumbents sought to professionalize to improve their status. In addition, they wanted to better their economic positions by securing occupational niches for their services (Ritzer and Walczak 1986). In the United States, at least, universities played the key role of transferring both the technical know-how and the culture of professionalism to new generations of professional aspirants (Bledstein 1976).

WHICH OCCUPATIONS ARE PROFESSIONS?

Today the term "profession" includes a range of occupations arrayed along a continuum of high to medium levels of prestige. At the high end of the continuum are the classic, or "status," professions of medicine, law, clergy, and university teaching. Incumbents in these occupations usually receive high incomes, exercise job autonomy, and receive deference from the public and those lower in the status hierarchy. Although women have begun to gain entry into some of the professions, most professions remain predominantly male: in 1998, women's representation among physicians, lawyers, and the clergy was 27, 28, and 12 percent, respectively. Women have made more progress moving in to college and university teaching, representing 42 percent of incumbents by 1998 (all 1998 data are from U.S. Bureau of Labor Statistics 1999, Table 11).

Somewhat lower on the continuum are the "newer" professions such as dentistry, engineering, accounting, and architecture, which also command respect and relatively high salaries. Men also predominate in these occupations: 20, 11, and 18 percent of dentists, engineers, and architects, respectively, were women in 1998. Only in accounting have women made significant inroads: 58 percent of all accountants and auditors were women in 1998. This feminization is attributable largely to accounting's dramatic occupational growth in the 1970s (Reskin and Roos 1990, pp. 40–41).

Still lower on the professional continuum are the "marginal professions" (e.g., pharmacy, chiropractic) and the "semiprofessions" (e.g., nursing, public school teaching, social work, librarianship). These occupations exhibit some characteristics of the classic professions but have not acquired full professional status because of opposition from established professions and an inability to convince the public that they command unique expertise. These occupations are less prestigious and their incumbents are paid less than those in either the classic or the new professions. Moreover, because they are concentrated in bureaucratic settings, these professionals exercise less job autonomy than higher-status professionals. An important difference between the marginal professions and the semiprofessions is that males are in the majority in the former (although pharmacy, an occupation that has feminized rapidly in recent years, is now 44 percent female), whereas semiprofessions have long been predominantly female (in 1998 women composed 92, 75, 68, and 83 percent of nurses, public school teachers, social workers, and librarians, respectively).

Paraprofessionals work with, but as subordinates to, members of the other professions. They are generally technicians associated with various professional occupations. Paralegals, for example, work closely with lawyers, and physicians delegate certain tasks and responsibilities to physicians' assistants. As in the semiprofessions, women tend to predominate in paraprofessional occupations. These data clearly show the sex-stratified nature of professional occupations, but these occupations are also stratified by race: in 1998, for instance, 5 percent of physicians were black, 6 percent of college and university teachers, 4 percent of lawyers, and 9 percent of clergy, notably less than their 11 percent representation in the labor force as a whole. Blacks are overrepresented, relative to their labor-force representation, in the following professions: dietitians (18 percent); respiratory therapists (12 percent); prekindergarten and kindergarten teachers (14 percent); educational and vocational counselors (13 percent); social workers (23 percent); recreation workers (16 percent); athletes (13 percent).

THE PROCESS OF PROFESSIONALIZATION

Given the stratification of the U.S. occupational structure, it is clear why workers desire to professionalize. Professionalization brings higher income, higher prestige, greater job autonomy, and higher job satisfaction. It also protects incumbents from competition. The "process of professionalization" posits a common sequence of development that occupations undergo. Some scholars accept Harold Wilensky's depiction of this process (1964). First, people begin to work full time at a specific set of tasks that will form the new occupation's core jurisdiction. Second, those in the occupation establish a university-affiliated training program, and some incumbents undertake the responsibility for training new generations of practitioners. Third, practitioners and teachers combine to form a professional association that identifies the occupation's core tasks and makes claims regarding skill jurisdiction. Fourth, occupational incumbents seek to protect their jurisdictional claims by political means. Professionals lobby for legal protection, in the form of licensing and certification requirements, to generate labor-market shelters that ensure their monopoly of skills. Finally, incumbents develop a formal code of ethics that embodies rules to protect clients, eliminate the unqualified, and spell out the occupation's service ideal. As we shall see, later theorists have come to question this linear sequence of events.

APPROACHES TO THE STUDY OF THE PROFESSIONS

What distinguishes the professions from other occupations? Theoretical approaches in studying this question have changed over time and remain in flux. Scholars have also developed new methods to address these questions.

The Trait Approach. After World War II, the trait approach was dominant in scholarship on the professions (Freidson 1986). Scholars—mostly American academics—tried to define the professions by generating an exhaustive list of characteristics. These traits, scholars hoped, would distinguish professions from nonprofessions and higher-status professions from those of lower status. The main method used was the case study.

Scholars carefully scrutinized particular occupations to determine how well they approximated the four major criteria, or traits, of the ideal-typical profession (Hodson and Sullivan 1990). First, professionals are experts with abstract, esoteric knowledge and skills that set them apart from others. Second, because of their unique expertise, professionals exercise autonomy on the job. Codes of ethics help to ensure autonomy from outside control by permitting professionals to police misconduct internally. Third, their esoteric knowledge allows professionals to claim authority over their clients and subordinate occupational groups. Finally, the professions are altruistic, that is, service-rather than profit-oriented. Underlying these four traits is a fifth: the public must recognize the occupation as a profession. Regardless of an occupation's claim of unique expertise, if the public does not view the occupation's knowledge as abstract, it is difficult for those working in it to claim professional status and the perquisites that accompany it.

Scholars used these criteria to differentiate among the professions, most particularly in comparing the female semiprofessions to the typically male status professions. While the semiprofessions have a body of knowledge, they lack a monopoly over that knowledge. They also have a difficult time convincing the public that their skills are professional. The public is less likely to recognize their expertise (e.g., teaching children, servicing library patrons) as particularly esoteric. Semiprofessionals typically work in bureaucratic settings and, as a consequence, are subject to heteronomy, or supervision by organizational superiors and professional colleagues. Their ability to claim autonomy is limited.

The Power Approach. In the 1960s, scholars in the United States and Great Britain began to criticize the trait approach as static and ideological. Recognizing the salience of culture and social structure, power theorists also shifted to historical methods to understand the sources of professional power. They argued that occupations we view as professions do not necessarily exhibit the requisite traits, but rather have the power to convince the public that they do. Power theorists viewed the professions as monopolistic organizations intent on gaining and retaining professional control and ensuring their status in the stratification system. Eliot Freidson (1986), for example, focused on how professions establish protected labor markets for their services. Magali Sarfatti Larson (1977) argued that the professions are market organizations in the capitalist economy, explicitly seeking to dominate the market for their expertise.

For these theorists, the so-called objective characteristics of the trait approach are ideological attempts to preserve the professions' status and privilege (Freidson 1986). Rather than being truly altruistic, professional incumbents create the myth

of service orientation to gain public goodwill, enhance their status, and minimize external control. According to this view, professionals sometimes abuse their autonomy by failing to police themselves, and incompetent doctors and lawyers fleece the public with little fear of reprisal from their peers. Finally, the professional's authority over clients has also declined in recent years as a more educated public has become active in activities seen as the province of professionals (e.g., getting second opinions on medical recommendations and becoming more educated consumers regarding medical and legal issues).

The historical battles between physicians, on the one hand, and pharmacists and chiropractors on the other, illustrate how an established profession exercises power against competing occupations (Starr 1982). When the pharmacist's traditional task of compounding drugs shifted to pharmaceutical companies, they lost their diagnostic expertise (and hence monopoly over their knowledge). With respect to chiropractors, the American Medical Association restricted access through licensing laws or blocked reimbursement from private insurance companies. As a consequence, pharmacy and chiropractic have yet to become fully professional.

What enables professions to wield power? Theorists point to the occupational characteristics indeterminancy and uncertainty (Ritzer and Walczak 1986). The professions that have achieved and maintained power are those whose tasks cannot be broken down or otherwise routinized (indeterminancy). Similarly, those that deal with areas of uncertainty are also likely to preserve their power. As Wilensky (1964) described it, professional knowledge involves a "tacit" dimension, in Polanyi's (1967) terminology. Their lengthy training and years of practical application ensure that physicians "know" what treatments to use for which symptoms. Similarly, lawyers "know" what legal strategies work best and college professors "know" what instructional strategies are most effective in enhancing student learning. Reading a textbook or consulting computerized data bases is not equivalent to tacit knowledge. This kind of knowledge—expertise refined by years of experience—is not easily routinized. Physicians and lawyers also deal with areas of high uncertainty for their clients, the former with physical health and the latter with legal affairs. Clients need these professionals to translate medical and legal jargon into everyday language they can more readily understand.

The System of Professions. Andrew Abbott's (1988, 1995) theory of professions critiqued the notion that professions undergo a common process of development. Employing historical and comparative methods, Abbott provided a wealth of evidence that the history of the professions is much more complicated than that represented in a linear process of professionalization. Rather than a history of professions that established systems of control (e.g., schools, professional associations, licensing and certification), Abbott's account is of ongoing interprofessional competitions, squabbles over jurisdictions, and professional births and deaths.

Abbott contended that professions make up an interdependent "system of professions." Understanding modern professions entails articulating their histories of conflict with other professions. Comprehending the realities of modern medicine, for example, depends more on investigating its historical conflicts with closely related professions such as psychiatry and chiropractic than on the particulars of medieval or nineteenth-century medicine.

Recognizing the interdependence of professions is important because it clarifies that professions emerge, grow, change, and die within the historical context of competition with other professions. This competition takes the form of jurisdictional disputes over the control of abstract knowledge. Professionals can use their abstract knowledge to define a core set of tasks (their jurisdiction), defend that jurisdiction from others, or appropriate the tasks of others. Interprofessional boundary wars reflect professions' attempts to "enclose" jurisdictional tasks within the boundaries of their profession's sphere of influence (Abbott 1995, p. 553; see also Witz 1992). One recent example of such a jurisdictional dispute was pediatric medicine's partially successful attempt to expand their sphere of influence to include children's psychosocial disorders (Halpern 1990). Whether professions succeed or fail in such jurisdictional disputes, any changes reverberate throughout the system. The professions reequilibrate, with some occupations accepting a subordinate or advisory role, some agreeing to split jurisdictions or clients, and others exiting the professions altogether. To

adequately theorize and model jurisdictional disputes, Abbott (1993, p. 205) advocated a multilevel analysis that links micro-level information on careers, to meso-level data on the network structure of careers and jobs, to the macro-level work and occupational structures.

SEX DIFFERENCES IN THE PROFESSIONS

In 1998, women composed 46 percent of the employed labor force and 53 percent of professionals, suggesting that women do quite well in the professions. However, a closer look reveals a different story. As noted, women are heavily concentrated in the semiprofessions (as nurses, public school teachers, social workers, and librarians) and men in the higher-status professions (as physicians, lawyers, and engineers). Incumbents in the former earn less and exercise less autonomy than in the latter. As in the occupational structure as a whole, the professions are highly segregated by sex.

Even within the higher-prestige professions, women work in different, lower-paying, and less prestigious jobs than men. Women lawyers, for example, work in government jobs, in research rather than litigation, and in certain specialties such as trust and estates; women physicians are more likely than men to specialize in pediatrics and to work in health maintenance organizations (HMOs); female clergy specialize in music or education (Reskin and Phipps 1988; see also Tang and Smith 1996).

Part of the reason for this differential job distribution by sex has to do with a characteristic unique to the professions. The high level of uncertainty inherent in prestigious professional jobs means that employers are careful to choose recruits who "fit in" with those already on the job. Thus, as Rosabeth Moss Kanter (1977) suggested, employers tend to recruit people much like themselves, a process she calls "homosocial reproduction." The predominance of males in the status professions thus helps to reproduce sex segregation.

Other factors reducing women's access to high-status professions are entrance restrictions such as certification and licensing. Physicians, for example, consolidated their control over medical jurisdictions by successfully pressing for legislation to outlaw midwives and prohibit the licensing of those trained at "irregular" schools, activities that disproportionately affected women. In 1872, the Supreme Court restricted women's ability to practice law, arguing that "the natural and proper timidity and delicacy which belongs to the female sex unfits it for many of the occupations of civil life" (Reskin and Phipps 1988, p. 192). Male professionals were thus able to establish labor-market shelters to protect themselves from competition from women as well as other "undesirables."

Since 1970, women have gained greater entry into some of the professions, including occupations such as medicine, law, and pharmacy. Indications are, however, that internal differentiation within the professions perpetuates job segregation by sex (Reskin and Roos 1990). For example, Polly Phipps (1990) found that women's representation in pharmacy nearly tripled (from 12 to 32 percent) between 1970 and 1988, and has continued to increase since then, reaching 44 percent by 1998. However, women pharmacists concentrate in the lower-paying hospital sector, while men predominate in the higher-paying retail sector. Similar ghettoization exists in other professions that are admitting more women (see, for example, Reskin [1990] on book editors; Donato [1990] on public relations specialists; Roos and Jones [1993] on academic sociologists; and Roos and Manley [1996] on human resource managers and professionals).

THE CHANGING PROFESSIONS

Some view the future of the professions as bleak, predicting that ongoing proletarianization or deprofessionalization will eliminate the professions' unique traits. The proletarianization thesis argues that an increasing division of labor and a bureaucratization within the professions are routinizing knowledge and transferring authority from professionals to organizational superiors. The deprofessionalization thesis documents declines in the professions' monopolistic control over their knowledge, their exercise of autonomy on the job, their ability to protect their jurisdiction from encroachments, and the public's deference to professional authority (Ritzer and Walczak 1986).

Some occupations, of course, have lost some of their professional status. As noted, as pharmaceutical companies increasingly absorbed the compounding of drugs, and as chains replaced independent pharmacies, pharmacists lost some of

their autonomy and monopoly of their knowledge to physicians. Taking a broad view of the professions, however, Freidson (1984; 1994, p. 9) argued that professionalism has been "reborn" in a hierarchical form in which bureaucratization and professionalization are often quite compatible. Working in organizations, he argued, has been the norm for many professions from their inception, with engineers the most obvious example. In addition, organizations that employ professionals tend to diverge enough from the ideal-typical bureaucracy to protect professional privilege. For example, professionals in organizations often exercise a lot of autonomy, working under senior members of their own profession rather than nonprofessional managers. Freidson thus portrayed most organizations as working to accommodate professionals, and operating under an "occupational principle" of authority, as opposed to an "administrative principle" of organizing and controlling work (1994, p. 61). Wallace (1995) also described how some bureaucratic work systems—specifically a "corporatist" model of control—can be quite compatible with professionals' self interests.

Like Freidson and Abbott, Brint (1994) viewed the professions as social forms that evolve historically in conjunction with other occupations and work organizations. Rather than look to professions interacting through jurisdictional disputes, however, Brint contextualized changes in the professions within the workplace itself, in the occupationally and organizationally based ties professionals have, and the markets in which they work (see also Leicht and Fennell 1997). He described the ascendance of a new, organizationally based profession—expert professions—that relaxes traditional assumptions about professional work. Pursuing profits, closer interconnections with business, and lesser attention to larger public interests, are all hallmarks of "expert professionalism" (Brint 1994, p. 8), which Brint juxtaposed with "social trustee professionalism," the traditional conception of professions as the trustees of socially important knowledge (p. 4). In Brint's view, the professional class has splintered into highly skilled experts in resource-rich organizations as opposed to professionals with less marketable skills in resource-poor organizations, especially in the public and nonprofit sectors (p. 11). These differing organizational locations have predictable consequences for incumbents' political and social views.

Even with such changes, Freidson (1984, 1994) found no evidence that the prestige of the professions as a whole has declined. Nor did he find that public trust in professionals has deteriorated relative to other American institutions. Moreover, the professions' continuing ability to erect labor-market barriers to competition is important evidence of their enduring power. Professionals today remain strong enough to exert their will against others lower in the occupational hierarchy. Professional privilege remains intact in the American occupational structure.

As the professions change, theorizing must evolve as well. Some have begun to call for a broader, synthetic theory of occupations, one that situates the professions in a comparative way within the larger occupational structure (e.g., Abbott 1993; Freidson 1994). Central to such a broader theory is a method that sets occupations not only in their historical, comparative contexts, but also in the organizational and market context in which occupational incumbents work (e.g., Brint 1994). Freidson (1994, p. 21) has argued for moving beyond a theory that defines professions by fiat, to one that recognizes the professional aspirations of a variety of other nonprofessional occupations. In Freidson's terminology, how do ordinary occupational incumbents invoke their day-to-day work activities so as to claim professional status, regardless of whether the larger public would recognize them as professionals? Such a conceptualization opens up the possibility that other occupations can organize in their own self-interest to generate their own "professional projects." Claiming a unique expertise or specialized knowledge, developing professional associations, and convincing the state that certification is appropriate are first steps toward claiming professional status. Ultimately, the true test of professional status will be to convince others that the expertise one has entitles one to professional privilege, and to the right to establish labor market shelters. Only then will professional status and earnings rise to accompany claims of professional privilege.

REFERENCES

Abbott, Andrew 1988 *The System of Professions: An Essay on the Division of Expert Labor.* Chicago: University of Chicago Press.

—— 1993 "The Sociology of Work and Occupations." *Annual Review of Sociology* 19:187–209.

—— 1995 "Boundaries of Social Work or Social Work of Boundaries." *Social Service Review* 4:545–562.

Bledstein, Burton J. 1976 *The Culture of Professionalism: The Middle Class and the Development of Higher Education in America.* New York: W. W. Norton.

Brint, Steven 1994 *In an Age of Experts: The Changing Role of Professionals in Politics and Public Life.* Princeton: Princeton University Press.

Carr-Saunders, A. M., and P. A. Wilson 1937 "Professions." In Edwin R. A. Seligman and Alvin Johnson, eds., *Encyclopaedia of the Social Sciences.* New York: Macmillan.

Dingwall, Robert, and Philip Lewis 1983 *The Sociology of the Professions: Lawyers, Doctors and Others.* London: Macmillan.

Donato, Katharine M. 1990 "Keepers of the Corporate Image: Women in Public Relations." In Barbara F. Reskin and Patricia A. Roos, eds., *Job Queues, Gender Queues: Explaining Women's Inroads into Male Occupations.* Philadelphia, Pa.: Temple University Press.

Freidson, Eliot 1984 "The Changing Nature of Professional Control." *Annual Review of Sociology* 10:1–20.

—— 1986 *Professional Powers: A Study of the Institutionalization of Formal Knowledge.* Chicago: University of Chicago Press.

—— 1994 *Professionalism Reborn: Theory, Prophecy, and Policy.* Chicago: University of Chicago Press.

Halpern, Sydney 1990 "Medicalization as Professional Process: Postwar Trends in Pediatrics." *Journal of Health and Social Behavior* 31:28–42.

Hodson, Randy, and Teresa A. Sullivan 1990 *The Social Organization of Work.* Belmont, Calif.: Wadsworth.

Kanter, Rosabeth Moss 1977 *Men and Women of the Corporation.* New York: Harper and Row.

Larson, Magali Sarfatti 1977 *The Rise of Professionalism: A Sociological Analysis.* Berkeley: University of California Press.

Leicht, Kevin T., and Mary L. Fennell 1997 "The Changing Organizational Context of Professional Work." *Annual Review of Sociology* 23:215–231.

Phipps, Polly A. 1990 "Industrial and Occupational Change in Pharmacy: Prescription for Feminization." In Barbara F. Reskin and Patricia A. Roos, eds., *Job Queues, Gender Queues: Explaining Women's Inroads into Male Occupations.* Philadelphia, Pa.: Temple University Press.

Polanyi, Michael 1967 *The Tacit Dimension.* Garden City, N.Y.: Anchor.

Reskin, Barbara F. 1990 "Culture, Commerce, and Gender: The Feminization of Book Editing." In Barbara F. Reskin and Patricia A. Roos, eds, *Job Queues, Gender*

Queues: Explaining Women's Inroads into Male Occupations. Philadelphia, Pa.: Temple University Press.

———, and Polly A. Phipps 1988 "Women in Male-Dominated Professional and Managerial Occupations." In Ann H. Stromberg and Shirley Harkess, eds., *Women Working. Theories and Facts in Perspective.* Mountain View, Calif.: Mayfield.

Reskin, Barbara F., and Patricia A. Roos 1990 *Job Queues, Gender Queues: Explaining Women's Inroads into Male Occupations.* Philadelphia, Pa.: Temple University Press.

Ritzer, George, and David Walczak 1986 *Working. Conflict and Change,* 3rd ed. Englewood Cliffs, N.J.: Prentice-Hall.

Roos, Patricia A., and Katharine Jones 1993 "Shifting Gender Boundaries: Women's Inroads into Academic Sociology." *Work and Occupations* 20:395–428.

Roos, Patricia A., and Joan E. Manley 1996 "Staffing Personnel: Feminization and Change in Human Resource Management." *Sociological Focus* 29:245–261.

Starr, Paul 1982 *The Social Transformation of American Medicine: The Rise of a Sovereign Profession and the Making of a Vast Industry.* New York: Basic.

Tang, Joyce, and Earl Smith (eds.) 1996 *Women and Minorities in American Professions.* Albany, N.Y.: State University of New York Press.

U.S. Bureau of Labor Statistics 1999 *Employment and Earnings,* vol. 46. Washington, D.C.: U.S. Government Printing Office.

Wallace, Jean E. 1995 "Corporatist Control and Organizational Commitment among Professions: the Case of Lawyers Working in Law Firms." *Social Forces* 73:811–839.

Wilensky, Harold L. 1964 "The Professionalization of Everyone?" *American Journal of Sociology* 70:137–158.

Witz, Anne 1992 *Professions and Patriarchy.* New York: Routledge.

PATRICIA A. ROOS

PROSTITUTION

See Sexual Behavior Patterns; Legislation of Morality; Sexual Violence and Exploitation.

PROTEST MOVEMENTS

Protest movements have been of high interest to sociological research since the inception of the discipline in the mid-nineteenth century, during the periods of great industrial and urban development in Europe and North America. In the context of massive changes in the economic structure and mass rural-to-urban and cross-national migration, a variety of protest movements developed. They caught the attention of Comte, Le Bon, Weber, and other early sociological analysts. In the United States, the first widely used introductory sociology textbook, developed by Chicago School sociologists Robert Park and Ernest Burgess in the 1920s, was organized around the concepts of collective behavior. Protest movements occupied a substantive part of the text.

Sociologists' interest in protest movements reflects the high interest of many who are not sociologists and are not research oriented. Such movements have the potential of affecting lives in substantial ways. This is particularly so when a protest touches on wide public concerns. In American society, the recognition of the potential impact of protest movements is encompassed within the framework of the U.S. Constitution's First Amendment guarantee of the right of the people peaceably to assemble and to petition the government for redress of grievances.

The language of the First Amendment, including the right to "peaceably" protest, is in recognition that protest movements can turn violent. Rebellion on taxes and other violent protest in the 1780s had strongly influenced the desire of those at the Constitutional Convention in 1787 to expand democratic public expression while outlawing violent means of bringing about protest movement changes. The language of the First Amendment reflects the potential power of protest ideas. Any consideration of protest movements needs to include the effects of those, like James Madison and Thomas Jefferson in the case of the amendment language, whose articulated ideas about grievances provide a key element in active protest emergence.

While most protest movements in the United States and in other democratically based societies have been mostly peaceful, there is a stream of protests which have not been peaceful. There are many examples of protest movements with no or little violence, including the multiple women's protests for more rights and opportunities throughout the nineteenth and twentieth centuries; the food and drug protection movement in the early twentieth century; the early- and late-twentieth century environmental protest movements for cleaner air, water, and protection of endangered species and open spaces; and the protest marches of 1998 in many communities and in Washington, D.C., which resulted in new record public expenditures for cancer research at a time of budget cutbacks in most government programs. In contrast, examples of protest movements that generated periodic violence include the labor movement protests to nonresponsive corporations and legislatures from the late nineteenth century through the 1930s, the racial- and ethnic-led civil rights protest since the mid-twentieth century, and the anti–Vietnam War protest movement of the late 1960s and the early 1970s.

As not all protest movements succeed, or may succeed at a frustratingly slow pace for participants, protest activists in these protests went beyond democratically legitimate means of protest. When that occurs generally, the basis exists for violent protest episodes. Protest movements may also generate violence in opposition to a protest movement from those whose perceived vested interests and way of life are threatened. Such violence may occur to intimidate people and prevent them from engaging in protests, one clear aim of the hundreds of lynchings of black citizens in the first half of the twentieth century. Violence may occur in the context of a counterprotest movement to reverse a successful movement, as in the case of the bombings and physician killings at abortion clinics following the successful establishment of the legal right of women to seek and have an abortion.

Whether violent or nonviolent, protest movements have the potential of being an interim form of collective challenge to some aspect of the social status quo. The protest continuum ranges from localized groups and crowds that organize around specific and short-term delimited grievances to mass protest movements about social conditions and perceived injustices. These mass protests are designed to generate comprehensive and fundamental changes in a society and sometimes across societies. More so than localized acting crowds and less so than systemic social movements, protest movements encompass mass behavior that extends beyond a localized situation, and they have the potential of generating social movements

when a variety of conducive conditions exists (Gusfield 1968; Smelser 1962; Tilly 1978).

The twentieth century has been characterized by a wide variety of protest movements. In the United States, industrial protests were common for the first third of the century, as were anti-immigration protests. The suffragette protest movement early in the century was a precursor to the women's movement for equal treatment and opportunity in the last third of the century. The civil rights movement, led by blacks in the 1950s and 1960s, precipitated countermovements—a common characteristic of protest movements—including the White Citizen's Council protests and the reemergence of the Ku Klux Klan. Poor people in Chile, El Salvador, Nicaragua, and other Latin American countries have protested the privileges of an elite economic class as vestiges of an unproductive and rigid class colonial structure. Such protest movements are evident globally, with protest occurrences in Africa, the Middle East, and Asia.

A common thread through the wide variety of protest movements is their political nature. In various ways governmental authority is challenged, changed, supported, or resisted in specific protest movements. To advance their prospects for success, protest movement leaders often engage in coalition politics with more powerful individuals and groups who, for their own interests and values, support the challenge raised by the movement. When protest movements succeed in generating sufficient public support to secure all or most of their goals, governments may offer policy legitimization of the movement as a means of adapting to, coopting, or modifying a movement's challenge to the state of premovement affairs.

Such political legitimation has taken a variety of forms. The labor protest movements culminated in the passage of the National Labor Relations Act of 1935, which legitimized labor-management collective bargaining and negotiated agreements. The suffragette movement resulted in passage of the Nineteenth Amendment to the Constitution, guaranteeing that the right to vote in the United States could not be denied or abridged on account of sex. The civil rights movement attained support with passage of the comprehensive Civil Rights Act in 1964 and then the Economic Opportunity Act and the Elementary and Secondary Education Act, both in 1965. All these system-modifying acts, which affect the lives of millions in American society, have continued in effect during relatively high and low periods of public support. This gives evidence of the long-term societal legitimation of these acts, which grew out of protest movements.

Success of these and other movements is often tempered by countermovements, participants in which perceive their relative positions and interests to be threatened. For instance, the women's movement experienced a series of challenges from religious groups, often fundamentalist, that adhered to a male-dominated patriarchy. As a consequence, women's progress was slowed in winning various forms of equal treatment and opportunity in educational, economic, political, and social areas of life, and in the 1970s and the 1980s Congress failed to pass the Equal Rights Amendment (ERA) to the U.S. Constitution, which was supported by the women's movement.

More generally, after passage of civil rights legislation in the mid-1960s, a series of protest movements within the Democratic and, more extensively, the Republican parties resulted in growing administrative, legislative, and judicial resistance to equality in educational, occupational, and housing opportunities. The countermovement result has been a reentrenchment of a long-established economic structure of racism and low-income class rigidity that functions independently of personalized racist feelings and beliefs (Wilson 1987). A reflection of such countermovement pressure is the growth in perception among white males that affirmative action educational and occupational policies directed toward racial and ethnic minorities and women constitute a form of reverse, or affirmative, discrimination (Glazer 1989).

Countermovements have generated their own counterprotest movements. This countermovement variation of Hegelian dialectic does not result in a return to whatever constituted premovement normalcy. In conventional political terms the results are more conservative, reactionary, liberal, or radical than what existed before the protest movement. When protests and counterprotests result in social change, such change generally affects the participants in a specific protest movement as well as established authorities in ways often not fully anticipated. While a predominant orientation may exist among protest activists and another among established authorities, in complex, mass modern societies, a range of political orientations is usually contending among protestors and their supporters and among established authorities and their supporters, against whom the protest is directed.

The U.S. civil rights movement of the 1950s and 1960s can be viewed in historical terms, if not contemporary terms, as a primarily conservative movement. The predominant, although not all-encompassing, aim of activists and organizations was to enable blacks and other minorities to break into the democratically value-based, but not fully practiced, political and economic system. Most protest leaders and participants did not aim to break the established system. In contrast, the late 1980s and early 1990s liberal to radical protest movements in Poland, Hungary, Rumania, and other eastern European countries did have as their goal the breakdown of the system of exclusive authoritarian political and economic domination.

In the United States, protest ideologies are largely reminiscent of established, liberal, democratic political ideals. This is evidenced in the way many protest groups adopt language from the Declaration of Independence to advance their aims. For example, the Black Panthers, popularly perceived as a radical group, adopted a statement of purpose that held, "We hold these truths to be self-evident, that all black and white [sic] men are created equal and endowed by their creator with certain unalienable rights." Similarly, the National Organization for Women inserted into its declaration of purposes the wording that "men and women" are created equal.

Protest movements attain mixed and sometimes changed results. These results occur because of institutional inertia, in which certain things have been done certain ways over a long period of time, and because of countermovements within institutional centers such as schools; businesses; and local, state, and national government offices. In the United States, reactions to the civil rights movement have resulted in private and public attitudes and behavior that have combined to support inclusion of some minority members while disadvantaging more severely the lowest-income racial and ethnic minorities (Wilson 1987). The result is that the countermovement resistance to educational, economic, and political advances for minority status groups has adversely affected the poorest racial and ethnic minority members. At the same time, census bureau reports document a growing number and proportion of blacks, women, and other minority group members moving into educational institutions, occupational settings, and political positions from which they were formerly excluded de jure or de facto.

Examples from history and other cultures demonstrate the mixed potential and results of protest movements. The German Nazi protest movement in the 1920s illustrated that a movement could be radical *and* reactionary, in that case toward further destabilization of the Weimar Republic's democratic government, which was perceived as being decreasingly effective and legitimate by growing sectors of the German public (Shirer 1960). After the Nazis succeeded in countering various democratic and communist protest movements, Germany saw a more comprehensive institutionalization of Nazi ideological and authoritarian control during the 1930s. An historic, more recent example is the 1989 Chinese student democratic movement in Tianenmen Square that resulted in a government-sponsored countermovement that physically shattered the student protest and created a system of political, economic, and educational controls that were more comprehensively rigid than those that existed before the protest movement. Yet, the underlying educational, economic, and political forces that generated the Chinese student activists continued to affect the dynamics of Chinese society, with the potential for further protest activation.

In these and other protest movements, there is a wide range of participants and of protest methods employed. Along with the nature of the social context and historical influences, the characteristics of protest participants and the methods they employ are consequential and have been central concerns of research on such movements.

PROTEST PARTICIPANTS AND METHODS OF PROTEST

If protest participants could alleviate their grievances or sense of injustice individually, there would be no likely motivation for them to become active in a protest movement. Protest participants thus have two central characteristics: (1) they have insufficient influence to gain a desired change in their circumstances, and (2) they seek active association with relatively like-minded persons to gain relief from their aggrieved state.

These two characteristics can be seen among protest participants over time and in different locales. In the 1960s civil rights movements in the United States, leading activists—including blacks, Hispanics, Native Americans, and women—expressed a strong sense of unequal treatment and opportunity while associating with and supporting activists to achieve equal opportunities in schools, jobs, elected offices, and other social settings. College students, the most active participants in the civil rights movement, could not generally be characterized in these minority status terms. Yet, they were not yet an established part of the economic and political order being challenged and were in a position to be critical of that order (Lipset 1971). Other participant supporters, such as labor unions, selected corporate leaders, and religiously motivated persons, often saw protest-related change needed in terms of their own long-term interests and worked either to help the civil rights movement succeed or to preempt or coopt it (Gamson 1990, pp. 28–31). The broad political support base for the comprehensive 1964 Civil Rights Act had all these protest movement participant elements.

The individuals who are most likely to initiate and support a protest movement tend to be those with long-developed grievances within a society. A case in point is Solidarity, the labor group that precipitated the successful 1980s protest movement against communist rule in Poland and that helped precipitate other successful eastern European protest movements. The initial work stoppage, instrumental in offering a political challenge to Polish and Soviet authority, occurred at the Lenin shipyard in Gdansk, a center of Cassubian ethnic residence. For generations Cassubians have held a minority status in Polish society (Lorentz 1935). As the protest movement proceeded to secure broad-based support among Polish citizens, it was no accident that Cassubians, who have experienced prejudice and discrimination beyond communist rule in Poland, would be at the forefront. It is not surprising that Solidarity was led by a Cassub, Lech Walesa. It is also noteworthy that the protest movement received strong support from another Cassub, Pope John Paul II, whose original name of Karol Wojtyla ends with a Cassubian "a" rather than the more typical Polish "ski."

In the United States, the civil rights movement was manifestly initiated and led by blacks. Jews, who have experienced more prejudice and discrimination than most other whites in American society, where they constitute less than 2 percent of the population, composed the largest group of whites in the movement. In the Congress of Racial Equality (CORE), one of the leading mass civil rights protest organizations, almost one-half of the white participants identified themselves as Jewish or as secularists whose parents were Jewish (Bell 1968).

The methods employed by protest participants and leaders tend to reflect a lack of institutionalized power. When such institutionalized power is available, it can be exercised to redress grievances without resorting to mass protests. Within democratic political processes in the United States and in other democratic societies much organized protest on such issues as trade policies, road construction and placement, and taxation can be viewed in more normative, adaptive terms.

When such normative activities do not result in a resolution of grievances, the potential for a protest movement increases. In such a context, legitimized guarantees of the right to protest, as embedded in the U.S. Constitution's First Amendment guarantee of the right to assemble and petition for redress of grievances, do not preclude protest strategies that go beyond legal or normative boundaries of protest behavior.

Methods of protest are related to prospects of success and levels of frustration. When a protest movement or a countermovement has broad public support and is likely to receive a positive response from targeted authorities, protest activities are likely to be peaceful and accepted by such authorities. Such is the case with pro-choice protest on the abortion issue; protest for clean air; and protest in support of Christian, Jewish, and other minority religious status groups in the Soviet Union. All these protest activities have relatively broad American support, even when they experience a minority activist opposition.

A variety of nonlegitimate strategies are used when protest movements address issues and involve participants with relatively little initial public support and active opposition. One such nonlegitimate strategy is Ghandi's nonviolent protest confrontation with British authorities in India. Adapted by Martin Luther King, Jr., and most other black civil rights protest leaders in the 1950s and early 1960s, the strategy of nonviolence was designed to call general public attention in a nonthreatening manner to perceived injustices experienced by blacks. With such techniques as sit-ins at racially segregated lunch counters and boycotts of segregated public buses, this nonviolent method generated conflict by breaking down established social practices. The aim of such nonviolent methods is to advance conflict resolution by negotiating a change in practices that produced the protest. A particularly famous case is the 1955 Montgomery, Alabama, bus boycott, which was one of several major precipitants of the national black-led civil rights movement.

Other, violent forms of protest include both planned strategies and unplanned spontaneous crowd action. In either case such activity tends to be perceived by authorities and their supporters as disorderly and lawless mob behavior. Masses of protest participants are likely to be drawn to violent action when the general perception, or emerging norm (Turner and Killian 1986, pp. 21–25), develops that redress of felt grievances is believed to be unattainable either in normal conditions before protest activation or by peaceful means. The history of violent protest is extensive in many societies, as exemplified by the forcible occupation of farms and fields by landless French peasants in the eighteenth century, American attacks on British possessions and military posts prior to the Declaration of Independence, and bread riots by Russian urban dwellers in World War I. The particular centuries-long history of violent protest movements in American society was documented in context of the urban race riots and anti–Vietnam War protest in the 1960s by the presidentially appointed National Commission on the Causes and Prevention of Violence in the United States (Graham and Gurr 1969).

Violent protests usually concern specific issues such as taxes, conscription into the military, and food shortages, issues that are confined to particular situations and times. Although these types of protest do not evolve into major social movements, they may have severe and immediate consequences. In 1863, for instance, during the Civil War, Irish Catholics protested what they perceived as the unfair nature of the military draft in New York City. This protest left several hundred dead. Likewise, many college students in the late 1960s and the early 1970s revolted against the draft during the unpopular Vietnam War, and the results included loss of student lives at Kent State University.

Unplanned violence may also be a form of protest. As reported by the National Advisory Commission on Civil Disorders and other research on over two dozen urban racial riots in the 1960s in the United States, these riots, which resulted in over a hundred deaths and over $100 million in property damage, were disorganized extensions of the black civil rights movement. These violent events closely fit Davie's J-curve thesis (1974), which argues that rising expectations, such as those generated by legal successes in mid-1960s by the black civil rights movement, were frustrated by the declining urban ghetto environments and growing Vietnam War tensions, both of which were related to the fact that large numbers of blacks were being drafted while most white college students were exempted.

Overall, protest movements are more frequent in societies that legitimize the right of protest. In such societies, social conflict generated by protest movements is often functional in resolving conflict over issues between challenging and target groups (Coser 1956). Still, urban and campus riots of the 1960s illustrate that formal rights of protest do not deter democratic authorities and their public supporters from responding with police force or from beginning a countermovement. Authoritarian societies may experience fewer protest movements, but when they do occur, such movements are far more likely to be intense and to have the potential for massive social movements designed to transform the society. This could be seen in widely disparate societies, including most eastern European nations and the Soviet Union, El Salvador, Nicaragua, South Africa, Iran, and mainland China.

CONSEQUENCES OF PROTEST MOVEMENTS

Given the long and continuing history of protest movements, there has been growing interest in the long-term consequences of such movements. Some assessments concentrate on historical, comparative analysis such as Snyder and Tilly's analysis (1972) of French collective violence in response to government-sponsored repression between 1830 and 1968, or Bohstedt and Williams's analysis (1988) of the diffusion of riotous protests in Devonshire, England, between 1766 and 1801. Other studies of long-term consequences make empirical assessments of the aftermath of more contemporary protest movements. Examples include Gordon's community-based assessment (1983) of black and white leadership accommodations in the decade following the Detroit race riots of 1967 and Morris's assessment (1980) of the decade-long impact on national public values of the environmental movement of the late 1960s.

The need for more short- and long-term assessment of the consequences of protest movements is evident in reviews of past movements. William Gamson's consideration of fifty-three protest movements in the United States between the 1830s and 1930s illustrates the need. Gamson categorized each movement's own specific goals in one of four ways: coopted, preempted, full response success, and collapsed failure (Gamson 1990, pp. 145–453). Gamson assessed each protest movement's success in achieving its goals during its own period of organized activity. For instance, Gamson assessed such groups as the German American Fund (1936–1943), the American Proportional Representation League (1893–1932), and the Dairyman's League (1907–1920).

Of the fifty-three identified protest movements, twenty-two, the largest single proportion, were categorized as being collapsed failures, twenty as achieving full response success, six as being preempted, and five as being coopted. Protest movements categorized as collapsed failures and full response successes demonstrate the need for assessment of protest movements long beyond their activist periods. Listed under collapsed failures were major long-term successful movements including the abolitionist North Carolina Manumission Society (1816–1834) and the American Anti-Slavery Society (1833–1840). In contrast, among full response success movements was the American Committee for the Outlawry of War (1921–1929), a major force in the achievement of the international Kellogg-Briand Pact of 1928, which outlawed war between nations, a short-lived success that for at least most of the rest of the twentieth century proved a grand failure.

Successful or unsuccessful in the short or the long term, protest movements are periodically a part of social change at local, national, and global levels and in situational, institutional, and cross-cultural contexts. In the United States and other modern mass urban societies, the long-term trend has been for protest movements to become more professionalized with increased mobilization of resources to more effectively challenge entrenched interests (Tilly 1978). Modern communication systems, global economic interdependence, and economical movement of masses of people over great distances assures that protest movements of the future will increasingly be characterized by a combination of ideas, people, and organization across all these areas of social life.

In contemporary terms, the historical end of the global Cold War at the end of the twentieth century with the collapse of the Soviet Union generated a basis for increased localized protest movements. This was initially evident in the former Soviet Union's sphere of influence in eastern European societies and within Russia itself. On the eve of the twenty-first century, evidence of this broadening localized protest activism was to be seen in many societies as exemplified by student-led protests in Indonesia, Chiapas Indian revitalization protests in Mexico, the Quebec separatist movement in Canada, the Queens' Borough protest to separate from New York City in the United States, and many others. In this context, the supply of localized protest issues is likely to proliferate. At the same time, some issues—such as protests associated with such transnational issues involving the environment and health—may touch upon many localized issues that coalesce into becoming national and global protest activities. Given massive economic, political, and social change forces in modern society and the potential for protest movements to directly affect the lives of many people, the concern of research specialists and publics with such movements can be expected to continue and to increase.

(SEE ALSO: *Segregation and Desegregation; Social Movements; Student Movements*)

REFERENCES

Bell, Inge Powell 1968 *CORE and the Strategy of Non-Violence*. New York: Random House.

Bohstedt, John, and Dale E. Williams 1988 "The Diffusion of Riots: The Patterns of 1966, 1795, and 1801 in Devonshire." *Journal of Interdisciplinary History* 19(1):1–24.

Coser, Lewis 1956 *The Functions of Social Conflict*. New York: Free Press.

Davies, James C. 1974 "The J-Curve and Power Struggle Theories of Collective Violence." *American Sociological Review* 39:607–612.

Fogelson, Robert 1971 *Violence as Protest: A Study of Riots*. New York: Anchor.

Gamson, William A. 1990 *The Strategy of Social Protest*. Homewood, Ill.: Dorsey.

Glazer, Nathan 1989 *Affirmative Discrimination*. Cambridge, Mass.: Harvard University Press.

Gordon, Leonard 1983 "Aftermath of a Race Riot: The Emergent Norm Process among Black and White Community Leaders." *Sociological Perspectives* 26:115–135.

Graham, Hugh D., and Ted Gurr (eds.) 1969 *The History of Violence in America: Report of the National Commission on the Causes and Preventions of Violence*. New York: Bantam.

Lipset, Seymour M. 1971 *Rebellion in the University*. Boston: Little, Brown.

Lorentz, Friedrich 1935 *The Cassubian Civilization*. London: Faber and Faber.

Morris, Aldon D. 1984 *The Origins of the Civil Rights Movement: Black Communities Organizing for Change*. New York: Free Press.

Morris, Denton 1980 "The Soft Cutting Edge of Environmentalism: Why and How the Appropriate Technology Notion Is Changing the Movement." *Natural Resources Journal* 20:275–298.

Mueller, Carol, and Charles Judd 1981 "Belief Consequences and Belief Constraint." *Social Forces* 60:182–187.

Shirer, William 1960 *The Rise and Fall of the Third Reich*. New York: Simon and Schuster.

Smelser, Neil J. 1962 *Theory of Collective Behavior*. New York: Free Press.

Snyder, David, and Charles Tilly 1972 "Hardship and Collective Violence in France: 1830 to 1960." *American Sociological Review* 37:520–532.

Tilly, Charles 1978 *From Mobilization to Rebellion*. New York: McGraw-Hill.

Turner, Ralph, and Lewis M. Killian 1986 *Collective Behavior*. Englewood Cliffs, N.J.: Prentice-Hall.

Wilson, William J. 1987 *The Truly Disadvantaged: The Inner City, The Underclass, and Public Policy*. Chicago: University of Chicago Press.

RECOMMENDED READINGS

Gamson, William A. 1990 *The Strategy of Social Protest.* Homewood, Ill.: Dorsey.

Tilly, Charles 1978 *From Mobilization to Rebellion.* New York: McGraw Hill.

LEONARD GORDON

PUBLIC OPINION

Public opinion is characterized, on the one hand, by its form as elementary collective behavior (Blumer 1972) and, on the other, by its functions as a means of social control (Ross 1901). It comes into play in situations that are problematical or normatively ambiguous in one or more of several senses: The situation is novel and unprecedented, so that established ways of coping no longer prove adequate, people actively disagree over which of several conventionally acceptable practices should apply, or the conventions themselves have come under serious challenge by a dissident group. In the extreme case, controversy over what should be done can heat up to a point where order gives way to violent group conflict.

Interest in public opinion is historically linked to the rise of popular government. Although rulers have always had to display some minimum sensitivity to the needs and demands of their subjects, they felt little need, unlike most contemporary governments that must face voters in mandated elections, to anticipate their constituents' reactions to events that were yet to occur or to policies still to be implemented. But public opinion operates equally outside the relationship between citizens and the state. Its influence is felt throughout civil society, where, on many matters, including personal taste in dress, music, and house furnishings, people remain sensitive to the changing opinions of peers and neighbors. They court approval by showing themselves in step with the times.

Opinions have behind them neither the sanctity of tradition nor the sanctions of law. They derive their force from agreement, which is more tenuous than either of these. People do change their minds. Moreover, to label something as "opinion" implies a certain willingness to acknowledge the potential validity of contrary views. Issues are settled by discussion and bargaining. Those who pay at least some attention and are ready to take sides make up a public. It expands in size as an issue heats up, only to contract again as the focus shifts to new problems. There are, in fact, as many publics as there are issues.

Social control through public opinion functions in subtle ways. All but the most intransigent partisans will recognize when an issue is settled to a point where further debate becomes not only superfluous but possibly disruptive of an underlying consensus. There are times when the need to display unity, perhaps in coping with a crisis, or moral fervor, whipped up in crusades against internal enemies, may unduly narrow the range of public discourse. Dissidents come under pressure to conform, at least outwardly, but not as completely as in the regimes that suppress public opinion by seeking control over all conversational channels through which ideologically deviant tendencies could spread.

Studies of public opinion have to contend with a broad range of beliefs. Located at one extreme are beliefs anchored in longstanding allegiances; at the other, the often fluctuating "gut" responses to whatever is current. The more general ideas that underlie the legitimacy of the political system have the greatest stability. They build on childhood experiences within the family, where children tend to adopt the views of their parents. Then, as the children become adults, these early beliefs are elaborated and modified in sustained contact with other major institutions, like school and church, and also (especially during major catastrophes affecting their country or its leaders) by the news media (Renshaw 1977). The content of the political culture from which opinions are derived differs from milieu to milieu.

Endemic cleavages related to position in social structure and in historical time are highlighted during controversies. Hence, public opinion often divides in predictable ways—by region, race, religion, ethnicity, class background, educational attainment, and so forth. If the differences in experience are sharp enough and each side raises nondebatable demands, public discourse can escalate to a point where the polity splits apart into two irreconcilable camps. Instead of reaching agreement, the more powerful group imposes its will.

Acquiescence does not qualify as rule by public opinion.

In the center of early sociological study of public opinion has been the question of competence. Analysts have sought to distinguish conceptually between the reasoned opinions developed in discussion and the clamor of a feared "mob" acting under the sway of emotion. Two works, one in Germany and one in America, coincidentally published the same year, analyzed the problem in structural terms.

Tönnies (1922) pointed to the press and to associations that usurped for themselves the role of articulating public opinion. He would have been even more critical of the public relations industry that has flourished since. For Lippmann (1922) there was a still more fundamental obstacle. He rejected as a false ideal the notion that ordinary citizens—even the most well-educated—had the time and incentive to acquire the expertise to grasp the complex problems of the day in the detail necessary to direct the course of public policy. Drawing on a wide range of literature, he showed how the public perceived the world through the stereotypes fed them by the press. This meant, he argued, that whenever the public attempted to intervene in the course of events, it inevitably did so as the dupe or unconscious ally of elite interests. Its role was properly limited to identifying the problem areas in need of remedial action and to deciding which party, institution, or agency should be entrusted with the solution. But the public was a potentially effective "reserve force" most effectively mobilized in support of the procedural norms of democracy. Contemporary contractualists, like Buchanan and Congleton (1998), have come to share Lippmann's emphasis on generalized procedures about which near unanimity is more easily achieved than about policies that inevitably produce winners and losers.

The list of social scientists pointing from different perspectives to the limits of "rule by public opinion" under modern conditions includes Mannheim (1940), Schumpeter (1942), Schattschneider (1960), Bogart (1972), and Ginsberg (1986). An all-too-obvious gap between the expectation of an informed citizenry put forward by democratic theory and the discomforting reality revealed by systematic survey interviewing is identified by Neuman (1986) as the "paradox of mass politics." Where pluralists see a public made up of many competing interests, each with its own leadership, Neuman discriminates among three levels of competence: an uncomfortably tiny percentage of citizens with some input into policy; uninterested and inactive know-nothings, who make up roughly one-fifth of the potential electorate; and a large middle mass whose members, if they vote, do so largely out of a sense of duty but with only a very limited understanding of the issues their vote is meant to decide. This discrepancy from the ideal, apparent in many polls on specific issues, can hardly be attributed to flaws in the method by which public opinion is ascertained.

PUBLIC OPINION POLLING

There are nevertheless some real questions about the momentary numerical majorities obtained in an opinion poll as a valid measure of public opinion. For one thing, polls vary in quality. How closely any particular poll reflects the distribution of opinion within a larger population hinges on three general factors: (1) who is interviewed, (2) the situation in which the interview takes place, and (3) the questions asked. Insofar as elections also provide a public record of "opinion," the utility of polls as a research tool can be tested against the actual vote count.

Two fiascoes in polling history have been painstakingly diagnosed. Never again will we see anything like the wildly incorrect 1936 forecast by the *Literary Digest* that Franklin D. Roosevelt, who won reelection by a landslide, would be voted out of office. It was based on 2.3 million returns from over 10 million straw ballots mailed to names on automobile registration lists and in telephone books. Poll takers learned the hard way that, especially when respondents are self-selected, sheer numbers do not guarantee accuracy. For one thing, the well-to-do, who owned cars and lived in homes with telephones, were somewhat less supportive of Roosevelt and his New Deal than those too poor to have either or both such conveniences. A second, actually more important, source of bias was self-selection; Republicans were more strongly motivated than Democrats to mail in their straw ballot as a protest against the party in power.

When in 1948 the pollsters, despite more rigorous sampling and face-to-face interviews,

wrongly predicted the defeat of incumbent President Harry Truman, this became the occasion for one of the most extensive inquiries into polling practices by a committee of the Social Science Research Council (Mosteller et al. 1949). Its report stressed the importance of random selection, in which every voter stands the same chance of being contacted, an objective often difficult to implement. Polling techniques have come a long way since and errors of such magnitude have not reoccurred. But, as shown by an investigation by Crespi (1988) of the factors associated with accurate prediction in 430 preelection polls during the 1980s, the extra effort invested in callbacks still pays off in greater accuracy. Persons missed because they are hard to reach or because they refuse to answer often differ from the rest in ways difficult to estimate.

As to the interview situation, answering the questions of a poll taker is hardly the same as casting a vote, all the more so when the election is months away. The large margins by which Truman had been trailing in the early fall of 1948 caused several pollsters to cease polling weeks before voting day. Thus, they never registered the strong Democratic rally taking place toward the end of the campaign. Another problem is determining how firm respondents are in their convictions and who will actually vote on election day. Despite refined techniques to ferret out likely nonvoters, predicting the outcome of a low-turnout election with little-known candidates and in referendums on questions beyond the understanding of many voters can be hazardous.

Public opinion research covers much more than elections, where the "issue" boils down to a clear split between parties, candidates, or those for or against a measure on the ballot. Issues come and go, and people do not necessarily have preconstructed views on everything about which polls may ask but tend to construct their answers in an ad hoc manner from information that, at the moment, strikes them as salient (Zaller 1992). Just as pollster have learned to omit from their tabulations of preelection surveys the likely nonvoters, so various "filters" are used to screen out persons who are generally unconcerned about politics, have given the particular subject little thought, and may not have even been aware of it except for the questions put to them. To avoid eliciting

"nonattitudes," as responses from such persons are called, they should be asked no further questions about the matter. This still leaves those reluctant to admit their unfamiliarity or lack of concern. One survey that deliberately inserted a question about a nonexistent bill allegedly under consideration by Congress had significant minorities respond that they had heard of it, with some even willing to fabricate an opinion about it.

Insofar as responses depend on how a question is phrased, different polls can provide dramatically different readings of where the public stands. Various polls on impeachment during Watergate, all about the same time, recorded levels of support ranging from a high of 53 percent on a question with the condition "if it were "decided that President Nixon was involved in the coverup" attached to a low of 10 percent on a question that offered resignation as an alternative to impeachment. Similarly, after Gallup modified its original question, which had coupled "impeachment *and* removal from office," by first explaining impeachment and then asking, "Given the various charges brought against the president, do you think impeachment charges should be brought against him or not?" support for impeachment jumped from 37 to 53 percent.

Views on many subjects are too nuanced to be caught in response to a single question. Few people are absolutists on most issues. On abortion, a highly contentious issue, it is not just being "pro choice" or "pro life" in all situations. One can deny that abortion is a constitutional right and still allow it under certain circumstances—when conception has resulted from rape or when abortion is necessary to save the life of the mother. Some legal restrictions are likewise acceptable for supporters of *Roe v. Wade*. Similar distinctions are called for in polling on "affirmative action," a term that stands for a welter of different policies. Explicit preferences, even as a redress for past discrimination, are endorsed by no more than a minority, but outreach programs to locate qualified minorities and/or women enjoy wide support. To correctly assess what is on people's mind requires a series of probing questions.

Nor do apparent majorities always speak as clearly as the student of public opinion would like. In a 1971 poll, a time when concern over American

involvement in Vietnam was higher than any other issue on the public agenda, two out of three respondents answered the question, "Do you favor or oppose the withdrawal of all American troops from Vietnam by the end of the year?" by declaring themselves in favor of withdrawal. But on another question in the same survey, about withdrawing all troops "regardless of how the war was going," these same respondents split with a plurality of 44 percent against and only 41 percent still for withdrawal. Does this 25-point difference between the 66 percent in favor of withdrawing on the first question and the 41 percent on the second identify a group ready to take back an off-the-cuff answer when reminded of the possible consequences of such a move? Or were those giving a "consistent" response confident that South Vietnam would not fall? There is still a third possibility: A lot of people no longer cared whether or not America was forced to withdraw in defeat. An undetermined number among them may, in fact, have welcomed such an outcome.

Sometimes the public does indeed hold views that seem contradictory, but the logic people follow may differ from that of the analyst, as it did during Vietnam, when polls were recording, at one and the same time, majorities in support of both immediate withdrawal and a stepped-up air war on the North. Others who considered American intervention in Vietnam a mistake still spoke out in favor of President Lyndon Johnson's Vietnam policy. Nor, for that matter, were self-styled "doves" necessarily in sympathy with student protests against the war.

For all their potential pitfalls, polls are one of the best ways for political leaders to maintain contact with their increasingly large and diverse constituencies—a more reliable reading for sure than such alternative indicators of public opinion as letters, telegrams, phone calls, and petitions to political leaders, which may reflect nothing more than the effort of a well-organized interest group. Yet even minorities, if implacable enough, should not always be ignored. A rise in the number who refuse draft calls or desert from the armed forces; a rise in certain crimes; and an increase in demonstrations, strikes, and other forms of protest are important clues, not necessarily to general opinion but at least to the unwillingness of the groups most affected by some problem to settle for the status quo (Tilly 1978). They signal problems or injustice that call for recognition by the rest of society.

DYNAMICS OF PUBLIC OPINION

Changes in the basic attitudes that underlie public opinion usually occur slowly, partly through replacement and partly through the diffusion of new experience. Differential birth rates, migration, social mobility, and the succession of generations are processes that disturb the existing balance without any change on the individual level and despite evidence of significant political continuity between parents and offspring. Distinct intergenerational differences are believed to develop in response to certain critical experiences, like the encounter, in early adulthood before one's outlook has fully crystallized, with general poverty and war, or participation in social struggles (Sigel 1989).

Attitudes on race are a good example of how diffusion and replacement operate in conjunction with each other. Surveys taken over time show a distinct movement toward greater racial tolerance (Schuman and Bobo 1985). All groups moved in the same direction, even if at different speeds. The younger generation showed the way, often with tacit support from sympathetic parents not yet ready themselves to join a radical challenge to segregation. Rising levels of education and the increase in certain kinds of intergroup contact also contributed to the shift, as did mortality among the older, more conservative cohorts. Especially noteworthy is that, in regions where segregationist practices were most firmly entrenched, opinion changed more rapidly than in the rest of the country, once the full force of national public opinion had been brought to bear on them through television. The pervasive coverage the national media gave the campaign for civil rights conveyed to even the most intransigent southerners how the rest of the country viewed their continuing resistance. While issues relating to race continue to divide the polity, the terms in which they are debated were never to be the same again.

The day-to-day shifts in public opinion on matters great and small are even more subject to influence by the media of mass communication. Most of the public is not issue-oriented but reacts to the general image of presidential performance. "Good" news of any kind tends to bolster that image, with one major exception: a national crisis. Such events typically generate a rally to the flag; critical voices are stilled, at least temporarily, in a show of patriotic unity. Effective political leadership under any condition requires access to the news media.

In their comprehensive review of American policy preferences over a half-century, Page and Shapiro (1992) show that, on thirty-two foreign and forty-eight domestic issues for which there were adequate data, the media coverage explained a large part of the movement of opinion in polls. However, they go on to note that opinions on none of these issues changed very much. The main influence of heightened media coverage, as repeatedly documented by communication research, is to move an issue or a problem into the public sphere, followed by an increase of concern and discussion, which then puts pressure on government to do something. When the press plays up crime, this helps create the impression of a crime wave, just as vivid details about a disaster drive home its magnitude. Serious discussion about the nature, causes, and consequence in the media of what came to be called "child abuse" facilitated its recognition as a social problem calling for intervention (Nelson 1984).

Once there is concern, the issue itself undergoes change. The actions of the principal actors involved in Watergate, as reported by the media, moved the debate away from Nixon's involvement in the illegal break-in into Democratic headquarters to his obstruction of justice, abuse of power, and contempt of Congress—the three counts on which the House Judiciary Committee voted for impeachment (Lang and Lang 1983). A similar kind of shift occurred in the "sex" scandal surrounding Bill Clinton. What began as the exposé of an improper affair with a White House intern was progressively redefined into whether the president had perjured himself and whether this felony, if committed by a president in connection with a civil suit later found without merit, rose to the level of an impeachable offense.

Media power is nevertheless limited. First of all, opinions, once they have crystalized, respond more to actual changes in circumstances than to media messages. Second, the potential influence of the media varies according what they report about. It is obviously greater when they expose widespread corruption in high places, report on a mishap in foreign relations, or highlight something that hardly anyone would ever know about unless alerted by the news media. Far less dependent on media recognition are inflation, shortages, a severe economic downturn, and other events. Neither they nor specific grievances anchored in shared group experience will go away for mere lack of mention. Third, media managers are less than fully independent. They have to accommodate other actors intent on publicizing only those issues (or aspects of issues) that work in their favor. While competition among the various practitioners of the highly developed art of news management introduce some balance, public discussion, and (indirectly) public opinion do respond to media strategies not so much aimed at persuasion as bent upon seizing the right issues.

PUBLIC OPINION AND POLICY

As to the effects of opinion change, leaders of major institutions, whether elected or not, have proved distinctly sensitive to trends in public opinion. The measure most consistently repeated over the most years is the presidential approval ratings. Most presidents have experienced a gradual slide during their terms in office, which Mueller (1973) attributes to a coalition of all the minorities that, over the years, will have been antagonized by the many decisions a president as the chief executive is forced to make. At least two American presidents have been driven from office by clear evidence of a loss of public support. Lyndon Johnson, with the failure of his Vietnam policy glaringly evident to all, took himself out of the race for reelection, even though as an incumbent president he would have been assured renomination as the standard bearer of his party (Schandler 1977). Public outrage during Watergate forced Richard Nixon to make several concessions and, ultimately, to resign after the Supreme Court forced the release of tapes with the incriminating evidence that made his impeachment and subsequent removal from office a near certainty (Lang and Lang 1983). Twenty-five years later, a president's high approval, despite his publicly acknowledged wrongdoing, caused Republicans in both houses of Congress, who wanted to hold him responsible, to frame the issue in the most narrow legal terms lest their moves backfire.

Congress, knowing that public opinion responds to events, sometimes even to the turn of a debate, often moves cautiously on potentially divisive issues. When Franklin Roosevelt tried to pack the Supreme Court and Nixon resisted the full exposure of Watergate, legislators were inclined to wait, watching to see which way the public tilted. And when it came to civil rights, major legislation was passed only after mass demonstration and media attention to discriminatory practices had created public concern and support for the principle had reached or exceeded the two-thirds mark. Laws subsequent to the initial pathbreaking legislation could then be enacted without direct pressure from below. But none of these things could have been achieved without effective political leadership responsive to the just demands of an obvious minority, which Johnson, still enjoying the honeymoon bequeathed an incoming president, was able to provide.

The accumulating evidence points to a basic congruence between public opinion on basic issues and legislative action (cf. Monroe 1998; Page and Shapiro 1983). Even the decisions of a judiciary with lifelong tenure are not entirely insulated from the political cross-currents that affect representative institutions. The U.S. Supreme Court, the most august of judicial bodies, as Marshall (1989) concludes, has been an essentially majoritarian institution. Of 142 decisions from the mid-1930s to the mid-1980s for which there existed corresponding opinion data, over four-fifths have been consistent with preferences expressed in polls. The linkage, strongest in times of crisis, reflects more the court's sensitivity to legislative and executive concerns that incorporate public opinion than direct to public pressure on the judges.

It is on the constitutional rights of dissident minorities that the Supreme Court has most consistently set itself against majority opinion. Other countermajority opinions have either articulated a rising trend, strengthened by the voice of the court, or been modified by later decisions that, in an apparent response to public opinion, carved out exceptions and introduced qualifications to the broad rule laid down in the original case. Public opinion continues to play a role in how

these court decisions are implemented. Following a decade of increasingly liberal attitudes toward abortion, the issue seemed settled once and for all by *Roe v. Wade*. Though the massive campaign prolifers have mounted since has had little impact nationally, states vary in their laws and practices. The states in which opposition to abortion has been strong have generally adopted more restrictive policies, resulting in lower abortion rates, than states in which the weight of public opinion was to make it a matter of choice (Wetstein 1996).

THE ERA OF POLLS

Elites have always been under some constraints, even in dealing with the more obscure issues typically resolved through specialized networks. Sheer prudence nevertheless commands that appearances be managed. This is done today, more than ever before, on the basis of increasingly accurate information from polls. Experts on polling have become members of the advisory staff not only of candidates for major offices but also of national party organizations. They also work in the White House and are consulted by presidents about proprietary polls which, unlike those sponsored by the media, especially during election season, the public rarely sees. There is little persuasive evidence so far about how the current high volume of polling activity has affected the political process.

One perhaps not very obvious consequence is the dissemination of a view on public opinion as statistics on a set of questions instead of a process to determine of what people will ultimately settle for. The public, too, is somewhat suspicious of polls. A large proportion of those queried on the subject believe that polls have effects and, particularly, that the majorities they record generate bandwagons even though these same people vehemently deny that the polls would have any effect on themselves. Nor has the variety of split-ballot polls and experiments, in which only one of two matched samples is informed about of the majority viewpoint, turned up differences large enough to support what many apparently fear. Noelle-Neumann (1984), in a more elaborate formulation, has shifted the emphasis away from direct bandwagons (i.e., people rushing to join the majority) to more complex sequences of events. She reasons that people who perceive themselves as being in the minority, even if falsely, are reluctant to speak out against the dominant opinion, thereby creating a spiral of silence through which the apparent majority gains extra strength. Such spirals have no doubt occurred, for example during the repressive era remembered as McCarthyism. But to generalize from this and other instances is to overlook situations in which committed minorities have raised their voices to compensate for what they lack in number. Polls do function as a corrective by reporting on opinions that, although underrepresented in the forums which most public discourse takes place, are too important to ignore.

Polls have other significant consequences insofar as those who rely on them react strategically. They certainly influence the choice of candidates, the platform and program on which a candidate or party stands for election, and the policies an administration pursues. Candidates who can demonstrate electability attract the financial support, endorsements, and media coverage necessary for an effective campaign. Citizens, too, vote strategically whenever they abandon a likely loser in favor of a minimally acceptable second choice. This is what gives a front-runner in the polls the momentum to increase his or her distance from the pack of competitors early in the primary season (Bartels 1988). A strong showing can also have a potential downside: A victory by less than the anticipated margin, even in a small state with low turnout and therefore difficult to predict, has sometimes been read as a defeat. Hence, candidates often work to lower expectations regardless of what their own polls may show.

Polls on the concerns and issue preferences of the electorate allow campaign managers to maximize their candidates' appeal. Political actors who act rationally, rather than ideologically, will moderate the more doctrinaire positions cherished by their loyal followers, who have no other place to go. According to the spatial model of politics first outlined by Downs (1957), parties and candidates are impelled to move toward the political center to reach out to the still uncommitted. More and more do the modern catch-all parties, competing for an ever-larger share of the electorate, rely on general promises and finely honed advertisements. They differentiate themselves more by the image the party seeks to project than by any clearly defined policies. Practices of this sort are bound to feed voter cynicism about the political system. One would also expect adverse effect on traditional party loyalties.

Republican leaders who heralded their success in 1994, an off-year election in which they took over both houses of Congress, as an endorsement of the party's Contract with America, quickly learned about the danger of being taken in by their own campaign slogans. At least their managers must have known that, as late as two weeks before the election, 65 percent of the public polled by the Gallup Organization had not yet even heard of the contract and that, according to another poll just days before the election, only 7 percent of those interviewed said they would be more likely to vote for the Republican candidate for Congress if he or she supported the contract. Acting as if they had a clear mandate, the Republicans in Congress made this their legislative agenda and, when embroiled in a budget dispute with the Democratic president, forced three closedowns of government. President Clinton's approval ratings rose sharply, and Republicans, who had misread the election results, lost credibility. By the same token, Democratic gains in 1998 plus polls showing clear majorities opposed to impeachment apparently misled the Clinton White House to underestimate the determination of House Republicans to bring down the president. Electoral results are not carbon copies of the public mood.

There is no question that elites are now in a better position than ever before to anticipate the public reaction to whatever they may do. Accurate information is all the more vital when the loosening of ideological bonds has forced an elected leader to engage in a continuous campaign for popularity. Such a leader has good reason to adopt the majority point of view on issues about which the public feels strongly and to save his political capital for other less salient issues, on which views have not yet crystalized. This is where Geer (1996) locates the opportunities for effective leadership. Informed by polls, a president now is in a better position to identify these issues than were presidents in previous eras, several of whom exercised what Geer calls "leadership by mistake." But although a democratic leader must accede to at least some of the wishes of his followers, failure to lead when possible would amount to more than a missed opportunity; it would be a serious mistake, because it cedes the territory to the opposition, which presumably has access to the same information and no hesitation to exploit it.

Still, what counts in the long run are the results. A leadership too sensitive to what a majority prefers at a given moment may sidestep a problem that cries for remedies the public is not yet prepared to approve. The absence of serious policy debates becomes an open invitation to topple a leader with personal attacks on his character and by grasping at every sign of a possible scandal. Other complications stem from the fact that governing majorities are coalitions of sometimes rather diverse interests, many of them organized and in possession of expertise beyond the comprehension of most citizens. Things of overriding importance to one interest may be anathema to all the others. The voice of the people comes across most clearly when the multitude is truly stirred by an all too apparent failure of policy or misbehavior in high places. It is on these occasions that the power of the public as a "reserve force," wisely or otherwise, is felt most directly.

REFERENCES

Bartels, Larry M. 1988 *Presidential Primaries and the Dynamics of Public Choice*. Princeton, N.J.: Princeton University Press.

Blumer, Herbert 1972 "Outline of Collective Behavior." In Robert R. Evans, ed., *Readings in Collective Behavior*. Chicago: Rand McNally.

Bogart, Leo 1972 *Polls and the Awareness of Public Opinion*. New York: John Wiley.

Buchanan, James M., and Roger D. Congleton 1998 *Politics by Principle: Toward Nondiscriminatory Democracy*. New York: Cambridge University Press.

Crespi, Irving 1988 *Pre-Election Polling: Sources of Accuracy and Error*. New York: Russell Sage.

Downs, Anthony 1957 *An Economic Theory of Democracy*. New York: Harper.

Ginsberg, Benjamin 1986 *The Captive Public: How Mass Opinion Promotes State Power*. New York: Basic Books.

Lang, Gladys Engel, and Kurt Lang 1983 *The Battle for Public Opinion: The President, the Press, and the Polls During Watergate*. New York: Columbia University Press.

Lippmann, Walter 1922 *Public Opinion*. New York: Macmillan.

Mannheim, Karl 1940 *Man and Society in an Age of Reconstruction*. New York: Harcourt, Brace.

Marshall, Thomas 1989 *Public Opinion and the Supreme Court*. Boston: Unwin Hyman.

Monroe, Alan D. 1998 "Public Opinion and Public Policy, 1980–1993." *Public Opinion Quarterly* 62:6–28.

Mosteller, Frederick, Herbert Hyman, Philip J. McCarthy, Eli S. Marks, and David B. Truman 1949 *The Preelection Polls of 1948*, Bulletin 68. New York: Social Science Research Council.

Mueller, John E. 1973 *War, Presidents, and Public Opinion*. New York: John Wiley.

Nelson, Barbara 1984 *Making an Issue of Child Abuse: Agenda Setting for Social Problems*. Chicago: University of Chicago Press.

Neuman, W. Russell 1986 *The Paradox of Mass Politics: Knowledge and Opinion in the American Electorate*. Cambridge, Mass.: Harvard University Press.

Noelle-Neumann, Elisabeth 1984 *The Spiral of Silence*. Chicago: University of Chicago Press.

Page, Benjamin I., and Robert Y. Shapiro 1983 "The Effects of Public Opinion on Policy." *American Political Science Review* 77:175–190.

—— 1992 *The Rational Public: Fifty Years of Trends in Americans' Policy Preferences*. Chicago: University of Chicago Press.

Renshaw, Stanley A. (ed.) 1977 *A Handbook of Political Socialization*. New York: Free Press.

Ross, Edward A. 1901 *Social Control: A Survey of the Social Foundations of Order*. New York: Macmillan.

Schandler, Herbert J. 1977 *The Unmaking of a President: Lyndon B. Johnson and Vietnam*. Princeton N.J.: Princeton University Press.

Schattschneider, E. E. 1960 *The Semisovereign People: A Realist's View of Democracy in America*. Hinsdale, Ill.: Dryden Press.

Schuman, Howard, and Lawrence Bobo 1985 *Racial Attitudes: Trends and Interpretations*. Cambridge, Mass.: Harvard University Press.

Schumpeter, Joseph A. 1942 *Capitalism, Socialism, and Democracy*. New York: Harper and Row.

Sigel, Roberta S. (ed.) 1989 *Political Learning in Adulthood: A Sourcebook of Theory and Research*. Chicago: University of Chicago Press.

Tilly, Charles 1978 *From Mobilization to Revolution*. New York: Random House.

Tönnies, Ferdinand 1922 *Kritik der öffentlichen Meinung*. Berlin: Springer.

Wetstein, Matthew E. 1996 *Abortion Rates in the United States: The Influence of Opinion and Policy*. Albany: State University of New York Press.

Zaller, John 1992 *The Nature and Origin of Mass Opinion*. New York: Cambridge University Press.

KURT LANG

PUBLIC POLICY ANALYSIS

Public policy analysis is a large, sprawling intellectual enterprise involving numerous academic disciplines, private research organizations, and governmental agencies each sharing a common concern with the formulation, implementation, or consequences of public policy decisions. There are approximately thirty journals published in the English language alone and nearly twenty professional associations that are devoted more or less exclusively to policy analysis. Departments, centers, and institutes dealing in whole or in part with policy analysis can be found at over forty American universities.

As currently practiced, policy analysis involves contributions from the entire gamut of scientific disciplines. Much present-day public policy analysis is undertaken by scholars from the various applied physical and biological sciences (for example, environmental impact studies, technology assessments, seismic risk analyses, and the like). The focus here, however, is on public policy analysis as it is conducted within the social and behavioral sciences, principally economics, political science, and sociology.

The diversity of research work conducted under the rubric of "public policy analysis," even when restricted to the social science component, is perhaps the distinguishing characteristic of the subject; in the space available here we can do little more than indicate the range of topics and approaches with which policy analysts are concerned. Rogers (1989) has developed a typology of public policy research that is useful for this purpose; the following is adapted from his discussion.

PROBLEM DEFINITION OR NEEDS ASSESSMENT

Public policy usually addresses real or sensed problems, and a great deal of public policy analysis is therefore devoted to defining or clarifying problems and assessing needs. What are the health care needs of a particular neighborhood? What are the housing or nutritional needs of the nation's poverty population? What social services do homeless persons require? It is obvious that the development and formulation of public policy will be enhanced when underlying needs have been adequately described and analyzed. There is a large literature on the theory and practice of problem definition and needs assessment; students seeking additional information will find Johnson and colleagues (1987) invaluable.

VALUE EXPLORATION OR CLARIFICATION

Given a demonstrated need, any number of policies might be developed to address it. Which policies, goals, or outcomes are most desirable? If an area is found to have unmet health needs, is it better to open freestanding clinics or to provide subsidized health insurance? Are the housing needs of the poor best addressed through public housing projects or through housing vouchers that can be used in lieu of rent? Should our policies with respect to the homeless attempt to ameliorate the conditions of a homeless existence, or prevent people from becoming homeless in the first place?

Assessing the relative desirability of policy options is only rarely an empirical matter; such decisions are more often ethical or ideological. MacRae (1985) stresses the unavoidable role of values in the process of policy analysis and the ensuing conflicts for the policy analyst. He identifies four principal "end values" widely shared throughout American society and against which policy decisions can be compared: economic benefit, subjective well-being, equity, and social integration. Sadly, policies that maximize equity may not maximize net economic benefit; those that enhance social integration may destroy subjective well-being. Thus, public policy analysis is not an arena for those who wish to pursue "value-neutral" science nor is it one for the morally or ideologically faint of heart.

CONCEPTUAL DEVELOPMENT

Much work in the area of public policy analysis consists of developing conceptual schemes or typologies that help sort out various kinds of policies or analyses of policies (such as the typology we are presently using). Nagel (1984) and Dubnick and Bardes (1983) review numerous conceptual schemes for typifying policies and policy analyses, with useful suggestions for synthesis; the former is an especially good overview of the field as a whole.

POLICY DESCRIPTION

Adequate description of public policy is essential for proper evaluation and understanding, but many public policies prove frustratingly complex, especially as delivered in the field. "Poverty policy" in the United States consists of a vast congeries of federal, state, and local programs each focused on different aspects of the poverty problem (income, employment, housing, nutrition) or on different segments of the poverty population (women, children, women with children, the disabled, the elderly). The same can obviously be said of housing policy, tax policy, environmental policy, health policy, and on through a very long list. Even a single element of poverty policy such as Temporary Assistance to Needy Families (TANF) has different eligibility requirements, administrative procedures, and payment levels in each of the fifty states. Thus, accurate policy description is by no means a straightforward task. Outstanding examples of policy description, both focused on poverty policy, are Haveman (1977) and Levitan (1985).

POLICY FORMULATION

Social science has a role to play in the formulation of policy as well as its description or evaluation. Most of the issues that policy attempts to address have been the focus of a great deal of basic social science research: poverty, ill health, homelessness, crime, violence, and so on. Although the once-obligatory discussion of "policy implications" of basic research has abated in recent years, few social scientists who work on policy-relevant issues can resist the urge to comment on the possible implications of the results for policy formulation. Much more work of this sort needs to be done, as it is evident that many policies are formulated and enacted in utter disregard for the extant state of knowledge about the topic. Indeed, Peter Rossi has hypothesized that the major reason social programs fail is that they are typically designed by amateurs who are largely innocent of social science theory, concepts, and results. Various job programs, mental health interventions, and crime reduction policies represent obvious cases in point.

METHODOLOGICAL RESEARCH

Unlike much basic disciplinary research in the social and behavioral sciences, whose results are largely inconsequential except to a handful of specialists, the results of policy studies will often influence peoples' lives and well-being and the cost of being wrong can run into millions or billions of dollars. Thus issues of internal and external validity, errors of measurement and specification, proper statistical modeling, and the like are more than methodological niceties to the policy analyst; they are worrisome, ever-present and potentially consequential threats to the accuracy of one's conclusions and to the policy decisions that ensue. A technical error in a journal article can be corrected in a simple retraction; an equivalent error in a policy analysis might result in wrong-headed or counterproductive policies being pursued.

Much of the literature on public policy analysis, and especially on impact evaluation (see below), is therefore mainly methodological in character; indeed, many recent innovations in research procedure have been developed by scholars working on applied, as opposed to basic, problems. There are many texts available on the methodology of public policy analysis. Rossi and colleagues (1998) provide a comprehensive overview; Judd and Kenny (1981) are highly recommended for the more advanced student.

POLICY EXPLANATION

Much public policy analysis undertaken by political scientists focuses on the processes by which policy is made at federal, state, and local levels. Classic examples are Marmor's analysis of the passage of Medicare (1970) and Moynihan's study of the ill-fated Family Assistance Plan proposed early in the Nixon administration but never enacted (1973).

Explanations of how public policy is made are invariably replete with the "dirty linen" of the political process: competing and often warring constituencies, equally legitimate but contradictory objectives and values, vote trading, compromises and deals, political posturing by key actors, intrusions by lobbying, advocacy and special interest groups, manipulation of public sentiment and understanding—in short, the "booming, buzzing confusion" of a fractious, pluralistic political system. For those whose understanding of such matters does not extend much beyond the obligatory high school civics lesson in "how a bill becomes a law," the policy explanation literature is a revelation.

POLITICAL INTELLIGENCE OR PUBLIC OPINION

In a democratic society, public opinion is supposed to "count" in the policy formation process. Sometimes it does; often it does not. Policy analysis thus sometimes involves plumbing the depths and sources of support or opposition to various policy initiatives, and in a larger sense, explicating the process by which policy becomes legitimated.

There is no easy answer to the question whether (or under what conditions) public opinion dictates the direction of public policy. It is evident that policy makers are sensitive to public opinion; many presidents, for example, are morbidly fascinated by their standing in the polls (e.g., Sussman 1988). It is equally evident, however, that many policies with strong majority support are never enacted into law. An interesting study of the effects of public opinion on policy formation is Verba and Nie (1975).

EVALUATION RESEARCH

The ultimate analytic question to be asked about any public policy is whether it produced (or will produce) its intended effects (or any effects, whether intended or not). The search for bottom-line effects—impact assessment—is one of two major activities subsumed under the rubric of evaluation research. The other is so-called process evaluation, discussed below under "Implementation Analysis."

There are many formidable barriers to be overcome in deciding whether a policy or program has produced its intended (or any) effects. First, the notion of "intended effects" presupposes clearly defined and articulated program goals, but many policies are enacted without a clear statement of the goals to be achieved. Thus, many texts in evaluation research recommend an assessment of the "evaluability" of the program prior to initiating the evaluation itself. A second barrier is the often-pronounced difference between the program-as-designed and the program-as-delivered. This

is the issue of program implementation, discussed below.

The most troublesome methodological issue in evaluation research lies in establishing the *ceteris paribus* (or "all else equal") condition, or in other words, in estimating what might have happened in the absence of the program to be evaluated. In an era of declining birthrates, any fertility reduction program will appear to be successful; in an era of declining crime rates, any crime reduction program will appear to be successful. How, then, can one differentiate between program effects and things that would have happened anyway owing to exogenous conditions? (Students of logic will see the problem here as the *post hoc, ergo propter hoc* fallacy.)

Because of this *ceteris paribus* problem, many evaluations are designed as experiments or quasi-experiments. In the former case, subjects are randomly assigned to various treatment and control conditions, and outcomes are monitored. Randomization in essence "initializes" all the starting conditions to the same values (except for the vagaries of chance). In the recent history of evaluation research, the various negative income tax experiments (see Rossi and Lyall 1976) are the best-known examples of large-scale field experiments of this general sort. *Quasi-experiments* are any of a number of research designs that do not involve randomization but use other methods to establish the *ceteris paribus* condition; the definitive statement on quasi-experiments is Cook and Campbell (1979).

Nowhere is the trade-off between internal and external validity more vexing than in the design of program evaluations. Evaluation designs with high internal validity, such as randomized experiments, are excellent in detecting program effects but the experimental conditions may not generalize to real-world settings. Thus, one telling critique of the Negative Income Tax (NIT) experiments is that participants knew from the beginning that the program would end in three (or in some cases five) years, so the labor-force response may have been very different than it would have been if negative income taxation became a permanent element of national income policy. Likewise, as the research setting comes to more closely mimic real-world conditions (that is, as it develops high external validity), the ability to detect real effects often declines.

A final problem in doing evaluation research is that most policies or programs are relatively small interventions intended to address rather large, complex social issues. The poverty rate, to illustrate, is a complex function of the rate of employment, trends in the world economy, prevailing wage rates, the provisions of the social welfare system, and a host of additional macrostructural factors. Any given antipoverty program, in contrast, will be a relatively small-scale intervention focused on one or a few components of the larger problem, often restricted to one or a few segments of the population. Often, the overall effects of the various large-scale, macrostructural factors will completely swamp the program effects—not because the program effects were not present or meritorious but because they are very small relative to exogenous effects.

The literature on the theory and practice of evaluation research is expansive; students seeking additional information will find themselves well served by Chambers and colleagues (1992), and by Rossi and colleagues (1998).

OUTCOME ANALYSIS

Assuming that a program has been adequately evaluated and an effect documented, one can then analyze that effect (or outcome) to determine whether it was worth the money and effort necessary to produce it. Outcome analysis thus examines the cost effectiveness or cost beneficiality of a given policy, program, or intervention.

Cost-benefit and cost-effectiveness analysis are intrinsically complex, technically demanding subjects. One complication lies in assessing the so-called opportunity costs. A dollar spent in one way is a dollar no longer available to use in some other way. Investing the dollar in any particular intervention thus means that one has lost the "opportunity" to invest that dollar in something that may have been far more beneficial.

A second complication is in the "accounting perspective" one chooses to assess benefits and costs. Consider the Food Stamp program. A recipient receives a benefit (a coupon that can be redeemed for food) at no cost; from the accounting perspective of that recipient, the benefit-cost ratio is thus infinite. The Food Stamp program is administered by the United States Department of Agriculture (USDA). From the USDA perspective, the benefit of the program presumably lies in the contribution it makes to relieving hunger and malnutrition in the population; the cost lies in whatever it takes to administer the program, redeem the coupons once submitted by food outlets, etc. Accounted against the USDA perspective, the benefit-cost ratio will be very different, and it will be different again when accounted against the perspective of society as a whole. The latter accounting, of course, requires asking what it is worth to us as a nation to provide food to those who might otherwise have to go without, clearly a moral question more than an empirical or analytic one.

This last example illustrates another thorny problem in doing cost-benefit analyses, namely, the incommensurability of benefits and costs. The dollar costs of most programs or policies can be reasonably well estimated. (The dollar costs are usually not the only costs. There may also be ethical or political costs that cannot be translated into dollars and cents but that are, nonetheless, real. Let us ignore the nondollar costs, however.) Unfortunately, the benefits of most interventions cannot be readily expressed in dollars; they are expressed, rather, in less tangible (but equally real) terms: lives saved, improvements in the quality of life, reductions of hunger, and the like. If the outcome cannot be converted to a dollar value, then a strict comparison to the dollar costs cannot be made and a true benefit-cost ratio cannot be calculated.

Cost effectiveness analysis, in contrast, compares the benefits of one program (expressed in any unit) at one cost to the benefits of another program (expressed in the same unit) at a different cost. Thus, a program that spends $10,000 to save one life is more cost effective than another program that spends $20,000 to save one life. Whether either program is cost beneficial, however, cannot be determined unless one is willing to assign a dollar value to a human life.

Many texts by economists deal at length with these and related complexities; accessible overviews include Levin (1975) and Yates (1996).

IMPLEMENTATION ANALYSIS

"Much is the slippage between the spoon and the mouth." A program as it is delivered in the field is rarely identical to the program as designed in the policy making process; sometimes, there is only a superficial resemblance. Since slippage between design and implementation might provide one explanation for the failure to achieve significant program effects, implementation analysis is an essential component of all capable policy evaluations.

There are many reasons why programs-as-delivered differ from programs-as-designed: technical impossibility, bureaucratic inertia, unanticipated conditions, exogenous influences. An elegantly designed policy experiment can fail at the point of randomization if program personnel let their own sentiments about "worthy" and "unworthy" clients override the randomizing process. Many educational policy initiatives are subverted because teachers persist in their same old ways despite the program admonition to do things differently. Welfare reform will mean little if caseworkers continue to apply the same standards and procedures as in the past. More generally, the real world finds ways to impinge in unexpected and often unwanted ways on any policy initiative; failure to anticipate these impingements has caused many a policy experiment to fail.

Loftin and McDowell (1981) provide a classic example of the utility of implementation analysis in their evaluation of the effects of the Detroit mandatory sentencing law. The policy-as-designed required a mandatory two-year "add on" to the prison sentence of any person convicted of a felony involving a firearm. Contrary to expectation, the rate of firearms crime did not decline after the law was enacted. Implementation analysis provided the reason. Judges, well aware of the overcrowded conditions in the state's prisons, were loath to increase average prison sentences. Yet, state law required that two years be added to the charge. To resolve the dilemma, judges in firearms cases would begin by reducing the main sentence by two or so years and then adding the mandated two-year add-on, so that the overall sentence remained about the same even as the judges remained in technical compliance with policy. A more thorough discussion of the implementation problem can be found in Chambers and colleagues (1992, chap. 1).

UTILIZATION

A consistent frustration expressed throughout the literature is that policy analysis seems only rarely to have any impact on actual policy. Utilization is an ongoing problem in the field of evaluation research. A more detailed treatment of the utilization problem can be found in Chambers and colleagues (1992, chapter 1), Shadish and colleagues (1991, chapters 6, 7), and Weiss (1988). For examples of ways in which evaluation can impact practice, see articles by Gueron, Lipsey, and Wholey in *New Directions for Evaluation* (1997).

Many reasons for nonutilization have been identified. One of the most important is timeliness. Good research takes time, whereas policy decisions are often made quickly, well before the results of the analysis are in. The negative income tax experiments mentioned earlier were stimulated in substantial part by a Nixon administration proposal for a modified negative income tax to replace the then-current welfare system. The shortest of the experiments ran for three years; several ran for five years; none were completed by the time the Nixon proposal was killed mainly on political grounds.

A second factor in the nonutilization of policy studies is that research is seldom unequivocal. Even the best-designed and best-executed policy researches will be accompanied by numerous caveats, conditions, and qualifications that strictly limit the safe policy inferences one may draw from them. Policy makers, of course, prefer simple declarative conclusions; policy research rarely allows one to make such statements.

Finally, even under the most favorable conditions, the scientific results of policy analyses are but one among many inputs into the policy-making process. There are, in addition, normative, economic, political, ethical, pragmatic, and ideological inputs that must be accommodated. In the process of accommodation, the influence of scientific research is often obscured to the point where it can no longer be recognized. It should not be inferred from this that policy analysis is not utilized, only that the research results are but one voice in the cacophony of the policy-making process.

Weiss has written extensively on the utilization problem and ways in which evaluation can be used effectively to change policy. She argues that "in its ideal form, evaluation is conducted for a client who has decisions to make and who looks to the evaluation for answers on which to base his decisions" (1972, p. 6). This is often not the case, however, as evaluation results seldom influence important decisions regarding programs and policies. Weiss's general conclusion regarding utilization is that evaluation results affect public policy by serving as the impetus for public discourse and debate that form social policy, rather than through extensive program reform or termination.

REFERENCES

Chambers, K., K. R. Wedel, and M. K. Rodwell 1992 *Evaluating Social Programs*. Boston: Allyn and Bacon.

Cook, Thomas, and Donald Campbell 1979 *Quasi-Experimentation*. Chicago: Rand McNally.

Dubnick, Melvin, and Barbara Bardes 1983 *Thinking about Public Policy: A Problem Solving Approach*. New York: John Wiley.

Gueron, Judith M. 1997 "Learning about Welfare Reform: Lessons from State-Based Evaluations." *New Directions for Evaluation* 76:79–94. (Edited by D. Rog and D. Fournier)

Haveman, Robert 1977 *A Decade of Federal Antipoverty Programs: Achievements, Failures, and Lessons*. New York: Academic.

Johnson, D., L. Meiller, L. Miller, and G. Summers 1987 *Needs Assessment: Theory and Methods*. Ames: Iowa State University Press.

Judd, Charles, and David Kenny 1981 *Estimating the Effects of Social Interventions*. New York: Cambridge University Press.

Levin, Henry 1975 "Cost-Effectiveness Analysis in Evaluation Research." In M. Guttentag and E. Struening, eds., *Handbook of Evaluation Research*. Newbury Park, Calif.: Sage.

Levitan, Sar 1985 *Programs in Aid of the Poor*. Baltimore, Md.: Johns Hopkins University Press.

Lipsey, Mark W. 1997 "What Can You Build with Thousands of Bricks? Musings on the Cumulation of Knowledge in Program Evaluation." *New Directions for Evaluation* 76:7–24. (Edited by D. Rog and D. Fournier.)

Loftin, Colin, and David McDowell 1981 "One with a Gun Gets You Two: Mandatory Sentencing and Firearms Violence in Detroit." *Annals of the American Academy of Political and Social Science* 455:150–168.

MacRae, Duncan 1985 *Policy Indicators: Links between Social Science and Public Debate*. Chapel Hill, N.C.: University of North Carolina Press.

Marmor, Theodore 1970 *The Politics of Medicare*. New York: Aldine.

Moynihan, Daniel 1973 *The Politics of a Guaranteed Annual Income: The Nixon Administration and the Family Assistance Plan*. New York: Vintage.

Nagel, Stuart 1984 *Contemporary Public Policy Analysis*. Birmingham: University of Alabama Press.

Rogers, James 1989 "Social Science Disciplines and Policy Research: The Case of Political Science." *Policy Studies Review* 9:13–28.

Rossi, Peter, Howard Freeman, and Mark Lipsey 1998 *Evaluation: A Systematic Approach*, 6th ed. Newbury Park, Calif.: Sage.

Rossi, Peter, and Kathryn Lyall 1976 *Reforming Public Welfare*. New York: Russell Sage.

Shadish, William R., Jr., T. D. Cook, and L. C. Leviton 1991 *Foundations of Program Evaluation*. Newbury Park, Calif.: Sage.

Sussman, Barry 1988 *What Americans Really Think and Why Our Politicians Pay No Attention*. New York: Pantheon.

Verba, Sidney, and Norman Nie 1975 *Participation in America: Political Democracy and Social Equality*. New York: Harper and Row.

Weiss, Carol H. 1972 *Evaluation Research: Methods for Assessing Program Effectiveness*. Englewood Cliffs, N.J.: Prentice-Hall.

—— 1988 "Evaluation for Decisions: Is Anybody There? Does Anybody Care?" *Evaluation Practice* 9:15–28.

Wholey, Joseph S. 1997 "Clarifying Goals, Reporting Results." *New Directions for Evaluation* 76:95–106. (Edited by D. Rog and D. Fournier.)

Yates, Brian T. 1996 *Analyzing Costs, Procedures, Processes, and Outcomes in Human Services*. Thousand Oaks, Calif.: Sage.

JAMES D. WRIGHT

ISBN 0-02-864851-X

90000